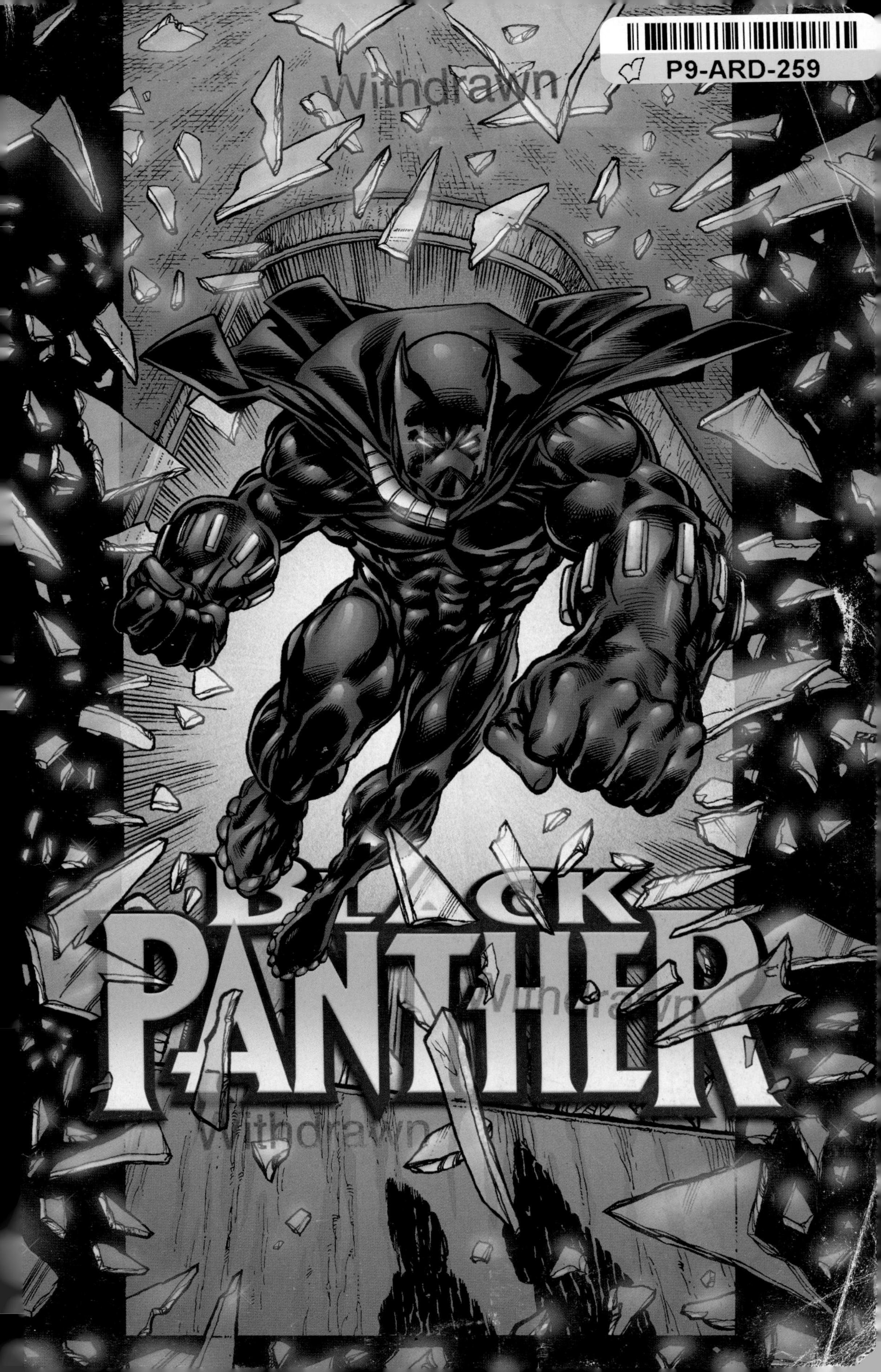
BLACK
PANTHER

WRITER **CHRISTOPHER PRIEST**

PENCILERS **JOE QUESADA, MARK TEXEIRA, VINCE EVANS, JOE JUSKO, MIKE MANLEY, MARK BRIGHT** & **SAL VELLUTO** WITH **AMANDA CONNER**

INKERS **MARK TEXEIRA, ALITHA MARTINEZ, VINCE EVANS, JOE JUSKO, JIMMY PALMIOTTI, MIKE MANLEY, NELSON DeCASTRO** & **BOB ALMOND**

COLORISTS **BRIAN HABERLIN, AVALON STUDIOS, ELIZABETH LEWIS, CHRIS SOTOMAYOR** & **BRAD VANCATA** WITH **DREW YACKEY** & **MATT YACKEY**

LETTERERS **RICHARD STARKINGS** & **COMICRAFT INC'S SIOBHAN HANNA, WES ABBOTT, JASON LEVINE** & **LIZ AGRAPHIOTIS;** AND **SHARPEFONT** & **PAUL TUTRONE**

ASSISTANT EDITORS **KELLY LAMY** & **FRANK DUNKERLEY** WITH **GREGG SCHIGIEL**

MANAGING EDITOR **NANCI DAKESIAN**

EDITORS **JOE QUESADA, JIMMY PALMIOTTI** & **RUBEN DIAZ** WITH **TOM BREVOORT**

BLACK PANTHER CREATED BY STAN LEE & JACK KIRBY

FRONT COVER ARTISTS: **JOE QUESADA** & **JIMMY PALMIOTTI**
BACK COVER ARTISTS: **JOE JUSKO** & **ELIZABETH LEWIS**

COLLECTION EDITOR **MARK D. BEAZLEY** ASSOCIATE EDITOR **SARAH BRUNSTAD**
ASSOCIATE MANAGING EDITOR **ALEX STARBUCK** EDITOR, SPECIAL PROJECTS **JENNIFER GRÜNWALD**
VP, PRODCUTION & SPECIAL PROJECTS **JEFF YOUNGQUIST** RESEARCH & LAYOUT **JEPH YORK**
PRODUCTION: **RYAN DEVALL** BOOK DESIGNER: **JAY BOWEN**
SVP PRINT, SALES & MARKETING: **DAVID GABRIEL**

EDITOR IN CHIEF: **AXEL ALONSO** CHIEF CREATIVE OFFICER: **JOE QUESADA**
PUBLISHER: **DAN BUCKLEY** EXECUTIVE PRODUCER: **ALAN FINE**

SPECIAL THANKS TO BOB ALMOND, MIKE HANSEN
AND MILE HIGH COMICS' CHUCK ROZANSKI & CHRIS BOYD

BLACK PANTHER BY CHRISTOPHER PRIEST: THE COMPLETE COLLECTION VOL. 1. Contains material originally published in magazine form as BLACK PANTHER #1-17. Second printing 2016. ISBN# 978-0-7851-926
Published by MARVEL WORLDWIDE, INC., a subsidiary of MARVEL ENTERTAINMENT, LLC. OFFICE OF PUBLICATION: 135 West 50th Street, New York, NY 10020. Copyright © 2015 MARVEL No similarity between any of
names, characters, persons, and/or institutions in this magazine with those of any living or dead person or institution is intended, and any such similarity which may exist is purely coincidental. **Printed in the U.S.A.** A
FINE, President, Marvel Entertainment; DAN BUCKLEY, President, TV, Publishing & Brand Management; JOE QUESADA, Chief Creative Officer; TOM BREVOORT, SVP of Publishing; DAVID BOGART, SVP of Business A
& Operations, Publishing & Partnership; C.B. CEBULSKI, VP of Brand Management & Development, Asia; DAVID GABRIEL, SVP of Sales & Marketing, Publishing; JEFF YOUNGQUIST, VP of Production & Special Proj
DAN CARR, Executive Director of Publishing Technology; ALEX MORALES, Director of Publishing Operations; SUSAN CRESPI, Production Manager; STAN LEE, Chairman Emeritus. For information regarding advertisi
Marvel Comics or on Marvel.com, please contact Vit DeBellis, Integrated Sales Manager, at vdebellis@marvel.com. For Marvel subscription inquiries, please call 888-511-5480. **Manufactured between 4/27/2016**
5/23/2016 by R.R. DONNELLEY, INC., OWENSVILLE, MO, USA.

10 9 8 7 6 5 4 3 2

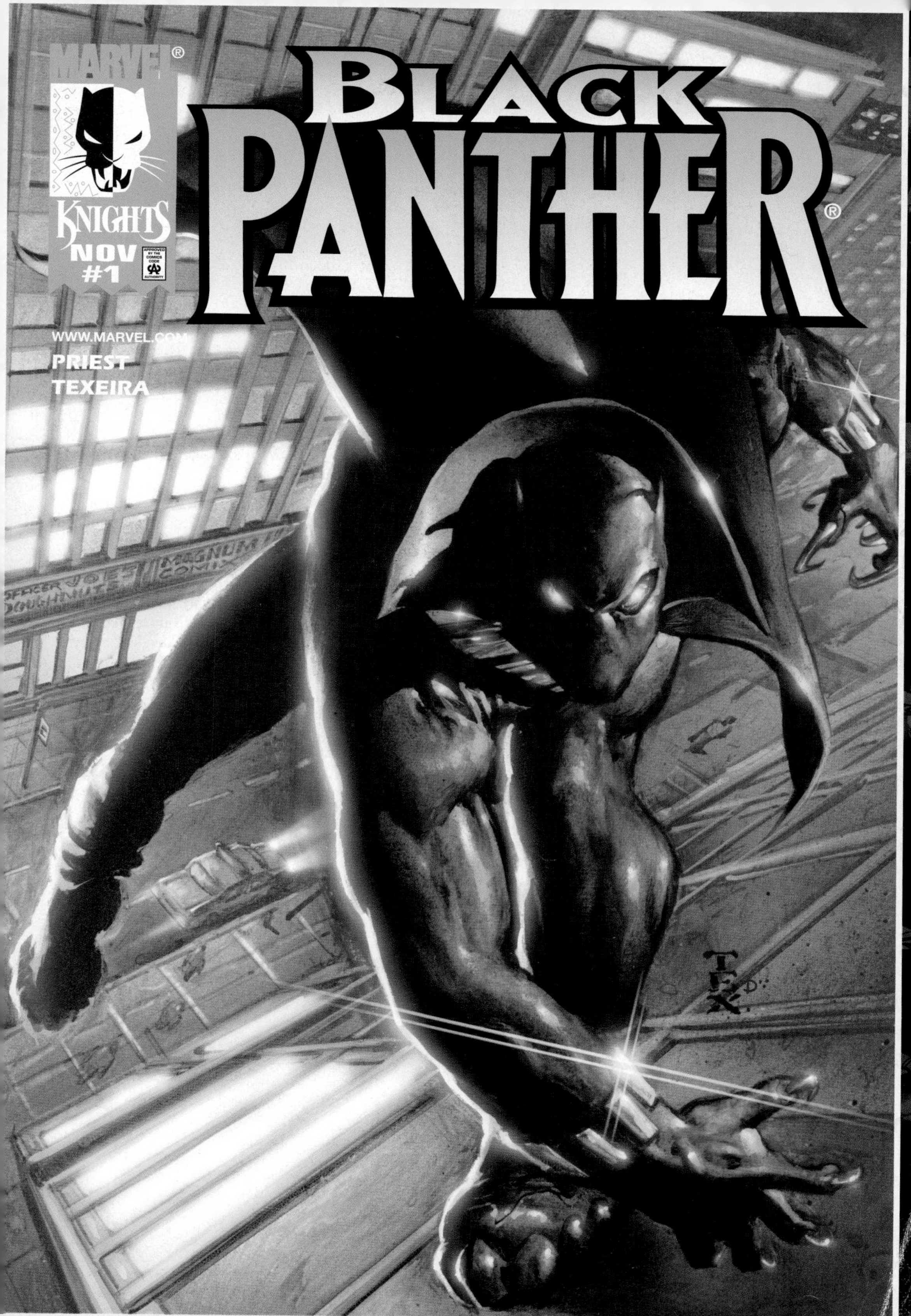
MARVEL
KNIGHTS
NOV
#1
APPROVED BY THE COMICS CODE AUTHORITY
BLACK
PANTHER
WWW.MARVEL.COM
PRIEST
TEXEIRA
MAGNUM COMIX

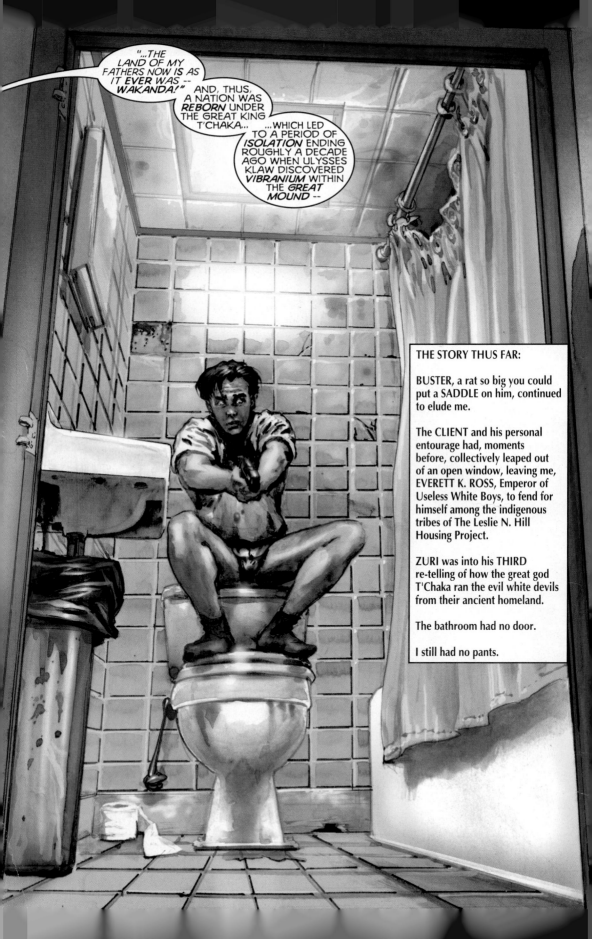

"...THE LAND OF MY FATHERS NOW IS AS IT *EVER WAS* -- *WAKANDA!*" AND, THUS, A NATION WAS *REBORN* UNDER THE GREAT KING T'CHAKA...

...WHICH LED TO A PERIOD OF *ISOLATION* ENDING ROUGHLY A DECADE AGO WHEN ULYSSES KLAW DISCOVERED *VIBRANIUM* WITHIN THE *GREAT MOUND* --

THE STORY THUS FAR:

BUSTER, a rat so big you could put a SADDLE on him, continued to elude me.

The CLIENT and his personal entourage had, moments before, collectively leaped out of an open window, leaving me, EVERETT K. ROSS, Emperor of Useless White Boys, to fend for himself among the indigenous tribes of The Leslie N. Hill Housing Project.

ZURI was into his THIRD re-telling of how the great god T'Chaka ran the evil white devils from their ancient homeland.

The bathroom had no door.

I still had no pants.

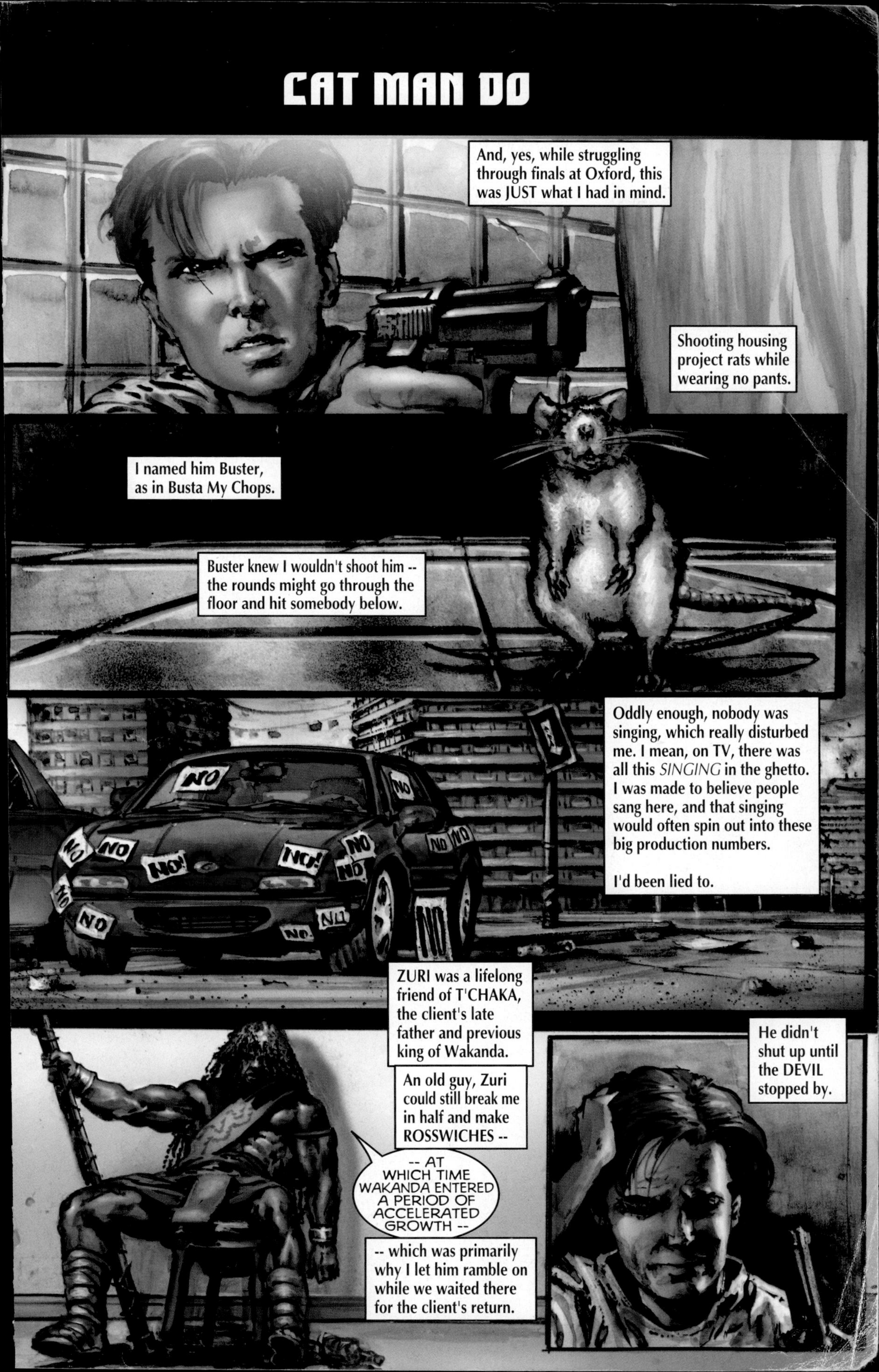
CAT MAN DO
And, yes, while struggling through finals at Oxford, this was JUST what I had in mind.
Shooting housing project rats while wearing no pants.
I named him Buster, as in Busta My Chops.
Buster knew I wouldn't shoot him -- the rounds might go through the floor and hit somebody below.
Oddly enough, nobody was singing, which really disturbed me. I mean, on TV, there was all this SINGING in the ghetto. I was made to believe people sang here, and that singing would often spin out into these big production numbers.
I'd been lied to.
NO
NO
NO
NO!
ZURI was a lifelong friend of T'CHAKA, the client's late father and previous king of Wakanda.
An old guy, Zuri could still break me in half and make ROSSWICHES --
-- AT WHICH TIME WAKANDA ENTERED A PERIOD OF ACCELERATED GROWTH --
-- which was primarily why I let him ramble on while we waited there for the client's return.
He didn't shut up until the DEVIL stopped by.

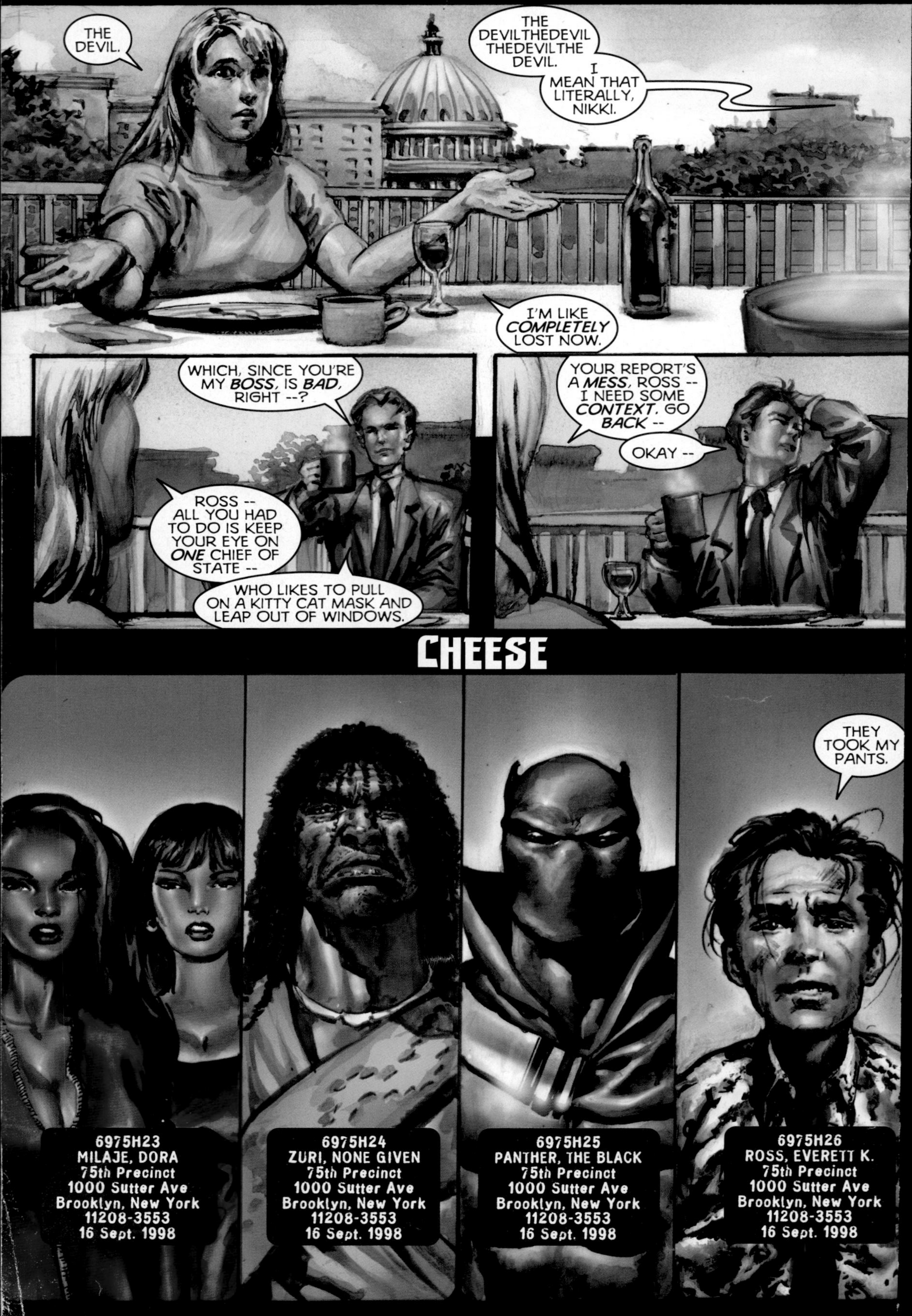
THE DEVIL.
THE DEVILTHEDEVIL THEDEVILTHE DEVIL.
I MEAN THAT LITERALLY, NIKKI.
I'M LIKE COMPLETELY LOST NOW.
WHICH, SINCE YOU'RE MY BOSS, IS BAD, RIGHT --?
ROSS -- ALL YOU HAD TO DO IS KEEP YOUR EYE ON ONE CHIEF OF STATE --
WHO LIKES TO PULL ON A KITTY CAT MASK AND LEAP OUT OF WINDOWS.
YOUR REPORT'S A MESS, ROSS -- I NEED SOME CONTEXT. GO BACK --
OKAY --
CHEESE
6975H23 MILAJE, DORA 75th Precinct 1000 Sutter Ave Brooklyn, New York 11208-3553 16 Sept. 1998
6975H24 ZURI, NONE GIVEN 75th Precinct 1000 Sutter Ave Brooklyn, New York 11208-3553 16 Sept. 1998
6975H25 PANTHER, THE BLACK 75th Precinct 1000 Sutter Ave Brooklyn, New York 11208-3553 16 Sept. 1998
THEY TOOK MY PANTS.
6975H26 ROSS, EVERETT K. 75th Precinct 1000 Sutter Ave Brooklyn, New York 11208-3553 16 Sept. 1998

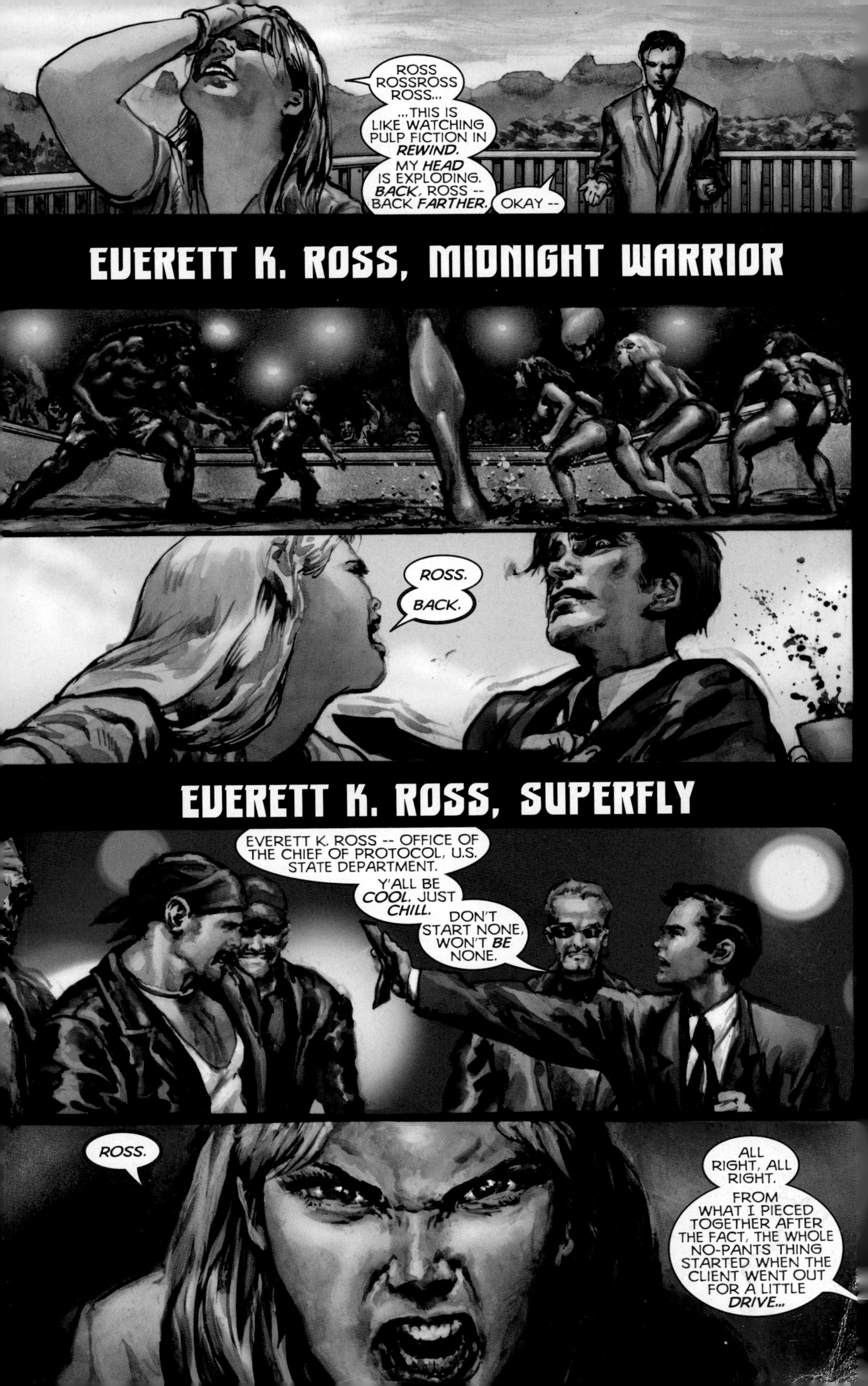
ROSS ROSSROSS ROSS... ...THIS IS LIKE WATCHING PULP FICTION IN *REWIND.* MY *HEAD* IS EXPLODING. *BACK,* ROSS -- BACK *FARTHER.*
OKAY --
EVERETT K. ROSS, MIDNIGHT WARRIOR
ROSS. *BACK.*
EVERETT K. ROSS, SUPERFLY
EVERETT K. ROSS -- OFFICE OF THE CHIEF OF PROTOCOL, U.S. STATE DEPARTMENT. Y'ALL BE *COOL.* JUST *CHILL.* DON'T START NONE, WON'T *BE* NONE.
ROSS.
ALL RIGHT, ALL RIGHT. FROM WHAT I PIECED TOGETHER AFTER THE FACT, THE WHOLE NO-PANTS THING STARTED WHEN THE CLIENT WENT OUT FOR A LITTLE *DRIVE...*

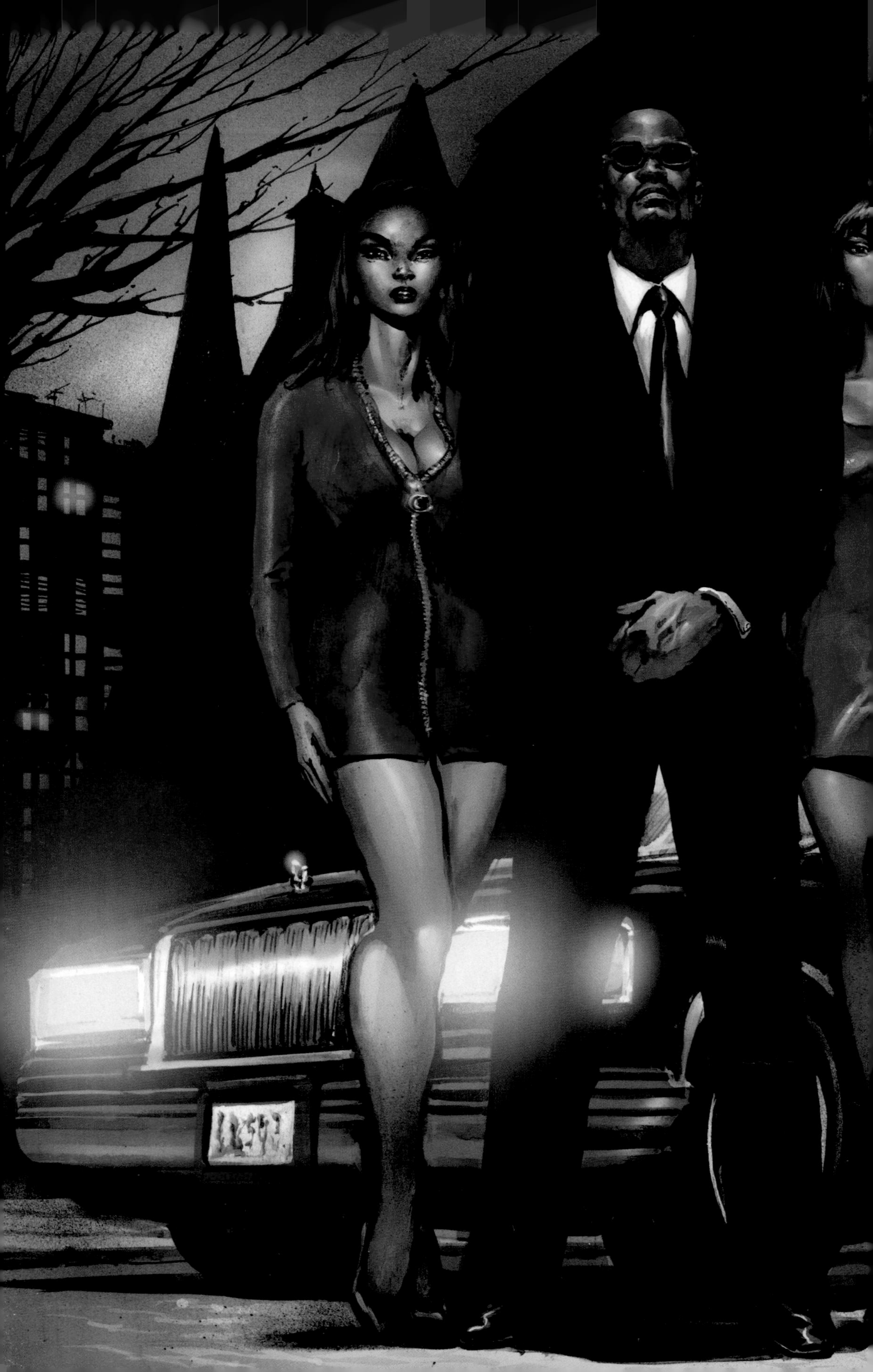

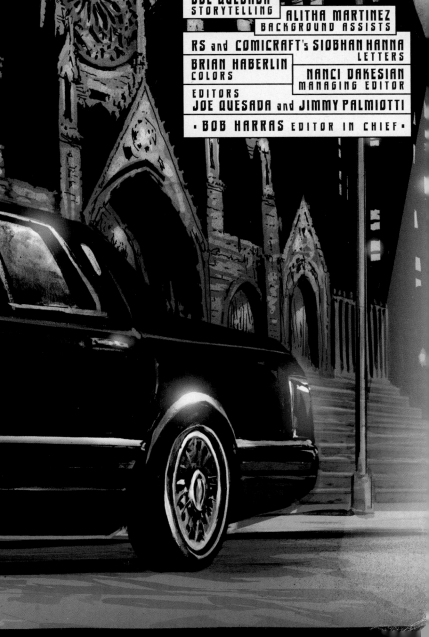

STAN LEE PROUDLY PRESENTS:
THE TRIUMPHANT RETURN OF
BLACK PANTHER IN

THE CLIENT

BY
CHRISTOPHER **PRIEST**
AND
MARK **TEXEIRA**
SCRIBES

JOE QUESADA
STORYTELLING

ALITHA MARTINEZ
BACKGROUND ASSISTS

RS and COMICRAFT's SIOBHAN HANNA
LETTERS

BRIAN HABERLIN
COLORS

NANCI DAKESIAN
MANAGING EDITOR

EDITORS
JOE QUESADA and JIMMY PALMIOTTI

• BOB HARRAS EDITOR IN CHIEF •

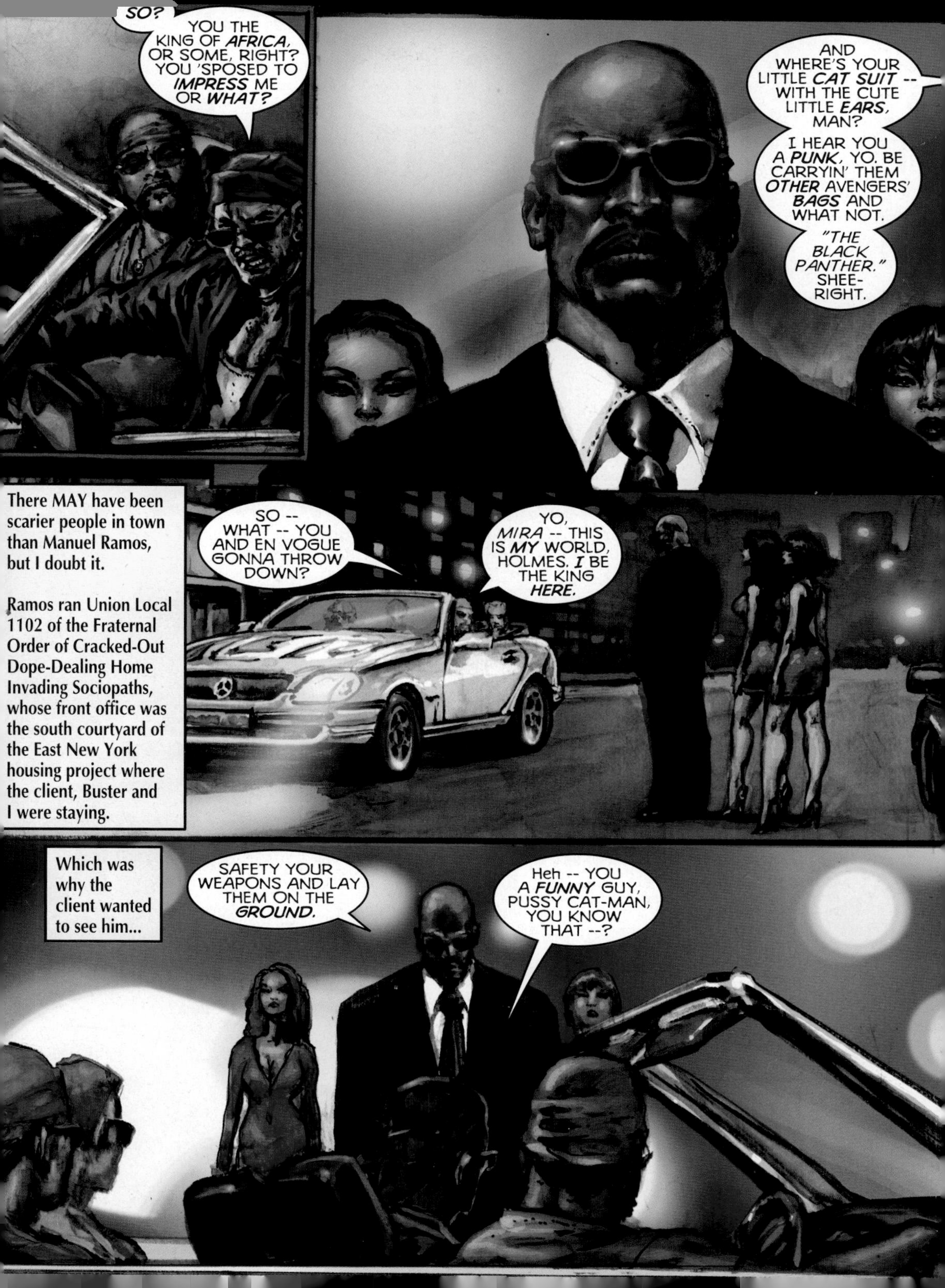
SO?
YOU THE KING OF *AFRICA*, OR SOME, RIGHT? YOU 'SPOSED TO *IMPRESS* ME OR *WHAT?*
AND WHERE'S YOUR LITTLE *CAT SUIT* -- WITH THE CUTE LITTLE *EARS*, MAN?
I HEAR YOU A *PUNK*, YO. BE CARRYIN' THEM *OTHER* AVENGERS' *BAGS* AND WHAT NOT.
"THE BLACK PANTHER." SHEE-RIGHT.
There MAY have been scarier people in town than Manuel Ramos, but I doubt it.
Ramos ran Union Local 1102 of the Fraternal Order of Cracked-Out Dope-Dealing Home Invading Sociopaths, whose front office was the south courtyard of the East New York housing project where the client, Buster and I were staying.
SO -- WHAT -- YOU AND EN VOGUE GONNA THROW DOWN?
YO, *MIRA* -- THIS IS *MY* WORLD, HOLMES. *I* BE THE KING *HERE.*
Which was why the client wanted to see him...
SAFETY YOUR WEAPONS AND LAY THEM ON THE *GROUND.*
Heh -- YOU A *FUNNY* GUY, PUSSY CAT-MAN, YOU KNOW THAT --?

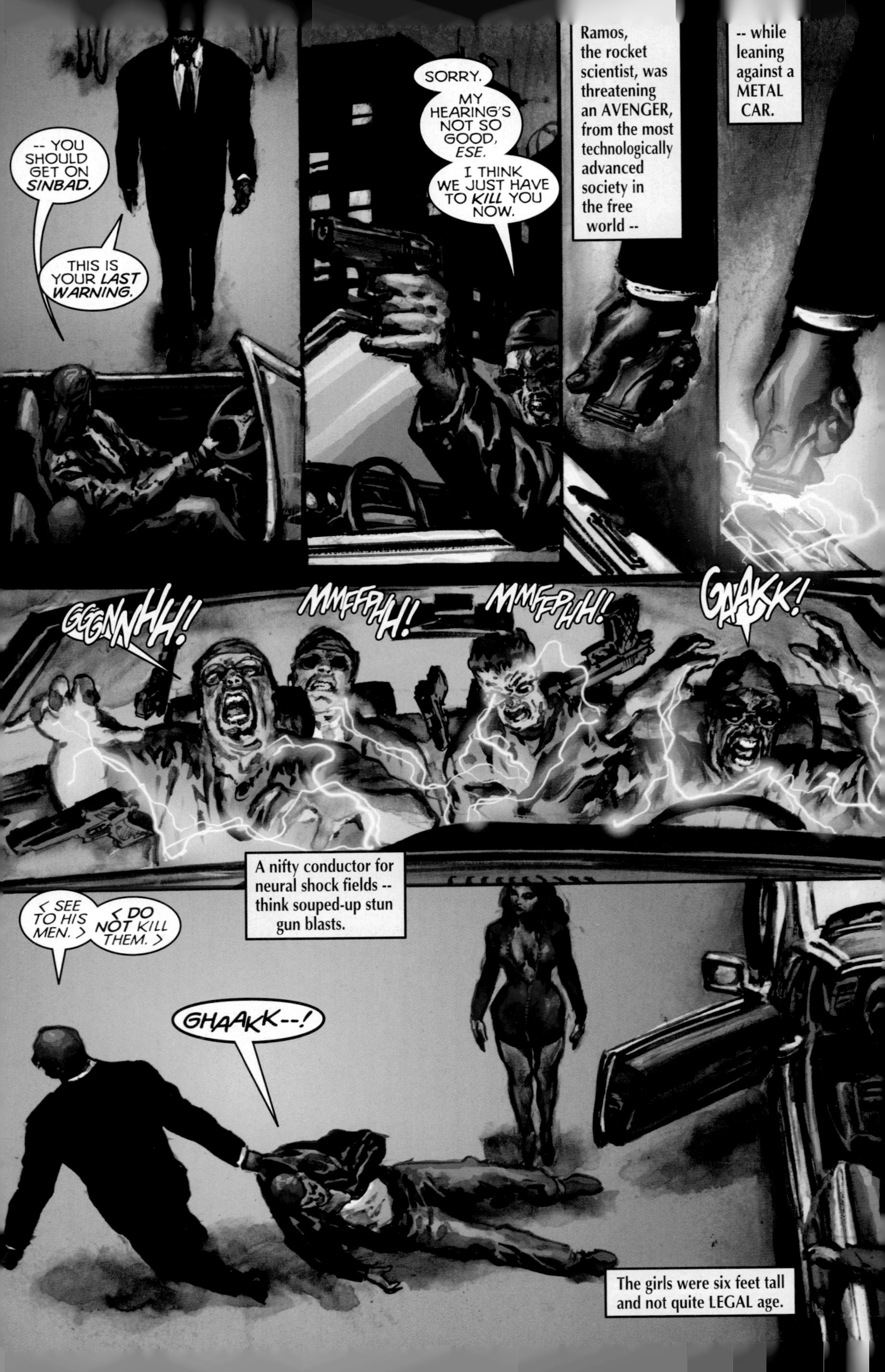

-- YOU SHOULD GET ON SINBAD.
THIS IS YOUR LAST WARNING.
SORRY.
MY HEARING'S NOT SO GOOD, ESE.
I THINK WE JUST HAVE TO KILL YOU NOW.
Ramos, the rocket scientist, was threatening an AVENGER, from the most technologically advanced society in the free world --
-- while leaning against a METAL CAR.
GGGNNHH!
MMFFPHH!
MMFFPHH!
GAAKK!
A nifty conductor for neural shock fields -- think souped-up stun gun blasts.
< SEE TO HIS MEN. >
< DO NOT KILL THEM. >
GHAAKK--!
The girls were six feet tall and not quite LEGAL age.

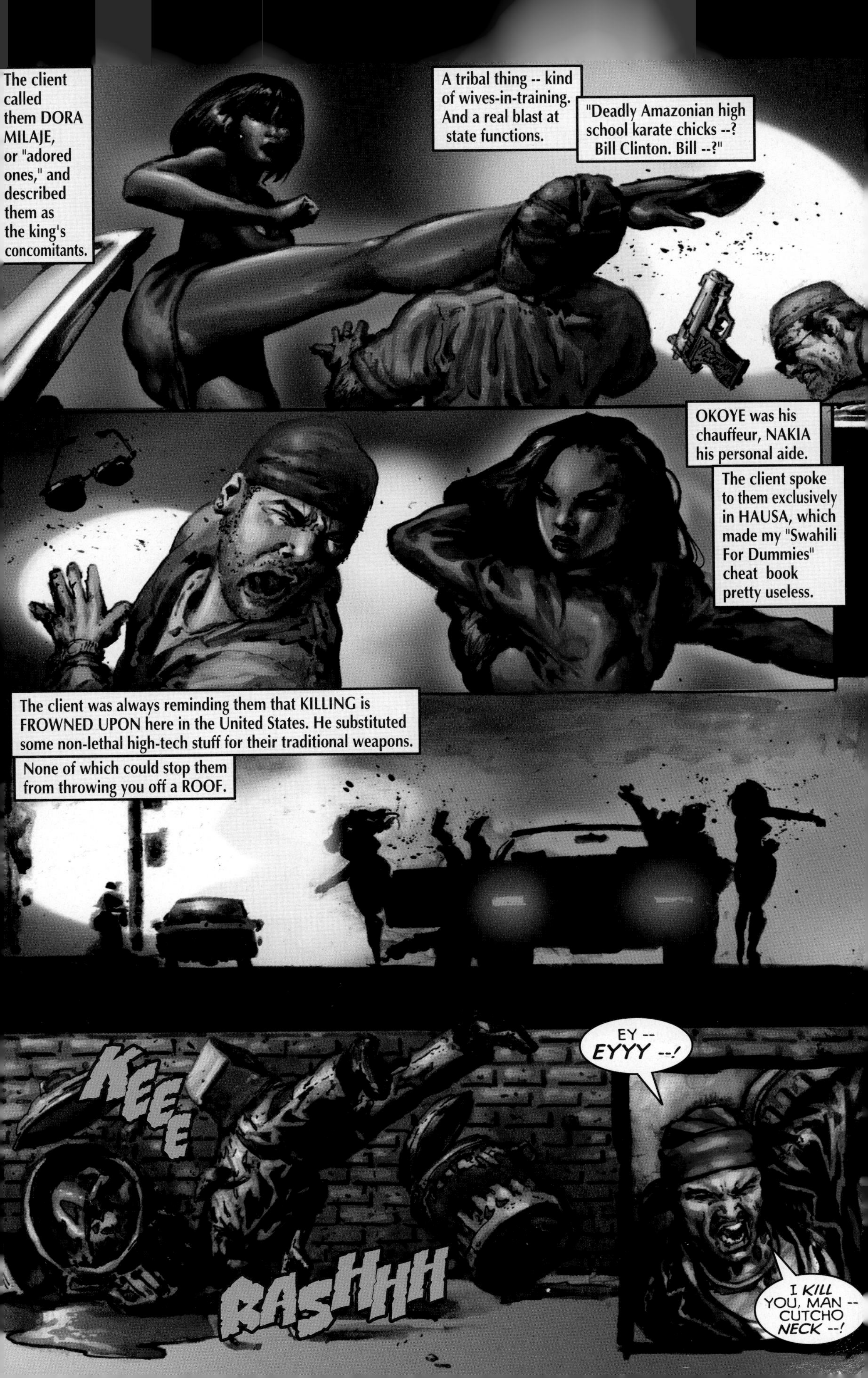

The client called them DORA MILAJE, or "adored ones," and described them as the king's concomitants.
A tribal thing -- kind of wives-in-training. And a real blast at state functions.
"Deadly Amazonian high school karate chicks --? Bill Clinton. Bill --?"
OKOYE was his chauffeur, NAKIA his personal aide.
The client spoke to them exclusively in HAUSA, which made my "Swahili For Dummies" cheat book pretty useless.
The client was always reminding them that KILLING is FROWNED UPON here in the United States. He substituted some non-lethal high-tech stuff for their traditional weapons.
None of which could stop them from throwing you off a ROOF.
KEEE
RASHHH
EY -- EYYY --!
I KILL YOU, MAN -- CUTCHO NECK --!

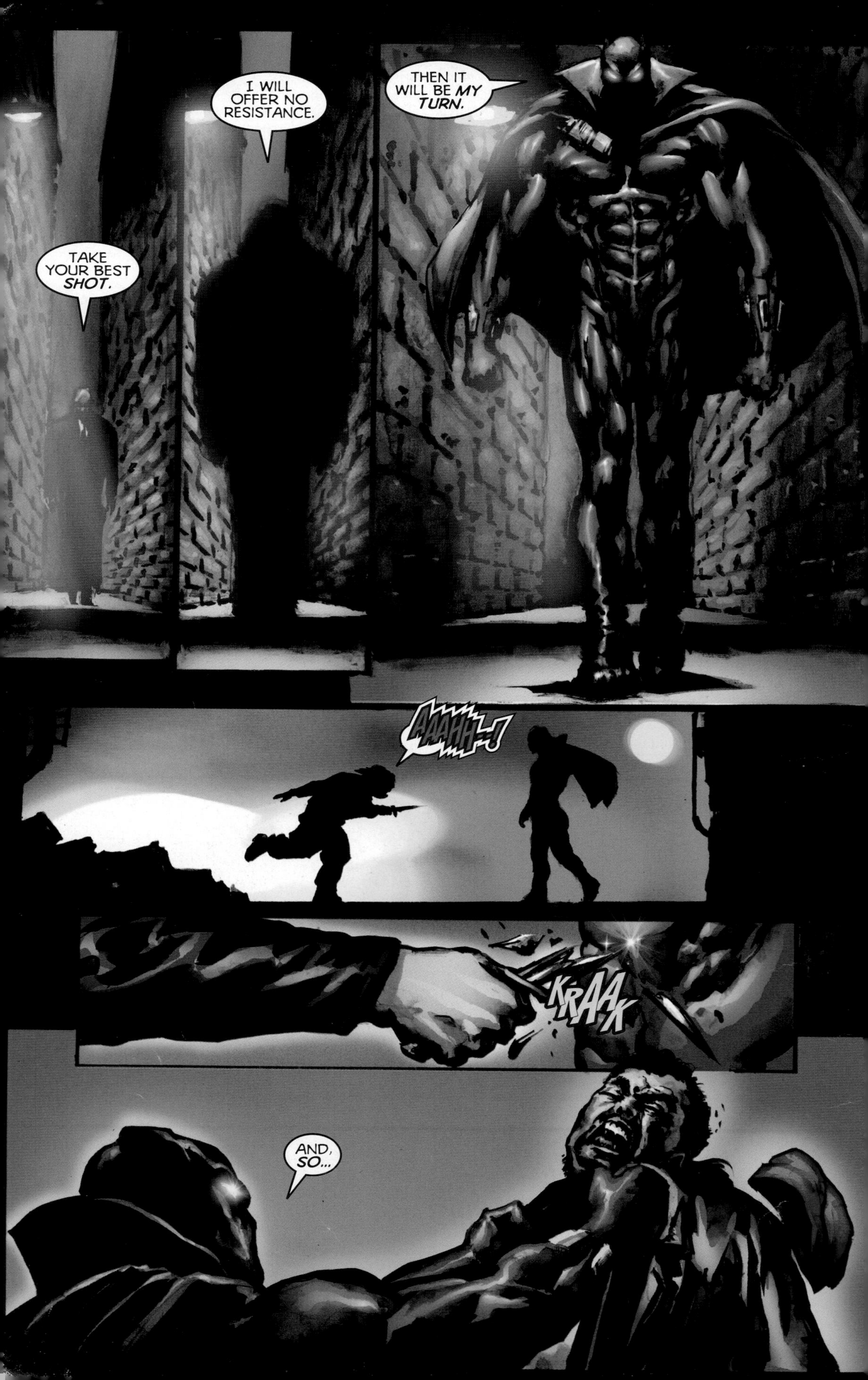
TAKE YOUR BEST SHOT.
I WILL OFFER NO RESISTANCE.
THEN IT WILL BE MY TURN.
AAAHH--!
KRAAK
AND, SO...

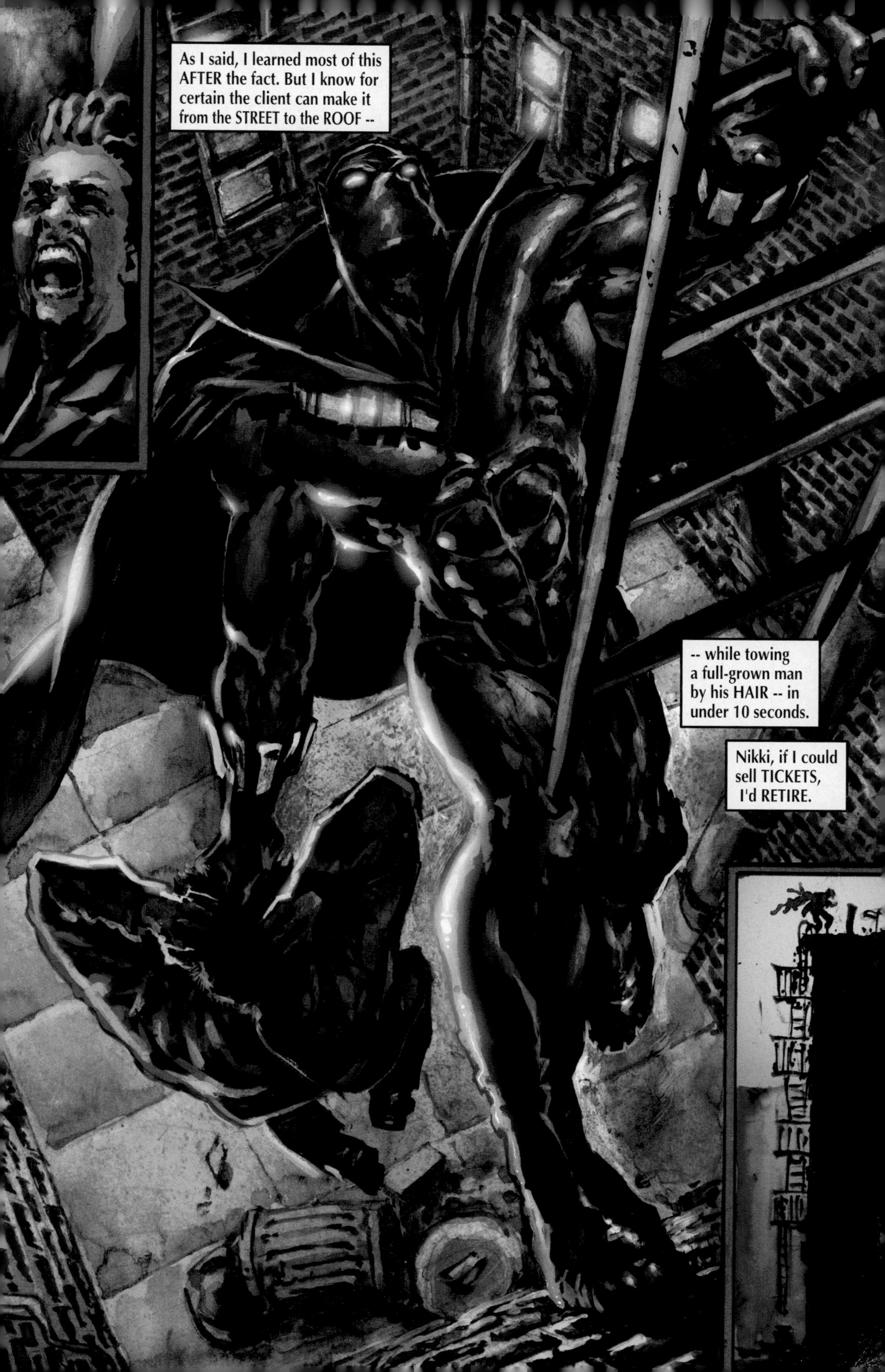
As I said, I learned most of this AFTER the fact. But I know for certain the client can make it from the STREET to the ROOF --
-- while towing a full-grown man by his HAIR -- in under 10 seconds.
Nikki, if I could sell TICKETS, I'd RETIRE.

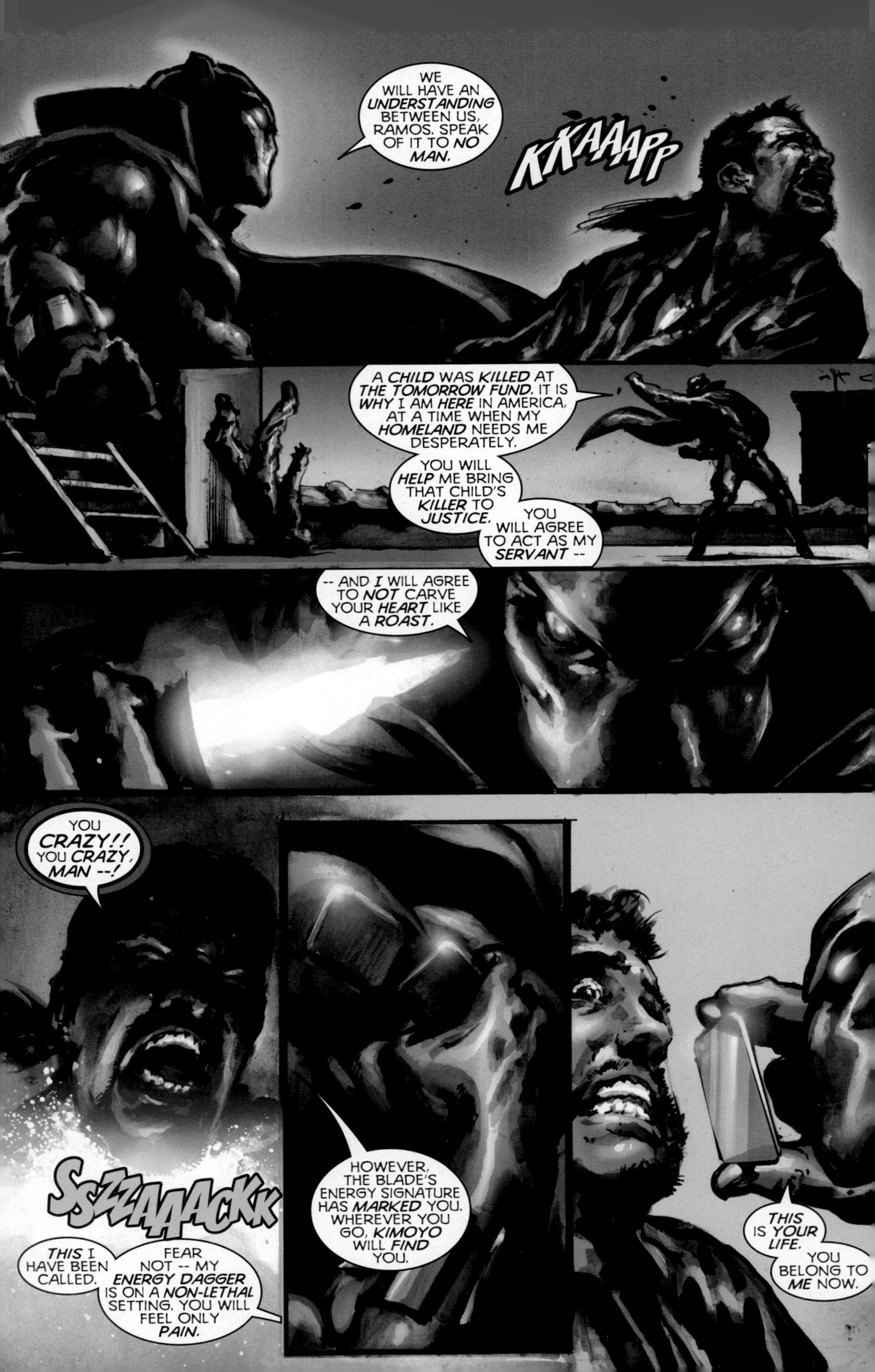
WE WILL HAVE AN UNDERSTANDING BETWEEN US, RAMOS. SPEAK OF IT TO NO MAN.
KKAAAPP
A CHILD WAS KILLED AT THE TOMORROW FUND. IT IS WHY I AM HERE IN AMERICA, AT A TIME WHEN MY HOMELAND NEEDS ME DESPERATELY.
YOU WILL HELP ME BRING THAT CHILD'S KILLER TO JUSTICE.
YOU WILL AGREE TO ACT AS MY SERVANT --
-- AND I WILL AGREE TO NOT CARVE YOUR HEART LIKE A ROAST.
YOU CRAZY!! YOU CRAZY, MAN --!
SSZZAAACKK
THIS I HAVE BEEN CALLED.
FEAR NOT -- MY ENERGY DAGGER IS ON A NON-LETHAL SETTING. YOU WILL FEEL ONLY PAIN.
HOWEVER, THE BLADE'S ENERGY SIGNATURE HAS MARKED YOU. WHEREVER YOU GO, KIMOYO WILL FIND YOU.
THIS IS YOUR LIFE.
YOU BELONG TO ME NOW.

AGING Mr. TARANTINO

GIANT RATS. TEENAGE AMAZONS. THE CLIENT TOSSING DRUG DEALERS.

AND SATAN. YOU LEFT OUT SATAN. THAT'S IMPORTANT.

AND THEN YOU LOST YOUR *PANTS.*

WRONG. FIRST WE WENT OUT FOR CHINESE TAKE-OUT.

THEN I LOST MY PANTS.

KUMUSTA KA

SPEAK LOUD!
PAY IN ADVANCE!
NO FOOD STAMPS!
NO CREDIT!
PUT MONEY IN SLOT!!

WHAT --?!

ROSS. THE *BEGINNING,* ROSS.

ALL RIGHT, ALL RIGHT -- HOW ABOUT --

EVERETT K. ROSS AND THE GANG

GET DOWN
JUNGLE
ET DOWN

GET DOWN
BOOGIE!
GET DOWN

SPLAASSH

OKAY.

IT ALL STARTED A FEW WEEKS AGO, AFTER I FINISHED UP THE McAFREE THING. WE WERE AT *MY PLACE...*

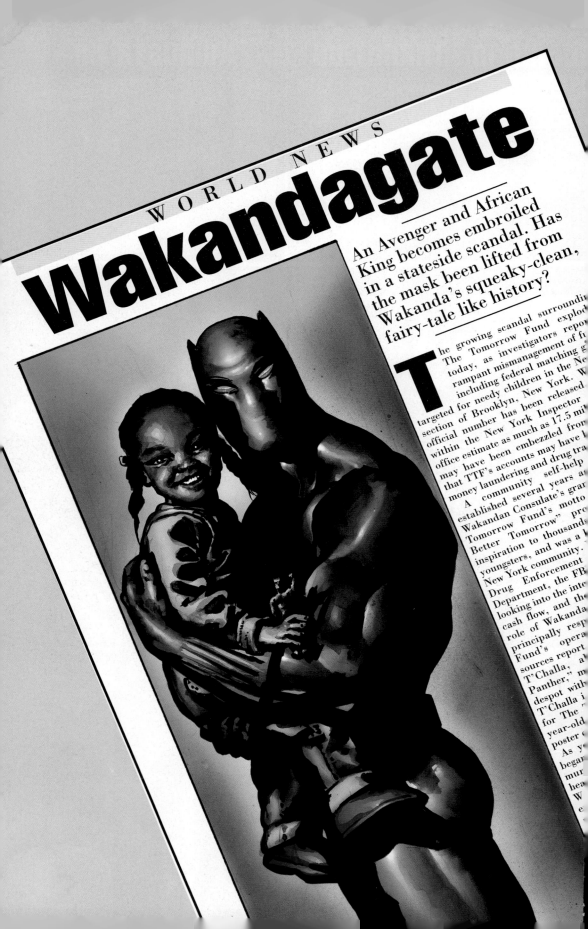

Wakandagate

An Avenger and African King becomes embroiled in a stateside scandal. Has the mask been lifted from Wakanda's squeaky-clean, fairy-tale like history?

The growing scandal surroundi The Tomorrow Fund explod today, as investigators repo rampant mismanagement of fu including federal matching g targeted for needy children in the Ne section of Brooklyn, New York. W official number has been released within the New York Inspector office estimate as much as 17.5 mi may have been embezzled from that TTF's accounts may have b money laundering and drug tra

A community self-help established several years a Wakandan Consulate's grar Tomorrow Fund's motto Better Tomorrow", pro inspiration to thousands youngsters, and was a l New York community.

Drug Enforcement Department, the FB looking into the inte cash flow, and the role of Wakanda Fund's principally resp sources report T'Challa, a Panther," m despot with T'Challa i for The year-old poster

As y began mu hea W

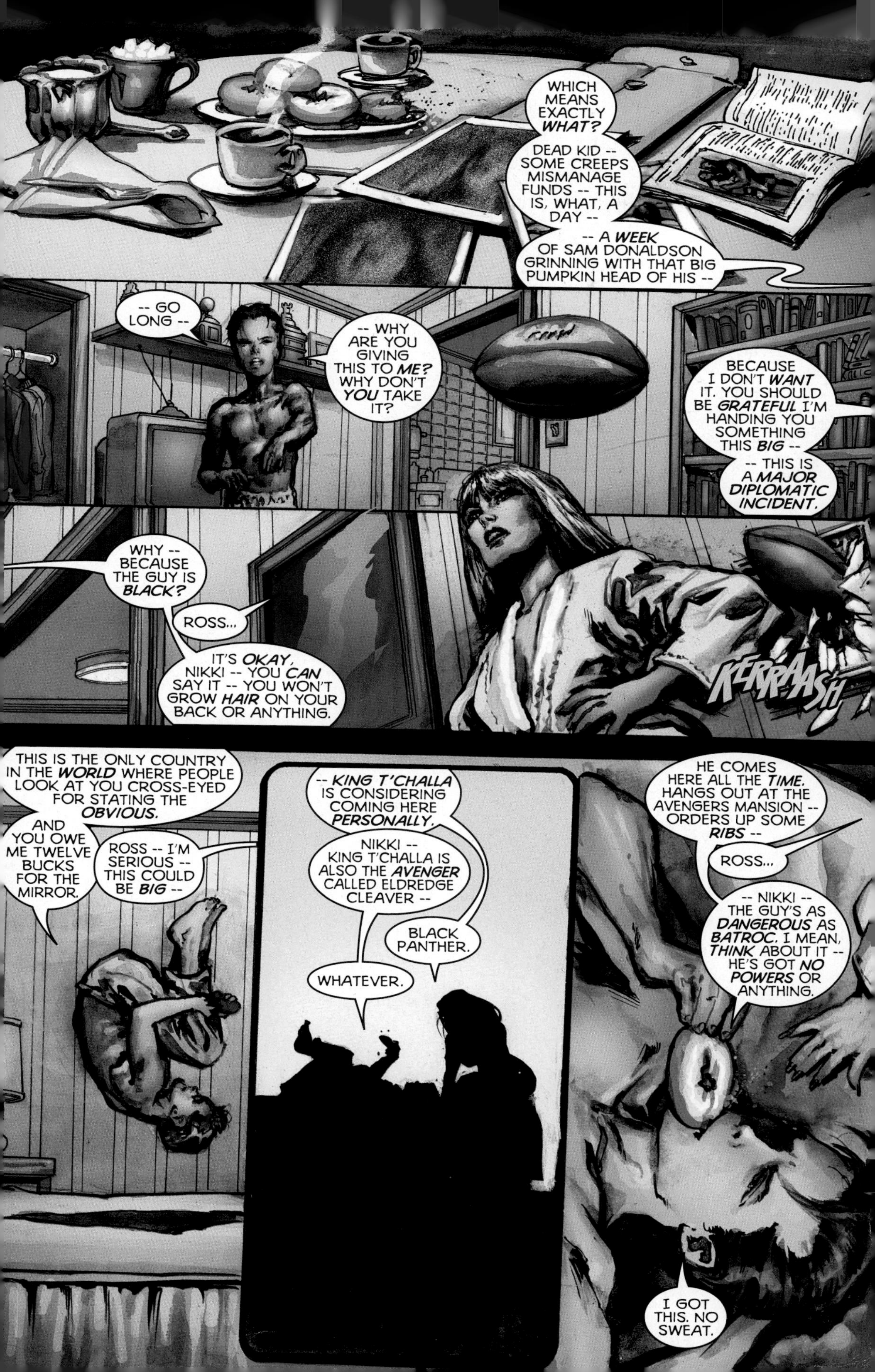

WHICH MEANS EXACTLY *WHAT?*
DEAD KID -- SOME CREEPS MISMANAGE FUNDS -- THIS IS, WHAT, A DAY --
-- A *WEEK* OF SAM DONALDSON GRINNING WITH THAT BIG PUMPKIN HEAD OF HIS --
-- GO LONG --
-- WHY ARE YOU GIVING THIS TO *ME?* WHY DON'T *YOU* TAKE IT?
BECAUSE I DON'T *WANT* IT. YOU SHOULD BE *GRATEFUL* I'M HANDING YOU SOMETHING THIS *BIG* --
-- THIS IS A *MAJOR DIPLOMATIC INCIDENT.*
WHY -- BECAUSE THE GUY IS *BLACK?*
ROSS...
IT'S *OKAY,* NIKKI -- YOU *CAN* SAY IT -- YOU WON'T GROW *HAIR* ON YOUR BACK OR ANYTHING.
KERRAASH
THIS IS THE ONLY COUNTRY IN THE *WORLD* WHERE PEOPLE LOOK AT YOU CROSS-EYED FOR STATING THE *OBVIOUS.*
AND YOU OWE ME TWELVE BUCKS FOR THE MIRROR.
ROSS -- I'M SERIOUS -- THIS COULD BE *BIG* --
-- *KING T'CHALLA* IS CONSIDERING COMING HERE *PERSONALLY.*
NIKKI -- KING T'CHALLA IS ALSO THE *AVENGER* CALLED ELDREDGE CLEAVER --
BLACK PANTHER.
WHATEVER.
HE COMES HERE ALL THE *TIME.* HANGS OUT AT THE AVENGERS MANSION -- ORDERS UP SOME *RIBS* --
ROSS...
-- NIKKI -- THE GUY'S AS *DANGEROUS* AS *BATROC.* I MEAN, *THINK* ABOUT IT -- HE'S GOT *NO POWERS* OR ANYTHING.
I GOT THIS. NO SWEAT.

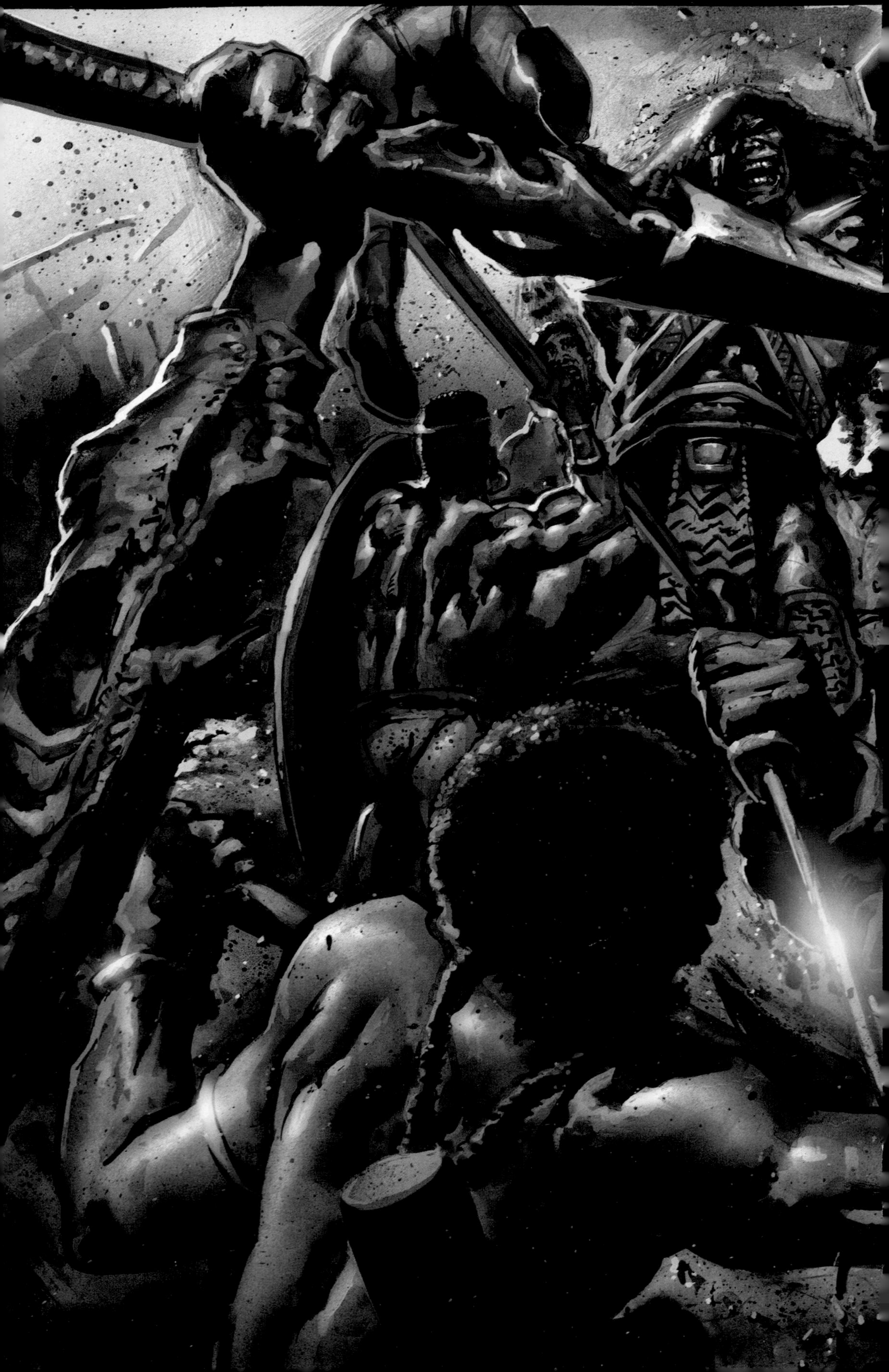

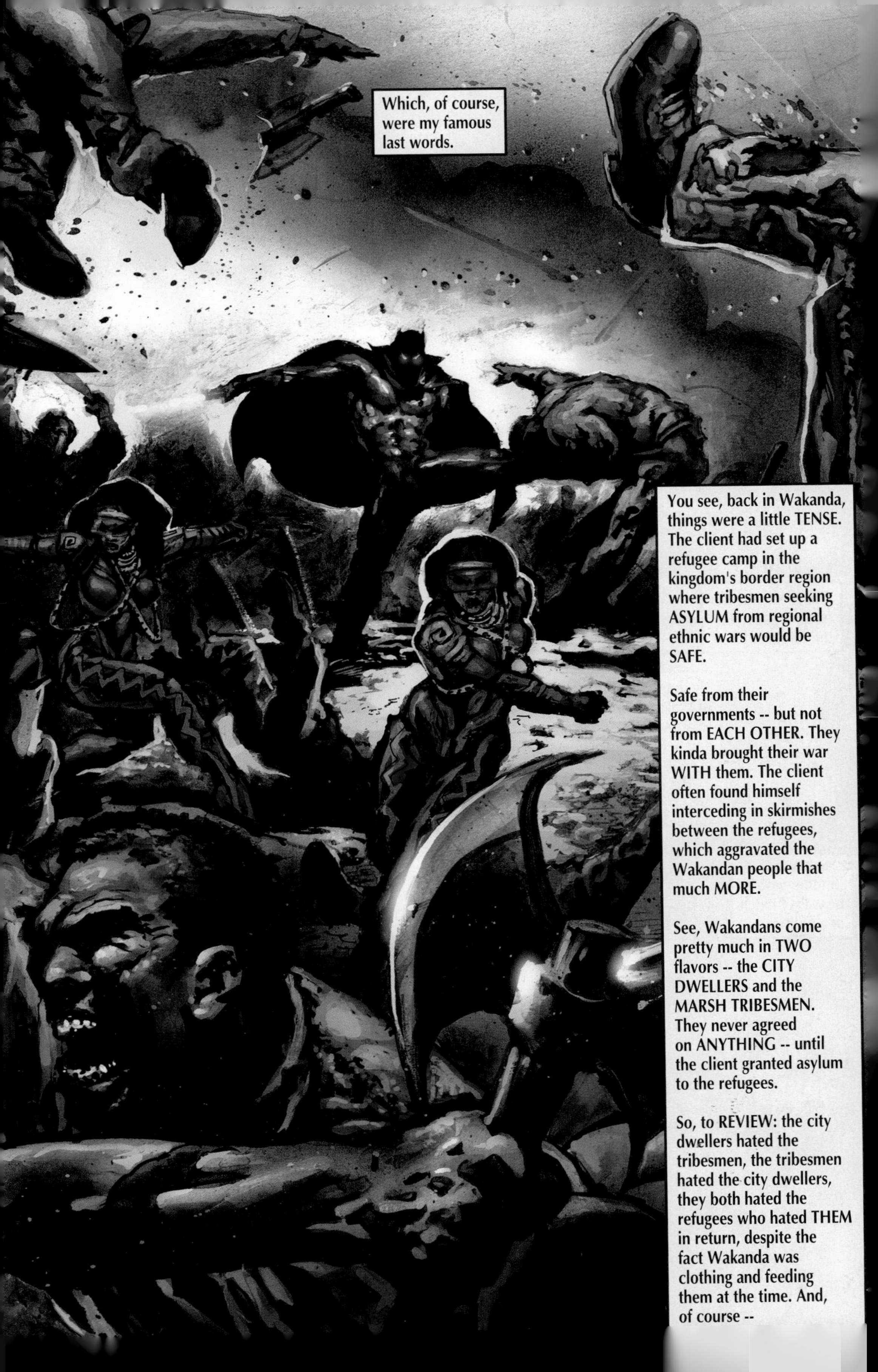
Which, of course, were my famous last words.
You see, back in Wakanda, things were a little TENSE. The client had set up a refugee camp in the kingdom's border region where tribesmen seeking ASYLUM from regional ethnic wars would be SAFE.
Safe from their governments -- but not from EACH OTHER. They kinda brought their war WITH them. The client often found himself interceding in skirmishes between the refugees, which aggravated the Wakandan people that much MORE.
See, Wakandans come pretty much in TWO flavors -- the CITY DWELLERS and the MARSH TRIBESMEN. They never agreed on ANYTHING -- until the client granted asylum to the refugees.
So, to REVIEW: the city dwellers hated the tribesmen, the tribesmen hated the city dwellers, they both hated the refugees who hated THEM in return, despite the fact Wakanda was clothing and feeding them at the time. And, of course --

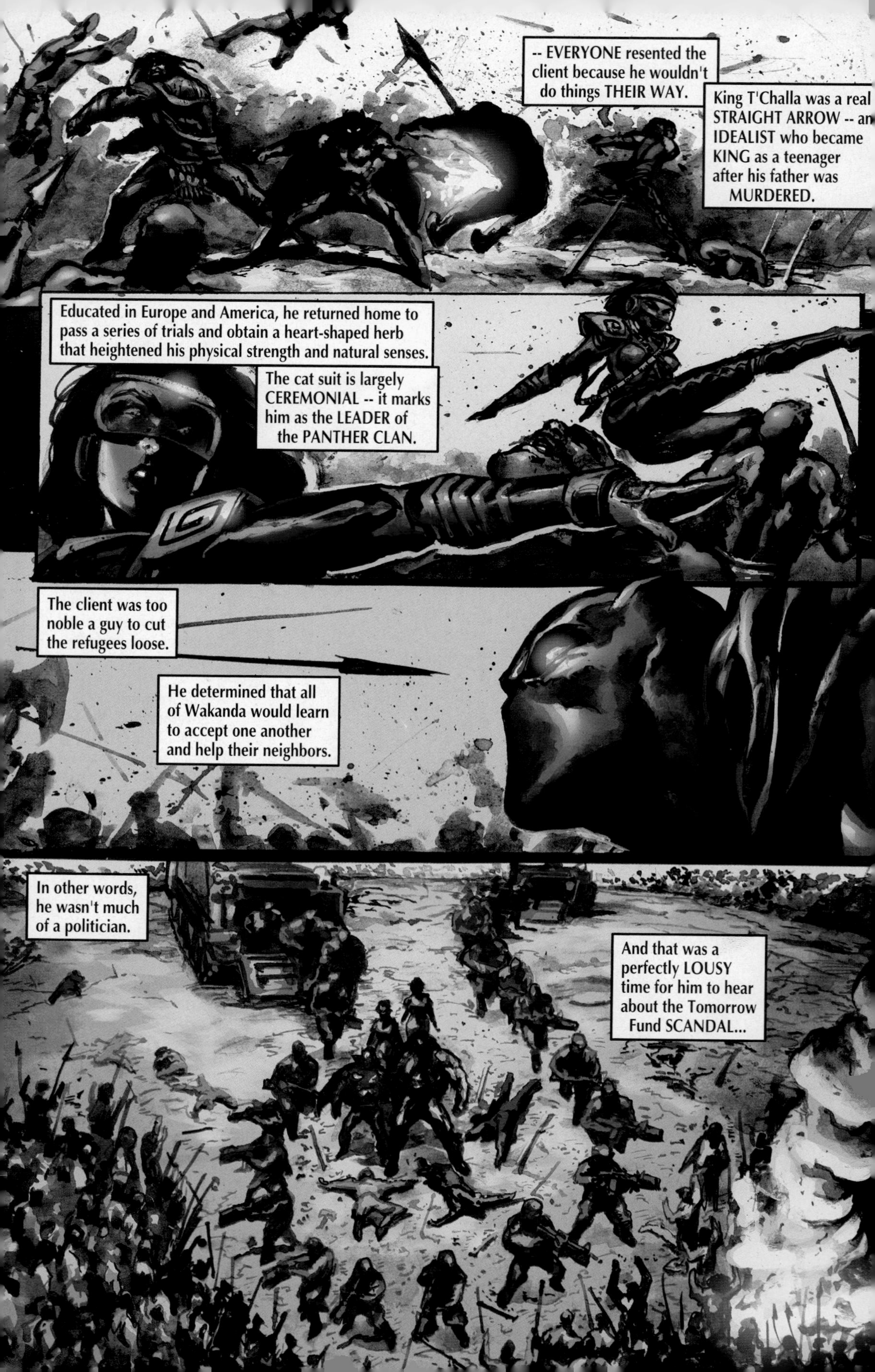
-- EVERYONE resented the client because he wouldn't do things THEIR WAY.
King T'Challa was a real STRAIGHT ARROW -- an IDEALIST who became KING as a teenager after his father was MURDERED.
Educated in Europe and America, he returned home to pass a series of trials and obtain a heart-shaped herb that heightened his physical strength and natural senses.
The cat suit is largely CEREMONIAL -- it marks him as the LEADER of the PANTHER CLAN.
The client was too noble a guy to cut the refugees loose.
He determined that all of Wakanda would learn to accept one another and help their neighbors.
In other words, he wasn't much of a politician.
And that was a perfectly LOUSY time for him to hear about the Tomorrow Fund SCANDAL...

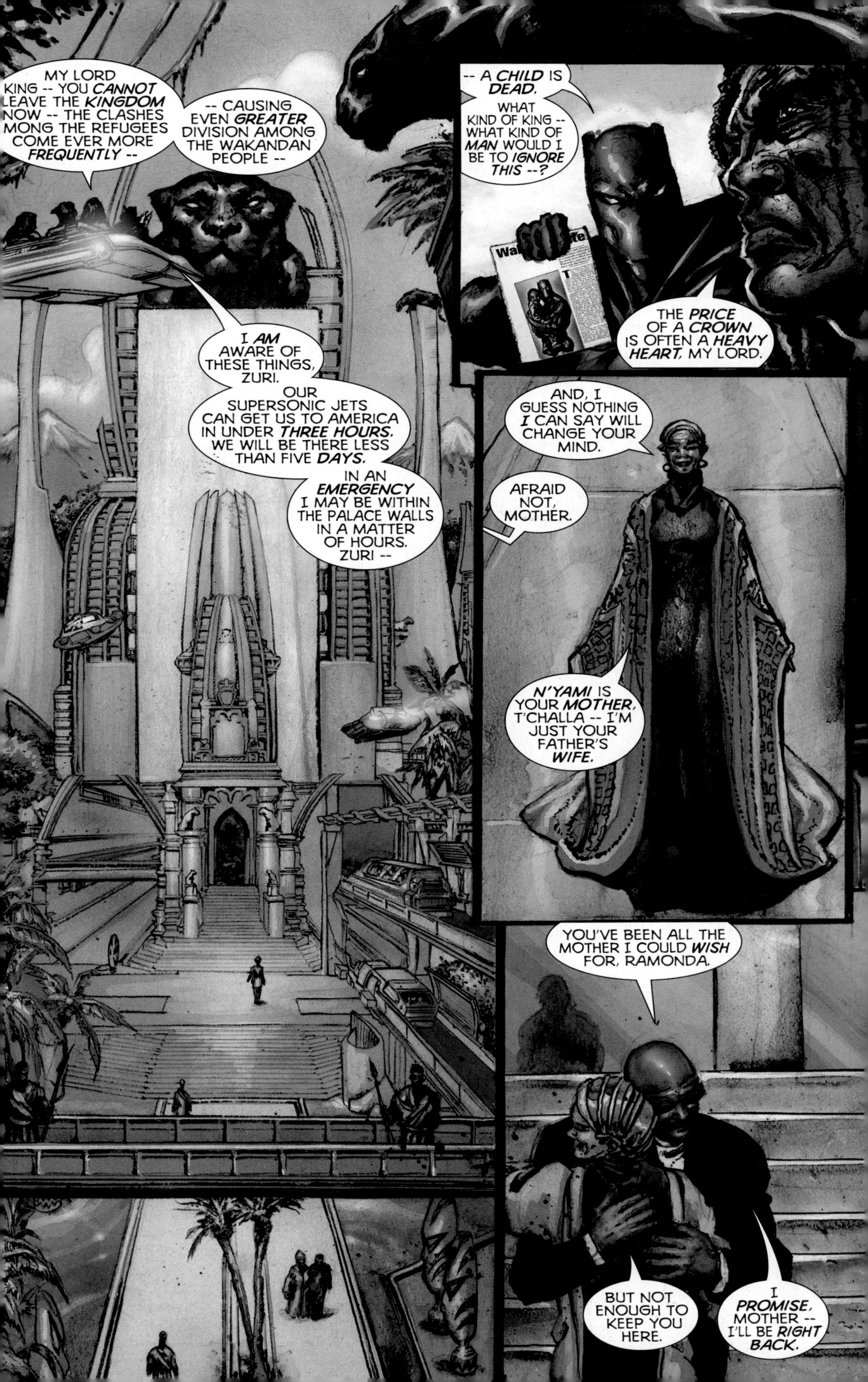
MY LORD KING -- YOU CANNOT LEAVE THE KINGDOM NOW -- THE CLASHES MONG THE REFUGEES COME EVER MORE FREQUENTLY --
-- CAUSING EVEN GREATER DIVISION AMONG THE WAKANDAN PEOPLE --
I AM AWARE OF THESE THINGS, ZURI.
OUR SUPERSONIC JETS CAN GET US TO AMERICA IN UNDER THREE HOURS. WE WILL BE THERE LESS THAN FIVE DAYS.
IN AN EMERGENCY I MAY BE WITHIN THE PALACE WALLS IN A MATTER OF HOURS. ZURI --
-- A CHILD IS DEAD.
WHAT KIND OF KING -- WHAT KIND OF MAN WOULD I BE TO IGNORE THIS --?
THE PRICE OF A CROWN IS OFTEN A HEAVY HEART, MY LORD.
AND, I GUESS NOTHING I CAN SAY WILL CHANGE YOUR MIND.
AFRAID NOT, MOTHER.
N'YAMI IS YOUR MOTHER, T'CHALLA -- I'M JUST YOUR FATHER'S WIFE.
YOU'VE BEEN ALL THE MOTHER I COULD WISH FOR, RAMONDA.
BUT NOT ENOUGH TO KEEP YOU HERE.
I PROMISE, MOTHER -- I'LL BE RIGHT BACK.

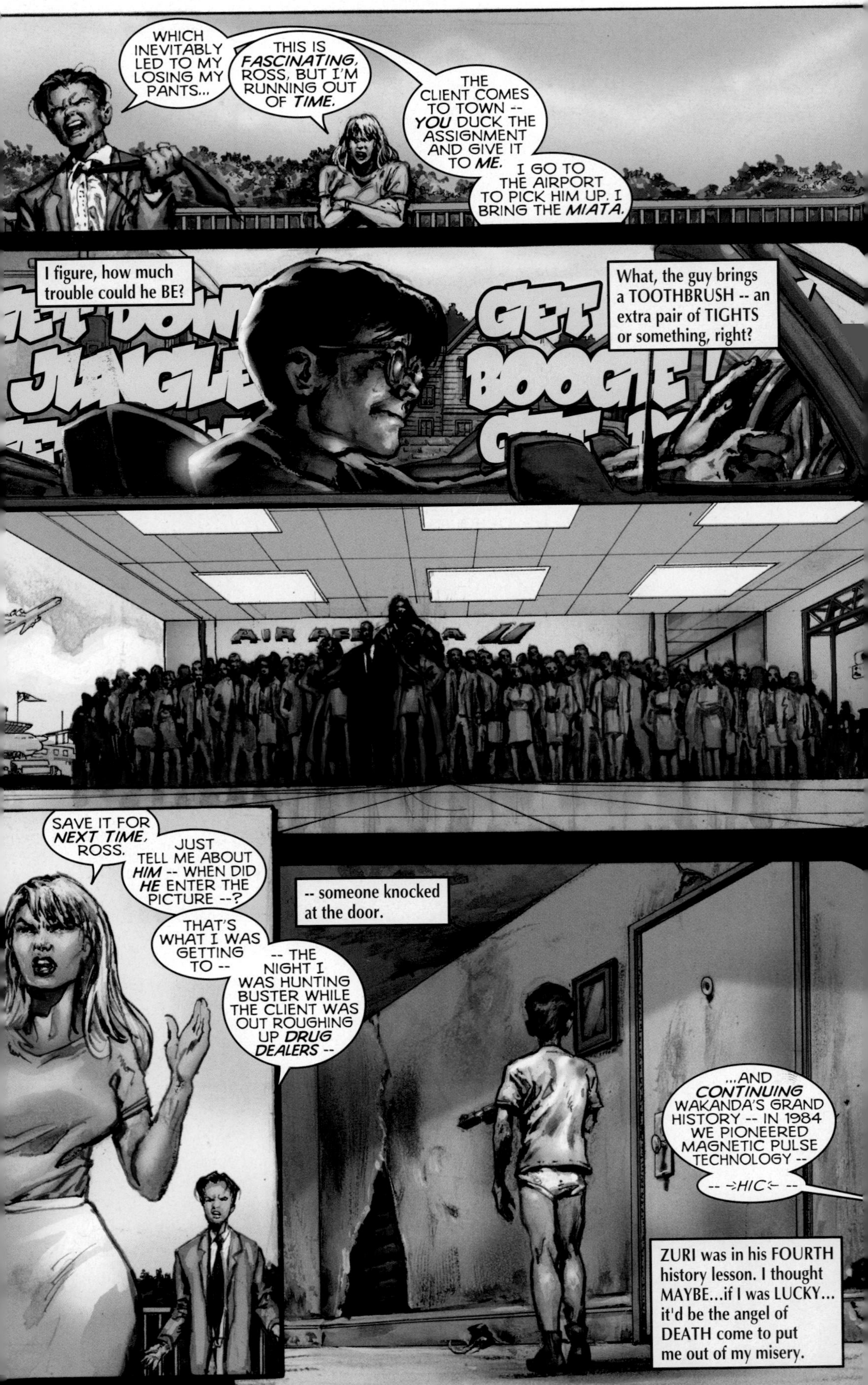

WHICH INEVITABLY LED TO MY LOSING MY PANTS...
THIS IS FASCINATING, ROSS, BUT I'M RUNNING OUT OF TIME.
THE CLIENT COMES TO TOWN -- YOU DUCK THE ASSIGNMENT AND GIVE IT TO ME.
I GO TO THE AIRPORT TO PICK HIM UP. I BRING THE MIATA.
I figure, how much trouble could he BE?
JUNGLE
GET
BOOGIE!
What, the guy brings a TOOTHBRUSH -- an extra pair of TIGHTS or something, right?
SAVE IT FOR NEXT TIME, ROSS.
JUST TELL ME ABOUT HIM -- WHEN DID HE ENTER THE PICTURE --?
THAT'S WHAT I WAS GETTING TO --
-- THE NIGHT I WAS HUNTING BUSTER WHILE THE CLIENT WAS OUT ROUGHING UP DRUG DEALERS --
-- someone knocked at the door.
...AND CONTINUING WAKANDA'S GRAND HISTORY -- IN 1984 WE PIONEERED MAGNETIC PULSE TECHNOLOGY --
-- ->HIC<- --
ZURI was in his FOURTH history lesson. I thought MAYBE...if I was LUCKY... it'd be the angel of DEATH come to put me out of my misery.

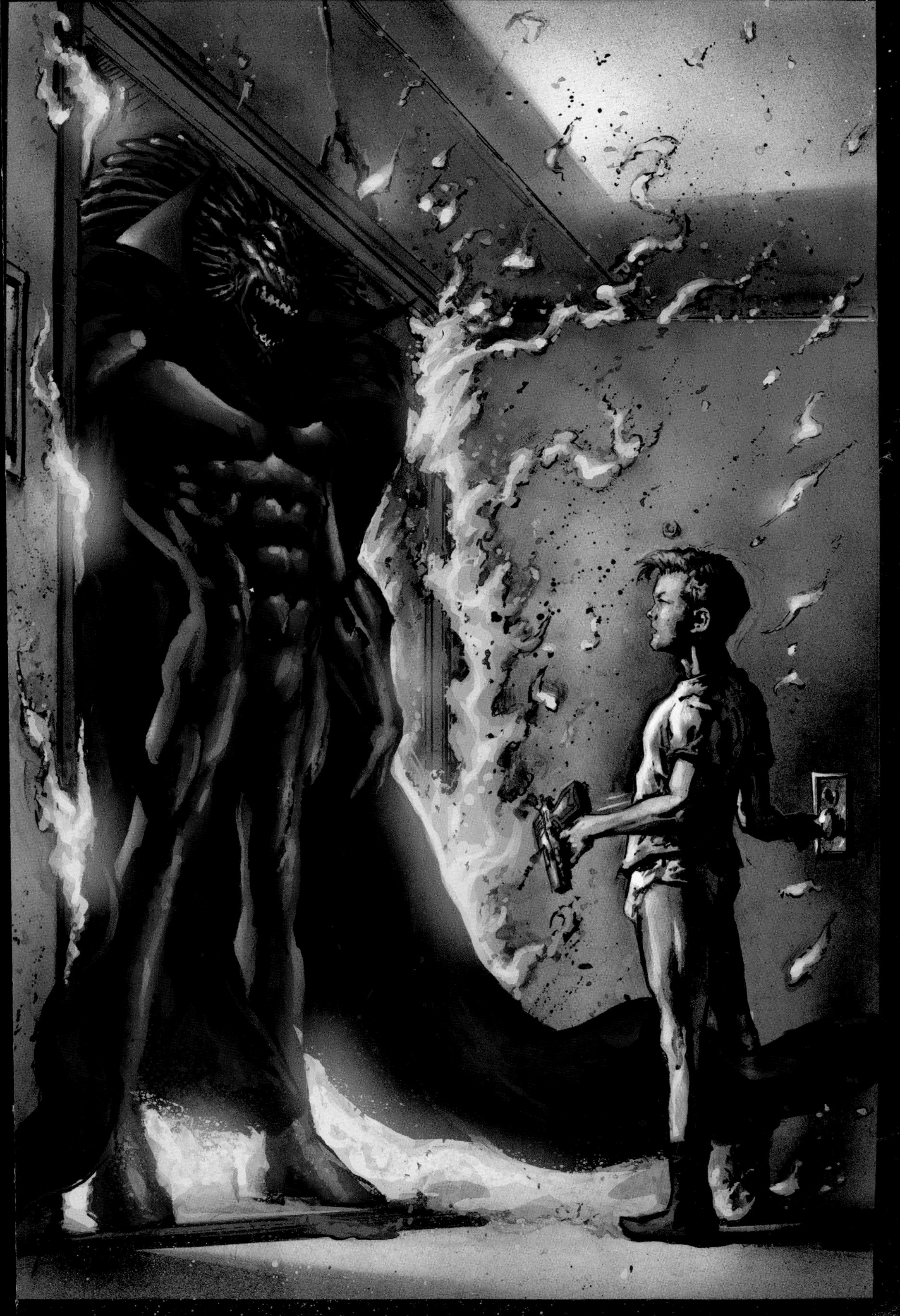

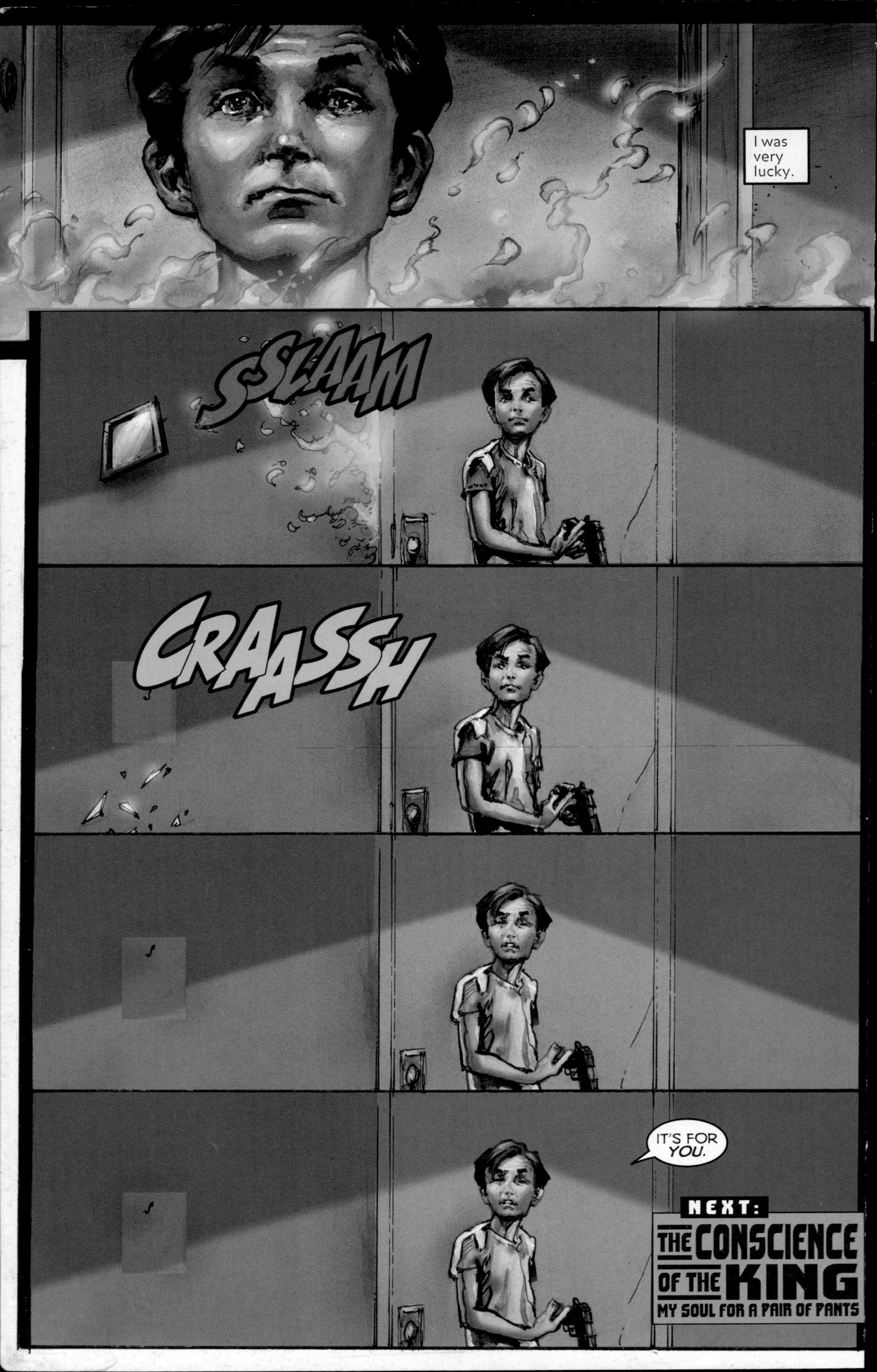
I was very lucky.
SSLAAM
CRAASSH
IT'S FOR YOU.
NEXT:
THE CONSCIENCE OF THE KING
MY SOUL FOR A PAIR OF PANTS

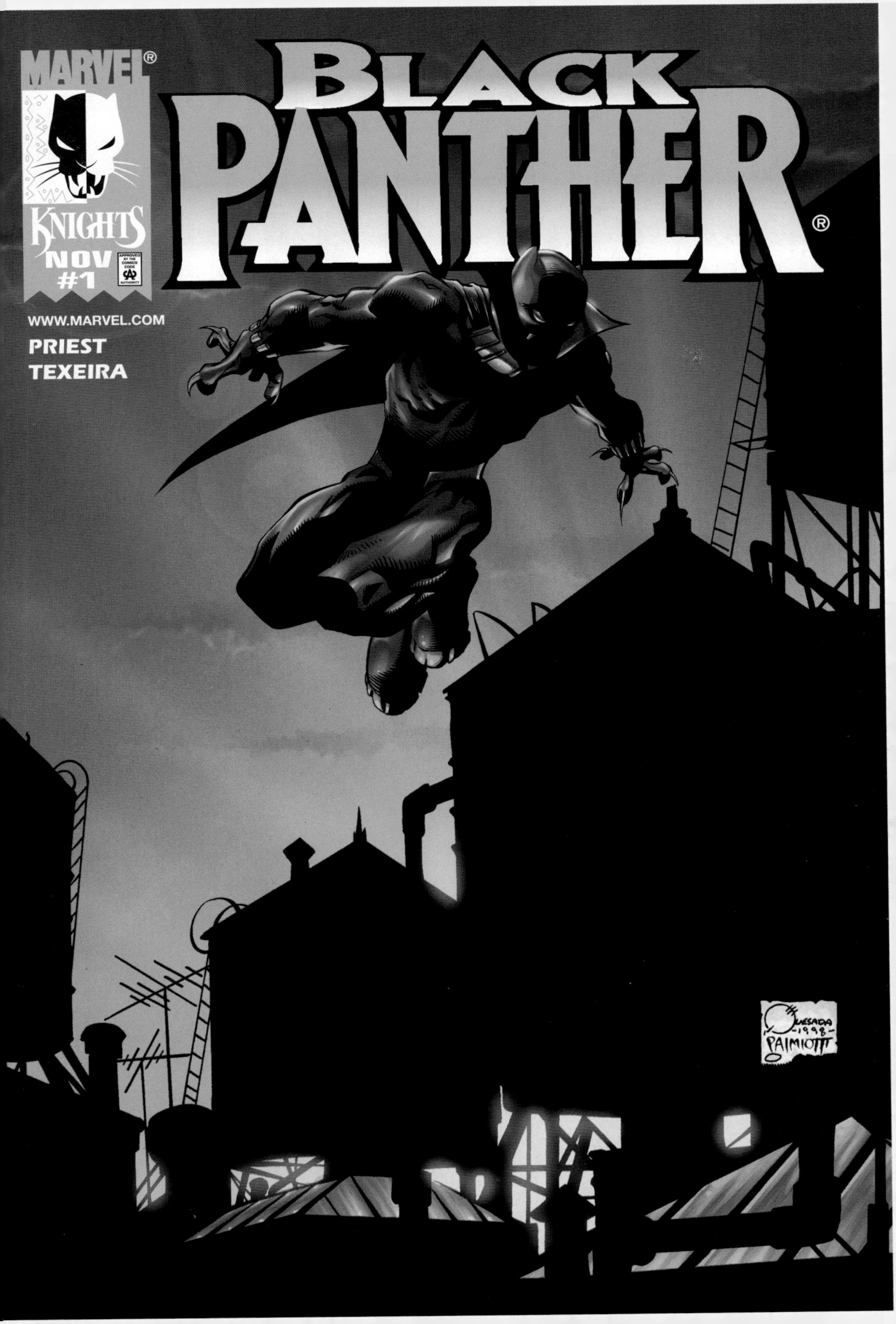
MARVEL®
BLACK PANTHER®
KNIGHTS
NOV
#1
APPROVED BY THE COMICS CODE AUTHORITY
WWW.MARVEL.COM
PRIEST
TEXEIRA

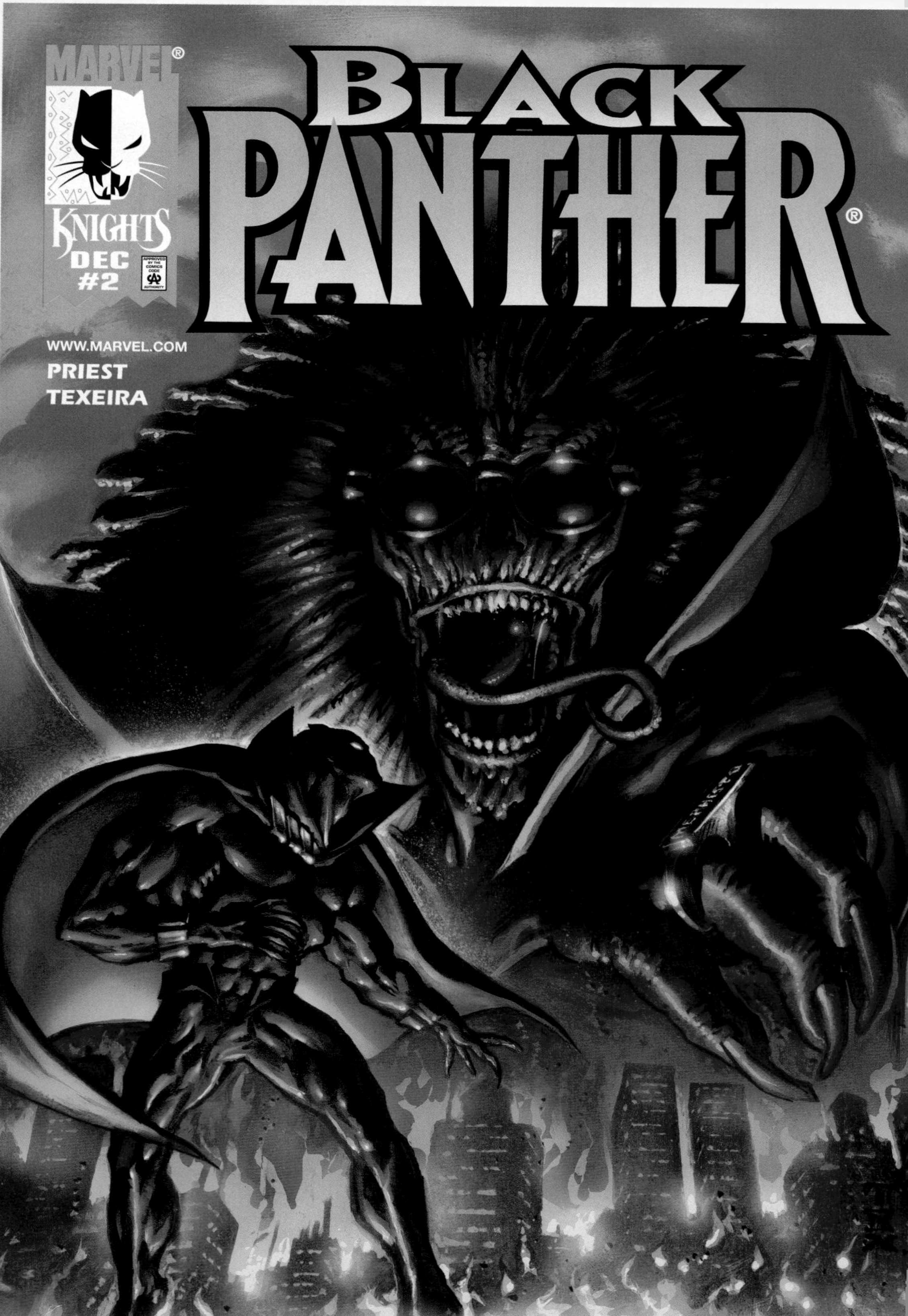

MARVEL®
KNIGHTS
DEC
#2
APPROVED BY THE COMICS CODE AUTHORITY
BLACK PANTHER®
WWW.MARVEL.COM
PRIEST
TEXEIRA

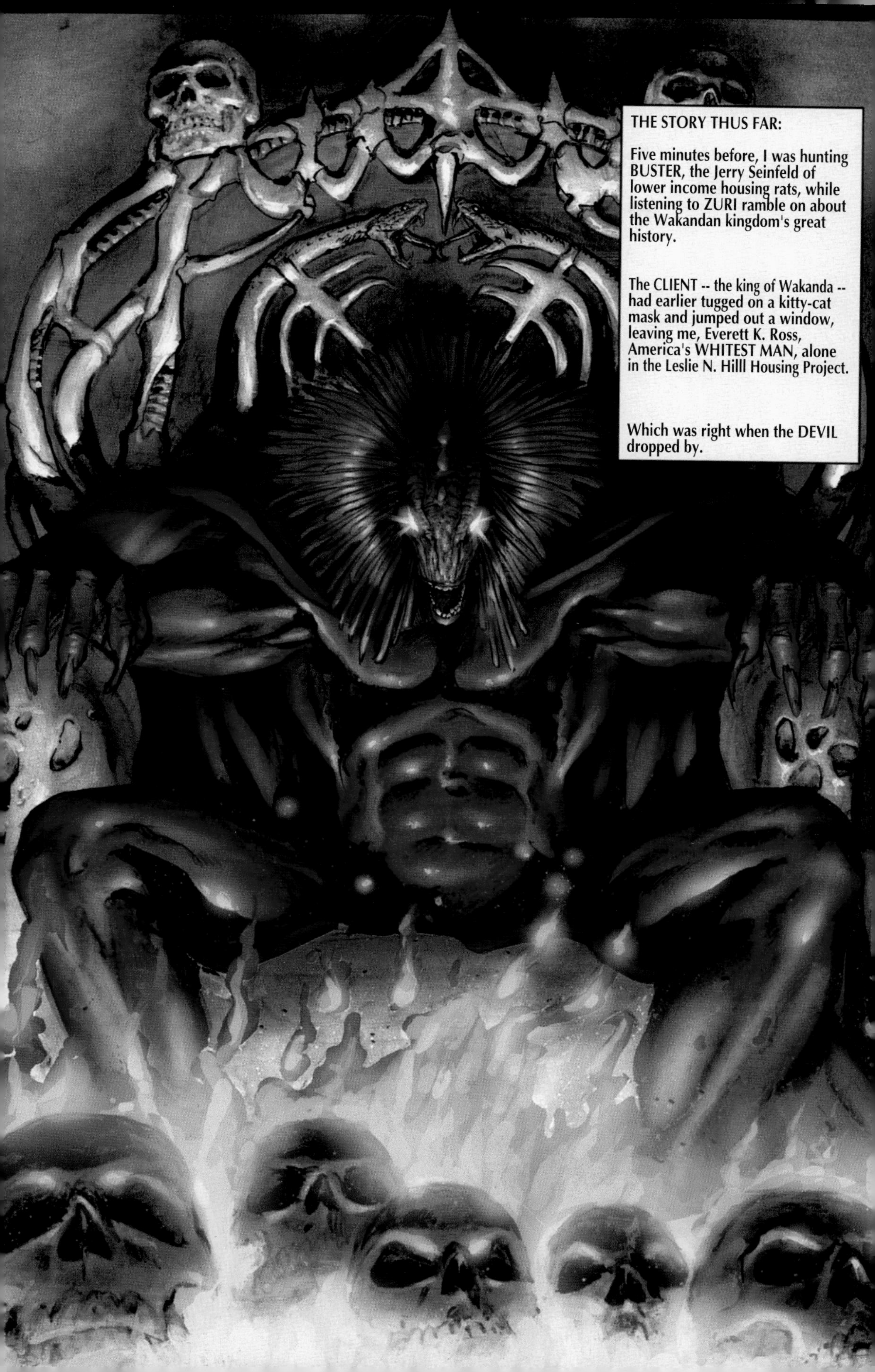
THE STORY THUS FAR:
Five minutes before, I was hunting BUSTER, the Jerry Seinfeld of lower income housing rats, while listening to ZURI ramble on about the Wakandan kingdom's great history.
The CLIENT -- the king of Wakanda -- had earlier tugged on a kitty-cat mask and jumped out a window, leaving me, Everett K. Ross, America's WHITEST MAN, alone in the Leslie N. Hilll Housing Project.
Which was right when the DEVIL dropped by.

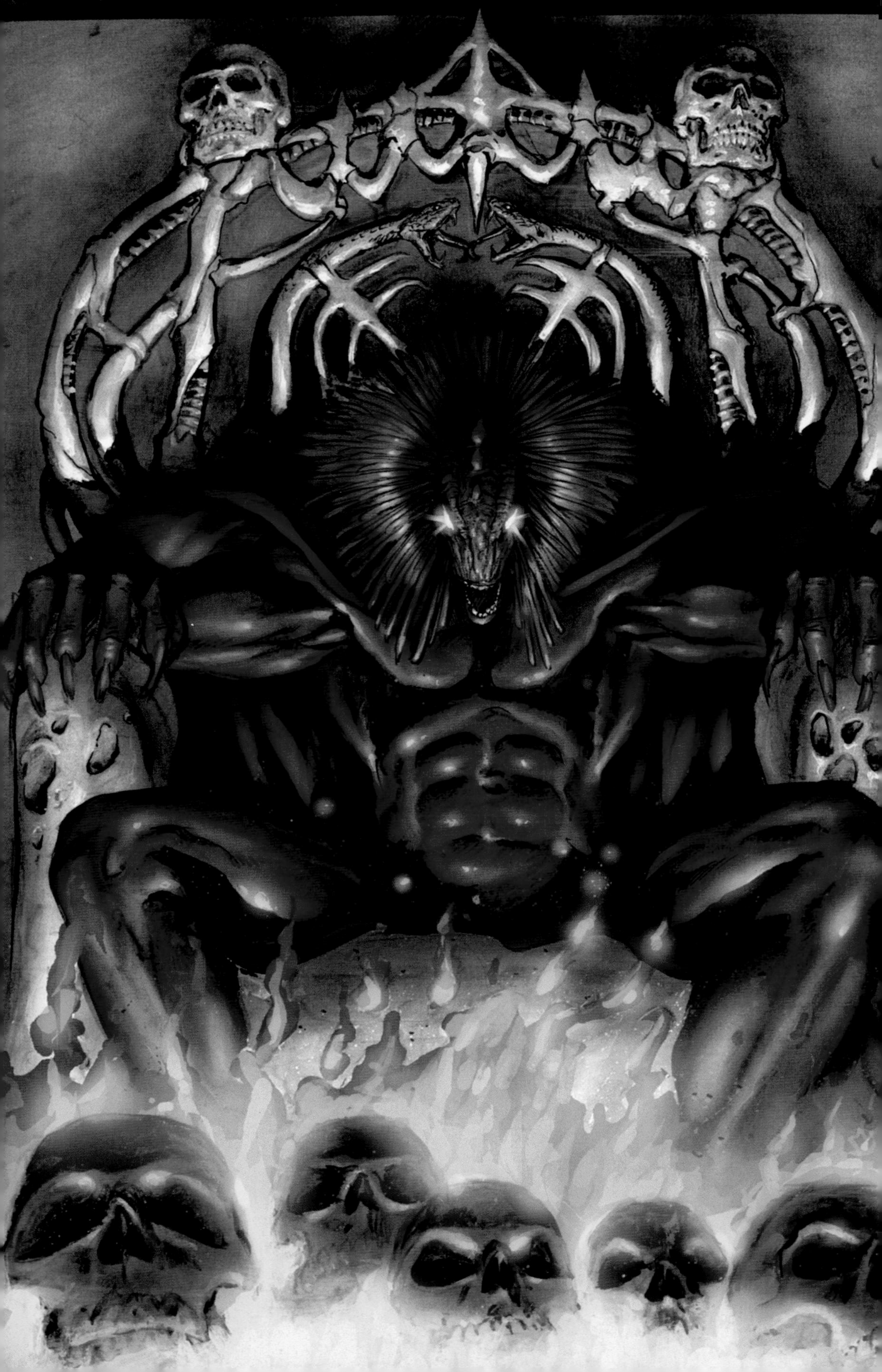

STAN LEE PRESENTS: BLACK PANTHER IN

INVASION

BY CHRISTOPHER PRIEST AND MARK TEXEIRA

STORY AND ART

JOE QUESADA
STORYTELLING

ALITHA MARTINEZ
BACKGROUND ASSISTS

AVALON COLOR
COLORS

RICH S AND COMICRAFT's
SIOBHAN HANNA
LETTERS

NANCI DAKESIAN
MANAGING EDITOR

JOE QUESADA AND
JIMMMY PALMIOTTI
EDITORS

BOB HARRAS
EDITOR IN CHIEF

ll had
pants.

TPPTAPTAPPTPATT

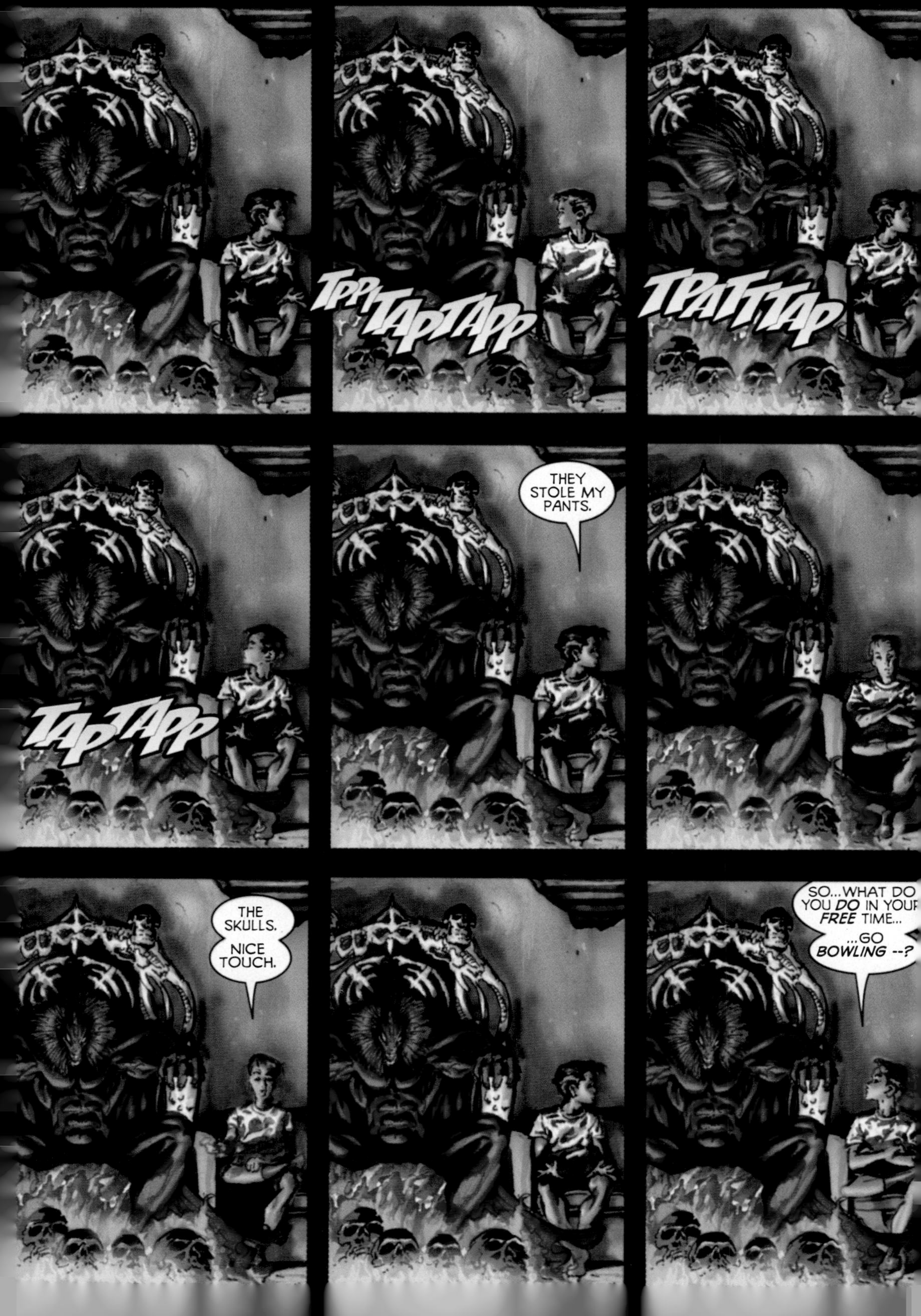
TPPITAPTAPP
TPATTTAP
TAPTAPP
THEY STOLE MY PANTS.
THE SKULLS. NICE TOUCH.
SO...WHAT DO YOU DO IN YOUR FREE TIME... ...GO BOWLING --?

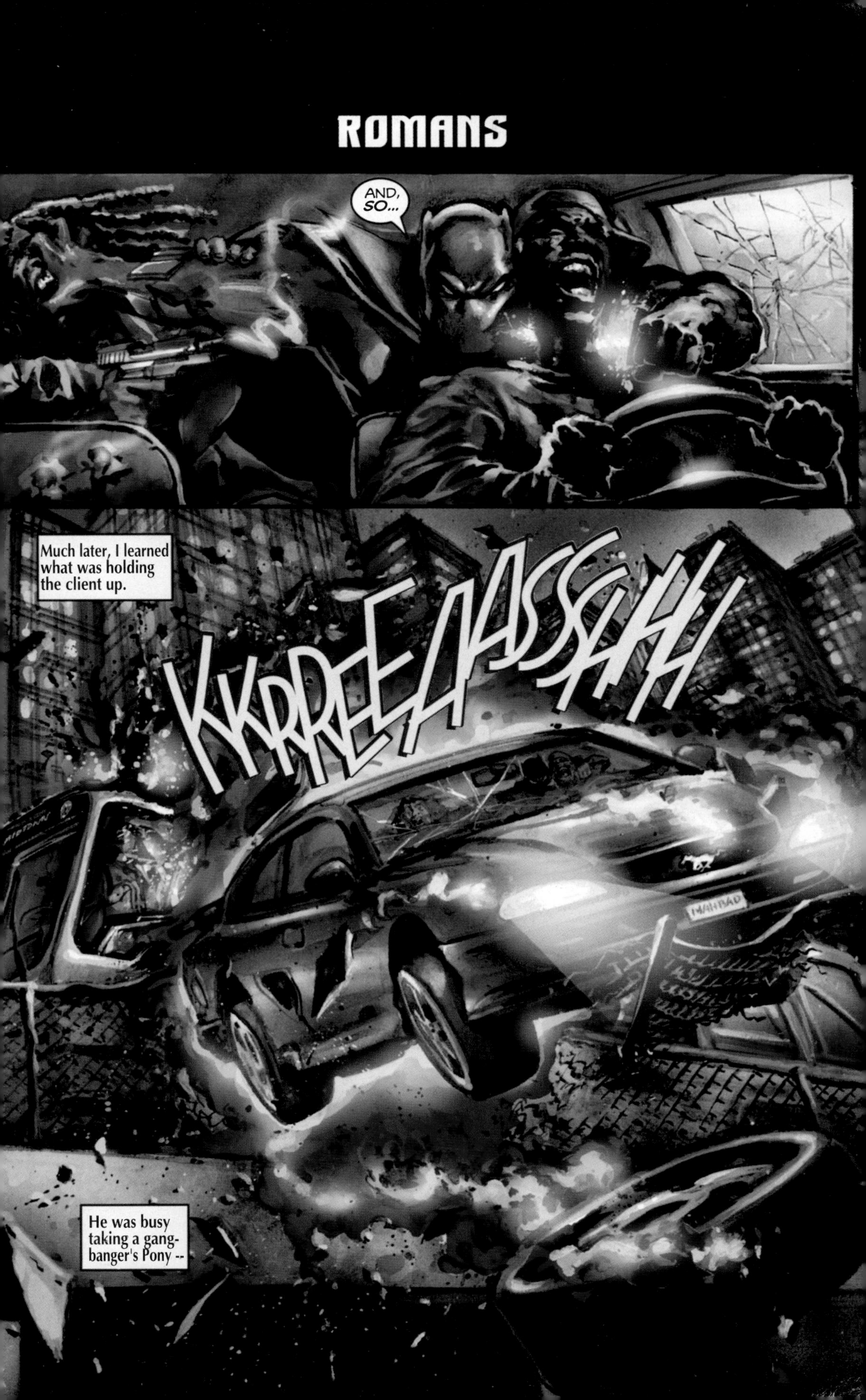
ROMANS
AND, SO...
Much later, I learned what was holding the client up.
KKRREEAASSHH
He was busy taking a gang-banger's Pony --

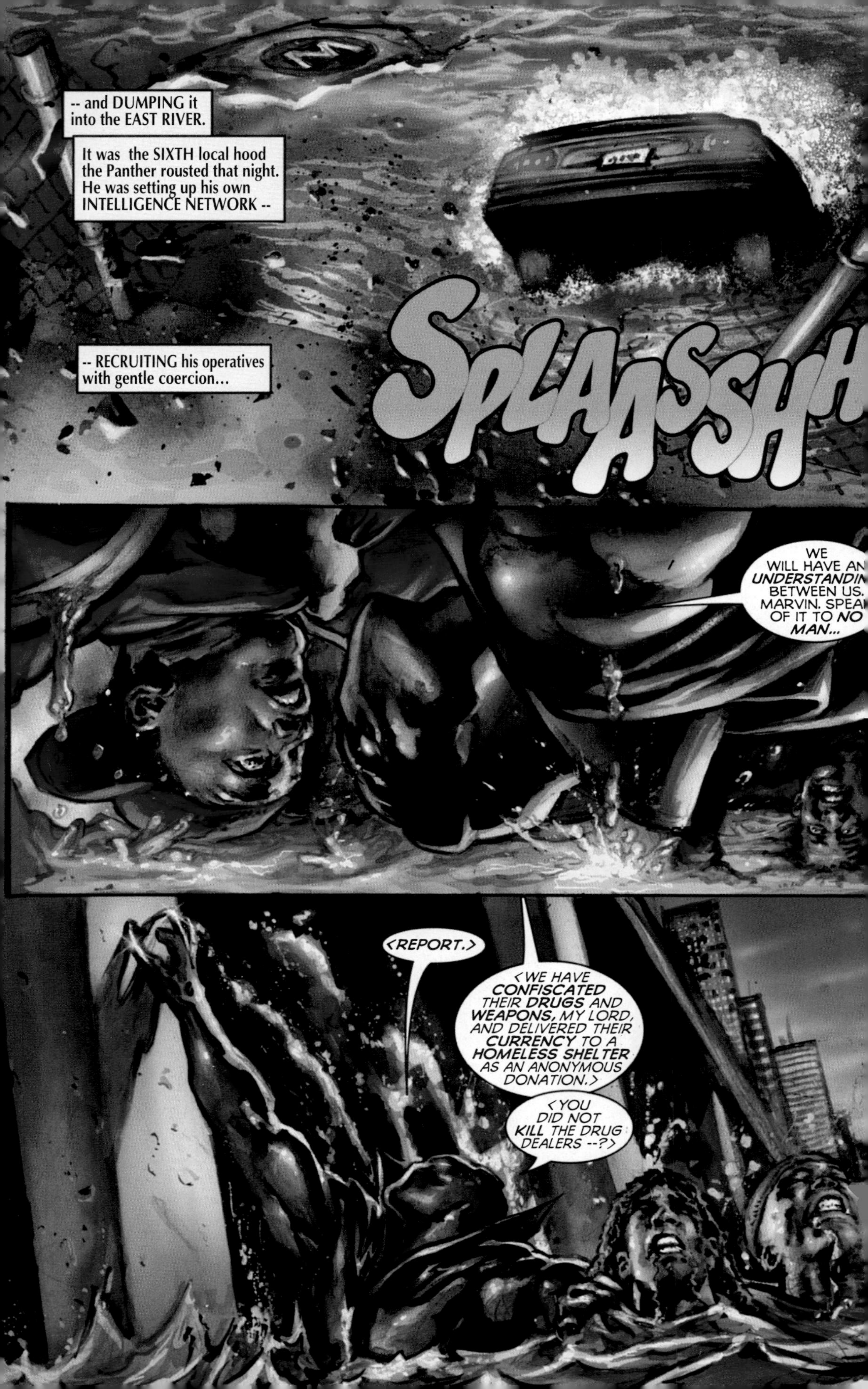
-- and DUMPING it into the EAST RIVER.
It was the SIXTH local hood the Panther rousted that night. He was setting up his own INTELLIGENCE NETWORK --
-- RECRUITING his operatives with gentle coercion...
SPLAASSHH
WE WILL HAVE AN UNDERSTANDIN BETWEEN US. MARVIN. SPEA OF IT TO NO MAN...
<REPORT.>
<WE HAVE CONFISCATED THEIR DRUGS AND WEAPONS, MY LORD, AND DELIVERED THEIR CURRENCY TO A HOMELESS SHELTER AS AN ANONYMOUS DONATION.>
<YOU DID NOT KILL THE DRUG DEALERS --?>

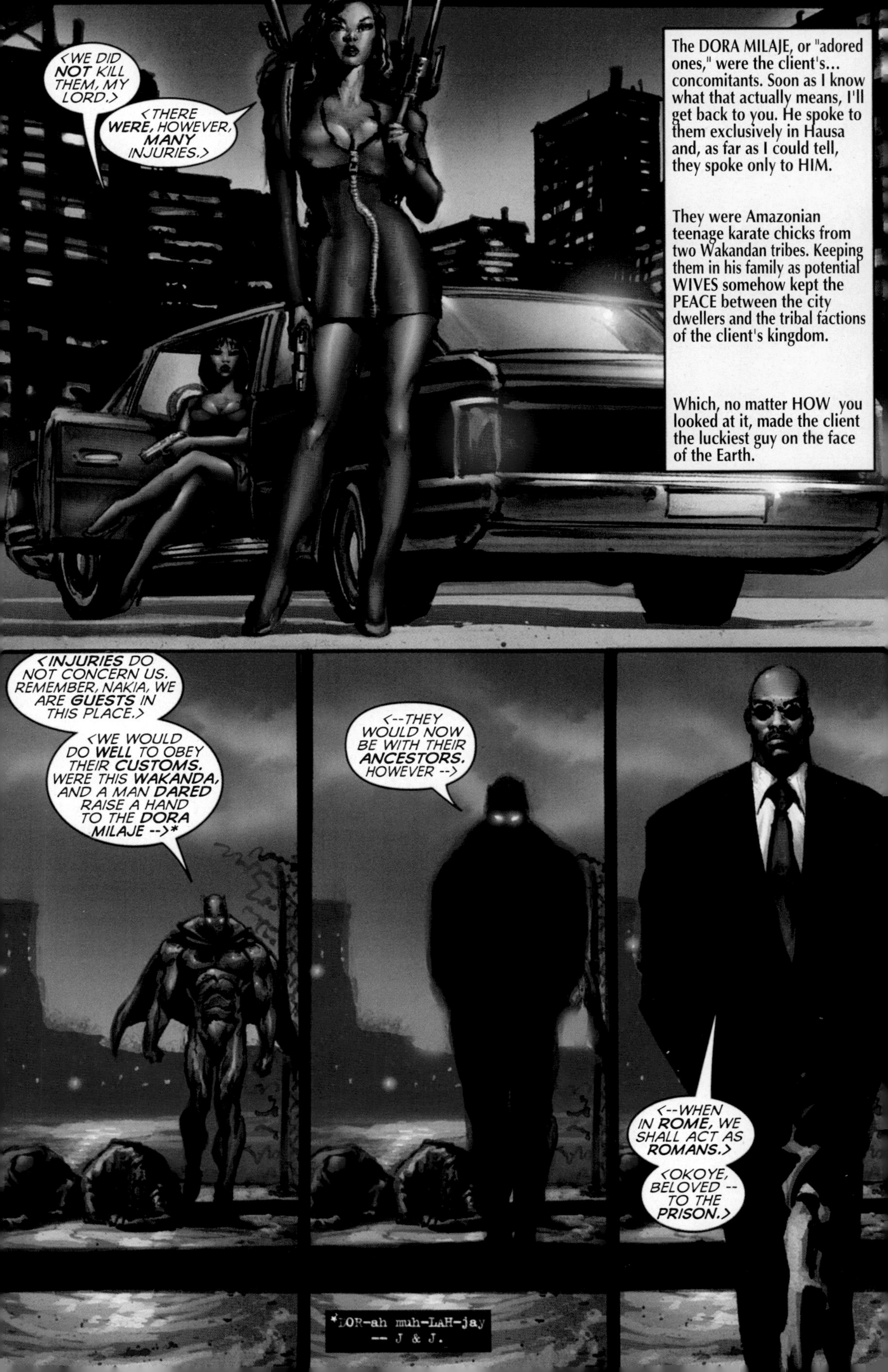

<WE DID NOT KILL THEM, MY LORD.>
<THERE WERE, HOWEVER, MANY INJURIES.>
The DORA MILAJE, or "adored ones," were the client's... concomitants. Soon as I know what that actually means, I'll get back to you. He spoke to them exclusively in Hausa and, as far as I could tell, they spoke only to HIM.
They were Amazonian teenage karate chicks from two Wakandan tribes. Keeping them in his family as potential WIVES somehow kept the PEACE between the city dwellers and the tribal factions of the client's kingdom.
Which, no matter HOW you looked at it, made the client the luckiest guy on the face of the Earth.
<INJURIES DO NOT CONCERN US. REMEMBER, NAKIA, WE ARE GUESTS IN THIS PLACE.>
<WE WOULD DO WELL TO OBEY THEIR CUSTOMS. WERE THIS WAKANDA, AND A MAN DARED RAISE A HAND TO THE DORA MILAJE -->*
<--THEY WOULD NOW BE WITH THEIR ANCESTORS. HOWEVER -->
<--WHEN IN ROME, WE SHALL ACT AS ROMANS.>
<OKOYE, BELOVED -- TO THE PRISON.>
*DOR-ah muh-LAH-jay -- J & J.

NOT TODAY

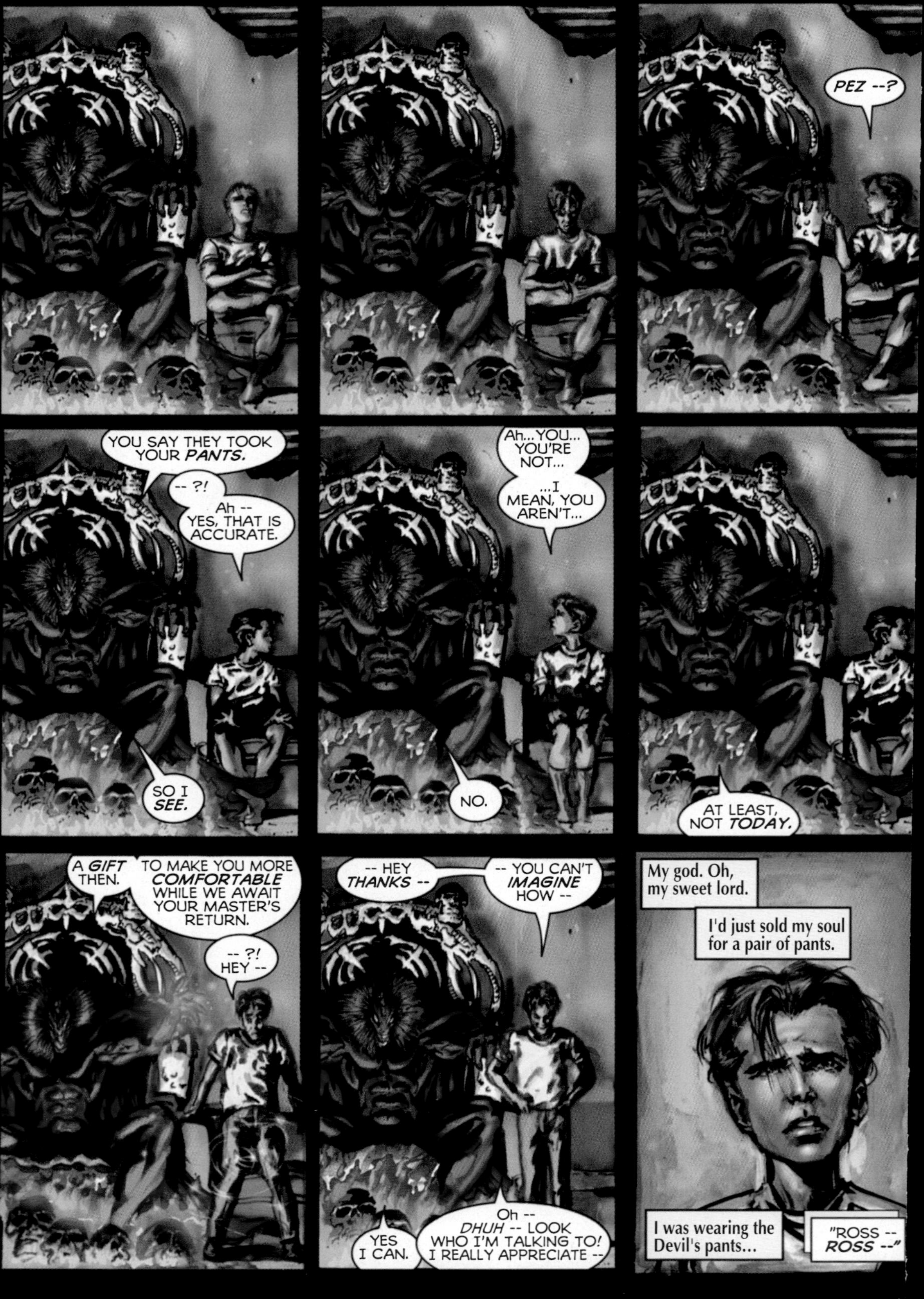

PEZ --?
YOU SAY THEY TOOK YOUR *PANTS.*
-- ?!
Ah -- YES, THAT IS ACCURATE.
SO I *SEE.*
Ah... YOU... YOU'RE NOT...
...I MEAN, YOU AREN'T...
NO.
AT LEAST, NOT *TODAY.*
A *GIFT* THEN.
TO MAKE YOU MORE *COMFORTABLE* WHILE WE AWAIT YOUR MASTER'S RETURN.
-- ?! HEY --
-- HEY *THANKS* --
-- YOU CAN'T *IMAGINE* HOW --
YES I CAN.
Oh -- *DHUH* -- LOOK WHO I'M TALKING TO! I REALLY APPRECIATE --
My god. Oh, my sweet lord.
I'd just sold my soul for a pair of pants.
I was wearing the Devil's pants...
"ROSS -- *ROSS* --"

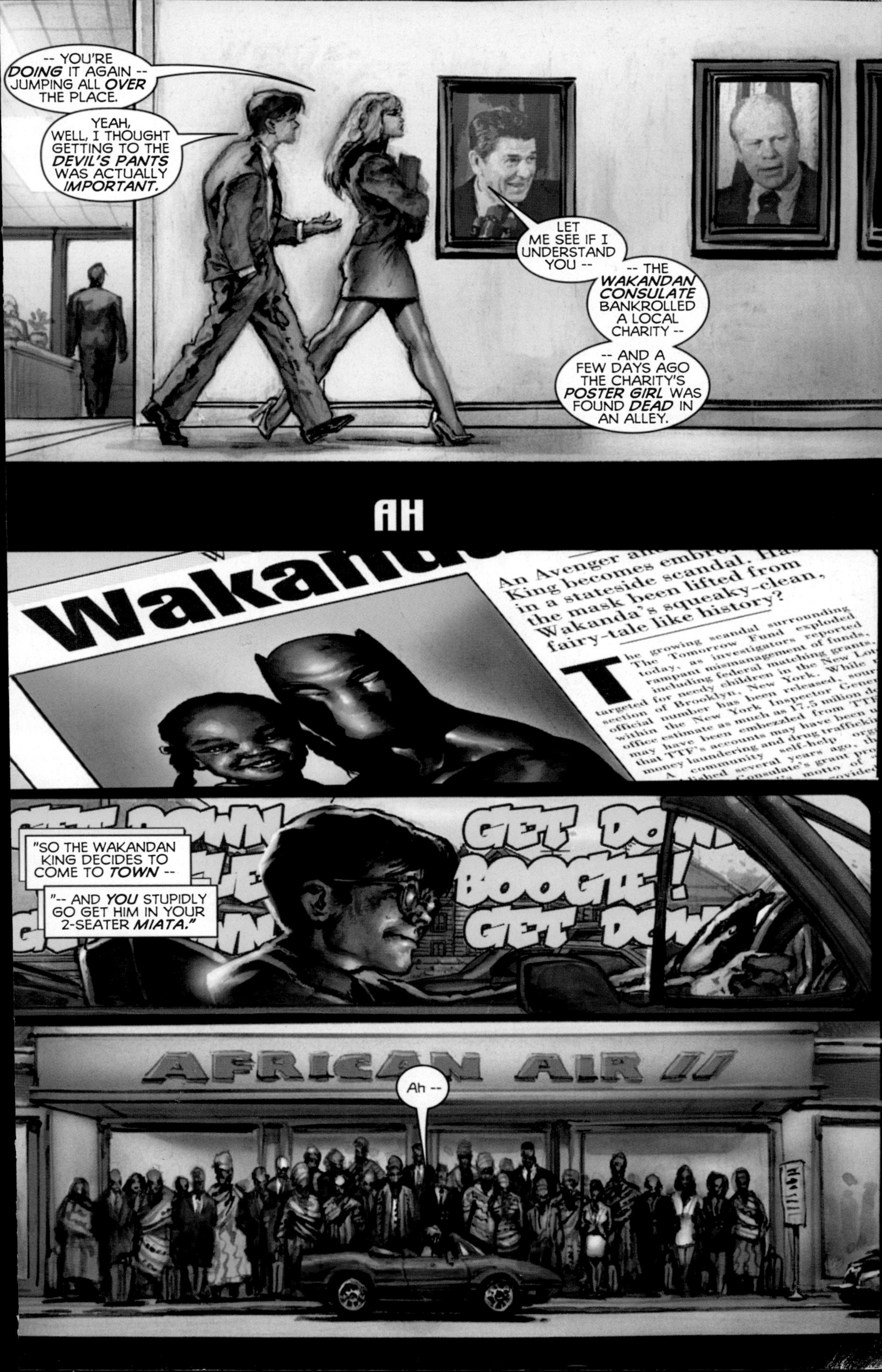

-- YOU'RE DOING IT AGAIN -- JUMPING ALL OVER THE PLACE.
YEAH, WELL, I THOUGHT GETTING TO THE DEVIL'S PANTS WAS ACTUALLY IMPORTANT.
LET ME SEE IF I UNDERSTAND YOU --
-- THE WAKANDAN CONSULATE BANKROLLED A LOCAL CHARITY --
-- AND A FEW DAYS AGO THE CHARITY'S POSTER GIRL WAS FOUND DEAD IN AN ALLEY.
AH
Wakand
in a stateside scandal. Has
the mask been lifted from
Wakanda's squeaky-clean,
fairy-tale like history?
GET DOWN
BOOGIE!
"SO THE WAKANDAN KING DECIDES TO COME TO TOWN --
"-- AND YOU STUPIDLY GO GET HIM IN YOUR 2-SEATER MIATA."
AFRICAN AIR
Ah --

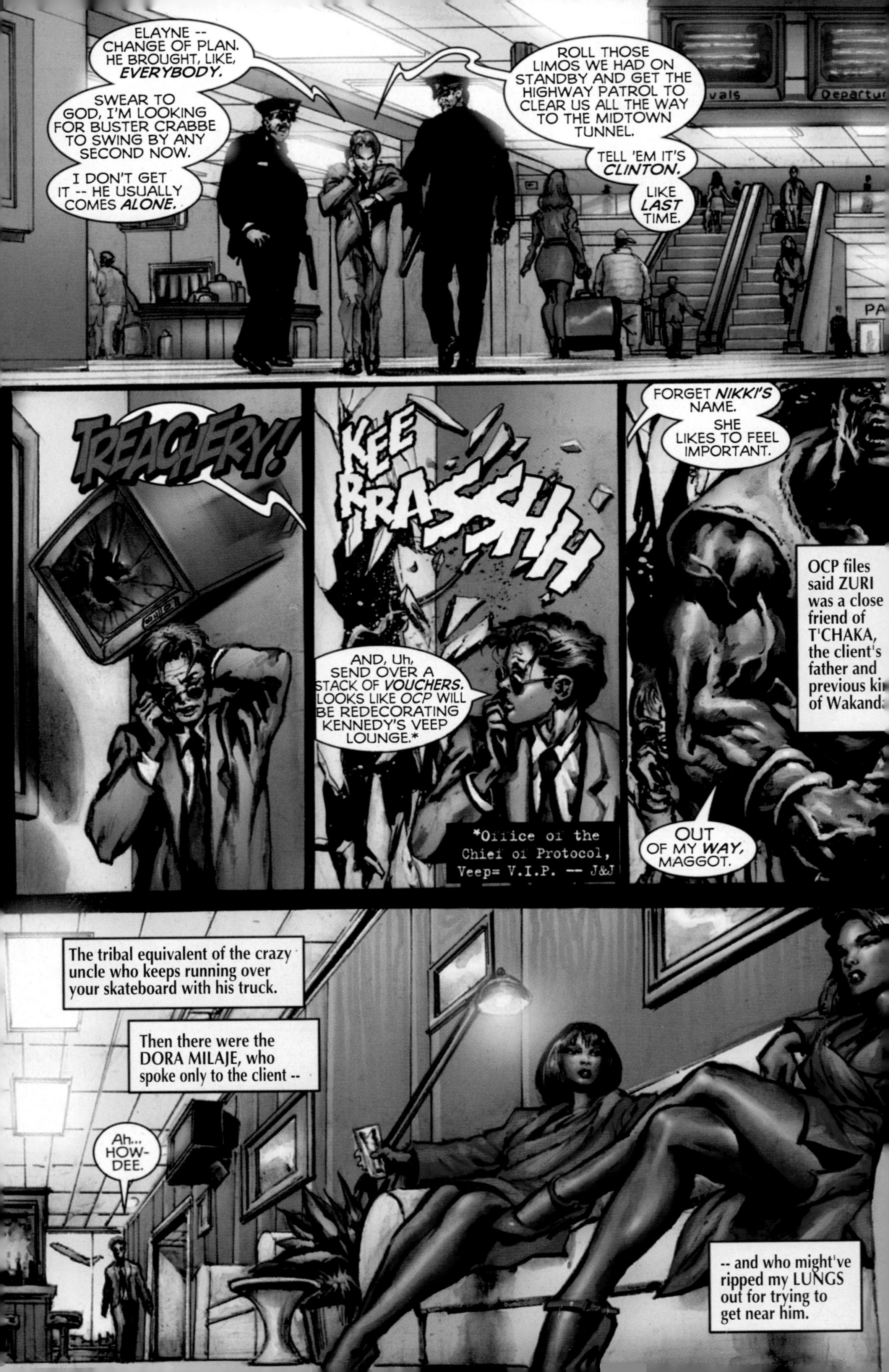
ELAYNE -- CHANGE OF PLAN. HE BROUGHT, LIKE, EVERYBODY.
SWEAR TO GOD, I'M LOOKING FOR BUSTER CRABBE TO SWING BY ANY SECOND NOW.
I DON'T GET IT -- HE USUALLY COMES ALONE.
ROLL THOSE LIMOS WE HAD ON STANDBY AND GET THE HIGHWAY PATROL TO CLEAR US ALL THE WAY TO THE MIDTOWN TUNNEL.
TELL 'EM IT'S CLINTON.
LIKE LAST TIME.
TREACHERY!
KEE RRASSHH
AND, Uh, SEND OVER A STACK OF VOUCHERS. LOOKS LIKE OCP WILL BE REDECORATING KENNEDY'S VEEP LOUNGE.*
*Office of the Chief of Protocol, Veep= V.I.P. -- J&J
FORGET NIKKI'S NAME.
SHE LIKES TO FEEL IMPORTANT.
OCP files said ZURI was a close friend of T'CHAKA, the client's father and previous ki of Wakanda
OUT OF MY WAY, MAGGOT.
The tribal equivalent of the crazy uncle who keeps running over your skateboard with his truck.
Then there were the DORA MILAJE, who spoke only to the client --
Ah... HOW-DEE.
-- and who might've ripped my LUNGS out for trying to get near him.

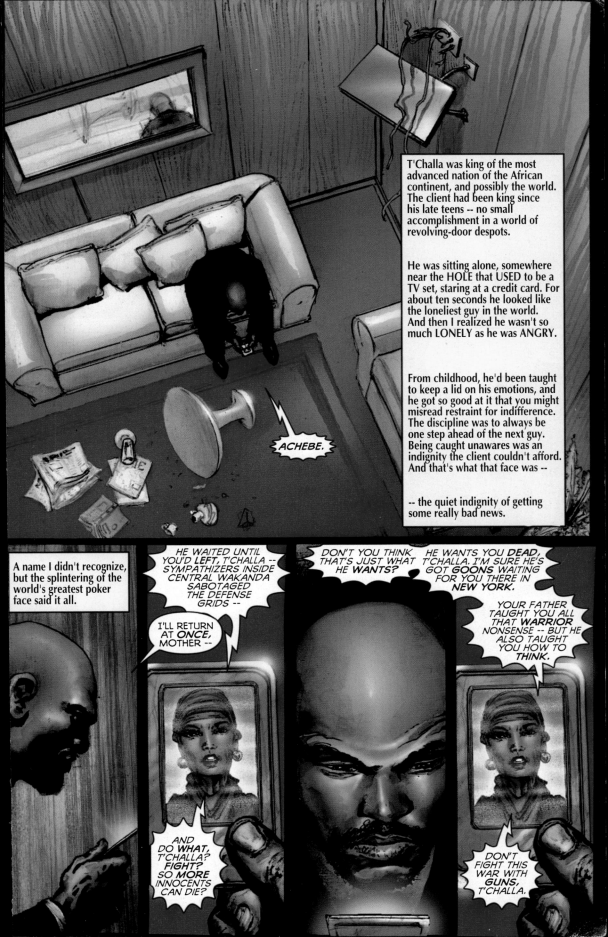

ACHEBE.

T'Challa was king of the most advanced nation of the African continent, and possibly the world. The client had been king since his late teens -- no small accomplishment in a world of revolving-door despots.

He was sitting alone, somewhere near the HOLE that USED to be a TV set, staring at a credit card. For about ten seconds he looked like the loneliest guy in the world. And then I realized he wasn't so much LONELY as he was ANGRY.

From childhood, he'd been taught to keep a lid on his emotions, and he got so good at it that you might misread restraint for indifference. The discipline was to always be one step ahead of the next guy. Being caught unawares was an indignity the client couldn't afford. And that's what that face was --

-- the quiet indignity of getting some really bad news.

A name I didn't recognize, but the splintering of the world's greatest poker face said it all.

HE WAITED UNTIL YOU'D *LEFT*, T'CHALLA -- SYMPATHIZERS INSIDE CENTRAL WAKANDA SABOTAGED THE DEFENSE GRIDS --

I'LL RETURN AT *ONCE*, MOTHER --

AND DO *WHAT*, T'CHALLA? *FIGHT*? SO *MORE* INNOCENTS CAN DIE?

DON'T YOU THINK THAT'S JUST WHAT HE *WANTS*?

HE WANTS YOU *DEAD*, T'CHALLA. I'M SURE HE'S GOT *GOONS* WAITING FOR YOU THERE IN *NEW YORK.*

YOUR FATHER TAUGHT YOU ALL THAT *WARRIOR* NONSENSE -- BUT HE ALSO TAUGHT YOU HOW TO *THINK.*

DON'T FIGHT THIS WAR WITH *GUNS*, T'CHALLA.

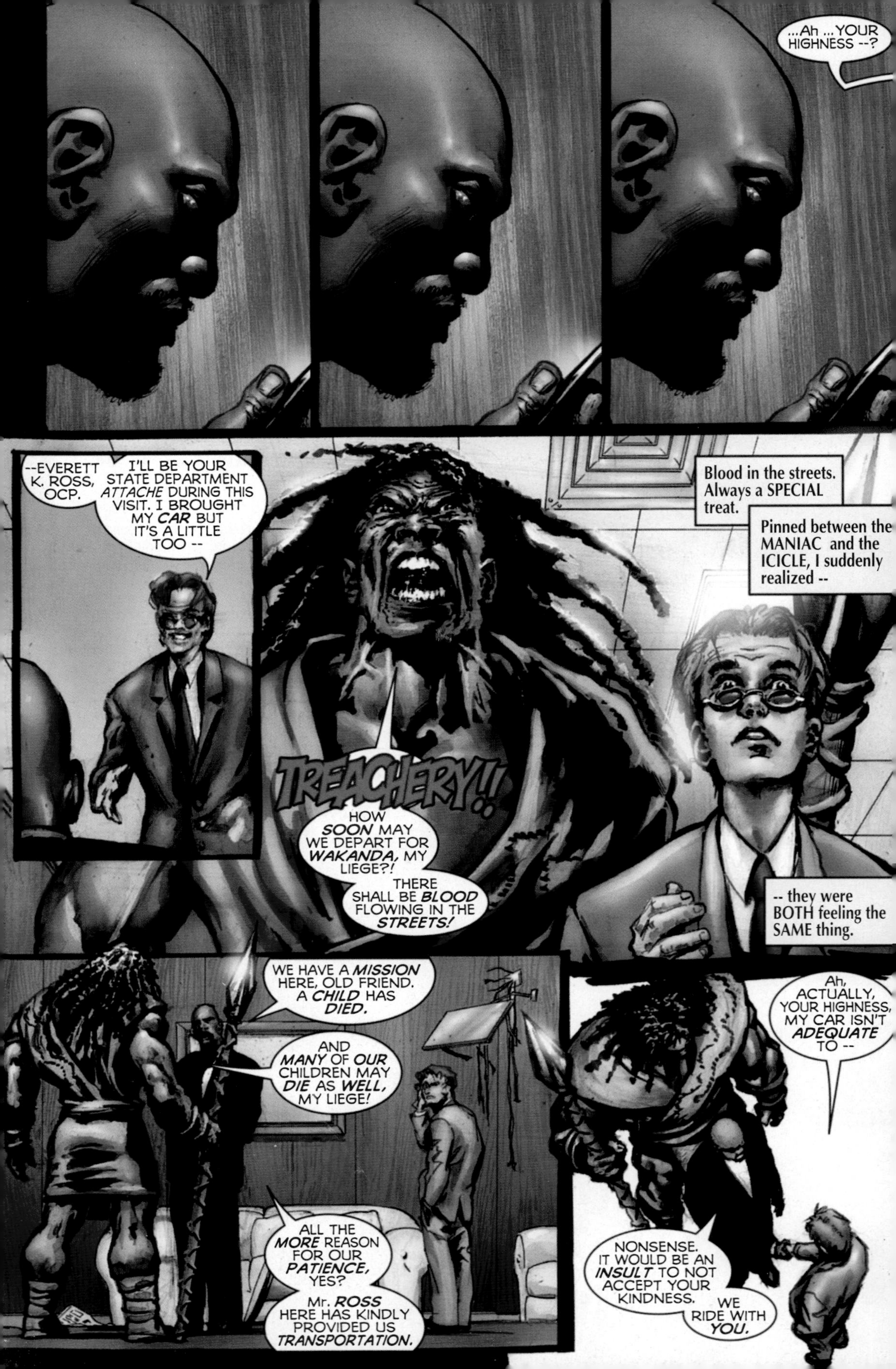
...Ah ...YOUR HIGHNESS --?
--EVERETT K. ROSS, OCP.
I'LL BE YOUR STATE DEPARTMENT ATTACHE DURING THIS VISIT. I BROUGHT MY CAR BUT IT'S A LITTLE TOO --
TREACHERY!!
HOW SOON MAY WE DEPART FOR WAKANDA, MY LIEGE?!
THERE SHALL BE BLOOD FLOWING IN THE STREETS!
Blood in the streets. Always a SPECIAL treat.
Pinned between the MANIAC and the ICICLE, I suddenly realized --
-- they were BOTH feeling the SAME thing.
WE HAVE A MISSION HERE, OLD FRIEND. A CHILD HAS DIED.
AND MANY OF OUR CHILDREN MAY DIE AS WELL, MY LIEGE!
ALL THE MORE REASON FOR OUR PATIENCE, YES?
Mr. ROSS HERE HAS KINDLY PROVIDED US TRANSPORTATION.
Ah, ACTUALLY, YOUR HIGHNESS, MY CAR ISN'T ADEQUATE TO --
NONSENSE. IT WOULD BE AN INSULT TO NOT ACCEPT YOUR KINDNESS.
WE RIDE WITH YOU.

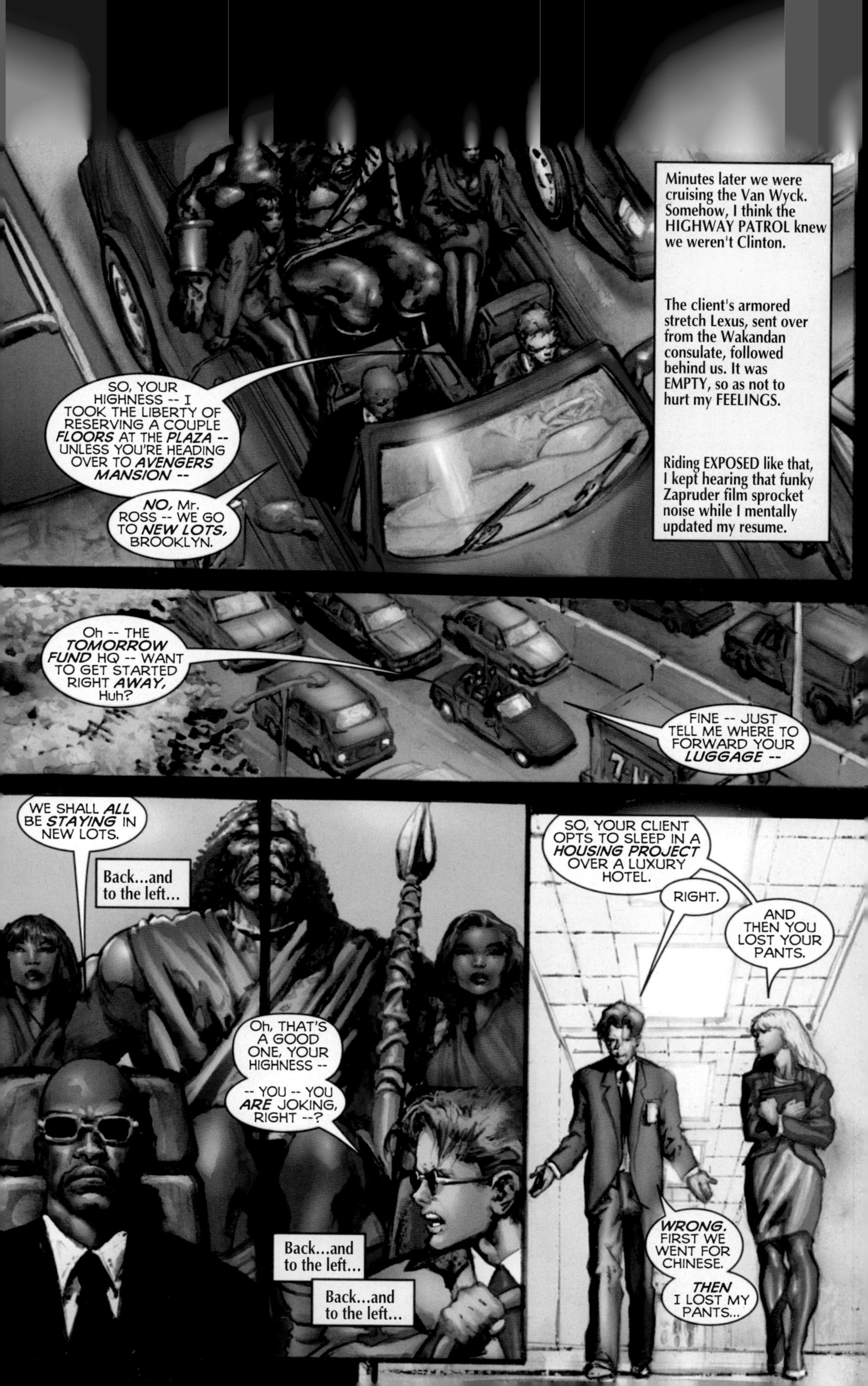

Minutes later we were cruising the Van Wyck. Somehow, I think the HIGHWAY PATROL knew we weren't Clinton.
The client's armored stretch Lexus, sent over from the Wakandan consulate, followed behind us. It was EMPTY, so as not to hurt my FEELINGS.
SO, YOUR HIGHNESS -- I TOOK THE LIBERTY OF RESERVING A COUPLE FLOORS AT THE PLAZA -- UNLESS YOU'RE HEADING OVER TO AVENGERS MANSION --
NO, Mr. ROSS -- WE GO TO NEW LOTS, BROOKLYN.
Riding EXPOSED like that, I kept hearing that funky Zapruder film sprocket noise while I mentally updated my resume.
Oh -- THE TOMORROW FUND HQ -- WANT TO GET STARTED RIGHT AWAY, Huh?
FINE -- JUST TELL ME WHERE TO FORWARD YOUR LUGGAGE --
WE SHALL ALL BE STAYING IN NEW LOTS.
Back...and to the left...
Oh, THAT'S A GOOD ONE, YOUR HIGHNESS --
-- YOU -- YOU ARE JOKING, RIGHT --?
Back...and to the left...
Back...and to the left...
SO, YOUR CLIENT OPTS TO SLEEP IN A HOUSING PROJECT OVER A LUXURY HOTEL.
RIGHT.
AND THEN YOU LOST YOUR PANTS.
WRONG. FIRST WE WENT FOR CHINESE.
THEN I LOST MY PANTS...

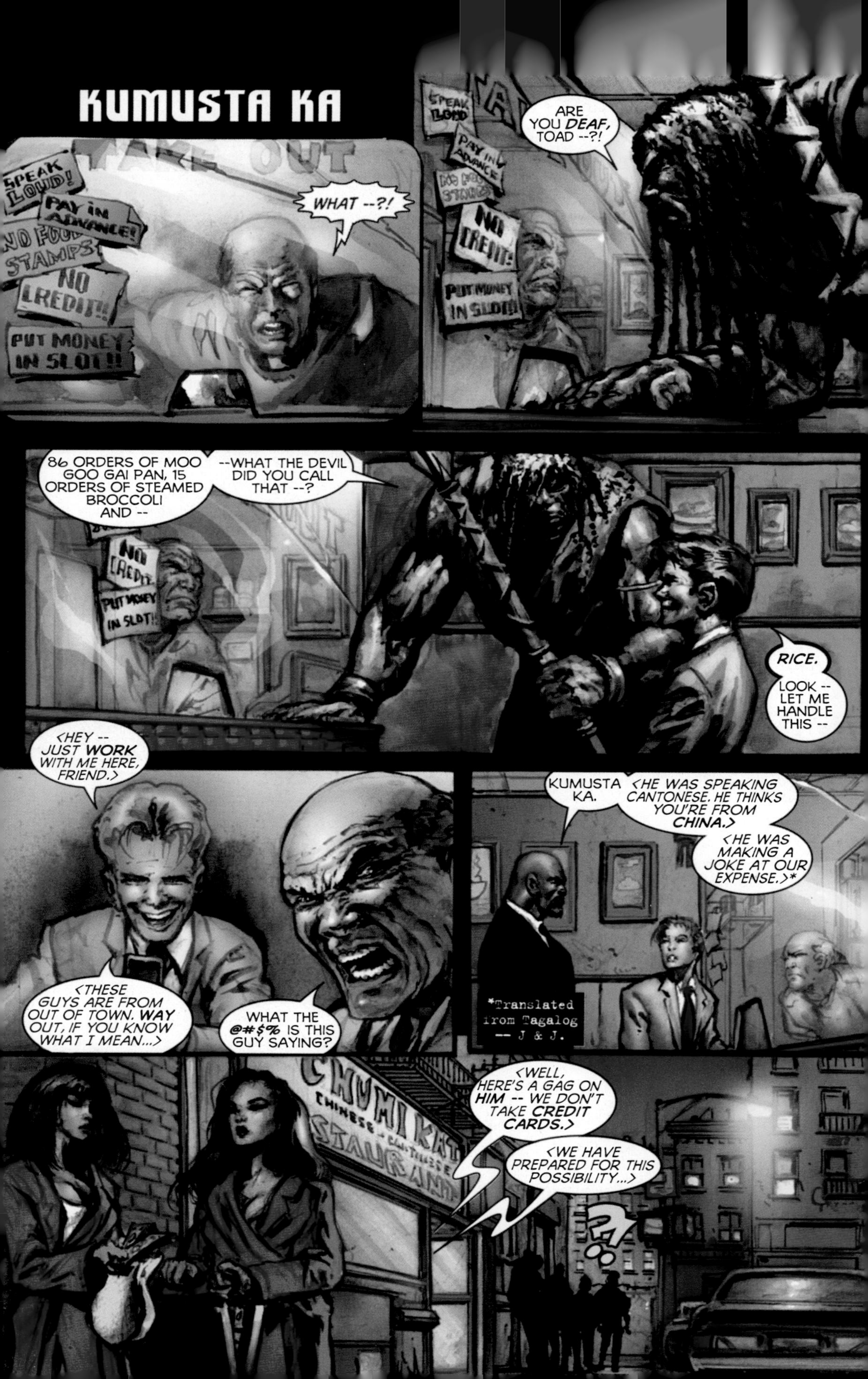
KUMUSTA KA
SPEAK LOUD!
PAY IN ADVANCE!
NO FOOD STAMPS
NO CREDIT!!
PUT MONEY IN SLOT!!
WHAT --?!
ARE YOU DEAF, TOAD --?!
86 ORDERS OF MOO GOO GAI PAN, 15 ORDERS OF STEAMED BROCCOLI AND --
--WHAT THE DEVIL DID YOU CALL THAT --?
RICE.
LOOK -- LET ME HANDLE THIS --
<HEY -- JUST WORK WITH ME HERE, FRIEND.>
<THESE GUYS ARE FROM OUT OF TOWN. WAY OUT, IF YOU KNOW WHAT I MEAN...>
WHAT THE @#$% IS THIS GUY SAYING?
KUMUSTA KA.
<HE WAS SPEAKING CANTONESE. HE THINKS YOU'RE FROM CHINA.>
<HE WAS MAKING A JOKE AT OUR EXPENSE.>*
*Translated from Tagalog -- J & J.
CHUMI KAT CHINESE - CANTONESE RESTAURANT
<WELL, HERE'S A GAG ON HIM -- WE DON'T TAKE CREDIT CARDS.>
<WE HAVE PREPARED FOR THIS POSSIBILITY...>

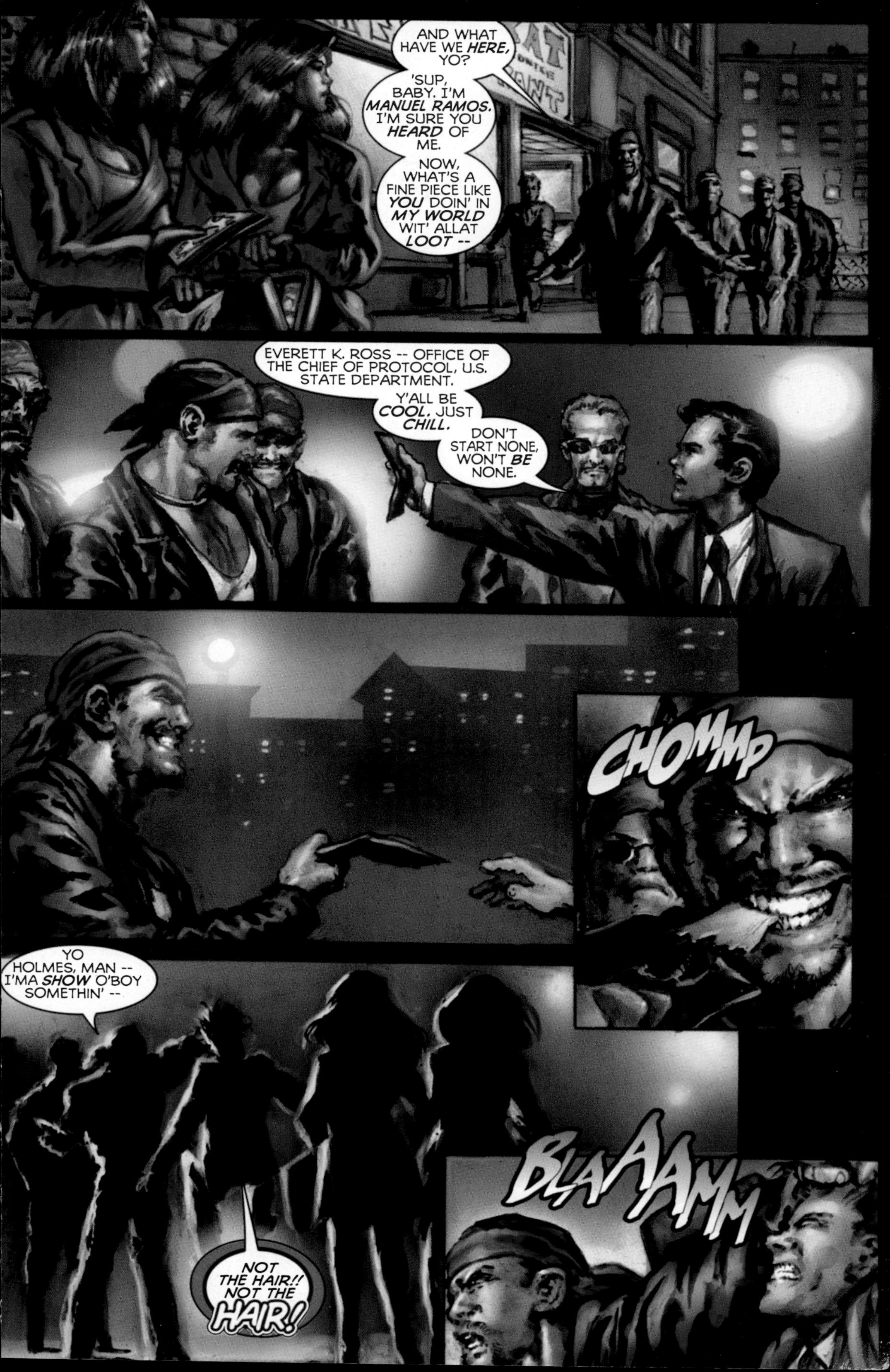
AND WHAT HAVE WE HERE, YO?
'SUP, BABY. I'M MANUEL RAMOS. I'M SURE YOU HEARD OF ME.
NOW, WHAT'S A FINE PIECE LIKE YOU DOIN' IN MY WORLD WIT' ALLAT LOOT --
EVERETT K. ROSS -- OFFICE OF THE CHIEF OF PROTOCOL, U.S. STATE DEPARTMENT.
Y'ALL BE COOL. JUST CHILL.
DON'T START NONE, WON'T BE NONE.
CHOMMP
YO HOLMES, MAN -- I'MA SHOW O'BOY SOMETHIN' --
NOT THE HAIR!! NOT THE HAIR!
BLAAAMM

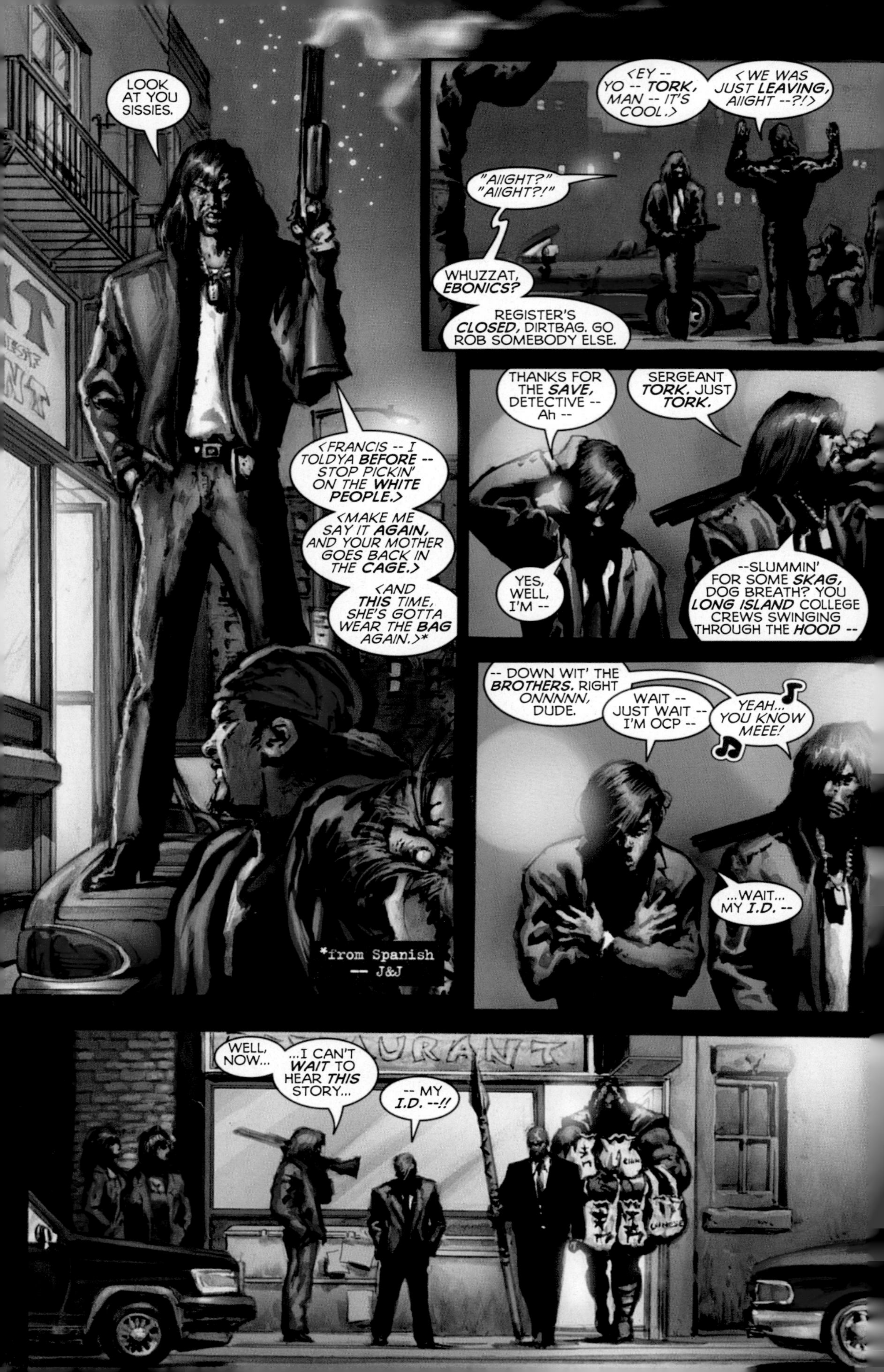
LOOK AT YOU SISSIES.
<EY -- YO -- TORK, MAN -- IT'S COOL.>
< WE WAS JUST LEAVING, AIIGHT --?!>
"AIIGHT?" "AIIGHT?!"
WHUZZAT, EBONICS?
REGISTER'S CLOSED, DIRTBAG. GO ROB SOMEBODY ELSE.
<FRANCIS -- I TOLDYA BEFORE -- STOP PICKIN' ON THE WHITE PEOPLE.>
<MAKE ME SAY IT AGAIN, AND YOUR MOTHER GOES BACK IN THE CAGE.>
<AND THIS TIME, SHE'S GOTTA WEAR THE BAG AGAIN.>*
*from Spanish — J&J
THANKS FOR THE SAVE, DETECTIVE -- Ah --
SERGEANT TORK. JUST TORK.
YES, WELL, I'M --
--SLUMMIN' FOR SOME SKAG, DOG BREATH? YOU LONG ISLAND COLLEGE CREWS SWINGING THROUGH THE HOOD --
-- DOWN WIT' THE BROTHERS. RIGHT ONNNNN, DUDE.
WAIT -- JUST WAIT -- I'M OCP --
YEAH... YOU KNOW MEEE!
...WAIT... MY I.D. --
WELL, NOW...
...I CAN'T WAIT TO HEAR THIS STORY...
-- MY I.D. --!!

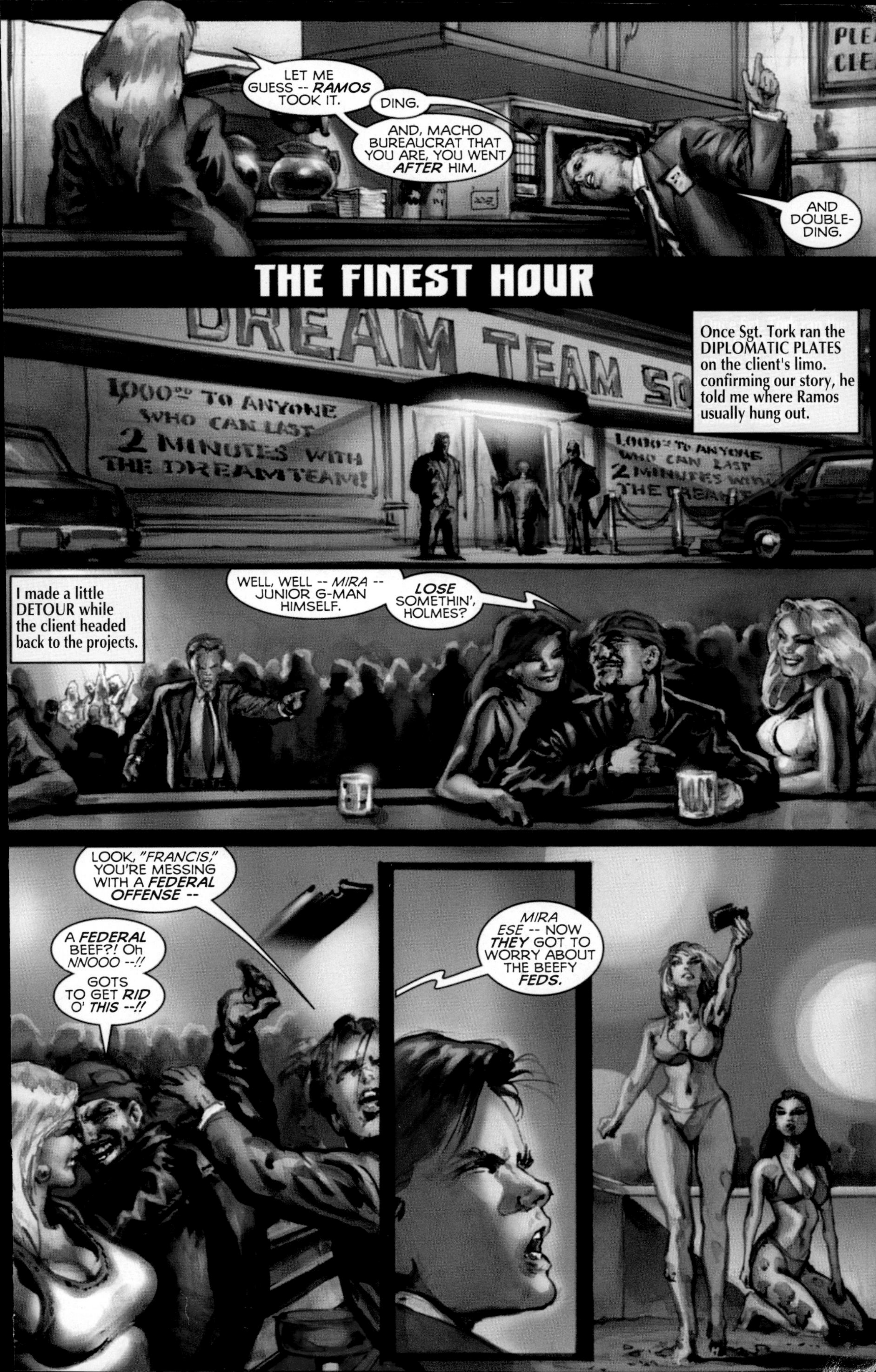
LET ME GUESS -- *RAMOS* TOOK IT.
DING.
AND, MACHO BUREAUCRAT THAT YOU ARE, YOU WENT *AFTER* HIM.
AND DOUBLE-DING.
THE FINEST HOUR
Once Sgt. Tork ran the DIPLOMATIC PLATES on the client's limo. confirming our story, he told me where Ramos usually hung out.
DREAM TEAM
1000[00] TO ANYONE WHO CAN LAST 2 MINUTES WITH THE DREAMTEAM!
I made a little DETOUR while the client headed back to the projects.
WELL, WELL -- *MIRA* -- JUNIOR G-MAN HIMSELF.
LOSE SOMETHIN', HOLMES?
LOOK, *"FRANCIS,"* YOU'RE MESSING WITH A *FEDERAL OFFENSE* --
A *FEDERAL* BEEF?! Oh *NNOOO* --!!
GOTS TO GET *RID* O' *THIS* --!!
MIRA ESE -- NOW *THEY* GOT TO WORRY ABOUT THE BEEFY *FEDS.*

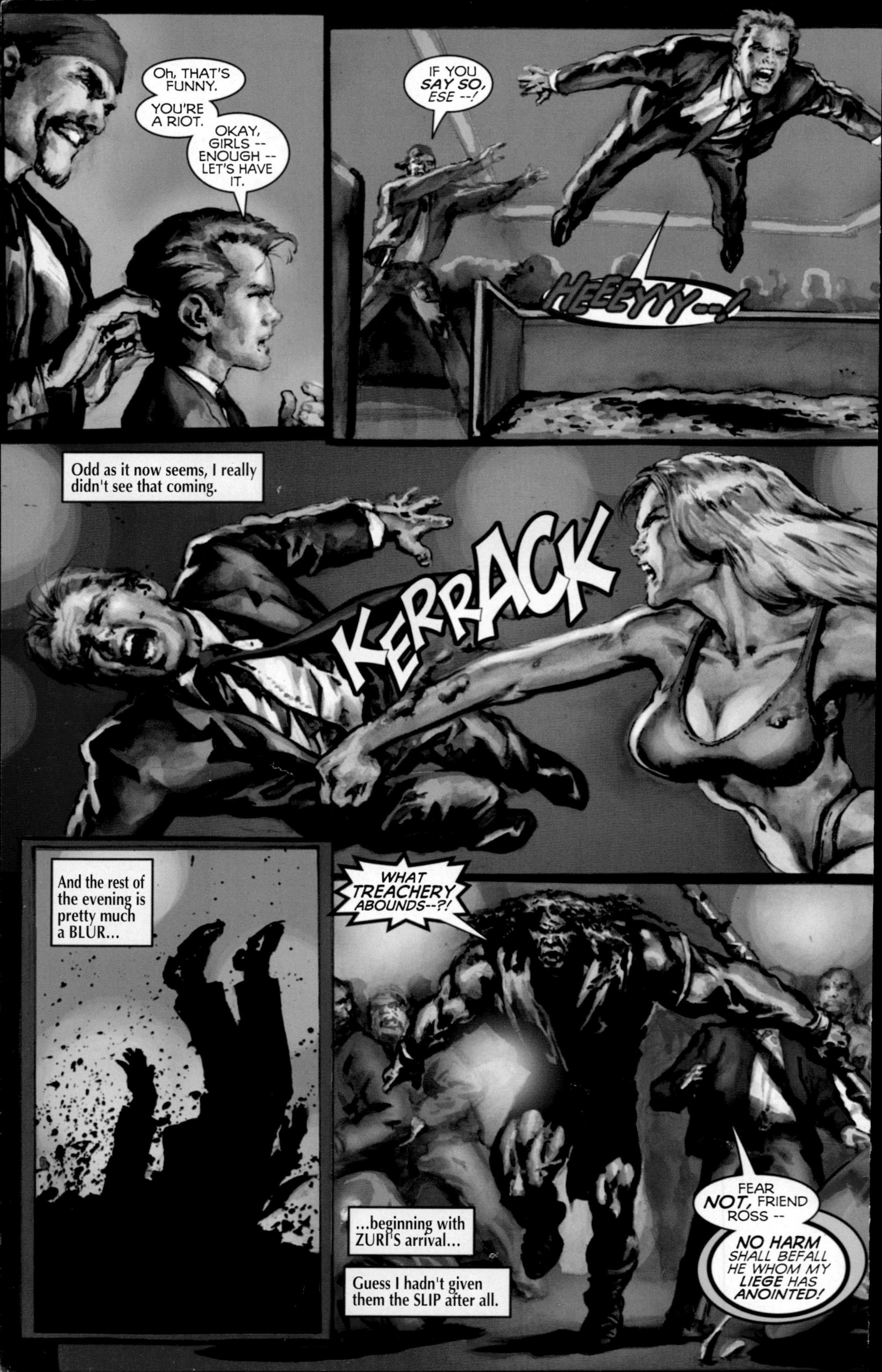

Oh, THAT'S FUNNY.
YOU'RE A RIOT.
OKAY, GIRLS -- ENOUGH -- LET'S HAVE IT.
IF YOU SAY SO, ESE --!
HEEEYYY--!
Odd as it now seems, I really didn't see that coming.
KERRACK
And the rest of the evening is pretty much a BLUR...
WHAT TREACHERY ABOUNDS--?!
...beginning with ZURI'S arrival...
Guess I hadn't given them the SLIP after all.
FEAR NOT, FRIEND ROSS --
NO HARM SHALL BEFALL HE WHOM MY LIEGE HAS ANOINTED!

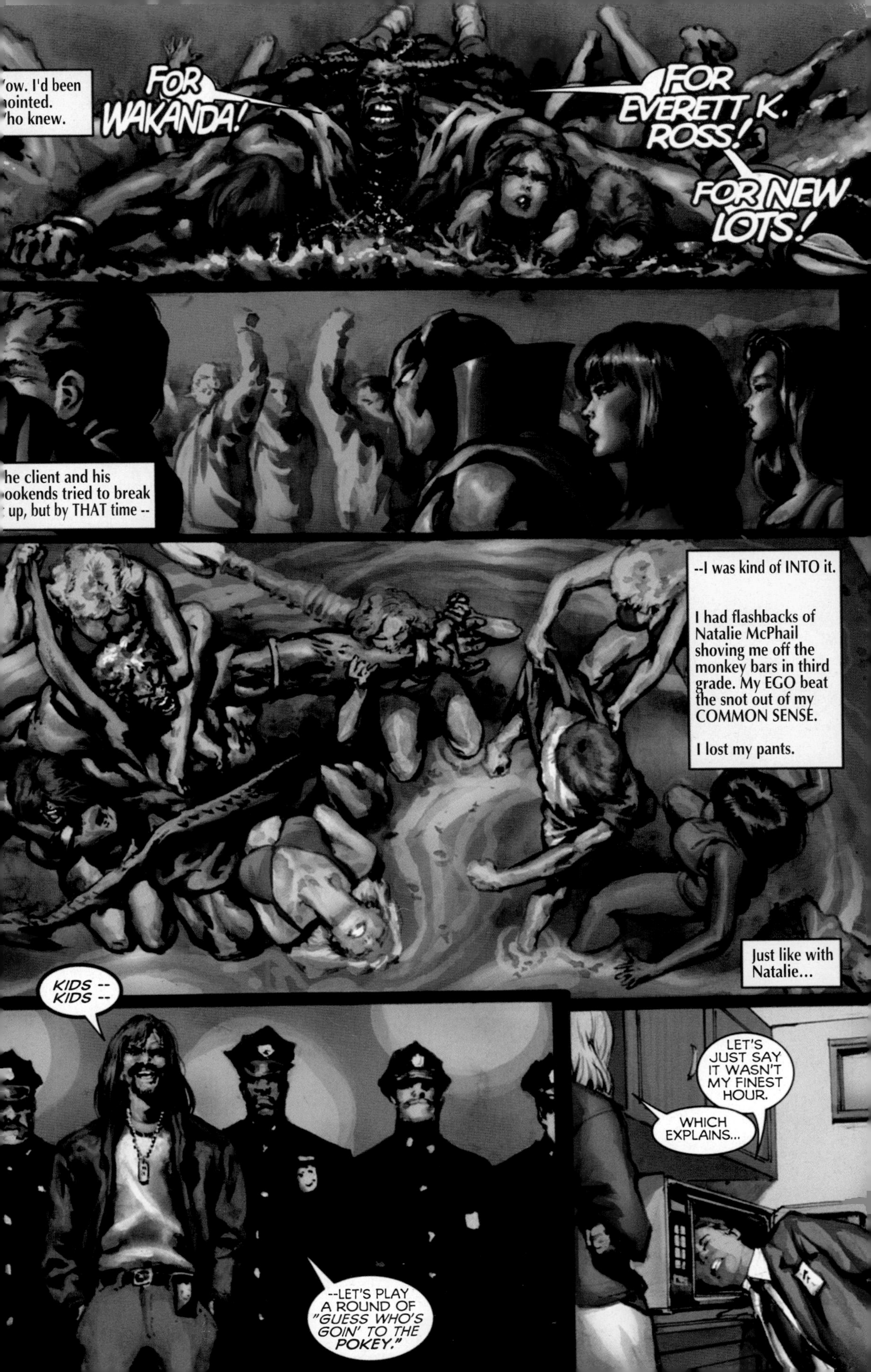
'ow. I'd been
iointed.
'ho knew.
FOR WAKANDA!
FOR EVERETT K. ROSS!
FOR NEW LOTS!
he client and his
ookends tried to break
: up, but by THAT time --
--I was kind of INTO it.
I had flashbacks of Natalie McPhail shoving me off the monkey bars in third grade. My EGO beat the snot out of my COMMON SENSE.
I lost my pants.
Just like with Natalie...
KIDS -- KIDS --
--LET'S PLAY A ROUND OF "GUESS WHO'S GOIN' TO THE POKEY."
LET'S JUST SAY IT WASN'T MY FINEST HOUR.
WHICH EXPLAINS...

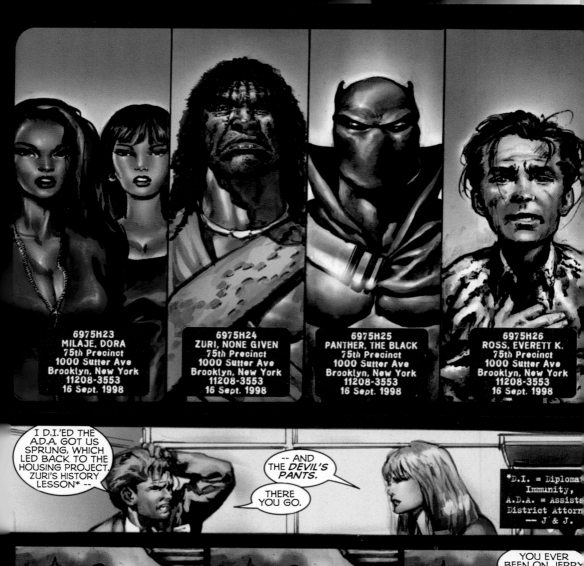

6975H23
MILAJE, DORA
75th Precinct
1000 Sutter Ave
Brooklyn, New York
11208-3553
16 Sept. 1998

6975H24
ZURI, NONE GIVEN
75th Precinct
1000 Sutter Ave
Brooklyn, New York
11208-3553
16 Sept. 1998

6975H25
PANTHER, THE BLACK
75th Precinct
1000 Sutter Ave
Brooklyn, New York
11208-3553
16 Sept. 1998

6975H26
ROSS, EVERETT K.
75th Precinct
1000 Sutter Ave
Brooklyn, New York
11208-3553
16 Sept. 1998

I D.I.'ED THE A.D.A. GOT US SPRUNG, WHICH LED BACK TO THE HOUSING PROJECT. ZURI'S HISTORY LESSON* --

-- AND THE *DEVIL'S PANTS.*

THERE YOU GO.

*D.I. = Diplomat' Immunity, A.D.A. = Assista District Attorn -- J & J.

YOU EVER BEEN ON JERRY SPRINGER --?

SO -- WHERE *WAS* THE CLIENT --?

STILL INVESTIGATING THE *TOMORROW FUND* THING.

HE DECIDED TO PAY A VISIT TO THE FUND'S *DIRECTOR* -- *AFTER* VISITING HOURS...

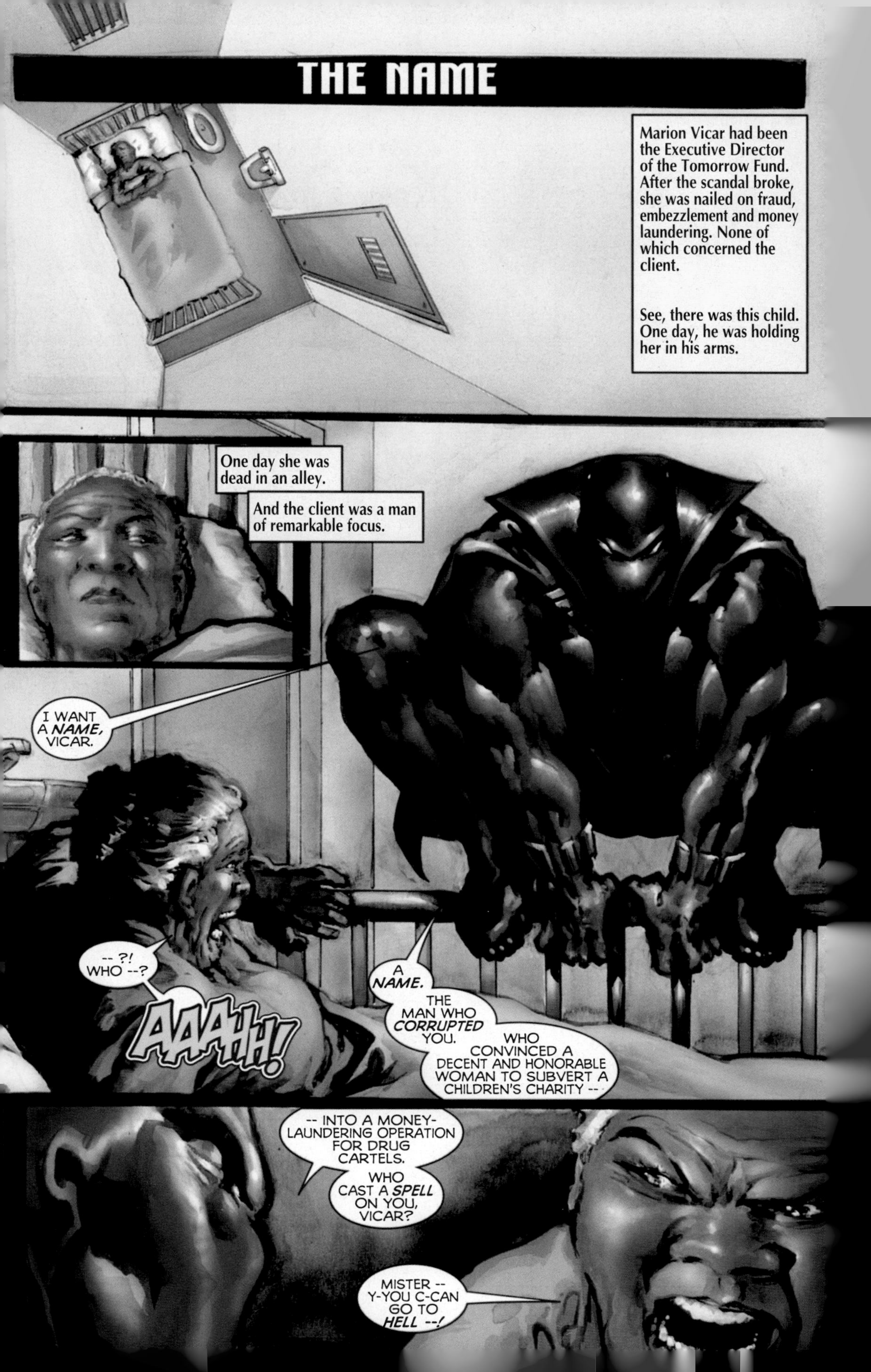
THE NAME
Marion Vicar had been the Executive Director of the Tomorrow Fund. After the scandal broke, she was nailed on fraud, embezzlement and money laundering. None of which concerned the client.
See, there was this child. One day, he was holding her in his arms.
One day she was dead in an alley.
And the client was a man of remarkable focus.
I WANT A NAME, VICAR.
-- ?! WHO --?
AAAHH!
A NAME.
THE MAN WHO CORRUPTED YOU.
WHO CONVINCED A DECENT AND HONORABLE WOMAN TO SUBVERT A CHILDREN'S CHARITY --
-- INTO A MONEY-LAUNDERING OPERATION FOR DRUG CARTELS.
WHO CAST A SPELL ON YOU, VICAR?
MISTER -- Y-YOU C-CAN GO TO HELL --!

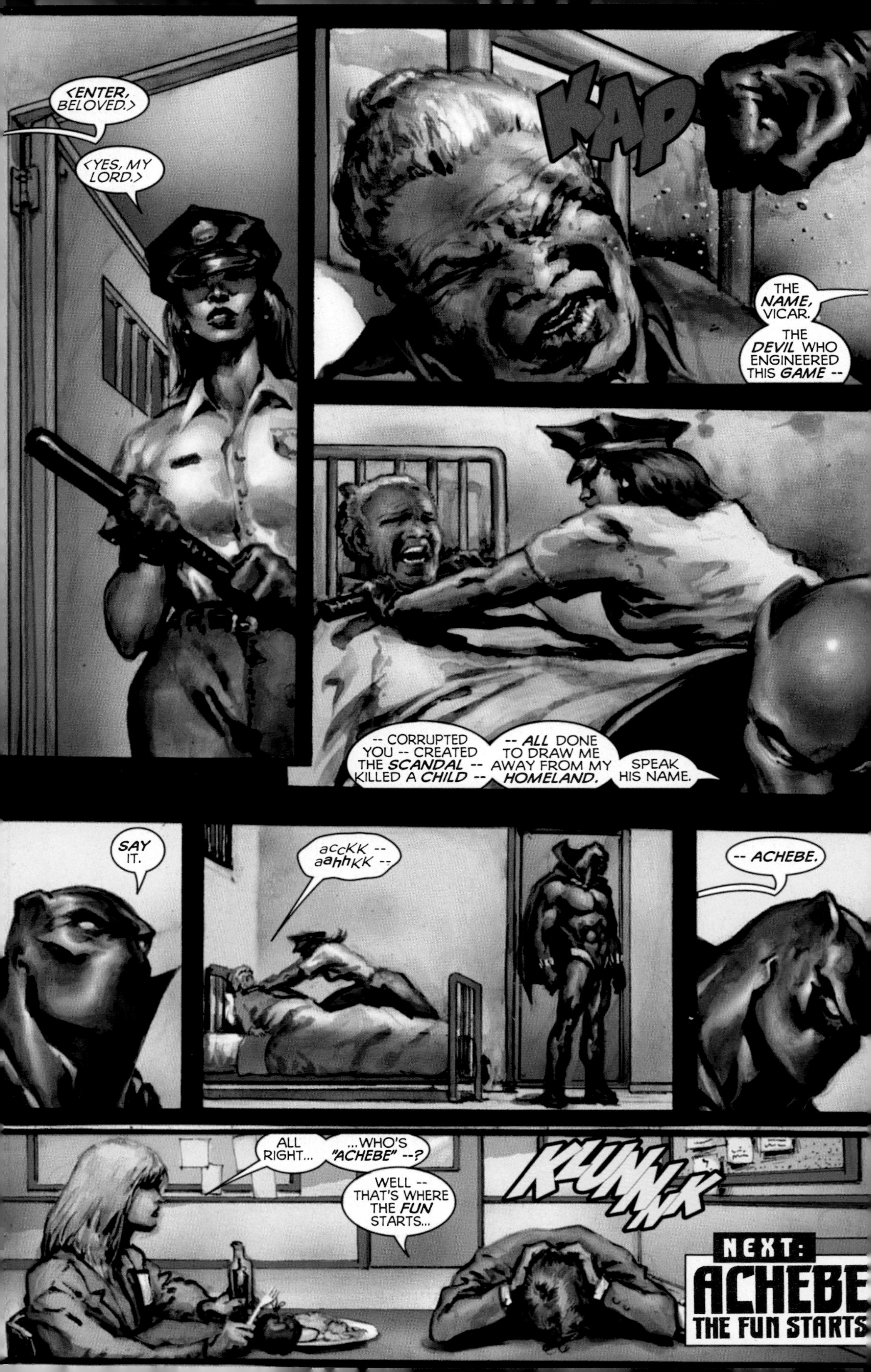
<ENTER, BELOVED.>
<YES, MY LORD.>
KAP
THE NAME, VICAR.
THE DEVIL WHO ENGINEERED THIS GAME --
-- CORRUPTED YOU -- CREATED THE SCANDAL -- KILLED A CHILD --
-- ALL DONE TO DRAW ME AWAY FROM MY HOMELAND.
SPEAK HIS NAME.
SAY IT.
acckk -- aahhkk --
-- ACHEBE.
ALL RIGHT...
...WHO'S "ACHEBE" --?
WELL -- THAT'S WHERE THE FUN STARTS...
KLUNNNK
NEXT:
ACHEBE
THE FUN STARTS

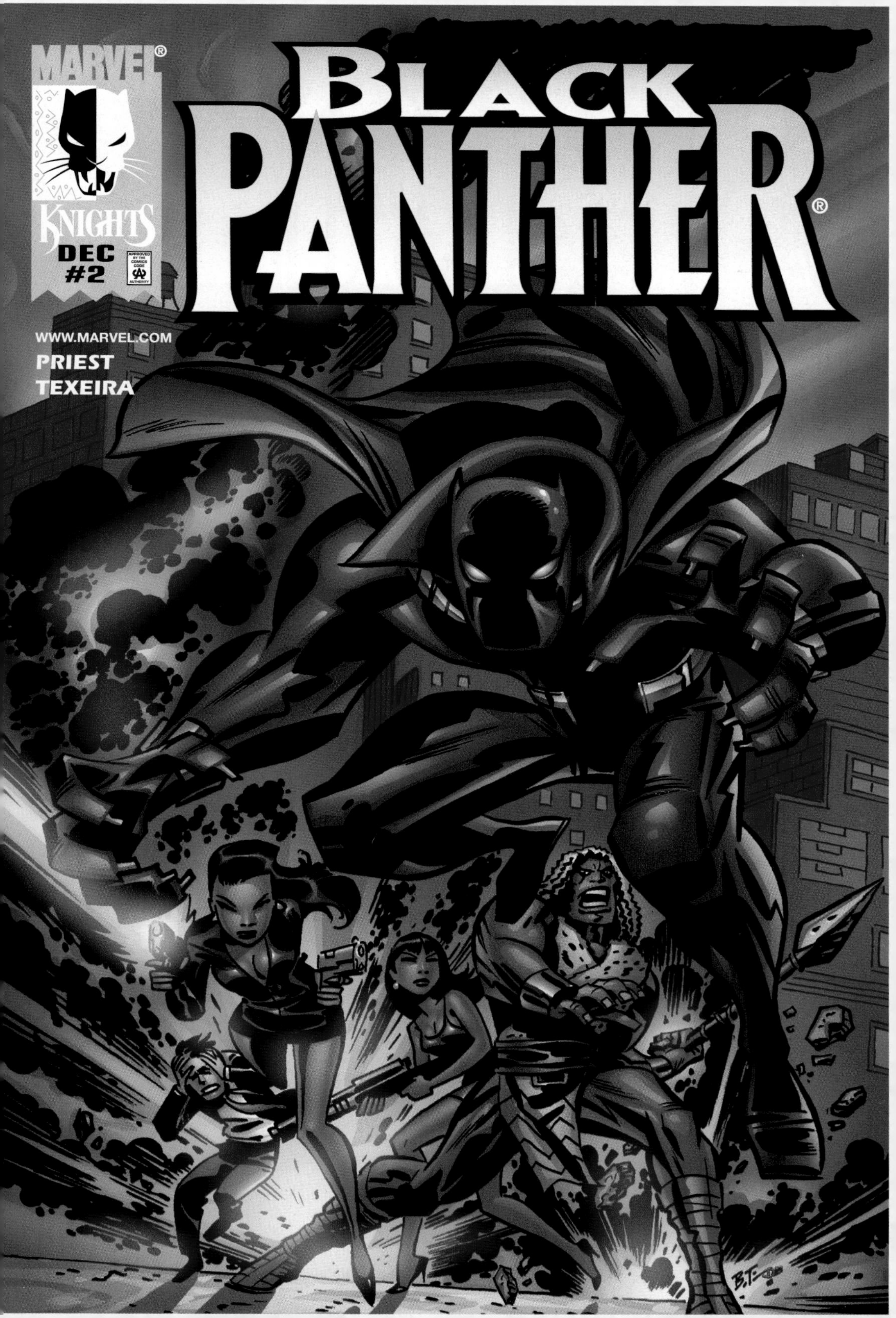

MARVEL®
KNIGHTS
DEC
#2
APPROVED BY THE COMICS CODE AUTHORITY
BLACK PANTHER®
WWW.MARVEL.COM
PRIEST
TEXEIRA

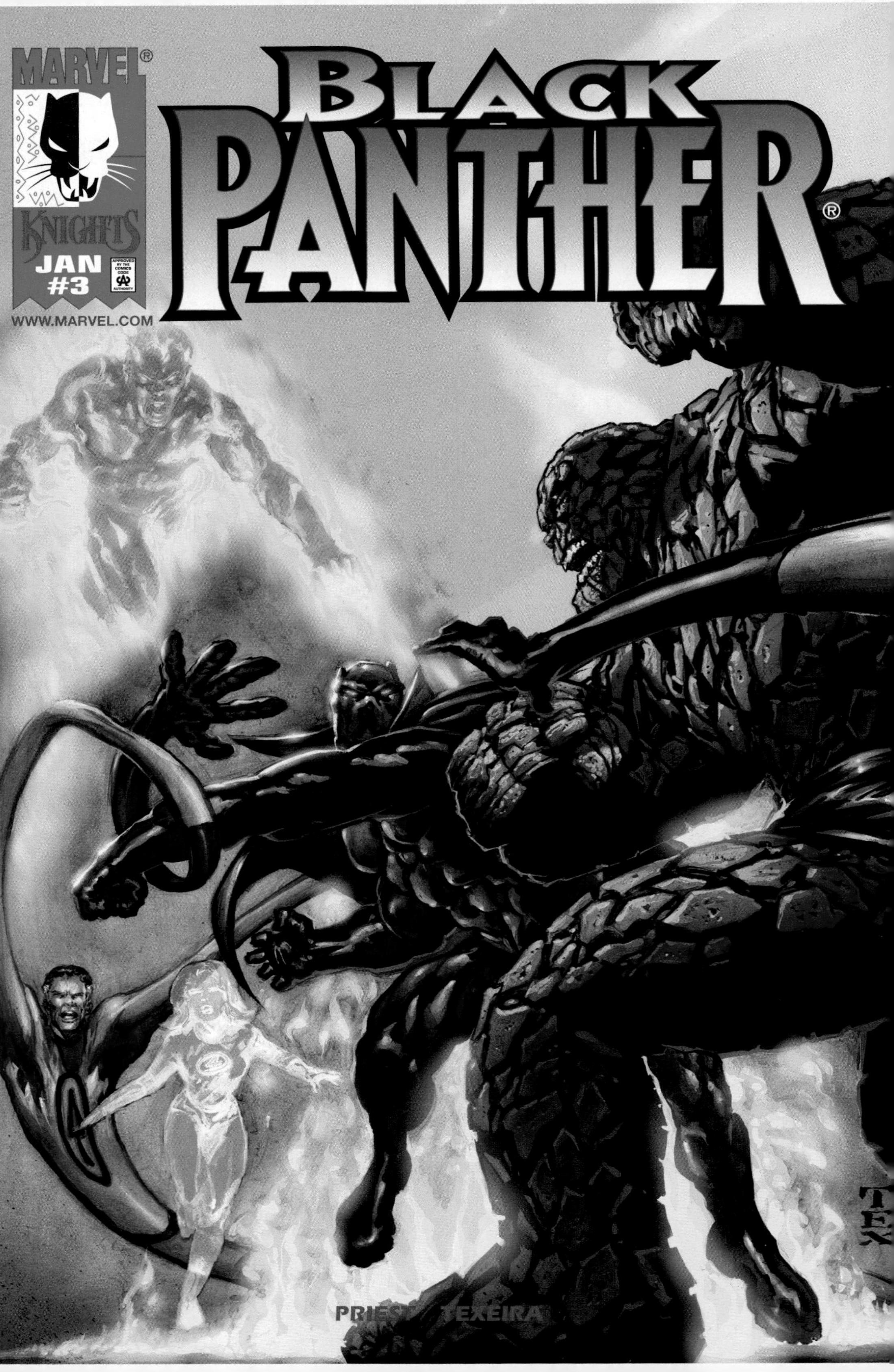
MARVEL
KNIGHTS
JAN
#3
APPROVED BY THE COMICS CODE AUTHORITY
WWW.MARVEL.COM
BLACK PANTHER
PRIEST
TEXEIRA

HEART AND SOLE

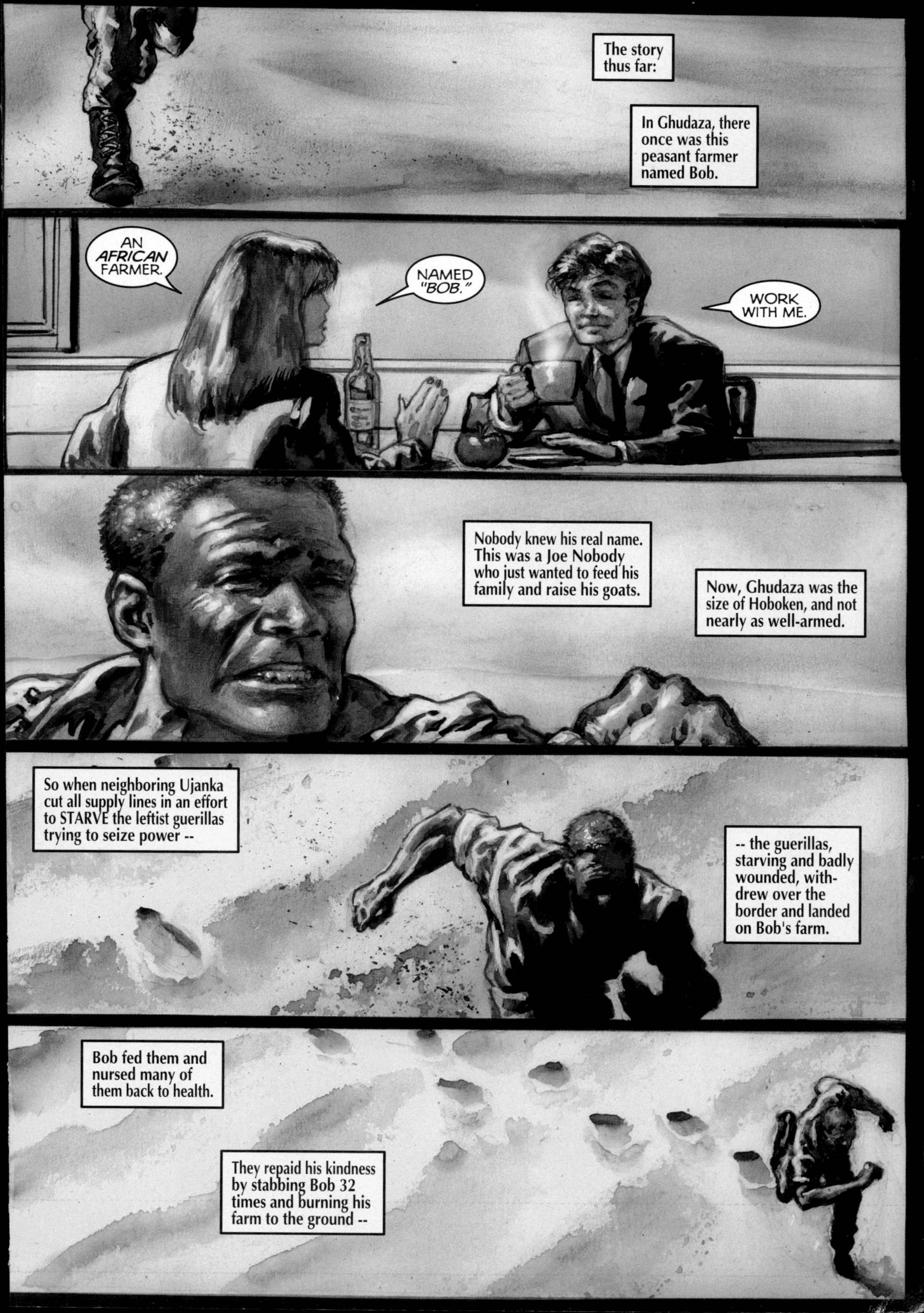

The story thus far:
In Ghudaza, there once was this peasant farmer named Bob.
AN *AFRICAN* FARMER.
NAMED *"BOB."*
WORK WITH ME.
Nobody knew his real name. This was a Joe Nobody who just wanted to feed his family and raise his goats.
Now, Ghudaza was the size of Hoboken, and not nearly as well-armed.
So when neighboring Ujanka cut all supply lines in an effort to STARVE the leftist guerillas trying to seize power --
-- the guerillas, starving and badly wounded, withdrew over the border and landed on Bob's farm.
Bob fed them and nursed many of them back to health.
They repaid his kindness by stabbing Bob 32 times and burning his farm to the ground --

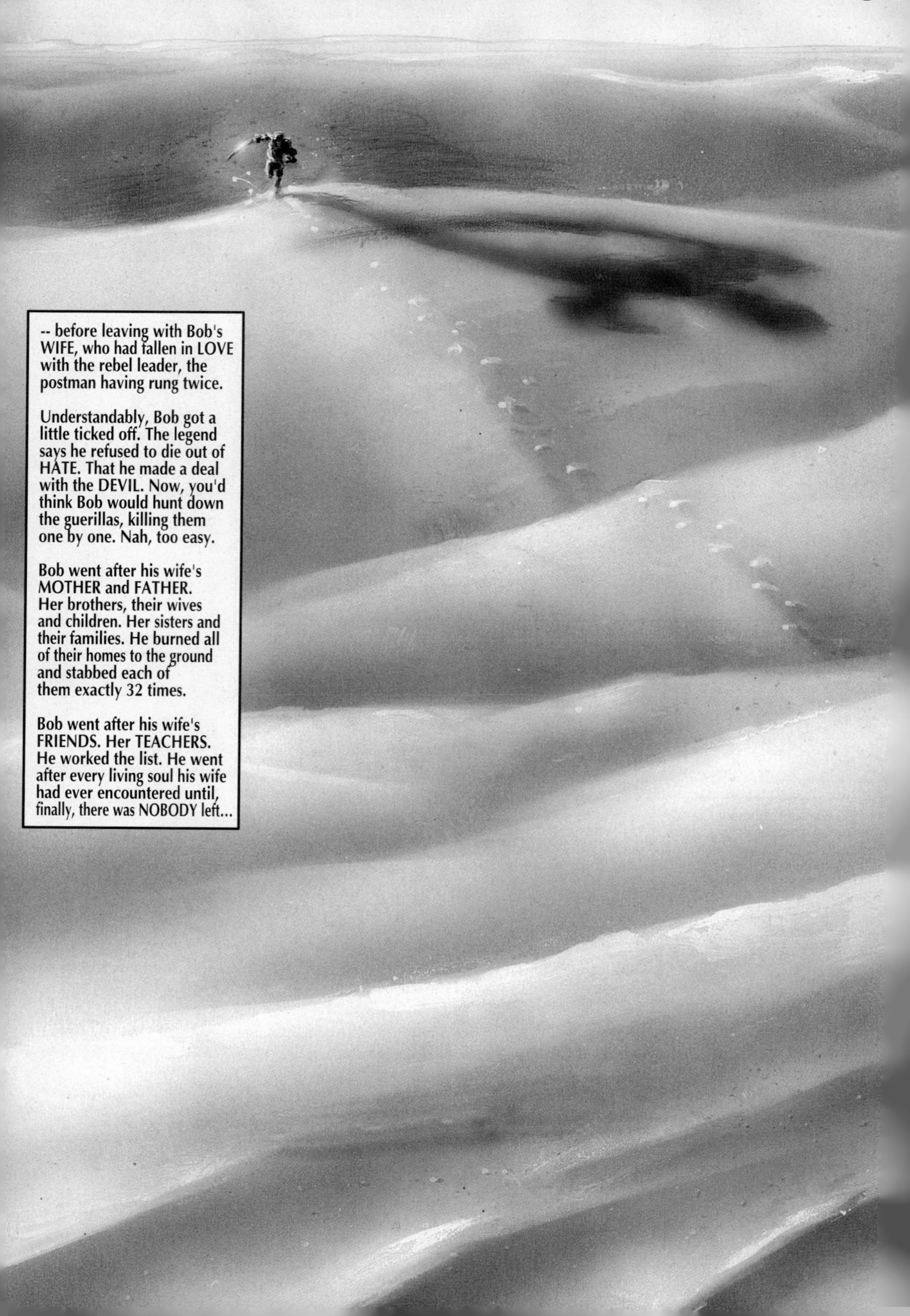
-- before leaving with Bob's WIFE, who had fallen in LOVE with the rebel leader, the postman having rung twice.
Understandably, Bob got a little ticked off. The legend says he refused to die out of HATE. That he made a deal with the DEVIL. Now, you'd think Bob would hunt down the guerillas, killing them one by one. Nah, too easy.
Bob went after his wife's MOTHER and FATHER. Her brothers, their wives and children. Her sisters and their families. He burned all of their homes to the ground and stabbed each of them exactly 32 times.
Bob went after his wife's FRIENDS. Her TEACHERS. He worked the list. He went after every living soul his wife had ever encountered until, finally, there was NOBODY left...

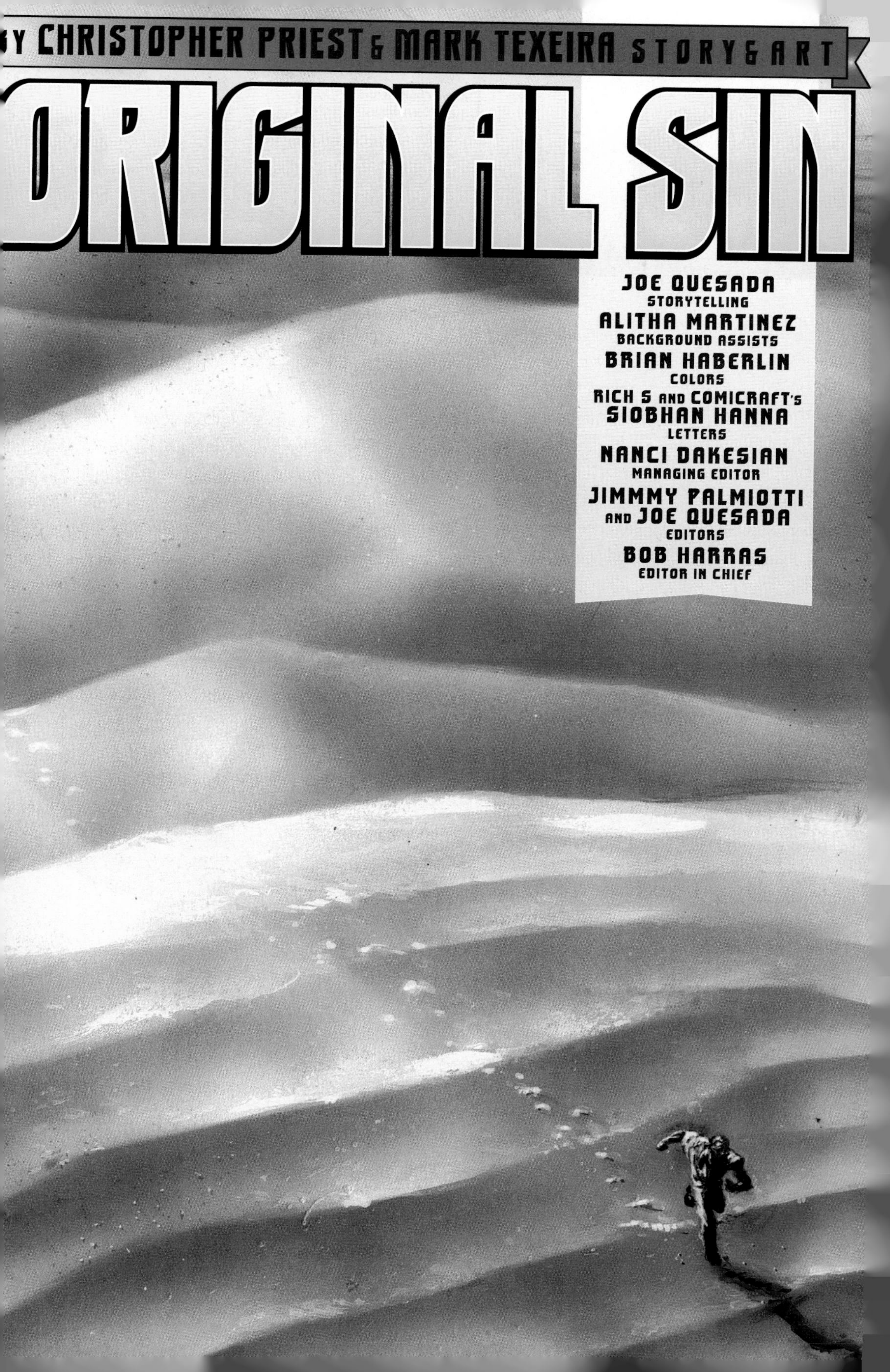
BY CHRISTOPHER PRIEST & MARK TEXEIRA STORY & ART
ORIGINAL SIN
JOE QUESADA
STORYTELLING
ALITHA MARTINEZ
BACKGROUND ASSISTS
BRIAN HABERLIN
COLORS
RICH S AND COMICRAFT'S
SIOBHAN HANNA
LETTERS
NANCI DAKESIAN
MANAGING EDITOR
JIMMMY PALMIOTTI
AND JOE QUESADA
EDITORS
BOB HARRAS
EDITOR IN CHIEF

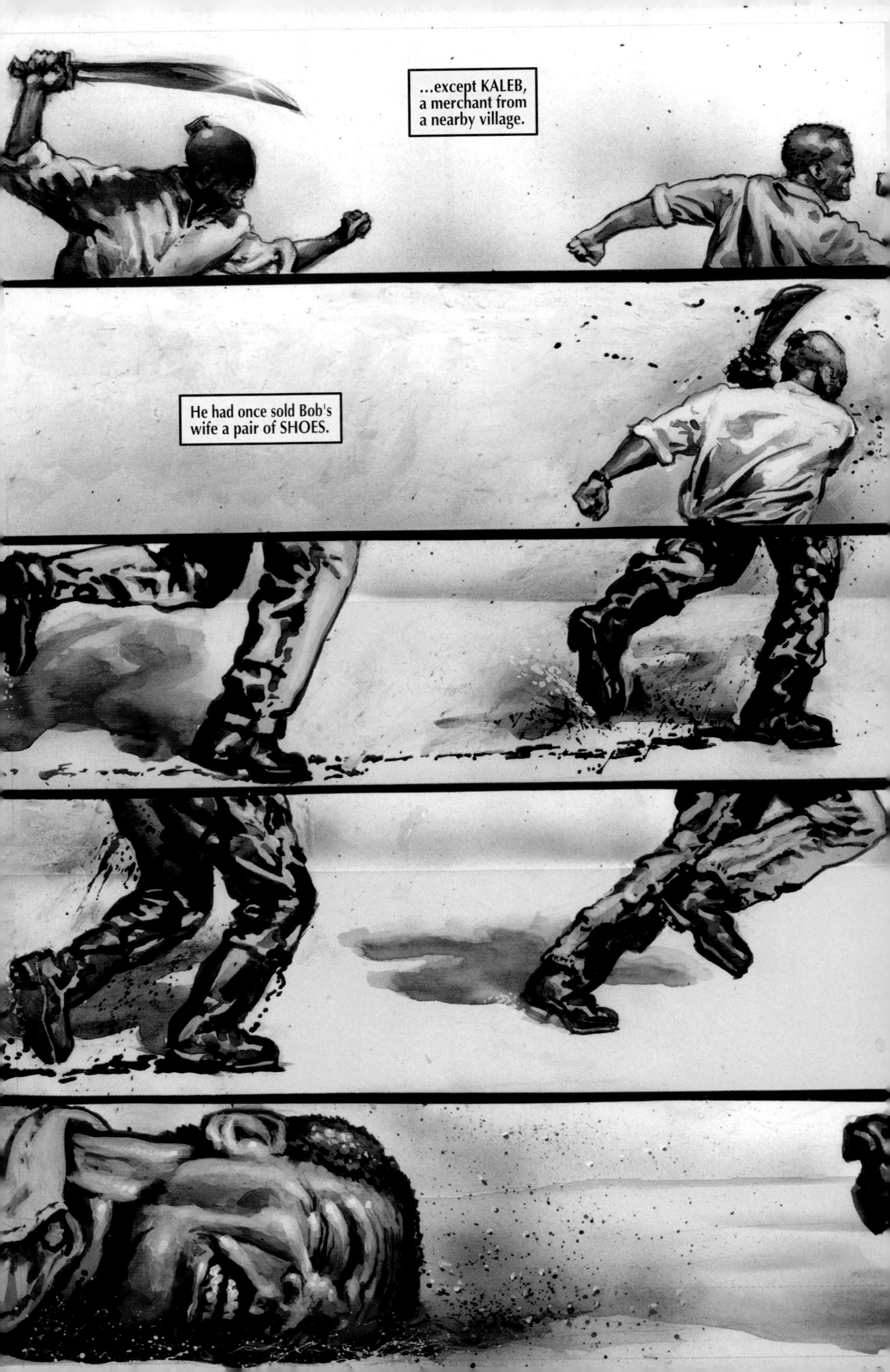
...except KALEB, a merchant from a nearby village.
He had once sold Bob's wife a pair of SHOES.

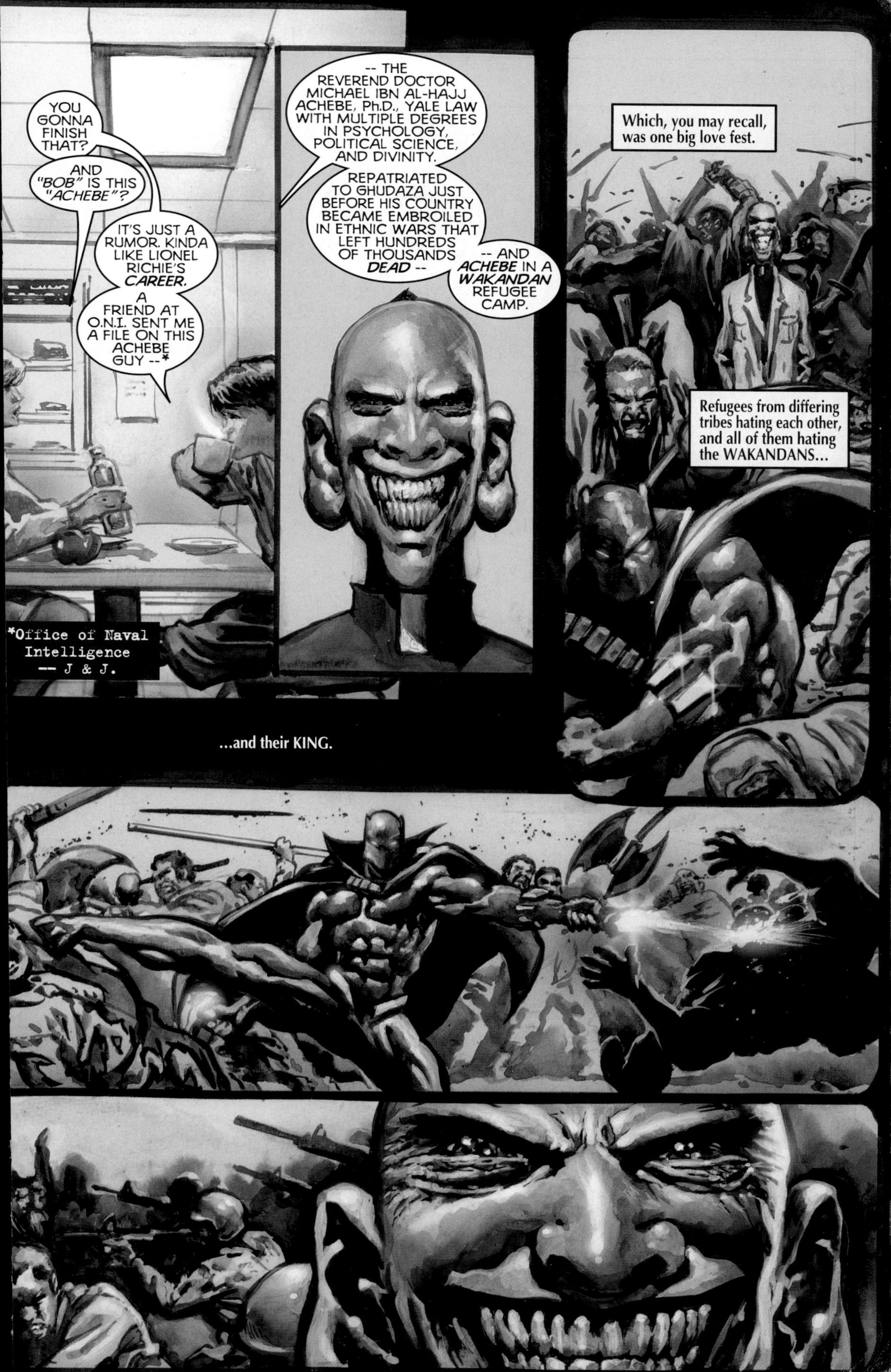
YOU GONNA FINISH THAT?
AND "BOB" IS THIS "ACHEBE"?
IT'S JUST A RUMOR. KINDA LIKE LIONEL RICHIE'S CAREER.
A FRIEND AT O.N.I. SENT ME A FILE ON THIS ACHEBE GUY --*
*Office of Naval Intelligence -- J & J.
-- THE REVEREND DOCTOR MICHAEL IBN AL-HAJJ ACHEBE, Ph.D., YALE LAW WITH MULTIPLE DEGREES IN PSYCHOLOGY, POLITICAL SCIENCE, AND DIVINITY.
REPATRIATED TO GHUDAZA JUST BEFORE HIS COUNTRY BECAME EMBROILED IN ETHNIC WARS THAT LEFT HUNDREDS OF THOUSANDS DEAD --
-- AND ACHEBE IN A WAKANDAN REFUGEE CAMP.
Which, you may recall, was one big love fest.
Refugees from differing tribes hating each other, and all of them hating the WAKANDANS...
...and their KING.

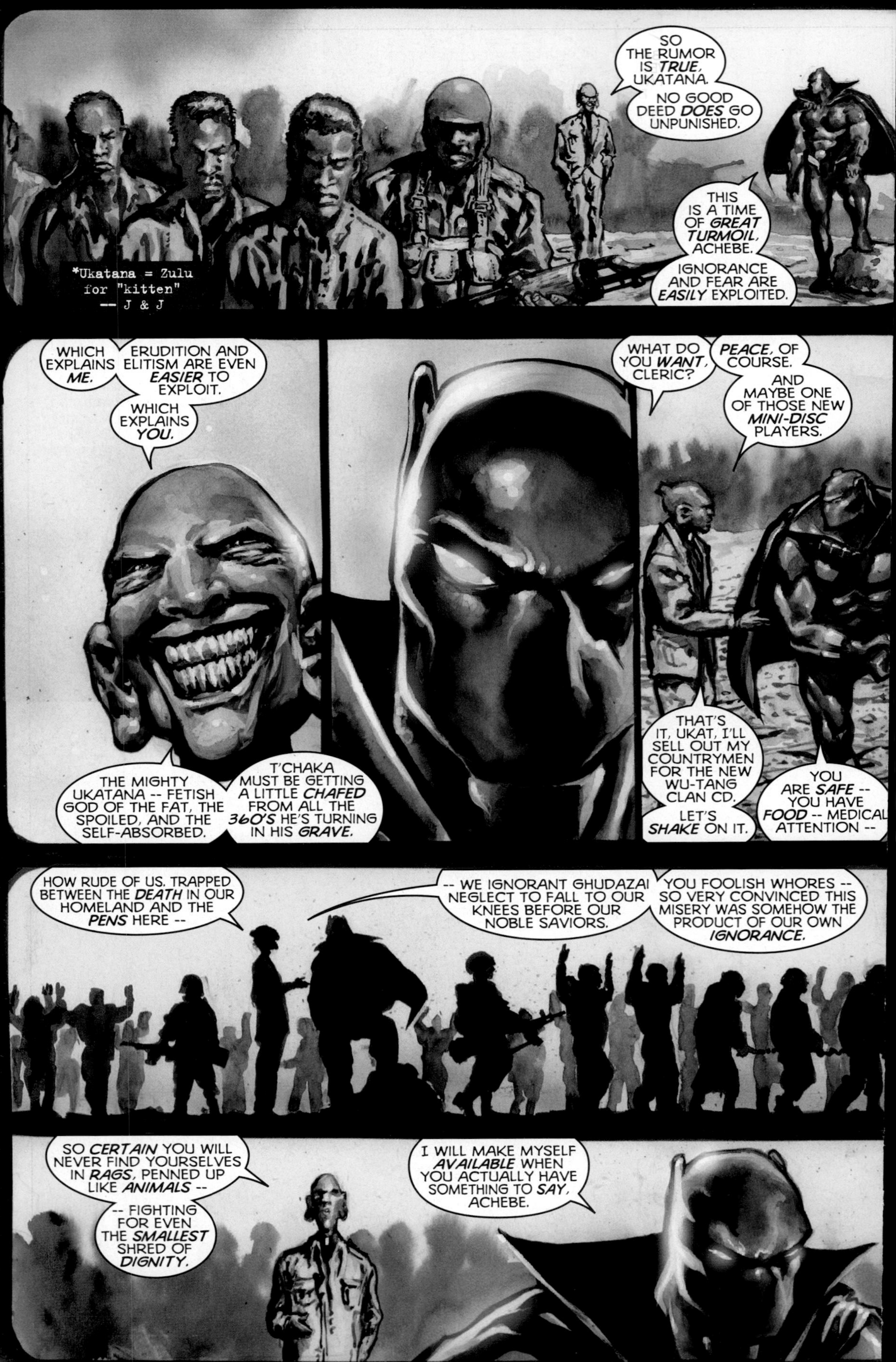
SO THE RUMOR IS TRUE, UKATANA.
NO GOOD DEED DOES GO UNPUNISHED.
THIS IS A TIME OF GREAT TURMOIL, ACHEBE.
IGNORANCE AND FEAR ARE EASILY EXPLOITED.
*Ukatana = Zulu for "kitten" -- J & J
WHICH EXPLAINS ME.
ERUDITION AND ELITISM ARE EVEN EASIER TO EXPLOIT.
WHICH EXPLAINS YOU.
THE MIGHTY UKATANA -- FETISH GOD OF THE FAT, THE SPOILED, AND THE SELF-ABSORBED.
T'CHAKA MUST BE GETTING A LITTLE CHAFED FROM ALL THE 360'S HE'S TURNING IN HIS GRAVE.
WHAT DO YOU WANT, CLERIC?
PEACE, OF COURSE.
AND MAYBE ONE OF THOSE NEW MINI-DISC PLAYERS.
THAT'S IT, UKAT, I'LL SELL OUT MY COUNTRYMEN FOR THE NEW WU-TANG CLAN CD.
LET'S SHAKE ON IT.
YOU ARE SAFE -- YOU HAVE FOOD -- MEDICAL ATTENTION --
HOW RUDE OF US. TRAPPED BETWEEN THE DEATH IN OUR HOMELAND AND THE PENS HERE --
-- WE IGNORANT GHUDAZAI NEGLECT TO FALL TO OUR KNEES BEFORE OUR NOBLE SAVIORS.
YOU FOOLISH WHORES -- SO VERY CONVINCED THIS MISERY WAS SOMEHOW THE PRODUCT OF OUR OWN IGNORANCE.
SO CERTAIN YOU WILL NEVER FIND YOURSELVES IN RAGS, PENNED UP LIKE ANIMALS --
-- FIGHTING FOR EVEN THE SMALLEST SHRED OF DIGNITY.
I WILL MAKE MYSELF AVAILABLE WHEN YOU ACTUALLY HAVE SOMETHING TO SAY, ACHEBE.

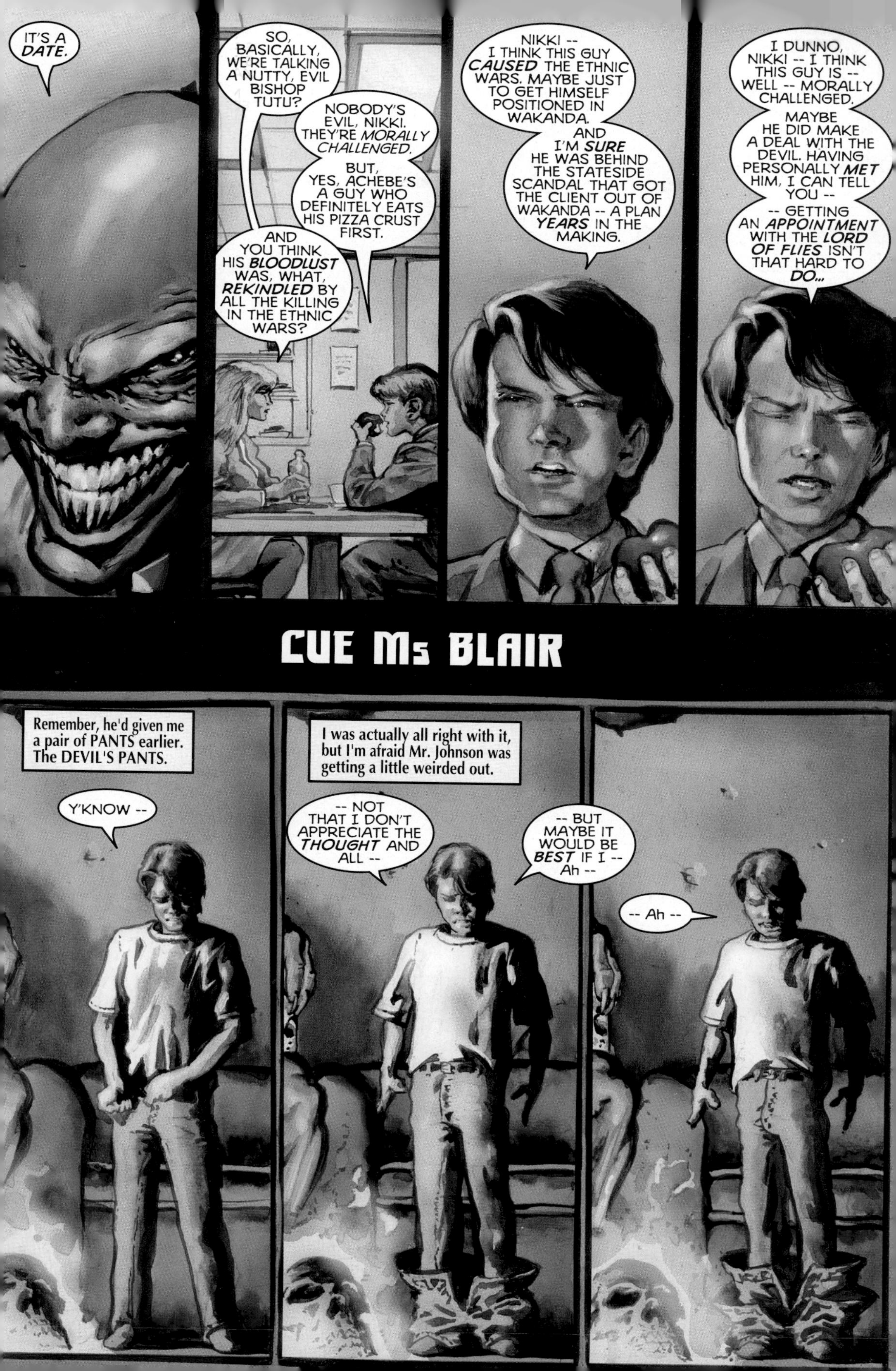
IT'S A DATE.
SO, BASICALLY, WE'RE TALKING A NUTTY, EVIL BISHOP TUTU?
NOBODY'S EVIL, NIKKI. THEY'RE MORALLY CHALLENGED.
BUT, YES, ACHEBE'S A GUY WHO DEFINITELY EATS HIS PIZZA CRUST FIRST.
AND YOU THINK HIS BLOODLUST WAS, WHAT, REKINDLED BY ALL THE KILLING IN THE ETHNIC WARS?
NIKKI -- I THINK THIS GUY CAUSED THE ETHNIC WARS. MAYBE JUST TO GET HIMSELF POSITIONED IN WAKANDA.
AND I'M SURE HE WAS BEHIND THE STATESIDE SCANDAL THAT GOT THE CLIENT OUT OF WAKANDA -- A PLAN YEARS IN THE MAKING.
I DUNNO, NIKKI -- I THINK THIS GUY IS -- WELL -- MORALLY CHALLENGED.
MAYBE HE DID MAKE A DEAL WITH THE DEVIL. HAVING PERSONALLY MET HIM, I CAN TELL YOU --
-- GETTING AN APPOINTMENT WITH THE LORD OF FLIES ISN'T THAT HARD TO DO...
CUE Ms BLAIR
Remember, he'd given me a pair of PANTS earlier. The DEVIL'S PANTS.
Y'KNOW --
I was actually all right with it, but I'm afraid Mr. Johnson was getting a little weirded out.
-- NOT THAT I DON'T APPRECIATE THE THOUGHT AND ALL --
-- BUT MAYBE IT WOULD BE BEST IF I -- Ah --
-- Ah --

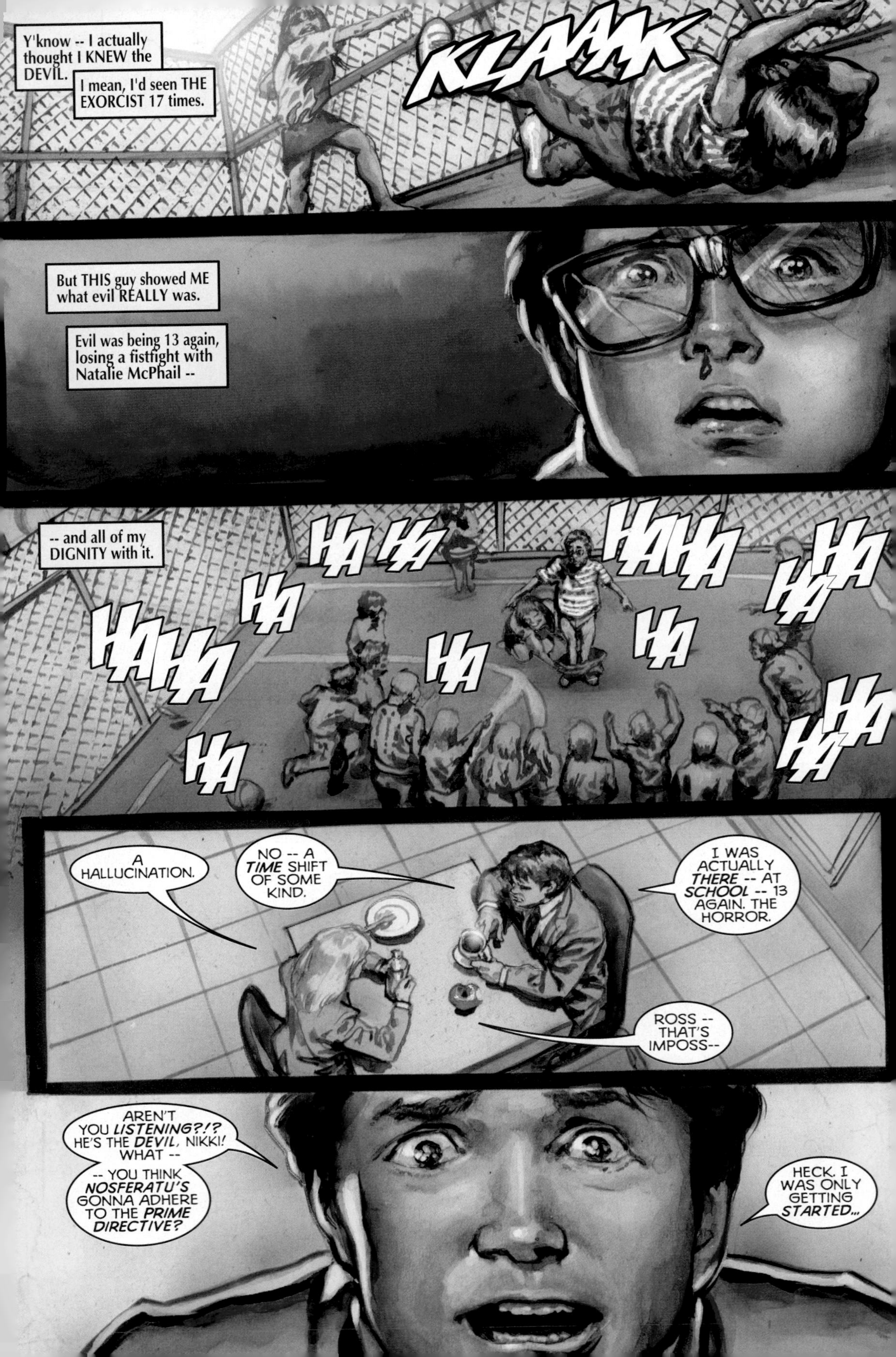
Y'know -- I actually thought I KNEW the DEVIL.
I mean, I'd seen THE EXORCIST 17 times.
KLAAAK
But THIS guy showed ME what evil REALLY was.
Evil was being 13 again, losing a fistfight with Natalie McPhail --
-- and all of my DIGNITY with it.
HA HA
HA
HAHAHA
HA
HA
HA
HAHAHA
HA
HAHA
HAHA
A HALLUCINATION.
NO -- A *TIME* SHIFT OF SOME KIND.
I WAS ACTUALLY *THERE* -- AT *SCHOOL* -- 13 AGAIN. THE HORROR.
ROSS -- THAT'S IMPOSS--
AREN'T YOU *LISTENING?!?* HE'S THE *DEVIL*, NIKKI! WHAT --
-- YOU THINK *NOSFERATU'S* GONNA ADHERE TO THE *PRIME DIRECTIVE?*
HECK. I WAS ONLY GETTING *STARTED...*

THE BEGINNING

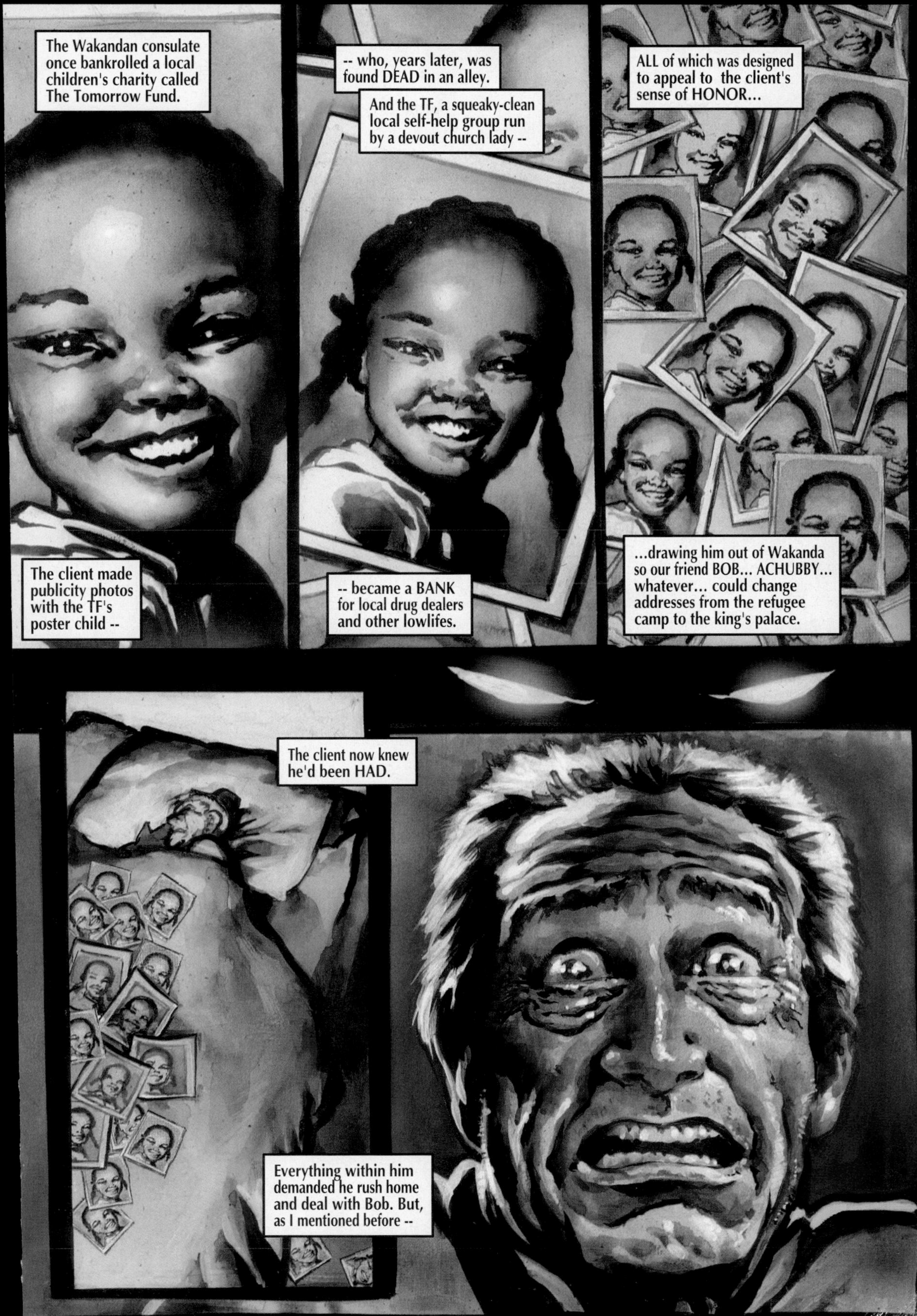
The Wakandan consulate once bankrolled a local children's charity called The Tomorrow Fund.
The client made publicity photos with the TF's poster child --
-- who, years later, was found DEAD in an alley.
And the TF, a squeaky-clean local self-help group run by a devout church lady --
-- became a BANK for local drug dealers and other lowlifes.
ALL of which was designed to appeal to the client's sense of HONOR...
...drawing him out of Wakanda so our friend BOB... ACHUBBY... whatever... could change addresses from the refugee camp to the king's palace.
The client now knew he'd been HAD.
Everything within him demanded he rush home and deal with Bob. But, as I mentioned before --

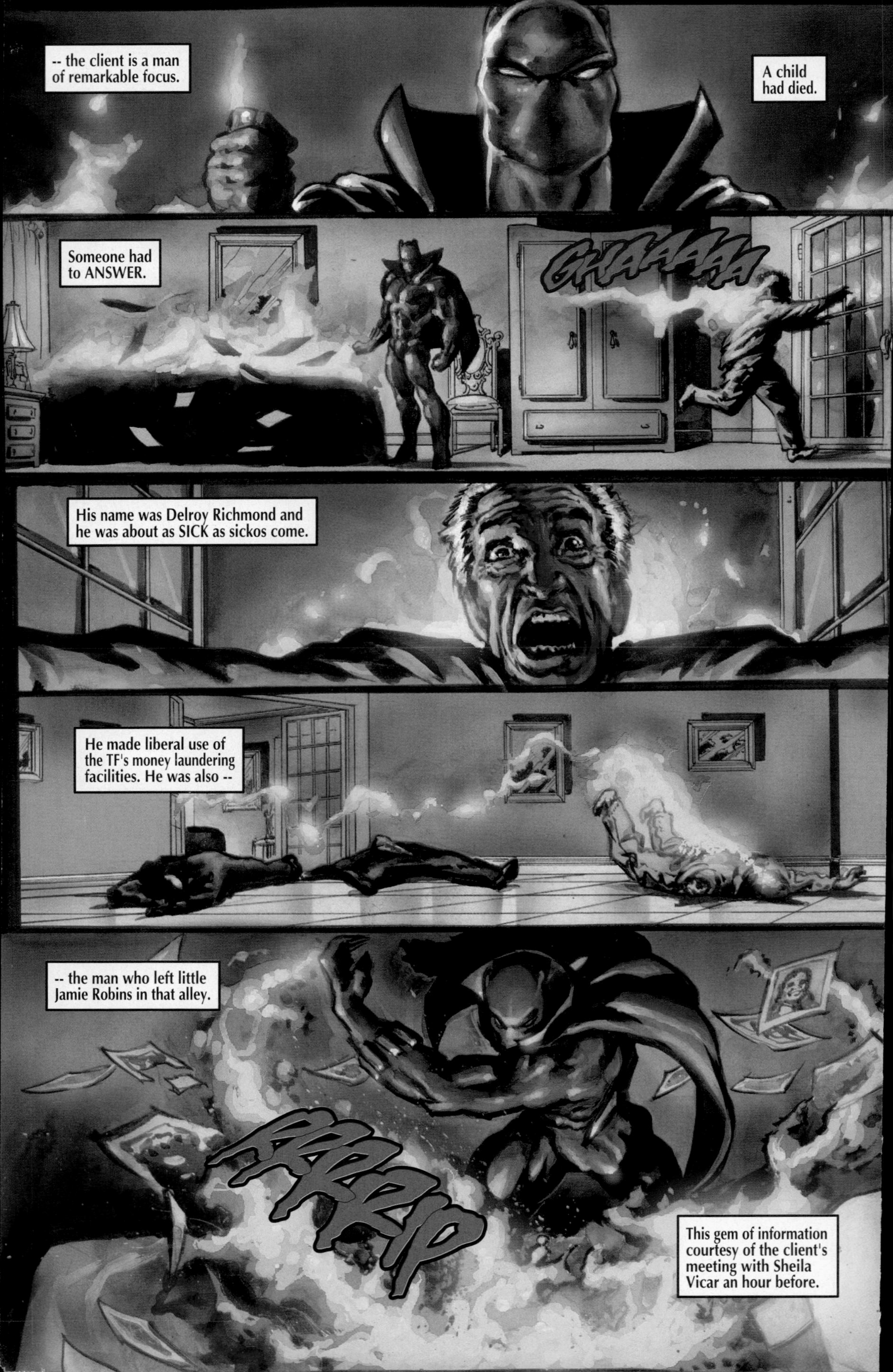
-- the client is a man of remarkable focus.
A child had died.
Someone had to ANSWER.
GHAAAAA
His name was Delroy Richmond and he was about as SICK as sickos come.
He made liberal use of the TF's money laundering facilities. He was also --
-- the man who left little Jamie Robins in that alley.
RRRIP
This gem of information courtesy of the client's meeting with Sheila Vicar an hour before.

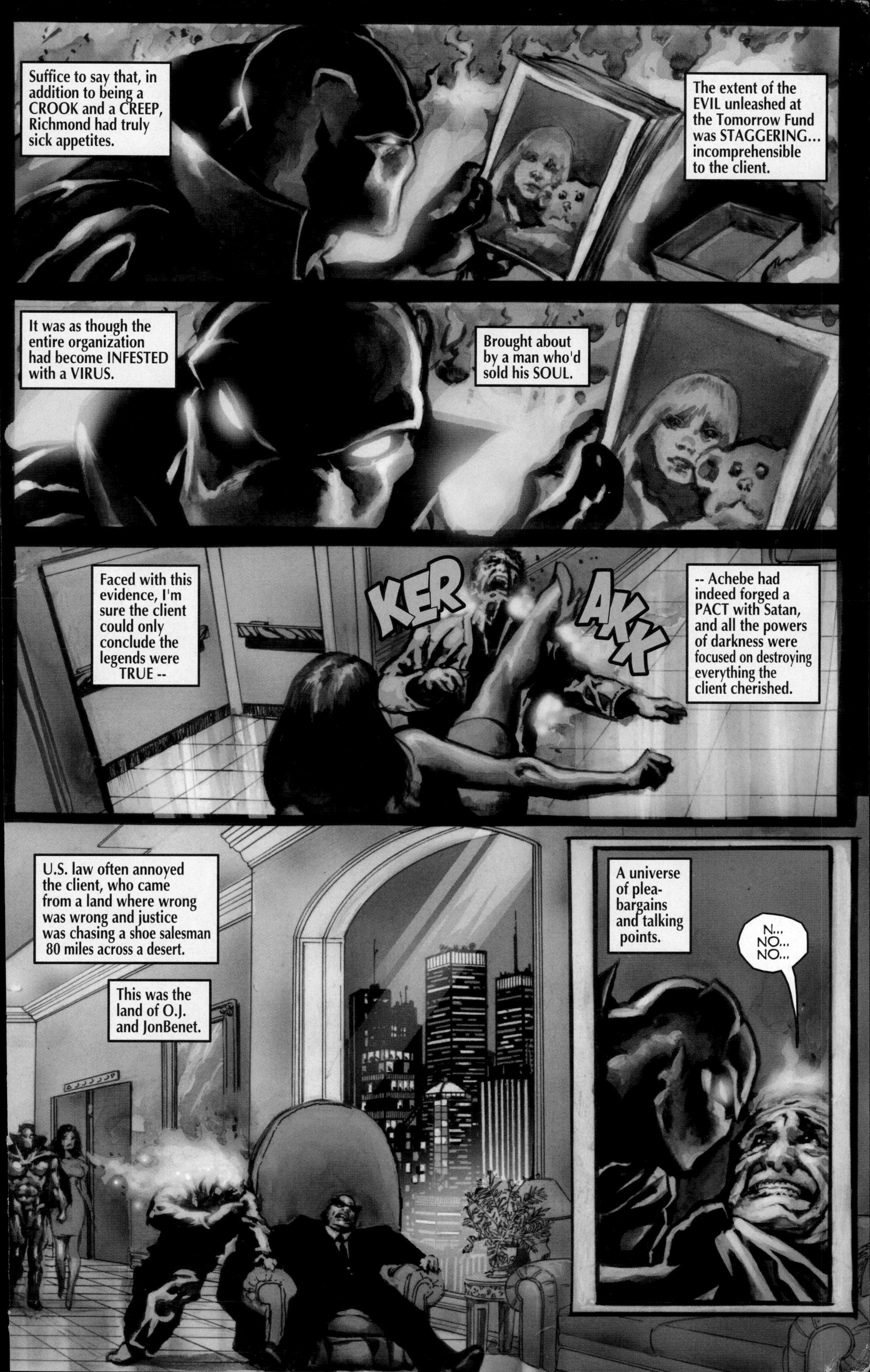

Suffice to say that, in addition to being a CROOK and a CREEP, Richmond had truly sick appetites.
The extent of the EVIL unleashed at the Tomorrow Fund was STAGGERING... incomprehensible to the client.
It was as though the entire organization had become INFESTED with a VIRUS.
Brought about by a man who'd sold his SOUL.
Faced with this evidence, I'm sure the client could only conclude the legends were TRUE --
KER
AKK
-- Achebe had indeed forged a PACT with Satan, and all the powers of darkness were focused on destroying everything the client cherished.
U.S. law often annoyed the client, who came from a land where wrong was wrong and justice was chasing a shoe salesman 80 miles across a desert.
This was the land of O.J. and JonBenet.
A universe of plea-bargains and talking points.
N... NO... NO...

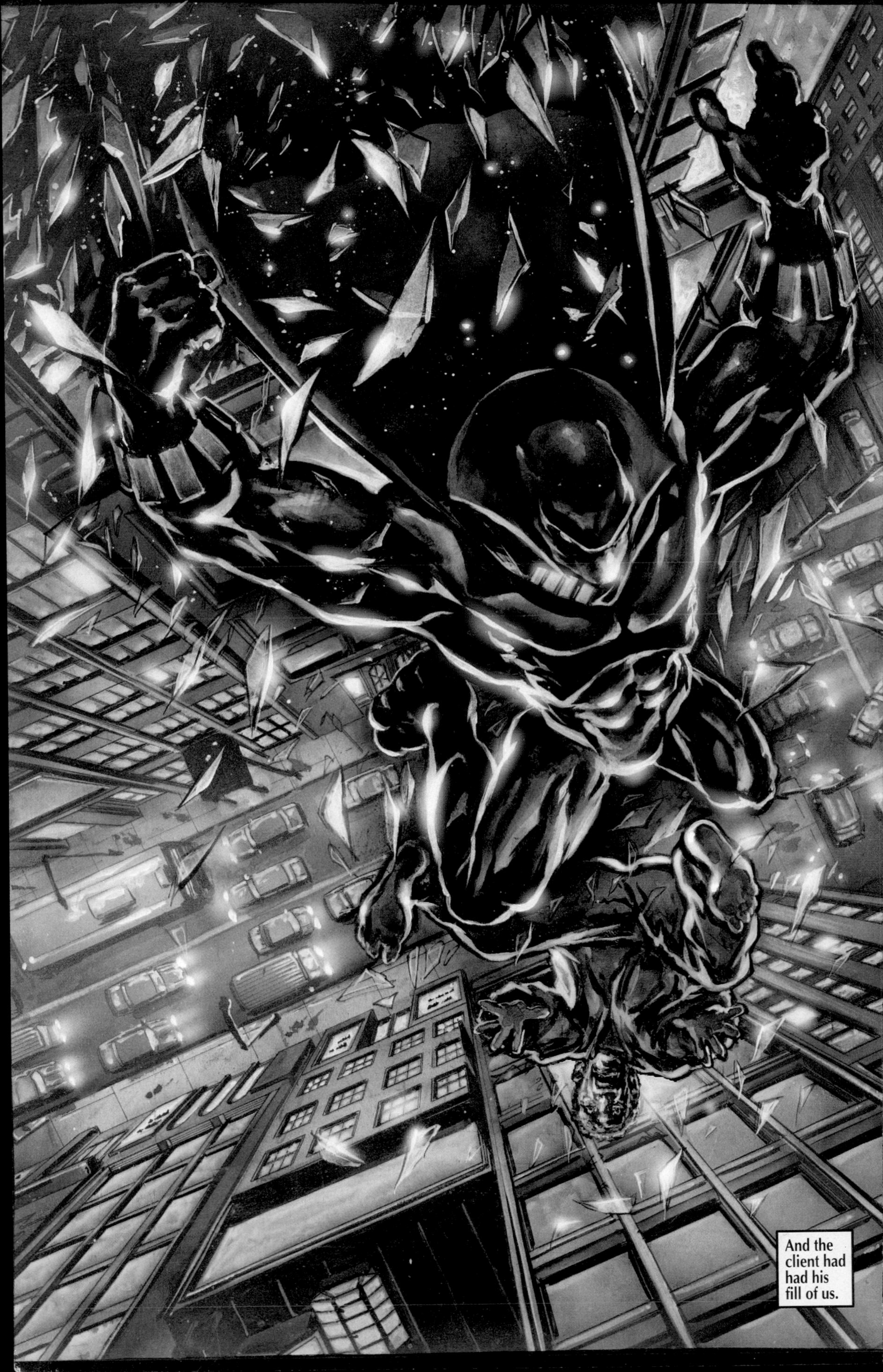
And the client had had his fill of us.

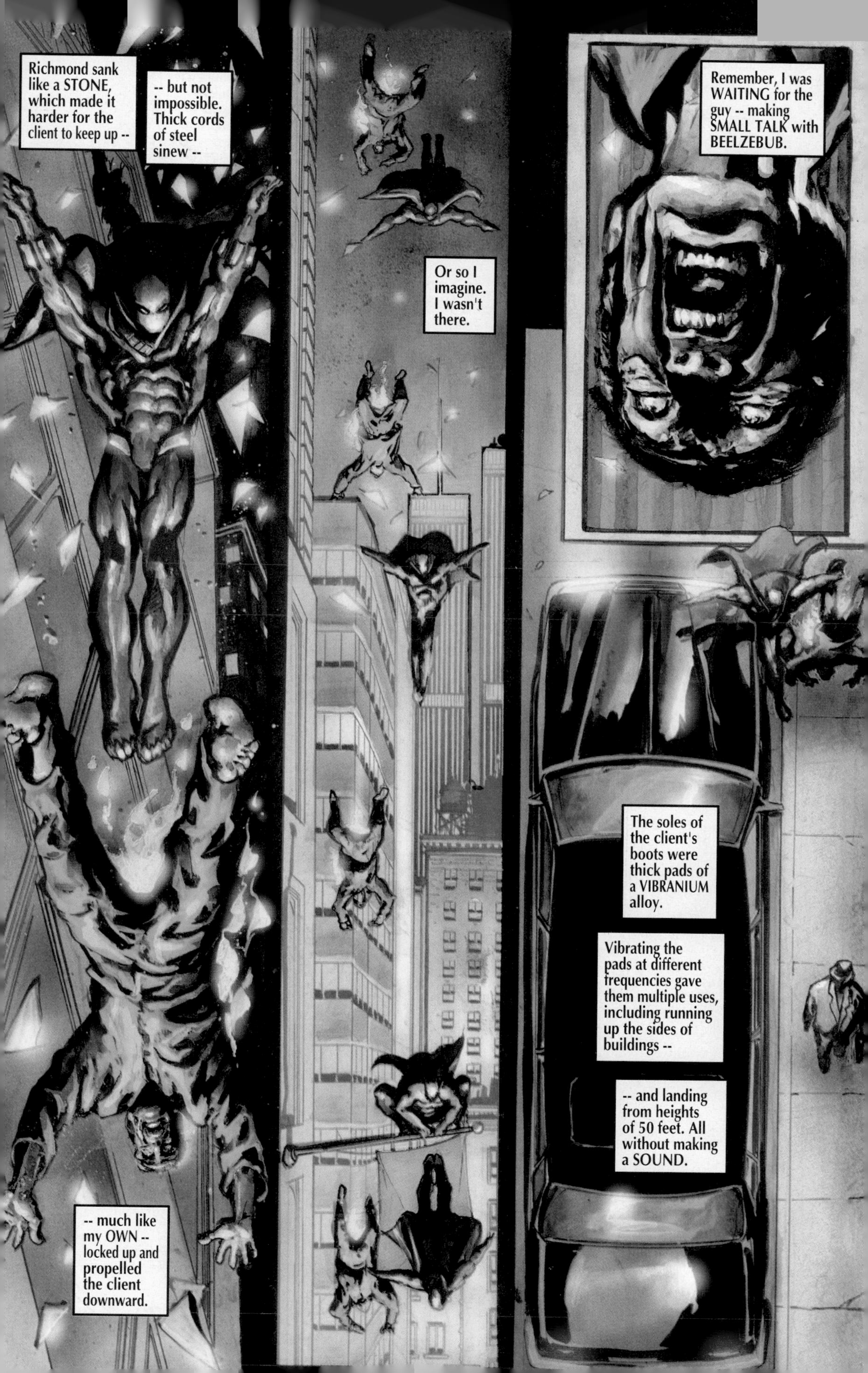
Richmond sank like a STONE, which made it harder for the client to keep up --
-- but not impossible. Thick cords of steel sinew --
-- much like my OWN -- locked up and propelled the client downward.
Or so I imagine. I wasn't there.
Remember, I was WAITING for the guy -- making SMALL TALK with BEELZEBUB.
The soles of the client's boots were thick pads of a VIBRANIUM alloy.
Vibrating the pads at different frequencies gave them multiple uses, including running up the sides of buildings --
-- and landing from heights of 50 feet. All without making a SOUND.

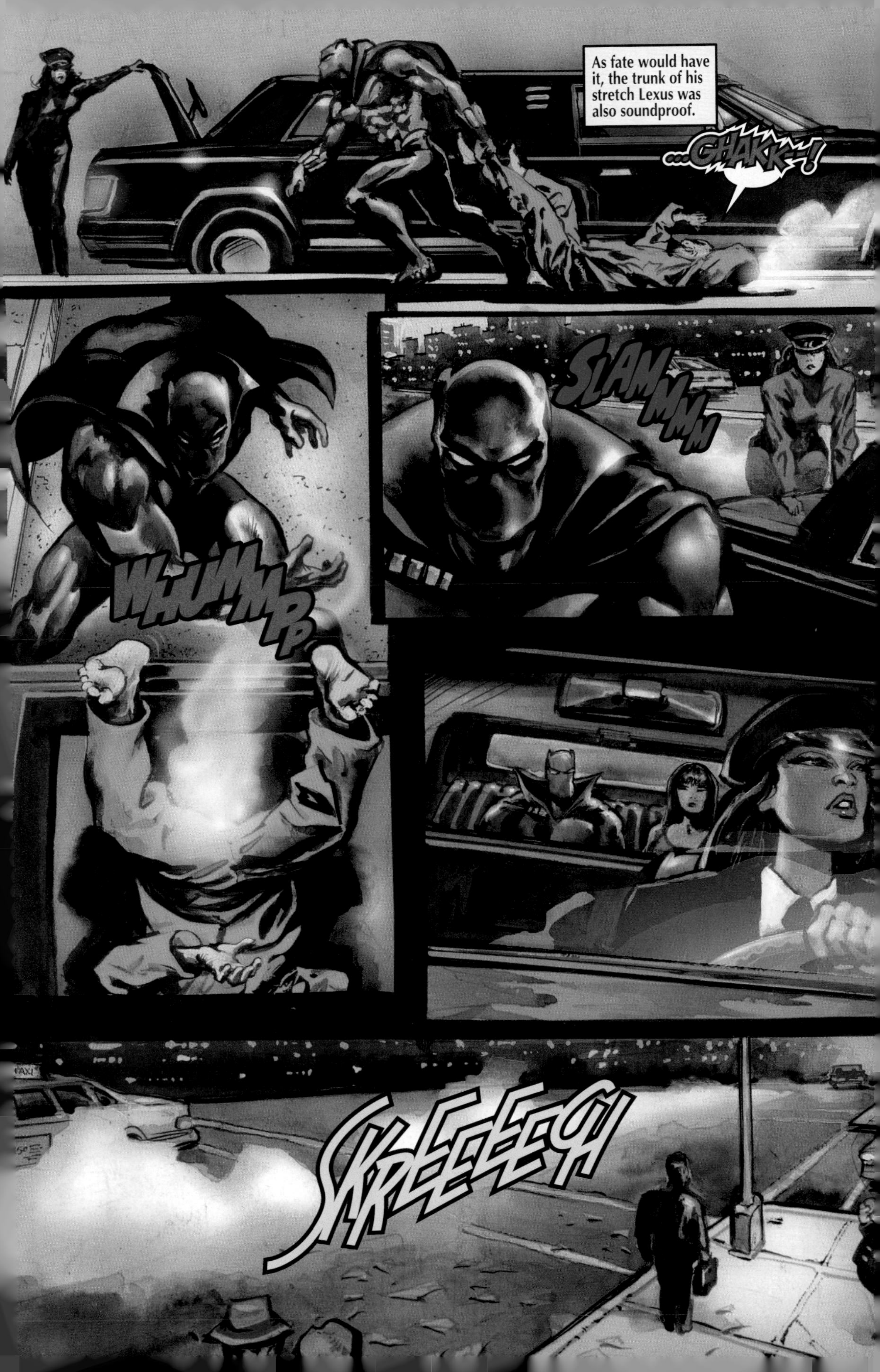

As fate would have it, the trunk of his stretch Lexus was also soundproof.
...GHAKK--!
WHUMMPP
SLAMMMM
SKREEEEGH

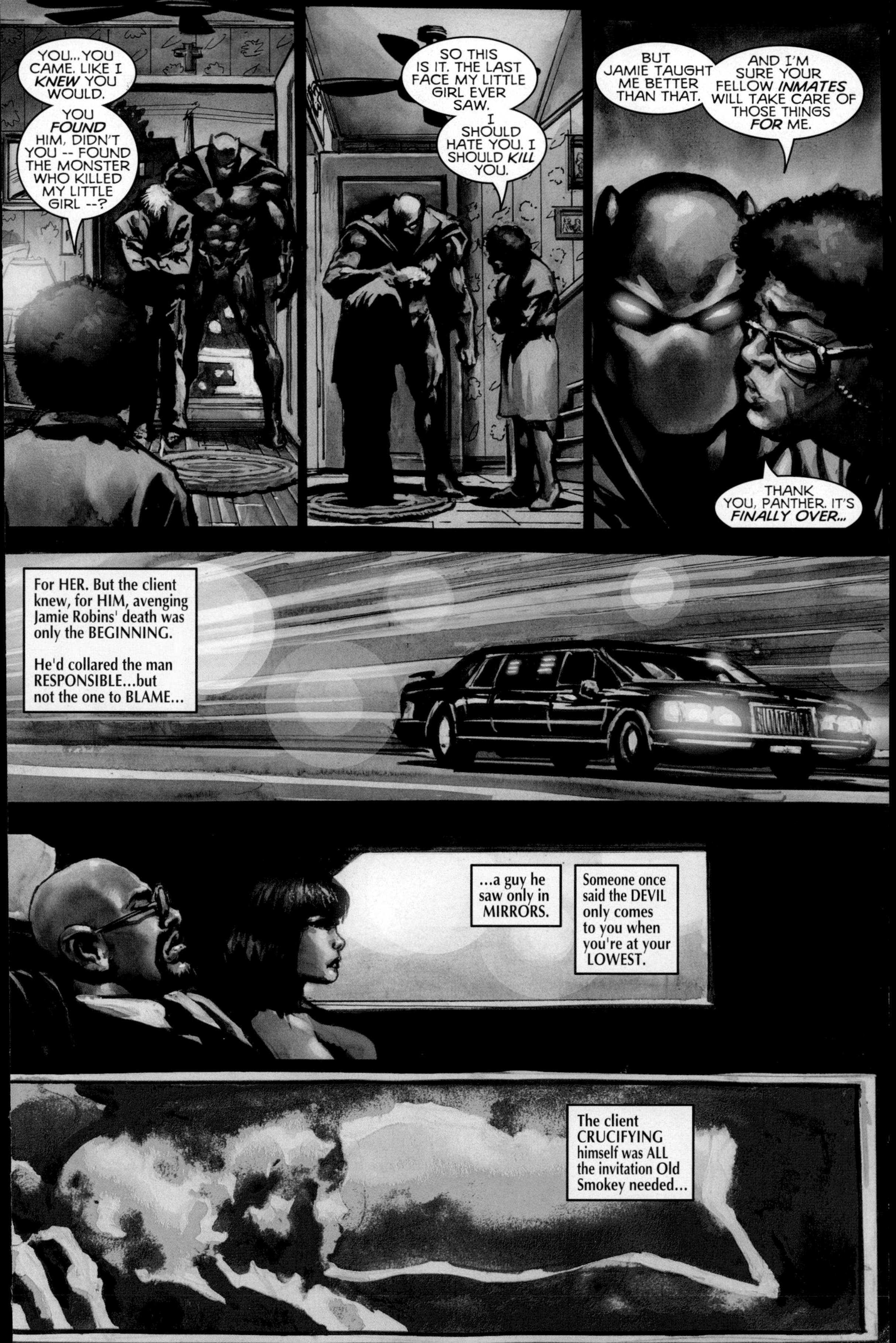

YOU...YOU CAME. LIKE I *KNEW* YOU WOULD.
YOU *FOUND* HIM, DIDN'T YOU -- FOUND THE MONSTER WHO KILLED MY LITTLE GIRL --?
SO THIS IS IT. THE LAST FACE MY LITTLE GIRL EVER SAW.
I SHOULD HATE YOU. I SHOULD *KILL* YOU.
BUT JAMIE TAUGHT ME BETTER THAN THAT.
AND I'M SURE YOUR FELLOW *INMATES* WILL TAKE CARE OF THOSE THINGS *FOR* ME.
THANK YOU, PANTHER. IT'S *FINALLY OVER...*
For HER. But the client knew, for HIM, avenging Jamie Robins' death was only the BEGINNING.
He'd collared the man RESPONSIBLE...but not the one to BLAME...
...a guy he saw only in MIRRORS.
Someone once said the DEVIL only comes to you when you're at your LOWEST.
The client CRUCIFYING himself was ALL the invitation Old Smokey needed...

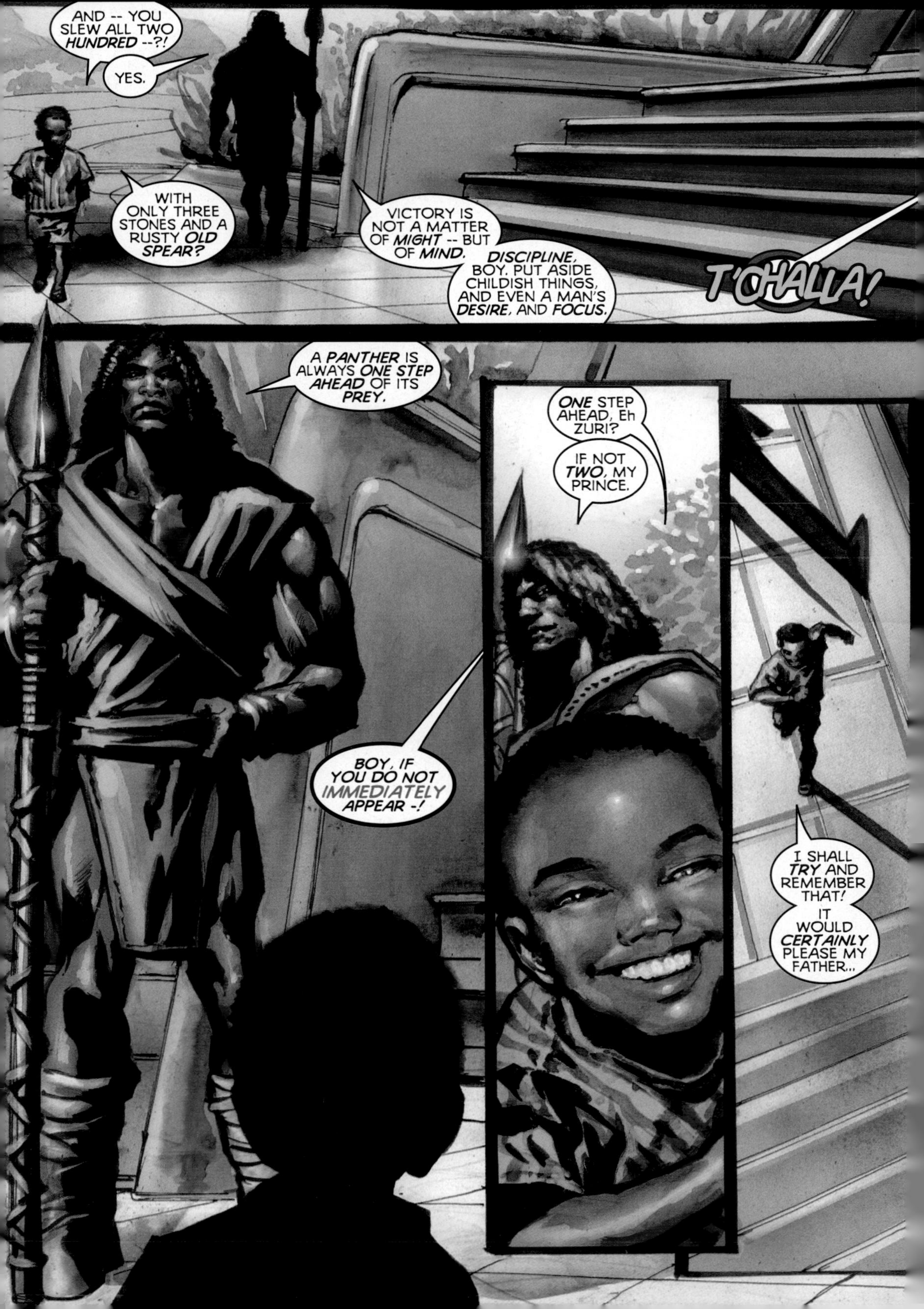
AND -- YOU SLEW ALL TWO *HUNDRED* --?!
YES.
WITH ONLY THREE STONES AND A RUSTY *OLD SPEAR?*
VICTORY IS NOT A MATTER OF *MIGHT* -- BUT OF *MIND.*
DISCIPLINE, BOY. PUT ASIDE CHILDISH THINGS, AND EVEN A MAN'S *DESIRE,* AND *FOCUS.*
T'CHALLA!
A *PANTHER* IS ALWAYS *ONE STEP AHEAD* OF ITS *PREY.*
ONE STEP AHEAD, Eh ZURI?
IF NOT *TWO,* MY PRINCE.
BOY, IF YOU DO NOT IMMEDIATELY APPEAR -!
I SHALL *TRY* AND REMEMBER THAT!
IT WOULD *CERTAINLY* PLEASE MY FATHER...

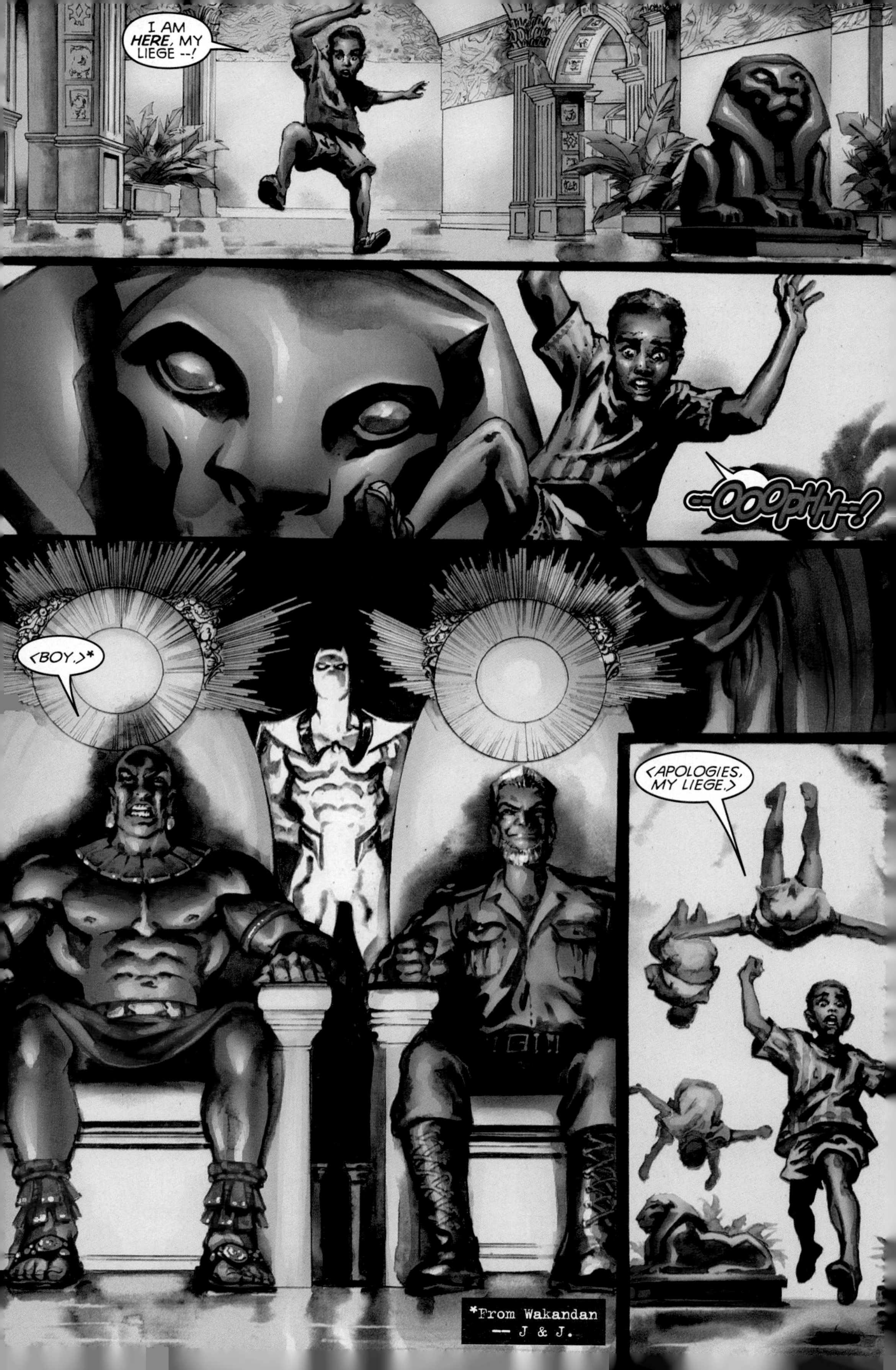
I AM HERE, MY LIEGE --!
--OOOPHH--!
<BOY,>*
<APOLOGIES, MY LIEGE.>
*From Wakandan -- J & J.

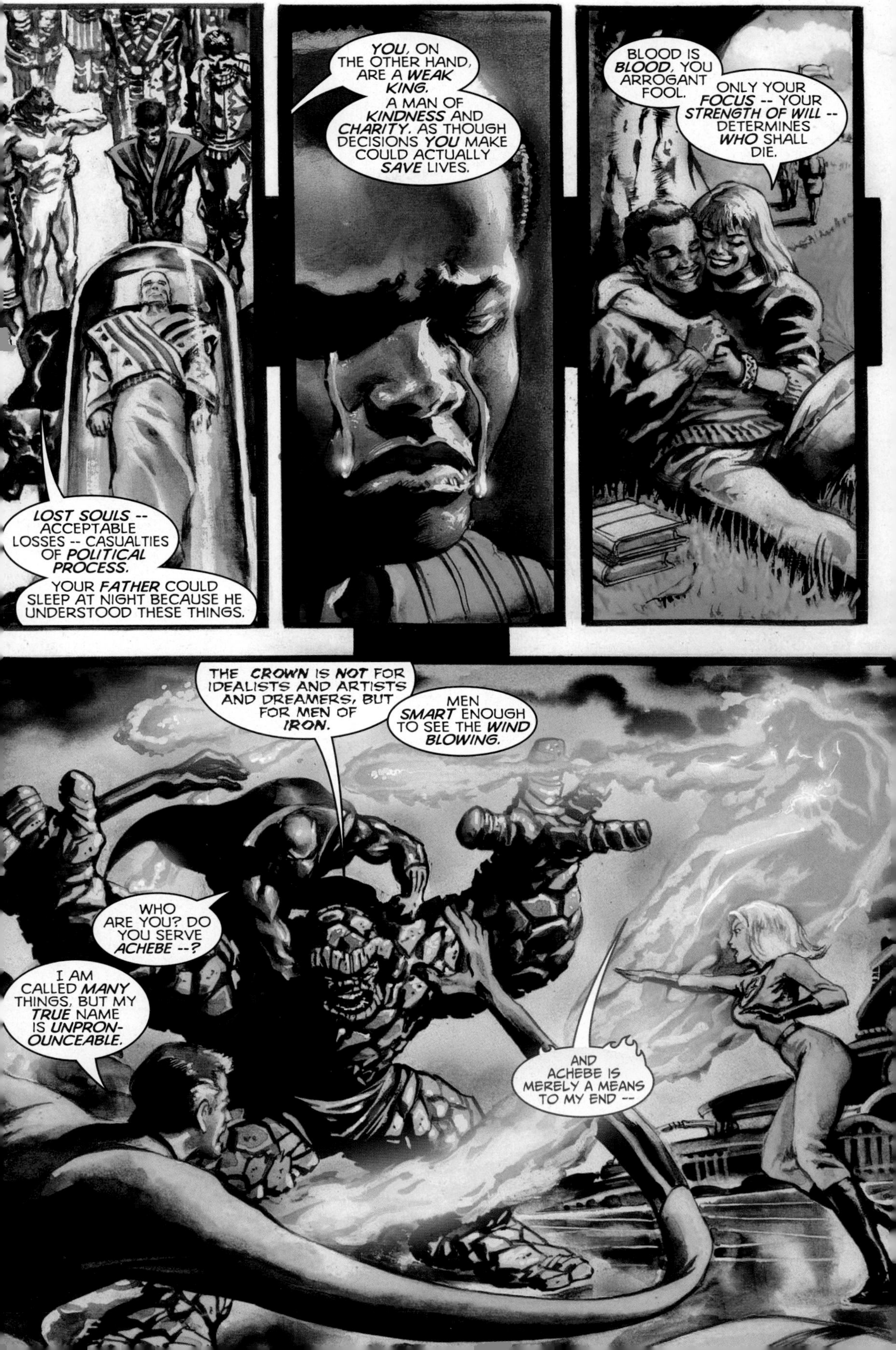
LOST SOULS -- ACCEPTABLE LOSSES -- CASUALTIES OF POLITICAL PROCESS.
YOUR FATHER COULD SLEEP AT NIGHT BECAUSE HE UNDERSTOOD THESE THINGS.
YOU, ON THE OTHER HAND, ARE A WEAK KING.
A MAN OF KINDNESS AND CHARITY. AS THOUGH DECISIONS YOU MAKE COULD ACTUALLY SAVE LIVES.
BLOOD IS BLOOD, YOU ARROGANT FOOL.
ONLY YOUR FOCUS -- YOUR STRENGTH OF WILL -- DETERMINES WHO SHALL DIE.
THE CROWN IS NOT FOR IDEALISTS AND ARTISTS AND DREAMERS, BUT FOR MEN OF IRON.
MEN SMART ENOUGH TO SEE THE WIND BLOWING.
WHO ARE YOU? DO YOU SERVE ACHEBE --?
I AM CALLED MANY THINGS, BUT MY TRUE NAME IS UNPRONOUNCEABLE.
AND ACHEBE IS MERELY A MEANS TO MY END --

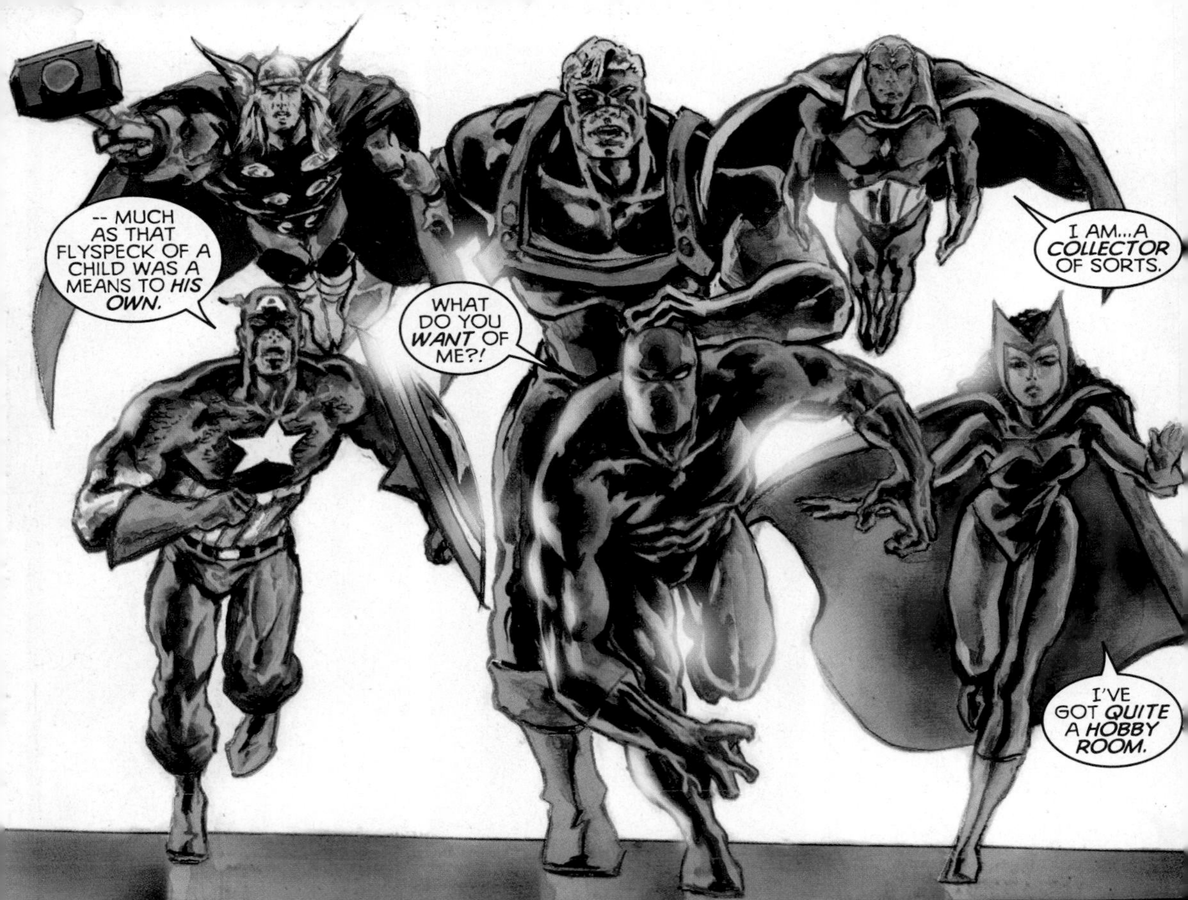
-- MUCH AS THAT FLYSPECK OF A CHILD WAS A MEANS TO HIS OWN.
WHAT DO YOU WANT OF ME?!
I AM...A COLLECTOR OF SORTS.
I'VE GOT QUITE A HOBBY ROOM.

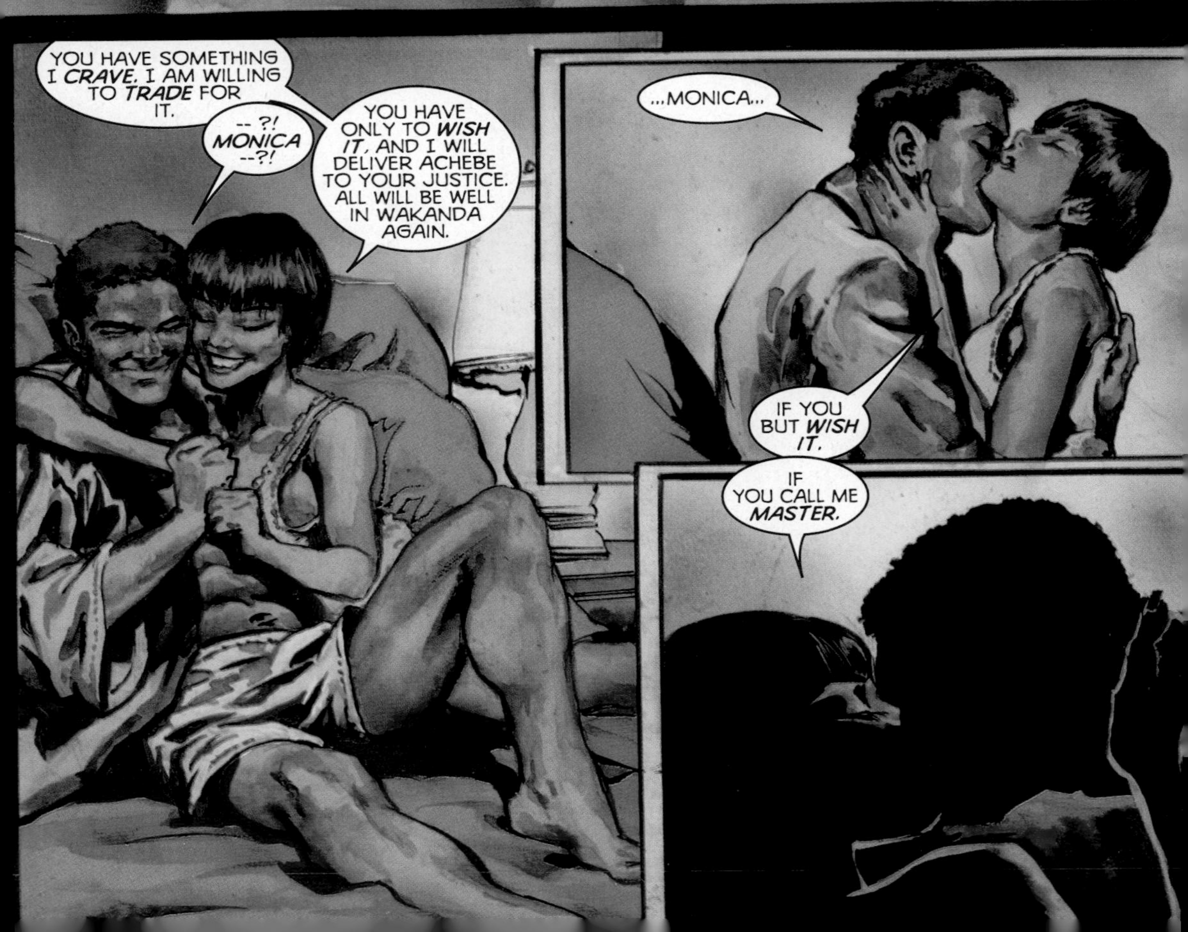
YOU HAVE SOMETHING I CRAVE. I AM WILLING TO TRADE FOR IT.
-- ?! MONICA --?!
YOU HAVE ONLY TO WISH IT, AND I WILL DELIVER ACHEBE TO YOUR JUSTICE. ALL WILL BE WELL IN WAKANDA AGAIN.
...MONICA...
IF YOU BUT WISH IT.
IF YOU CALL ME MASTER.

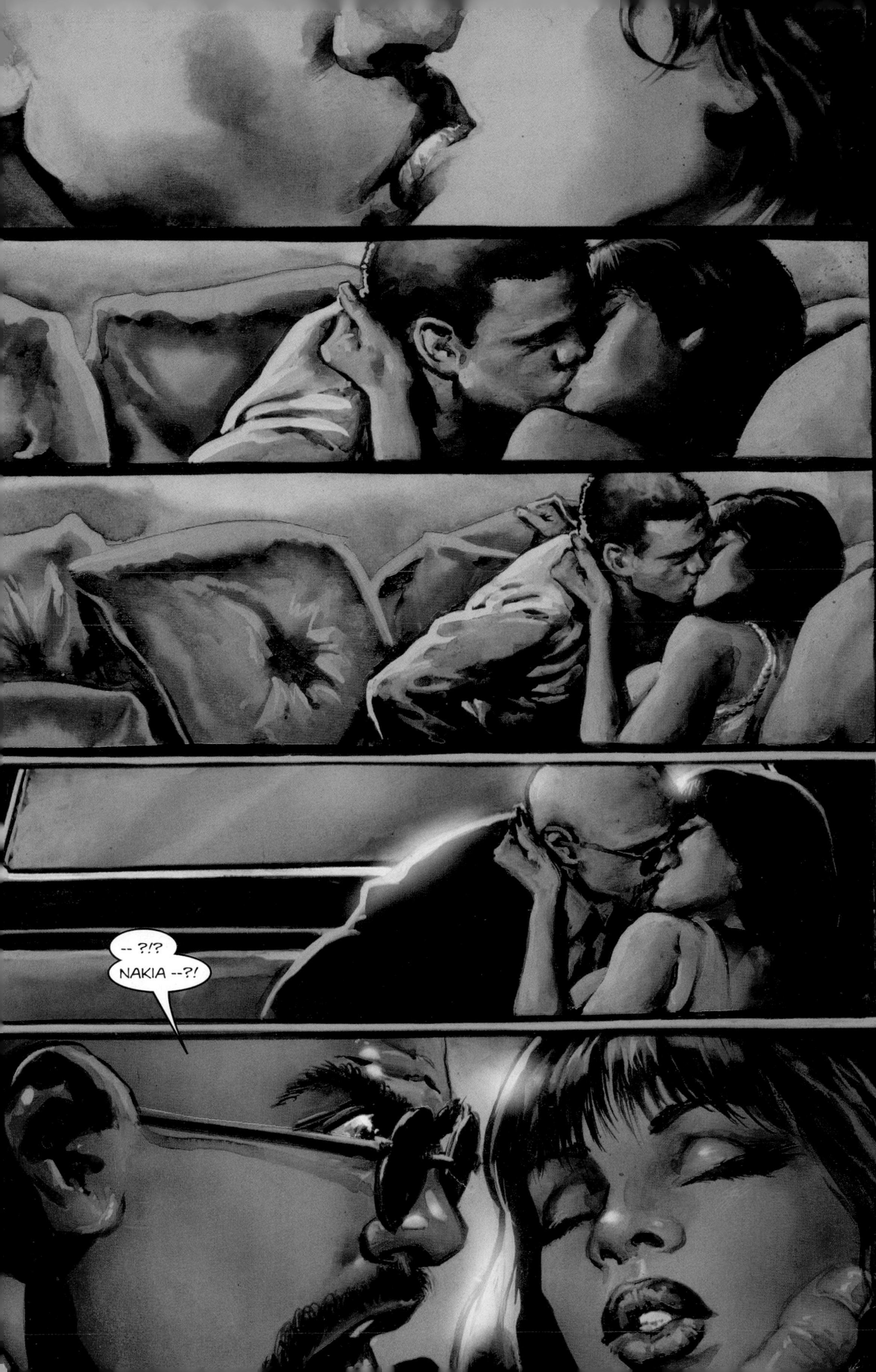
-- ?!?
NAKIA --?!

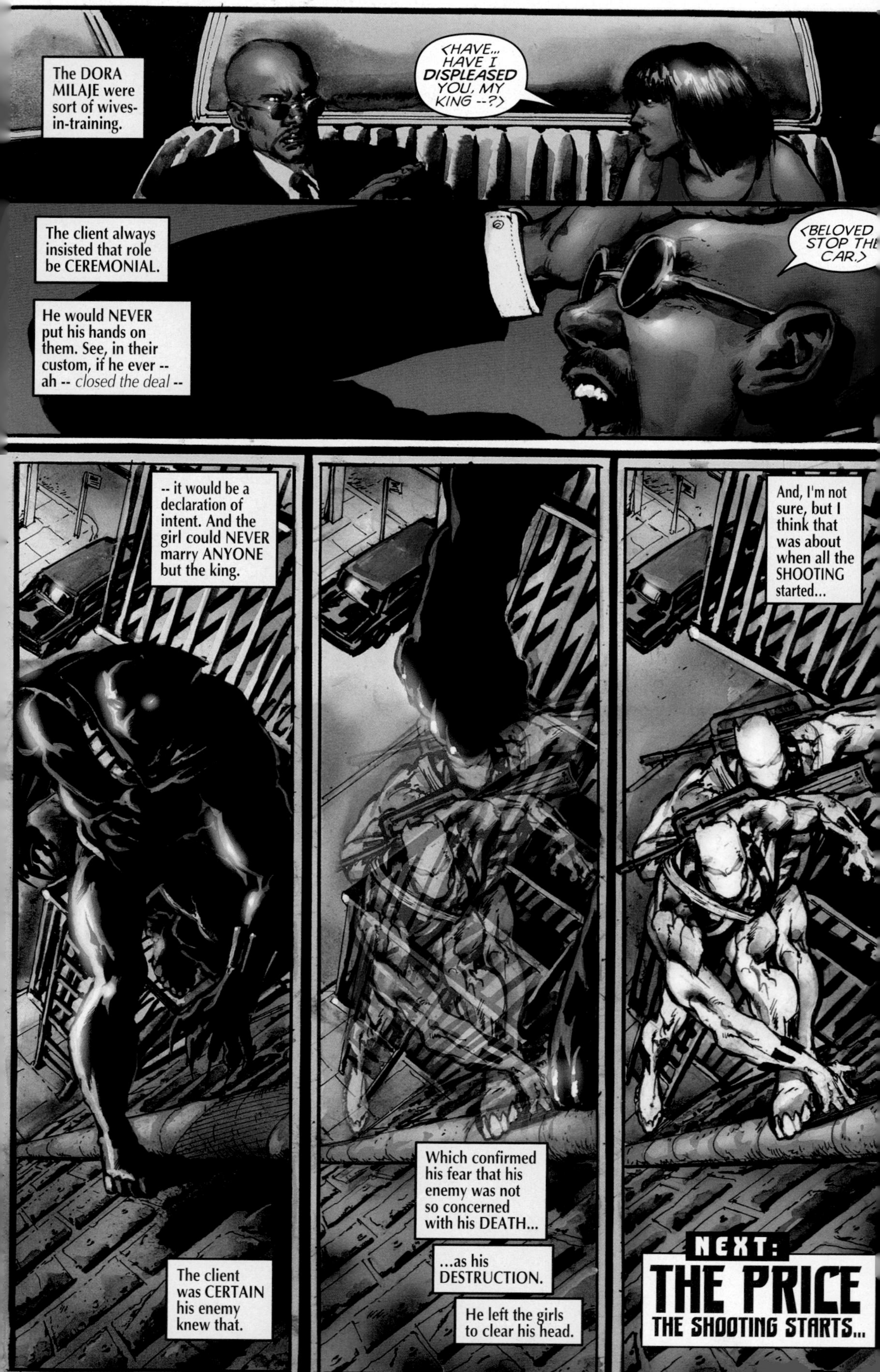

The DORA MILAJE were sort of wives-in-training.
<HAVE... HAVE I DISPLEASED YOU, MY KING --?>
The client always insisted that role be CEREMONIAL.
He would NEVER put his hands on them. See, in their custom, if he ever -- ah -- closed the deal --
<BELOVED STOP THE CAR.>
-- it would be a declaration of intent. And the girl could NEVER marry ANYONE but the king.
The client was CERTAIN his enemy knew that.
Which confirmed his fear that his enemy was not so concerned with his DEATH...
...as his DESTRUCTION.
He left the girls to clear his head.
And, I'm not sure, but I think that was about when all the SHOOTING started...
NEXT:
THE PRICE
THE SHOOTING STARTS...

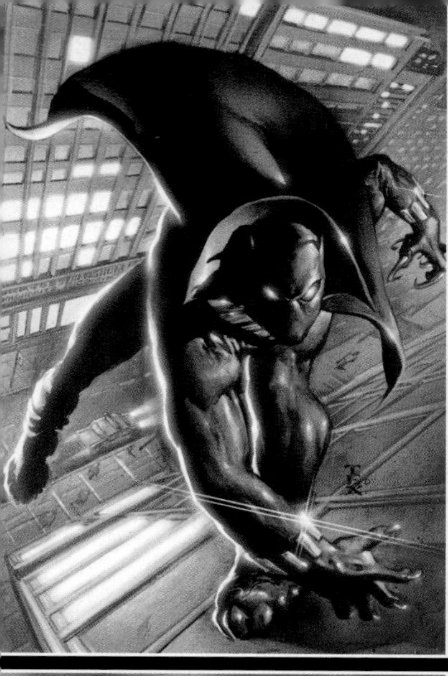
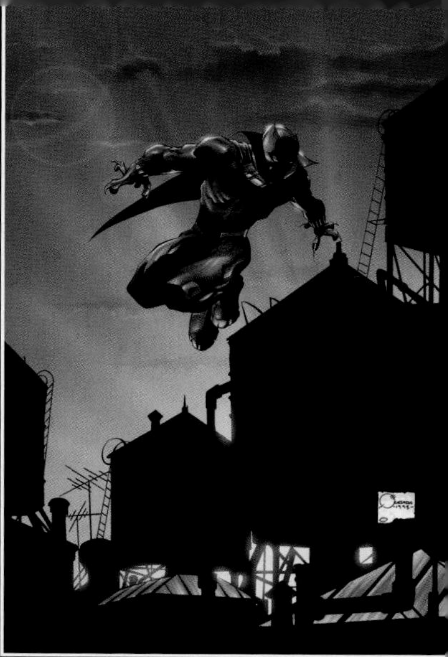
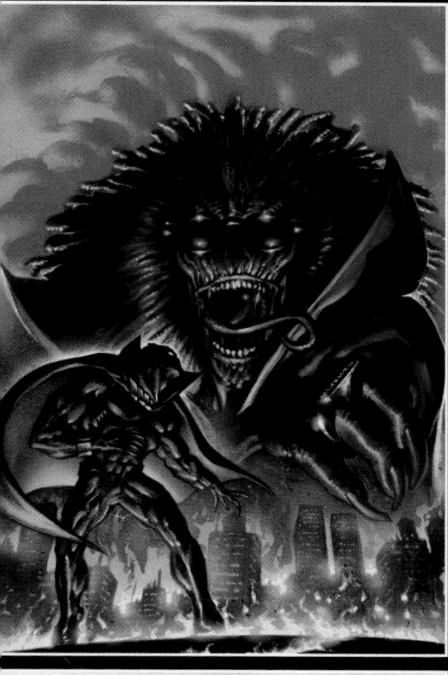
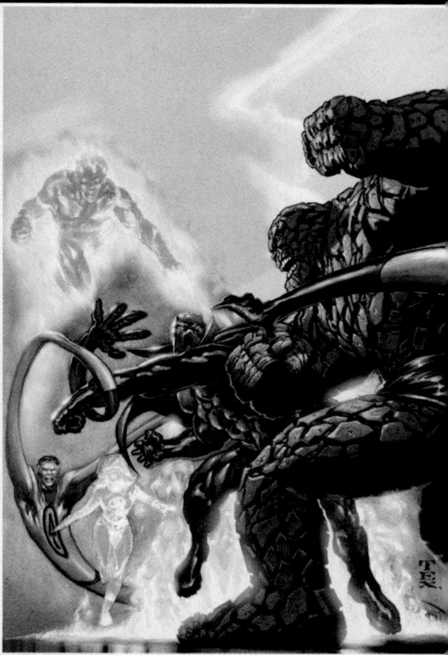
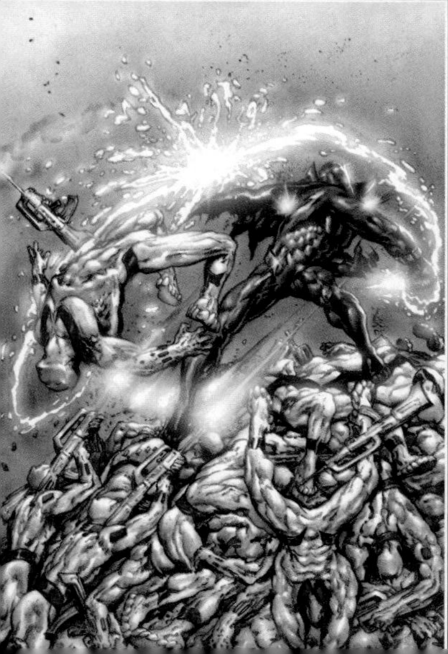
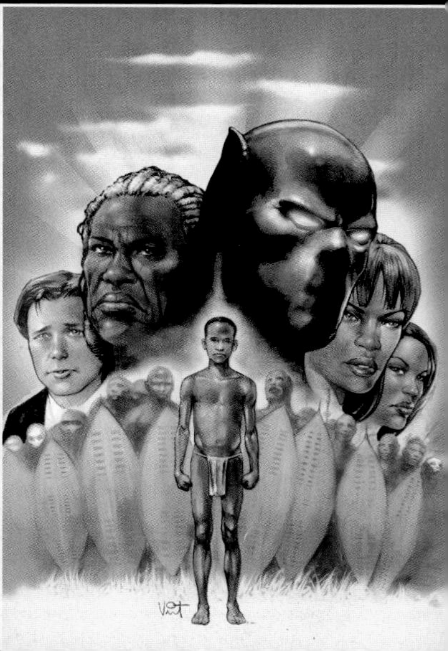

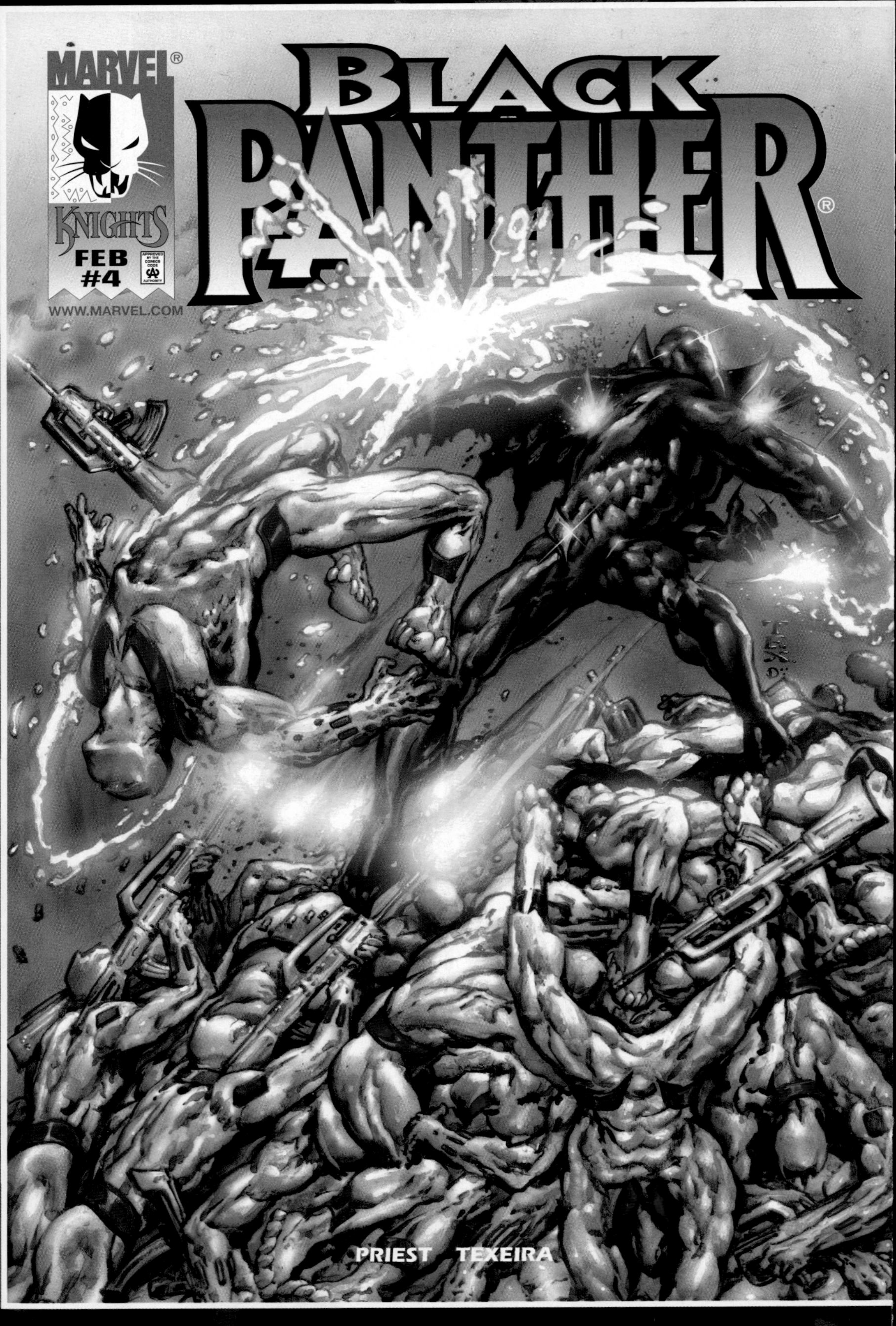
MARVEL®
KNIGHTS
FEB
#4
APPROVED BY THE COMICS CODE AUTHORITY
WWW.MARVEL.COM
BLACK PANTHER®
PRIEST TEXEIRA

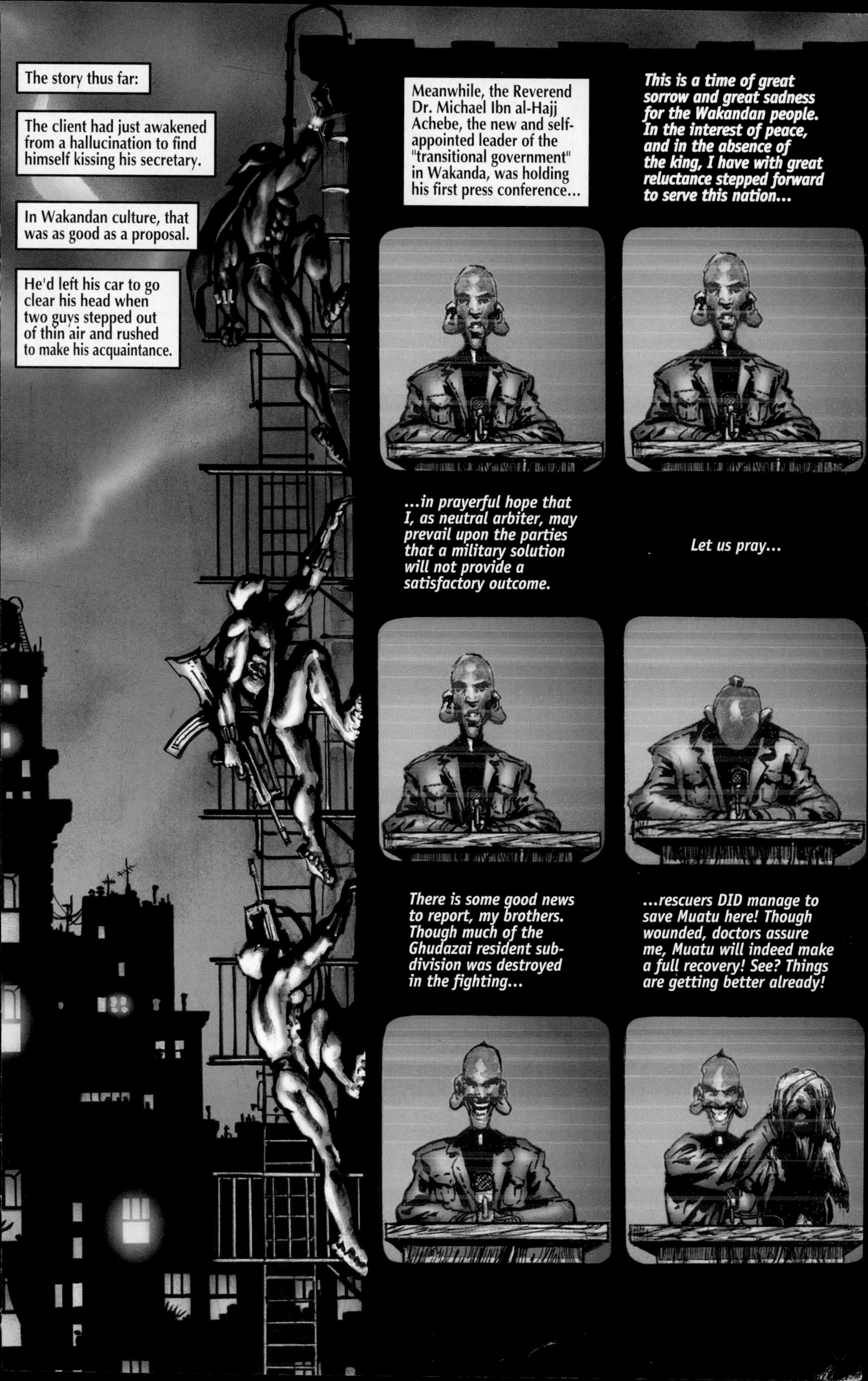
The story thus far:
The client had just awakened from a hallucination to find himself kissing his secretary.
In Wakandan culture, that was as good as a proposal.
He'd left his car to go clear his head when two guys stepped out of thin air and rushed to make his acquaintance.
Meanwhile, the Reverend Dr. Michael Ibn al-Hajj Achebe, the new and self-appointed leader of the "transitional government" in Wakanda, was holding his first press conference...
This is a time of great sorrow and great sadness for the Wakandan people. In the interest of peace, and in the absence of the king, I have with great reluctance stepped forward to serve this nation...
...in prayerful hope that I, as neutral arbiter, may prevail upon the parties that a military solution will not provide a satisfactory outcome.
Let us pray...
There is some good news to report, my brothers. Though much of the Ghudazai resident sub-division was destroyed in the fighting...
...rescuers DID manage to save Muatu here! Though wounded, doctors assure me, Muatu will indeed make a full recovery! See? Things are getting better already!

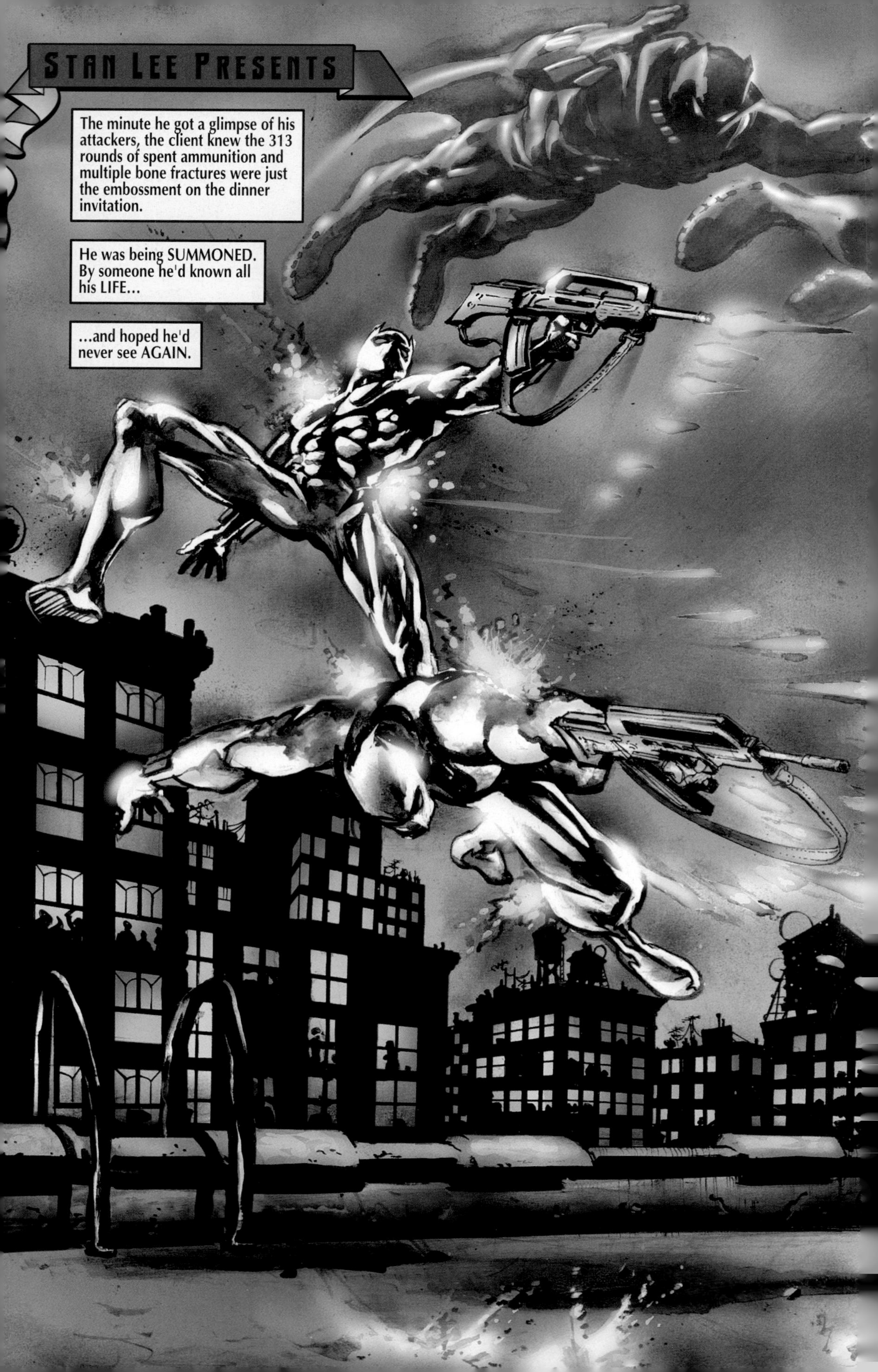
STAN LEE PRESENTS
The minute he got a glimpse of his attackers, the client knew the 313 rounds of spent ammunition and multiple bone fractures were just the embossment on the dinner invitation.
He was being SUMMONED. By someone he'd known all his LIFE...
...and hoped he'd never see AGAIN.

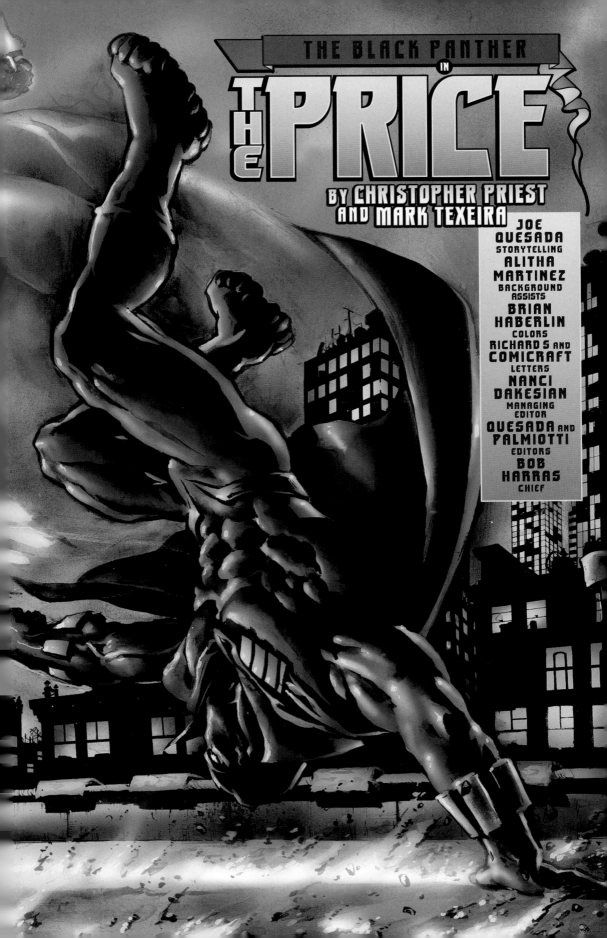

THE BLACK PANTHER
IN
THE PRICE

BY CHRISTOPHER PRIEST
AND MARK TEXEIRA

JOE QUESADA
STORYTELLING
ALITHA MARTINEZ
BACKGROUND ASSISTS
BRIAN HABERLIN
COLORS
RICHARD S AND COMICRAFT
LETTERS
NANCI DAKESIAN
MANAGING EDITOR
QUESADA AND PALMIOTTI
EDITORS
BOB HARRAS
CHIEF

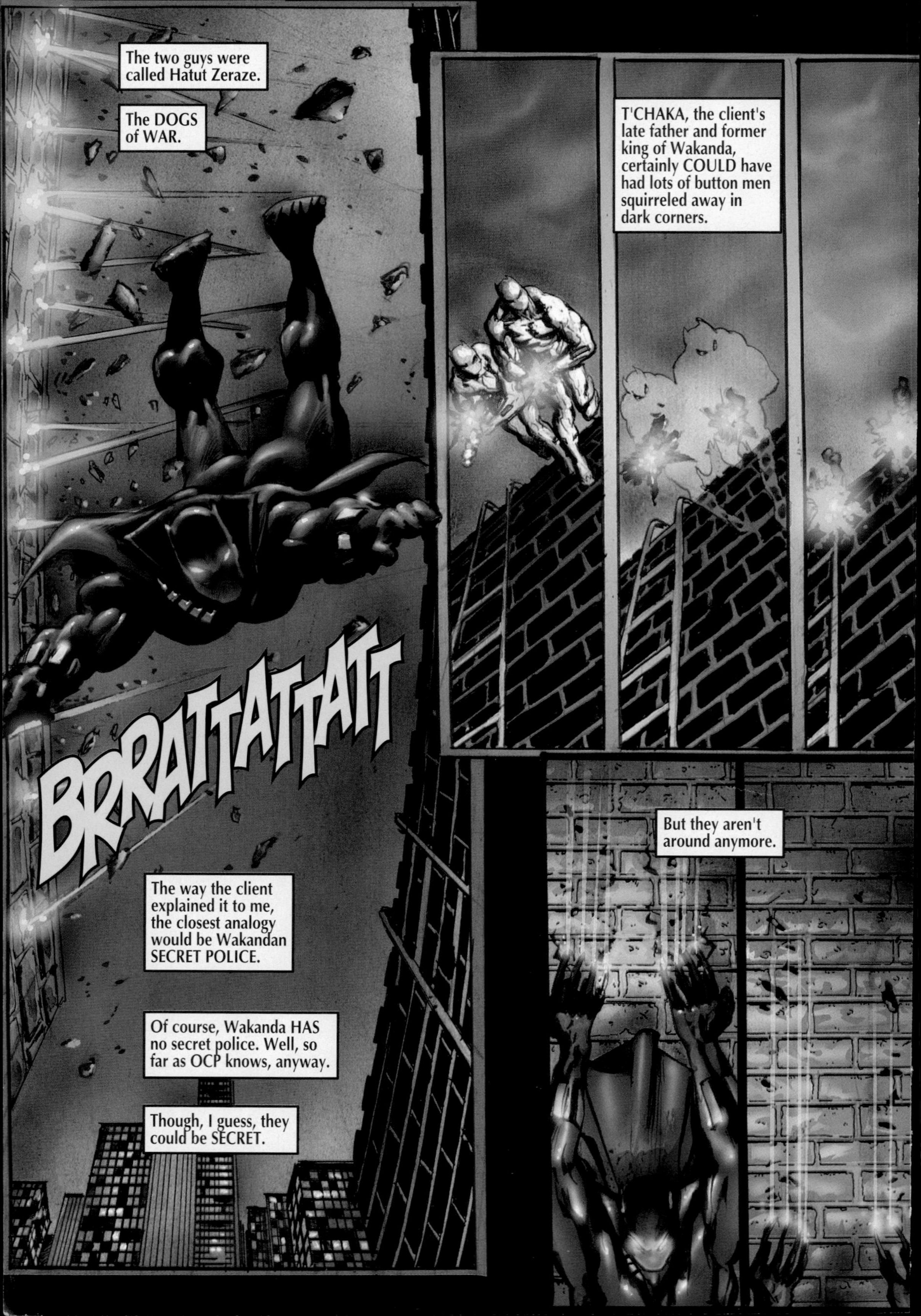

The two guys were called Hatut Zeraze.
The DOGS of WAR.
T'CHAKA, the client's late father and former king of Wakanda, certainly COULD have had lots of button men squirreled away in dark corners.
BRRATTATTATT
The way the client explained it to me, the closest analogy would be Wakandan SECRET POLICE.
Of course, Wakanda HAS no secret police. Well, so far as OCP knows, anyway.
Though, I guess, they could be SECRET.
But they aren't around anymore.

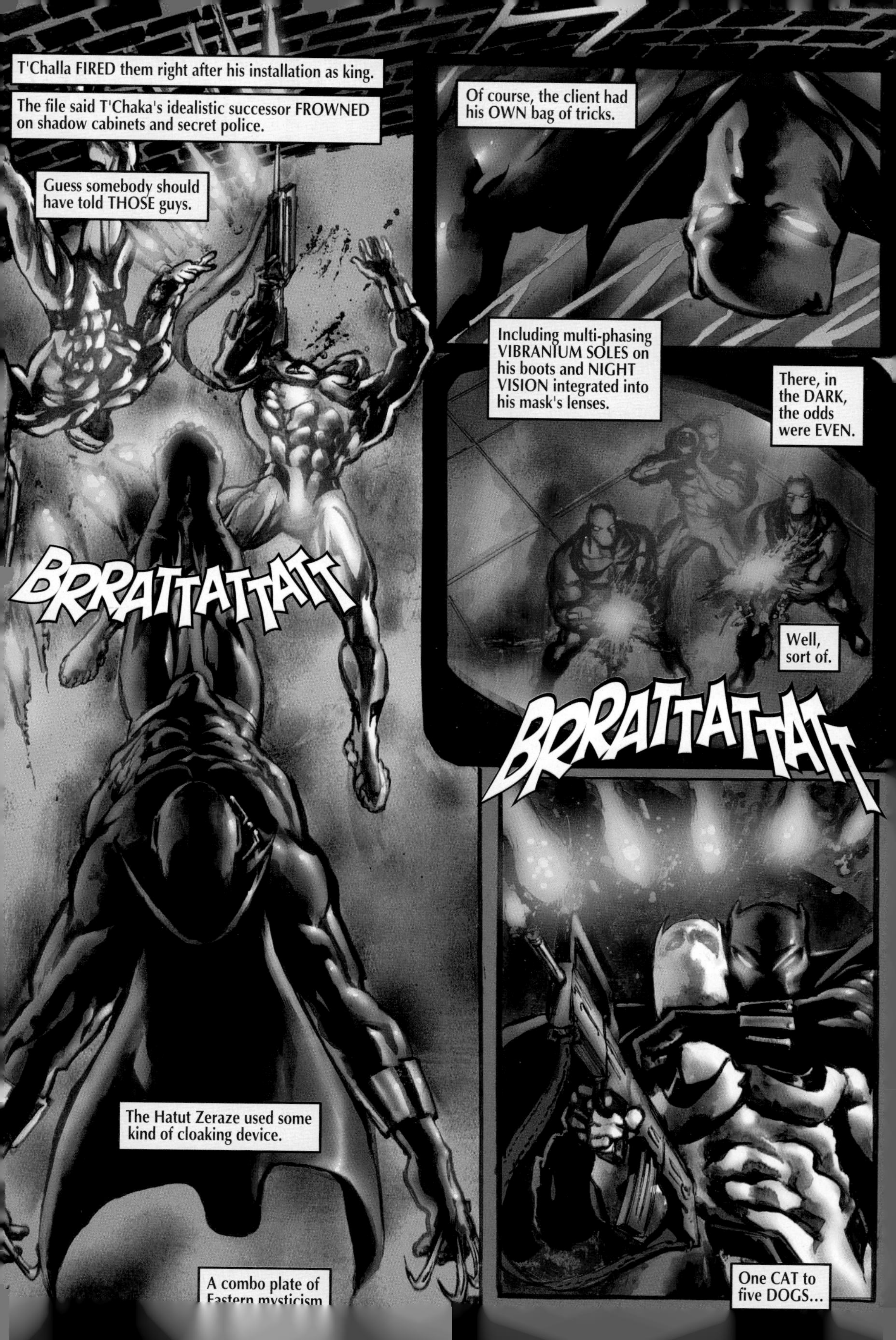
T'Challa FIRED them right after his installation as king.
The file said T'Chaka's idealistic successor FROWNED on shadow cabinets and secret police.
Guess somebody should have told THOSE guys.
BRRATTATTATT
The Hatut Zeraze used some kind of cloaking device.
A combo plate of
Of course, the client had his OWN bag of tricks.
Including multi-phasing VIBRANIUM SOLES on his boots and NIGHT VISION integrated into his mask's lenses.
There, in the DARK, the odds were EVEN.
Well, sort of.
BRRATTATTATT
One CAT to five DOGS...

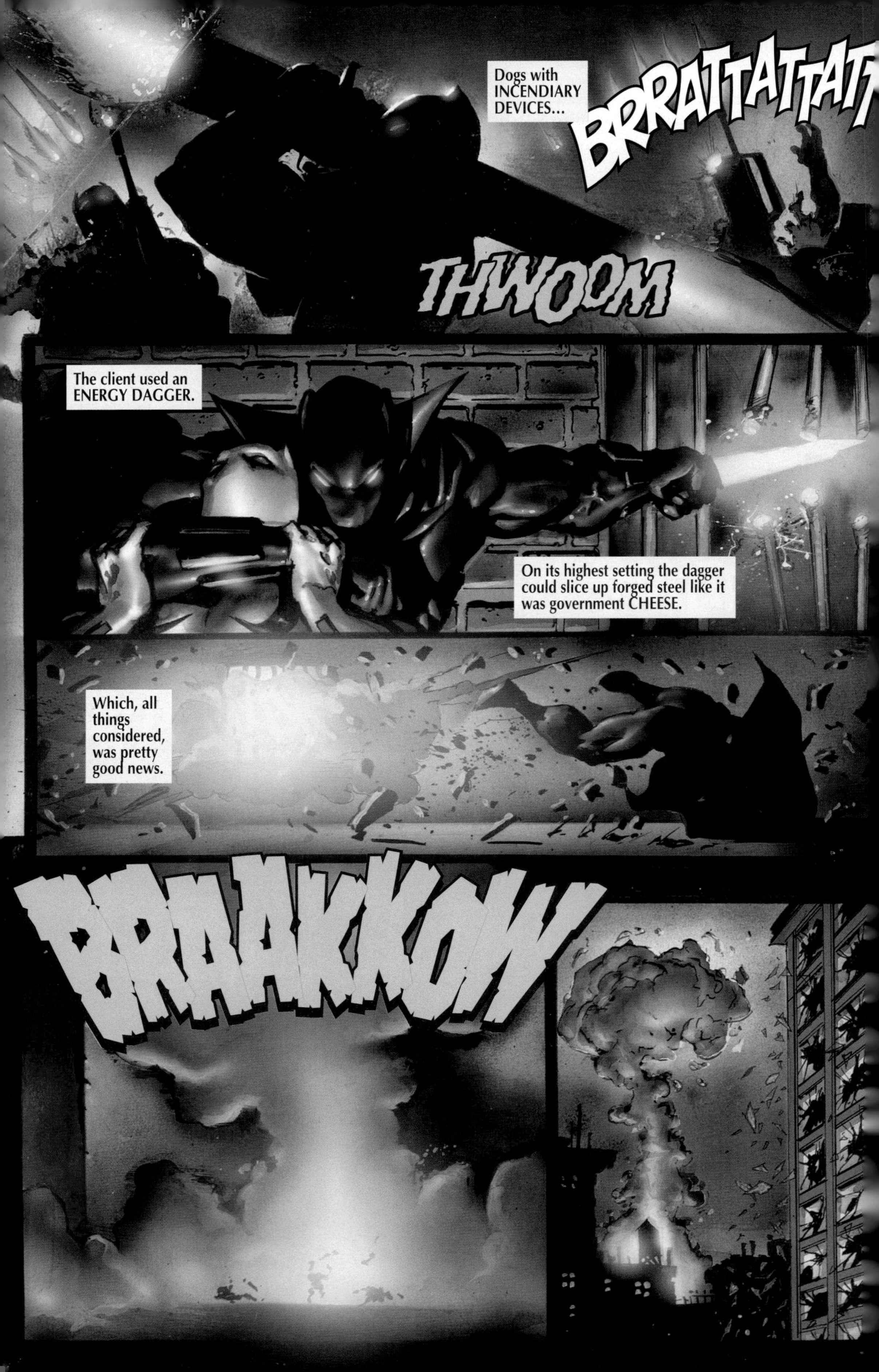
Dogs with INCENDIARY DEVICES...
BRRATTATTATT
THWOOM
The client used an ENERGY DAGGER.
On its highest setting the dagger could slice up forged steel like it was government CHEESE.
Which, all things considered, was pretty good news.
BRAAKKOW

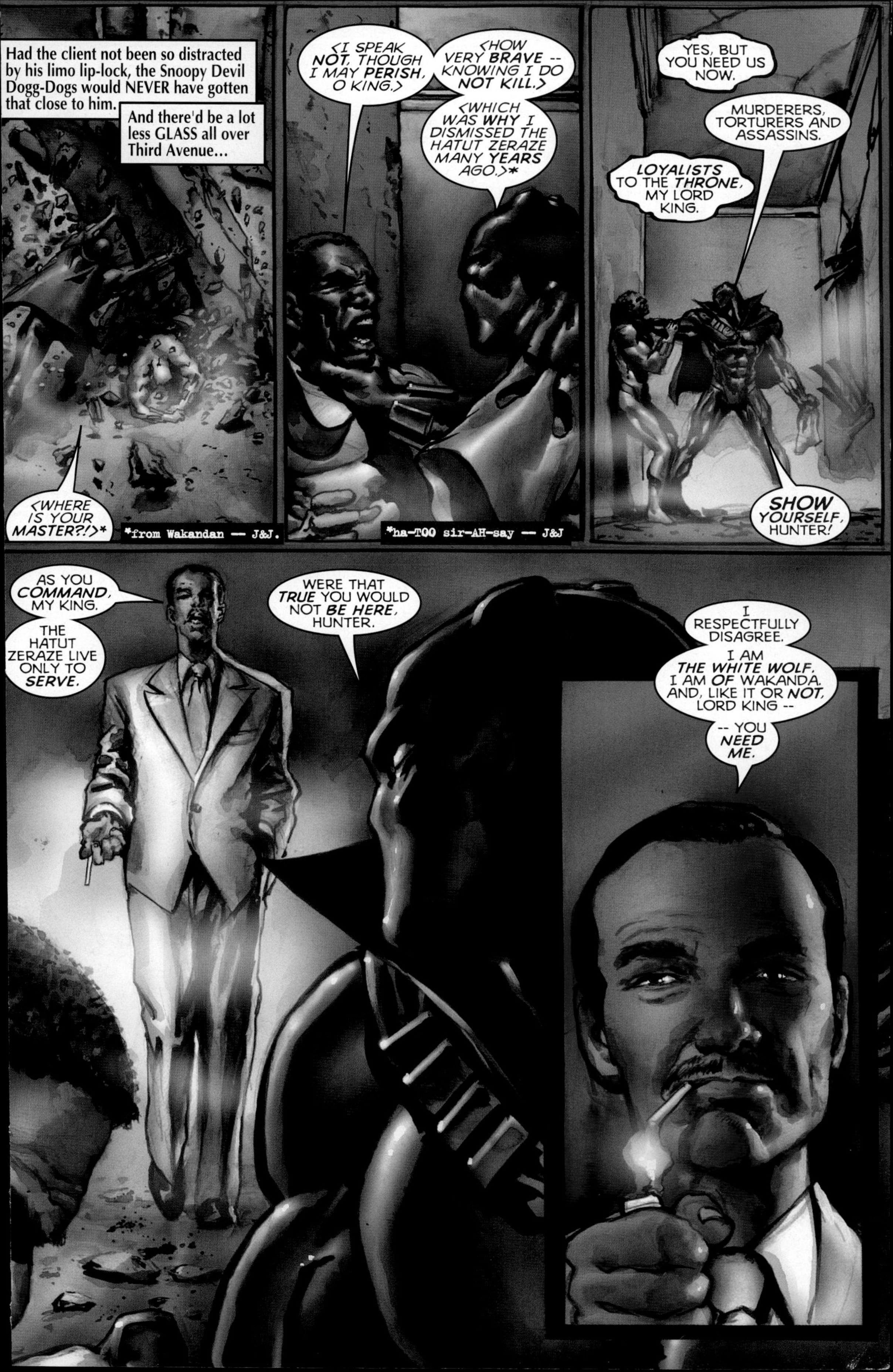
Had the client not been so distracted by his limo lip-lock, the Snoopy Devil Dogg-Dogs would NEVER have gotten that close to him.
And there'd be a lot less GLASS all over Third Avenue...
<WHERE IS YOUR MASTER?!>*
*from Wakandan -- J&J.
<I SPEAK NOT, THOUGH I MAY PERISH, O KING.>
<HOW VERY BRAVE -- KNOWING I DO NOT KILL.>
<WHICH WAS WHY I DISMISSED THE HATUT ZERAZE MANY YEARS AGO.>*
*ha-TOO sir-AH-say -- J&J
YES, BUT YOU NEED US NOW.
MURDERERS, TORTURERS AND ASSASSINS.
LOYALISTS TO THE THRONE, MY LORD KING.
SHOW YOURSELF, HUNTER!
AS YOU COMMAND, MY KING.
THE HATUT ZERAZE LIVE ONLY TO SERVE.
WERE THAT TRUE YOU WOULD NOT BE HERE, HUNTER.
I RESPECTFULLY DISAGREE.
I AM THE WHITE WOLF. I AM OF WAKANDA. AND, LIKE IT OR NOT, LORD KING --
-- YOU NEED ME.

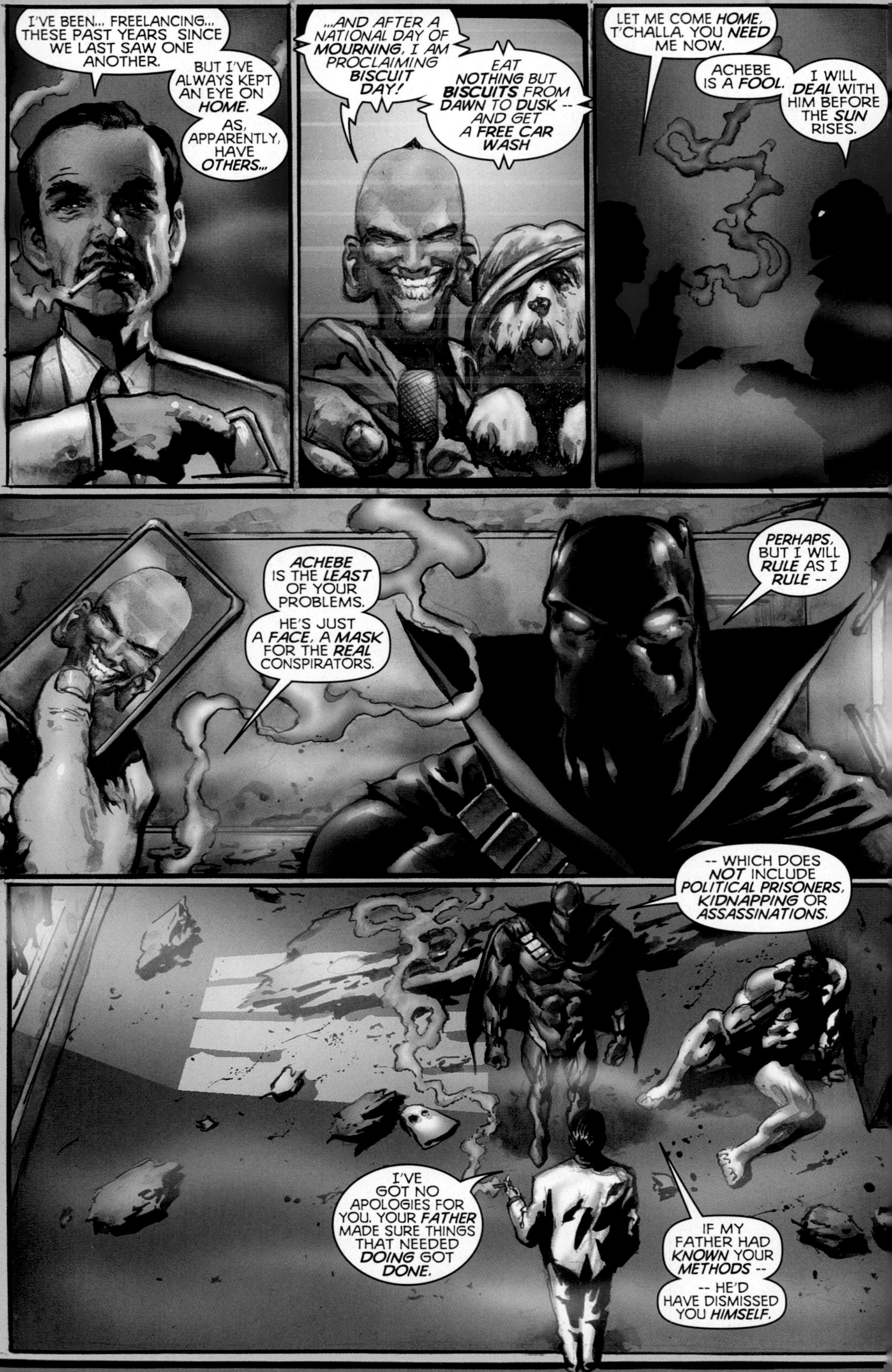
I'VE BEEN... FREELANCING... THESE PAST YEARS SINCE WE LAST SAW ONE ANOTHER.
BUT I'VE ALWAYS KEPT AN EYE ON HOME.
AS, APPARENTLY, HAVE OTHERS...
...AND AFTER A NATIONAL DAY OF MOURNING, I AM PROCLAIMING BISCUIT DAY!
EAT NOTHING BUT BISCUITS FROM DAWN TO DUSK -- AND GET A FREE CAR WASH
LET ME COME HOME, T'CHALLA. YOU NEED ME NOW.
ACHEBE IS A FOOL.
I WILL DEAL WITH HIM BEFORE THE SUN RISES.
ACHEBE IS THE LEAST OF YOUR PROBLEMS.
HE'S JUST A FACE, A MASK FOR THE REAL CONSPIRATORS.
PERHAPS, BUT I WILL RULE AS I RULE --
-- WHICH DOES NOT INCLUDE POLITICAL PRISONERS, KIDNAPPING OR ASSASSINATIONS.
I'VE GOT NO APOLOGIES FOR YOU. YOUR FATHER MADE SURE THINGS THAT NEEDED DOING GOT DONE.
IF MY FATHER HAD KNOWN YOUR METHODS --
-- HE'D HAVE DISMISSED YOU HIMSELF.

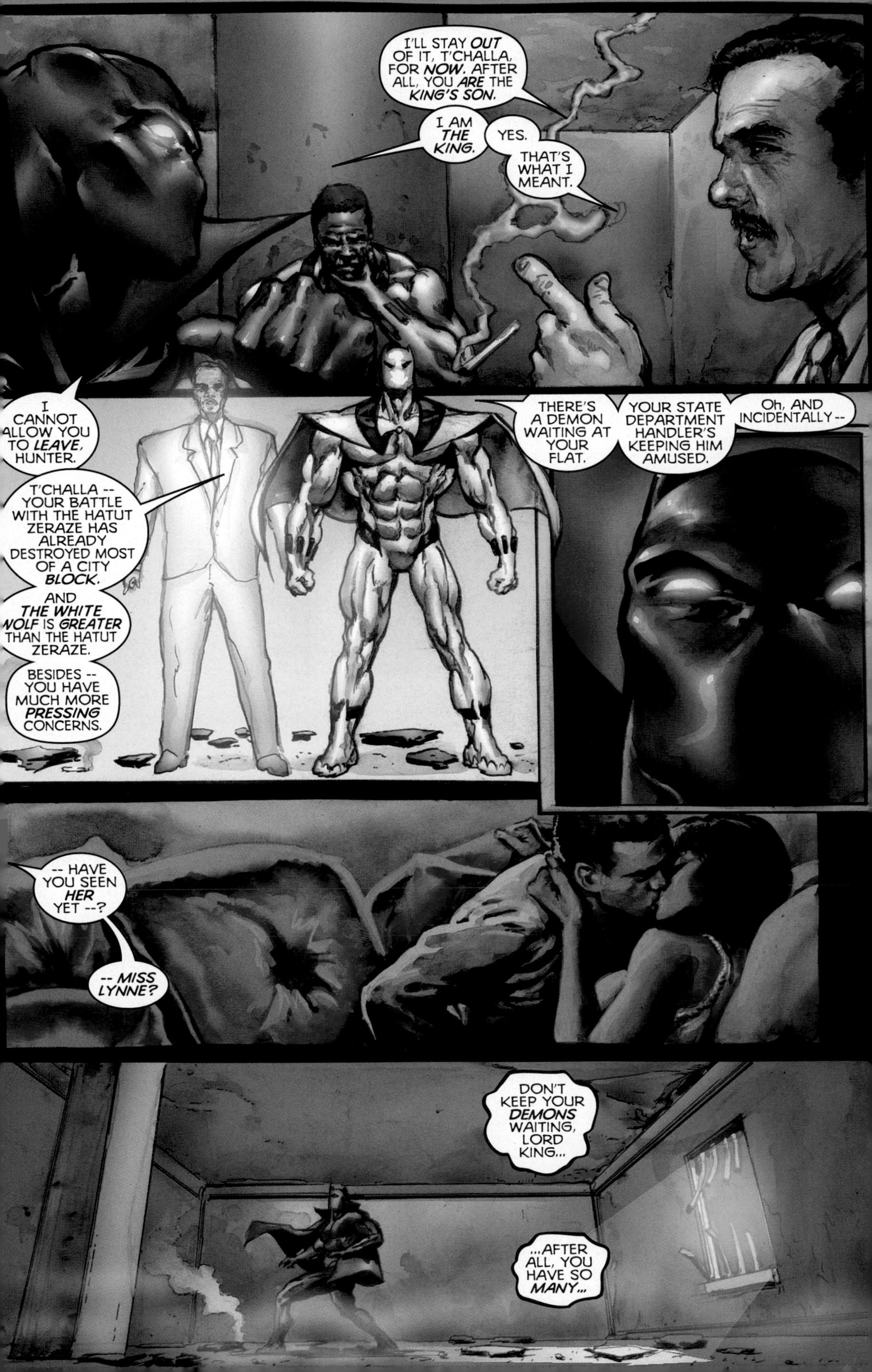
I'LL STAY OUT OF IT, T'CHALLA, FOR NOW. AFTER ALL, YOU ARE THE KING'S SON.
I AM THE KING.
YES.
THAT'S WHAT I MEANT.
I CANNOT ALLOW YOU TO LEAVE, HUNTER.
T'CHALLA -- YOUR BATTLE WITH THE HATUT ZERAZE HAS ALREADY DESTROYED MOST OF A CITY BLOCK.
AND THE WHITE WOLF IS GREATER THAN THE HATUT ZERAZE.
BESIDES -- YOU HAVE MUCH MORE PRESSING CONCERNS.
THERE'S A DEMON WAITING AT YOUR FLAT.
YOUR STATE DEPARTMENT HANDLER'S KEEPING HIM AMUSED.
Oh, AND INCIDENTALLY --
-- HAVE YOU SEEN HER YET --?
-- MISS LYNNE?
DON'T KEEP YOUR DEMONS WAITING, LORD KING...
...AFTER ALL, YOU HAVE SO MANY...

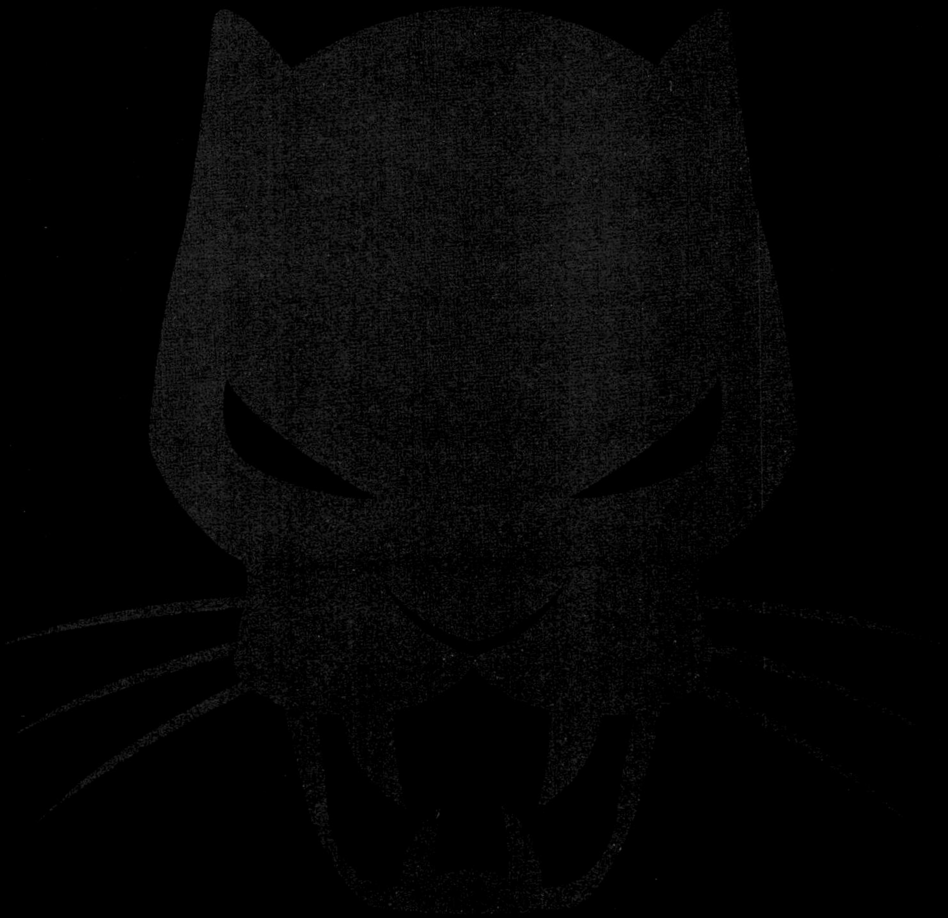

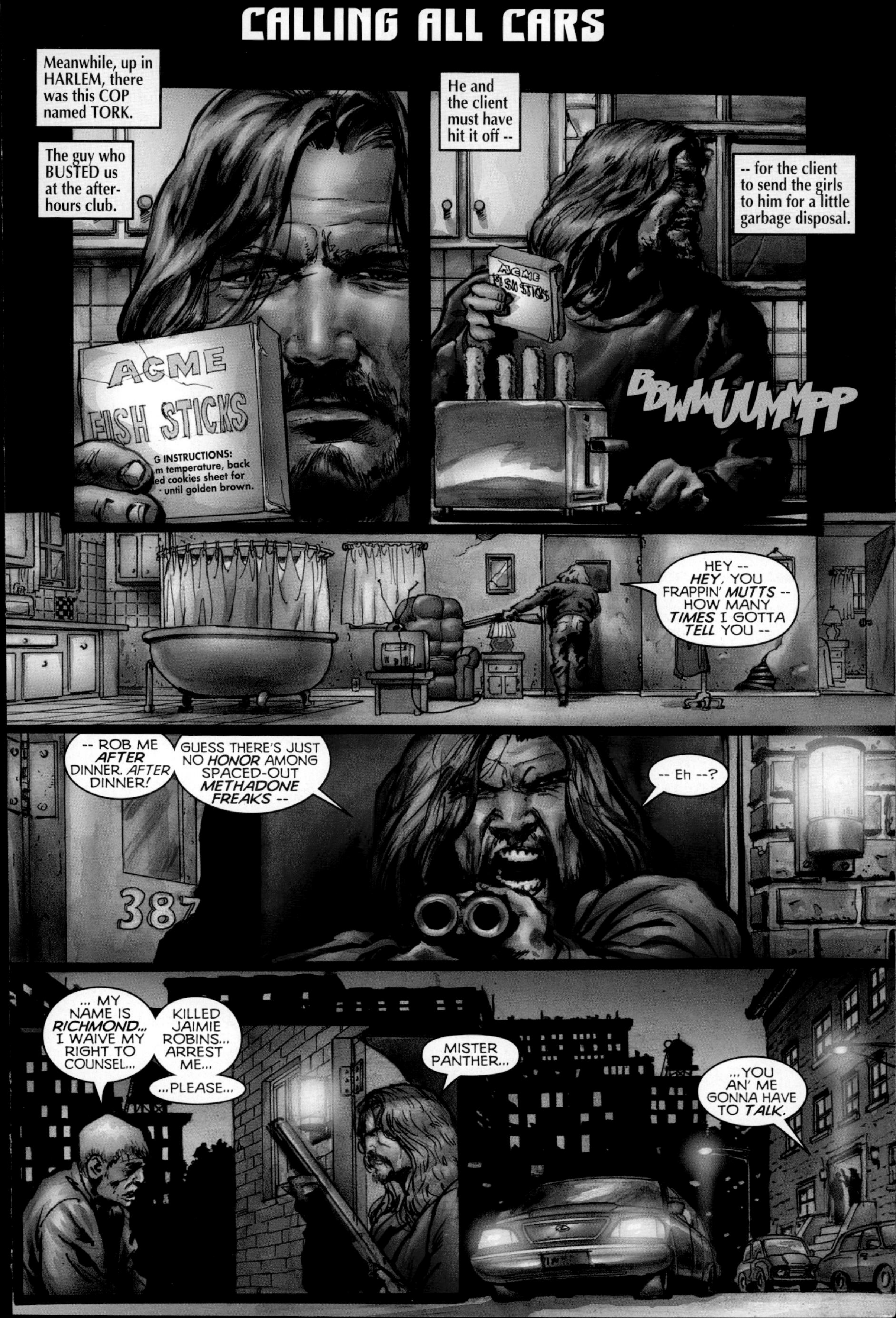

CALLING ALL CARS
Meanwhile, up in HARLEM, there was this COP named TORK.
The guy who BUSTED us at the after-hours club.
ACME
FISH STICKS
G INSTRUCTIONS:
m temperature, back
ed cookies sheet for
- until golden brown.
He and the client must have hit it off --
-- for the client to send the girls to him for a little garbage disposal.
ACME
BBWWUUMMPP
HEY -- HEY, YOU FRAPPIN' MUTTS -- HOW MANY TIMES I GOTTA TELL YOU --
-- ROB ME AFTER DINNER. AFTER DINNER!
GUESS THERE'S JUST NO HONOR AMONG SPACED-OUT METHADONE FREAKS --
-- Eh --?
387
... MY NAME IS RICHMOND... I WAIVE MY RIGHT TO COUNSEL...
KILLED JAIMIE ROBINS... ARREST ME...
...PLEASE...
MISTER PANTHER...
...YOU AN' ME GONNA HAVE TO TALK.

HEE HAW WAS NEVER LIKE THIS

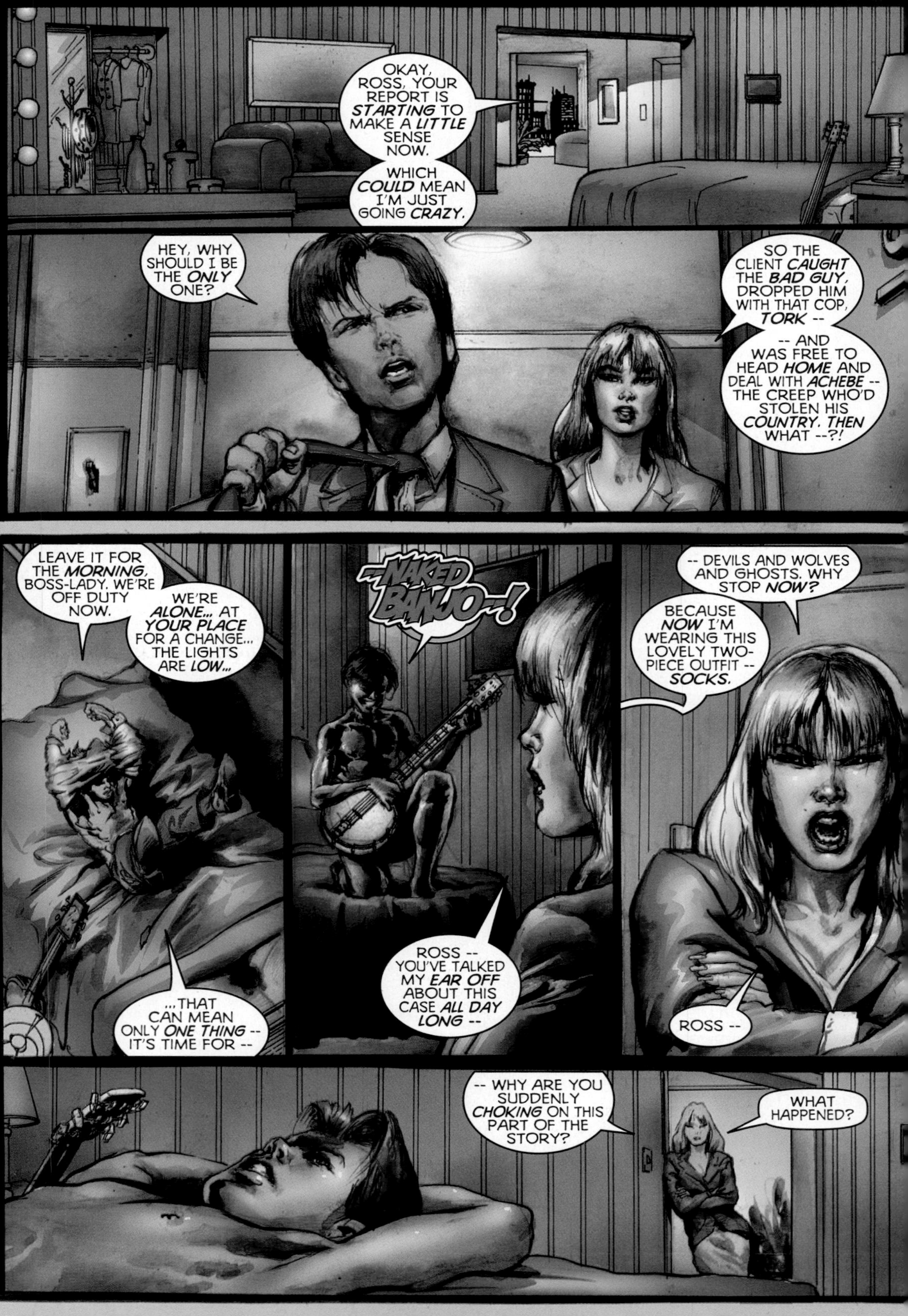

OKAY, ROSS, YOUR REPORT IS STARTING TO MAKE A LITTLE SENSE NOW.
WHICH COULD MEAN I'M JUST GOING CRAZY.
HEY, WHY SHOULD I BE THE ONLY ONE?
SO THE CLIENT CAUGHT THE BAD GUY, DROPPED HIM WITH THAT COP, TORK --
-- AND WAS FREE TO HEAD HOME AND DEAL WITH ACHEBE -- THE CREEP WHO'D STOLEN HIS COUNTRY. THEN WHAT --?!
LEAVE IT FOR THE MORNING, BOSS-LADY. WE'RE OFF DUTY NOW.
WE'RE ALONE... AT YOUR PLACE FOR A CHANGE... THE LIGHTS ARE LOW...
...THAT CAN MEAN ONLY ONE THING -- IT'S TIME FOR --
--NAKED BANJO--!
ROSS -- YOU'VE TALKED MY EAR OFF ABOUT THIS CASE ALL DAY LONG --
-- DEVILS AND WOLVES AND GHOSTS. WHY STOP NOW?
BECAUSE NOW I'M WEARING THIS LOVELY TWO-PIECE OUTFIT -- SOCKS.
ROSS --
-- WHY ARE YOU SUDDENLY CHOKING ON THIS PART OF THE STORY?
WHAT HAPPENED?

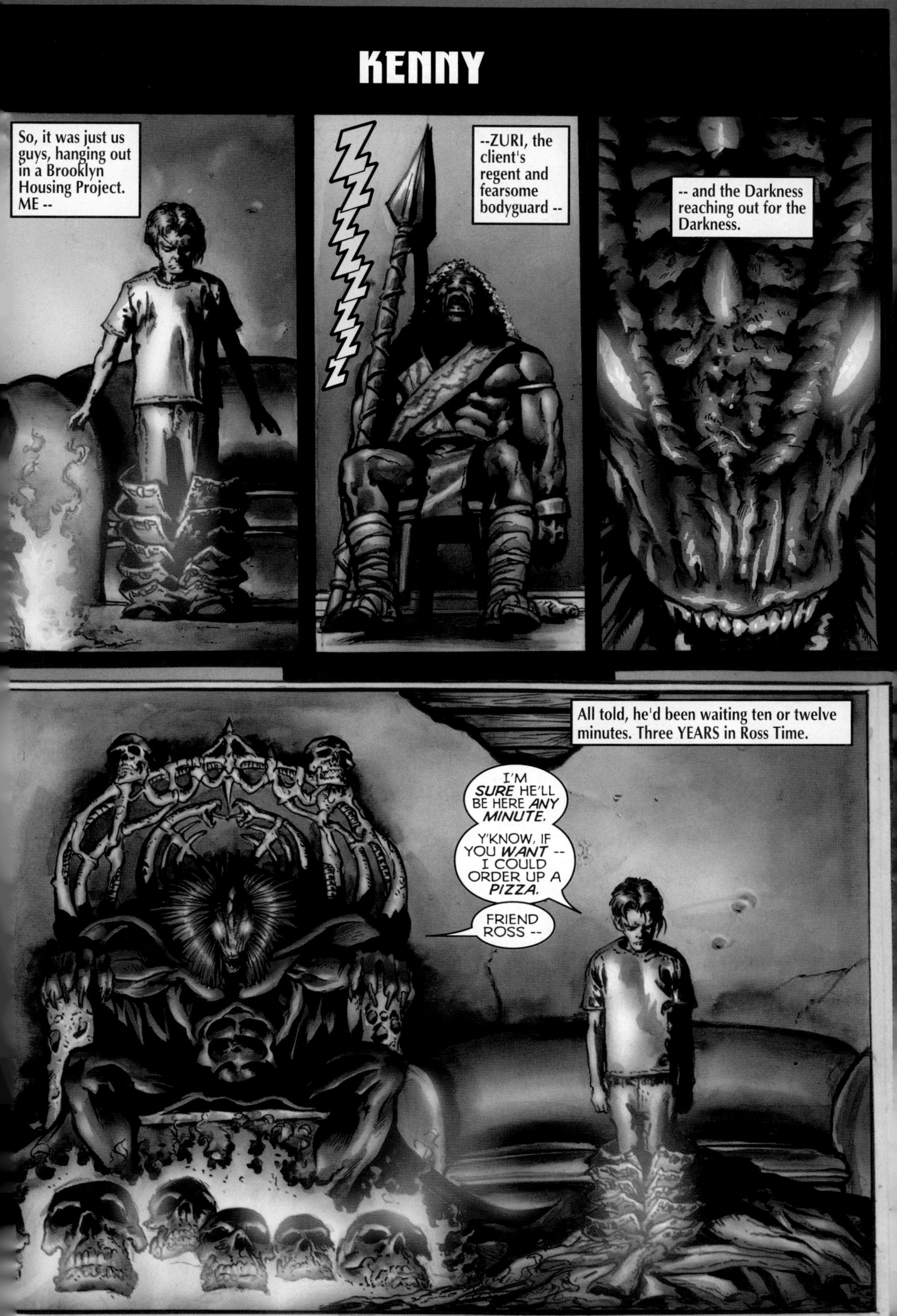
KENNY
So, it was just us guys, hanging out in a Brooklyn Housing Project. ME --
--ZURI, the client's regent and fearsome bodyguard --
ZZZZZZZZ
-- and the Darkness reaching out for the Darkness.
All told, he'd been waiting ten or twelve minutes. Three YEARS in Ross Time.
I'M SURE HE'LL BE HERE ANY MINUTE.
Y'KNOW, IF YOU WANT -- I COULD ORDER UP A PIZZA.
FRIEND ROSS --

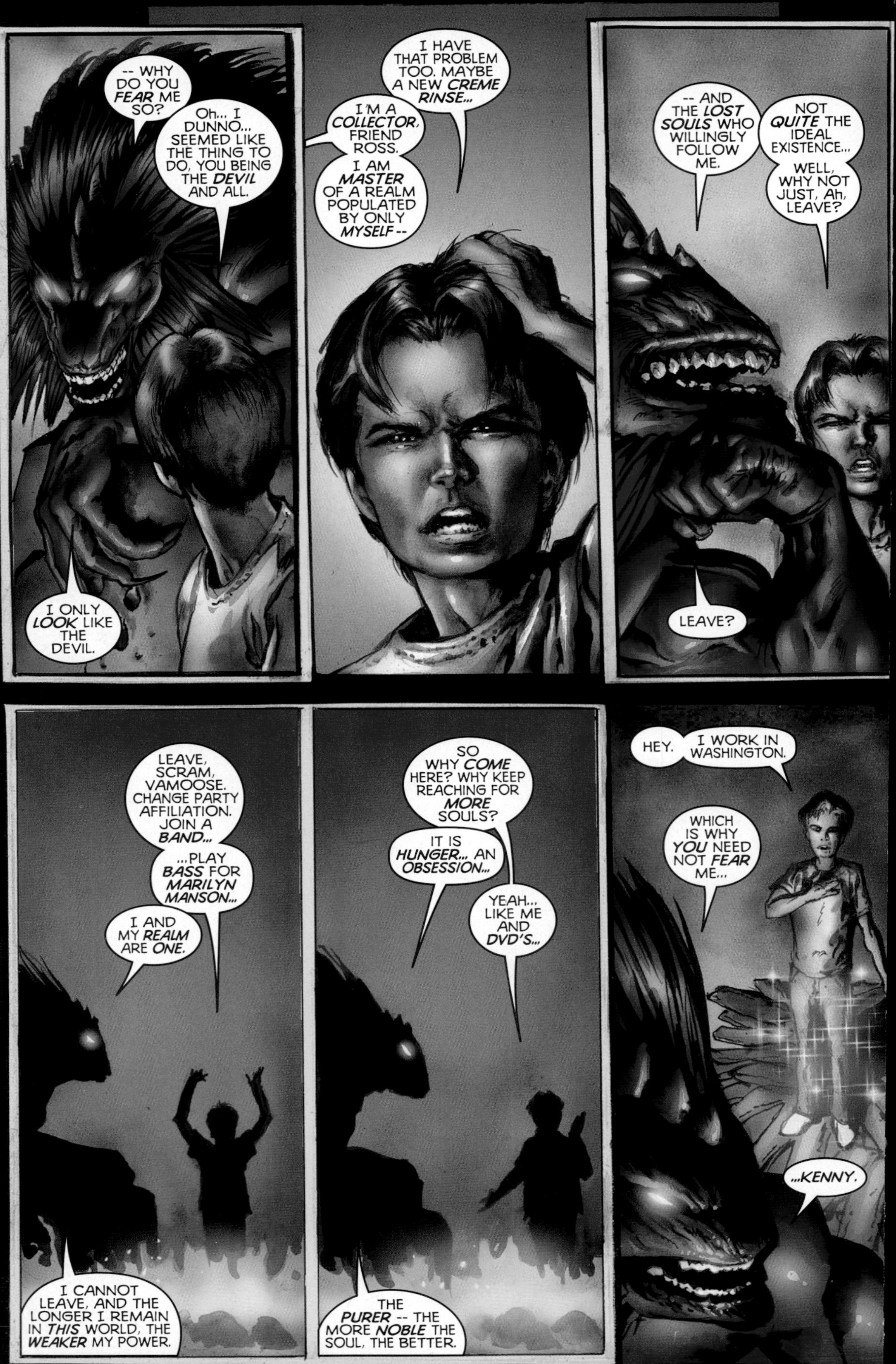
-- WHY DO YOU FEAR ME SO?
Oh... I DUNNO... SEEMED LIKE THE THING TO DO, YOU BEING THE DEVIL AND ALL.
I ONLY LOOK LIKE THE DEVIL.
I HAVE THAT PROBLEM TOO. MAYBE A NEW CREME RINSE...
I'M A COLLECTOR, FRIEND ROSS.
I AM MASTER OF A REALM POPULATED BY ONLY MYSELF --
-- AND THE LOST SOULS WHO WILLINGLY FOLLOW ME.
NOT QUITE THE IDEAL EXISTENCE...
WELL, WHY NOT JUST, Ah, LEAVE?
LEAVE?
LEAVE, SCRAM, VAMOOSE. CHANGE PARTY AFFILIATION. JOIN A BAND...
...PLAY BASS FOR MARILYN MANSON...
I AND MY REALM ARE ONE.
I CANNOT LEAVE, AND THE LONGER I REMAIN IN THIS WORLD, THE WEAKER MY POWER.
SO WHY COME HERE? WHY KEEP REACHING FOR MORE SOULS?
IT IS HUNGER... AN OBSESSION...
YEAH... LIKE ME AND DVD'S...
THE PURER -- THE MORE NOBLE THE SOUL, THE BETTER.
HEY.
I WORK IN WASHINGTON.
WHICH IS WHY YOU NEED NOT FEAR ME...
...KENNY.

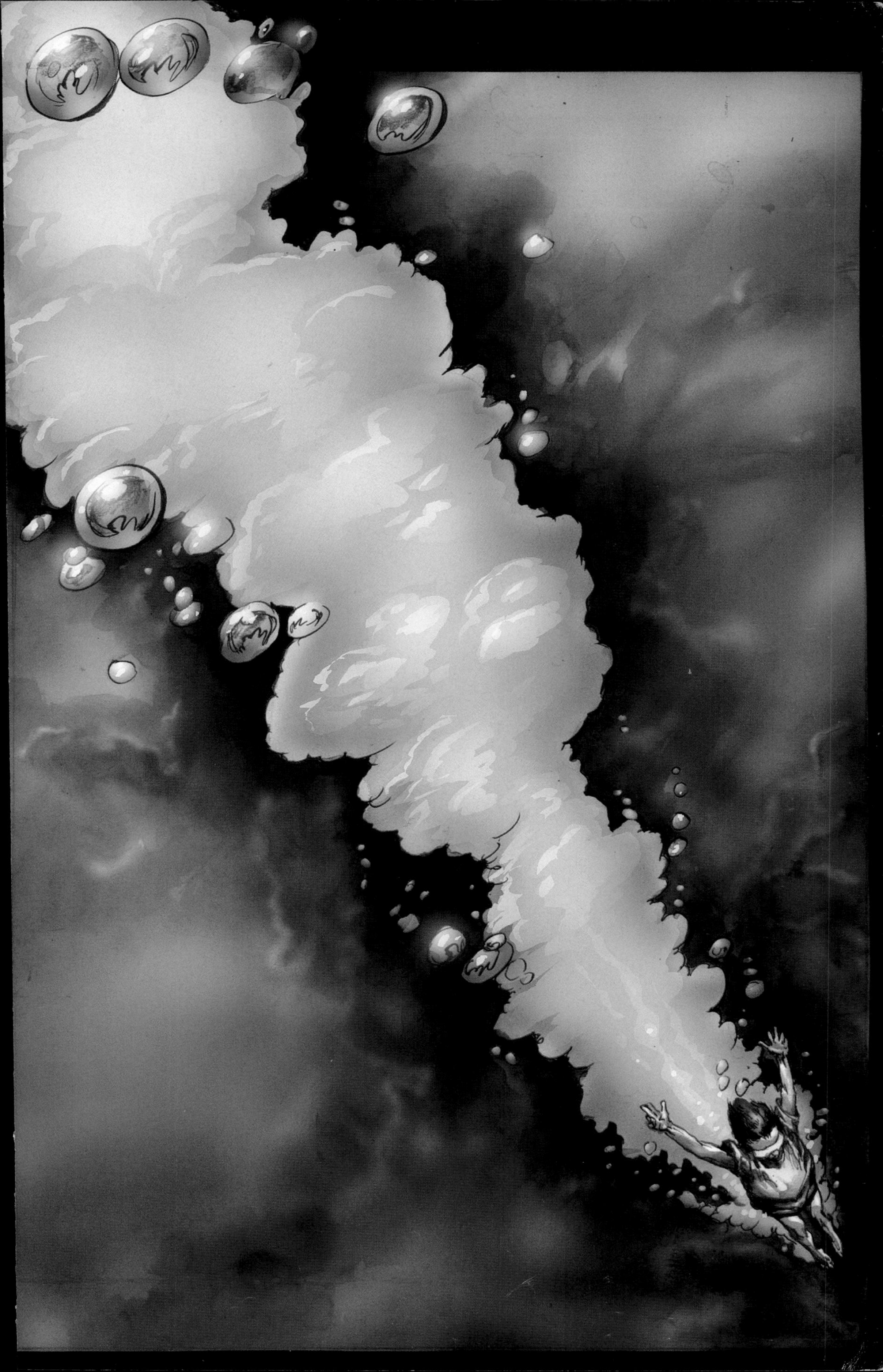

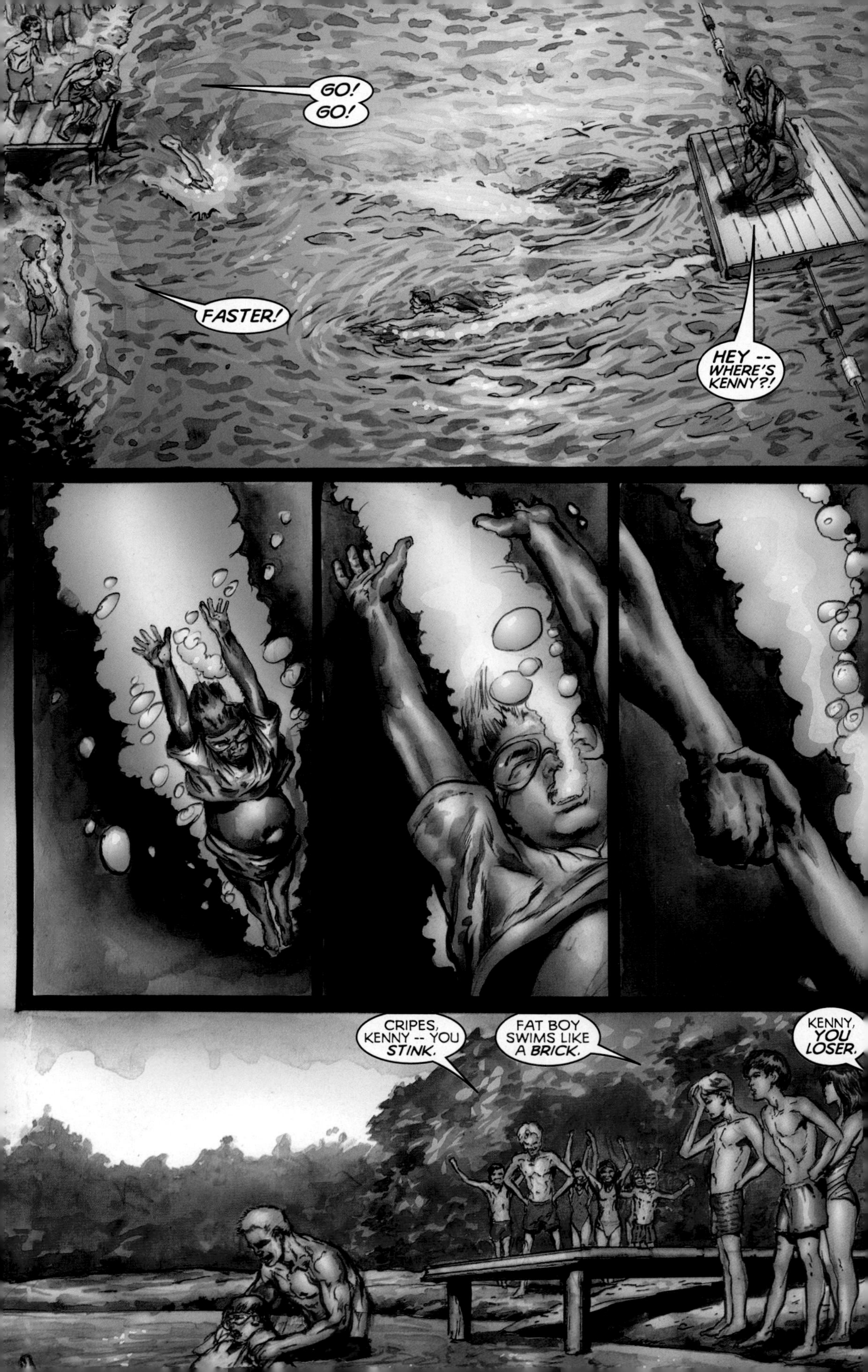
GO! GO!
FASTER!
HEY -- WHERE'S KENNY?!
CRIPES, KENNY -- YOU STINK.
FAT BOY SWIMS LIKE A BRICK.
KENNY, YOU LOSER.

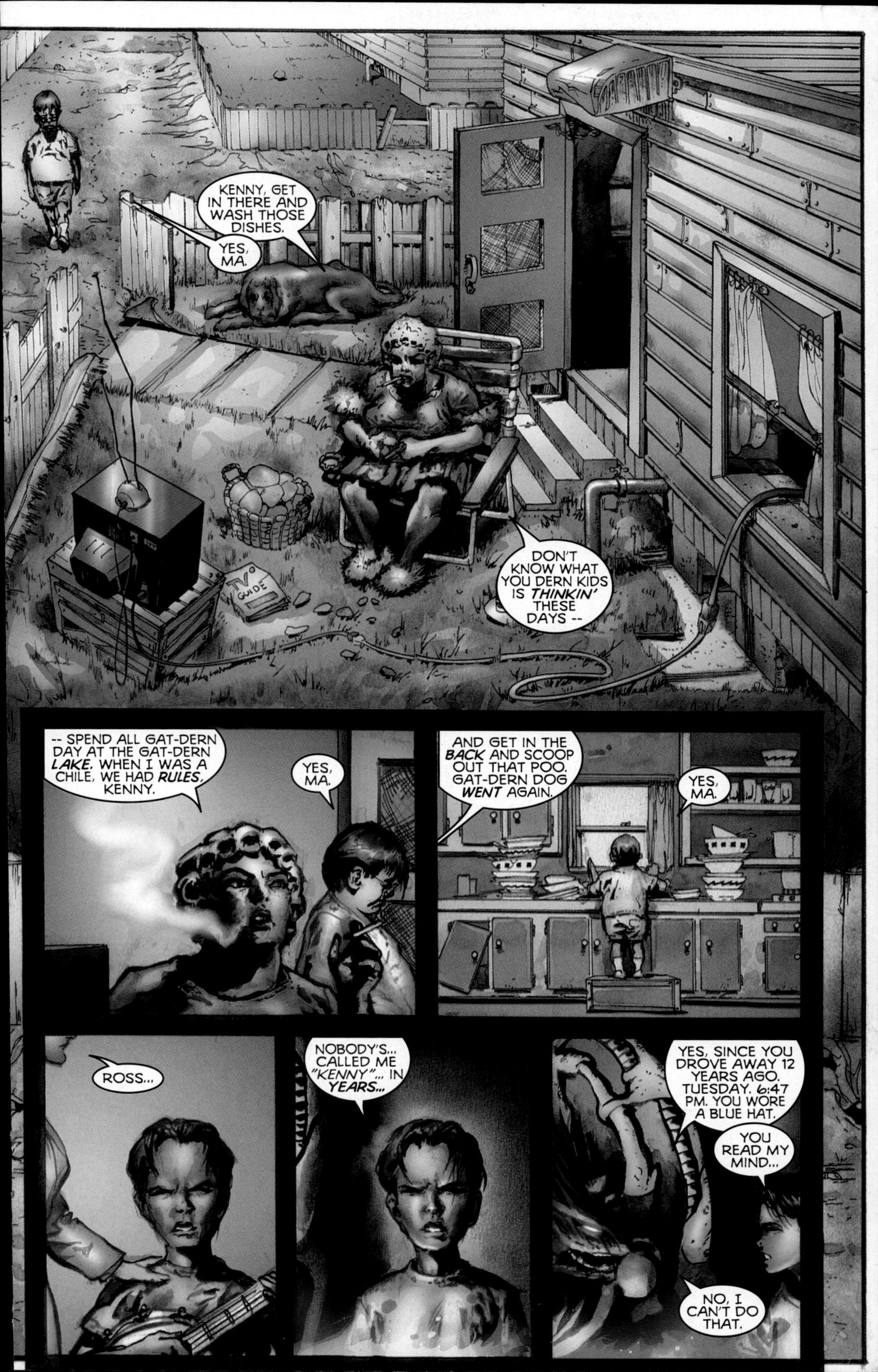
KENNY, GET IN THERE AND WASH THOSE DISHES.
YES, MA.
DON'T KNOW WHAT YOU DERN KIDS IS THINKIN' THESE DAYS --
-- SPEND ALL GAT-DERN DAY AT THE GAT-DERN LAKE. WHEN I WAS A CHILE, WE HAD RULES, KENNY.
YES, MA.
AND GET IN THE BACK AND SCOOP OUT THAT POO. GAT-DERN DOG WENT AGAIN.
YES, MA.
ROSS...
NOBODY'S... CALLED ME "KENNY"... IN YEARS...
YES, SINCE YOU DROVE AWAY 12 YEARS AGO. TUESDAY. 6:47 PM. YOU WORE A BLUE HAT.
YOU READ MY MIND...
NO, I CAN'T DO THAT.

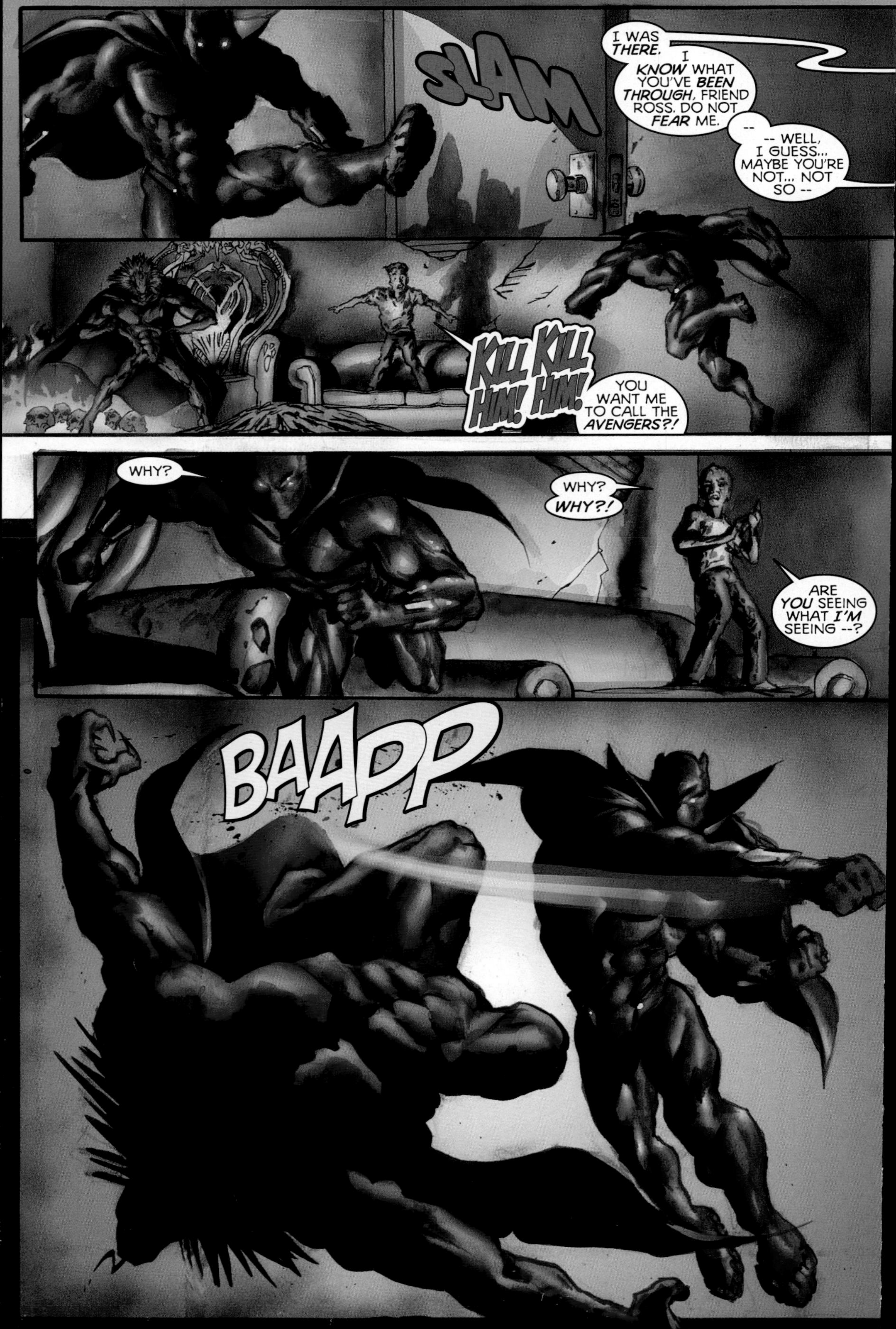
SLAM
I WAS THERE.
I KNOW WHAT YOU'VE BEEN THROUGH, FRIEND ROSS. DO NOT FEAR ME.
--
-- WELL, I GUESS... MAYBE YOU'RE NOT... NOT SO --
KILL HIM! KILL HIM!
YOU WANT ME TO CALL THE AVENGERS?!
WHY?
WHY? WHY?!
ARE YOU SEEING WHAT I'M SEEING --?
BAAPP

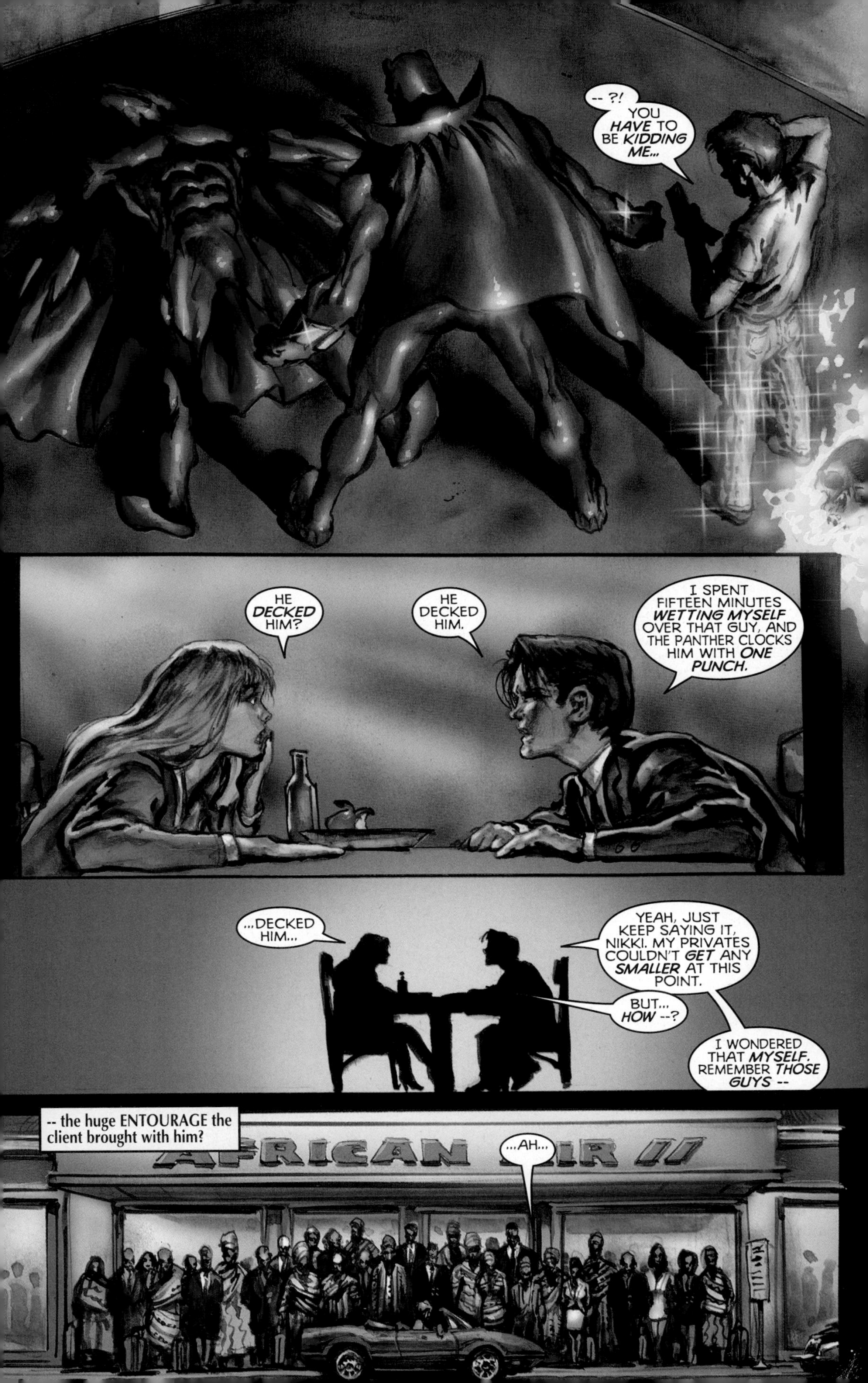
-- ?! YOU HAVE TO BE KIDDING ME...
HE DECKED HIM?
HE DECKED HIM.
I SPENT FIFTEEN MINUTES WETTING MYSELF OVER THAT GUY, AND THE PANTHER CLOCKS HIM WITH ONE PUNCH.
...DECKED HIM...
YEAH, JUST KEEP SAYING IT, NIKKI. MY PRIVATES COULDN'T GET ANY SMALLER AT THIS POINT.
BUT... HOW --?
I WONDERED THAT MYSELF. REMEMBER THOSE GUYS --
-- the huge ENTOURAGE the client brought with him?
AFRICAN AIR II
...AH...

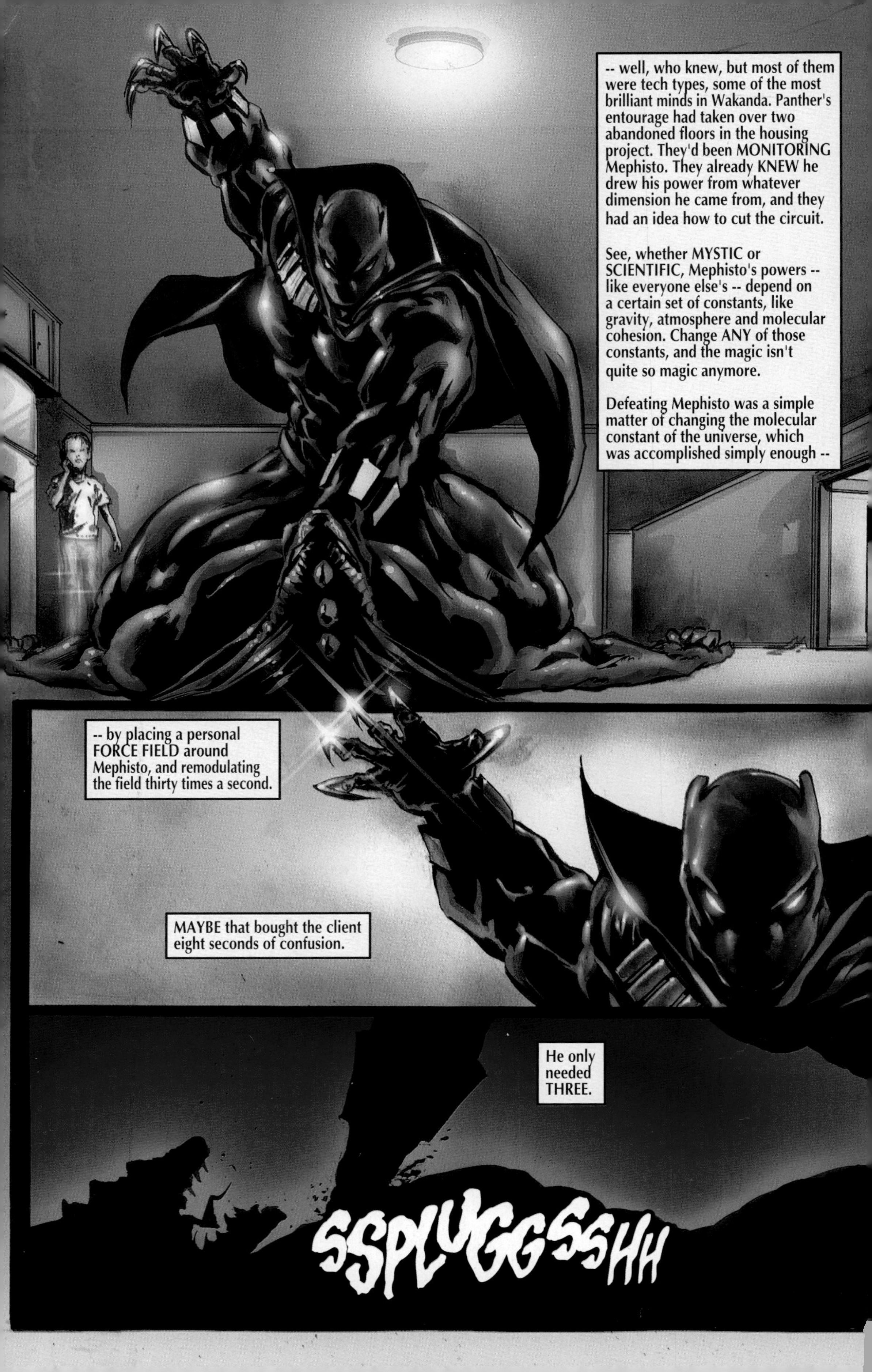
-- well, who knew, but most of them were tech types, some of the most brilliant minds in Wakanda. Panther's entourage had taken over two abandoned floors in the housing project. They'd been MONITORING Mephisto. They already KNEW he drew his power from whatever dimension he came from, and they had an idea how to cut the circuit.
See, whether MYSTIC or SCIENTIFIC, Mephisto's powers -- like everyone else's -- depend on a certain set of constants, like gravity, atmosphere and molecular cohesion. Change ANY of those constants, and the magic isn't quite so magic anymore.
Defeating Mephisto was a simple matter of changing the molecular constant of the universe, which was accomplished simply enough --
-- by placing a personal FORCE FIELD around Mephisto, and remodulating the field thirty times a second.
MAYBE that bought the client eight seconds of confusion.
He only needed THREE.
SSPLUGGSSHH

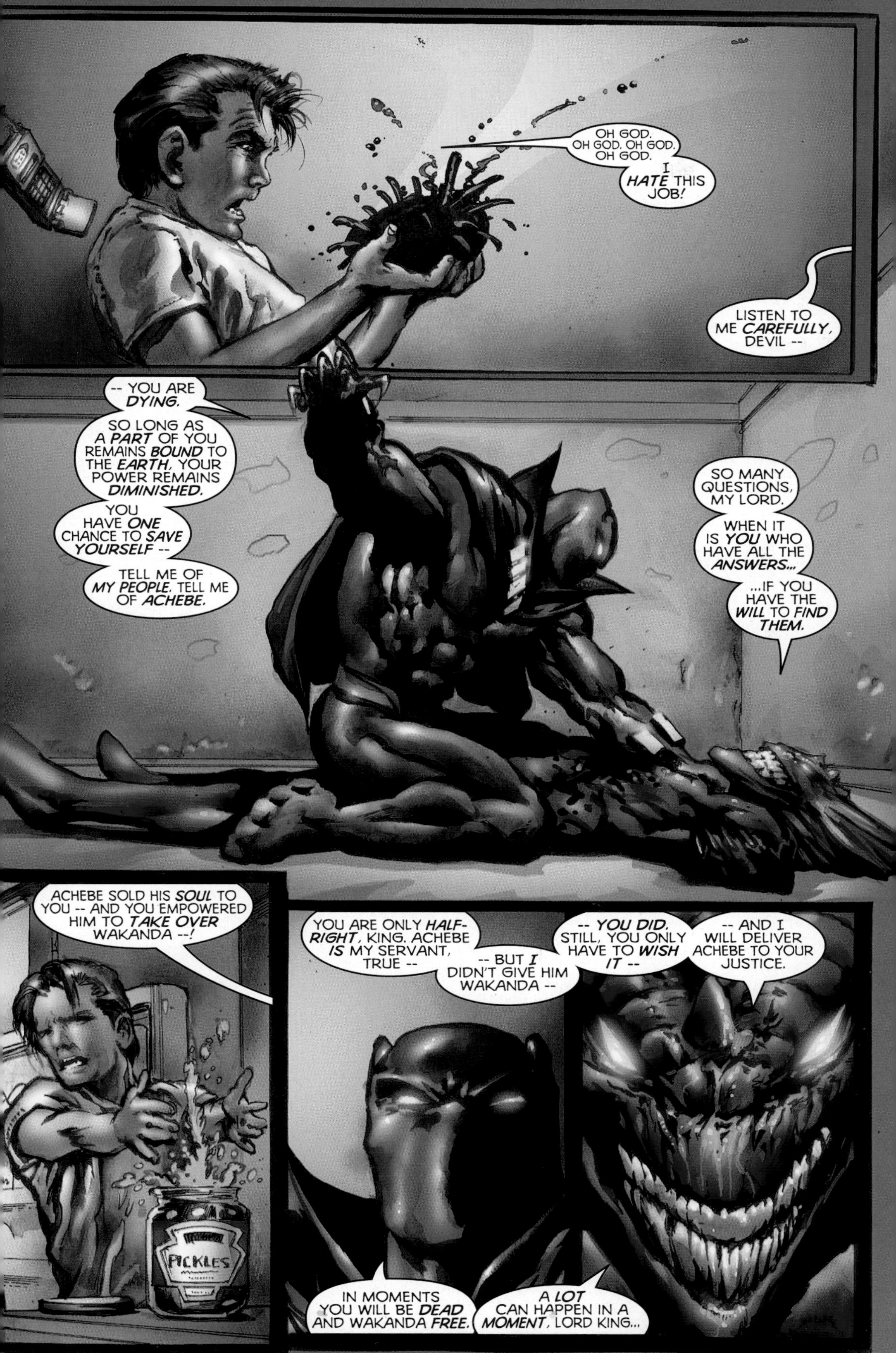

OH GOD. OH GOD. OH GOD. OH GOD. I HATE THIS JOB!
LISTEN TO ME CAREFULLY, DEVIL --
-- YOU ARE DYING.
SO LONG AS A PART OF YOU REMAINS BOUND TO THE EARTH, YOUR POWER REMAINS DIMINISHED.
YOU HAVE ONE CHANCE TO SAVE YOURSELF --
TELL ME OF MY PEOPLE. TELL ME OF ACHEBE.
SO MANY QUESTIONS, MY LORD.
WHEN IT IS YOU WHO HAVE ALL THE ANSWERS...
...IF YOU HAVE THE WILL TO FIND THEM.
ACHEBE SOLD HIS SOUL TO YOU -- AND YOU EMPOWERED HIM TO TAKE OVER WAKANDA --!
PICKLES
YOU ARE ONLY HALF-RIGHT, KING. ACHEBE IS MY SERVANT, TRUE --
-- BUT I DIDN'T GIVE HIM WAKANDA --
-- YOU DID. STILL, YOU ONLY HAVE TO WISH IT --
-- AND I WILL DELIVER ACHEBE TO YOUR JUSTICE.
IN MOMENTS YOU WILL BE DEAD AND WAKANDA FREE.
A LOT CAN HAPPEN IN A MOMENT, LORD KING...

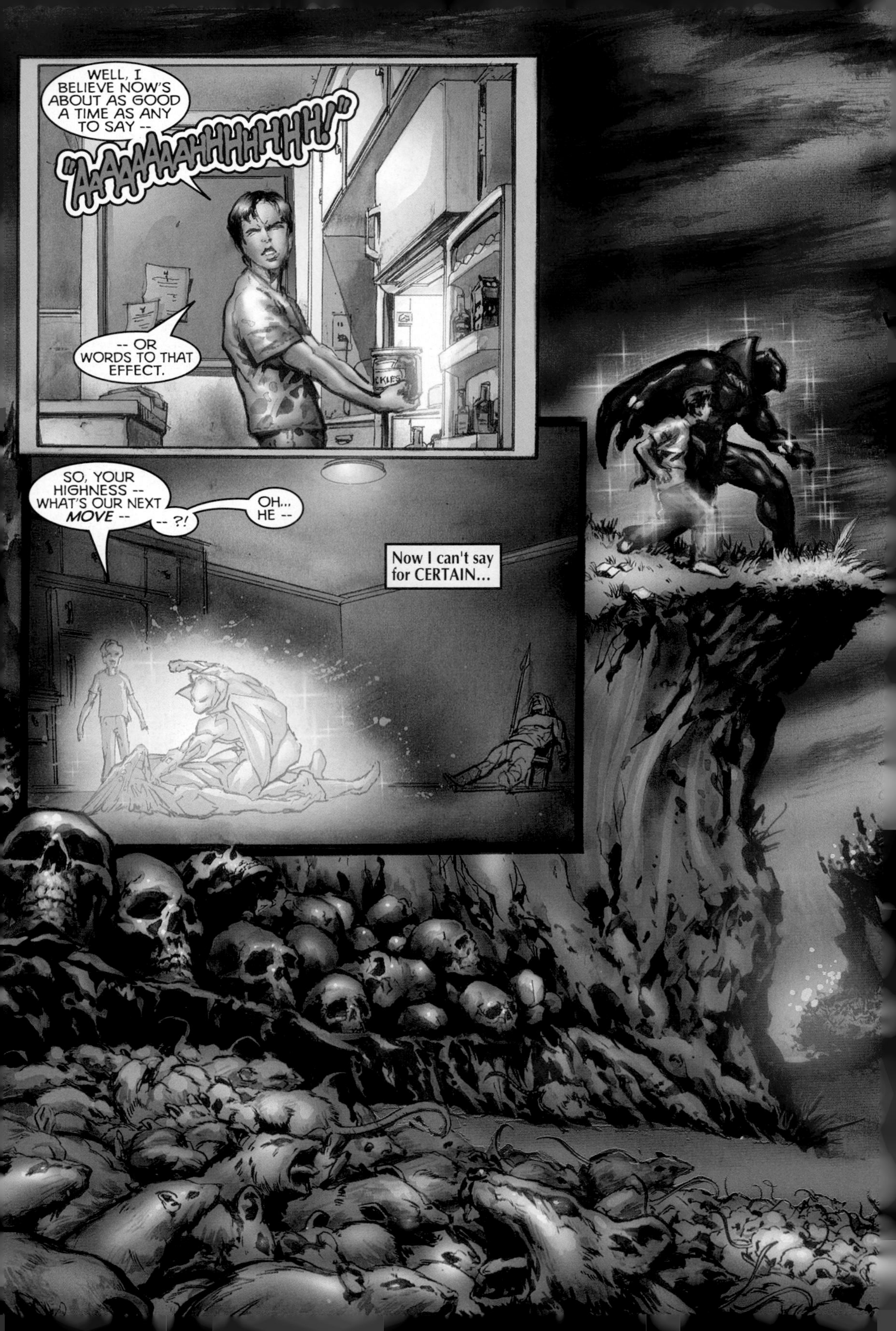
WELL, I BELIEVE NOW'S ABOUT AS GOOD A TIME AS ANY TO SAY --
"AAAAAAAHHHHHHH!"
-- OR WORDS TO THAT EFFECT.
SO, YOUR HIGHNESS -- WHAT'S OUR NEXT *MOVE* --
-- ?!
OH... HE --
Now I can't say for CERTAIN...

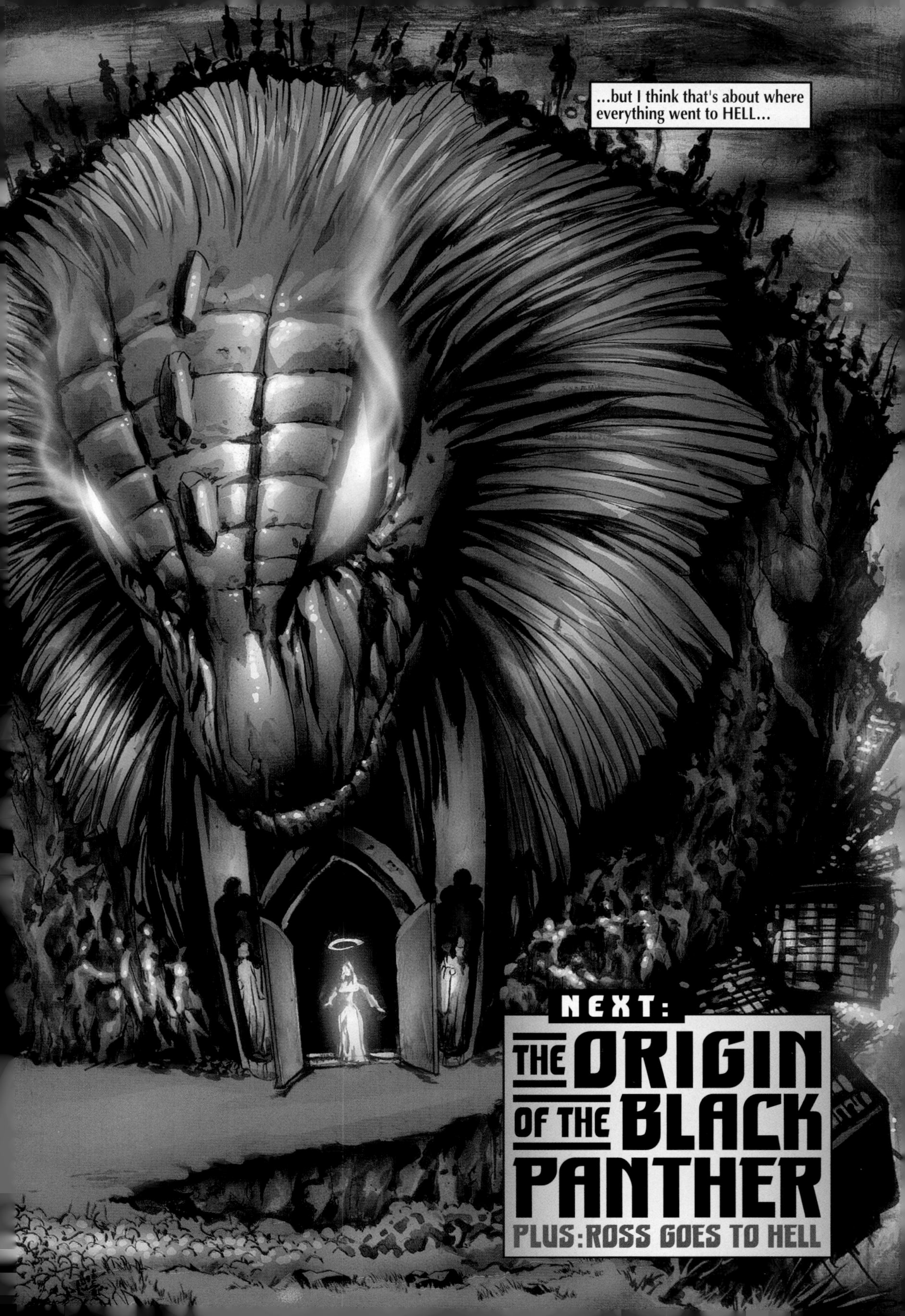
...but I think that's about where everything went to HELL...
NEXT:
THE ORIGIN OF THE BLACK PANTHER
PLUS: ROSS GOES TO HELL

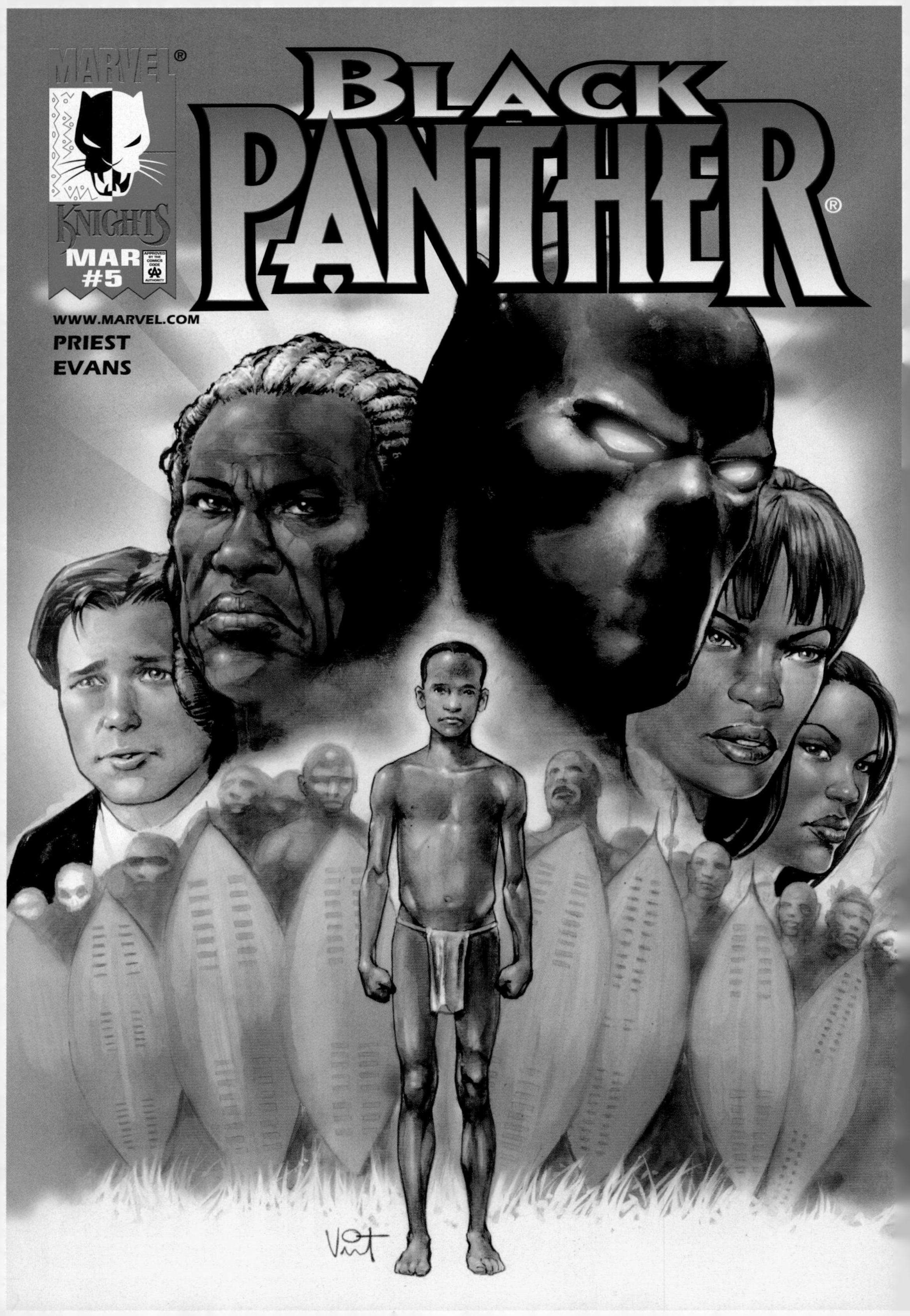
MARVEL®
KNIGHTS
MAR
#5
APPROVED BY THE COMICS CODE AUTHORITY
BLACK PANTHER®
WWW.MARVEL.COM
PRIEST
EVANS

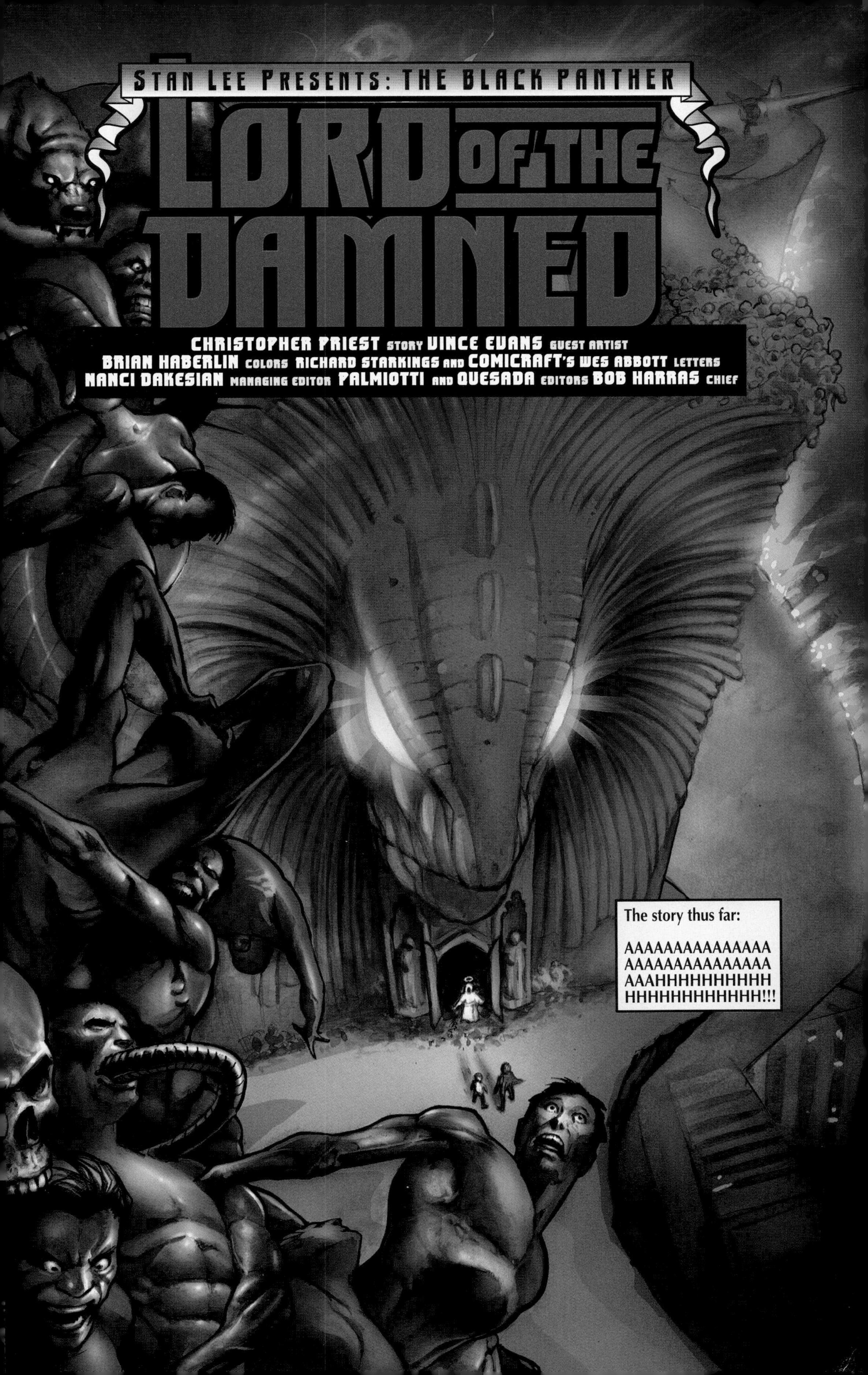
STAN LEE PRESENTS: THE BLACK PANTHER
LORD OF THE DAMNED
CHRISTOPHER PRIEST STORY VINCE EVANS GUEST ARTIST
BRIAN HABERLIN COLORS RICHARD STARKINGS AND COMICRAFT'S WES ABBOTT LETTERS
NANCI DAKESIAN MANAGING EDITOR PALMIOTTI AND QUESADA EDITORS BOB HARRAS CHIEF
The story thus far:
AAAAAAAAAAAAAAA
AAAAAAAAAAAAAAA
AAAHHHHHHHHHH
HHHHHHHHHHHH!!!

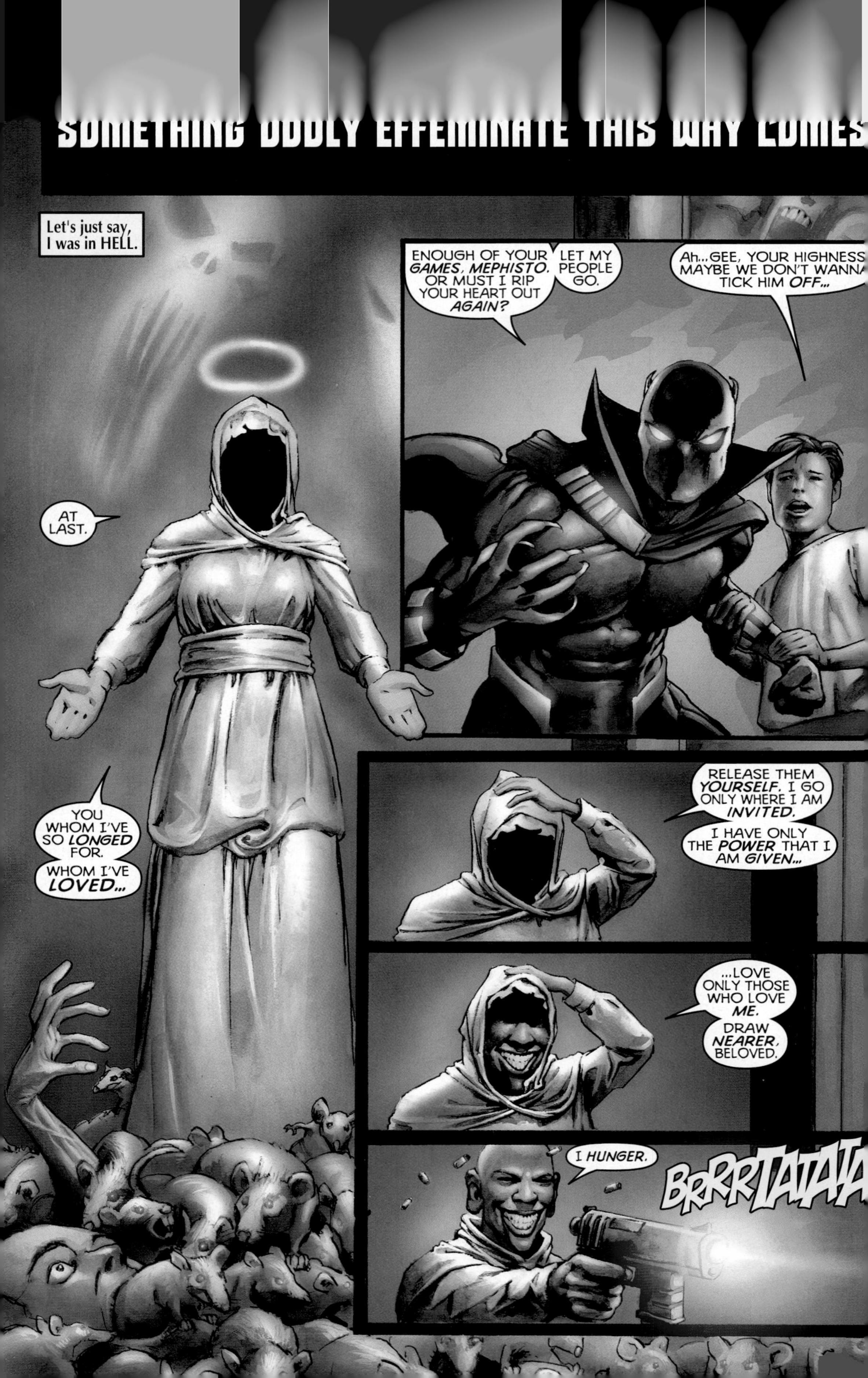
SOMETHING ODDLY EFFEMINATE THIS WAY COMES
Let's just say, I was in HELL.
AT LAST.
YOU WHOM I'VE SO LONGED FOR.
WHOM I'VE LOVED...
ENOUGH OF YOUR GAMES, MEPHISTO. OR MUST I RIP YOUR HEART OUT AGAIN?
LET MY PEOPLE GO.
Ah...GEE, YOUR HIGHNESS MAYBE WE DON'T WANNA TICK HIM OFF...
RELEASE THEM YOURSELF. I GO ONLY WHERE I AM INVITED.
I HAVE ONLY THE POWER THAT I AM GIVEN...
...LOVE ONLY THOSE WHO LOVE ME.
DRAW NEARER, BELOVED.
I HUNGER.
BRRRTATATA

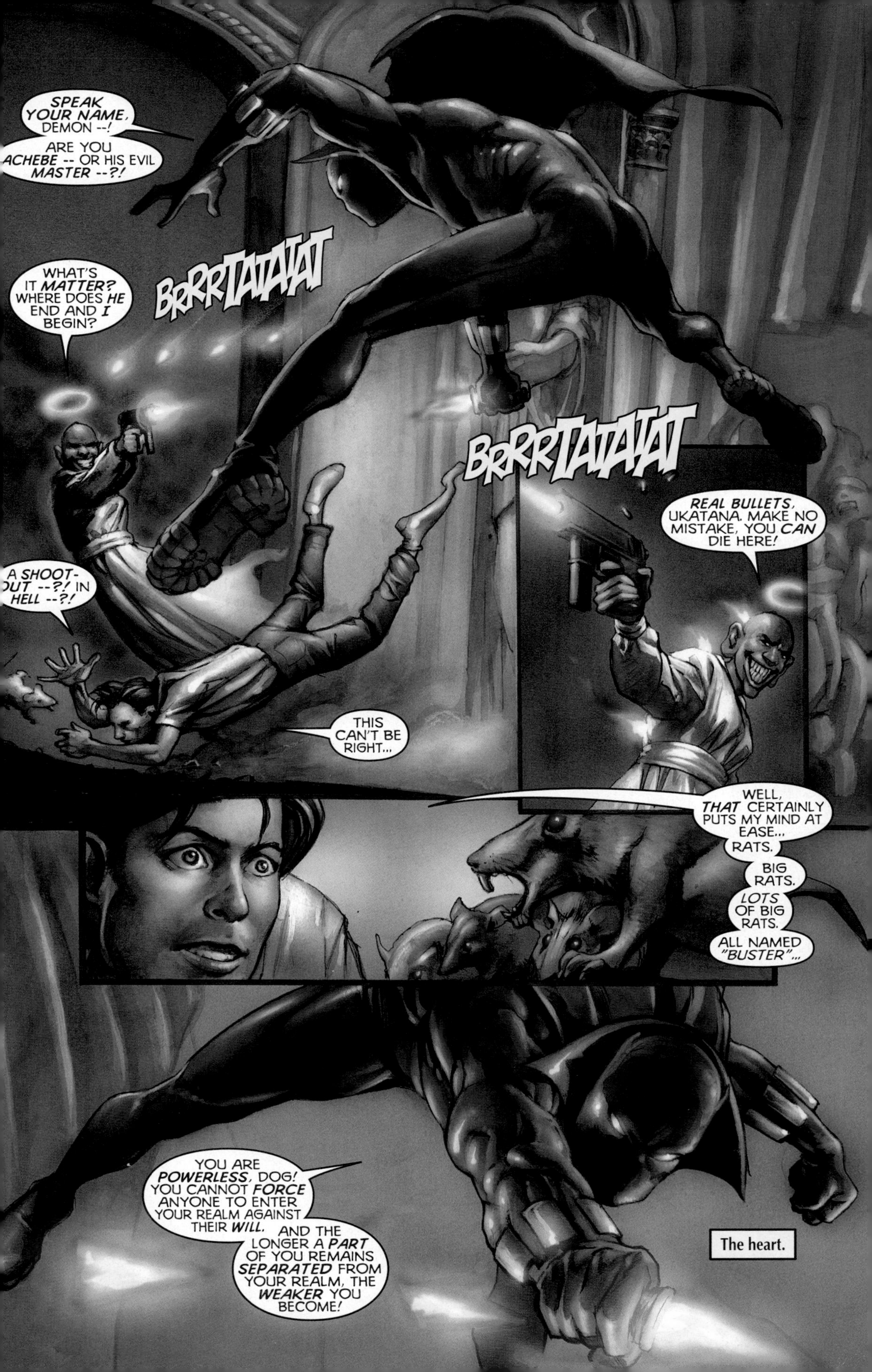

SPEAK YOUR NAME, DEMON --!
ARE YOU ACHEBE -- OR HIS EVIL MASTER --?!
BRRRTATATAT
WHAT'S IT MATTER? WHERE DOES HE END AND I BEGIN?
BRRRTATATAT
A SHOOT-OUT --?! IN HELL --?!
THIS CAN'T BE RIGHT...
REAL BULLETS, UKATANA. MAKE NO MISTAKE, YOU CAN DIE HERE!
WELL, THAT CERTAINLY PUTS MY MIND AT EASE...
RATS.
BIG RATS.
LOTS OF BIG RATS.
ALL NAMED "BUSTER"...
YOU ARE POWERLESS, DOG! YOU CANNOT FORCE ANYONE TO ENTER YOUR REALM AGAINST THEIR WILL.
AND THE LONGER A PART OF YOU REMAINS SEPARATED FROM YOUR REALM, THE WEAKER YOU BECOME!
The heart.

LEFTOVERS

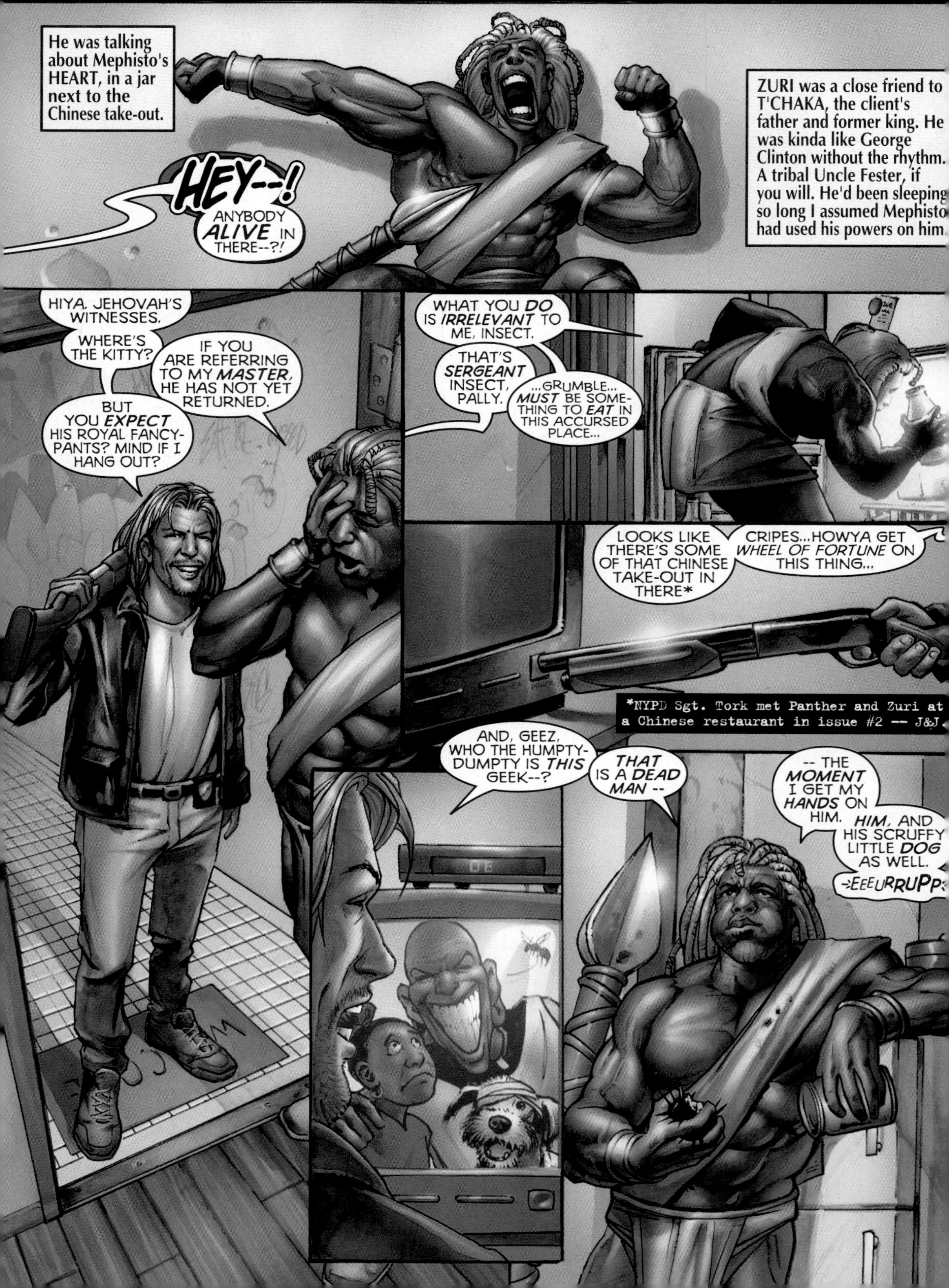

He was talking about Mephisto's HEART, in a jar next to the Chinese take-out.
ZURI was a close friend to T'CHAKA, the client's father and former king. He was kinda like George Clinton without the rhythm. A tribal Uncle Fester, if you will. He'd been sleeping so long I assumed Mephisto had used his powers on him.
HEY--! ANYBODY ALIVE IN THERE--?!
HIYA. JEHOVAH'S WITNESSES.
WHERE'S THE KITTY?
IF YOU ARE REFERRING TO MY MASTER, HE HAS NOT YET RETURNED.
BUT YOU EXPECT HIS ROYAL FANCY-PANTS? MIND IF I HANG OUT?
WHAT YOU DO IS IRRELEVANT TO ME, INSECT.
THAT'S SERGEANT INSECT, PALLY.
...GRUMBLE... MUST BE SOME-THING TO EAT IN THIS ACCURSED PLACE...
LOOKS LIKE THERE'S SOME OF THAT CHINESE TAKE-OUT IN THERE*
CRIPES...HOWYA GET WHEEL OF FORTUNE ON THIS THING...
*NYPD Sgt. Tork met Panther and Zuri at a Chinese restaurant in issue #2 -- J&J.
AND, GEEZ, WHO THE HUMPTY-DUMPTY IS THIS GEEK--?
THAT IS A DEAD MAN --
-- THE MOMENT I GET MY HANDS ON HIM. HIM, AND HIS SCRUFFY LITTLE DOG AS WELL.
EEEURRUPP

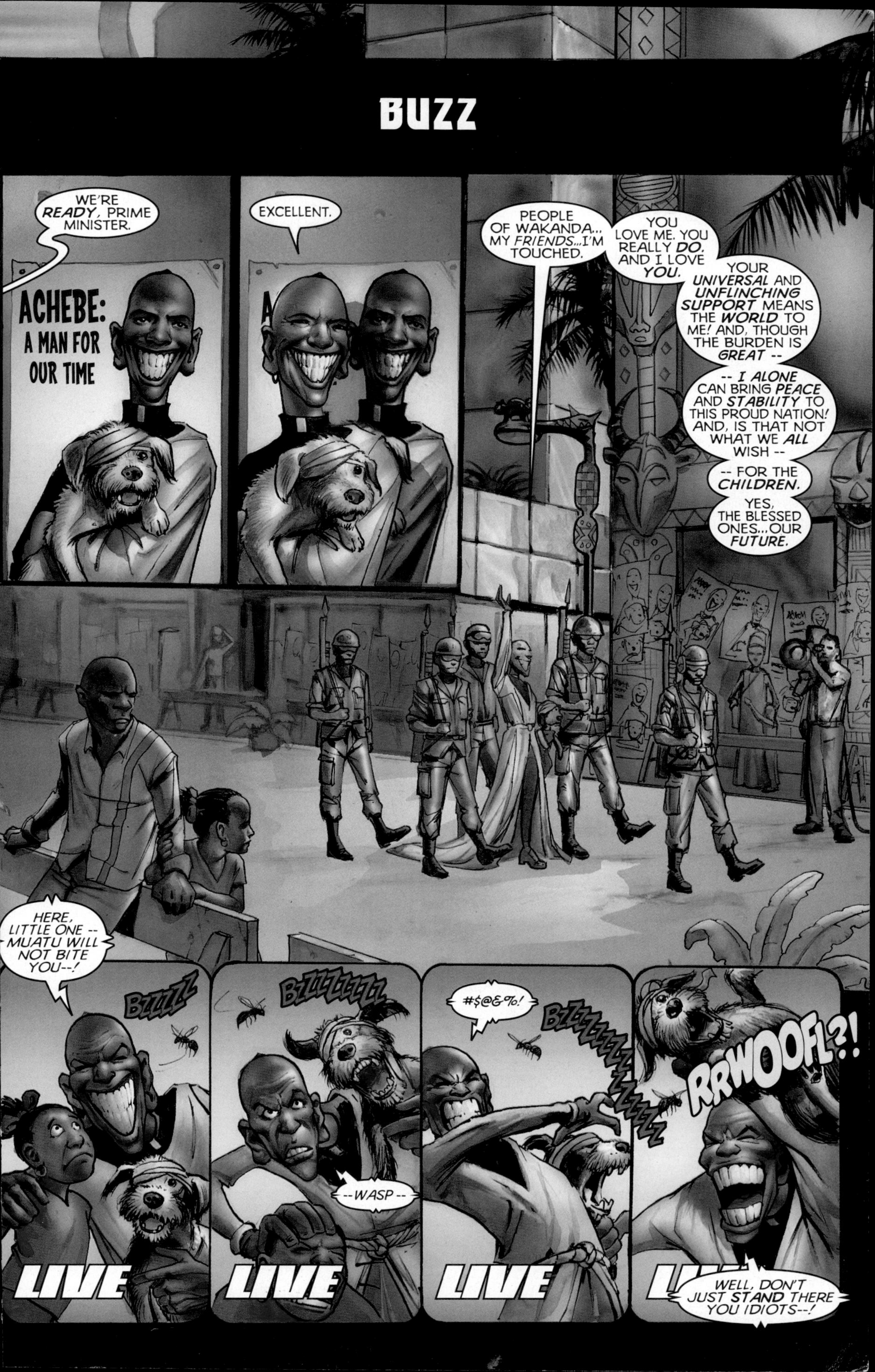
BUZZ
WE'RE READY, PRIME MINISTER.
ACHEBE: A MAN FOR OUR TIME
EXCELLENT.
PEOPLE OF WAKANDA... MY FRIENDS...I'M TOUCHED.
YOU LOVE ME. YOU REALLY DO. AND I LOVE YOU.
YOUR UNIVERSAL AND UNFLINCHING SUPPORT MEANS THE WORLD TO ME! AND, THOUGH THE BURDEN IS GREAT --
-- I ALONE CAN BRING PEACE AND STABILITY TO THIS PROUD NATION! AND, IS THAT NOT WHAT WE ALL WISH --
-- FOR THE CHILDREN.
YES, THE BLESSED ONES...OUR FUTURE.
HERE, LITTLE ONE -- MUATU WILL NOT BITE YOU--!
BZZZZZ
LIVE
BZZZZZZZZZ
--WASP--
LIVE
#$@&%!
BZZZZZZZZZZZZZ
LIVE
RRWOOFL?!
WELL, DON'T JUST STAND THERE YOU IDIOTS--!

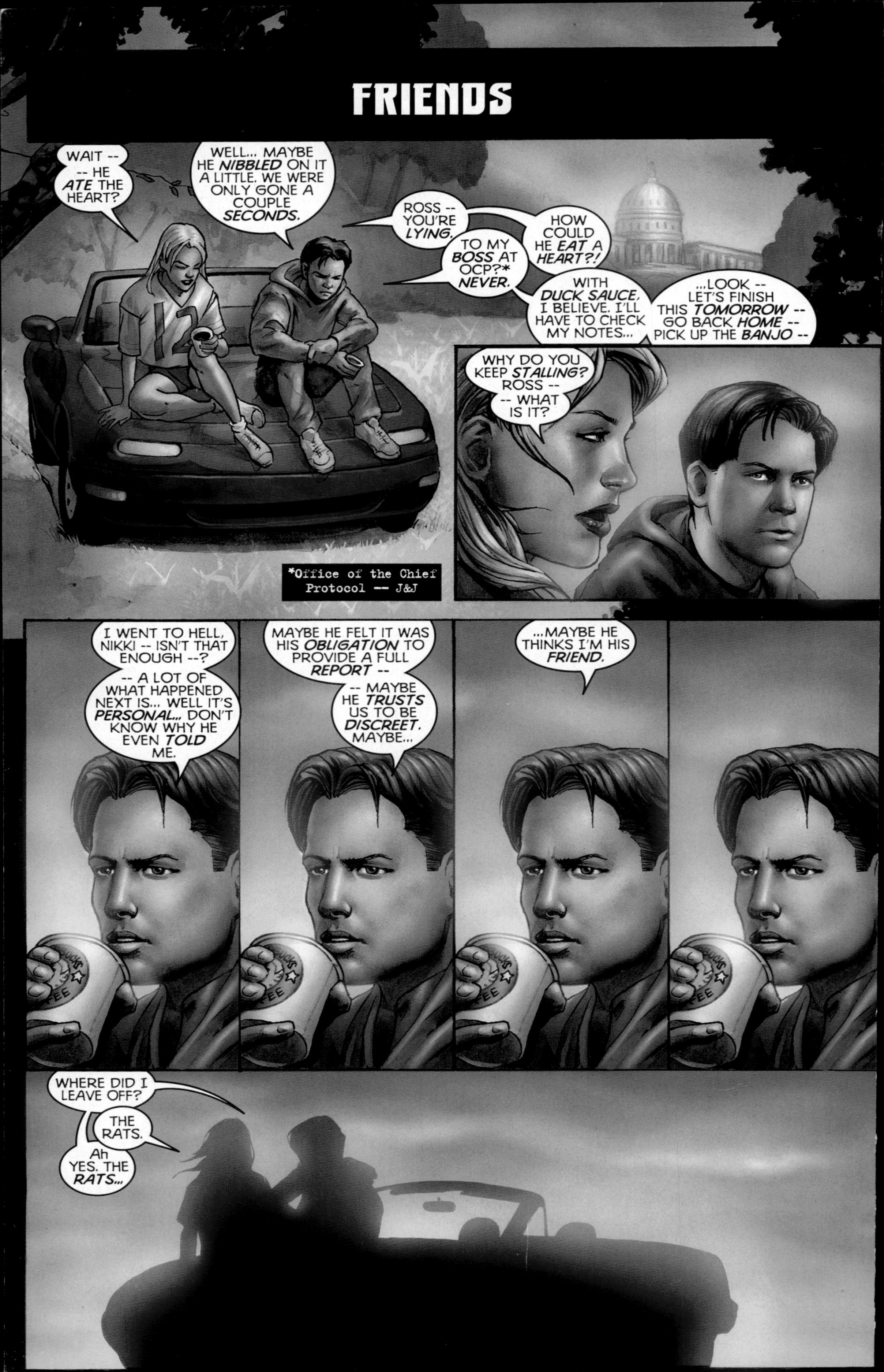
FRIENDS
WAIT -- -- HE ATE THE HEART?
WELL... MAYBE HE NIBBLED ON IT A LITTLE. WE WERE ONLY GONE A COUPLE SECONDS.
ROSS -- YOU'RE LYING.
TO MY BOSS AT OCP?* NEVER.
HOW COULD HE EAT A HEART?!
WITH DUCK SAUCE, I BELIEVE. I'LL HAVE TO CHECK MY NOTES...
...LOOK -- LET'S FINISH THIS TOMORROW -- GO BACK HOME -- PICK UP THE BANJO --
*Office of the Chief Protocol -- J&J
WHY DO YOU KEEP STALLING? ROSS --
-- WHAT IS IT?
I WENT TO HELL, NIKKI -- ISN'T THAT ENOUGH --?
-- A LOT OF WHAT HAPPENED NEXT IS... WELL IT'S PERSONAL... DON'T KNOW WHY HE EVEN TOLD ME.
MAYBE HE FELT IT WAS HIS OBLIGATION TO PROVIDE A FULL REPORT --
-- MAYBE HE TRUSTS US TO BE DISCREET. MAYBE...
...MAYBE HE THINKS I'M HIS FRIEND.
WHERE DID I LEAVE OFF?
THE RATS.
Ah YES. THE RATS...

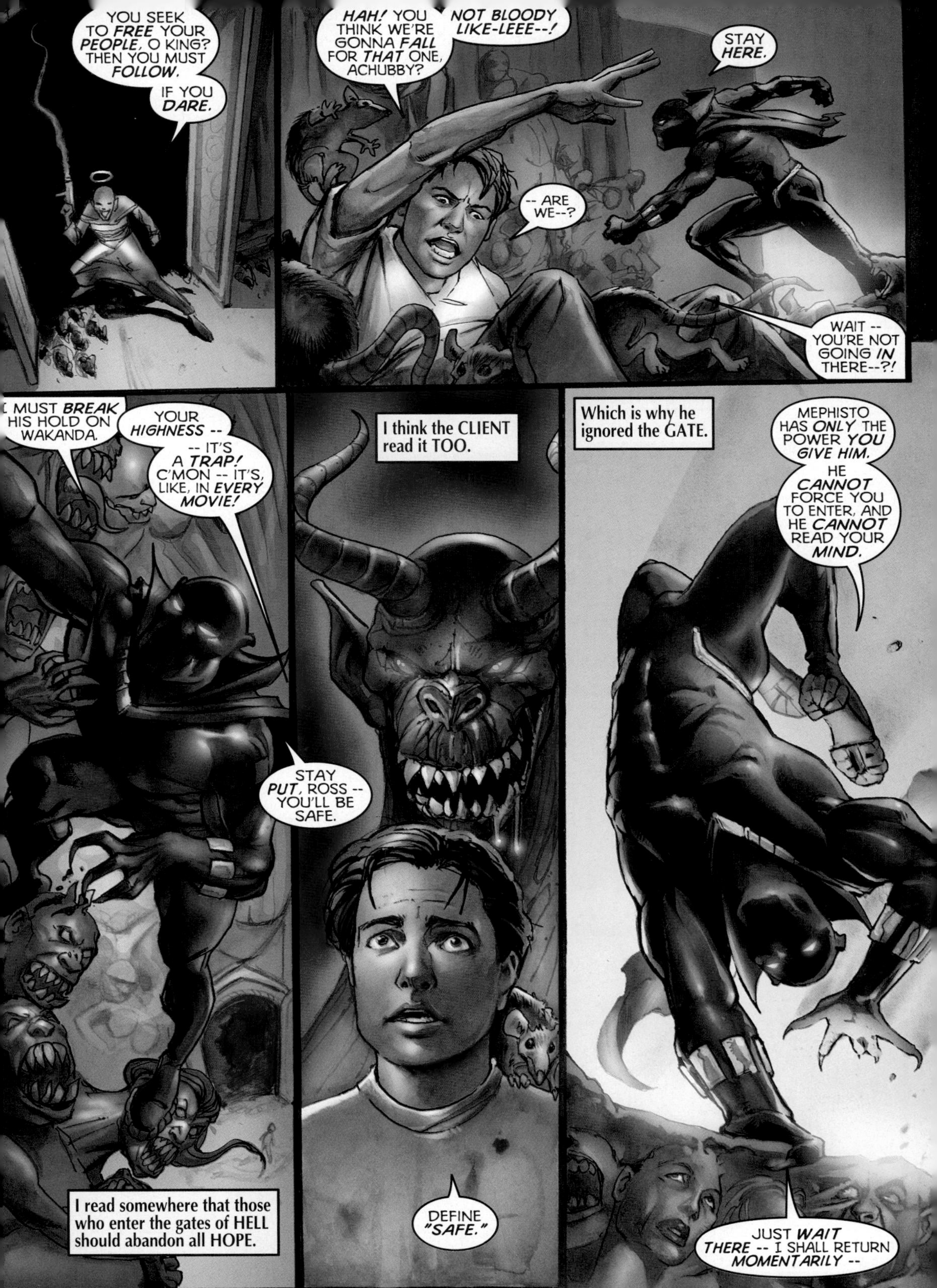
YOU SEEK TO FREE YOUR PEOPLE, O KING? THEN YOU MUST FOLLOW.
IF YOU DARE.
HAH! YOU THINK WE'RE GONNA FALL FOR THAT ONE, ACHUBBY?
NOT BLOODY LIKE-LEEE--!
STAY HERE.
-- ARE WE--?
WAIT -- YOU'RE NOT GOING IN THERE--?!
I MUST BREAK HIS HOLD ON WAKANDA.
YOUR HIGHNESS --
-- IT'S A TRAP! C'MON -- IT'S, LIKE, IN EVERY MOVIE!
STAY PUT, ROSS -- YOU'LL BE SAFE.
I read somewhere that those who enter the gates of HELL should abandon all HOPE.
I think the CLIENT read it TOO.
DEFINE "SAFE."
Which is why he ignored the GATE.
MEPHISTO HAS ONLY THE POWER YOU GIVE HIM.
HE CANNOT FORCE YOU TO ENTER, AND HE CANNOT READ YOUR MIND.
JUST WAIT THERE -- I SHALL RETURN MOMENTARILY --

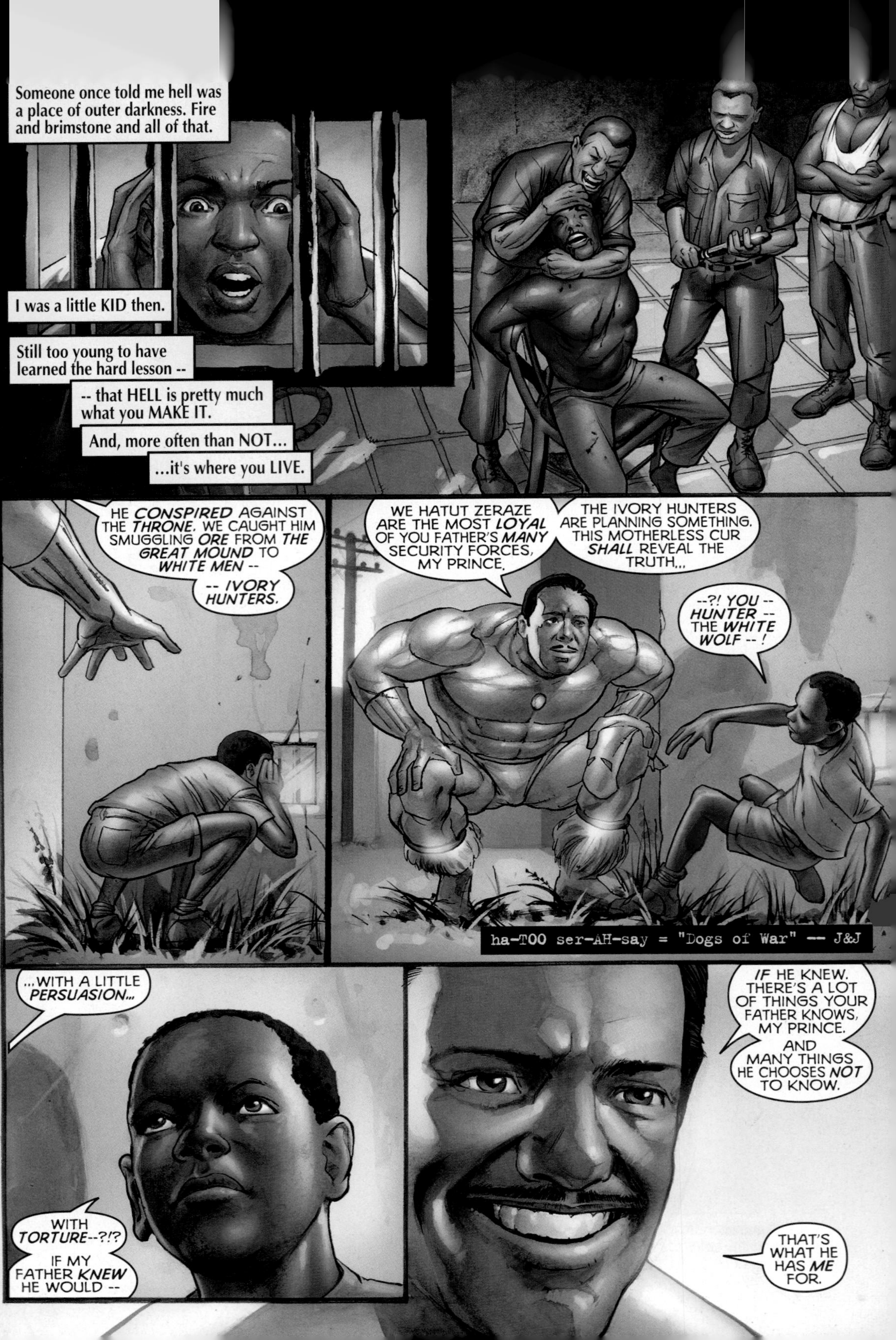
Someone once told me hell was a place of outer darkness. Fire and brimstone and all of that.
I was a little KID then.
Still too young to have learned the hard lesson --
-- that HELL is pretty much what you MAKE IT.
And, more often than NOT...
...it's where you LIVE.
HE CONSPIRED AGAINST THE THRONE. WE CAUGHT HIM SMUGGLING ORE FROM THE GREAT MOUND TO WHITE MEN --
-- IVORY HUNTERS.
WE HATUT ZERAZE ARE THE MOST LOYAL OF YOU FATHER'S MANY SECURITY FORCES, MY PRINCE.
THE IVORY HUNTERS ARE PLANNING SOMETHING. THIS MOTHERLESS CUR SHALL REVEAL THE TRUTH...
--?! YOU -- HUNTER -- THE WHITE WOLF -- !
ha-TOO ser-AH-say = "Dogs of War" -- J&J
...WITH A LITTLE PERSUASION...
WITH TORTURE--?!?
IF MY FATHER KNEW HE WOULD --
IF HE KNEW. THERE'S A LOT OF THINGS YOUR FATHER KNOWS, MY PRINCE.
AND MANY THINGS HE CHOOSES NOT TO KNOW.
THAT'S WHAT HE HAS ME FOR.

APOCALYPSE THEN

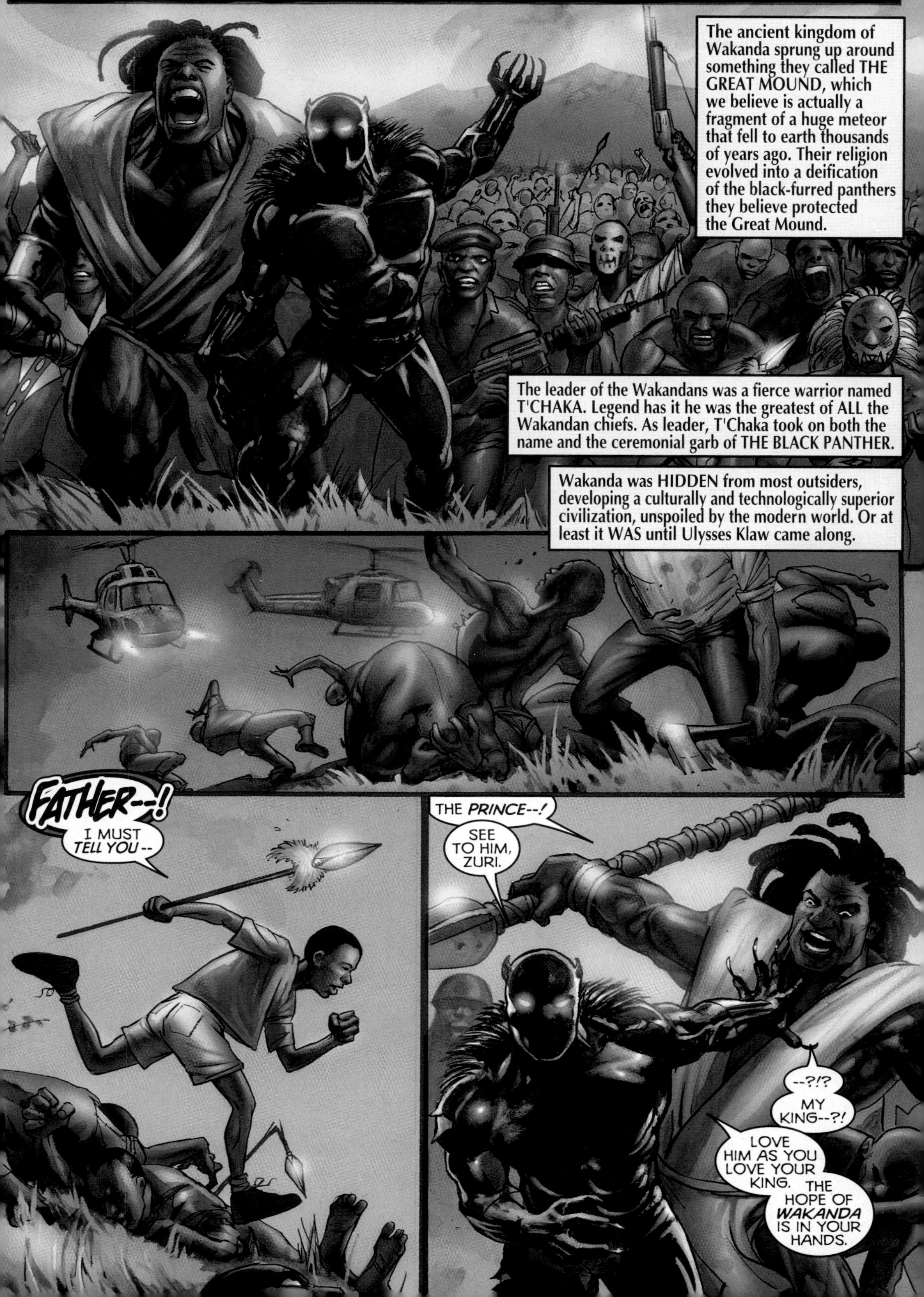

The ancient kingdom of Wakanda sprung up around something they called THE GREAT MOUND, which we believe is actually a fragment of a huge meteor that fell to earth thousands of years ago. Their religion evolved into a deification of the black-furred panthers they believe protected the Great Mound.
The leader of the Wakandans was a fierce warrior named T'CHAKA. Legend has it he was the greatest of ALL the Wakandan chiefs. As leader, T'Chaka took on both the name and the ceremonial garb of THE BLACK PANTHER.
Wakanda was HIDDEN from most outsiders, developing a culturally and technologically superior civilization, unspoiled by the modern world. Or at least it WAS until Ulysses Klaw came along.
FATHER--!
I MUST TELL YOU --
THE PRINCE--!
SEE TO HIM, ZURI.
--?!?
MY KING--?!
LOVE HIM AS YOU LOVE YOUR KING.
THE HOPE OF WAKANDA IS IN YOUR HANDS.

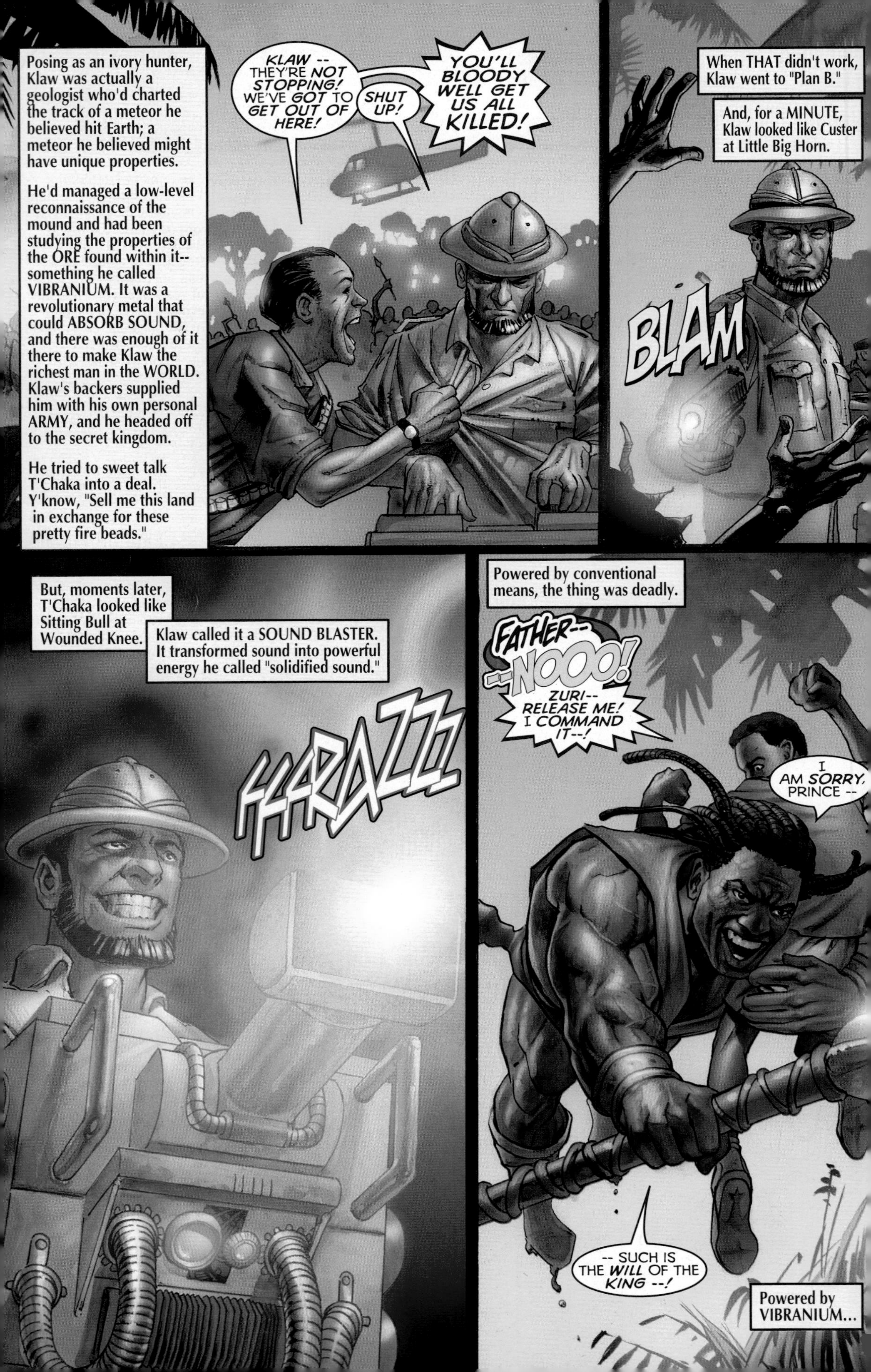

Posing as an ivory hunter, Klaw was actually a geologist who'd charted the track of a meteor he believed hit Earth; a meteor he believed might have unique properties.
He'd managed a low-level reconnaissance of the mound and had been studying the properties of the ORE found within it--something he called VIBRANIUM. It was a revolutionary metal that could ABSORB SOUND, and there was enough of it there to make Klaw the richest man in the WORLD. Klaw's backers supplied him with his own personal ARMY, and he headed off to the secret kingdom.
He tried to sweet talk T'Chaka into a deal. Y'know, "Sell me this land in exchange for these pretty fire beads."
KLAW -- THEY'RE NOT STOPPING! WE'VE GOT TO GET OUT OF HERE!
SHUT UP!
YOU'LL BLOODY WELL GET US ALL KILLED!
When THAT didn't work, Klaw went to "Plan B."
And, for a MINUTE, Klaw looked like Custer at Little Big Horn.
BLAM
But, moments later, T'Chaka looked like Sitting Bull at Wounded Knee.
Klaw called it a SOUND BLASTER. It transformed sound into powerful energy he called "solidified sound."
FFFRAZZZ
Powered by conventional means, the thing was deadly.
FATHER-- --NOOO!
ZURI-- RELEASE ME! I COMMAND IT--!
I AM SORRY, PRINCE --
-- SUCH IS THE WILL OF THE KING --!
Powered by VIBRANIUM...

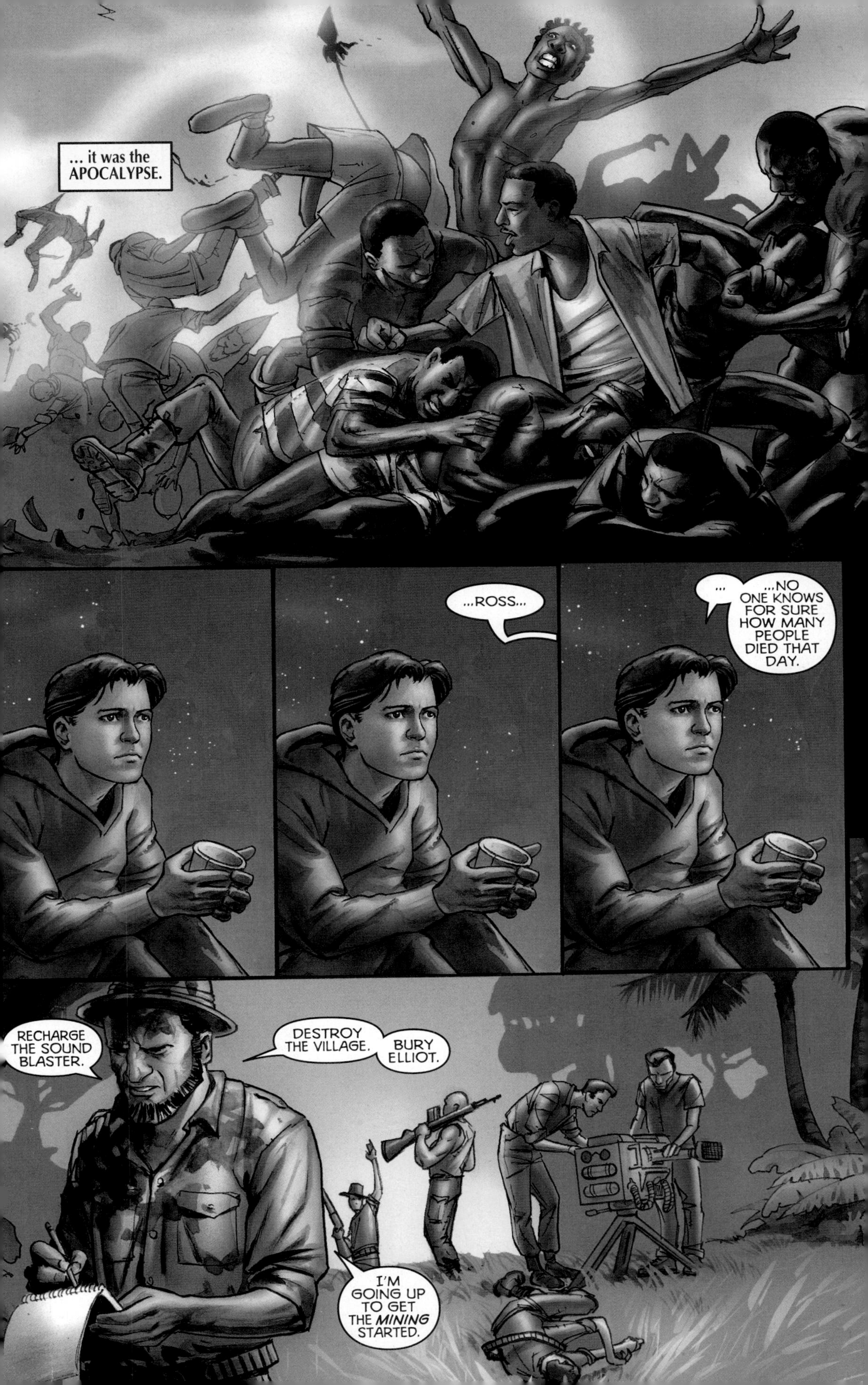
... it was the APOCALYPSE.
...ROSS...
... ...NO ONE KNOWS FOR SURE HOW MANY PEOPLE DIED THAT DAY.
RECHARGE THE SOUND BLASTER.
DESTROY THE VILLAGE.
BURY ELLIOT.
I'M GOING UP TO GET THE *MINING* STARTED.

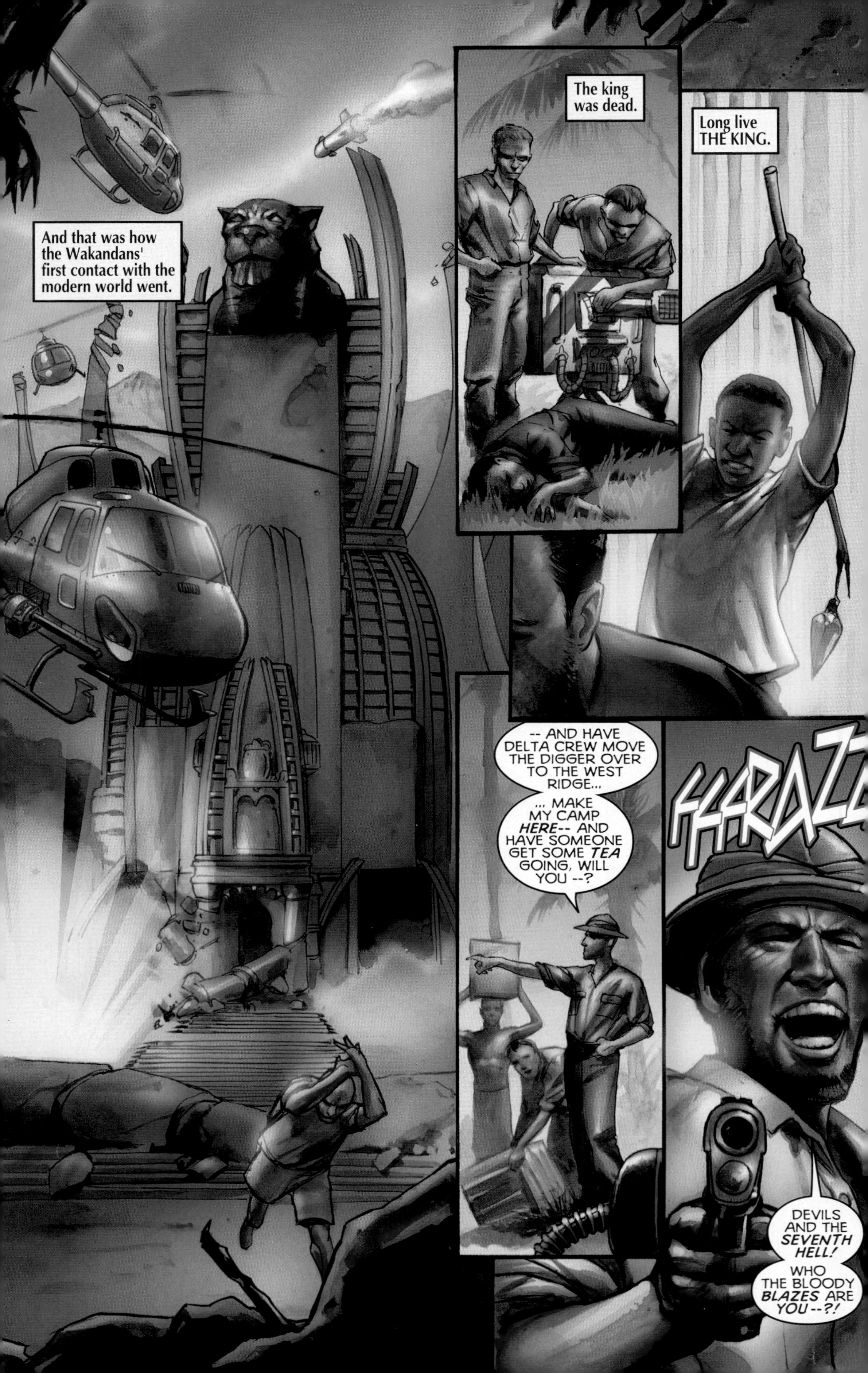
And that was how the Wakandans' first contact with the modern world went.
The king was dead.
Long live THE KING.
-- AND HAVE DELTA CREW MOVE THE DIGGER OVER TO THE WEST RIDGE...
... MAKE MY CAMP *HERE*-- AND HAVE SOMEONE GET SOME *TEA* GOING, WILL YOU --?
DEVILS AND THE *SEVENTH HELL!*
WHO THE BLOODY *BLAZES* ARE *YOU* --?!

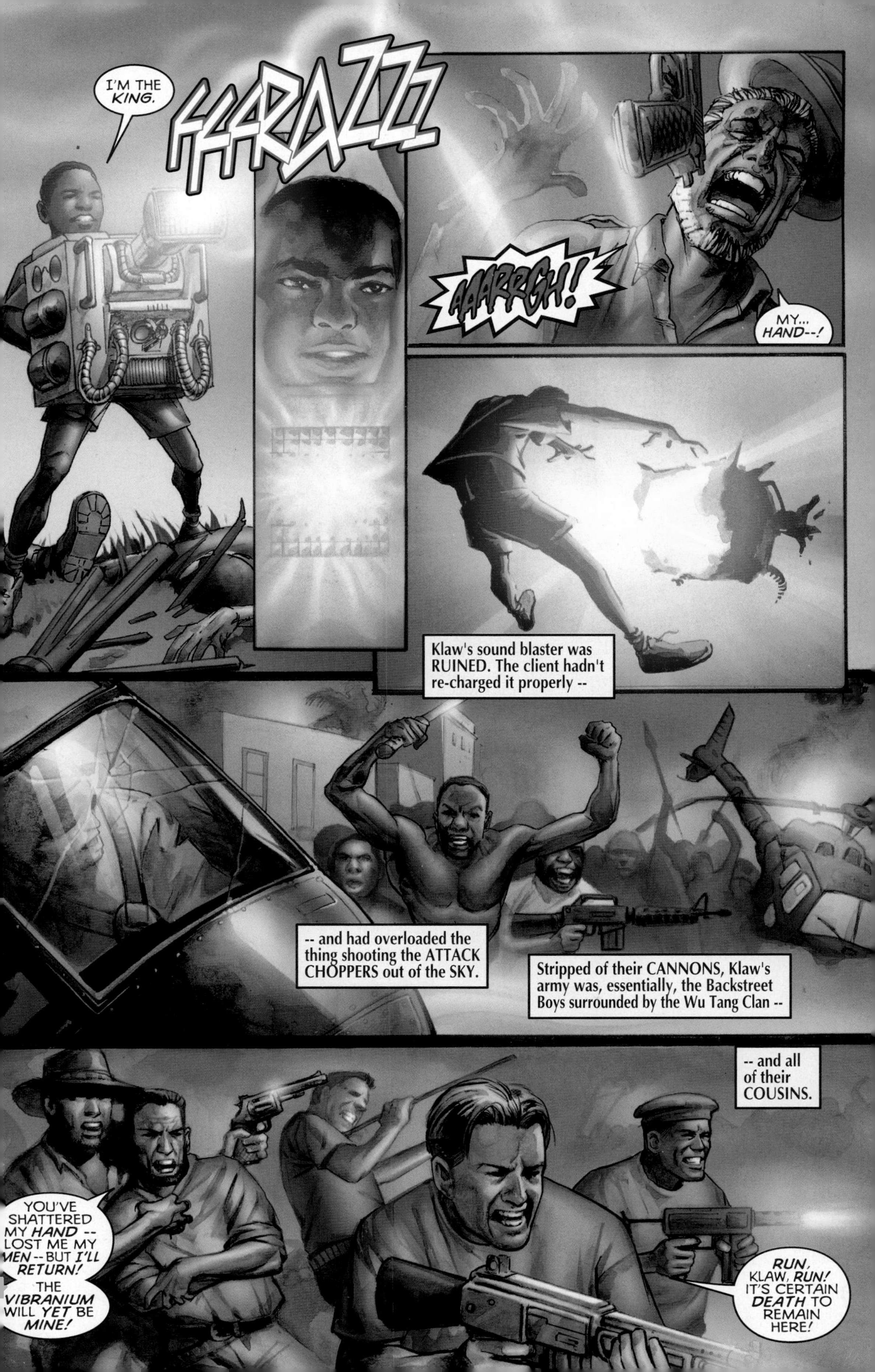
I'M THE KING.
FFFRAZZZ
AAARRGH!
MY... HAND--!
Klaw's sound blaster was RUINED. The client hadn't re-charged it properly --
-- and had overloaded the thing shooting the ATTACK CHOPPERS out of the SKY.
Stripped of their CANNONS, Klaw's army was, essentially, the Backstreet Boys surrounded by the Wu Tang Clan --
-- and all of their COUSINS.
YOU'VE SHATTERED MY HAND -- LOST ME MY MEN -- BUT I'LL RETURN!
THE VIBRANIUM WILL YET BE MINE!
RUN, KLAW, RUN! IT'S CERTAIN DEATH TO REMAIN HERE!

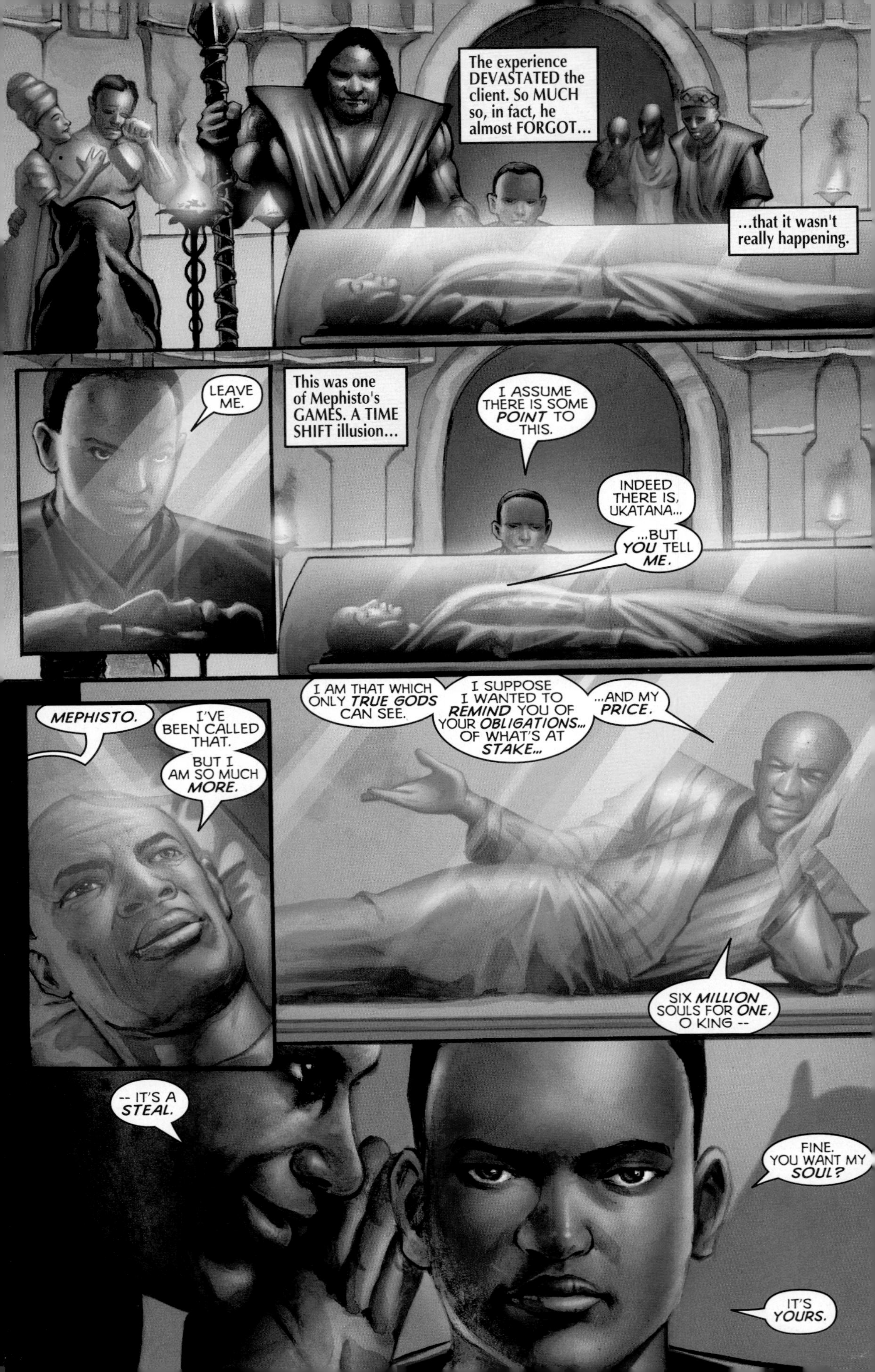
The experience DEVASTATED the client. So MUCH so, in fact, he almost FORGOT...
...that it wasn't really happening.
LEAVE ME.
This was one of Mephisto's GAMES. A TIME SHIFT illusion...
I ASSUME THERE IS SOME POINT TO THIS.
INDEED THERE IS, UKATANA...
...BUT YOU TELL ME.
MEPHISTO.
I'VE BEEN CALLED THAT.
BUT I AM SO MUCH MORE.
I AM THAT WHICH ONLY TRUE GODS CAN SEE.
I SUPPOSE I WANTED TO REMIND YOU OF YOUR OBLIGATIONS... OF WHAT'S AT STAKE...
...AND MY PRICE.
SIX MILLION SOULS FOR ONE, O KING --
-- IT'S A STEAL.
FINE. YOU WANT MY SOUL?
IT'S YOURS.

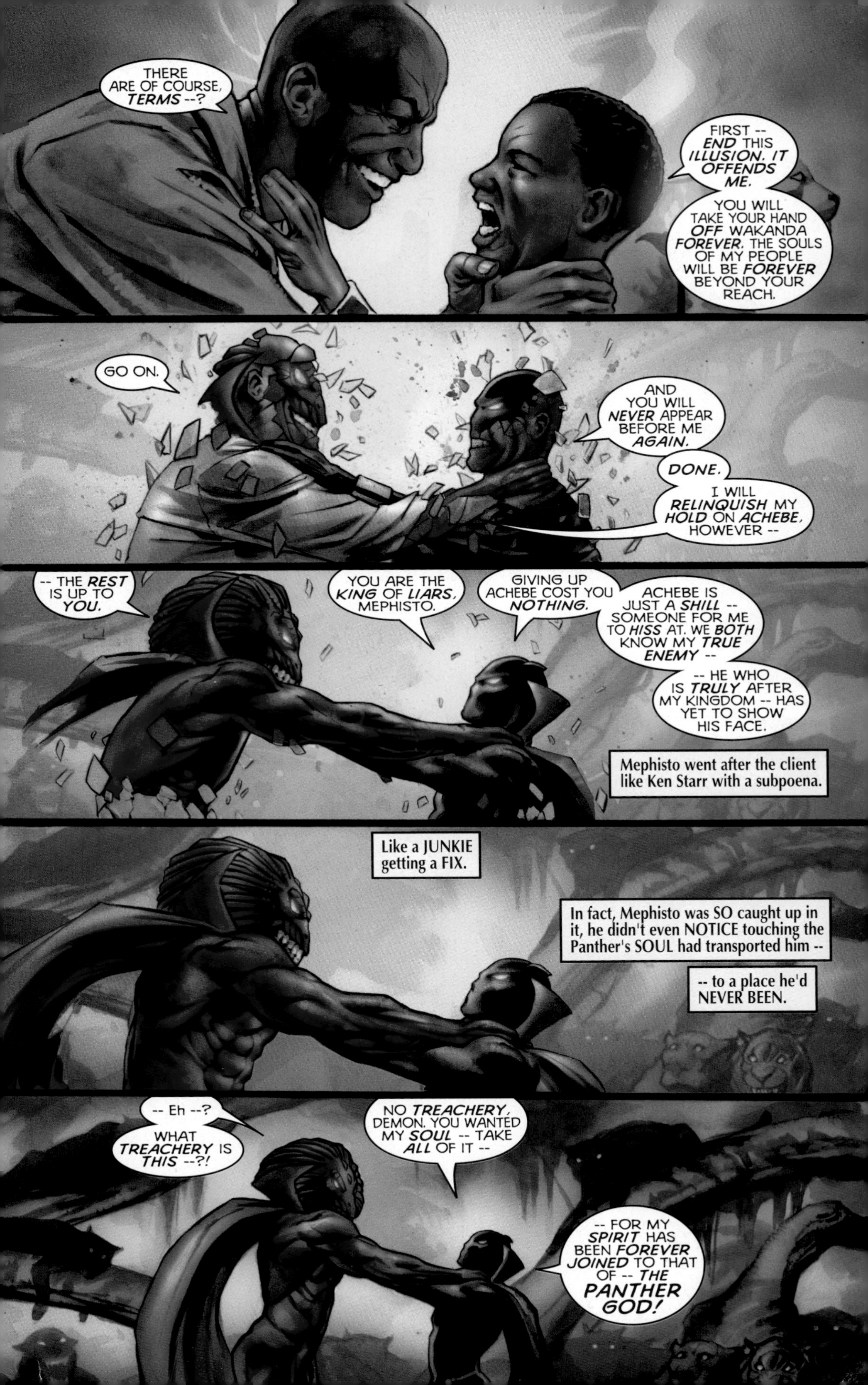
THERE ARE OF COURSE, TERMS --?
FIRST -- END THIS ILLUSION. IT OFFENDS ME.
YOU WILL TAKE YOUR HAND OFF WAKANDA FOREVER. THE SOULS OF MY PEOPLE WILL BE FOREVER BEYOND YOUR REACH.
GO ON.
AND YOU WILL NEVER APPEAR BEFORE ME AGAIN.
DONE.
I WILL RELINQUISH MY HOLD ON ACHEBE, HOWEVER --
-- THE REST IS UP TO YOU.
YOU ARE THE KING OF LIARS, MEPHISTO.
GIVING UP ACHEBE COST YOU NOTHING.
ACHEBE IS JUST A SHILL -- SOMEONE FOR ME TO HISS AT. WE BOTH KNOW MY TRUE ENEMY --
-- HE WHO IS TRULY AFTER MY KINGDOM -- HAS YET TO SHOW HIS FACE.
Mephisto went after the client like Ken Starr with a subpoena.
Like a JUNKIE getting a FIX.
In fact, Mephisto was SO caught up in it, he didn't even NOTICE touching the Panther's SOUL had transported him --
-- to a place he'd NEVER BEEN.
-- Eh --?
WHAT TREACHERY IS THIS --?!
NO TREACHERY, DEMON. YOU WANTED MY SOUL -- TAKE ALL OF IT --
-- FOR MY SPIRIT HAS BEEN FOREVER JOINED TO THAT OF -- THE PANTHER GOD!

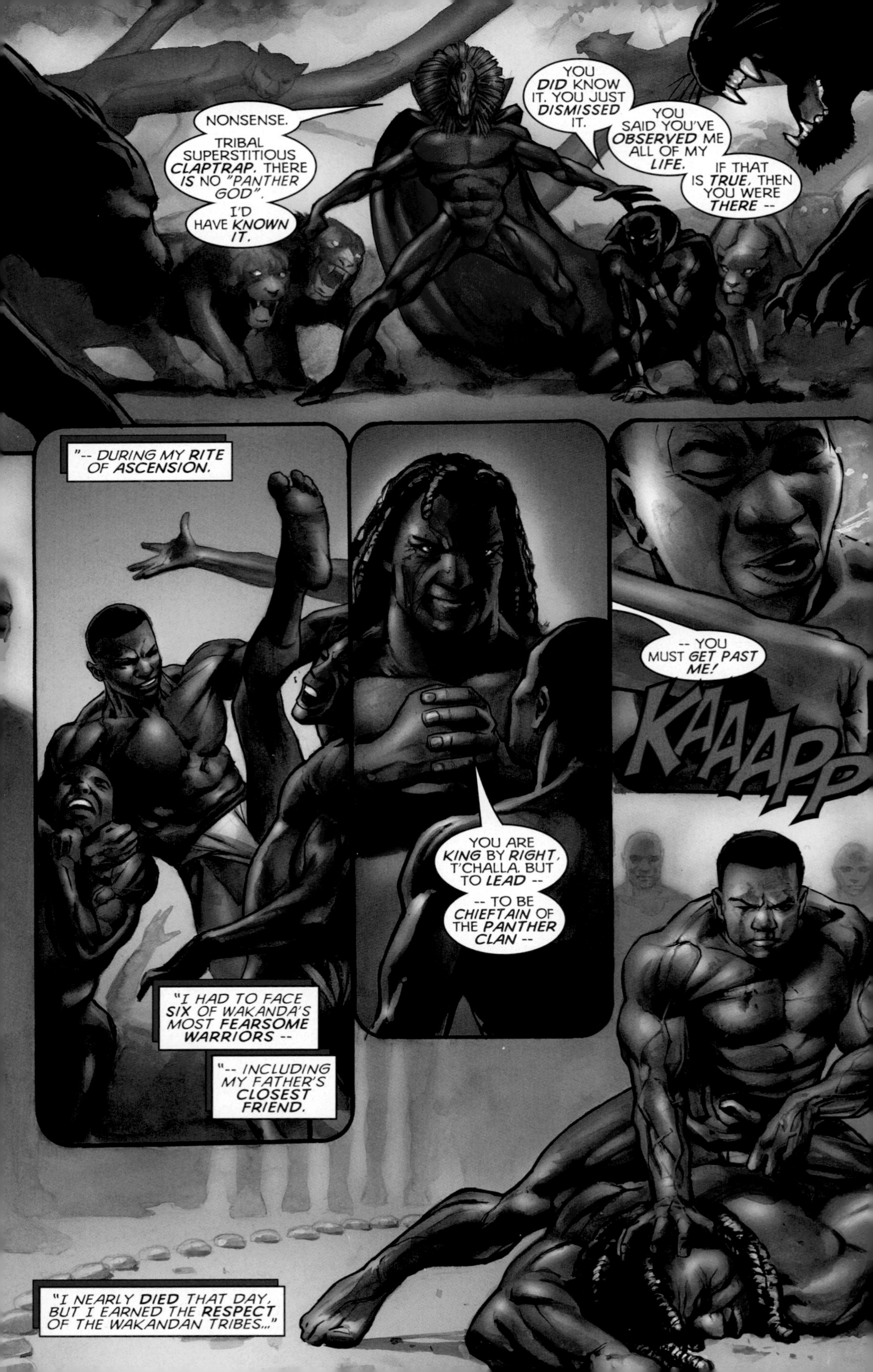
NONSENSE.
TRIBAL SUPERSTITIOUS CLAPTRAP. THERE IS NO "PANTHER GOD".
I'D HAVE KNOWN IT.
YOU DID KNOW IT. YOU JUST DISMISSED IT.
YOU SAID YOU'VE OBSERVED ME ALL OF MY LIFE.
IF THAT IS TRUE, THEN YOU WERE THERE --
"-- DURING MY RITE OF ASCENSION.
"I HAD TO FACE SIX OF WAKANDA'S MOST FEARSOME WARRIORS --
"-- INCLUDING MY FATHER'S CLOSEST FRIEND.
YOU ARE KING BY RIGHT, T'CHALLA. BUT TO LEAD --
-- TO BE CHIEFTAIN OF THE PANTHER CLAN --
-- YOU MUST GET PAST ME!
KAAAPP
"I NEARLY DIED THAT DAY, BUT I EARNED THE RESPECT OF THE WAKANDAN TRIBES..."

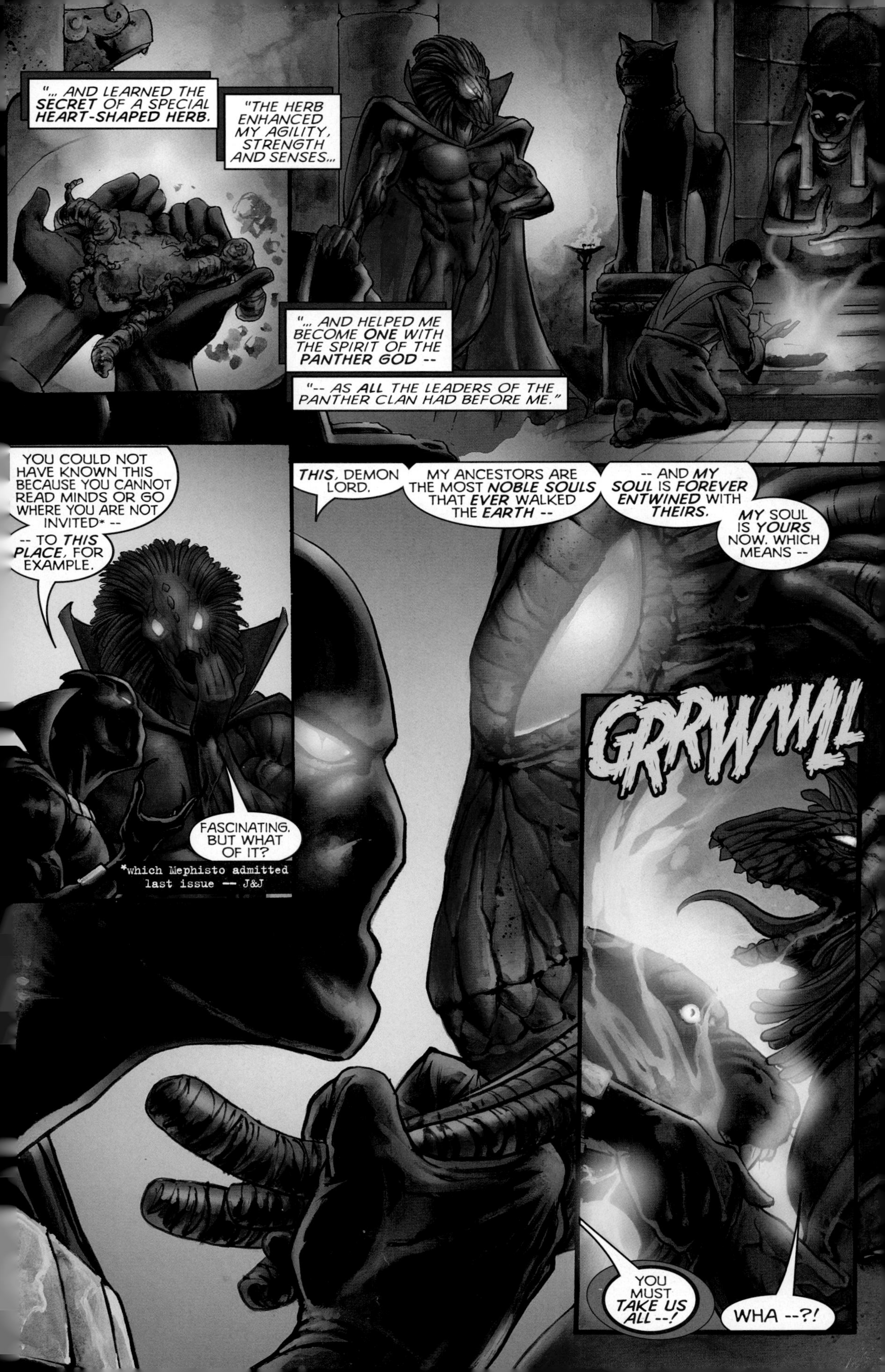
"... AND LEARNED THE SECRET OF A SPECIAL HEART-SHAPED HERB.
"THE HERB ENHANCED MY AGILITY, STRENGTH AND SENSES...
"... AND HELPED ME BECOME ONE WITH THE SPIRIT OF THE PANTHER GOD --
"-- AS ALL THE LEADERS OF THE PANTHER CLAN HAD BEFORE ME."
YOU COULD NOT HAVE KNOWN THIS BECAUSE YOU CANNOT READ MINDS OR GO WHERE YOU ARE NOT INVITED* --
-- TO THIS PLACE, FOR EXAMPLE.
FASCINATING. BUT WHAT OF IT?
*which Mephisto admitted last issue -- J&J
THIS, DEMON LORD.
MY ANCESTORS ARE THE MOST NOBLE SOULS THAT EVER WALKED THE EARTH --
-- AND MY SOUL IS FOREVER ENTWINED WITH THEIRS.
MY SOUL IS YOURS NOW. WHICH MEANS --
GRRWWL
YOU MUST TAKE US ALL --!
WHA --?!

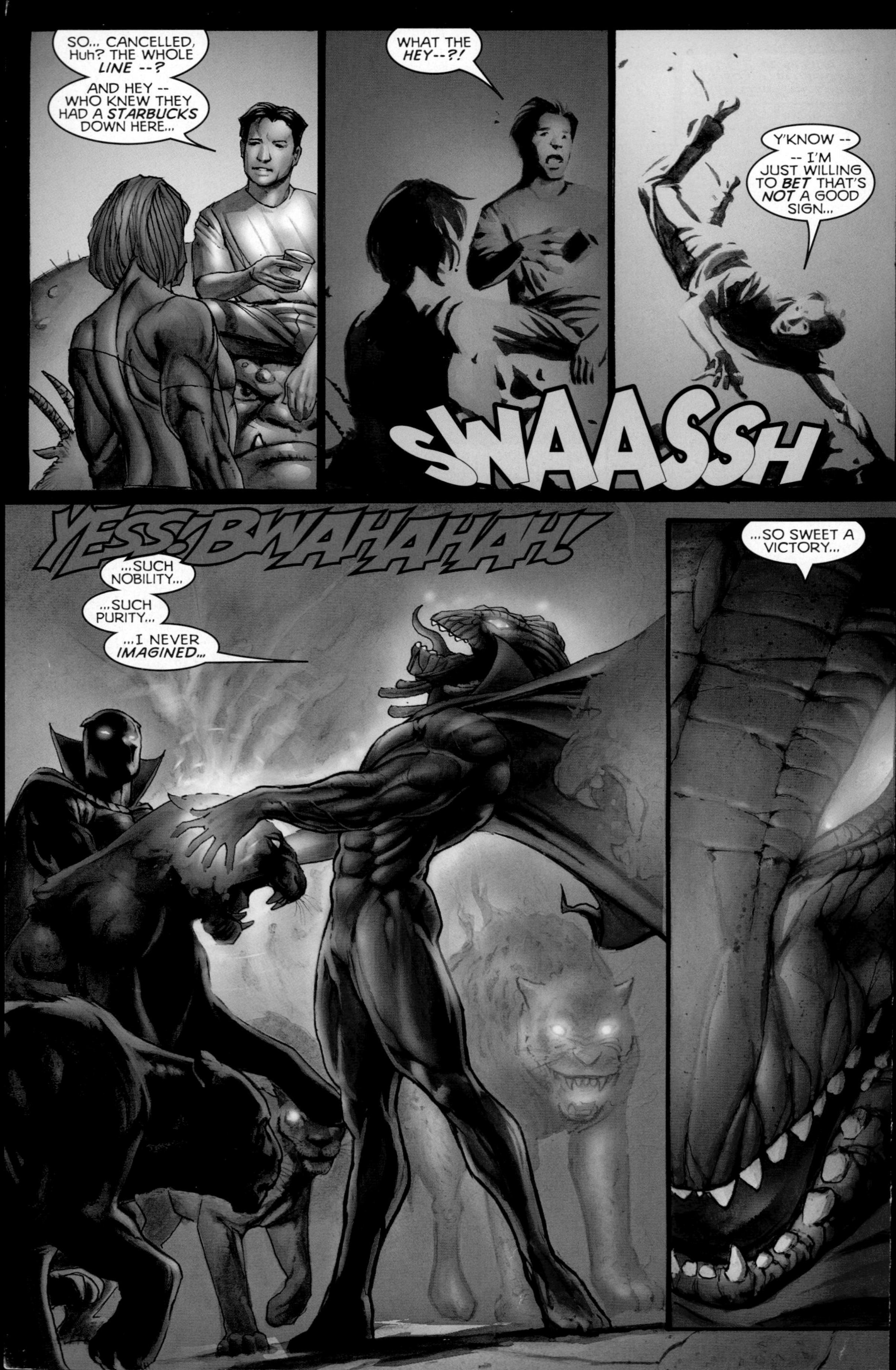
SO... CANCELLED, Huh? THE WHOLE LINE --?
AND HEY -- WHO KNEW THEY HAD A STARBUCKS DOWN HERE...
WHAT THE HEY--?!
Y'KNOW --
-- I'M JUST WILLING TO BET THAT'S NOT A GOOD SIGN...
SWAASSH
YESS! BWAHAHAH!
...SUCH NOBILITY...
...SUCH PURITY...
...I NEVER IMAGINED...
...SO SWEET A VICTORY...

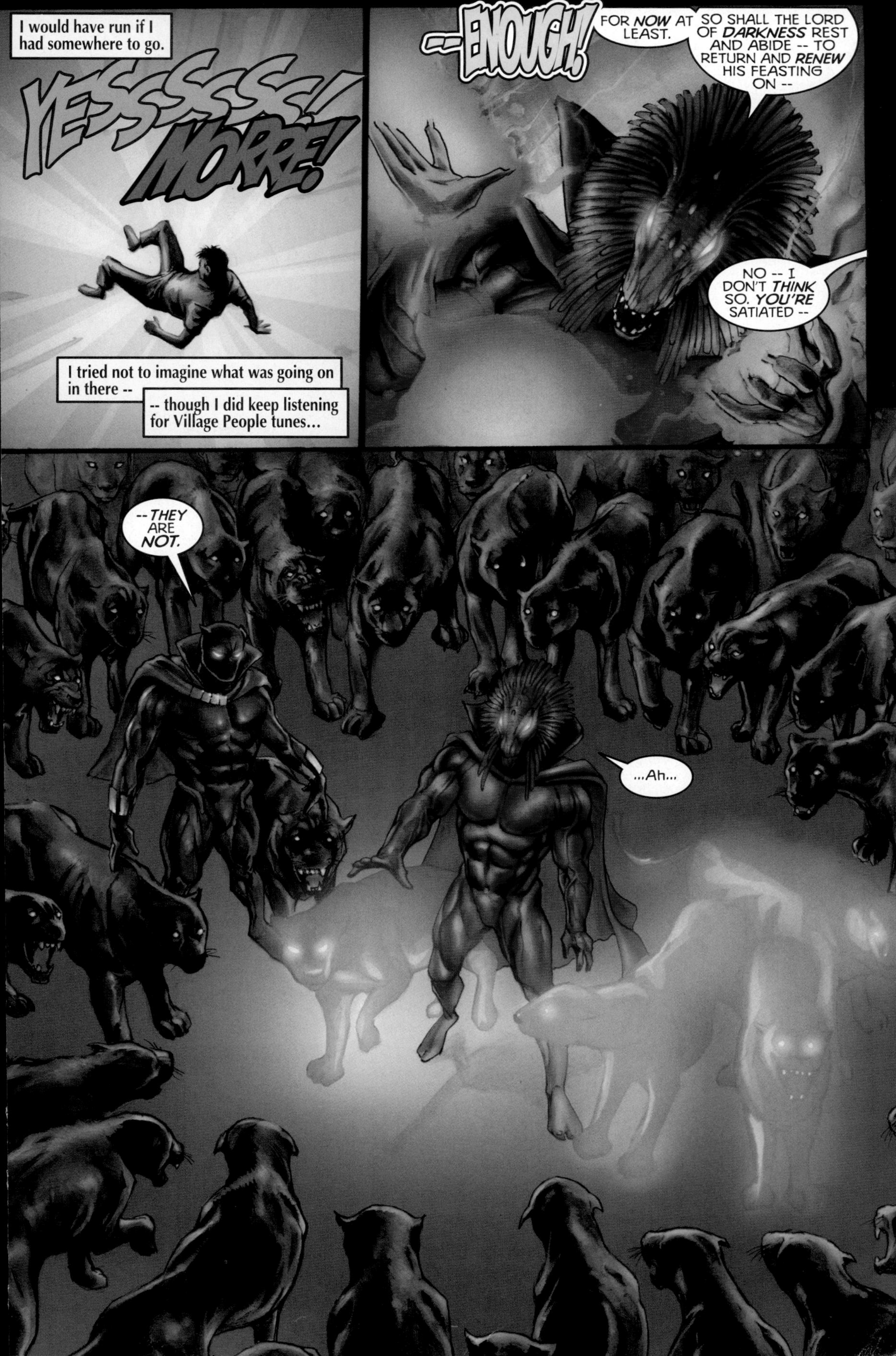

I would have run if I had somewhere to go.
YESSSSSSS!! MORRE!
I tried not to imagine what was going on in there --
-- though I did keep listening for Village People tunes...
--ENOUGH!
FOR NOW AT LEAST.
SO SHALL THE LORD OF DARKNESS REST AND ABIDE -- TO RETURN AND RENEW HIS FEASTING ON --
NO -- I DON'T THINK SO. YOU'RE SATIATED --
--THEY ARE NOT.
...Ah...

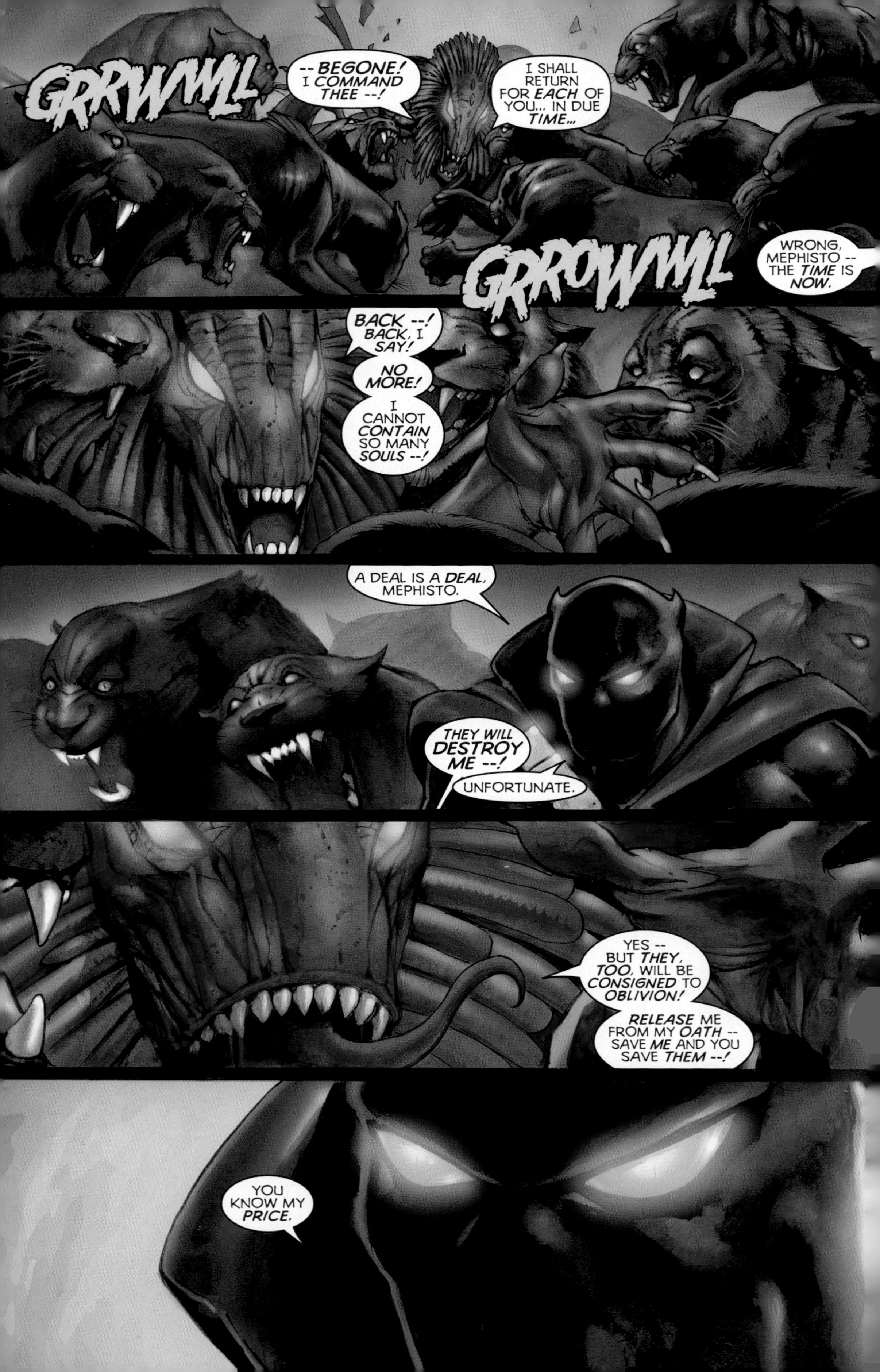
GRRWML
-- BEGONE! I COMMAND THEE --!
I SHALL RETURN FOR EACH OF YOU..., IN DUE TIME...
GRROWML
WRONG, MEPHISTO -- THE TIME IS NOW.
BACK --! BACK, I SAY!
NO MORE!
I CANNOT CONTAIN SO MANY SOULS --!
A DEAL IS A DEAL, MEPHISTO.
THEY WILL DESTROY ME --!
UNFORTUNATE.
YES -- BUT THEY, TOO, WILL BE CONSIGNED TO OBLIVION!
RELEASE ME FROM MY OATH -- SAVE ME AND YOU SAVE THEM --!
YOU KNOW MY PRICE.

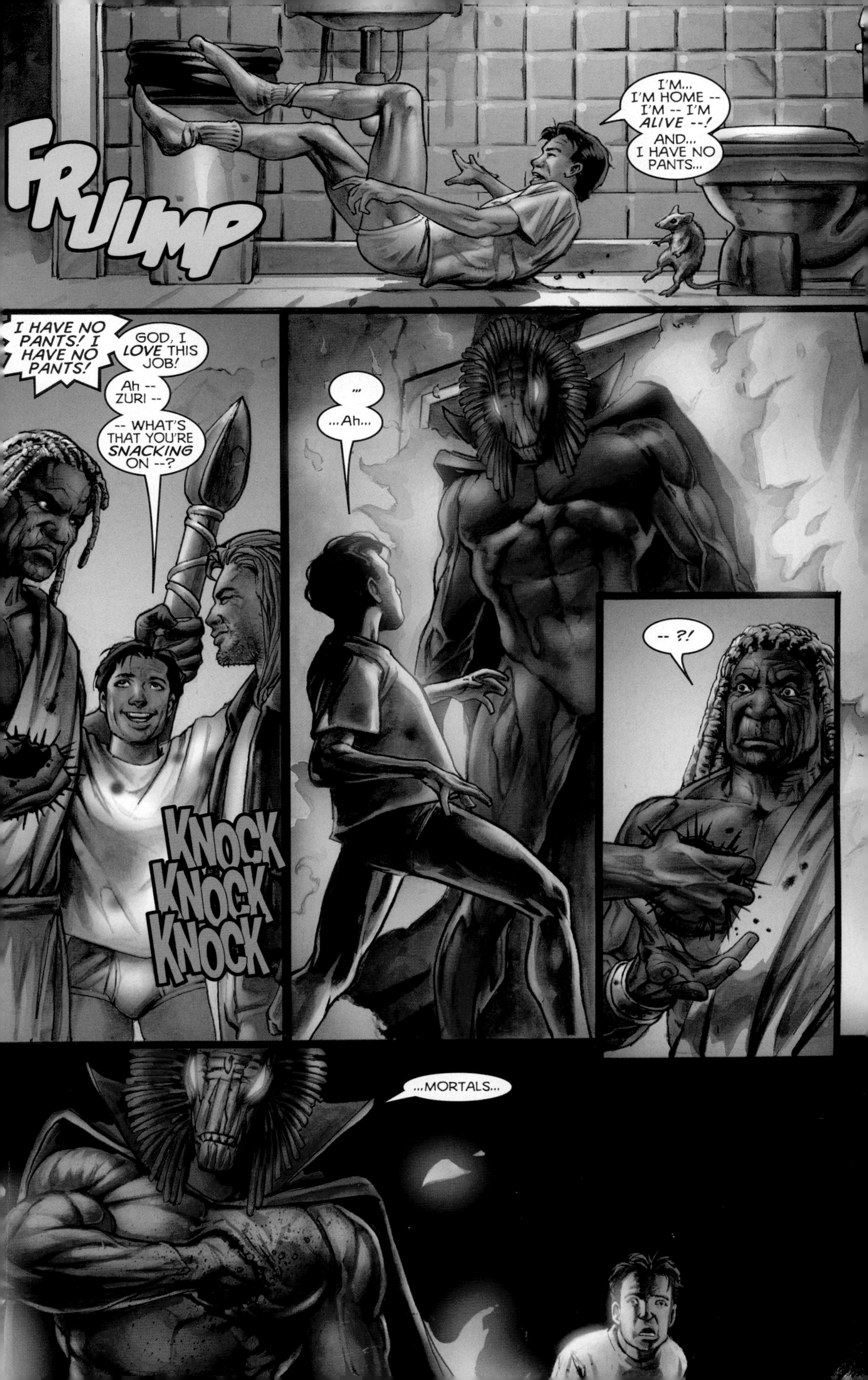
FRUUMP
I'M... I'M HOME -- I'M -- I'M *ALIVE* --!
AND... I HAVE NO PANTS...
I HAVE NO PANTS! I HAVE NO PANTS!
GOD, I *LOVE* THIS JOB!
Ah -- ZURI --
-- WHAT'S THAT YOU'RE *SNACKING* ON --?
KNOCK KNOCK KNOCK
...
...Ah...
-- ?!
...MORTALS...

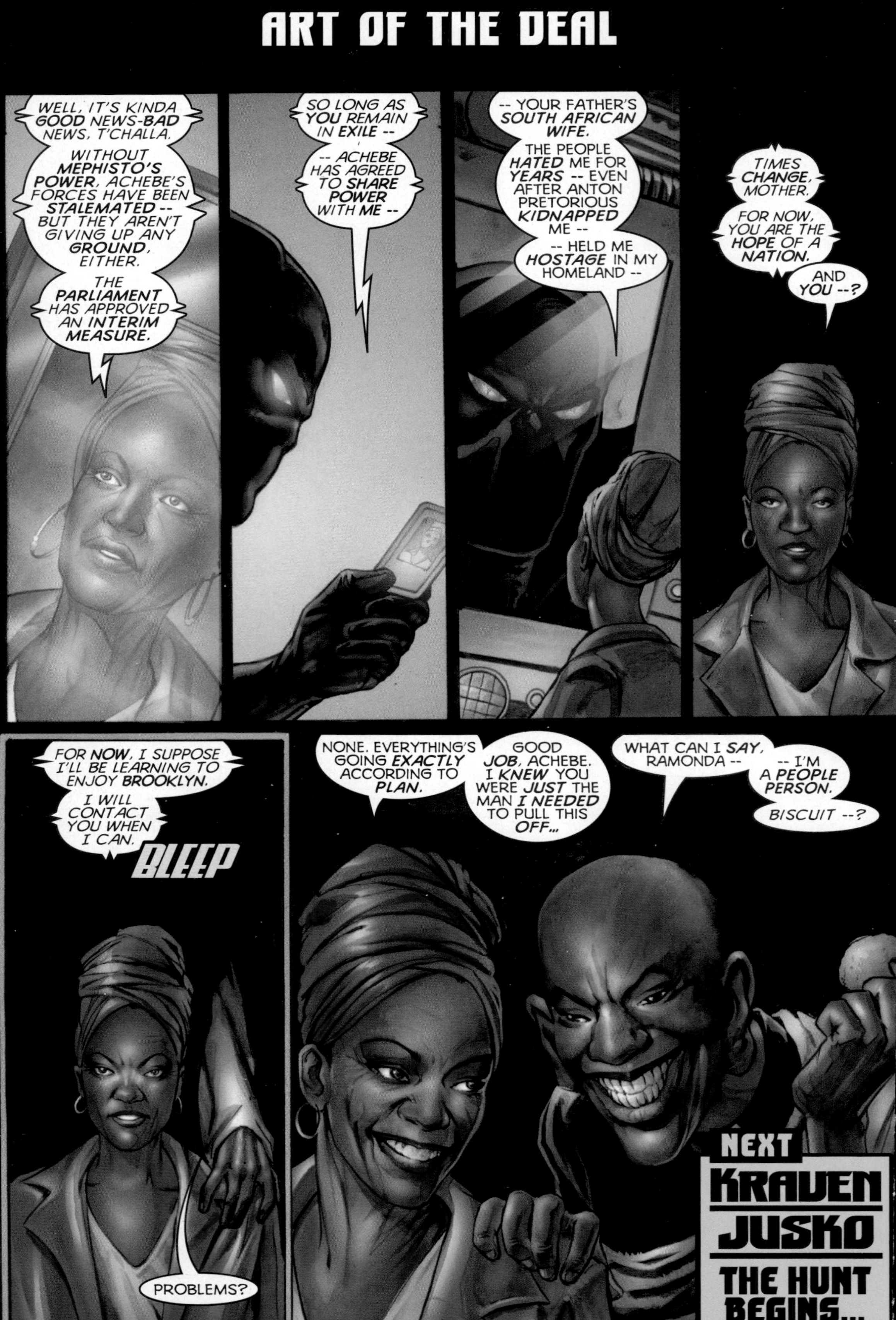
ART OF THE DEAL
WELL, IT'S KINDA GOOD NEWS-BAD NEWS, T'CHALLA.
WITHOUT MEPHISTO'S POWER, ACHEBE'S FORCES HAVE BEEN STALEMATED -- BUT THEY AREN'T GIVING UP ANY GROUND, EITHER.
THE PARLIAMENT HAS APPROVED AN INTERIM MEASURE.
SO LONG AS YOU REMAIN IN EXILE --
-- ACHEBE HAS AGREED TO SHARE POWER WITH ME --
-- YOUR FATHER'S SOUTH AFRICAN WIFE.
THE PEOPLE HATED ME FOR YEARS -- EVEN AFTER ANTON PRETORIOUS KIDNAPPED ME --
-- HELD ME HOSTAGE IN MY HOMELAND --
TIMES CHANGE, MOTHER.
FOR NOW, YOU ARE THE HOPE OF A NATION.
AND YOU --?
FOR NOW, I SUPPOSE I'LL BE LEARNING TO ENJOY BROOKLYN.
I WILL CONTACT YOU WHEN I CAN.
BLEEP
PROBLEMS?
NONE. EVERYTHING'S GOING EXACTLY ACCORDING TO PLAN.
GOOD JOB, ACHEBE. I KNEW YOU WERE JUST THE MAN I NEEDED TO PULL THIS OFF...
WHAT CAN I SAY, RAMONDA --
-- I'M A PEOPLE PERSON.
BISCUIT --?
NEXT
KRAVEN
JUSKO
THE HUNT BEGINS...

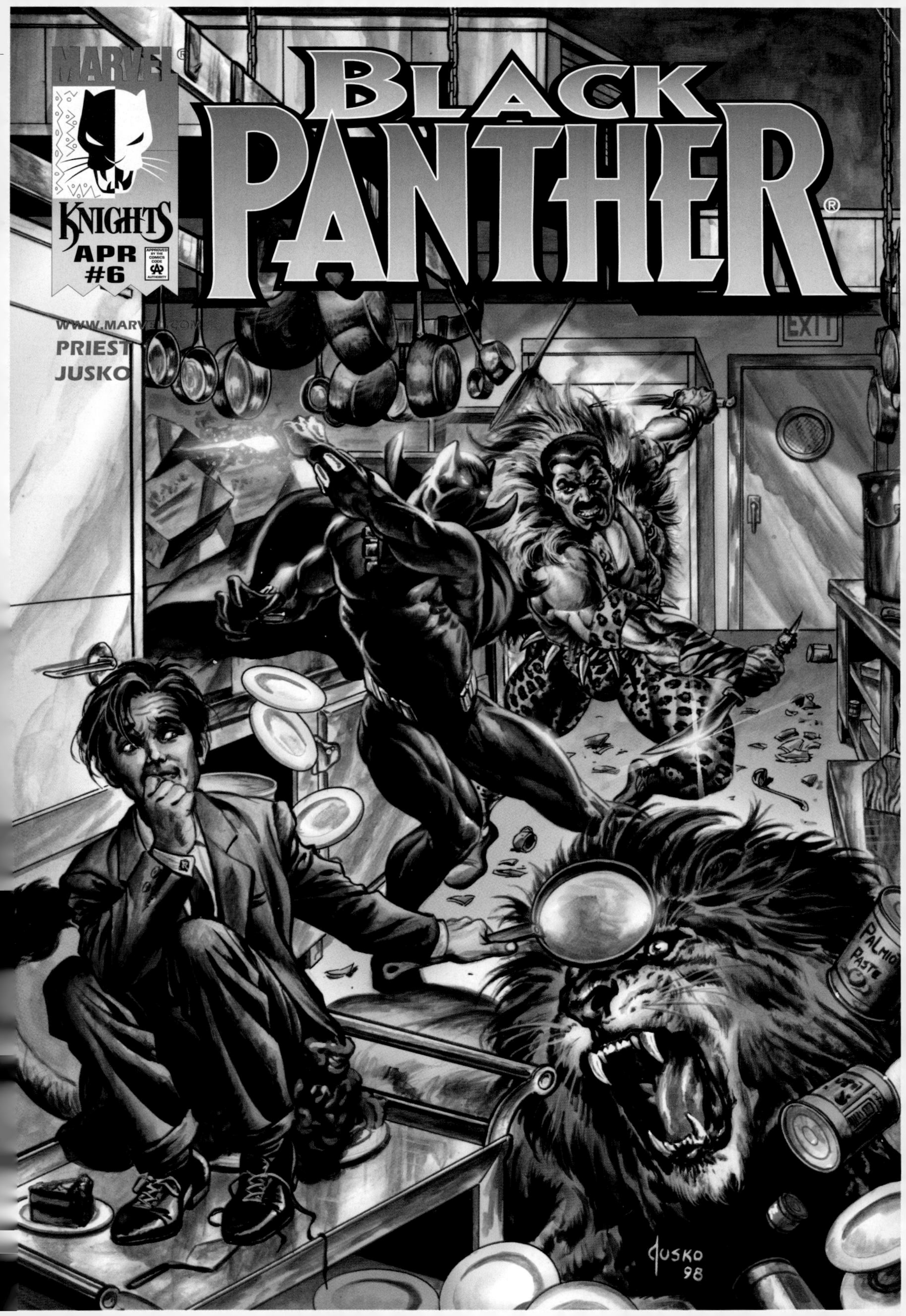
MARVEL
BLACK PANTHER
KNIGHTS
APR
#6
APPROVED BY THE COMICS CODE AUTHORITY
PRIEST
JUSKO
EXIT
PASTE
JUSKO 98

GREAT BALLS OF SPIT

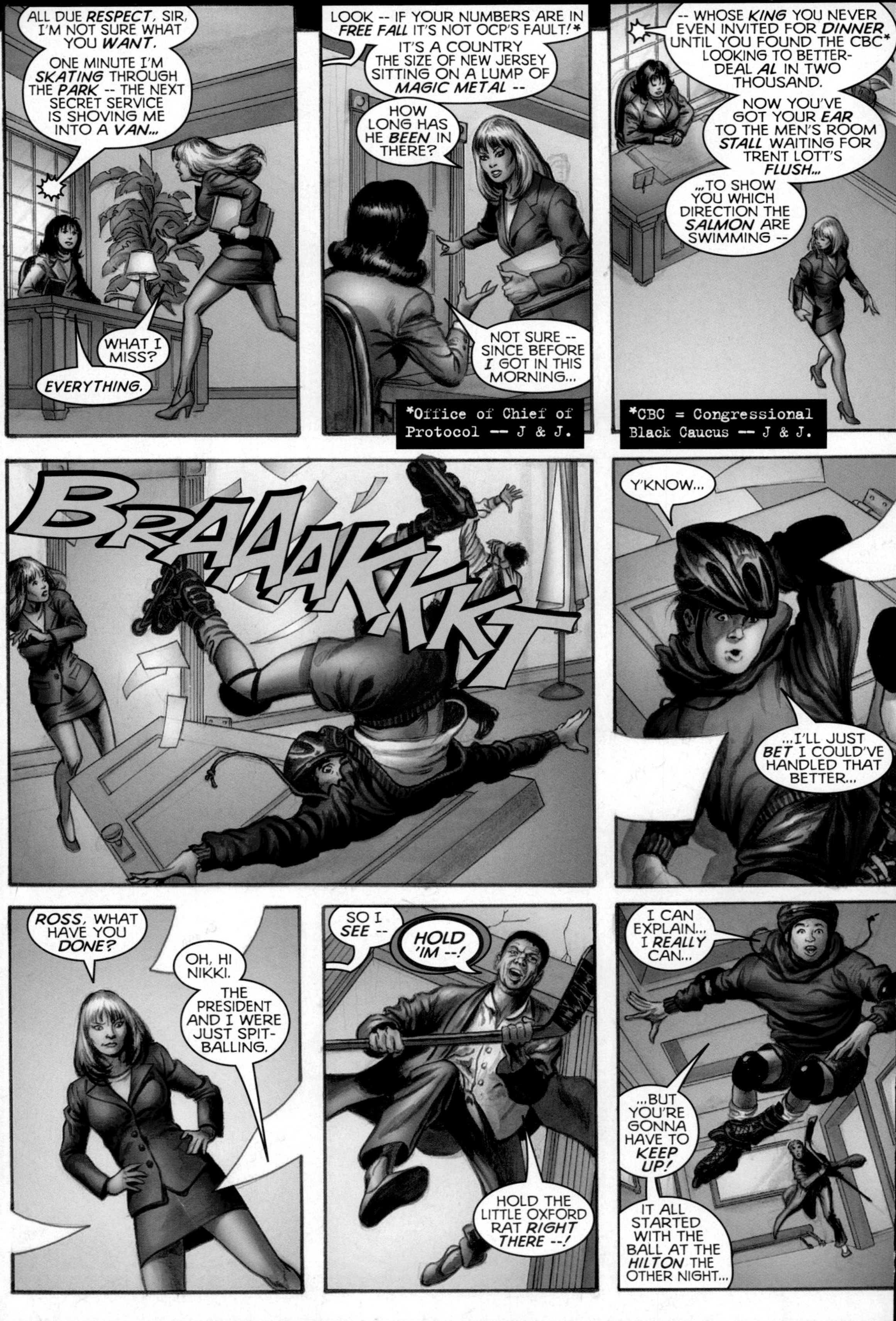

ALL DUE RESPECT, SIR, I'M NOT SURE WHAT YOU WANT.
ONE MINUTE I'M SKATING THROUGH THE PARK -- THE NEXT SECRET SERVICE IS SHOVING ME INTO A VAN...
WHAT I MISS?
EVERYTHING.
LOOK -- IF YOUR NUMBERS ARE IN FREE FALL IT'S NOT OCP'S FAULT!*
IT'S A COUNTRY THE SIZE OF NEW JERSEY SITTING ON A LUMP OF MAGIC METAL --
HOW LONG HAS HE BEEN IN THERE?
NOT SURE -- SINCE BEFORE I GOT IN THIS MORNING...
*Office of Chief of Protocol -- J & J.
-- WHOSE KING YOU NEVER EVEN INVITED FOR DINNER UNTIL YOU FOUND THE CBC* LOOKING TO BETTER-DEAL AL IN TWO THOUSAND.
NOW YOU'VE GOT YOUR EAR TO THE MEN'S ROOM STALL WAITING FOR TRENT LOTT'S FLUSH...
...TO SHOW YOU WHICH DIRECTION THE SALMON ARE SWIMMING --
*CBC = Congressional Black Caucus -- J & J.
BRAAAKKKT
Y'KNOW...
...I'LL JUST BET I COULD'VE HANDLED THAT BETTER...
ROSS, WHAT HAVE YOU DONE?
OH, HI NIKKI.
THE PRESIDENT AND I WERE JUST SPIT-BALLING.
SO I SEE --
HOLD 'IM --!
HOLD THE LITTLE OXFORD RAT RIGHT THERE --!
I CAN EXPLAIN... I REALLY CAN...
...BUT YOU'RE GONNA HAVE TO KEEP UP!
IT ALL STARTED WITH THE BALL AT THE HILTON THE OTHER NIGHT...

DUCK TIME

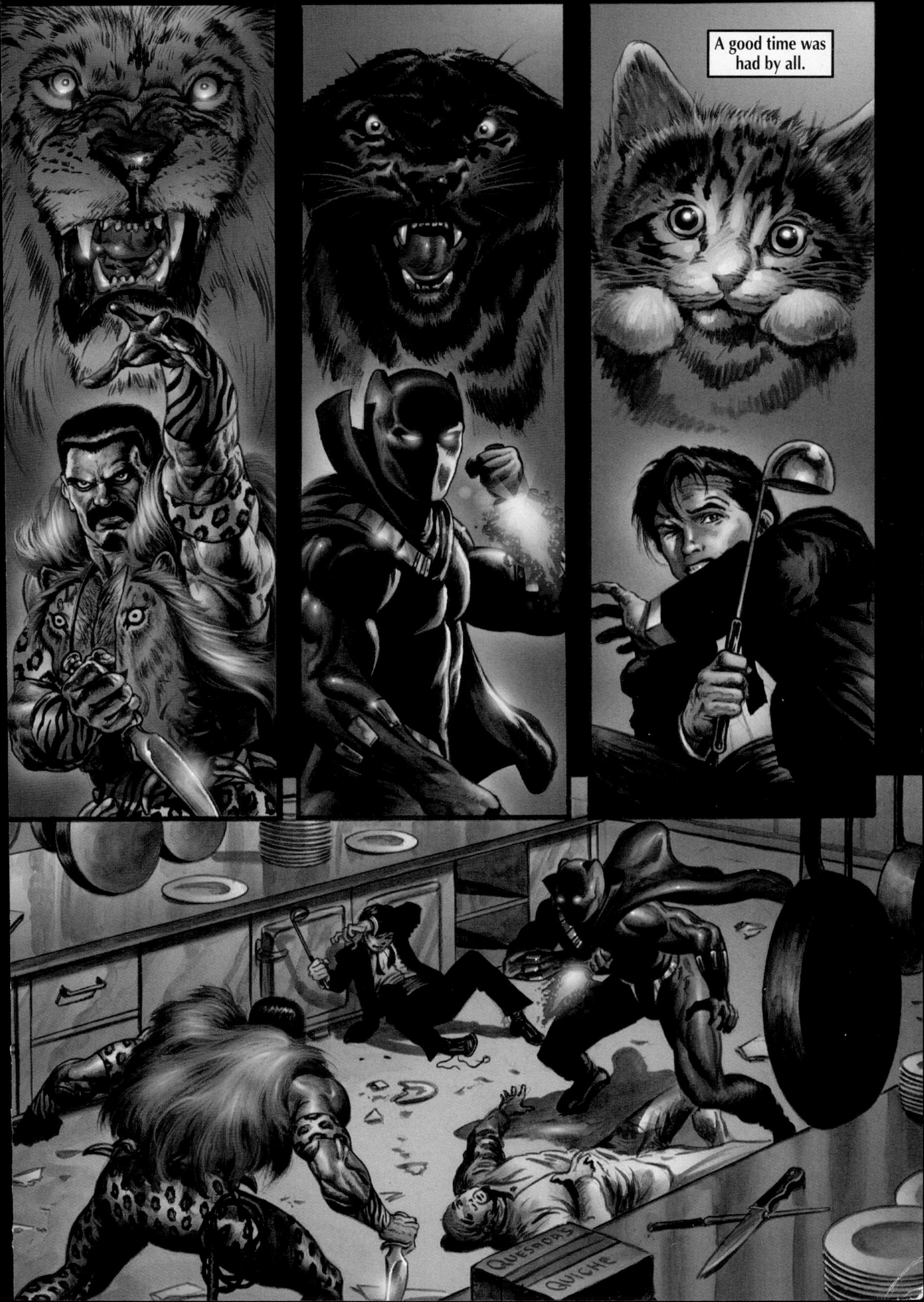
A good time was had by all.
QUICHE

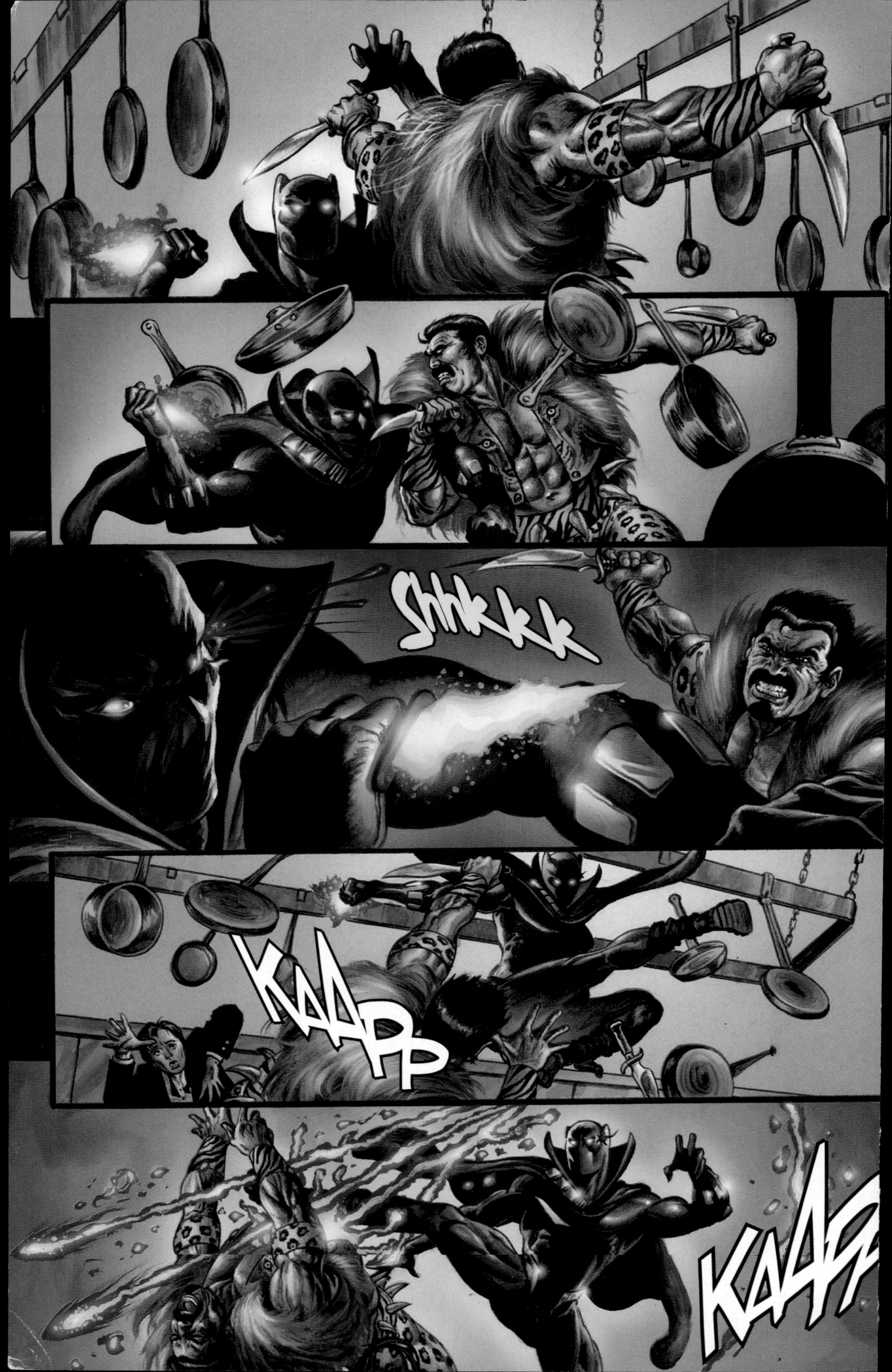
SHNKKK
KRAPP
KRAS

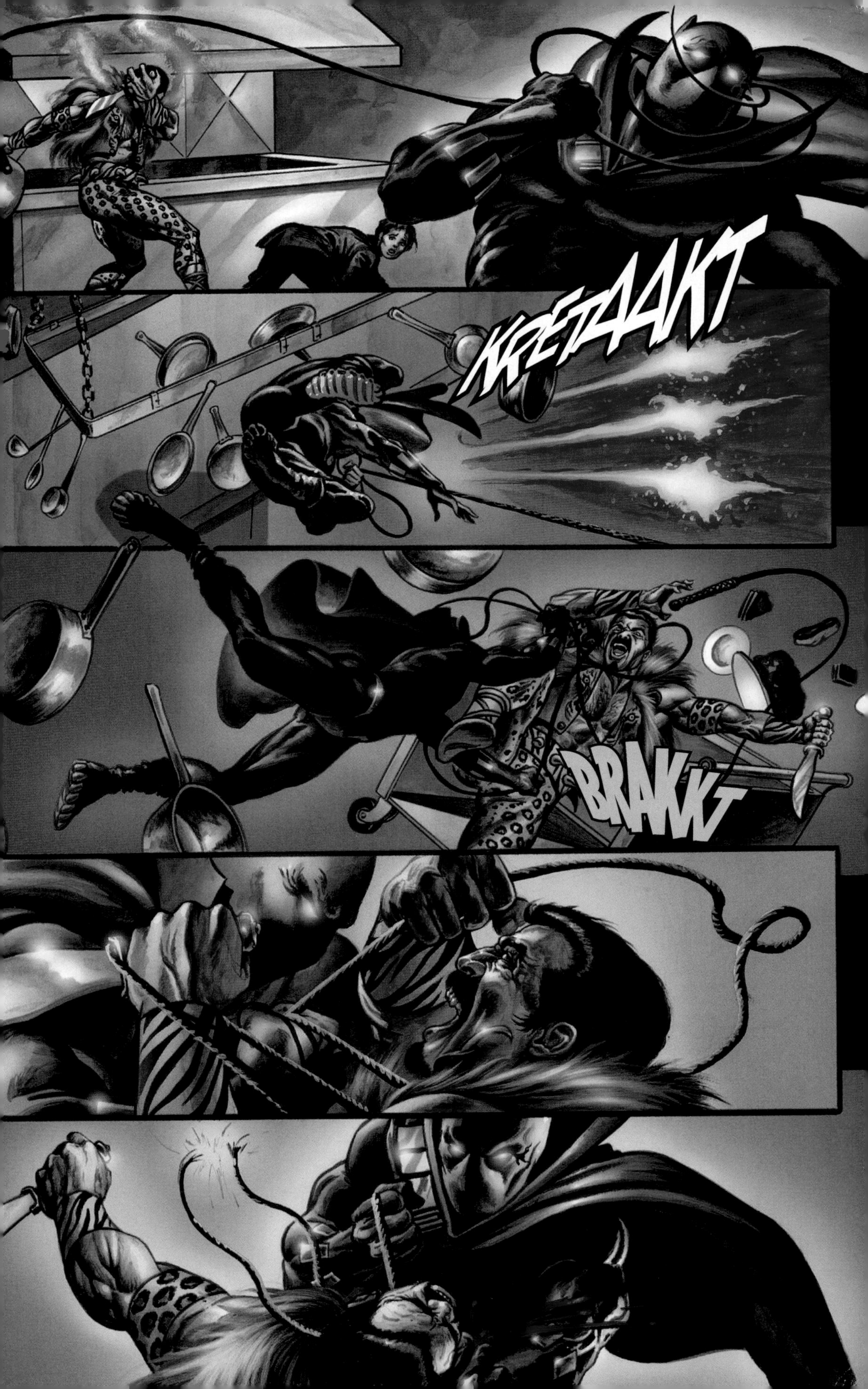
KRETAAKT
BRAKKT

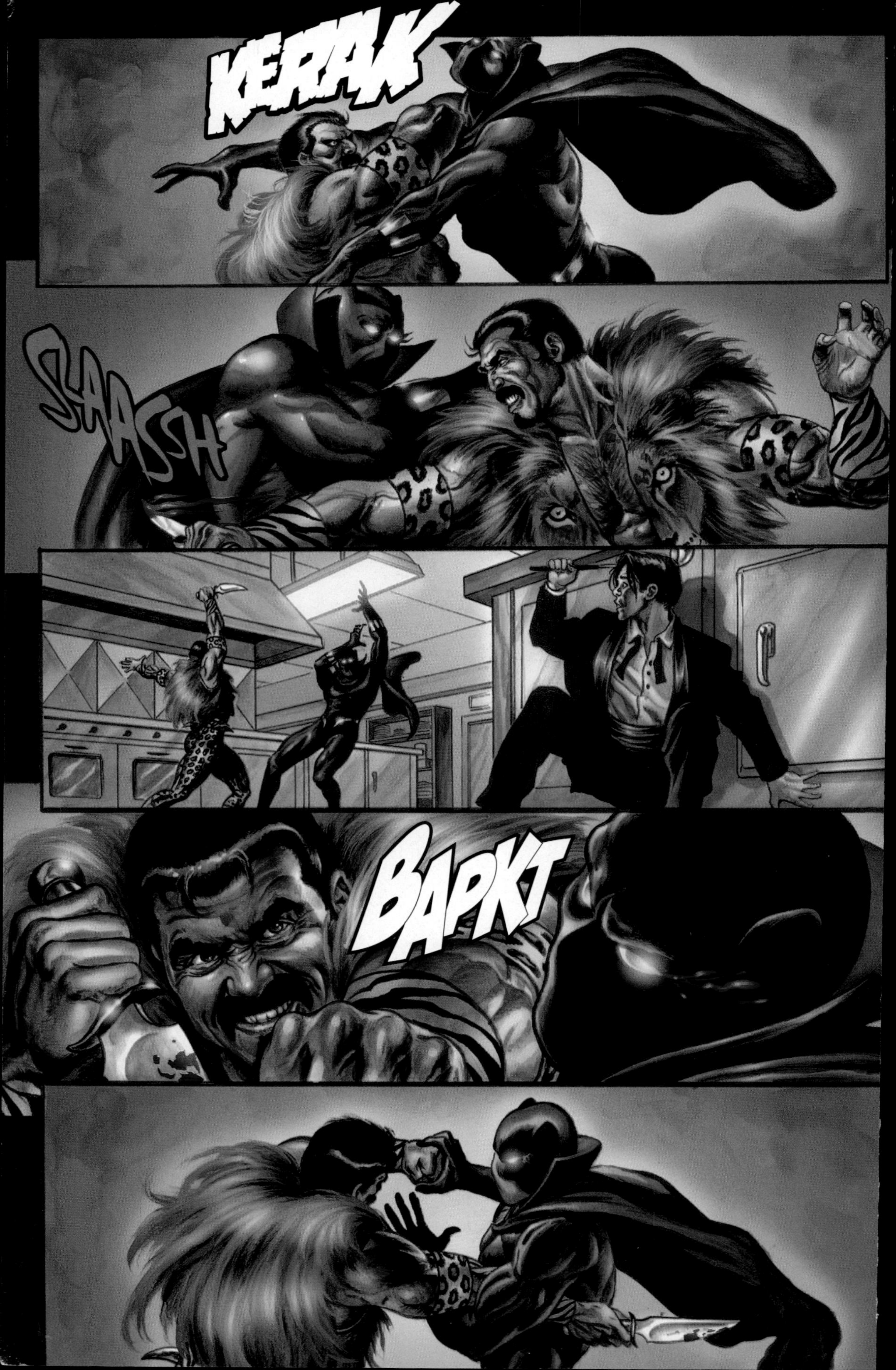
KERAK
SLASH
BAPKT

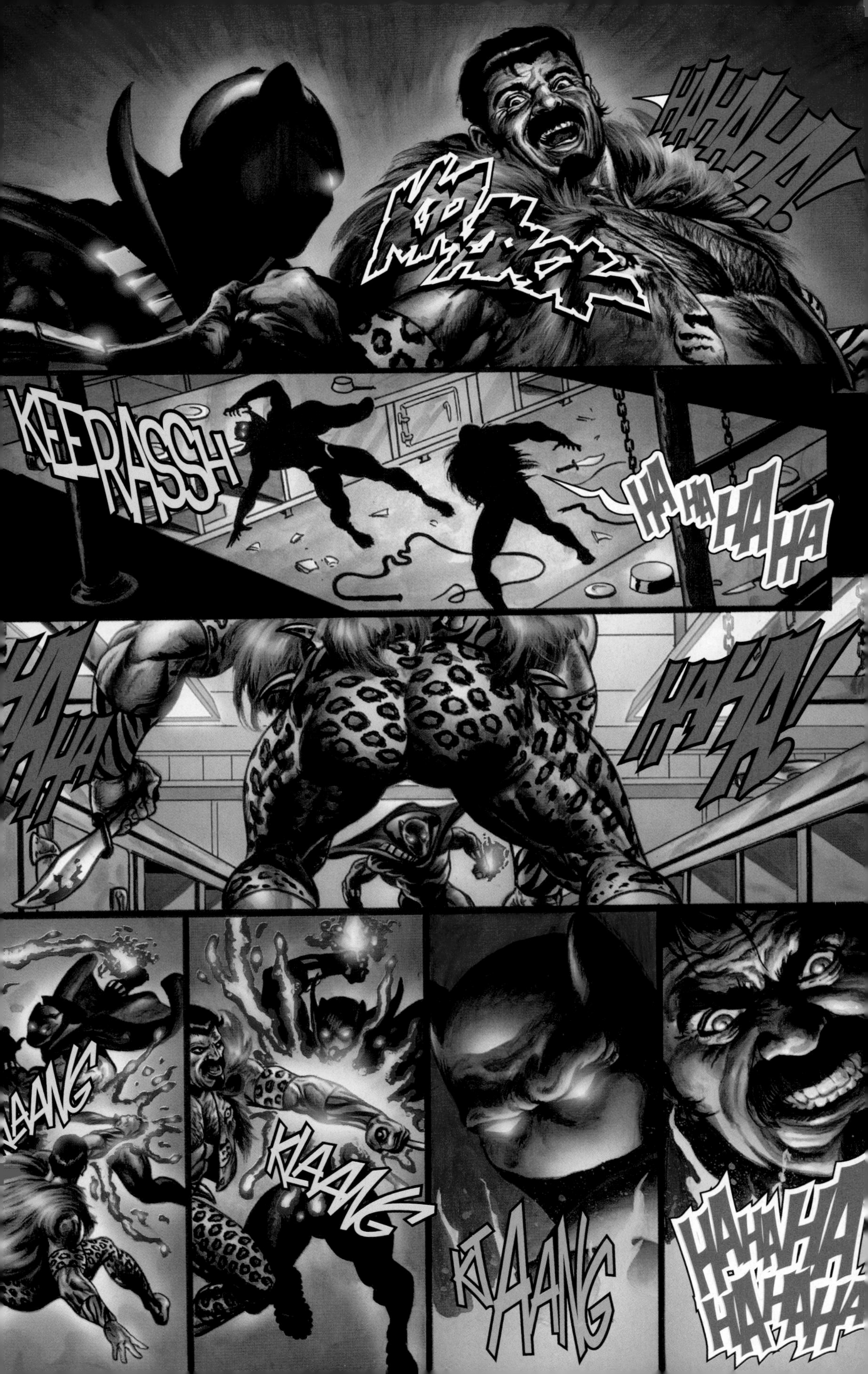
HAHAHA!
KEERASSH
HA HA HA HA
HAHA!
HAHA!
KLAANG
KLAANG
KLAANG
HAHAHAHA
HAHAHAHA

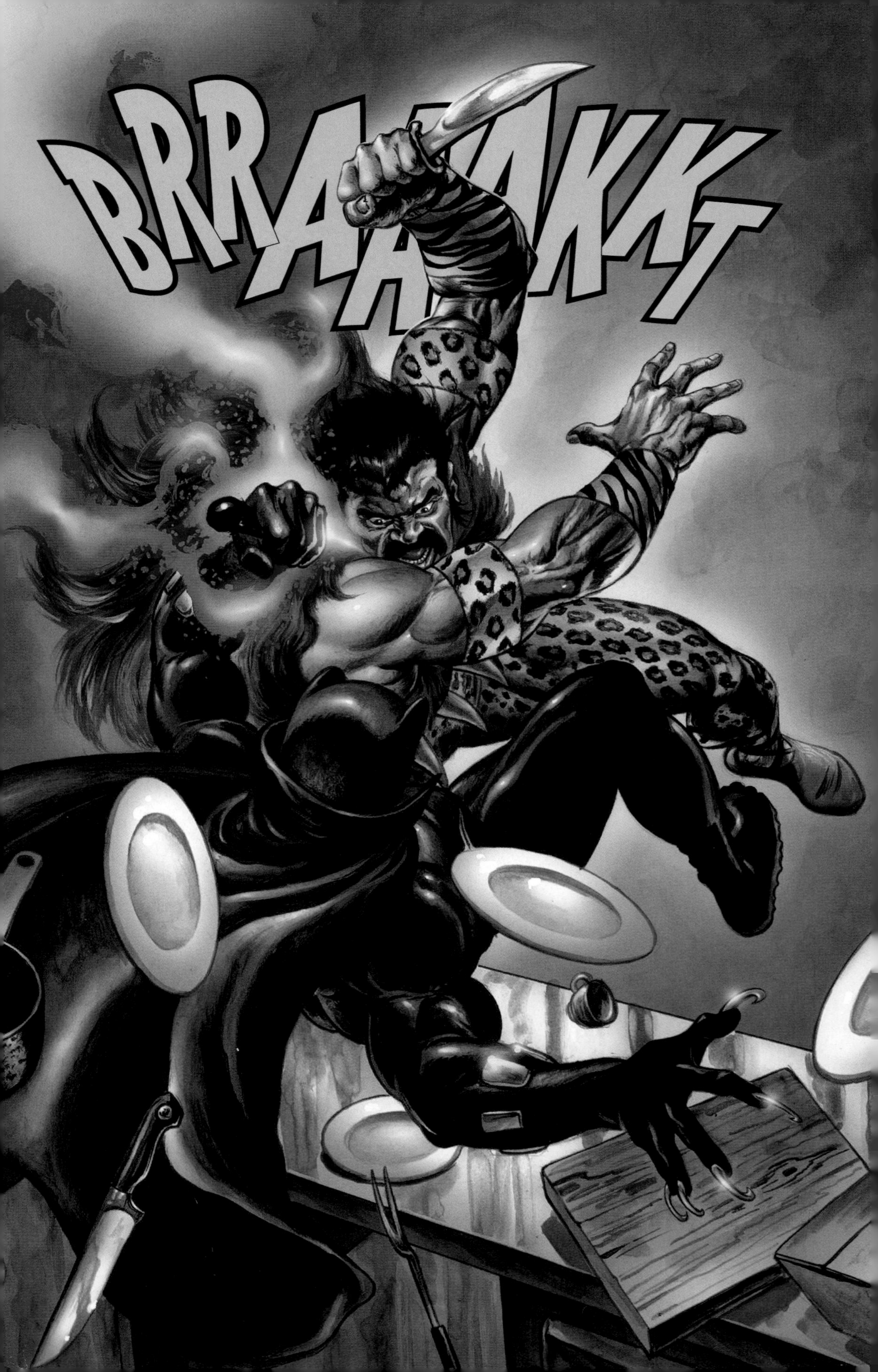
BRRAAAKKT

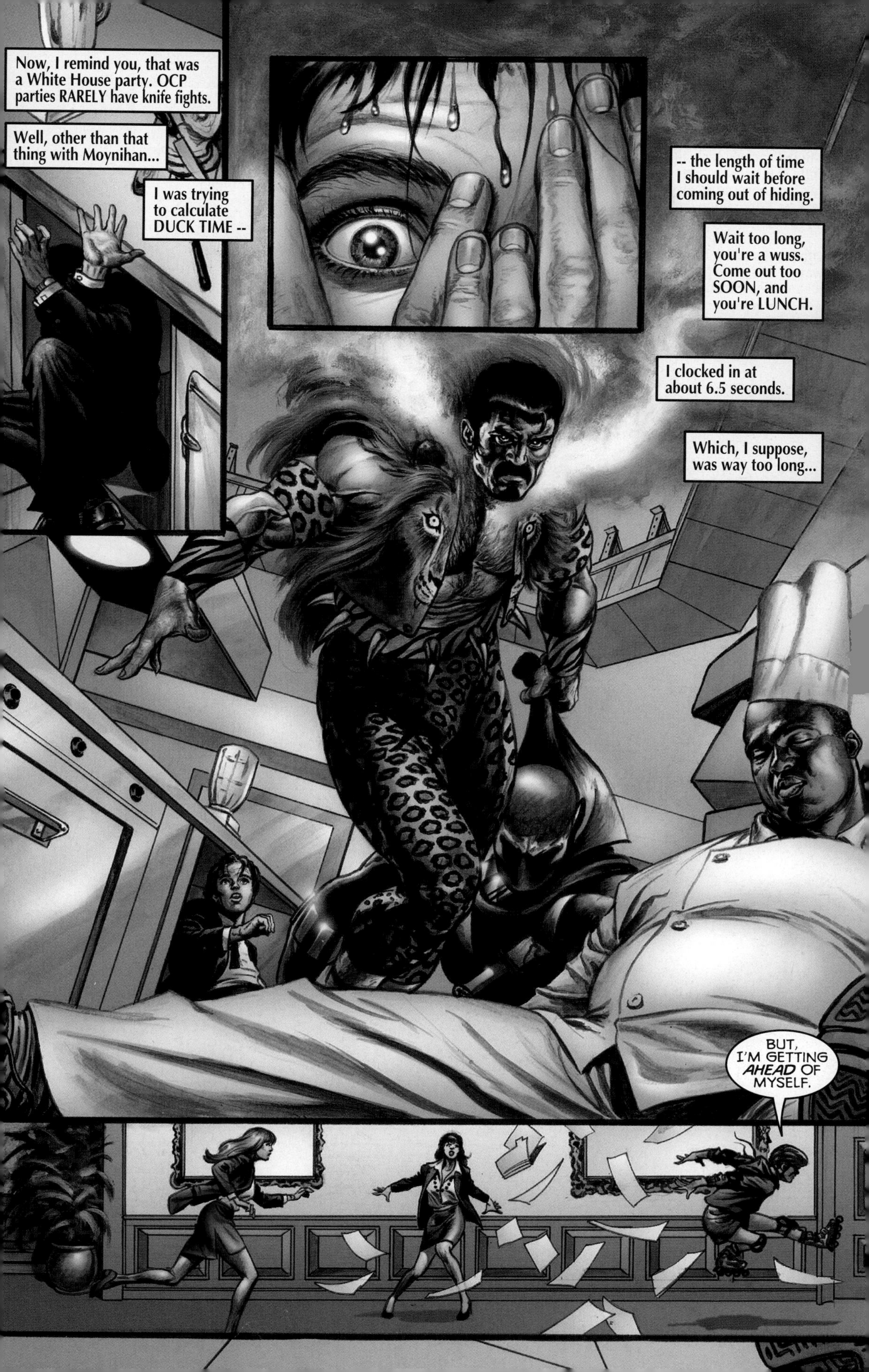
Now, I remind you, that was a White House party. OCP parties RARELY have knife fights.
Well, other than that thing with Moynihan...
I was trying to calculate DUCK TIME --
-- the length of time I should wait before coming out of hiding.
Wait too long, you're a wuss. Come out too SOON, and you're LUNCH.
I clocked in at about 6.5 seconds.
Which, I suppose, was way too long...
BUT, I'M GETTING AHEAD OF MYSELF.

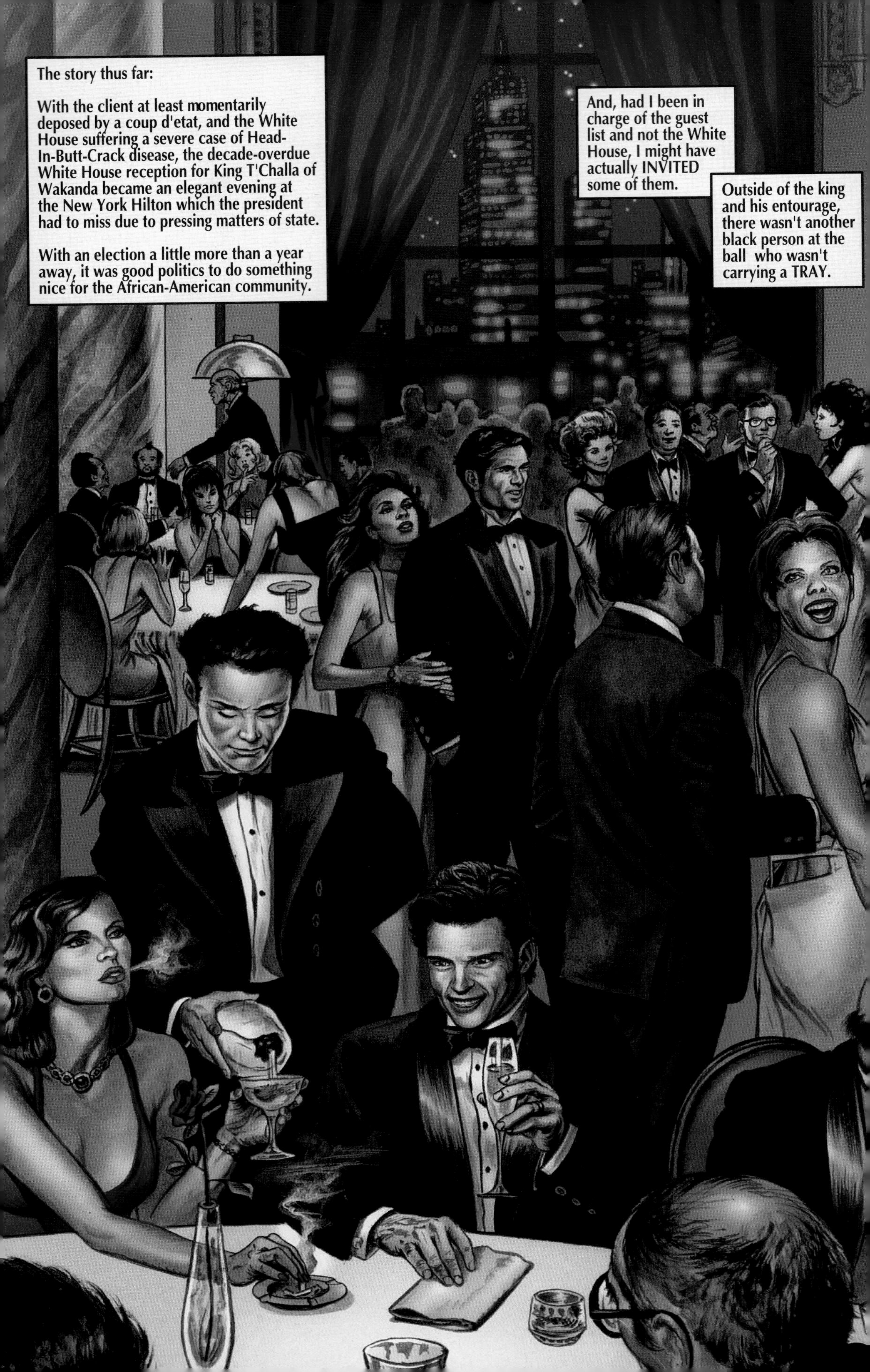

The story thus far:
With the client at least momentarily deposed by a coup d'etat, and the White House suffering a severe case of Head-In-Butt-Crack disease, the decade-overdue White House reception for King T'Challa of Wakanda became an elegant evening at the New York Hilton which the president had to miss due to pressing matters of state.
With an election a little more than a year away, it was good politics to do something nice for the African-American community.
Outside of the king and his entourage, there wasn't another black person at the ball who wasn't carrying a TRAY.
And, had I been in charge of the guest list and not the White House, I might have actually INVITED some of them.

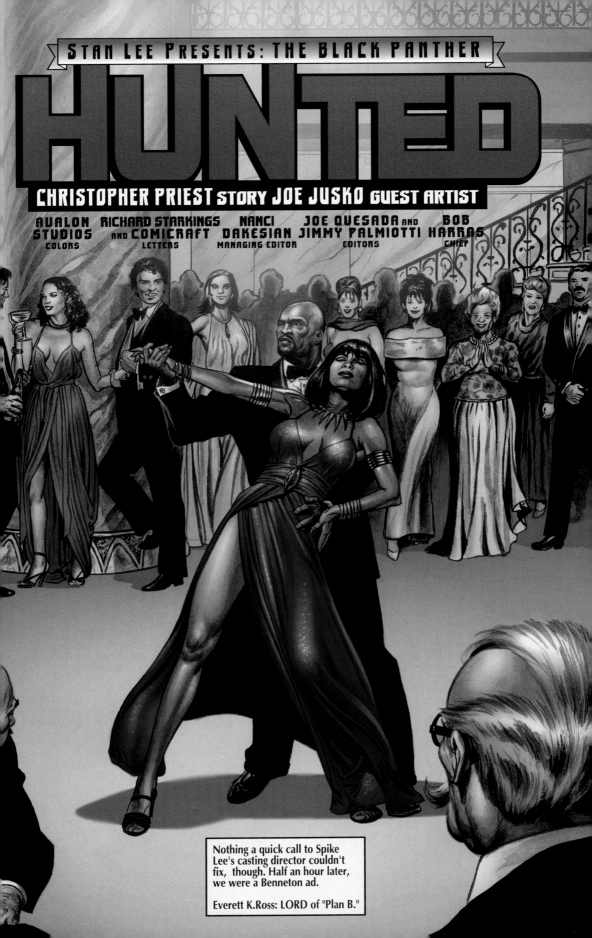

STAN LEE PRESENTS: THE BLACK PANTHER

HUNTED

CHRISTOPHER PRIEST STORY JOE JUSKO GUEST ARTIST

AVALON STUDIOS COLORS

RICHARD STARKINGS AND COMICRAFT LETTERS

NANCI DAKESIAN MANAGING EDITOR

JOE QUESADA AND JIMMY PALMIOTTI EDITORS

BOB HARRAS CHIEF

Nothing a quick call to Spike Lee's casting director couldn't fix, though. Half an hour later, we were a Benneton ad.

Everett K.Ross: LORD of "Plan B."

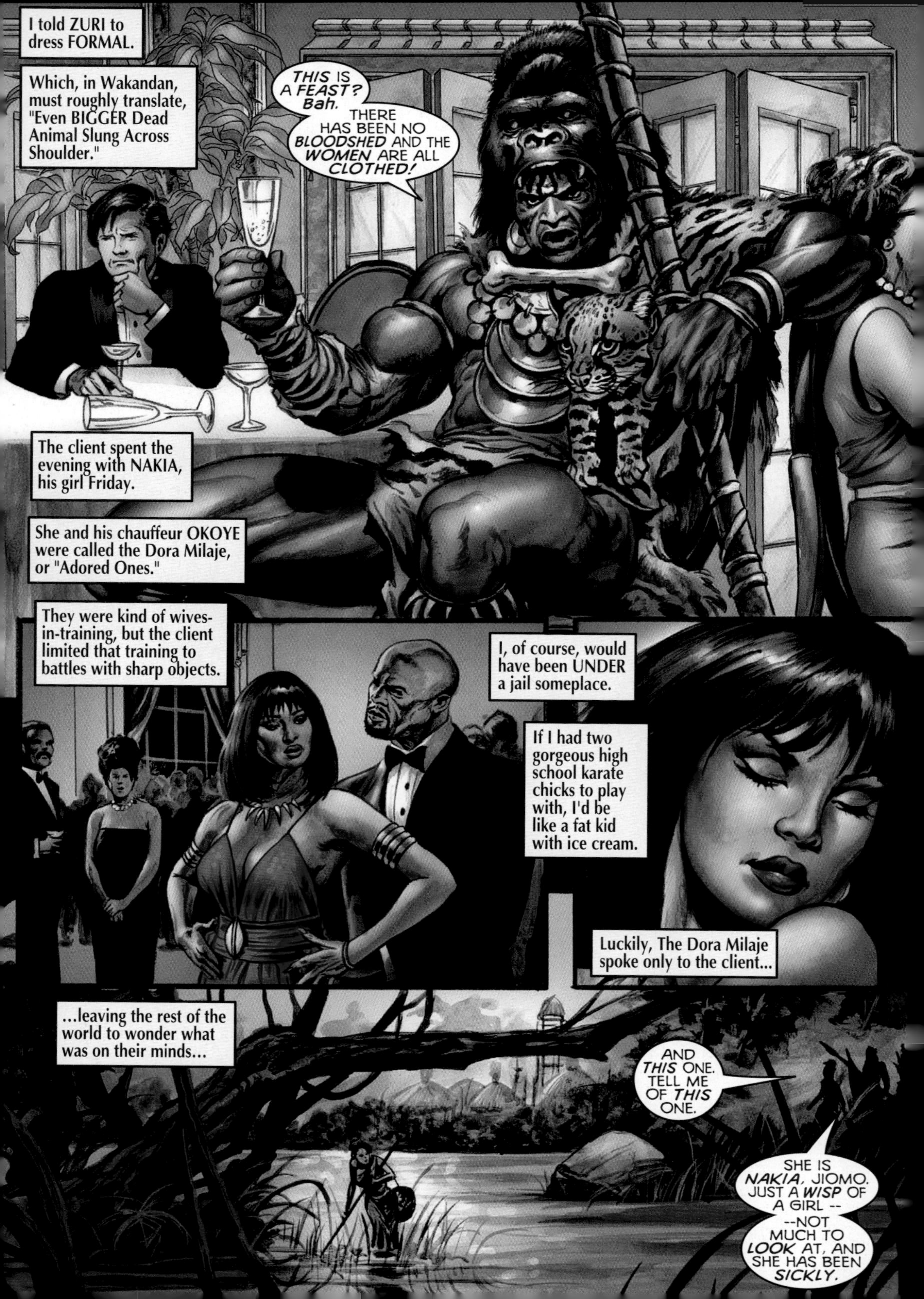
I told ZURI to dress FORMAL.
Which, in Wakandan, must roughly translate, "Even BIGGER Dead Animal Slung Across Shoulder."
THIS IS A FEAST? Bah.
THERE HAS BEEN NO BLOODSHED AND THE WOMEN ARE ALL CLOTHED!
The client spent the evening with NAKIA, his girl Friday.
She and his chauffeur OKOYE were called the Dora Milaje, or "Adored Ones."
They were kind of wives-in-training, but the client limited that training to battles with sharp objects.
I, of course, would have been UNDER a jail someplace.
If I had two gorgeous high school karate chicks to play with, I'd be like a fat kid with ice cream.
Luckily, The Dora Milaje spoke only to the client...
...leaving the rest of the world to wonder what was on their minds...
AND THIS ONE. TELL ME OF THIS ONE.
SHE IS NAKIA, JIOMO. JUST A WISP OF A GIRL --
--NOT MUCH TO LOOK AT, AND SHE HAS BEEN SICKLY.

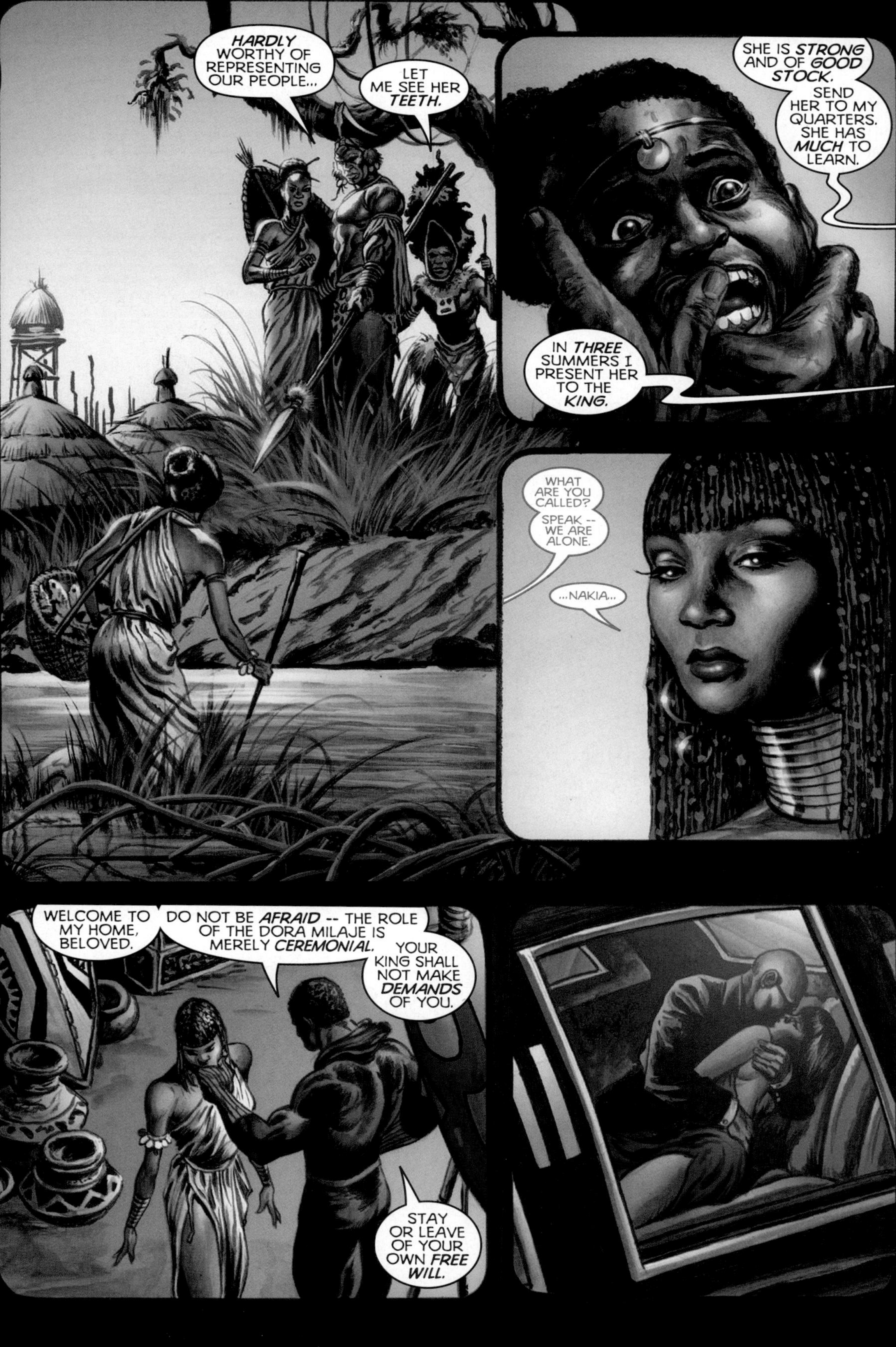
HARDLY WORTHY OF REPRESENTING OUR PEOPLE...
LET ME SEE HER TEETH.
SHE IS STRONG AND OF GOOD STOCK.
SEND HER TO MY QUARTERS. SHE HAS MUCH TO LEARN.
IN THREE SUMMERS I PRESENT HER TO THE KING.
WHAT ARE YOU CALLED?
SPEAK -- WE ARE ALONE.
...NAKIA...
WELCOME TO MY HOME, BELOVED.
DO NOT BE AFRAID -- THE ROLE OF THE DORA MILAJE IS MERELY CEREMONIAL.
YOUR KING SHALL NOT MAKE DEMANDS OF YOU.
STAY OR LEAVE OF YOUR OWN FREE WILL.

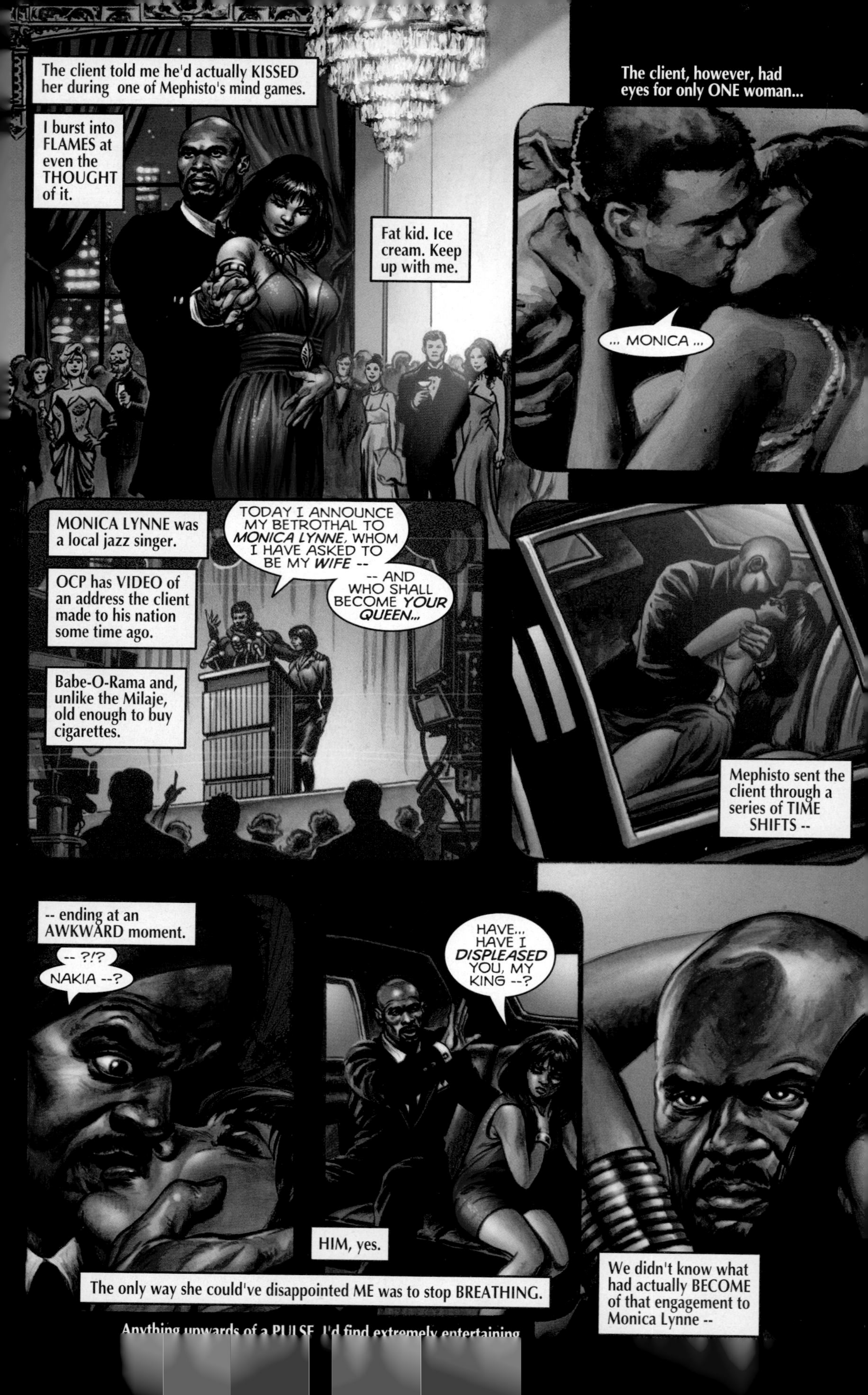

The client told me he'd actually KISSED her during one of Mephisto's mind games.
I burst into FLAMES at even the THOUGHT of it.
Fat kid. Ice cream. Keep up with me.
The client, however, had eyes for only ONE woman...
... MONICA ...
MONICA LYNNE was a local jazz singer.
OCP has VIDEO of an address the client made to his nation some time ago.
Babe-O-Rama and, unlike the Milaje, old enough to buy cigarettes.
TODAY I ANNOUNCE MY BETROTHAL TO MONICA LYNNE, WHOM I HAVE ASKED TO BE MY WIFE --
-- AND WHO SHALL BECOME YOUR QUEEN...
Mephisto sent the client through a series of TIME SHIFTS --
-- ending at an AWKWARD moment.
-- ?!?
NAKIA --?
HAVE... HAVE I DISPLEASED YOU, MY KING --?
HIM, yes.
The only way she could've disappointed ME was to stop BREATHING.
We didn't know what had actually BECOME of that engagement to Monica Lynne --

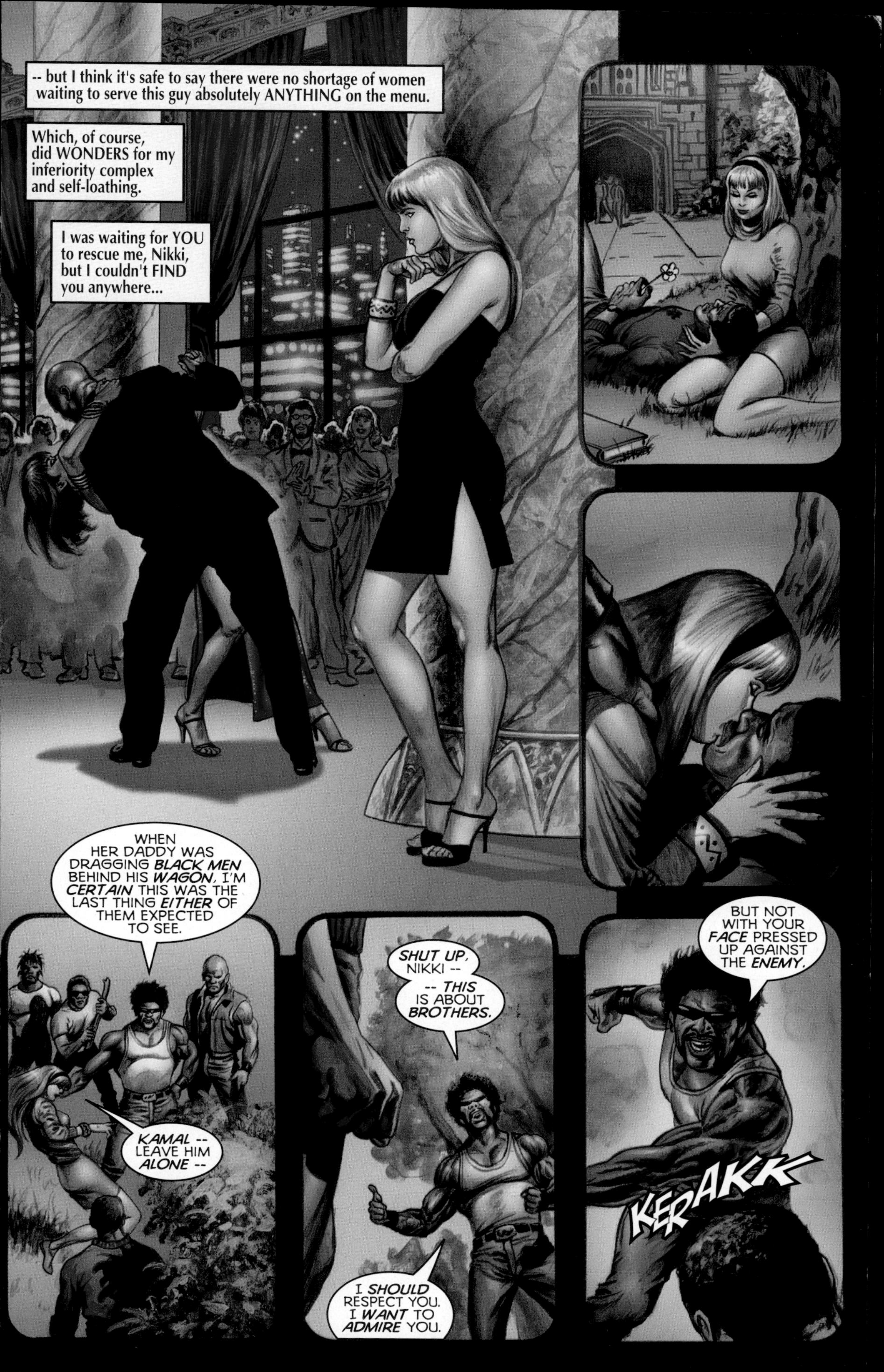

-- but I think it's safe to say there were no shortage of women waiting to serve this guy absolutely ANYTHING on the menu.
Which, of course, did WONDERS for my inferiority complex and self-loathing.
I was waiting for YOU to rescue me, Nikki, but I couldn't FIND you anywhere...
WHEN HER DADDY WAS DRAGGING BLACK MEN BEHIND HIS WAGON, I'M CERTAIN THIS WAS THE LAST THING EITHER OF THEM EXPECTED TO SEE.
KAMAL -- LEAVE HIM ALONE --
SHUT UP, NIKKI --
-- THIS IS ABOUT BROTHERS.
I SHOULD RESPECT YOU. I WANT TO ADMIRE YOU.
BUT NOT WITH YOUR FACE PRESSED UP AGAINST THE ENEMY.
KERAKK

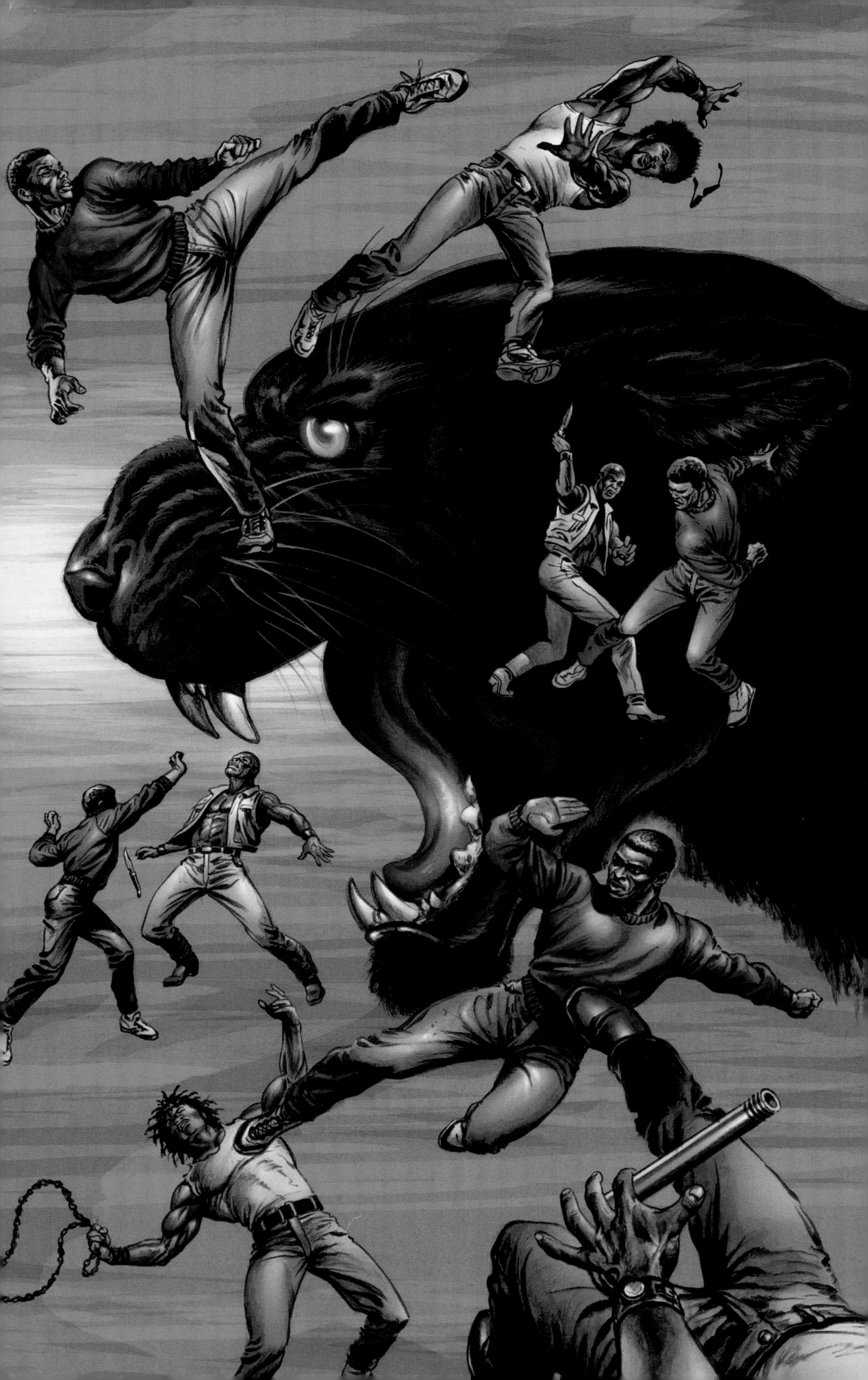

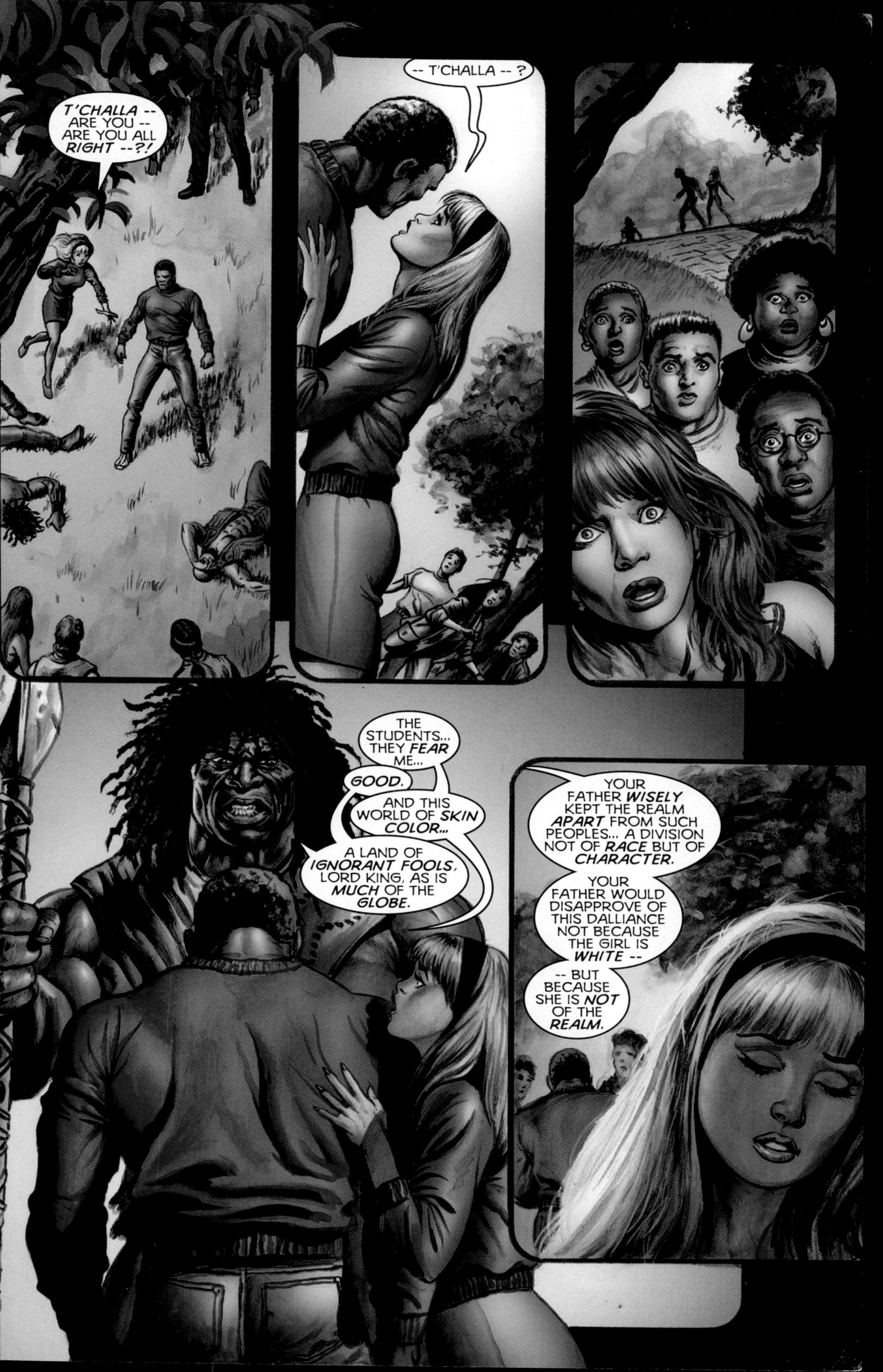
T'CHALLA -- ARE YOU -- ARE YOU ALL RIGHT --?!
-- T'CHALLA -- ?
THE STUDENTS... THEY FEAR ME...
GOOD.
AND THIS WORLD OF SKIN COLOR...
A LAND OF IGNORANT FOOLS, LORD KING, AS IS MUCH OF THE GLOBE.
YOUR FATHER WISELY KEPT THE REALM APART FROM SUCH PEOPLES... A DIVISION NOT OF RACE BUT OF CHARACTER.
YOUR FATHER WOULD DISAPPROVE OF THIS DALLIANCE NOT BECAUSE THE GIRL IS WHITE --
-- BUT BECAUSE SHE IS NOT OF THE REALM.

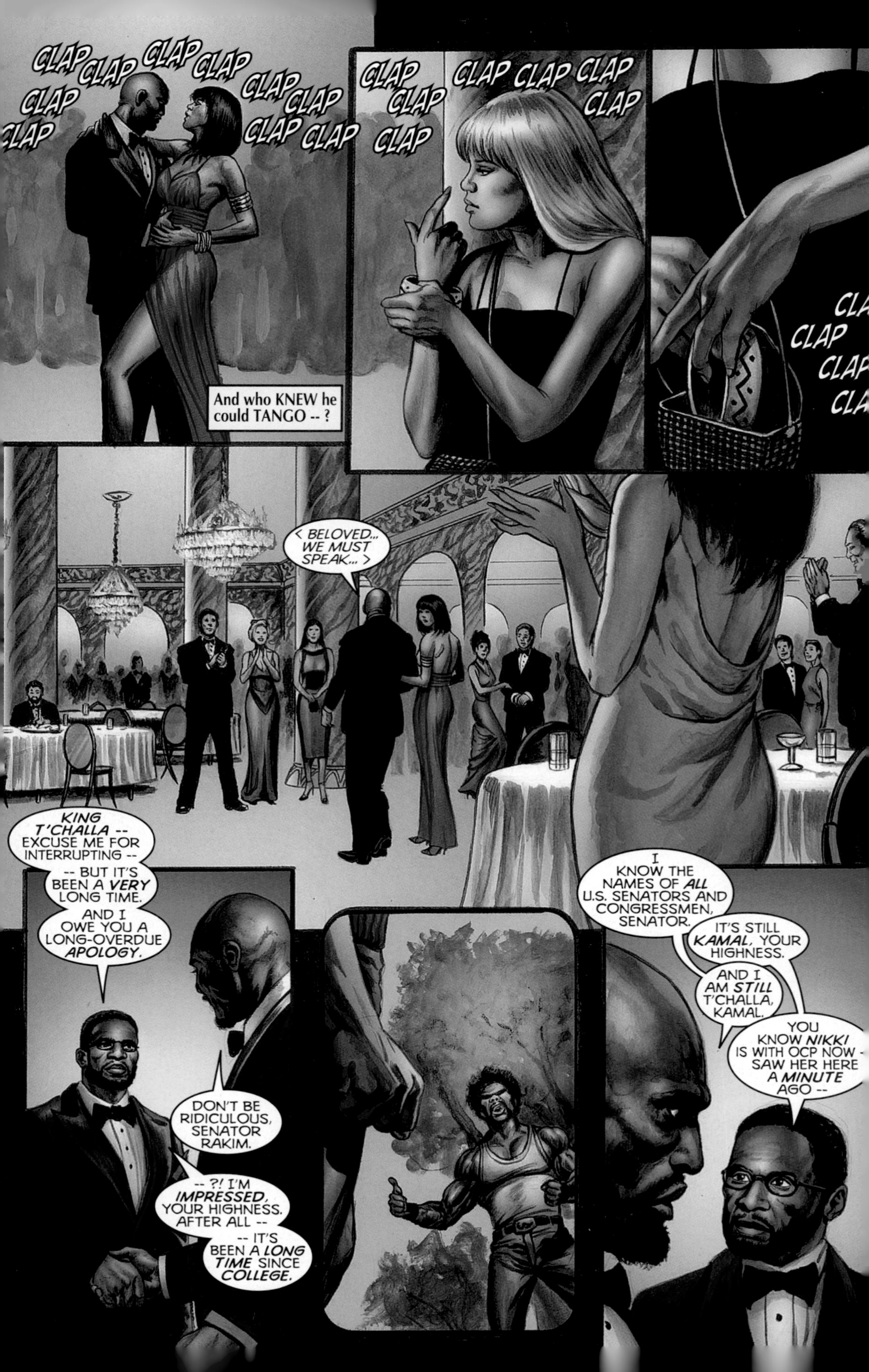
CLAP CLAP CLAP CLAP CLAP CLAP CLAP CLAP CLAP CLAP
And who KNEW he could TANGO -- ?
CLAP CLAP CLAP CLAP CLAP CLAP CLAP
CLAP CLAP CLAP
< BELOVED... WE MUST SPEAK... >
KING T'CHALLA -- EXCUSE ME FOR INTERRUPTING --
-- BUT IT'S BEEN A VERY LONG TIME.
AND I OWE YOU A LONG-OVERDUE APOLOGY.
DON'T BE RIDICULOUS, SENATOR RAKIM.
-- ?! I'M IMPRESSED, YOUR HIGHNESS. AFTER ALL --
-- IT'S BEEN A LONG TIME SINCE COLLEGE.
I KNOW THE NAMES OF ALL U.S. SENATORS AND CONGRESSMEN, SENATOR.
IT'S STILL KAMAL, YOUR HIGHNESS.
AND I AM STILL T'CHALLA, KAMAL.
YOU KNOW NIKKI IS WITH OCP NOW - SAW HER HERE A MINUTE AGO --

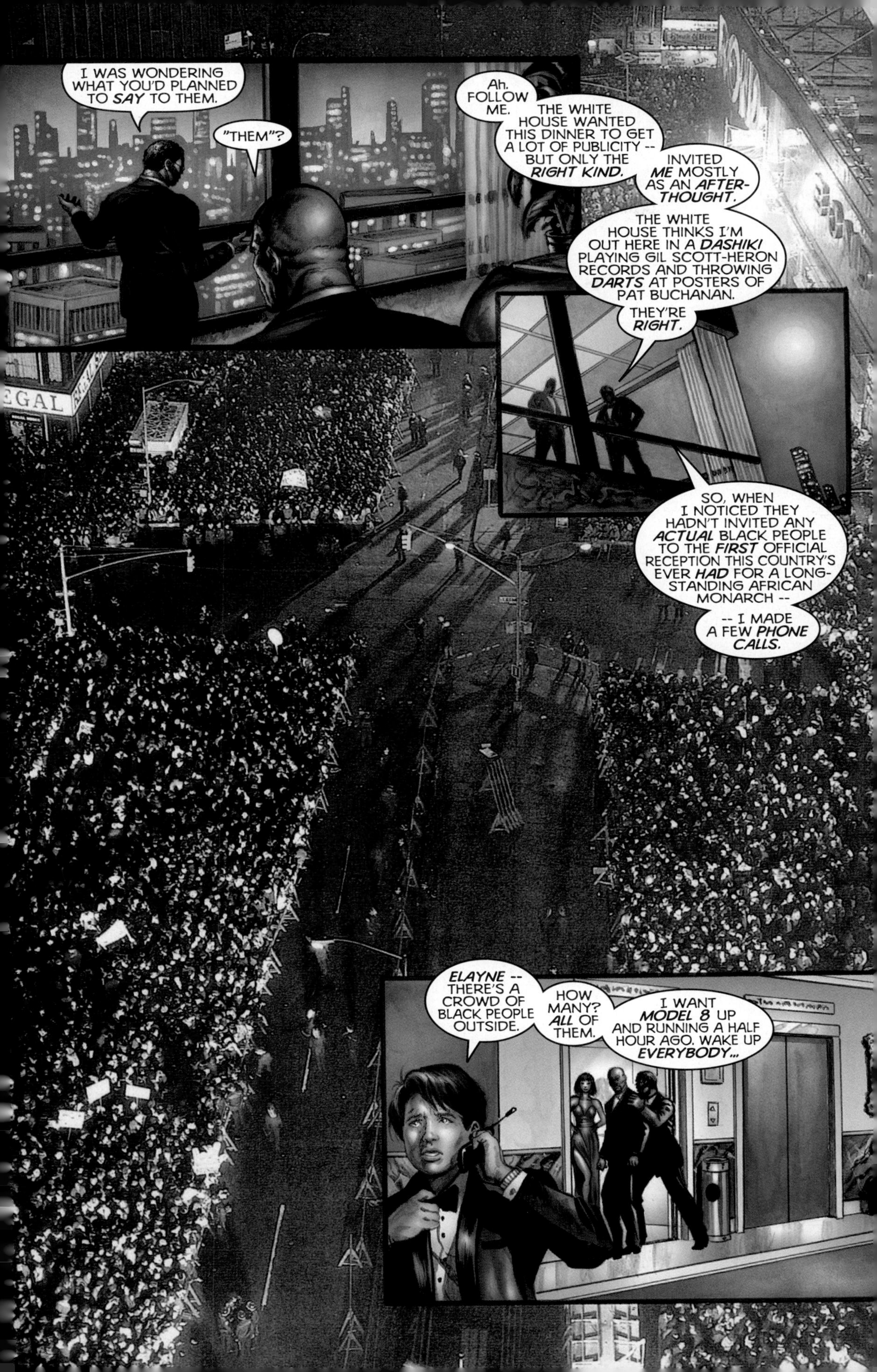
I WAS WONDERING WHAT YOU'D PLANNED TO SAY TO THEM.
"THEM"?
Ah. FOLLOW ME.
THE WHITE HOUSE WANTED THIS DINNER TO GET A LOT OF PUBLICITY -- BUT ONLY THE RIGHT KIND.
INVITED ME MOSTLY AS AN AFTER-THOUGHT.
THE WHITE HOUSE THINKS I'M OUT HERE IN A DASHIKI PLAYING GIL SCOTT-HERON RECORDS AND THROWING DARTS AT POSTERS OF PAT BUCHANAN.
THEY'RE RIGHT.
SO, WHEN I NOTICED THEY HADN'T INVITED ANY ACTUAL BLACK PEOPLE TO THE FIRST OFFICIAL RECEPTION THIS COUNTRY'S EVER HAD FOR A LONG-STANDING AFRICAN MONARCH --
-- I MADE A FEW PHONE CALLS.
ELAYNE -- THERE'S A CROWD OF BLACK PEOPLE OUTSIDE.
HOW MANY? ALL OF THEM.
I WANT MODEL 8 UP AND RUNNING A HALF HOUR AGO. WAKE UP EVERYBODY...

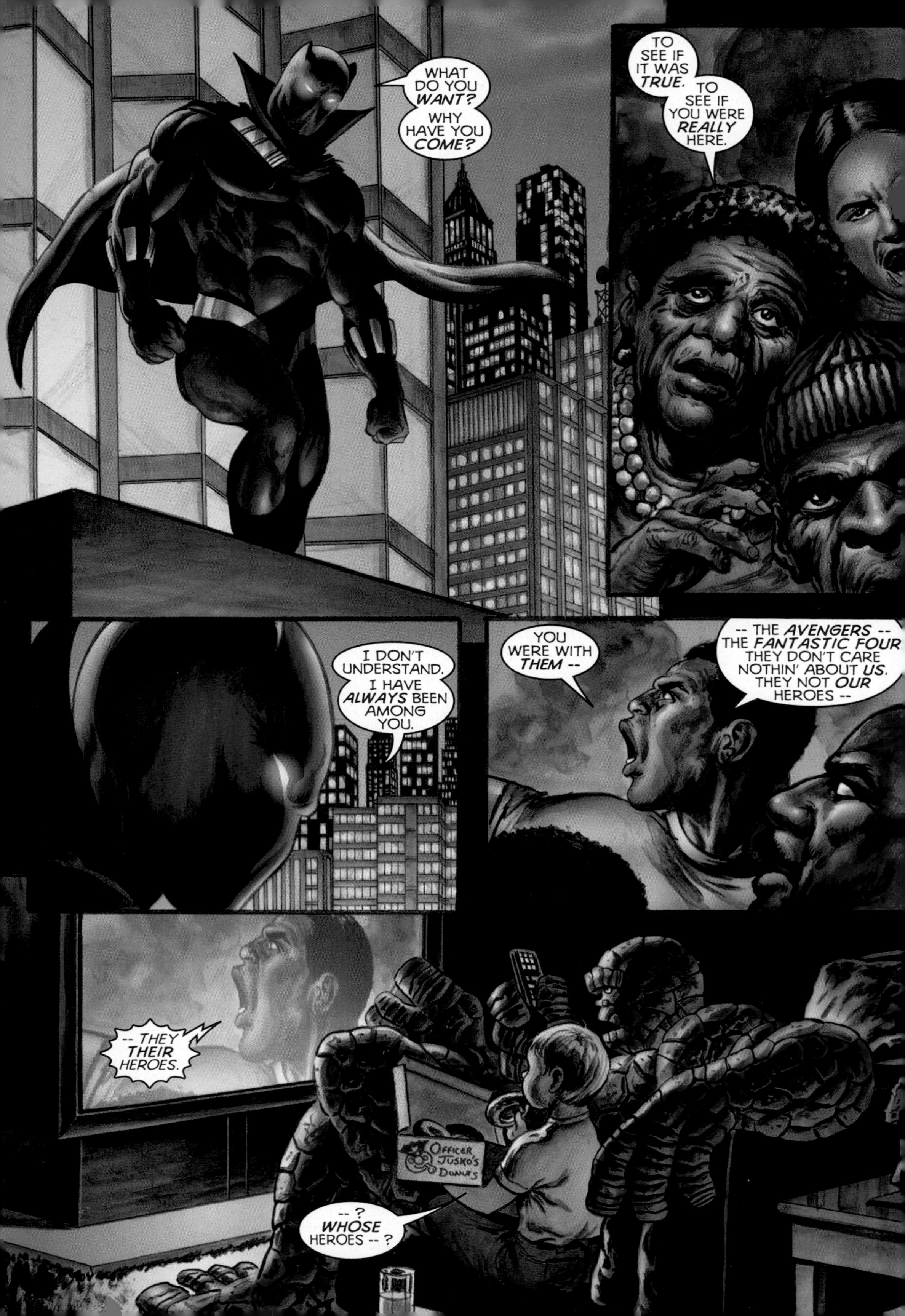
WHAT DO YOU WANT? WHY HAVE YOU COME?
TO SEE IF IT WAS TRUE.
TO SEE IF YOU WERE REALLY HERE.
I DON'T UNDERSTAND. I HAVE ALWAYS BEEN AMONG YOU.
YOU WERE WITH THEM --
-- THE AVENGERS -- THE FANTASTIC FOUR THEY DON'T CARE NOTHIN' ABOUT US. THEY NOT OUR HEROES --
-- THEY THEIR HEROES.
OFFICER JUSKO'S DONUTS
-- ? WHOSE HEROES -- ?

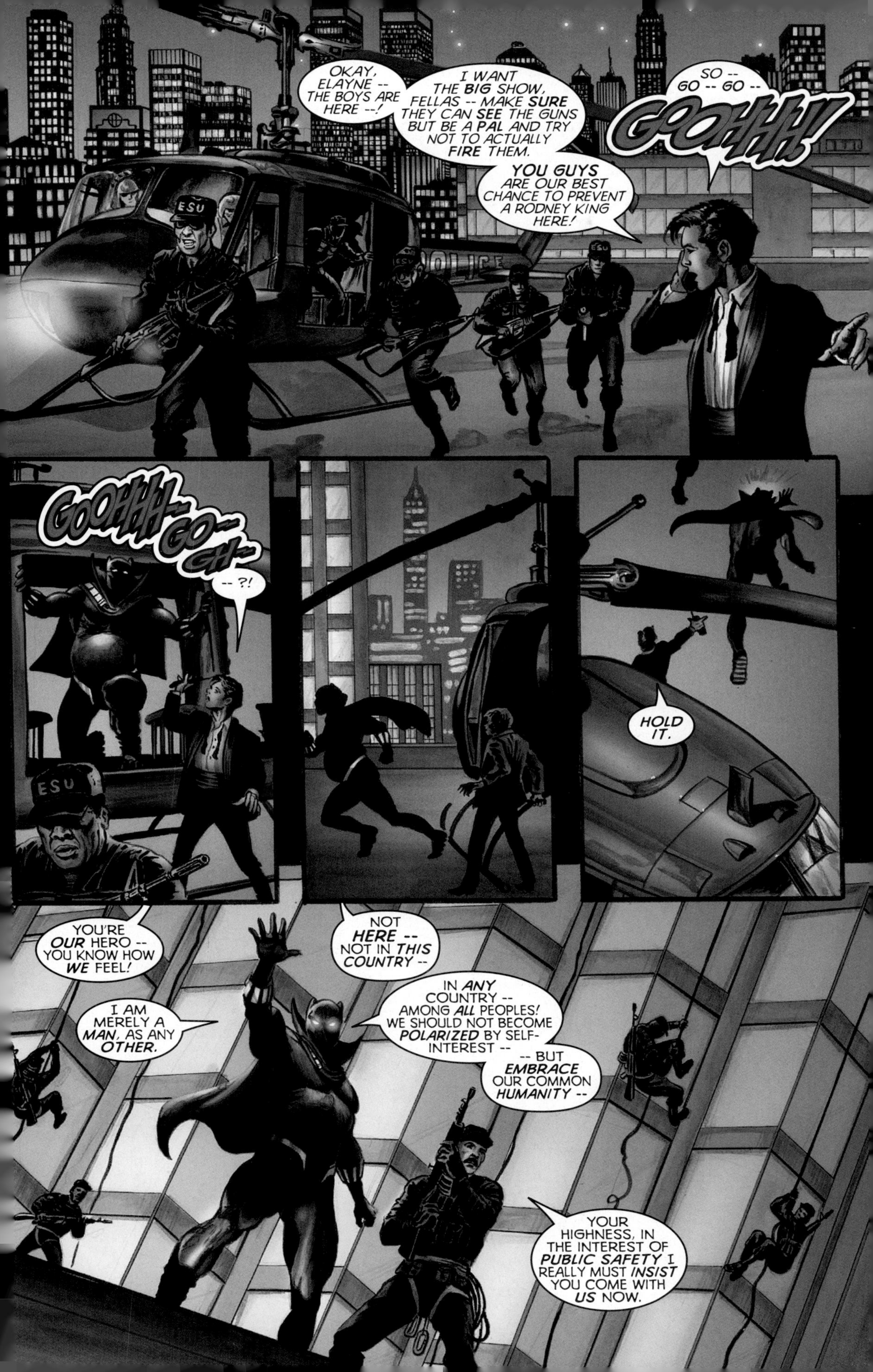
OKAY, ELAYNE -- THE BOYS ARE HERE --!
I WANT THE BIG SHOW, FELLAS -- MAKE SURE THEY CAN SEE THE GUNS BUT BE A PAL AND TRY NOT TO ACTUALLY FIRE THEM.
YOU GUYS ARE OUR BEST CHANCE TO PREVENT A RODNEY KING HERE!
SO -- GO -- GO --
GOOHHH!
GOOHHH-- GO-- GH--
-- ?!
HOLD IT.
YOU'RE OUR HERO -- YOU KNOW HOW WE FEEL!
I AM MERELY A MAN, AS ANY OTHER.
NOT HERE -- NOT IN THIS COUNTRY --
IN ANY COUNTRY -- AMONG ALL PEOPLES! WE SHOULD NOT BECOME POLARIZED BY SELF-INTEREST --
-- BUT EMBRACE OUR COMMON HUMANITY --
YOUR HIGHNESS, IN THE INTEREST OF PUBLIC SAFETY I REALLY MUST INSIST YOU COME WITH US NOW.

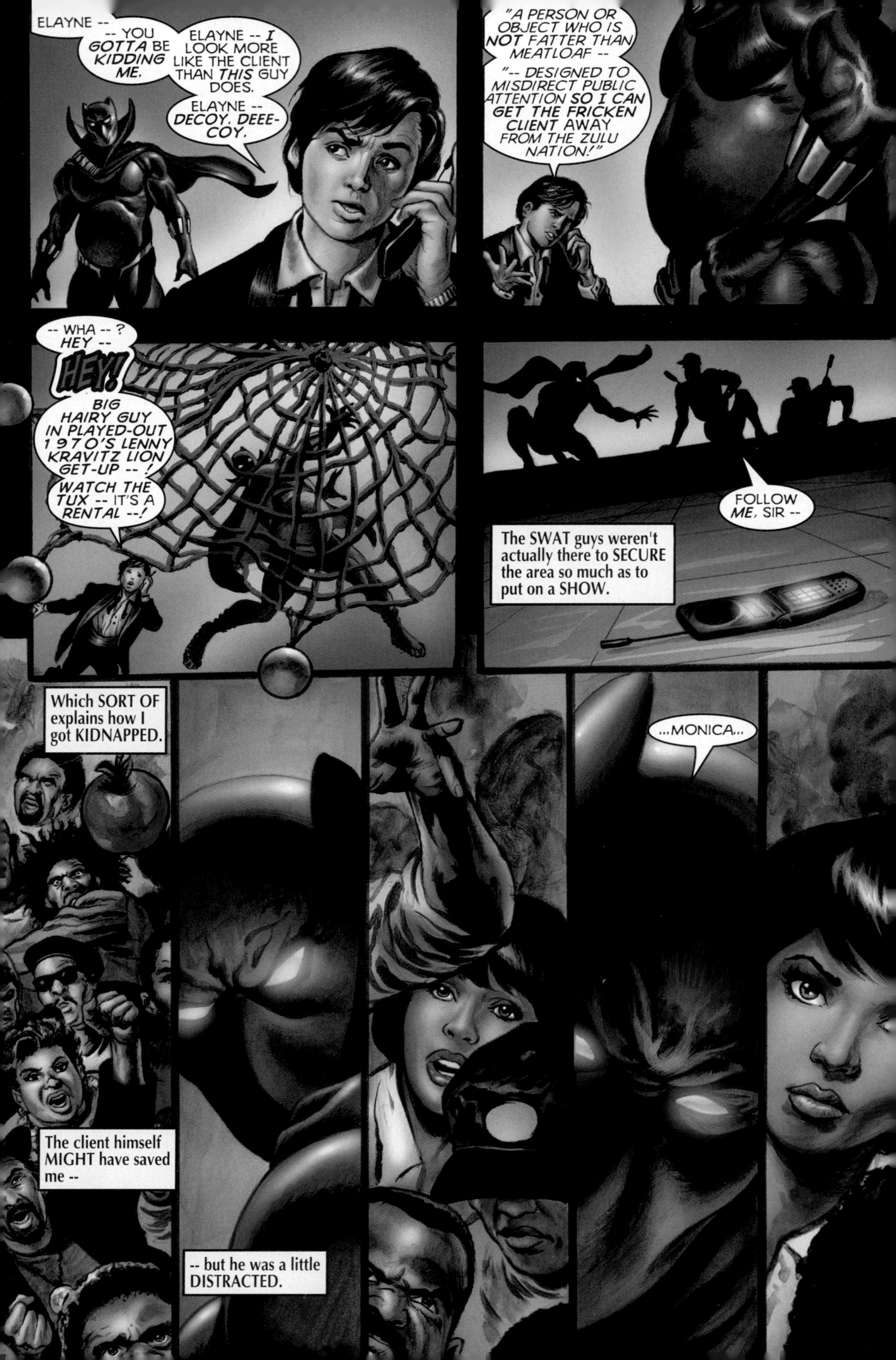
ELAYNE --
-- YOU GOTTA BE KIDDING ME.
ELAYNE -- I LOOK MORE LIKE THE CLIENT THAN THIS GUY DOES.
ELAYNE -- DECOY. DEEE-COY.
"A PERSON OR OBJECT WHO IS NOT FATTER THAN MEATLOAF --
"-- DESIGNED TO MISDIRECT PUBLIC ATTENTION SO I CAN GET THE FRICKEN CLIENT AWAY FROM THE ZULU NATION!"
-- WHA -- ? HEY --
HEY!
BIG HAIRY GUY IN PLAYED-OUT 1970'S LENNY KRAVITZ LION GET-UP -- !
WATCH THE TUX -- IT'S A RENTAL --!
FOLLOW ME, SIR --
The SWAT guys weren't actually there to SECURE the area so much as to put on a SHOW.
Which SORT OF explains how I got KIDNAPPED.
...MONICA...
The client himself MIGHT have saved me --
-- but he was a little DISTRACTED.

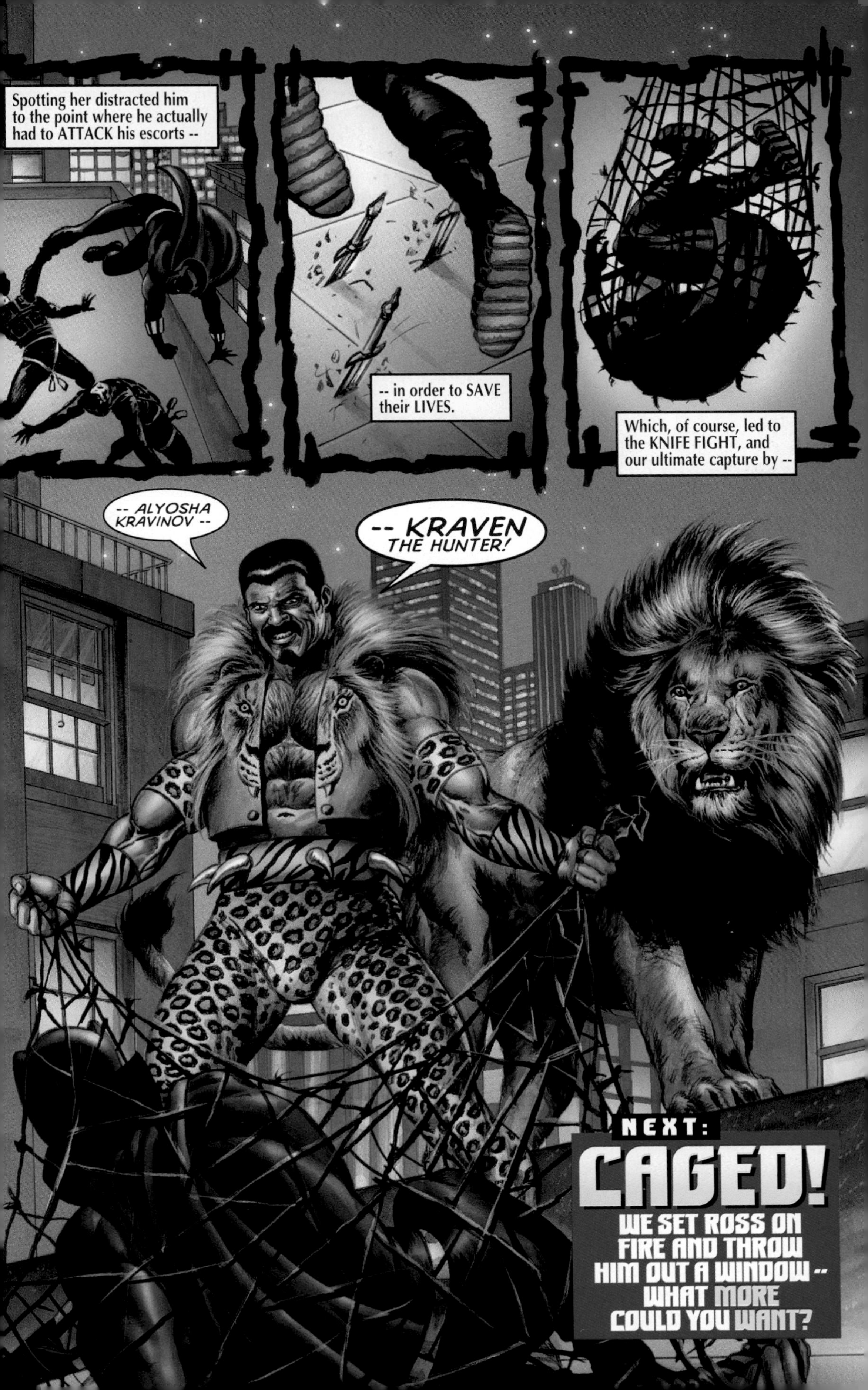
Spotting her distracted him to the point where he actually had to ATTACK his escorts --
-- in order to SAVE their LIVES.
Which, of course, led to the KNIFE FIGHT, and our ultimate capture by --
-- ALYOSHA KRAVINOV --
-- KRAVEN THE HUNTER!
NEXT:
CAGED!
WE SET ROSS ON FIRE AND THROW HIM OUT A WINDOW -- WHAT MORE COULD YOU WANT?

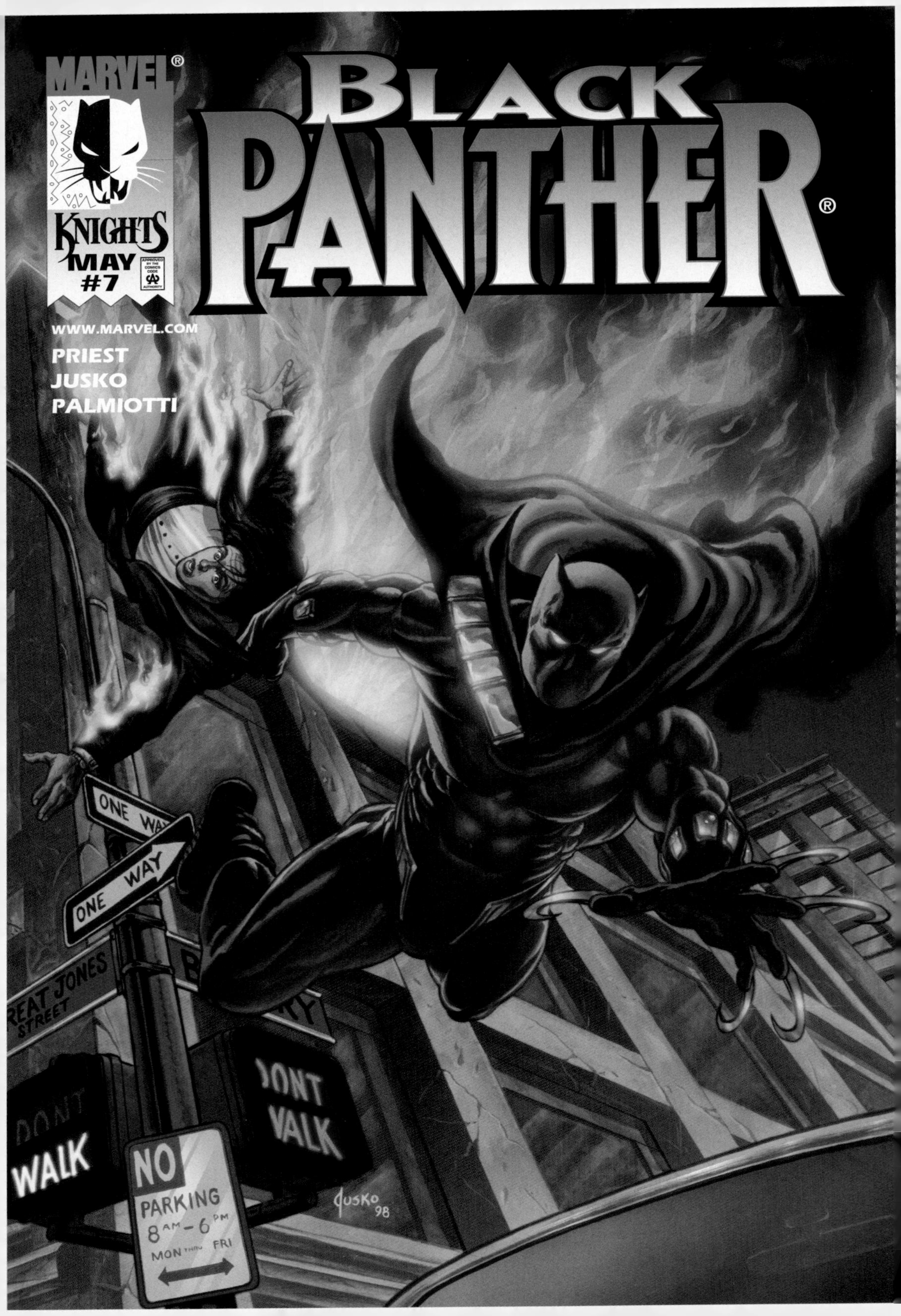

MARVEL
KNIGHTS
MAY
#7
APPROVED BY THE COMICS CODE AUTHORITY
BLACK PANTHER
WWW.MARVEL.COM
PRIEST
JUSKO
PALMIOTTI
ONE WAY
ONE WAY
GREAT JONES STREET
DONT WALK
WALK
NO PARKING 8AM-6PM MON THRU FRI
JUSKO 98

MAYBE WE DO STILL HAVE HIM TO KICK AROUND

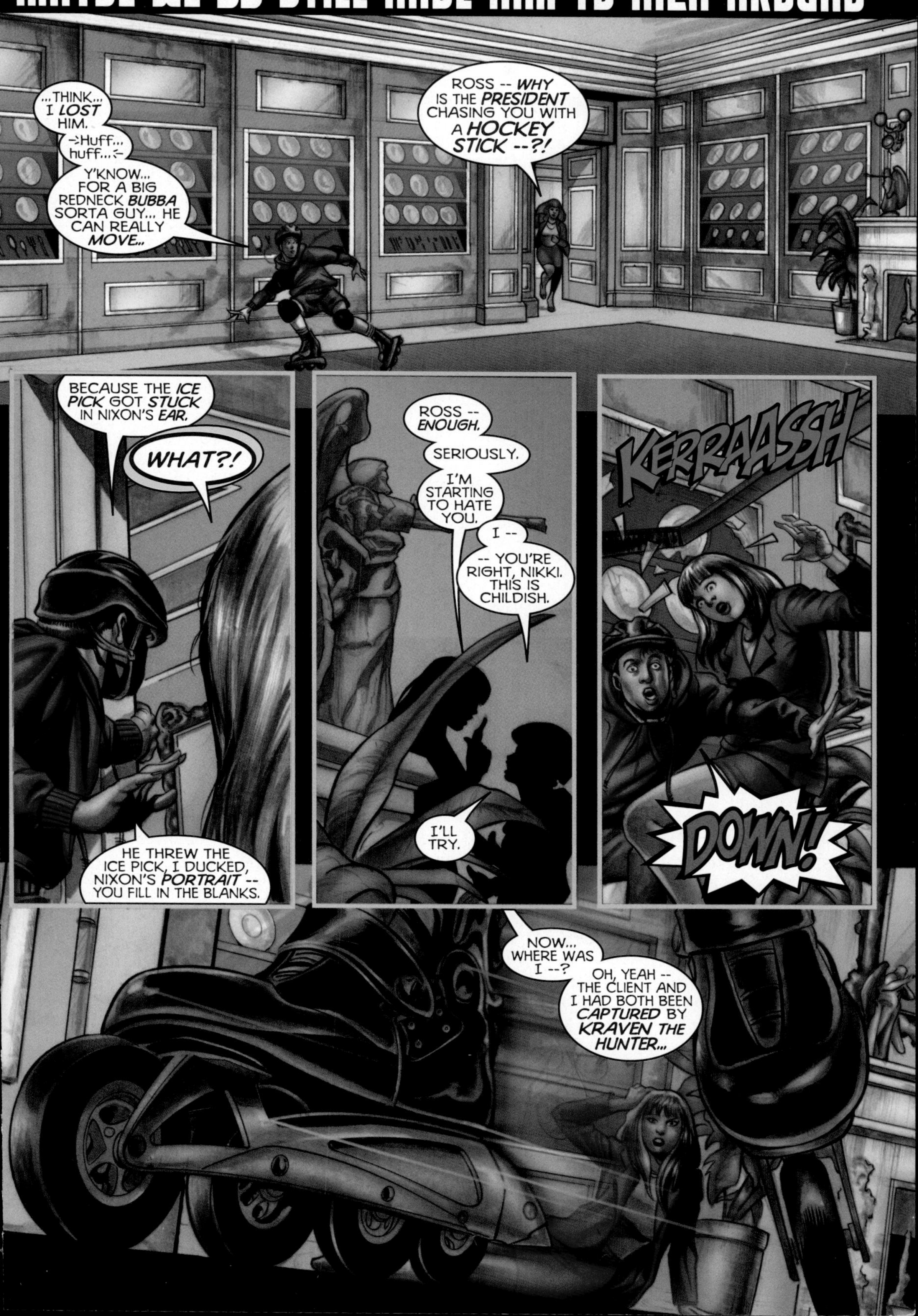
...THINK... I LOST HIM.
-Huff... huff...-
Y'KNOW... FOR A BIG REDNECK BUBBA SORTA GUY... HE CAN REALLY MOVE...
ROSS -- WHY IS THE PRESIDENT CHASING YOU WITH A HOCKEY STICK --?!
BECAUSE THE ICE PICK GOT STUCK IN NIXON'S EAR.
WHAT?!
HE THREW THE ICE PICK, I DUCKED, NIXON'S PORTRAIT -- YOU FILL IN THE BLANKS.
ROSS -- ENOUGH.
SERIOUSLY.
I'M STARTING TO HATE YOU.
I --
-- YOU'RE RIGHT, NIKKI. THIS IS CHILDISH.
I'LL TRY.
KERRAASSH
DOWN!
NOW... WHERE WAS I --?
OH, YEAH -- THE CLIENT AND I HAD BOTH BEEN CAPTURED BY KRAVEN THE HUNTER...

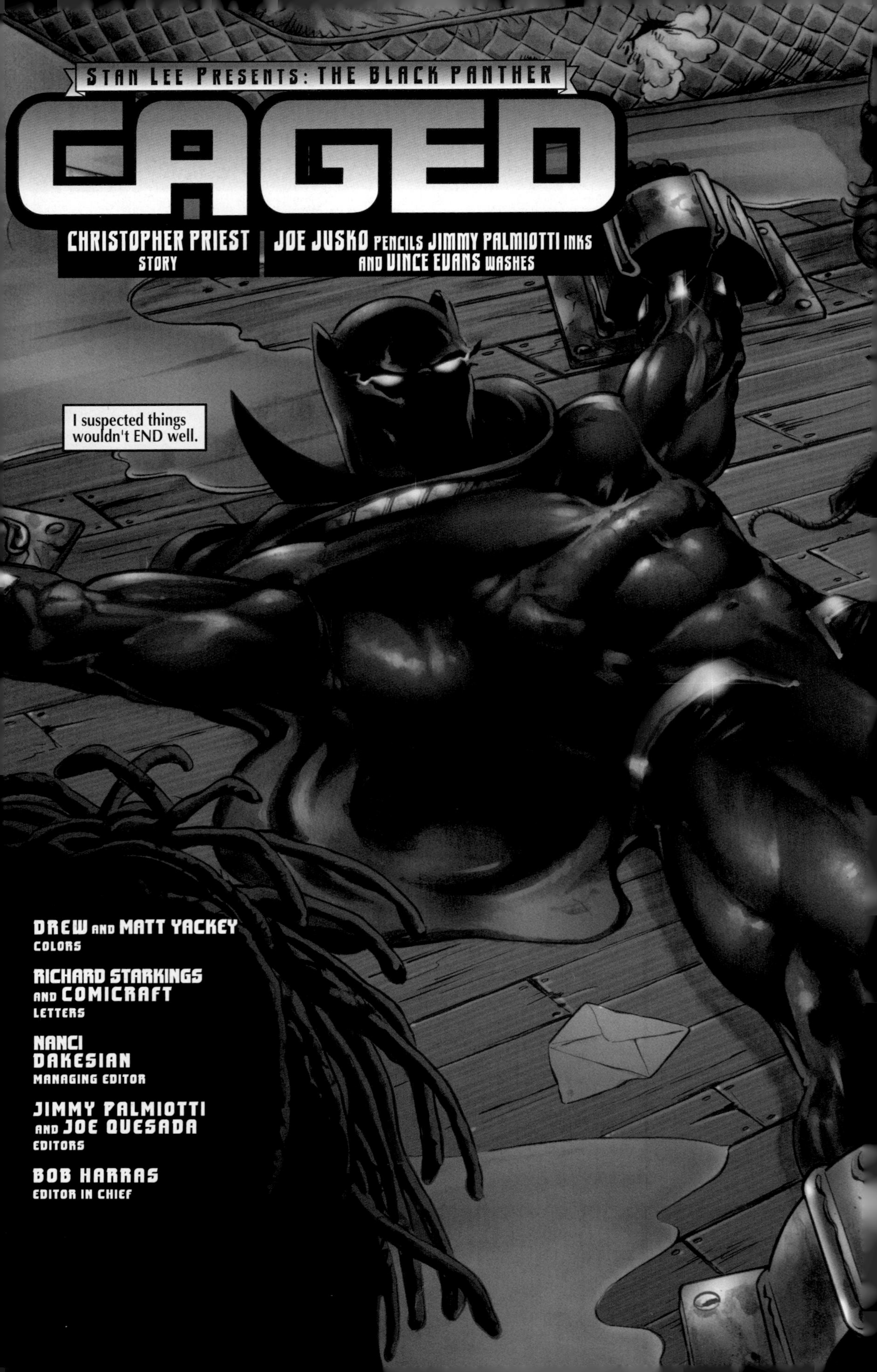
STAN LEE PRESENTS: THE BLACK PANTHER
CAGED
CHRISTOPHER PRIEST STORY
JOE JUSKO PENCILS JIMMY PALMIOTTI INKS AND VINCE EVANS WASHES
I suspected things wouldn't END well.
DREW AND MATT YACKEY COLORS
RICHARD STARKINGS AND COMICRAFT LETTERS
NANCI DAKESIAN MANAGING EDITOR
JIMMY PALMIOTTI AND JOE QUESADA EDITORS
BOB HARRAS EDITOR IN CHIEF

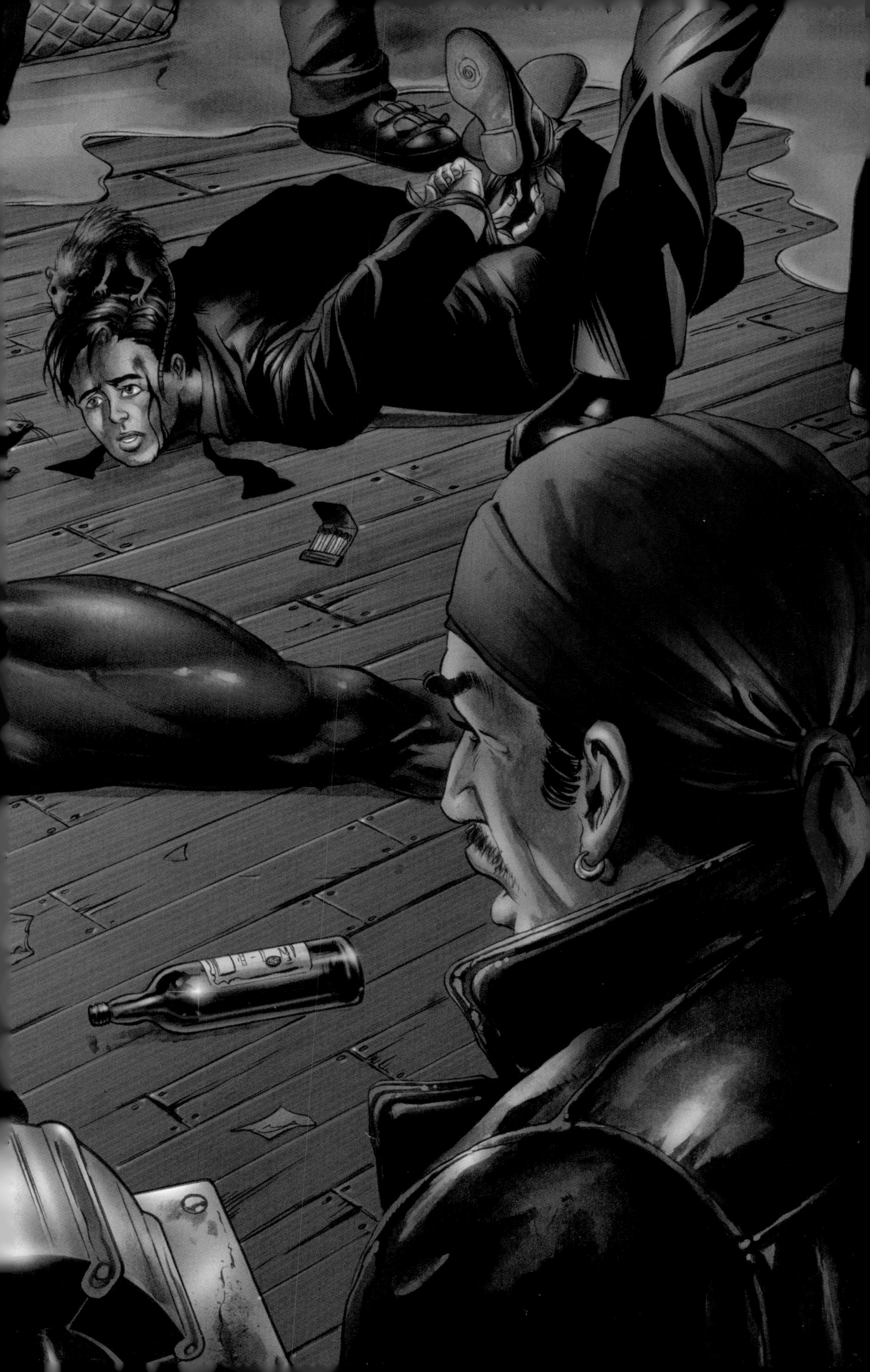

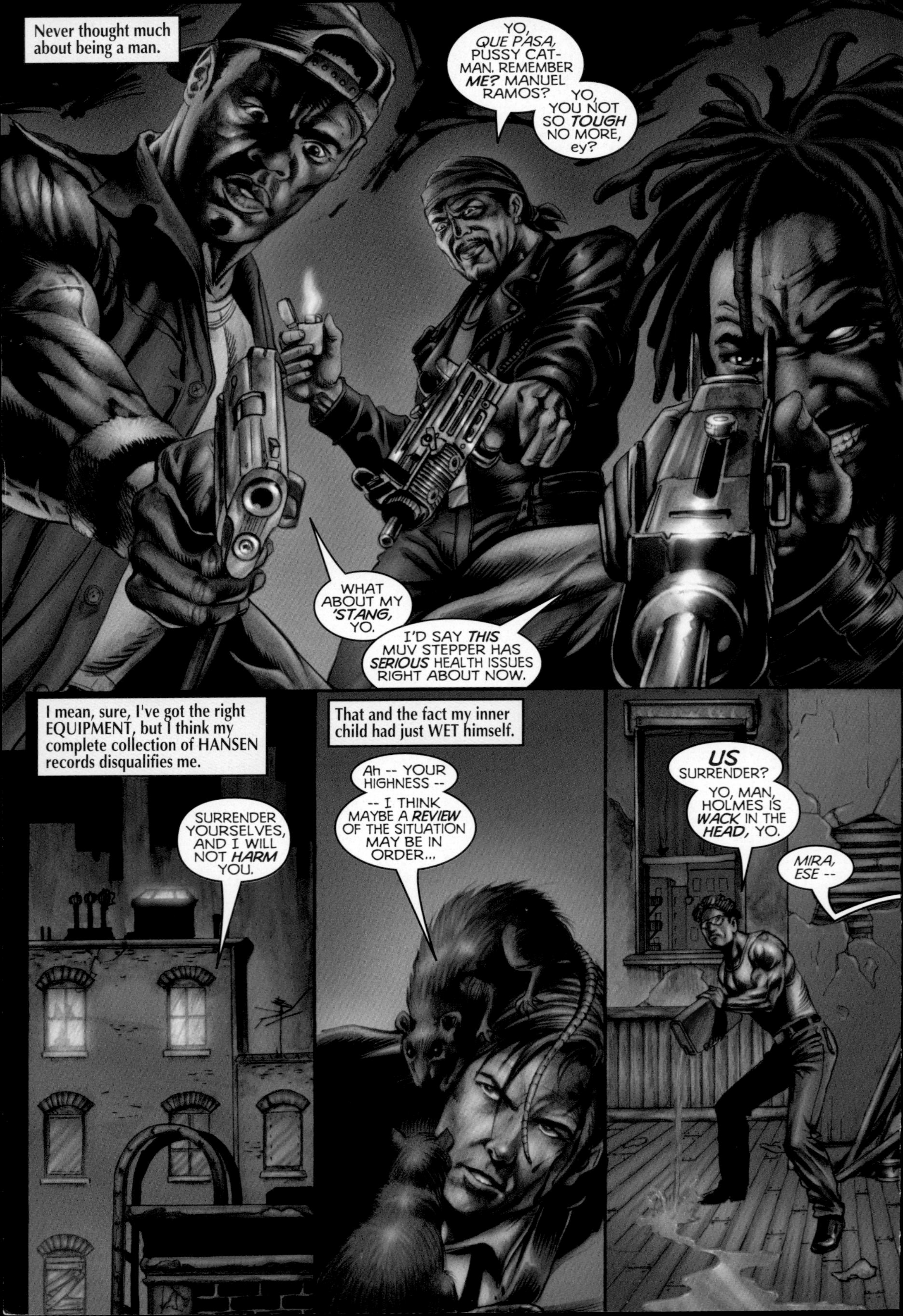
Never thought much about being a man.
YO, QUE PASA, PUSSY CAT-MAN. REMEMBER ME? MANUEL RAMOS?
YO, YOU NOT SO TOUGH NO MORE, ey?
WHAT ABOUT MY 'STANG, YO.
I'D SAY THIS MUV STEPPER HAS SERIOUS HEALTH ISSUES RIGHT ABOUT NOW.
I mean, sure, I've got the right EQUIPMENT, but I think my complete collection of HANSEN records disqualifies me.
SURRENDER YOURSELVES, AND I WILL NOT HARM YOU.
That and the fact my inner child had just WET himself.
Ah -- YOUR HIGHNESS --
-- I THINK MAYBE A REVIEW OF THE SITUATION MAY BE IN ORDER...
US SURRENDER?
YO, MAN, HOLMES IS WACK IN THE HEAD, YO.
MIRA, ESE --

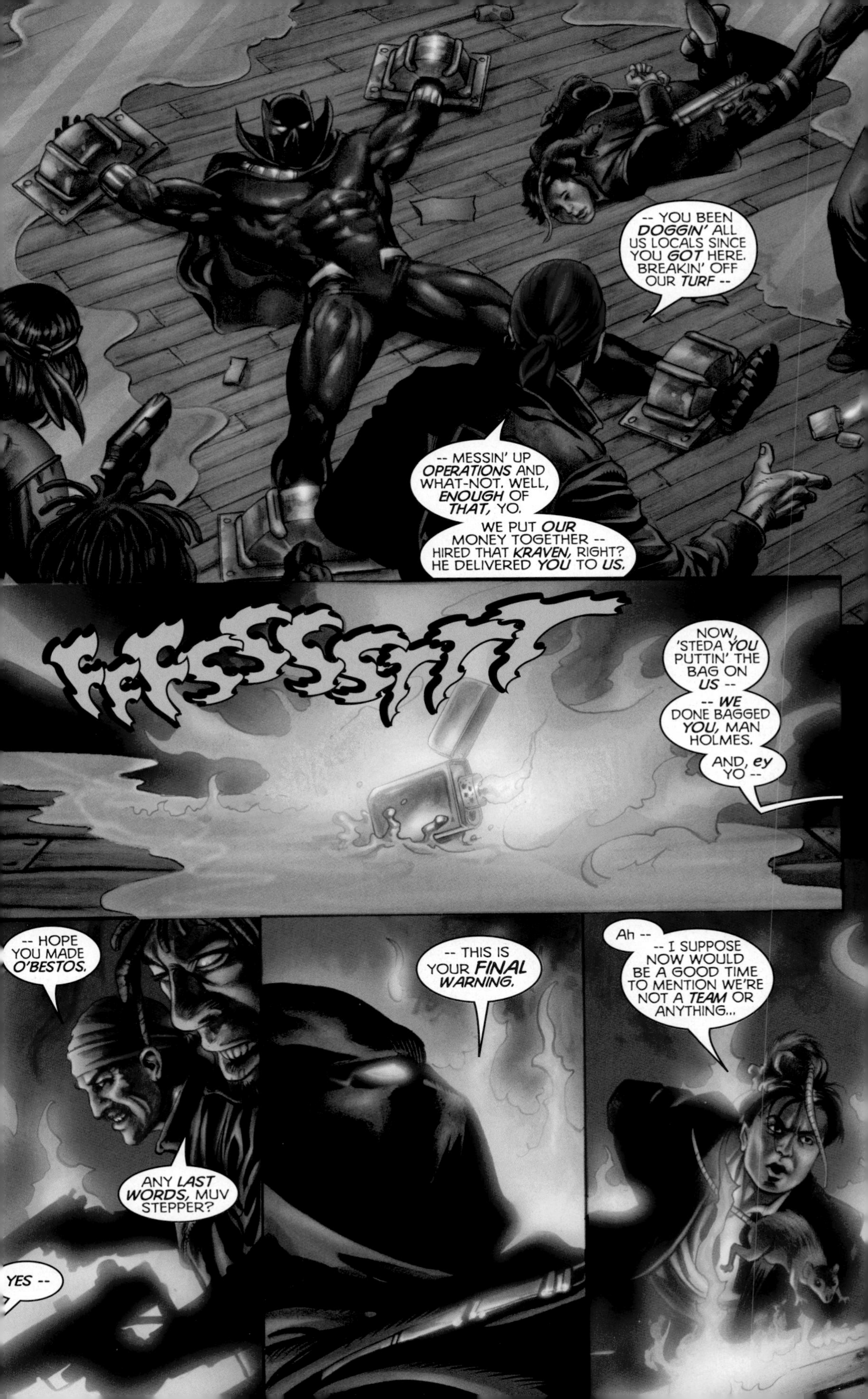
-- YOU BEEN DOGGIN' ALL US LOCALS SINCE YOU GOT HERE. BREAKIN' OFF OUR TURF --
-- MESSIN' UP OPERATIONS AND WHAT-NOT. WELL, ENOUGH OF THAT, YO.
WE PUT OUR MONEY TOGETHER -- HIRED THAT KRAVEN, RIGHT? HE DELIVERED YOU TO US.
FFFSSSSHHT
NOW, 'STEDA YOU PUTTIN' THE BAG ON US --
-- WE DONE BAGGED YOU, MAN HOLMES.
AND, ey YO --
-- HOPE YOU MADE O'BESTOS.
ANY LAST WORDS, MUV STEPPER?
YES --
-- THIS IS YOUR FINAL WARNING.
Ah --
-- I SUPPOSE NOW WOULD BE A GOOD TIME TO MENTION WE'RE NOT A TEAM OR ANYTHING...

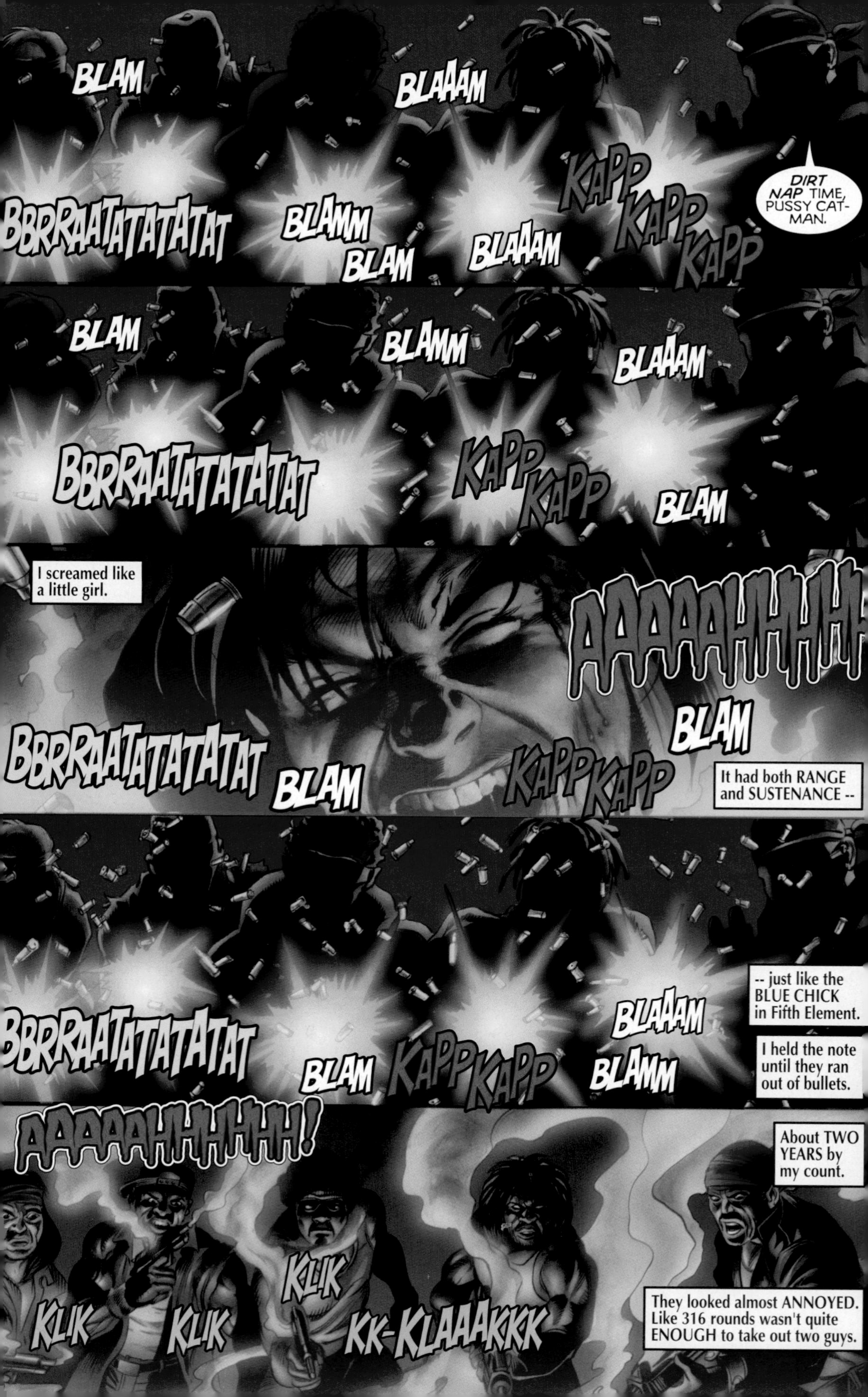
BLAM
BLAAAM
DIRT NAP TIME, PUSSY CAT-MAN.
BBRRAATATATATAT
BLAMM
BLAM
BLAAAM
KAPP KAPP KAPP
BLAM
BLAMM
BLAAAM
BBRRAATATATATAT
KAPP KAPP
BLAM
I screamed like a little girl.
AAAAAHHHHH
BBRRAATATATATAT
BLAM
KAPP KAPP
BLAM
It had both RANGE and SUSTENANCE --
BBRRAATATATATAT
BLAM
KAPP KAPP
BLAAAM
BLAMM
-- just like the BLUE CHICK in Fifth Element.
I held the note until they ran out of bullets.
AAAAAHHHHHH!
About TWO YEARS by my count.
KLIK
KLIK
KLIK
KK-KLAAAKKK
They looked almost ANNOYED. Like 316 rounds wasn't quite ENOUGH to take out two guys.

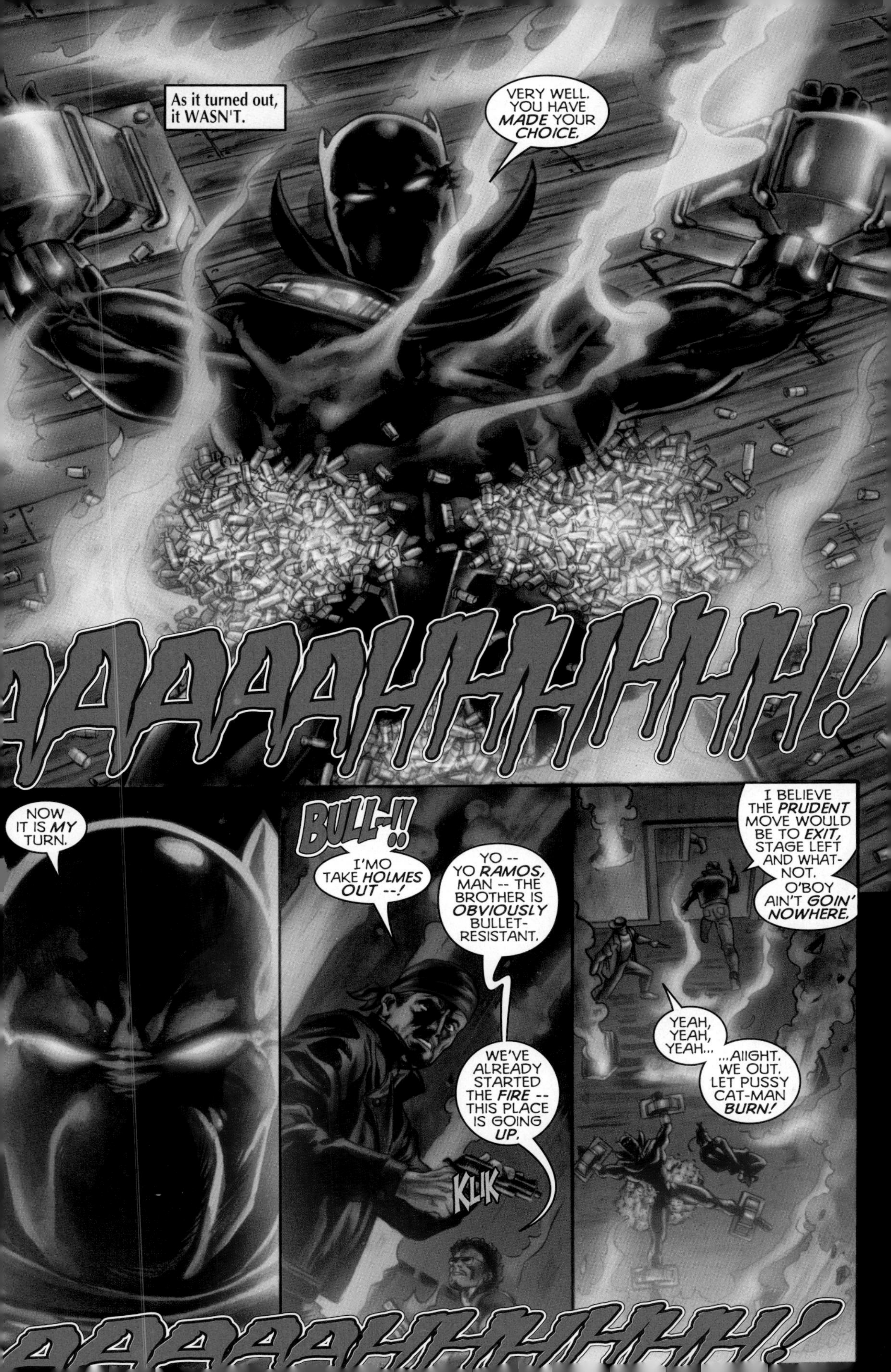
As it turned out, it WASN'T.
VERY WELL. YOU HAVE MADE YOUR CHOICE.
AAAAAAHHHHHHHH!
NOW IT IS MY TURN.
BULL--!!
I'MO TAKE HOLMES OUT --!
YO -- YO RAMOS, MAN -- THE BROTHER IS OBVIOUSLY BULLET-RESISTANT.
WE'VE ALREADY STARTED THE FIRE -- THIS PLACE IS GOING UP.
KLIK
I BELIEVE THE PRUDENT MOVE WOULD BE TO EXIT, STAGE LEFT AND WHAT-NOT.
O'BOY AIN'T GOIN' NOWHERE.
YEAH, YEAH, YEAH...
...AIIGHT. WE OUT. LET PUSSY CAT-MAN BURN!
AAAAAAHHHHHHHH!

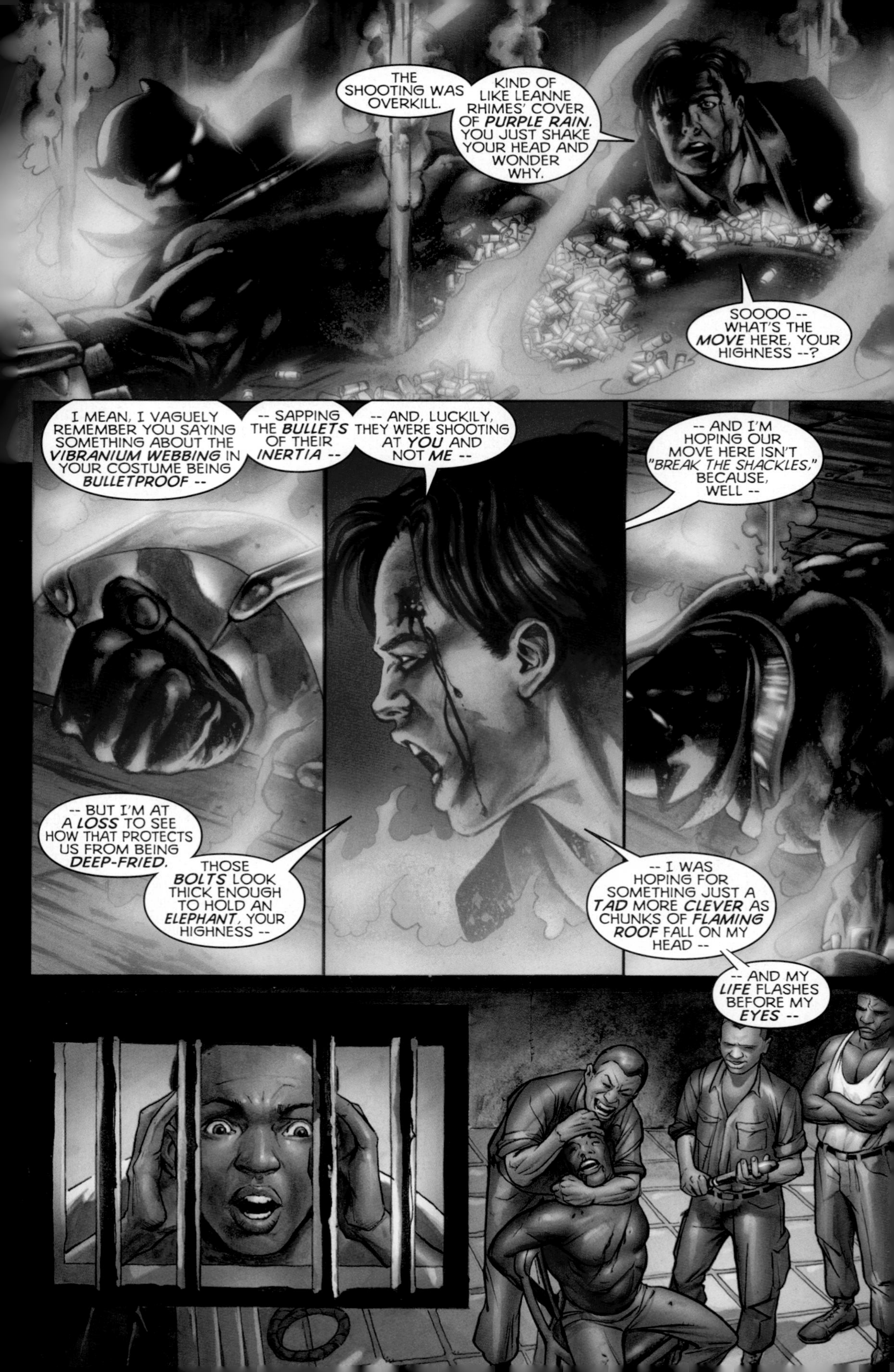
THE SHOOTING WAS OVERKILL.
KIND OF LIKE LEANNE RHIMES' COVER OF PURPLE RAIN. YOU JUST SHAKE YOUR HEAD AND WONDER WHY.
SOOOO -- WHAT'S THE MOVE HERE, YOUR HIGHNESS --?
I MEAN, I VAGUELY REMEMBER YOU SAYING SOMETHING ABOUT THE VIBRANIUM WEBBING IN YOUR COSTUME BEING BULLETPROOF --
-- SAPPING THE BULLETS OF THEIR INERTIA --
-- AND, LUCKILY, THEY WERE SHOOTING AT YOU AND NOT ME --
-- AND I'M HOPING OUR MOVE HERE ISN'T "BREAK THE SHACKLES," BECAUSE, WELL --
-- BUT I'M AT A LOSS TO SEE HOW THAT PROTECTS US FROM BEING DEEP-FRIED.
THOSE BOLTS LOOK THICK ENOUGH TO HOLD AN ELEPHANT, YOUR HIGHNESS --
-- I WAS HOPING FOR SOMETHING JUST A TAD MORE CLEVER AS CHUNKS OF FLAMING ROOF FALL ON MY HEAD --
-- AND MY LIFE FLASHES BEFORE MY EYES --

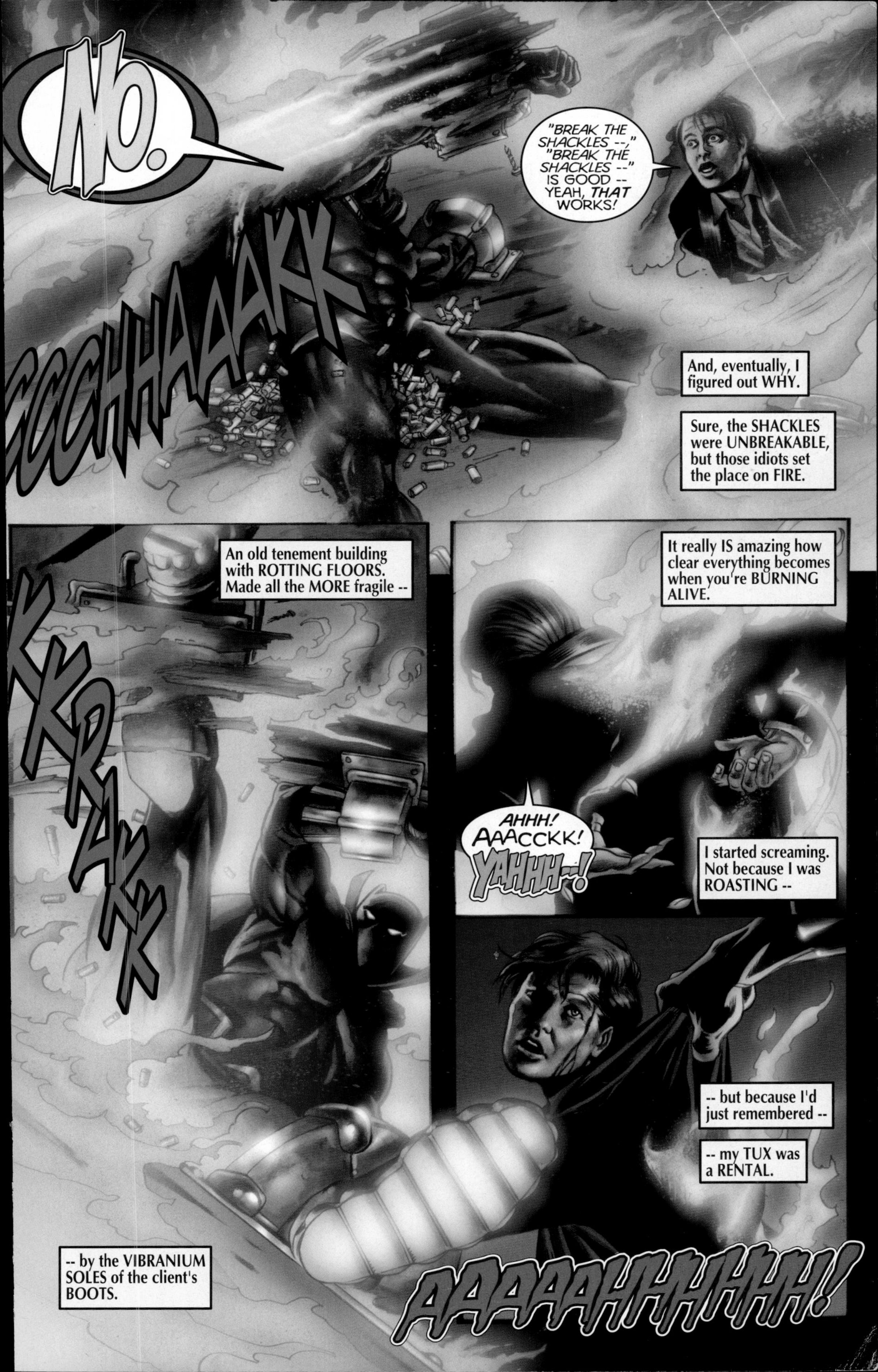
NO.
"BREAK THE SHACKLES --," "BREAK THE SHACKLES --" IS GOOD -- YEAH, THAT WORKS!
CCHHAAAKK
And, eventually, I figured out WHY.
Sure, the SHACKLES were UNBREAKABLE, but those idiots set the place on FIRE.
An old tenement building with ROTTING FLOORS. Made all the MORE fragile --
KKRAKK
-- by the VIBRANIUM SOLES of the client's BOOTS.
It really IS amazing how clear everything becomes when you're BURNING ALIVE.
AHHH! AAACCKK! YAHHH--!
I started screaming. Not because I was ROASTING --
-- but because I'd just remembered --
-- my TUX was a RENTAL.
AAAAAHHHHHH!

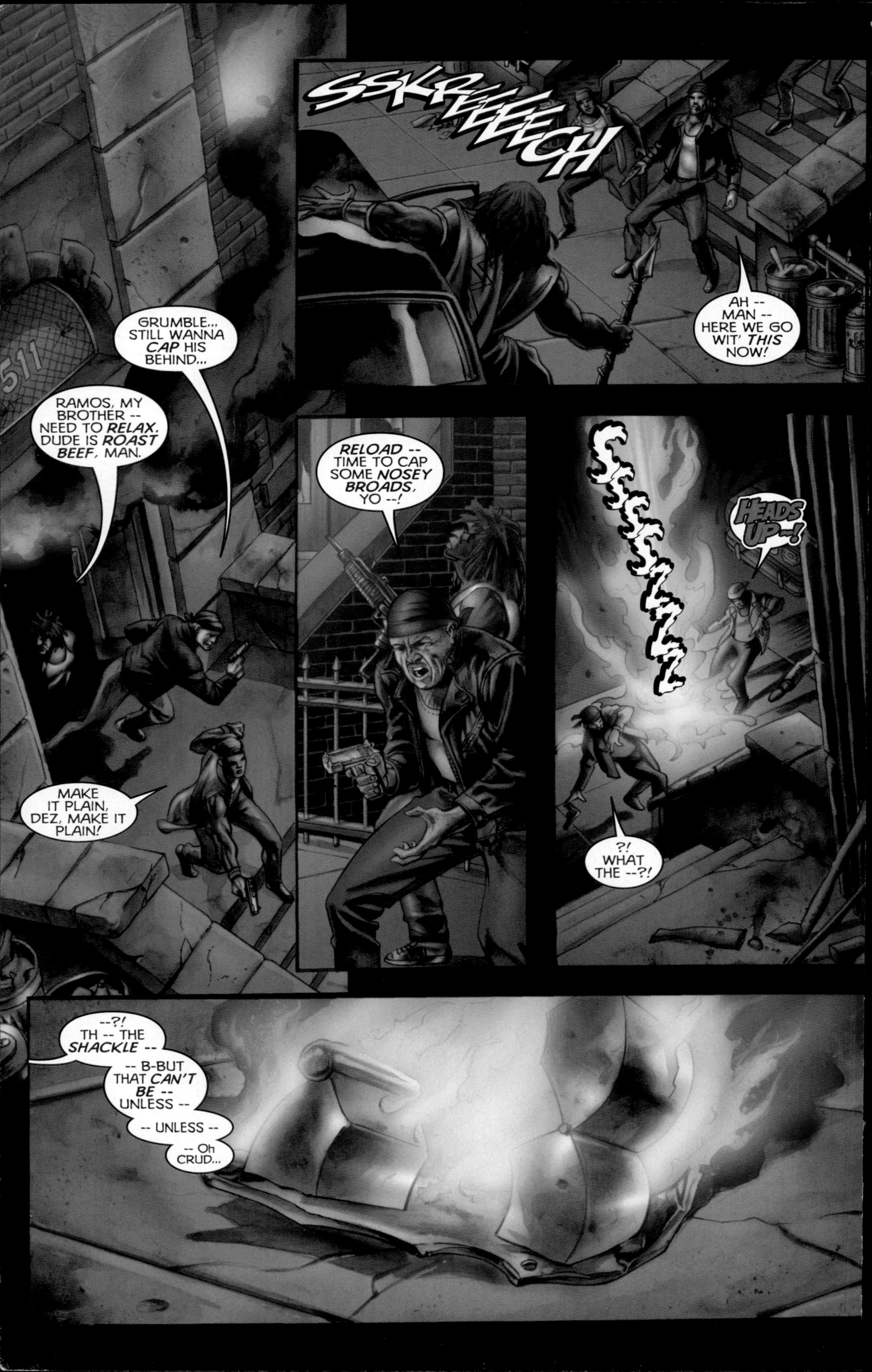

SSKREEEEECH
AH -- MAN -- HERE WE GO WIT' THIS NOW!
GRUMBLE... STILL WANNA CAP HIS BEHIND...
RAMOS, MY BROTHER -- NEED TO RELAX. DUDE IS ROAST BEEF, MAN.
MAKE IT PLAIN, DEZ, MAKE IT PLAIN!
RELOAD -- TIME TO CAP SOME NOSEY BROADS, YO --!
SSSSZZZZZ
HEADS UP--!
?! WHAT THE --?!
--?! TH -- THE SHACKLE --
-- B-BUT THAT CAN'T BE -- UNLESS --
-- UNLESS --
-- Oh CRUD...

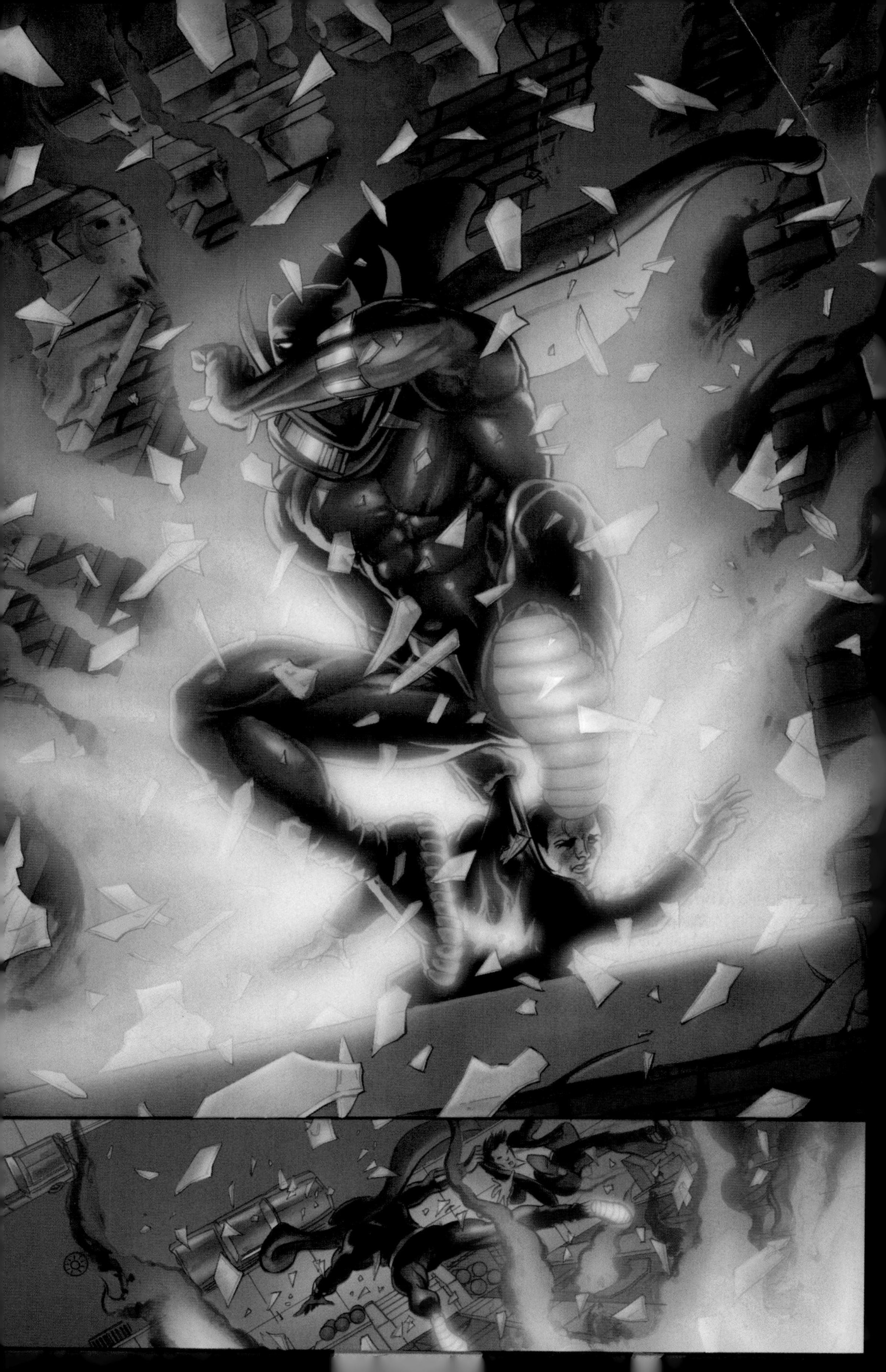

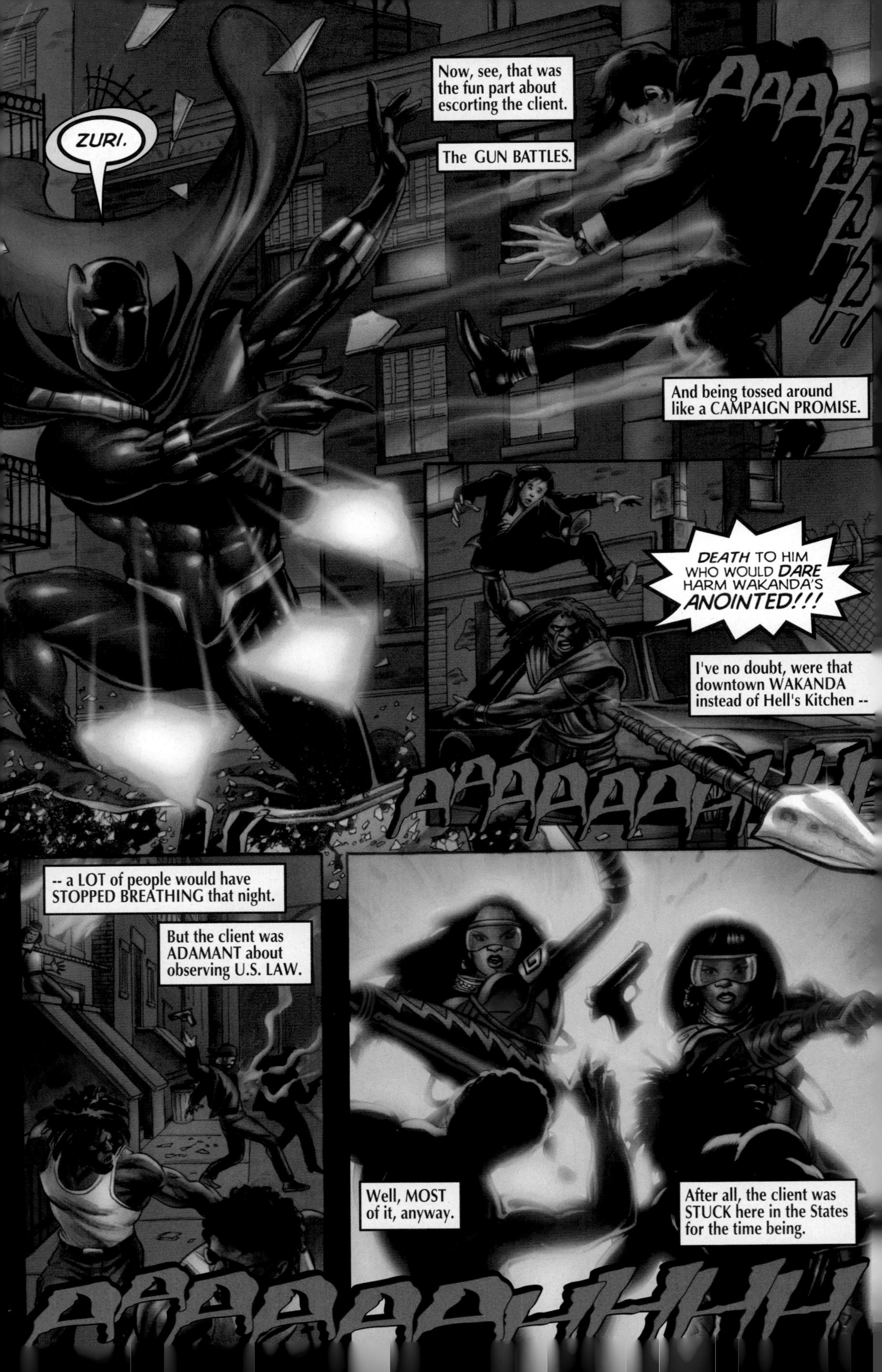

ZURI.
Now, see, that was the fun part about escorting the client.
The GUN BATTLES.
AAAAAAAHHH
And being tossed around like a CAMPAIGN PROMISE.
DEATH TO HIM WHO WOULD DARE HARM WAKANDA'S ANOINTED!!!
I've no doubt, were that downtown WAKANDA instead of Hell's Kitchen --
AAAAAAHHH
-- a LOT of people would have STOPPED BREATHING that night.
But the client was ADAMANT about observing U.S. LAW.
Well, MOST of it, anyway.
After all, the client was STUCK here in the States for the time being.
AAAAAAHHHH

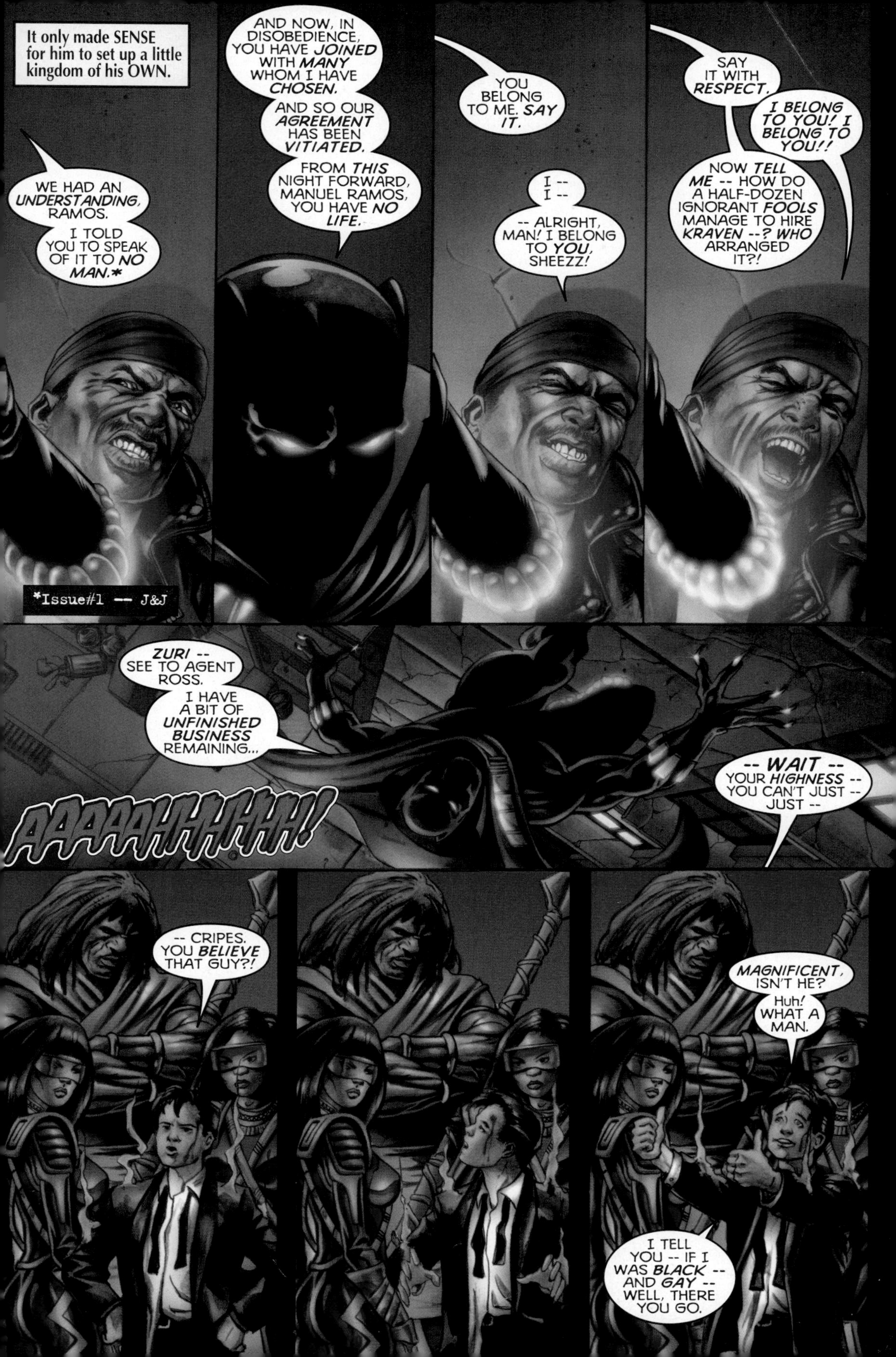

It only made SENSE for him to set up a little kingdom of his OWN.
WE HAD AN UNDERSTANDING, RAMOS.
I TOLD YOU TO SPEAK OF IT TO NO MAN.*
*Issue#1 -- J&J
AND NOW, IN DISOBEDIENCE, YOU HAVE JOINED WITH MANY WHOM I HAVE CHOSEN.
AND SO OUR AGREEMENT HAS BEEN VITIATED.
FROM THIS NIGHT FORWARD, MANUEL RAMOS, YOU HAVE NO LIFE.
YOU BELONG TO ME. SAY IT.
I -- I --
-- ALRIGHT, MAN! I BELONG TO YOU, SHEEZZ!
SAY IT WITH RESPECT.
I BELONG TO YOU! I BELONG TO YOU!!
NOW TELL ME -- HOW DO A HALF-DOZEN IGNORANT FOOLS MANAGE TO HIRE KRAVEN --? WHO ARRANGED IT?!
ZURI -- SEE TO AGENT ROSS.
I HAVE A BIT OF UNFINISHED BUSINESS REMAINING...
AAAAAHHHHHH!
-- WAIT -- YOUR HIGHNESS -- YOU CAN'T JUST -- JUST --
-- CRIPES. YOU BELIEVE THAT GUY?!
MAGNIFICENT, ISN'T HE?
Huh! WHAT A MAN.
I TELL YOU -- IF I WAS BLACK -- AND GAY -- WELL, THERE YOU GO.

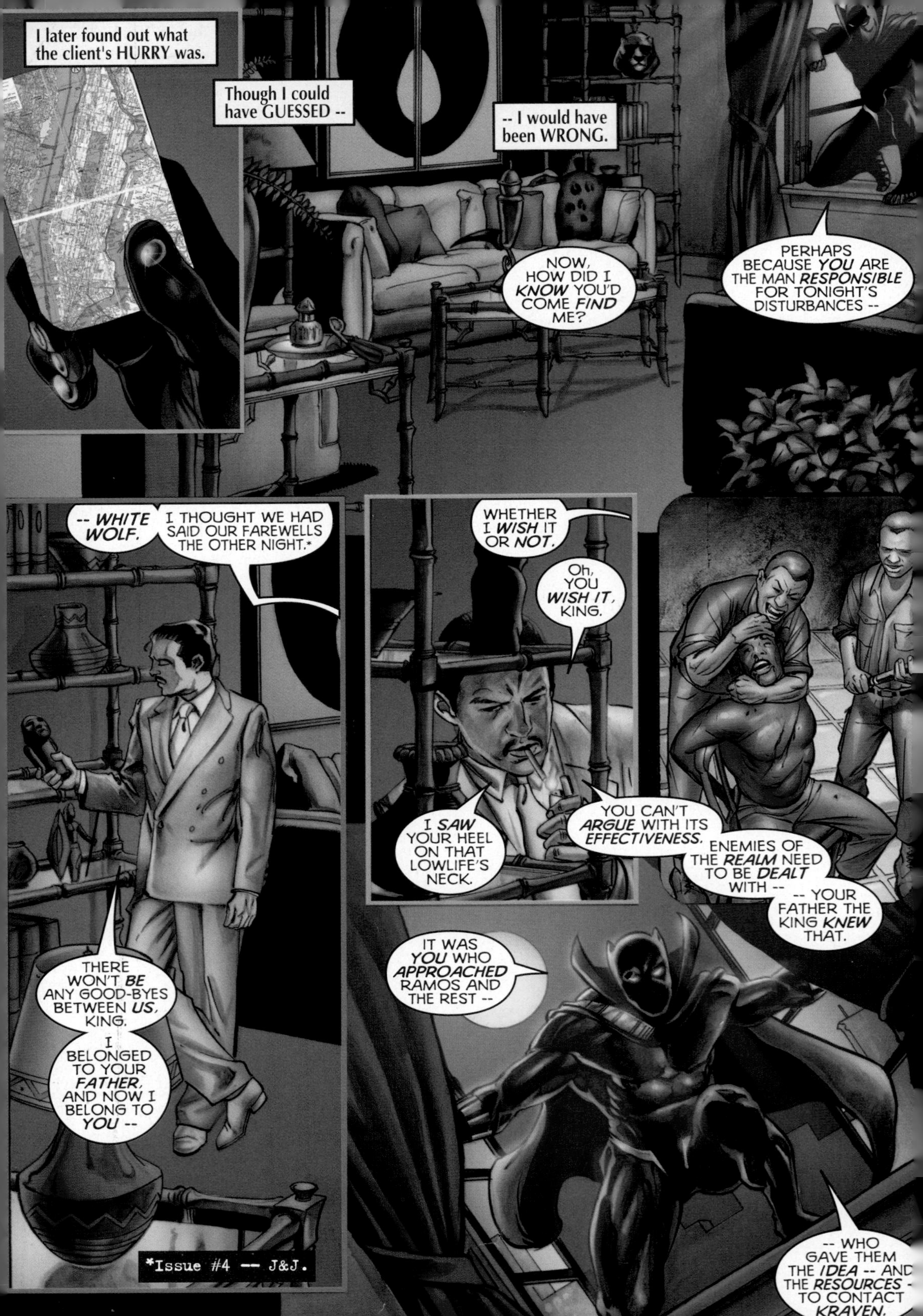

I later found out what the client's HURRY was.
Though I could have GUESSED --
-- I would have been WRONG.
NOW, HOW DID I KNOW YOU'D COME FIND ME?
PERHAPS BECAUSE YOU ARE THE MAN RESPONSIBLE FOR TONIGHT'S DISTURBANCES --
-- WHITE WOLF.
I THOUGHT WE HAD SAID OUR FAREWELLS THE OTHER NIGHT.*
THERE WON'T BE ANY GOOD-BYES BETWEEN US, KING.
I BELONGED TO YOUR FATHER, AND NOW I BELONG TO YOU --
WHETHER I WISH IT OR NOT.
Oh, YOU WISH IT, KING.
I SAW YOUR HEEL ON THAT LOWLIFE'S NECK.
YOU CAN'T ARGUE WITH ITS EFFECTIVENESS.
ENEMIES OF THE REALM NEED TO BE DEALT WITH --
-- YOUR FATHER THE KING KNEW THAT.
IT WAS YOU WHO APPROACHED RAMOS AND THE REST --
-- WHO GAVE THEM THE IDEA -- AND THE RESOURCES -- TO CONTACT KRAVEN.
*Issue #4 -- J&J.

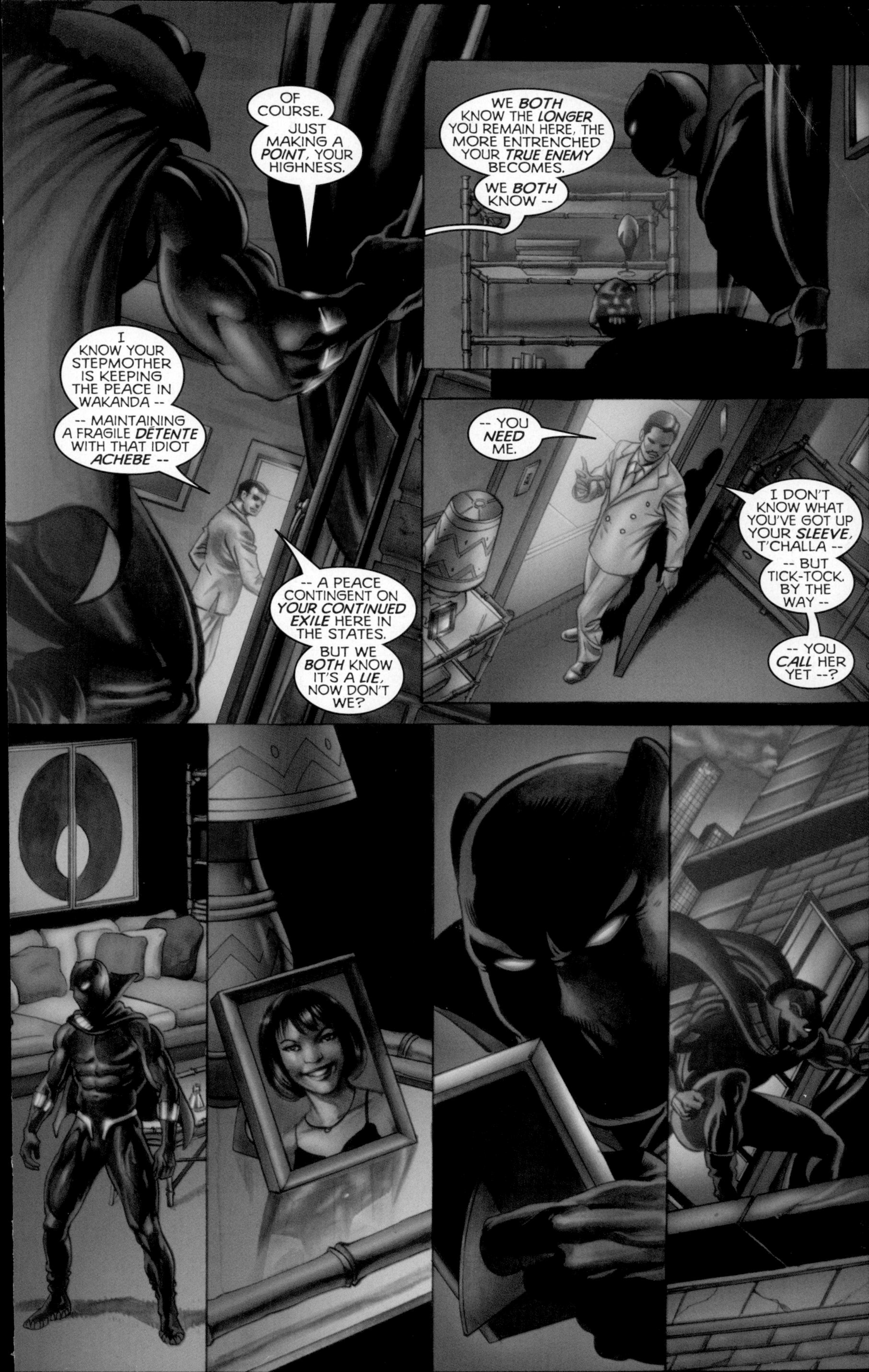
OF COURSE.
JUST MAKING A POINT, YOUR HIGHNESS.
WE BOTH KNOW THE LONGER YOU REMAIN HERE, THE MORE ENTRENCHED YOUR TRUE ENEMY BECOMES.
WE BOTH KNOW --
I KNOW YOUR STEPMOTHER IS KEEPING THE PEACE IN WAKANDA --
-- MAINTAINING A FRAGILE DÉTENTE WITH THAT IDIOT ACHEBE --
-- A PEACE CONTINGENT ON YOUR CONTINUED EXILE HERE IN THE STATES.
BUT WE BOTH KNOW IT'S A LIE, NOW DON'T WE?
-- YOU NEED ME.
I DON'T KNOW WHAT YOU'VE GOT UP YOUR SLEEVE, T'CHALLA --
-- BUT TICK-TOCK. BY THE WAY --
-- YOU CALL HER YET --?

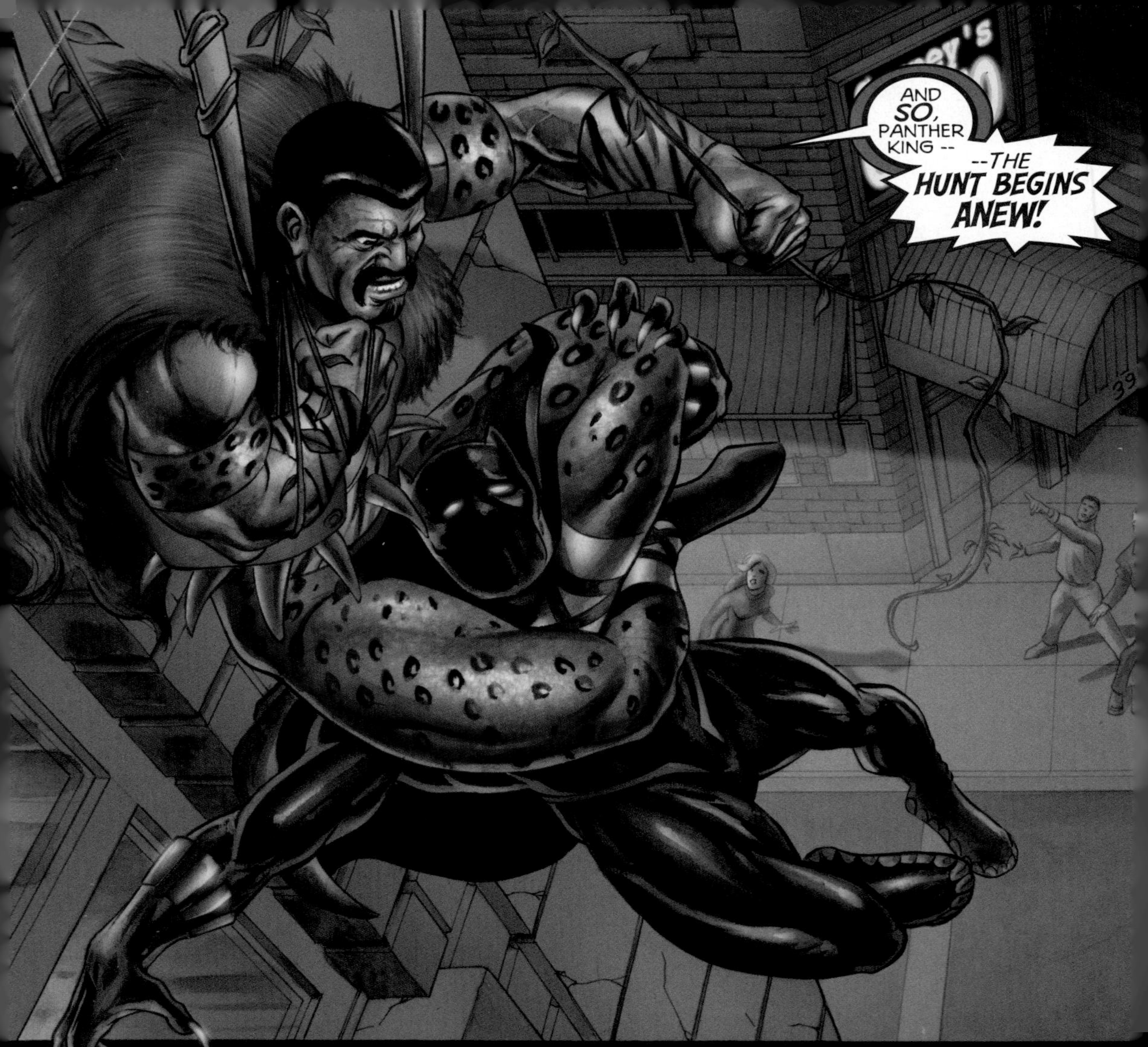
AND SO, PANTHER KING --
--THE HUNT BEGINS ANEW!

DON'T DROP THE SOAP

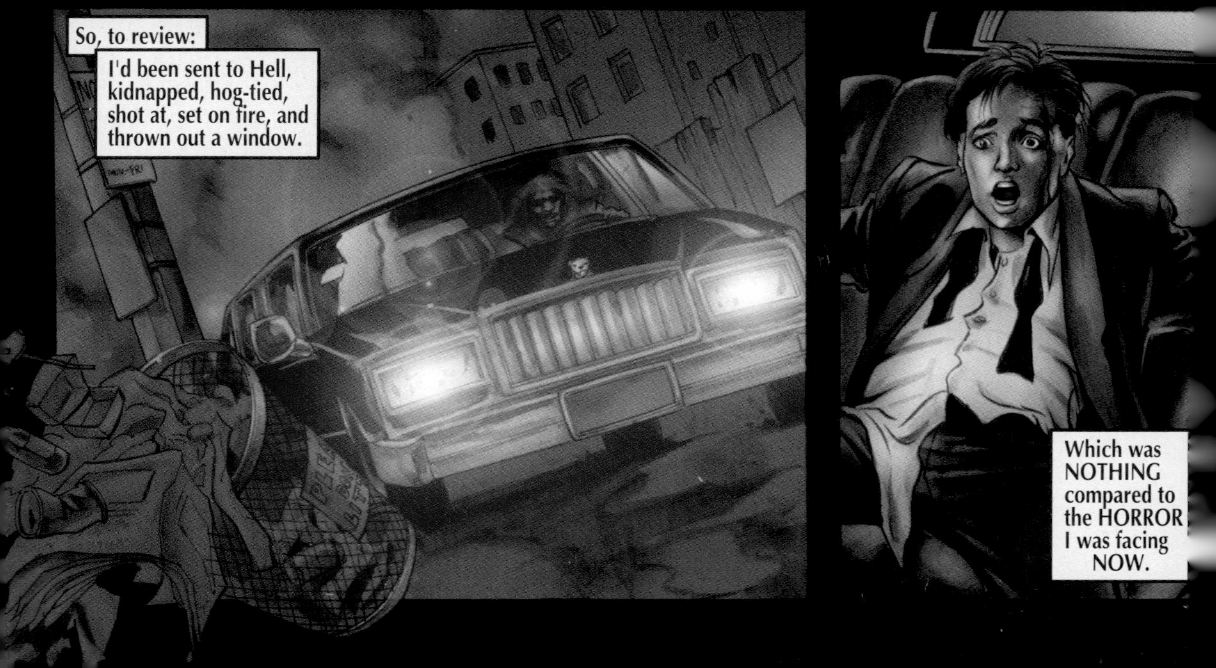
So, to review:
I'd been sent to Hell, kidnapped, hog-tied, shot at, set on fire, and thrown out a window.
Which was NOTHING compared to the HORROR I was facing NOW.

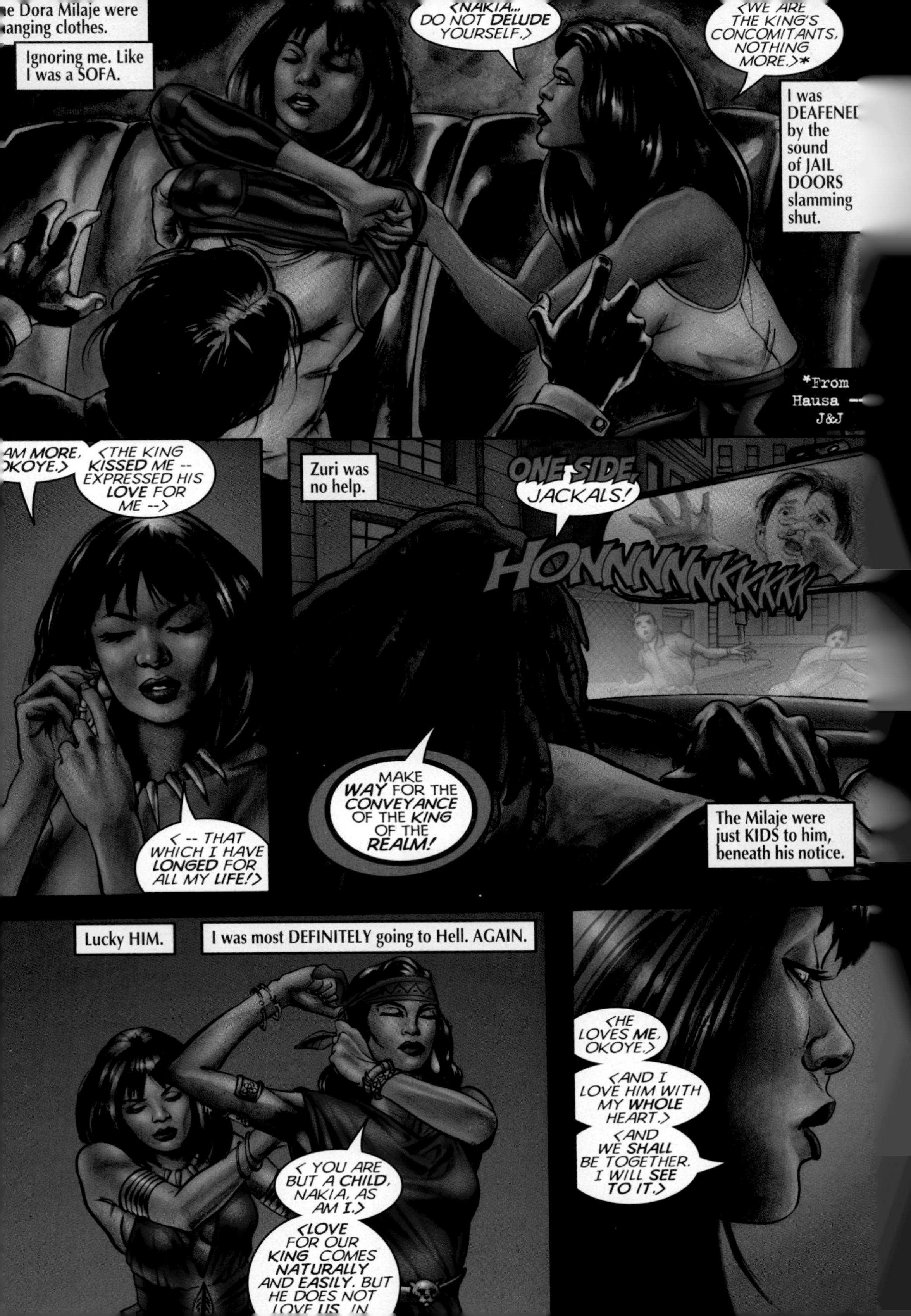

e Dora Milaje were
anging clothes.
Ignoring me. Like I was a SOFA.
<NAKIA... DO NOT DELUDE YOURSELF.>
<WE ARE THE KING'S CONCOMITANTS, NOTHING MORE.>*
I was DEAFENED by the sound of JAIL DOORS slamming shut.
*From Hausa -- J&J
AM MORE, OKOYE.>
<THE KING KISSED ME -- EXPRESSED HIS LOVE FOR ME -->
<-- THAT WHICH I HAVE LONGED FOR ALL MY LIFE!>
Zuri was no help.
ONE SIDE, JACKALS!
HONNNNNKKKK!
MAKE WAY FOR THE CONVEYANCE OF THE KING OF THE REALM!
The Milaje were just KIDS to him, beneath his notice.
Lucky HIM.
I was most DEFINITELY going to Hell. AGAIN.
< YOU ARE BUT A CHILD, NAKIA, AS AM I.>
<LOVE FOR OUR KING COMES NATURALLY AND EASILY. BUT HE DOES NOT LOVE US, IN
<HE LOVES ME, OKOYE.>
<AND I LOVE HIM WITH MY WHOLE HEART.>
<AND WE SHALL BE TOGETHER. I WILL SEE TO IT.>

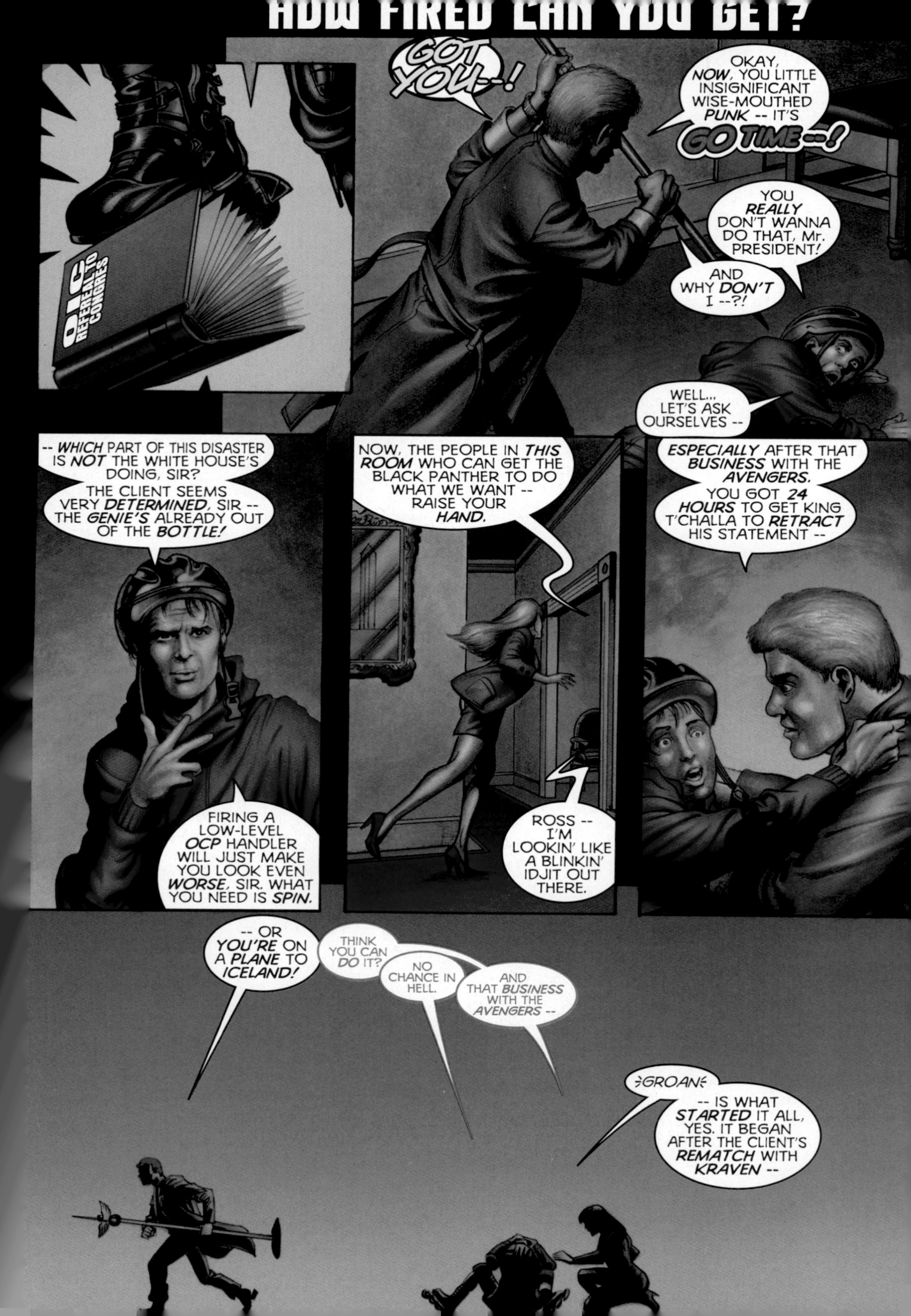

HOW FIRED CAN YOU GET?
OIC REFEREAL TO CONGRES
GOT YOU--!
OKAY, NOW, YOU LITTLE INSIGNIFICANT WISE-MOUTHED PUNK -- IT'S GO TIME--!
YOU REALLY DON'T WANNA DO THAT, Mr. PRESIDENT!
AND WHY DON'T I --?!
WELL... LET'S ASK OURSELVES --
-- WHICH PART OF THIS DISASTER IS NOT THE WHITE HOUSE'S DOING, SIR?
THE CLIENT SEEMS VERY DETERMINED, SIR -- THE GENIE'S ALREADY OUT OF THE BOTTLE!
FIRING A LOW-LEVEL OCP HANDLER WILL JUST MAKE YOU LOOK EVEN WORSE, SIR. WHAT YOU NEED IS SPIN.
NOW, THE PEOPLE IN THIS ROOM WHO CAN GET THE BLACK PANTHER TO DO WHAT WE WANT -- RAISE YOUR HAND.
ROSS -- I'M LOOKIN' LIKE A BLINKIN' IDJIT OUT THERE.
ESPECIALLY AFTER THAT BUSINESS WITH THE AVENGERS.
YOU GOT 24 HOURS TO GET KING T'CHALLA TO RETRACT HIS STATEMENT --
-- OR YOU'RE ON A PLANE TO ICELAND!
THINK YOU CAN DO IT?
NO CHANCE IN HELL.
AND THAT BUSINESS WITH THE AVENGERS --
GROAN
-- IS WHAT STARTED IT ALL, YES. IT BEGAN AFTER THE CLIENT'S REMATCH WITH KRAVEN --

THE LESSON

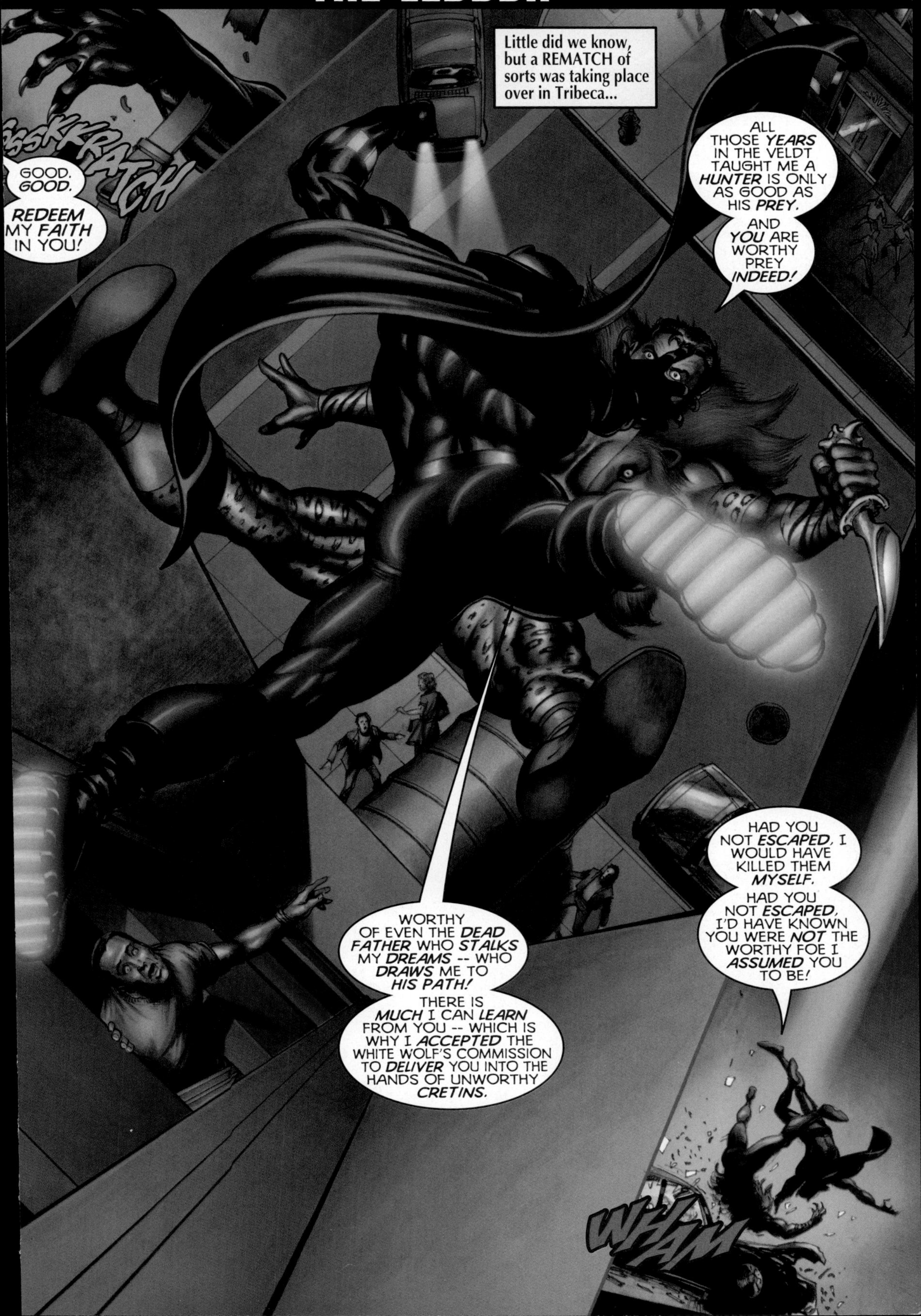

Little did we know, but a REMATCH of sorts was taking place over in Tribeca...
SSSKKRATCH
GOOD. GOOD.
REDEEM MY FAITH IN YOU!
ALL THOSE YEARS IN THE VELDT TAUGHT ME A HUNTER IS ONLY AS GOOD AS HIS PREY.
AND YOU ARE WORTHY PREY INDEED!
WORTHY OF EVEN THE DEAD FATHER WHO STALKS MY DREAMS -- WHO DRAWS ME TO HIS PATH!
THERE IS MUCH I CAN LEARN FROM YOU -- WHICH IS WHY I ACCEPTED THE WHITE WOLF'S COMMISSION TO DELIVER YOU INTO THE HANDS OF UNWORTHY CRETINS.
HAD YOU NOT ESCAPED, I WOULD HAVE KILLED THEM MYSELF.
HAD YOU NOT ESCAPED, I'D HAVE KNOWN YOU WERE NOT THE WORTHY FOE I ASSUMED YOU TO BE!
WHAM

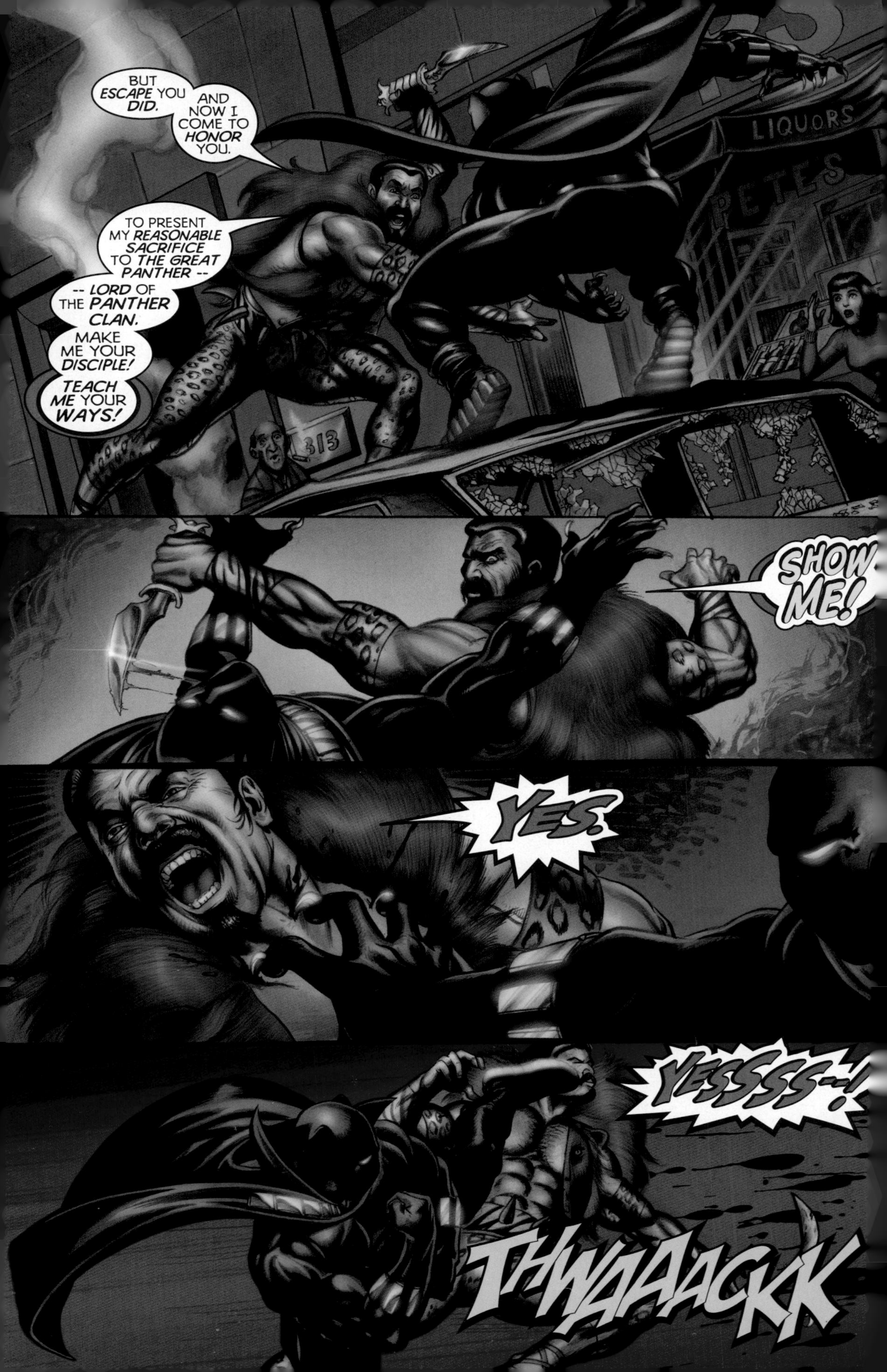

BUT ESCAPE YOU DID.
AND NOW I COME TO HONOR YOU.
TO PRESENT MY REASONABLE SACRIFICE TO THE GREAT PANTHER --
-- LORD OF THE PANTHER CLAN.
MAKE ME YOUR DISCIPLE!
TEACH ME YOUR WAYS!
LIQUORS
PETES
313
SHOW ME!
YES.
YESSSS--!
THWAAACKK

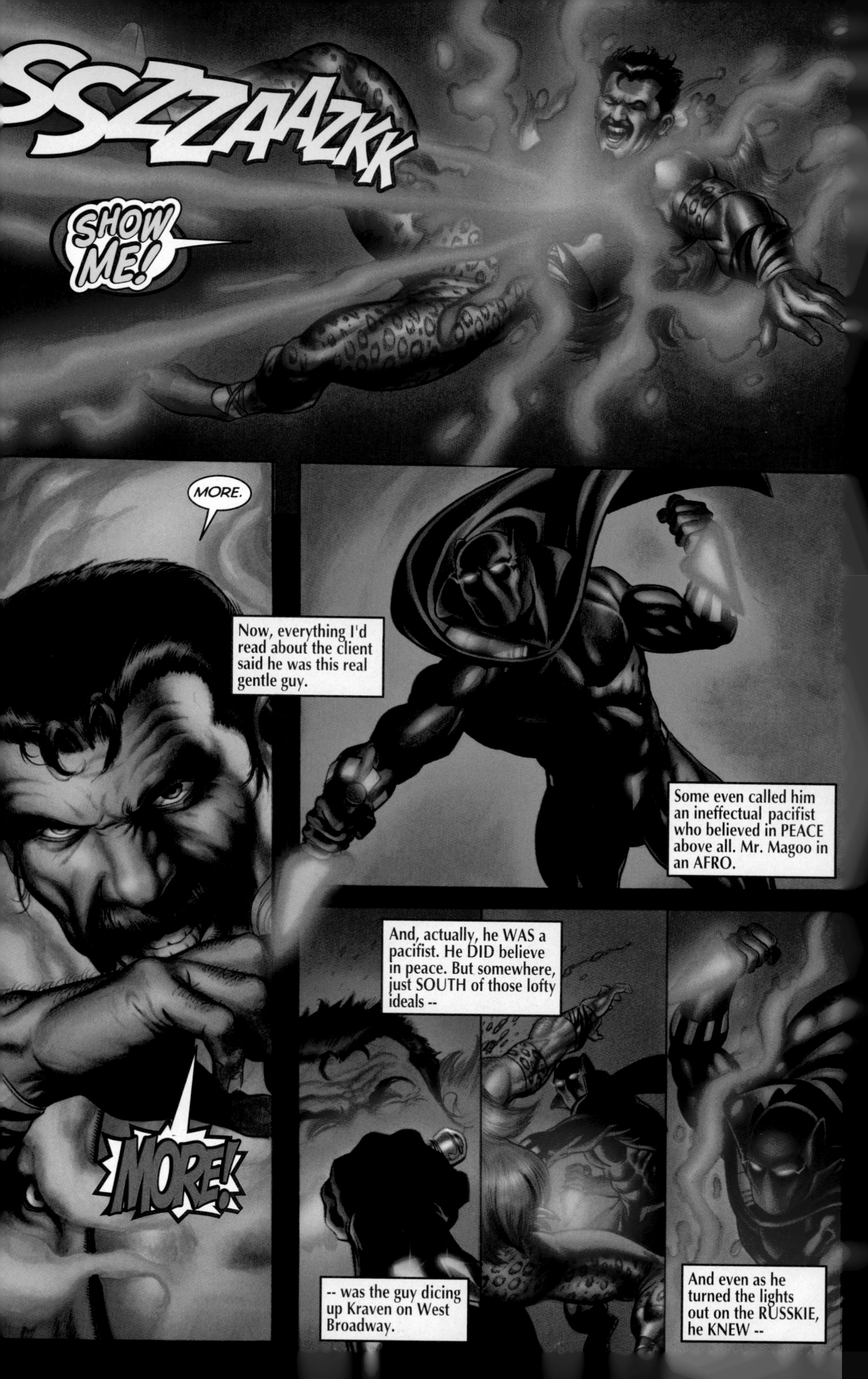
SSZZAAZKK
SHOW ME!
MORE.
Now, everything I'd read about the client said he was this real gentle guy.
Some even called him an ineffectual pacifist who believed in PEACE above all. Mr. Magoo in an AFRO.
MORE!
And, actually, he WAS a pacifist. He DID believe in peace. But somewhere, just SOUTH of those lofty ideals --
-- was the guy dicing up Kraven on West Broadway.
And even as he turned the lights out on the RUSSKIE, he KNEW --

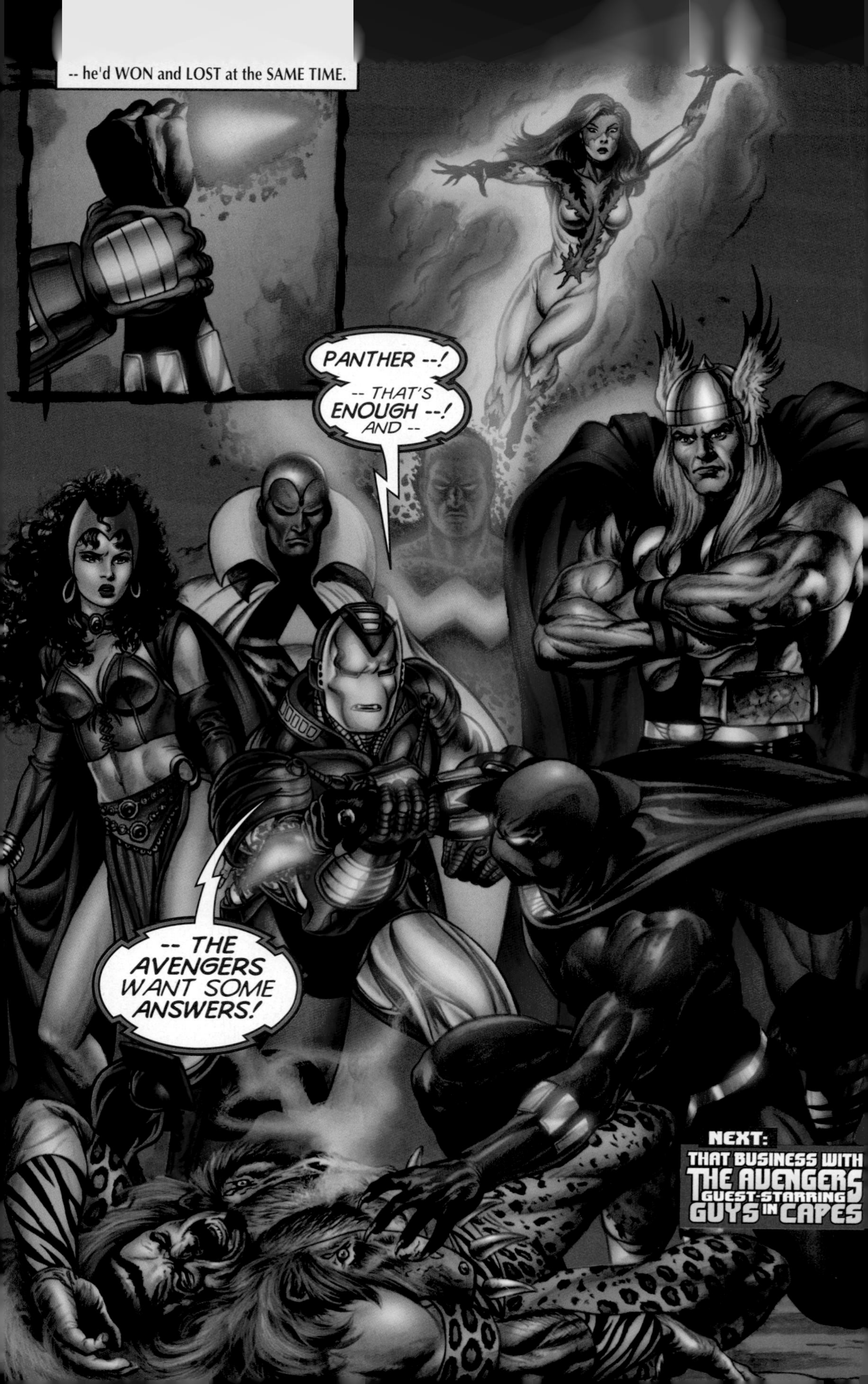
-- he'd WON and LOST at the SAME TIME.
PANTHER --! -- THAT'S ENOUGH --! AND --
-- THE AVENGERS WANT SOME ANSWERS!
NEXT:
THAT BUSINESS WITH THE AVENGERS GUEST-STARRING GUYS IN CAPES

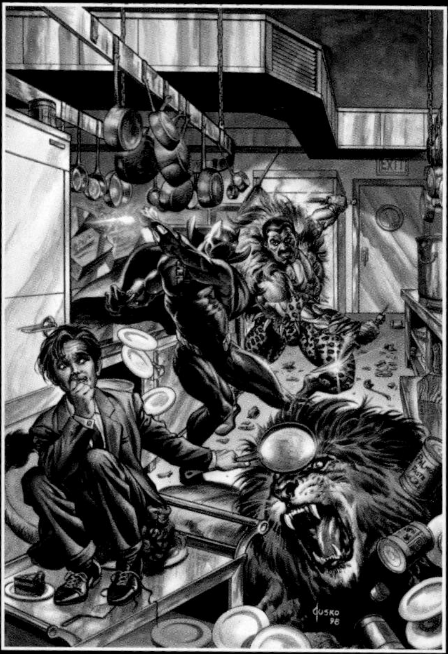
EXIT
JUSKO 98

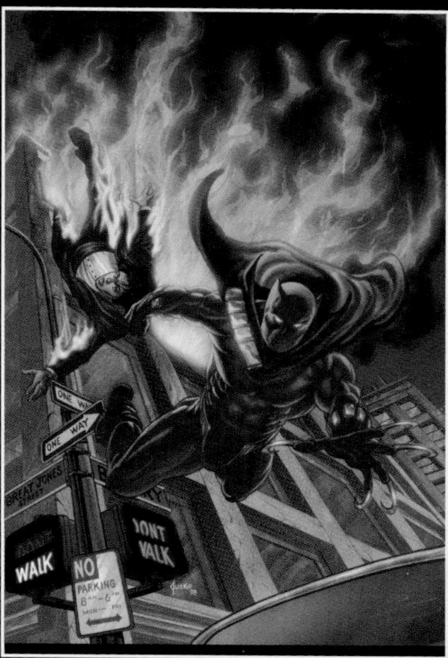
ONE WAY
ONE WAY
GREAT JONES
DONT WALK
WALK
NO PARKING

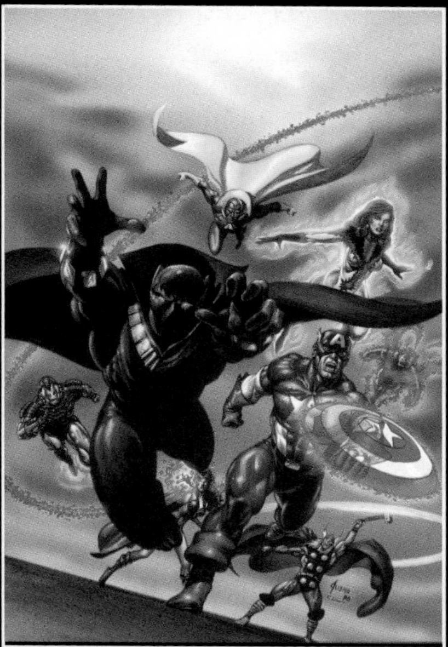

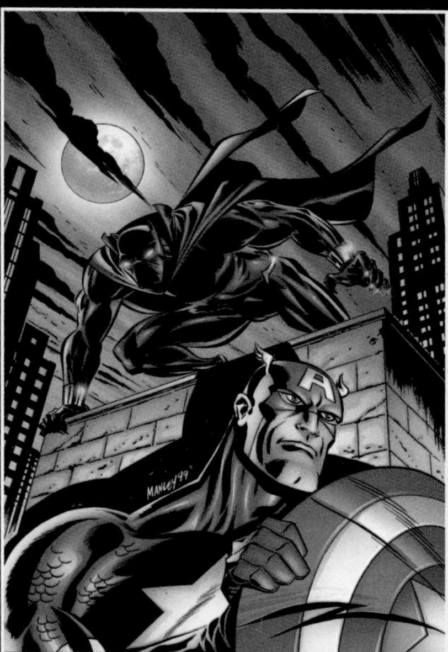
MANLEY 99

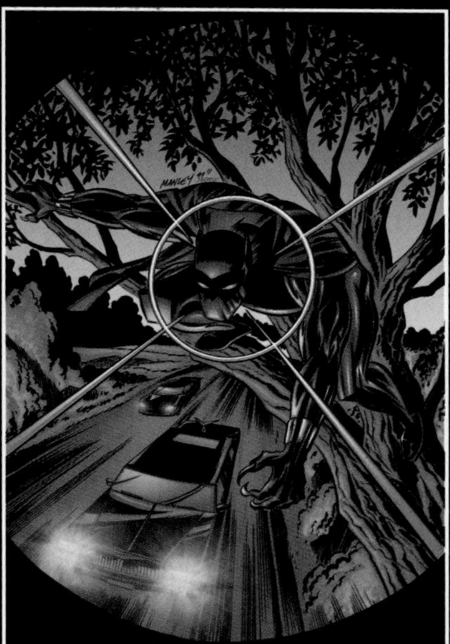

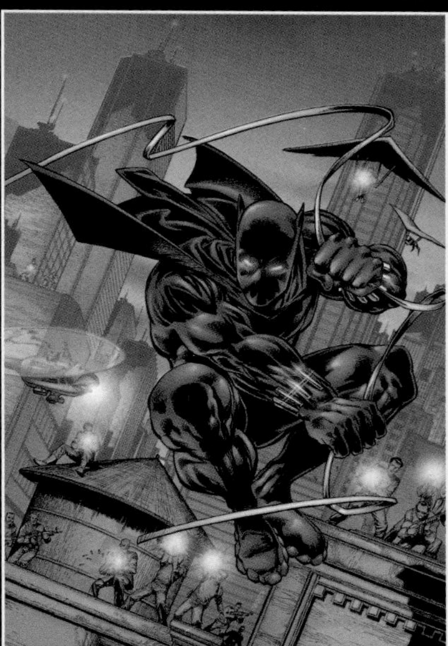

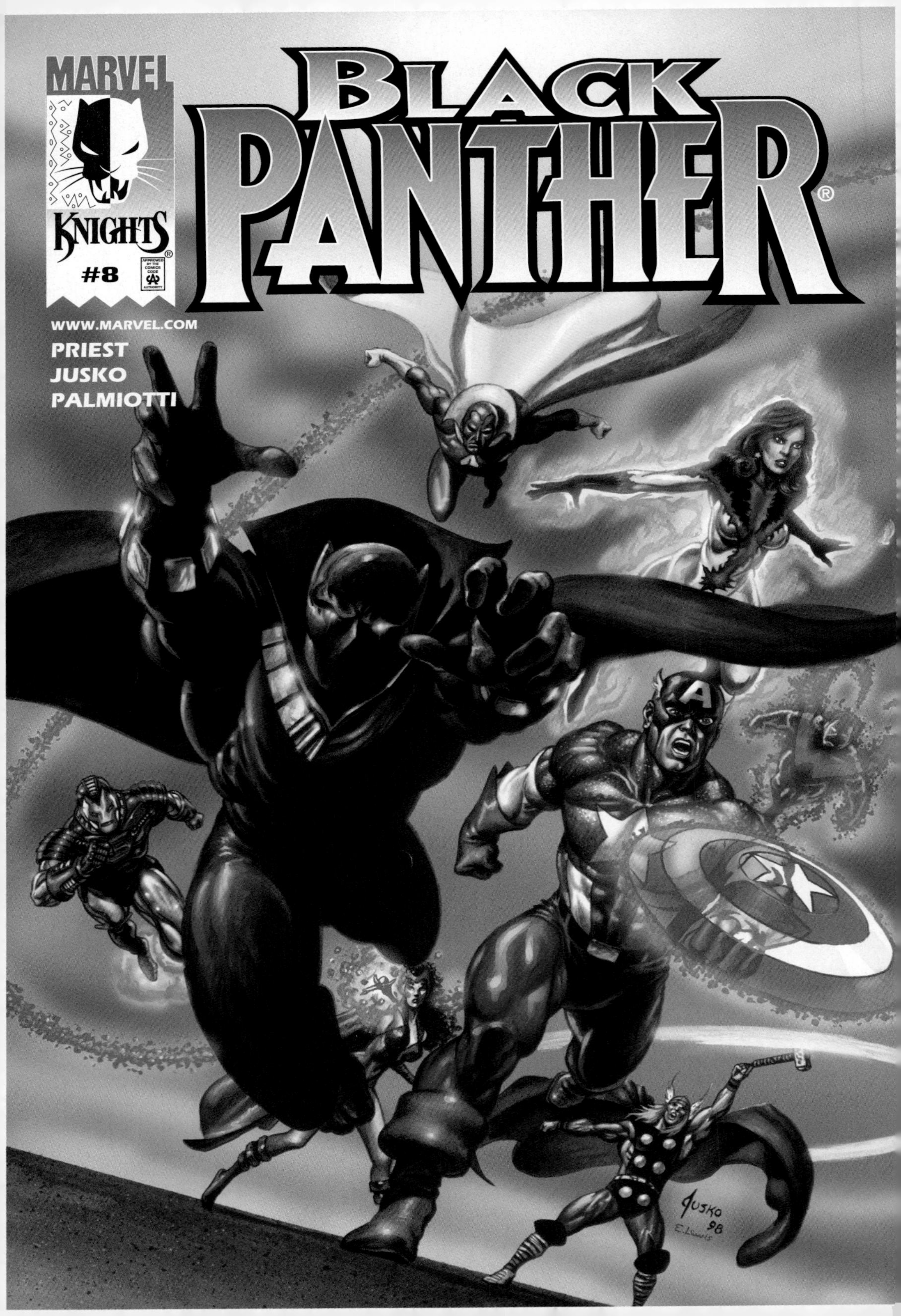
MARVEL
KNIGHTS
BLACK PANTHER
#8
APPROVED BY THE COMICS CODE AUTHORITY
WWW.MARVEL.COM
PRIEST
JUSKO
PALMIOTTI
JUSKO 98
E. Lewis

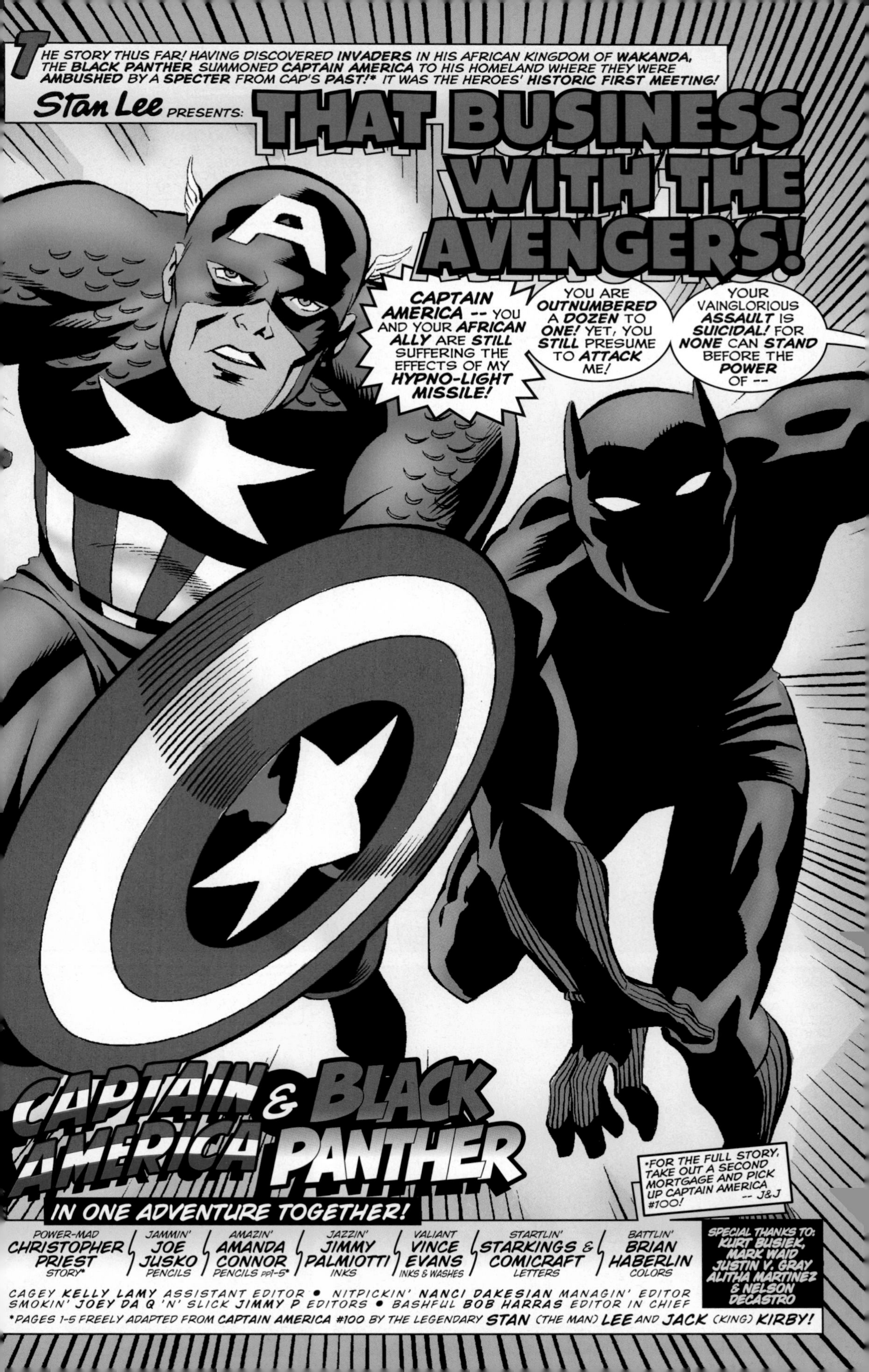
THE STORY THUS FAR! HAVING DISCOVERED INVADERS IN HIS AFRICAN KINGDOM OF WAKANDA, THE BLACK PANTHER SUMMONED CAPTAIN AMERICA TO HIS HOMELAND WHERE THEY WERE AMBUSHED BY A SPECTER FROM CAP'S PAST!* IT WAS THE HEROES' HISTORIC FIRST MEETING!
Stan Lee PRESENTS: THAT BUSINESS WITH THE AVENGERS!
CAPTAIN AMERICA -- YOU AND YOUR AFRICAN ALLY ARE STILL SUFFERING THE EFFECTS OF MY HYPNO-LIGHT MISSILE!
YOU ARE OUTNUMBERED A DOZEN TO ONE! YET, YOU STILL PRESUME TO ATTACK ME!
YOUR VAINGLORIOUS ASSAULT IS SUICIDAL! FOR NONE CAN STAND BEFORE THE POWER OF --
CAPTAIN AMERICA & BLACK PANTHER
IN ONE ADVENTURE TOGETHER!
*FOR THE FULL STORY, TAKE OUT A SECOND MORTGAGE AND PICK UP CAPTAIN AMERICA #100! -- J&J
POWER-MAD CHRISTOPHER PRIEST STORY*
JAMMIN' JOE JUSKO PENCILS
AMAZIN' AMANDA CONNOR PENCILS pp1-5*
JAZZIN' JIMMY PALMIOTTI INKS
VALIANT VINCE EVANS INKS & WASHES
STARTLIN' STARKINGS & COMICRAFT LETTERS
BATTLIN' BRIAN HABERLIN COLORS
SPECIAL THANKS TO: KURT BUSIEK, MARK WAID JUSTIN V. GRAY ALITHA MARTINEZ & NELSON DECASTRO
CAGEY KELLY LAMY ASSISTANT EDITOR • NITPICKIN' NANCI DAKESIAN MANAGIN' EDITOR
SMOKIN' JOEY DA Q 'N' SLICK JIMMY P EDITORS • BASHFUL BOB HARRAS EDITOR IN CHIEF
*PAGES 1-5 FREELY ADAPTED FROM CAPTAIN AMERICA #100 BY THE LEGENDARY STAN (THE MAN) LEE AND JACK (KING) KIRBY!

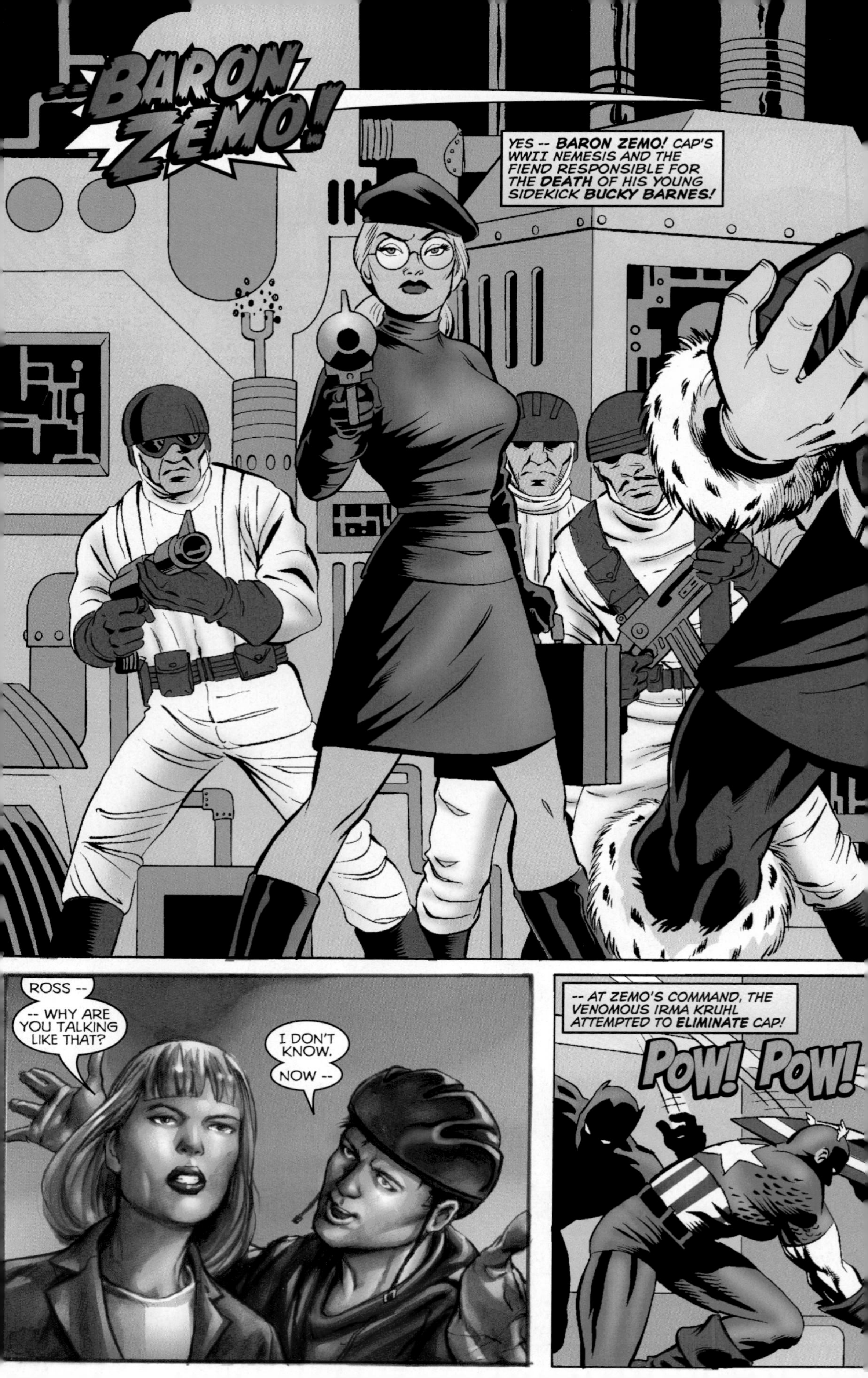
-- BARON ZEMO!
YES -- BARON ZEMO! CAP'S WWII NEMESIS AND THE FIEND RESPONSIBLE FOR THE DEATH OF HIS YOUNG SIDEKICK BUCKY BARNES!
ROSS --
-- WHY ARE YOU TALKING LIKE THAT?
I DON'T KNOW.
NOW --
-- AT ZEMO'S COMMAND, THE VENOMOUS IRMA KRUHL ATTEMPTED TO ELIMINATE CAP!
POW! POW!

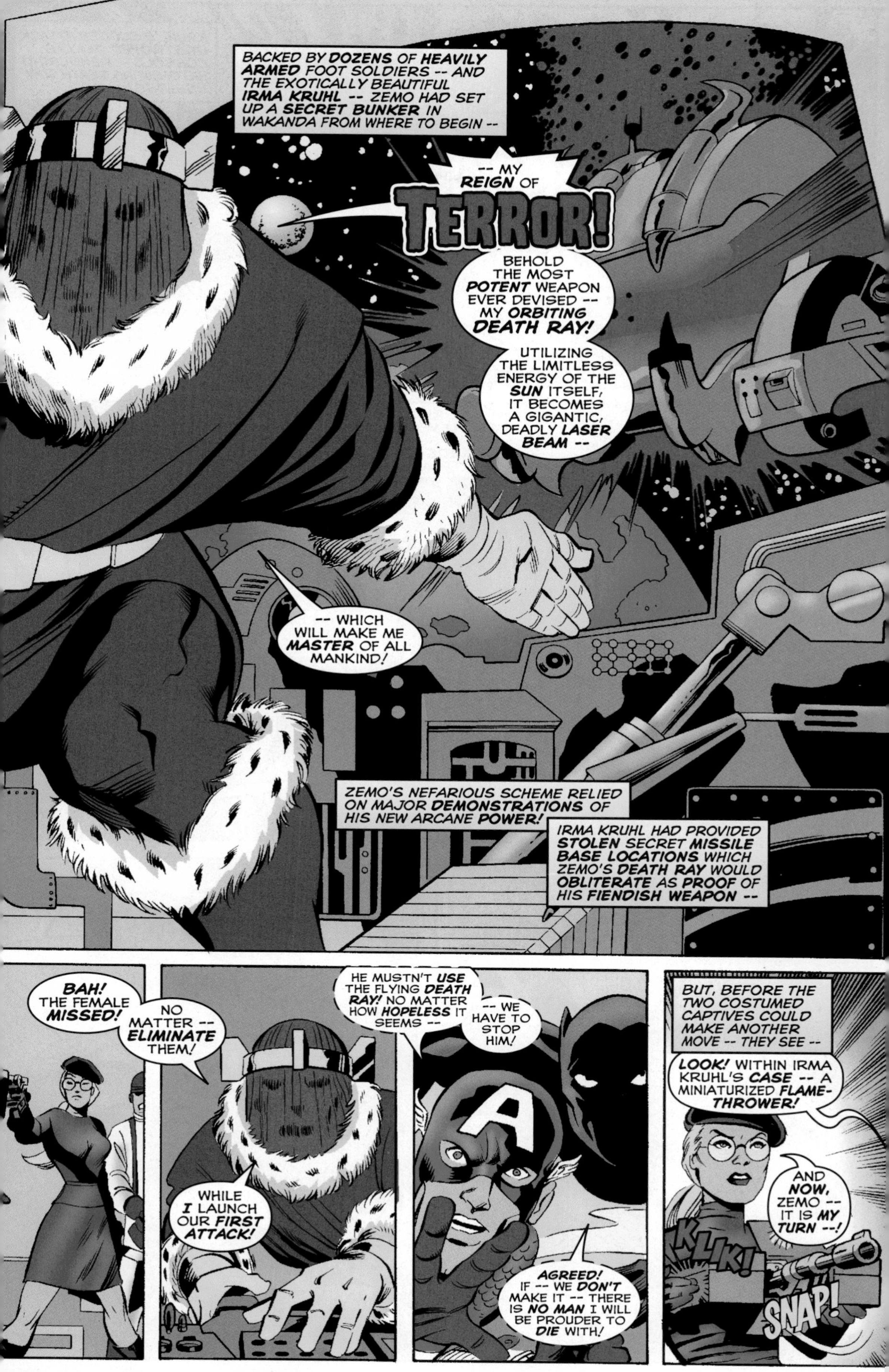
BACKED BY DOZENS OF HEAVILY ARMED FOOT SOLDIERS -- AND THE EXOTICALLY BEAUTIFUL IRMA KRUHL -- ZEMO HAD SET UP A SECRET BUNKER IN WAKANDA FROM WHERE TO BEGIN --
-- MY REIGN OF TERROR!
BEHOLD THE MOST POTENT WEAPON EVER DEVISED -- MY ORBITING DEATH RAY!
UTILIZING THE LIMITLESS ENERGY OF THE SUN ITSELF, IT BECOMES A GIGANTIC, DEADLY LASER BEAM --
-- WHICH WILL MAKE ME MASTER OF ALL MANKIND!
ZEMO'S NEFARIOUS SCHEME RELIED ON MAJOR DEMONSTRATIONS OF HIS NEW ARCANE POWER!
IRMA KRUHL HAD PROVIDED STOLEN SECRET MISSILE BASE LOCATIONS WHICH ZEMO'S DEATH RAY WOULD OBLITERATE AS PROOF OF HIS FIENDISH WEAPON --
BAH! THE FEMALE MISSED!
NO MATTER -- ELIMINATE THEM!
WHILE I LAUNCH OUR FIRST ATTACK!
HE MUSTN'T USE THE FLYING DEATH RAY! NO MATTER HOW HOPELESS IT SEEMS --
-- WE HAVE TO STOP HIM!
AGREED! IF -- WE DON'T MAKE IT -- THERE IS NO MAN I WILL BE PROUDER TO DIE WITH!
BUT, BEFORE THE TWO COSTUMED CAPTIVES COULD MAKE ANOTHER MOVE -- THEY SEE --
LOOK! WITHIN IRMA KRUHL'S CASE -- A MINIATURIZED FLAME-THROWER!
AND NOW, ZEMO -- IT IS MY TURN --!
KLIK!
SNAP!

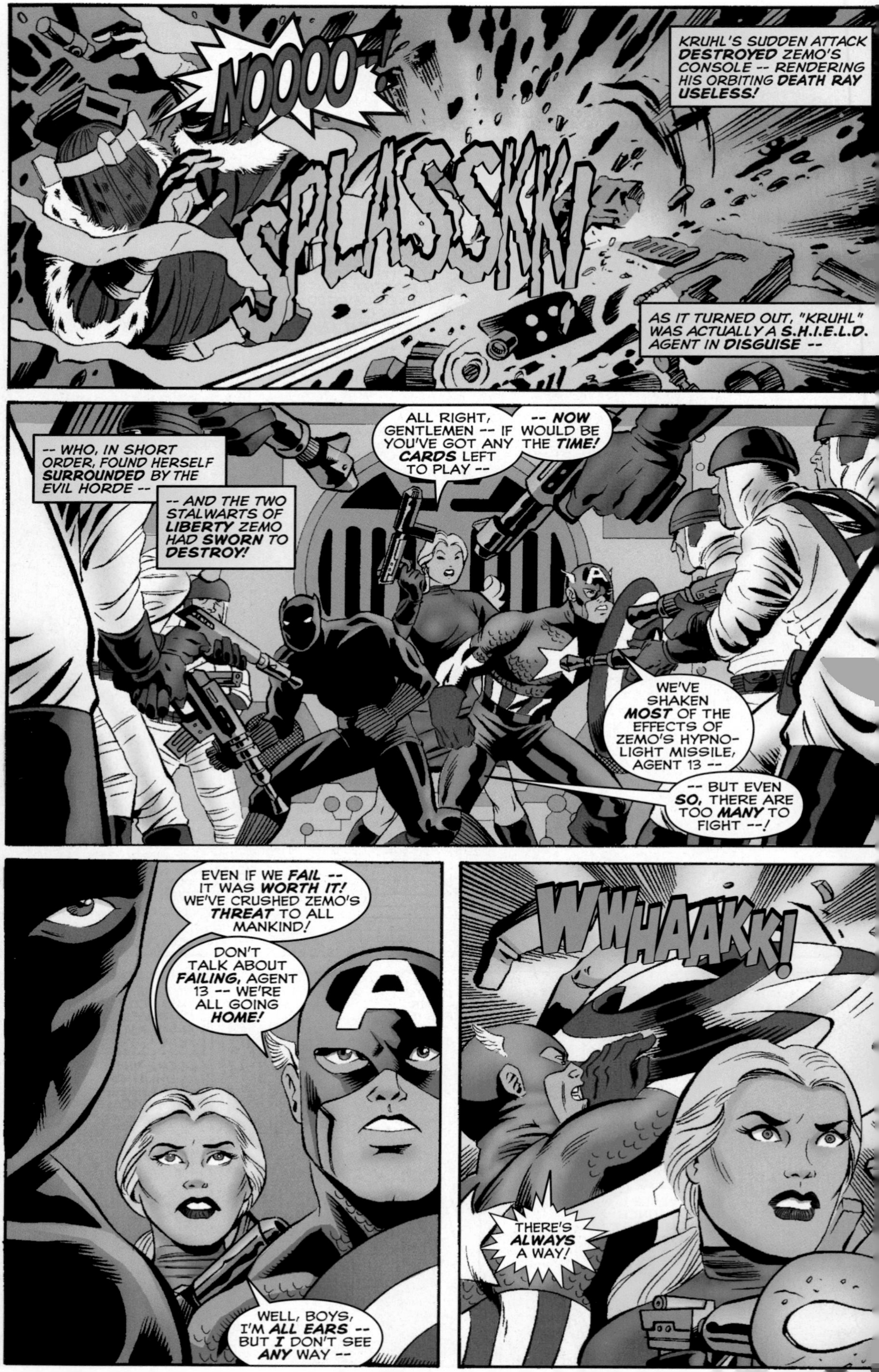

NOOOO--!
KRUHL'S SUDDEN ATTACK DESTROYED ZEMO'S CONSOLE -- RENDERING HIS ORBITING DEATH RAY USELESS!
SPLASSKK!
AS IT TURNED OUT, "KRUHL" WAS ACTUALLY A S.H.I.E.L.D. AGENT IN DISGUISE --
-- WHO, IN SHORT ORDER, FOUND HERSELF SURROUNDED BY THE EVIL HORDE --
-- AND THE TWO STALWARTS OF LIBERTY ZEMO HAD SWORN TO DESTROY!
ALL RIGHT, GENTLEMEN -- IF YOU'VE GOT ANY CARDS LEFT TO PLAY --
-- NOW WOULD BE THE TIME!
WE'VE SHAKEN MOST OF THE EFFECTS OF ZEMO'S HYPNO-LIGHT MISSILE, AGENT 13 --
-- BUT EVEN SO, THERE ARE TOO MANY TO FIGHT --!
EVEN IF WE FAIL -- IT WAS WORTH IT! WE'VE CRUSHED ZEMO'S THREAT TO ALL MANKIND!
DON'T TALK ABOUT FAILING, AGENT 13 -- WE'RE ALL GOING HOME!
WELL, BOYS, I'M ALL EARS -- BUT I DON'T SEE ANY WAY --
WWHAAKK!
THERE'S ALWAYS A WAY!

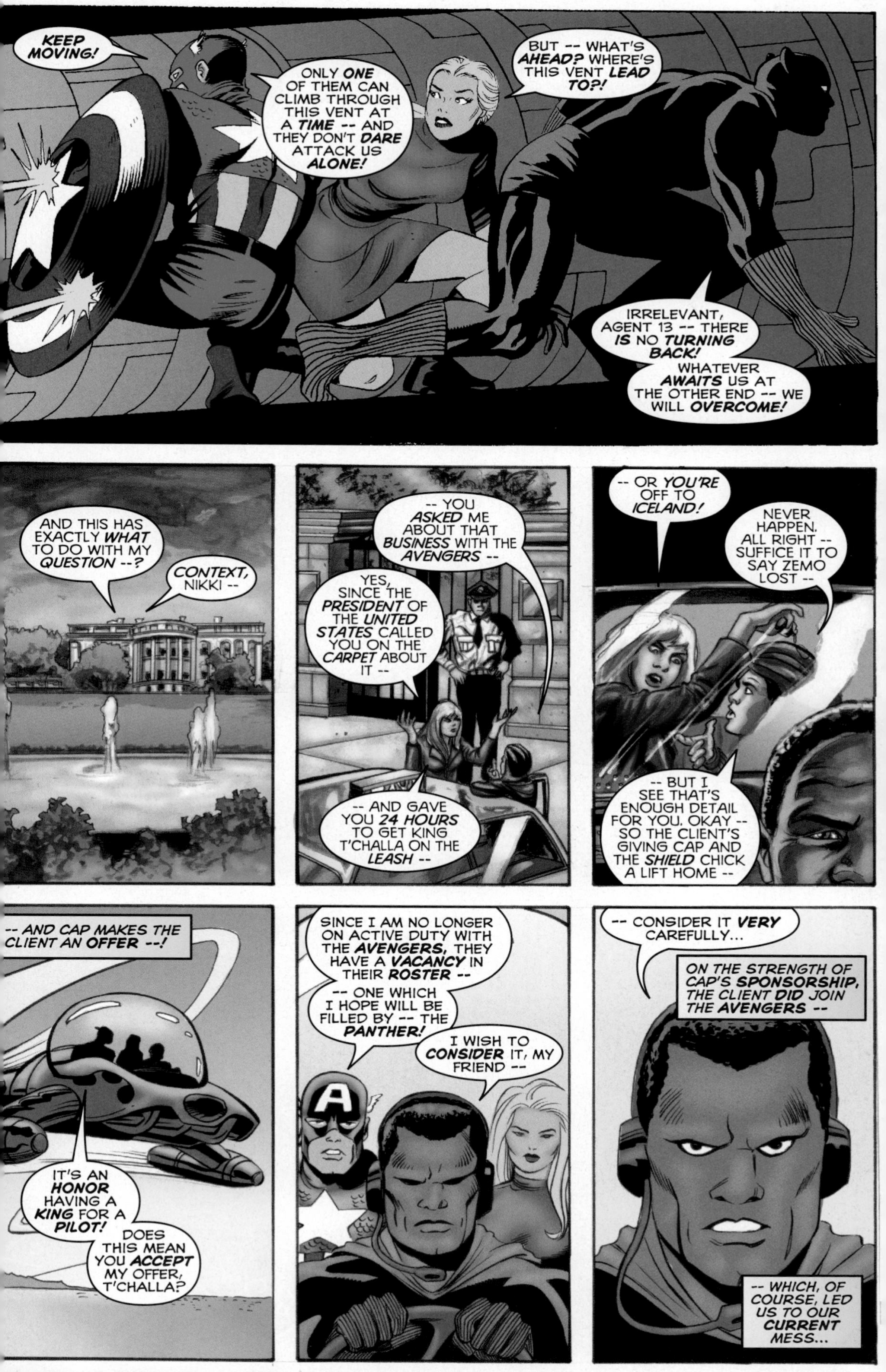
KEEP MOVING!
ONLY ONE OF THEM CAN CLIMB THROUGH THIS VENT AT A TIME -- AND THEY DON'T DARE ATTACK US ALONE!
BUT -- WHAT'S AHEAD? WHERE'S THIS VENT LEAD TO?!
IRRELEVANT, AGENT 13 -- THERE IS NO TURNING BACK!
WHATEVER AWAITS US AT THE OTHER END -- WE WILL OVERCOME!
AND THIS HAS EXACTLY WHAT TO DO WITH MY QUESTION --?
CONTEXT, NIKKI --
-- YOU ASKED ME ABOUT THAT BUSINESS WITH THE AVENGERS --
YES, SINCE THE PRESIDENT OF THE UNITED STATES CALLED YOU ON THE CARPET ABOUT IT --
-- AND GAVE YOU 24 HOURS TO GET KING T'CHALLA ON THE LEASH --
-- OR YOU'RE OFF TO ICELAND!
NEVER HAPPEN. ALL RIGHT -- SUFFICE IT TO SAY ZEMO LOST --
-- BUT I SEE THAT'S ENOUGH DETAIL FOR YOU. OKAY -- SO THE CLIENT'S GIVING CAP AND THE SHIELD CHICK A LIFT HOME --
-- AND CAP MAKES THE CLIENT AN OFFER --!
IT'S AN HONOR HAVING A KING FOR A PILOT!
DOES THIS MEAN YOU ACCEPT MY OFFER, T'CHALLA?
SINCE I AM NO LONGER ON ACTIVE DUTY WITH THE AVENGERS, THEY HAVE A VACANCY IN THEIR ROSTER --
-- ONE WHICH I HOPE WILL BE FILLED BY -- THE PANTHER!
I WISH TO CONSIDER IT, MY FRIEND --
-- CONSIDER IT VERY CAREFULLY...
ON THE STRENGTH OF CAP'S SPONSORSHIP, THE CLIENT DID JOIN THE AVENGERS --
-- WHICH, OF COURSE, LED US TO OUR CURRENT MESS...

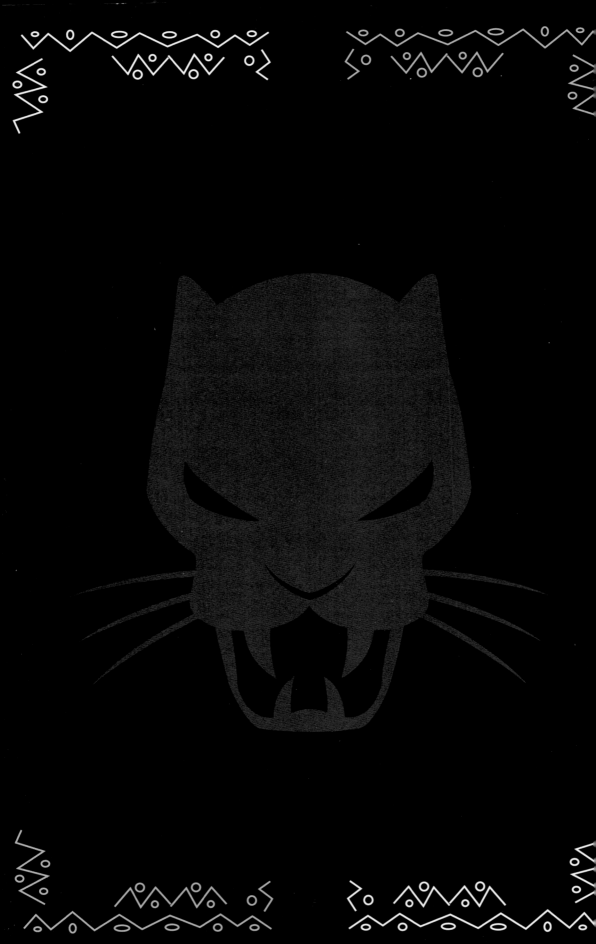

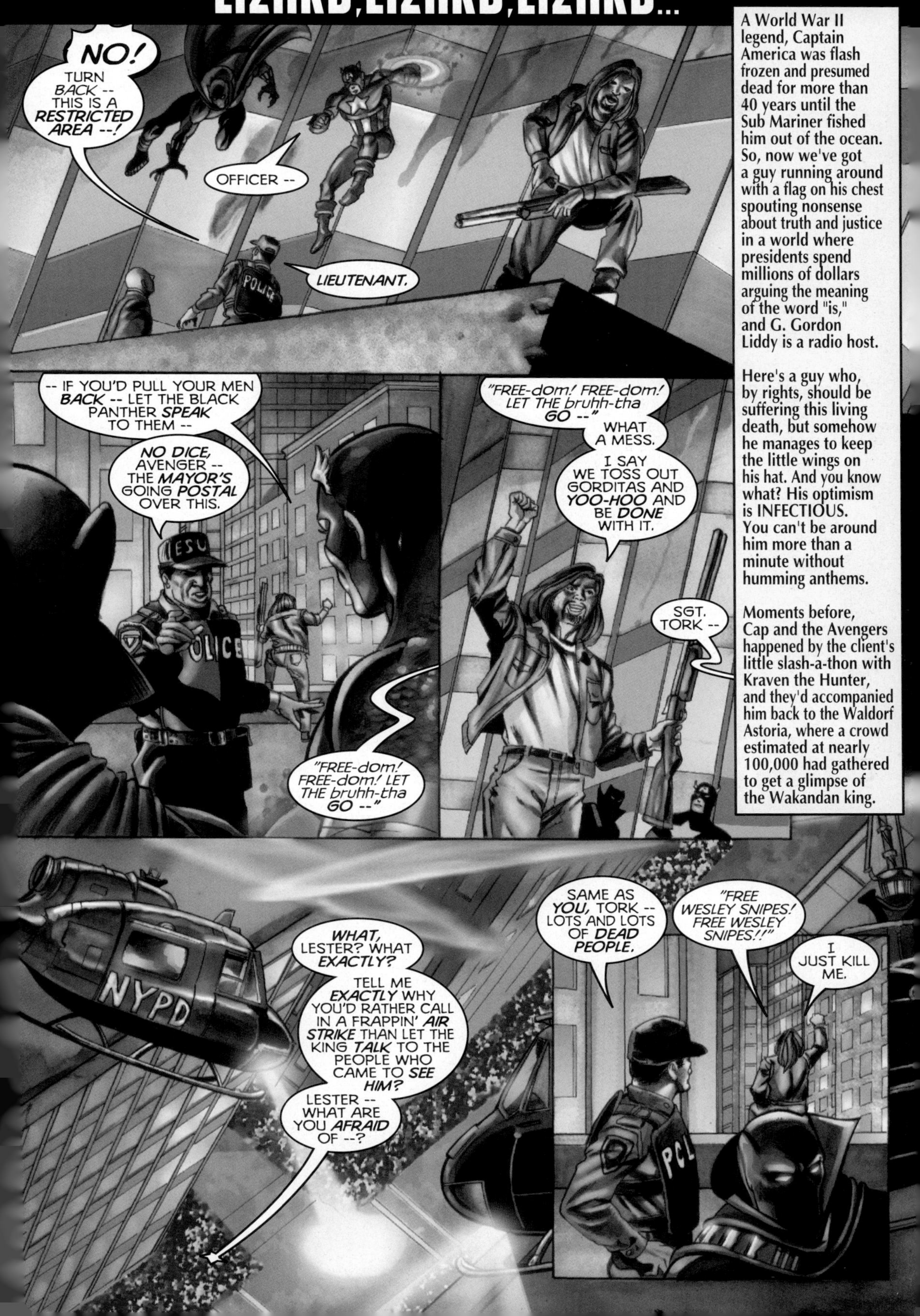

A World War II legend, Captain America was flash frozen and presumed dead for more than 40 years until the Sub Mariner fished him out of the ocean. So, now we've got a guy running around with a flag on his chest spouting nonsense about truth and justice in a world where presidents spend millions of dollars arguing the meaning of the word "is," and G. Gordon Liddy is a radio host.
Here's a guy who, by rights, should be suffering this living death, but somehow he manages to keep the little wings on his hat. And you know what? His optimism is INFECTIOUS. You can't be around him more than a minute without humming anthems.
Moments before, Cap and the Avengers happened by the client's little slash-a-thon with Kraven the Hunter, and they'd accompanied him back to the Waldorf Astoria, where a crowd estimated at nearly 100,000 had gathered to get a glimpse of the Wakandan king.
NO! TURN BACK -- THIS IS A RESTRICTED AREA --!
OFFICER --
LIEUTENANT.
-- IF YOU'D PULL YOUR MEN BACK -- LET THE BLACK PANTHER SPEAK TO THEM --
NO DICE, AVENGER -- THE MAYOR'S GOING POSTAL OVER THIS.
"FREE-dom! FREE-dom! LET THE bruhh-tha GO --"
"FREE-dom! FREE-dom! LET THE bruhh-tha GO --"
WHAT A MESS.
I SAY WE TOSS OUT GORDITAS AND YOO-HOO AND BE DONE WITH IT.
SGT. TORK --
NYPD
WHAT, LESTER? WHAT EXACTLY?
TELL ME EXACTLY WHY YOU'D RATHER CALL IN A FRAPPIN' AIR STRIKE THAN LET THE KING TALK TO THE PEOPLE WHO CAME TO SEE HIM?
LESTER -- WHAT ARE YOU AFRAID OF --?
SAME AS YOU, TORK -- LOTS AND LOTS OF DEAD PEOPLE.
"FREE WESLEY SNIPES! FREE WESLEY SNIPES!!"
I JUST KILL ME.

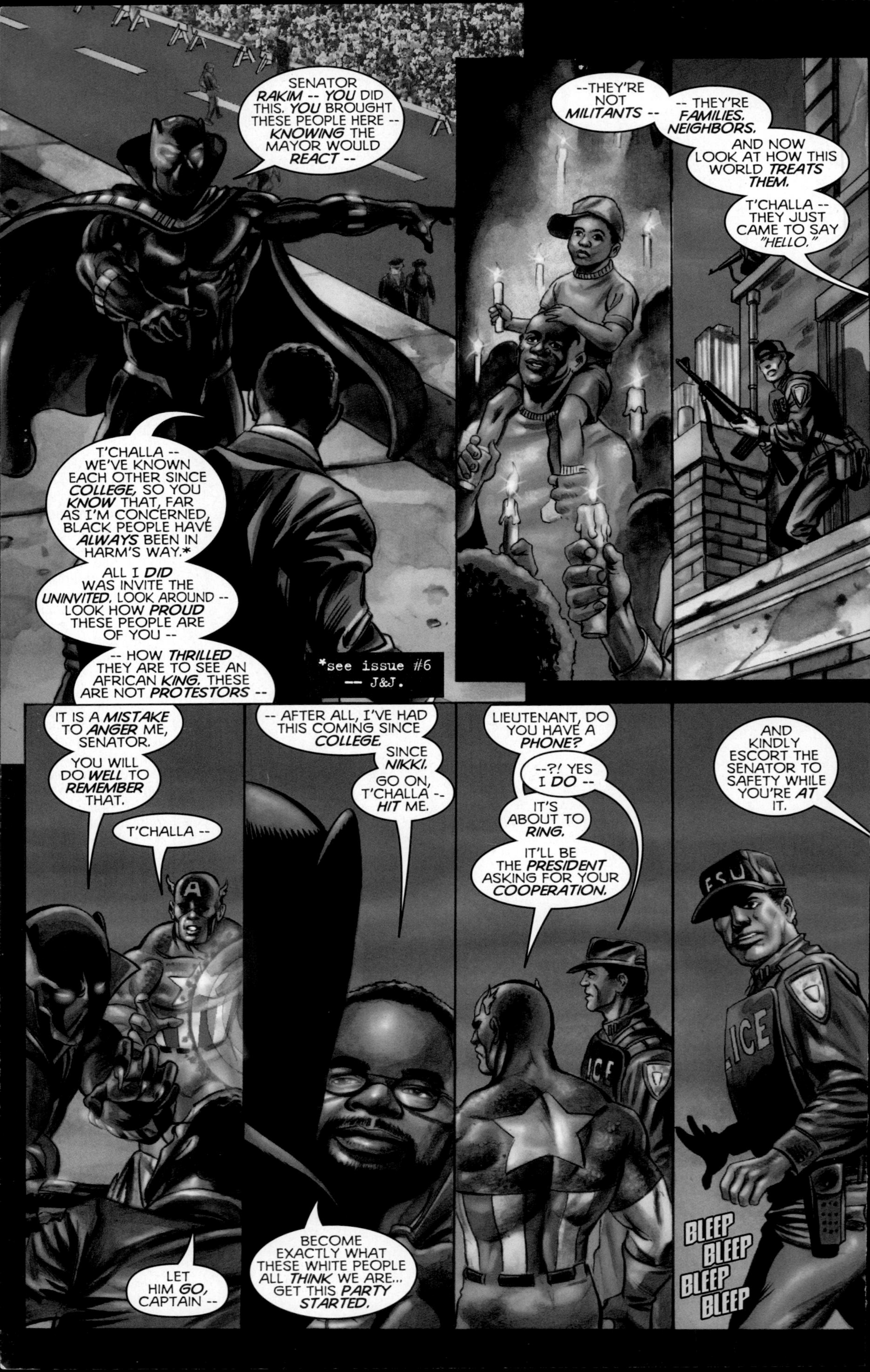
SENATOR RAKIM -- YOU DID THIS. YOU BROUGHT THESE PEOPLE HERE -- KNOWING THE MAYOR WOULD REACT --
T'CHALLA -- WE'VE KNOWN EACH OTHER SINCE COLLEGE, SO YOU KNOW THAT, FAR AS I'M CONCERNED, BLACK PEOPLE HAVE ALWAYS BEEN IN HARM'S WAY.*
ALL I DID WAS INVITE THE UNINVITED. LOOK AROUND -- LOOK HOW PROUD THESE PEOPLE ARE OF YOU --
-- HOW THRILLED THEY ARE TO SEE AN AFRICAN KING. THESE ARE NOT PROTESTORS --
*see issue #6 -- J&J.
--THEY'RE NOT MILITANTS --
-- THEY'RE FAMILIES, NEIGHBORS.
AND NOW LOOK AT HOW THIS WORLD TREATS THEM.
T'CHALLA -- THEY JUST CAME TO SAY "HELLO."
IT IS A MISTAKE TO ANGER ME, SENATOR.
YOU WILL DO WELL TO REMEMBER THAT.
T'CHALLA --
LET HIM GO, CAPTAIN --
-- AFTER ALL, I'VE HAD THIS COMING SINCE COLLEGE.
SINCE NIKKI.
GO ON, T'CHALLA -- HIT ME.
BECOME EXACTLY WHAT THESE WHITE PEOPLE ALL THINK WE ARE... GET THIS PARTY STARTED.
LIEUTENANT, DO YOU HAVE A PHONE?
--?! YES I DO --
IT'S ABOUT TO RING.
IT'LL BE THE PRESIDENT ASKING FOR YOUR COOPERATION.
AND KINDLY ESCORT THE SENATOR TO SAFETY WHILE YOU'RE AT IT.
BLEEP BLEEP BLEEP BLEEP

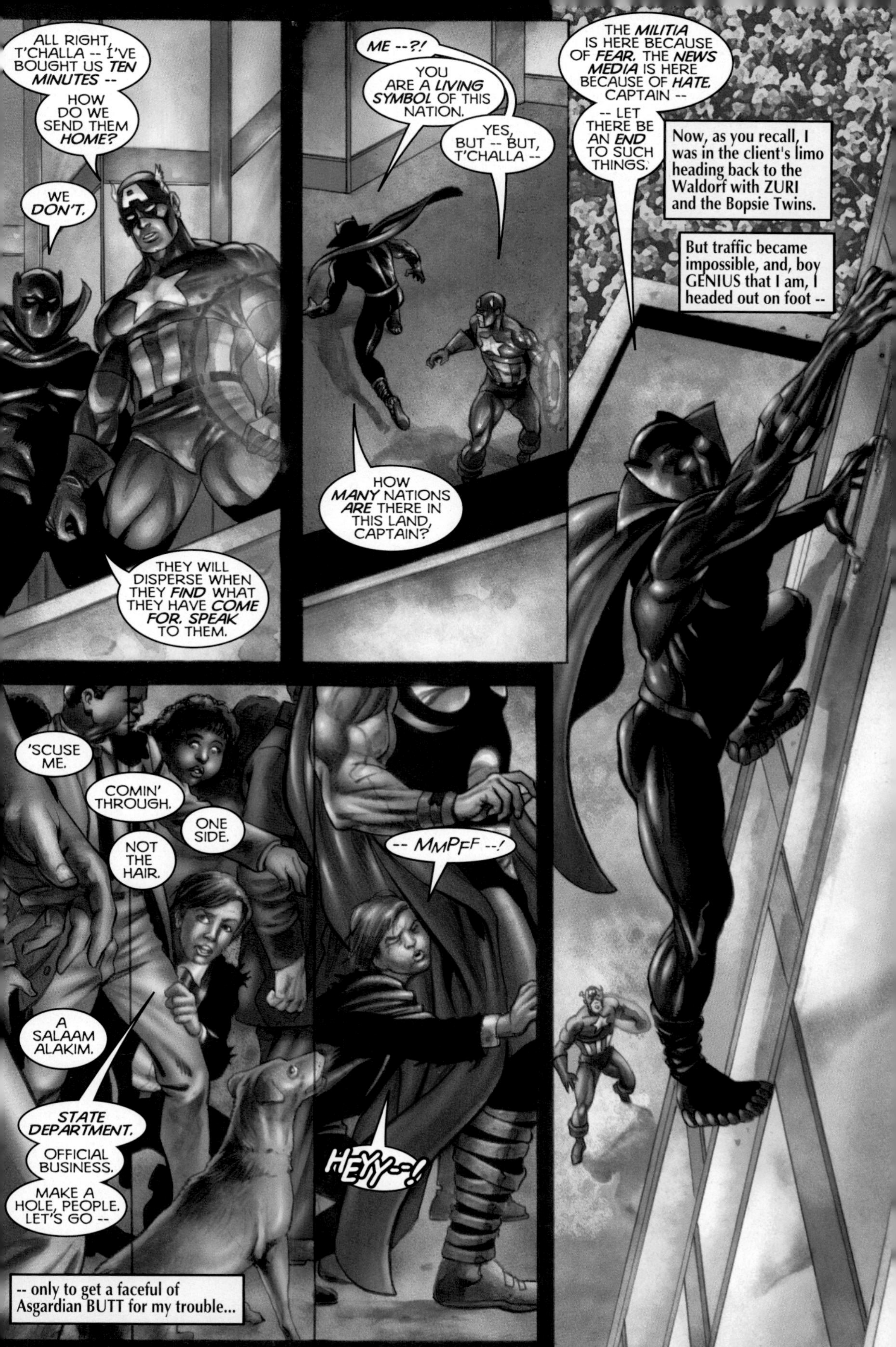
ALL RIGHT, T'CHALLA -- I'VE BOUGHT US TEN MINUTES --
HOW DO WE SEND THEM HOME?
WE DON'T.
THEY WILL DISPERSE WHEN THEY FIND WHAT THEY HAVE COME FOR. SPEAK TO THEM.
ME --?!
YOU ARE A LIVING SYMBOL OF THIS NATION.
YES, BUT -- BUT, T'CHALLA --
HOW MANY NATIONS ARE THERE IN THIS LAND, CAPTAIN?
THE MILITIA IS HERE BECAUSE OF FEAR. THE NEWS MEDIA IS HERE BECAUSE OF HATE, CAPTAIN --
-- LET THERE BE AN END TO SUCH THINGS.
Now, as you recall, I was in the client's limo heading back to the Waldorf with ZURI and the Bopsie Twins.
But traffic became impossible, and, boy GENIUS that I am, I headed out on foot --
'SCUSE ME.
COMIN' THROUGH.
ONE SIDE.
NOT THE HAIR.
A SALAAM ALAKIM.
STATE DEPARTMENT.
OFFICIAL BUSINESS.
MAKE A HOLE, PEOPLE. LET'S GO --
-- MMPFF --!
HEYY--!
-- only to get a faceful of Asgardian BUTT for my trouble...

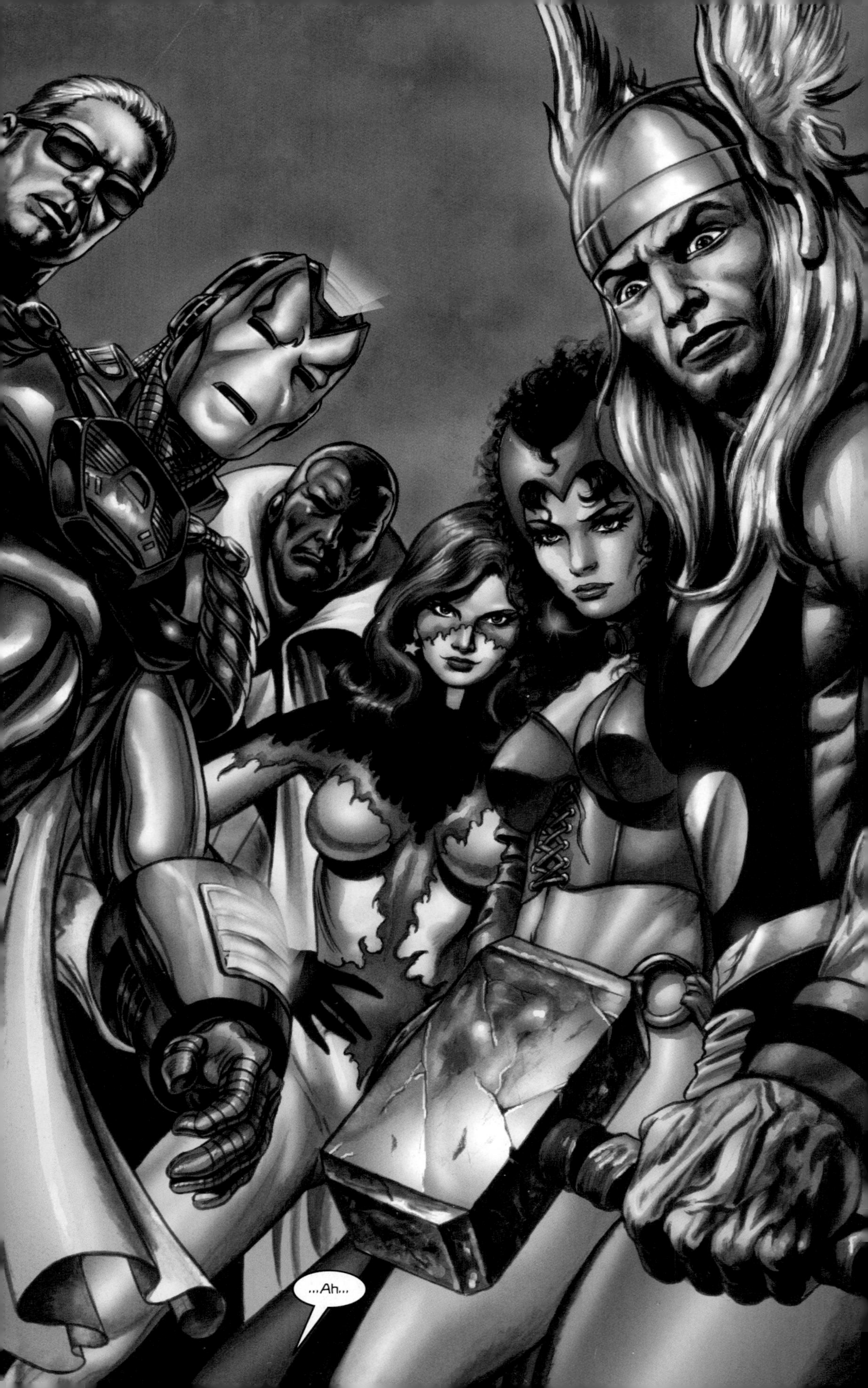
...Ah...

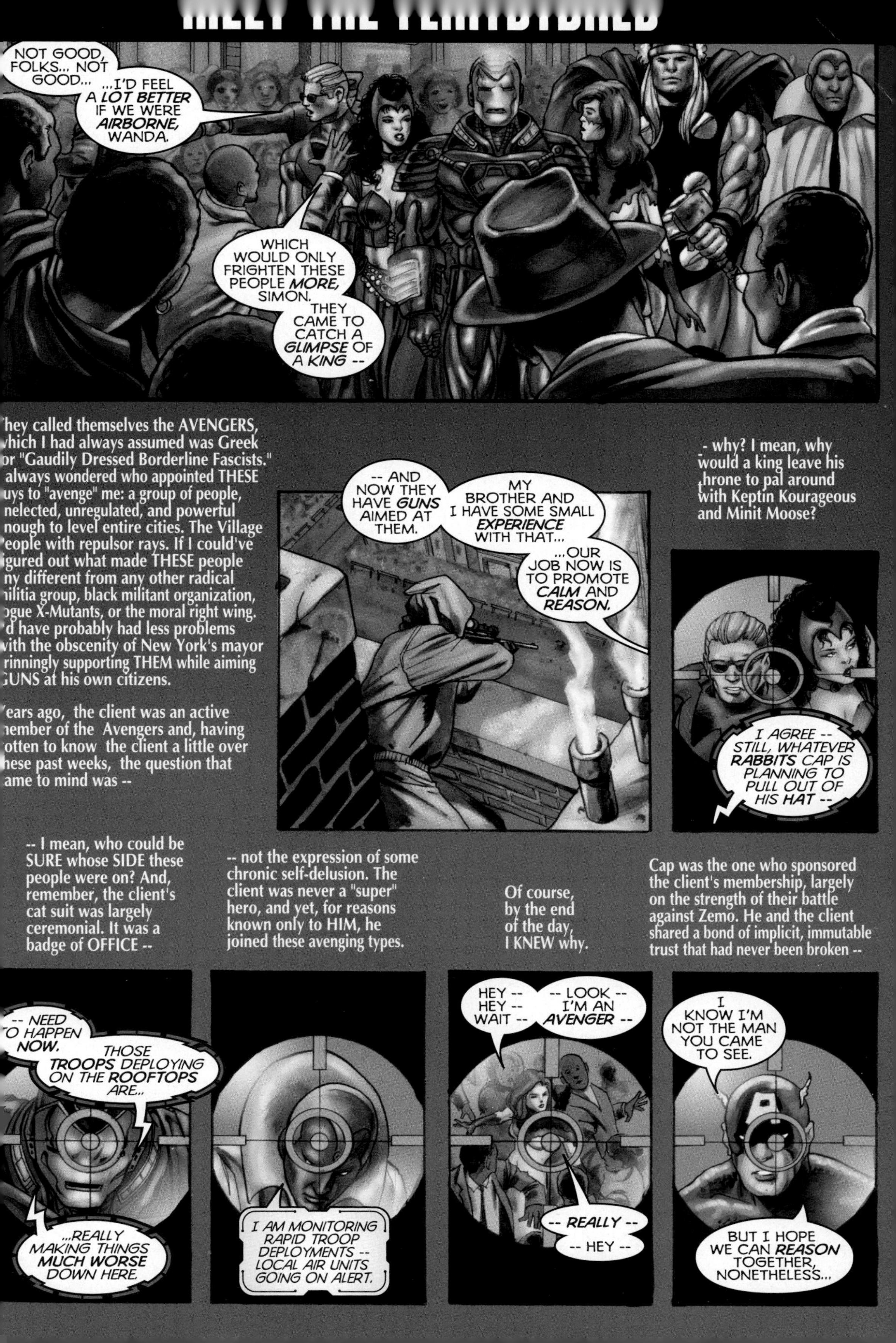

NOT GOOD, FOLKS... NOT GOOD...
...I'D FEEL A LOT BETTER IF WE WERE AIRBORNE, WANDA.
WHICH WOULD ONLY FRIGHTEN THESE PEOPLE MORE, SIMON.
THEY CAME TO CATCH A GLIMPSE OF A KING --
'hey called themselves the AVENGERS, vhich I had always assumed was Greek or "Gaudily Dressed Borderline Fascists." always wondered who appointed THESE uys to "avenge" me: a group of people, nelected, unregulated, and powerful nough to level entire cities. The Village 'eople with repulsor rays. If I could've igured out what made THESE people ny different from any other radical nilitia group, black militant organization, ogue X-Mutants, or the moral right wing. 'd have probably had less problems vith the obscenity of New York's mayor rinningly supporting THEM while aiming GUNS at his own citizens.
'ears ago, the client was an active nember of the Avengers and, having otten to know the client a little over hese past weeks, the question that ame to mind was --
-- AND NOW THEY HAVE GUNS AIMED AT THEM.
MY BROTHER AND I HAVE SOME SMALL EXPERIENCE WITH THAT...
...OUR JOB NOW IS TO PROMOTE CALM AND REASON.
- why? I mean, why would a king leave his hrone to pal around with Keptin Kourageous and Minit Moose?
I AGREE -- STILL, WHATEVER RABBITS CAP IS PLANNING TO PULL OUT OF HIS HAT --
-- I mean, who could be SURE whose SIDE these people were on? And, remember, the client's cat suit was largely ceremonial. It was a badge of OFFICE --
-- not the expression of some chronic self-delusion. The client was never a "super" hero, and yet, for reasons known only to HIM, he joined these avenging types.
Of course, by the end of the day, I KNEW why.
Cap was the one who sponsored the client's membership, largely on the strength of their battle against Zemo. He and the client shared a bond of implicit, immutable trust that had never been broken --
-- NEED 'O HAPPEN NOW.
THOSE TROOPS DEPLOYING ON THE ROOFTOPS ARE...
...REALLY MAKING THINGS MUCH WORSE DOWN HERE.
I AM MONITORING RAPID TROOP DEPLOYMENTS -- LOCAL AIR UNITS GOING ON ALERT.
HEY -- HEY -- WAIT --
-- LOOK -- I'M AN AVENGER --
-- REALLY --
-- HEY --
I KNOW I'M NOT THE MAN YOU CAME TO SEE.
BUT I HOPE WE CAN REASON TOGETHER, NONETHELESS...

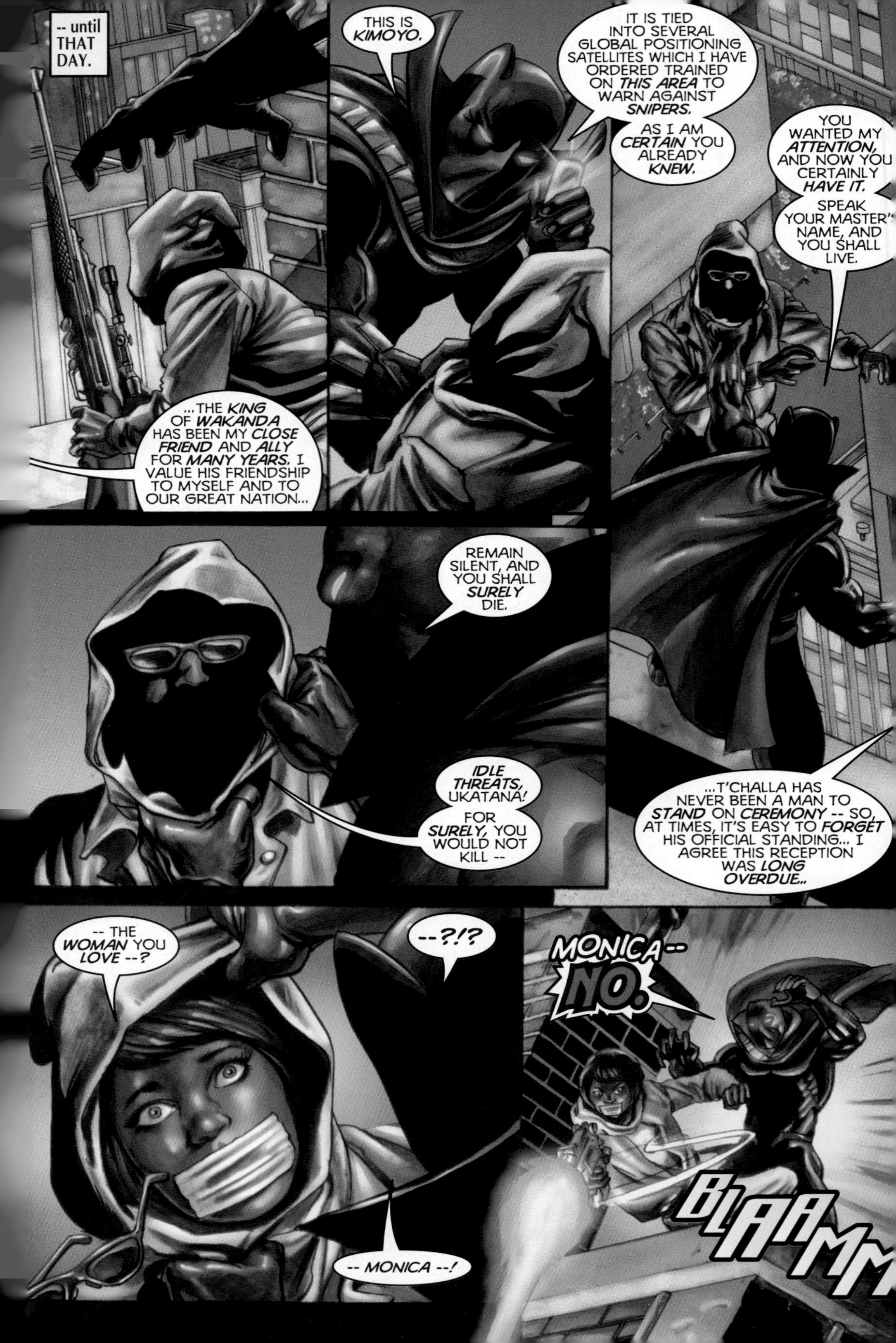
-- until THAT DAY.
...THE KING OF WAKANDA HAS BEEN MY CLOSE FRIEND AND ALLY FOR MANY YEARS. I VALUE HIS FRIENDSHIP TO MYSELF AND TO OUR GREAT NATION...
THIS IS KIMOYO.
IT IS TIED INTO SEVERAL GLOBAL POSITIONING SATELLITES WHICH I HAVE ORDERED TRAINED ON THIS AREA TO WARN AGAINST SNIPERS.
AS I AM CERTAIN YOU ALREADY KNEW.
YOU WANTED MY ATTENTION, AND NOW YOU CERTAINLY HAVE IT.
SPEAK YOUR MASTER'S NAME, AND YOU SHALL LIVE.
REMAIN SILENT, AND YOU SHALL SURELY DIE.
IDLE THREATS, UKATANA!
FOR SURELY, YOU WOULD NOT KILL --
...T'CHALLA HAS NEVER BEEN A MAN TO STAND ON CEREMONY -- SO, AT TIMES, IT'S EASY TO FORGET HIS OFFICIAL STANDING... I AGREE THIS RECEPTION WAS LONG OVERDUE...
-- THE WOMAN YOU LOVE --?
--?!?
-- MONICA --!
MONICA-- NO.
BLAAMM

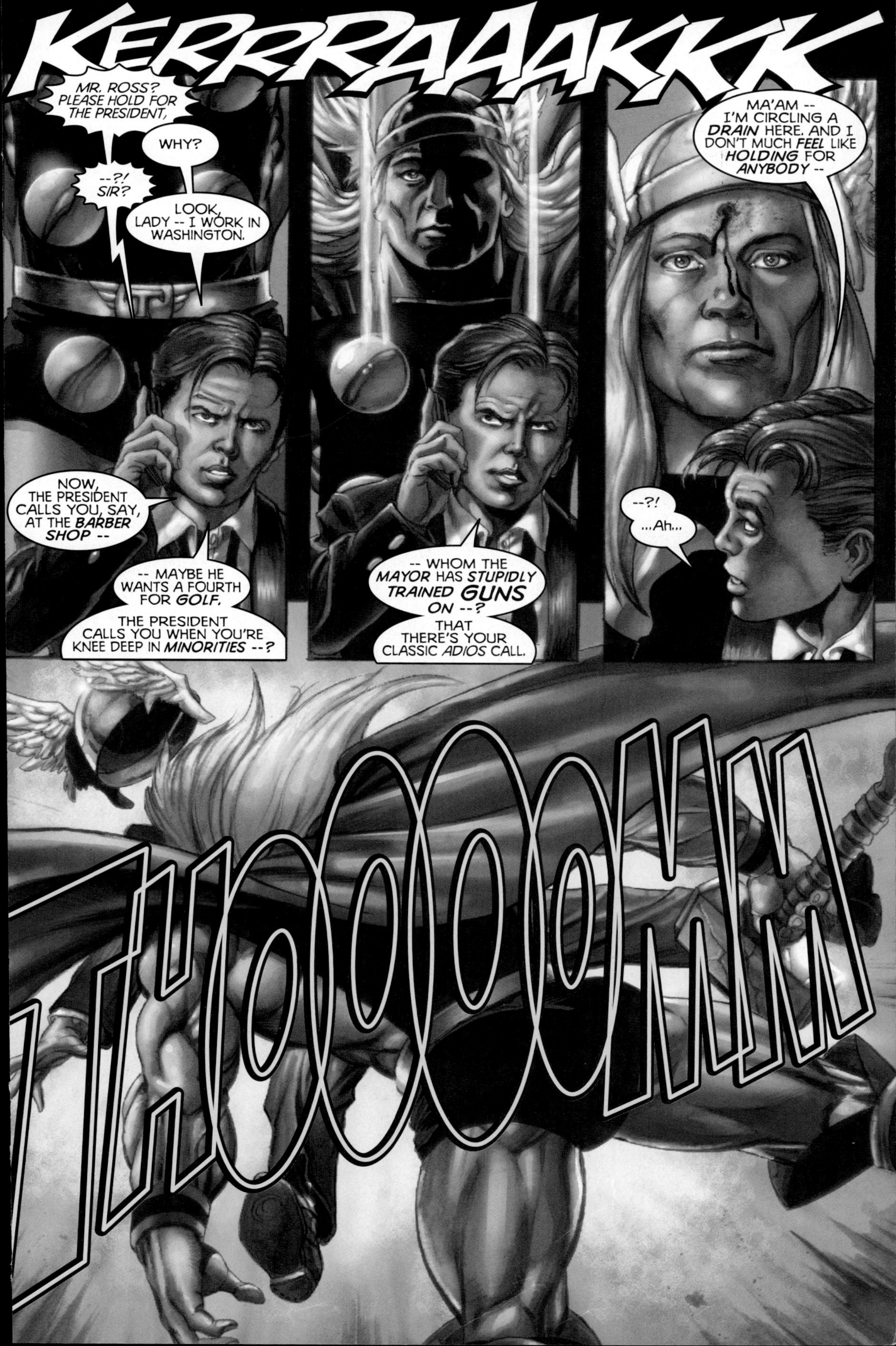
KERRRAAAKKK
MR. ROSS? PLEASE HOLD FOR THE PRESIDENT,
WHY?
--?! SIR?
LOOK, LADY -- I WORK IN WASHINGTON.
NOW, THE PRESIDENT CALLS YOU, SAY, AT THE BARBER SHOP --
-- MAYBE HE WANTS A FOURTH FOR GOLF.
THE PRESIDENT CALLS YOU WHEN YOU'RE KNEE DEEP IN MINORITIES --?
-- WHOM THE MAYOR HAS STUPIDLY TRAINED GUNS ON --?
THAT THERE'S YOUR CLASSIC ADIOS CALL.
MA'AM -- I'M CIRCLING A DRAIN HERE. AND I DON'T MUCH FEEL LIKE HOLDING FOR ANYBODY --
--?!
...Ah...
THOOOOOMM

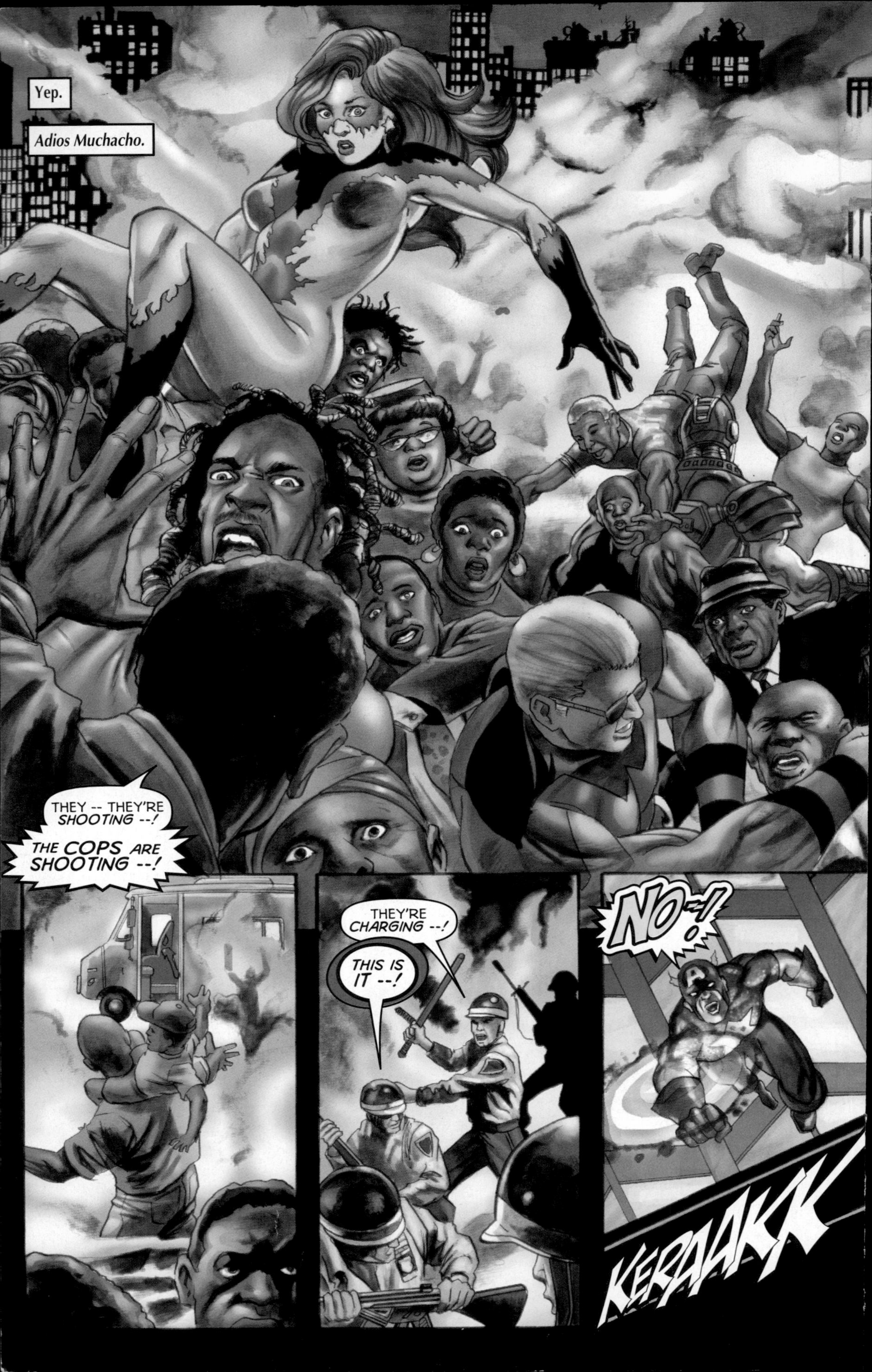
Yep.
Adios Muchacho.
THEY -- THEY'RE SHOOTING --!
THE COPS ARE SHOOTING --!
THEY'RE CHARGING --!
THIS IS IT --!
NO--!
KERAAKK

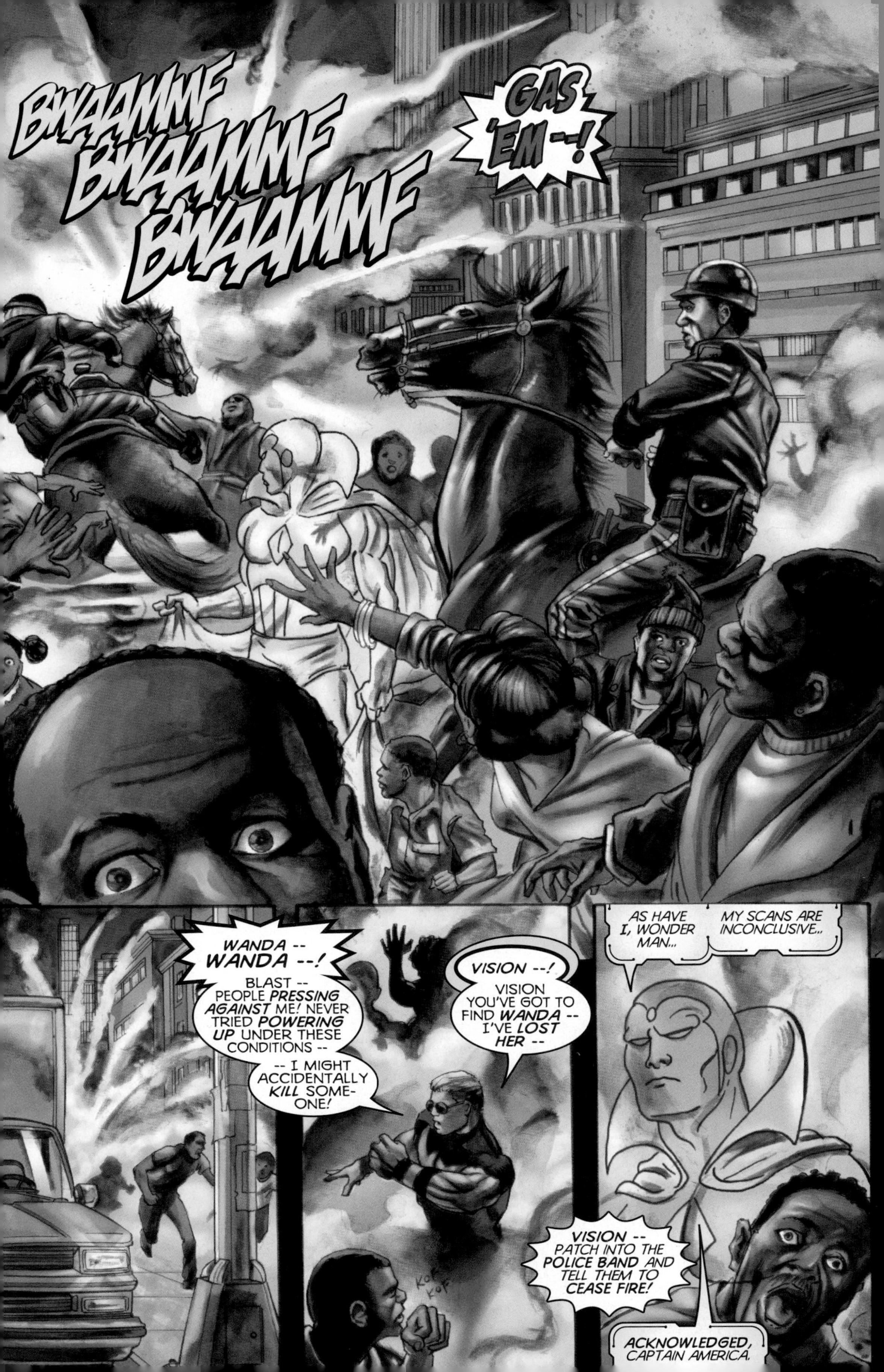
BWAAMMF
BWAAMMF
BWAAMMF
GAS 'EM --!
WANDA -- WANDA --!
BLAST -- PEOPLE PRESSING AGAINST ME! NEVER TRIED POWERING UP UNDER THESE CONDITIONS --
-- I MIGHT ACCIDENTALLY KILL SOME-ONE!
KOF KOF
VISION --!
VISION YOU'VE GOT TO FIND WANDA -- I'VE LOST HER --
AS HAVE I, WONDER MAN...
MY SCANS ARE INCONCLUSIVE...
VISION -- PATCH INTO THE POLICE BAND AND TELL THEM TO CEASE FIRE!
ACKNOWLEDGED, CAPTAIN AMERICA.

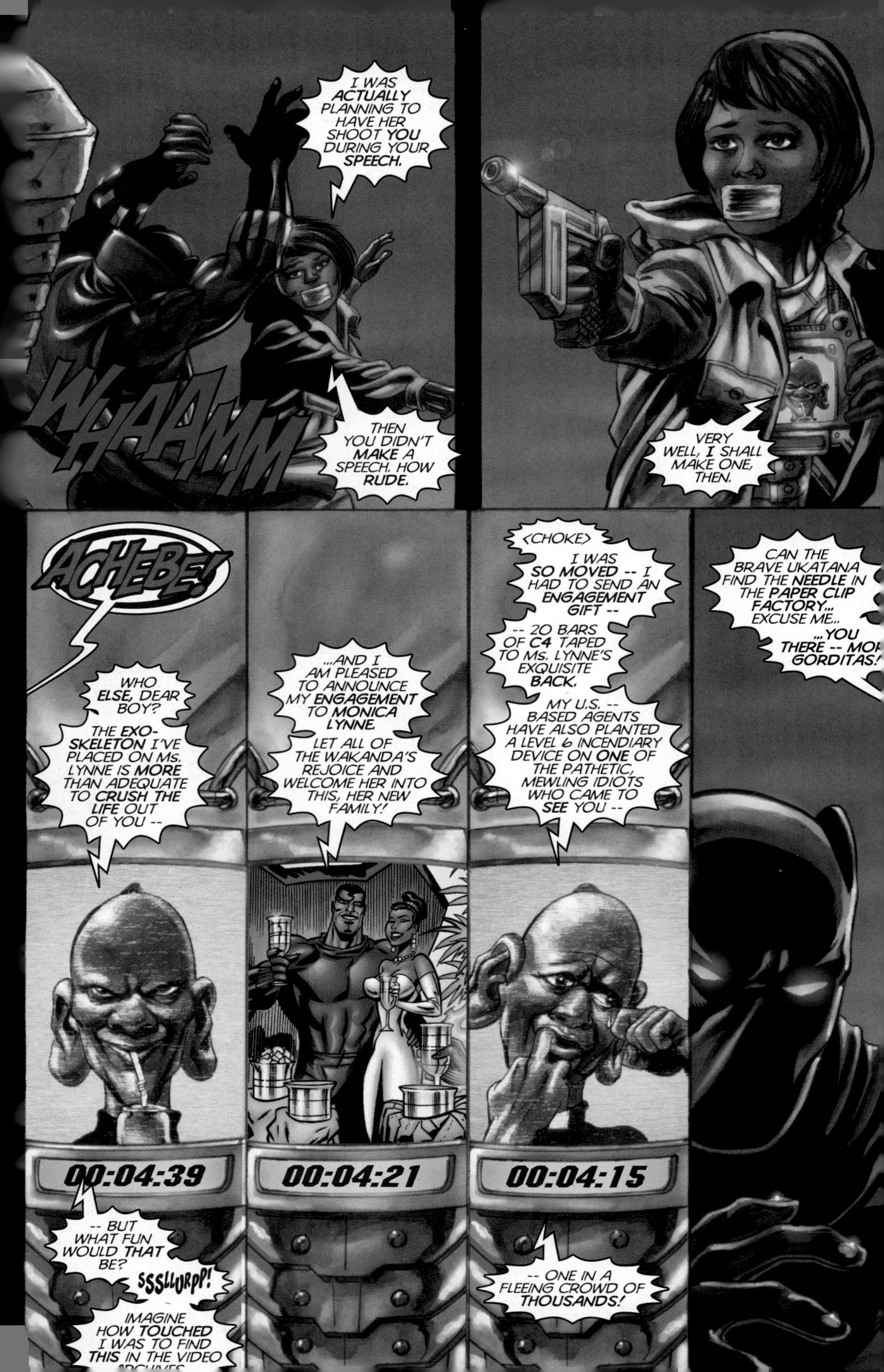

I WAS ACTUALLY PLANNING TO HAVE HER SHOOT YOU DURING YOUR SPEECH.
WHAAMM
THEN YOU DIDN'T MAKE A SPEECH. HOW RUDE.
VERY WELL, I SHALL MAKE ONE, THEN.
ACHEBE!
WHO ELSE, DEAR BOY?
THE EXO-SKELETON I'VE PLACED ON Ms. LYNNE IS MORE THAN ADEQUATE TO CRUSH THE LIFE OUT OF YOU --
00:04:39
-- BUT WHAT FUN WOULD THAT BE?
SSSLLURPP!
IMAGINE HOW TOUCHED I WAS TO FIND THIS IN THE VIDEO
...AND I AM PLEASED TO ANNOUNCE MY ENGAGEMENT TO MONICA LYNNE.
LET ALL OF THE WAKANDA'S REJOICE AND WELCOME HER INTO THIS, HER NEW FAMILY!
00:04:21
<CHOKE>
I WAS SO MOVED -- I HAD TO SEND AN ENGAGEMENT GIFT --
-- 20 BARS OF C4 TAPED TO Ms. LYNNE'S EXQUISITE BACK.
MY U.S. -- BASED AGENTS HAVE ALSO PLANTED A LEVEL 6 INCENDIARY DEVICE ON ONE OF THE PATHETIC, MEWLING IDIOTS WHO CAME TO SEE YOU --
00:04:15
-- ONE IN A FLEEING CROWD OF THOUSANDS!
CAN THE BRAVE UKATANA FIND THE NEEDLE IN THE PAPER CLIP FACTORY...
EXCUSE ME...
...YOU THERE -- MO
GORDITAS!

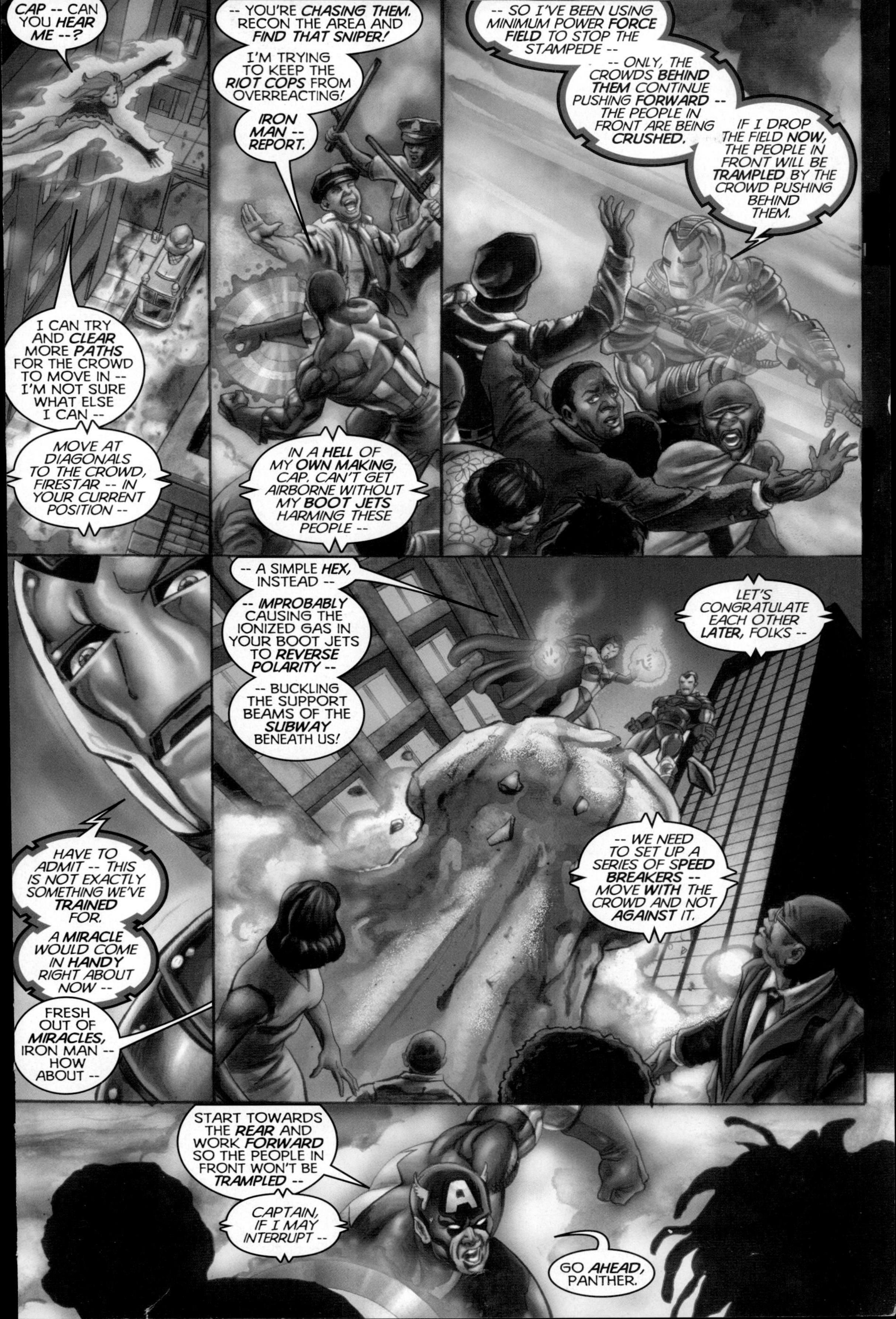
CAP -- CAN YOU HEAR ME --?
-- YOU'RE CHASING THEM. RECON THE AREA AND FIND THAT SNIPER!
I'M TRYING TO KEEP THE RIOT COPS FROM OVERREACTING!
IRON MAN -- REPORT.
-- SO I'VE BEEN USING MINIMUM POWER FORCE FIELD TO STOP THE STAMPEDE --
-- ONLY, THE CROWDS BEHIND THEM CONTINUE PUSHING FORWARD -- THE PEOPLE IN FRONT ARE BEING CRUSHED.
IF I DROP THE FIELD NOW, THE PEOPLE IN FRONT WILL BE TRAMPLED BY THE CROWD PUSHING BEHIND THEM.
I CAN TRY AND CLEAR MORE PATHS FOR THE CROWD TO MOVE IN -- I'M NOT SURE WHAT ELSE I CAN --
MOVE AT DIAGONALS TO THE CROWD, FIRESTAR -- IN YOUR CURRENT POSITION --
IN A HELL OF MY OWN MAKING, CAP. CAN'T GET AIRBORNE WITHOUT MY BOOT JETS HARMING THESE PEOPLE --
HAVE TO ADMIT -- THIS IS NOT EXACTLY SOMETHING WE'VE TRAINED FOR.
A MIRACLE WOULD COME IN HANDY RIGHT ABOUT NOW --
FRESH OUT OF MIRACLES, IRON MAN -- HOW ABOUT --
-- A SIMPLE HEX, INSTEAD --
-- IMPROBABLY CAUSING THE IONIZED GAS IN YOUR BOOT JETS TO REVERSE POLARITY --
-- BUCKLING THE SUPPORT BEAMS OF THE SUBWAY BENEATH US!
LET'S CONGRATULATE EACH OTHER LATER, FOLKS --
-- WE NEED TO SET UP A SERIES OF SPEED BREAKERS -- MOVE WITH THE CROWD AND NOT AGAINST IT.
START TOWARDS THE REAR AND WORK FORWARD SO THE PEOPLE IN FRONT WON'T BE TRAMPLED --
CAPTAIN, IF I MAY INTERRUPT --
GO AHEAD, PANTHER.

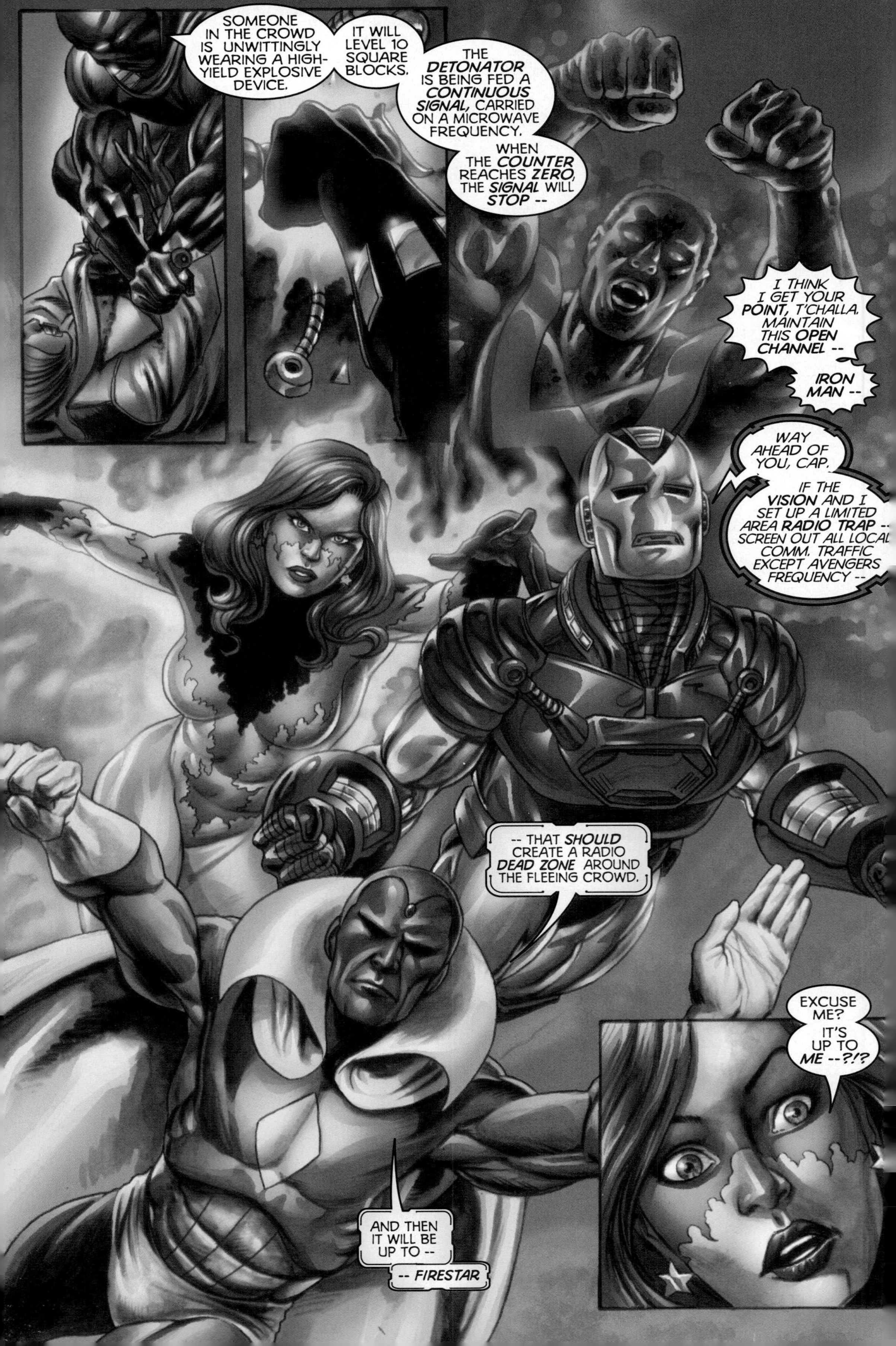
SOMEONE IN THE CROWD IS UNWITTINGLY WEARING A HIGH-YIELD EXPLOSIVE DEVICE.
IT WILL LEVEL 10 SQUARE BLOCKS.
THE DETONATOR IS BEING FED A CONTINUOUS SIGNAL, CARRIED ON A MICROWAVE FREQUENCY.
WHEN THE COUNTER REACHES ZERO, THE SIGNAL WILL STOP --
I THINK I GET YOUR POINT, T'CHALLA. MAINTAIN THIS OPEN CHANNEL --
IRON MAN --
WAY AHEAD OF YOU, CAP.
IF THE VISION AND I SET UP A LIMITED AREA RADIO TRAP -- SCREEN OUT ALL LOCAL COMM. TRAFFIC EXCEPT AVENGERS FREQUENCY --
-- THAT SHOULD CREATE A RADIO DEAD ZONE AROUND THE FLEEING CROWD.
AND THEN IT WILL BE UP TO --
-- FIRESTAR.
EXCUSE ME?
IT'S UP TO ME --?!?

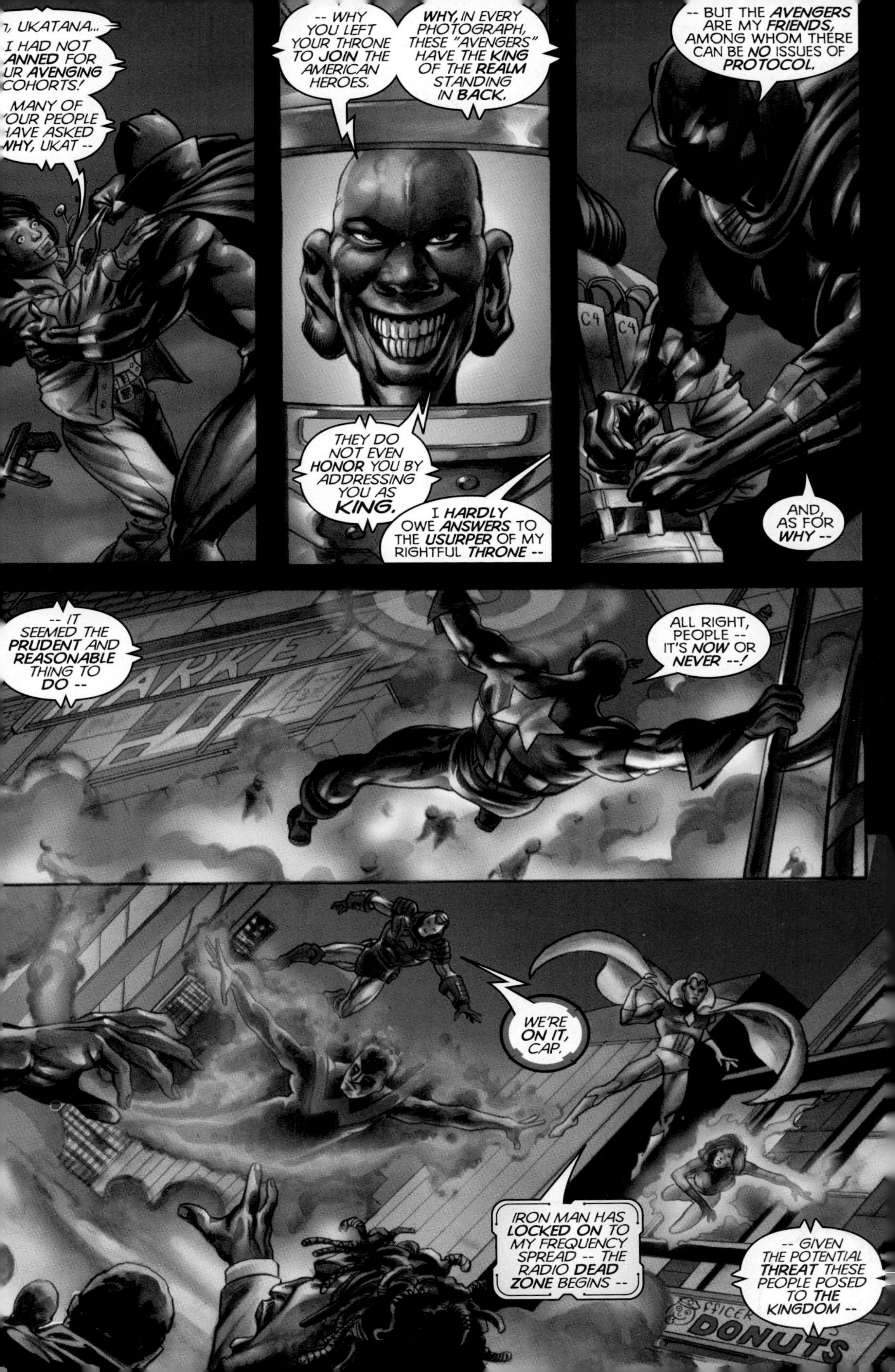

I HAD NOT ANNED FOR UR AVENGING COHORTS!
MANY OF YOUR PEOPLE HAVE ASKED WHY, UKAT --
-- WHY YOU LEFT YOUR THRONE TO JOIN THE AMERICAN HEROES.
WHY, IN EVERY PHOTOGRAPH, THESE "AVENGERS" HAVE THE KING OF THE REALM STANDING IN BACK.
THEY DO NOT EVEN HONOR YOU BY ADDRESSING YOU AS KING.
I HARDLY OWE ANSWERS TO THE USURPER OF MY RIGHTFUL THRONE --
-- BUT THE AVENGERS ARE MY FRIENDS, AMONG WHOM THERE CAN BE NO ISSUES OF PROTOCOL.
AND, AS FOR WHY --
-- IT SEEMED THE PRUDENT AND REASONABLE THING TO DO --
ALL RIGHT, PEOPLE -- IT'S NOW OR NEVER --!
WE'RE ON IT, CAP.
IRON MAN HAS LOCKED ON TO MY FREQUENCY SPREAD -- THE RADIO DEAD ZONE BEGINS --
-- GIVEN THE POTENTIAL THREAT THESE PEOPLE POSED TO THE KINGDOM --
DONUTS

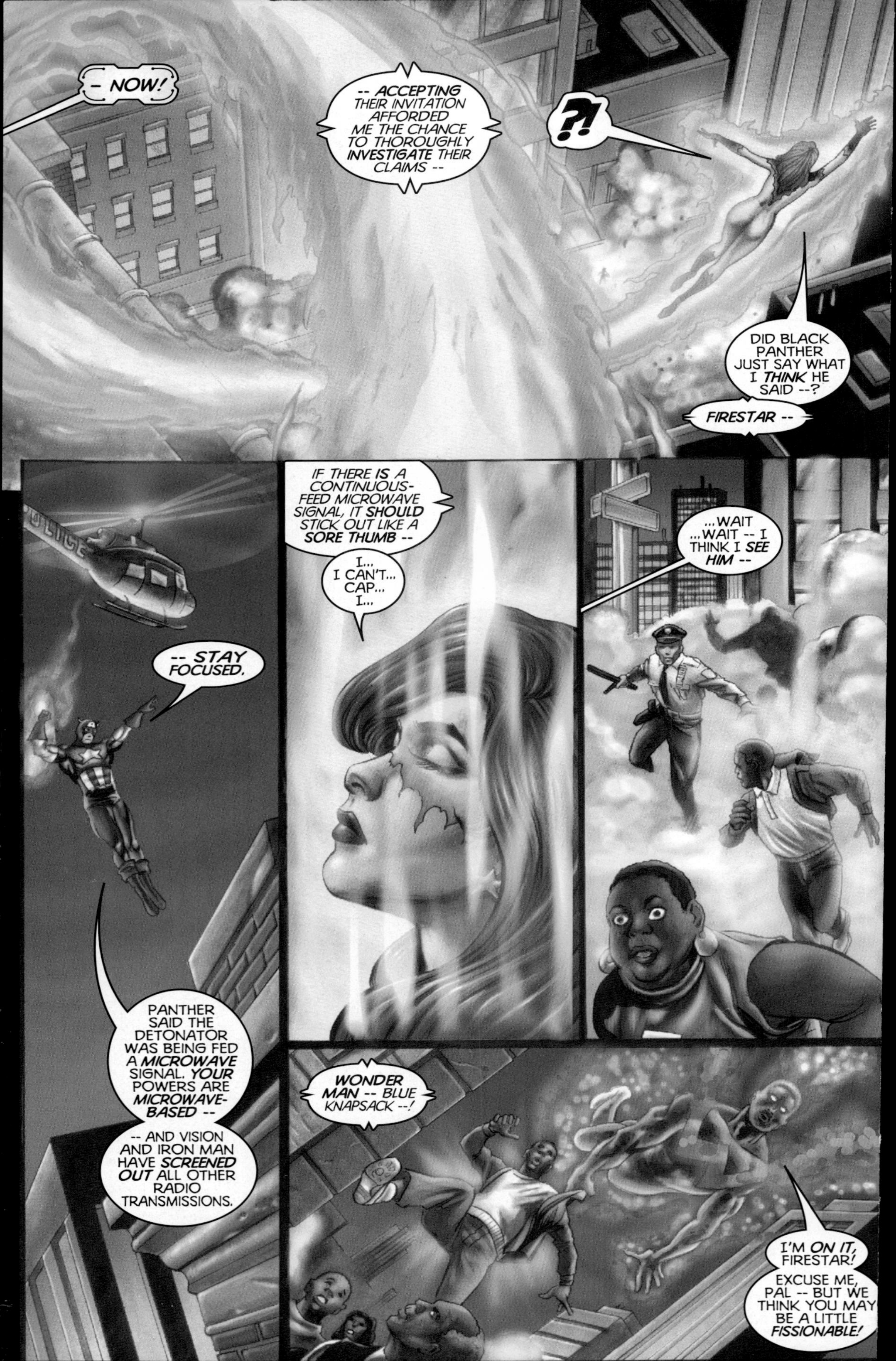
- NOW!
-- ACCEPTING THEIR INVITATION AFFORDED ME THE CHANCE TO THOROUGHLY INVESTIGATE THEIR CLAIMS --
?!
DID BLACK PANTHER JUST SAY WHAT I THINK HE SAID --?
FIRESTAR --
POLICE
-- STAY FOCUSED.
PANTHER SAID THE DETONATOR WAS BEING FED A MICROWAVE SIGNAL. YOUR POWERS ARE MICROWAVE-BASED --
-- AND VISION AND IRON MAN HAVE SCREENED OUT ALL OTHER RADIO TRANSMISSIONS.
IF THERE IS A CONTINUOUS-FEED MICROWAVE SIGNAL, IT SHOULD STICK OUT LIKE A SORE THUMB --
I... I CAN'T... CAP... I...
...WAIT ...WAIT -- I THINK I SEE HIM --
WONDER MAN -- BLUE KNAPSACK --!
I'M ON IT, FIRESTAR!
EXCUSE ME, PAL -- BUT WE THINK YOU MAY BE A LITTLE FISSIONABLE!

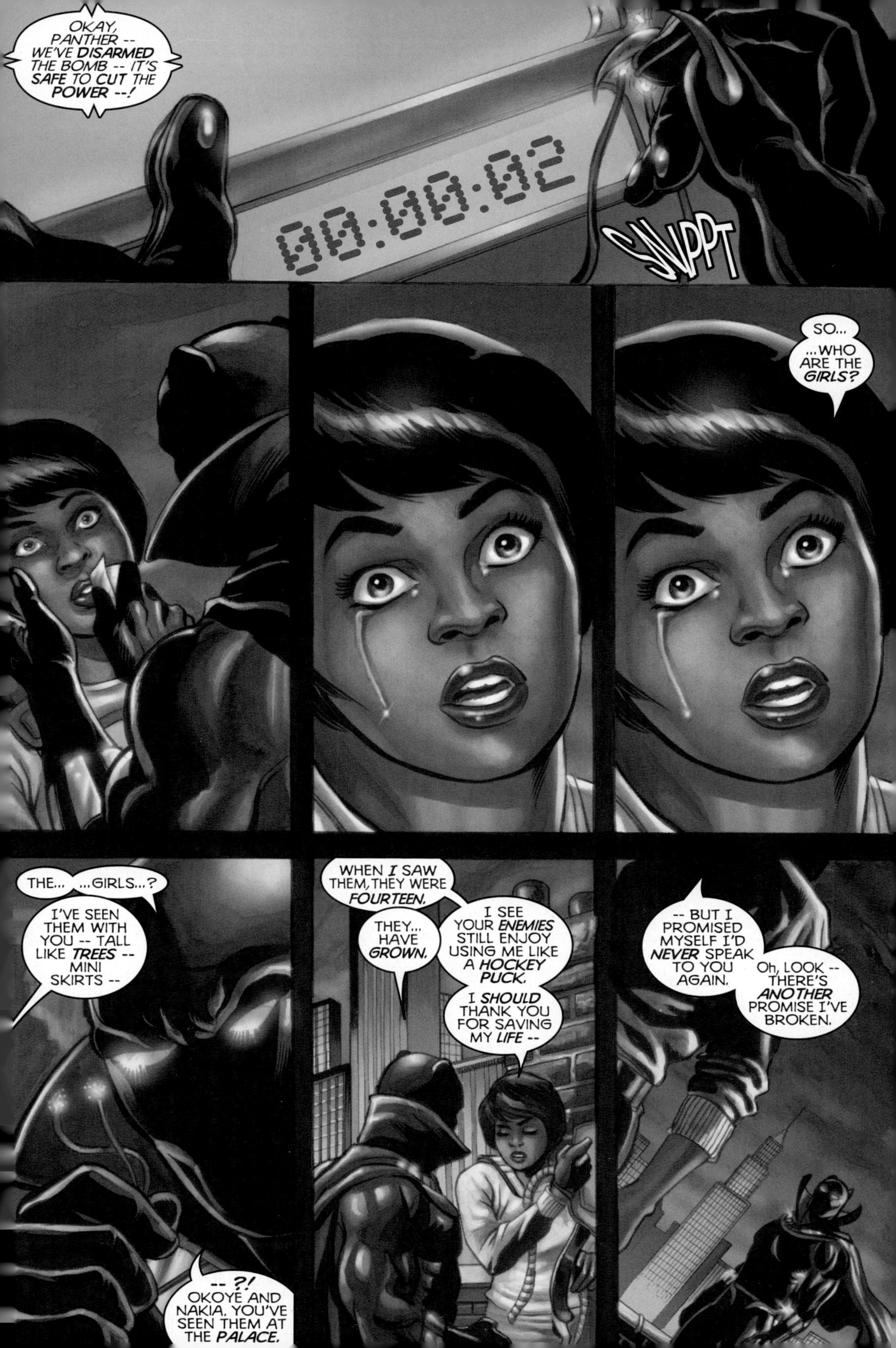
OKAY, PANTHER -- WE'VE DISARMED THE BOMB -- IT'S SAFE TO CUT THE POWER --!
00:00:02
SNPPT
SO... ...WHO ARE THE GIRLS?
THE... ...GIRLS...?
I'VE SEEN THEM WITH YOU -- TALL LIKE TREES -- MINI SKIRTS --
-- ?! OKOYE AND NAKIA. YOU'VE SEEN THEM AT THE PALACE.
WHEN I SAW THEM, THEY WERE FOURTEEN.
THEY... HAVE GROWN.
I SEE YOUR ENEMIES STILL ENJOY USING ME LIKE A HOCKEY PUCK.
I SHOULD THANK YOU FOR SAVING MY LIFE --
-- BUT I PROMISED MYSELF I'D NEVER SPEAK TO YOU AGAIN.
Oh, LOOK -- THERE'S ANOTHER PROMISE I'VE BROKEN.

JAIL HOUSE ROCK

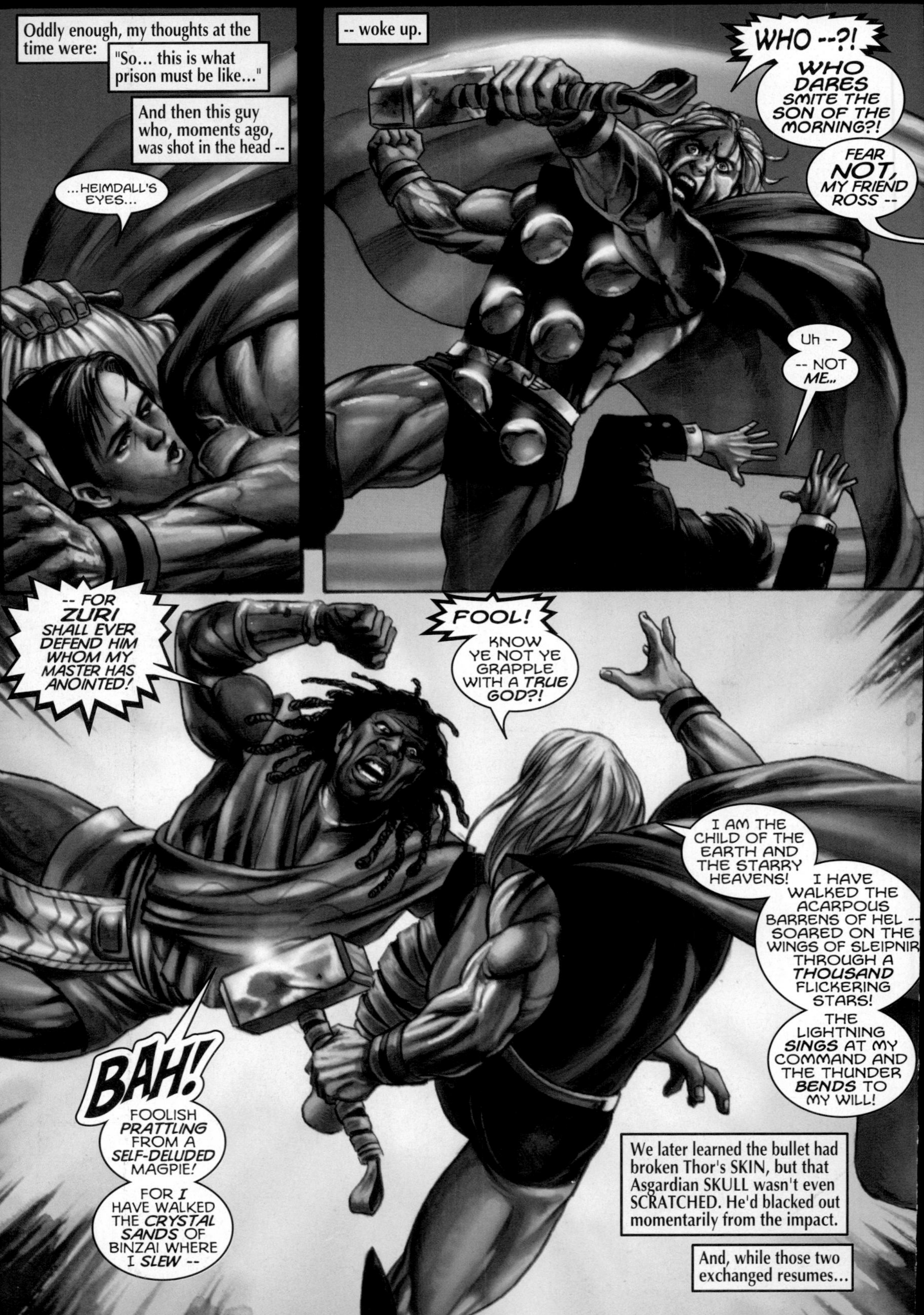

Oddly enough, my thoughts at the time were:
"So... this is what prison must be like..."
And then this guy who, moments ago, was shot in the head --
...HEIMDALL'S EYES...
-- woke up.
WHO --?!
WHO DARES SMITE THE SON OF THE MORNING?!
FEAR NOT, MY FRIEND ROSS --
Uh --
-- NOT ME...
-- FOR ZURI SHALL EVER DEFEND HIM WHOM MY MASTER HAS ANOINTED!
FOOL!
KNOW YE NOT YE GRAPPLE WITH A TRUE GOD?!
I AM THE CHILD OF THE EARTH AND THE STARRY HEAVENS!
I HAVE WALKED THE ACARPOUS BARRENS OF HEL -- SOARED ON THE WINGS OF SLEIPNIR THROUGH A THOUSAND FLICKERING STARS!
THE LIGHTNING SINGS AT MY COMMAND AND THE THUNDER BENDS TO MY WILL!
BAH!
FOOLISH PRATTLING FROM A SELF-DELUDED MAGPIE!
FOR I HAVE WALKED THE CRYSTAL SANDS OF BINZAI WHERE I SLEW --
We later learned the bullet had broken Thor's SKIN, but that Asgardian SKULL wasn't even SCRATCHED. He'd blacked out momentarily from the impact.
And, while those two exchanged resumes...

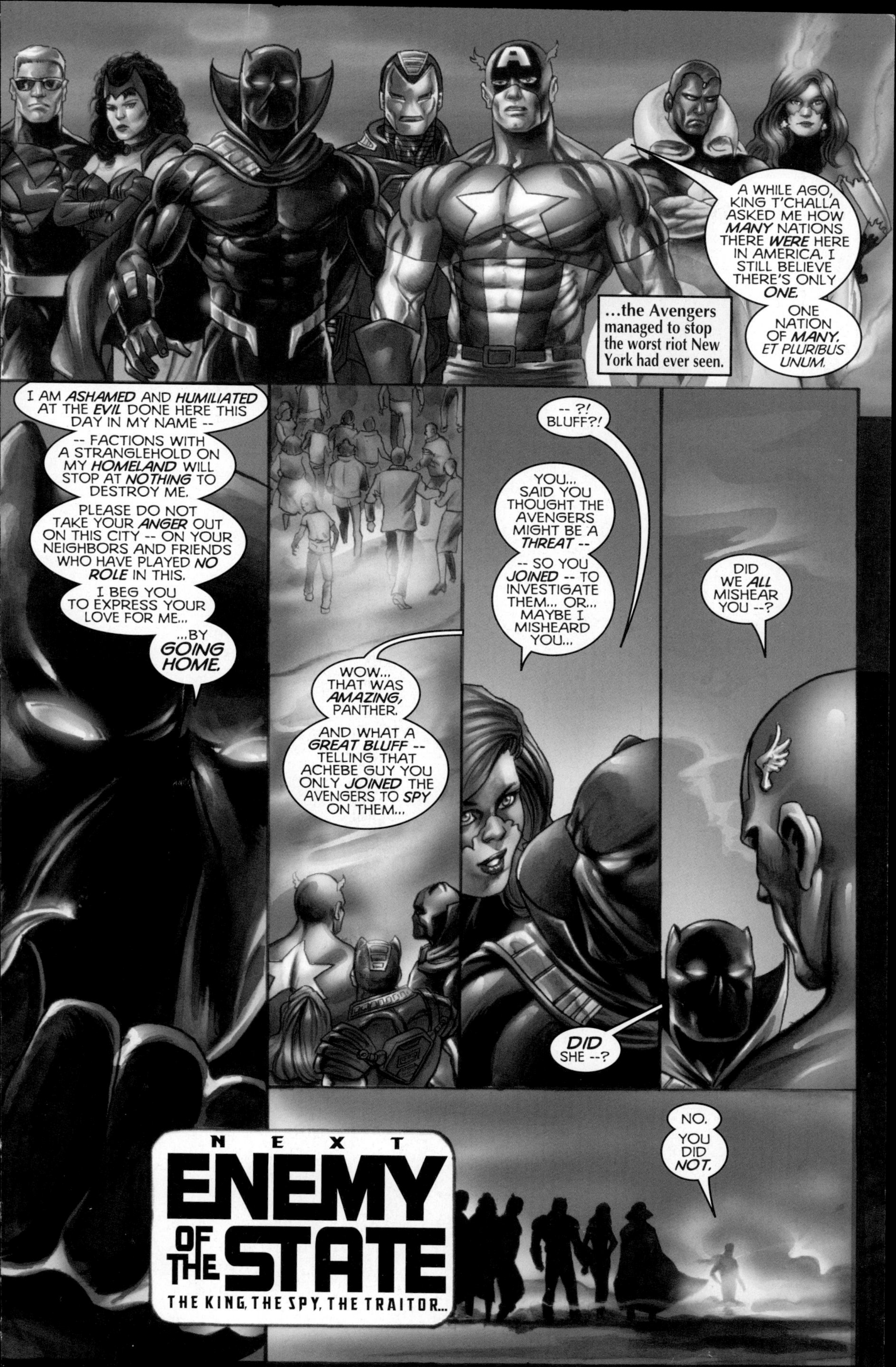
A WHILE AGO, KING T'CHALLA ASKED ME HOW MANY NATIONS THERE WERE HERE IN AMERICA. I STILL BELIEVE THERE'S ONLY ONE.
...the Avengers managed to stop the worst riot New York had ever seen.
ONE NATION OF MANY. ET PLURIBUS UNUM.
I AM ASHAMED AND HUMILIATED AT THE EVIL DONE HERE THIS DAY IN MY NAME --
-- FACTIONS WITH A STRANGLEHOLD ON MY HOMELAND WILL STOP AT NOTHING TO DESTROY ME.
PLEASE DO NOT TAKE YOUR ANGER OUT ON THIS CITY -- ON YOUR NEIGHBORS AND FRIENDS WHO HAVE PLAYED NO ROLE IN THIS.
I BEG YOU TO EXPRESS YOUR LOVE FOR ME...
...BY GOING HOME.
WOW... THAT WAS AMAZING, PANTHER.
AND WHAT A GREAT BLUFF -- TELLING THAT ACHEBE GUY YOU ONLY JOINED THE AVENGERS TO SPY ON THEM...
-- ?! BLUFF?!
YOU... SAID YOU THOUGHT THE AVENGERS MIGHT BE A THREAT --
-- SO YOU JOINED -- TO INVESTIGATE THEM... OR... MAYBE I MISHEARD YOU...
DID SHE --?
DID WE ALL MISHEAR YOU --?
NO. YOU DID NOT.
NEXT
ENEMY OF THE STATE
THE KING, THE SPY, THE TRAITOR...

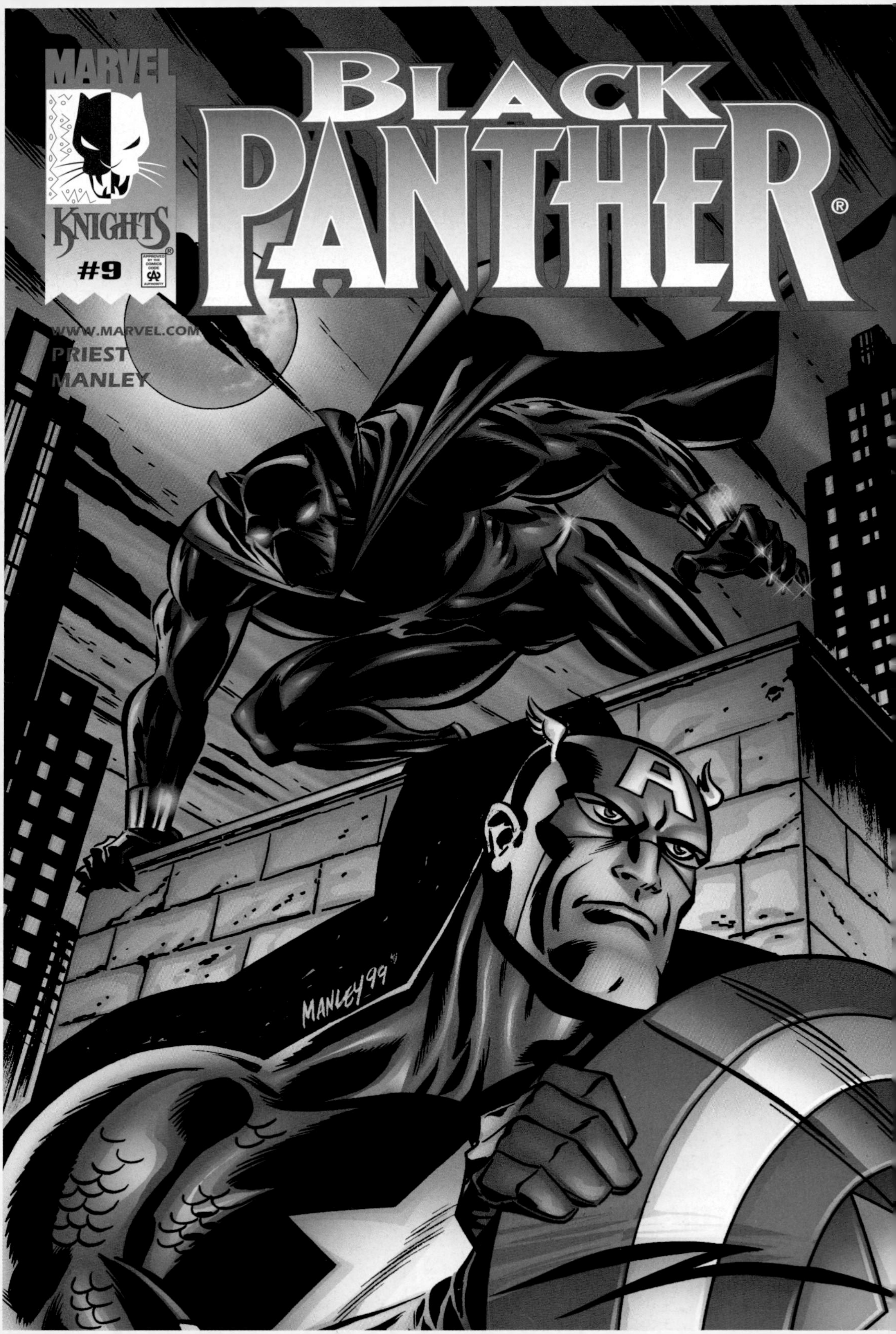
MARVEL
KNIGHTS
#9
APPROVED BY THE COMICS CODE AUTHORITY
BLACK PANTHER®
WWW.MARVEL.COM
PRIEST
MANLEY
MANLEY 99

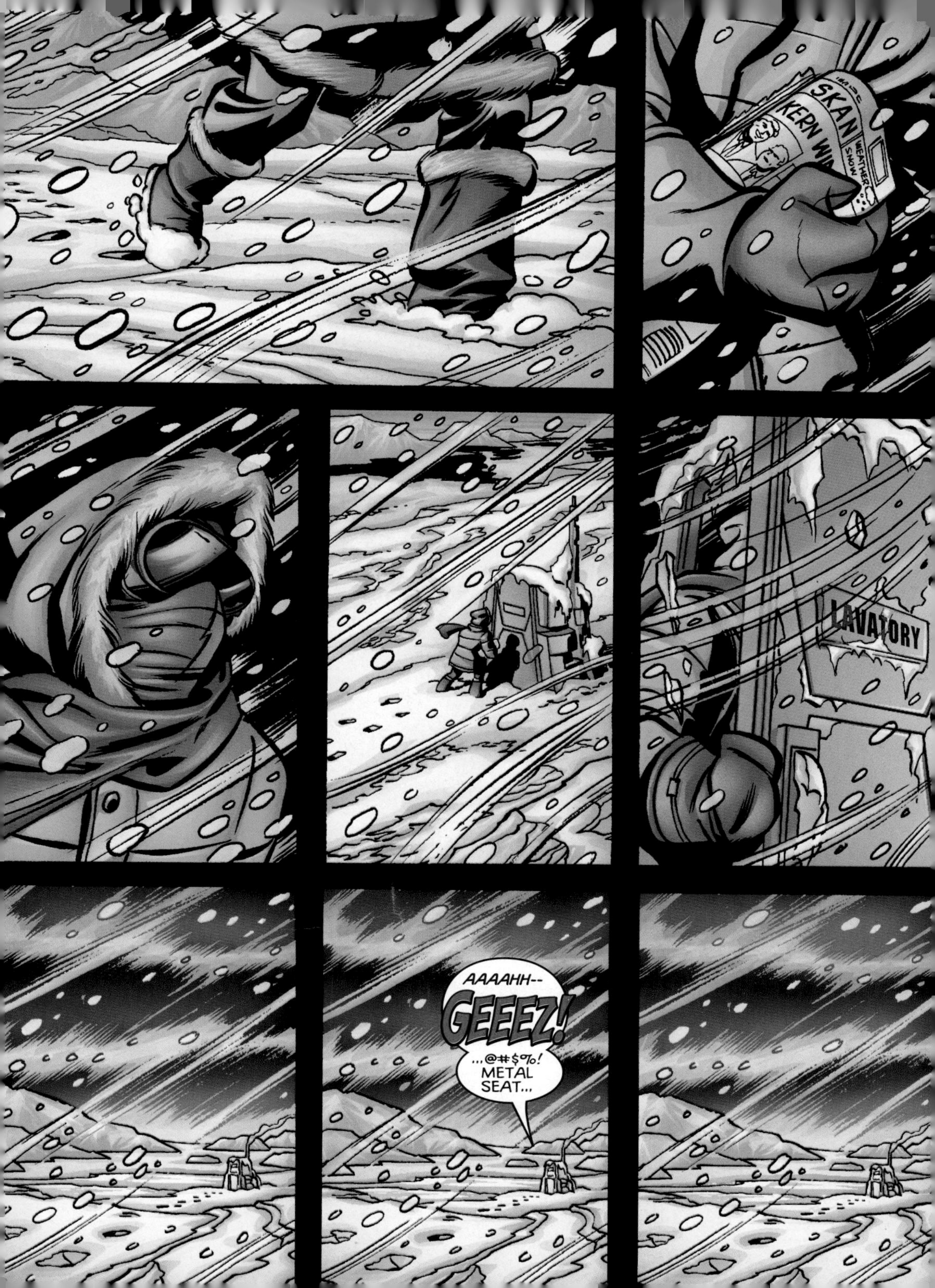
LAVATORY
AAAAHH--
GEEEZ!
...@#$%! METAL SEAT...

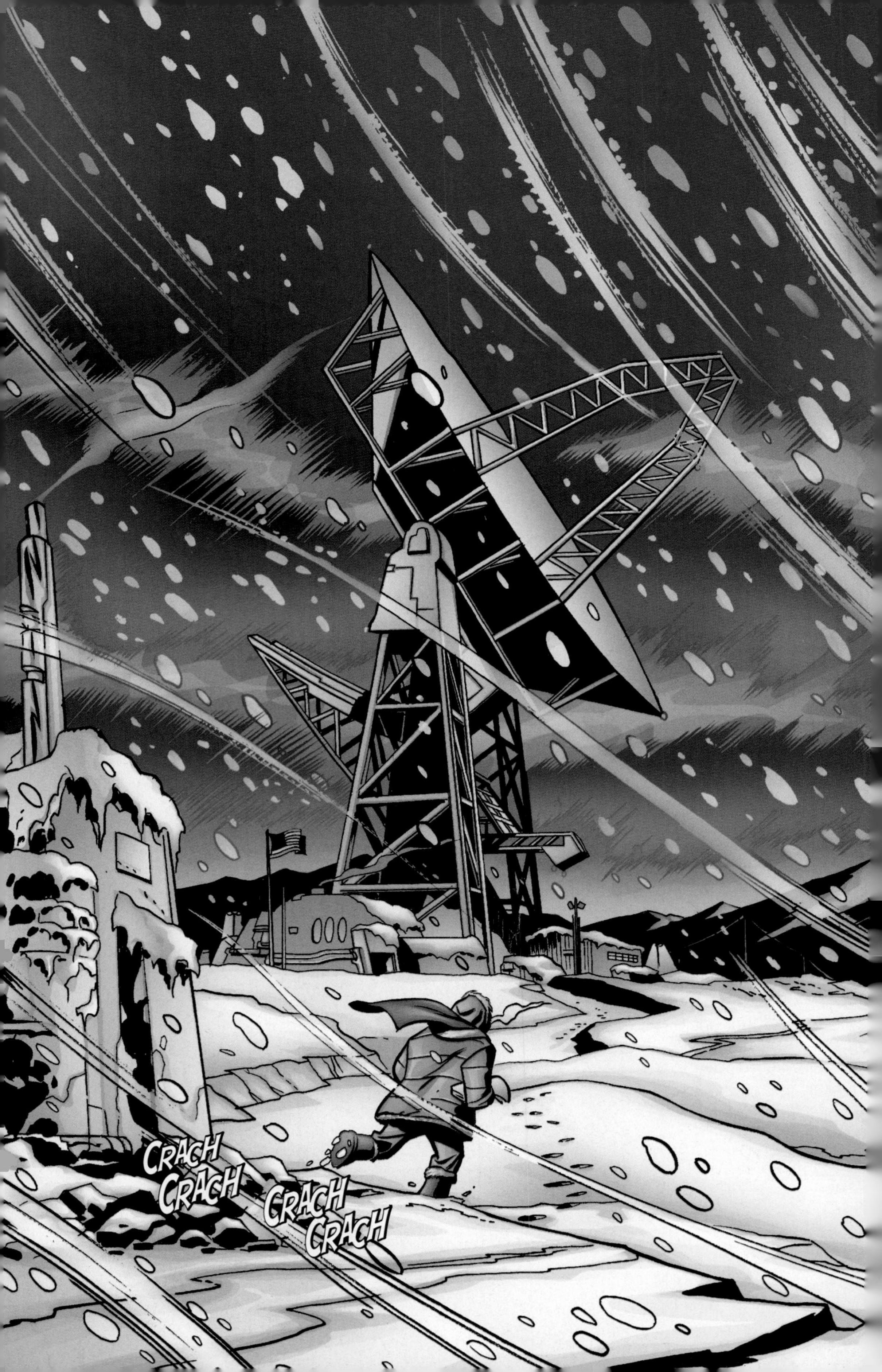
CRACH
CRACH
CRACH
CRACH

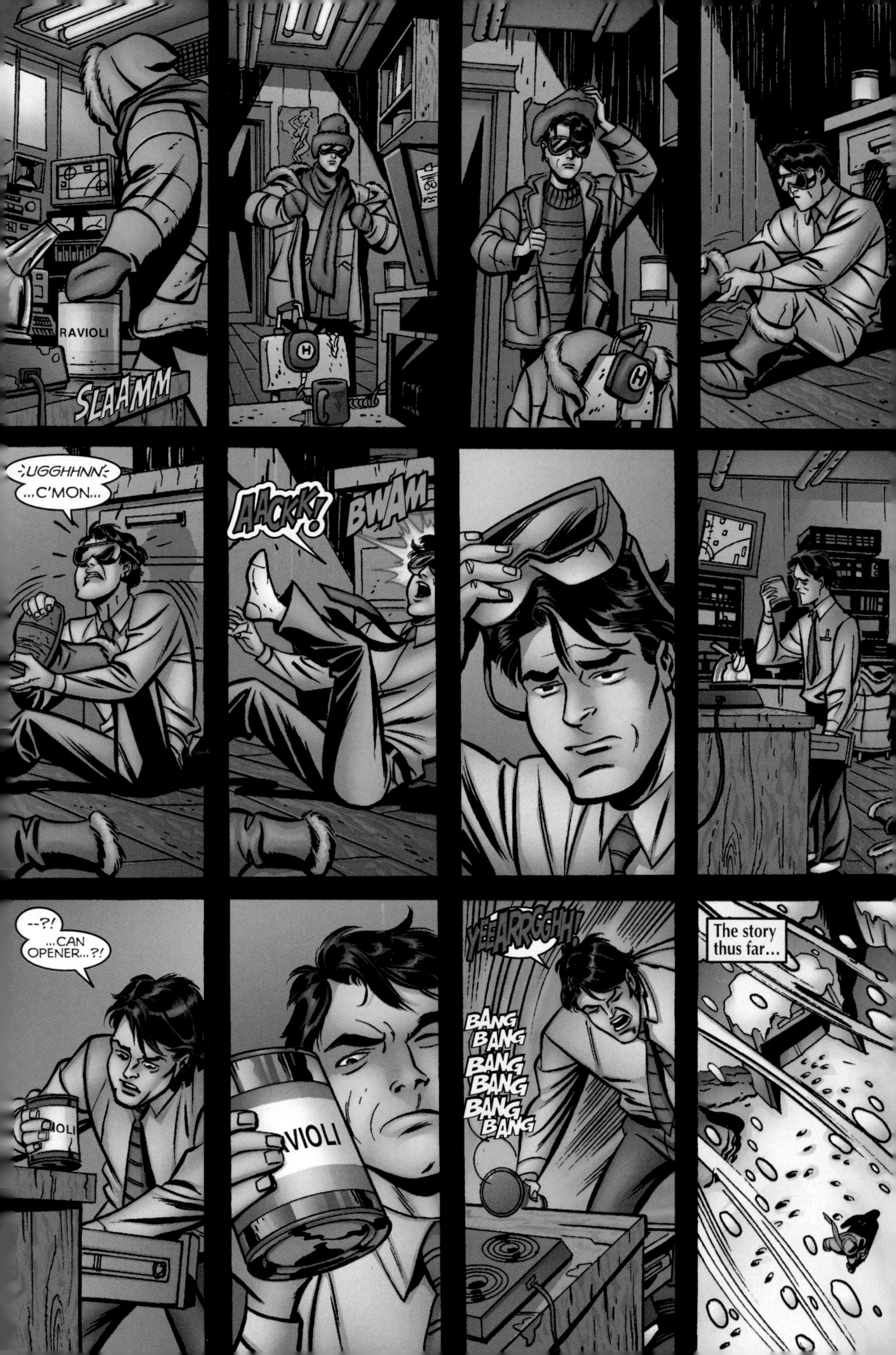
RAVIOLI
SLAAMM
UGGHHNN
...C'MON...
AACKK!
BWAM
--?!
...CAN OPENER...?!
RAVIOLI
YEEARRGGHH!
BANG BANG BANG BANG BANG BANG
The story thus far...

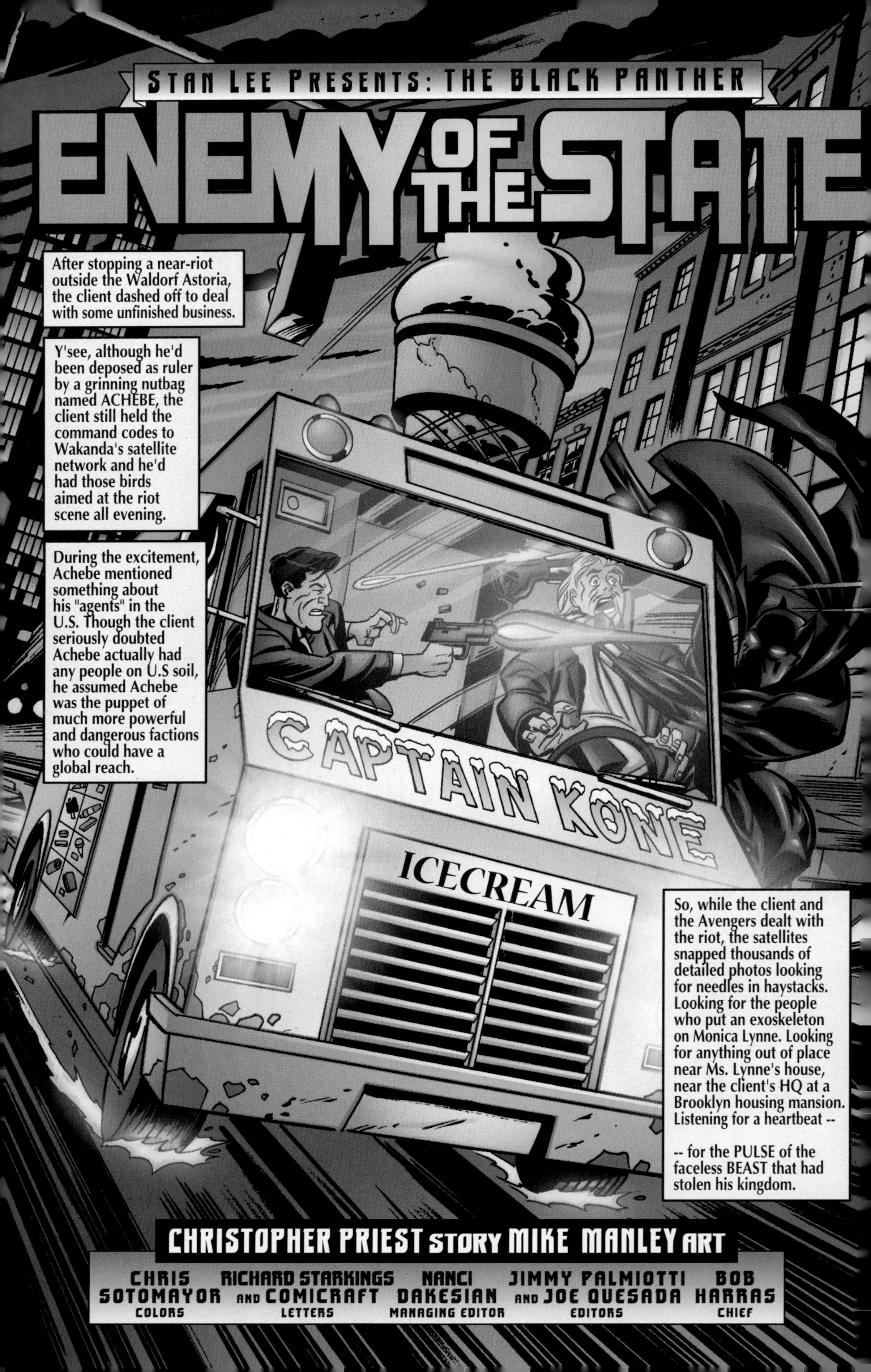
STAN LEE PRESENTS: THE BLACK PANTHER
ENEMY OF THE STATE
After stopping a near-riot outside the Waldorf Astoria, the client dashed off to deal with some unfinished business.
Y'see, although he'd been deposed as ruler by a grinning nutbag named ACHEBE, the client still held the command codes to Wakanda's satellite network and he'd had those birds aimed at the riot scene all evening.
During the excitement, Achebe mentioned something about his "agents" in the U.S. Though the client seriously doubted Achebe actually had any people on U.S soil, he assumed Achebe was the puppet of much more powerful and dangerous factions who could have a global reach.
CAPTAIN KONE
ICECREAM
So, while the client and the Avengers dealt with the riot, the satellites snapped thousands of detailed photos looking for needles in haystacks. Looking for the people who put an exoskeleton on Monica Lynne. Looking for anything out of place near Ms. Lynne's house, near the client's HQ at a Brooklyn housing mansion. Listening for a heartbeat --
-- for the PULSE of the faceless BEAST that had stolen his kingdom.
CHRISTOPHER PRIEST STORY MIKE MANLEY ART
CHRIS SOTOMAYOR COLORS
RICHARD STARKINGS AND COMICRAFT LETTERS
NANCI DAKESIAN MANAGING EDITOR
JIMMY PALMIOTTI AND JOE QUESADA EDITORS
BOB HARRAS CHIEF

LONG LIVE THE KING

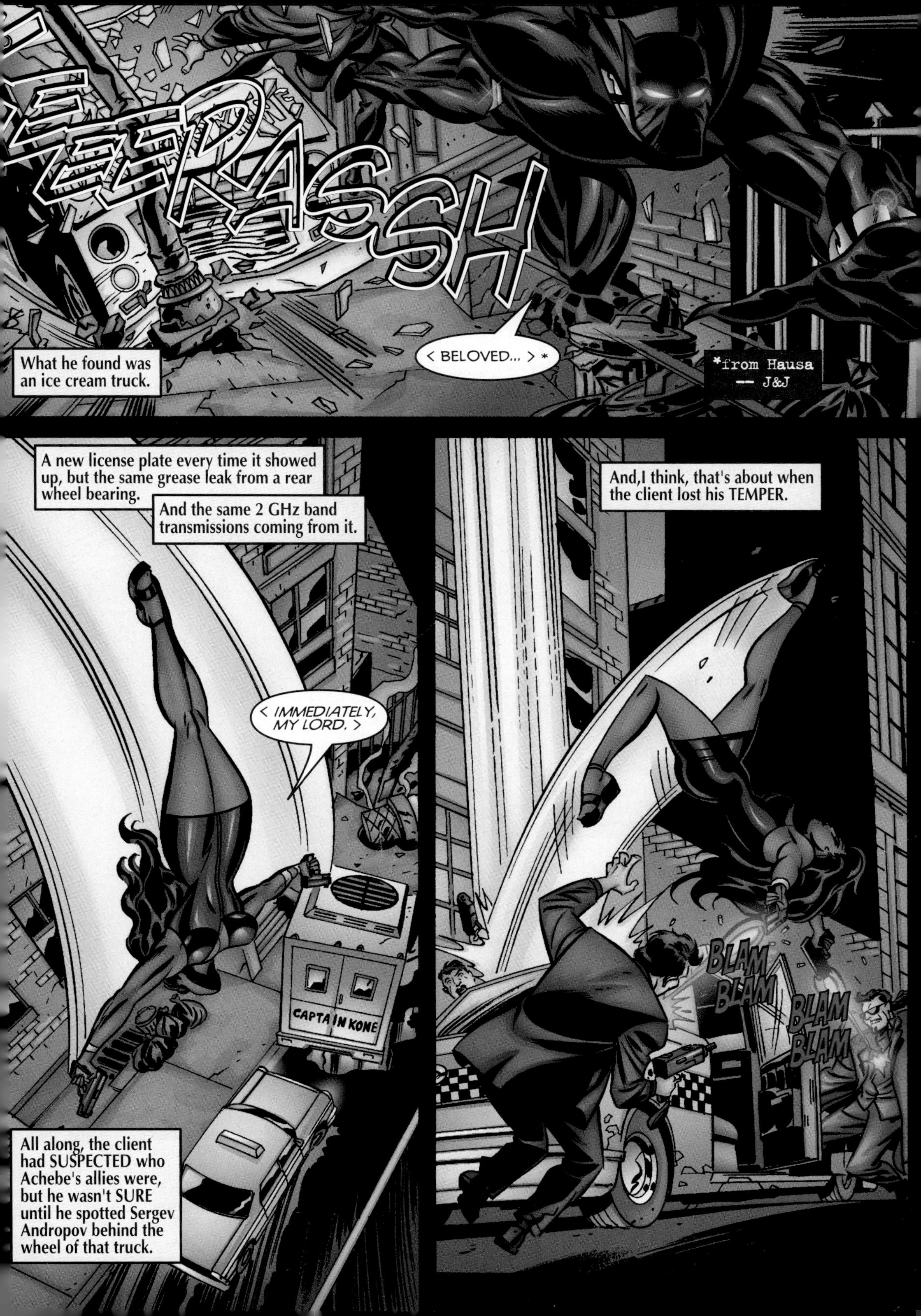

KEERASSH
What he found was an ice cream truck.
< BELOVED... > *
*from Hausa -- J&J
A new license plate every time it showed up, but the same grease leak from a rear wheel bearing.
And the same 2 GHz band transmissions coming from it.
< IMMEDIATELY, MY LORD. >
CAPTAIN KONE
All along, the client had SUSPECTED who Achebe's allies were, but he wasn't SURE until he spotted Sergev Andropov behind the wheel of that truck.
And,I think, that's about when the client lost his TEMPER.
BLAM BLAM
BLAM BLAM

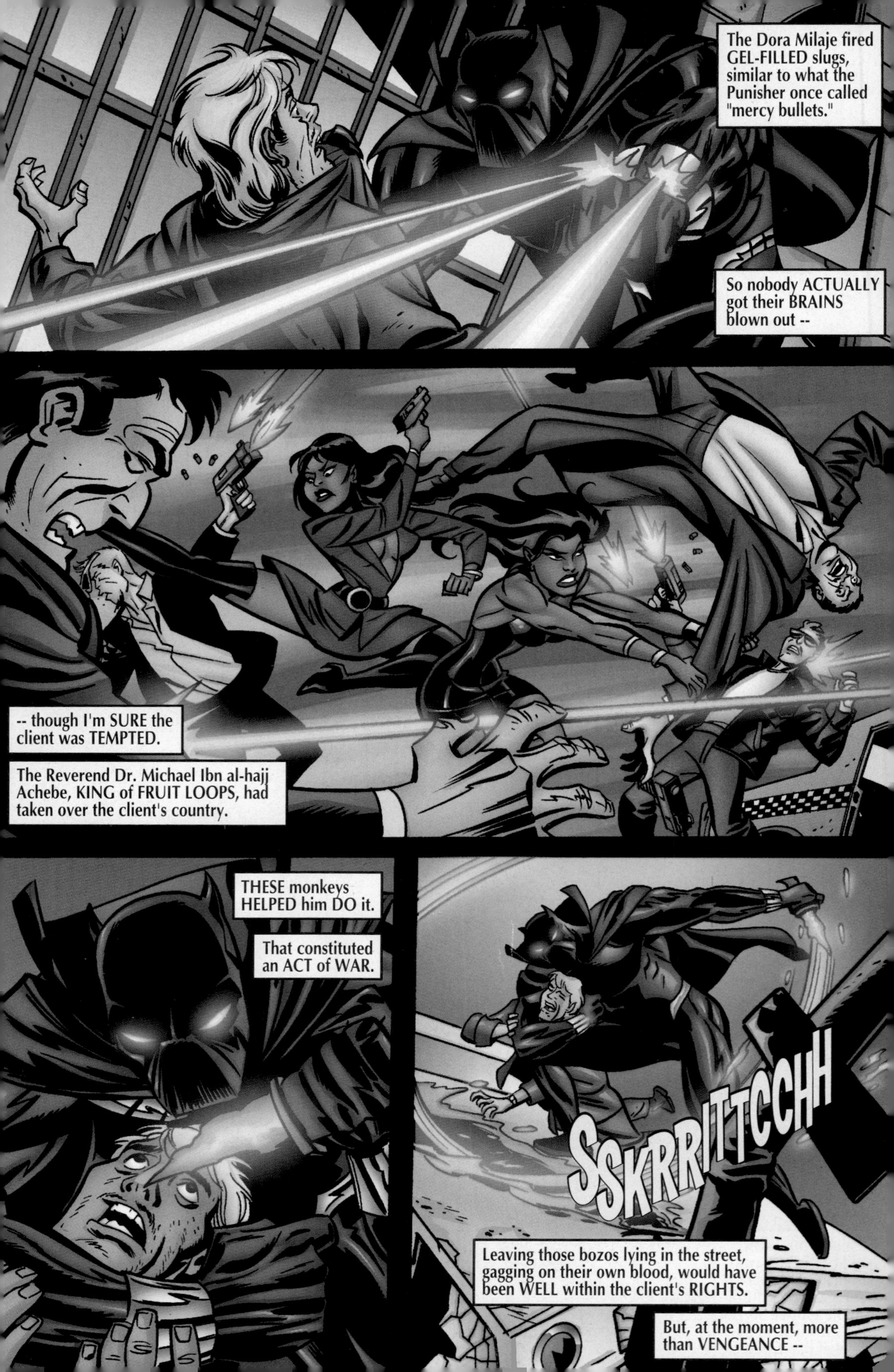

The Dora Milaje fired GEL-FILLED slugs, similar to what the Punisher once called "mercy bullets."
So nobody ACTUALLY got their BRAINS blown out --
-- though I'm SURE the client was TEMPTED.
The Reverend Dr. Michael Ibn al-hajj Achebe, KING of FRUIT LOOPS, had taken over the client's country.
THESE monkeys HELPED him DO it.
That constituted an ACT of WAR.
SSKRRITTCCHH
Leaving those bozos lying in the street, gagging on their own blood, would have been WELL within the client's RIGHTS.
But, at the moment, more than VENGEANCE --

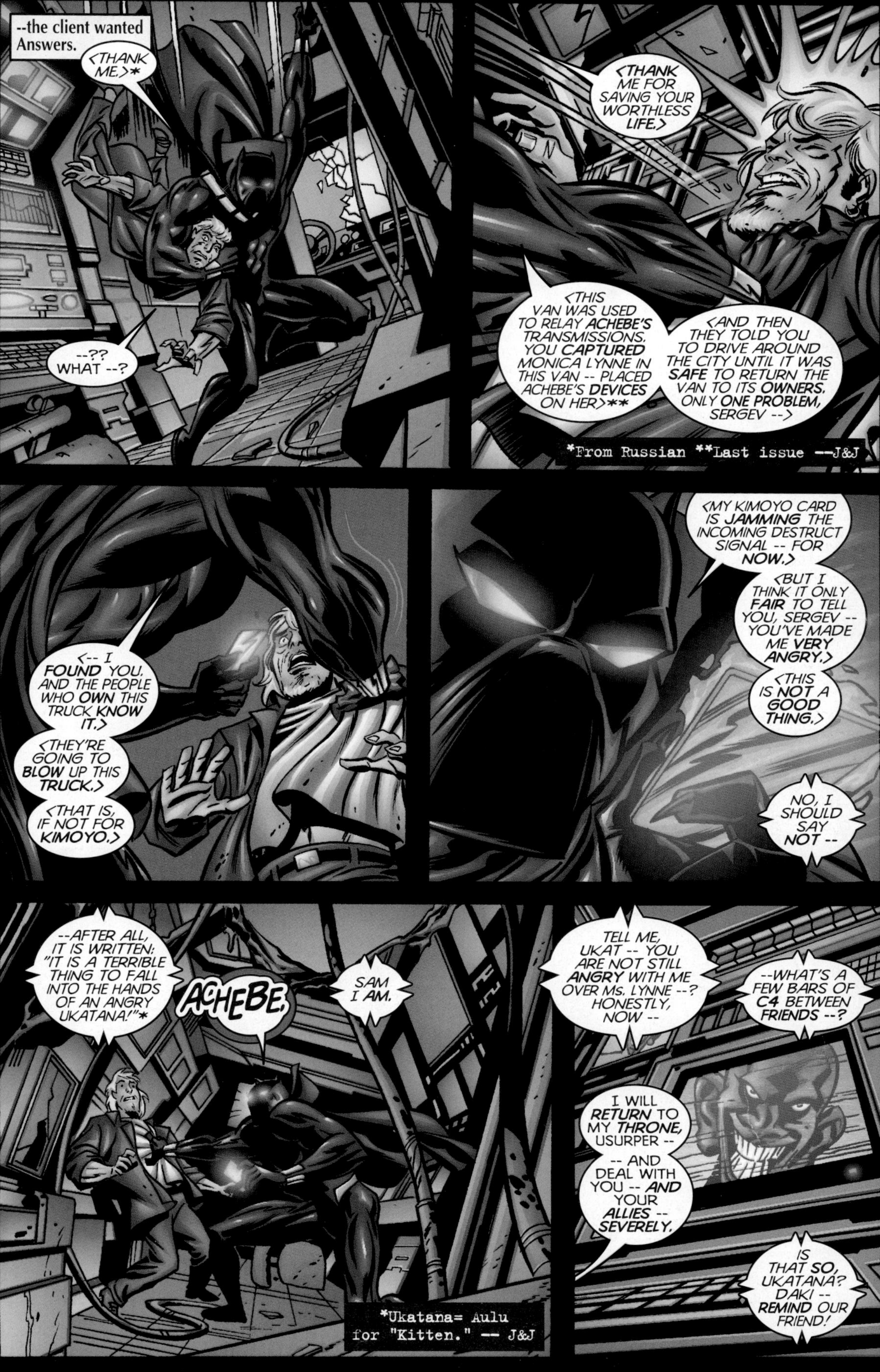
--the client wanted Answers.
<THANK ME.>*
--?? WHAT --?
<THANK ME FOR SAVING YOUR WORTHLESS LIFE.>
<THIS VAN WAS USED TO RELAY ACHEBE'S TRANSMISSIONS. YOU CAPTURED MONICA LYNNE IN THIS VAN -- PLACED ACHEBE'S DEVICES ON HER>**
<AND THEN THEY TOLD YOU TO DRIVE AROUND THE CITY UNTIL IT WAS SAFE TO RETURN THE VAN TO ITS OWNERS. ONLY ONE PROBLEM, SERGEV -->
*From Russian **Last issue --J&J
<-- I FOUND YOU. AND THE PEOPLE WHO OWN THIS TRUCK KNOW IT.>
<THEY'RE GOING TO BLOW UP THIS TRUCK.>
<THAT IS, IF NOT FOR KIMOYO.>
<MY KIMOYO CARD IS JAMMING THE INCOMING DESTRUCT SIGNAL -- FOR NOW.>
<BUT I THINK IT ONLY FAIR TO TELL YOU, SERGEV -- YOU'VE MADE ME VERY ANGRY.>
<THIS IS NOT A GOOD THING.>
NO, I SHOULD SAY NOT --
--AFTER ALL, IT IS WRITTEN: "IT IS A TERRIBLE THING TO FALL INTO THE HANDS OF AN ANGRY UKATANA!"*
ACHEBE.
SAM I AM.
*Ukatana= Aulu for "Kitten." -- J&J
TELL ME, UKAT -- YOU ARE NOT STILL ANGRY WITH ME OVER MS. LYNNE --? HONESTLY, NOW --
--WHAT'S A FEW BARS OF C4 BETWEEN FRIENDS --?
I WILL RETURN TO MY THRONE, USURPER --
-- AND DEAL WITH YOU -- AND YOUR ALLIES -- SEVERELY.
IS THAT SO, UKATANA? DAKI -- REMIND OUR FRIEND!

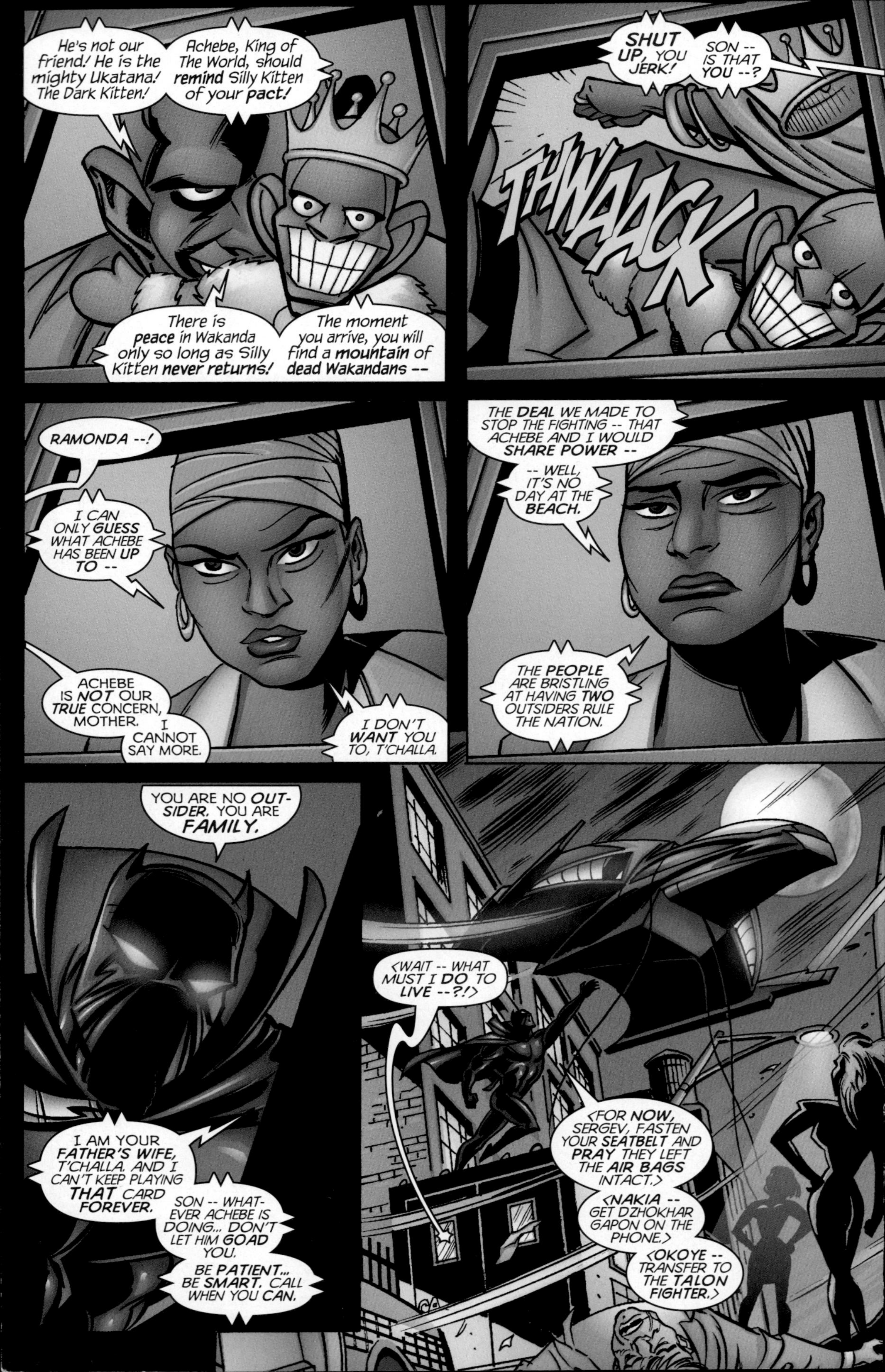

He's not our friend! He is the mighty Ukatana! The Dark Kitten!
Achebe, King of The World, should remind Silly Kitten of your pact!
There is peace in Wakanda only so long as Silly Kitten never returns!
The moment you arrive, you will find a mountain of dead Wakandans --
SHUT UP, YOU JERK!
SON -- IS THAT YOU --?
THWAACK
RAMONDA --!
I CAN ONLY GUESS WHAT ACHEBE HAS BEEN UP TO --
ACHEBE IS NOT OUR TRUE CONCERN, MOTHER.
I CANNOT SAY MORE.
I DON'T WANT YOU TO, T'CHALLA.
THE DEAL WE MADE TO STOP THE FIGHTING -- THAT ACHEBE AND I WOULD SHARE POWER --
-- WELL, IT'S NO DAY AT THE BEACH.
THE PEOPLE ARE BRISTLING AT HAVING TWO OUTSIDERS RULE THE NATION.
YOU ARE NO OUTSIDER. YOU ARE FAMILY.
I AM YOUR FATHER'S WIFE, T'CHALLA, AND I CAN'T KEEP PLAYING THAT CARD FOREVER.
SON -- WHATEVER ACHEBE IS DOING... DON'T LET HIM GOAD YOU.
BE PATIENT... BE SMART. CALL WHEN YOU CAN.
<WAIT -- WHAT MUST I DO TO LIVE --?!>
<FOR NOW, SERGEV, FASTEN YOUR SEATBELT AND PRAY THEY LEFT THE AIR BAGS INTACT.>
<NAKIA -- GET DZHOKHAR GAPON ON THE PHONE.>
<OKOYE -- TRANSFER TO THE TALON FIGHTER.>

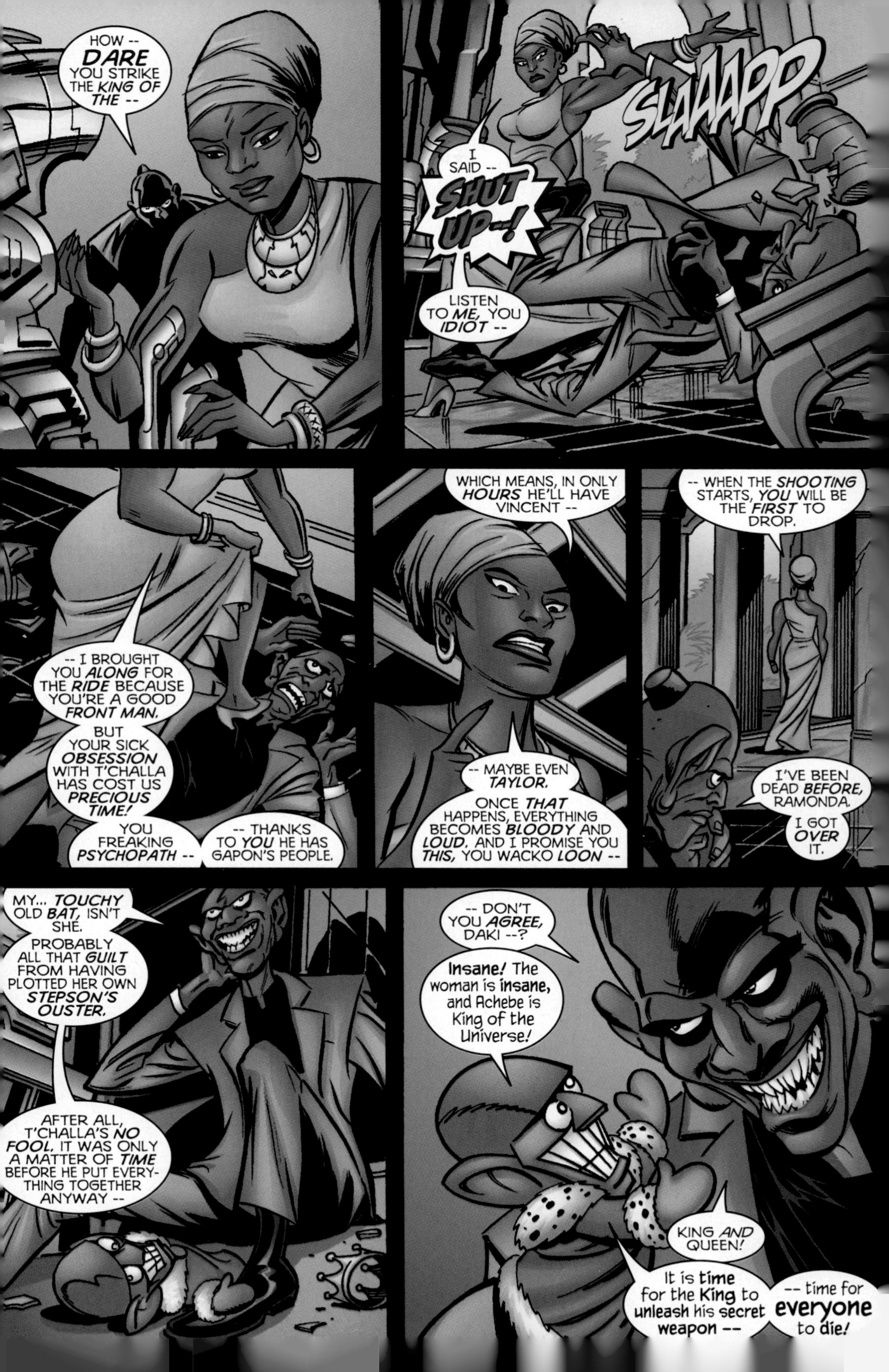

HOW -- DARE YOU STRIKE THE KING OF THE --
SLAAAPP
I SAID -- SHUT UP--!
LISTEN TO ME, YOU IDIOT --
-- I BROUGHT YOU ALONG FOR THE RIDE BECAUSE YOU'RE A GOOD FRONT MAN.
BUT YOUR SICK OBSESSION WITH T'CHALLA HAS COST US PRECIOUS TIME!
YOU FREAKING PSYCHOPATH --
-- THANKS TO YOU HE HAS GAPON'S PEOPLE.
WHICH MEANS, IN ONLY HOURS HE'LL HAVE VINCENT --
-- MAYBE EVEN TAYLOR.
ONCE THAT HAPPENS, EVERYTHING BECOMES BLOODY AND LOUD. AND I PROMISE YOU THIS, YOU WACKO LOON --
-- WHEN THE SHOOTING STARTS, YOU WILL BE THE FIRST TO DROP.
I'VE BEEN DEAD BEFORE, RAMONDA.
I GOT OVER IT.
MY... TOUCHY OLD BAT, ISN'T SHE.
PROBABLY ALL THAT GUILT FROM HAVING PLOTTED HER OWN STEPSON'S OUSTER.
AFTER ALL, T'CHALLA'S NO FOOL. IT WAS ONLY A MATTER OF TIME BEFORE HE PUT EVERY-THING TOGETHER ANYWAY --
-- DON'T YOU AGREE, DAKI --?
Insane! The woman is insane, and Achebe is King of the Universe!
KING AND QUEEN!
It is time for the King to unleash his secret weapon --
-- time for everyone to die!

MYSTERY DATE

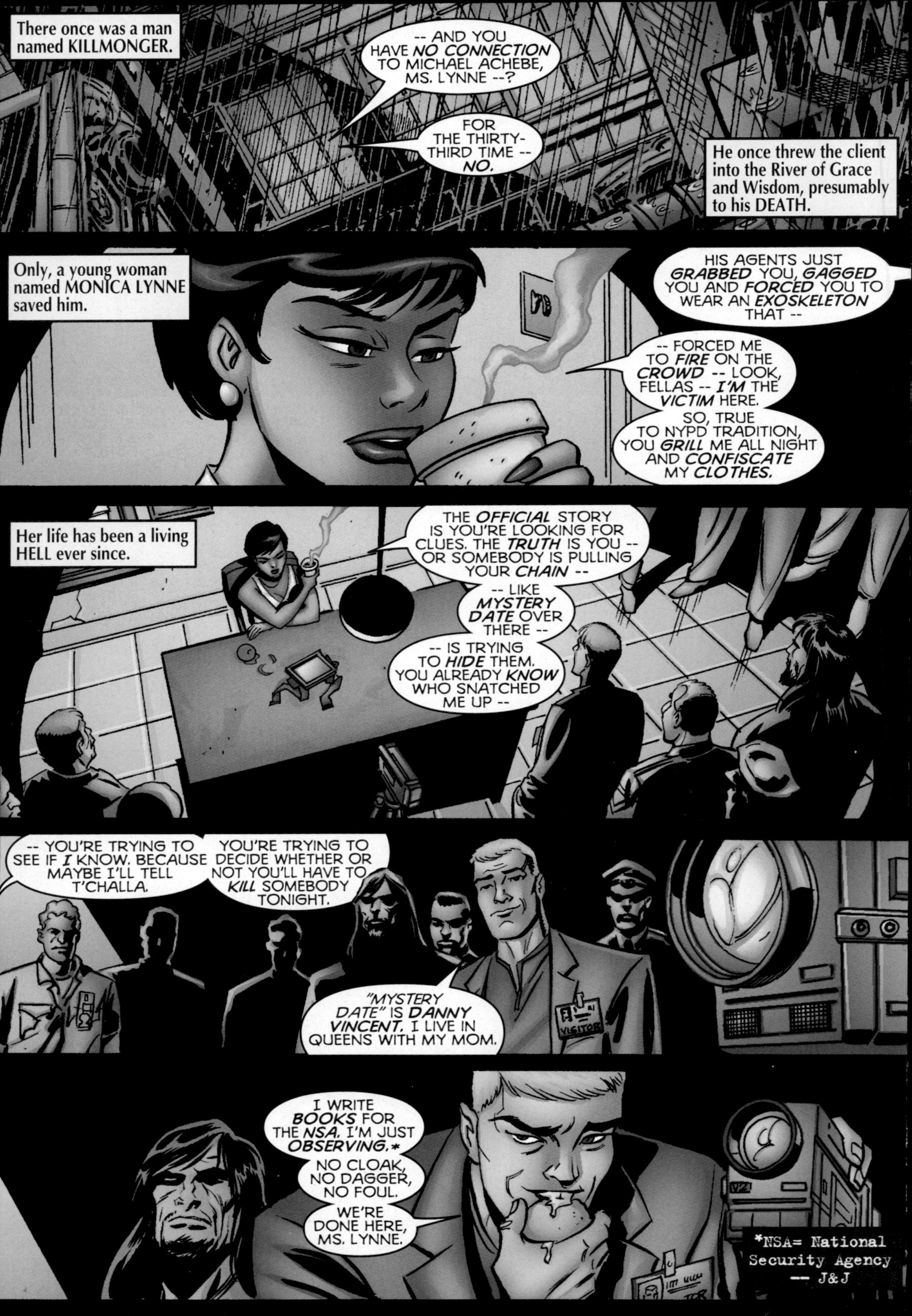

There once was a man named KILLMONGER.
-- AND YOU HAVE NO CONNECTION TO MICHAEL ACHEBE, MS. LYNNE --?
FOR THE THIRTY-THIRD TIME -- NO.
He once threw the client into the River of Grace and Wisdom, presumably to his DEATH.
Only, a young woman named MONICA LYNNE saved him.
HIS AGENTS JUST GRABBED YOU, GAGGED YOU AND FORCED YOU TO WEAR AN EXOSKELETON THAT --
-- FORCED ME TO FIRE ON THE CROWD -- LOOK, FELLAS -- I'M THE VICTIM HERE.
SO, TRUE TO NYPD TRADITION, YOU GRILL ME ALL NIGHT AND CONFISCATE MY CLOTHES.
Her life has been a living HELL ever since.
THE OFFICIAL STORY IS YOU'RE LOOKING FOR CLUES. THE TRUTH IS YOU -- OR SOMEBODY IS PULLING YOUR CHAIN --
-- LIKE MYSTERY DATE OVER THERE --
-- IS TRYING TO HIDE THEM. YOU ALREADY KNOW WHO SNATCHED ME UP --
-- YOU'RE TRYING TO SEE IF I KNOW. BECAUSE MAYBE I'LL TELL T'CHALLA.
YOU'RE TRYING TO DECIDE WHETHER OR NOT YOU'LL HAVE TO KILL SOMEBODY TONIGHT.
"MYSTERY DATE" IS DANNY VINCENT. I LIVE IN QUEENS WITH MY MOM.
VISITOR
I WRITE BOOKS FOR THE NSA. I'M JUST OBSERVING.*
NO CLOAK, NO DAGGER, NO FOUL.
WE'RE DONE HERE, MS. LYNNE.
*NSA= National Security Agency
-- J&J

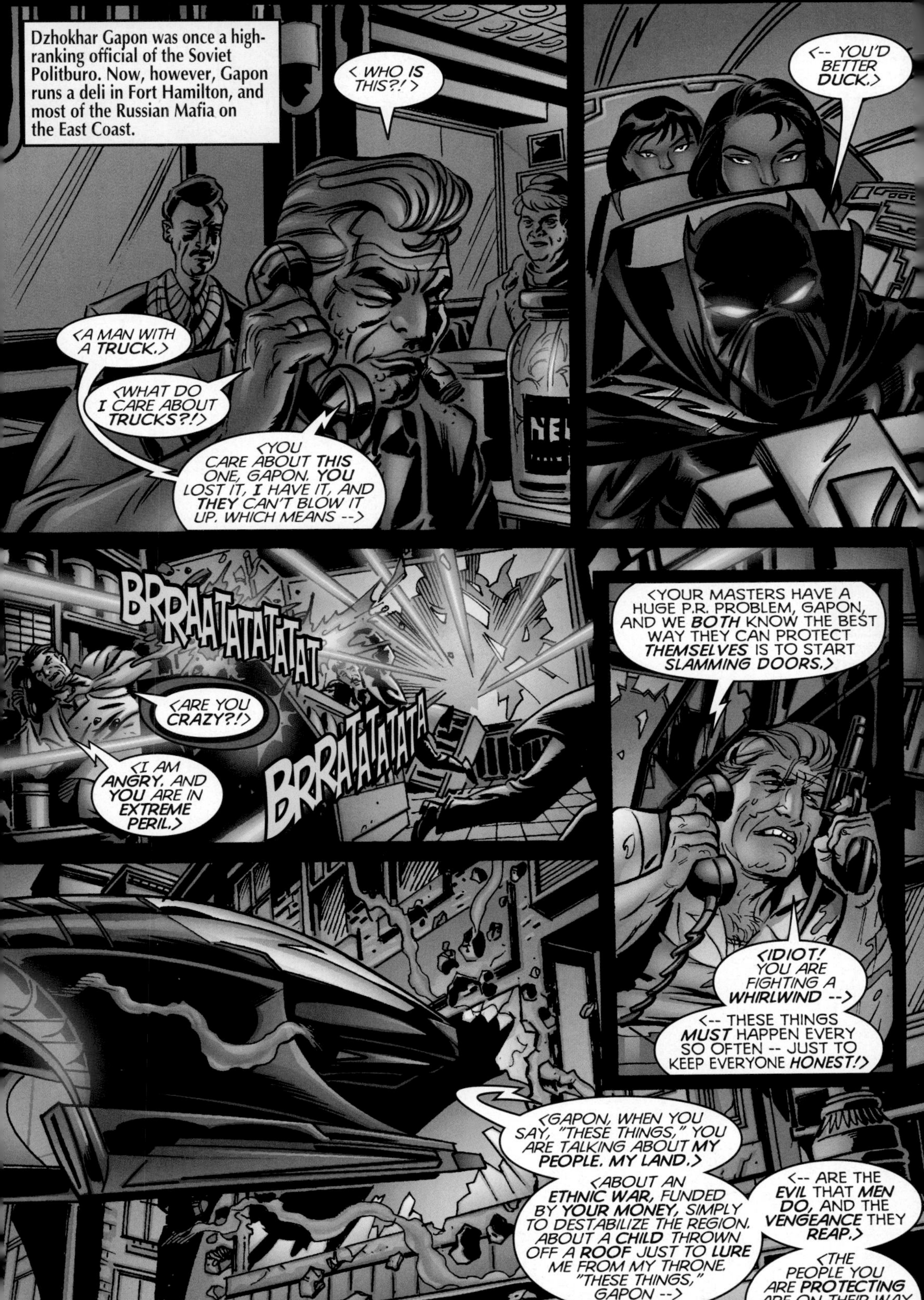
Dzhokhar Gapon was once a high-ranking official of the Soviet Politburo. Now, however, Gapon runs a deli in Fort Hamilton, and most of the Russian Mafia on the East Coast.
< WHO IS THIS?! >
<A MAN WITH A TRUCK.>
<WHAT DO I CARE ABOUT TRUCKS?!>
<YOU CARE ABOUT THIS ONE, GAPON. YOU LOST IT, I HAVE IT, AND THEY CAN'T BLOW IT UP. WHICH MEANS -->
<-- YOU'D BETTER DUCK.>
BRRAATATATATATAT
<ARE YOU CRAZY?!>
<I AM ANGRY. AND YOU ARE IN EXTREME PERIL.>
BRRATATATATA
<YOUR MASTERS HAVE A HUGE P.R. PROBLEM, GAPON, AND WE BOTH KNOW THE BEST WAY THEY CAN PROTECT THEMSELVES IS TO START SLAMMING DOORS.>
<IDIOT! YOU ARE FIGHTING A WHIRLWIND -->
<-- THESE THINGS MUST HAPPEN EVERY SO OFTEN -- JUST TO KEEP EVERYONE HONEST!>
<GAPON, WHEN YOU SAY, "THESE THINGS," YOU ARE TALKING ABOUT MY PEOPLE. MY LAND.>
<ABOUT AN ETHNIC WAR, FUNDED BY YOUR MONEY, SIMPLY TO DESTABILIZE THE REGION. ABOUT A CHILD THROWN OFF A ROOF JUST TO LURE ME FROM MY THRONE. "THESE THINGS," GAPON -->
<-- ARE THE EVIL THAT MEN DO, AND THE VENGEANCE THEY REAP.>
<THE PEOPLE YOU ARE PROTECTING ARE ON THEIR WAY TO KILL YOU. MAKE YOUR CHOICE.>

THE VERY BEST

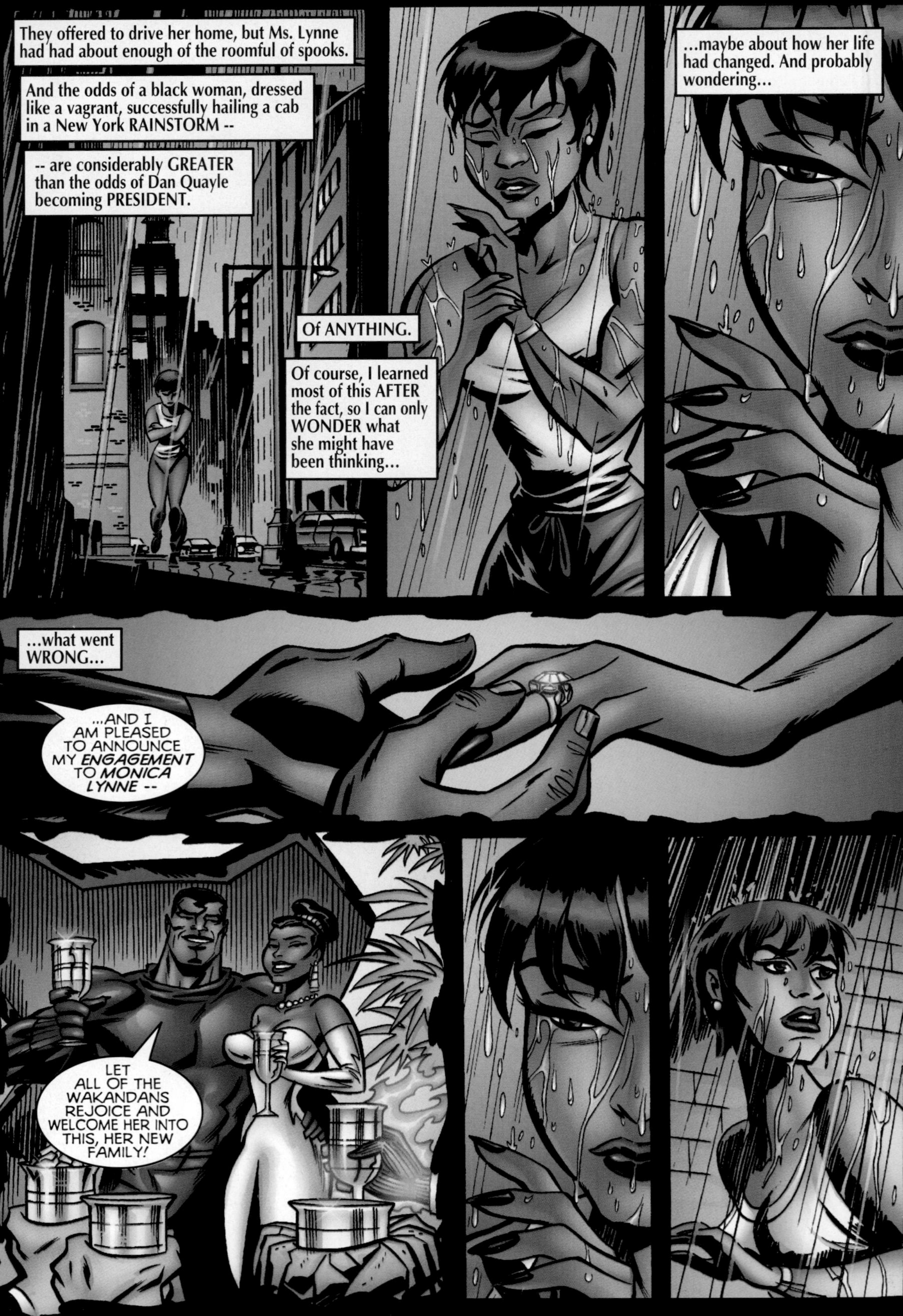

They offered to drive her home, but Ms. Lynne had had about enough of the roomful of spooks.
And the odds of a black woman, dressed like a vagrant, successfully hailing a cab in a New York RAINSTORM --
-- are considerably GREATER than the odds of Dan Quayle becoming PRESIDENT.
Of ANYTHING.
Of course, I learned most of this AFTER the fact, so I can only WONDER what she might have been thinking...
...maybe about how her life had changed. And probably wondering...
...what went WRONG...
...AND I AM PLEASED TO ANNOUNCE MY ENGAGEMENT TO MONICA LYNNE --
LET ALL OF THE WAKANDANS REJOICE AND WELCOME HER INTO THIS, HER NEW FAMILY!

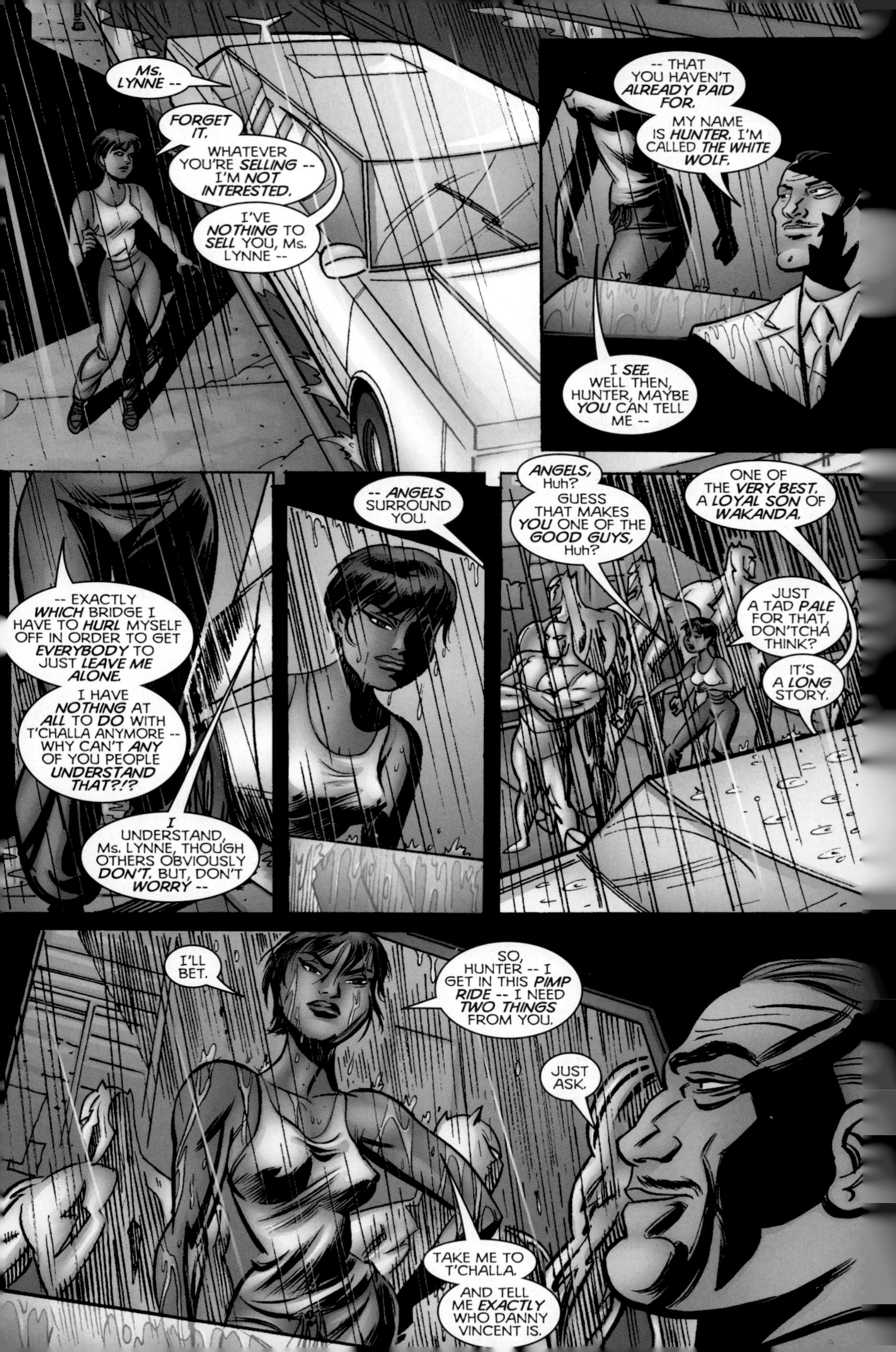
Ms. LYNNE --
FORGET IT.
WHATEVER YOU'RE SELLING -- I'M NOT INTERESTED.
I'VE NOTHING TO SELL YOU, Ms. LYNNE --
-- THAT YOU HAVEN'T ALREADY PAID FOR.
MY NAME IS HUNTER. I'M CALLED THE WHITE WOLF.
I SEE. WELL THEN, HUNTER, MAYBE YOU CAN TELL ME --
-- EXACTLY WHICH BRIDGE I HAVE TO HURL MYSELF OFF IN ORDER TO GET EVERYBODY TO JUST LEAVE ME ALONE.
I HAVE NOTHING AT ALL TO DO WITH T'CHALLA ANYMORE -- WHY CAN'T ANY OF YOU PEOPLE UNDERSTAND THAT?!?
I UNDERSTAND, Ms. LYNNE, THOUGH OTHERS OBVIOUSLY DON'T. BUT, DON'T WORRY --
-- ANGELS SURROUND YOU.
ANGELS, Huh? GUESS THAT MAKES YOU ONE OF THE GOOD GUYS, Huh?
ONE OF THE VERY BEST. A LOYAL SON OF WAKANDA.
JUST A TAD PALE FOR THAT, DON'TCHA THINK?
IT'S A LONG STORY.
I'LL BET.
SO, HUNTER -- I GET IN THIS PIMP RIDE -- I NEED TWO THINGS FROM YOU.
JUST ASK.
TAKE ME TO T'CHALLA.
AND TELL ME EXACTLY WHO DANNY VINCENT IS.

JACK BE QUICK

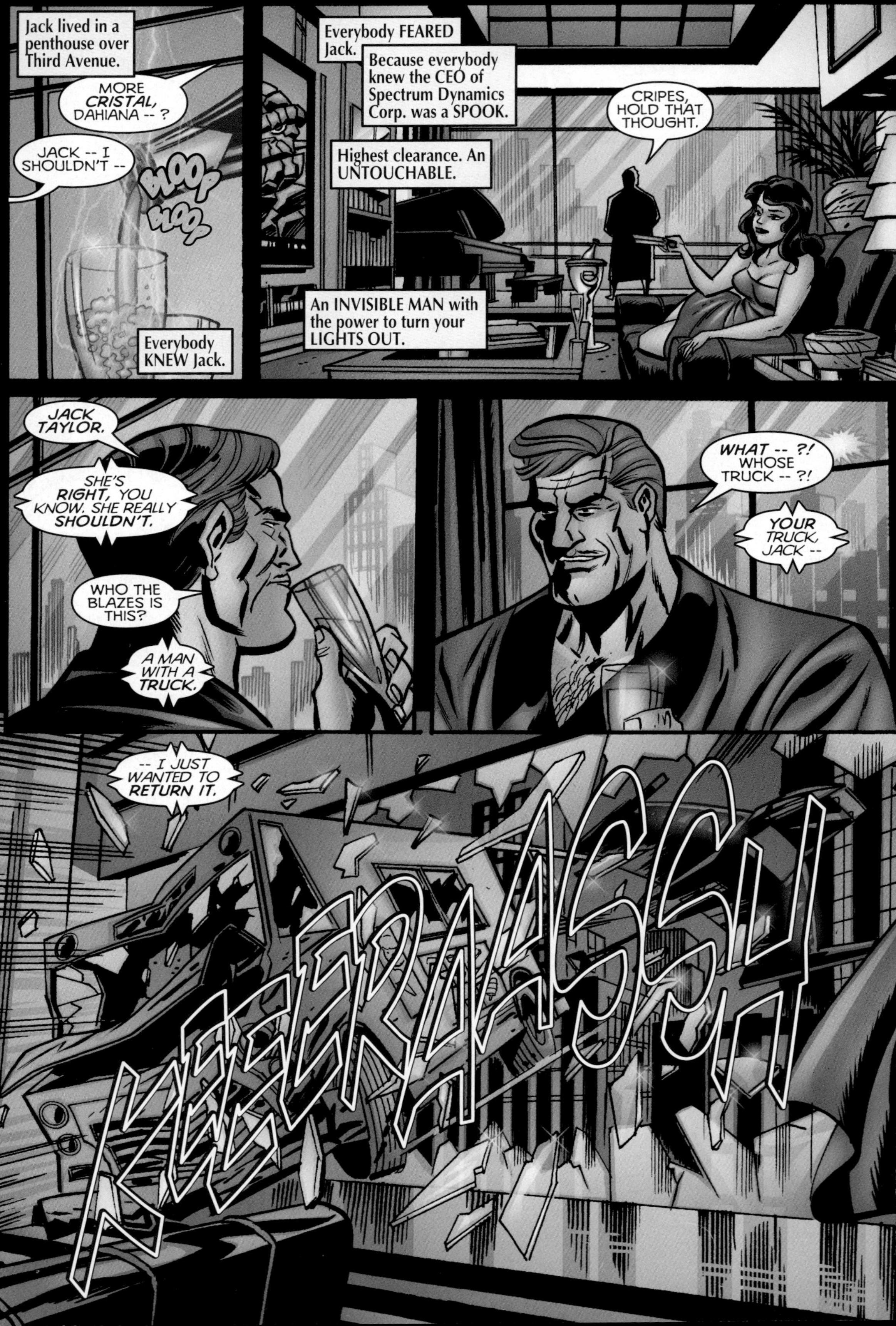

Jack lived in a penthouse over Third Avenue.
MORE CRISTAL, DAHIANA -- ?
JACK -- I SHOULDN'T --
BLOOP BLOOP
Everybody KNEW Jack.
Everybody FEARED Jack.
Because everybody knew the CEO of Spectrum Dynamics Corp. was a SPOOK.
Highest clearance. An UNTOUCHABLE.
An INVISIBLE MAN with the power to turn your LIGHTS OUT.
CRIPES, HOLD THAT THOUGHT.
JACK TAYLOR.
SHE'S RIGHT, YOU KNOW. SHE REALLY SHOULDN'T.
WHO THE BLAZES IS THIS?
A MAN WITH A TRUCK.
WHAT -- ?! WHOSE TRUCK -- ?!
YOUR TRUCK, JACK --
-- I JUST WANTED TO RETURN IT.
KKEERRAASSH

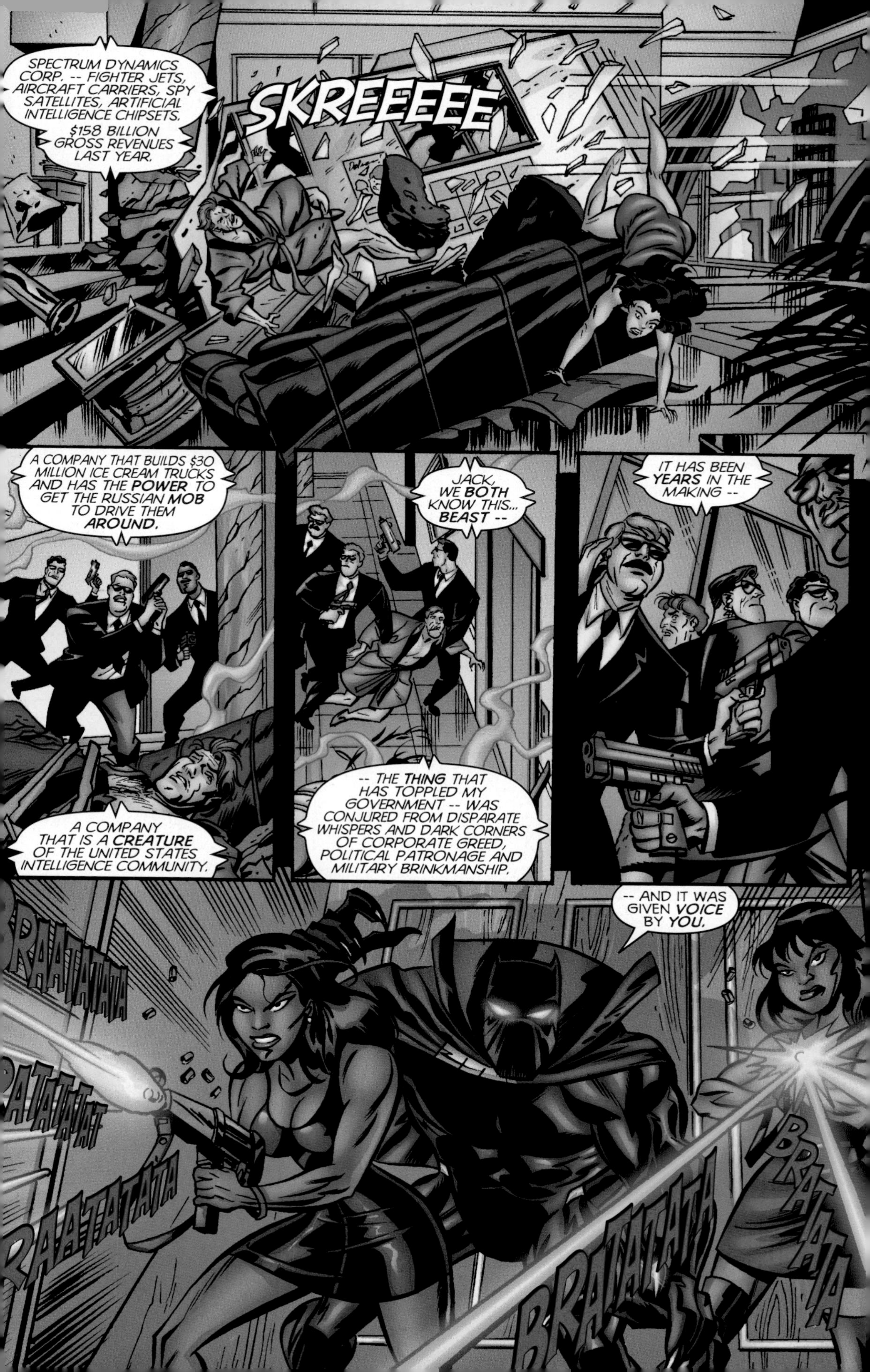
SPECTRUM DYNAMICS CORP. -- FIGHTER JETS, AIRCRAFT CARRIERS, SPY SATELLITES, ARTIFICIAL INTELLIGENCE CHIPSETS. $158 BILLION GROSS REVENUES LAST YEAR.
SKREEEEEE
A COMPANY THAT BUILDS $30 MILLION ICE CREAM TRUCKS AND HAS THE POWER TO GET THE RUSSIAN MOB TO DRIVE THEM AROUND.
A COMPANY THAT IS A CREATURE OF THE UNITED STATES INTELLIGENCE COMMUNITY.
JACK, WE BOTH KNOW THIS... BEAST --
-- THE THING THAT HAS TOPPLED MY GOVERNMENT -- WAS CONJURED FROM DISPARATE WHISPERS AND DARK CORNERS OF CORPORATE GREED, POLITICAL PATRONAGE AND MILITARY BRINKMANSHIP.
IT HAS BEEN YEARS IN THE MAKING --
-- AND IT WAS GIVEN VOICE BY YOU.
BRAATATATATA
BRATATATATAT
BRAATATATATA
BRATATATATA
BRATATATATA

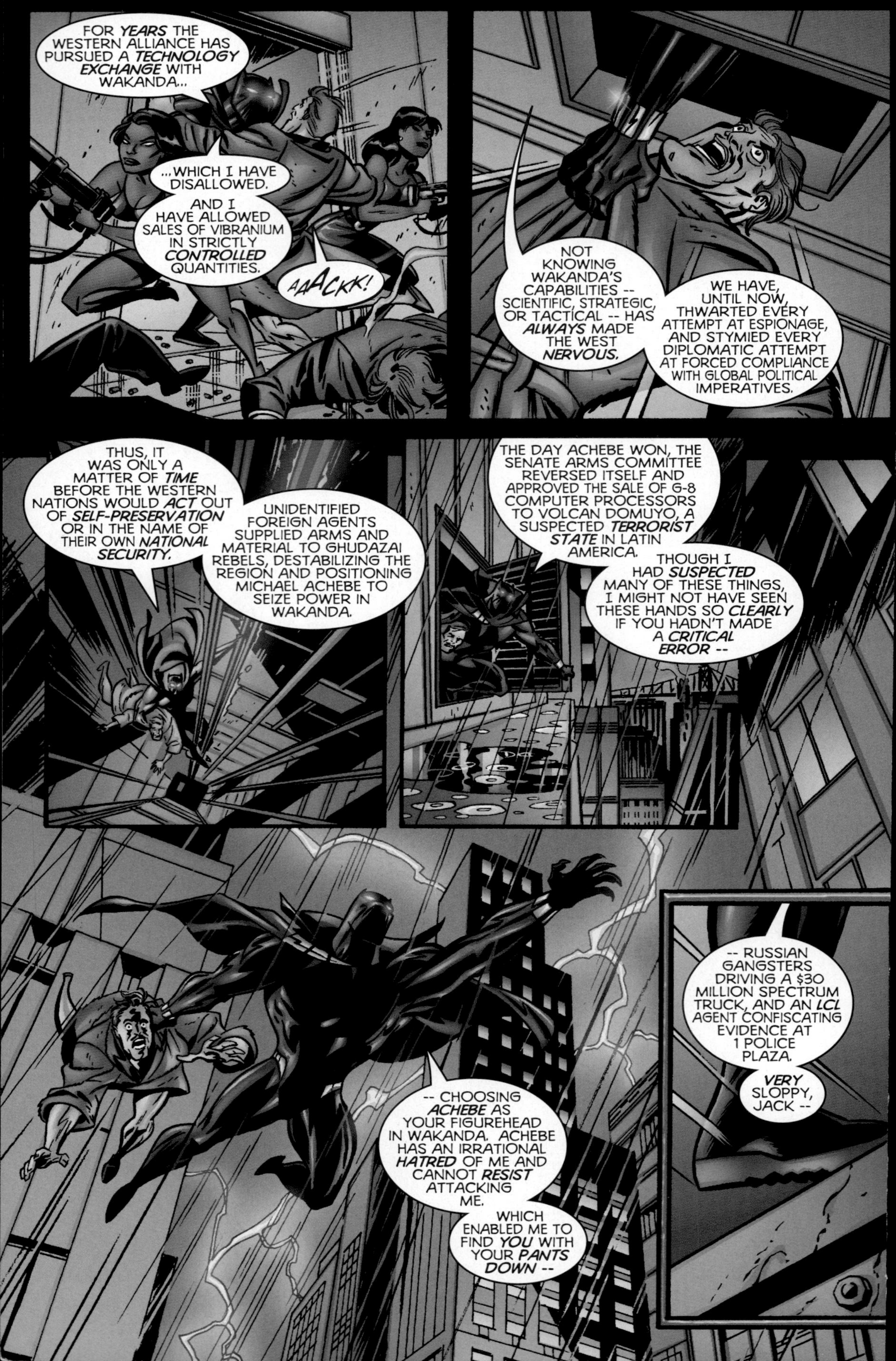
FOR YEARS THE WESTERN ALLIANCE HAS PURSUED A TECHNOLOGY EXCHANGE WITH WAKANDA...
...WHICH I HAVE DISALLOWED.
AND I HAVE ALLOWED SALES OF VIBRANIUM IN STRICTLY CONTROLLED QUANTITIES.
AAACKK!
NOT KNOWING WAKANDA'S CAPABILITIES -- SCIENTIFIC, STRATEGIC, OR TACTICAL -- HAS ALWAYS MADE THE WEST NERVOUS.
WE HAVE, UNTIL NOW, THWARTED EVERY ATTEMPT AT ESPIONAGE, AND STYMIED EVERY DIPLOMATIC ATTEMPT AT FORCED COMPLIANCE WITH GLOBAL POLITICAL IMPERATIVES.
THUS, IT WAS ONLY A MATTER OF TIME BEFORE THE WESTERN NATIONS WOULD ACT OUT OF SELF-PRESERVATION OR IN THE NAME OF THEIR OWN NATIONAL SECURITY.
UNIDENTIFIED FOREIGN AGENTS SUPPLIED ARMS AND MATERIAL TO GHUDAZAI REBELS, DESTABILIZING THE REGION AND POSITIONING MICHAEL ACHEBE TO SEIZE POWER IN WAKANDA.
THE DAY ACHEBE WON, THE SENATE ARMS COMMITTEE REVERSED ITSELF AND APPROVED THE SALE OF G-8 COMPUTER PROCESSORS TO VOLCAN DOMUYO, A SUSPECTED TERRORIST STATE IN LATIN AMERICA.
THOUGH I HAD SUSPECTED MANY OF THESE THINGS, I MIGHT NOT HAVE SEEN THESE HANDS SO CLEARLY IF YOU HADN'T MADE A CRITICAL ERROR --
-- CHOOSING ACHEBE AS YOUR FIGUREHEAD IN WAKANDA. ACHEBE HAS AN IRRATIONAL HATRED OF ME AND CANNOT RESIST ATTACKING ME.
WHICH ENABLED ME TO FIND YOU WITH YOUR PANTS DOWN --
-- RUSSIAN GANGSTERS DRIVING A $30 MILLION SPECTRUM TRUCK, AND AN LCL AGENT CONFISCATING EVIDENCE AT 1 POLICE PLAZA.
VERY SLOPPY, JACK --

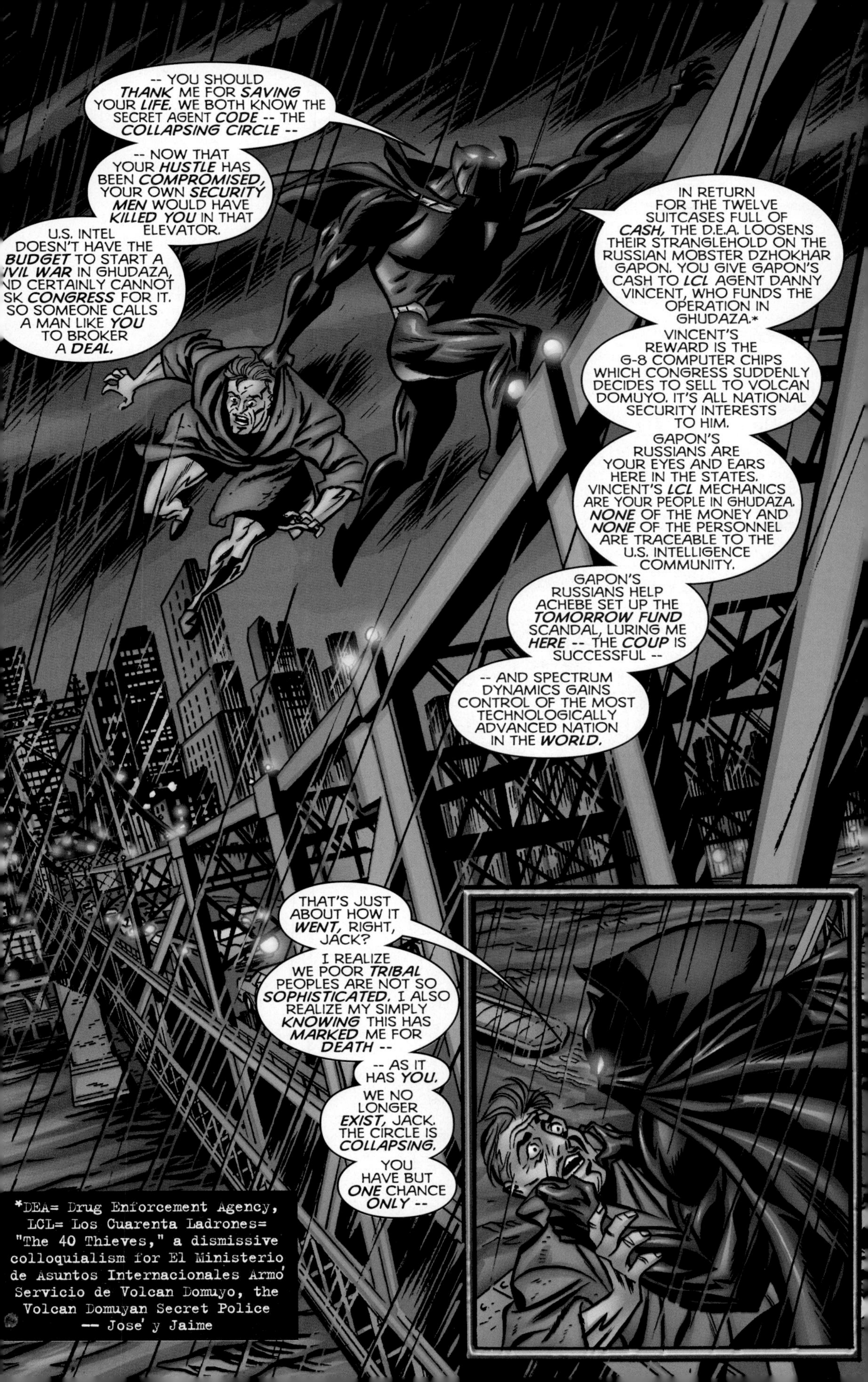

-- YOU SHOULD *THANK* ME FOR *SAVING* YOUR *LIFE.* WE BOTH KNOW THE SECRET AGENT *CODE* -- THE *COLLAPSING CIRCLE* --
-- NOW THAT YOUR *HUSTLE* HAS BEEN *COMPROMISED,* YOUR OWN *SECURITY MEN* WOULD HAVE *KILLED YOU* IN THAT ELEVATOR.
U.S. INTEL DOESN'T HAVE THE *BUDGET* TO START A *IVIL WAR* IN GHUDAZA, ND CERTAINLY CANNOT SK *CONGRESS* FOR IT. SO SOMEONE CALLS A MAN LIKE *YOU* TO BROKER A *DEAL.*
IN RETURN FOR THE TWELVE SUITCASES FULL OF *CASH,* THE D.E.A. LOOSENS THEIR STRANGLEHOLD ON THE RUSSIAN MOBSTER DZHOKHAR GAPON. YOU GIVE GAPON'S CASH TO *LCL* AGENT DANNY VINCENT, WHO FUNDS THE OPERATION IN GHUDAZA.*
VINCENT'S REWARD IS THE G-8 COMPUTER CHIPS WHICH CONGRESS SUDDENLY DECIDES TO SELL TO VOLCAN DOMUYO. IT'S ALL NATIONAL SECURITY INTERESTS TO HIM.
GAPON'S RUSSIANS ARE YOUR EYES AND EARS HERE IN THE STATES. VINCENT'S *LCL* MECHANICS ARE YOUR PEOPLE IN GHUDAZA. *NONE* OF THE MONEY AND *NONE* OF THE PERSONNEL ARE TRACEABLE TO THE U.S. INTELLIGENCE COMMUNITY.
GAPON'S RUSSIANS HELP ACHEBE SET UP THE *TOMORROW FUND* SCANDAL, LURING ME *HERE* -- THE *COUP* IS SUCCESSFUL --
-- AND SPECTRUM DYNAMICS GAINS CONTROL OF THE MOST TECHNOLOGICALLY ADVANCED NATION IN THE *WORLD.*
THAT'S JUST ABOUT HOW IT *WENT,* RIGHT, JACK?
I REALIZE WE POOR *TRIBAL* PEOPLES ARE NOT SO *SOPHISTICATED.* I ALSO REALIZE MY SIMPLY *KNOWING* THIS HAS *MARKED* ME FOR *DEATH* --
-- AS IT HAS *YOU.*
WE NO LONGER *EXIST,* JACK. THE CIRCLE IS *COLLAPSING.*
YOU HAVE BUT *ONE* CHANCE *ONLY* --
*DEA= Drug Enforcement Agency, LCL= Los Cuarenta Ladrones= "The 40 Thieves," a dismissive colloquialism for El Ministerio de Asuntos Internacionales Armo' Servicio de Volcan Domuyo, the Volcan Domuyan Secret Police -- Jose' y Jaime

158 BILLION REASONS

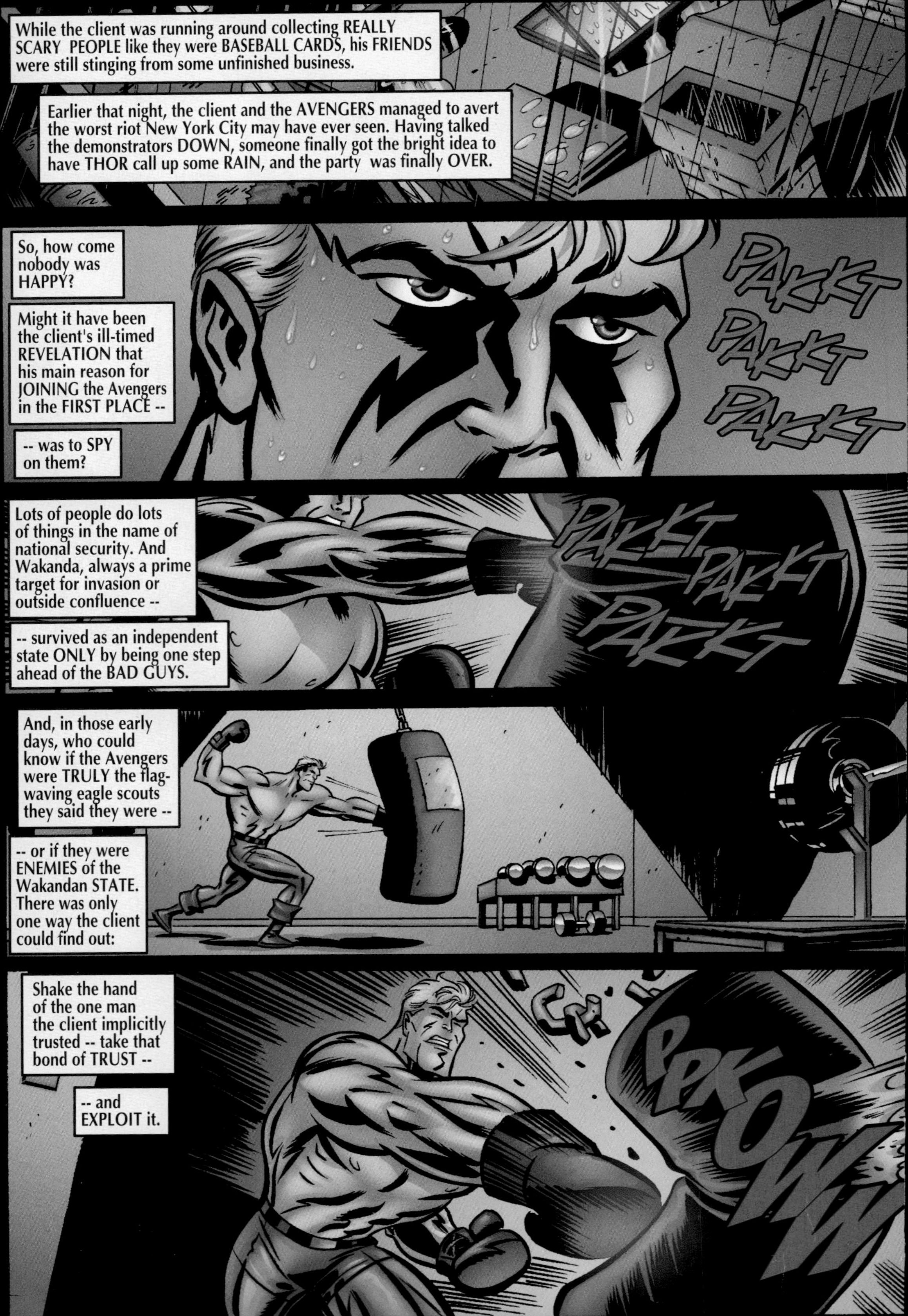

While the client was running around collecting REALLY SCARY PEOPLE like they were BASEBALL CARDS, his FRIENDS were still stinging from some unfinished business.
Earlier that night, the client and the AVENGERS managed to avert the worst riot New York City may have ever seen. Having talked the demonstrators DOWN, someone finally got the bright idea to have THOR call up some RAIN, and the party was finally OVER.
So, how come nobody was HAPPY?
Might it have been the client's ill-timed REVELATION that his main reason for JOINING the Avengers in the FIRST PLACE --
-- was to SPY on them?
PAKKT PAKKT PAKKT
Lots of people do lots of things in the name of national security. And Wakanda, always a prime target for invasion or outside confluence --
-- survived as an independent state ONLY by being one step ahead of the BAD GUYS.
PAKKT PAKKT PAKKT
And, in those early days, who could know if the Avengers were TRULY the flag-waving eagle scouts they said they were --
-- or if they were ENEMIES of the Wakandan STATE. There was only one way the client could find out:
Shake the hand of the one man the client implicitly trusted -- take that bond of TRUST --
-- and EXPLOIT it.
PPKOWW

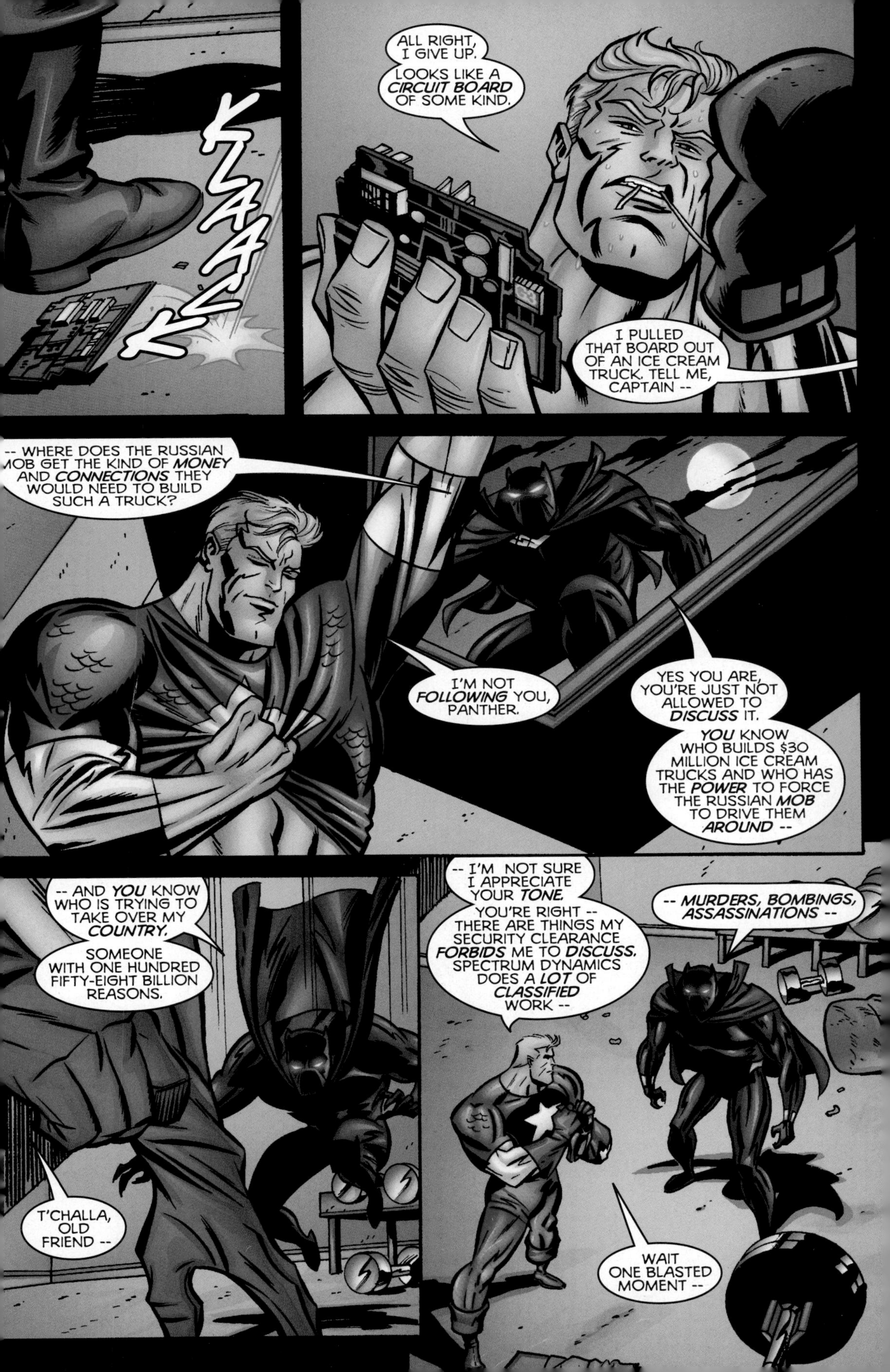
KLAAACK
ALL RIGHT, I GIVE UP.
LOOKS LIKE A *CIRCUIT BOARD* OF SOME KIND.
I PULLED THAT BOARD OUT OF AN ICE CREAM TRUCK. TELL ME, CAPTAIN --
-- WHERE DOES THE RUSSIAN MOB GET THE KIND OF *MONEY* AND *CONNECTIONS* THEY WOULD NEED TO BUILD SUCH A TRUCK?
I'M NOT *FOLLOWING* YOU, PANTHER.
YES YOU ARE, YOU'RE JUST NOT ALLOWED TO *DISCUSS* IT.
YOU KNOW WHO BUILDS $30 MILLION ICE CREAM TRUCKS AND WHO HAS THE *POWER* TO FORCE THE RUSSIAN *MOB* TO DRIVE THEM *AROUND* --
-- AND *YOU* KNOW WHO IS TRYING TO TAKE OVER MY *COUNTRY.*
SOMEONE WITH ONE HUNDRED FIFTY-EIGHT BILLION REASONS.
T'CHALLA, OLD FRIEND --
-- I'M NOT SURE I APPRECIATE YOUR *TONE.*
YOU'RE RIGHT -- THERE ARE THINGS MY SECURITY CLEARANCE *FORBIDS* ME TO *DISCUSS.* SPECTRUM DYNAMICS DOES A *LOT* OF *CLASSIFIED* WORK --
-- *MURDERS, BOMBINGS, ASSASSINATIONS* --
WAIT ONE BLASTED MOMENT --

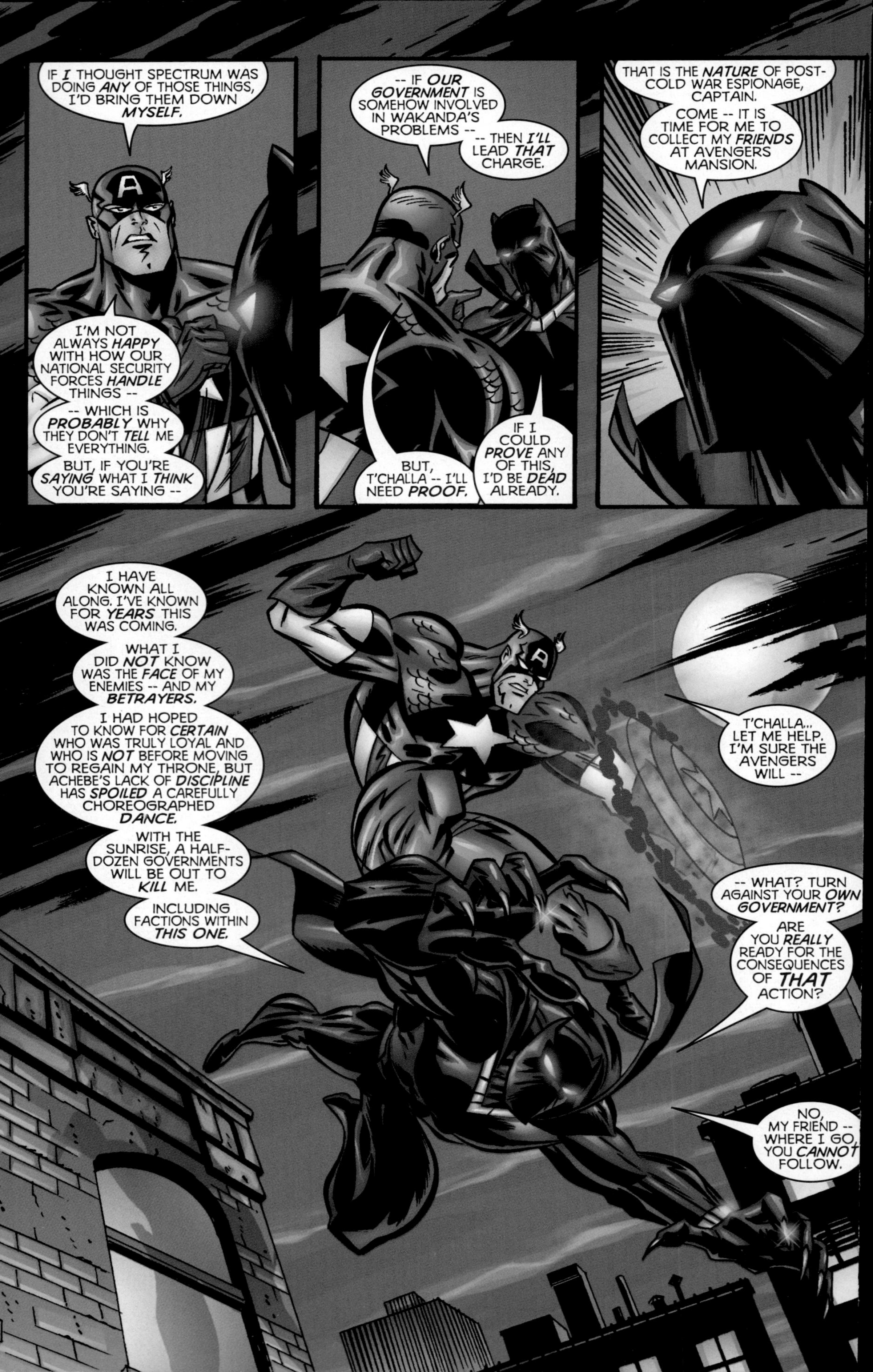

IF I THOUGHT SPECTRUM WAS DOING ANY OF THOSE THINGS, I'D BRING THEM DOWN MYSELF.
I'M NOT ALWAYS HAPPY WITH HOW OUR NATIONAL SECURITY FORCES HANDLE THINGS --
-- WHICH IS PROBABLY WHY THEY DON'T TELL ME EVERYTHING.
BUT, IF YOU'RE SAYING WHAT I THINK YOU'RE SAYING --
-- IF OUR GOVERNMENT IS SOMEHOW INVOLVED IN WAKANDA'S PROBLEMS --
-- THEN I'LL LEAD THAT CHARGE.
BUT, T'CHALLA -- I'LL NEED PROOF.
IF I COULD PROVE ANY OF THIS, I'D BE DEAD ALREADY.
THAT IS THE NATURE OF POST-COLD WAR ESPIONAGE, CAPTAIN.
COME -- IT IS TIME FOR ME TO COLLECT MY FRIENDS AT AVENGERS MANSION.
I HAVE KNOWN ALL ALONG. I'VE KNOWN FOR YEARS THIS WAS COMING.
WHAT I DID NOT KNOW WAS THE FACE OF MY ENEMIES -- AND MY BETRAYERS.
I HAD HOPED TO KNOW FOR CERTAIN WHO WAS TRULY LOYAL AND WHO IS NOT BEFORE MOVING TO REGAIN MY THRONE, BUT ACHEBE'S LACK OF DISCIPLINE HAS SPOILED A CAREFULLY CHOREOGRAPHED DANCE.
WITH THE SUNRISE, A HALF-DOZEN GOVERNMENTS WILL BE OUT TO KILL ME.
INCLUDING FACTIONS WITHIN THIS ONE.
T'CHALLA... LET ME HELP. I'M SURE THE AVENGERS WILL --
-- WHAT? TURN AGAINST YOUR OWN GOVERNMENT?
ARE YOU REALLY READY FOR THE CONSEQUENCES OF THAT ACTION?
NO, MY FRIEND -- WHERE I GO, YOU CANNOT FOLLOW.

COUSINS

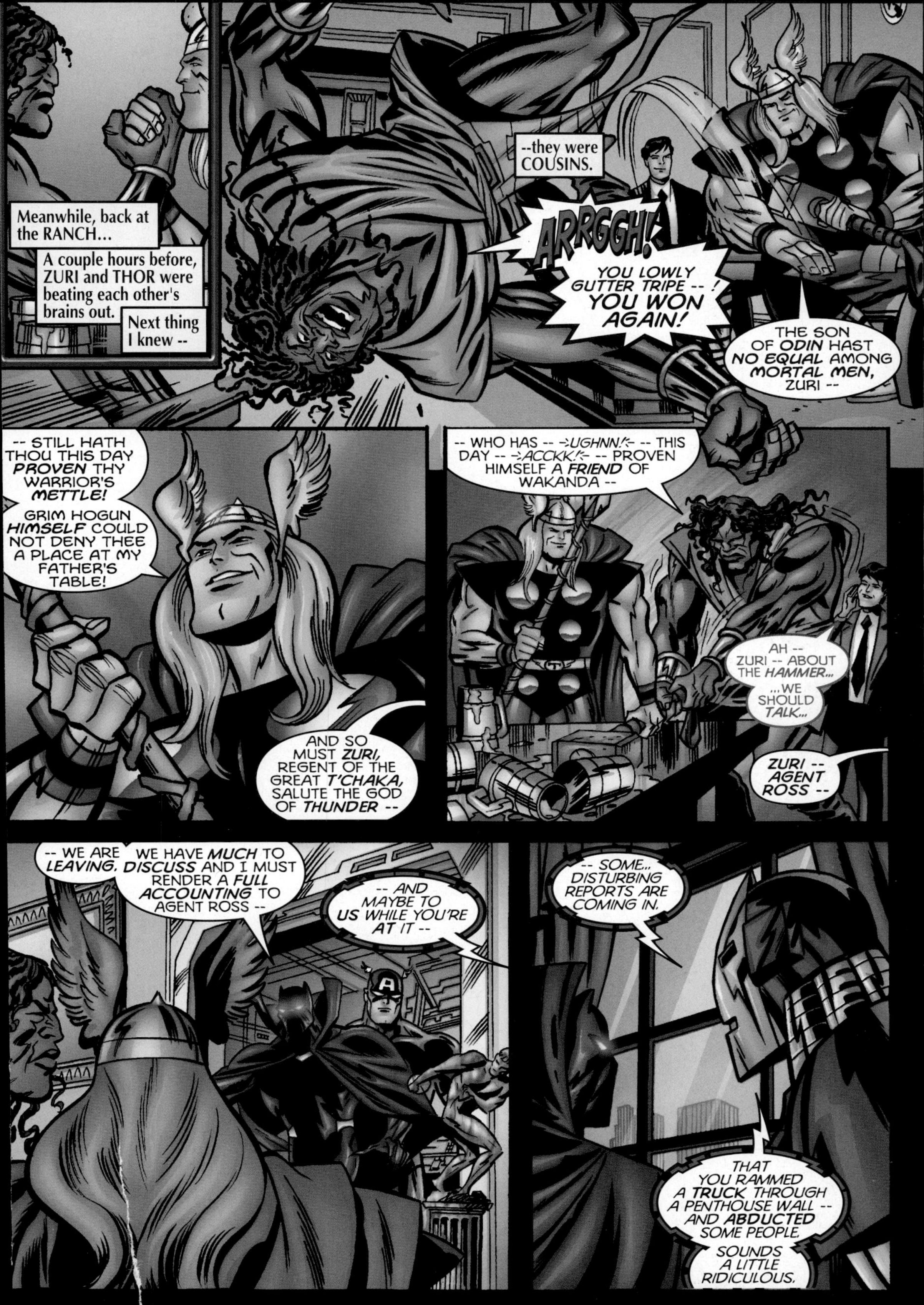

Meanwhile, back at the RANCH...
A couple hours before, ZURI and THOR were beating each other's brains out.
Next thing I knew --
--they were COUSINS.
ARRGGH!
YOU LOWLY GUTTER TRIPE -- ! YOU WON AGAIN!
THE SON OF ODIN HAST NO EQUAL AMONG MORTAL MEN, ZURI --
-- STILL HATH THOU THIS DAY PROVEN THY WARRIOR'S METTLE!
GRIM HOGUN HIMSELF COULD NOT DENY THEE A PLACE AT MY FATHER'S TABLE!
AND SO MUST ZURI, REGENT OF THE GREAT T'CHAKA, SALUTE THE GOD OF THUNDER --
-- WHO HAS -- ->UGHNN!<- -- THIS DAY -- ->ACCKK!<- -- PROVEN HIMSELF A FRIEND OF WAKANDA --
AH -- ZURI -- ABOUT THE HAMMER...
...WE SHOULD TALK...
ZURI -- AGENT ROSS --
-- WE ARE LEAVING.
WE HAVE MUCH TO DISCUSS AND I MUST RENDER A FULL ACCOUNTING TO AGENT ROSS --
-- AND MAYBE TO US WHILE YOU'RE AT IT --
-- SOME... DISTURBING REPORTS ARE COMING IN.
THAT YOU RAMMED A TRUCK THROUGH A PENTHOUSE WALL -- AND ABDUCTED SOME PEOPLE.
SOUNDS A LITTLE RIDICULOUS.

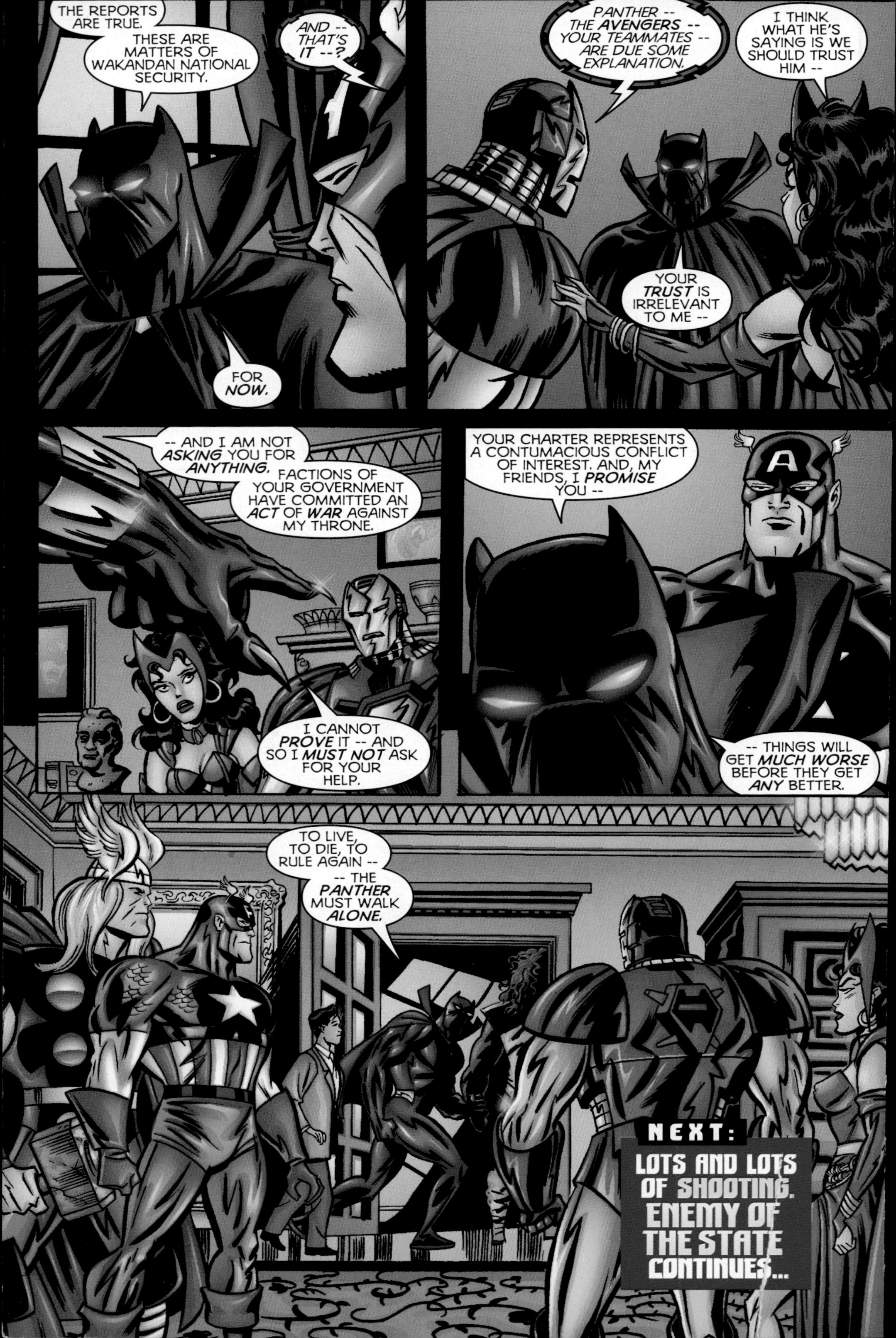
THE REPORTS ARE TRUE.
THESE ARE MATTERS OF WAKANDAN NATIONAL SECURITY.
AND -- THAT'S IT --?
FOR NOW.
PANTHER -- THE AVENGERS -- YOUR TEAMMATES -- ARE DUE SOME EXPLANATION.
I THINK WHAT HE'S SAYING IS WE SHOULD TRUST HIM --
YOUR TRUST IS IRRELEVANT TO ME --
-- AND I AM NOT ASKING YOU FOR ANYTHING.
FACTIONS OF YOUR GOVERNMENT HAVE COMMITTED AN ACT OF WAR AGAINST MY THRONE.
I CANNOT PROVE IT -- AND SO I MUST NOT ASK FOR YOUR HELP.
YOUR CHARTER REPRESENTS A CONTUMACIOUS CONFLICT OF INTEREST. AND, MY FRIENDS, I PROMISE YOU --
-- THINGS WILL GET MUCH WORSE BEFORE THEY GET ANY BETTER.
TO LIVE, TO DIE, TO RULE AGAIN --
-- THE PANTHER MUST WALK ALONE.
NEXT:
LOTS AND LOTS OF SHOOTING. ENEMY OF THE STATE CONTINUES...

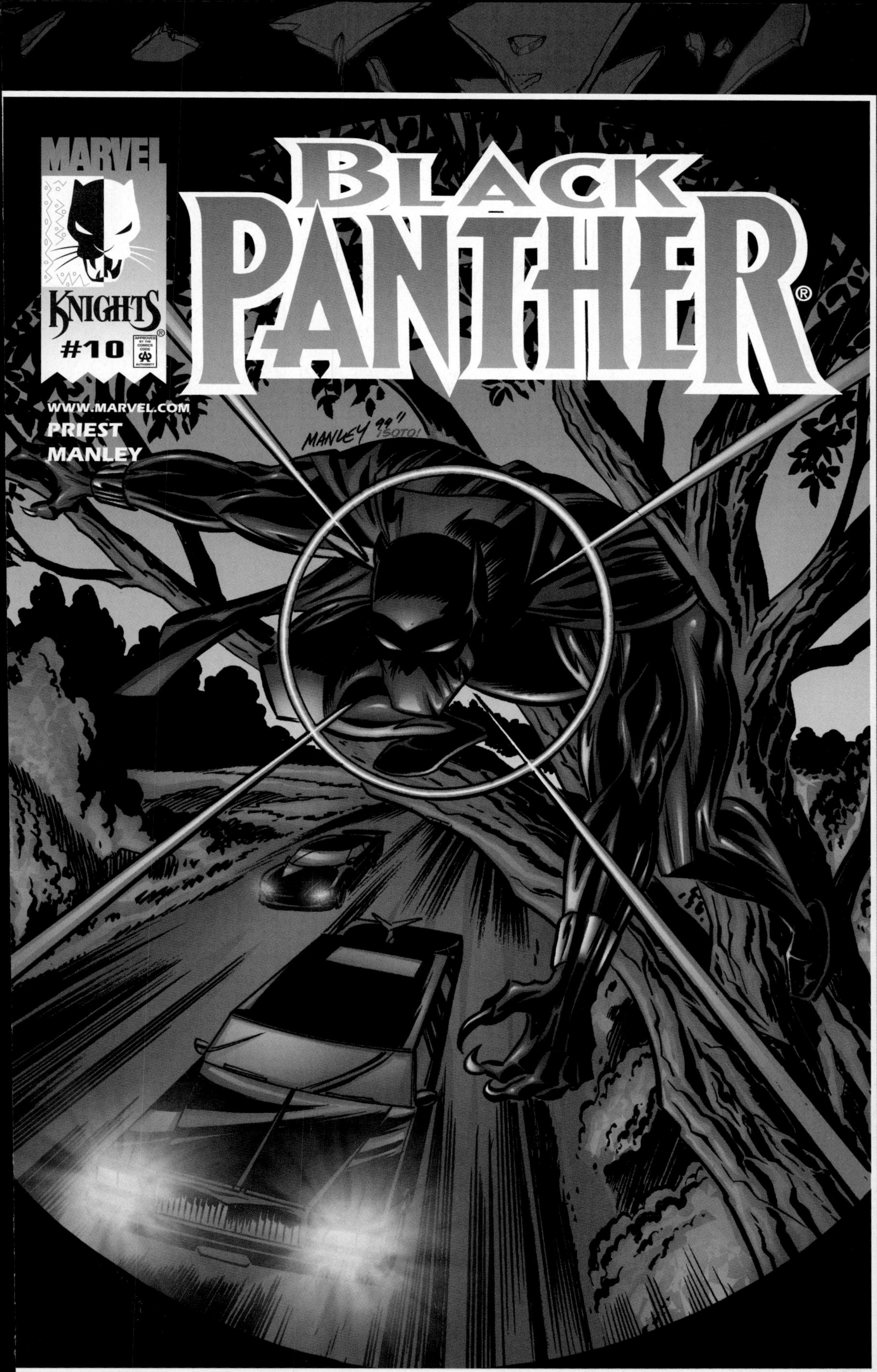
MARVEL
KNIGHTS
#10
APPROVED BY THE COMICS CODE AUTHORITY
BLACK PANTHER®
WWW.MARVEL.COM
PRIEST
MANLEY

THE UPPER HAND

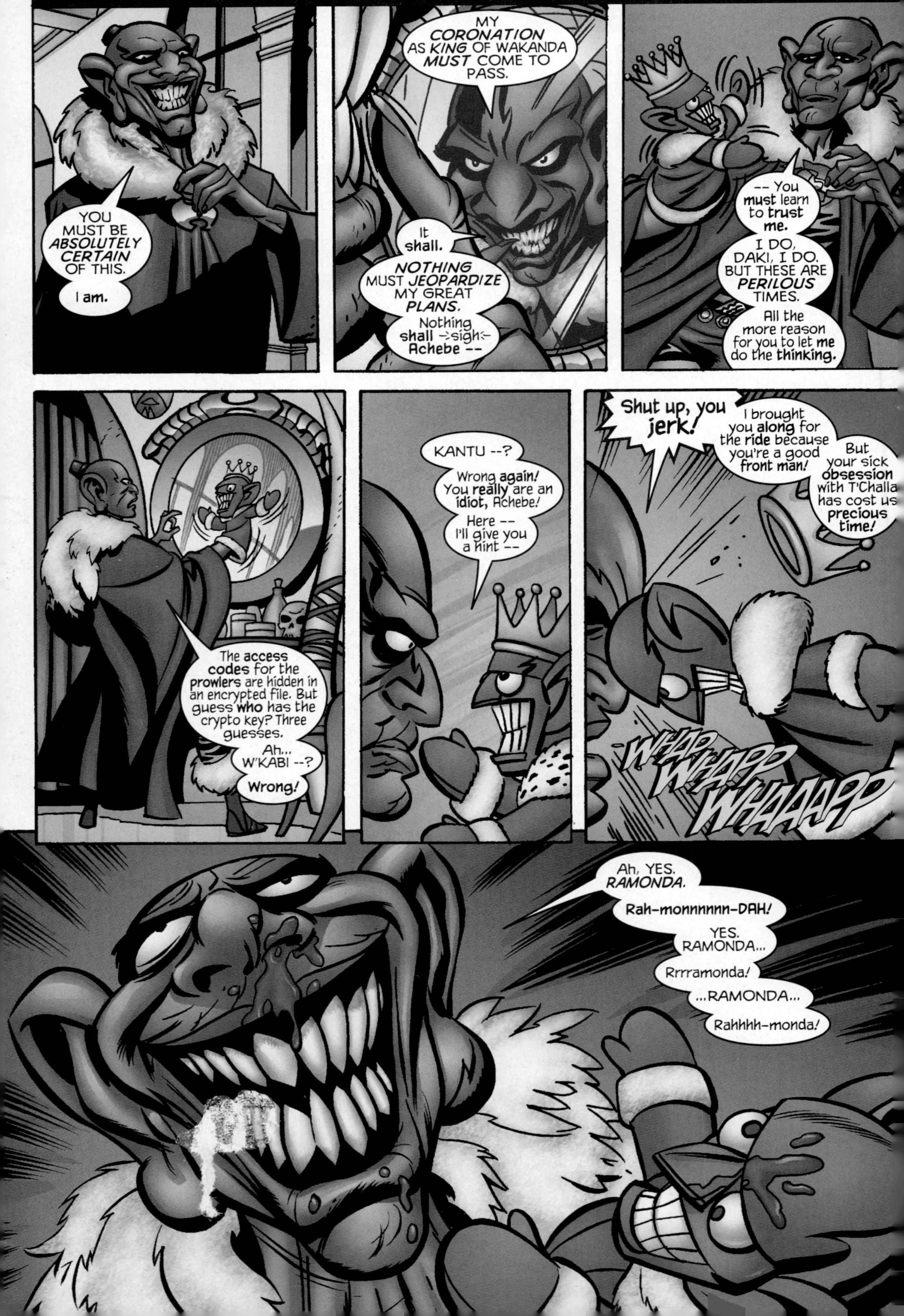

YOU MUST BE ABSOLUTELY CERTAIN OF THIS.
I am.
MY CORONATION AS KING OF WAKANDA MUST COME TO PASS.
It shall.
NOTHING MUST JEOPARDIZE MY GREAT PLANS.
Nothing shall -sigh- Achebe --
-- You must learn to trust me.
I DO, DAKI, I DO. BUT THESE ARE PERILOUS TIMES.
All the more reason for you to let me do the thinking.
The access codes for the prowlers are hidden in an encrypted file. But guess who has the crypto key? Three guesses.
Ah... W'KABI --?
Wrong!
KANTU --?
Wrong again! You really are an idiot, Achebe!
Here -- I'll give you a hint --
Shut up, you jerk!
I brought you along for the ride because you're a good front man!
But your sick obsession with T'Challa has cost us precious time!
WHAP WHAPP WHAAAPP
Ah, YES. RAMONDA.
Rah-monnnnnn-DAH!
YES. RAMONDA...
Rrrramonda!
...RAMONDA...
Rahhhh-monda!

STAN LEE PRESENTS: THE BLACK PANTHER

ENEMY OF THE STATE

BOOK TWO

The story thus far:

Having rounded up the Russian mobster and the American spook -- both semifinalists for the 1999 "Mr. Kill You Without A Second Thought" Image Award -- the client went out to QUEENS to make it a trifecta.

CHRISTOPHER PRIEST STORY **MIKE MANLEY** ART

| CHRIS SOMOMAYOR COLORS | RICHARD STARKINGS AND COMICRAFT/JL LETTERS | NANCI DAKESIAN MANAGING EDITOR | JIMMY PALMIOTTI AND JOE QUESADA EDITORS | BOB HARRAS CHIEF |

JUNTA

The client went for Danny Vincent.

¿DANNY -- CUÁNDO VA USTED ENCONTRAR A UNA MUCHACHA BUENA Y ESTABLECERSE?

TUESDAY, MA. IT'S IN MY *BOOK*.

RIGHT *BACK*, MA -- LEFT SOMETHING IN THE *CAR*.

Now, it was only a RUMOR, but word had it Danny Vincent's real name was Vicente, and Vicente was a high-ranking official of the LCL, the Volcan Domuyan Secret Service.

Danny helped arm extremist factions in Ghudaza as part of a dirty tricks campaign to bring down the client's government.

The Ghudaza civil war turned into an ethnic slaughter, but to Danny, it was just business --

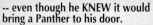

-- even though he KNEW it would bring a Panther to his door.

GUESS I SHOULD BE *SCARED* NOW. LOOK -- NOT FOR NOTHING -- BUT IF I HADN'T WORKED FOR GHUDAZA...

...JACK TAYLOR WOULDA JUST SUBBED THAT JOB OUT TO THE HAND OR MOSSAD OR SOMEBODY.

THE VOLCAN DOMUYO WOULDN'T GET THOSE G-8 CHIPS TAYLOR CARROT-AND-STICKED US WITH.

TO SERVE MY COUNTRY, I DO WHAT I *DO*. I SHOOK A *HAND* AND DID A PIECE OF *BUSINESS*.

IN THE TRUNK, I GOT A CROWBAR AND A ROLL OF *DUCT TAPE*. THAT'S ABOUT THE EXTENT OF MY HI-TECH WEAPONS' CACHE.

BUT, IN TERMS OF THE *TUNE-UP* THAT IS SURE TO BE THE *HIGH-LIGHT* OF TONIGHT'S PERFORMANCE --

-- HIGH ON THE *SHORT LIST* OF THINGS YOUR HIGHNESS NEEDS TO KNOW ABOUT ME IS I *DON'T* ROLL OVER. BAD FOR BUSINESS.

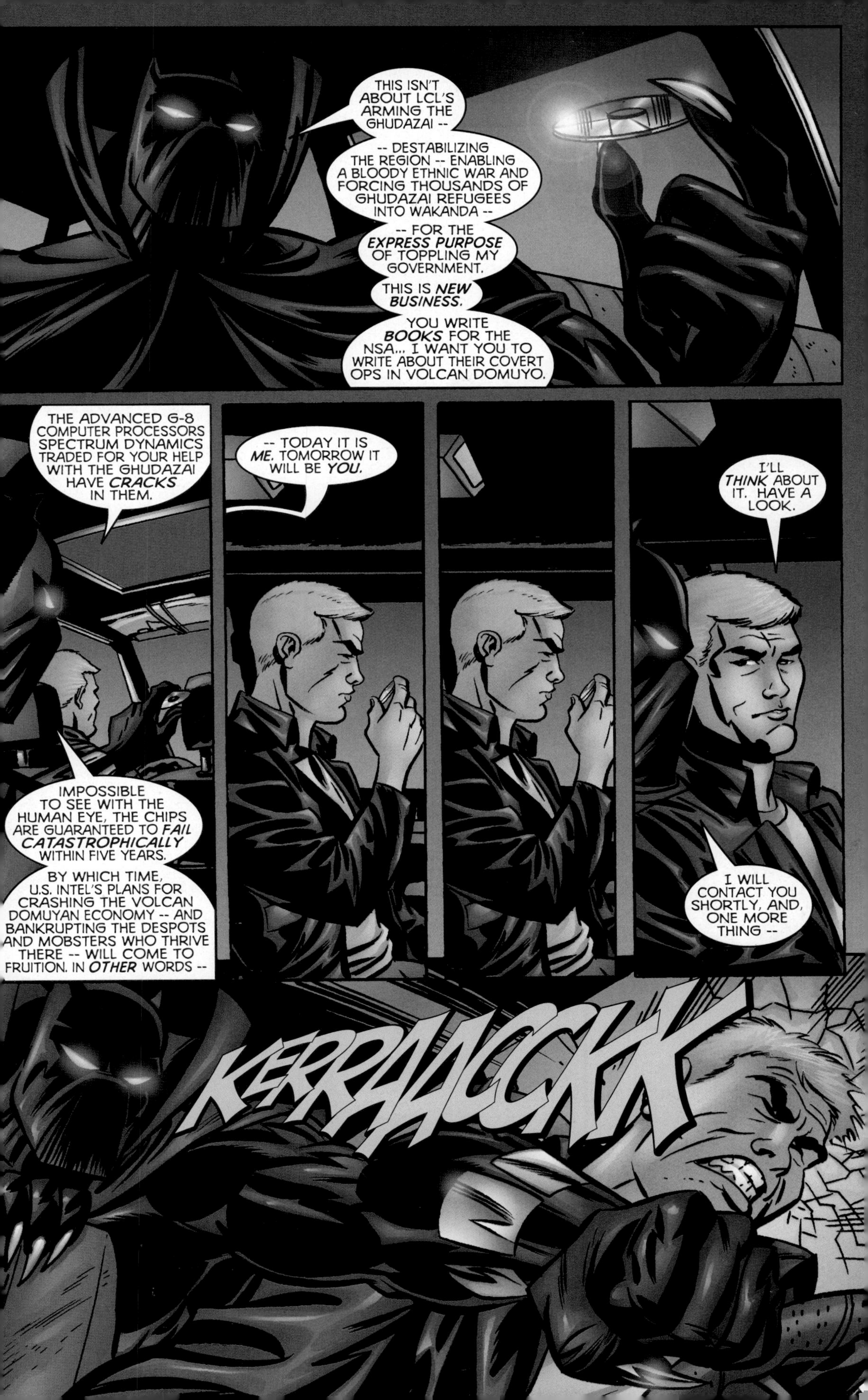
THIS ISN'T ABOUT LCL'S ARMING THE GHUDAZAI --
-- DESTABILIZING THE REGION -- ENABLING A BLOODY ETHNIC WAR AND FORCING THOUSANDS OF GHUDAZAI REFUGEES INTO WAKANDA --
-- FOR THE EXPRESS PURPOSE OF TOPPLING MY GOVERNMENT.
THIS IS NEW BUSINESS.
YOU WRITE BOOKS FOR THE NSA... I WANT YOU TO WRITE ABOUT THEIR COVERT OPS IN VOLCAN DOMUYO.
THE ADVANCED G-8 COMPUTER PROCESSORS SPECTRUM DYNAMICS TRADED FOR YOUR HELP WITH THE GHUDAZAI HAVE CRACKS IN THEM.
IMPOSSIBLE TO SEE WITH THE HUMAN EYE, THE CHIPS ARE GUARANTEED TO FAIL CATASTROPHICALLY WITHIN FIVE YEARS.
BY WHICH TIME, U.S. INTEL'S PLANS FOR CRASHING THE VOLCAN DOMUYAN ECONOMY -- AND BANKRUPTING THE DESPOTS AND MOBSTERS WHO THRIVE THERE -- WILL COME TO FRUITION. IN OTHER WORDS --
-- TODAY IT IS ME. TOMORROW IT WILL BE YOU.
I'LL THINK ABOUT IT. HAVE A LOOK.
I WILL CONTACT YOU SHORTLY, AND, ONE MORE THING --
KERRAACCKK

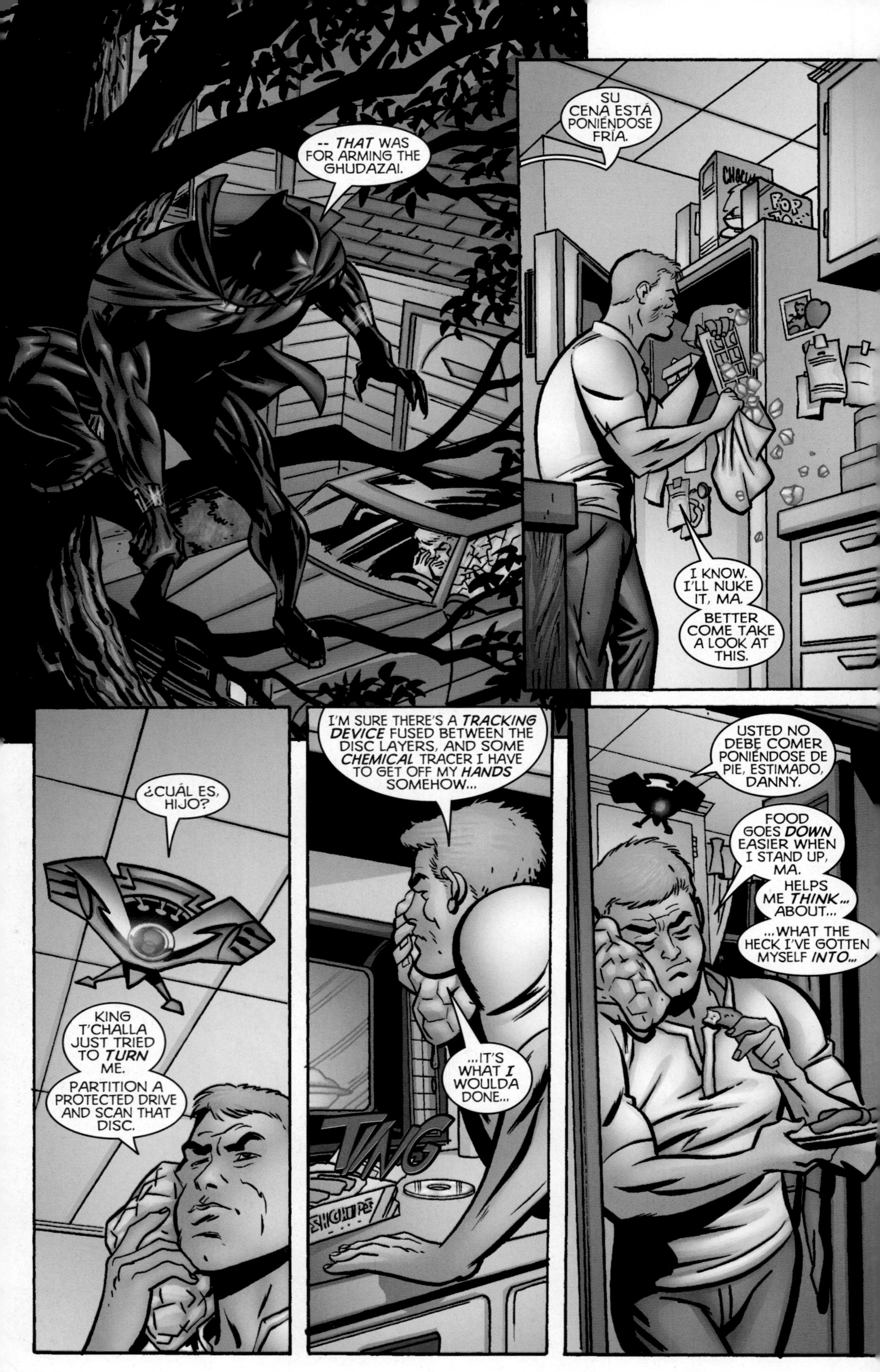
-- THAT WAS FOR ARMING THE GHUDAZAI.
SU CENA ESTÁ PONIÉNDOSE FRÍA.
I KNOW. I'LL NUKE IT, MA.
BETTER COME TAKE A LOOK AT THIS.
¿CUÁL ES, HIJO?
KING T'CHALLA JUST TRIED TO TURN ME.
PARTITION A PROTECTED DRIVE AND SCAN THAT DISC.
I'M SURE THERE'S A TRACKING DEVICE FUSED BETWEEN THE DISC LAYERS, AND SOME CHEMICAL TRACER I HAVE TO GET OFF MY HANDS SOMEHOW...
...IT'S WHAT I WOULDA DONE...
TNG
USTED NO DEBE COMER PONIÉNDOSE DE PIE, ESTIMADO, DANNY.
FOOD GOES DOWN EASIER WHEN I STAND UP, MA.
HELPS ME THINK... ABOUT...
...WHAT THE HECK I'VE GOTTEN MYSELF INTO...

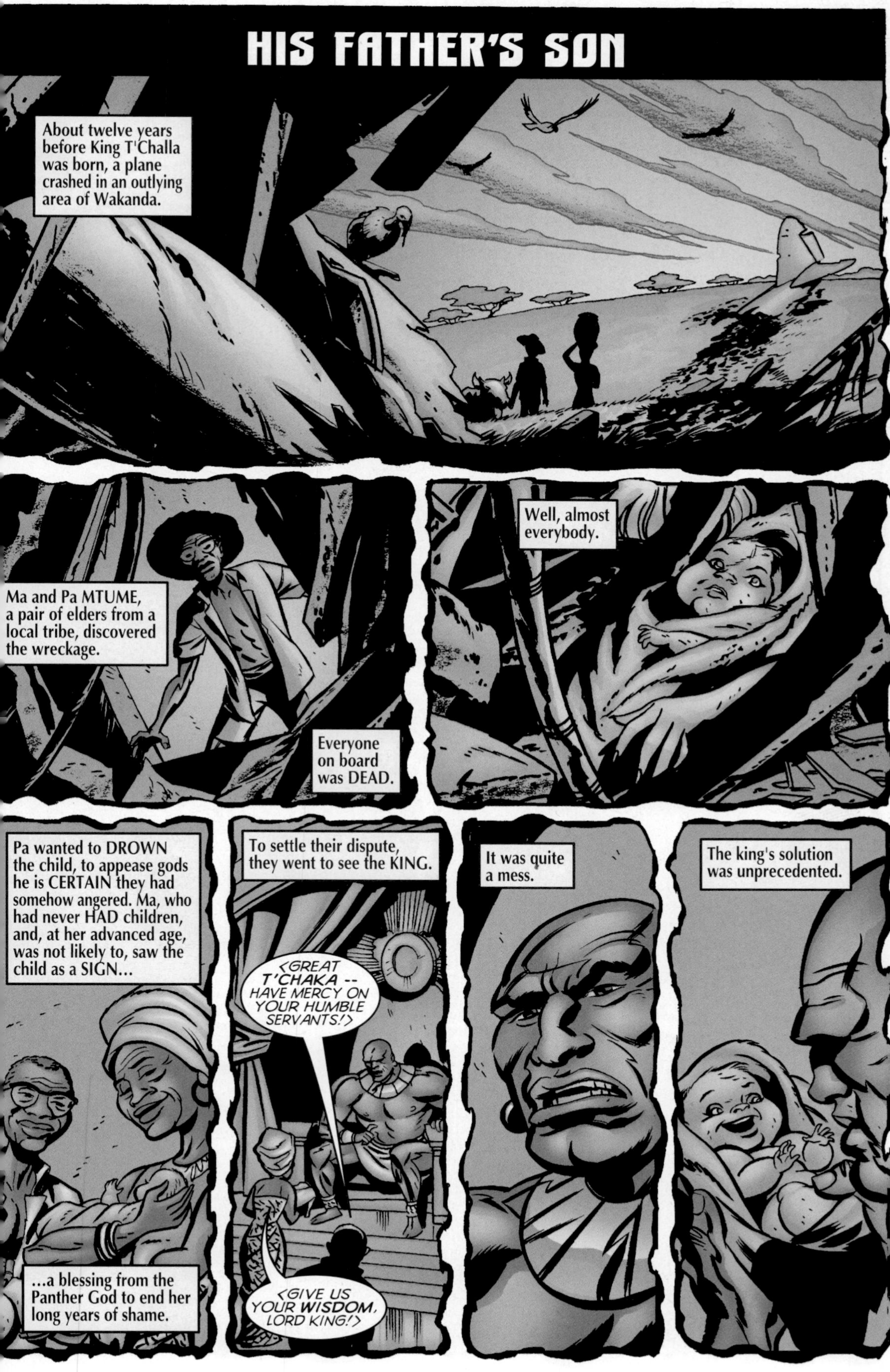

HIS FATHER'S SON
About twelve years before King T'Challa was born, a plane crashed in an outlying area of Wakanda.
Ma and Pa MTUME, a pair of elders from a local tribe, discovered the wreckage.
Everyone on board was DEAD.
Well, almost everybody.
Pa wanted to DROWN the child, to appease gods he is CERTAIN they had somehow angered. Ma, who had never HAD children, and, at her advanced age, was not likely to, saw the child as a SIGN...
...a blessing from the Panther God to end her long years of shame.
To settle their dispute, they went to see the KING.
<GREAT T'CHAKA -- HAVE MERCY ON YOUR HUMBLE SERVANTS!>
<GIVE US YOUR WISDOM, LORD KING!>
It was quite a mess.
The king's solution was unprecedented.

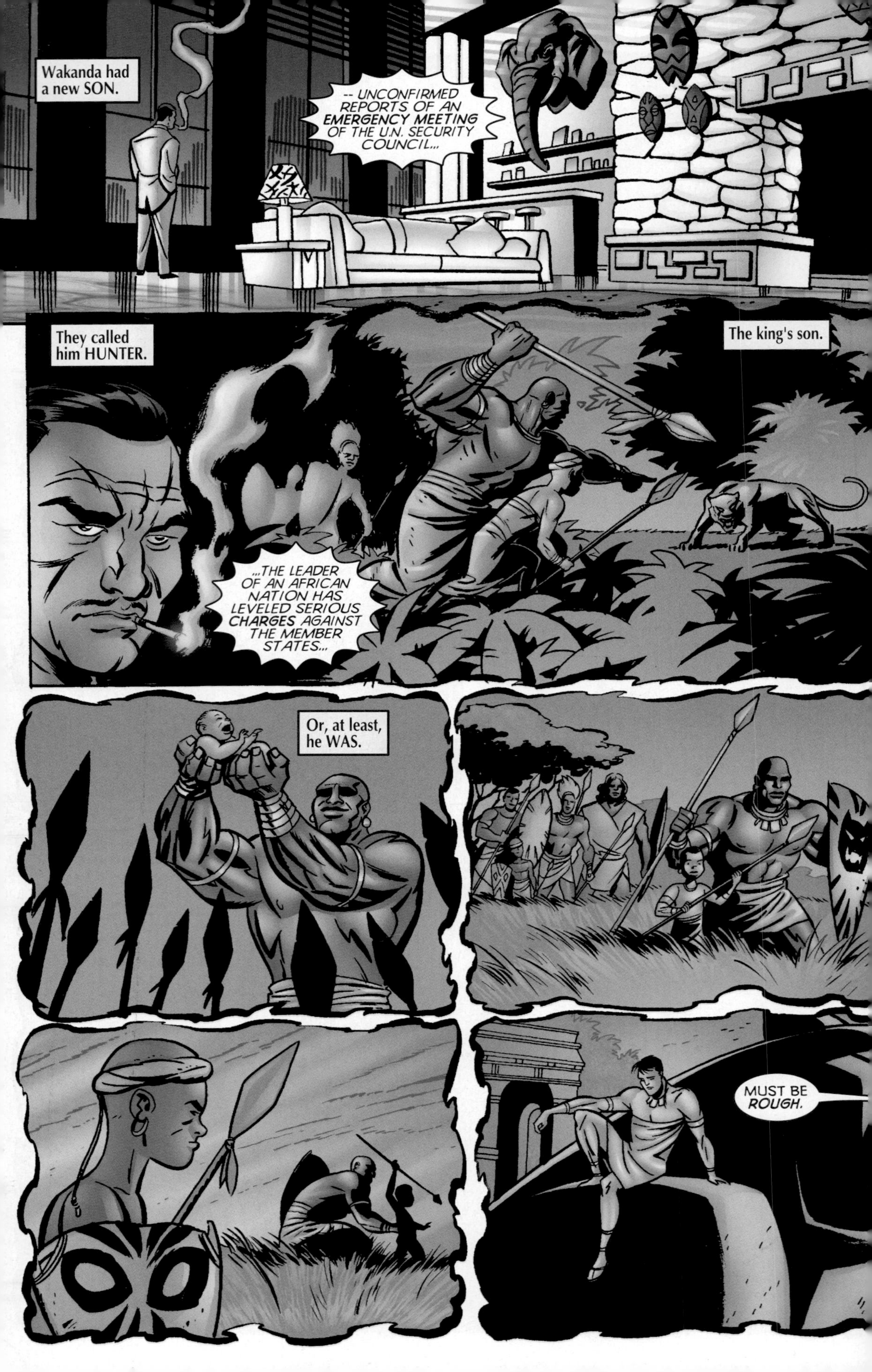

Wakanda had a new SON.
-- UNCONFIRMED REPORTS OF AN EMERGENCY MEETING OF THE U.N. SECURITY COUNCIL...
They called him HUNTER.
The king's son.
...THE LEADER OF AN AFRICAN NATION HAS LEVELED SERIOUS CHARGES AGAINST THE MEMBER STATES...
Or, at least, he WAS.
MUST BE ROUGH.

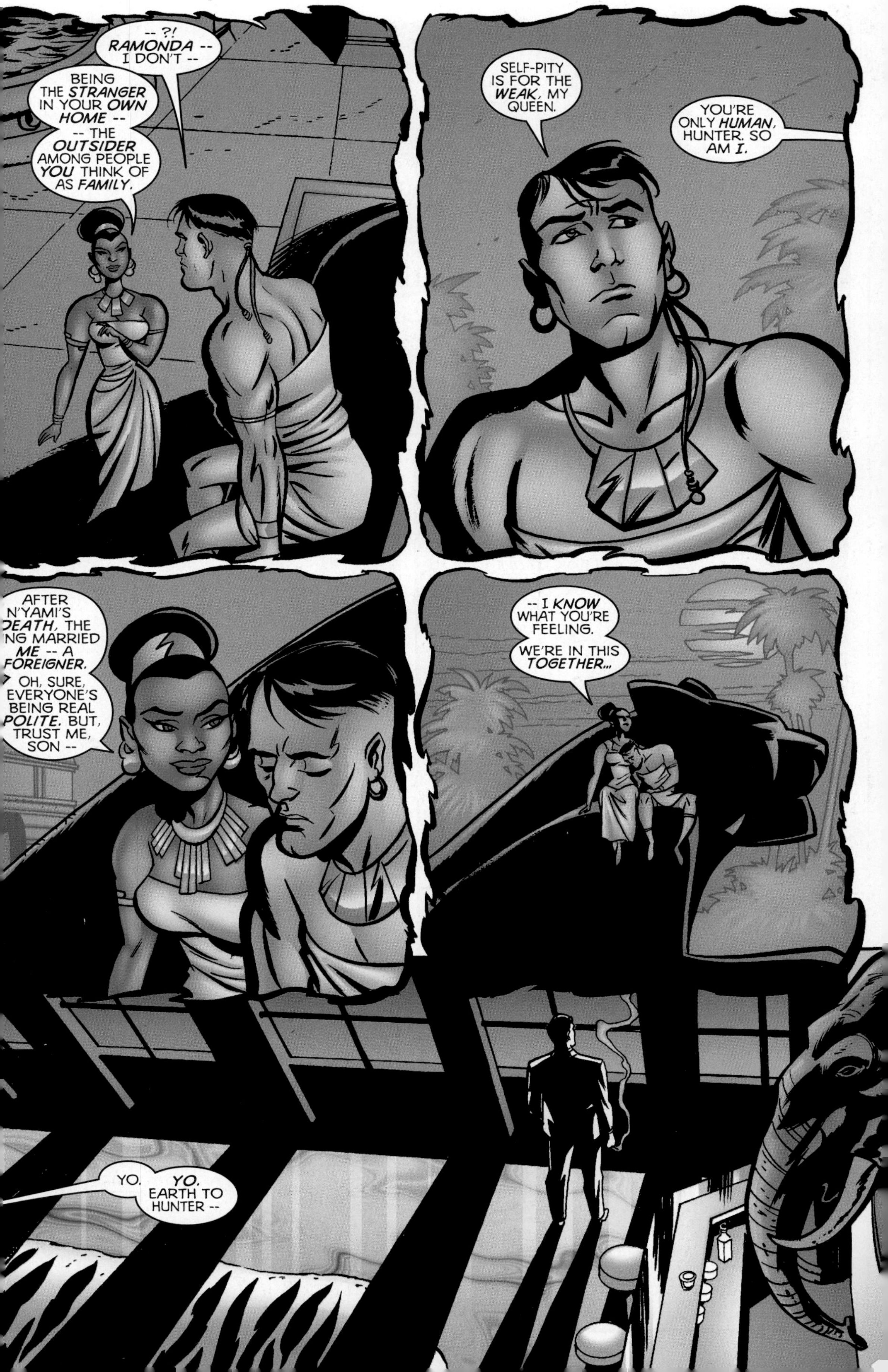
-- ?! RAMONDA -- I DON'T --
BEING THE STRANGER IN YOUR OWN HOME --
-- THE OUTSIDER AMONG PEOPLE YOU THINK OF AS FAMILY.
SELF-PITY IS FOR THE WEAK, MY QUEEN.
YOU'RE ONLY HUMAN, HUNTER. SO AM I.
AFTER N'YAMI'S DEATH, THE NG MARRIED ME -- A FOREIGNER.
OH, SURE, EVERYONE'S BEING REAL POLITE. BUT, TRUST ME, SON --
-- I KNOW WHAT YOU'RE FEELING.
WE'RE IN THIS TOGETHER...
YO. YO. EARTH TO HUNTER --

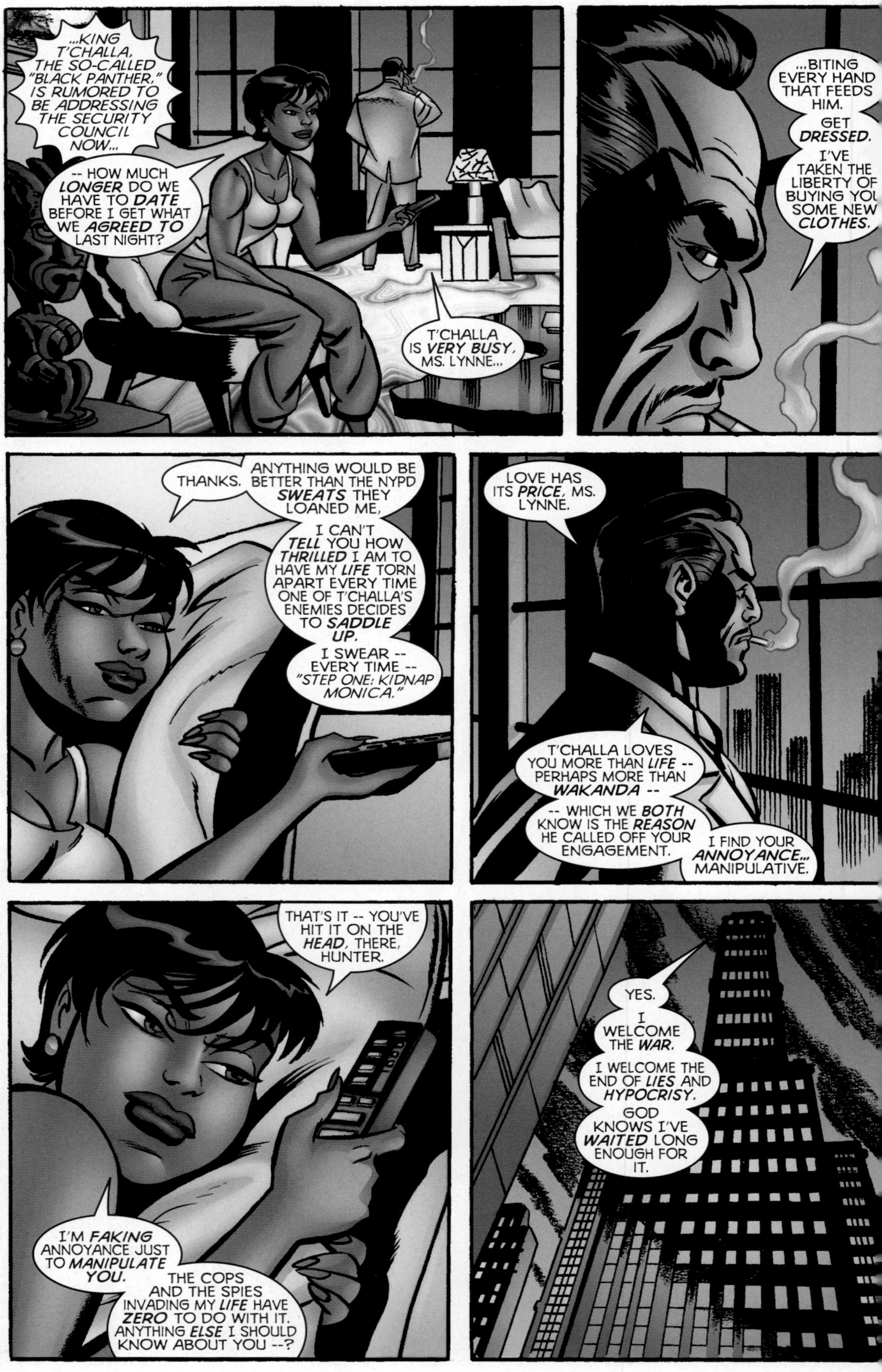
...KING T'CHALLA, THE SO-CALLED "BLACK PANTHER," IS RUMORED TO BE ADDRESSING THE SECURITY COUNCIL NOW...
-- HOW MUCH LONGER DO WE HAVE TO DATE BEFORE I GET WHAT WE AGREED TO LAST NIGHT?
T'CHALLA IS VERY BUSY, MS. LYNNE...
...BITING EVERY HAND THAT FEEDS HIM.
GET DRESSED.
I'VE TAKEN THE LIBERTY OF BUYING YOU SOME NEW CLOTHES.
THANKS.
ANYTHING WOULD BE BETTER THAN THE NYPD SWEATS THEY LOANED ME,
I CAN'T TELL YOU HOW THRILLED I AM TO HAVE MY LIFE TORN APART EVERY TIME ONE OF T'CHALLA'S ENEMIES DECIDES TO SADDLE UP.
I SWEAR -- EVERY TIME -- "STEP ONE: KIDNAP MONICA."
LOVE HAS ITS PRICE, MS. LYNNE.
T'CHALLA LOVES YOU MORE THAN LIFE -- PERHAPS MORE THAN WAKANDA --
-- WHICH WE BOTH KNOW IS THE REASON HE CALLED OFF YOUR ENGAGEMENT.
I FIND YOUR ANNOYANCE... MANIPULATIVE.
THAT'S IT -- YOU'VE HIT IT ON THE HEAD, THERE, HUNTER.
I'M FAKING ANNOYANCE JUST TO MANIPULATE YOU.
THE COPS AND THE SPIES INVADING MY LIFE HAVE ZERO TO DO WITH IT. ANYTHING ELSE I SHOULD KNOW ABOUT YOU --?
YES.
I WELCOME THE WAR.
I WELCOME THE END OF LIES AND HYPOCRISY.
GOD KNOWS I'VE WAITED LONG ENOUGH FOR IT.

Across town, I was working out...

NO -- NO -- NIKKI --

-- I DON'T *KNOW* WHAT IT MEANS. HE SNATCHED UP JACK TAYLOR -- *JACK TAYLOR* --!

I'M SCARED TO EVEN *SAY* THE MAN'S *NAME,* AND THE CLIENT JUST GRABS HIM UP LIKE HE'S *STYMIE* --

-- CRIPES...

...KNEW I SHOULDN'T HAVE SAID HIS NAME...

What I DIDN'T know was, across town, the client was getting an EARLY START on ending my CAREER...

NOW, THANKS LARGELY TO THE *FREELY OFFERED* COOPERATION OF *THESE MEN* --

...calling an EMERGENCY SESSION of the U.N. Security Council.

-- TO WHOM I HAVE GRANTED *POLITICAL ASYLUM* -- WE NOW HAVE CREDIBLE, SUBSTANTIAL EMPIRICAL EVIDENCE --

GAPON

TAYLOR

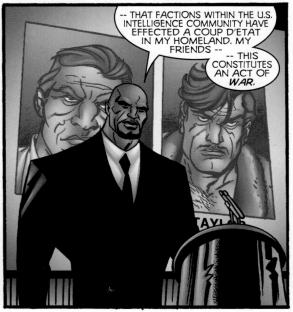

-- THAT FACTIONS WITHIN THE U.S. INTELLIGENCE COMMUNITY HAVE EFFECTED A COUP D'ETAT IN MY HOMELAND. MY FRIENDS --

-- THIS CONSTITUTES AN ACT OF *WAR.*

TAYLOR

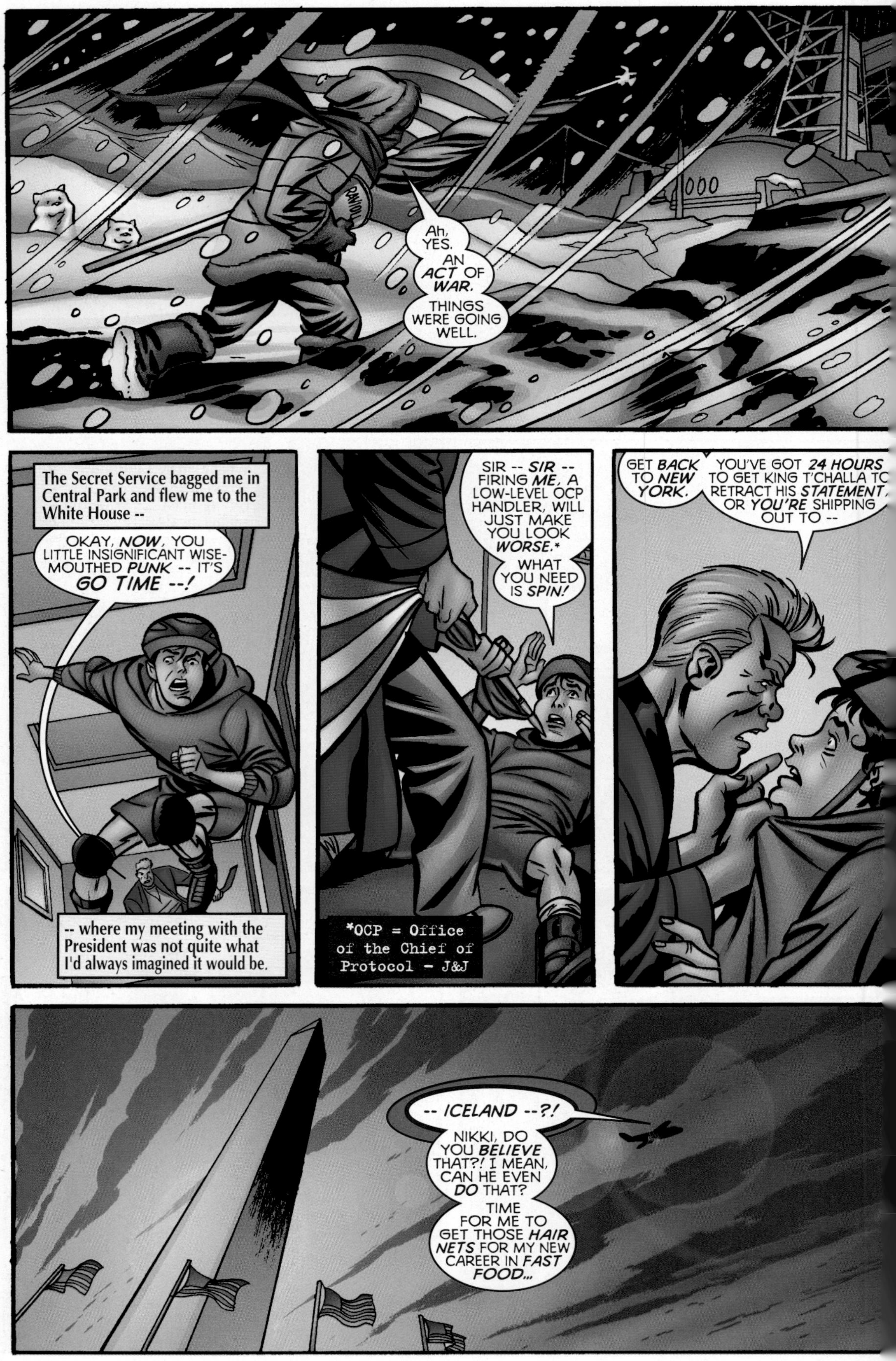

Ah, YES. AN ACT OF WAR.
THINGS WERE GOING WELL.
The Secret Service bagged me in Central Park and flew me to the White House --
OKAY, NOW, YOU LITTLE INSIGNIFICANT WISE-MOUTHED PUNK -- IT'S GO TIME --!
-- where my meeting with the President was not quite what I'd always imagined it would be.
SIR -- SIR -- FIRING ME, A LOW-LEVEL OCP HANDLER, WILL JUST MAKE YOU LOOK WORSE.*
WHAT YOU NEED IS SPIN!
*OCP = Office of the Chief of Protocol - J&J
GET BACK TO NEW YORK.
YOU'VE GOT 24 HOURS TO GET KING T'CHALLA TO RETRACT HIS STATEMENT, OR YOU'RE SHIPPING OUT TO --
-- ICELAND --?!
NIKKI, DO YOU BELIEVE THAT?! I MEAN, CAN HE EVEN DO THAT?
TIME FOR ME TO GET THOSE HAIR NETS FOR MY NEW CAREER IN FAST FOOD...

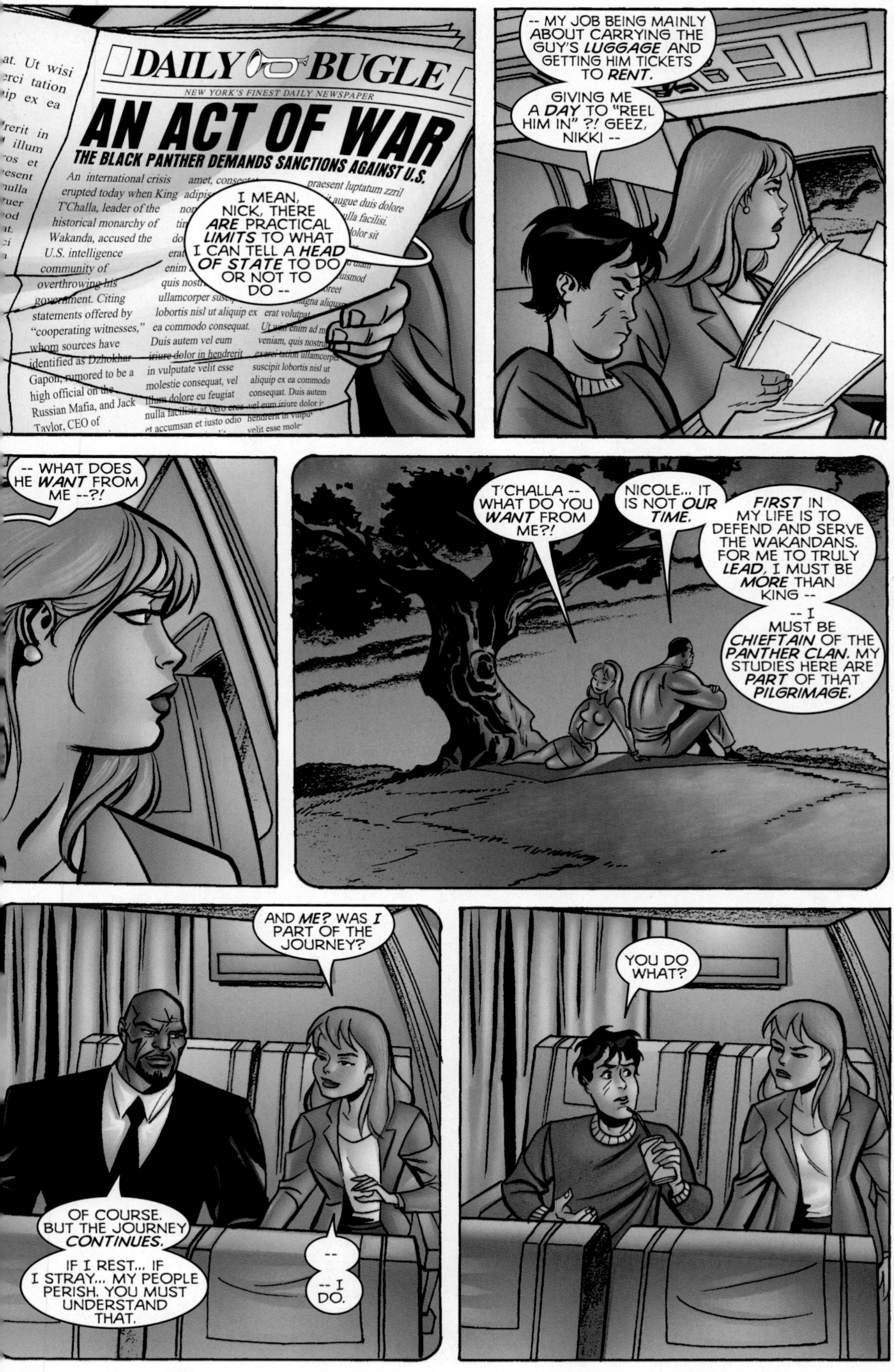

DAILY BUGLE
NEW YORK'S FINEST DAILY NEWSPAPER
AN ACT OF WAR
THE BLACK PANTHER DEMANDS SANCTIONS AGAINST U.S.
An international crisis erupted today when King T'Challa, leader of the historical monarchy of Wakanda, accused the U.S. intelligence community of overthrowing his government. Citing statements offered by "cooperating witnesses," whom sources have identified as Dzhokhar Gapon, rumored to be a high official on the Russian Mafia, and Jack Taylor, CEO of
I MEAN, NICK, THERE ARE PRACTICAL LIMITS TO WHAT I CAN TELL A HEAD OF STATE TO DO OR NOT TO DO --
-- MY JOB BEING MAINLY ABOUT CARRYING THE GUY'S LUGGAGE AND GETTING HIM TICKETS TO RENT.
GIVING ME A DAY TO "REEL HIM IN" ?! GEEZ, NIKKI --
-- WHAT DOES HE WANT FROM ME --?!
T'CHALLA -- WHAT DO YOU WANT FROM ME?!
NICOLE... IT IS NOT OUR TIME.
FIRST IN MY LIFE IS TO DEFEND AND SERVE THE WAKANDANS. FOR ME TO TRULY LEAD, I MUST BE MORE THAN KING --
-- I MUST BE CHIEFTAIN OF THE PANTHER CLAN. MY STUDIES HERE ARE PART OF THAT PILGRIMAGE.
AND ME? WAS I PART OF THE JOURNEY?
OF COURSE. BUT THE JOURNEY CONTINUES.
IF I REST... IF I STRAY... MY PEOPLE PERISH. YOU MUST UNDERSTAND THAT.
--
-- I DO.
YOU DO WHAT?

ARE YOU EVEN *LISTENING* TO ME?

LOOK -- I THINK *YOU* NEED TO RUN WITH THE BALL FOR AWHILE.

TOSS ME WHATEVER'S ON YOUR DESK AND *YOU* HANDLE KING T'CHALLA.

NO.

ROSS, MUCH AS I ENJOY *KISSING* YOU, I'M STILL *YOUR BOSS.*

HE'S *ONE GUY.* KEEP HIM OUT OF TROUBLE FOR TWENTY-FOUR *HOURS.*

HOW *HARD* COULD THAT *BE?!*

LESS THAN AN HOUR LATER

YYYEEEEAAAAHHH!

BOOOM BOOOM BOOOM

BRAAAAATATATATATATATAT

SEVENTEEN HOURS AFTER THAT

-- WHICH, OF COURSE, BROUGHT ME *HERE.*

BUT, I'M GETTING *AHEAD* OF MYSELF AGAIN.

STAY WITH ME... THIS GETS A LITTLE COMPLICATED...

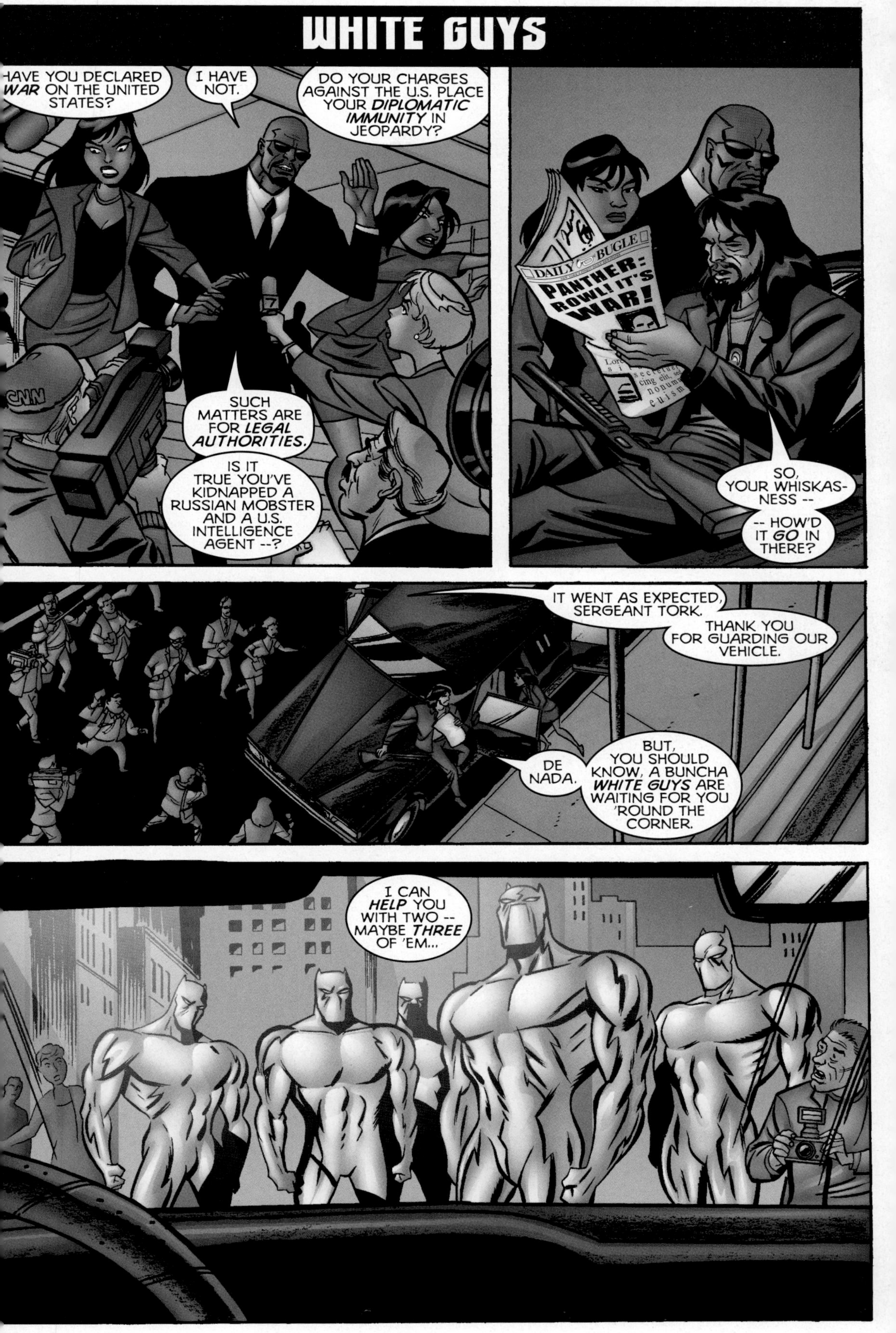
WHITE GUYS
HAVE YOU DECLARED WAR ON THE UNITED STATES?
I HAVE NOT.
DO YOUR CHARGES AGAINST THE U.S. PLACE YOUR DIPLOMATIC IMMUNITY IN JEOPARDY?
SUCH MATTERS ARE FOR LEGAL AUTHORITIES.
IS IT TRUE YOU'VE KIDNAPPED A RUSSIAN MOBSTER AND A U.S. INTELLIGENCE AGENT --?
CNN
DAILY BUGLE
PANTHER: ROWL! IT'S WAR!
SO, YOUR WHISKAS-NESS --
-- HOW'D IT GO IN THERE?
IT WENT AS EXPECTED, SERGEANT TORK.
THANK YOU FOR GUARDING OUR VEHICLE.
DE NADA.
BUT, YOU SHOULD KNOW, A BUNCHA WHITE GUYS ARE WAITING FOR YOU 'ROUND THE CORNER.
I CAN HELP YOU WITH TWO -- MAYBE THREE OF 'EM...

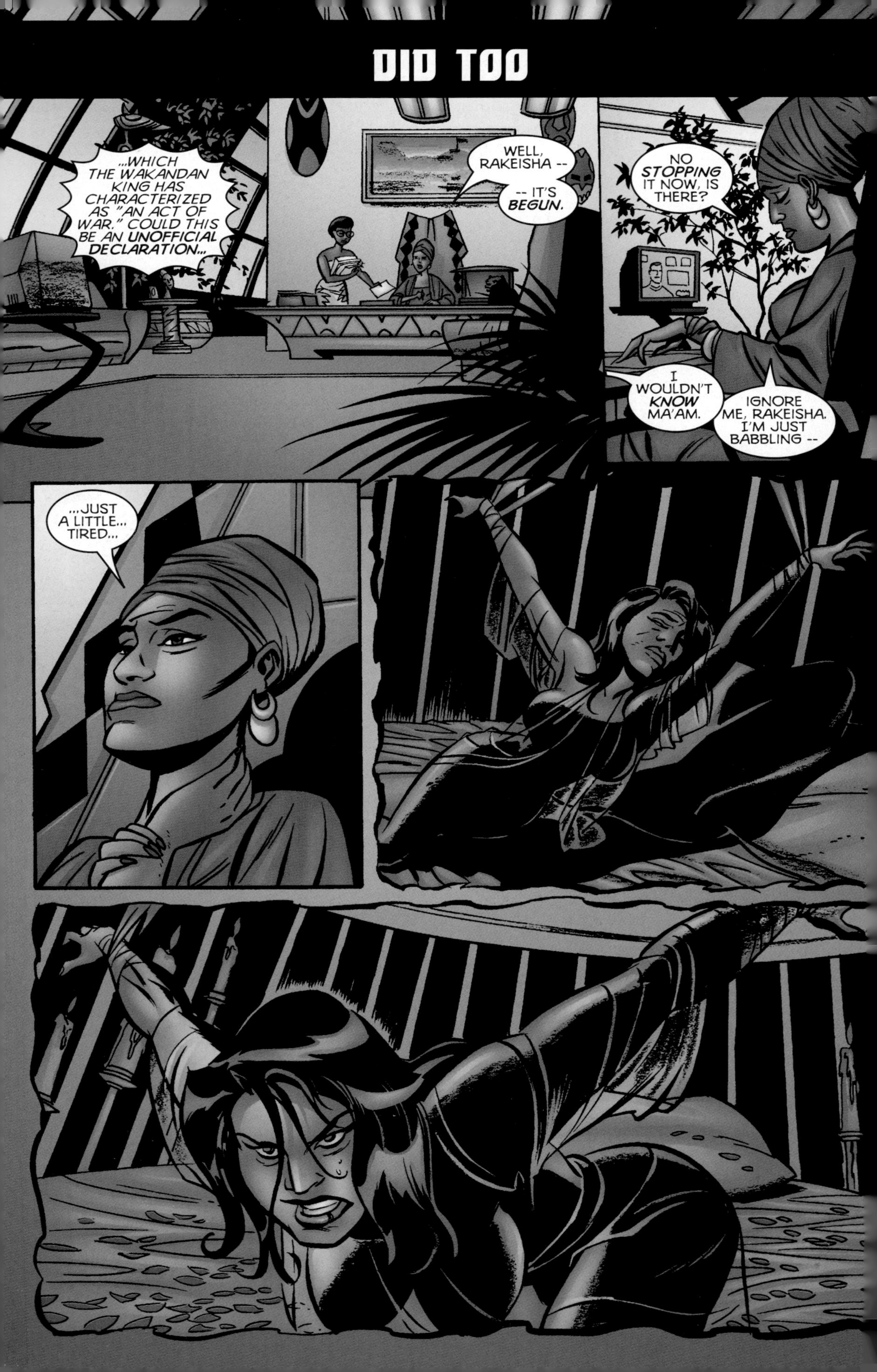
DID TOO
...WHICH THE WAKANDAN KING HAS CHARACTERIZED AS "AN ACT OF WAR." COULD THIS BE AN UNOFFICIAL DECLARATION...
WELL, RAKEISHA --
-- IT'S BEGUN.
NO STOPPING IT NOW, IS THERE?
I WOULDN'T KNOW MA'AM.
IGNORE ME, RAKEISHA. I'M JUST BABBLING --
...JUST A LITTLE... TIRED...

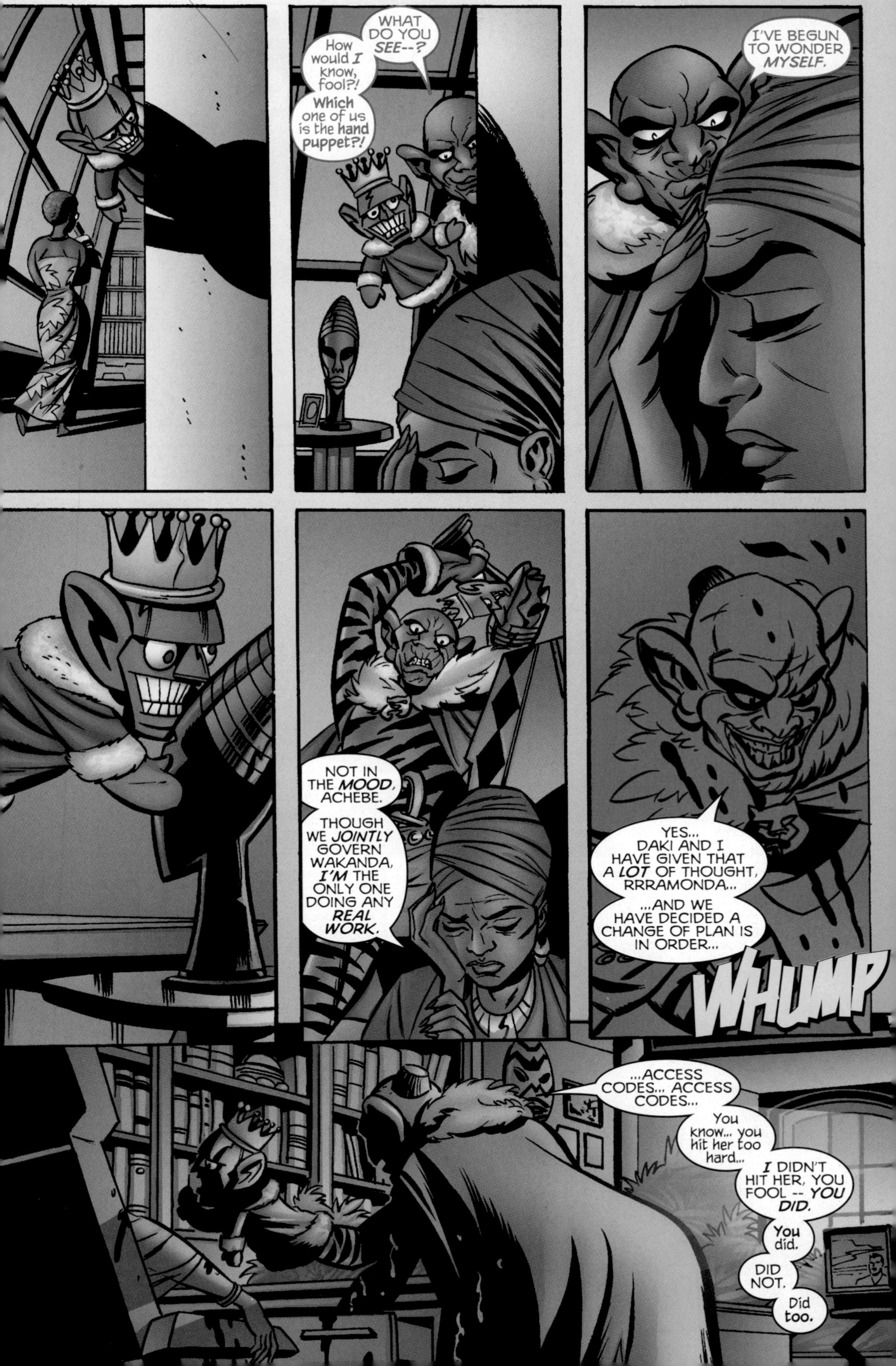
WHAT DO YOU SEE--?
How would I know, fool?!
Which one of us is the hand puppet?!
I'VE BEGUN TO WONDER MYSELF.
NOT IN THE MOOD, ACHEBE.
THOUGH WE JOINTLY GOVERN WAKANDA, I'M THE ONLY ONE DOING ANY REAL WORK.
YES... DAKI AND I HAVE GIVEN THAT A LOT OF THOUGHT, RRRAMONDA...
...AND WE HAVE DECIDED A CHANGE OF PLAN IS IN ORDER...
WHUMP
...ACCESS CODES... ACCESS CODES...
You know... you hit her too hard...
I DIDN'T HIT HER, YOU FOOL -- YOU DID.
You did.
DID NOT.
Did too.

THE HOCKEY PUCK

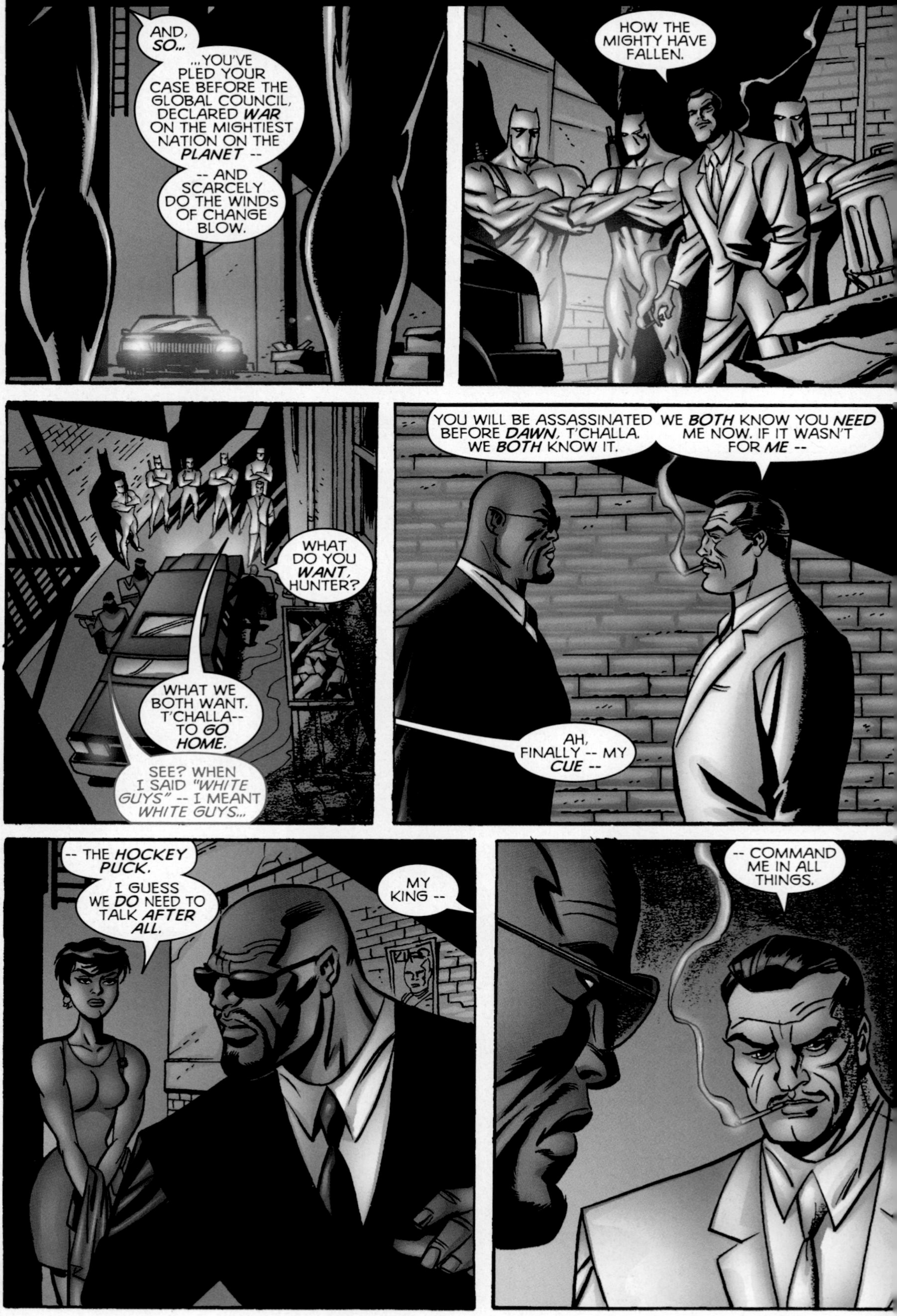
AND, SO...
...YOU'VE PLED YOUR CASE BEFORE THE GLOBAL COUNCIL, DECLARED WAR ON THE MIGHTIEST NATION ON THE PLANET --
-- AND SCARCELY DO THE WINDS OF CHANGE BLOW.
HOW THE MIGHTY HAVE FALLEN.
WHAT DO YOU WANT, HUNTER?
WHAT WE BOTH WANT. T'CHALLA-- TO GO HOME.
SEE? WHEN I SAID "WHITE GUYS" -- I MEANT WHITE GUYS...
YOU WILL BE ASSASSINATED BEFORE DAWN, T'CHALLA. WE BOTH KNOW IT.
WE BOTH KNOW YOU NEED ME NOW. IF IT WASN'T FOR ME --
AH, FINALLY -- MY CUE --
-- THE HOCKEY PUCK.
I GUESS WE DO NEED TO TALK AFTER ALL.
MY KING --
-- COMMAND ME IN ALL THINGS.

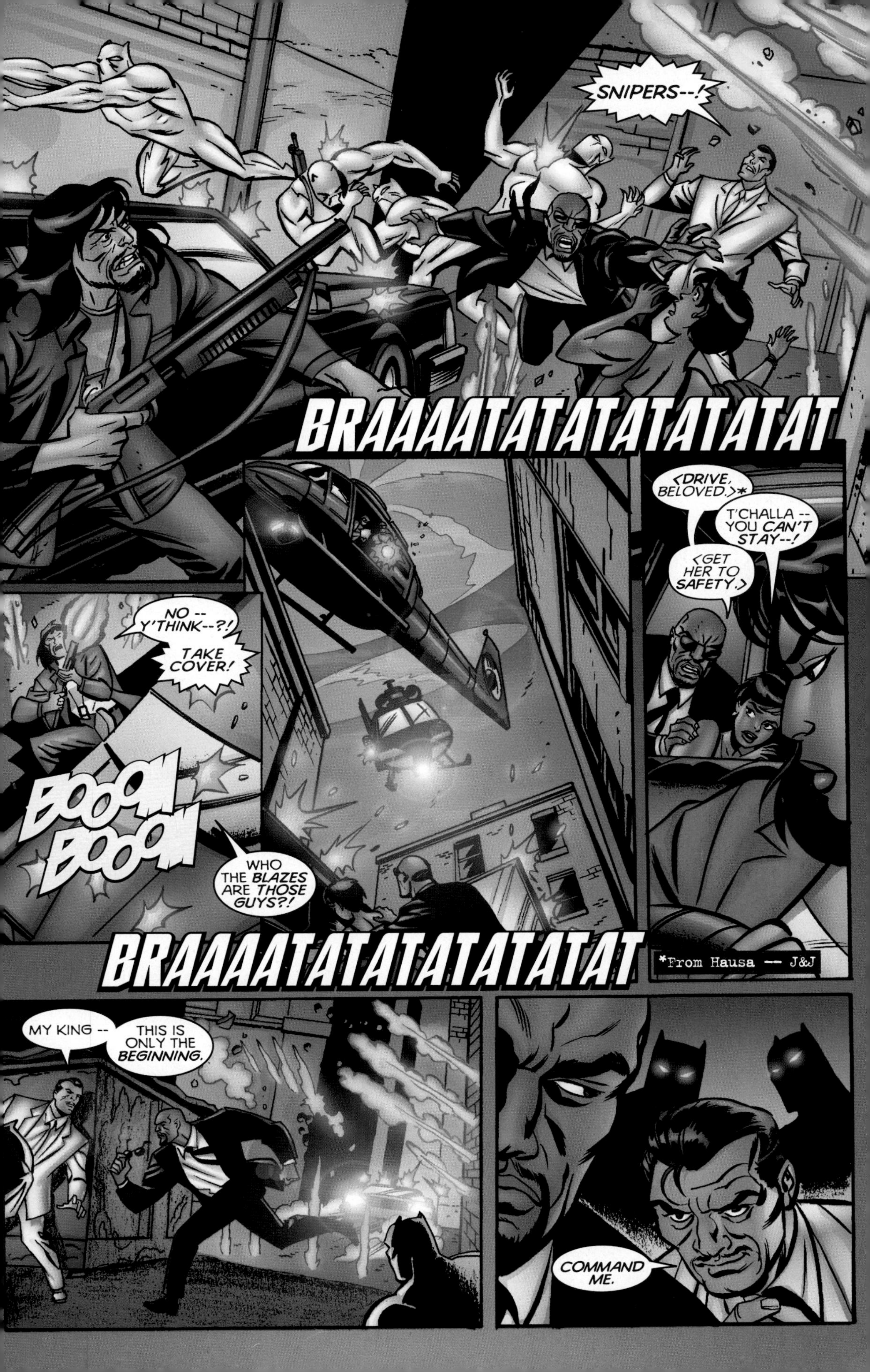
SNIPERS--!
BRAAAATATATATATATAT
<DRIVE, BELOVED.>*
T'CHALLA -- YOU CAN'T STAY--!
<GET HER TO SAFETY.>
NO -- Y'THINK--?!
TAKE COVER!
BOOOM
BOOOM
WHO THE BLAZES ARE THOSE GUYS?!
BRAAAATATATATATATAT
*From Hausa -- J&J
MY KING --
THIS IS ONLY THE BEGINNING.
COMMAND ME.

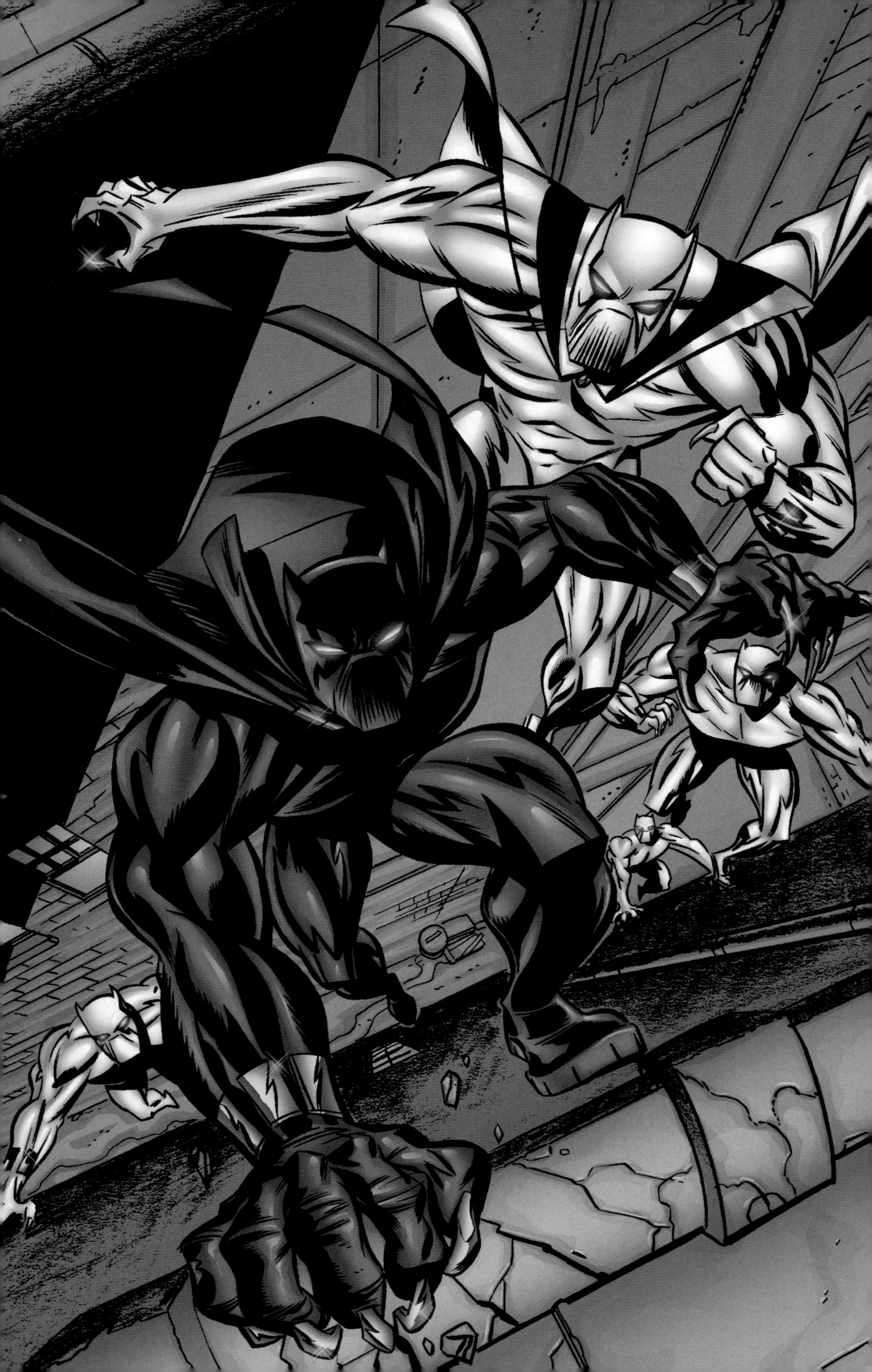

r plane had just gotten in, d I'd double-timed it to the N.

I felt like I'd walked in on the MIDDLE of a Van Damme flick.

--?!?

WHAT'D I MISS?! WHAT'D I MISS--?!

SHADDUP, YOU LITTLE WEASEL, AND *GET IN HERE*!!

--?! WHY?!

THAT'S WHY!

THETUNNEL THETUNNELTHETUNNEL THETUNNELTHETUNNEL THETUNNEL.

LOAD THIS.

--?! ARE YOU *KIDDING* ME--?!

BRAAAAATATATATATAT

BRAAAAATATATATATATATAT

Yup.

Things were going well.

SKKREEEEECHH

PROWLERS

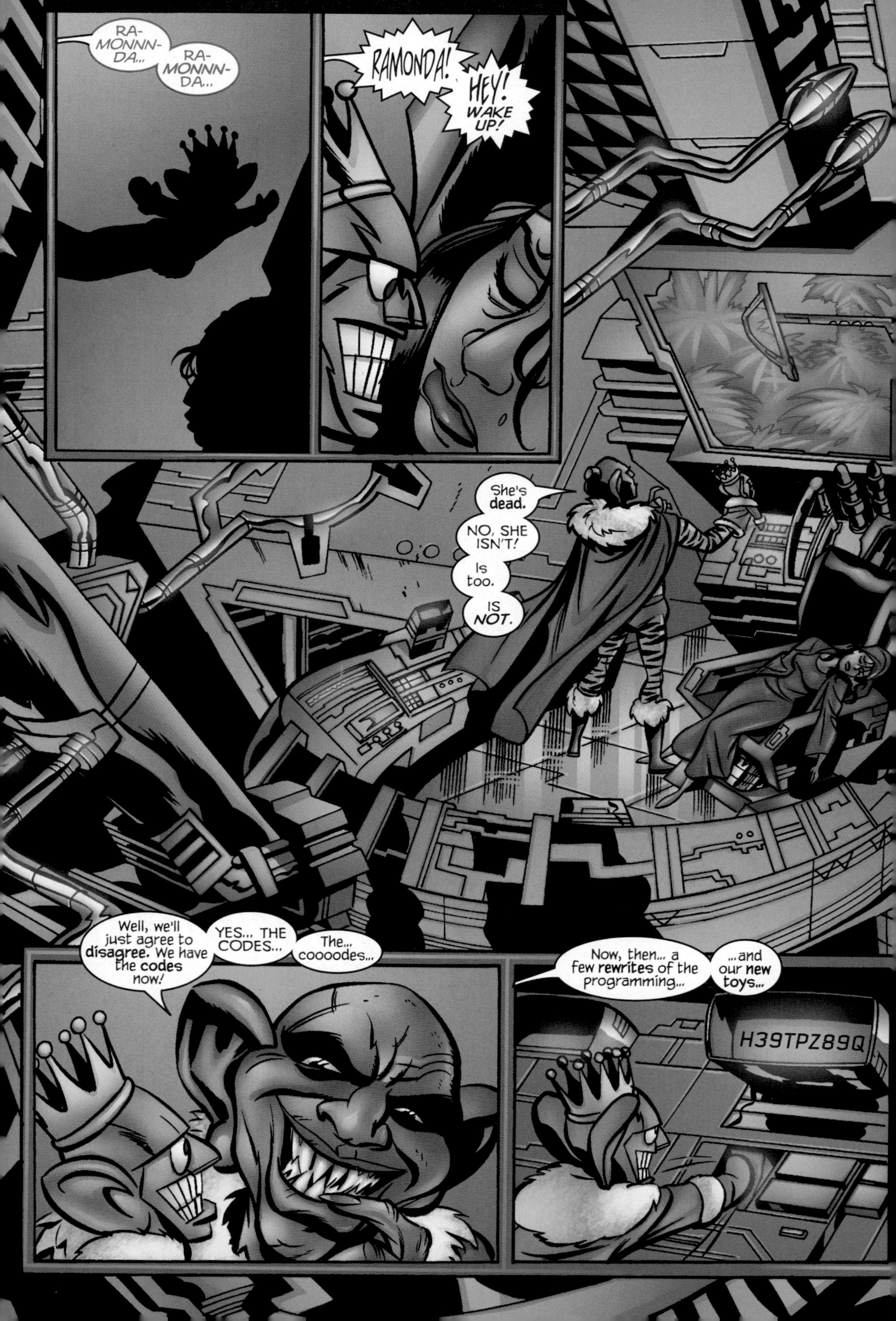

RA-MONNN-DA...
RA-MONNN-DA...
RAMONDA!
HEY! WAKE UP!
She's dead.
NO, SHE ISN'T!
Is too.
IS NOT.
Well, we'll just agree to disagree. We have the codes now!
YES... THE CODES...
The... coooodes...
Now, then... a few rewrites of the programming...
...and our new toys...
H39TPZ89Q

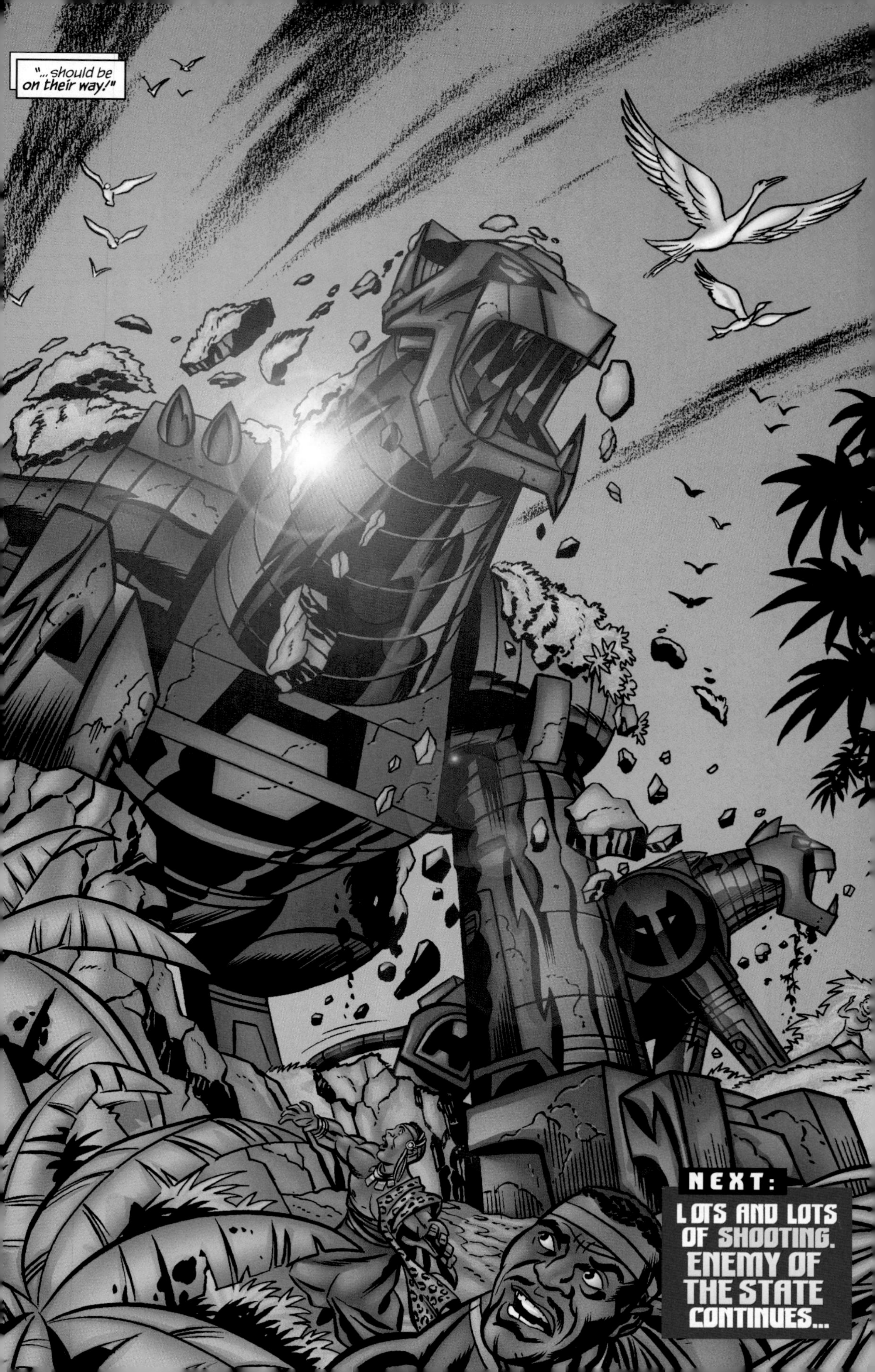
"...should be on their way!"
NEXT:
LOTS AND LOTS OF SHOOTING. ENEMY OF THE STATE CONTINUES...

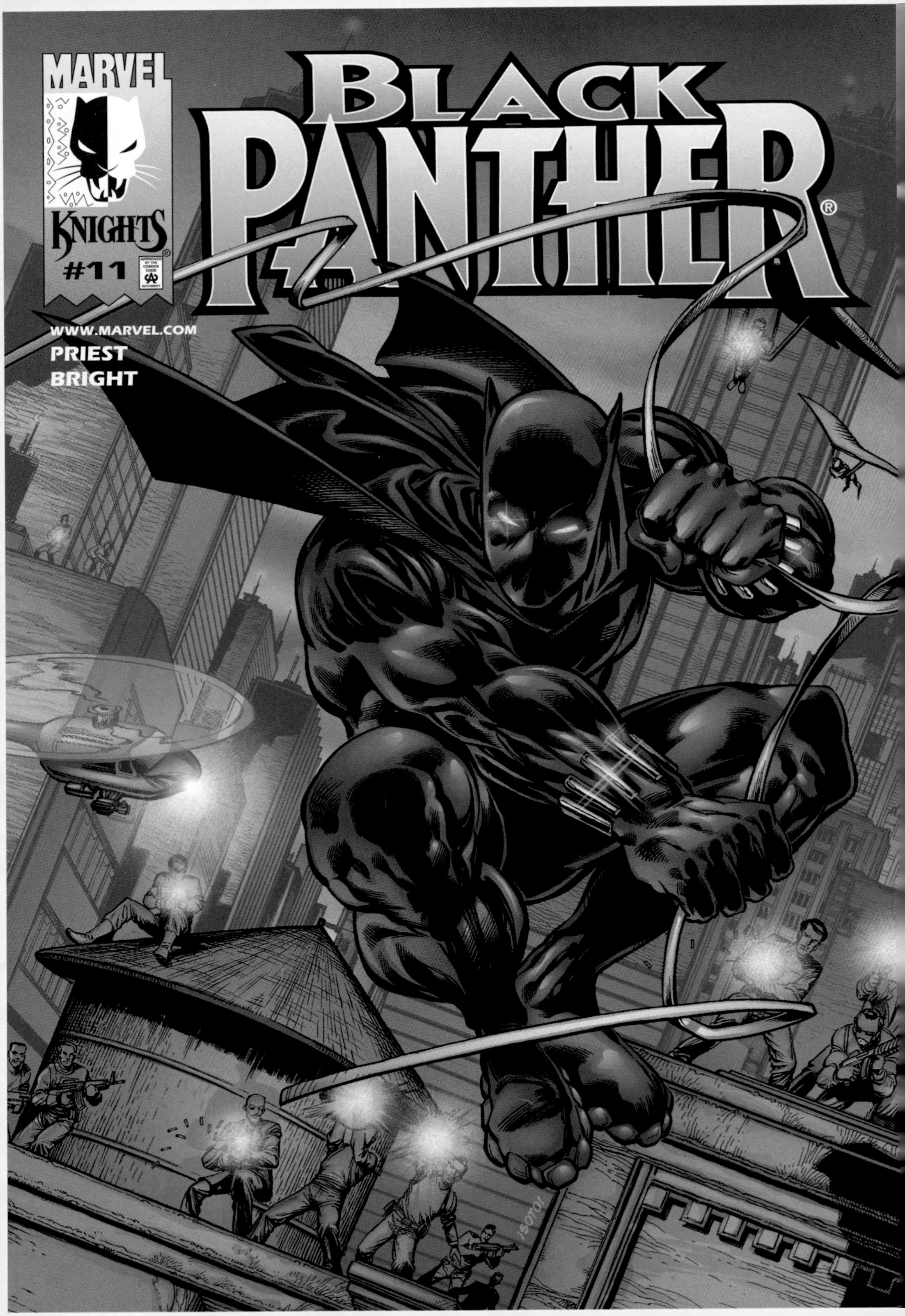
MARVEL
KNIGHTS
#11
APPROVED BY THE COMICS CODE AUTHORITY
BLACK PANTHER®
WWW.MARVEL.COM
PRIEST
BRIGHT

WITH THE SLEEKNESS OF THE JUNGLE CAT WHOSE NAME HE BEARS, T-CHALLA - KING OF WAKANDA - STALKS BOTH THE CONCRETE CITY AND THE UNDERGROWTH OF THE VELDT. SO IT HAS BEEN FOR COUNTLESS GENERATIONS OF WARRIOR KINGS, SO IT IS TODAY, AND SO IT SHALL BE FOR THE LAW OF THE JUNGLE DICTATES THAT ONLY THE SWIFT, THE SMART, AND THE STRONG SURVIVE! NOBLE CHAMPION. VIGILANT PROTECTOR. STAN LEE PRESENTS: **BLACK PANTHER**

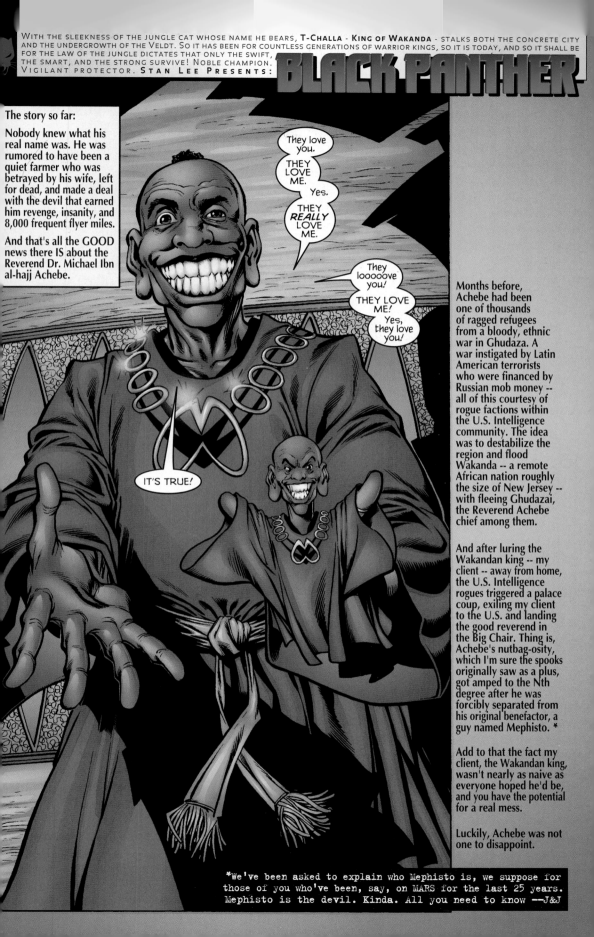

The story so far:

Nobody knew what his real name was. He was rumored to have been a quiet farmer who was betrayed by his wife, left for dead, and made a deal with the devil that earned him revenge, insanity, and 8,000 frequent flyer miles.

And that's all the GOOD news there IS about the Reverend Dr. Michael Ibn al-hajj Achebe.

They love you.

THEY LOVE ME.

Yes.

THEY *REALLY* LOVE ME.

They looooove you!

THEY LOVE ME!

Yes, they love you!

IT'S TRUE!

Months before, Achebe had been one of thousands of ragged refugees from a bloody, ethnic war in Ghudaza. A war instigated by Latin American terrorists who were financed by Russian mob money -- all of this courtesy of rogue factions within the U.S. Intelligence community. The idea was to destabilize the region and flood Wakanda -- a remote African nation roughly the size of New Jersey -- with fleeing Ghudazai, the Reverend Achebe chief among them.

And after luring the Wakandan king -- my client -- away from home, the U.S. Intelligence rogues triggered a palace coup, exiling my client to the U.S. and landing the good reverend in the Big Chair. Thing is, Achebe's nutbag-osity, which I'm sure the spooks originally saw as a plus, got amped to the Nth degree after he was forcibly separated from his original benefactor, a guy named Mephisto. *

Add to that the fact my client, the Wakandan king, wasn't nearly as naive as everyone hoped he'd be, and you have the potential for a real mess.

Luckily, Achebe was not one to disappoint.

*We've been asked to explain who Mephisto is, we suppose for those of you who've been, say, on MARS for the last 25 years. Mephisto is the devil. Kinda. All you need to know —J&J

STAN LEE PRESENTS: THE BLACK PANTHER

ENEMY OF THE STATE

BOOK THREE

CHRISTOPHER PRIEST STORY **MARK BRIGHT** ART

NELSON DECASTRO	CHRIS SOTOMAYOR	RICHARD STARKINGS AND COMICRAFT/JL	NANCI DAKESIAN	JIMMY PALMIOTTI AND JOE QUESADA	BOB HARRAS
INKS	COLORS	LETTERS	MANAGING EDITOR	EDITORS	CHIEF

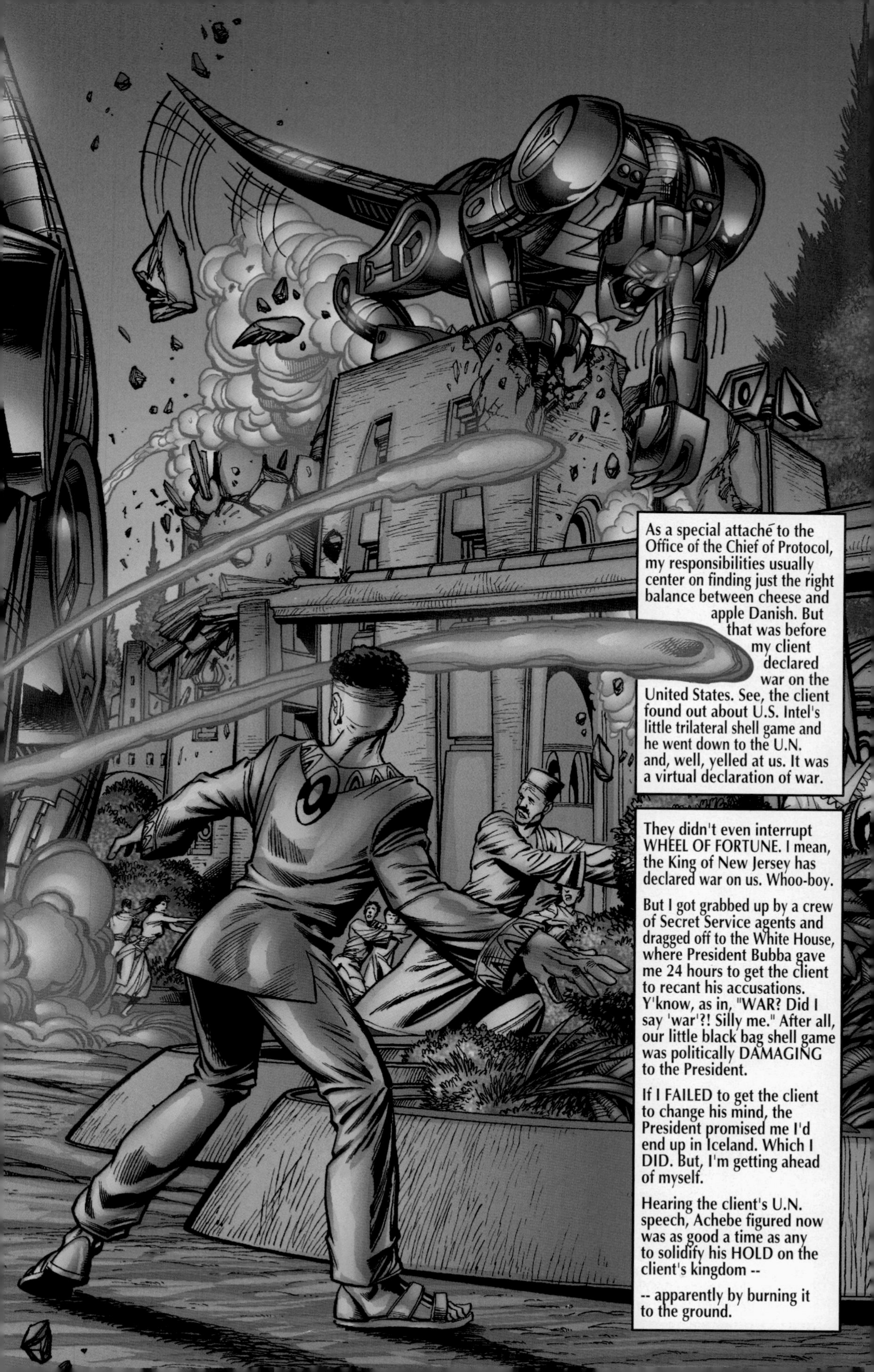
As a special attaché to the Office of the Chief of Protocol, my responsibilities usually center on finding just the right balance between cheese and apple Danish. But that was before my client declared war on the United States. See, the client found out about U.S. Intel's little trilateral shell game and he went down to the U.N. and, well, yelled at us. It was a virtual declaration of war.
They didn't even interrupt WHEEL OF FORTUNE. I mean, the King of New Jersey has declared war on us. Whoo-boy.
But I got grabbed up by a crew of Secret Service agents and dragged off to the White House, where President Bubba gave me 24 hours to get the client to recant his accusations. Y'know, as in, "WAR? Did I say 'war'?! Silly me." After all, our little black bag shell game was politically DAMAGING to the President.
If I FAILED to get the client to change his mind, the President promised me I'd end up in Iceland. Which I DID. But, I'm getting ahead of myself.
Hearing the client's U.N. speech, Achebe figured now was as good a time as any to solidify his HOLD on the client's kingdom --
-- apparently by burning it to the ground.

THE LAW

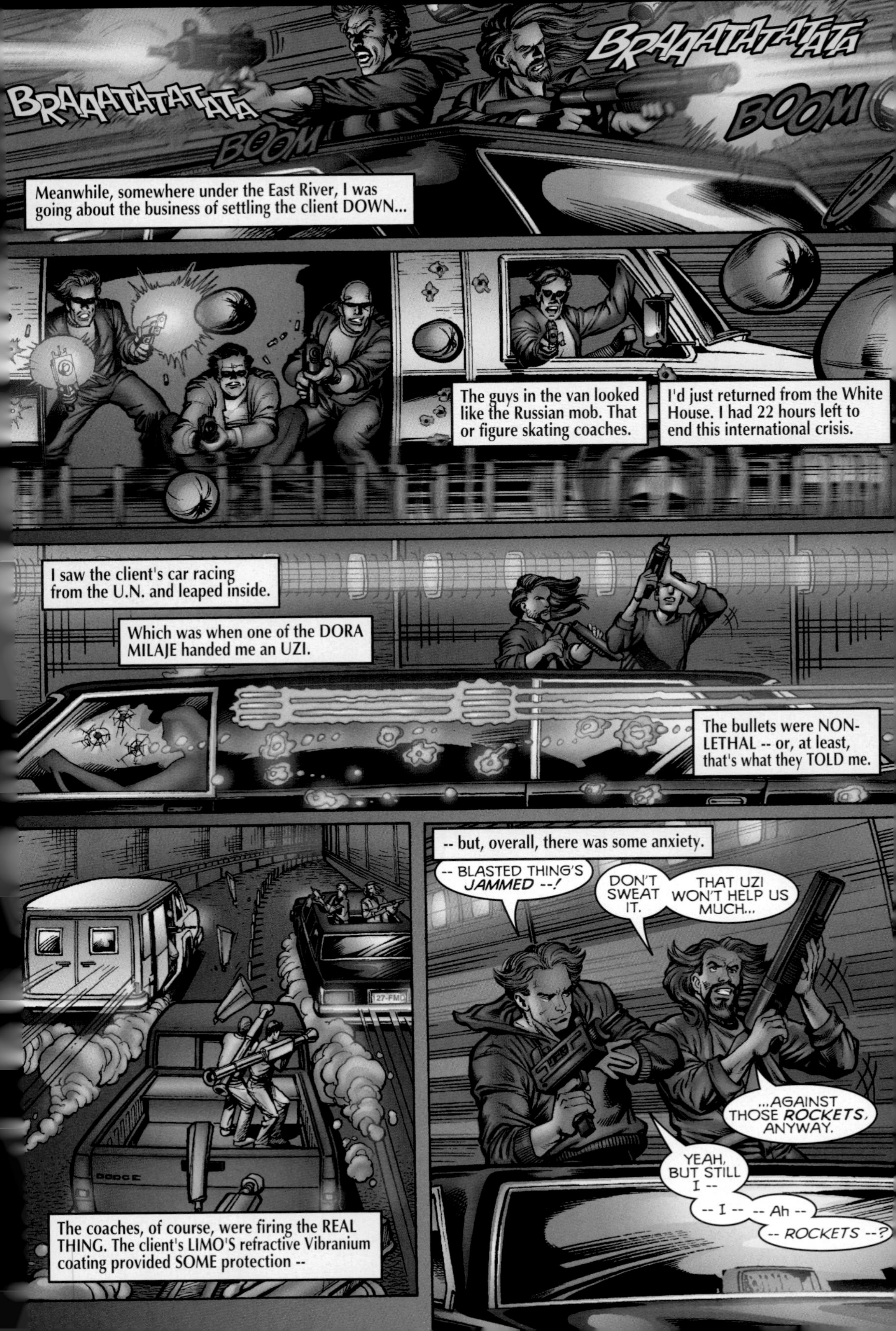

BRAAATATATATA
BOOM
BRAAATATATATA
BOOM
Meanwhile, somewhere under the East River, I was going about the business of settling the client DOWN...
The guys in the van looked like the Russian mob. That or figure skating coaches.
I'd just returned from the White House. I had 22 hours left to end this international crisis.
I saw the client's car racing from the U.N. and leaped inside.
Which was when one of the DORA MILAJE handed me an UZI.
The bullets were NON-LETHAL -- or, at least, that's what they TOLD me.
The coaches, of course, were firing the REAL THING. The client's LIMO'S refractive Vibranium coating provided SOME protection --
-- but, overall, there was some anxiety.
-- BLASTED THING'S JAMMED --!
DON'T SWEAT IT.
THAT UZI WON'T HELP US MUCH...
...AGAINST THOSE ROCKETS, ANYWAY.
YEAH, BUT STILL I --
-- I -- -- Ah --
-- ROCKETS --?

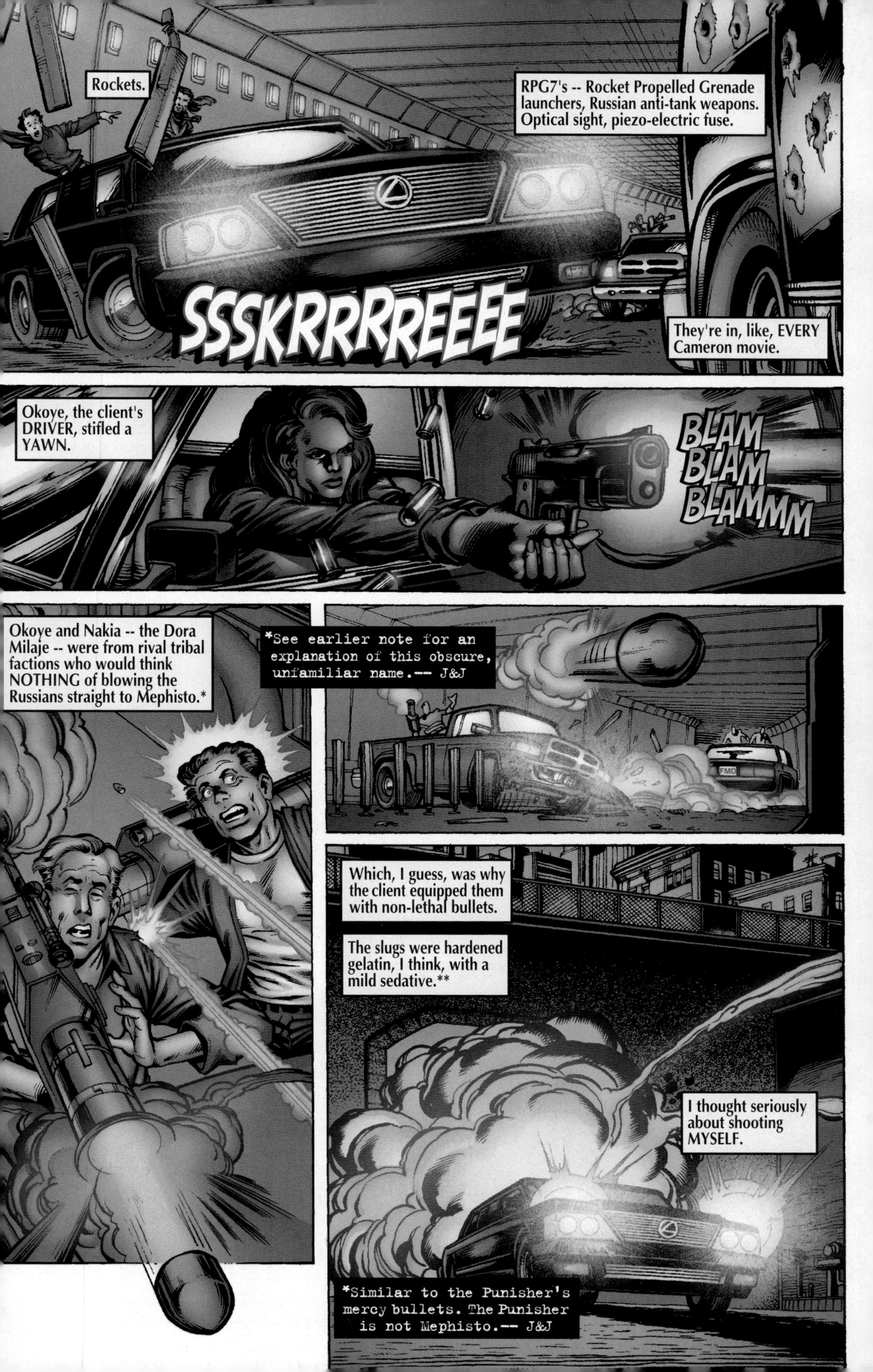

Rockets.
RPG7's -- Rocket Propelled Grenade launchers, Russian anti-tank weapons. Optical sight, piezo-electric fuse.
SSSKRRRRREEEE
They're in, like, EVERY Cameron movie.
Okoye, the client's DRIVER, stifled a YAWN.
BLAM BLAM BLAMMM
Okoye and Nakia -- the Dora Milaje -- were from rival tribal factions who would think NOTHING of blowing the Russians straight to Mephisto.*
*See earlier note for an explanation of this obscure, unfamiliar name.-- J&J
FMD
Which, I guess, was why the client equipped them with non-lethal bullets.
The slugs were hardened gelatin, I think, with a mild sedative.**
I thought seriously about shooting MYSELF.
*Similar to the Punisher's mercy bullets. The Punisher is not Mephisto.-- J&J

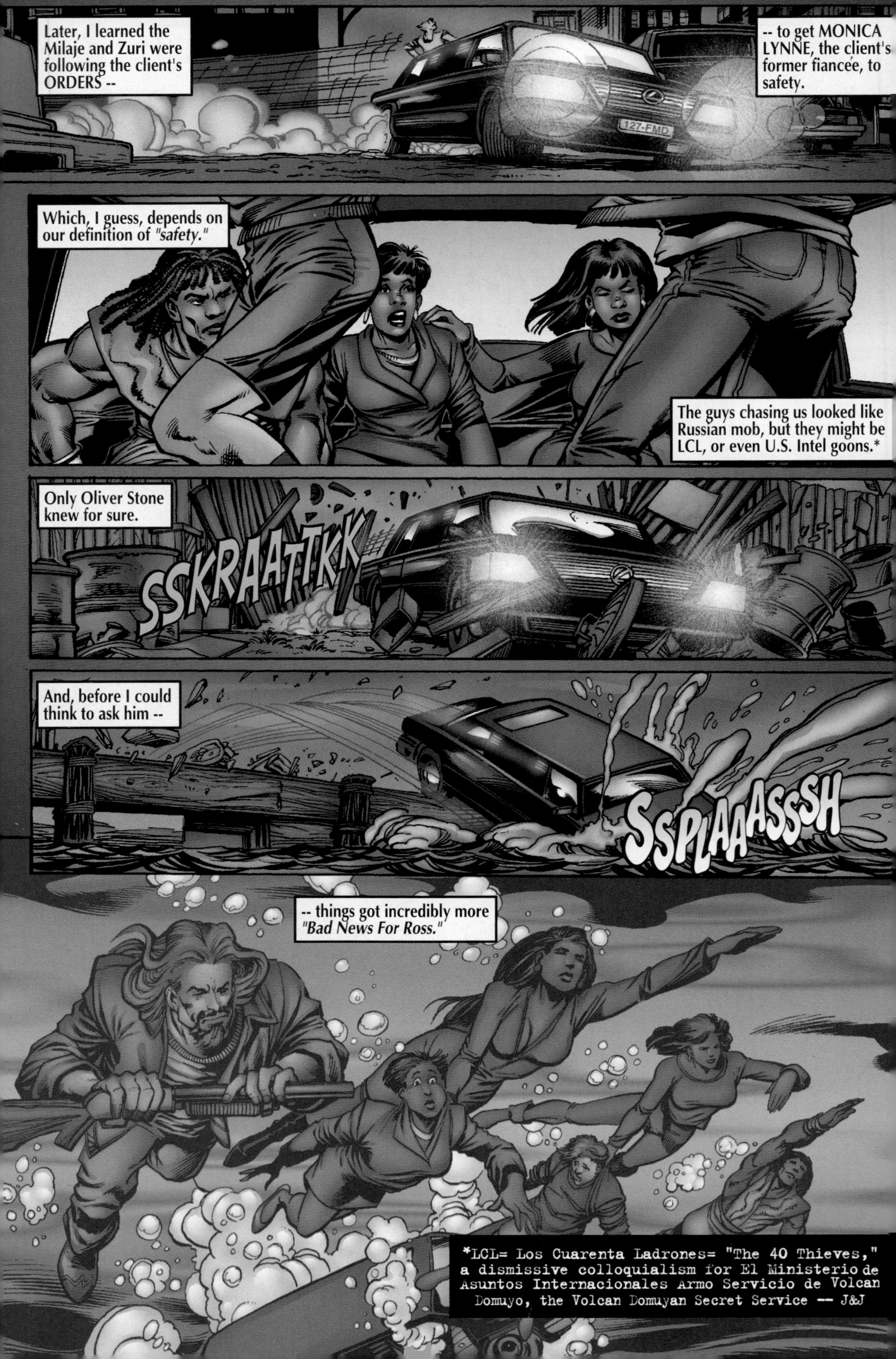
Later, I learned the Milaje and Zuri were following the client's ORDERS --
-- to get MONICA LYNNE, the client's former fiancée, to safety.
127-FMD
Which, I guess, depends on our definition of *"safety."*
The guys chasing us looked like Russian mob, but they might be LCL, or even U.S. Intel goons.*
Only Oliver Stone knew for sure.
SSKRAATTKK
And, before I could think to ask him --
SSPLAAASSSH
-- things got incredibly more *"Bad News For Ross."*
*LCL= Los Cuarenta Ladrones= "The 40 Thieves," a dismissive colloquialism for El Ministerio de Asuntos Internacionales Armo Servicio de Volcan Domuyo, the Volcan Domuyan Secret Service -- J&J

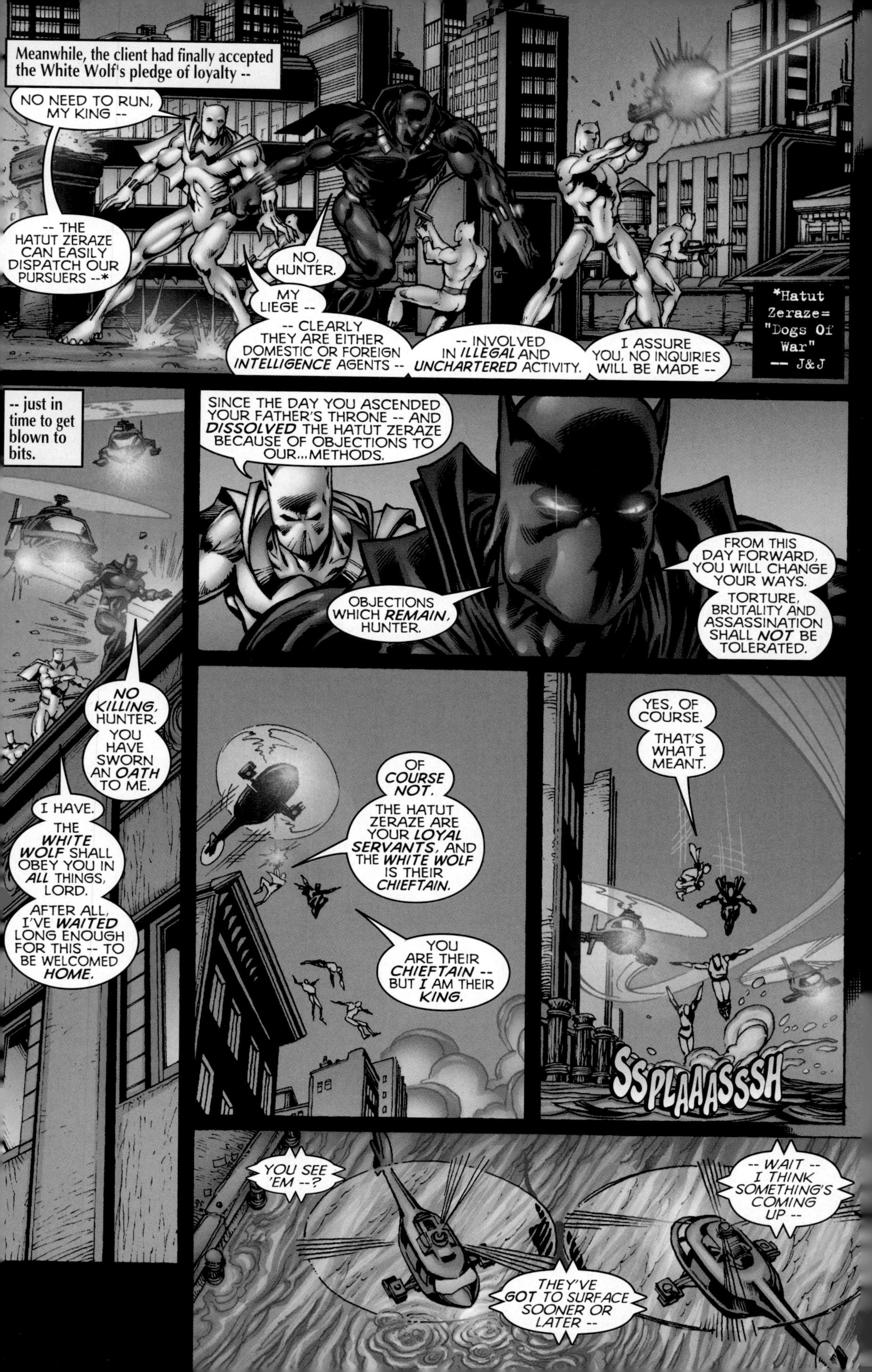
Meanwhile, the client had finally accepted the White Wolf's pledge of loyalty --
NO NEED TO RUN, MY KING --
-- THE HATUT ZERAZE CAN EASILY DISPATCH OUR PURSUERS --*
NO, HUNTER.
MY LIEGE --
-- CLEARLY THEY ARE EITHER DOMESTIC OR FOREIGN INTELLIGENCE AGENTS --
-- INVOLVED IN ILLEGAL AND UNCHARTERED ACTIVITY.
I ASSURE YOU, NO INQUIRIES WILL BE MADE --
*Hatut Zeraze= "Dogs Of War" -- J&J
-- just in time to get blown to bits.
SINCE THE DAY YOU ASCENDED YOUR FATHER'S THRONE -- AND DISSOLVED THE HATUT ZERAZE BECAUSE OF OBJECTIONS TO OUR...METHODS.
OBJECTIONS WHICH REMAIN, HUNTER.
FROM THIS DAY FORWARD, YOU WILL CHANGE YOUR WAYS.
TORTURE, BRUTALITY AND ASSASSINATION SHALL NOT BE TOLERATED.
NO KILLING, HUNTER.
YOU HAVE SWORN AN OATH TO ME.
I HAVE.
THE WHITE WOLF SHALL OBEY YOU IN ALL THINGS, LORD.
AFTER ALL, I'VE WAITED LONG ENOUGH FOR THIS -- TO BE WELCOMED HOME.
OF COURSE NOT.
THE HATUT ZERAZE ARE YOUR LOYAL SERVANTS, AND THE WHITE WOLF IS THEIR CHIEFTAIN.
YOU ARE THEIR CHIEFTAIN -- BUT I AM THEIR KING.
YES, OF COURSE.
THAT'S WHAT I MEANT.
SSPLAAASSSH
YOU SEE 'EM --?
-- WAIT -- I THINK SOMETHING'S COMING UP --
THEY'VE GOT TO SURFACE SOONER OR LATER --

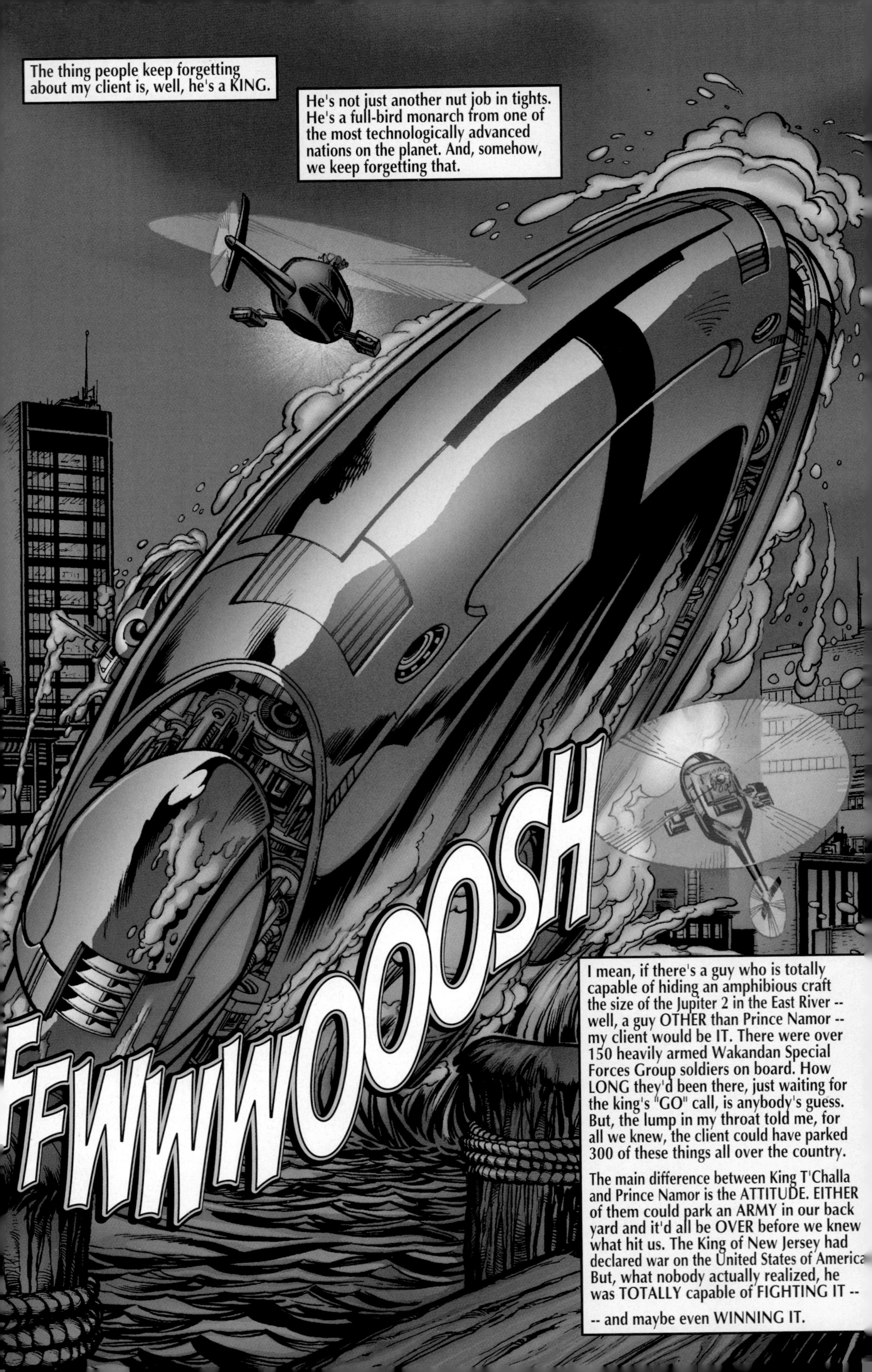

The thing people keep forgetting about my client is, well, he's a KING.
He's not just another nut job in tights. He's a full-bird monarch from one of the most technologically advanced nations on the planet. And, somehow, we keep forgetting that.
FWWWOOOOSH
I mean, if there's a guy who is totally capable of hiding an amphibious craft the size of the Jupiter 2 in the East River -- well, a guy OTHER than Prince Namor -- my client would be IT. There were over 150 heavily armed Wakandan Special Forces Group soldiers on board. How LONG they'd been there, just waiting for the king's "GO" call, is anybody's guess. But, the lump in my throat told me, for all we knew, the client could have parked 300 of these things all over the country.
The main difference between King T'Challa and Prince Namor is the ATTITUDE. EITHER of them could park an ARMY in our back yard and it'd all be OVER before we knew what hit us. The King of New Jersey had declared war on the United States of America But, what nobody actually realized, he was TOTALLY capable of FIGHTING IT --
-- and maybe even WINNING IT.

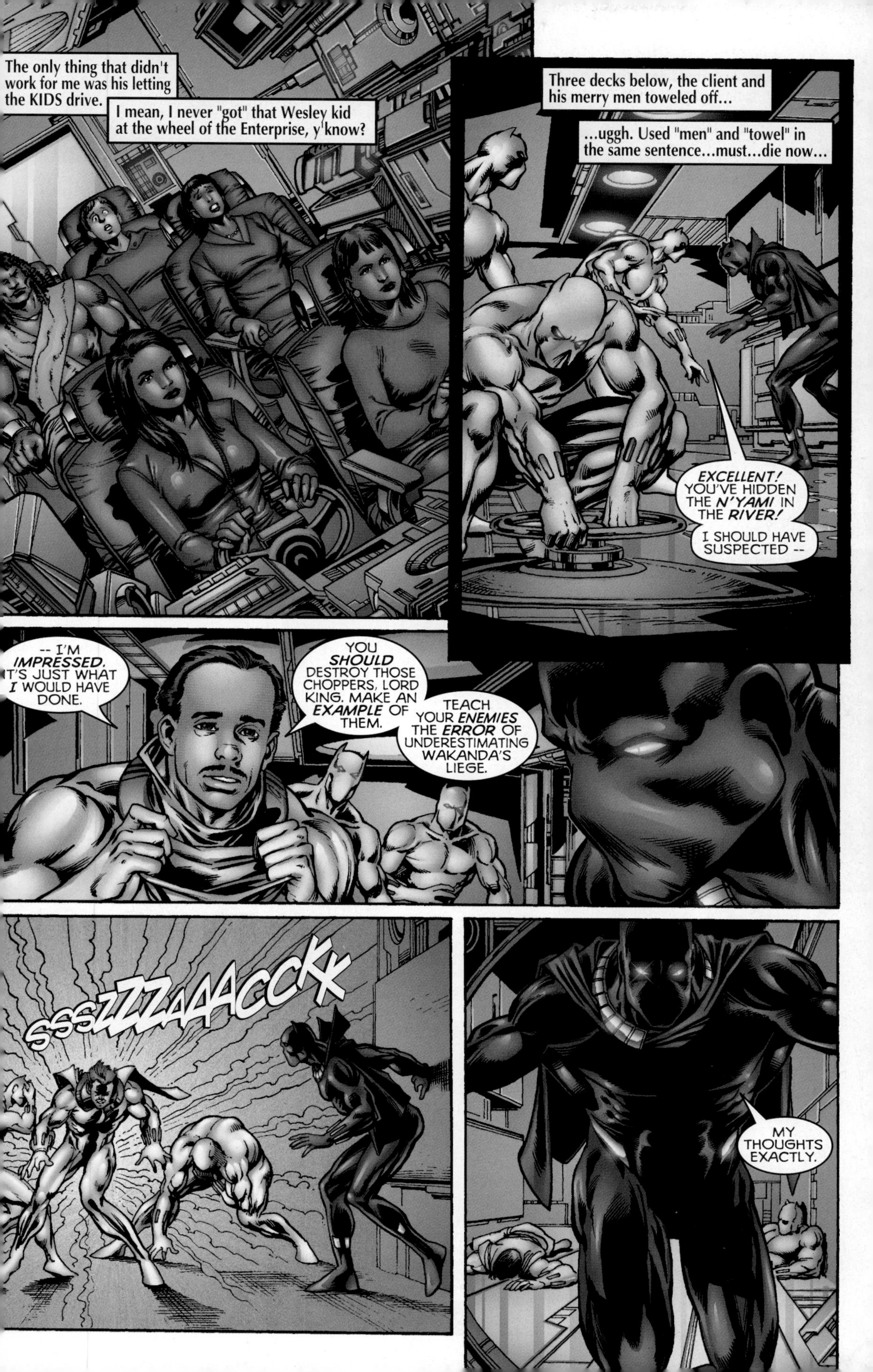

The only thing that didn't work for me was his letting the KIDS drive.
I mean, I never "got" that Wesley kid at the wheel of the Enterprise, y'know?
Three decks below, the client and his merry men toweled off...
...ugh. Used "men" and "towel" in the same sentence...must...die now...
EXCELLENT! YOU'VE HIDDEN THE N'YAMI IN THE RIVER!
I SHOULD HAVE SUSPECTED --
-- I'M IMPRESSED. IT'S JUST WHAT I WOULD HAVE DONE.
YOU SHOULD DESTROY THOSE CHOPPERS, LORD KING. MAKE AN EXAMPLE OF THEM.
TEACH YOUR ENEMIES THE ERROR OF UNDERESTIMATING WAKANDA'S LIEGE.
SSSZZZAAAACCKK
MY THOUGHTS EXACTLY.

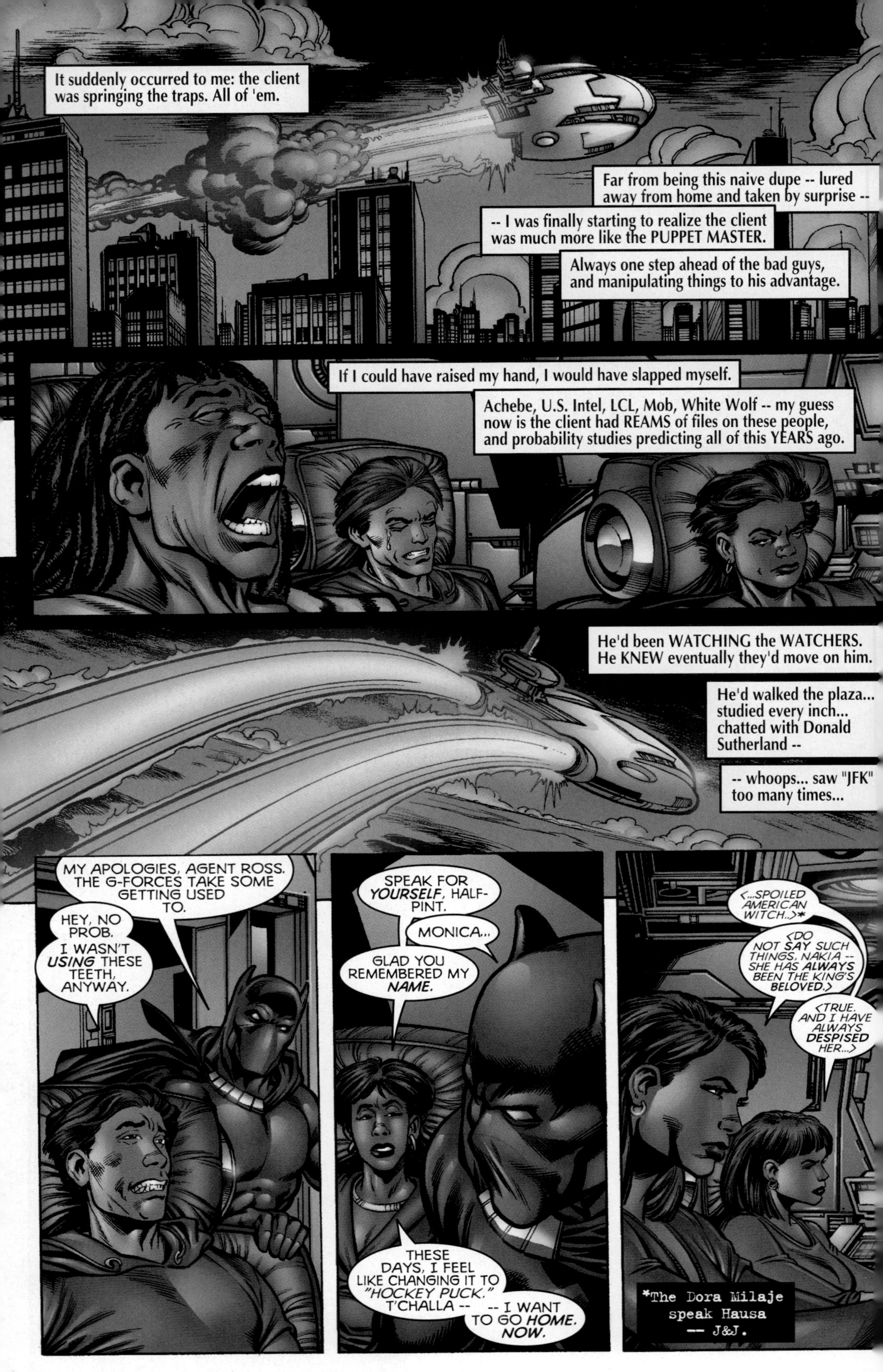
It suddenly occurred to me: the client was springing the traps. All of 'em.
Far from being this naive dupe -- lured away from home and taken by surprise --
-- I was finally starting to realize the client was much more like the PUPPET MASTER.
Always one step ahead of the bad guys, and manipulating things to his advantage.
If I could have raised my hand, I would have slapped myself.
Achebe, U.S. Intel, LCL, Mob, White Wolf -- my guess now is the client had REAMS of files on these people, and probability studies predicting all of this YEARS ago.
He'd been WATCHING the WATCHERS. He KNEW eventually they'd move on him.
He'd walked the plaza... studied every inch... chatted with Donald Sutherland --
-- whoops... saw "JFK" too many times...
MY APOLOGIES, AGENT ROSS. THE G-FORCES TAKE SOME GETTING USED TO.
HEY, NO PROB.
I WASN'T USING THESE TEETH, ANYWAY.
SPEAK FOR YOURSELF, HALF-PINT.
MONICA...
GLAD YOU REMEMBERED MY NAME.
THESE DAYS, I FEEL LIKE CHANGING IT TO "HOCKEY PUCK." T'CHALLA --
-- I WANT TO GO HOME. NOW.
<...SPOILED AMERICAN WITCH...>*
<DO NOT SAY SUCH THINGS, NAKIA -- SHE HAS ALWAYS BEEN THE KING'S BELOVED.>
<TRUE. AND I HAVE ALWAYS DESPISED HER...>
*The Dora Milaje speak Hausa -- J&J.

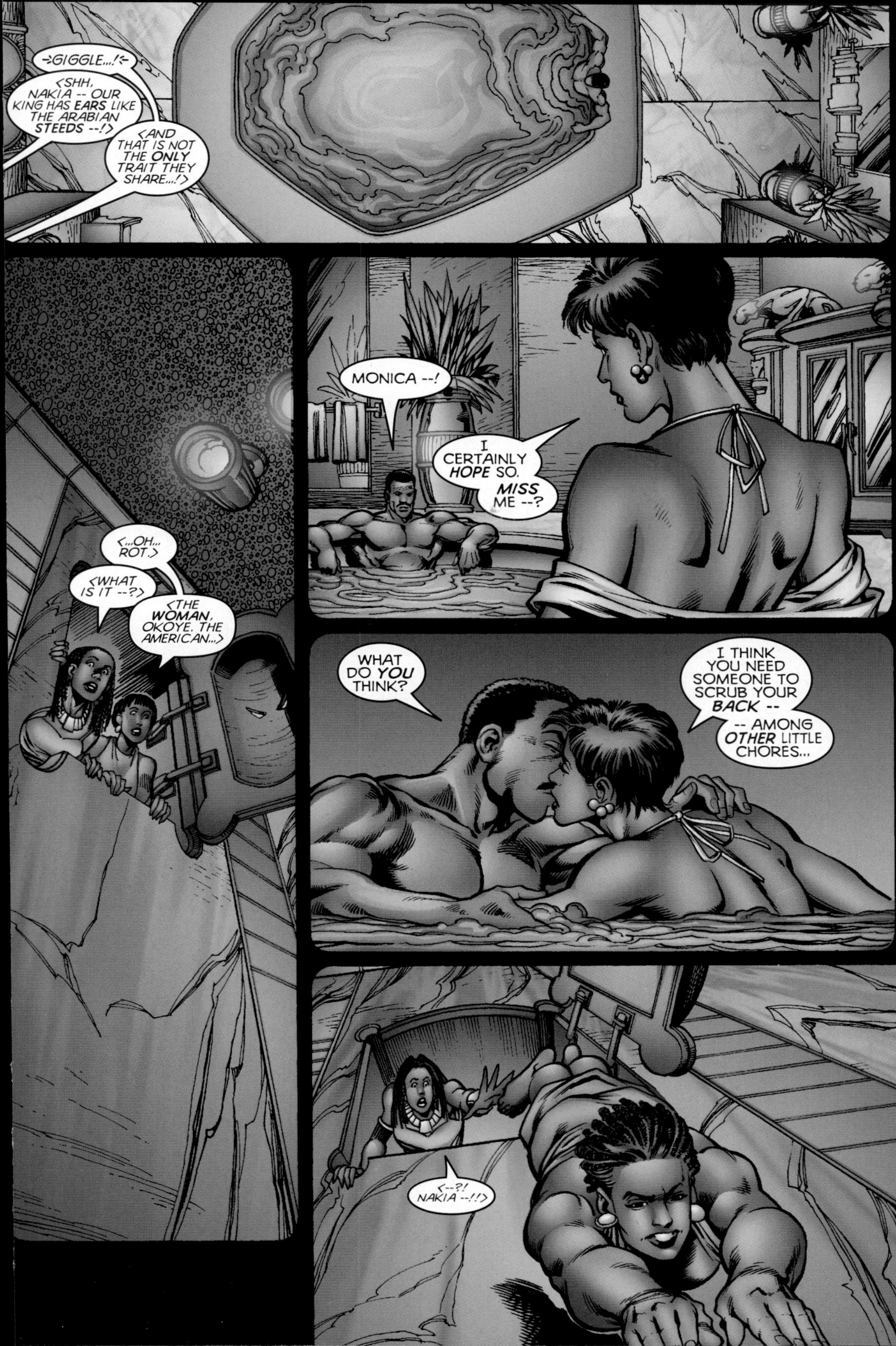

~GIGGLE...!~
<SHH, NAKIA -- OUR KING HAS EARS LIKE THE ARABIAN STEEDS --!>
<AND THAT IS NOT THE ONLY TRAIT THEY SHARE...!>
<...OH... ROT.>
<WHAT IS IT --?>
<THE WOMAN, OKOYE. THE AMERICAN...>
MONICA --!
I CERTAINLY HOPE SO. MISS ME --?
WHAT DO YOU THINK?
I THINK YOU NEED SOMEONE TO SCRUB YOUR BACK --
-- AMONG OTHER LITTLE CHORES...
<--?! NAKIA --!!>

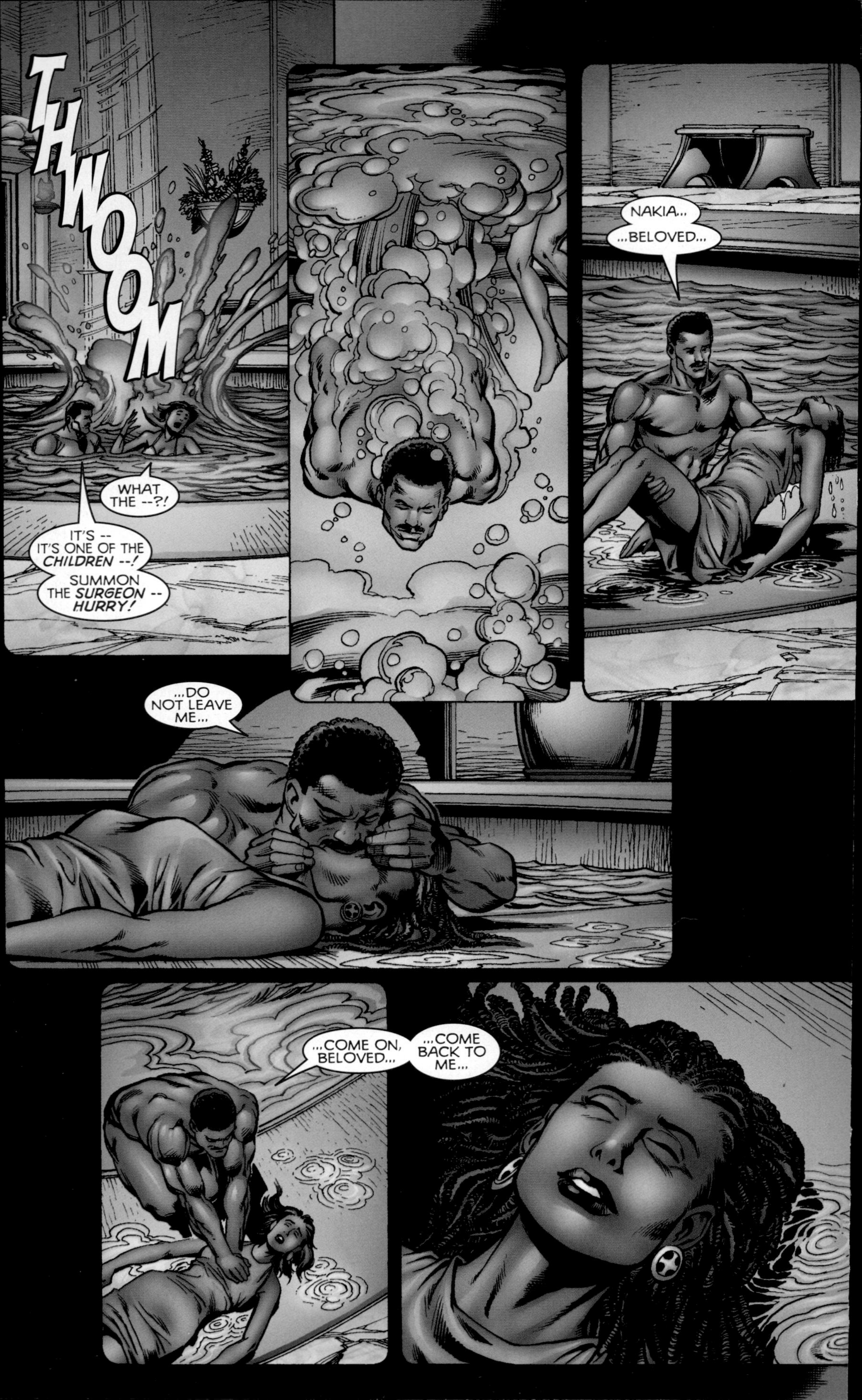
THWOOM
WHAT THE --?!
IT'S -- IT'S ONE OF THE CHILDREN --! SUMMON THE SURGEON -- HURRY!
NAKIA...
...BELOVED...
...DO NOT LEAVE ME...
...COME ON, BELOVED...
...COME BACK TO ME...

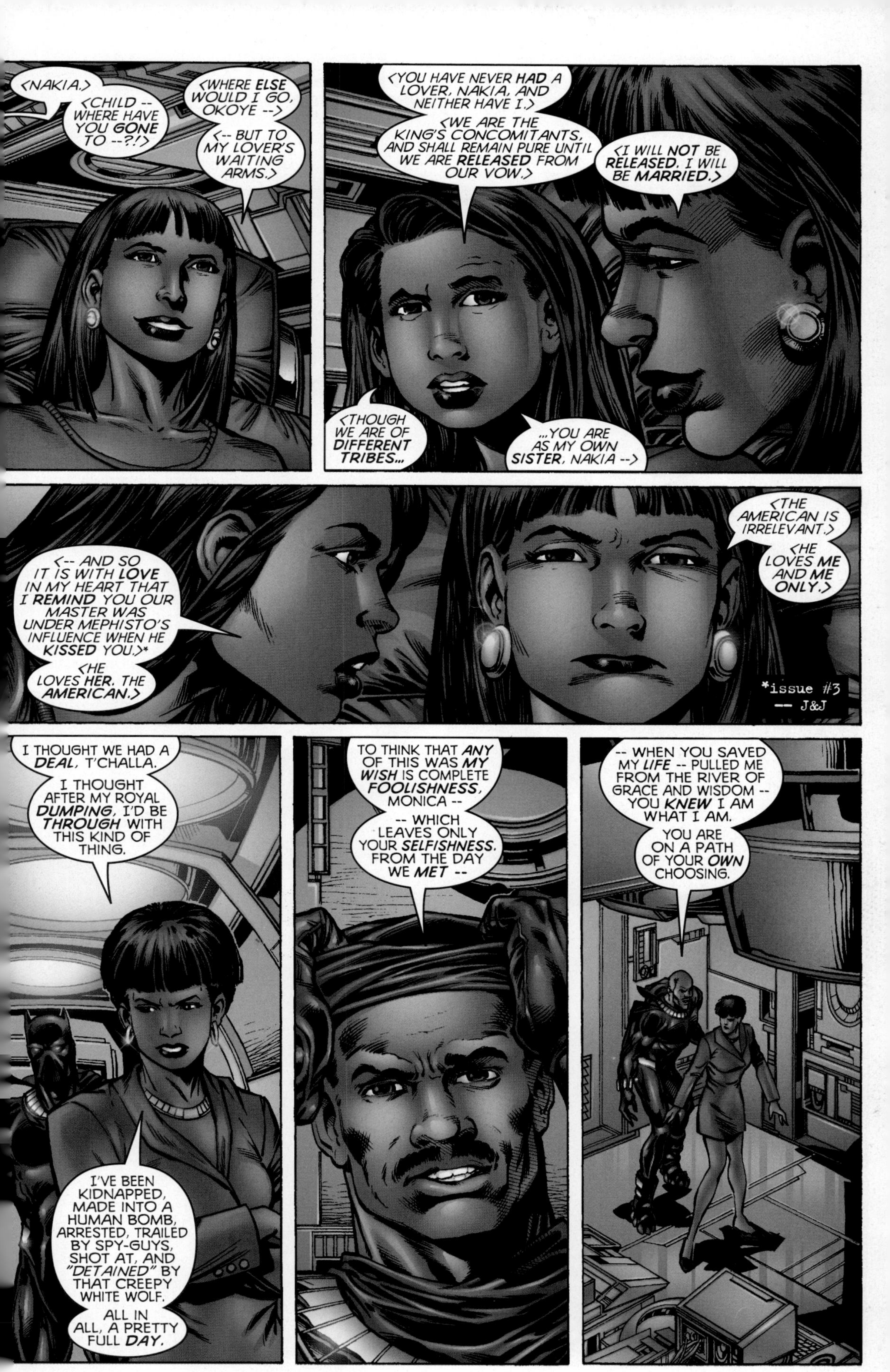

<NAKIA.>
<CHILD -- WHERE HAVE YOU GONE TO --?!>
<WHERE ELSE WOULD I GO, OKOYE -->
<-- BUT TO MY LOVER'S WAITING ARMS.>
<YOU HAVE NEVER HAD A LOVER, NAKIA, AND NEITHER HAVE I.>
<WE ARE THE KING'S CONCOMITANTS, AND SHALL REMAIN PURE UNTIL WE ARE RELEASED FROM OUR VOW.>
<I WILL NOT BE RELEASED. I WILL BE MARRIED.>
<THOUGH WE ARE OF DIFFERENT TRIBES...
...YOU ARE AS MY OWN SISTER, NAKIA -->
<-- AND SO IT IS WITH LOVE IN MY HEART THAT I REMIND YOU OUR MASTER WAS UNDER MEPHISTO'S INFLUENCE WHEN HE KISSED YOU.>*
<HE LOVES HER. THE AMERICAN.>
<THE AMERICAN IS IRRELEVANT.>
<HE LOVES ME AND ME ONLY.>
*issue #3 -- J&J
I THOUGHT WE HAD A DEAL, T'CHALLA.
I THOUGHT AFTER MY ROYAL DUMPING, I'D BE THROUGH WITH THIS KIND OF THING.
I'VE BEEN KIDNAPPED, MADE INTO A HUMAN BOMB, ARRESTED, TRAILED BY SPY-GUYS, SHOT AT, AND "DETAINED" BY THAT CREEPY WHITE WOLF.
ALL IN ALL, A PRETTY FULL DAY.
TO THINK THAT ANY OF THIS WAS MY WISH IS COMPLETE FOOLISHNESS, MONICA --
-- WHICH LEAVES ONLY YOUR SELFISHNESS. FROM THE DAY WE MET --
-- WHEN YOU SAVED MY LIFE -- PULLED ME FROM THE RIVER OF GRACE AND WISDOM -- YOU KNEW I AM WHAT I AM.
YOU ARE ON A PATH OF YOUR OWN CHOOSING.

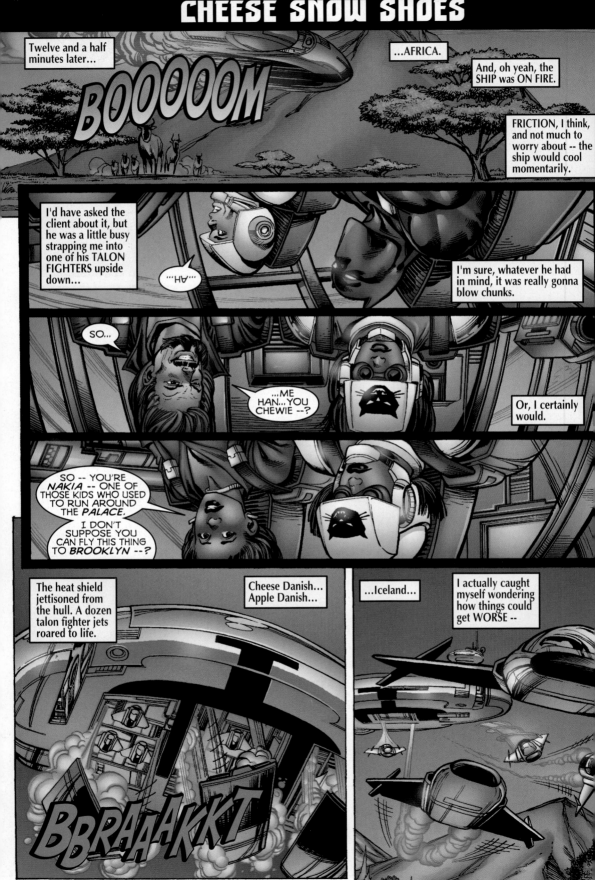

Twelve and a half minutes later...

BOOOOOM

...AFRICA.

And, oh yeah, the SHIP was ON FIRE.

FRICTION, I think, and not much to worry about -- the ship would cool momentarily.

I'd have asked the client about it, but he was a little busy strapping me into one of his TALON FIGHTERS upside down...

"'HA'"

I'm sure, whatever he had in mind, it was really gonna blow chunks.

SO...

...ME HAN...YOU CHEWIE --?

Or, I certainly would.

SO -- YOU'RE NAKIA -- ONE OF THOSE KIDS WHO USED TO RUN AROUND THE PALACE.

I DON'T SUPPOSE YOU CAN FLY THIS THING TO BROOKLYN --?

The heat shield jettisoned from the hull. A dozen talon fighter jets roared to life.

Cheese Danish... Apple Danish...

...Iceland...

I actually caught myself wondering how things could get WORSE --

BBRAAAKKT

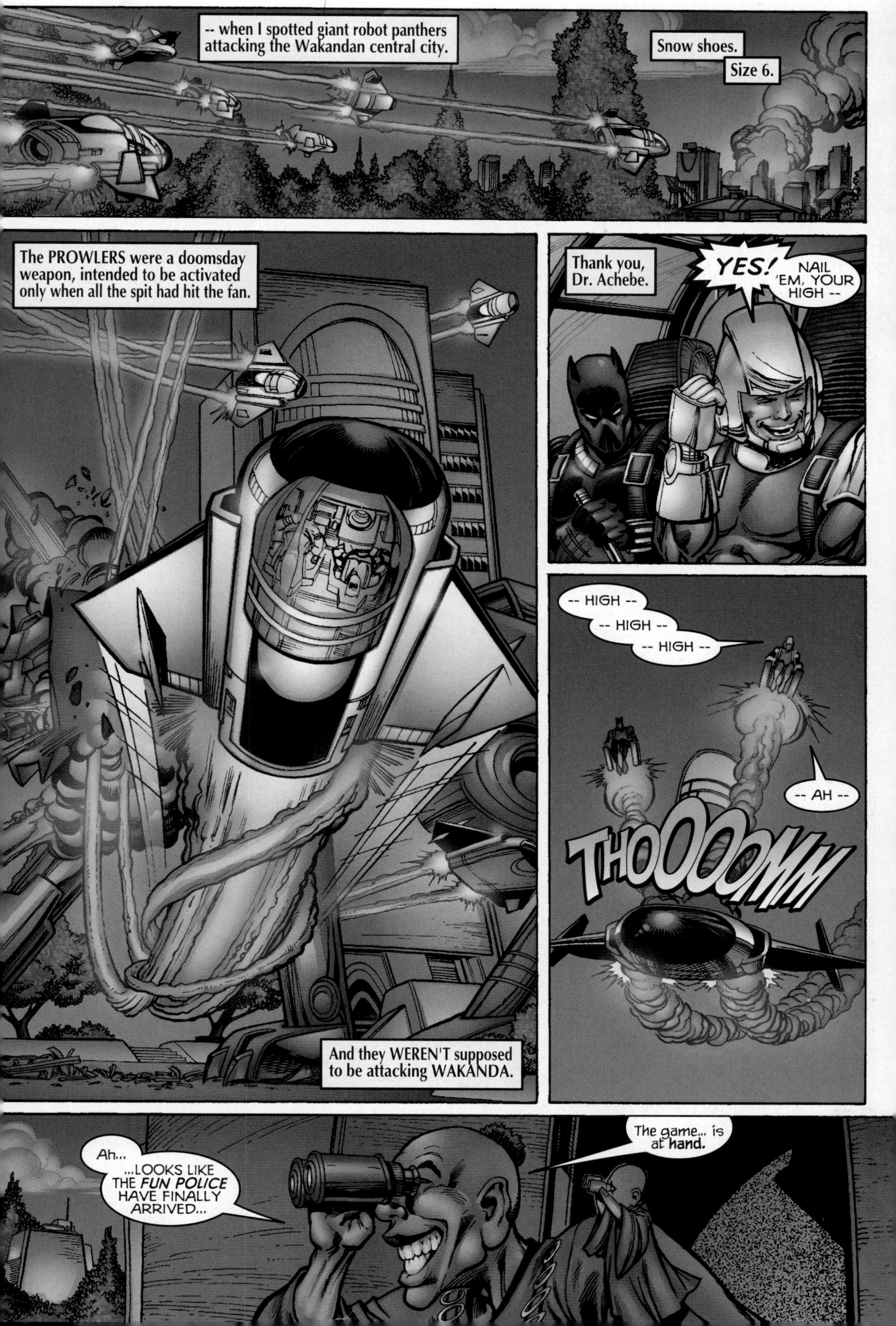
-- when I spotted giant robot panthers attacking the Wakandan central city.
Snow shoes.
Size 6.
The PROWLERS were a doomsday weapon, intended to be activated only when all the spit had hit the fan.
And they WEREN'T supposed to be attacking WAKANDA.
Thank you, Dr. Achebe.
YES!
NAIL 'EM, YOUR HIGH --
-- HIGH --
-- HIGH --
-- HIGH --
-- AH --
THOOOOMM
Ah...
...LOOKS LIKE THE FUN POLICE HAVE FINALLY ARRIVED...
The game... is at hand.

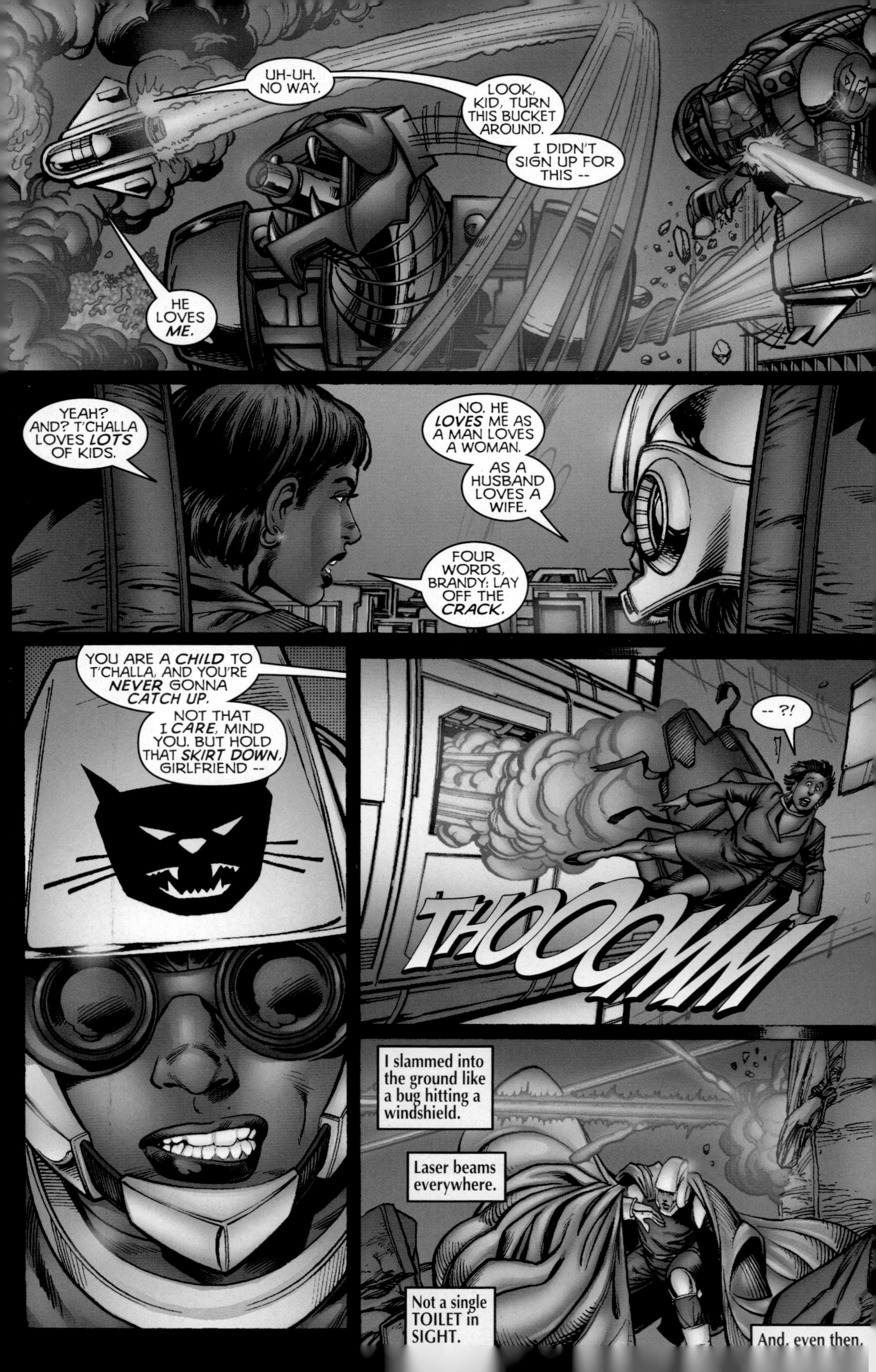
UH-UH. NO WAY.
LOOK, KID, TURN THIS BUCKET AROUND.
I DIDN'T SIGN UP FOR THIS --
HE LOVES ME.
YEAH? AND? T'CHALLA LOVES LOTS OF KIDS.
NO. HE LOVES ME AS A MAN LOVES A WOMAN.
AS A HUSBAND LOVES A WIFE.
FOUR WORDS, BRANDY: LAY OFF THE CRACK.
YOU ARE A CHILD TO T'CHALLA, AND YOU'RE NEVER GONNA CATCH UP.
NOT THAT I CARE, MIND YOU. BUT HOLD THAT SKIRT DOWN, GIRLFRIEND --
-- ?!
THOOOMM
I slammed into the ground like a bug hitting a windshield.
Laser beams everywhere.
Not a single TOILET in SIGHT.
And, even then.

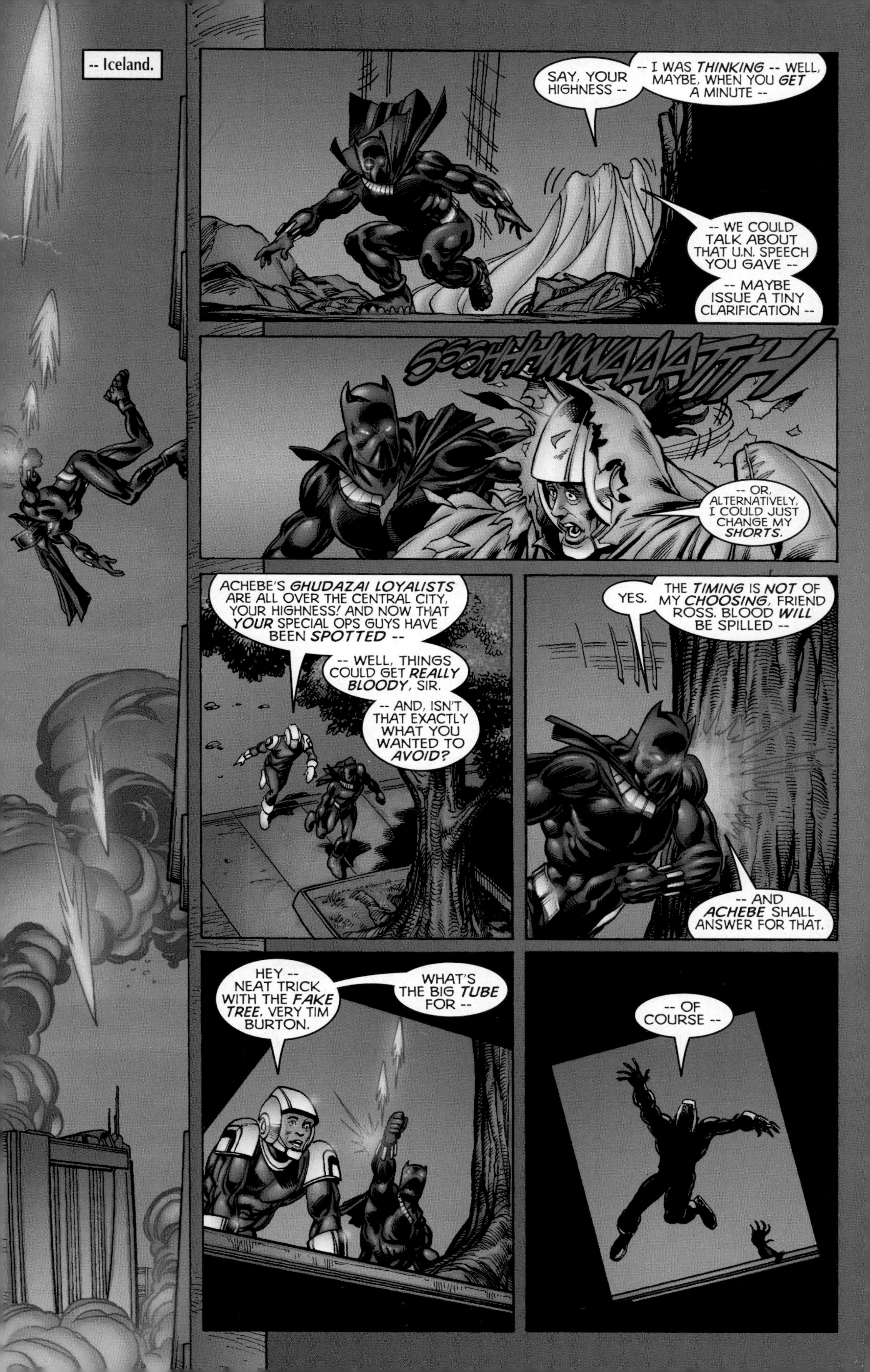
-- Iceland.
SAY, YOUR HIGHNESS --
-- I WAS THINKING -- WELL, MAYBE, WHEN YOU GET A MINUTE --
-- WE COULD TALK ABOUT THAT U.N. SPEECH YOU GAVE --
-- MAYBE ISSUE A TINY CLARIFICATION --
SSSHHHWWAAAATTH
-- OR, ALTERNATIVELY, I COULD JUST CHANGE MY SHORTS.
ACHEBE'S GHUDAZAI LOYALISTS ARE ALL OVER THE CENTRAL CITY, YOUR HIGHNESS! AND NOW THAT YOUR SPECIAL OPS GUYS HAVE BEEN SPOTTED --
-- WELL, THINGS COULD GET REALLY BLOODY, SIR.
-- AND, ISN'T THAT EXACTLY WHAT YOU WANTED TO AVOID?
YES.
THE TIMING IS NOT OF MY CHOOSING, FRIEND ROSS. BLOOD WILL BE SPILLED --
-- AND ACHEBE SHALL ANSWER FOR THAT.
HEY -- NEAT TRICK WITH THE FAKE TREE. VERY TIM BURTON.
WHAT'S THE BIG TUBE FOR --
-- OF COURSE --

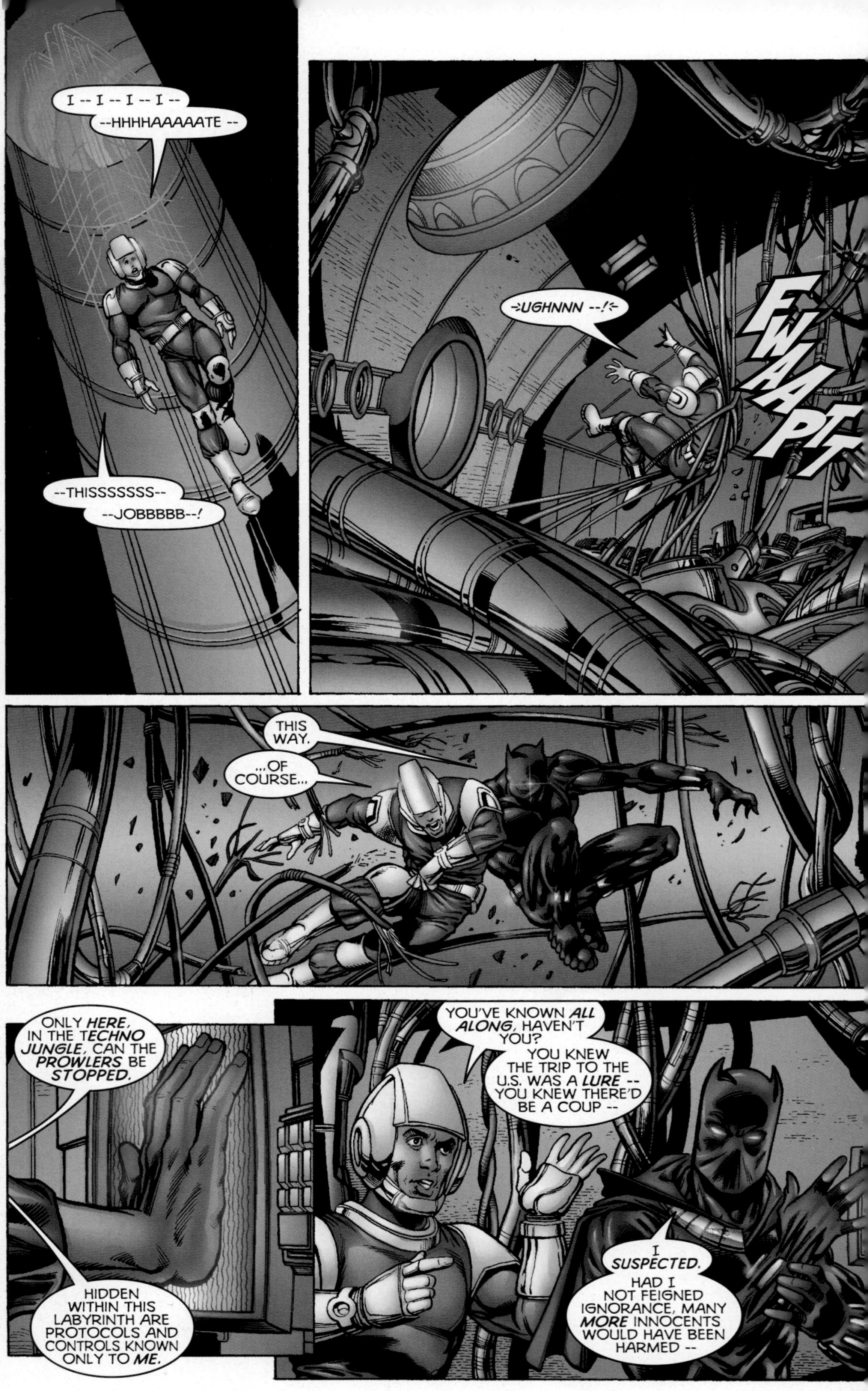

I -- I -- I -- I --
--HHHHAAAAATE --
--THISSSSSSS--
--JOBBBBB--!
‹UGHNNN --!›
FWAAPTT
THIS WAY.
...OF COURSE...
ONLY HERE, IN THE TECHNO JUNGLE, CAN THE PROWLERS BE STOPPED.
HIDDEN WITHIN THIS LABYRINTH ARE PROTOCOLS AND CONTROLS KNOWN ONLY TO ME.
YOU'VE KNOWN ALL ALONG, HAVEN'T YOU?
YOU KNEW THE TRIP TO THE U.S. WAS A LURE -- YOU KNEW THERE'D BE A COUP --
I SUSPECTED.
HAD I NOT FEIGNED IGNORANCE, MANY MORE INNOCENTS WOULD HAVE BEEN HARMED --

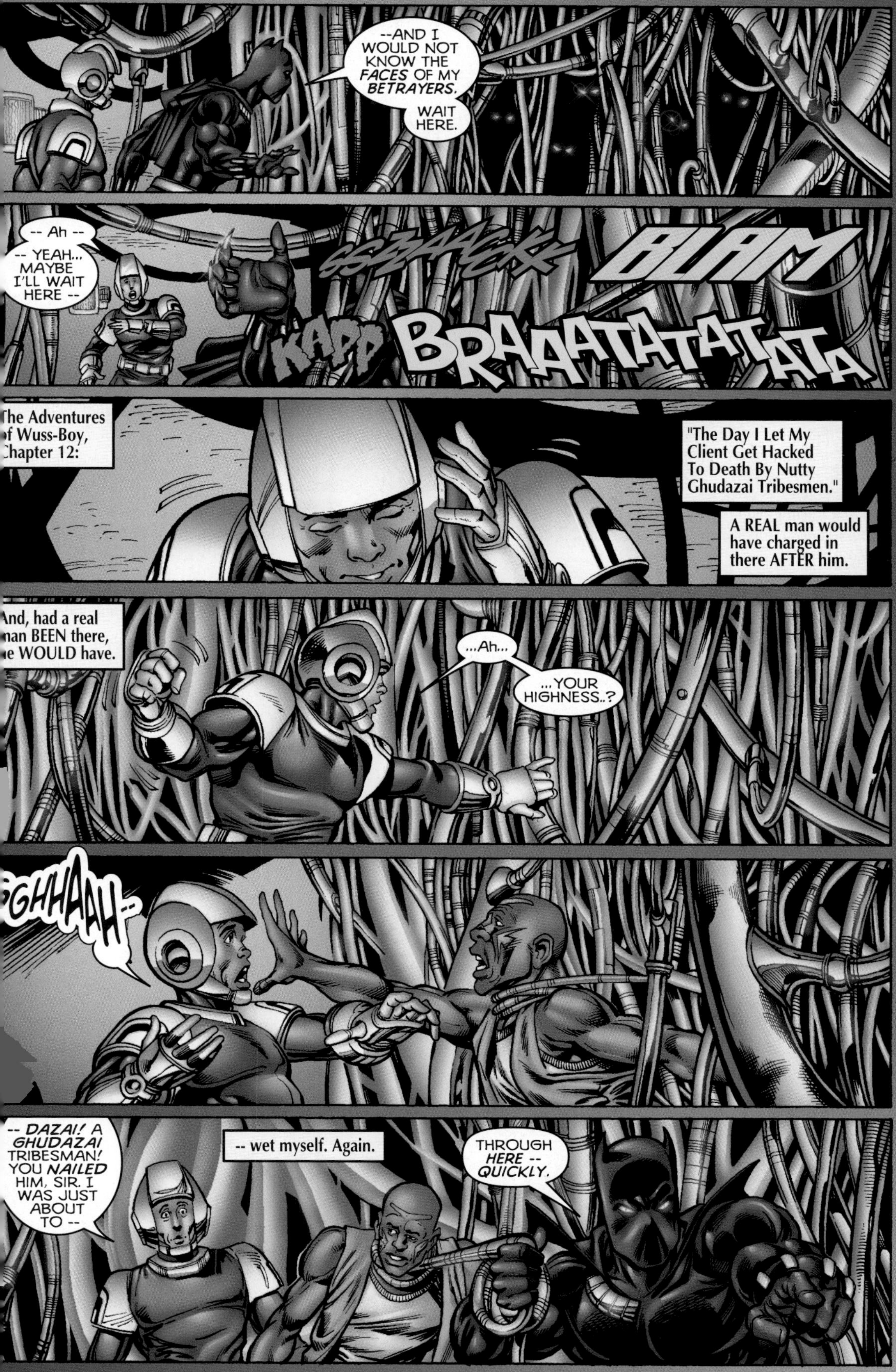
--AND I WOULD NOT KNOW THE FACES OF MY BETRAYERS.
WAIT HERE.
-- Ah --
-- YEAH... MAYBE I'LL WAIT HERE --
BLAM
BRAAATATATATA
The Adventures of Wuss-Boy, Chapter 12:
"The Day I Let My Client Get Hacked To Death By Nutty Ghudazai Tribesmen."
A REAL man would have charged in there AFTER him.
And, had a real man BEEN there, he WOULD have.
...Ah...
...YOUR HIGHNESS..?
-- DAZAI! A GHUDAZAI TRIBESMAN! YOU NAILED HIM, SIR. I WAS JUST ABOUT TO --
-- wet myself. Again.
THROUGH HERE -- QUICKLY.

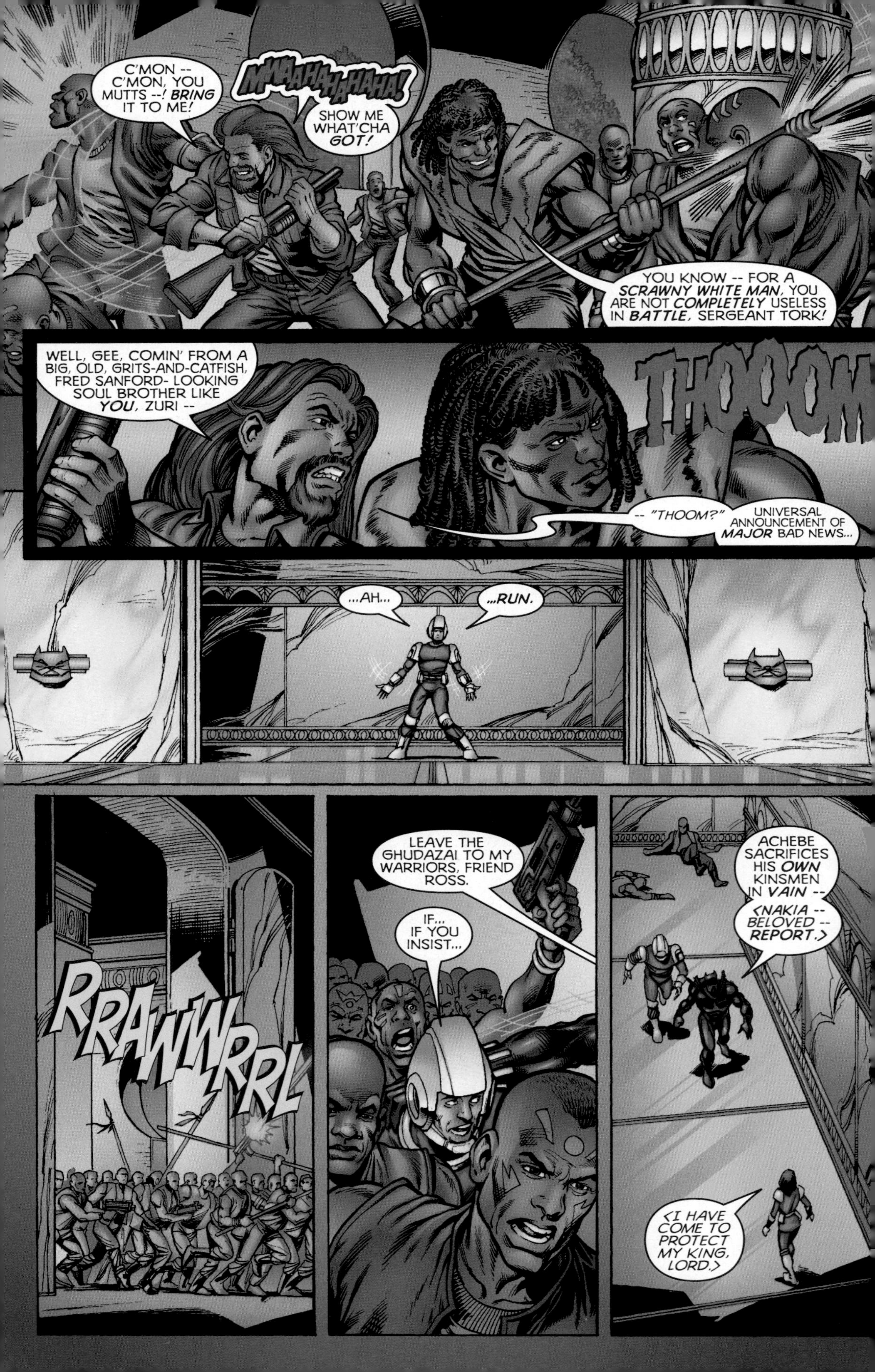
C'MON -- C'MON, YOU MUTTS --! BRING IT TO ME!
MWAAHAHAHAHA!
SHOW ME WHAT'CHA GOT!
YOU KNOW -- FOR A SCRAWNY WHITE MAN, YOU ARE NOT COMPLETELY USELESS IN BATTLE, SERGEANT TORK!
WELL, GEE, COMIN' FROM A BIG, OLD, GRITS-AND-CATFISH, FRED SANFORD- LOOKING SOUL BROTHER LIKE YOU, ZURI --
THOOOM
-- "THOOM?"
UNIVERSAL ANNOUNCEMENT OF MAJOR BAD NEWS...
...AH...
...RUN.
RRAWWRRL
LEAVE THE GHUDAZAI TO MY WARRIORS, FRIEND ROSS.
IF... IF YOU INSIST...
ACHEBE SACRIFICES HIS OWN KINSMEN IN VAIN --
<NAKIA -- BELOVED -- REPORT.>
<I HAVE COME TO PROTECT MY KING, LORD.>

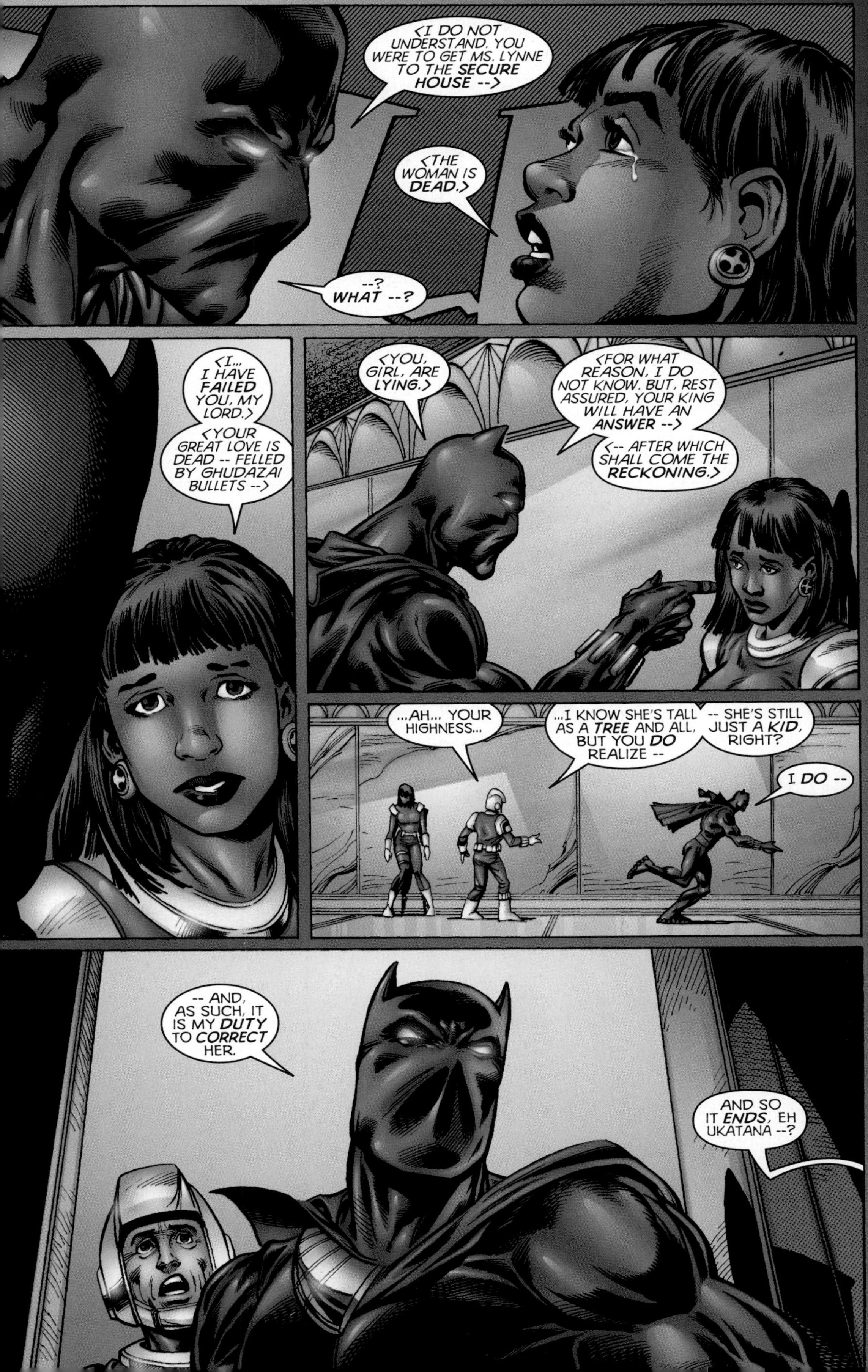

<I DO NOT UNDERSTAND. YOU WERE TO GET MS. LYNNE TO THE SECURE HOUSE -->
<THE WOMAN IS DEAD.>
--? WHAT --?
<I... I HAVE FAILED YOU, MY LORD.>
<YOUR GREAT LOVE IS DEAD -- FELLED BY GHUDAZAI BULLETS -->
<YOU, GIRL, ARE LYING.>
<FOR WHAT REASON, I DO NOT KNOW. BUT, REST ASSURED, YOUR KING WILL HAVE AN ANSWER -->
<-- AFTER WHICH SHALL COME THE RECKONING.>
...AH... YOUR HIGHNESS...
...I KNOW SHE'S TALL AS A TREE AND ALL, BUT YOU DO REALIZE --
-- SHE'S STILL JUST A KID, RIGHT?
I DO --
-- AND, AS SUCH, IT IS MY DUTY TO CORRECT HER.
AND SO IT ENDS, EH UKATANA --?

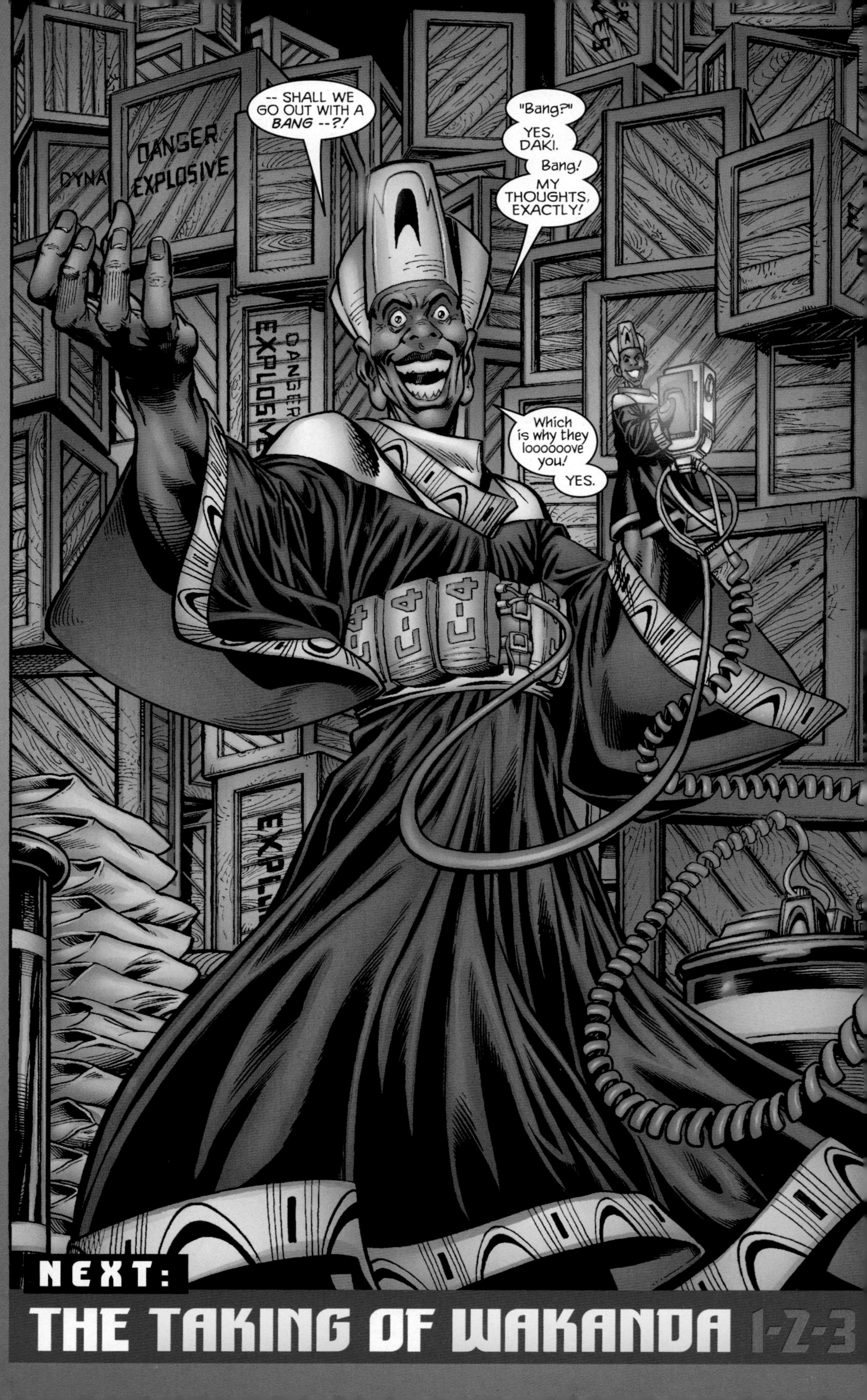
-- SHALL WE GO OUT WITH A *BANG* --?!
"Bang?"
YES, DAKI.
Bang!
MY THOUGHTS, EXACTLY!
Which is why they loooooove you!
YES.
DANGER EXPLOSIVE
C-4
NEXT:
THE TAKING OF WAKANDA 1-2-3

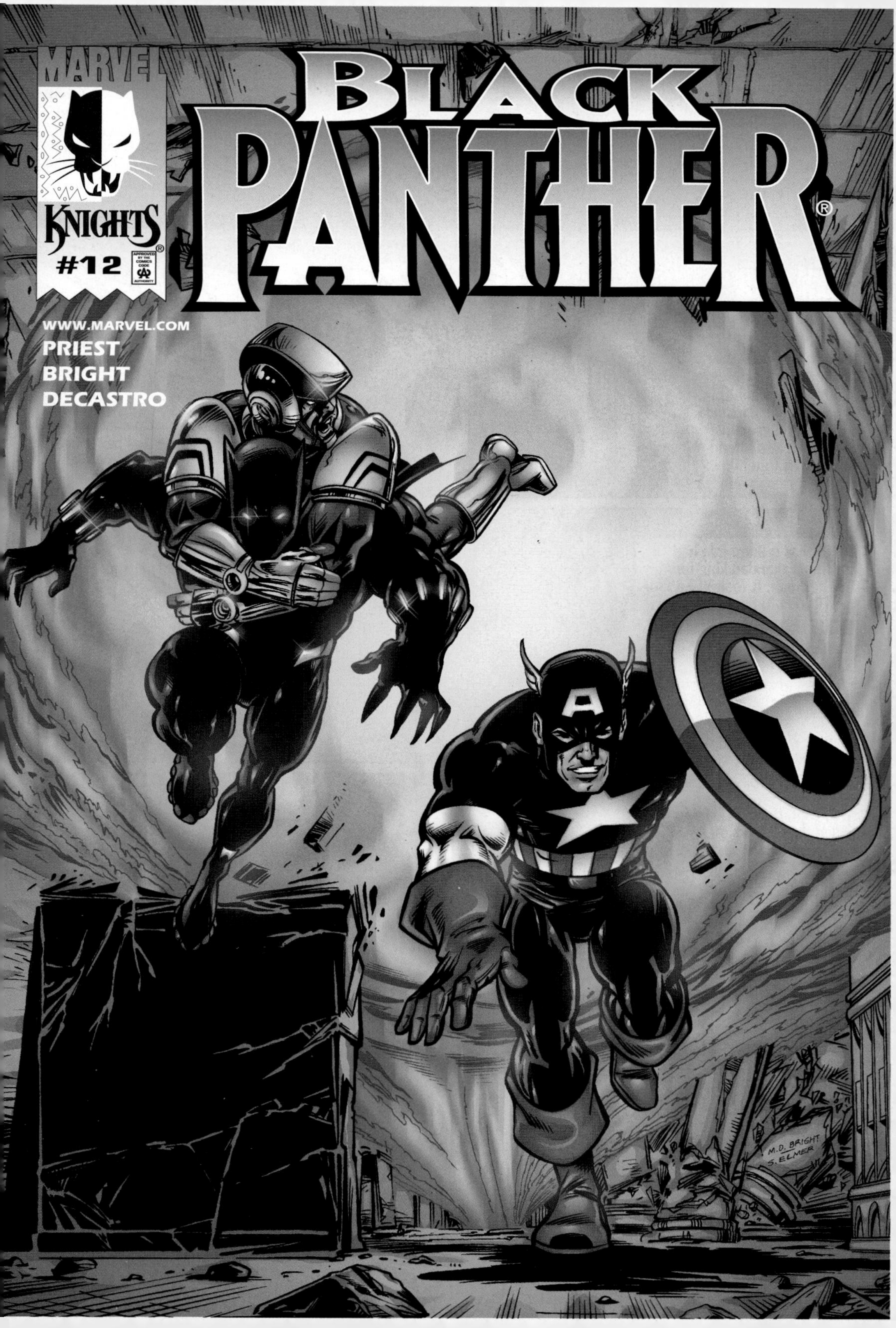
MARVEL
KNIGHTS
#12
APPROVED BY THE COMICS CODE AUTHORITY
BLACK PANTHER®
WWW.MARVEL.COM
PRIEST
BRIGHT
DECASTRO
M.D. BRIGHT
S. ELMER

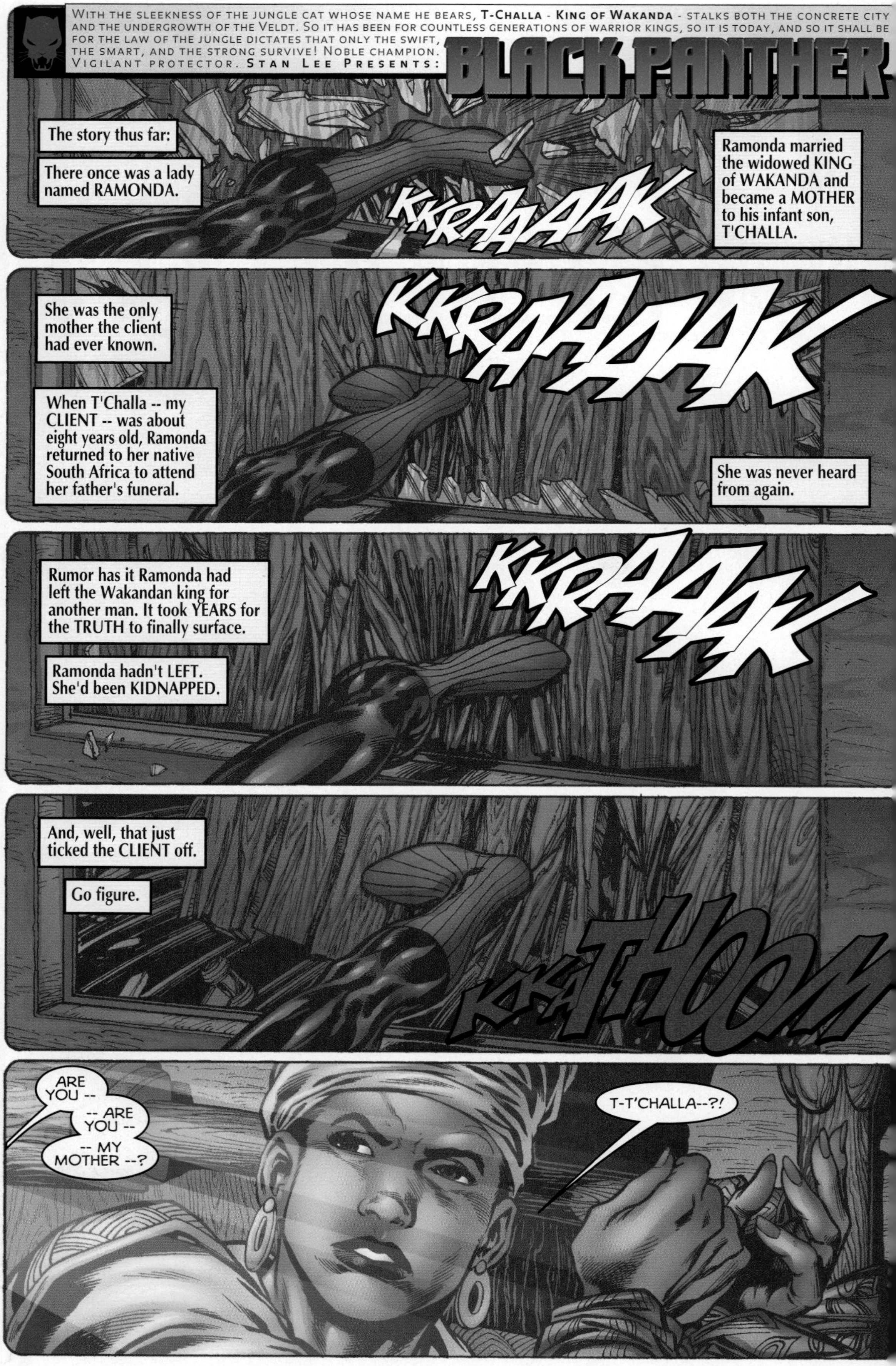

With the sleekness of the jungle cat whose name he bears, T-Challa - King of Wakanda - stalks both the concrete city and the undergrowth of the Veldt. So it has been for countless generations of warrior kings, so it is today, and so it shall be for the law of the jungle dictates that only the swift, the smart, and the strong survive! Noble champion. Vigilant protector. Stan Lee Presents:
BLACK PANTHER
The story thus far:
There once was a lady named RAMONDA.
KKRAAAAK
Ramonda married the widowed KING of WAKANDA and became a MOTHER to his infant son, T'CHALLA.
She was the only mother the client had ever known.
KKRAAAAK
When T'Challa -- my CLIENT -- was about eight years old, Ramonda returned to her native South Africa to attend her father's funeral.
She was never heard from again.
Rumor has it Ramonda had left the Wakandan king for another man. It took YEARS for the TRUTH to finally surface.
KKRAAAAK
Ramonda hadn't LEFT. She'd been KIDNAPPED.
And, well, that just ticked the CLIENT off.
Go figure.
KKATHOOM
ARE YOU --
-- ARE YOU --
-- MY MOTHER --?
T-T'CHALLA--?!

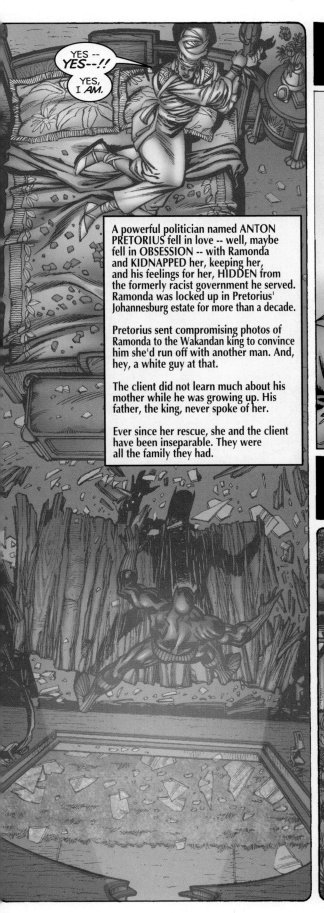

YES -- *YES*--!!

YES, I *AM*.

A powerful politician named ANTON PRETORIUS fell in love -- well, maybe fell in OBSESSION -- with Ramonda and KIDNAPPED her, keeping her, and his feelings for her, HIDDEN from the formerly racist government he served. Ramonda was locked up in Pretorius' Johannesburg estate for more than a decade.

Pretorius sent compromising photos of Ramonda to the Wakandan king to convince him she'd run off with another man. And, hey, a white guy at that.

The client did not learn much about his mother while he was growing up. His father, the king, never spoke of her.

Ever since her rescue, she and the client have been inseparable. They were all the family they had.

CAPTAIN REWIND

BUT, I'M GETTING AHEAD OF MYSELF AGAIN.

I KNOW... I KNOW, GUYS. IT'S A HARD HABIT TO BREAK.

I LEFT THIS PART OUT -- REMEMBER, EARLIER --

THE OTHER SON

Ramonda was mother to more than ONE son.

Remember I told you about HUNTER, the WHITE WOLF, orphaned when his parents' plane crashed in the jungle --

-- and ADOPTED by the Wakandan king?*

*see issue #10 for details -- J&J

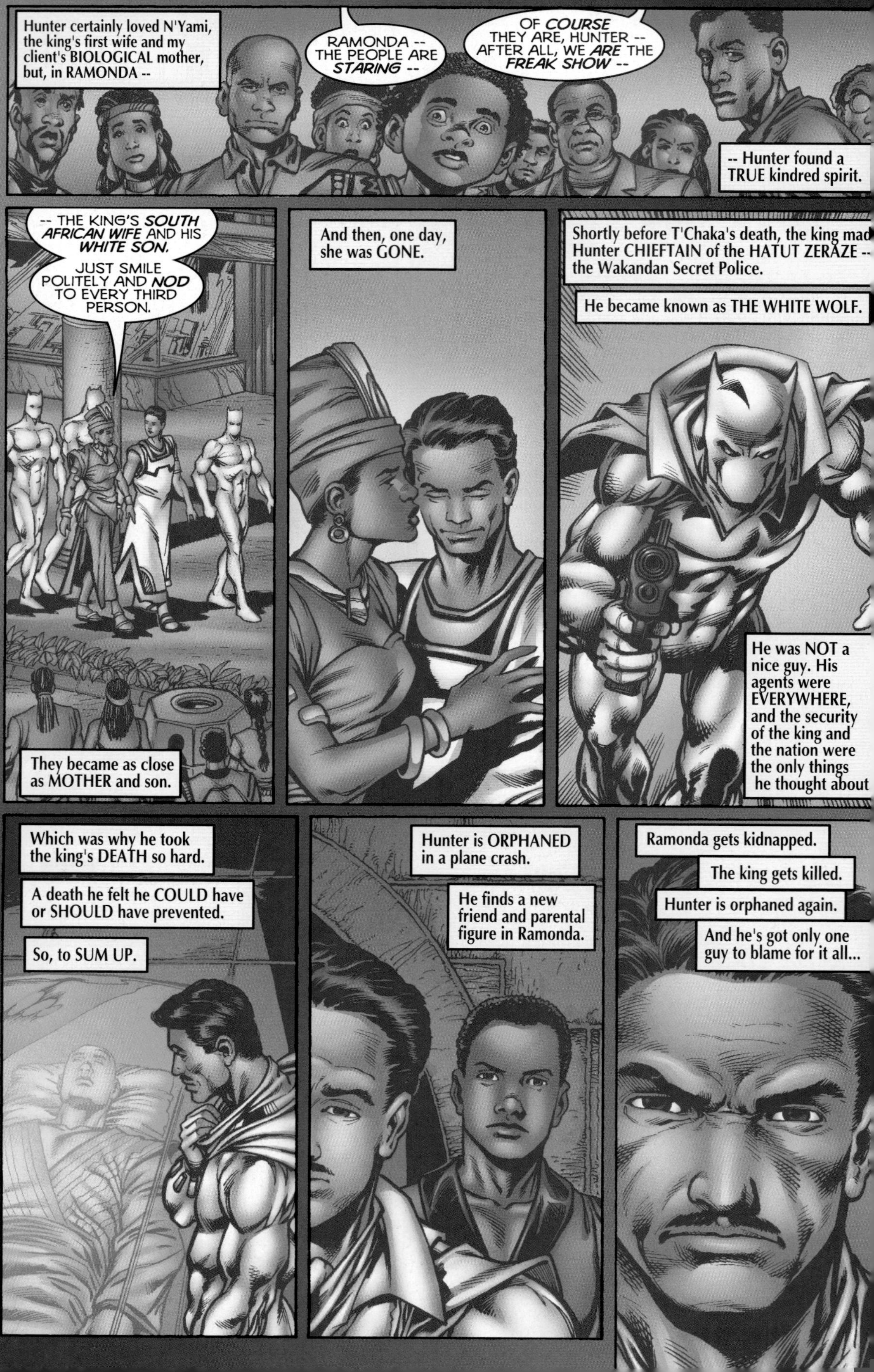
Hunter certainly loved N'Yami, the king's first wife and my client's BIOLOGICAL mother, but, in RAMONDA --
RAMONDA -- THE PEOPLE ARE STARING --
OF COURSE THEY ARE, HUNTER -- AFTER ALL, WE ARE THE FREAK SHOW --
-- Hunter found a TRUE kindred spirit.
-- THE KING'S SOUTH AFRICAN WIFE AND HIS WHITE SON.
JUST SMILE POLITELY AND NOD TO EVERY THIRD PERSON.
They became as close as MOTHER and son.
And then, one day, she was GONE.
Shortly before T'Chaka's death, the king mad Hunter CHIEFTAIN of the HATUT ZERAZE -- the Wakandan Secret Police.
He became known as THE WHITE WOLF.
He was NOT a nice guy. His agents were EVERYWHERE, and the security of the king and the nation were the only things he thought about
Which was why he took the king's DEATH so hard.
A death he felt he COULD have or SHOULD have prevented.
So, to SUM UP.
Hunter is ORPHANED in a plane crash.
He finds a new friend and parental figure in Ramonda.
Ramonda gets kidnapped.
The king gets killed.
Hunter is orphaned again.
And he's got only one guy to blame for it all...

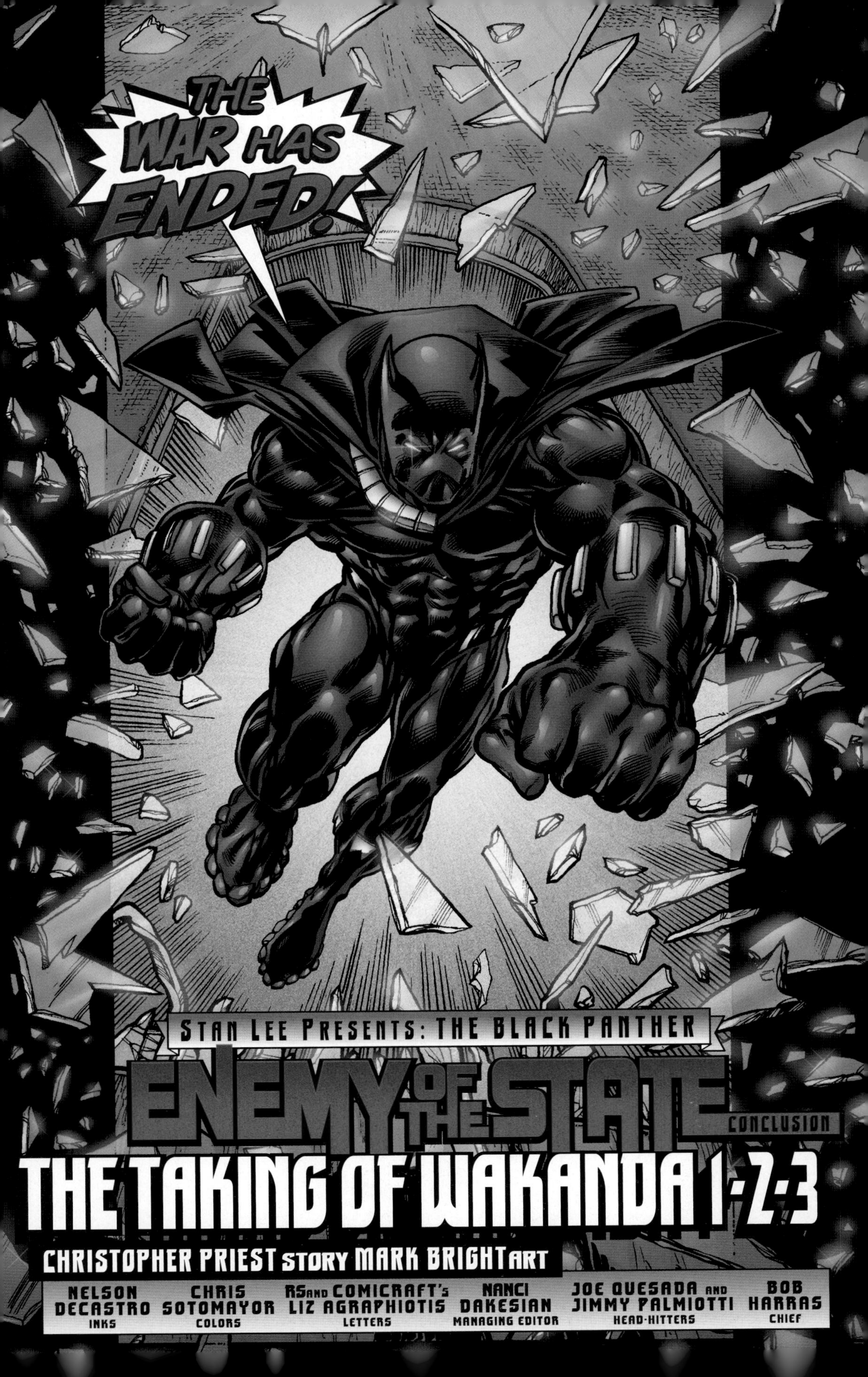
THE WAR HAS ENDED!
STAN LEE PRESENTS: THE BLACK PANTHER
ENEMY OF THE STATE CONCLUSION
THE TAKING OF WAKANDA 1-2-3
CHRISTOPHER PRIEST STORY MARK BRIGHT ART
NELSON DECASTRO INKS
CHRIS SOTOMAYOR COLORS
RS AND COMICRAFT'S LIZ AGRAPHIOTIS LETTERS
NANCI DAKESIAN MANAGING EDITOR
JOE QUESADA AND JIMMY PALMIOTTI HEAD-HITTERS
BOB HARRAS CHIEF

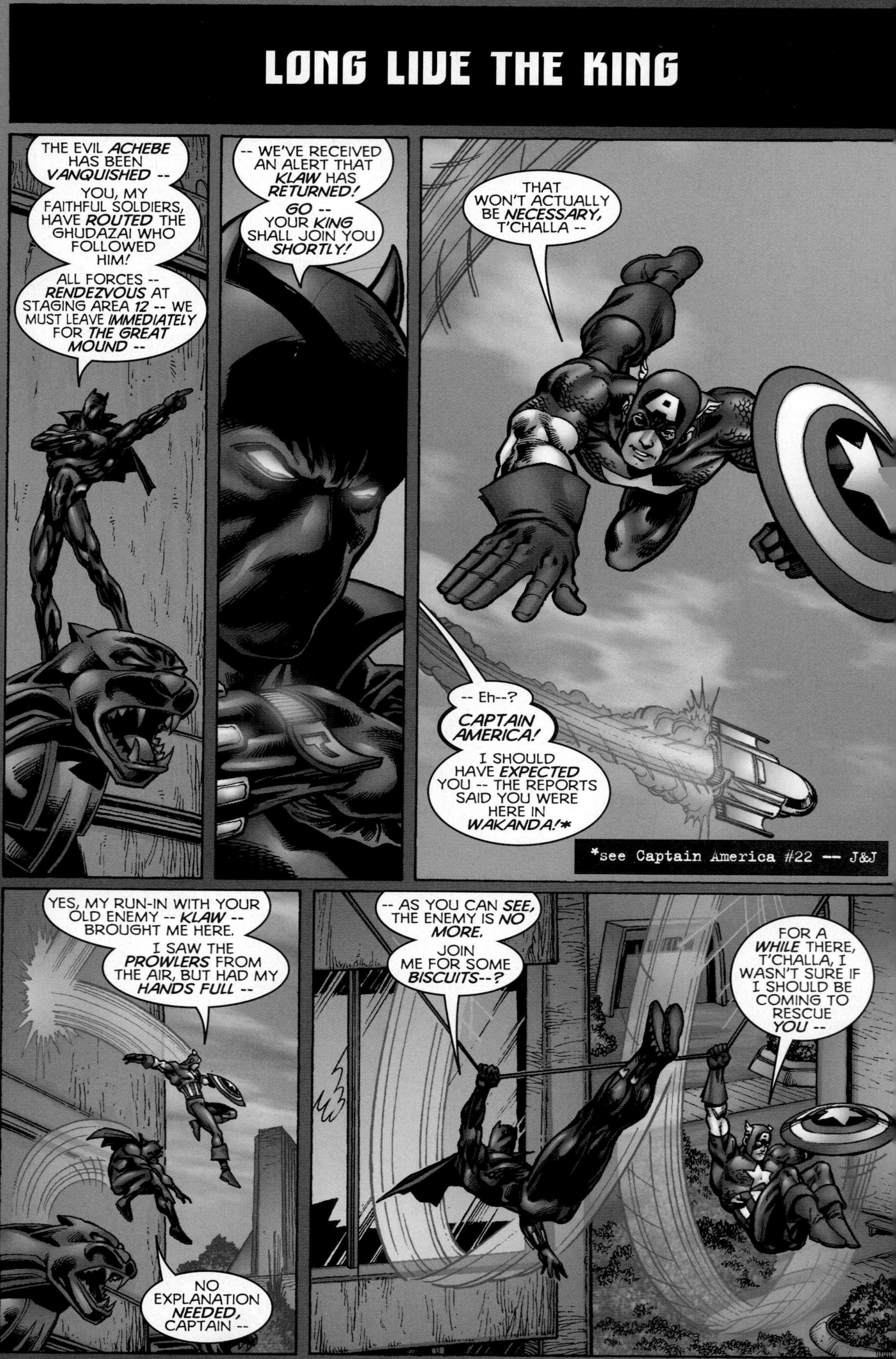
LONG LIVE THE KING
THE EVIL ACHEBE HAS BEEN VANQUISHED --
YOU, MY FAITHFUL SOLDIERS, HAVE ROUTED THE GHUDAZAI WHO FOLLOWED HIM!
ALL FORCES -- RENDEZVOUS AT STAGING AREA 12 -- WE MUST LEAVE IMMEDIATELY FOR THE GREAT MOUND --
-- WE'VE RECEIVED AN ALERT THAT KLAW HAS RETURNED!
GO -- YOUR KING SHALL JOIN YOU SHORTLY!
THAT WON'T ACTUALLY BE NECESSARY, T'CHALLA --
-- Eh--?
CAPTAIN AMERICA!
I SHOULD HAVE EXPECTED YOU -- THE REPORTS SAID YOU WERE HERE IN WAKANDA!*
*see Captain America #22 -- J&J
YES, MY RUN-IN WITH YOUR OLD ENEMY -- KLAW -- BROUGHT ME HERE.
I SAW THE PROWLERS FROM THE AIR, BUT HAD MY HANDS FULL --
NO EXPLANATION NEEDED, CAPTAIN --
-- AS YOU CAN SEE, THE ENEMY IS NO MORE.
JOIN ME FOR SOME BISCUITS--?
FOR A WHILE THERE, T'CHALLA, I WASN'T SURE IF I SHOULD BE COMING TO RESCUE YOU --

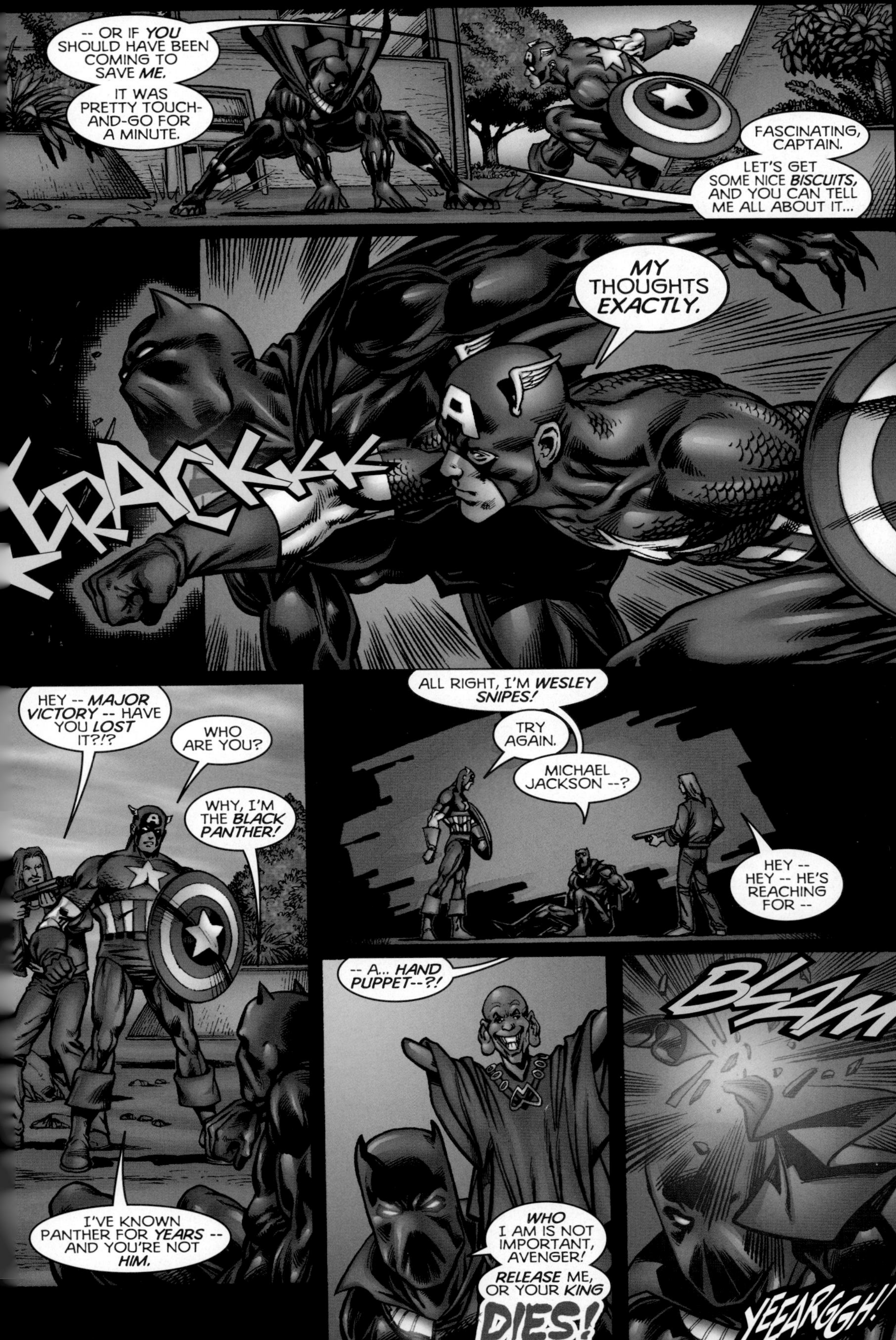
-- OR IF YOU SHOULD HAVE BEEN COMING TO SAVE ME.
IT WAS PRETTY TOUCH-AND-GO FOR A MINUTE.
FASCINATING, CAPTAIN.
LET'S GET SOME NICE BISCUITS, AND YOU CAN TELL ME ALL ABOUT IT...
MY THOUGHTS EXACTLY.
KRACKKK
HEY -- MAJOR VICTORY -- HAVE YOU LOST IT?!?
WHO ARE YOU?
WHY, I'M THE BLACK PANTHER!
I'VE KNOWN PANTHER FOR YEARS -- AND YOU'RE NOT HIM.
ALL RIGHT, I'M WESLEY SNIPES!
TRY AGAIN.
MICHAEL JACKSON --?
HEY -- HEY -- HE'S REACHING FOR --
-- A... HAND PUPPET--?!
WHO I AM IS NOT IMPORTANT, AVENGER!
RELEASE ME, OR YOUR KING DIES!
BLAM
YEEARGGH!

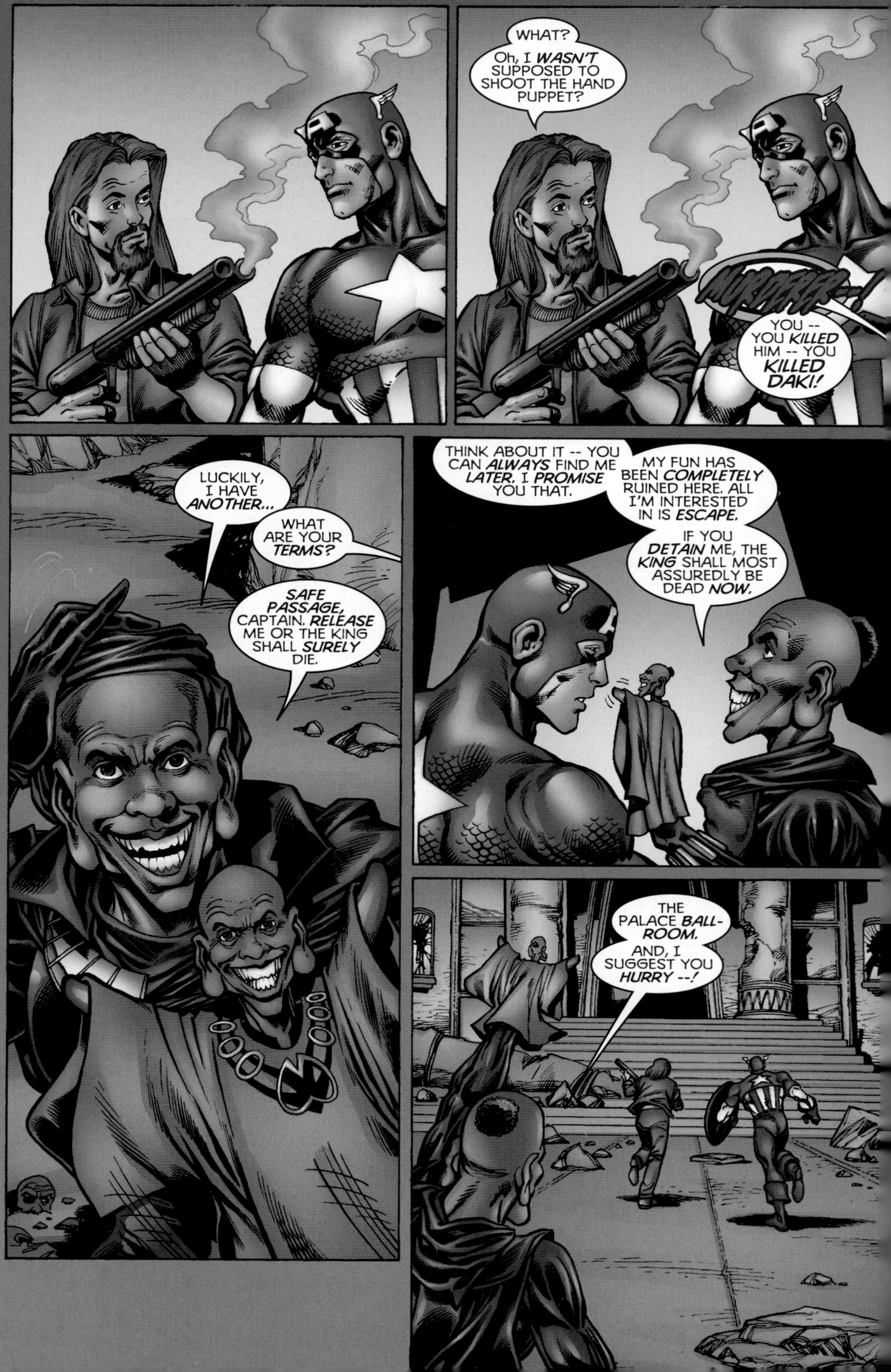
WHAT?
Oh, I *WASN'T* SUPPOSED TO SHOOT THE HAND PUPPET?
MURDERER--!
YOU -- YOU *KILLED* HIM -- YOU *KILLED DAKI!*
LUCKILY, I HAVE *ANOTHER*...
WHAT ARE YOUR *TERMS?*
SAFE PASSAGE, CAPTAIN. *RELEASE* ME OR THE KING SHALL *SURELY* DIE.
THINK ABOUT IT -- YOU CAN *ALWAYS* FIND ME *LATER.* I *PROMISE* YOU THAT.
MY FUN HAS BEEN *COMPLETELY* RUINED HERE. ALL I'M INTERESTED IN IS *ESCAPE.*
IF YOU *DETAIN* ME, THE *KING* SHALL MOST ASSUREDLY BE DEAD *NOW.*
THE PALACE *BALL-ROOM.*
AND, I SUGGEST YOU *HURRY --!*

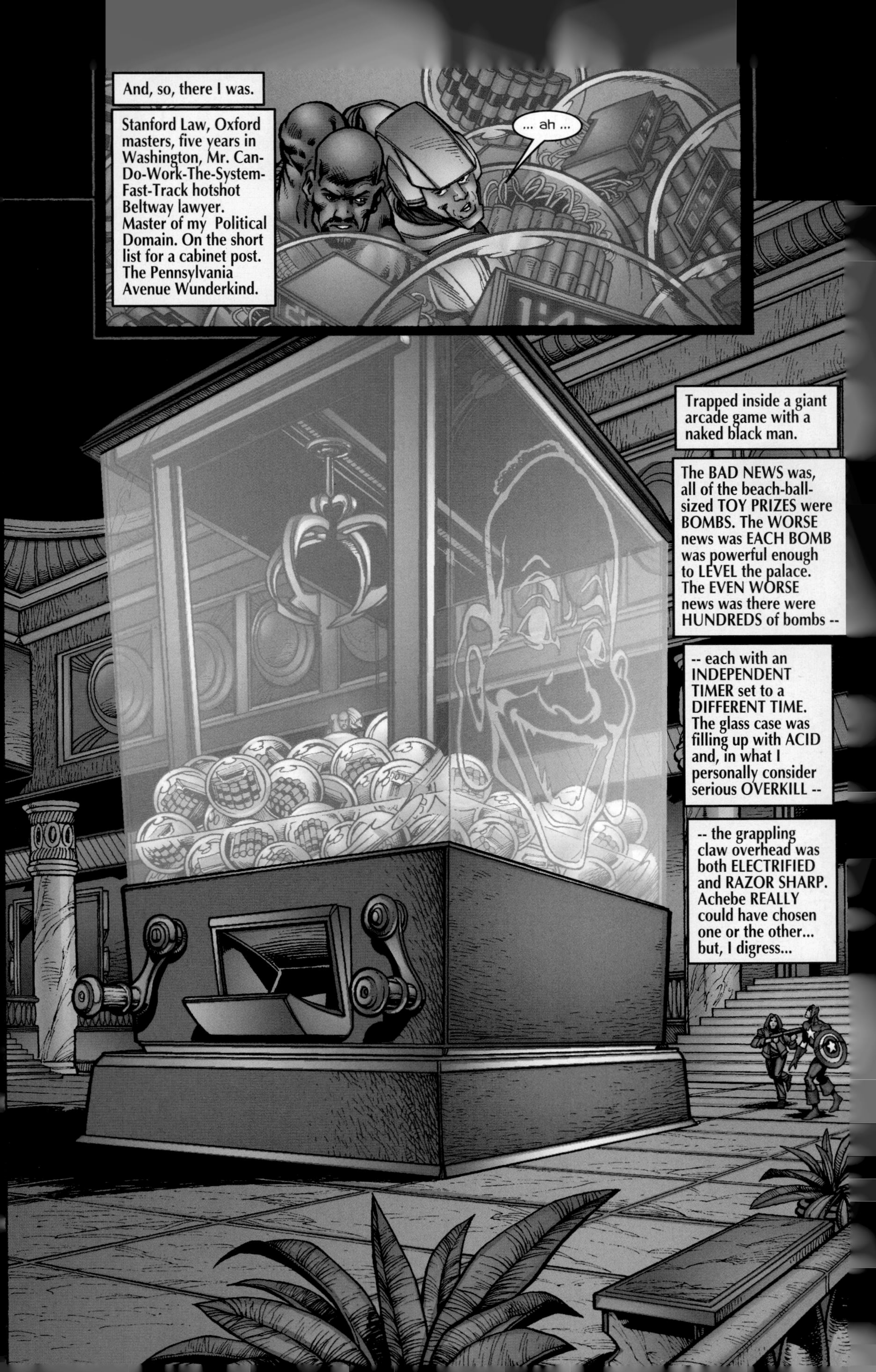

And, so, there I was.
Stanford Law, Oxford masters, five years in Washington, Mr. Can-Do-Work-The-System-Fast-Track hotshot Beltway lawyer. Master of my Political Domain. On the short list for a cabinet post. The Pennsylvania Avenue Wunderkind.
... ah ...
Trapped inside a giant arcade game with a naked black man.
The BAD NEWS was, all of the beach-ball-sized TOY PRIZES were BOMBS. The WORSE news was EACH BOMB was powerful enough to LEVEL the palace. The EVEN WORSE news was there were HUNDREDS of bombs --
-- each with an INDEPENDENT TIMER set to a DIFFERENT TIME. The glass case was filling up with ACID and, in what I personally consider serious OVERKILL --
-- the grappling claw overhead was both ELECTRIFIED and RAZOR SHARP. Achebe REALLY could have chosen one or the other... but, I digress...

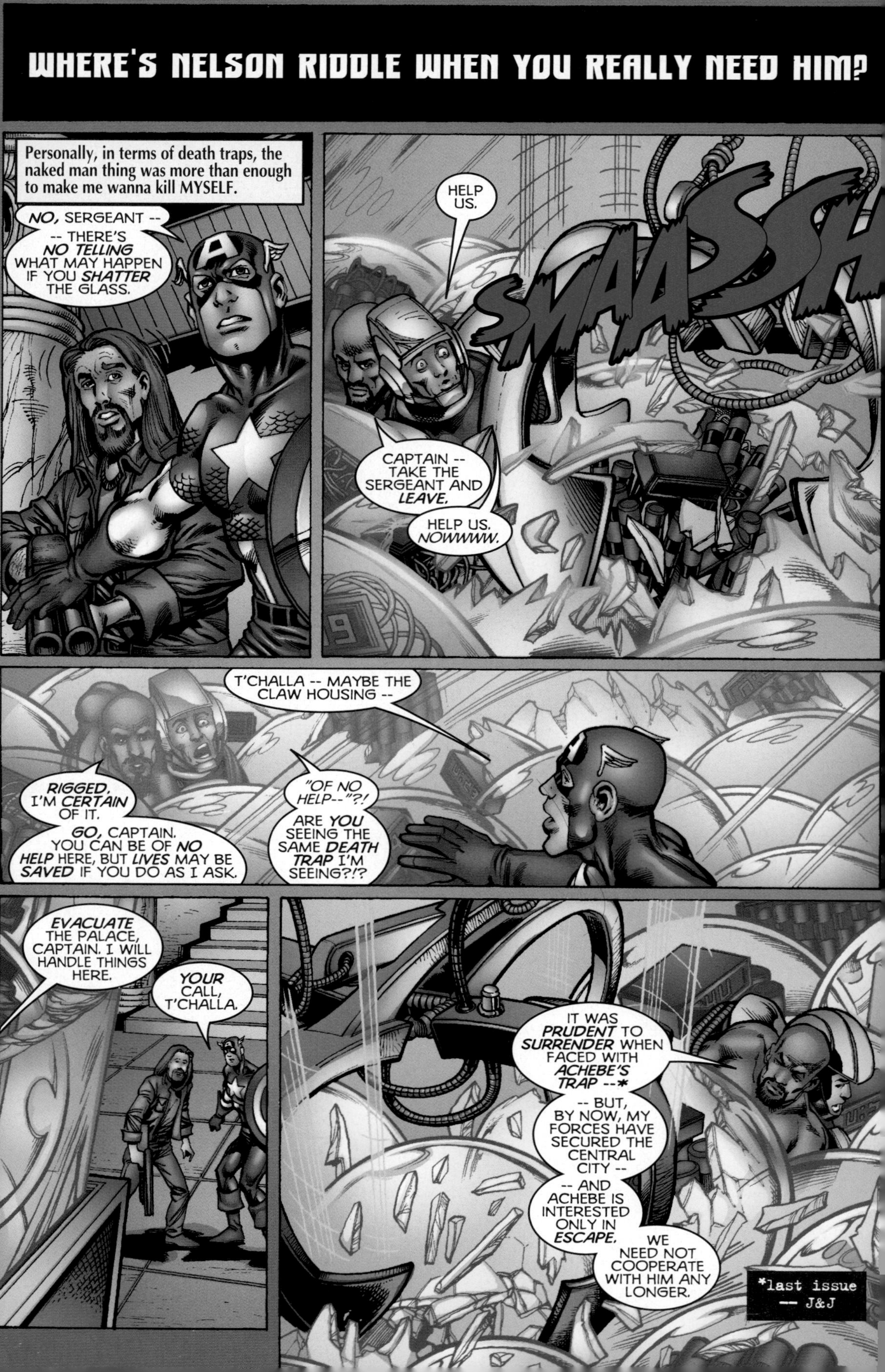
WHERE'S NELSON RIDDLE WHEN YOU REALLY NEED HIM?
Personally, in terms of death traps, the naked man thing was more than enough to make me wanna kill MYSELF.
NO, SERGEANT --
-- THERE'S NO TELLING WHAT MAY HAPPEN IF YOU SHATTER THE GLASS.
HELP US.
SMAASH
CAPTAIN -- TAKE THE SERGEANT AND LEAVE.
HELP US. NOWWWW.
T'CHALLA -- MAYBE THE CLAW HOUSING --
RIGGED, I'M CERTAIN OF IT.
GO, CAPTAIN. YOU CAN BE OF NO HELP HERE, BUT LIVES MAY BE SAVED IF YOU DO AS I ASK.
"OF NO HELP--"?!
ARE YOU SEEING THE SAME DEATH TRAP I'M SEEING?!?
EVACUATE THE PALACE, CAPTAIN. I WILL HANDLE THINGS HERE.
YOUR CALL, T'CHALLA.
IT WAS PRUDENT TO SURRENDER WHEN FACED WITH ACHEBE'S TRAP --*
-- BUT, BY NOW, MY FORCES HAVE SECURED THE CENTRAL CITY --
-- AND ACHEBE IS INTERESTED ONLY IN ESCAPE.
WE NEED NOT COOPERATE WITH HIM ANY LONGER.
*last issue -- J&J

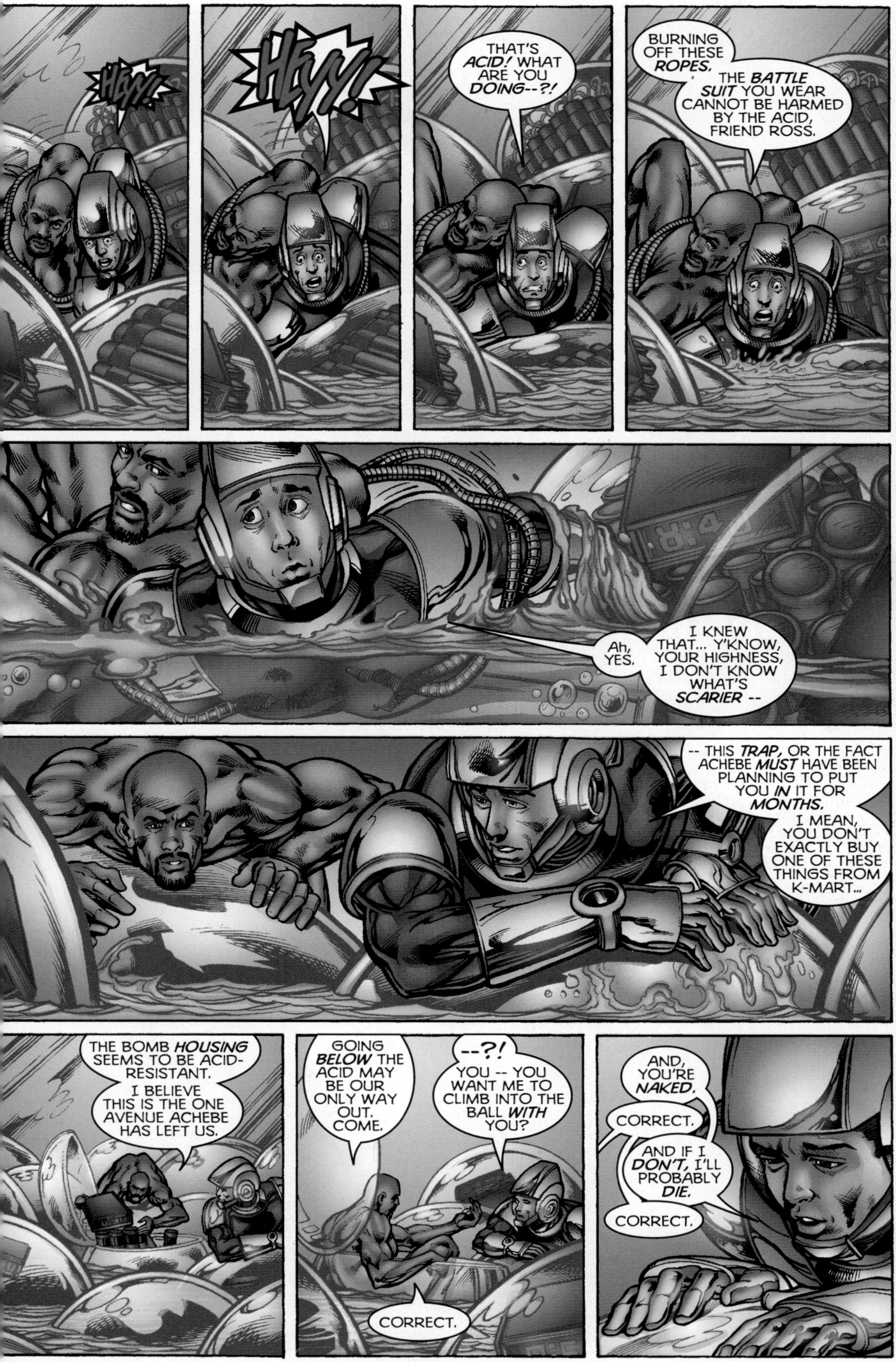
HEYY!
HEYYY!
THAT'S ACID! WHAT ARE YOU DOING--?!
BURNING OFF THESE ROPES.
THE BATTLE SUIT YOU WEAR CANNOT BE HARMED BY THE ACID, FRIEND ROSS.
Ah, YES.
I KNEW THAT... Y'KNOW, YOUR HIGHNESS, I DON'T KNOW WHAT'S SCARIER --
-- THIS TRAP, OR THE FACT ACHEBE MUST HAVE BEEN PLANNING TO PUT YOU IN IT FOR MONTHS.
I MEAN, YOU DON'T EXACTLY BUY ONE OF THESE THINGS FROM K-MART...
THE BOMB HOUSING SEEMS TO BE ACID-RESISTANT.
I BELIEVE THIS IS THE ONE AVENUE ACHEBE HAS LEFT US.
GOING BELOW THE ACID MAY BE OUR ONLY WAY OUT. COME.
--?!
YOU -- YOU WANT ME TO CLIMB INTO THE BALL WITH YOU?
CORRECT.
AND, YOU'RE NAKED.
CORRECT.
AND IF I DON'T, I'LL PROBABLY DIE.
CORRECT.

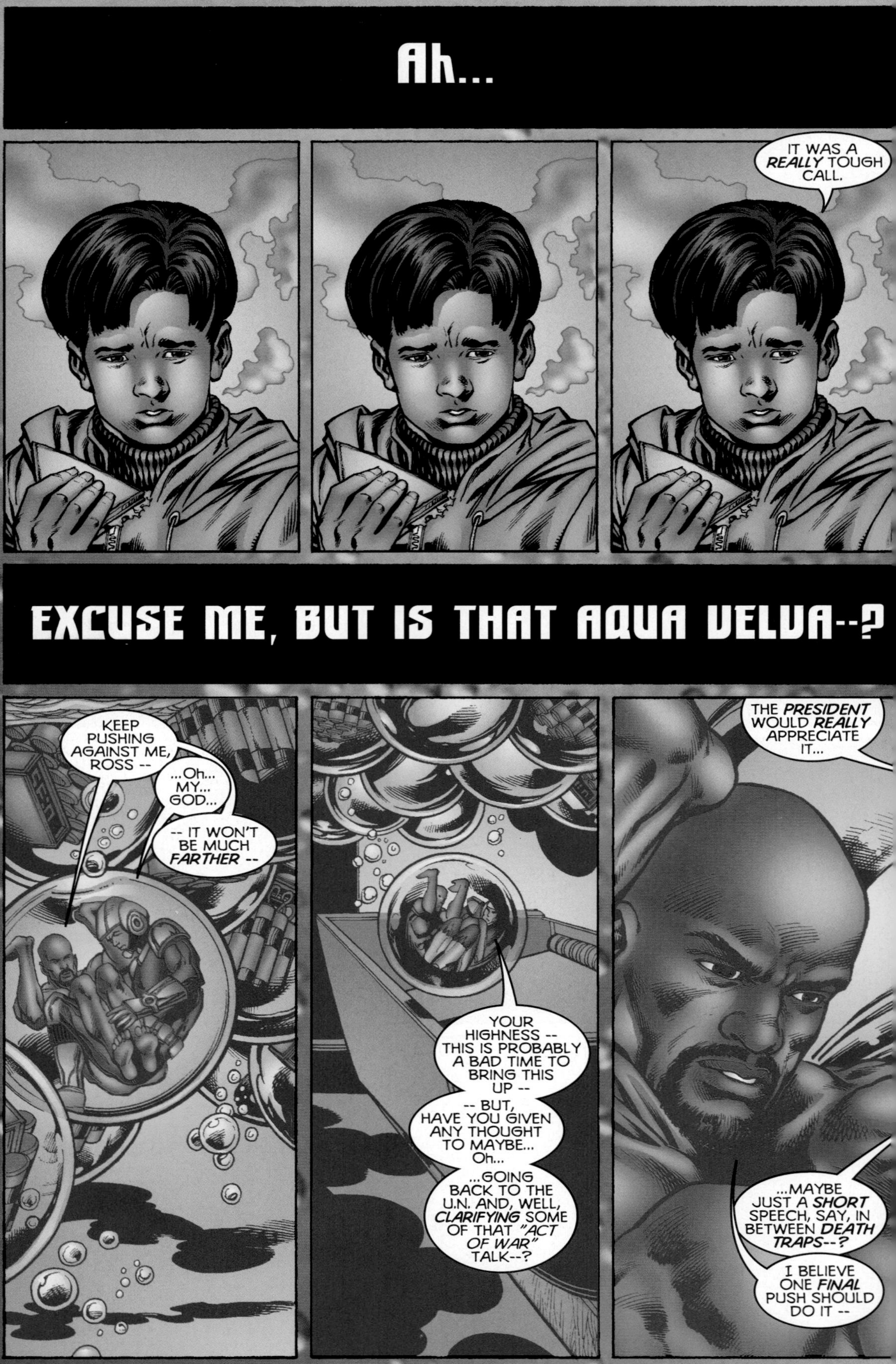
Ah...
IT WAS A REALLY TOUGH CALL.
EXCUSE ME, BUT IS THAT AQUA VELVA--?
KEEP PUSHING AGAINST ME, ROSS --
...Oh... MY... GOD...
-- IT WON'T BE MUCH FARTHER --
YOUR HIGHNESS -- THIS IS PROBABLY A BAD TIME TO BRING THIS UP --
-- BUT, HAVE YOU GIVEN ANY THOUGHT TO MAYBE... Oh...
...GOING BACK TO THE U.N. AND, WELL, CLARIFYING SOME OF THAT "ACT OF WAR" TALK--?
THE PRESIDENT WOULD REALLY APPRECIATE IT...
...MAYBE JUST A SHORT SPEECH, SAY, IN BETWEEN DEATH TRAPS--?
I BELIEVE ONE FINAL PUSH SHOULD DO IT --

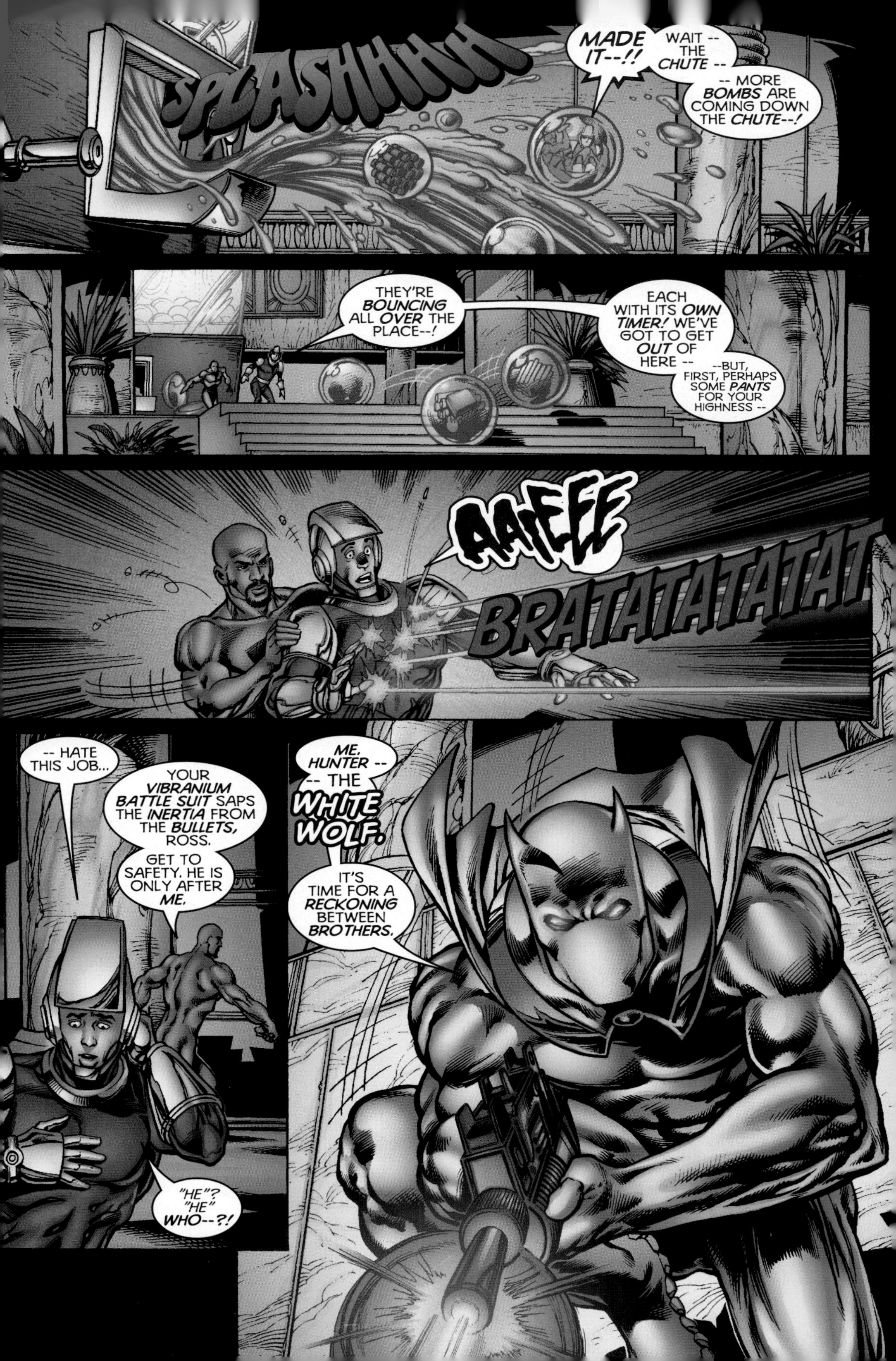
SPLASHHHH
MADE IT--!!
WAIT -- THE CHUTE --
-- MORE BOMBS ARE COMING DOWN THE CHUTE--!
THEY'RE BOUNCING ALL OVER THE PLACE--!
EACH WITH ITS OWN TIMER! WE'VE GOT TO GET OUT OF HERE --
--BUT, FIRST, PERHAPS SOME PANTS FOR YOUR HIGHNESS --
AAIEEE
BRATATATATAT
-- HATE THIS JOB...
YOUR VIBRANIUM BATTLE SUIT SAPS THE INERTIA FROM THE BULLETS, ROSS.
GET TO SAFETY. HE IS ONLY AFTER ME.
"HE"? "HE" WHO--?!
ME. HUNTER --
-- THE WHITE WOLF.
IT'S TIME FOR A RECKONING BETWEEN BROTHERS.

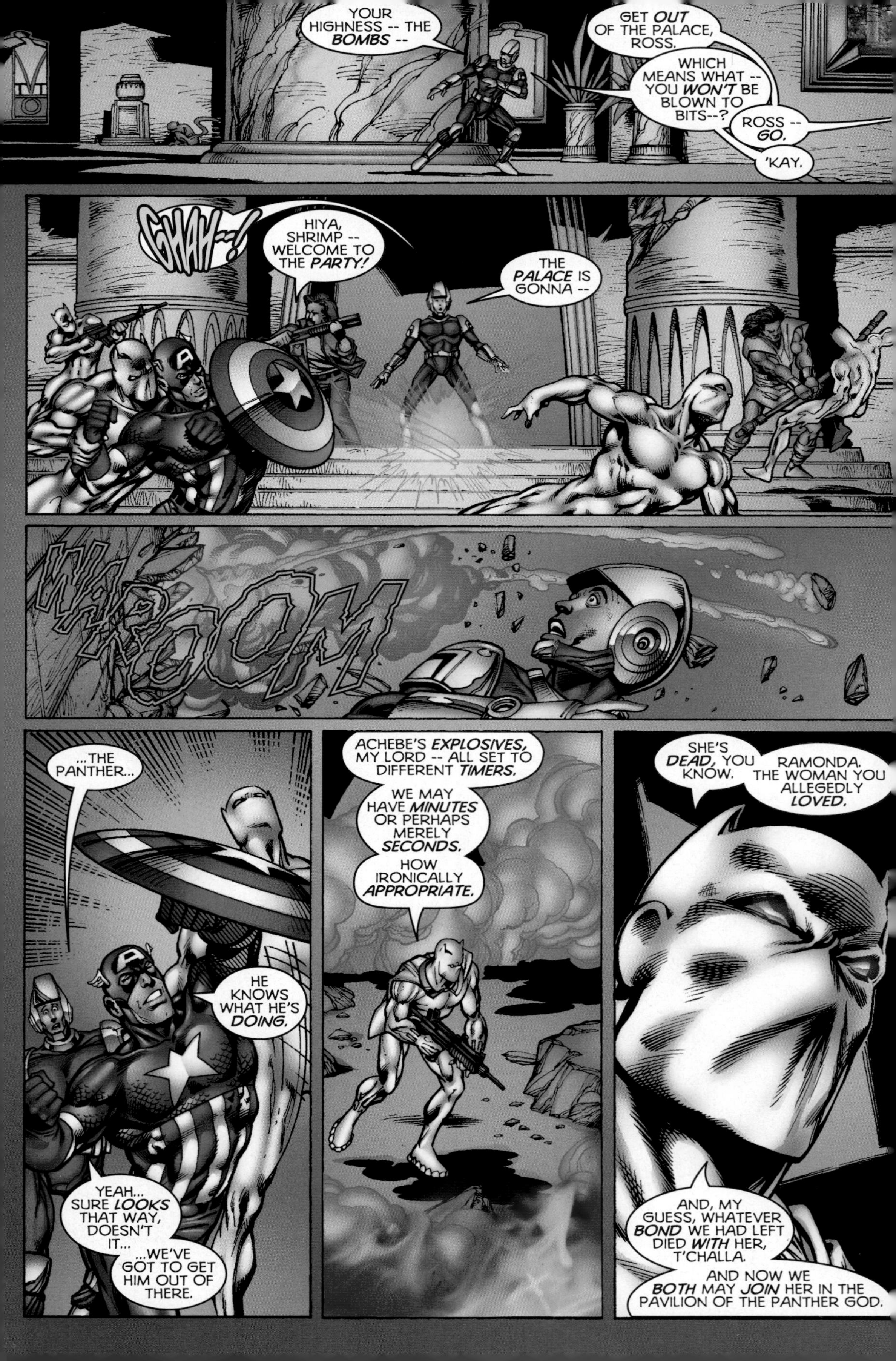
YOUR HIGHNESS -- THE BOMBS --
GET OUT OF THE PALACE, ROSS.
WHICH MEANS WHAT -- YOU WON'T BE BLOWN TO BITS--?
ROSS -- GO.
'KAY.
GWAH--!
HIYA, SHRIMP -- WELCOME TO THE PARTY!
THE PALACE IS GONNA --
WHABOOM
...THE PANTHER...
HE KNOWS WHAT HE'S DOING.
YEAH... SURE LOOKS THAT WAY, DOESN'T IT...
...WE'VE GOT TO GET HIM OUT OF THERE.
ACHEBE'S EXPLOSIVES, MY LORD -- ALL SET TO DIFFERENT TIMERS.
WE MAY HAVE MINUTES OR PERHAPS MERELY SECONDS.
HOW IRONICALLY APPROPRIATE.
SHE'S DEAD, YOU KNOW.
RAMONDA. THE WOMAN YOU ALLEGEDLY LOVED.
AND, MY GUESS, WHATEVER BOND WE HAD LEFT DIED WITH HER, T'CHALLA.
AND NOW WE BOTH MAY JOIN HER IN THE PAVILION OF THE PANTHER GOD.

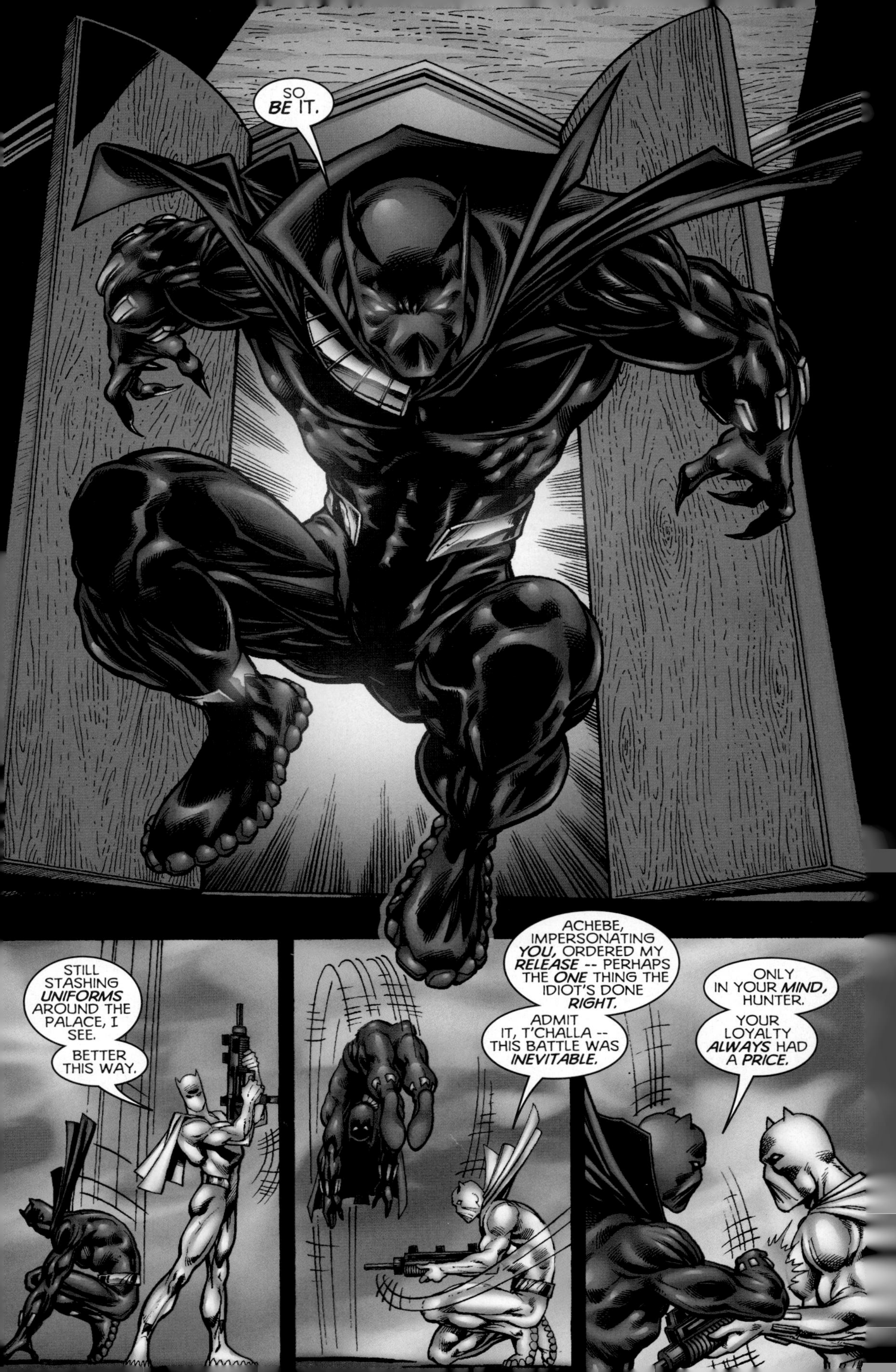
SO BE IT.
STILL STASHING UNIFORMS AROUND THE PALACE, I SEE.
BETTER THIS WAY.
ACHEBE, IMPERSONATING YOU, ORDERED MY RELEASE -- PERHAPS THE ONE THING THE IDIOT'S DONE RIGHT.
ADMIT IT, T'CHALLA -- THIS BATTLE WAS INEVITABLE.
ONLY IN YOUR MIND, HUNTER.
YOUR LOYALTY ALWAYS HAD A PRICE.

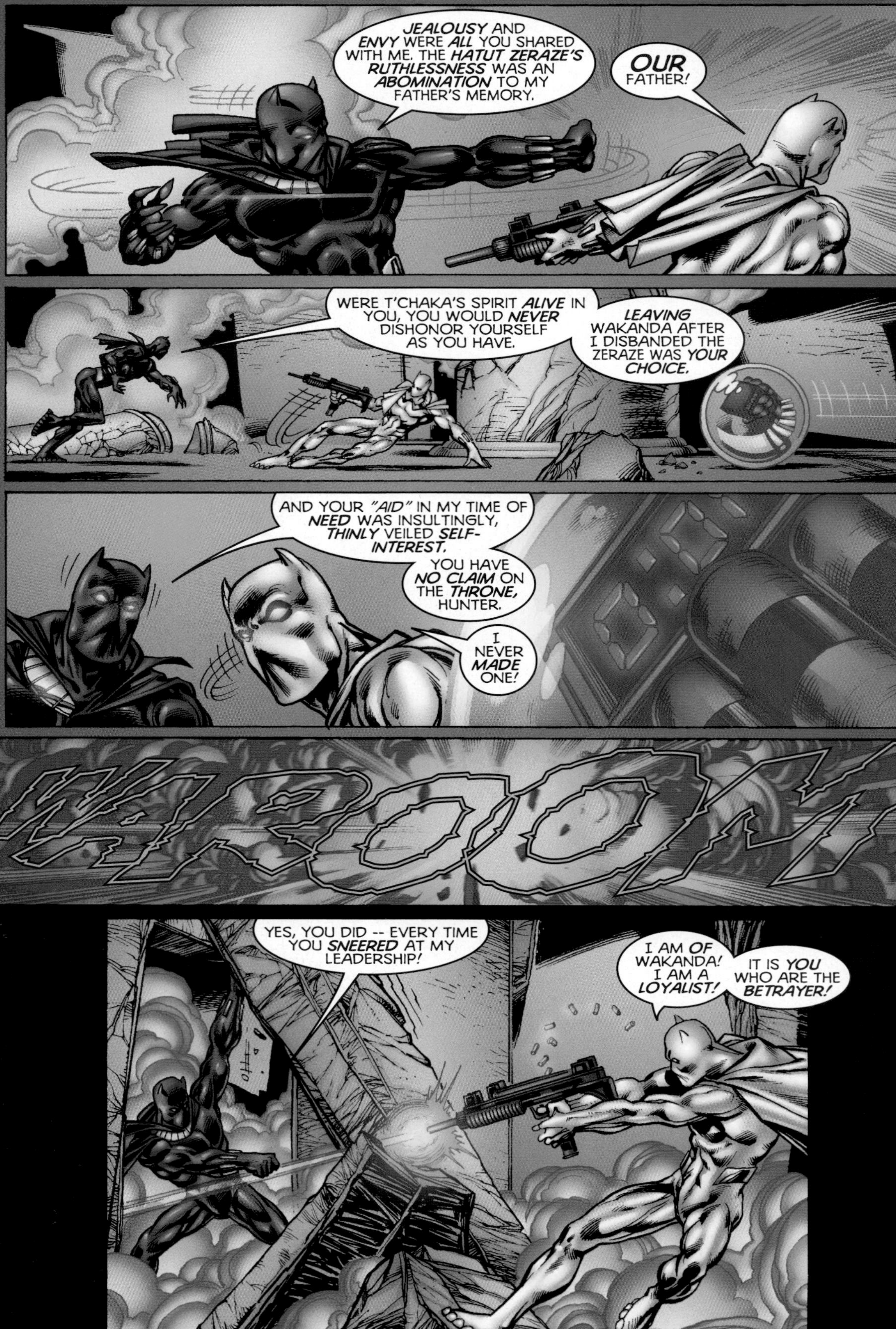

JEALOUSY AND ENVY WERE ALL YOU SHARED WITH ME. THE HATUT ZERAZE'S RUTHLESSNESS WAS AN ABOMINATION TO MY FATHER'S MEMORY.
OUR FATHER!
WERE T'CHAKA'S SPIRIT ALIVE IN YOU, YOU WOULD NEVER DISHONOR YOURSELF AS YOU HAVE.
LEAVING WAKANDA AFTER I DISBANDED THE ZERAZE WAS YOUR CHOICE.
AND YOUR "AID" IN MY TIME OF NEED WAS INSULTINGLY, THINLY VEILED SELF-INTEREST.
YOU HAVE NO CLAIM ON THE THRONE, HUNTER.
I NEVER MADE ONE!
WHROOM
YES, YOU DID -- EVERY TIME YOU SNEERED AT MY LEADERSHIP!
I AM OF WAKANDA! I AM A LOYALIST!
IT IS YOU WHO ARE THE BETRAYER!

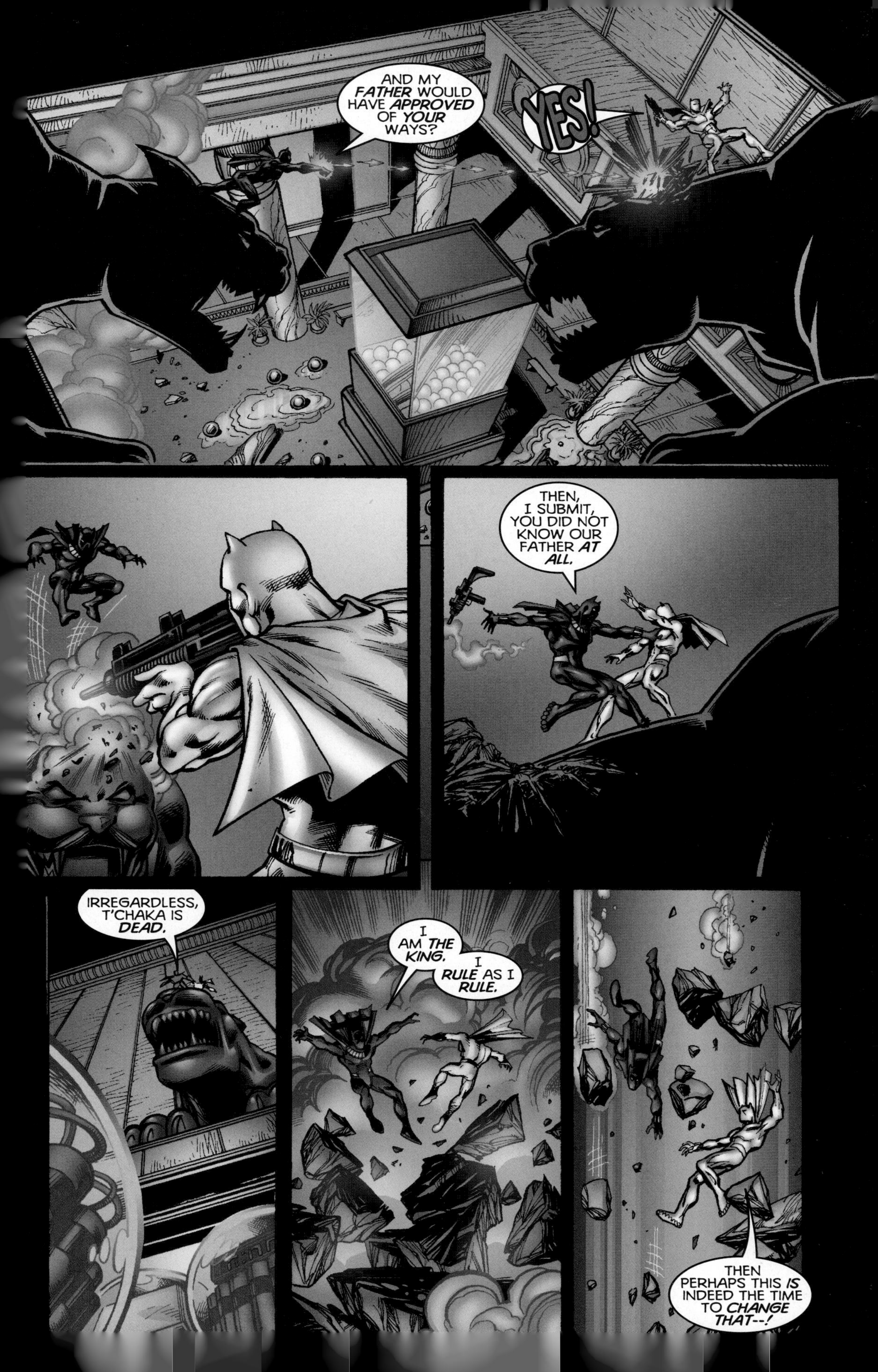
AND MY FATHER WOULD HAVE APPROVED OF YOUR WAYS?
YES!
THEN, I SUBMIT, YOU DID NOT KNOW OUR FATHER AT ALL.
IRREGARDLESS, T'CHAKA IS DEAD.
I AM THE KING.
I RULE AS I RULE.
THEN PERHAPS THIS IS INDEED THE TIME TO CHANGE THAT--!

Outside, the White Wolf's boys were making things fairly interesting.

...NOT THE HAIR... NOT THE HAIR...

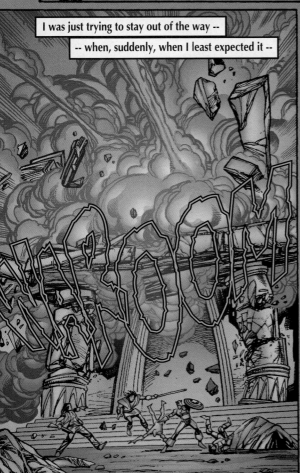

I was just trying to stay out of the way --

-- when, suddenly, when I least expected it --

SHKABOOM

-- I became a MAN.

ROSS -- NO -- IT'S *TOO DANGEROUS*--!

Don't ask me to EXPLAIN it, Nikki. It's just -- well -- I just couldn't LEAVE him in there.

WON'T... BE LONG *NOW*, MY LORD...

ACHEBE'S DEVILISH *HANDIWORK* HAS ALL BUT *LEVELED* YOUR GREAT HOME...

...TIME ... TO END THINGS BETWEEN US...

SO, HUNTER -- *THIS* -- THIS *TREACHERY* -- IS THE ACT OF A *LOYALIST* --?!

I AM *LOYAL* TO THE *THRONE*, T'CHALLA!

THIS IS A DISPUTE BETWEEN *BROTHERS!!*

COMMAND ME AS MY *KING* --

-- AND, OF COURSE, I WILL OBEY YOU.

THAT'S ALL IT WILL *TAKE*, T'CHALLA --

-- COMMAND ME.

COMMAND ME. I DEMAND IT!

YOU STUBBORN FOOL -- DON'T MAKE ME *KILL YOU* JUST TO *SPITE ME!*

I AM OF WAKANDA! BE *MY KING!*

I... SHALL *NEVER* BE KING... ... OF *YOUR* WAKANDA.

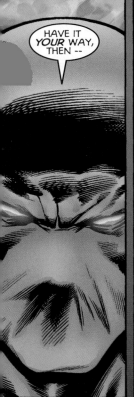

HAVE IT *YOUR* WAY, THEN --

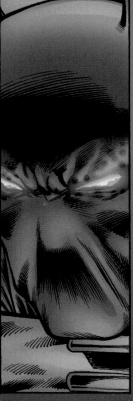

NNOOO!

LET HIM GO--! LET HIM GO, YOU *JERK*--!

THAT'S IT. YOU *DIE* --

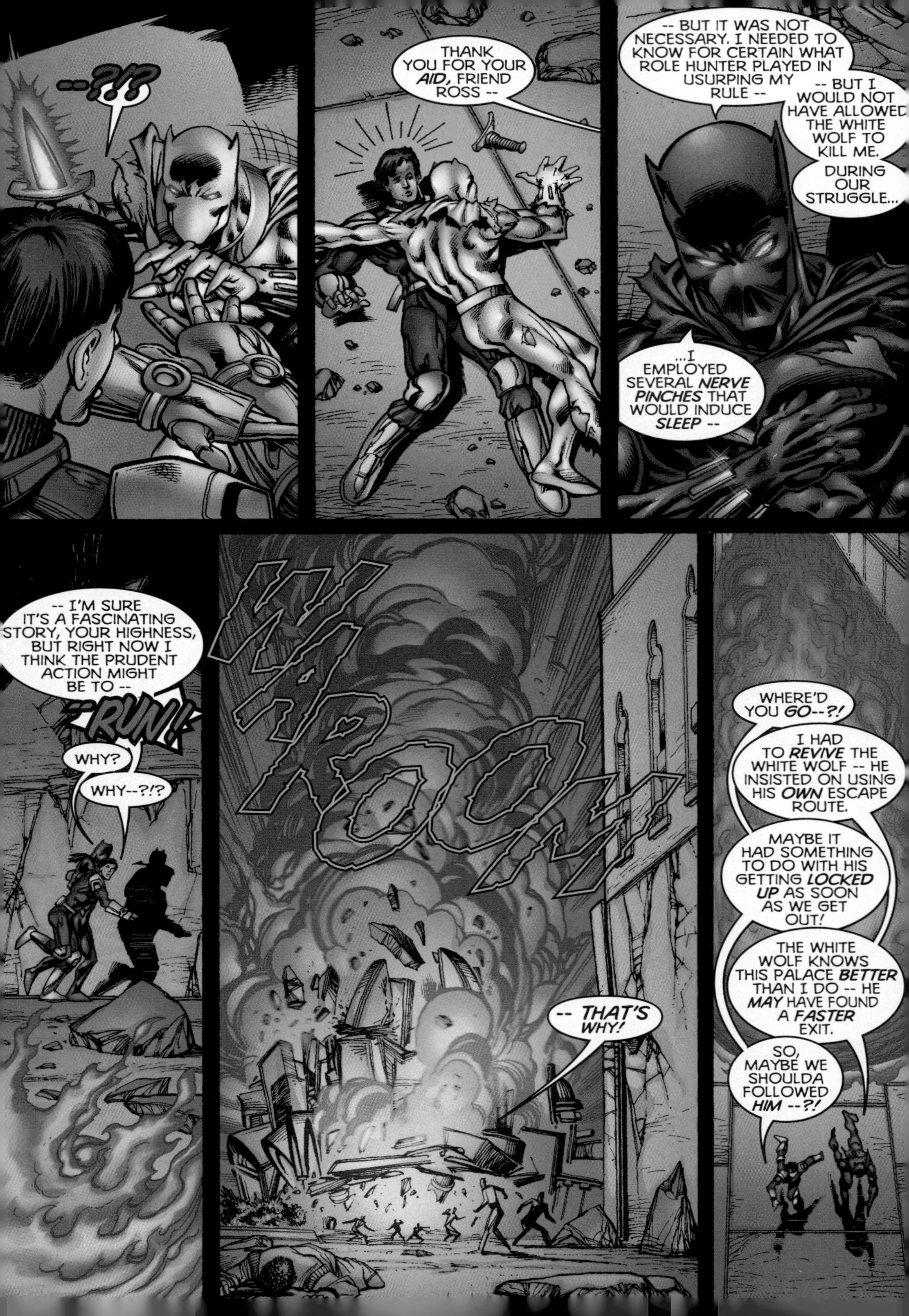
--?!?
THANK YOU FOR YOUR AID, FRIEND ROSS --
-- BUT IT WAS NOT NECESSARY. I NEEDED TO KNOW FOR CERTAIN WHAT ROLE HUNTER PLAYED IN USURPING MY RULE --
-- BUT I WOULD NOT HAVE ALLOWED THE WHITE WOLF TO KILL ME.
DURING OUR STRUGGLE...
...I EMPLOYED SEVERAL NERVE PINCHES THAT WOULD INDUCE SLEEP --
-- I'M SURE IT'S A FASCINATING STORY, YOUR HIGHNESS, BUT RIGHT NOW I THINK THE PRUDENT ACTION MIGHT BE TO --
--RUN!
WHY?
WHY--?!?
WHOOOM
-- THAT'S WHY!
WHERE'D YOU GO--?!
I HAD TO REVIVE THE WHITE WOLF -- HE INSISTED ON USING HIS OWN ESCAPE ROUTE.
MAYBE IT HAD SOMETHING TO DO WITH HIS GETTING LOCKED UP AS SOON AS WE GET OUT!
THE WHITE WOLF KNOWS THIS PALACE BETTER THAN I DO -- HE MAY HAVE FOUND A FASTER EXIT.
SO, MAYBE WE SHOULDA FOLLOWED HIM --?!

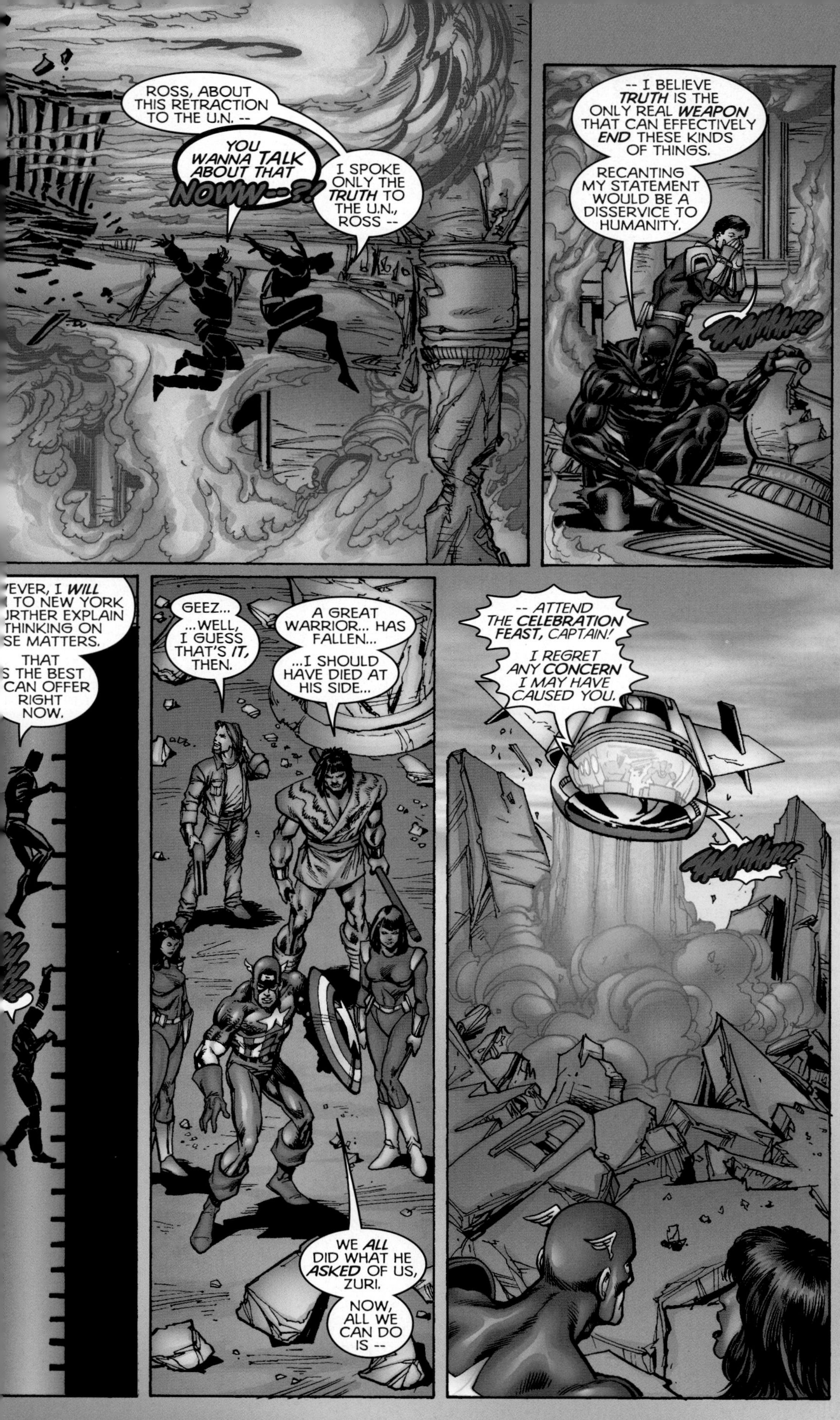
ROSS, ABOUT THIS RETRACTION TO THE U.N. --
YOU WANNA TALK ABOUT THAT NOWW--?!
I SPOKE ONLY THE TRUTH TO THE U.N., ROSS --
-- I BELIEVE TRUTH IS THE ONLY REAL WEAPON THAT CAN EFFECTIVELY END THESE KINDS OF THINGS.
RECANTING MY STATEMENT WOULD BE A DISSERVICE TO HUMANITY.
VEVER, I WILL
TO NEW YORK
URTHER EXPLAIN
THINKING ON
SE MATTERS.
THAT
S THE BEST
CAN OFFER
RIGHT
NOW.
GEEZ... ...WELL, I GUESS THAT'S IT, THEN.
A GREAT WARRIOR... HAS FALLEN...
...I SHOULD HAVE DIED AT HIS SIDE...
WE ALL DID WHAT HE ASKED OF US, ZURI.
NOW, ALL WE CAN DO IS --
-- ATTEND THE CELEBRATION FEAST, CAPTAIN!
I REGRET ANY CONCERN I MAY HAVE CAUSED YOU.

AWAKENINGS

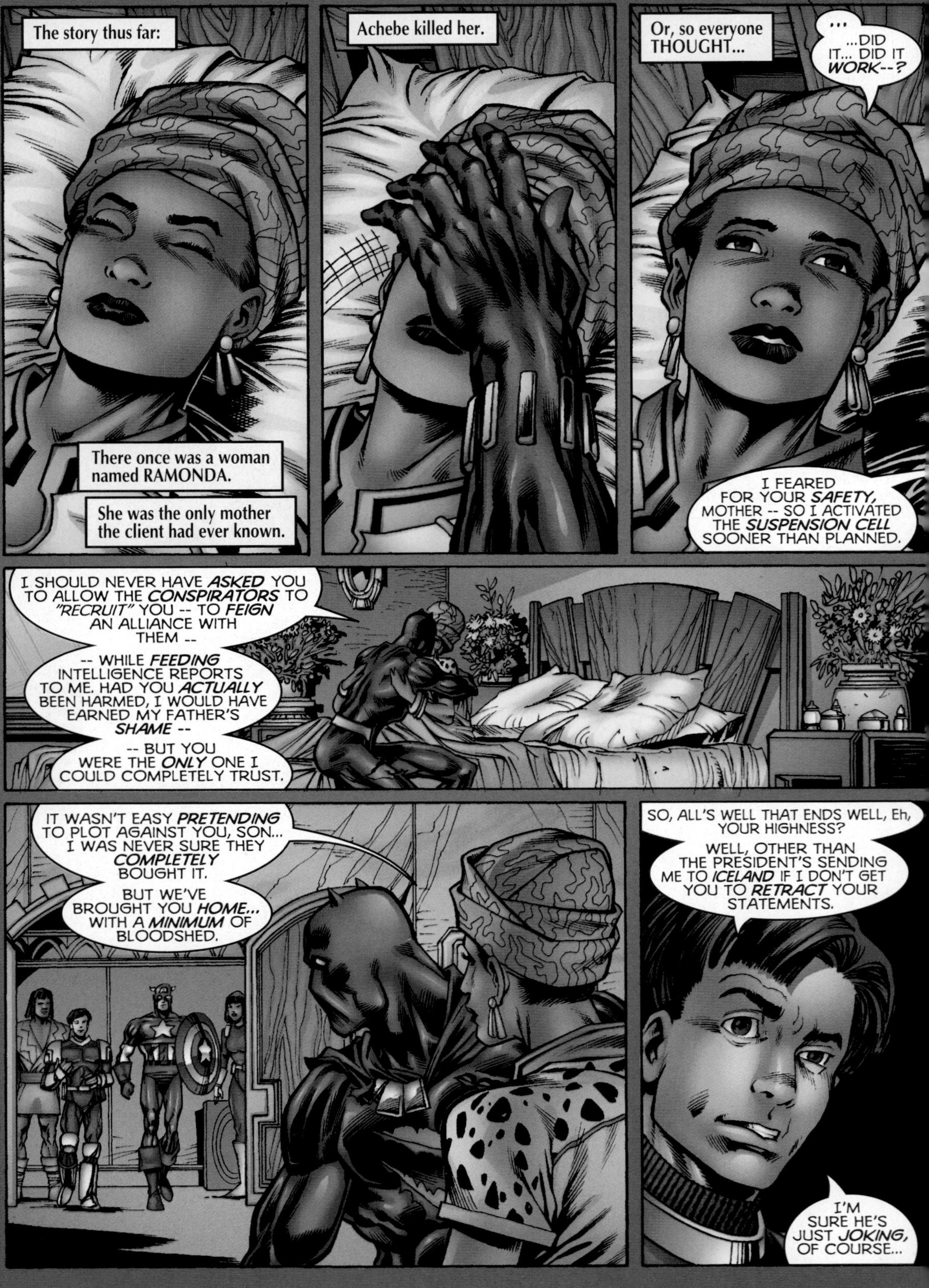
The story thus far:
There once was a woman named RAMONDA.
She was the only mother the client had ever known.
Achebe killed her.
Or, so everyone THOUGHT...
...
...DID IT... DID IT WORK--?
I FEARED FOR YOUR SAFETY, MOTHER -- SO I ACTIVATED THE SUSPENSION CELL SOONER THAN PLANNED.
I SHOULD NEVER HAVE ASKED YOU TO ALLOW THE CONSPIRATORS TO "RECRUIT" YOU -- TO FEIGN AN ALLIANCE WITH THEM --
-- WHILE FEEDING INTELLIGENCE REPORTS TO ME. HAD YOU ACTUALLY BEEN HARMED, I WOULD HAVE EARNED MY FATHER'S SHAME --
-- BUT YOU WERE THE ONLY ONE I COULD COMPLETELY TRUST.
IT WASN'T EASY PRETENDING TO PLOT AGAINST YOU, SON... I WAS NEVER SURE THEY COMPLETELY BOUGHT IT.
BUT WE'VE BROUGHT YOU HOME... WITH A MINIMUM OF BLOODSHED.
SO, ALL'S WELL THAT ENDS WELL, Eh, YOUR HIGHNESS?
WELL, OTHER THAN THE PRESIDENT'S SENDING ME TO ICELAND IF I DON'T GET YOU TO RETRACT YOUR STATEMENTS.
I'M SURE HE'S JUST JOKING, OF COURSE...

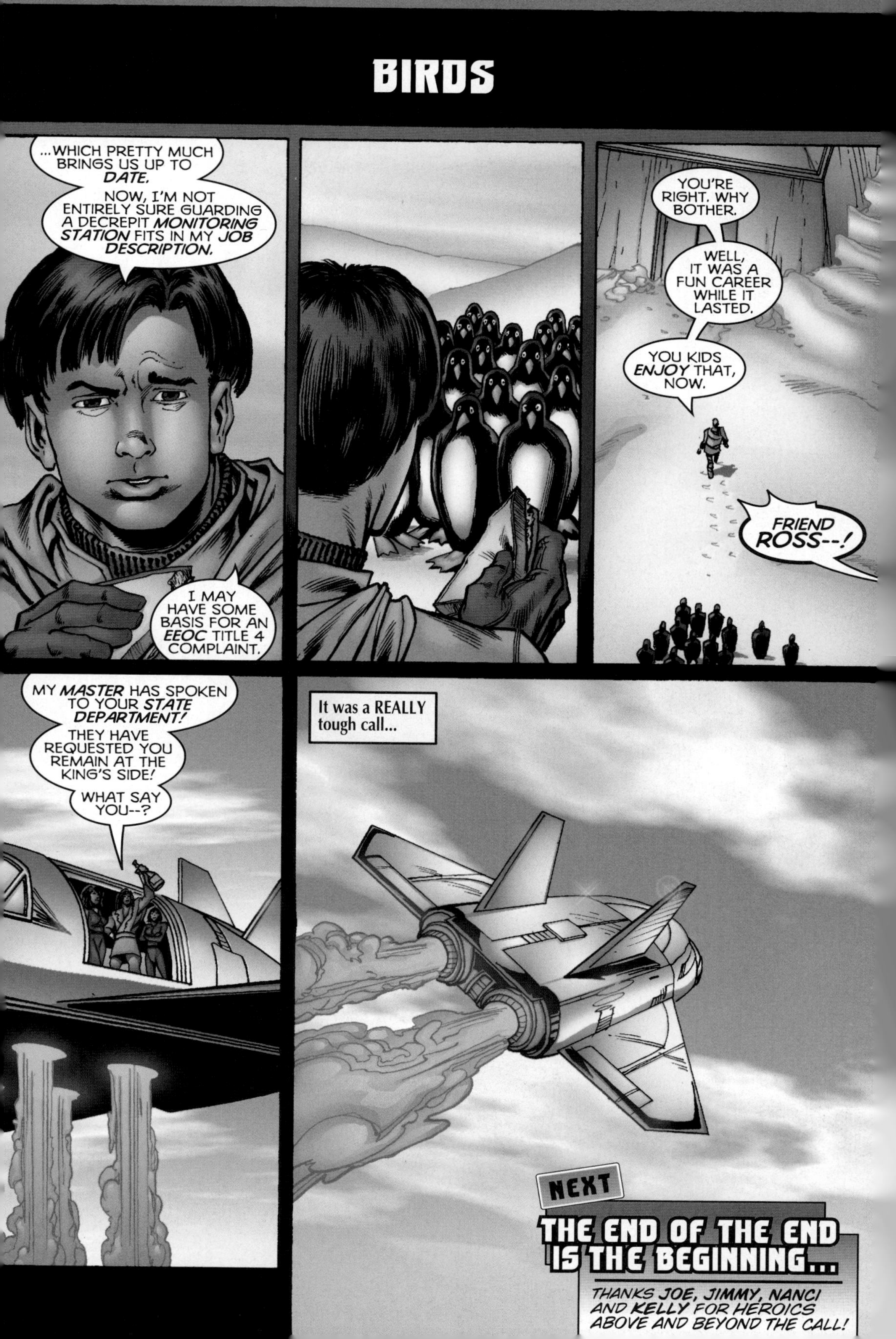
BIRDS
...WHICH PRETTY MUCH BRINGS US UP TO DATE.
NOW, I'M NOT ENTIRELY SURE GUARDING A DECREPIT MONITORING STATION FITS IN MY JOB DESCRIPTION.
I MAY HAVE SOME BASIS FOR AN EEOC TITLE 4 COMPLAINT.
YOU'RE RIGHT. WHY BOTHER.
WELL, IT WAS A FUN CAREER WHILE IT LASTED.
YOU KIDS ENJOY THAT, NOW.
FRIEND ROSS--!
MY MASTER HAS SPOKEN TO YOUR STATE DEPARTMENT!
THEY HAVE REQUESTED YOU REMAIN AT THE KING'S SIDE!
WHAT SAY YOU--?
It was a REALLY tough call...
NEXT
THE END OF THE END IS THE BEGINNING...
THANKS JOE, JIMMY, NANCI AND KELLY FOR HEROICS ABOVE AND BEYOND THE CALL!

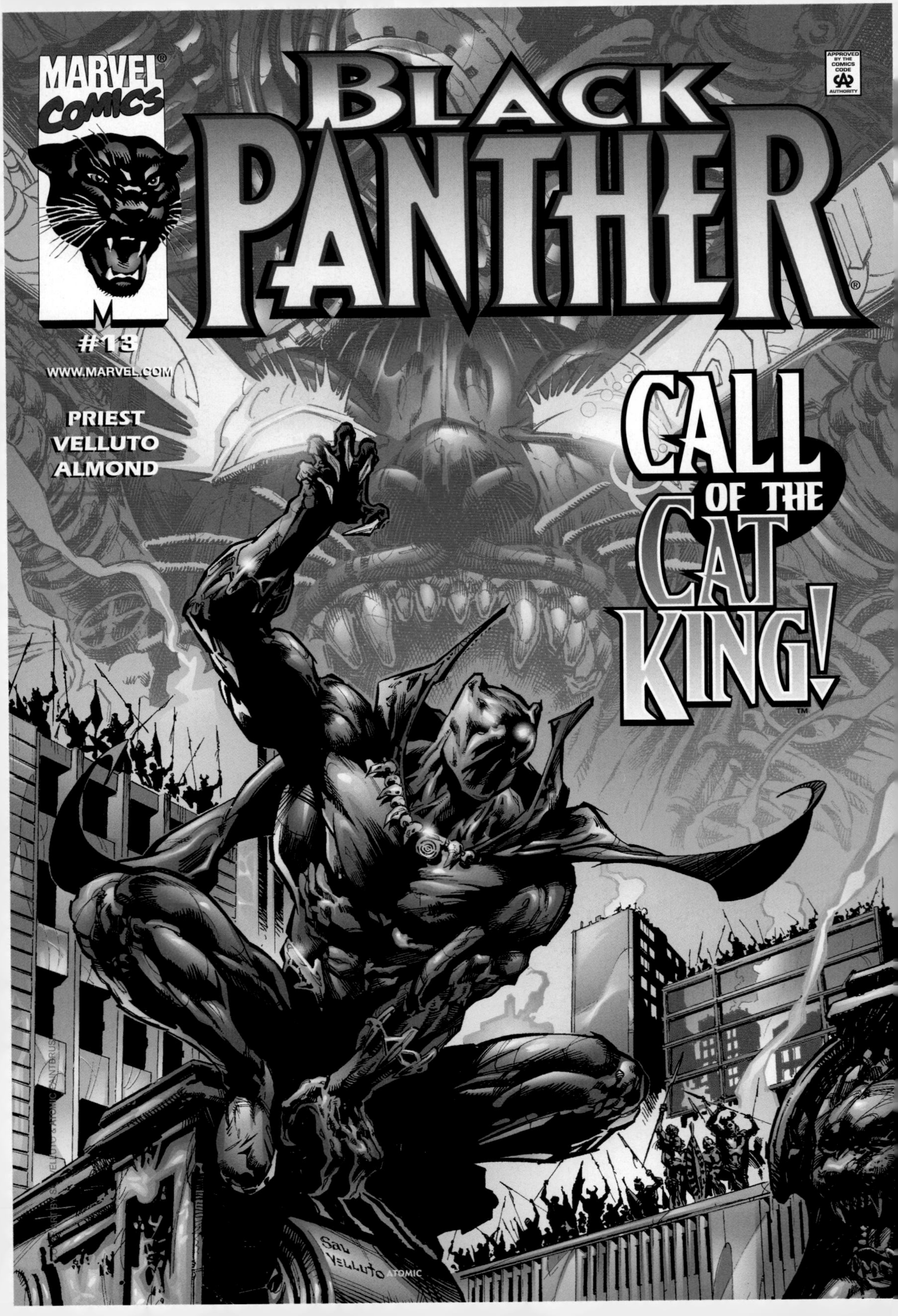
MARVEL COMICS
APPROVED BY THE COMICS CODE AUTHORITY
BLACK PANTHER
#13
WWW.MARVEL.COM
PRIEST
VELLUTO
ALMOND
CALL OF THE CAT KING!
Sal Velluto ATOMIC

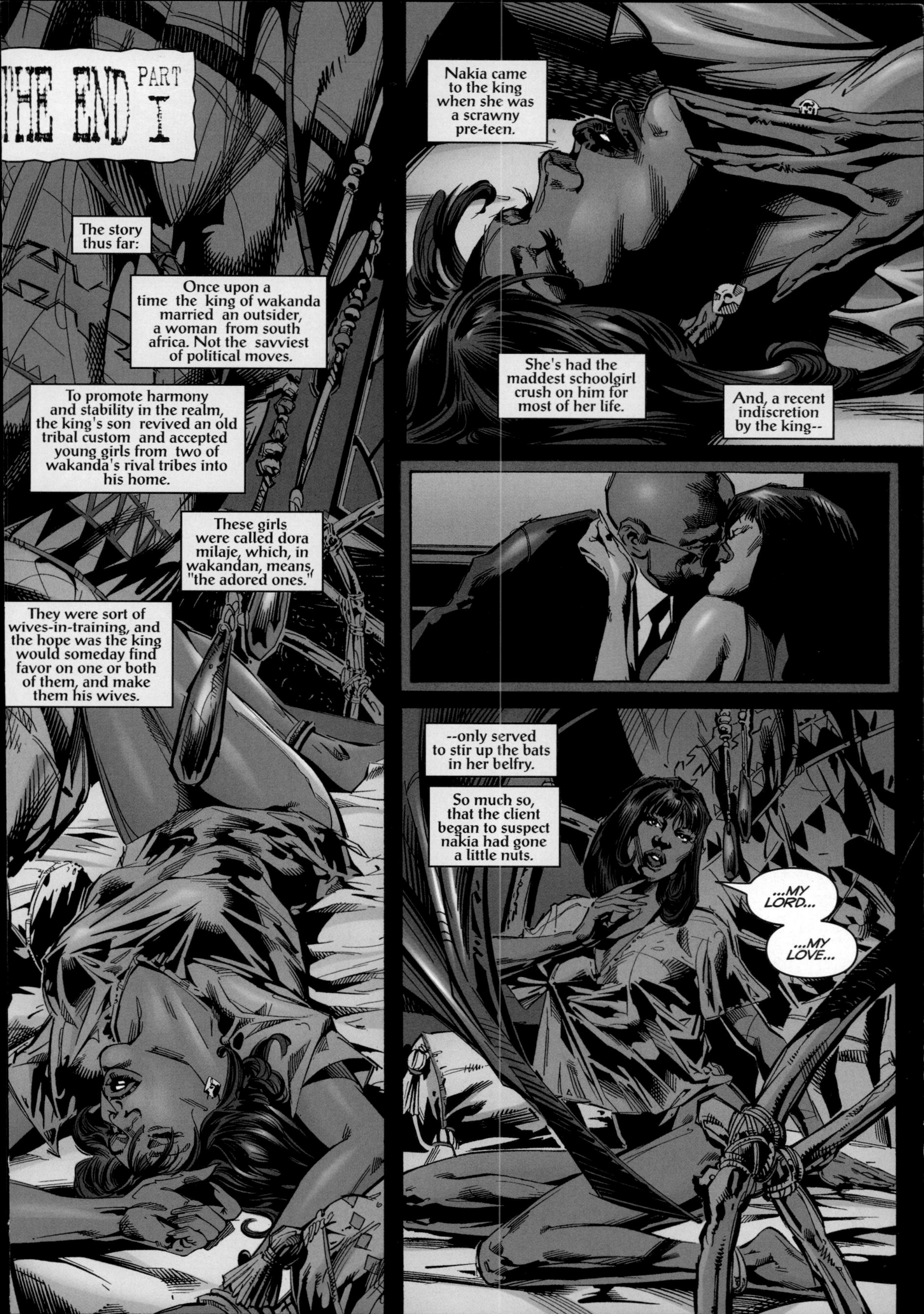
THE END PART I
The story thus far:
Once upon a time the king of wakanda married an outsider, a woman from south africa. Not the savviest of political moves.
To promote harmony and stability in the realm, the king's son revived an old tribal custom and accepted young girls from two of wakanda's rival tribes into his home.
These girls were called dora milaje, which, in wakandan, means, "the adored ones."
They were sort of wives-in-training, and the hope was the king would someday find favor on one or both of them, and make them his wives.
Nakia came to the king when she was a scrawny pre-teen.
She's had the maddest schoolgirl crush on him for most of her life.
And, a recent indiscretion by the king--
--only served to stir up the bats in her belfry.
So much so, that the client began to suspect nakia had gone a little nuts.
...MY LORD...
...MY LOVE...

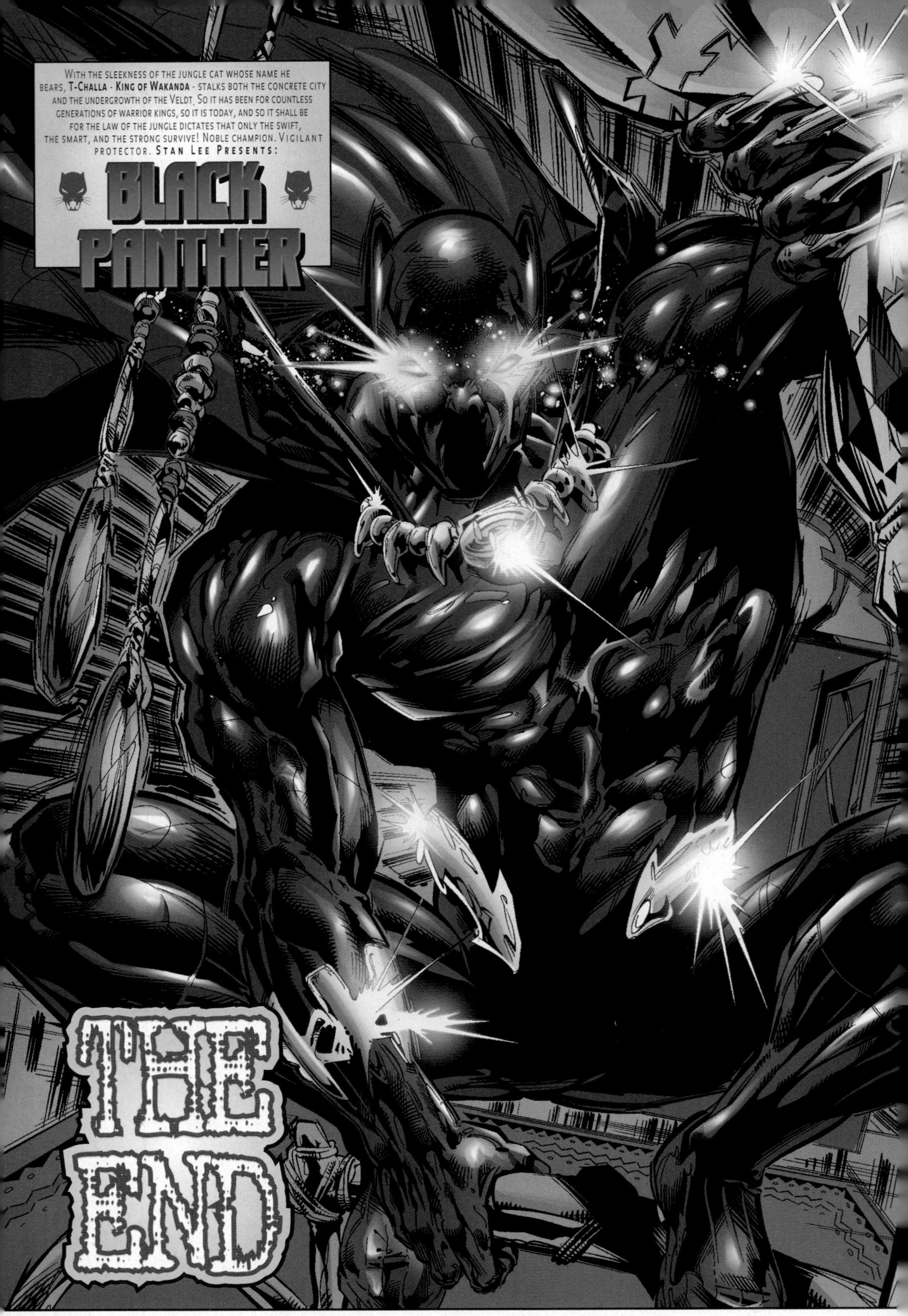

With the sleekness of the jungle cat whose name he bears, T-Challa - King of Wakanda - stalks both the concrete city and the undergrowth of the Veldt. So it has been for countless generations of warrior kings, so it is today, and so it shall be for the law of the jungle dictates that only the swift, the smart, and the strong survive! Noble champion. Vigilant protector. Stan Lee Presents:
BLACK PANTHER
THE END

Introducing the NEW creative team of
CHRISTOPHER PRIEST - writer * SAL VELLUTO - penciler * BOB ALMOND - inking
SHARPEFONT & PT - letters * BRAD VANCATA - colorist * RUBEN DIAZ - editor * BOB HARRAS - ch

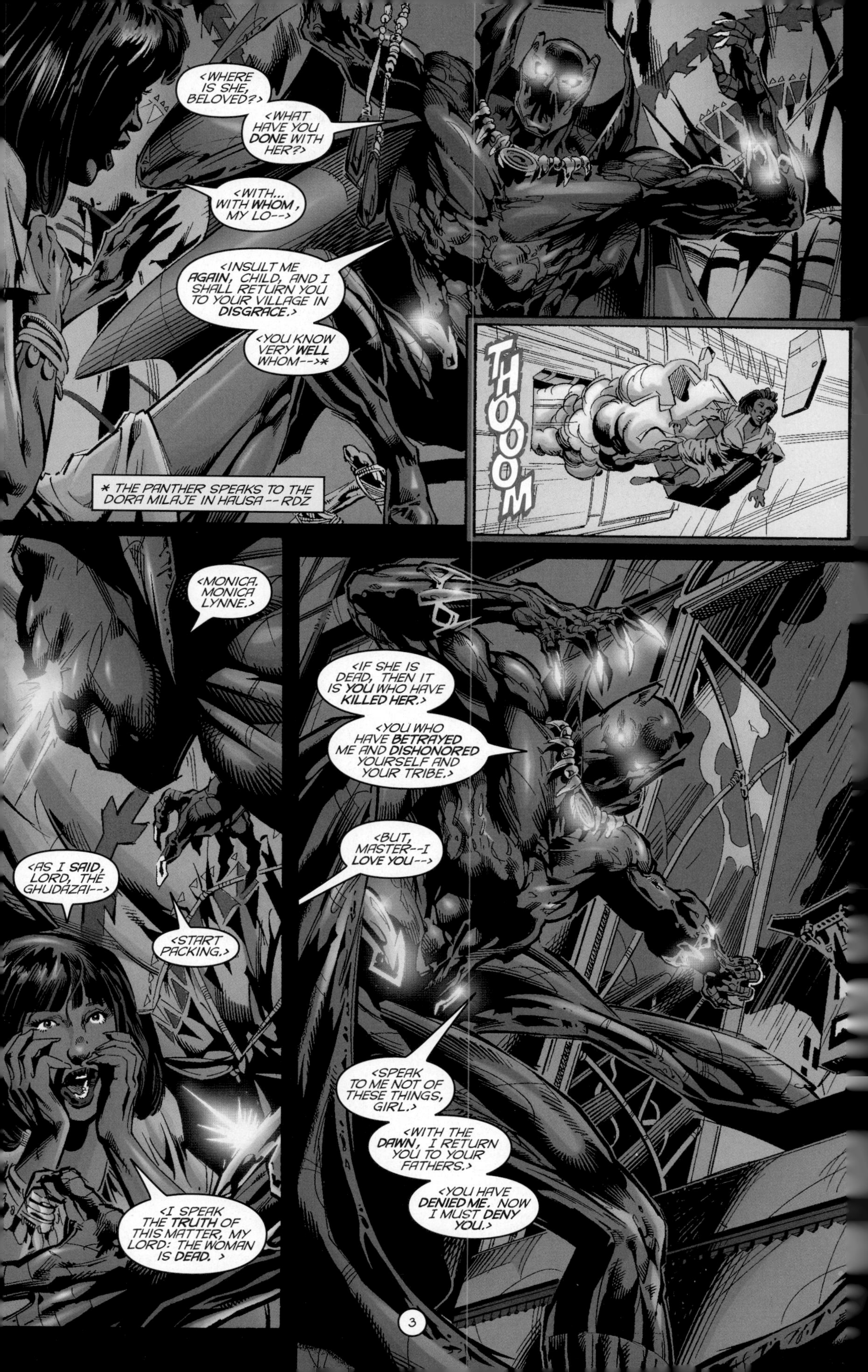

<WHERE IS SHE, BELOVED?>
<WHAT HAVE YOU DONE WITH HER?>
<WITH... WITH WHOM, MY LO-->
<INSULT ME AGAIN, CHILD, AND I SHALL RETURN YOU TO YOUR VILLAGE IN DISGRACE.>
<YOU KNOW VERY WELL WHOM-->*
* THE PANTHER SPEAKS TO THE DORA MILAJE IN HAUSA --RDZ
THOOOM
<MONICA. MONICA LYNNE.>
<AS I SAID, LORD, THE GHUDAZAI-->
<START PACKING.>
<I SPEAK THE TRUTH OF THIS MATTER, MY LORD: THE WOMAN IS DEAD.>
<IF SHE IS DEAD, THEN IT IS YOU WHO HAVE KILLED HER.>
<YOU WHO HAVE BETRAYED ME AND DISHONORED YOURSELF AND YOUR TRIBE.>
<BUT, MASTER--I LOVE YOU-->
<SPEAK TO ME NOT OF THESE THINGS, GIRL.>
<WITH THE DAWN, I RETURN YOU TO YOUR FATHERS.>
<YOU HAVE DENIED ME. NOW I MUST DENY YOU.>

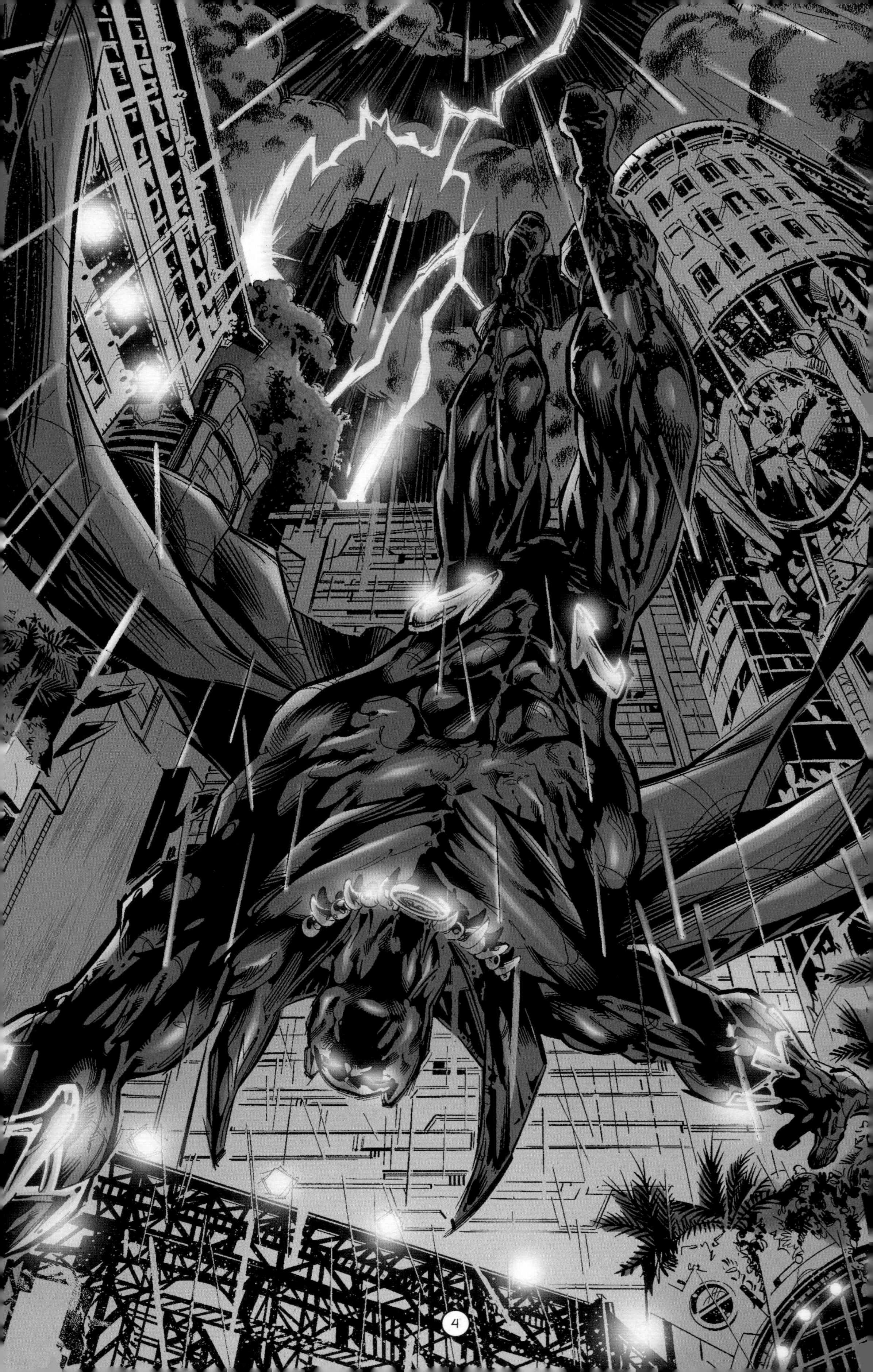

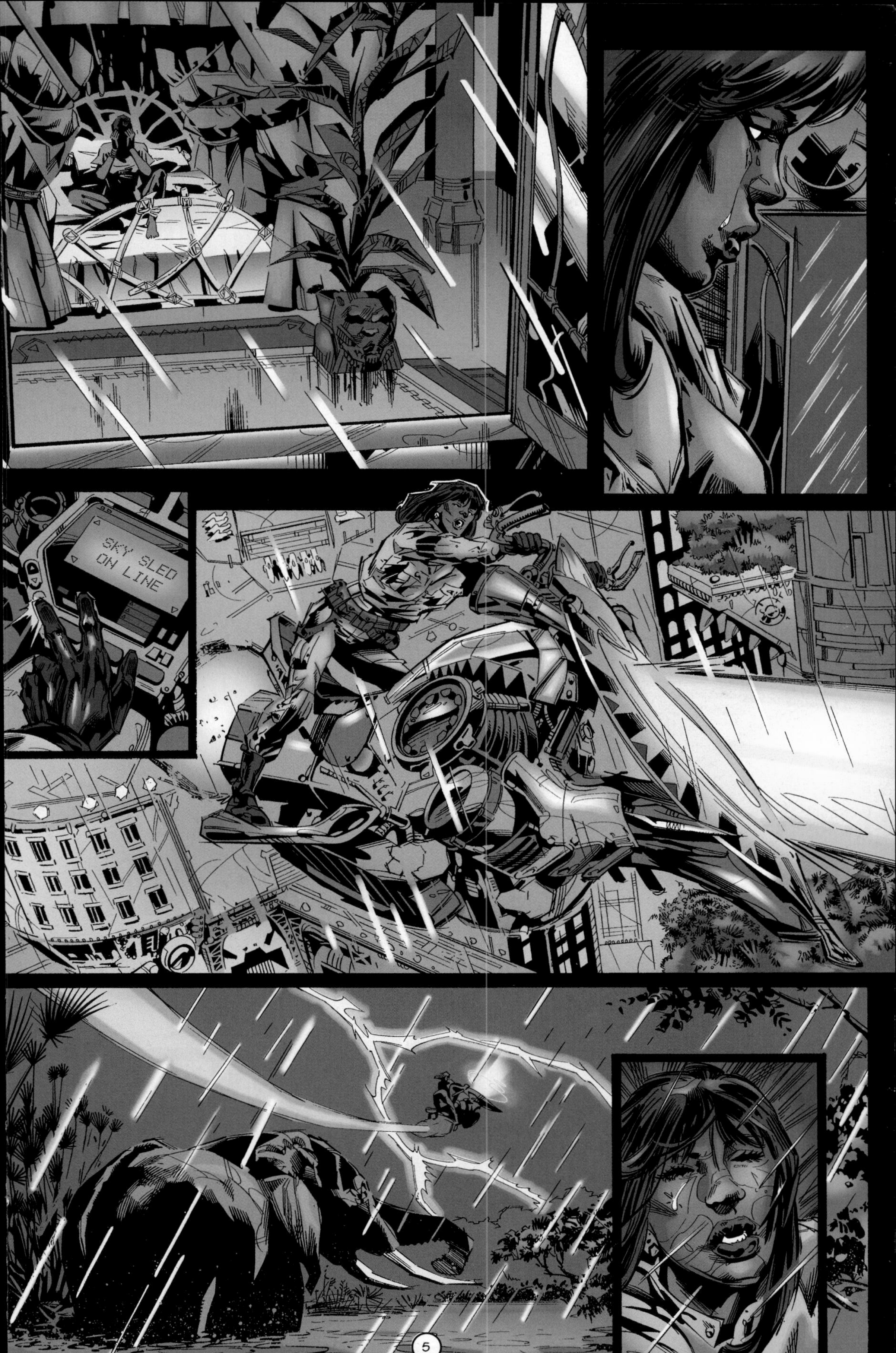
SKY SLED
ON LINE

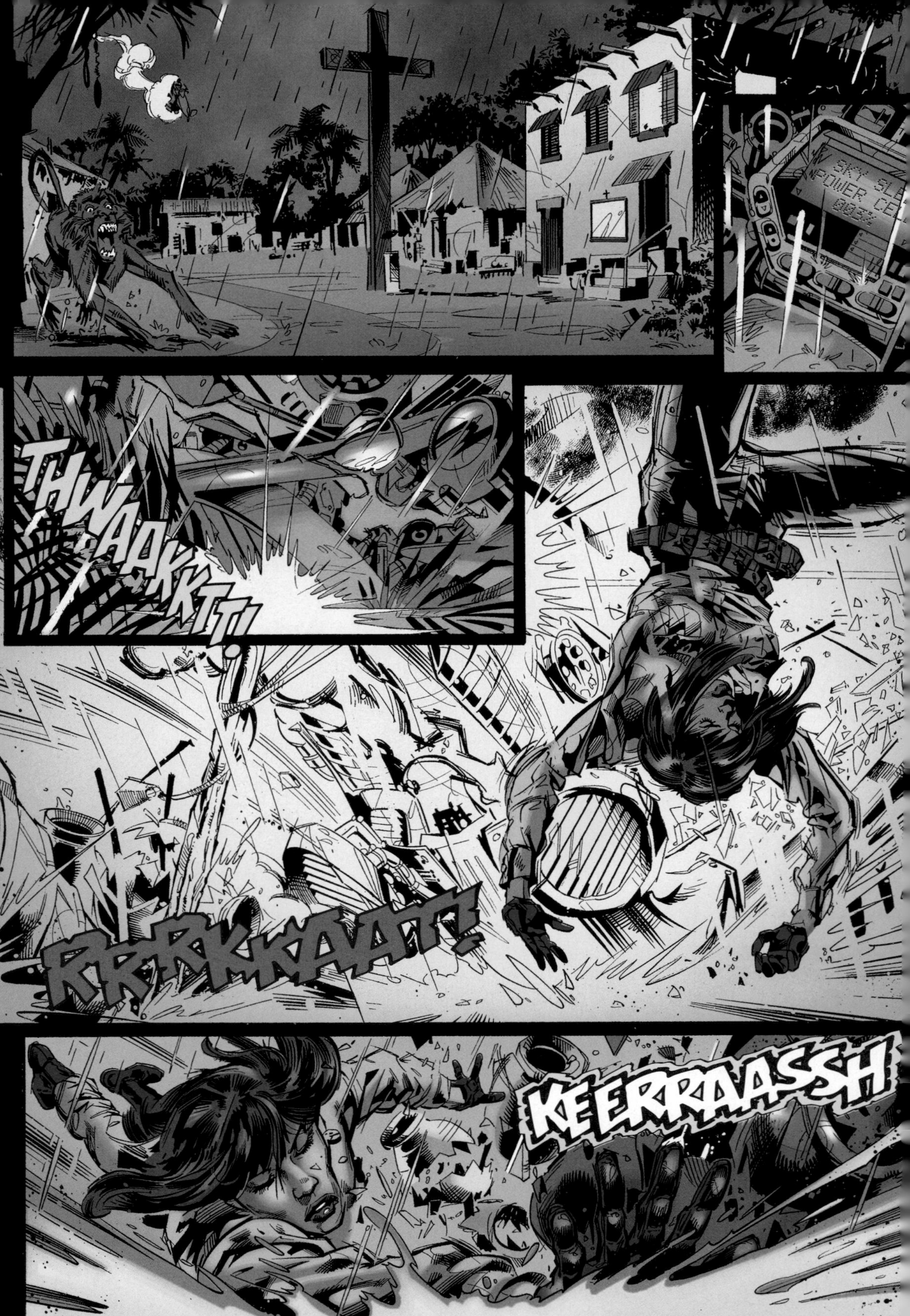
THWAAKKTT!
RRRKKAAATT!
KEERRAASSH

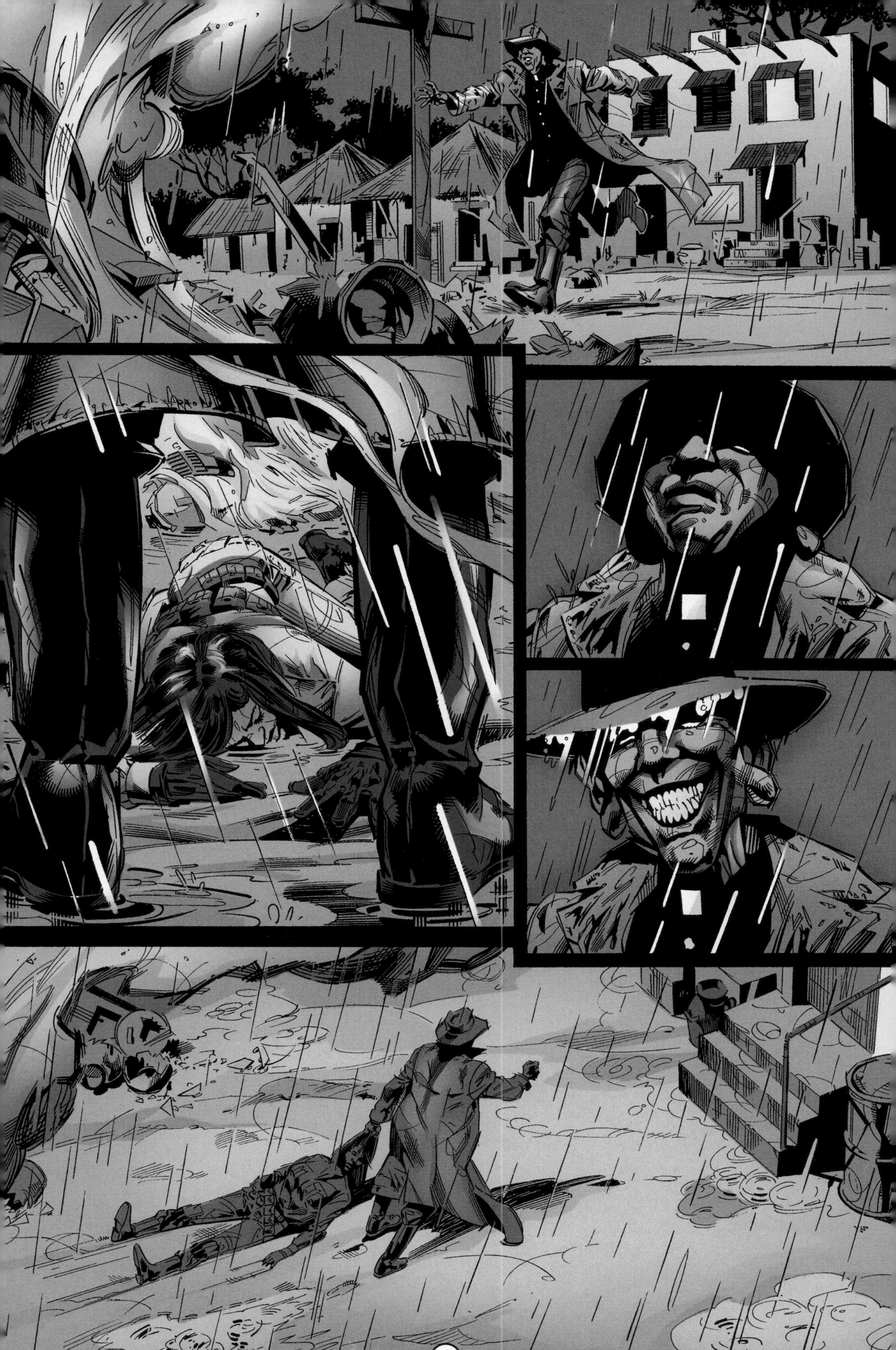

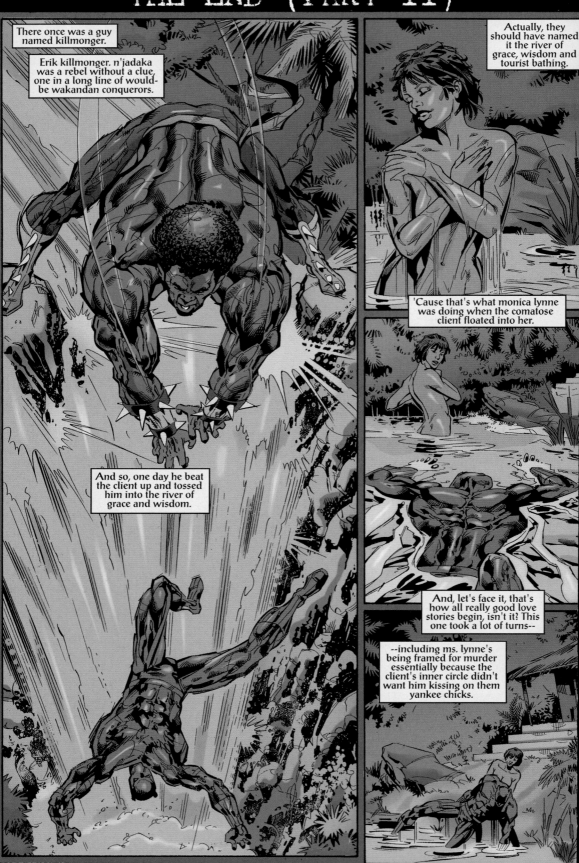

There once was a guy named killmonger.

Erik killmonger. n'jadaka was a rebel without a clue, one in a long line of would-be wakandan conquerors.

And so, one day he beat the client up and tossed him into the river of grace and wisdom.

Actually, they should have named it the river of grace, wisdom and tourist bathing.

'Cause that's what monica lynne was doing when the comatose client floated into her.

And, let's face it, that's how all really good love stories begin, isn't it? This one took a lot of turns--

--including ms. lynne's being framed for murder essentially because the client's inner circle didn't want him kissing on them yankee chicks.

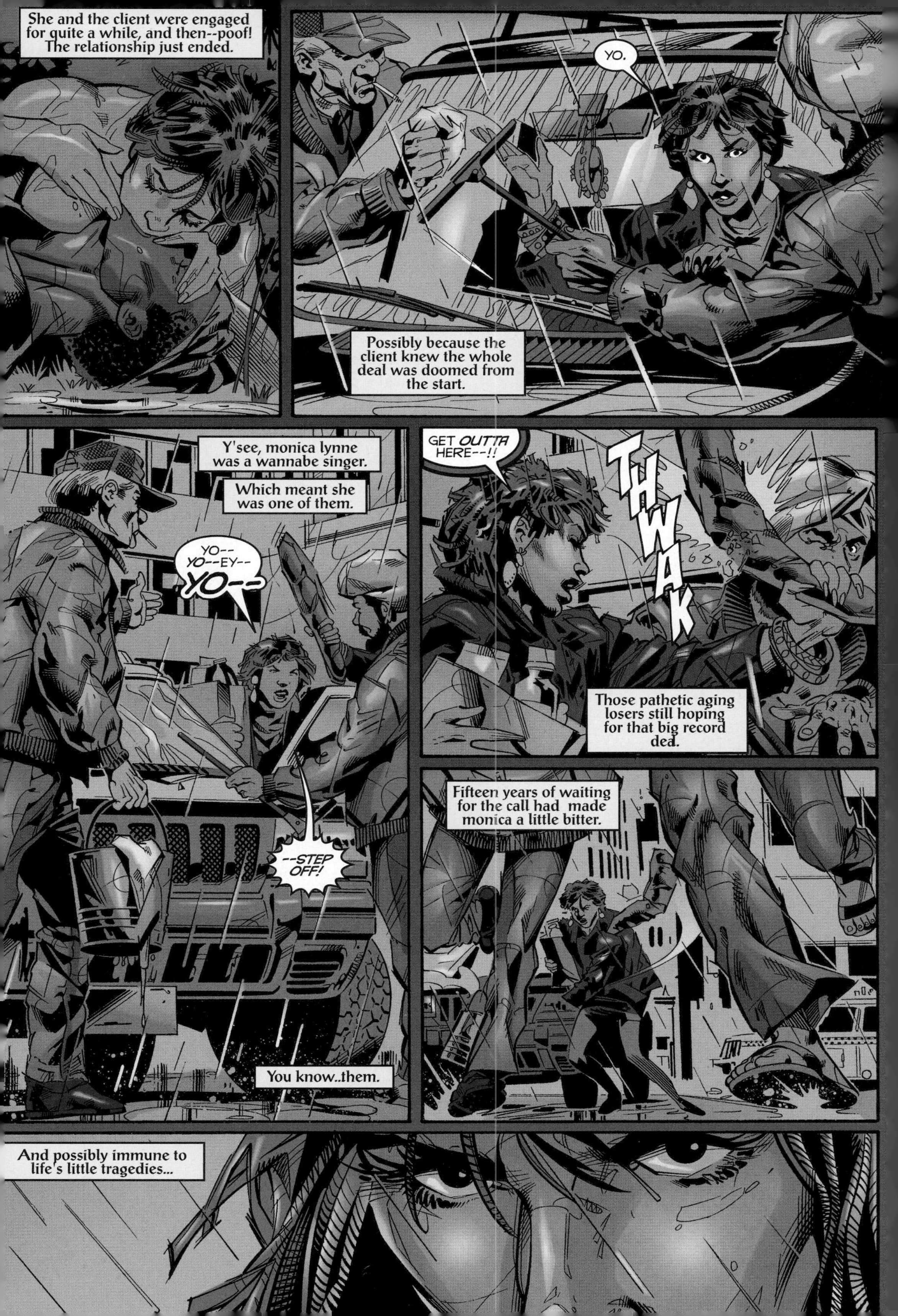
She and the client were engaged for quite a while, and then--poof! The relationship just ended.
YO.
Possibly because the client knew the whole deal was doomed from the start.
Y'see, monica lynne was a wannabe singer.
Which meant she was one of them.
YO-- YO--EY-- YO--
--STEP OFF!
You know..them.
GET OUTTA HERE--!!
THWAK
Those pathetic aging losers still hoping for that big record deal.
Fifteen years of waiting for the call had made monica a little bitter.
And possibly immune to life's little tragedies...

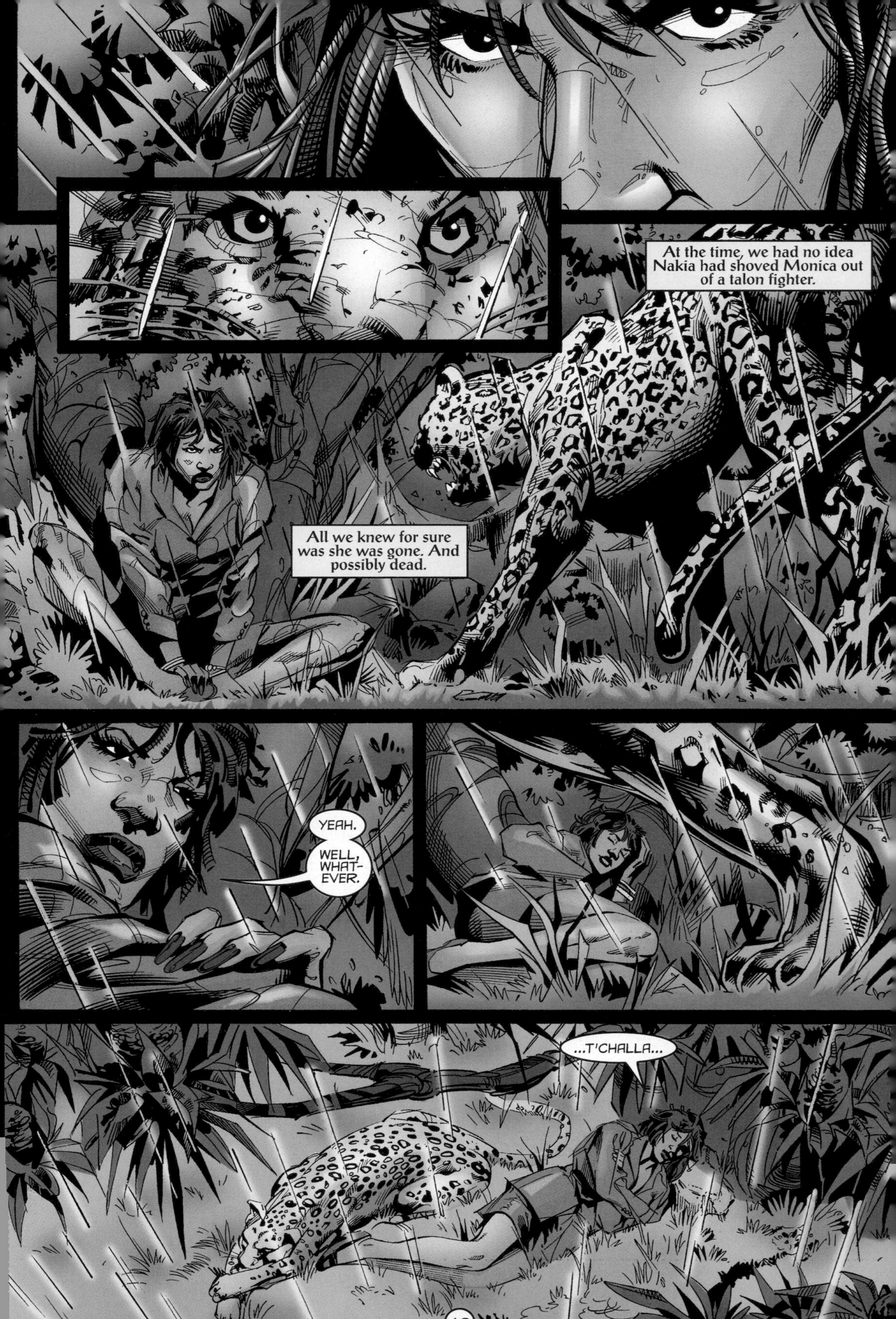

At the time, we had no idea Nakia had shoved Monica out of a talon fighter.
All we knew for sure was she was gone. And possibly dead.
YEAH.
WELL, WHAT-EVER.
...T'CHALLA...

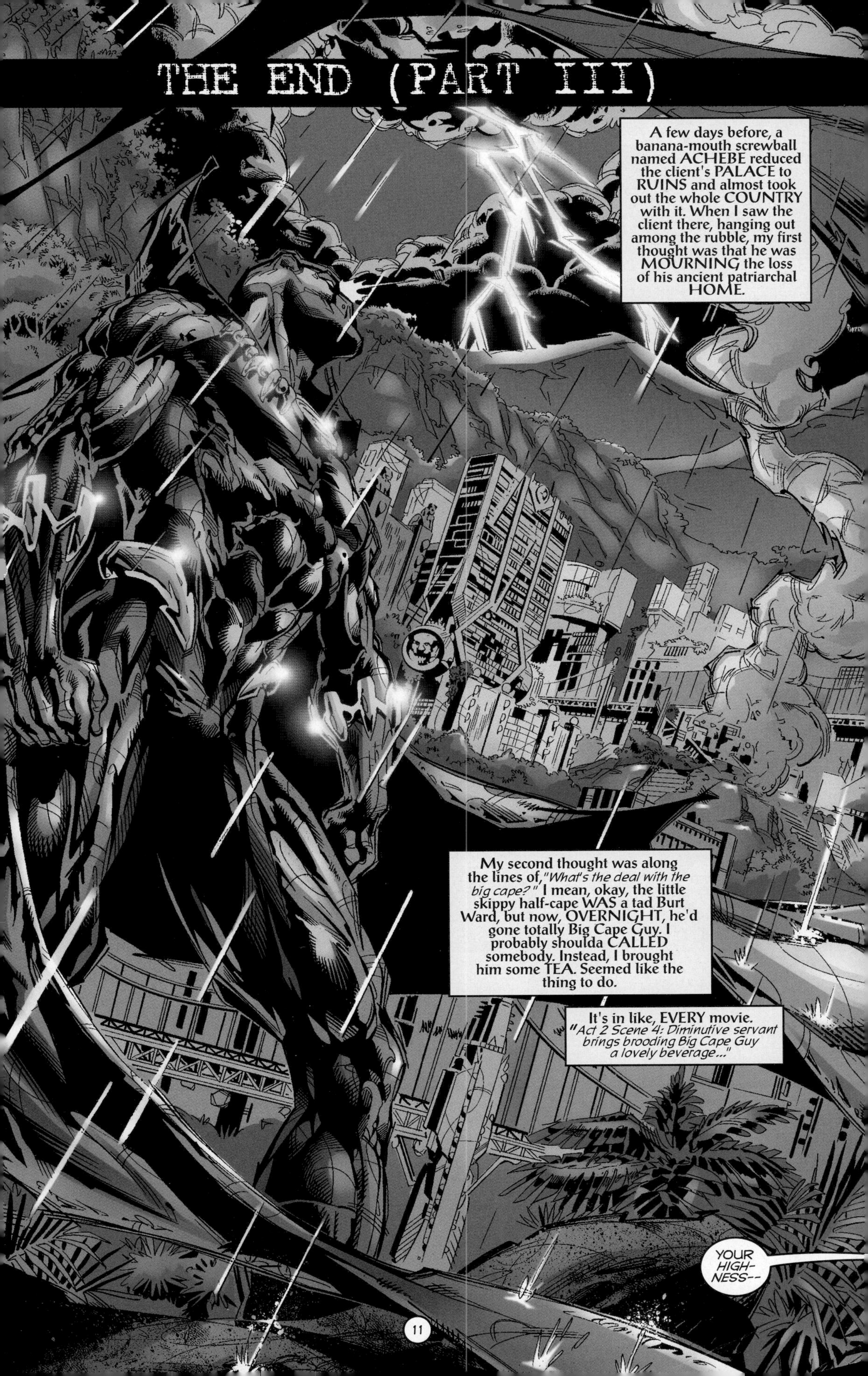
THE END (PART III)
A few days before, a banana-mouth screwball named ACHEBE reduced the client's PALACE to RUINS and almost took out the whole COUNTRY with it. When I saw the client there, hanging out among the rubble, my first thought was that he was MOURNING the loss of his ancient patriarchal HOME.
My second thought was along the lines of, "What's the deal with the big cape?" I mean, okay, the little skippy half-cape WAS a tad Burt Ward, but now, OVERNIGHT, he'd gone totally Big Cape Guy. I probably shoulda CALLED somebody. Instead, I brought him some TEA. Seemed like the thing to do.
It's in like, EVERY movie. "Act 2 Scene 4: Diminutive servant brings brooding Big Cape Guy a lovely beverage..."
YOUR HIGH-NESS--

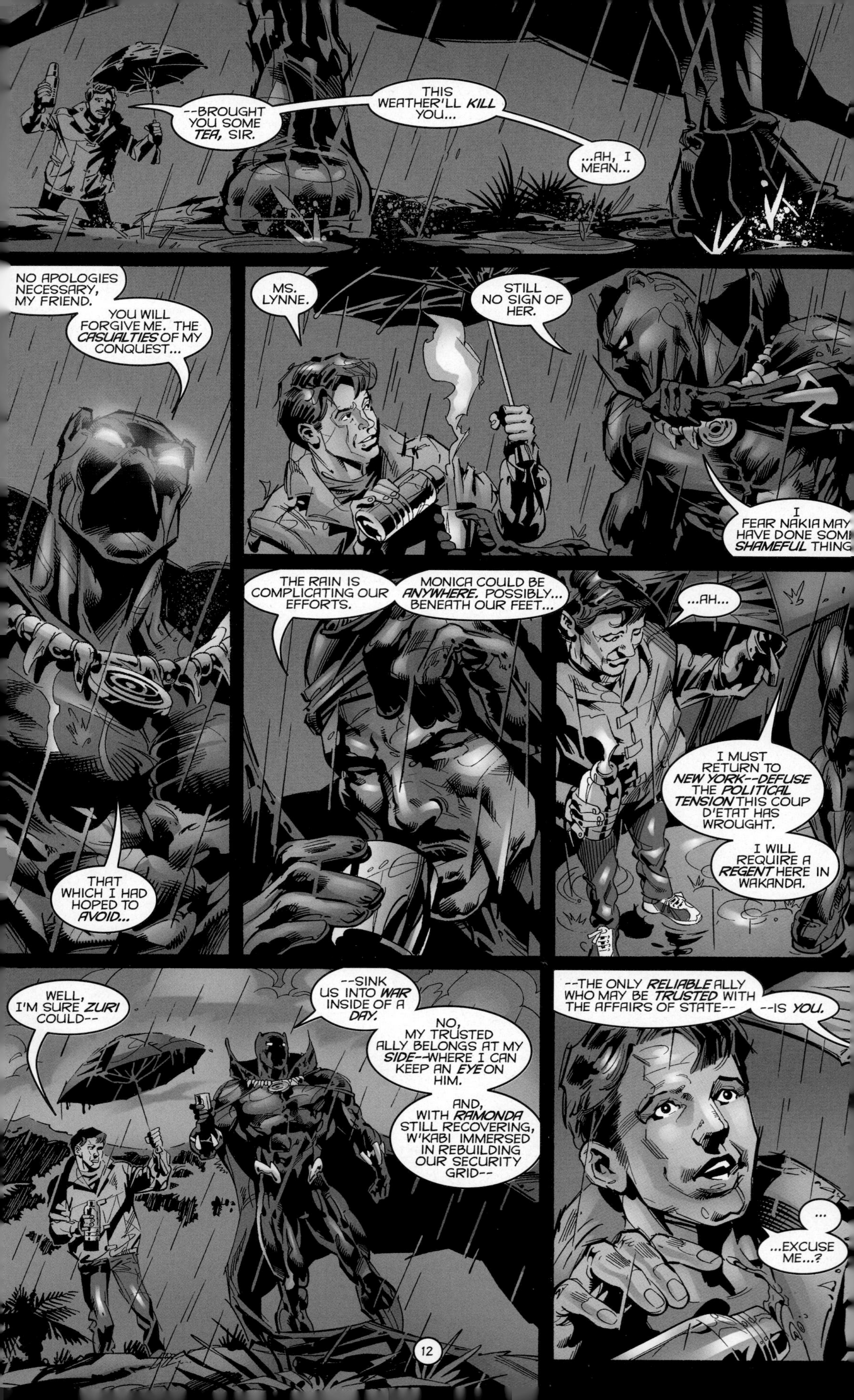

--BROUGHT YOU SOME TEA, SIR.
THIS WEATHER'LL KILL YOU...
...AH, I MEAN...
NO APOLOGIES NECESSARY, MY FRIEND.
YOU WILL FORGIVE ME. THE CASUALTIES OF MY CONQUEST...
THAT WHICH I HAD HOPED TO AVOID...
MS. LYNNE.
STILL NO SIGN OF HER.
I FEAR NAKIA MAY HAVE DONE SOME SHAMEFUL THING
THE RAIN IS COMPLICATING OUR EFFORTS.
MONICA COULD BE ANYWHERE. POSSIBLY... BENEATH OUR FEET...
...AH...
I MUST RETURN TO NEW YORK--DEFUSE THE POLITICAL TENSION THIS COUP D'ETAT HAS WROUGHT.
I WILL REQUIRE A REGENT HERE IN WAKANDA.
WELL, I'M SURE ZURI COULD--
--SINK US INTO WAR INSIDE OF A DAY.
NO, MY TRUSTED ALLY BELONGS AT MY SIDE--WHERE I CAN KEEP AN EYE ON HIM.
AND, WITH RAMONDA STILL RECOVERING, W'KABI IMMERSED IN REBUILDING OUR SECURITY GRID--
--THE ONLY RELIABLE ALLY WHO MAY BE TRUSTED WITH THE AFFAIRS OF STATE--
--IS YOU.
...
...EXCUSE ME...?

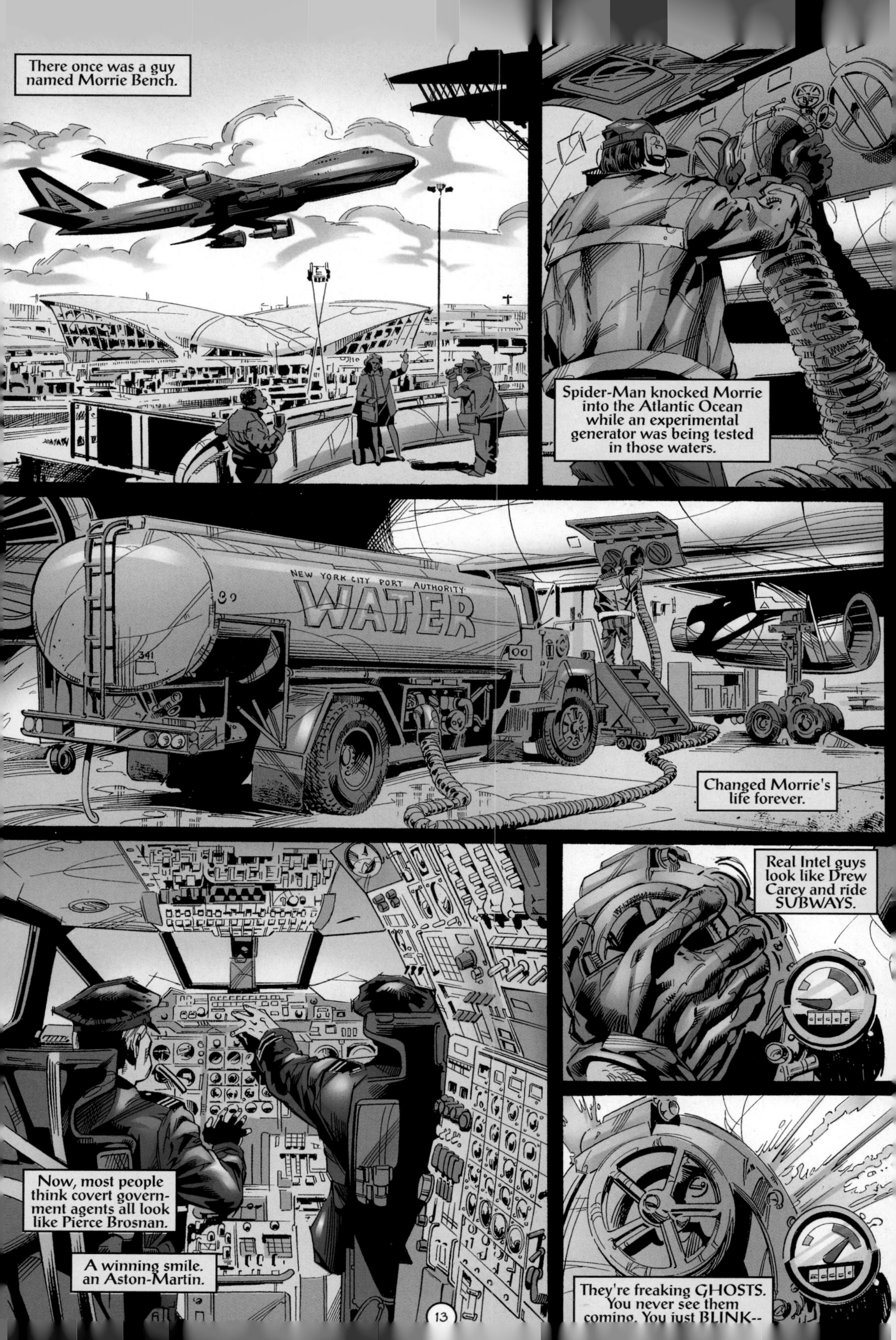
There once was a guy named Morrie Bench.
Spider-Man knocked Morrie into the Atlantic Ocean while an experimental generator was being tested in those waters.
NEW YORK CITY PORT AUTHORITY
WATER
Changed Morrie's life forever.
Now, most people think covert government agents all look like Pierce Brosnan.
A winning smile. an Aston-Martin.
Real Intel guys look like Drew Carey and ride SUBWAYS.
They're freaking GHOSTS. You never see them coming. You just BLINK--

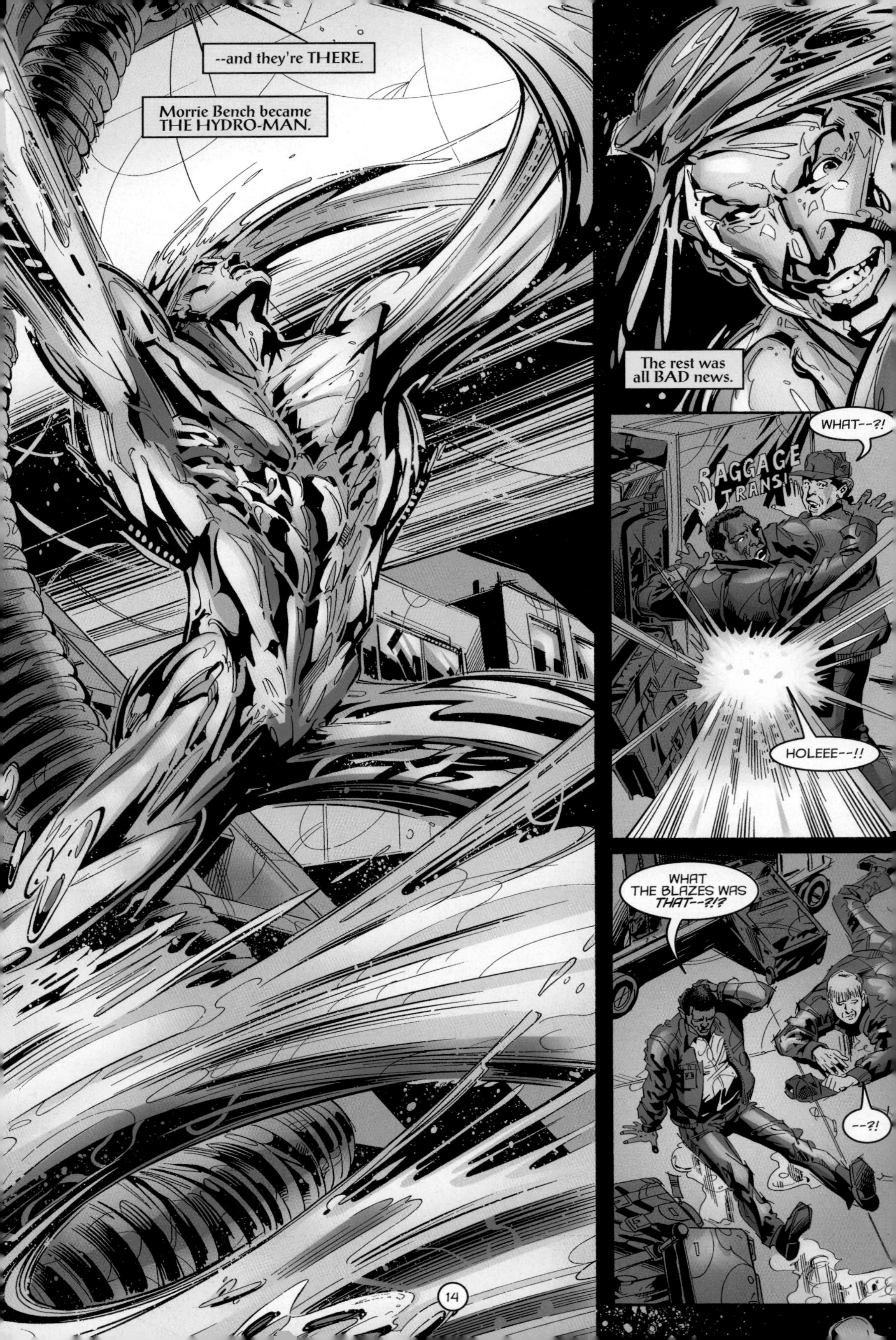
--and they're THERE.
Morrie Bench became THE HYDRO-MAN.
The rest was all BAD news.
WHAT--?!
BAGGAGE TRANS.
HOLEEE--!!
WHAT THE BLAZES WAS THAT--?!?
--?!

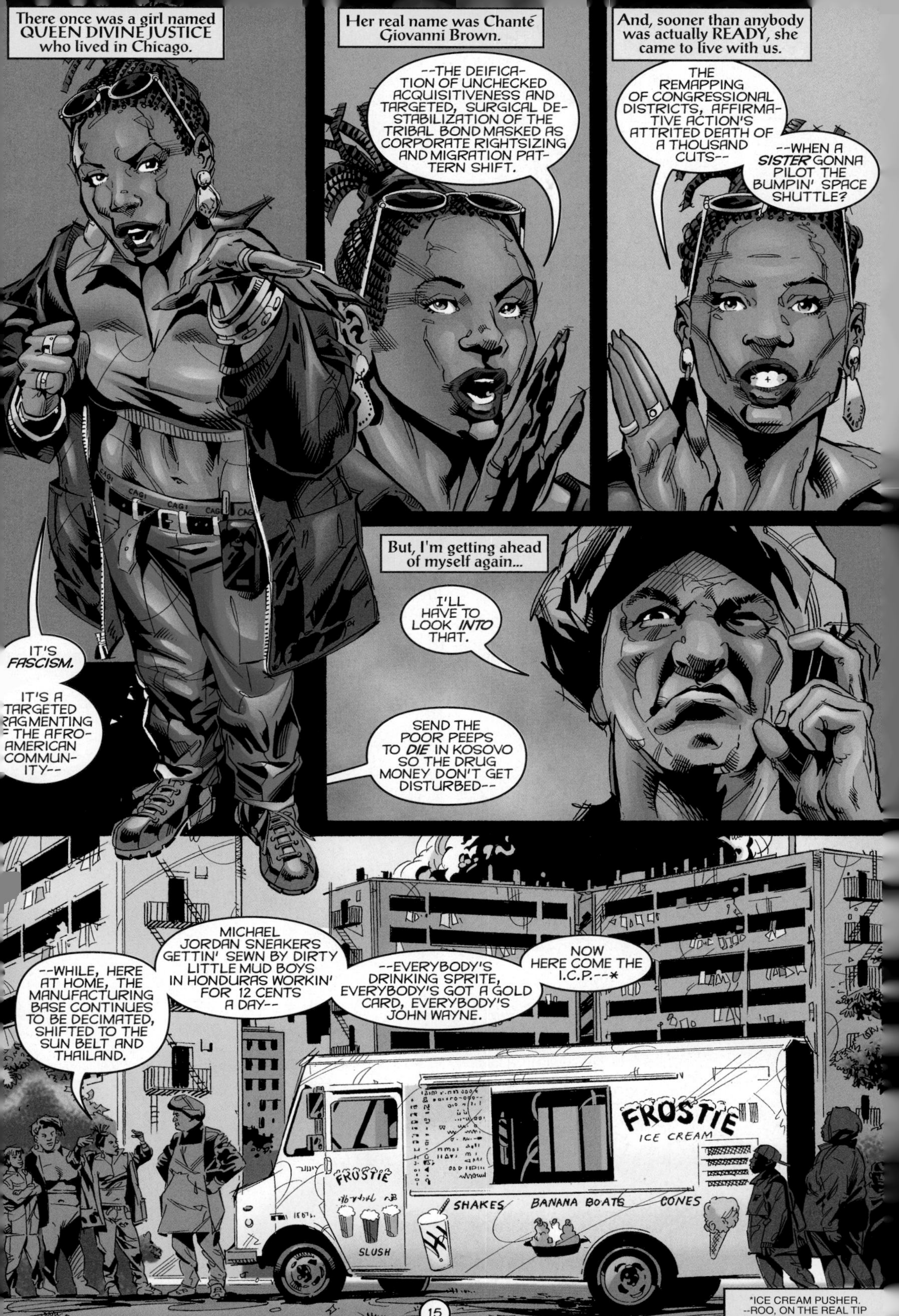
There once was a girl named QUEEN DIVINE JUSTICE who lived in Chicago.
IT'S FASCISM.
IT'S A TARGETED RAGMENTING F THE AFRO-AMERICAN COMMUN-ITY--
Her real name was Chanté Giovanni Brown.
--THE DEIFICA-TION OF UNCHECKED ACQUISITIVENESS AND TARGETED, SURGICAL DE-STABILIZATION OF THE TRIBAL BOND MASKED AS CORPORATE RIGHTSIZING AND MIGRATION PAT-TERN SHIFT.
And, sooner than anybody was actually READY, she came to live with us.
THE REMAPPING OF CONGRESSIONAL DISTRICTS, AFFIRMA-TIVE ACTION'S ATTRITED DEATH OF A THOUSAND CUTS--
--WHEN A SISTER GONNA PILOT THE BUMPIN' SPACE SHUTTLE?
But, I'm getting ahead of myself again...
I'LL HAVE TO LOOK INTO THAT.
SEND THE POOR PEEPS TO DIE IN KOSOVO SO THE DRUG MONEY DON'T GET DISTURBED--
--WHILE, HERE AT HOME, THE MANUFACTURING BASE CONTINUES TO BE DECIMATED, SHIFTED TO THE SUN BELT AND THAILAND.
MICHAEL JORDAN SNEAKERS GETTIN' SEWN BY DIRTY LITTLE MUD BOYS IN HONDURAS WORKIN' FOR 12 CENTS A DAY--
--EVERYBODY'S DRINKING SPRITE, EVERYBODY'S GOT A GOLD CARD, EVERYBODY'S JOHN WAYNE.
NOW HERE COME THE I.C.P.--*
FROSTIE ICE CREAM
FROSTIE
SHAKES
BANANA BOATS
CONES
SLUSH
*ICE CREAM PUSHER. --ROO, ON THE REAL TIP

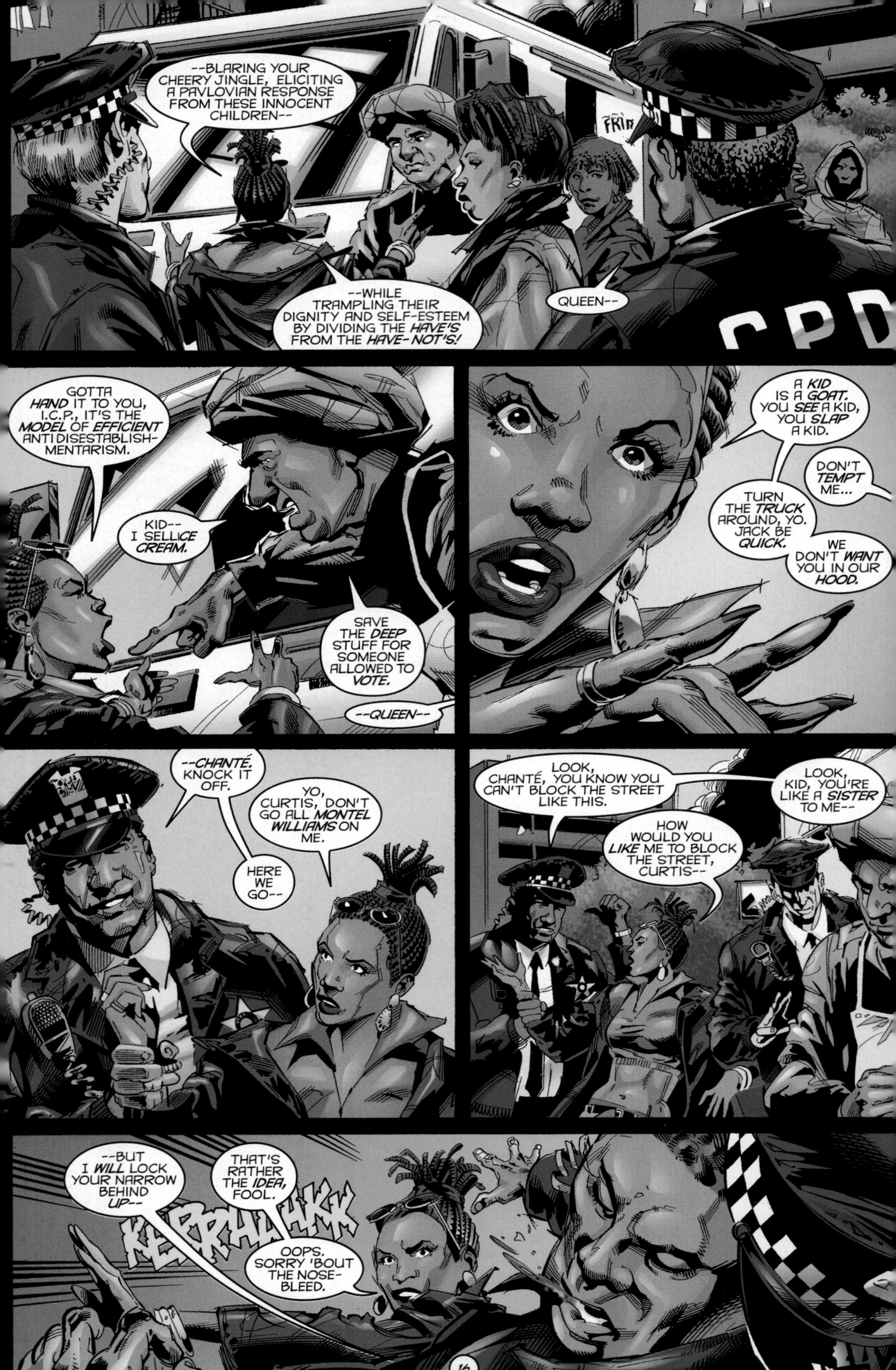
--BLARING YOUR CHEERY JINGLE, ELICITING A PAVLOVIAN RESPONSE FROM THESE INNOCENT CHILDREN--
--WHILE TRAMPLING THEIR DIGNITY AND SELF-ESTEEM BY DIVIDING THE HAVE'S FROM THE HAVE-NOT'S!
QUEEN--
CPD
GOTTA HAND IT TO YOU, I.C.P., IT'S THE MODEL OF EFFICIENT ANTI DISESTABLISH-MENTARISM.
KID-- I SELL ICE CREAM.
SAVE THE DEEP STUFF FOR SOMEONE ALLOWED TO VOTE.
--QUEEN--
A KID IS A GOAT. YOU SEE A KID, YOU SLAP A KID.
DON'T TEMPT ME...
TURN THE TRUCK AROUND, YO. JACK BE QUICK.
WE DON'T WANT YOU IN OUR HOOD.
--CHANTÉ. KNOCK IT OFF.
YO, CURTIS, DON'T GO ALL MONTEL WILLIAMS ON ME.
HERE WE GO--
LOOK, CHANTÉ, YOU KNOW YOU CAN'T BLOCK THE STREET LIKE THIS.
HOW WOULD YOU LIKE ME TO BLOCK THE STREET, CURTIS--
LOOK, KID, YOU'RE LIKE A SISTER TO ME--
--BUT I WILL LOCK YOUR NARROW BEHIND UP--
THAT'S RATHER THE IDEA, FOOL.
KERRCHUKK
OOPS. SORRY 'BOUT THE NOSE-BLEED.

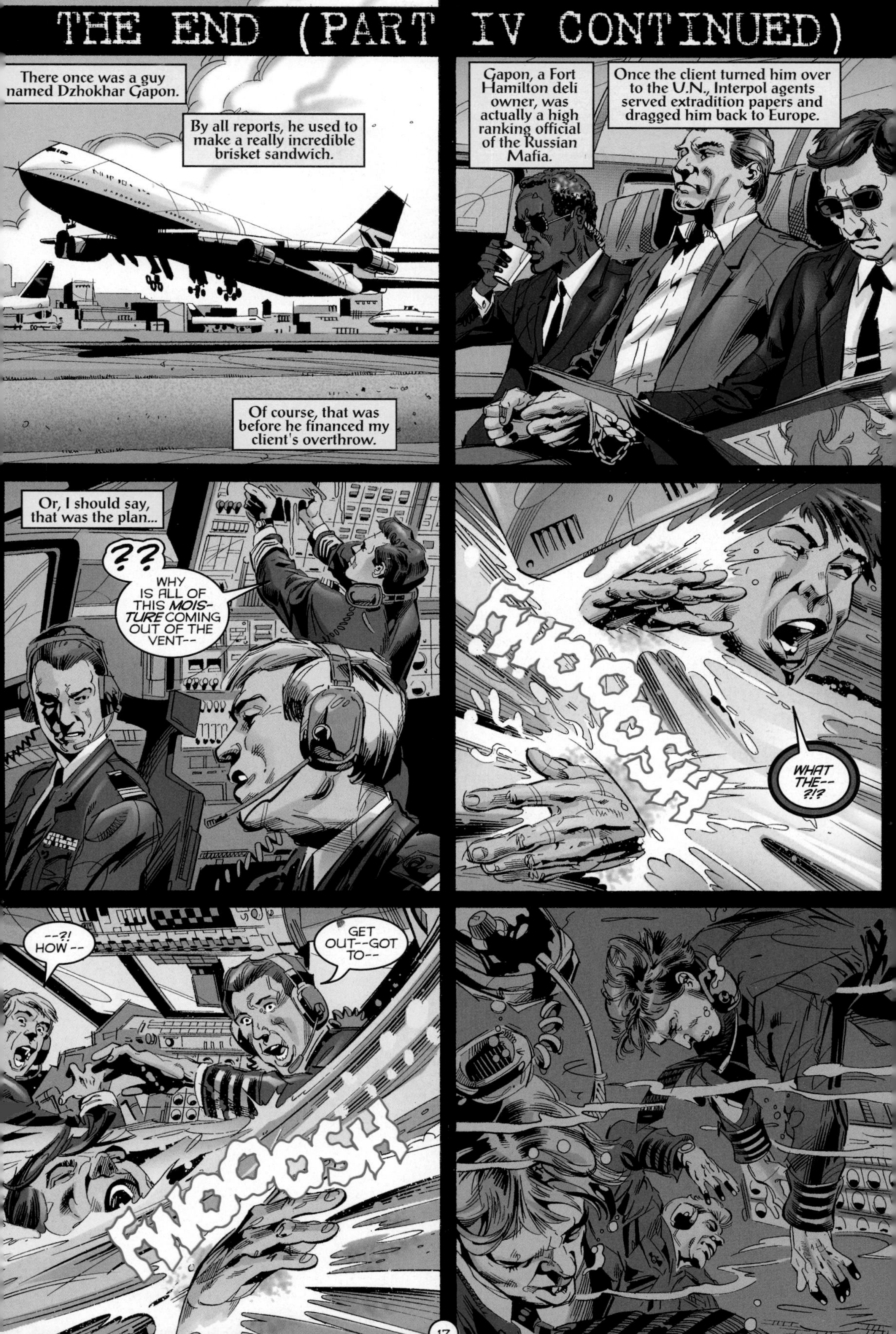
THE END (PART IV CONTINUED)
There once was a guy named Dzhokhar Gapon.
By all reports, he used to make a really incredible brisket sandwich.
Of course, that was before he financed my client's overthrow.
Gapon, a Fort Hamilton deli owner, was actually a high ranking official of the Russian Mafia.
Once the client turned him over to the U.N., Interpol agents served extradition papers and dragged him back to Europe.
Or, I should say, that was the plan...
??
WHY IS ALL OF THIS MOIS-TURE COMING OUT OF THE VENT--
FWOOOSH
WHAT THE--?!?
--?! HOW--
GET OUT--GOT TO--
FWOOOSH

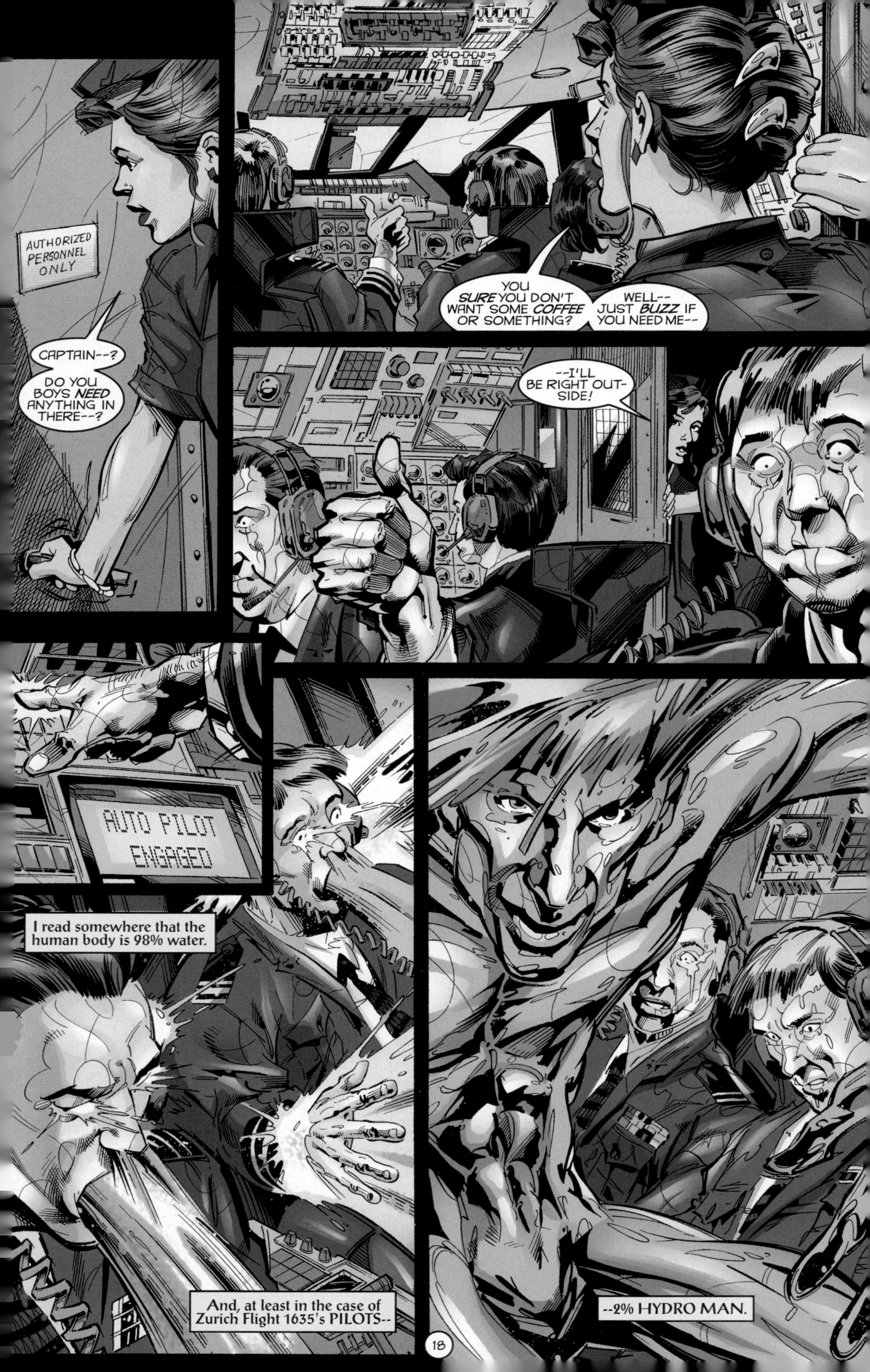
AUTHORIZED PERSONNEL ONLY
CAPTAIN--?
DO YOU BOYS *NEED* ANYTHING IN THERE--?
YOU *SURE* YOU DON'T WANT SOME *COFFEE* OR SOMETHING?
WELL-- JUST *BUZZ* IF YOU NEED ME--
--I'LL BE RIGHT OUT-SIDE!
AUTO PILOT ENGAGED
I read somewhere that the human body is 98% water.
And, at least in the case of Zurich Flight 1635's PILOTS--
--2% HYDRO MAN.

THE END (PART VI)

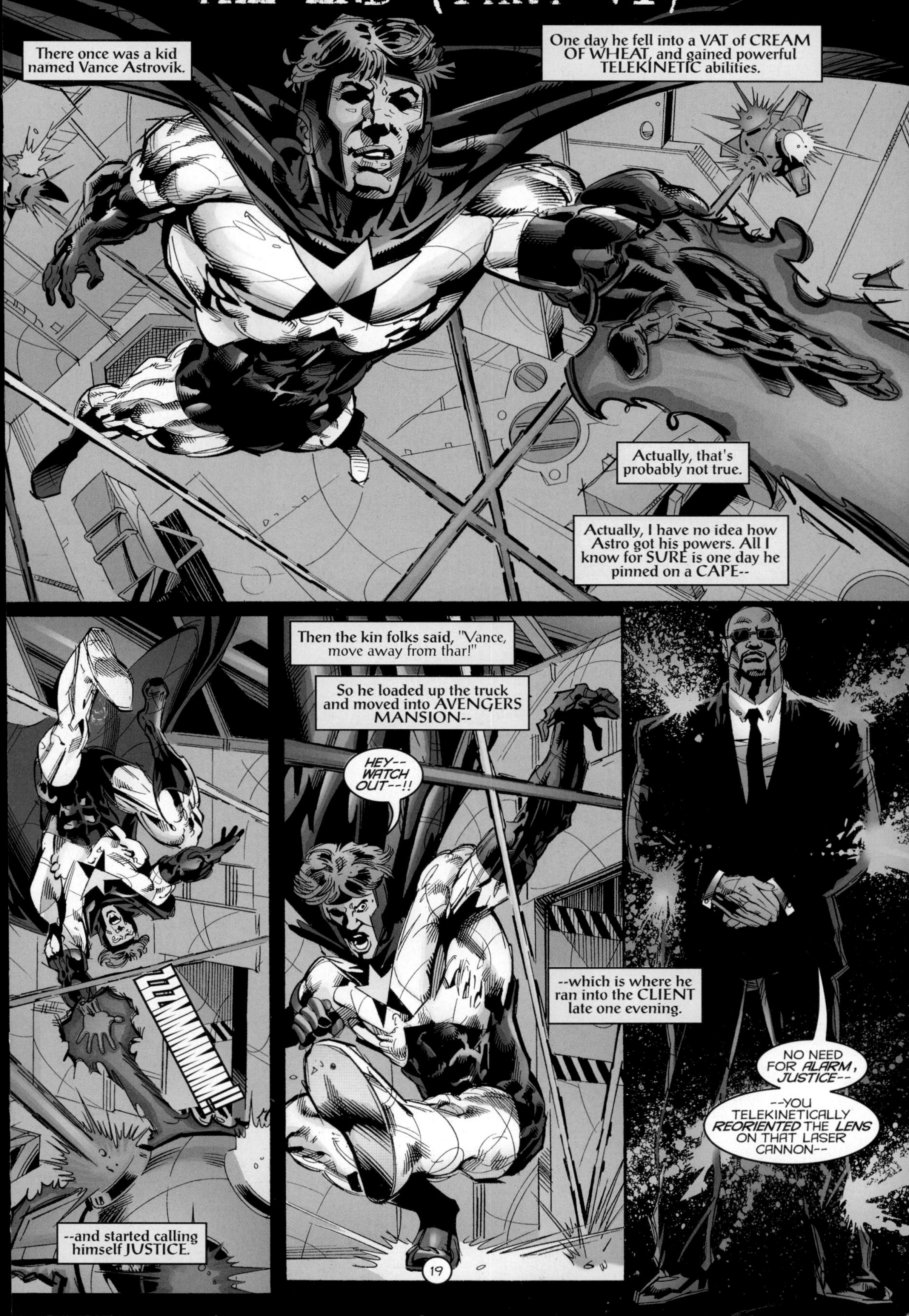
There once was a kid named Vance Astrovik.
One day he fell into a VAT of CREAM OF WHEAT, and gained powerful TELEKINETIC abilities.
Actually, that's probably not true.
Actually, I have no idea how Astro got his powers. All I know for SURE is one day he pinned on a CAPE--
--and started calling himself JUSTICE.
Then the kin folks said, "Vance, move away from thar!"
So he loaded up the truck and moved into AVENGERS MANSION--
HEY--WATCH OUT--!!
--which is where he ran into the CLIENT late one evening.
NO NEED FOR ALARM, JUSTICE--
--YOU TELEKINETICALLY REORIENTED THE LENS ON THAT LASER CANNON--

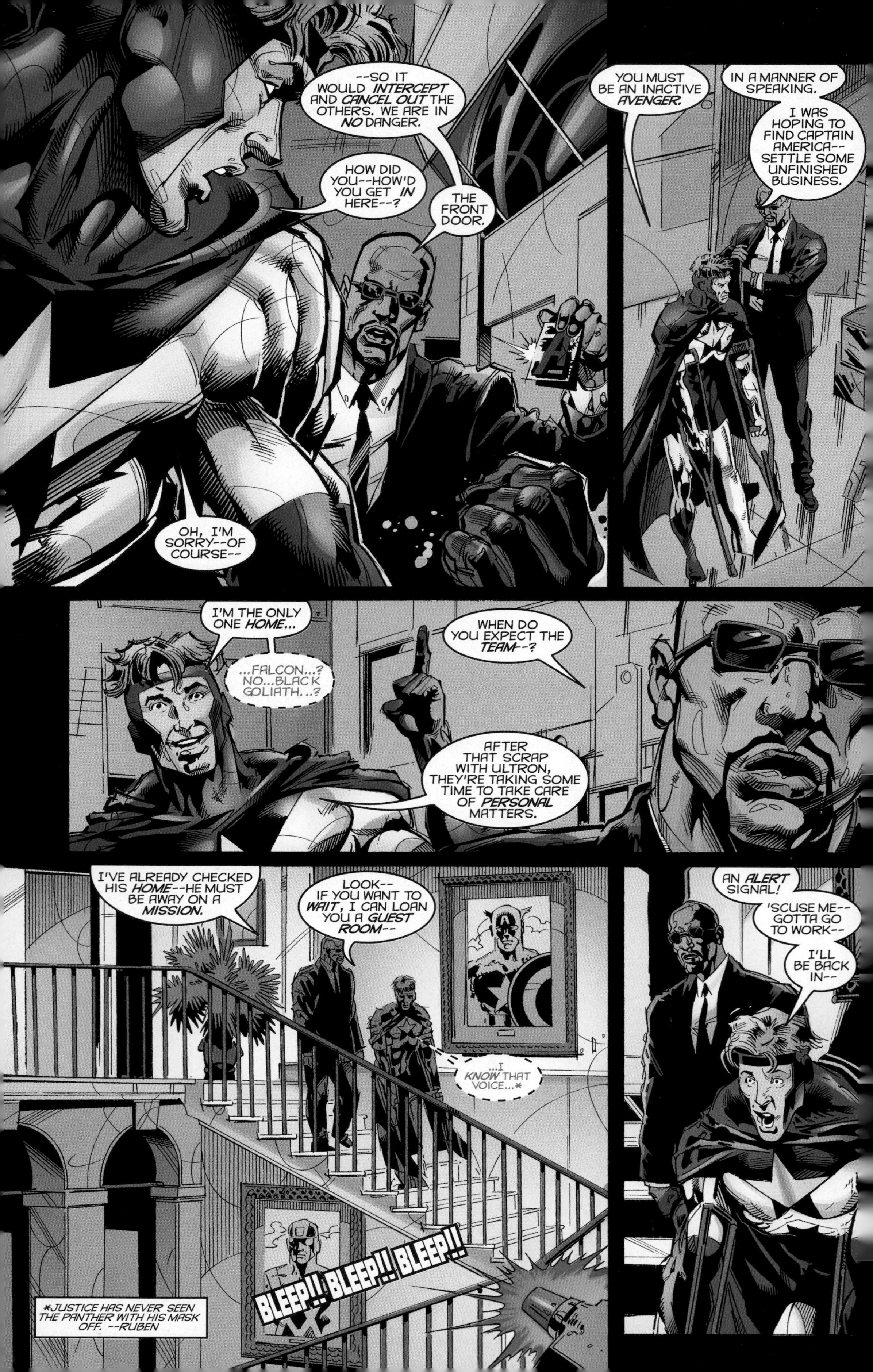
--SO IT WOULD INTERCEPT AND CANCEL OUT THE OTHERS. WE ARE IN NO DANGER.
HOW DID YOU--HOW'D YOU GET IN HERE--?
THE FRONT DOOR.
OH, I'M SORRY--OF COURSE--
YOU MUST BE AN INACTIVE AVENGER.
IN A MANNER OF SPEAKING.
I WAS HOPING TO FIND CAPTAIN AMERICA--SETTLE SOME UNFINISHED BUSINESS.
I'M THE ONLY ONE HOME...
...FALCON...? NO...BLACK GOLIATH...?
WHEN DO YOU EXPECT THE TEAM--?
AFTER THAT SCRAP WITH ULTRON, THEY'RE TAKING SOME TIME TO TAKE CARE OF PERSONAL MATTERS.
I'VE ALREADY CHECKED HIS HOME--HE MUST BE AWAY ON A MISSION.
LOOK--IF YOU WANT TO WAIT, I CAN LOAN YOU A GUEST ROOM--
...I KNOW THAT VOICE...*
BLEEP!! BLEEP!! BLEEP!!
*JUSTICE HAS NEVER SEEN THE PANTHER WITH HIS MASK OFF. --RUBEN
AN ALERT SIGNAL!
'SCUSE ME--GOTTA GO TO WORK--
I'LL BE BACK IN--

--A SEC...

...HOW...

I'VE SPENT MANY YEARS IN THIS MANSION, JUSTICE.

THERE ARE MANY SHORTCUTS.

BOEING 747

DZHOKHAR GAPON

DZHOKHAR

DZHOKHAR G

THIS PLANE HAS VEERED FAR OFF COURSE AND IS LOSING ALTITUDE.

IT IS NOT RESPONDING TO THE CONTROL TOWER.

I'D BETTER PUT OUT A GENERAL ALERT--

THAT WILL NOT BE NECESSARY.

I BELIEVE THE DISTRESS CALL--THE SUMMONS--WAS INTENDED FOR ONE MAN.

ME.

--?!?

-- YOU--?

YES.

DZHOKHAR GAPON'S PRESENCE IS PROOF OF THAT.

BUT--

I WILL EXPLAIN EN ROUTE. FOR NOW--

--WE MUST HURRY TO THE QUINJET HANGAR.

"...FALCON..." BOY I WOULD'VE NEVER HEARD THE END OF THAT ONE!

21

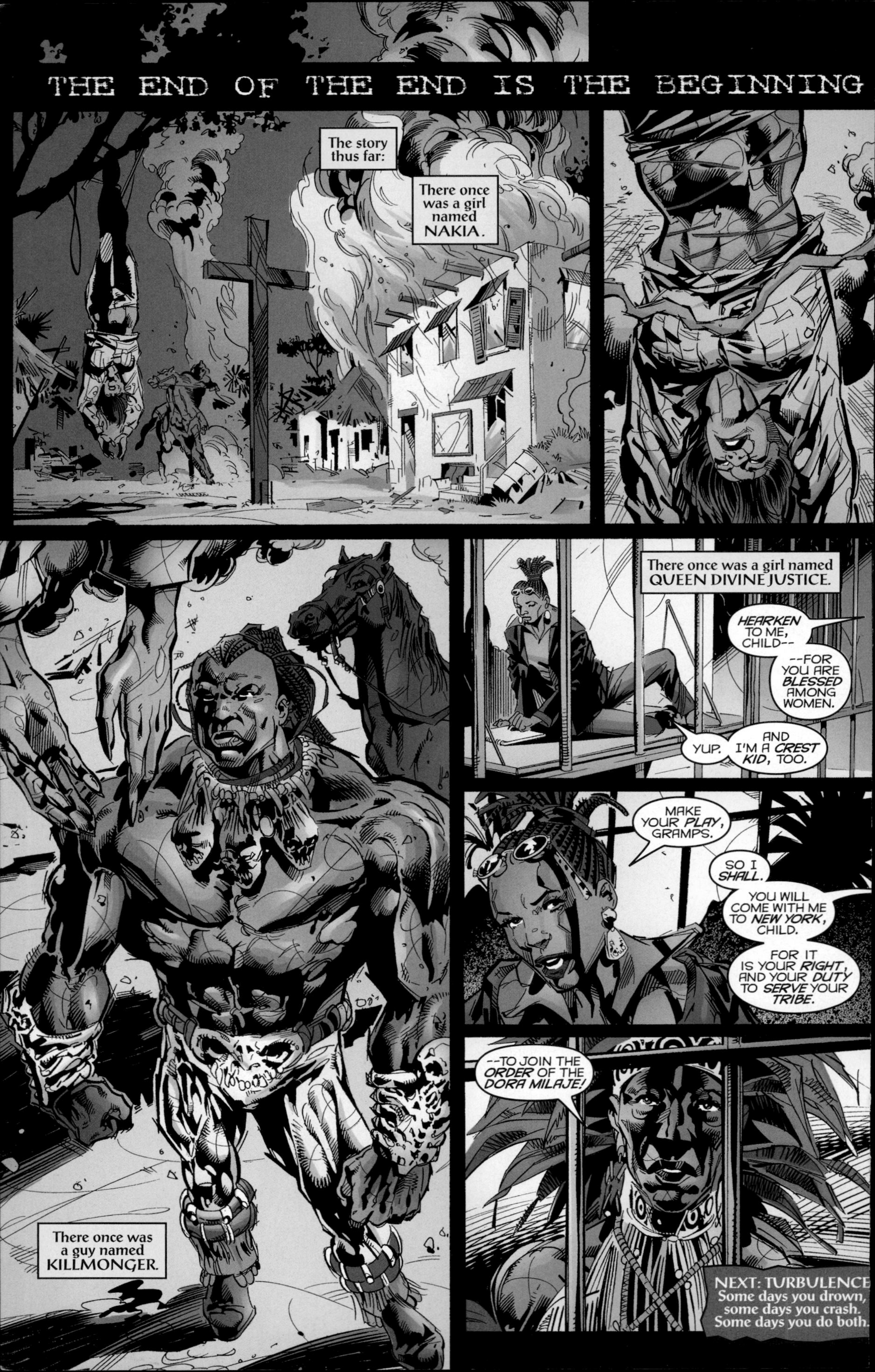
THE END OF THE END IS THE BEGINNING
The story thus far:
There once was a girl named NAKIA.
There once was a guy named KILLMONGER.
There once was a girl named QUEEN DIVINE JUSTICE.
HEARKEN TO ME, CHILD--
--FOR YOU ARE BLESSED AMONG WOMEN.
YUP.
AND I'M A CREST KID, TOO.
MAKE YOUR PLAY, GRAMPS.
SO I SHALL.
YOU WILL COME WITH ME TO NEW YORK, CHILD.
FOR IT IS YOUR RIGHT, AND YOUR DUTY TO SERVE YOUR TRIBE.
--TO JOIN THE ORDER OF THE DORA MILAJE!
NEXT: TURBULENCE
Some days you drown, some days you crash. Some days you do both.

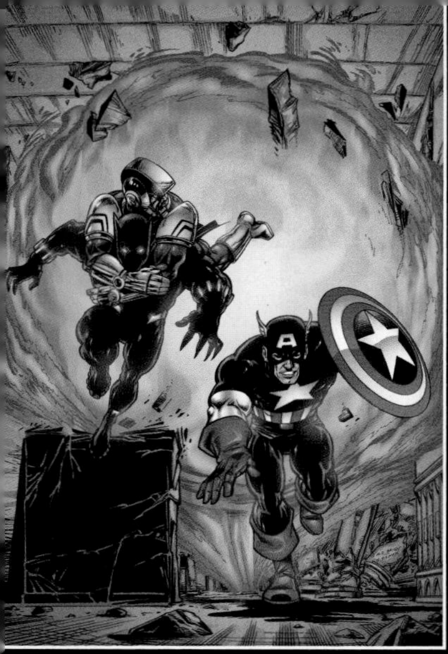
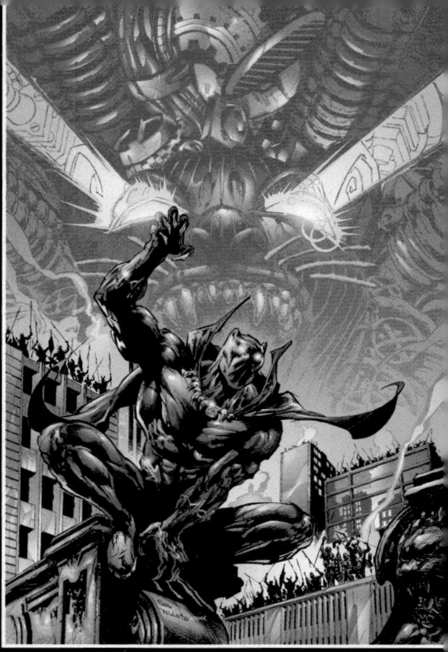
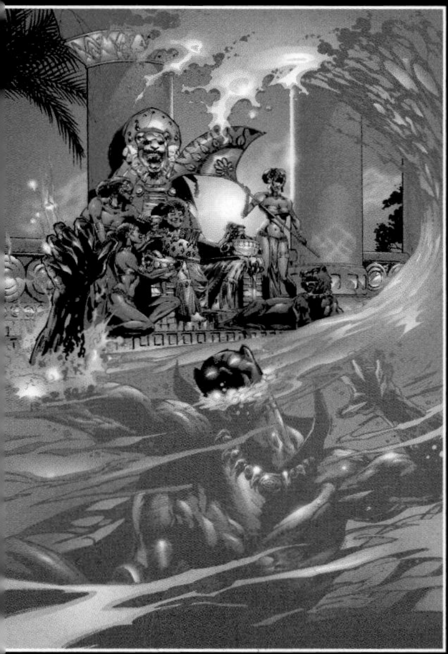
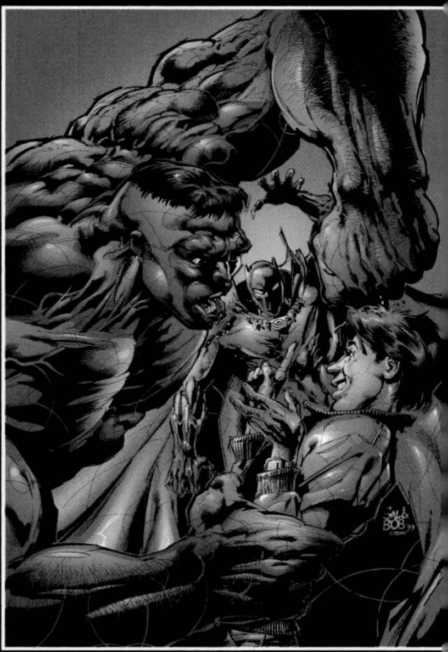
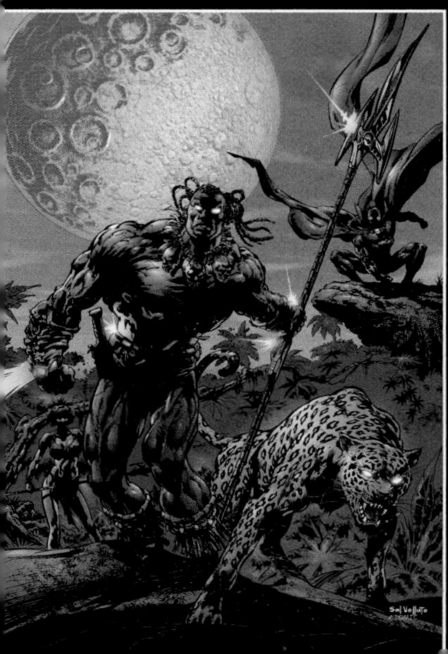
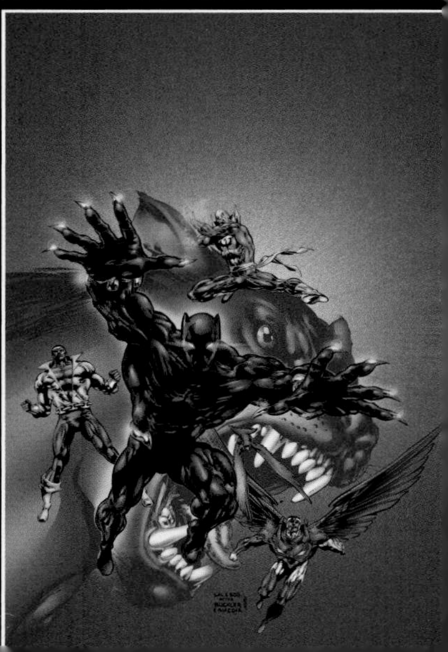

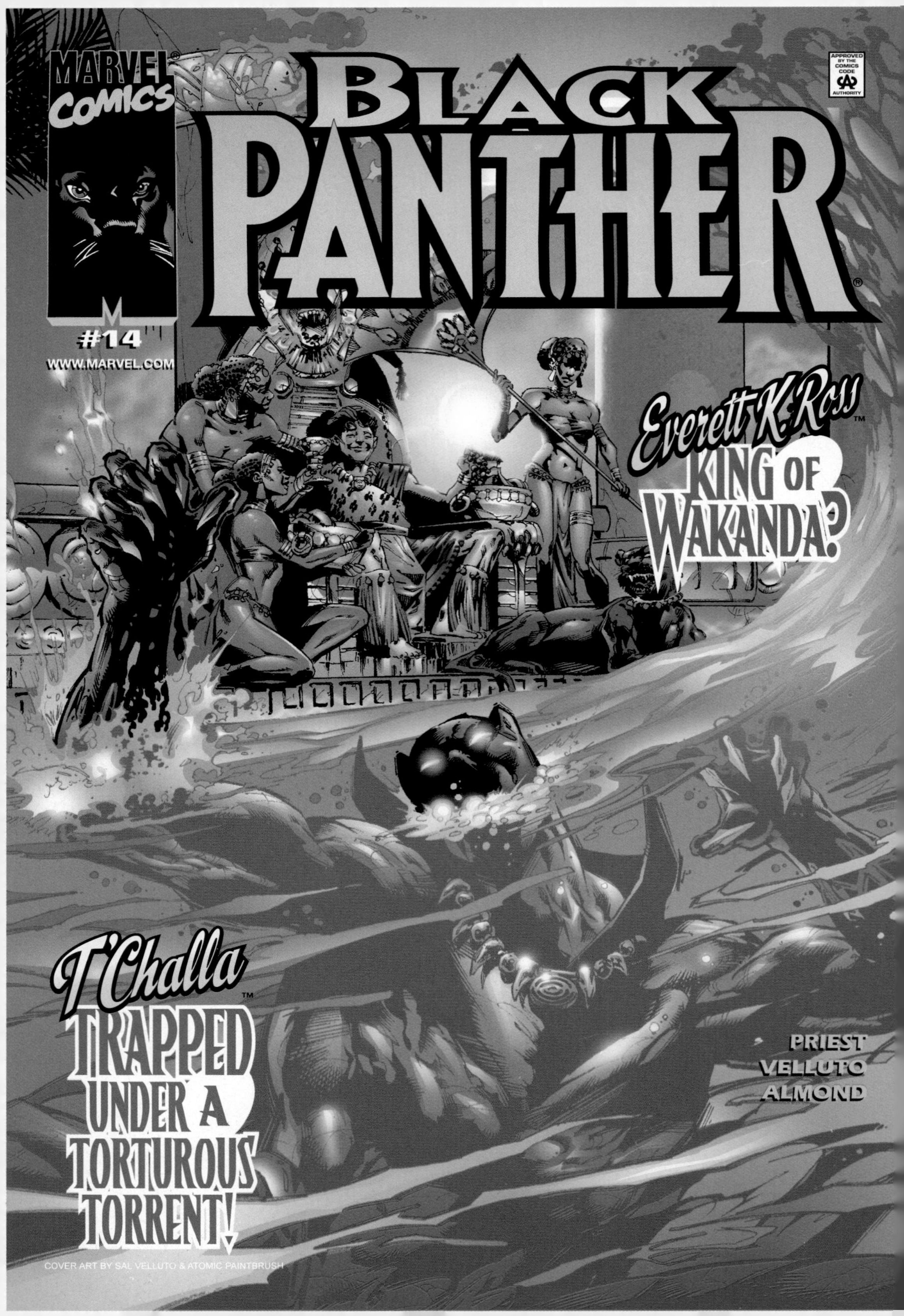
MARVEL COMICS
BLACK PANTHER
#14
WWW.MARVEL.COM
Everett K. Ross
KING OF WAKANDA?
T'Challa
TRAPPED UNDER A TORTUROUS TORRENT!
PRIEST
VELLUTO
ALMOND
COVER ART BY SAL VELLUTO & ATOMIC PAINTBRUSH

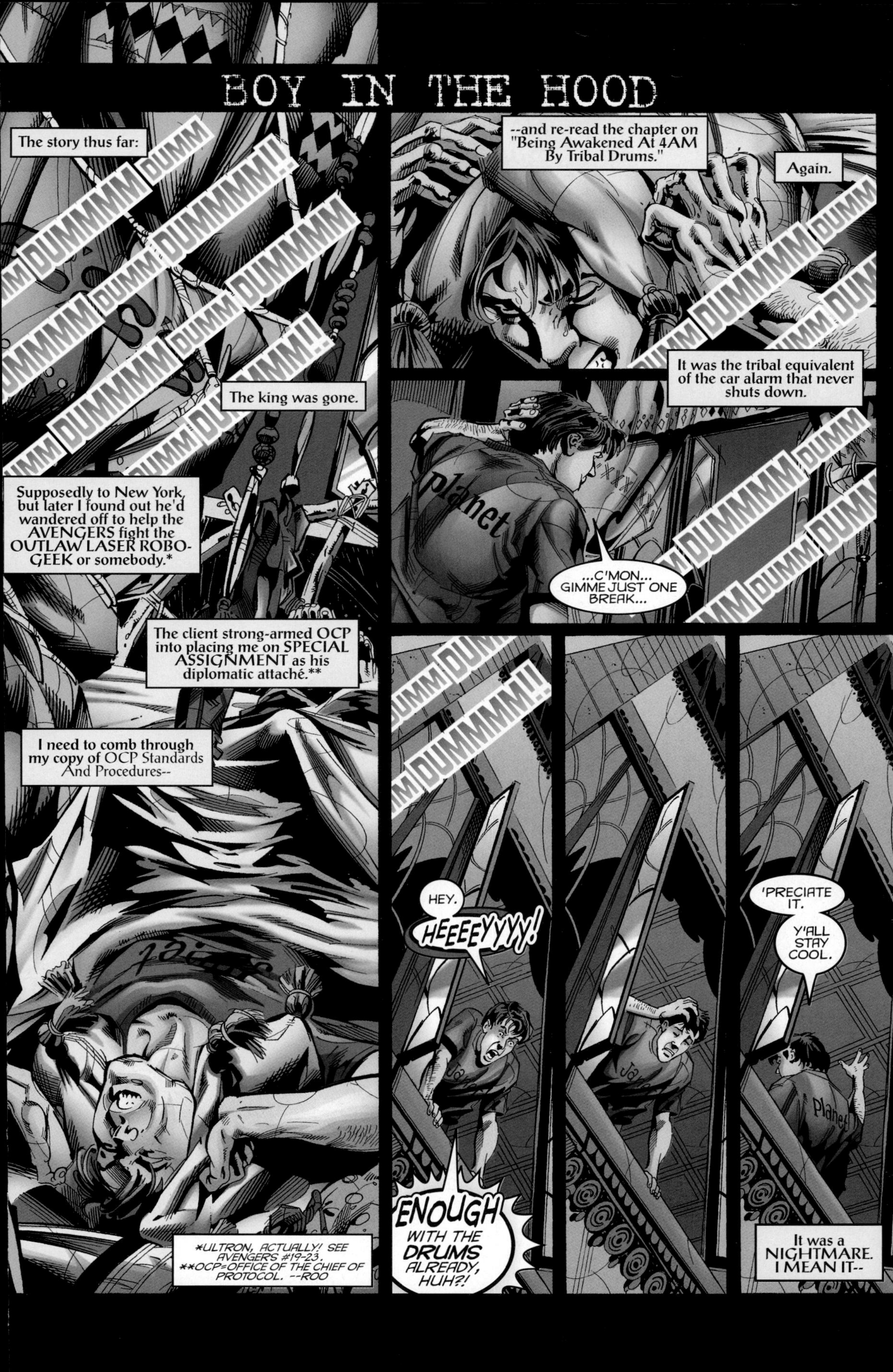
BOY IN THE HOOD
The story thus far:
DUMMM DUMM DUMMMM DUMMMM!! DUMMMM DUMM DUMMMMM
The king was gone.
Supposedly to New York, but later I found out he'd wandered off to help the AVENGERS fight the OUTLAW LASER ROBO-GEEK or somebody.*
The client strong-armed OCP into placing me on SPECIAL ASSIGNMENT as his diplomatic attaché.**
I need to comb through my copy of OCP Standards And Procedures--
*ULTRON, ACTUALLY! SEE AVENGERS #19-23.
**OCP=OFFICE OF THE CHIEF OF PROTOCOL. --ROO
--and re-read the chapter on "Being Awakened At 4AM By Tribal Drums."
Again.
It was the tribal equivalent of the car alarm that never shuts down.
...C'MON... GIMME JUST ONE BREAK...
DUMM DUMMMM!!
HEY.
HEEEEYYYY!
ENOUGH WITH THE DRUMS ALREADY, HUH?!
'PRECIATE IT.
Y'ALL STAY COOL.
It was a NIGHTMARE. I MEAN IT--

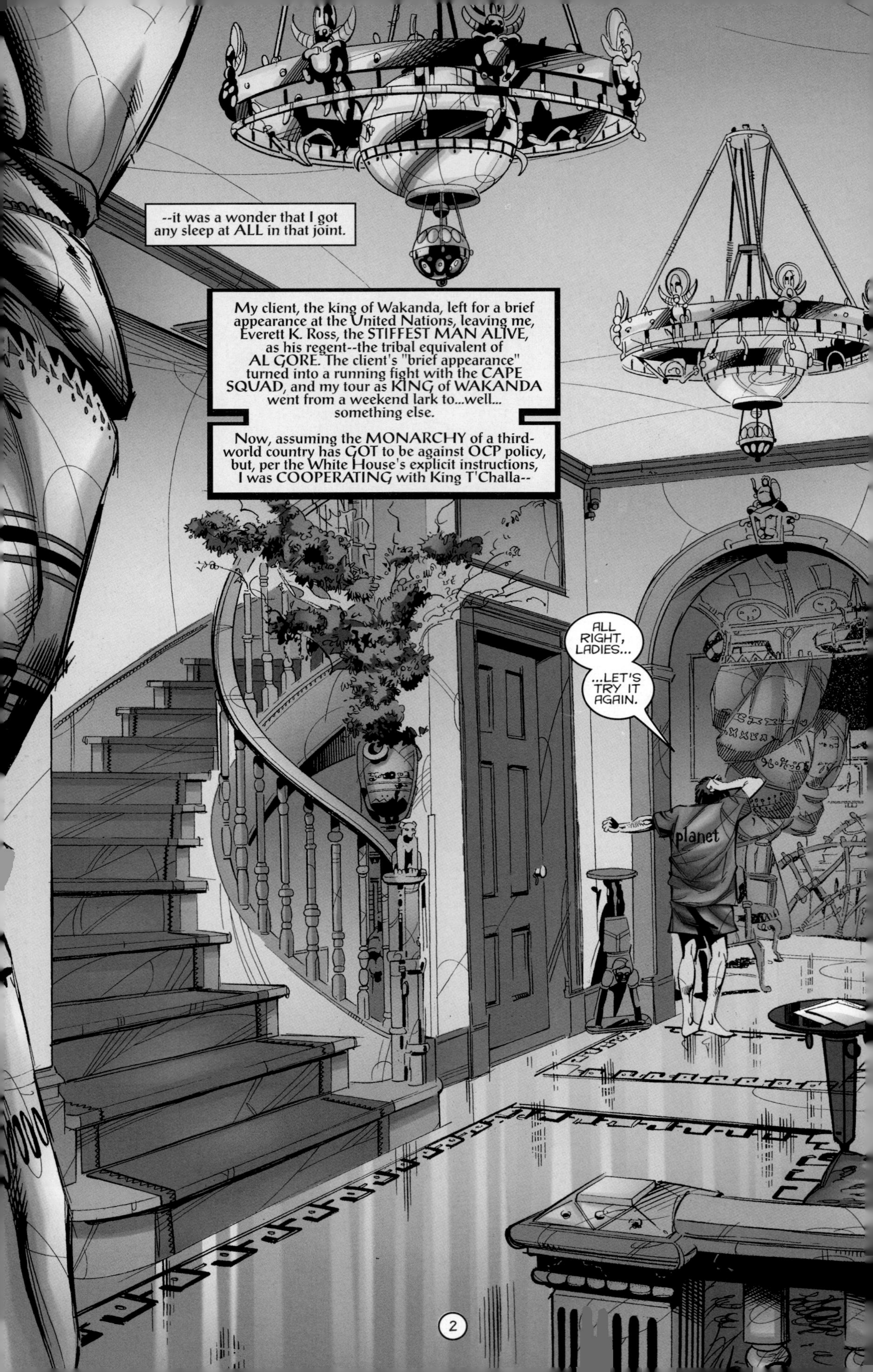
--it was a wonder that I got any sleep at ALL in that joint.
My client, the king of Wakanda, left for a brief appearance at the United Nations, leaving me, Everett K. Ross, the STIFFEST MAN ALIVE, as his regent--the tribal equivalent of AL GORE. The client's "brief appearance" turned into a running fight with the CAPE SQUAD, and my tour as KING of WAKANDA went from a weekend lark to...well... something else.
Now, assuming the MONARCHY of a third-world country has GOT to be against OCP policy, but, per the White House's explicit instructions, I was COOPERATING with King T'Challa--
ALL RIGHT, LADIES...
...LET'S TRY IT AGAIN.
planet

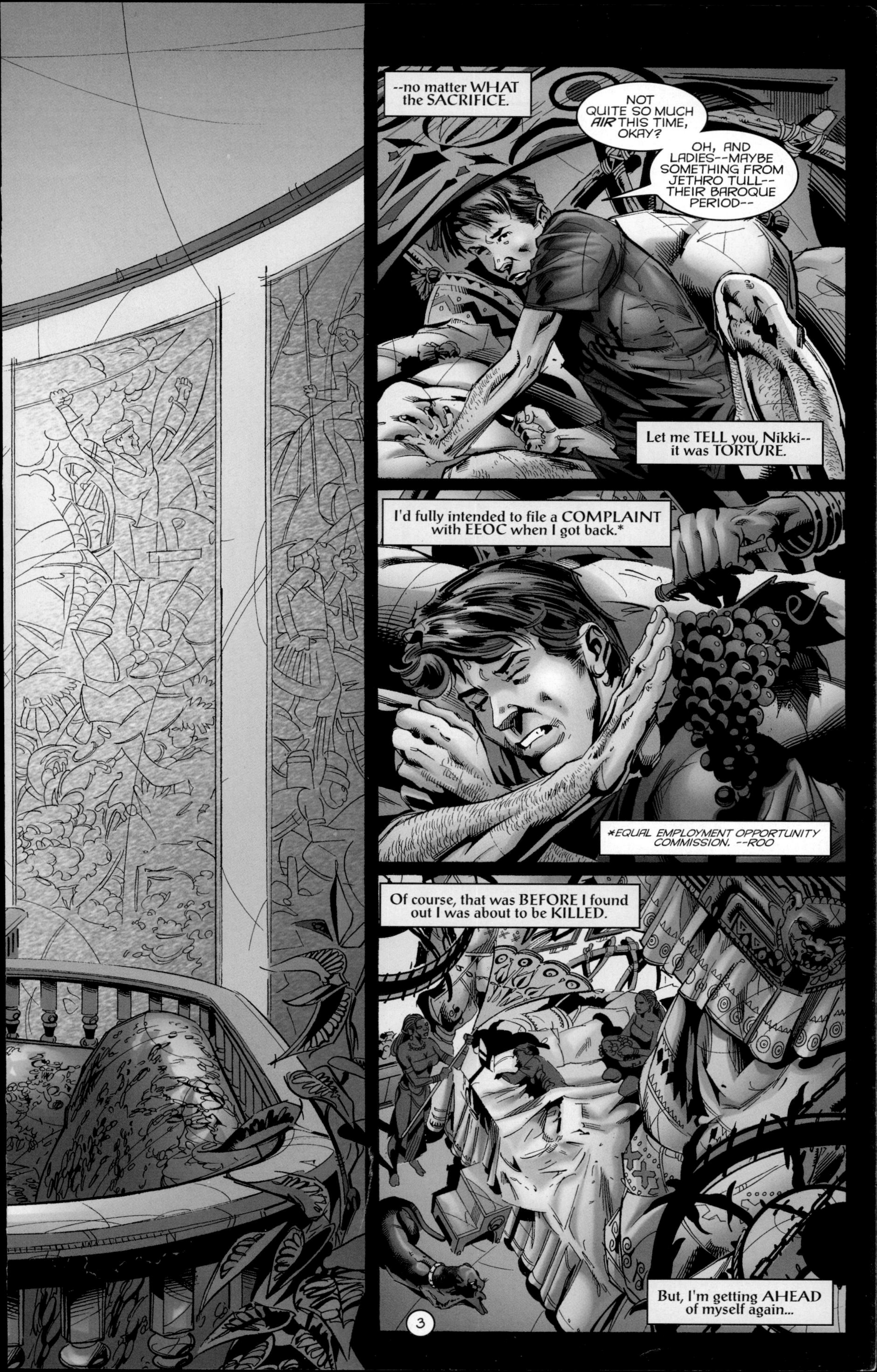
--no matter WHAT the SACRIFICE.
NOT QUITE SO MUCH AIR THIS TIME, OKAY?
OH, AND LADIES--MAYBE SOMETHING FROM JETHRO TULL--THEIR BAROQUE PERIOD--
Let me TELL you, Nikki--it was TORTURE.
I'd fully intended to file a COMPLAINT with EEOC when I got back.*
*EQUAL EMPLOYMENT OPPORTUNITY COMMISSION. --ROO
Of course, that was BEFORE I found out I was about to be KILLED.
But, I'm getting AHEAD of myself again...

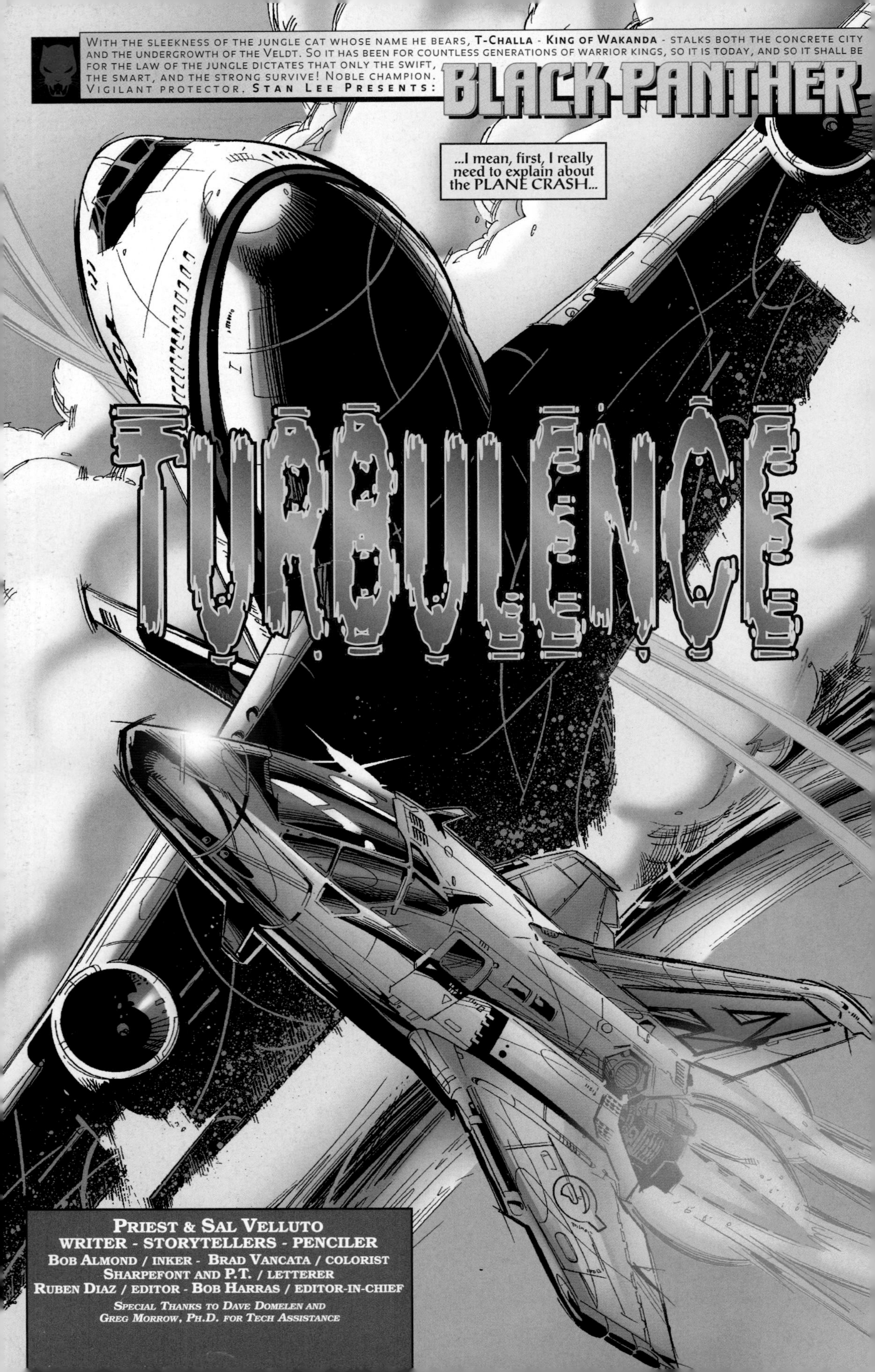

With the sleekness of the jungle cat whose name he bears, T-Challa - King of Wakanda - stalks both the concrete city and the undergrowth of the Veldt. So it has been for countless generations of warrior kings, so it is today, and so it shall be for the law of the jungle dictates that only the swift, the smart, and the strong survive! Noble champion. Vigilant protector. Stan Lee Presents:
BLACK PANTHER
...I mean, first, I really need to explain about the PLANE CRASH...
TURBULENCE
Priest & Sal Velluto
Writer - Storytellers - Penciler
Bob Almond / inker - Brad Vancata / colorist
Sharpefont and P.T. / letterer
Ruben Diaz / editor - Bob Harras / editor-in-chief
Special Thanks to Dave Domelen and Greg Morrow, Ph.D. for Tech Assistance

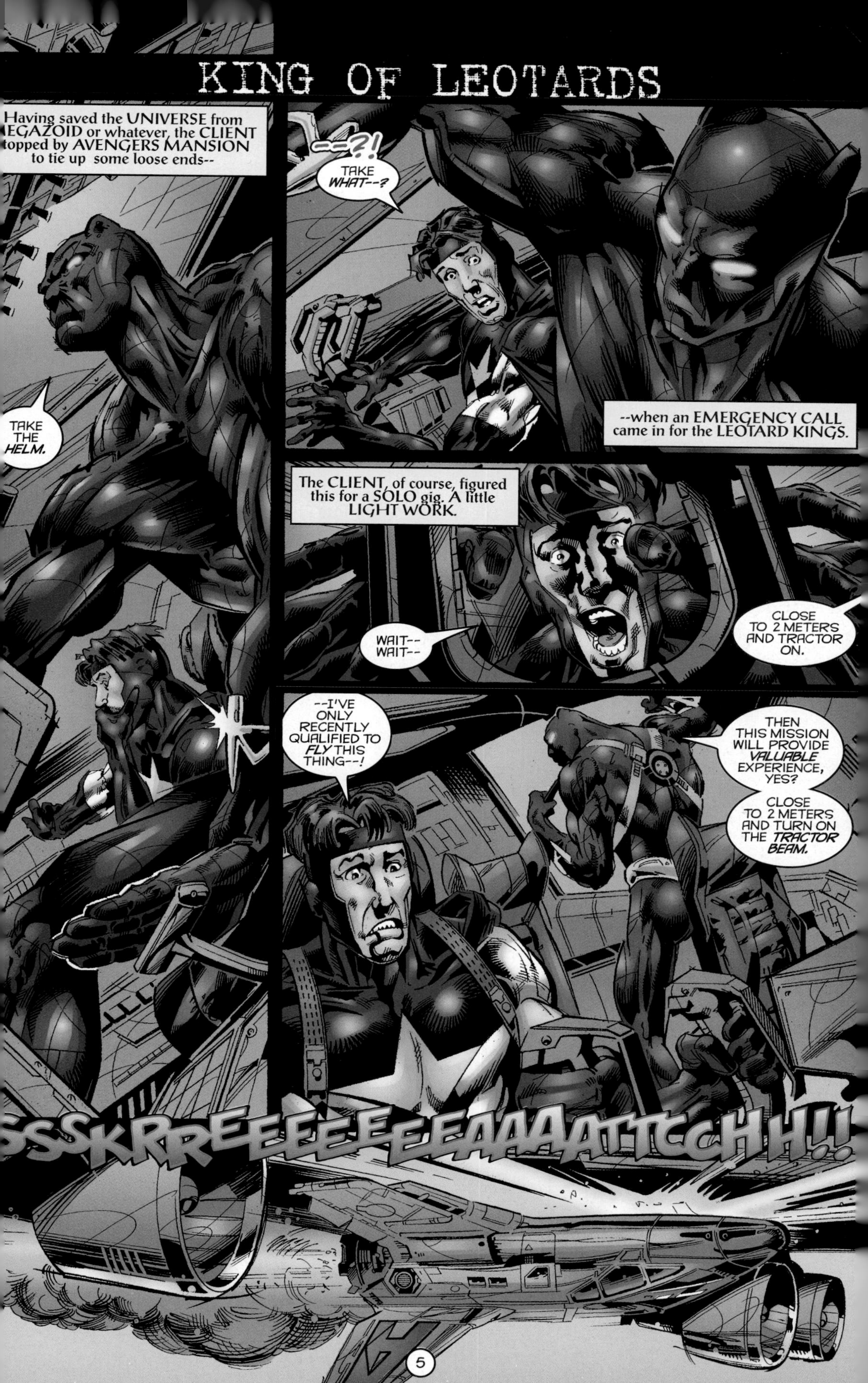

KING OF LEOTARDS
Having saved the UNIVERSE from MEGAZOID or whatever, the CLIENT stopped by AVENGERS MANSION to tie up some loose ends--
TAKE THE HELM.
--?!
TAKE WHAT--?
--when an EMERGENCY CALL came in for the LEOTARD KINGS.
The CLIENT, of course, figured this for a SOLO gig. A little LIGHT WORK.
WAIT-- WAIT--
CLOSE TO 2 METERS AND TRACTOR ON.
--I'VE ONLY RECENTLY QUALIFIED TO FLY THIS THING--!
THEN THIS MISSION WILL PROVIDE VALUABLE EXPERIENCE, YES?
CLOSE TO 2 METERS AND TURN ON THE TRACTOR BEAM.
SSKRREEEEEEEAAAATTCCHH!!

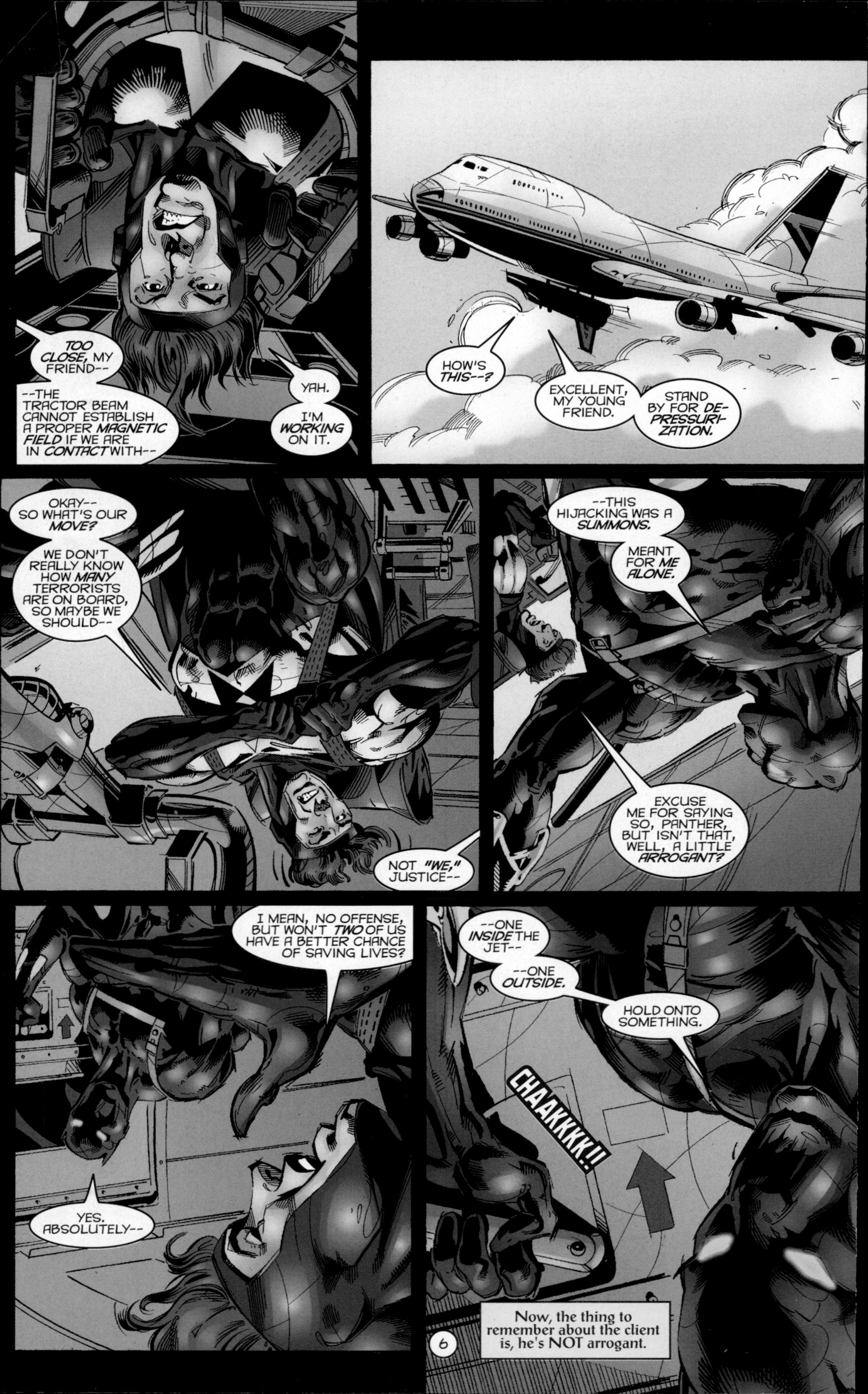
TOO CLOSE, MY FRIEND--
--THE TRACTOR BEAM CANNOT ESTABLISH A PROPER MAGNETIC FIELD IF WE ARE IN CONTACT WITH--
YAH.
I'M WORKING ON IT.
HOW'S THIS--?
EXCELLENT, MY YOUNG FRIEND.
STAND BY FOR DE-PRESSURI-ZATION.
OKAY-- SO WHAT'S OUR MOVE?
WE DON'T REALLY KNOW HOW MANY TERRORISTS ARE ON BOARD, SO MAYBE WE SHOULD--
NOT "WE," JUSTICE--
--THIS HIJACKING WAS A SUMMONS.
MEANT FOR ME ALONE.
EXCUSE ME FOR SAYING SO, PANTHER, BUT ISN'T THAT, WELL, A LITTLE ARROGANT?
I MEAN, NO OFFENSE, BUT WON'T TWO OF US HAVE A BETTER CHANCE OF SAVING LIVES?
YES. ABSOLUTELY--
--ONE INSIDE THE JET--
--ONE OUTSIDE.
HOLD ONTO SOMETHING.
CHAAKKKK!!
Now, the thing to remember about the client is, he's NOT arrogant.
6

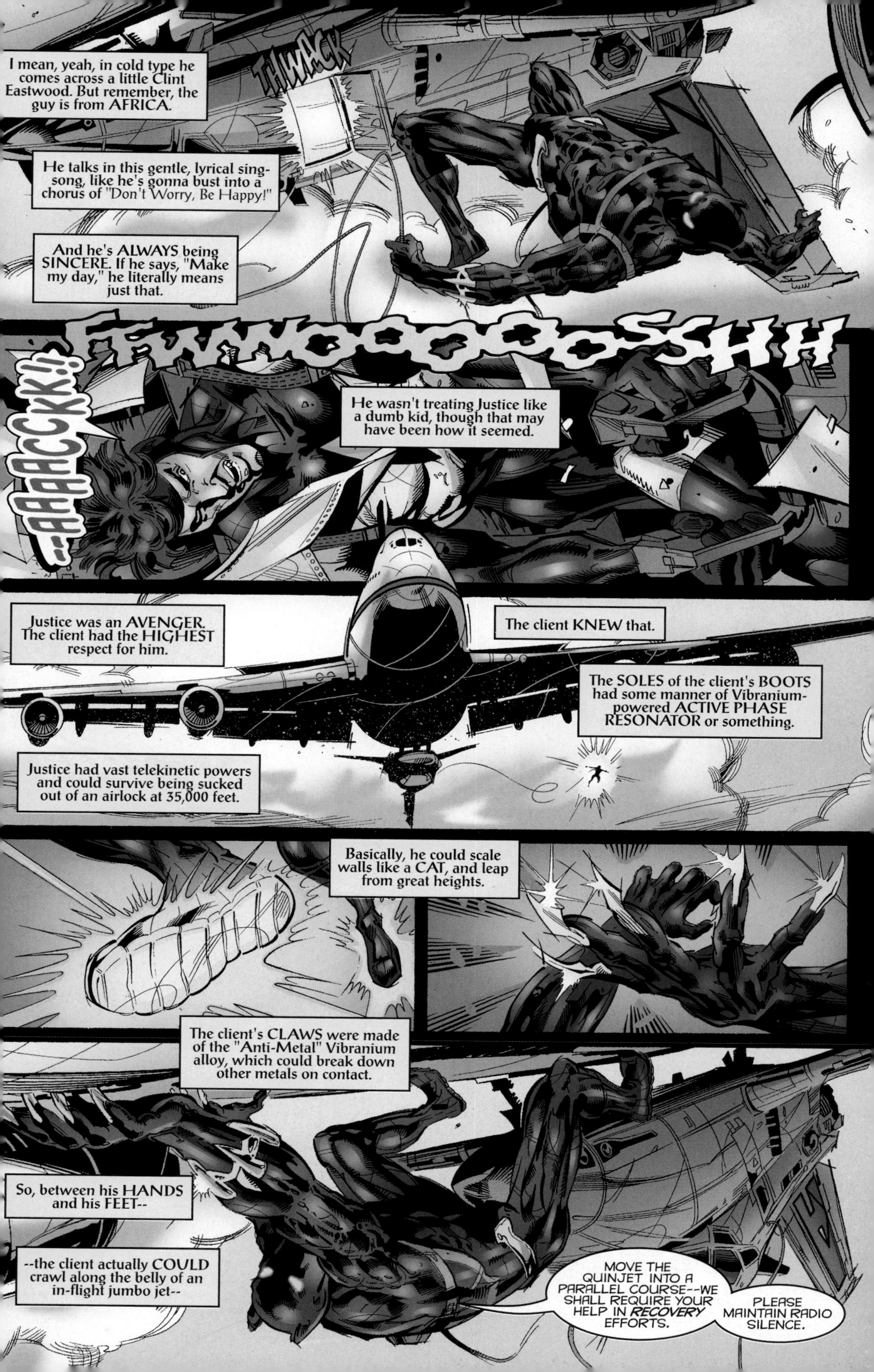
I mean, yeah, in cold type he comes across a little Clint Eastwood. But remember, the guy is from AFRICA.
THWACK
He talks in this gentle, lyrical sing-song, like he's gonna bust into a chorus of "Don't Worry, Be Happy!"
And he's ALWAYS being SINCERE. If he says, "Make my day," he literally means just that.
FFWWOOOOOSSHH
--AAAACKK!!
He wasn't treating Justice like a dumb kid, though that may have been how it seemed.
Justice was an AVENGER. The client had the HIGHEST respect for him.
The client KNEW that.
The SOLES of the client's BOOTS had some manner of Vibranium-powered ACTIVE PHASE RESONATOR or something.
Justice had vast telekinetic powers and could survive being sucked out of an airlock at 35,000 feet.
Basically, he could scale walls like a CAT, and leap from great heights.
The client's CLAWS were made of the "Anti-Metal" Vibranium alloy, which could break down other metals on contact.
So, between his HANDS and his FEET--
--the client actually COULD crawl along the belly of an in-flight jumbo jet--
MOVE THE QUINJET INTO A PARALLEL COURSE--WE SHALL REQUIRE YOUR HELP IN *RECOVERY* EFFORTS.
PLEASE MAINTAIN RADIO SILENCE.

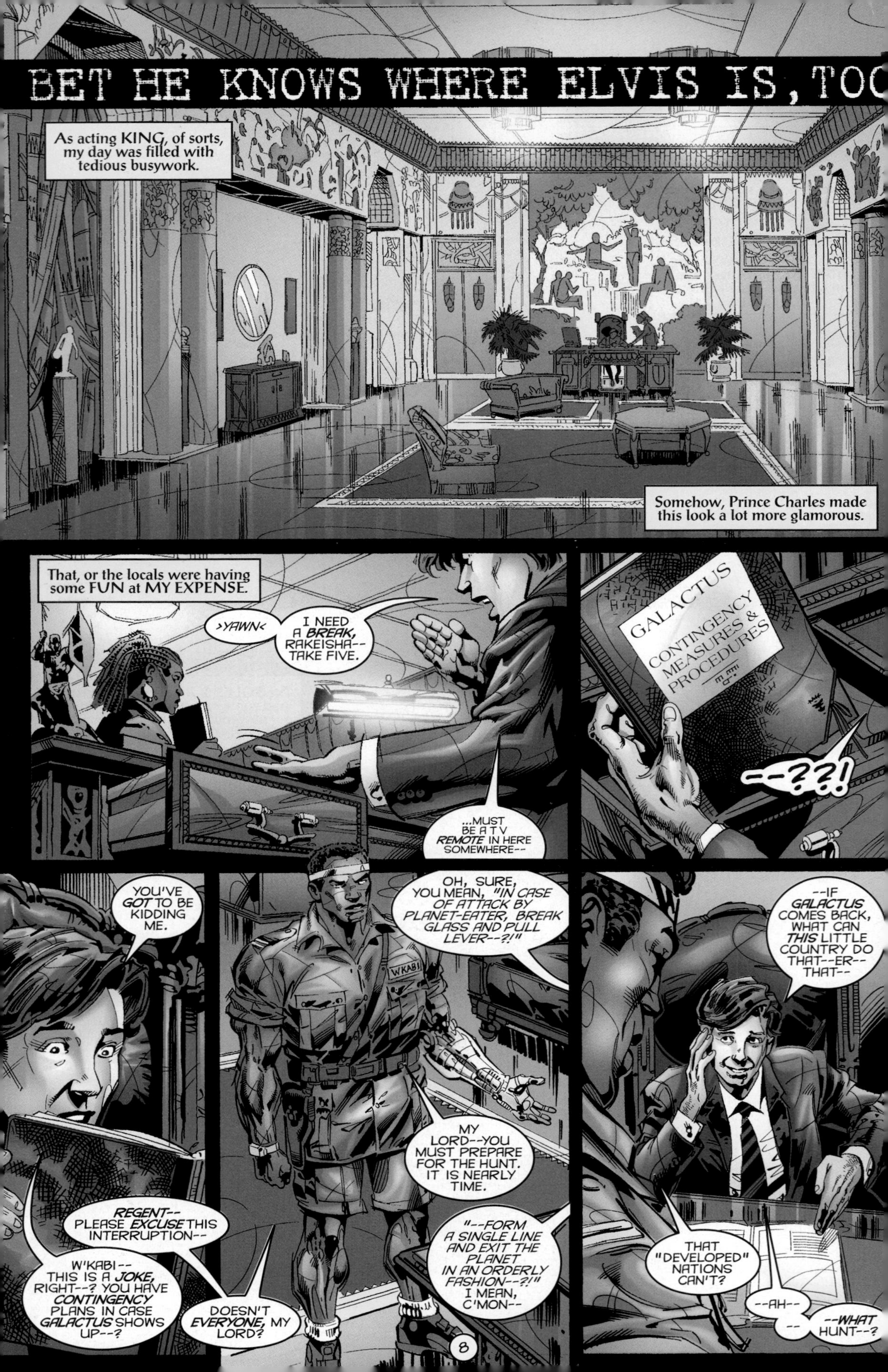
BET HE KNOWS WHERE ELVIS IS, TOO
As acting KING, of sorts, my day was filled with tedious busywork.
Somehow, Prince Charles made this look a lot more glamorous.
That, or the locals were having some FUN at MY EXPENSE.
>YAWN<
I NEED A BREAK, RAKEISHA-- TAKE FIVE.
...MUST BE A TV REMOTE IN HERE SOMEWHERE--
GALACTUS
CONTINGENCY MEASURES & PROCEDURES
--??!
YOU'VE GOT TO BE KIDDING ME.
OH, SURE, YOU MEAN, "IN CASE OF ATTACK BY PLANET-EATER, BREAK GLASS AND PULL LEVER--?!"
W'KABI
MY LORD--YOU MUST PREPARE FOR THE HUNT. IT IS NEARLY TIME.
REGENT-- PLEASE EXCUSE THIS INTERRUPTION--
W'KABI-- THIS IS A JOKE, RIGHT--? YOU HAVE CONTINGENCY PLANS IN CASE GALACTUS SHOWS UP--?
DOESN'T EVERYONE, MY LORD?
"--FORM A SINGLE LINE AND EXIT THE PLANET IN AN ORDERLY FASHION--?!" I MEAN, C'MON--
--IF GALACTUS COMES BACK, WHAT CAN THIS LITTLE COUNTRY DO THAT--ER-- THAT--
THAT "DEVELOPED" NATIONS CAN'T?
--AH--
-- --WHAT HUNT--?

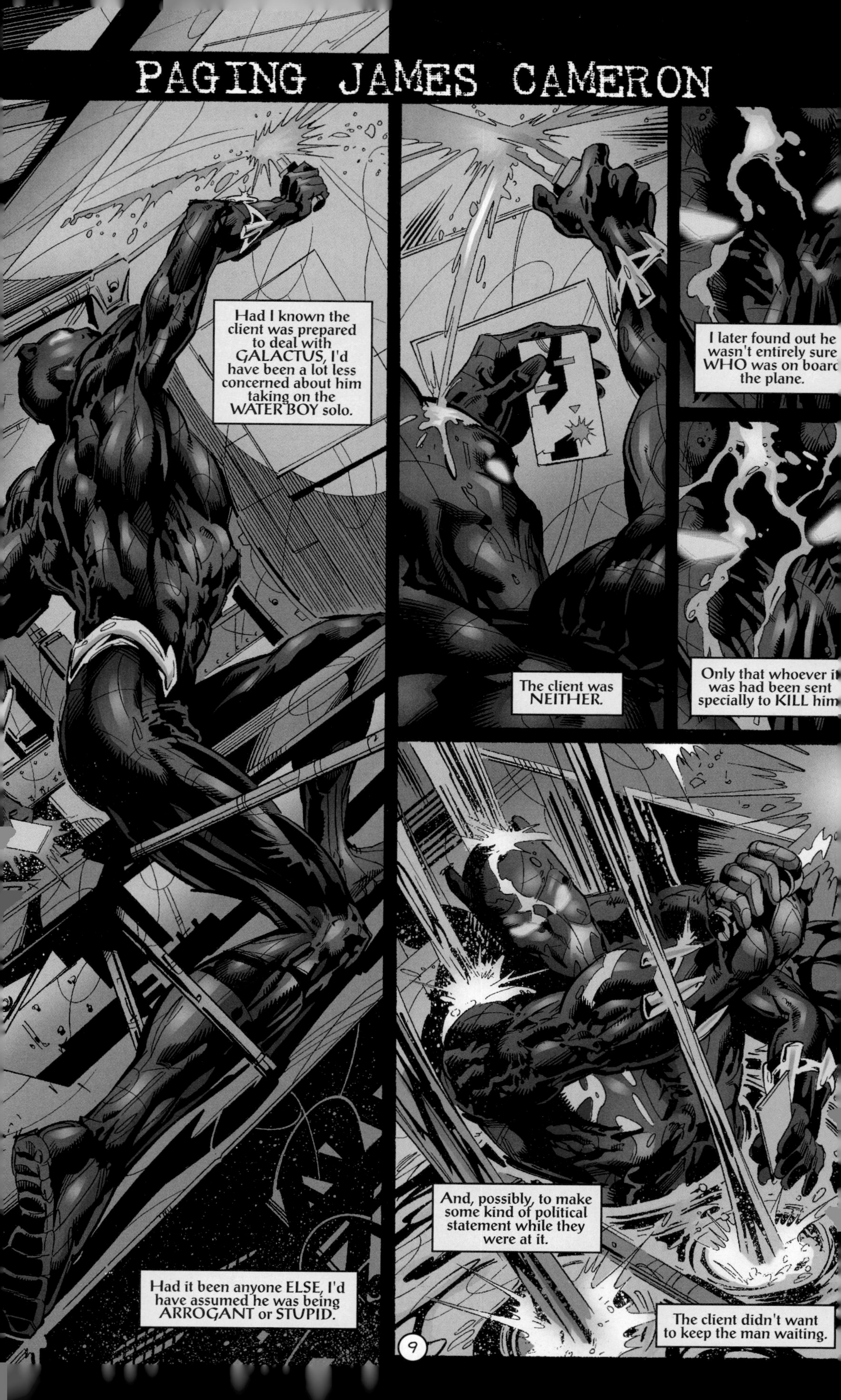

PAGING JAMES CAMERON
Had I known the client was prepared to deal with GALACTUS, I'd have been a lot less concerned about him taking on the WATER BOY solo.
Had it been anyone ELSE, I'd have assumed he was being ARROGANT or STUPID.
The client was NEITHER.
I later found out he wasn't entirely sure WHO was on board the plane.
Only that whoever it was had been sent specially to KILL him
And, possibly, to make some kind of political statement while they were at it.
The client didn't want to keep the man waiting.

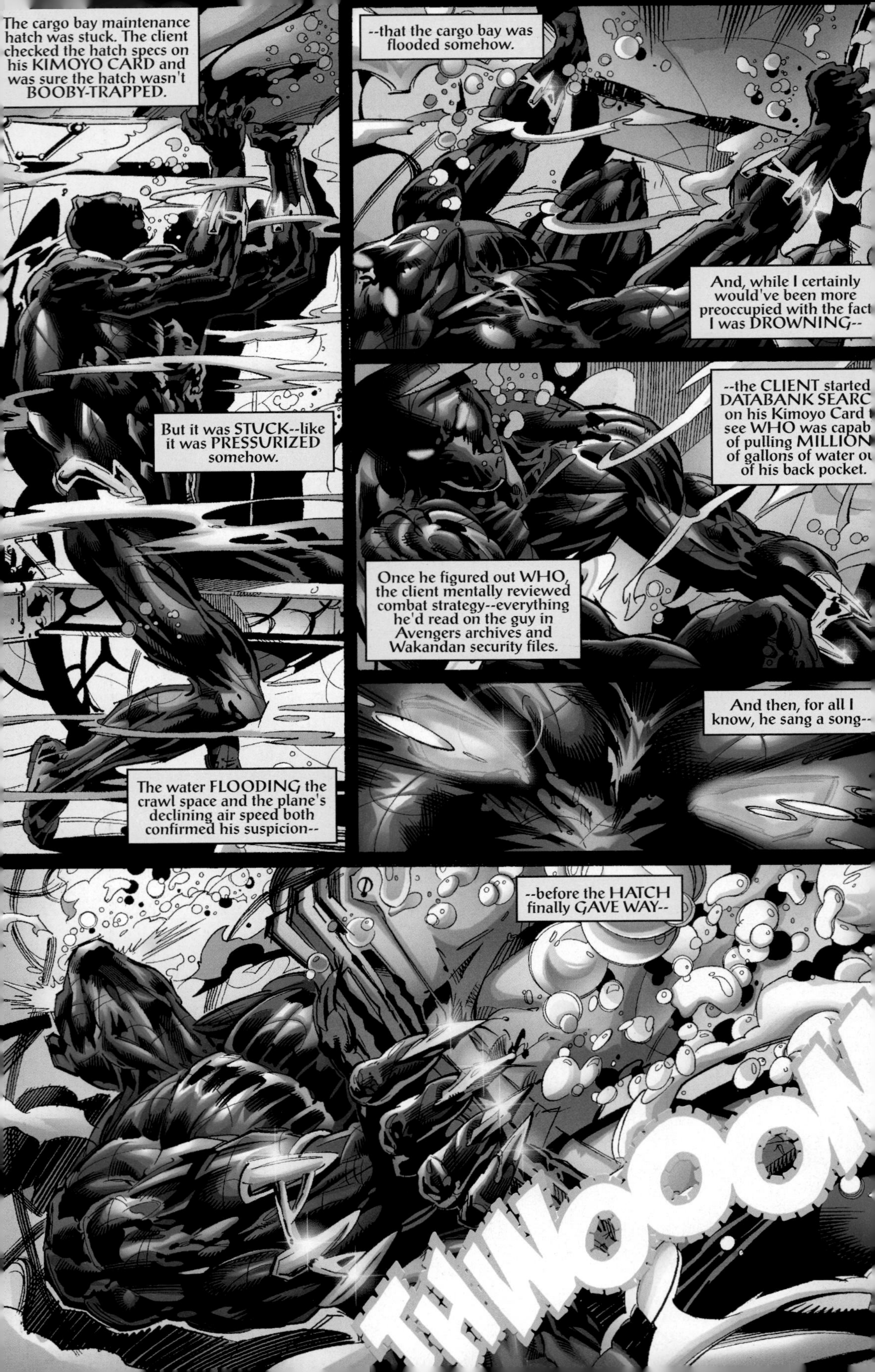
The cargo bay maintenance hatch was stuck. The client checked the hatch specs on his KIMOYO CARD and was sure the hatch wasn't BOOBY-TRAPPED.
But it was STUCK--like it was PRESSURIZED somehow.
The water FLOODING the crawl space and the plane's declining air speed both confirmed his suspicion--
--that the cargo bay was flooded somehow.
And, while I certainly would've been more preoccupied with the fact I was DROWNING--
--the CLIENT started DATABANK SEARC on his Kimoyo Card see WHO was capab of pulling MILLION of gallons of water ou of his back pocket.
Once he figured out WHO, the client mentally reviewed combat strategy--everything he'd read on the guy in Avengers archives and Wakandan security files.
And then, for all I know, he sang a song--
--before the HATCH finally GAVE WAY--
THWOOOOM

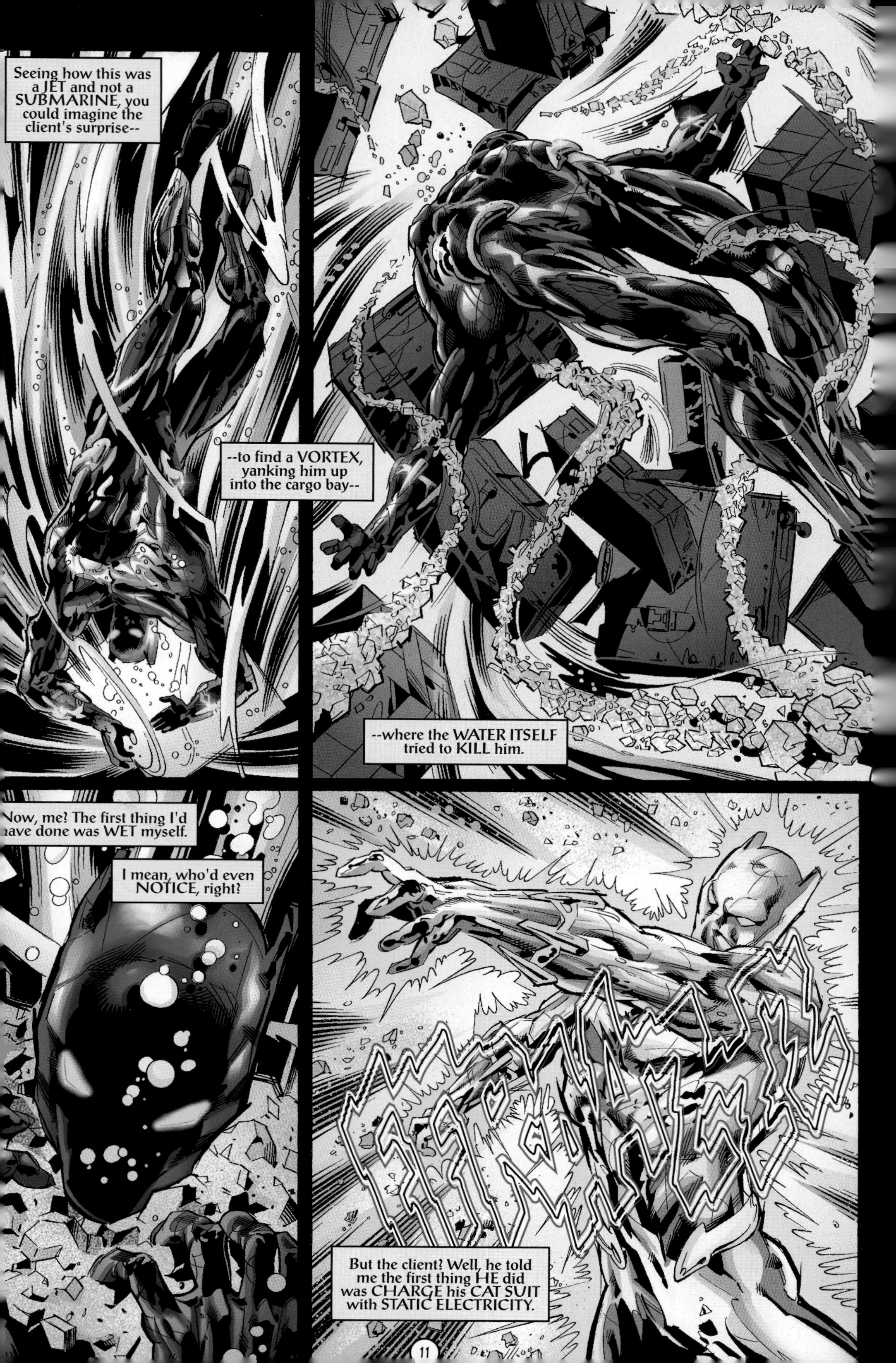

Seeing how this was a JET and not a SUBMARINE, you could imagine the client's surprise--
--to find a VORTEX, yanking him up into the cargo bay--
--where the WATER ITSELF tried to KILL him.
Now, me? The first thing I'd have done was WET myself.
I mean, who'd even NOTICE, right?
But the client? Well, he told me the first thing HE did was CHARGE his CAT SUIT with STATIC ELECTRICITY.

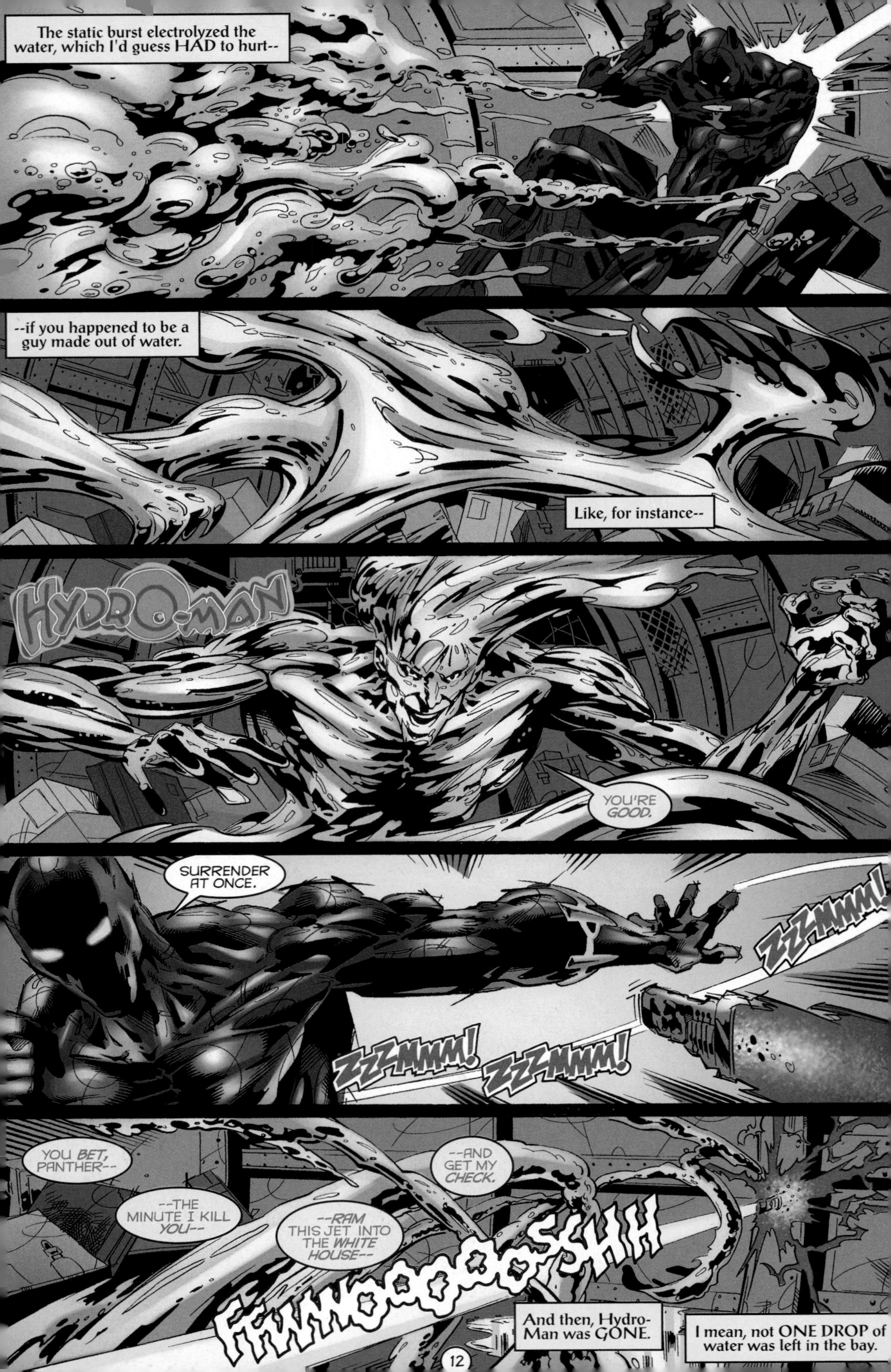
The static burst electrolyzed the water, which I'd guess HAD to hurt--
--if you happened to be a guy made out of water.
Like, for instance--
HYDRO-MAN
YOU'RE GOOD.
SURRENDER AT ONCE.
ZZZMMM!
ZZZMMM!
ZZZMMM!
YOU BET, PANTHER--
--THE MINUTE I KILL YOU--
--RAM THIS JET INTO THE WHITE HOUSE--
--AND GET MY CHECK.
FFWWOOOOOOSSHH
And then, Hydro-Man was GONE.
I mean, not ONE DROP of water was left in the bay.

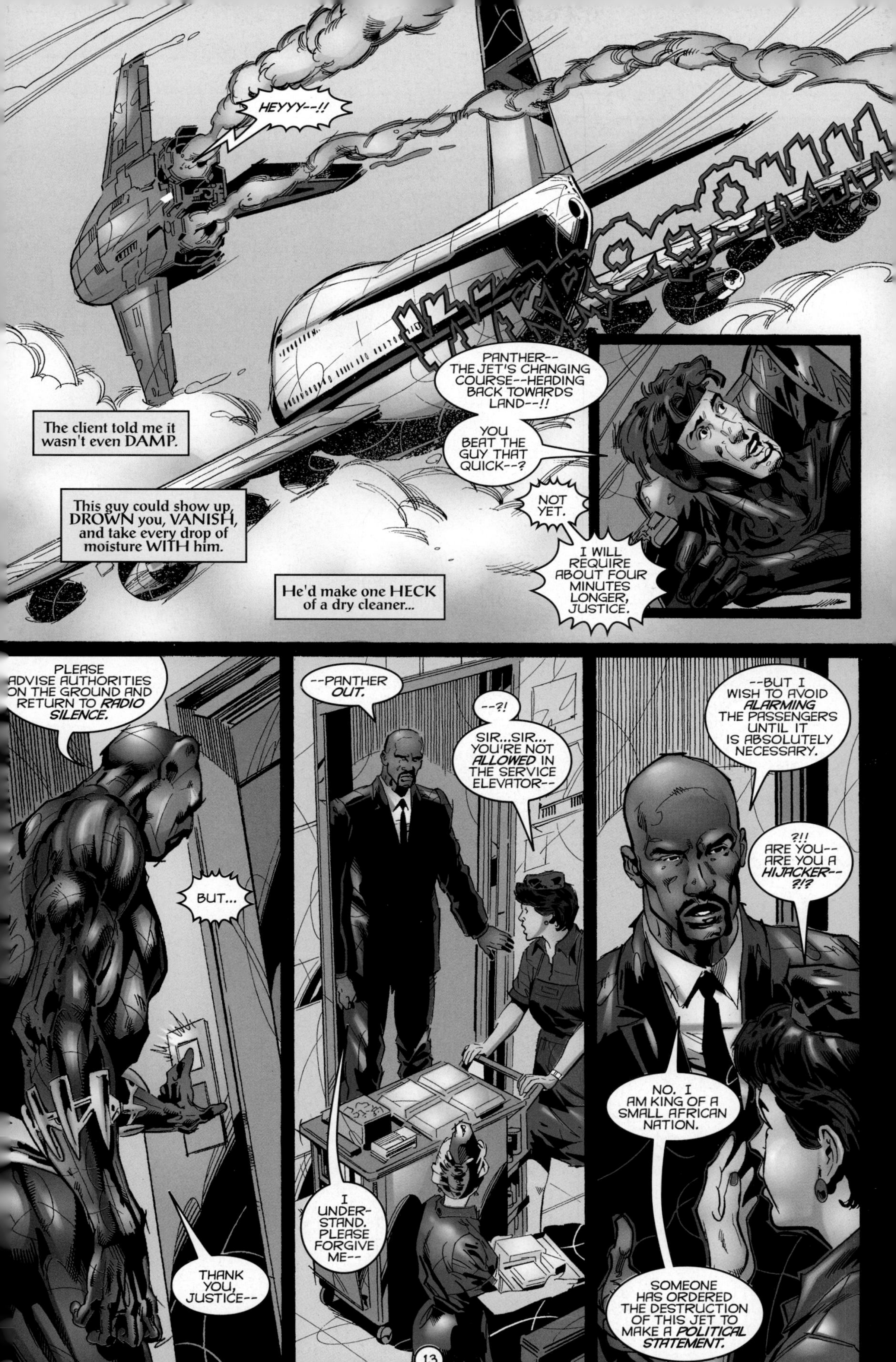
HEYYY--!!
PANTHER-- THE JET'S CHANGING COURSE--HEADING BACK TOWARDS LAND--!!
YOU BEAT THE GUY THAT QUICK--?
NOT YET.
I WILL REQUIRE ABOUT FOUR MINUTES LONGER, JUSTICE.
The client told me it wasn't even DAMP.
This guy could show up, DROWN you, VANISH, and take every drop of moisture WITH him.
He'd make one HECK of a dry cleaner...
PLEASE ADVISE AUTHORITIES ON THE GROUND AND RETURN TO *RADIO SILENCE.*
BUT...
THANK YOU, JUSTICE--
--PANTHER *OUT.*
--?!
SIR...SIR... YOU'RE NOT *ALLOWED* IN THE SERVICE ELEVATOR--
I UNDER-STAND. PLEASE FORGIVE ME--
--BUT I WISH TO AVOID *ALARMING* THE PASSENGERS UNTIL IT IS ABSOLUTELY NECESSARY.
?!! ARE YOU-- ARE YOU A *HIJACKER--* ?!?
NO. I AM KING OF A SMALL AFRICAN NATION.
SOMEONE HAS ORDERED THE DESTRUCTION OF THIS JET TO MAKE A *POLITICAL STATEMENT.*

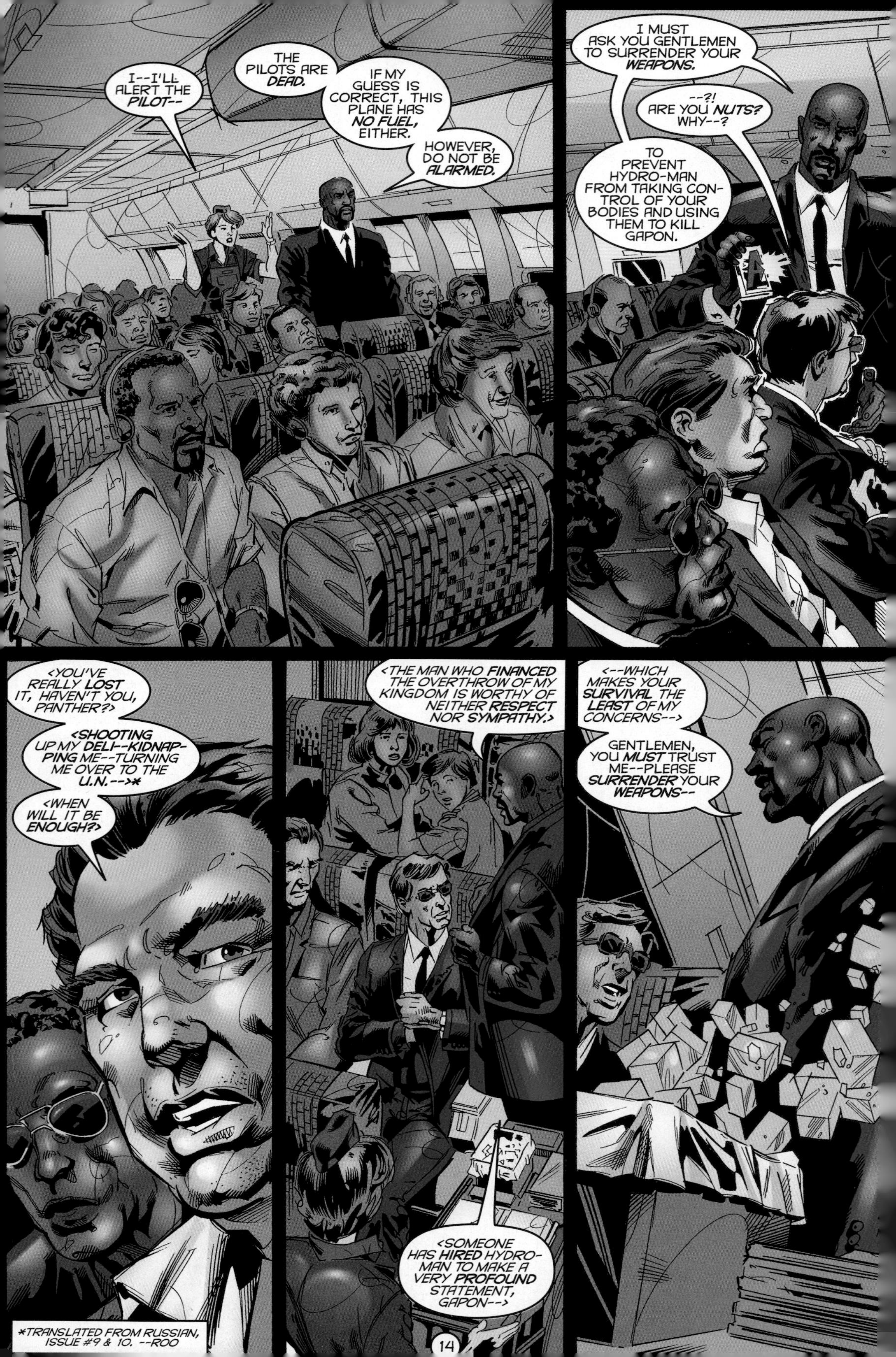
I--I'LL ALERT THE PILOT--
THE PILOTS ARE DEAD.
IF MY GUESS IS CORRECT, THIS PLANE HAS NO FUEL, EITHER.
HOWEVER, DO NOT BE ALARMED.
I MUST ASK YOU GENTLEMEN TO SURRENDER YOUR WEAPONS.
--?! ARE YOU NUTS? WHY--?
TO PREVENT HYDRO-MAN FROM TAKING CONTROL OF YOUR BODIES AND USING THEM TO KILL GAPON.
<YOU'VE REALLY LOST IT, HAVEN'T YOU, PANTHER?>
<SHOOTING UP MY DELI--KIDNAPPING ME--TURNING ME OVER TO THE U.N.-->*
<WHEN WILL IT BE ENOUGH?>
<THE MAN WHO FINANCED THE OVERTHROW OF MY KINGDOM IS WORTHY OF NEITHER RESPECT NOR SYMPATHY.>
<SOMEONE HAS HIRED HYDRO-MAN TO MAKE A VERY PROFOUND STATEMENT, GAPON-->
<--WHICH MAKES YOUR SURVIVAL THE LEAST OF MY CONCERNS-->
GENTLEMEN, YOU MUST TRUST ME--PLEASE SURRENDER YOUR WEAPONS--

*TRANSLATED FROM RUSSIAN, ISSUE #9 & 10. --ROO

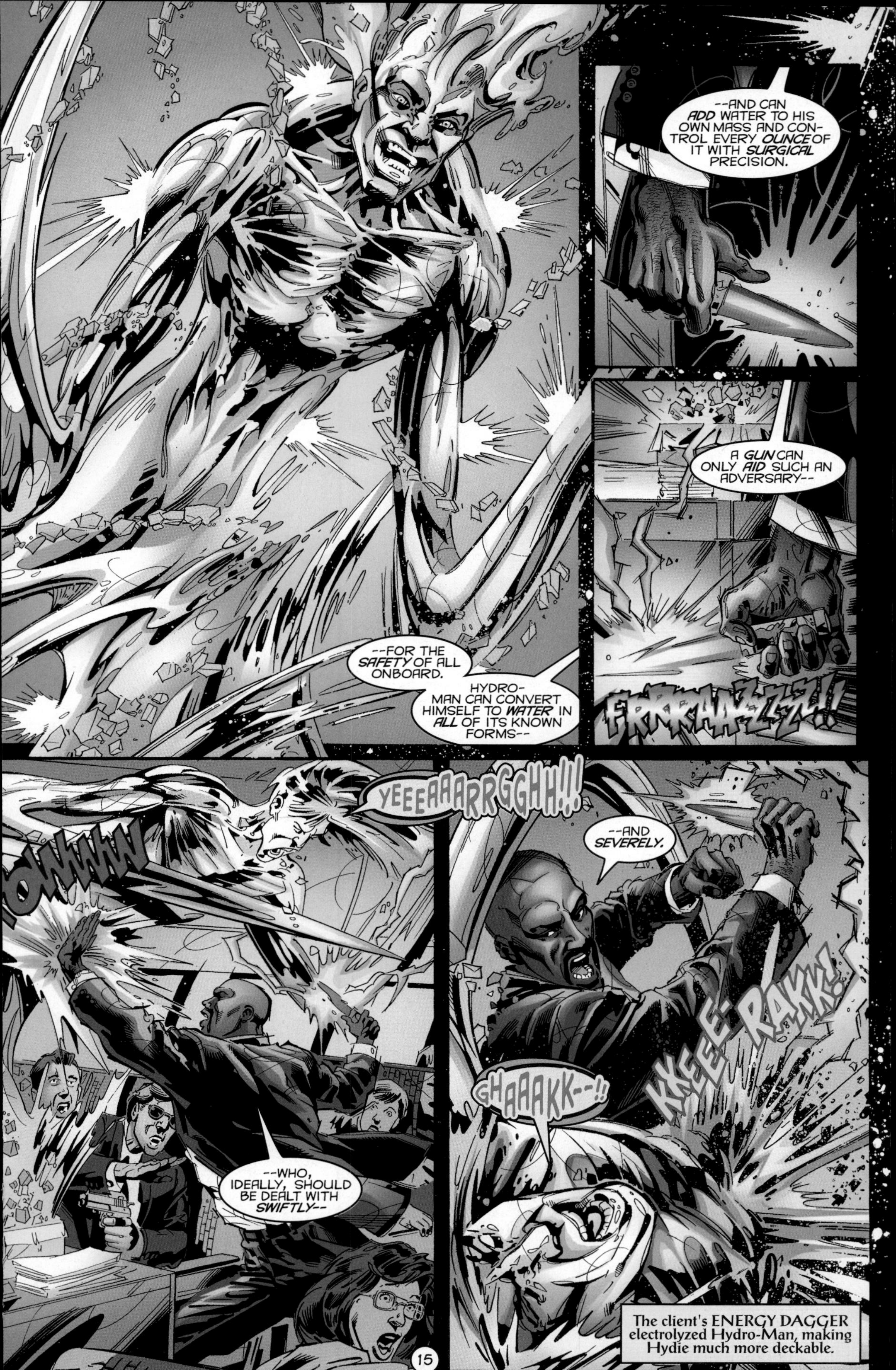
--FOR THE SAFETY OF ALL ONBOARD.
HYDRO-MAN CAN CONVERT HIMSELF TO WATER IN ALL OF ITS KNOWN FORMS--
--AND CAN ADD WATER TO HIS OWN MASS AND CONTROL EVERY OUNCE OF IT WITH SURGICAL PRECISION.
A GUN CAN ONLY AID SUCH AN ADVERSARY--
YEEEAAARRGGHH!!!
--WHO, IDEALLY, SHOULD BE DEALT WITH SWIFTLY--
--AND SEVERELY.
GHAAAKK--!!
The client's ENERGY DAGGER electrolyzed Hydro-Man, making Hydie much more deckable.

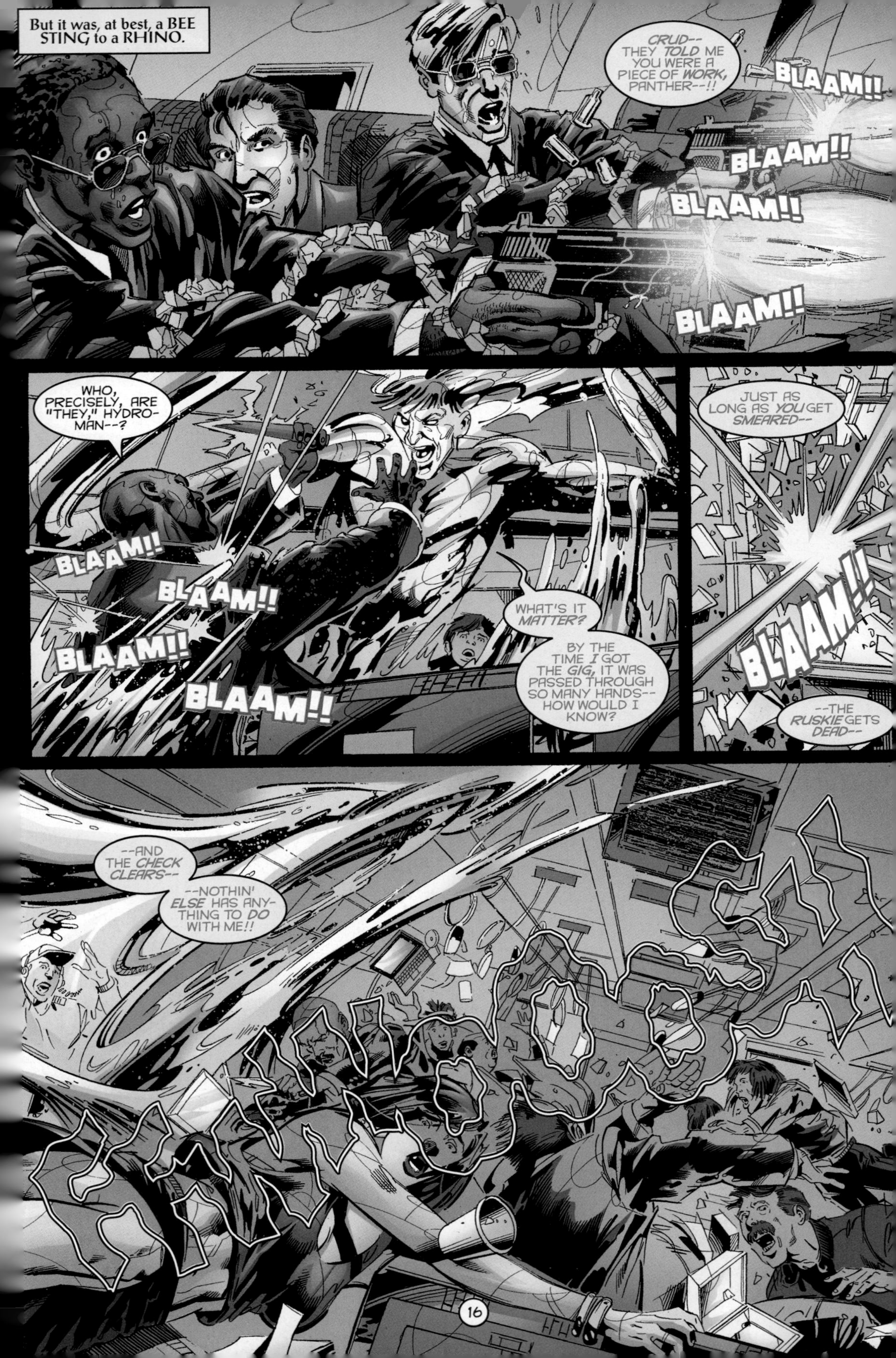

But it was, at best, a BEE STING to a RHINO.
CRUD-- THEY TOLD ME YOU WERE A PIECE OF WORK, PANTHER--!!
BLAAM!!
BLAAM!!
BLAAM!!
BLAAM!!
WHO, PRECISELY, ARE "THEY," HYDRO-MAN--?
BLAAM!!
BLAAM!!
BLAAM!!
BLAAM!!
WHAT'S IT MATTER?
BY THE TIME I GOT THE GIG, IT WAS PASSED THROUGH SO MANY HANDS--HOW WOULD I KNOW?
JUST AS LONG AS YOU GET SMEARED--
BLAAM!!
--THE RUSKIE GETS DEAD--
--AND THE CHECK CLEARS--
--NOTHIN' ELSE HAS ANY-THING TO DO WITH ME!!

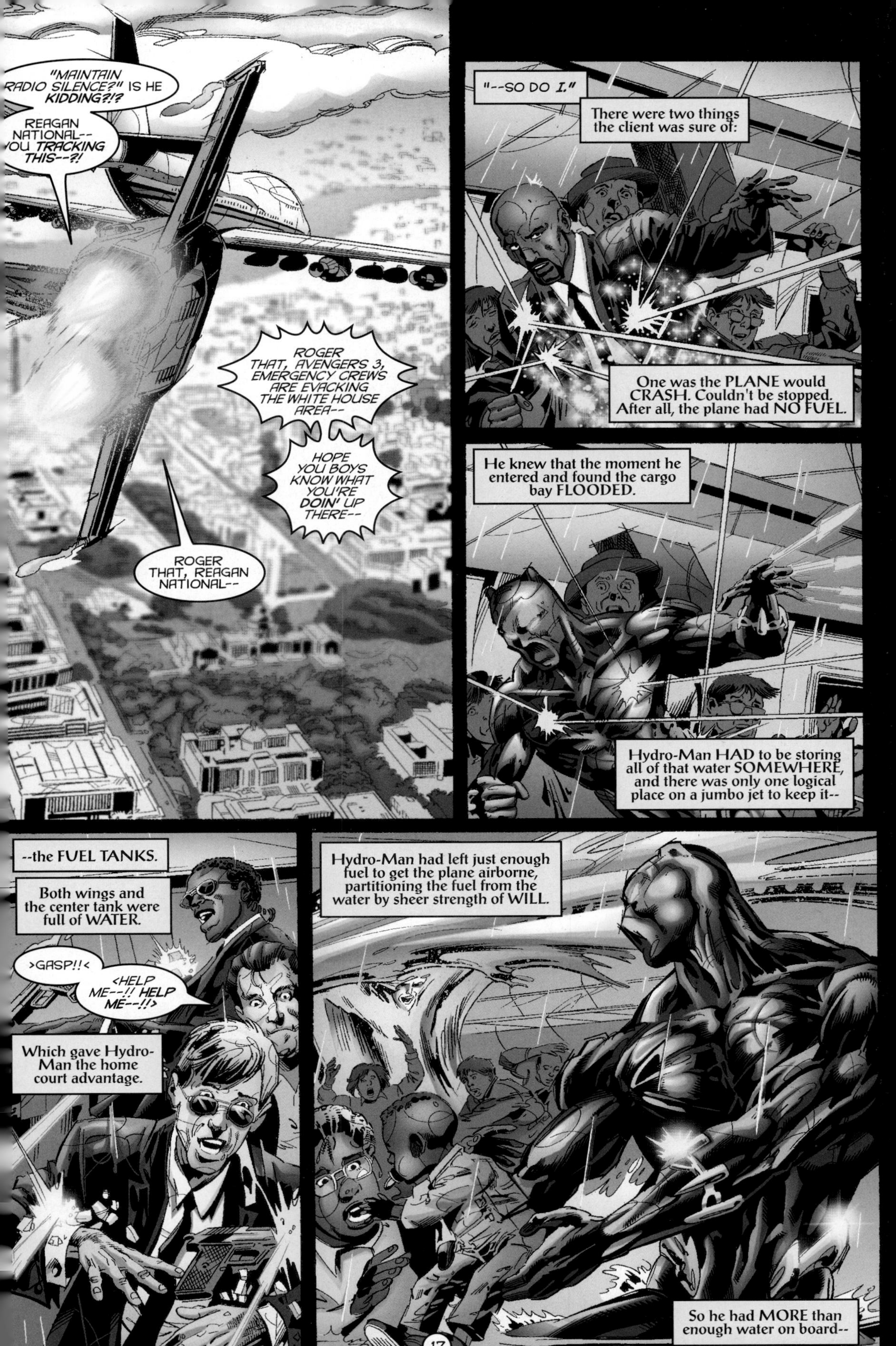
"MAINTAIN RADIO SILENCE?" IS HE KIDDING?!?
REAGAN NATIONAL-- YOU TRACKING THIS--?!
ROGER THAT, AVENGERS 3, EMERGENCY CREWS ARE EVACKING THE WHITE HOUSE AREA--
HOPE YOU BOYS KNOW WHAT YOU'RE DOIN' UP THERE--
ROGER THAT, REAGAN NATIONAL--
"--SO DO I."
There were two things the client was sure of:
One was the PLANE would CRASH. Couldn't be stopped. After all, the plane had NO FUEL.
He knew that the moment he entered and found the cargo bay FLOODED.
Hydro-Man HAD to be storing all of that water SOMEWHERE, and there was only one logical place on a jumbo jet to keep it--
--the FUEL TANKS.
Both wings and the center tank were full of WATER.
>GASP!!<
<HELP ME--!! HELP ME--!!>
Which gave Hydro-Man the home court advantage.
Hydro-Man had left just enough fuel to get the plane airborne, partitioning the fuel from the water by sheer strength of WILL.
So he had MORE than enough water on board--

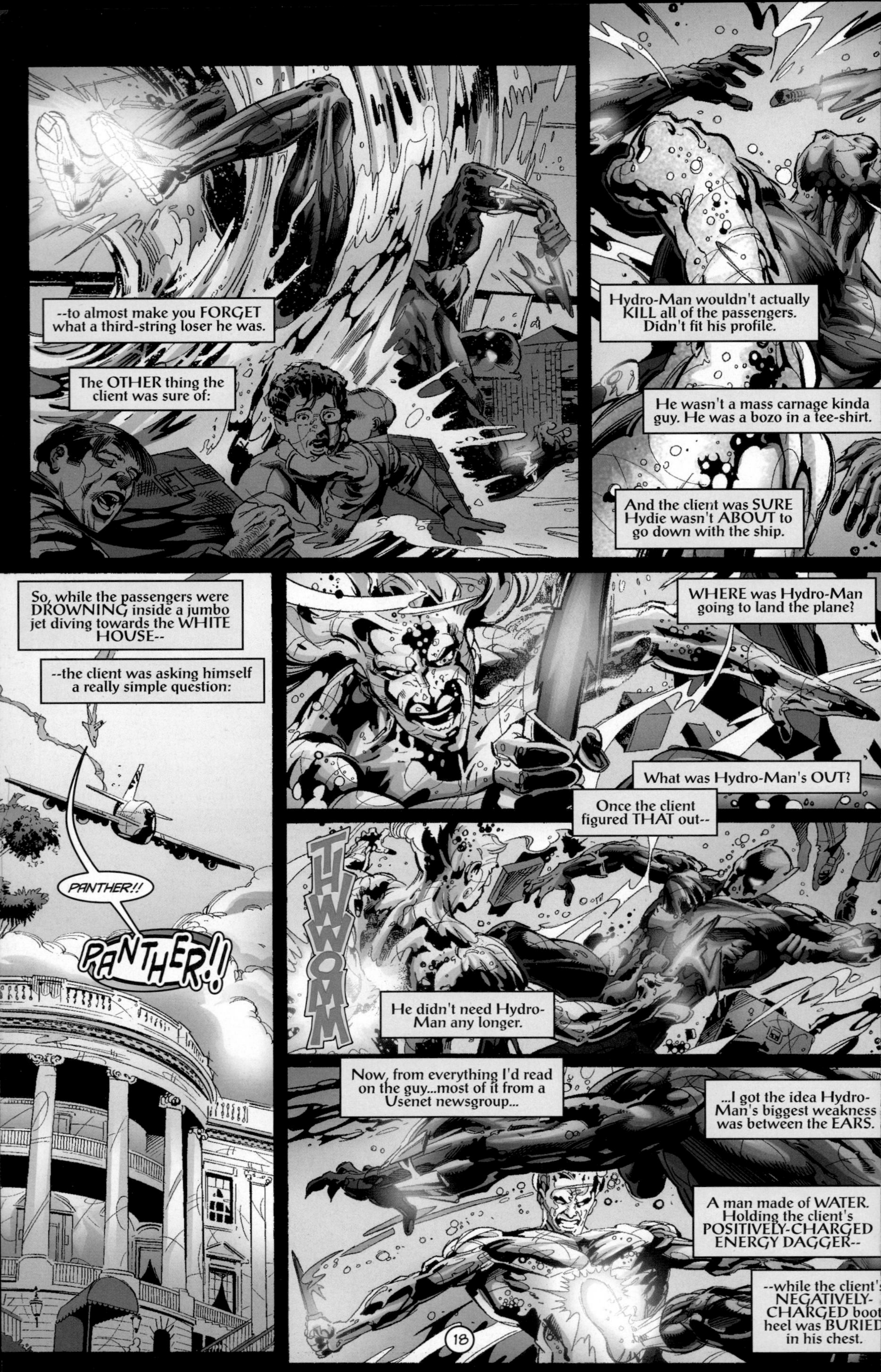

--to almost make you FORGET what a third-string loser he was.
The OTHER thing the client was sure of:
Hydro-Man wouldn't actually KILL all of the passengers. Didn't fit his profile.
He wasn't a mass carnage kinda guy. He was a bozo in a tee-shirt.
And the client was SURE Hydie wasn't ABOUT to go down with the ship.
So, while the passengers were DROWNING inside a jumbo jet diving towards the WHITE HOUSE--
--the client was asking himself a really simple question:
PANTHER!!
PANTHER!!
WHERE was Hydro-Man going to land the plane?
What was Hydro-Man's OUT?
Once the client figured THAT out--
THWOOM
He didn't need Hydro-Man any longer.
Now, from everything I'd read on the guy...most of it from a Usenet newsgroup...
...I got the idea Hydro-Man's biggest weakness was between the EARS.
A man made of WATER. Holding the client's POSITIVELY-CHARGED ENERGY DAGGER--
--while the client's NEGATIVELY-CHARGED boot heel was BURIED in his chest.

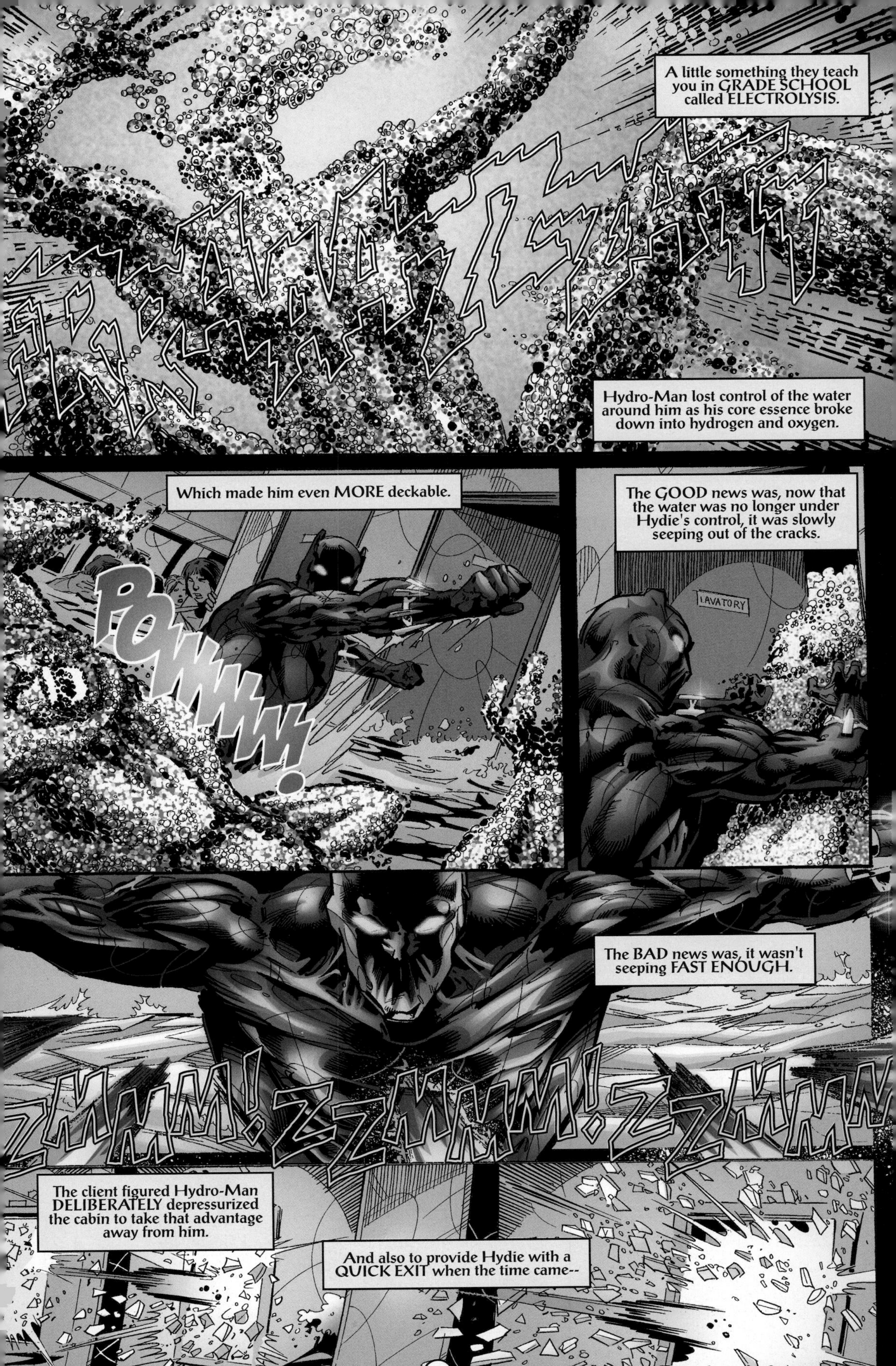

A little something they teach you in GRADE SCHOOL called ELECTROLYSIS.
Hydro-Man lost control of the water around him as his core essence broke down into hydrogen and oxygen.
Which made him even MORE deckable.
POWWWW!
The GOOD news was, now that the water was no longer under Hydie's control, it was slowly seeping out of the cracks.
LAVATORY
The BAD news was, it wasn't seeping FAST ENOUGH.
ZMMM! ZZMMM! ZZMMM
The client figured Hydro-Man DELIBERATELY depressurized the cabin to take that advantage away from him.
And also to provide Hydie with a QUICK EXIT when the time came--

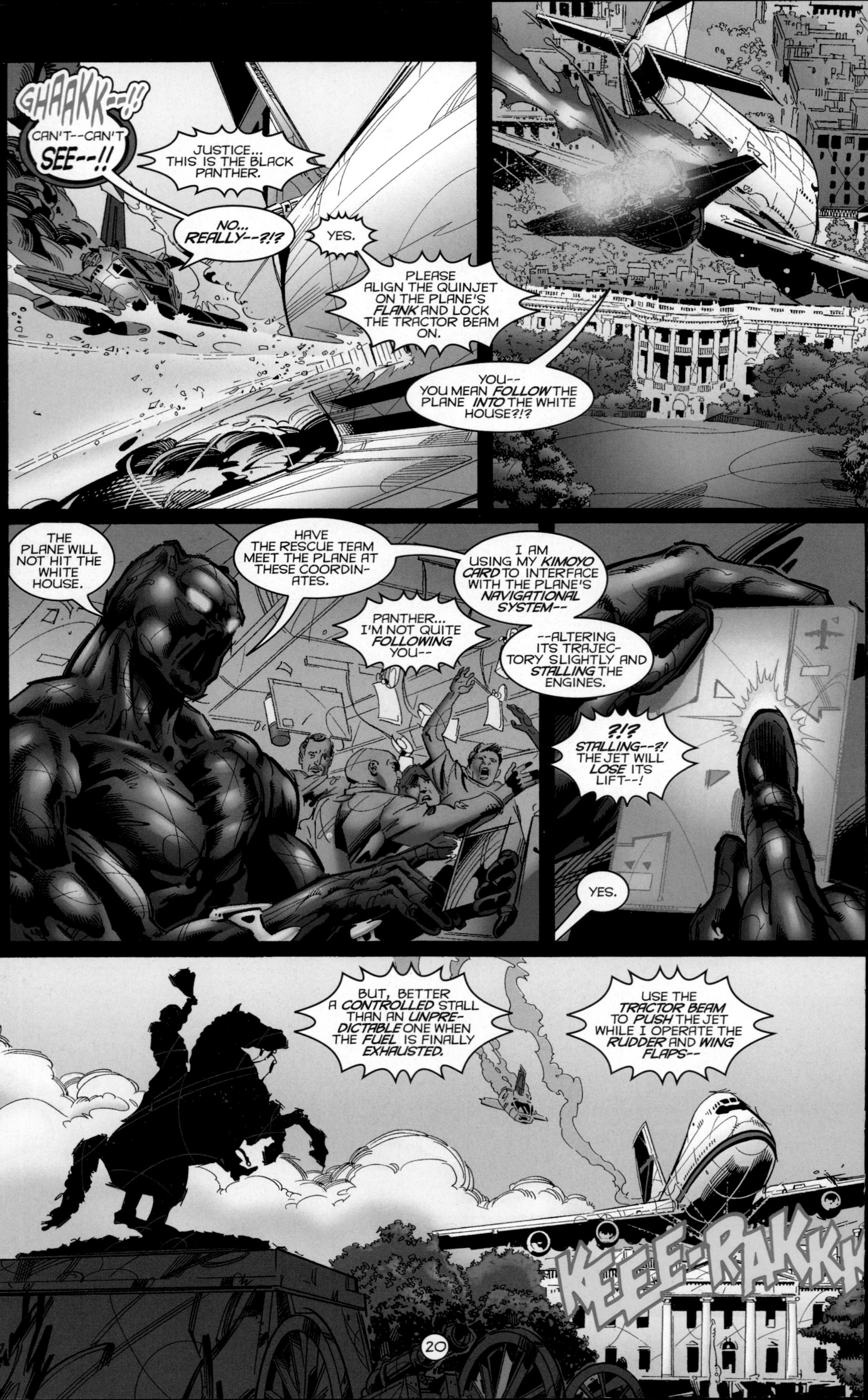
GHAAKK--!!
CAN'T--CAN'T SEE--!!
JUSTICE... THIS IS THE BLACK PANTHER.
NO... REALLY--?!?
YES.
PLEASE ALIGN THE QUINJET ON THE PLANE'S FLANK AND LOCK THE TRACTOR BEAM ON.
YOU-- YOU MEAN FOLLOW THE PLANE INTO THE WHITE HOUSE?!?
THE PLANE WILL NOT HIT THE WHITE HOUSE.
HAVE THE RESCUE TEAM MEET THE PLANE AT THESE COORDINATES.
PANTHER... I'M NOT QUITE FOLLOWING YOU--
I AM USING MY KIMOYO CARD TO INTERFACE WITH THE PLANE'S NAVIGATIONAL SYSTEM--
--ALTERING ITS TRAJECTORY SLIGHTLY AND STALLING THE ENGINES.
?!? STALLING--?! THE JET WILL LOSE ITS LIFT--!
YES.
BUT, BETTER A CONTROLLED STALL THAN AN UNPREDICTABLE ONE WHEN THE FUEL IS FINALLY EXHAUSTED.
USE THE TRACTOR BEAM TO PUSH THE JET WHILE I OPERATE THE RUDDER AND WING FLAPS--
KEEE-RAKK

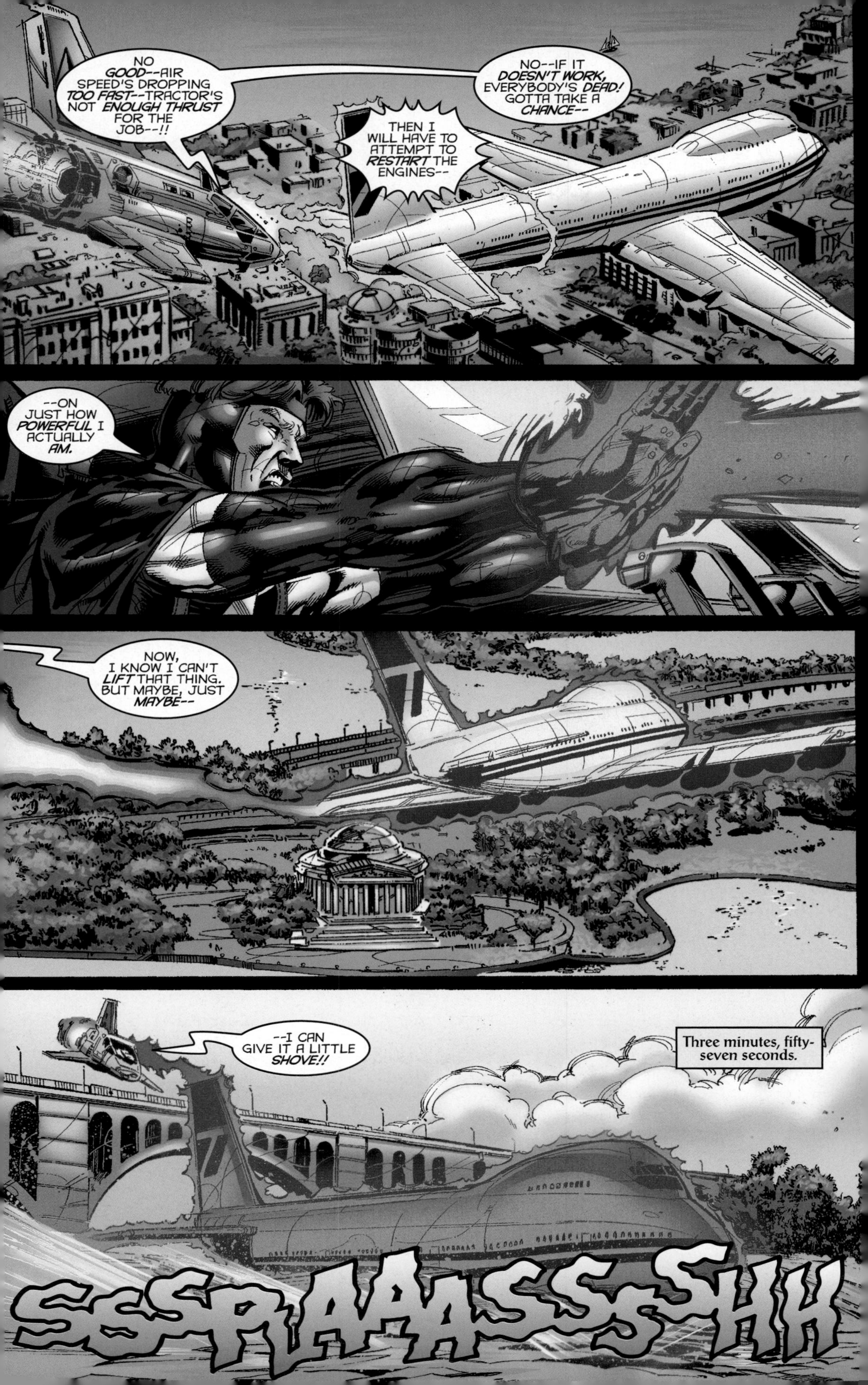
NO GOOD--AIR SPEED'S DROPPING TOO FAST--TRACTOR'S NOT ENOUGH THRUST FOR THE JOB--!!
THEN I WILL HAVE TO ATTEMPT TO RESTART THE ENGINES--
NO--IF IT DOESN'T WORK, EVERYBODY'S DEAD! GOTTA TAKE A CHANCE--
--ON JUST HOW POWERFUL I ACTUALLY AM.
NOW, I KNOW I CAN'T LIFT THAT THING. BUT MAYBE, JUST MAYBE--
--I CAN GIVE IT A LITTLE SHOVE!!
Three minutes, fifty-seven seconds.
SSSRAAASSSSHK

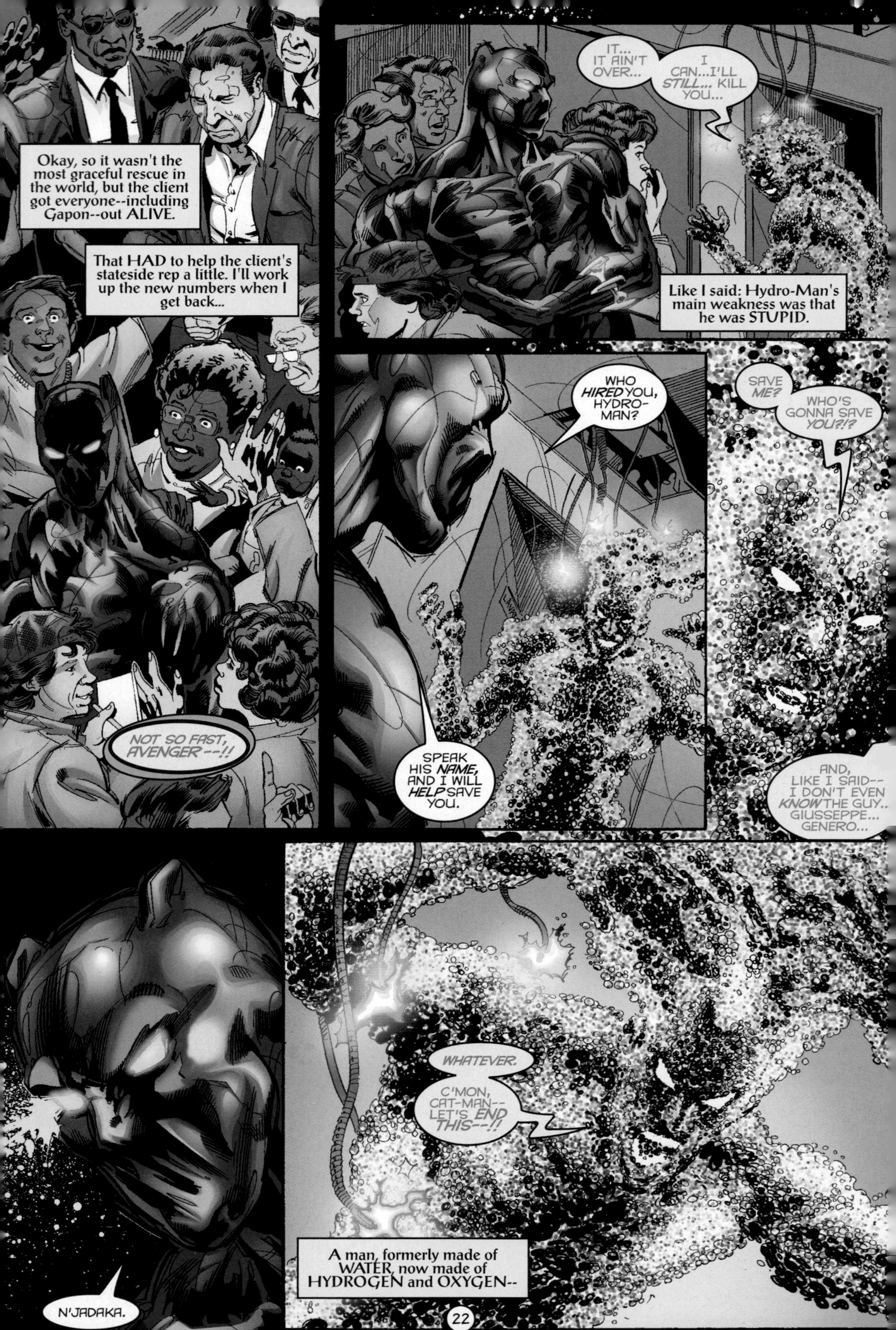

Okay, so it wasn't the most graceful rescue in the world, but the client got everyone--including Gapon--out ALIVE.
That HAD to help the client's stateside rep a little. I'll work up the new numbers when I get back...
NOT SO FAST, AVENGER--!!
IT... IT AIN'T OVER...
I CAN...I'LL STILL... KILL YOU...
Like I said: Hydro-Man's main weakness was that he was STUPID.
WHO HIRED YOU, HYDRO-MAN?
SPEAK HIS NAME, AND I WILL HELP SAVE YOU.
SAVE ME?
WHO'S GONNA SAVE YOU?!?
AND, LIKE I SAID-- I DON'T EVEN KNOW THE GUY.. GIUSSEPPE... GENERO...
WHATEVER.
C'MON, CAT-MAN-- LET'S END THIS--!!
A man, formerly made of WATER, now made of HYDROGEN and OXYGEN--
N'JADAKA.

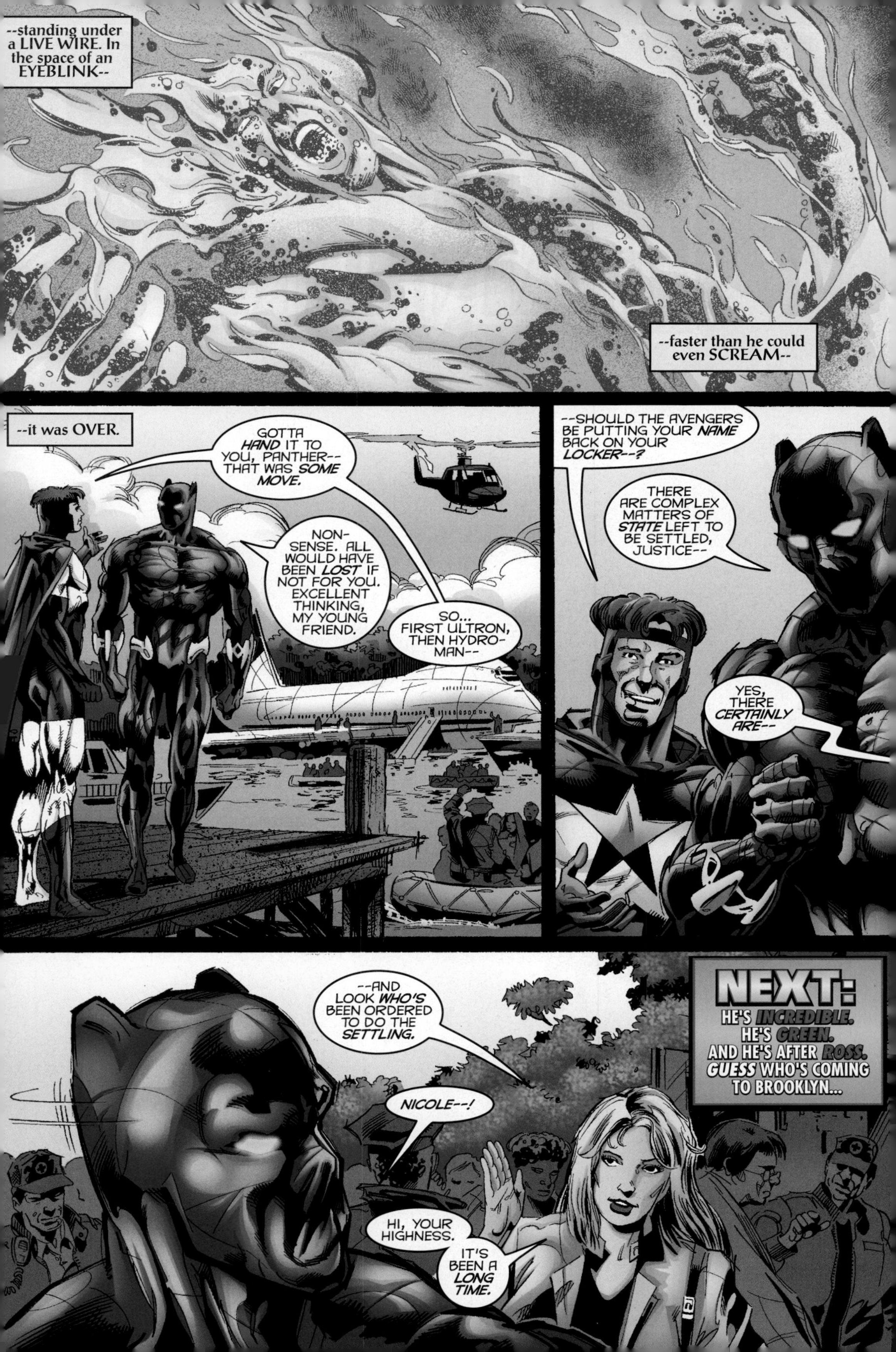
--standing under a LIVE WIRE. In the space of an EYEBLINK--
--faster than he could even SCREAM--
--it was OVER.
GOTTA HAND IT TO YOU, PANTHER--THAT WAS SOME MOVE.
NON-SENSE. ALL WOULD HAVE BEEN LOST IF NOT FOR YOU. EXCELLENT THINKING, MY YOUNG FRIEND.
SO... FIRST ULTRON, THEN HYDRO-MAN--
--SHOULD THE AVENGERS BE PUTTING YOUR NAME BACK ON YOUR LOCKER--?
THERE ARE COMPLEX MATTERS OF STATE LEFT TO BE SETTLED, JUSTICE--
YES, THERE CERTAINLY ARE--
--AND LOOK WHO'S BEEN ORDERED TO DO THE SETTLING.
NICOLE--!
HI, YOUR HIGHNESS.
IT'S BEEN A LONG TIME.
NEXT:
HE'S INCREDIBLE.
HE'S GREEN.
AND HE'S AFTER ROSS.
GUESS WHO'S COMING TO BROOKLYN...

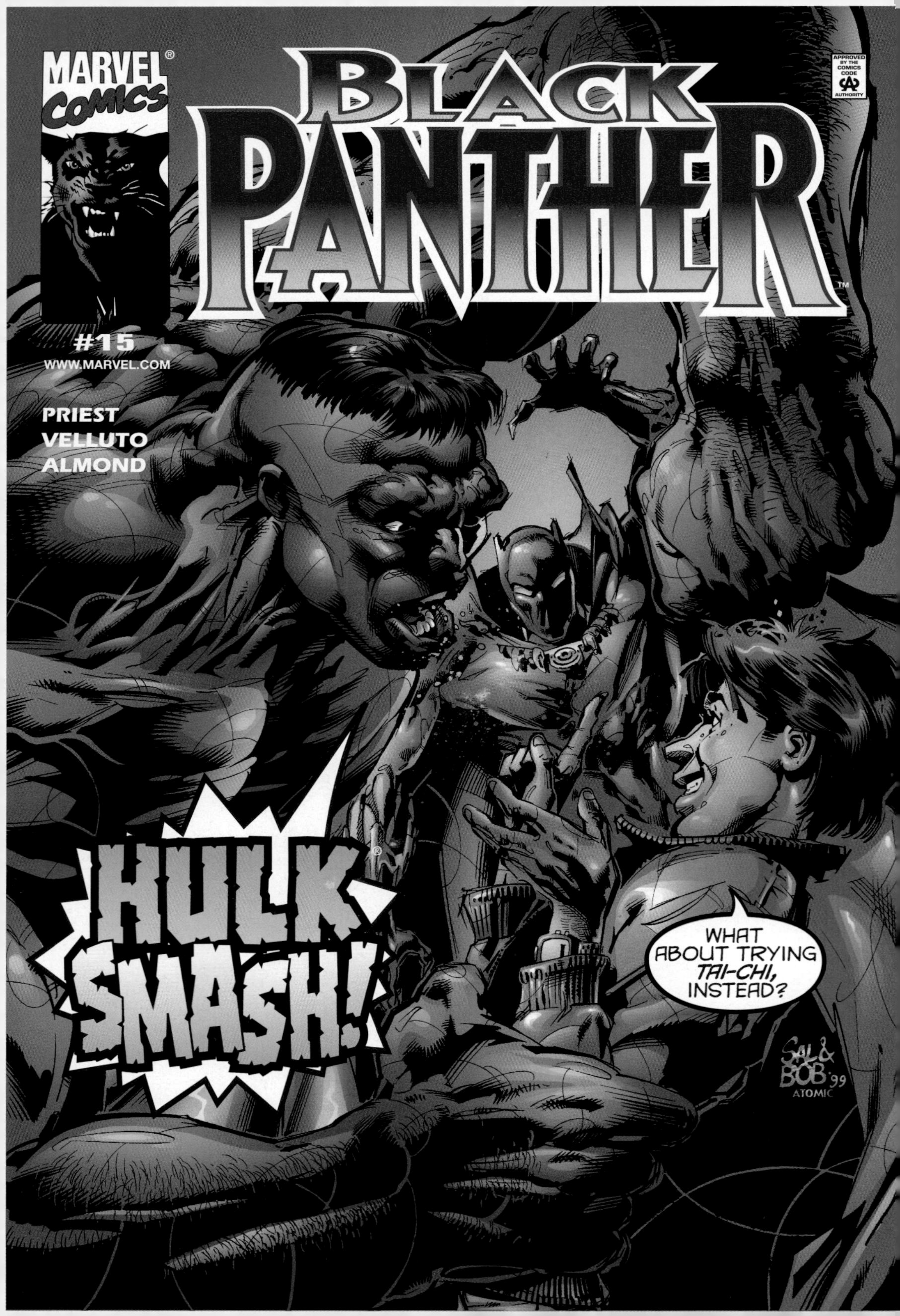

MARVEL® COMICS
BLACK PANTHER™
APPROVED BY THE COMICS CODE CA AUTHORITY
#15
WWW.MARVEL.COM
PRIEST
VELLUTO
ALMOND
HULK® SMASH!
WHAT ABOUT TRYING TAI-CHI, INSTEAD?
SAL & BOB '99
ATOMIC

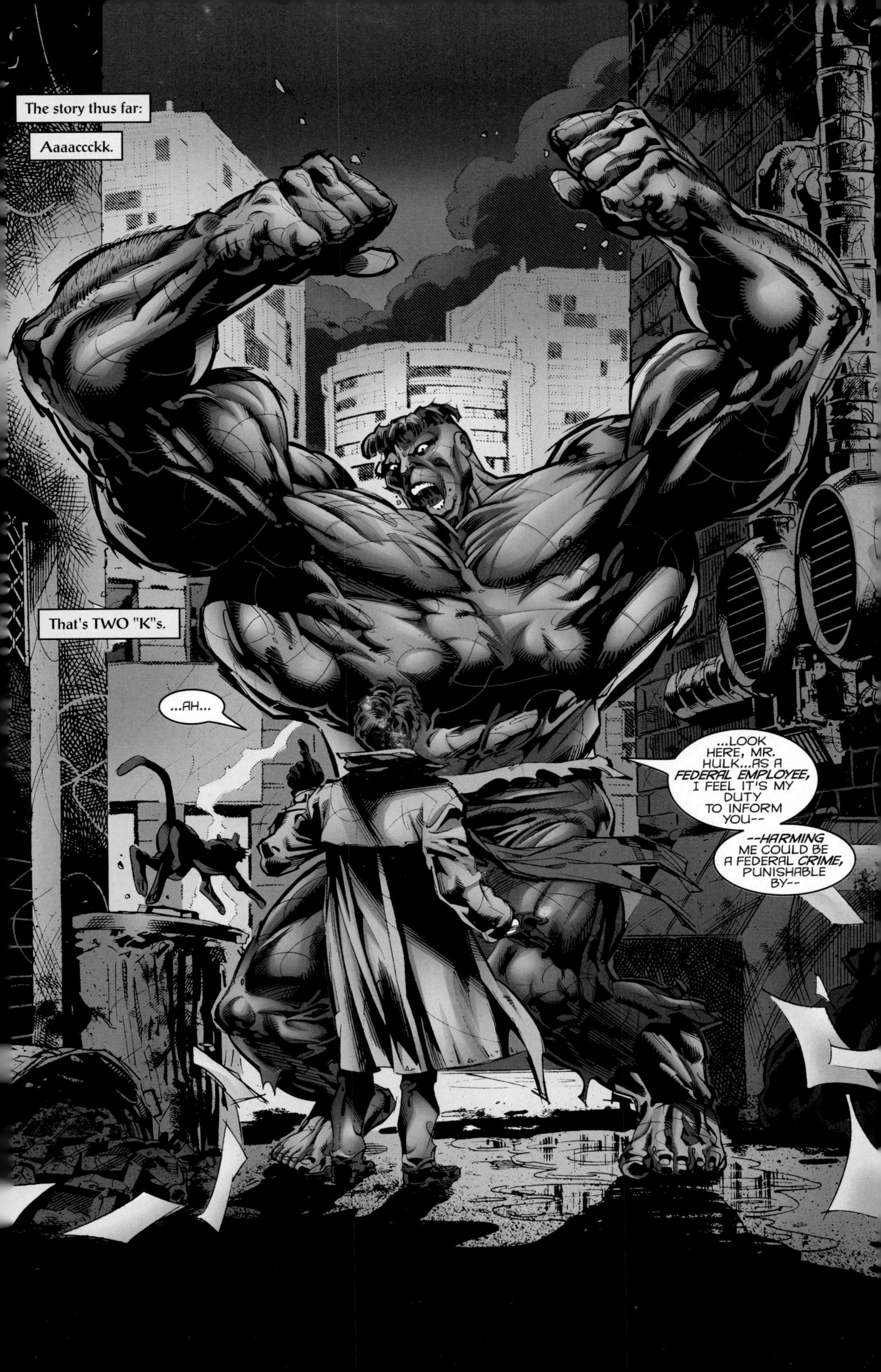
The story thus far:
Aaaaccckk.
That's TWO "K"s.
...AH...
...LOOK HERE, MR. HULK...AS A *FEDERAL EMPLOYEE,* I FEEL IT'S MY DUTY TO INFORM YOU--
--*HARMING* ME COULD BE A FEDERAL *CRIME,* PUNISHABLE BY--

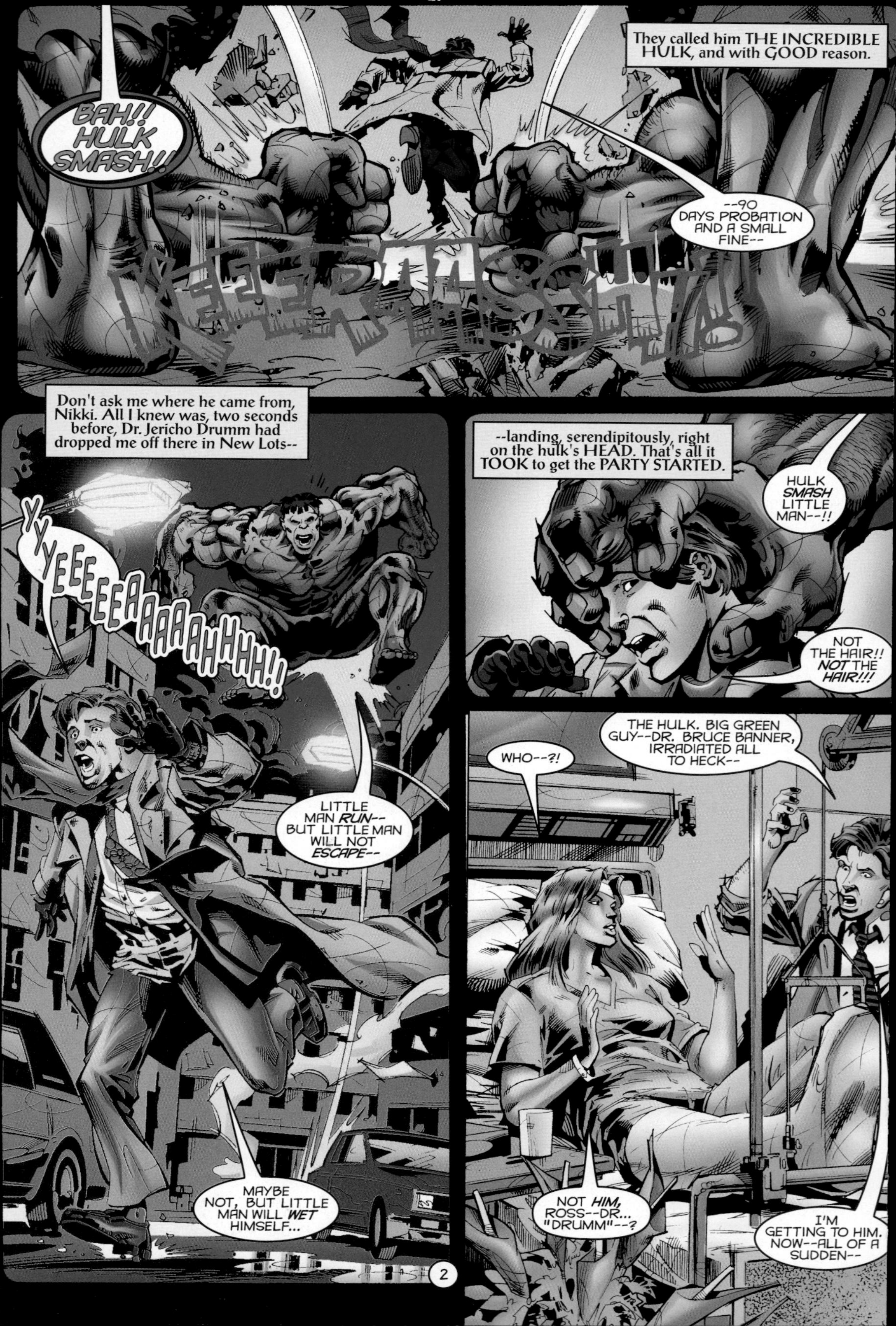
BAH!! HULK SMASH!!
They called him THE INCREDIBLE HULK, and with GOOD reason.
--90 DAYS PROBATION AND A SMALL FINE--
Don't ask me where he came from, Nikki. All I knew was, two seconds before, Dr. Jericho Drumm had dropped me off there in New Lots--
YYYEEEEEEAAAAAHHHH!!
LITTLE MAN RUN-- BUT LITTLE MAN WILL NOT ESCAPE--
MAYBE NOT, BUT LITTLE MAN WILL WET HIMSELF...
2
--landing, serendipitously, right on the hulk's HEAD. That's all it TOOK to get the PARTY STARTED.
HULK SMASH LITTLE MAN--!!
NOT THE HAIR!! NOT THE HAIR!!!
WHO--?!
THE HULK. BIG GREEN GUY--DR. BRUCE BANNER, IRRADIATED ALL TO HECK--
NOT HIM, ROSS--DR... "DRUMM"--?
I'M GETTING TO HIM. NOW--ALL OF A SUDDEN--

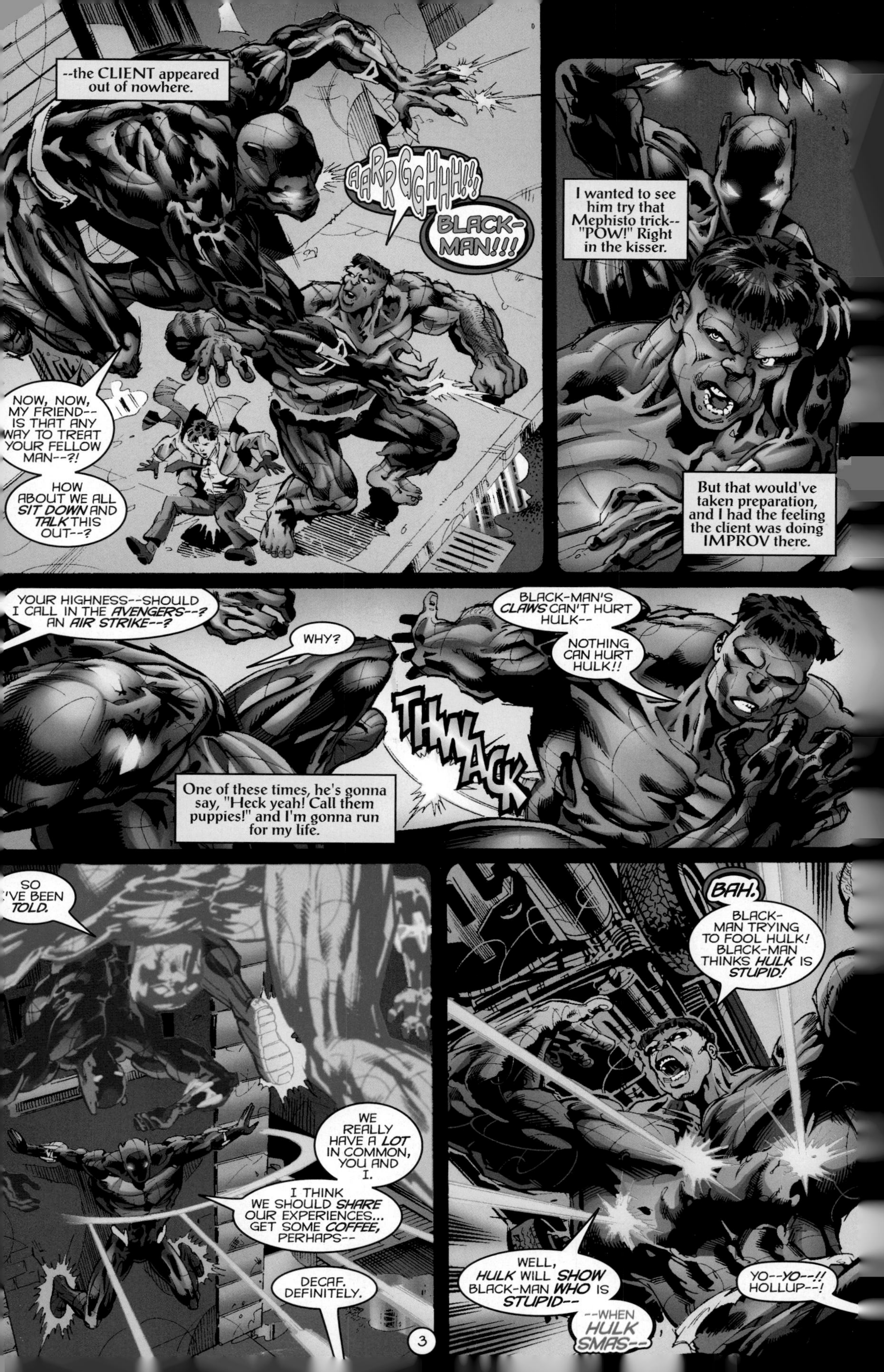
--the CLIENT appeared out of nowhere.
AARRGGHHH!!!
BLACK-MAN!!!
NOW, NOW, MY FRIEND-- IS THAT ANY WAY TO TREAT YOUR FELLOW MAN--?!
HOW ABOUT WE ALL SIT DOWN AND TALK THIS OUT--?
I wanted to see him try that Mephisto trick-- "POW!" Right in the kisser.
But that would've taken preparation, and I had the feeling the client was doing IMPROV there.
YOUR HIGHNESS--SHOULD I CALL IN THE AVENGERS--? AN AIR STRIKE--?
WHY?
BLACK-MAN'S CLAWS CAN'T HURT HULK--
NOTHING CAN HURT HULK!!
THWACK
One of these times, he's gonna say, "Heck yeah! Call them puppies!" and I'm gonna run for my life.
SO I'VE BEEN TOLD.
WE REALLY HAVE A LOT IN COMMON, YOU AND I.
I THINK WE SHOULD SHARE OUR EXPERIENCES... GET SOME COFFEE, PERHAPS--
DECAF. DEFINITELY.
BAH.
BLACK-MAN TRYING TO FOOL HULK! BLACK-MAN THINKS HULK IS STUPID!
WELL, HULK WILL SHOW BLACK-MAN WHO IS STUPID--
--WHEN HULK SMAS--
YO--YO--!! HOLLUP--!

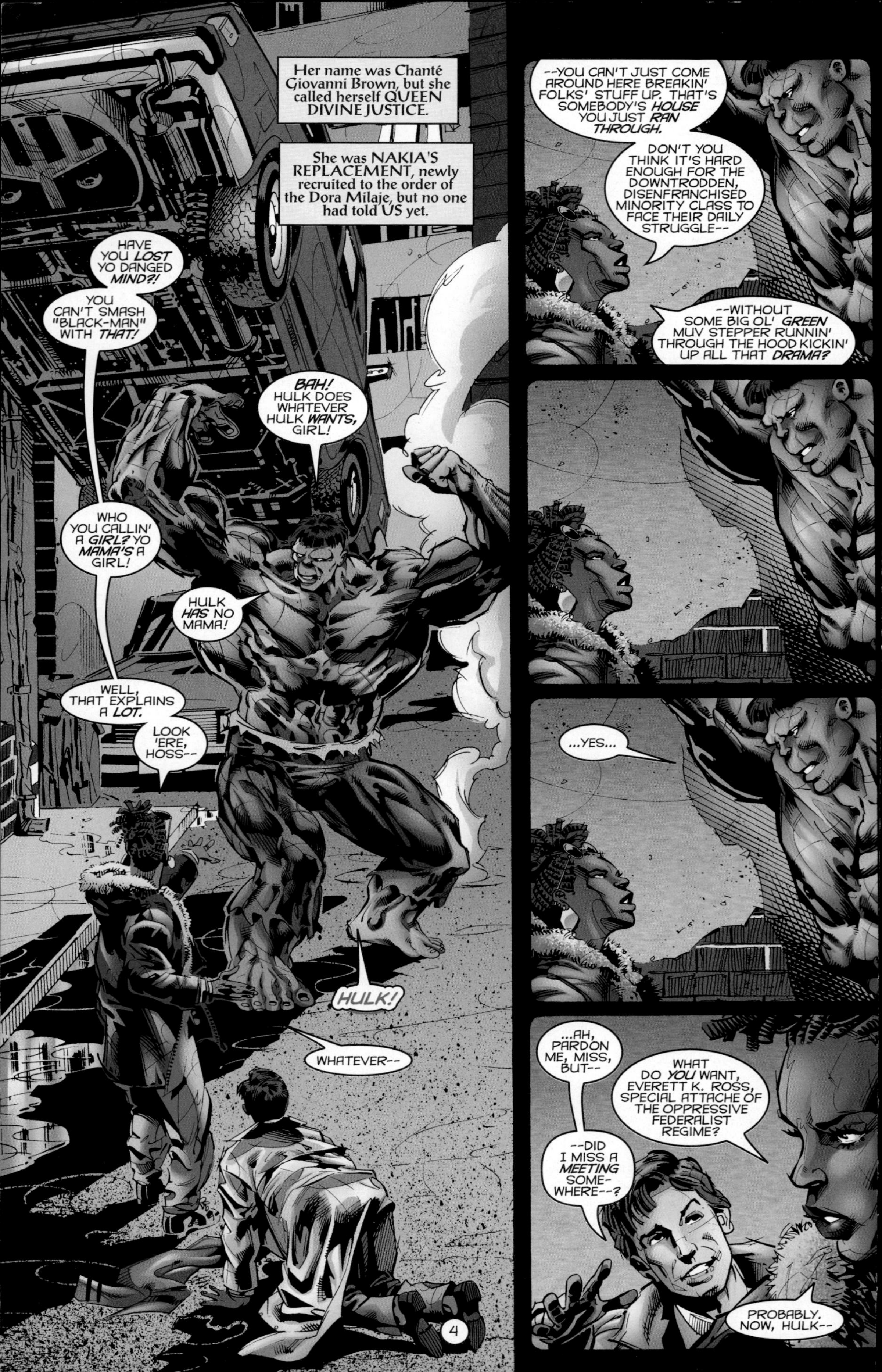
Her name was Chanté Giovanni Brown, but she called herself QUEEN DIVINE JUSTICE.
She was NAKIA'S REPLACEMENT, newly recruited to the order of the Dora Milaje, but no one had told US yet.
HAVE YOU LOST YO DANGED MIND?!
YOU CAN'T SMASH "BLACK-MAN" WITH THAT!
BAH! HULK DOES WHATEVER HULK WANTS, GIRL!
WHO YOU CALLIN' A GIRL? YO MAMA'S A GIRL!
HULK HAS NO MAMA!
WELL, THAT EXPLAINS A LOT.
LOOK 'ERE, HOSS--
HULK!
WHATEVER--
--YOU CAN'T JUST COME AROUND HERE BREAKIN' FOLKS' STUFF UP. THAT'S SOMEBODY'S HOUSE YOU JUST RAN THROUGH.
DON'T YOU THINK IT'S HARD ENOUGH FOR THE DOWNTRODDEN, DISENFRANCHISED MINORITY CLASS TO FACE THEIR DAILY STRUGGLE--
--WITHOUT SOME BIG OL' GREEN MUV STEPPER RUNNIN' THROUGH THE HOOD KICKIN' UP ALL THAT DRAMA?
...YES...
...AH, PARDON ME, MISS, BUT--
WHAT DO YOU WANT, EVERETT K. ROSS, SPECIAL ATTACHE OF THE OPPRESSIVE FEDERALIST REGIME?
--DID I MISS A MEETING SOME-WHERE--?
PROBABLY. NOW, HULK--
4

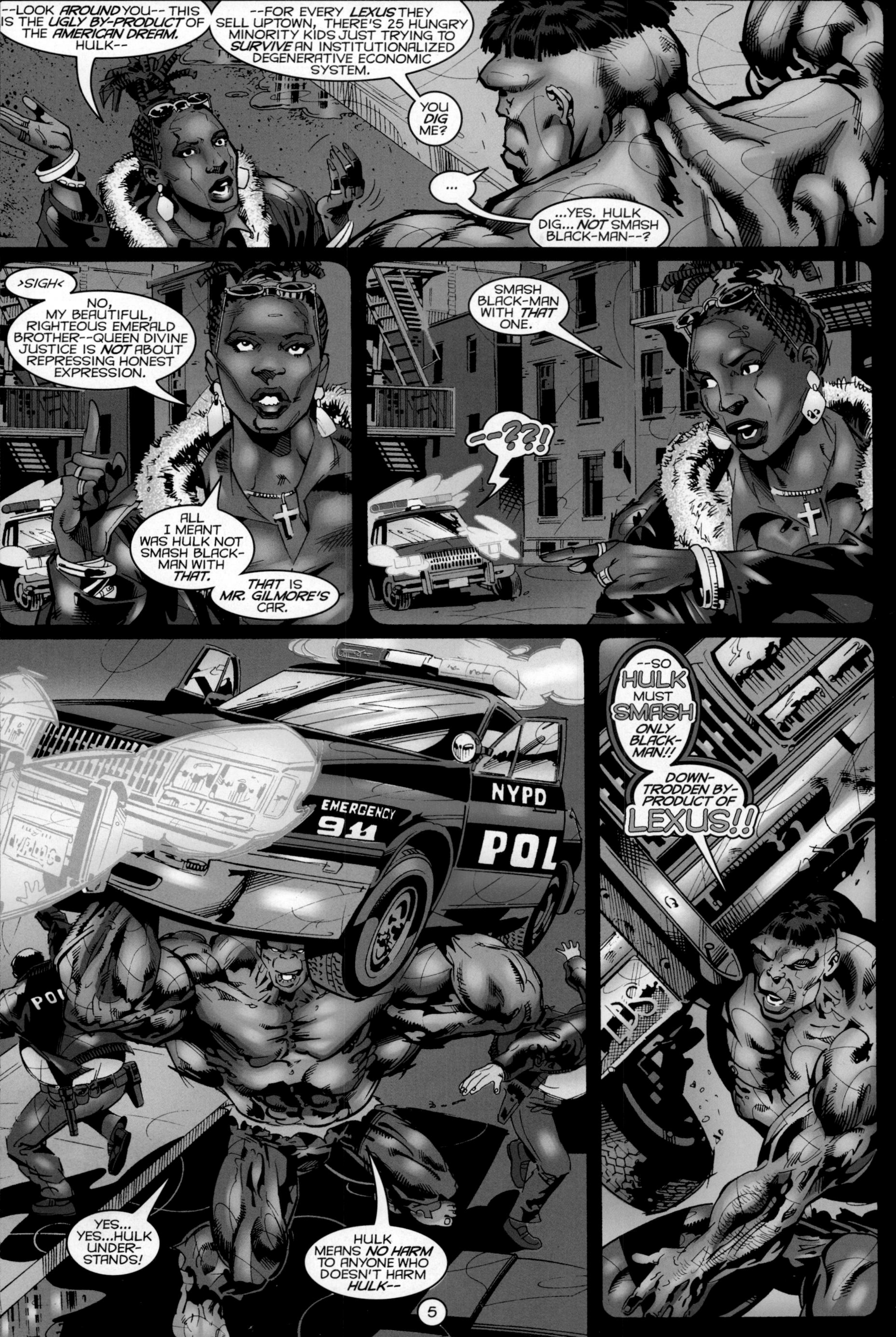
--LOOK AROUND YOU-- THIS IS THE UGLY BY-PRODUCT OF THE AMERICAN DREAM. HULK--
--FOR EVERY LEXUS THEY SELL UPTOWN, THERE'S 25 HUNGRY MINORITY KIDS JUST TRYING TO SURVIVE AN INSTITUTIONALIZED DEGENERATIVE ECONOMIC SYSTEM.
YOU DIG ME?
...
...YES. HULK DIG... NOT SMASH BLACK-MAN--?
>SIGH<
NO, MY BEAUTIFUL, RIGHTEOUS EMERALD BROTHER--QUEEN DIVINE JUSTICE IS NOT ABOUT REPRESSING HONEST EXPRESSION.
ALL I MEANT WAS HULK NOT SMASH BLACK-MAN WITH THAT.
THAT IS MR. GILMORE'S CAR.
SMASH BLACK-MAN WITH THAT ONE.
--??!
EMERGENCY
911
NYPD
POL
POL
YES... YES...HULK UNDER-STANDS!
HULK MEANS NO HARM TO ANYONE WHO DOESN'T HARM HULK--
--SO HULK MUST SMASH ONLY BLACK-MAN!!
DOWN-TRODDEN BY-PRODUCT OF LEXUS!!

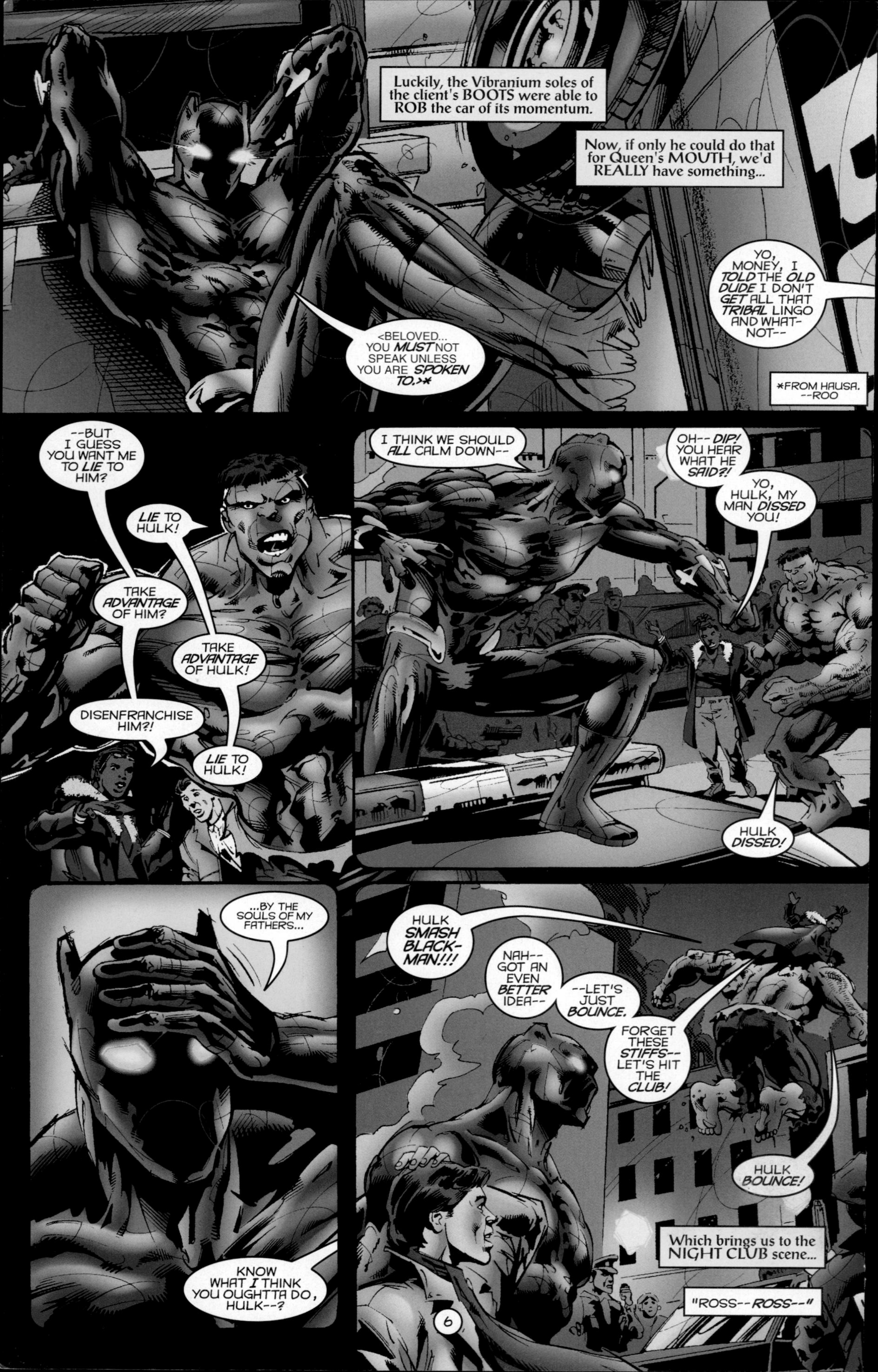

Luckily, the Vibranium soles of the client's BOOTS were able to ROB the car of its momentum.
Now, if only he could do that for Queen's MOUTH, we'd REALLY have something...
<BELOVED... YOU MUST NOT SPEAK UNLESS YOU ARE SPOKEN TO.>*
YO, MONEY, I TOLD THE OLD DUDE I DON'T GET ALL THAT TRIBAL LINGO AND WHAT-NOT--
*FROM HAUSA. --ROO
--BUT I GUESS YOU WANT ME TO LIE TO HIM?
LIE TO HULK!
TAKE ADVANTAGE OF HIM?
TAKE ADVANTAGE OF HULK!
DISENFRANCHISE HIM?!
LIE TO HULK!
I THINK WE SHOULD ALL CALM DOWN--
OH-- DIP! YOU HEAR WHAT HE SAID?!
YO, HULK, MY MAN DISSED YOU!
HULK DISSED!
...BY THE SOULS OF MY FATHERS...
KNOW WHAT I THINK YOU OUGHTTA DO, HULK--?
HULK SMASH BLACK-MAN!!!
NAH-- GOT AN EVEN BETTER IDEA--
--LET'S JUST BOUNCE.
FORGET THESE STIFFS-- LET'S HIT THE CLUB!
HULK BOUNCE!
Which brings us to the NIGHT CLUB scene...
"ROSS--ROSS--"

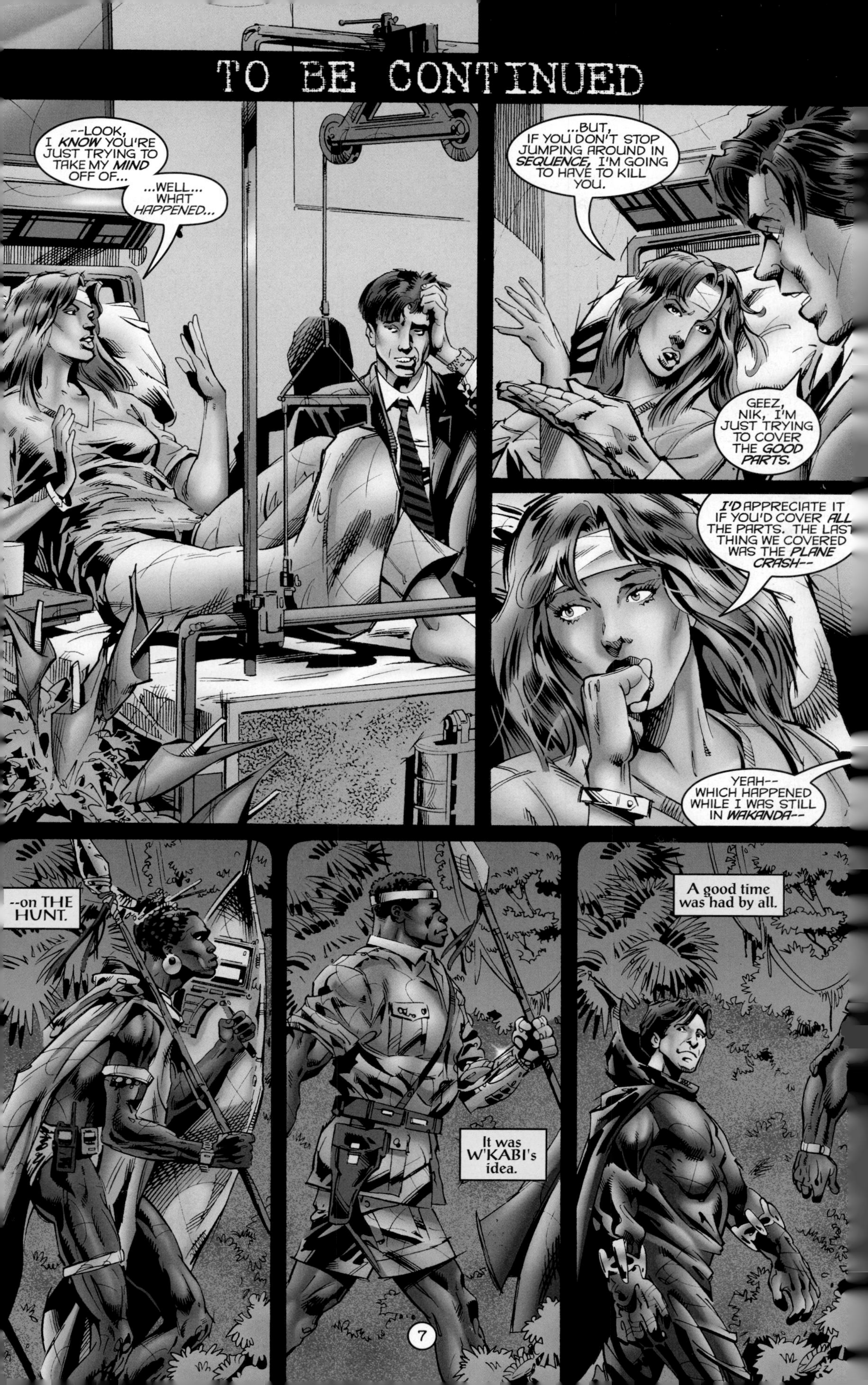
TO BE CONTINUED
--LOOK, I KNOW YOU'RE JUST TRYING TO TAKE MY MIND OFF OF...
...WELL... WHAT HAPPENED...
...BUT, IF YOU DON'T STOP JUMPING AROUND IN SEQUENCE, I'M GOING TO HAVE TO KILL YOU.
GEEZ, NIK, I'M JUST TRYING TO COVER THE GOOD PARTS.
I'D APPRECIATE IT IF YOU'D COVER ALL THE PARTS. THE LAST THING WE COVERED WAS THE PLANE CRASH--
YEAH-- WHICH HAPPENED WHILE I WAS STILL IN WAKANDA--
--on THE HUNT.
It was W'KABI's idea.
A good time was had by all.

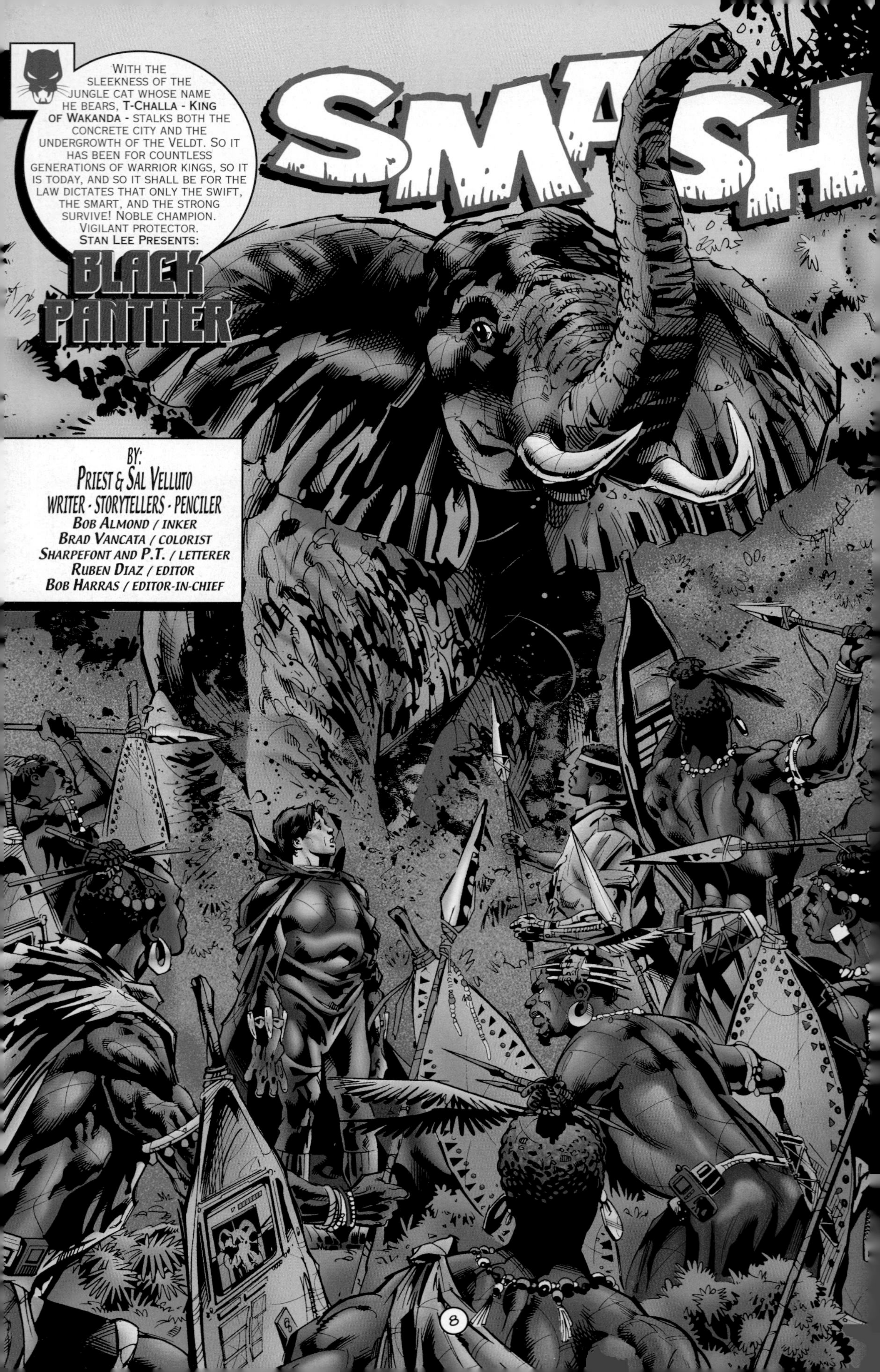

WITH THE SLEEKNESS OF THE JUNGLE CAT WHOSE NAME HE BEARS, T-CHALLA - KING OF WAKANDA - STALKS BOTH THE CONCRETE CITY AND THE UNDERGROWTH OF THE VELDT. SO IT HAS BEEN FOR COUNTLESS GENERATIONS OF WARRIOR KINGS, SO IT IS TODAY, AND SO IT SHALL BE FOR THE LAW DICTATES THAT ONLY THE SWIFT, THE SMART, AND THE STRONG SURVIVE! NOBLE CHAMPION. VIGILANT PROTECTOR.
STAN LEE PRESENTS:
BLACK PANTHER
SMASH
BY:
PRIEST & SAL VELLUTO
WRITER - STORYTELLERS - PENCILER
BOB ALMOND / INKER
BRAD VANCATA / COLORIST
SHARPEFONT AND P.T. / LETTERER
RUBEN DIAZ / EDITOR
BOB HARRAS / EDITOR-IN-CHIEF

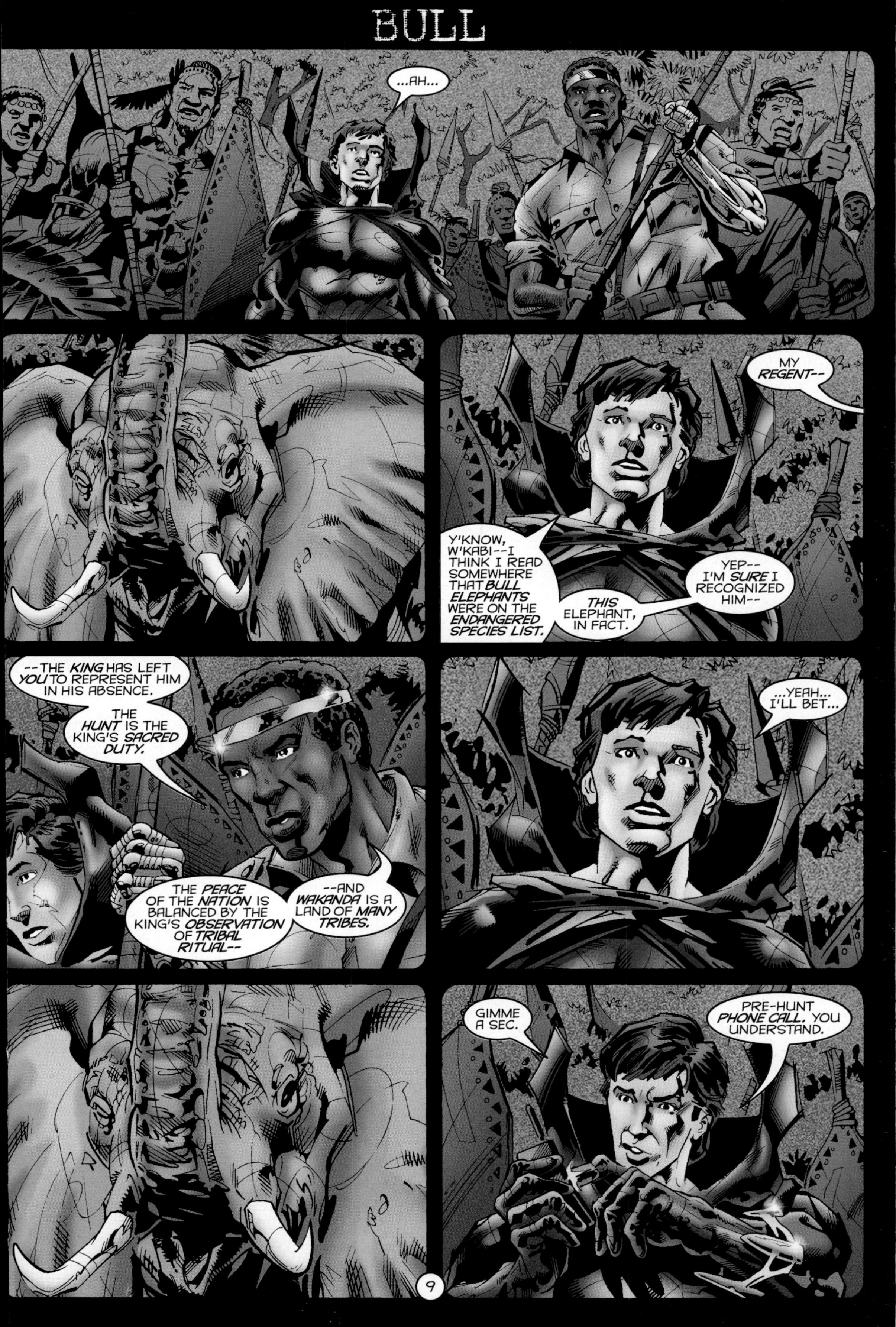
BULL
...AH...
MY REGENT--
Y'KNOW, W'KABI--I THINK I READ SOMEWHERE THAT BULL ELEPHANTS WERE ON THE ENDANGERED SPECIES LIST.
THIS ELEPHANT, IN FACT.
YEP-- I'M SURE I RECOGNIZED HIM--
--THE KING HAS LEFT YOU TO REPRESENT HIM IN HIS ABSENCE.
THE HUNT IS THE KING'S SACRED DUTY.
THE PEACE OF THE NATION IS BALANCED BY THE KING'S OBSERVATION OF TRIBAL RITUAL--
--AND WAKANDA IS A LAND OF MANY TRIBES.
...YEAH... I'LL BET...
GIMME A SEC.
PRE-HUNT PHONE CALL. YOU UNDERSTAND.

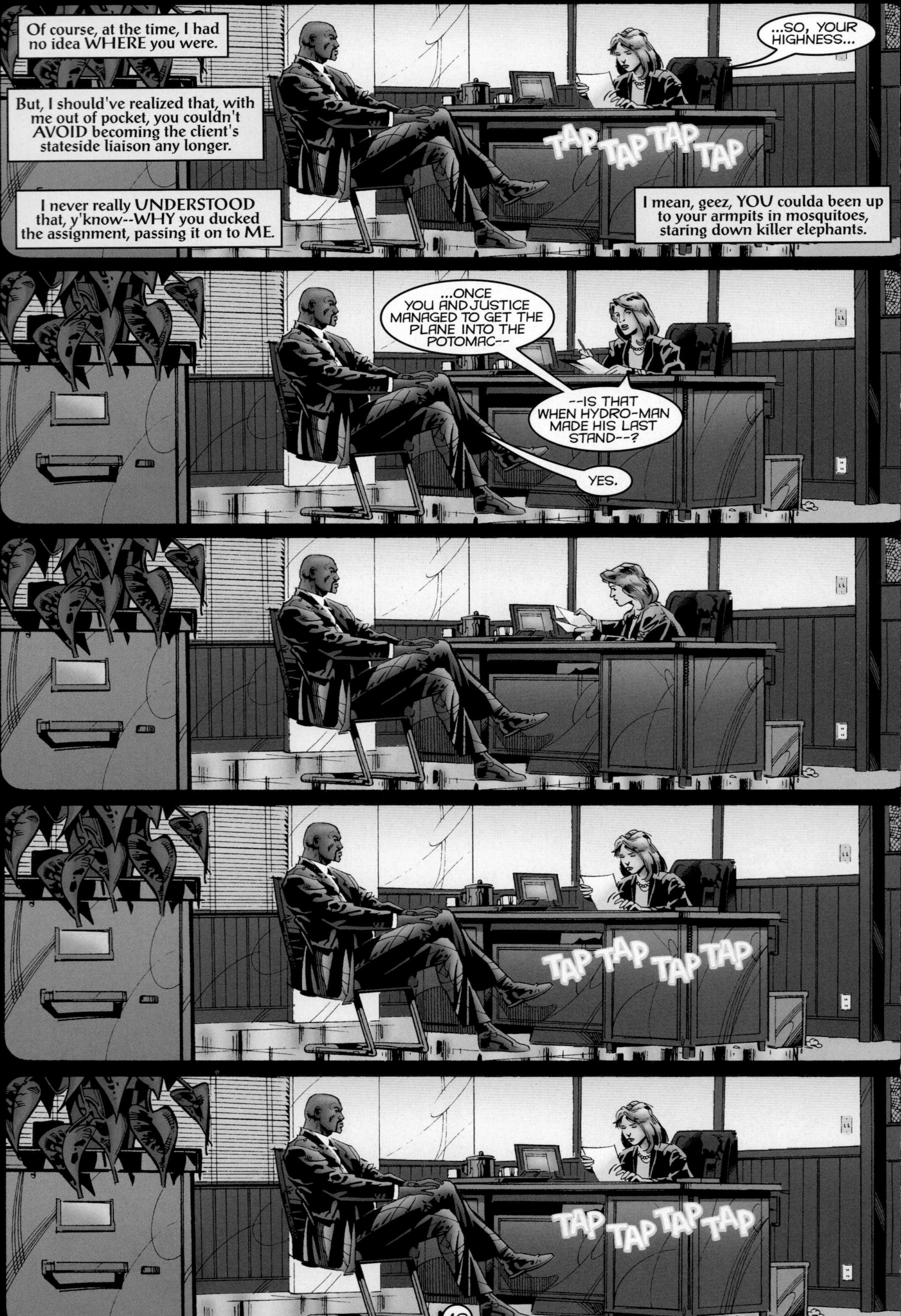
Of course, at the time, I had no idea WHERE you were.
But, I should've realized that, with me out of pocket, you couldn't AVOID becoming the client's stateside liaison any longer.
I never really UNDERSTOOD that, y'know--WHY you ducked the assignment, passing it on to ME.
...SO, YOUR HIGHNESS...
TAP TAP TAP TAP
I mean, geez, YOU coulda been up to your armpits in mosquitoes, staring down killer elephants.
...ONCE YOU AND JUSTICE MANAGED TO GET THE PLANE INTO THE POTOMAC--
--IS THAT WHEN HYDRO-MAN MADE HIS LAST STAND--?
YES.
TAP TAP TAP TAP
TAP TAP TAP TAP

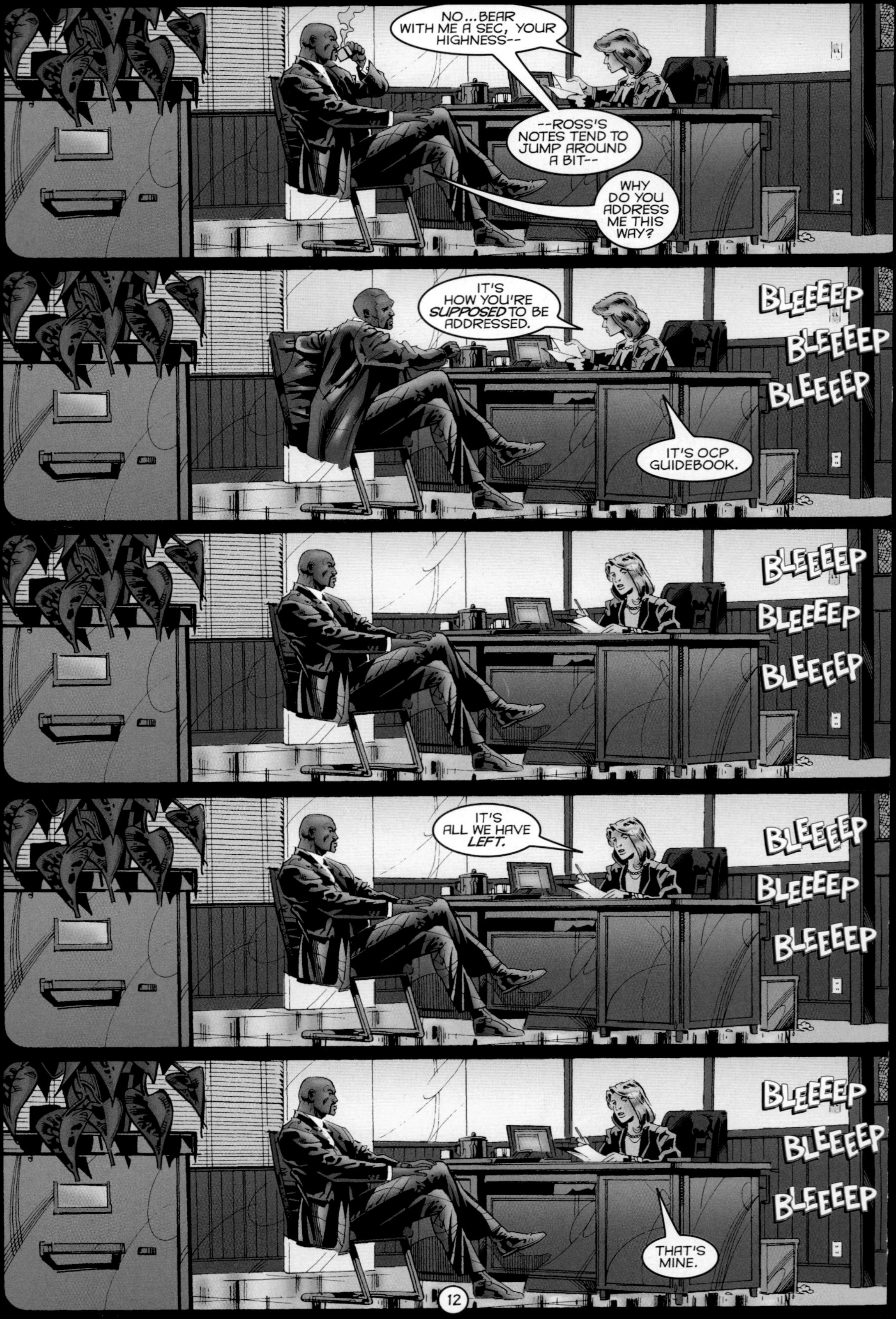
NO...BEAR WITH ME A SEC, YOUR HIGHNESS--
--ROSS'S NOTES TEND TO JUMP AROUND A BIT--
WHY DO YOU ADDRESS ME THIS WAY?
IT'S HOW YOU'RE SUPPOSED TO BE ADDRESSED.
BLEEEEP
BLEEEEP
BLEEEEP
IT'S OCP GUIDEBOOK.
BLEEEEP
BLEEEEP
BLEEEEP
IT'S ALL WE HAVE LEFT.
BLEEEEP
BLEEEEP
BLEEEEP
BLEEEEP
BLEEEEP
BLEEEEP
THAT'S MINE.

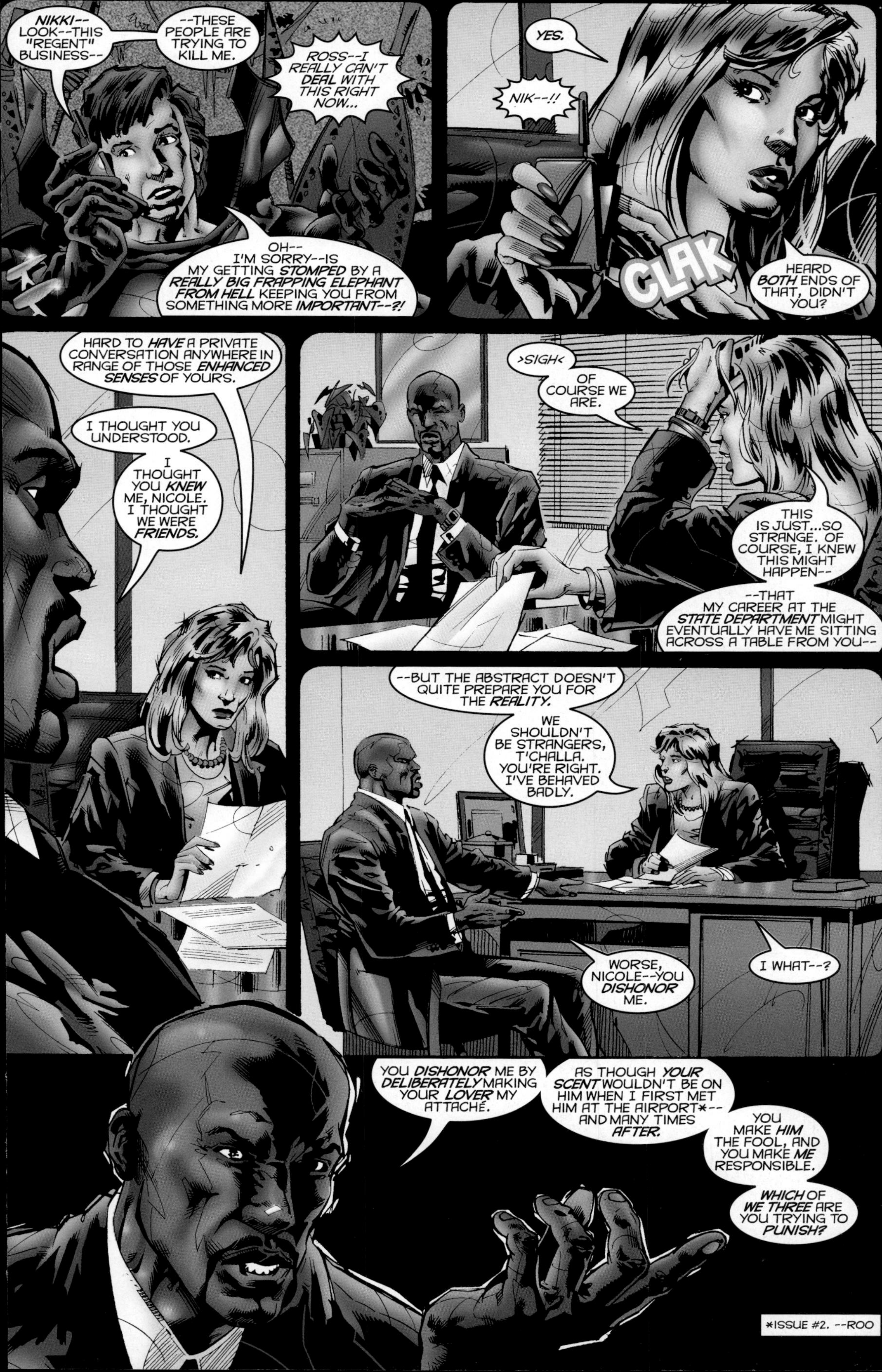
NIKKI-- LOOK--THIS "REGENT" BUSINESS--
--THESE PEOPLE ARE TRYING TO KILL ME.
ROSS--I REALLY CAN'T DEAL WITH THIS RIGHT NOW...
OH-- I'M SORRY--IS MY GETTING STOMPED BY A REALLY BIG FRAPPING ELEPHANT FROM HELL KEEPING YOU FROM SOMETHING MORE IMPORTANT--?!
YES.
NIK--!!
CLAK
HEARD BOTH ENDS OF THAT, DIDN'T YOU?
HARD TO HAVE A PRIVATE CONVERSATION ANYWHERE IN RANGE OF THOSE ENHANCED SENSES OF YOURS.
I THOUGHT YOU UNDERSTOOD.
I THOUGHT YOU KNEW ME, NICOLE. I THOUGHT WE WERE FRIENDS.
>SIGH<
OF COURSE WE ARE.
THIS IS JUST...SO STRANGE. OF COURSE, I KNEW THIS MIGHT HAPPEN--
--THAT MY CAREER AT THE STATE DEPARTMENT MIGHT EVENTUALLY HAVE ME SITTING ACROSS A TABLE FROM YOU--
--BUT THE ABSTRACT DOESN'T QUITE PREPARE YOU FOR THE REALITY.
WE SHOULDN'T BE STRANGERS, T'CHALLA. YOU'RE RIGHT. I'VE BEHAVED BADLY.
WORSE, NICOLE--YOU DISHONOR ME.
I WHAT--?
YOU DISHONOR ME BY DELIBERATELY MAKING YOUR LOVER MY ATTACHÉ.
AS THOUGH YOUR SCENT WOULDN'T BE ON HIM WHEN I FIRST MET HIM AT THE AIRPORT*-- AND MANY TIMES AFTER.
YOU MAKE HIM THE FOOL, AND YOU MAKE ME RESPONSIBLE.
WHICH OF WE THREE ARE YOU TRYING TO PUNISH?
*ISSUE #2. --ROO

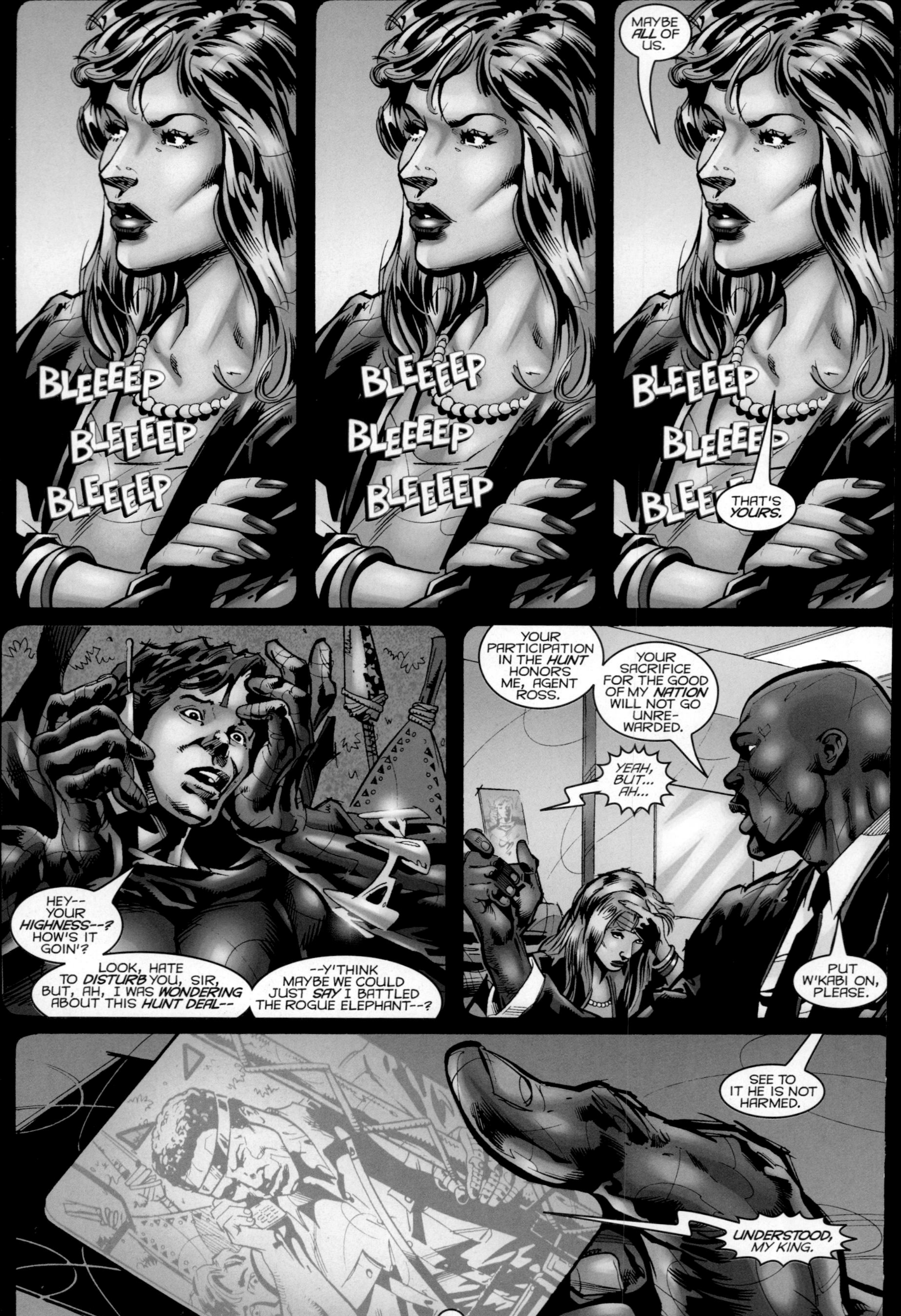

BLEEEEP
BLEEEEP
BLEEEEP
BLEEEEP
BLEEEEP
BLEEEEP
MAYBE ALL OF US.
BLEEEEP
BLEEEEP
BLEE
THAT'S YOURS.
HEY--YOUR HIGHNESS--? HOW'S IT GOIN'?
LOOK, HATE TO DISTURB YOU, SIR, BUT, AH, I WAS WONDERING ABOUT THIS HUNT DEAL--
--Y'THINK MAYBE WE COULD JUST SAY I BATTLED THE ROGUE ELEPHANT--?
YOUR PARTICIPATION IN THE HUNT HONORS ME, AGENT ROSS.
YOUR SACRIFICE FOR THE GOOD OF MY NATION WILL NOT GO UNRE-WARDED.
YEAH, BUT... AH...
PUT W'KABI ON, PLEASE.
SEE TO IT HE IS NOT HARMED.
UNDERSTOOD, MY KING.

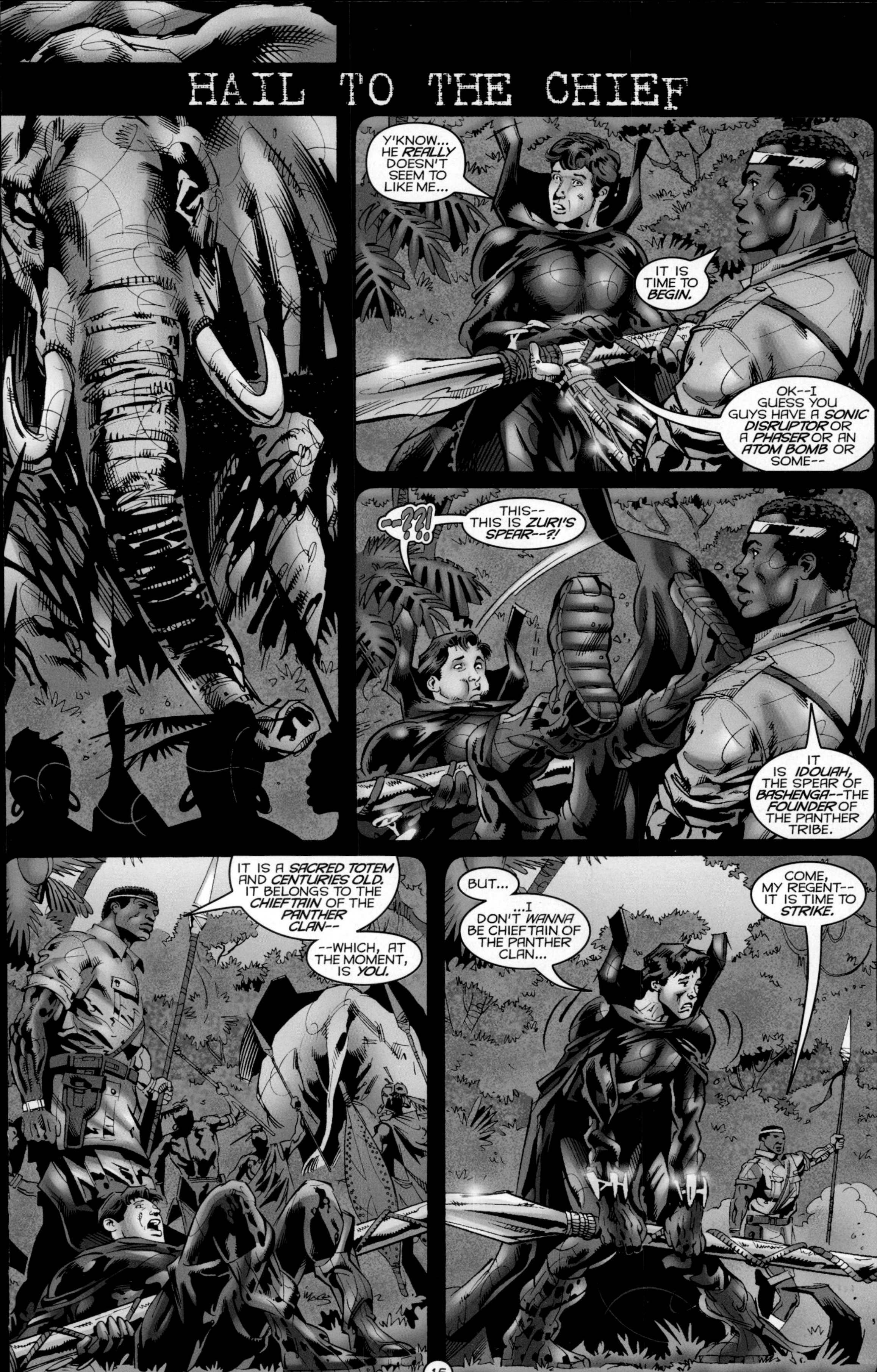
HAIL TO THE CHIEF
Y'KNOW... HE REALLY DOESN'T SEEM TO LIKE ME...
IT IS TIME TO BEGIN.
OK--I GUESS YOU GUYS HAVE A SONIC DISRUPTOR OR A PHASER OR AN ATOM BOMB OR SOME--
--??!
THIS-- THIS IS ZURI'S SPEAR--?!
IT IS IDOUAH, THE SPEAR OF BASHENGA--THE FOUNDER OF THE PANTHER TRIBE.
IT IS A SACRED TOTEM AND CENTURIES OLD. IT BELONGS TO THE CHIEFTAIN OF THE PANTHER CLAN--
--WHICH, AT THE MOMENT, IS YOU.
BUT...
...I DON'T WANNA BE CHIEFTAIN OF THE PANTHER CLAN...
COME, MY REGENT-- IT IS TIME TO STRIKE.

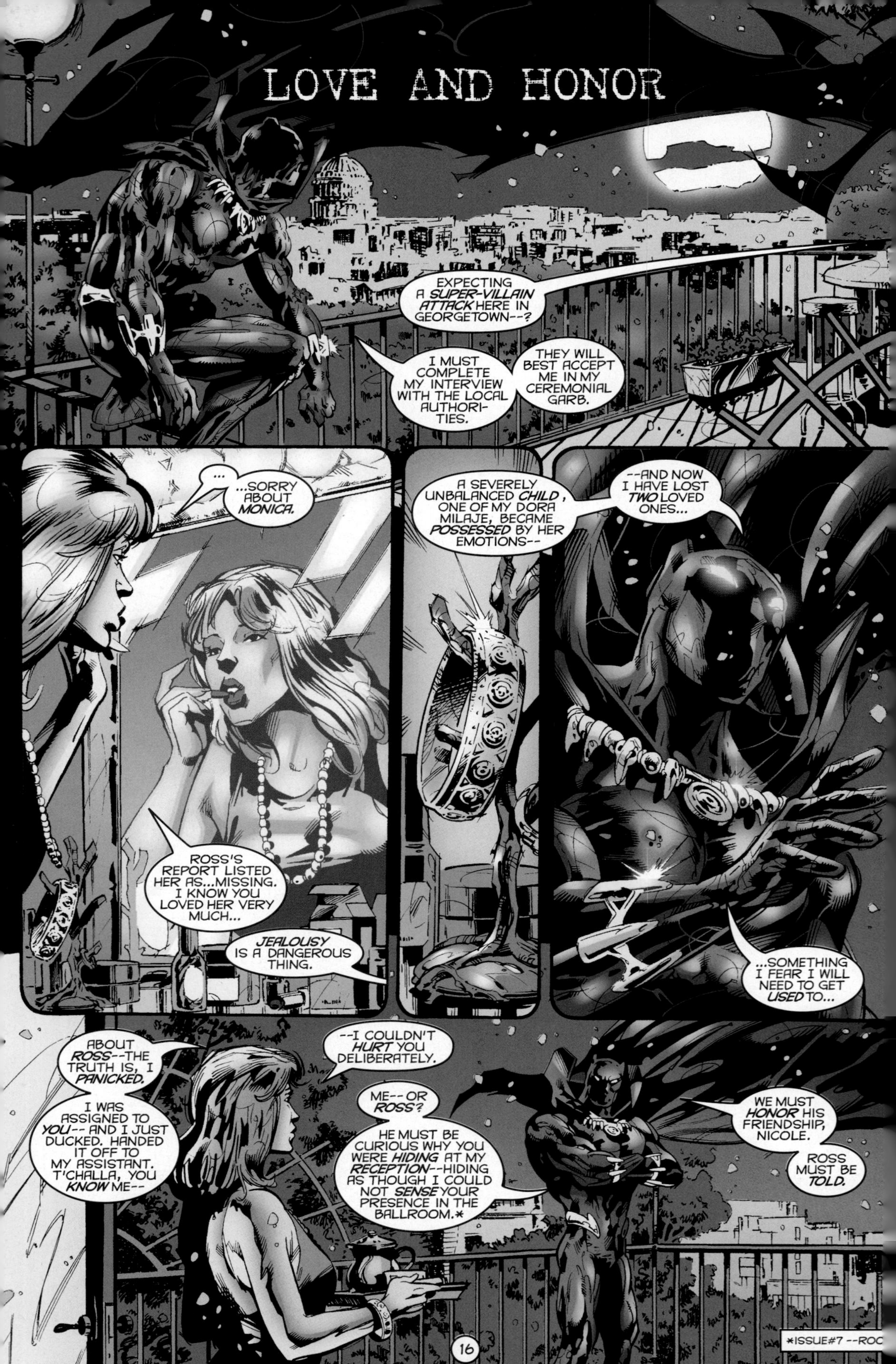

LOVE AND HONOR
EXPECTING A SUPER-VILLAIN ATTACK HERE IN GEORGETOWN--?
I MUST COMPLETE MY INTERVIEW WITH THE LOCAL AUTHORITIES.
THEY WILL BEST ACCEPT ME IN MY CEREMONIAL GARB.
...
...SORRY ABOUT MONICA.
ROSS'S REPORT LISTED HER AS...MISSING. I KNOW YOU LOVED HER VERY MUCH...
JEALOUSY IS A DANGEROUS THING.
A SEVERELY UNBALANCED CHILD, ONE OF MY DORA MILAJE, BECAME POSSESSED BY HER EMOTIONS--
--AND NOW I HAVE LOST TWO LOVED ONES...
...SOMETHING I FEAR I WILL NEED TO GET USED TO...
ABOUT ROSS--THE TRUTH IS, I PANICKED.
I WAS ASSIGNED TO YOU-- AND I JUST DUCKED. HANDED IT OFF TO MY ASSISTANT. T'CHALLA, YOU KNOW ME--
--I COULDN'T HURT YOU DELIBERATELY.
ME--OR ROSS?
HE MUST BE CURIOUS WHY YOU WERE HIDING AT MY RECEPTION--HIDING AS THOUGH I COULD NOT SENSE YOUR PRESENCE IN THE BALLROOM.*
WE MUST HONOR HIS FRIENDSHIP, NICOLE.
ROSS MUST BE TOLD.
*ISSUE#7 --ROC

HIS TURN

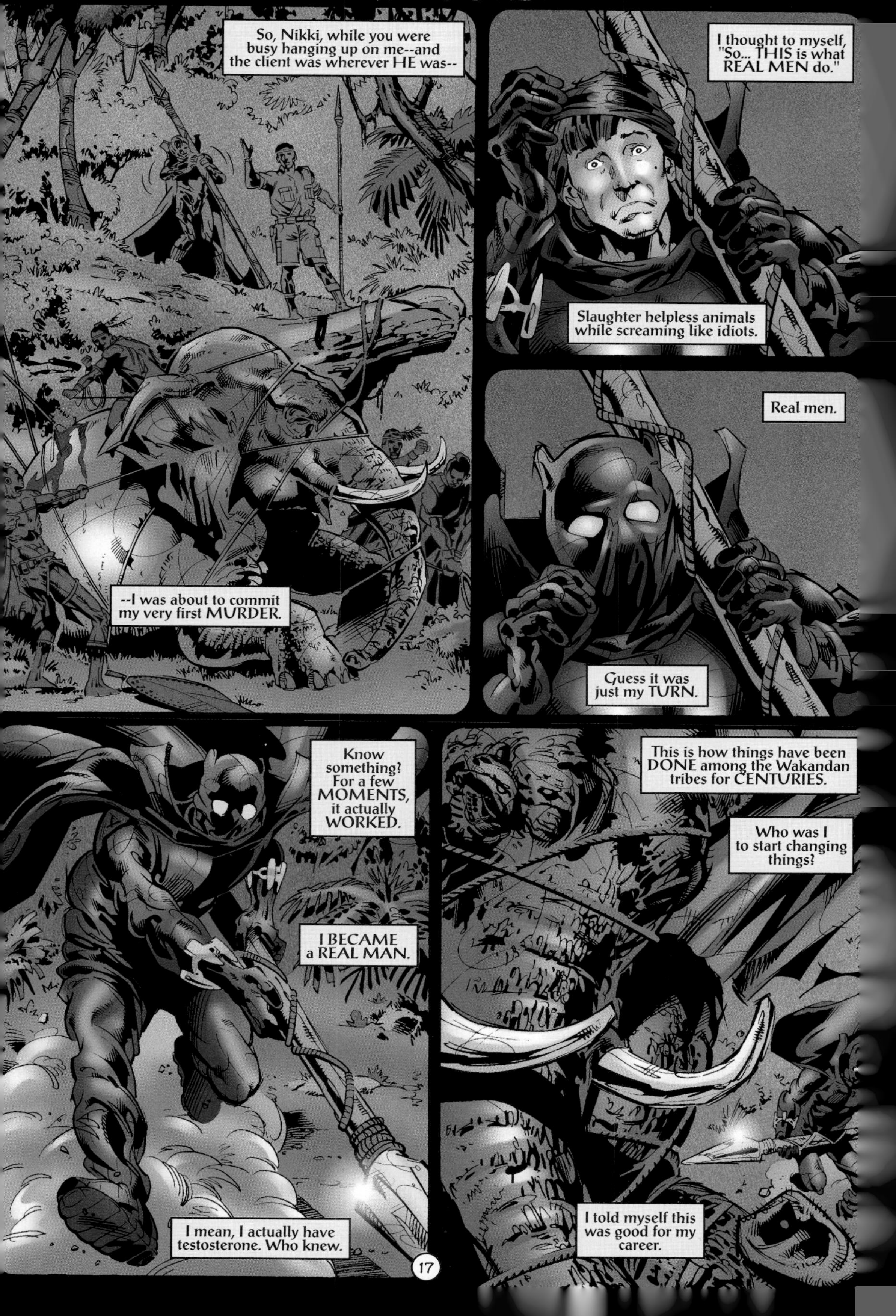

So, Nikki, while you were busy hanging up on me--and the client was wherever HE was--
--I was about to commit my very first MURDER.
I thought to myself, "So... THIS is what REAL MEN do."
Slaughter helpless animals while screaming like idiots.
Real men.
Guess it was just my TURN.
Know something? For a few MOMENTS, it actually WORKED.
I BECAME a REAL MAN.
I mean, I actually have testosterone. Who knew.
This is how things have been DONE among the Wakandan tribes for CENTURIES.
Who was I to start changing things?
I told myself this was good for my career.

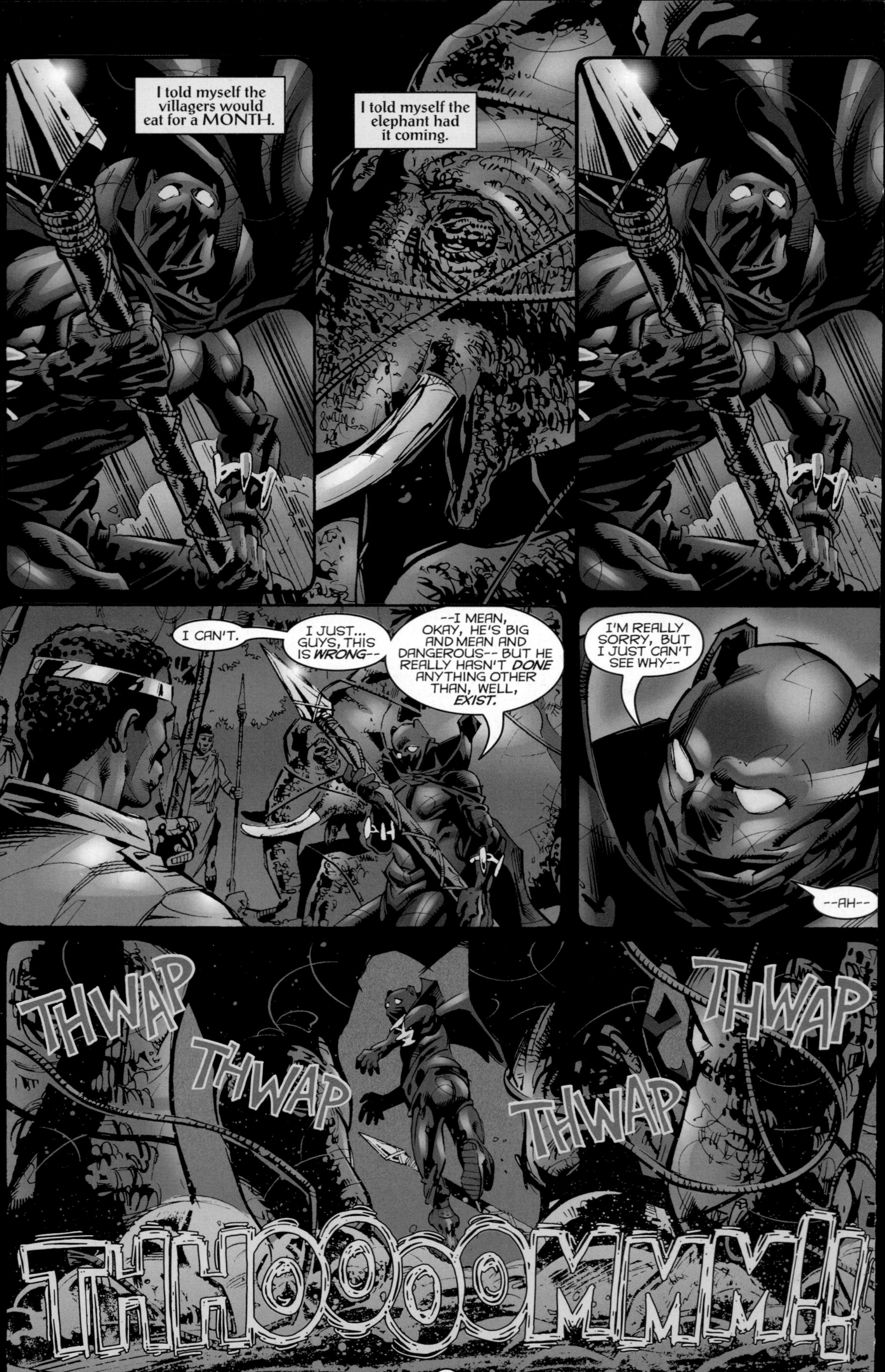
I told myself the villagers would eat for a MONTH.
I told myself the elephant had it coming.
I CAN'T.
I JUST... GUYS, THIS IS *WRONG*--
--I MEAN, OKAY, HE'S BIG AND MEAN AND DANGEROUS-- BUT HE REALLY HASN'T *DONE* ANYTHING OTHER THAN, WELL, *EXIST.*
I'M REALLY SORRY, BUT I JUST CAN'T SEE WHY--
--AH--
THWAP
THWAP
THWAP
THWAP
THHOOOOOMMMM!!

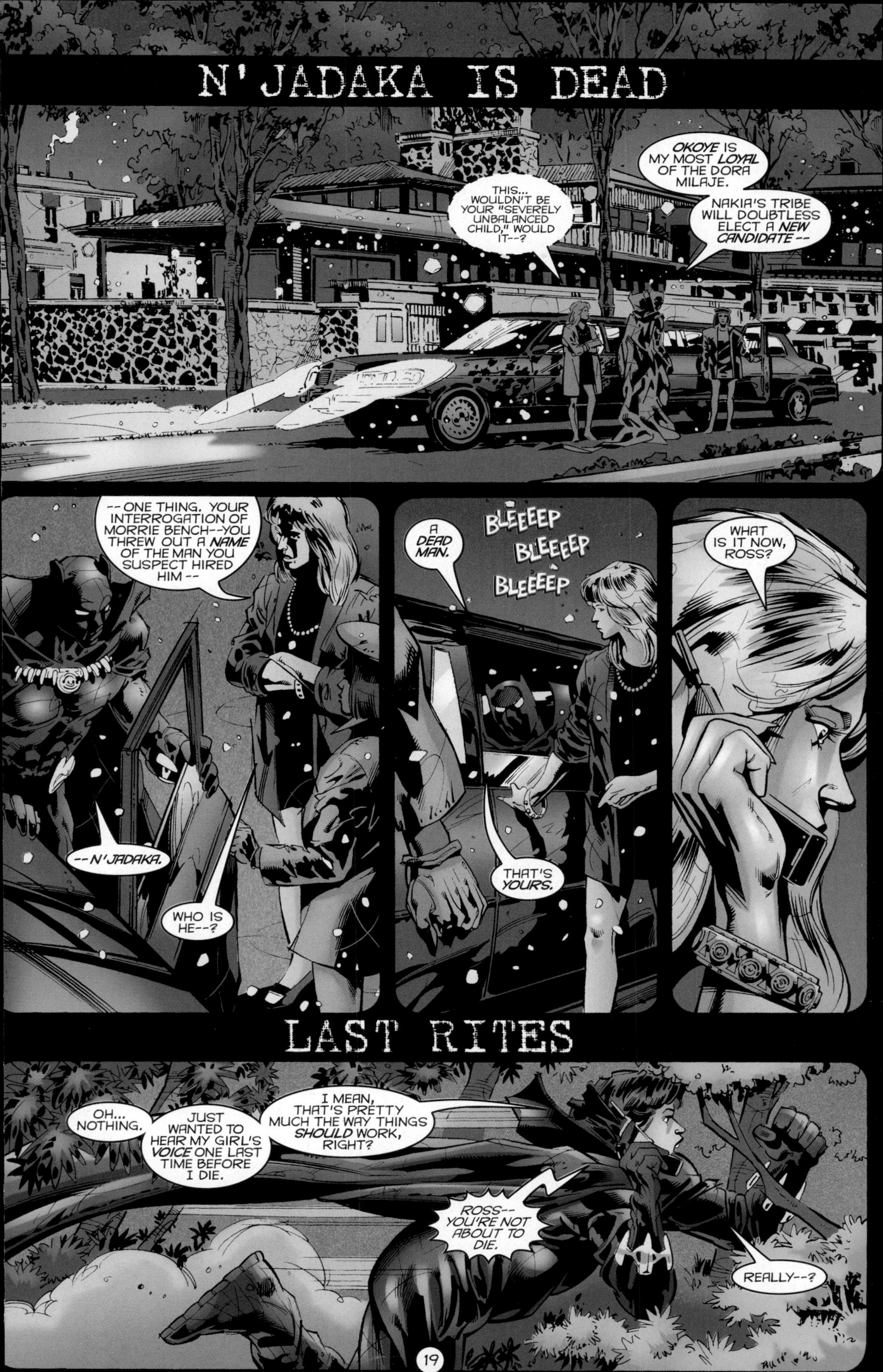
N'JADAKA IS DEAD
THIS... WOULDN'T BE YOUR "SEVERELY UNBALANCED CHILD," WOULD IT--?
OKOYE IS MY MOST LOYAL OF THE DORA MILAJE.
NAKIA'S TRIBE WILL DOUBTLESS ELECT A NEW CANDIDATE --
-- ONE THING. YOUR INTERROGATION OF MORRIE BENCH--YOU THREW OUT A NAME OF THE MAN YOU SUSPECT HIRED HIM --
--N'JADAKA.
WHO IS HE--?
A DEAD MAN.
BLEEEEP
BLEEEEP
BLEEEEP
THAT'S YOURS.
WHAT IS IT NOW, ROSS?
LAST RITES
OH... NOTHING.
JUST WANTED TO HEAR MY GIRL'S VOICE ONE LAST TIME BEFORE I DIE.
I MEAN, THAT'S PRETTY MUCH THE WAY THINGS SHOULD WORK, RIGHT?
ROSS-- YOU'RE NOT ABOUT TO DIE.
REALLY--?

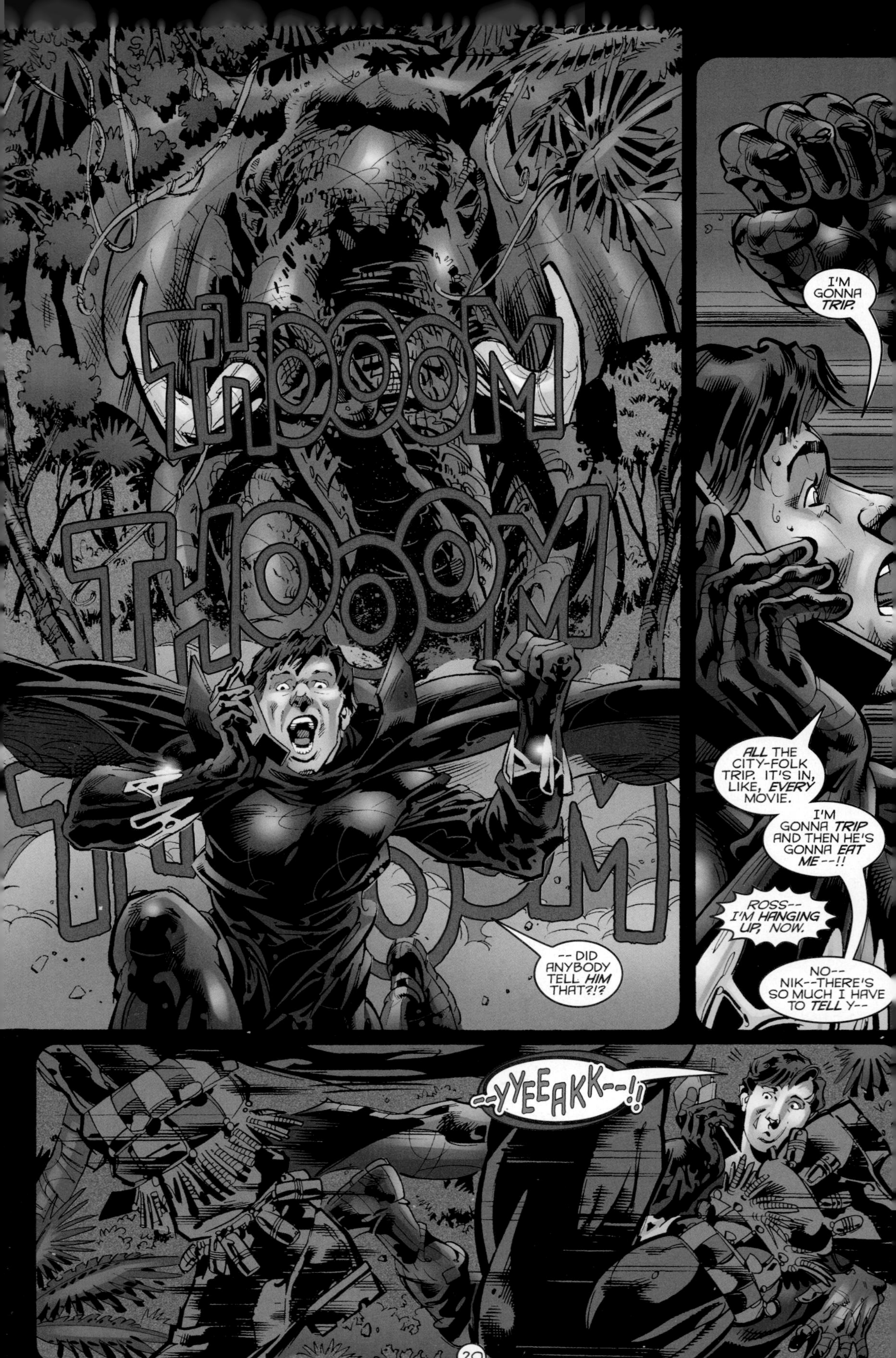
THOOOM
THOOOOM
THOOOM
-- DID ANYBODY TELL HIM THAT?!?
I'M GONNA TRIP.
ALL THE CITY-FOLK TRIP. IT'S IN, LIKE, EVERY MOVIE.
I'M GONNA TRIP AND THEN HE'S GONNA EAT ME --!!
ROSS-- I'M HANGING UP, NOW.
NO-- NIK--THERE'S SO MUCH I HAVE TO TELL Y--
--YYEEAKK--!!

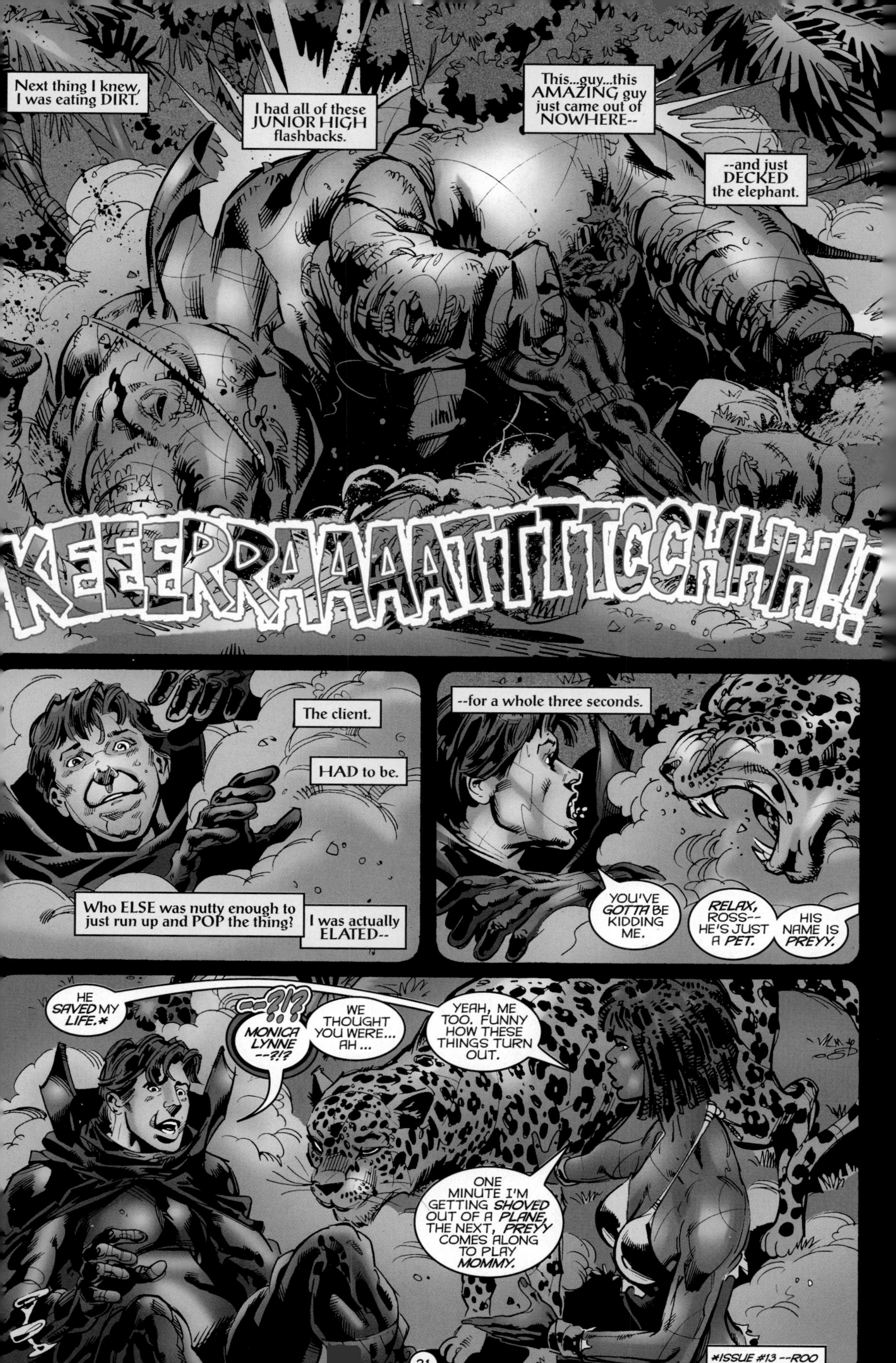

Next thing I knew, I was eating DIRT.
I had all of these JUNIOR HIGH flashbacks.
This...guy...this AMAZING guy just came out of NOWHERE--
--and just DECKED the elephant.
KEEERRAAAATTTTCCHHH!!
The client.
HAD to be.
Who ELSE was nutty enough to just run up and POP the thing?
I was actually ELATED--
--for a whole three seconds.
YOU'VE GOTTA BE KIDDING ME.
RELAX, ROSS-- HE'S JUST A PET.
HIS NAME IS PREYY.
HE SAVED MY LIFE.*
--?!?
MONICA LYNNE --?!?
WE THOUGHT YOU WERE... AH ...
YEAH, ME TOO. FUNNY HOW THESE THINGS TURN OUT.
ONE MINUTE I'M GETTING SHOVED OUT OF A PLANE, THE NEXT, PREYY COMES ALONG TO PLAY MOMMY.
*ISSUE #13 --ROO

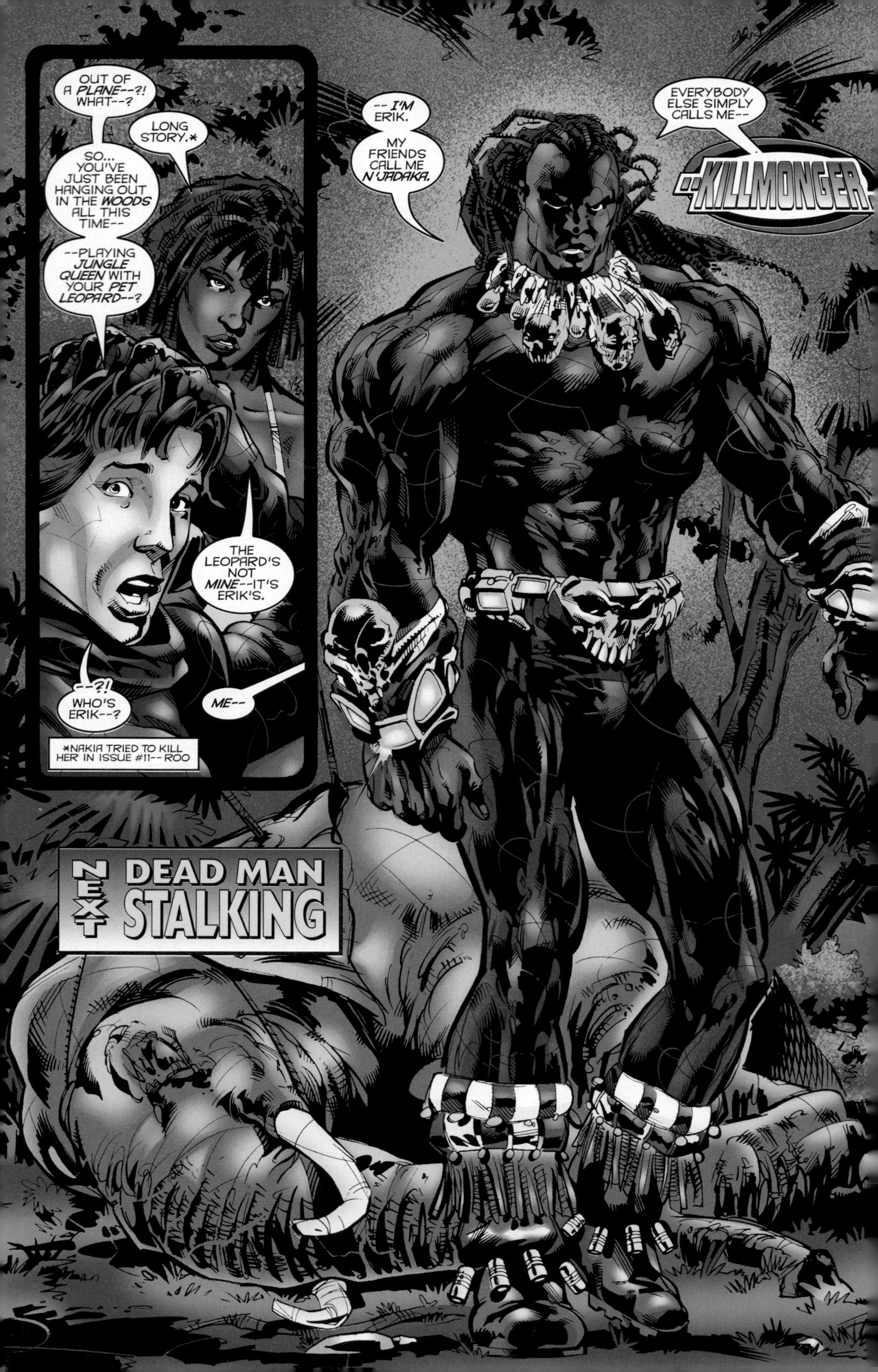
OUT OF A PLANE--?! WHAT--?
LONG STORY.*
SO... YOU'VE JUST BEEN HANGING OUT IN THE WOODS ALL THIS TIME--
--PLAYING JUNGLE QUEEN WITH YOUR PET LEOPARD--?
THE LEOPARD'S NOT MINE--IT'S ERIK'S.
--?! WHO'S ERIK--?
ME--
*NAKIA TRIED TO KILL HER IN ISSUE #11-- ROO
--I'M ERIK.
MY FRIENDS CALL ME N'JADAKA.
EVERYBODY ELSE SIMPLY CALLS ME--
--KILLMONGER
NEXT DEAD MAN STALKING

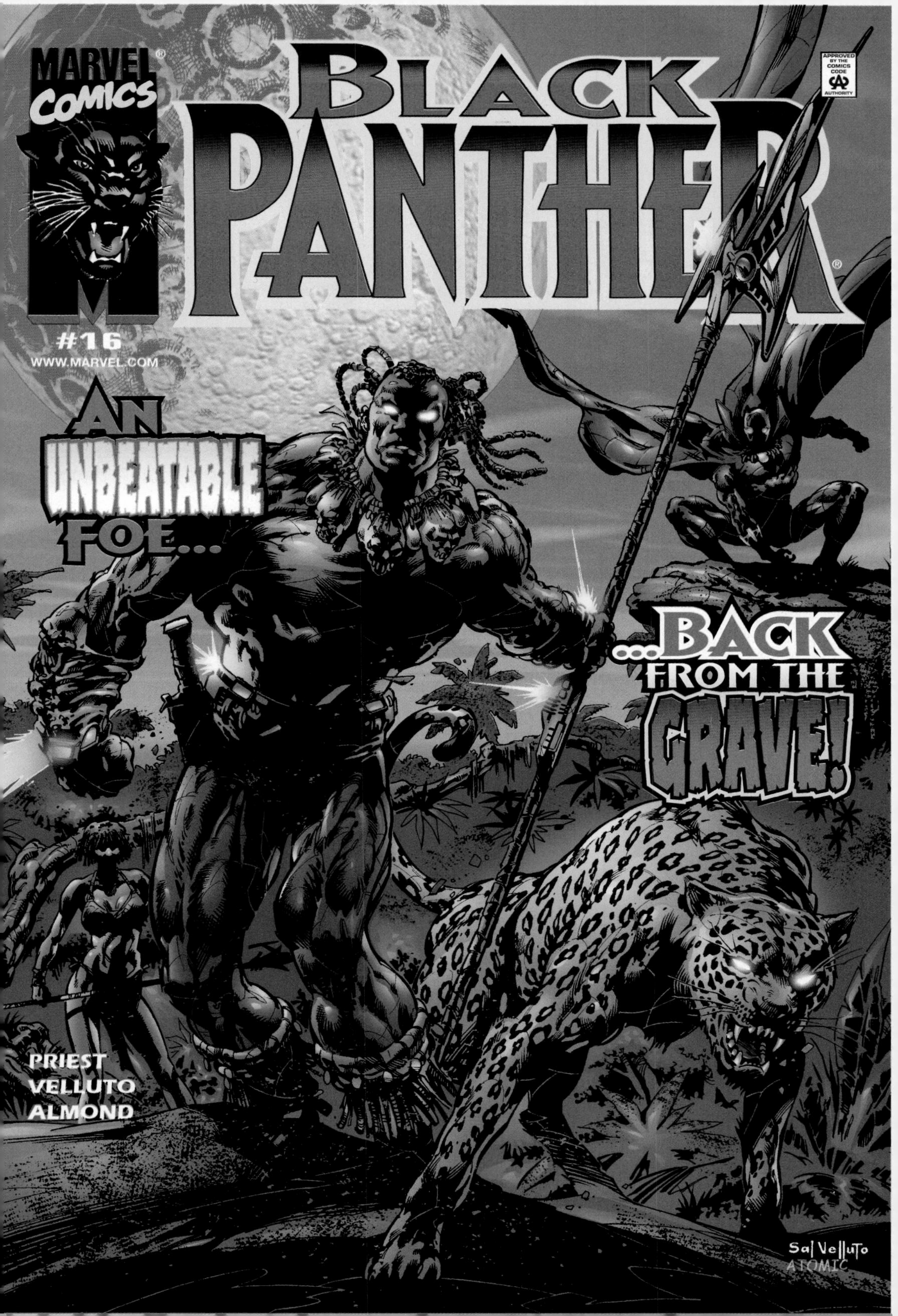
MARVEL COMICS
APPROVED BY THE COMICS CODE AUTHORITY
BLACK PANTHER
#16
WWW.MARVEL.COM
AN UNBEATABLE FOE...
...BACK FROM THE GRAVE!
PRIEST
VELLUTO
ALMOND
Sal Velluto
ATOMIC

QUERY

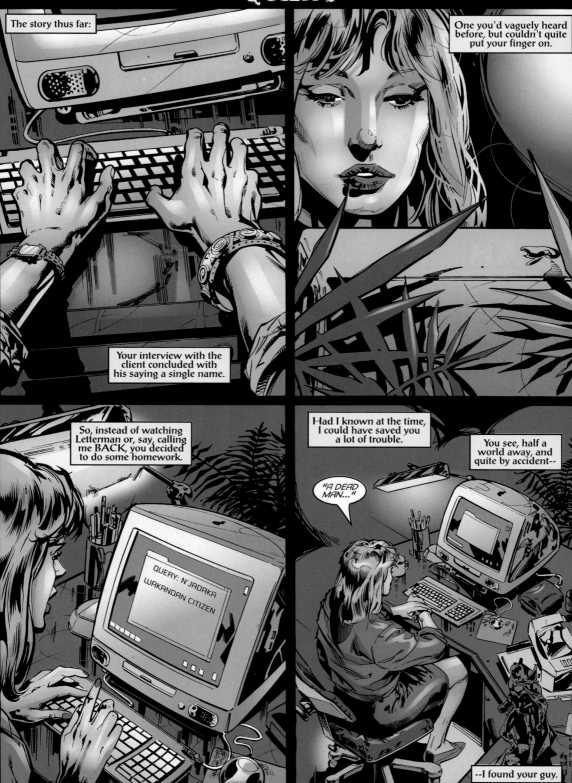

The story thus far:

One you'd vaguely heard before, but couldn't quite put your finger on.

Your interview with the client concluded with his saying a single name.

So, instead of watching Letterman or, say, calling me BACK, you decided to do some homework.

QUERY: N'JADAKA
WAKANDAN CITIZEN

Had I known at the time, I could have saved you a lot of trouble.

You see, half a world away, and quite by accident--

"A DEAD MAN..."

--I found your guy.

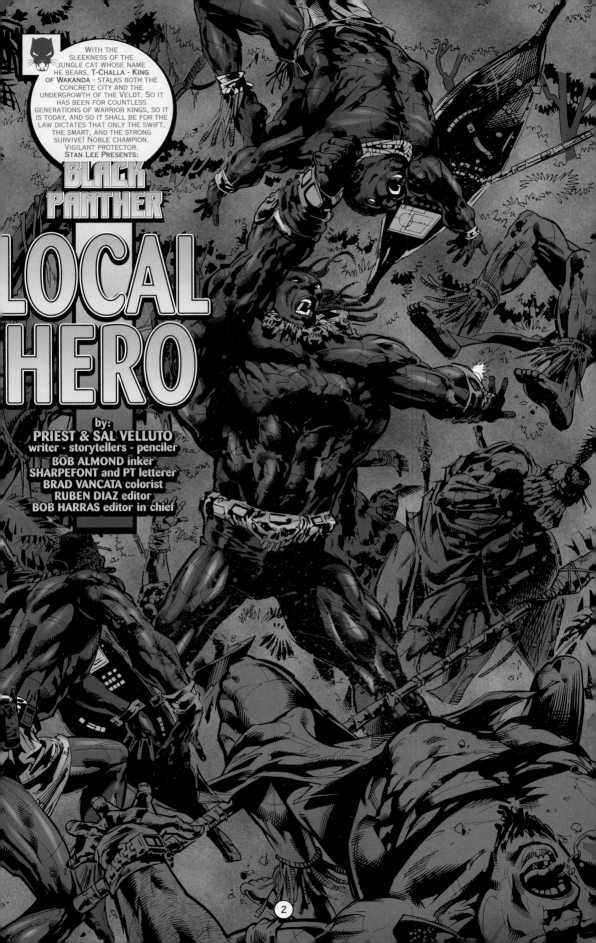

WITH THE SLEEKNESS OF THE JUNGLE CAT WHOSE NAME HE BEARS, T-CHALLA - KING OF WAKANDA - STALKS BOTH THE CONCRETE CITY AND THE UNDERGROWTH OF THE VELDT. SO IT HAS BEEN FOR COUNTLESS GENERATIONS OF WARRIOR KINGS, SO IT IS TODAY, AND SO IT SHALL BE FOR THE LAW DICTATES THAT ONLY THE SWIFT, THE SMART, AND THE STRONG SURVIVE! NOBLE CHAMPION. VIGILANT PROTECTOR. STAN LEE PRESENTS:

BLACK PANTHER
LOCAL HERO

by:
PRIEST & SAL VELLUTO
writer - storytellers - penciler
BOB ALMOND inker
SHARPEFONT and **PT** letterer
BRAD VANCATA colorist
RUBEN DIAZ editor
BOB HARRAS editor in chief

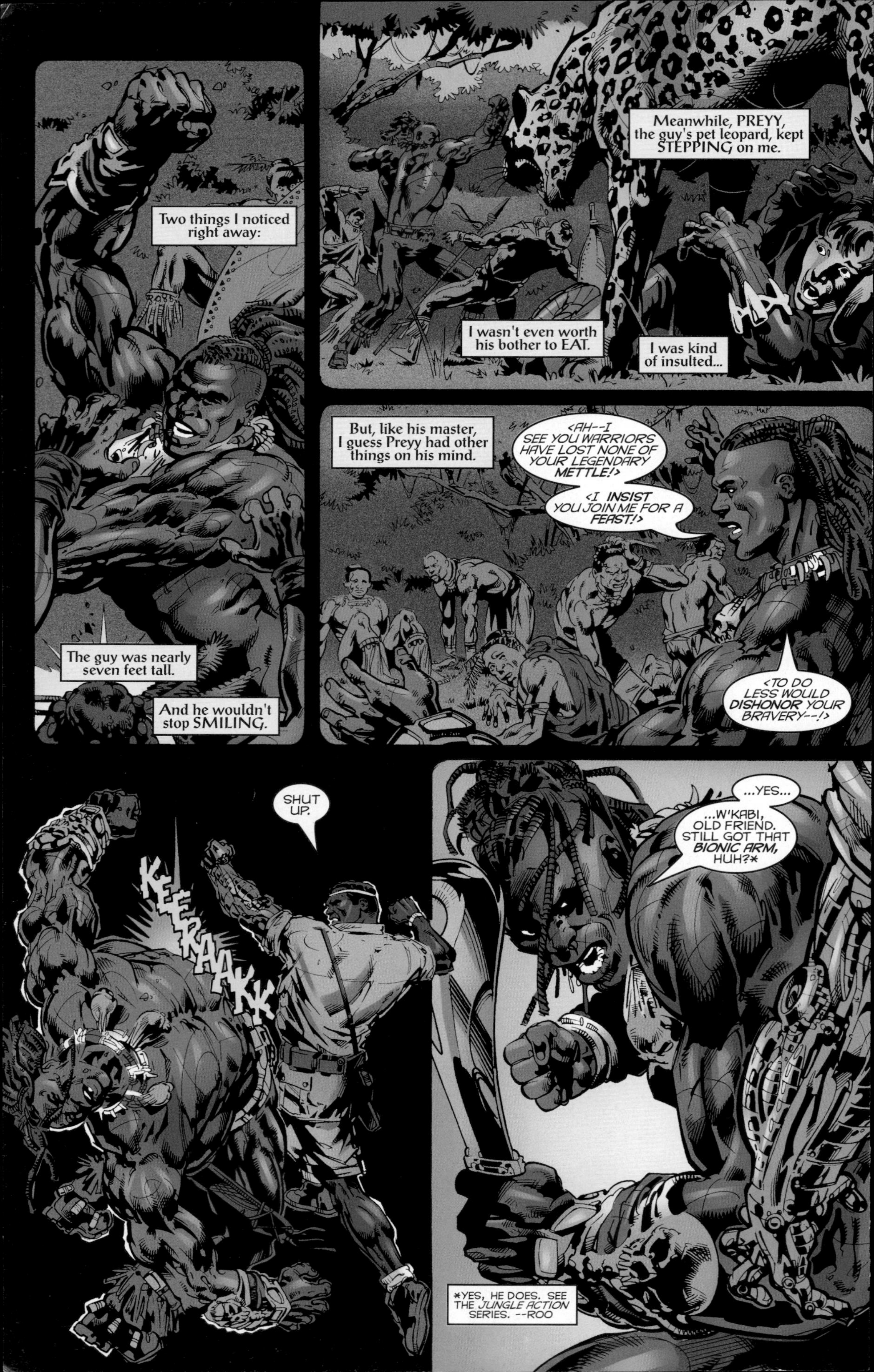

Two things I noticed right away:
The guy was nearly seven feet tall.
And he wouldn't stop SMILING.
Meanwhile, PREYY, the guy's pet leopard, kept STEPPING on me.
I wasn't even worth his bother to EAT.
I was kind of insulted...
But, like his master, I guess Preyy had other things on his mind.
<AH--I SEE YOU WARRIORS HAVE LOST NONE OF YOUR LEGENDARY METTLE!>
<I INSIST YOU JOIN ME FOR A FEAST!>
<TO DO LESS WOULD DISHONOR YOUR BRAVERY--!>
SHUT UP.
KEERAAAKK
...YES...
...W'KABI, OLD FRIEND. STILL GOT THAT BIONIC ARM, HUH?*
*YES, HE DOES. SEE THE JUNGLE ACTION SERIES. --ROO

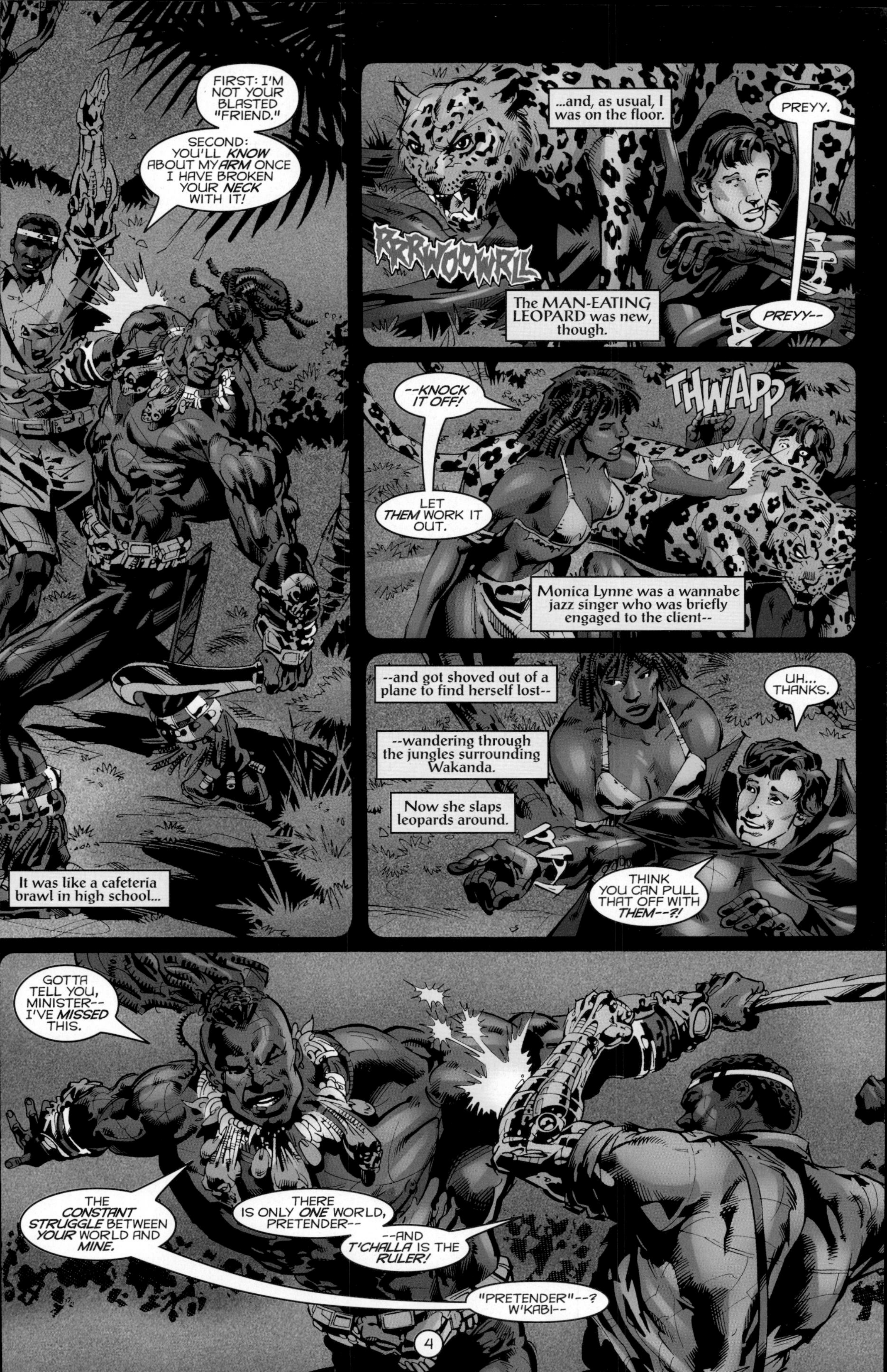

FIRST: I'M NOT YOUR BLASTED "FRIEND."
SECOND: YOU'LL KNOW ABOUT MY ARM ONCE I HAVE BROKEN YOUR NECK WITH IT!
It was like a cafeteria brawl in high school...
...and, as usual, I was on the floor.
PREYY.
RRRWOOWRLL
The MAN-EATING LEOPARD was new, though.
PREYY--
--KNOCK IT OFF!
THWAPP
LET THEM WORK IT OUT.
Monica Lynne was a wannabe jazz singer who was briefly engaged to the client--
--and got shoved out of a plane to find herself lost--
--wandering through the jungles surrounding Wakanda.
Now she slaps leopards around.
UH... THANKS.
THINK YOU CAN PULL THAT OFF WITH THEM--?!
GOTTA TELL YOU, MINISTER--I'VE MISSED THIS.
THE CONSTANT STRUGGLE BETWEEN YOUR WORLD AND MINE.
THERE IS ONLY ONE WORLD, PRETENDER--
--AND T'CHALLA IS THE RULER!
"PRETENDER"--? W'KABI--

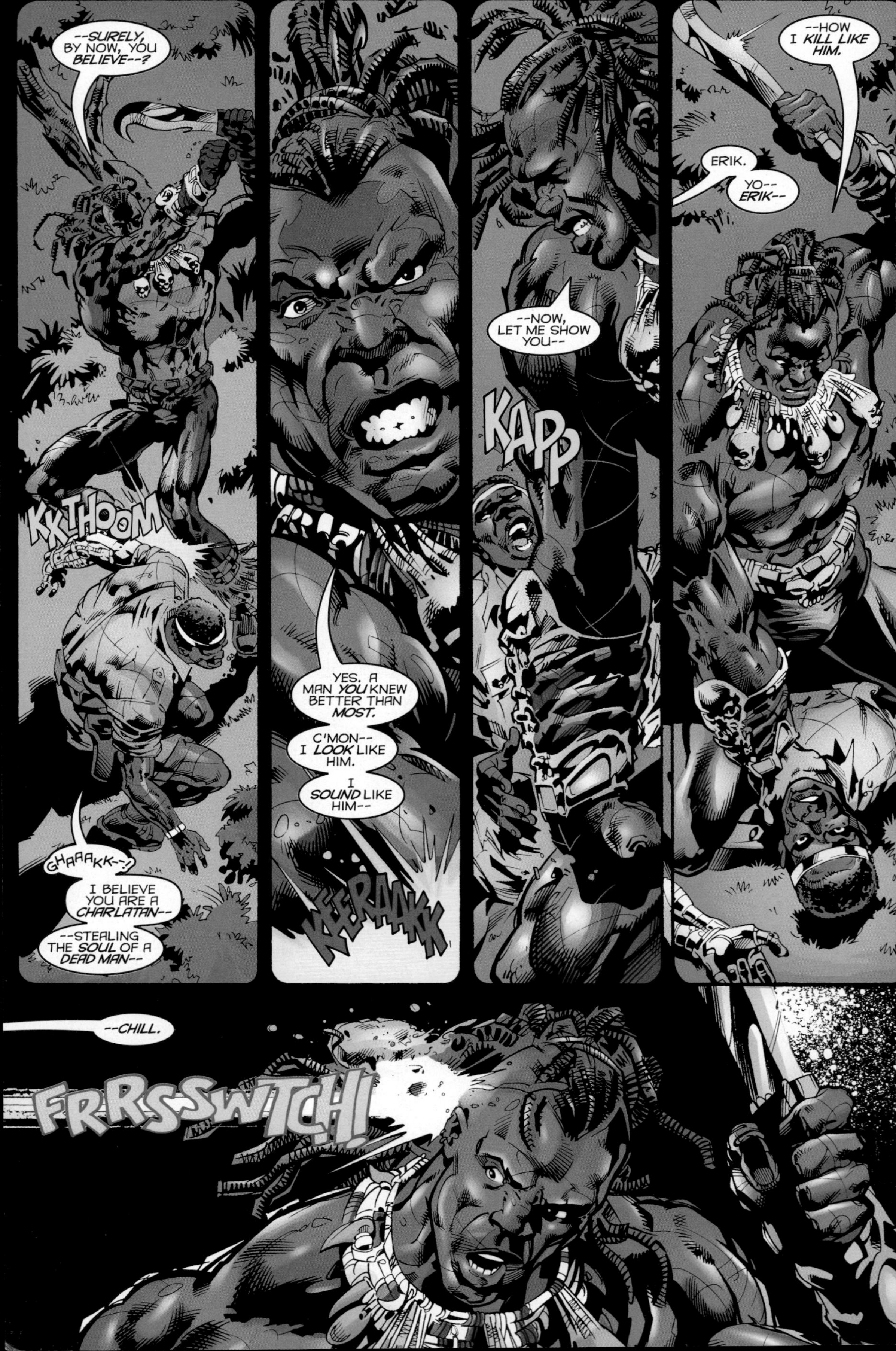
--SURELY, BY NOW, YOU BELIEVE--?
KKTHOOM
GHAAAKK--!
I BELIEVE YOU ARE A CHARLATAN--
--STEALING THE SOUL OF A DEAD MAN--
YES. A MAN YOU KNEW BETTER THAN MOST.
C'MON-- I LOOK LIKE HIM.
I SOUND LIKE HIM--
KEERAAKK
--NOW, LET ME SHOW YOU--
KAPP
--HOW I KILL LIKE HIM.
ERIK.
YO-- ERIK--
--CHILL.
FRRSSWTCH!

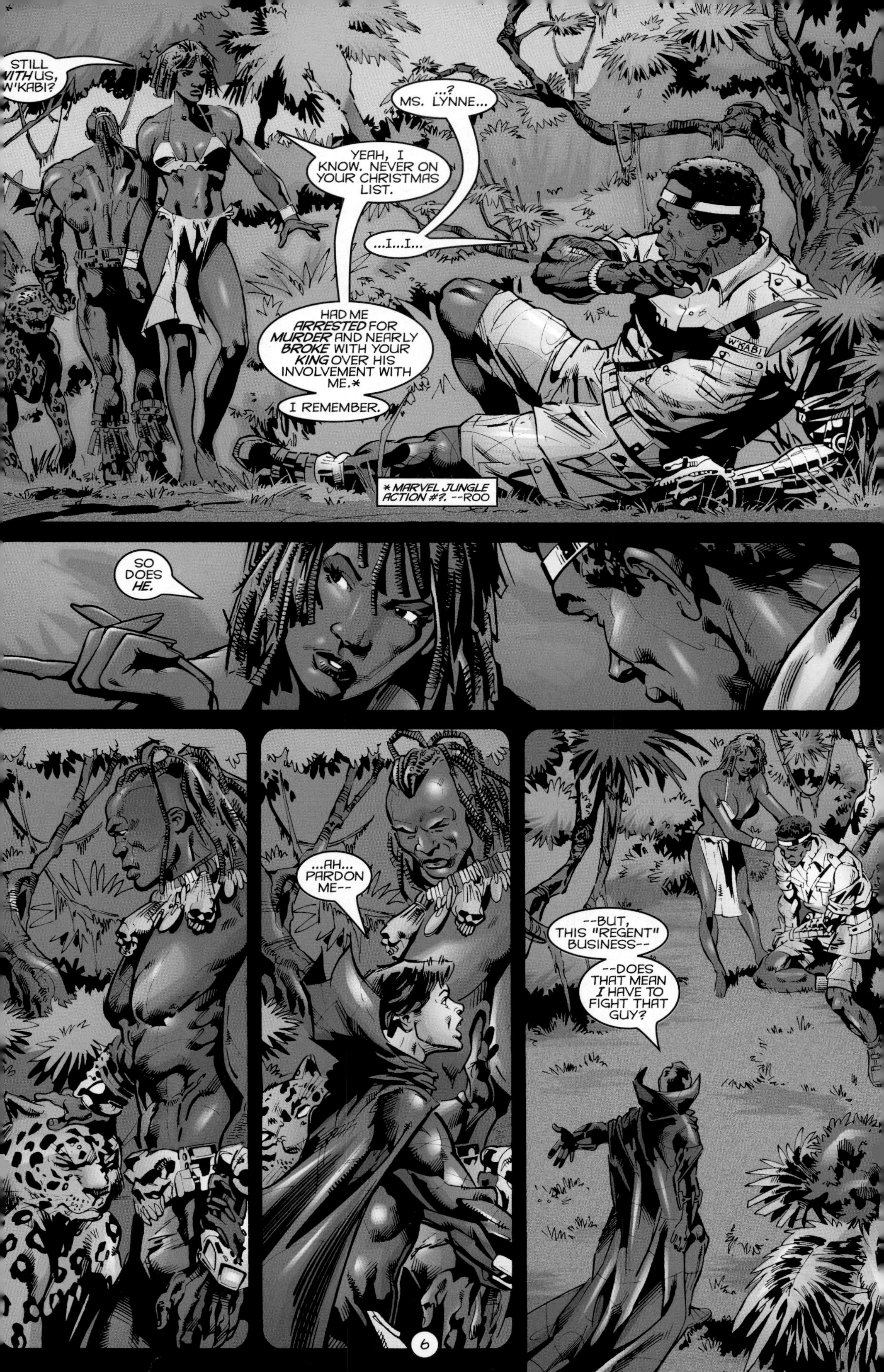
STILL WITH US, W'KABI?
...? MS. LYNNE...
YEAH, I KNOW. NEVER ON YOUR CHRISTMAS LIST.
...I...I...
HAD ME ARRESTED FOR MURDER AND NEARLY BROKE WITH YOUR KING OVER HIS INVOLVEMENT WITH ME.*
I REMEMBER.
W'KABI
*MARVEL JUNGLE ACTION #?. --ROO
SO DOES HE.
...AH... PARDON ME--
--BUT, THIS "REGENT" BUSINESS--
--DOES THAT MEAN I HAVE TO FIGHT THAT GUY?

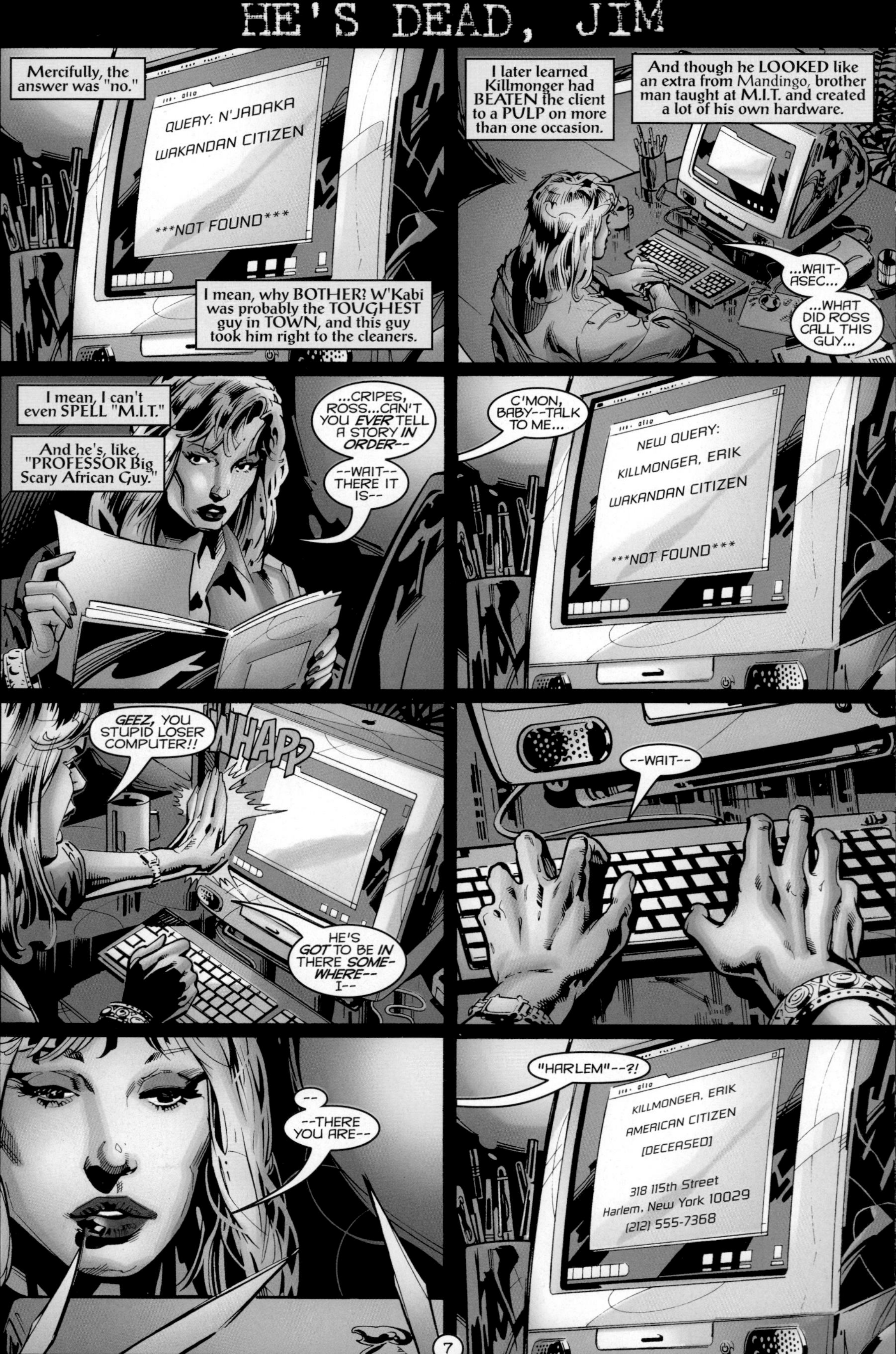
HE'S DEAD, JIM
Mercifully, the answer was "no."
QUERY: N'JADAKA
WAKANDAN CITIZEN
NOT FOUND
I mean, why BOTHER? W'Kabi was probably the TOUGHEST guy in TOWN, and this guy took him right to the cleaners.
I later learned Killmonger had BEATEN the client to a PULP on more than one occasion.
And though he LOOKED like an extra from Mandingo, brother man taught at M.I.T. and created a lot of his own hardware.
...WAIT-ASEC...
...WHAT DID ROSS CALL THIS GUY...
I mean, I can't even SPELL "M.I.T."
And he's, like, "PROFESSOR Big Scary African Guy."
...CRIPES, ROSS...CAN'T YOU EVER TELL A STORY IN ORDER--
--WAIT--THERE IT IS--
C'MON, BABY--TALK TO ME...
NEW QUERY:
KILLMONGER, ERIK
WAKANDAN CITIZEN
NOT FOUND
GEEZ, YOU STUPID LOSER COMPUTER!!
WHAPP
HE'S GOT TO BE IN THERE SOME-WHERE--I--
--WAIT--
--
--THERE YOU ARE--
"HARLEM"--?!
KILLMONGER, ERIK
AMERICAN CITIZEN
[DECEASED]
318 115th Street
Harlem, New York 10029
(212) 555-7368
7

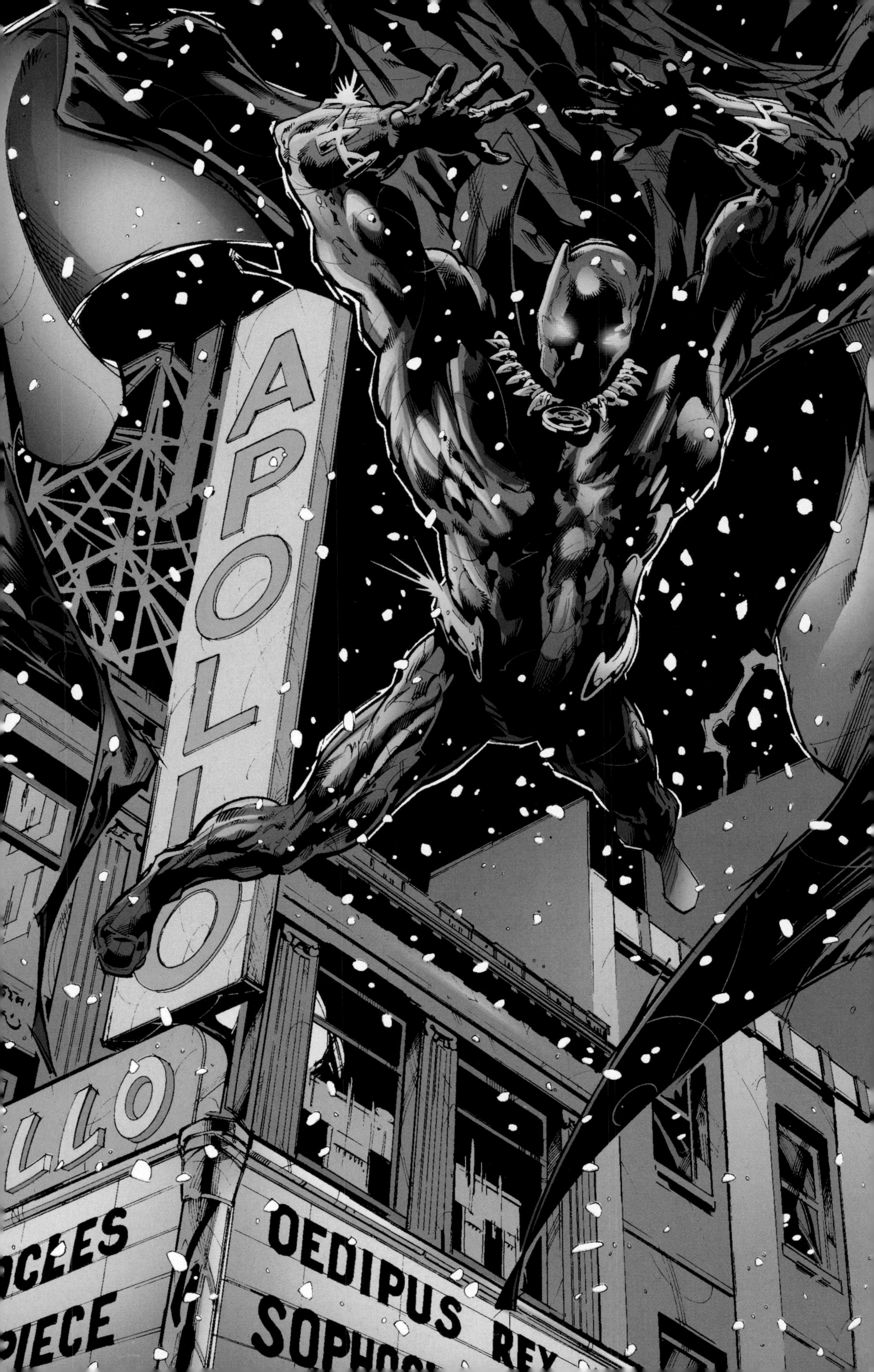

APOLLO
LLO
OCLES
PIECE
OEDIPUS
REX
SOPHOC

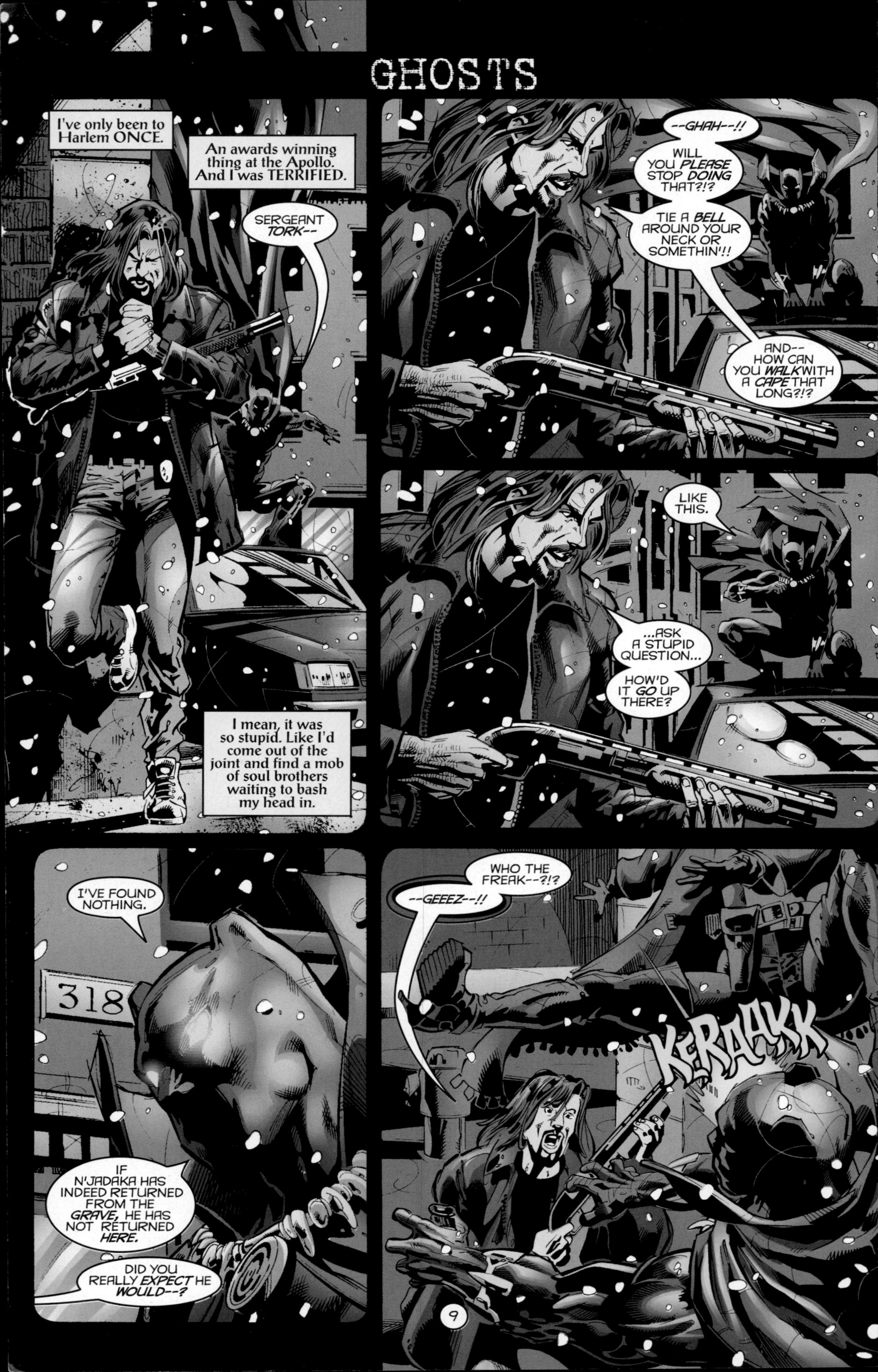
GHOSTS
I've only been to Harlem ONCE.
An awards winning thing at the Apollo. And I was TERRIFIED.
SERGEANT TORK--
I mean, it was so stupid. Like I'd come out of the joint and find a mob of soul brothers waiting to bash my head in.
--GHAH--!!
WILL YOU PLEASE STOP DOING THAT?!?
TIE A BELL AROUND YOUR NECK OR SOMETHIN'!!
AND-- HOW CAN YOU WALK WITH A CAPE THAT LONG?!?
LIKE THIS.
...ASK A STUPID QUESTION...
HOW'D IT GO UP THERE?
I'VE FOUND NOTHING.
318
IF N'JADAKA HAS INDEED RETURNED FROM THE GRAVE, HE HAS NOT RETURNED HERE.
DID YOU REALLY EXPECT HE WOULD--?
WHO THE FREAK--?!?
--GEEEZ--!!
KERAAKK
9

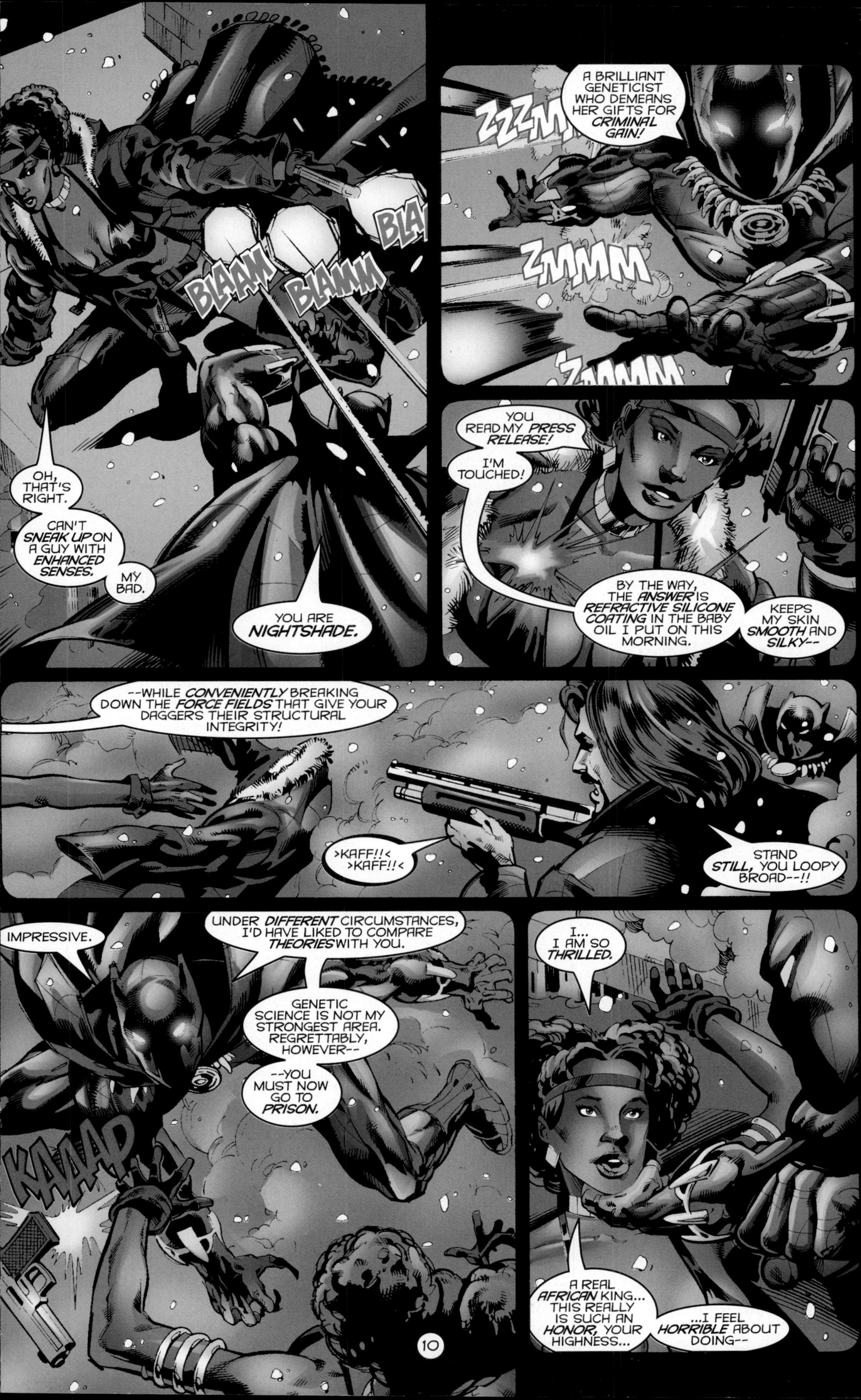
BLAAM
BLAMM
BLA
A BRILLIANT GENETICIST WHO DEMEANS HER GIFTS FOR CRIMINAL GAIN!
ZZZM
ZMMM
ZMMM
OH, THAT'S RIGHT.
CAN'T SNEAK UP ON A GUY WITH ENHANCED SENSES.
MY BAD.
YOU ARE NIGHTSHADE.
YOU READ MY PRESS RELEASE!
I'M TOUCHED!
BY THE WAY, THE ANSWER IS REFRACTIVE SILICONE COATING IN THE BABY OIL I PUT ON THIS MORNING.
KEEPS MY SKIN SMOOTH AND SILKY--
--WHILE CONVENIENTLY BREAKING DOWN THE FORCE FIELDS THAT GIVE YOUR DAGGERS THEIR STRUCTURAL INTEGRITY!
>KAFF!!< >KAFF!!<
STAND STILL, YOU LOOPY BROAD--!!
IMPRESSIVE.
UNDER DIFFERENT CIRCUMSTANCES, I'D HAVE LIKED TO COMPARE THEORIES WITH YOU.
GENETIC SCIENCE IS NOT MY STRONGEST AREA. REGRETTABLY, HOWEVER--
--YOU MUST NOW GO TO PRISON.
KAAAP
I... I AM SO THRILLED.
A REAL AFRICAN KING... THIS REALLY IS SUCH AN HONOR, YOUR HIGHNESS...
...I FEEL HORRIBLE ABOUT DOING--
10

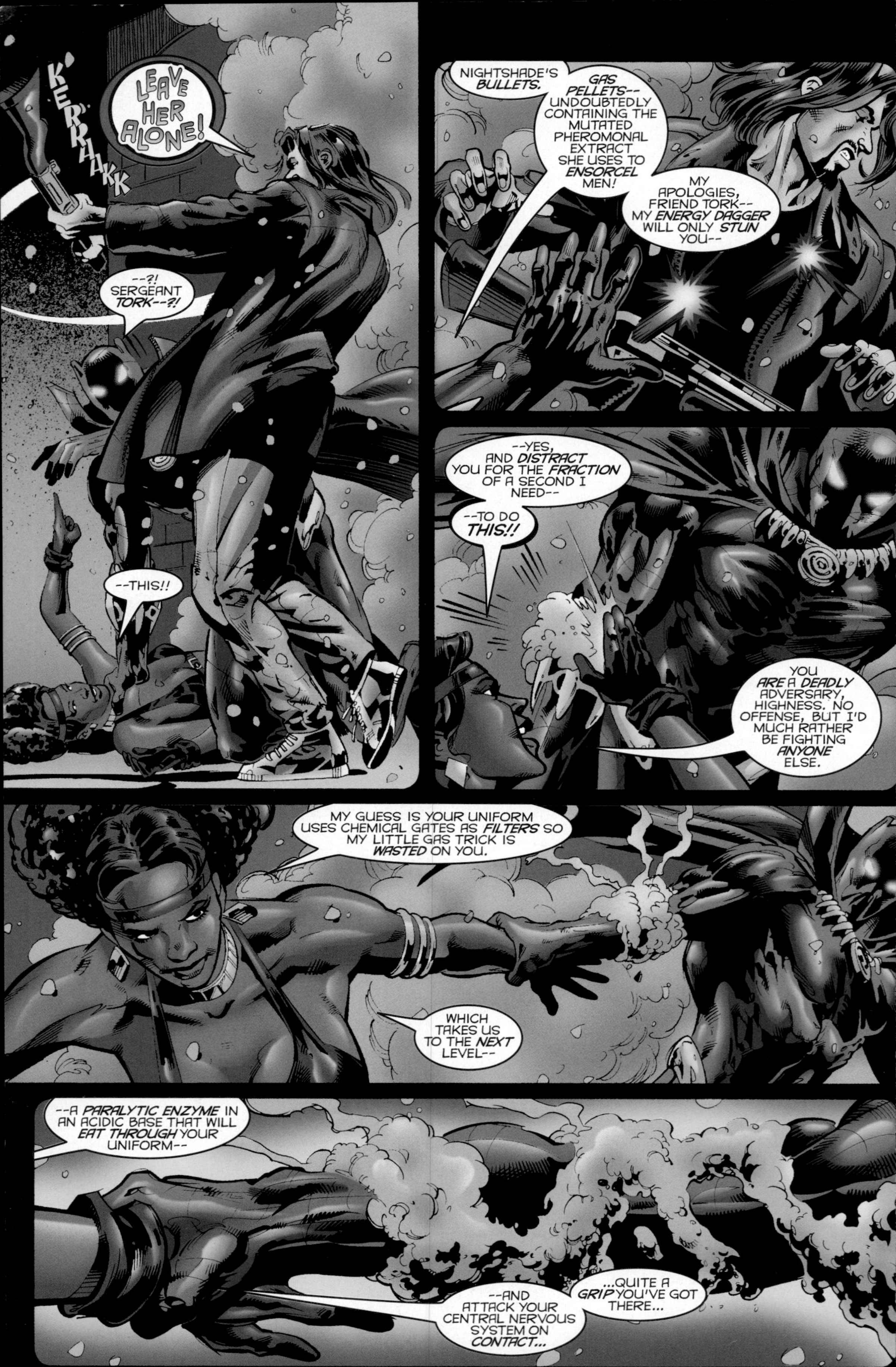

KERRRAKK
LEAVE HER ALONE!
--?! SERGEANT TORK--?!
--THIS!!
NIGHTSHADE'S BULLETS.
GAS PELLETS-- UNDOUBTEDLY CONTAINING THE MUTATED PHEROMONAL EXTRACT SHE USES TO ENSORCEL MEN!
MY APOLOGIES, FRIEND TORK-- MY ENERGY DAGGER WILL ONLY STUN YOU--
--YES, AND DISTRACT YOU FOR THE FRACTION OF A SECOND I NEED--
--TO DO THIS!!
YOU ARE A DEADLY ADVERSARY, HIGHNESS. NO OFFENSE, BUT I'D MUCH RATHER BE FIGHTING ANYONE ELSE.
MY GUESS IS YOUR UNIFORM USES CHEMICAL GATES AS FILTERS SO MY LITTLE GAS TRICK IS WASTED ON YOU.
WHICH TAKES US TO THE NEXT LEVEL--
--A PARALYTIC ENZYME IN AN ACIDIC BASE THAT WILL EAT THROUGH YOUR UNIFORM--
--AND ATTACK YOUR CENTRAL NERVOUS SYSTEM ON CONTACT...
...QUITE A GRIP YOU'VE GOT THERE...

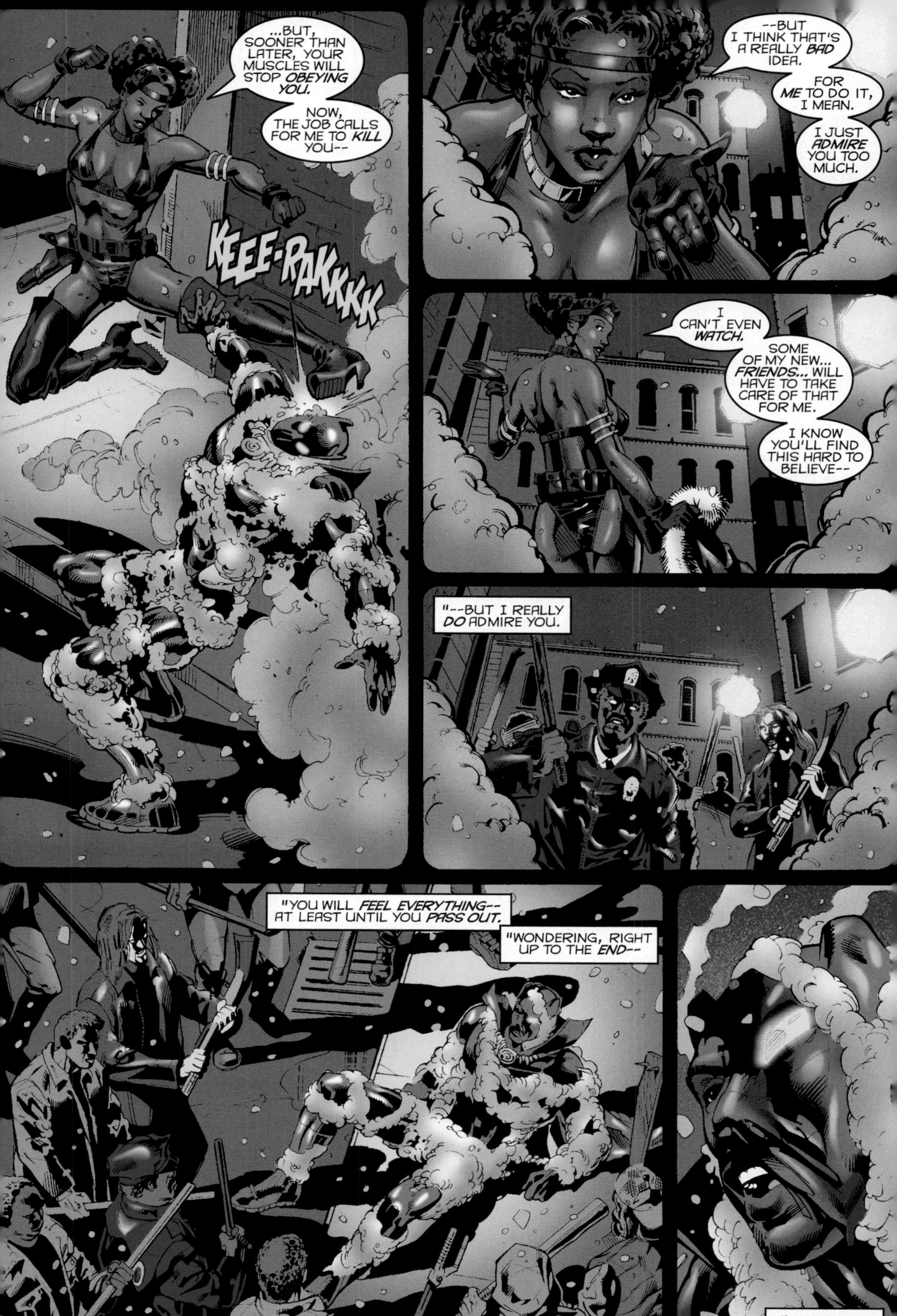
...BUT, SOONER THAN LATER, YOUR MUSCLES WILL STOP OBEYING YOU.
NOW, THE JOB CALLS FOR ME TO KILL YOU--
KEEE-RAKKKKK
--BUT I THINK THAT'S A REALLY BAD IDEA.
FOR ME TO DO IT, I MEAN.
I JUST ADMIRE YOU TOO MUCH.
I CAN'T EVEN WATCH.
SOME OF MY NEW... FRIENDS... WILL HAVE TO TAKE CARE OF THAT FOR ME.
I KNOW YOU'LL FIND THIS HARD TO BELIEVE--
"--BUT I REALLY DO ADMIRE YOU.
"YOU WILL FEEL EVERYTHING-- AT LEAST UNTIL YOU PASS OUT.
"WONDERING, RIGHT UP TO THE END--
"--WHO WILL SAVE YOU--?"

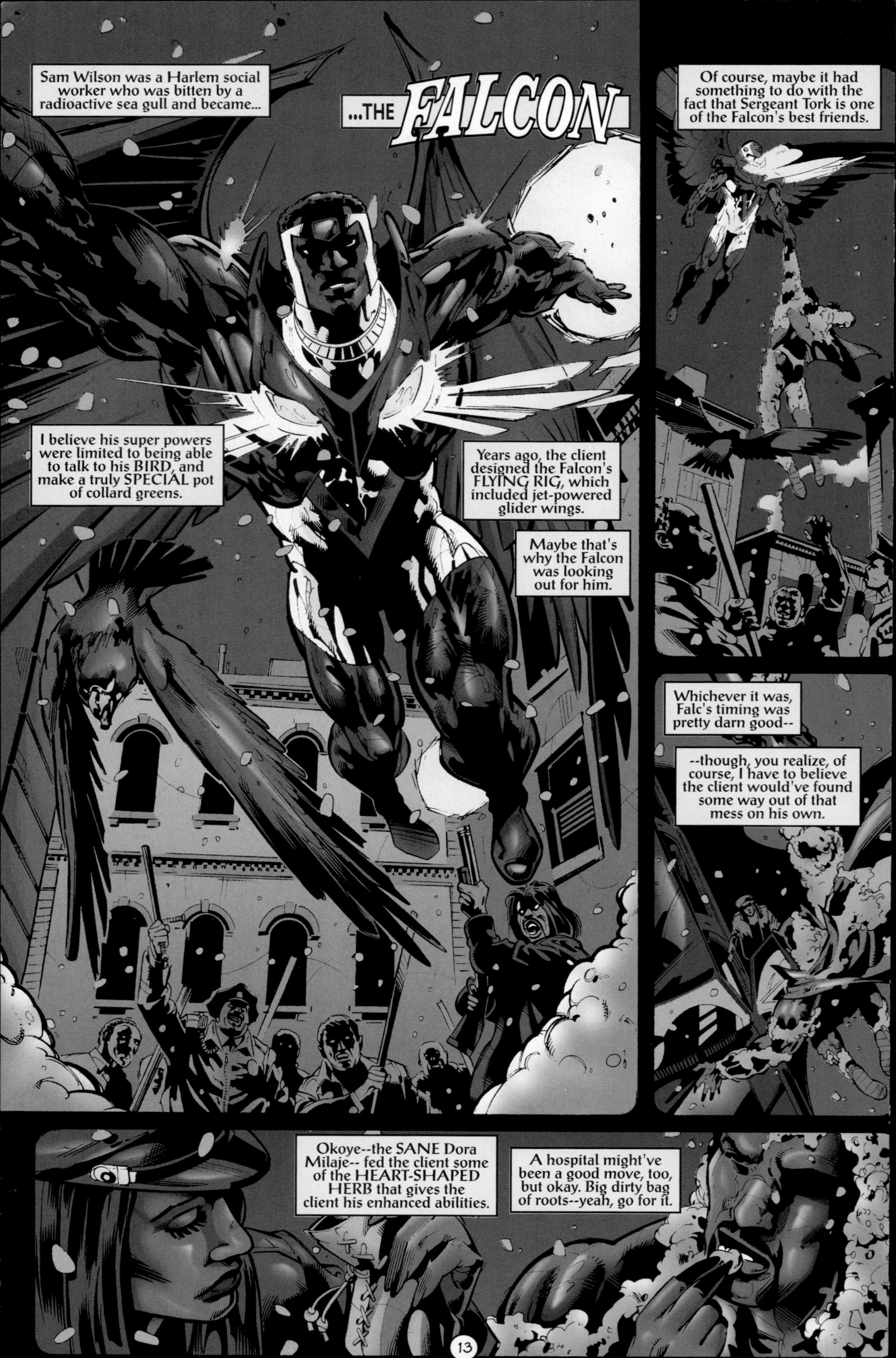

Sam Wilson was a Harlem social worker who was bitten by a radioactive sea gull and became...
...THE FALCON
I believe his super powers were limited to being able to talk to his BIRD, and make a truly SPECIAL pot of collard greens.
Years ago, the client designed the Falcon's FLYING RIG, which included jet-powered glider wings.
Maybe that's why the Falcon was looking out for him.
Of course, maybe it had something to do with the fact that Sergeant Tork is one of the Falcon's best friends.
Whichever it was, Falc's timing was pretty darn good--
--though, you realize, of course, I have to believe the client would've found some way out of that mess on his own.
Okoye--the SANE Dora Milaje-- fed the client some of the HEART-SHAPED HERB that gives the client his enhanced abilities.
A hospital might've been a good move, too, but okay. Big dirty bag of roots--yeah, go for it.

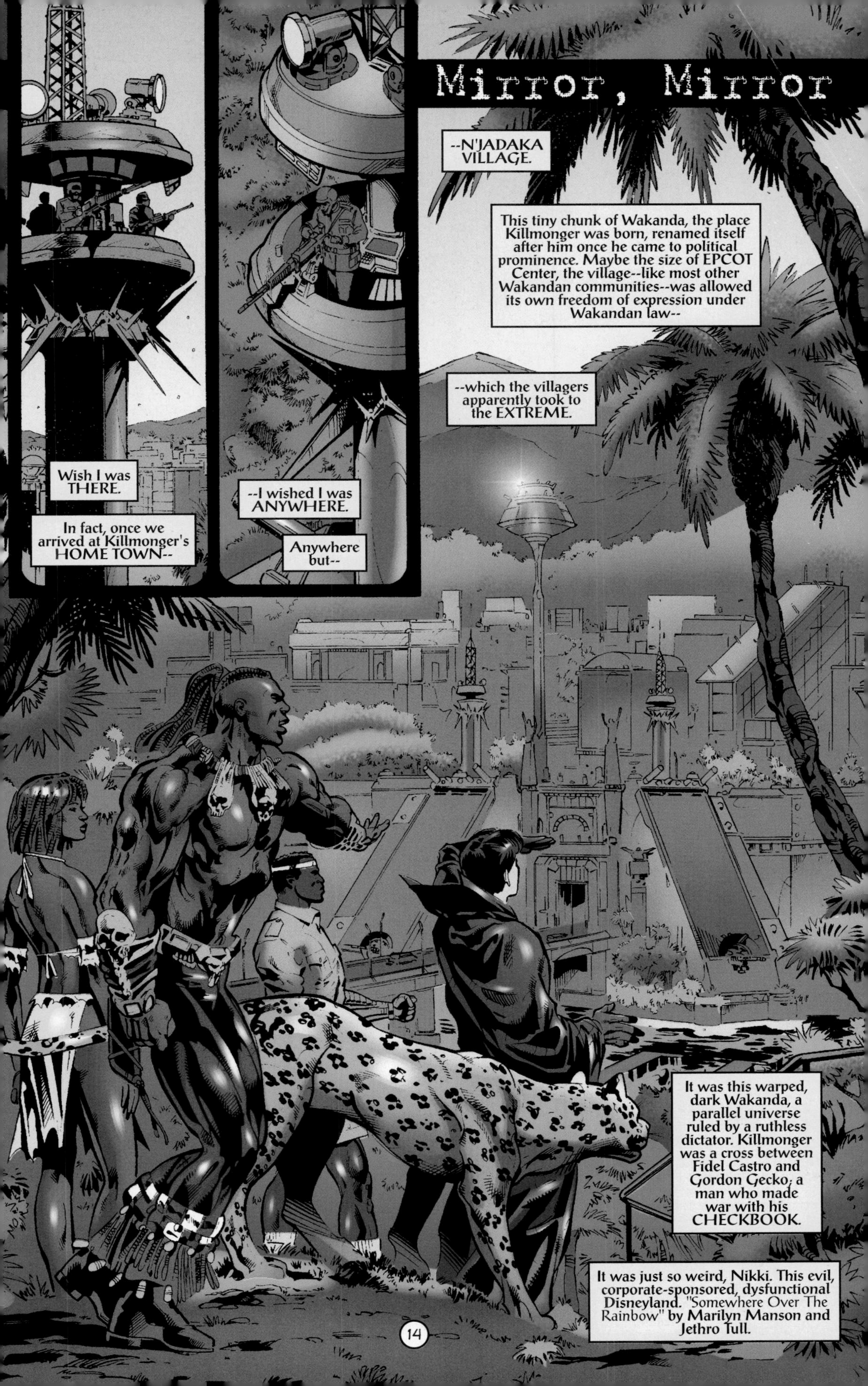

Mirror, Mirror
--N'JADAKA VILLAGE.
This tiny chunk of Wakanda, the place Killmonger was born, renamed itself after him once he came to political prominence. Maybe the size of EPCOT Center, the village--like most other Wakandan communities--was allowed its own freedom of expression under Wakandan law--
--which the villagers apparently took to the EXTREME.
Wish I was THERE.
In fact, once we arrived at Killmonger's HOME TOWN--
--I wished I was ANYWHERE.
Anywhere but--
It was this warped, dark Wakanda, a parallel universe ruled by a ruthless dictator. Killmonger was a cross between Fidel Castro and Gordon Gecko; a man who made war with his CHECKBOOK.
It was just so weird, Nikki. This evil, corporate-sponsored, dysfunctional Disneyland. "Somewhere Over The Rainbow" by Marilyn Manson and Jethro Tull.

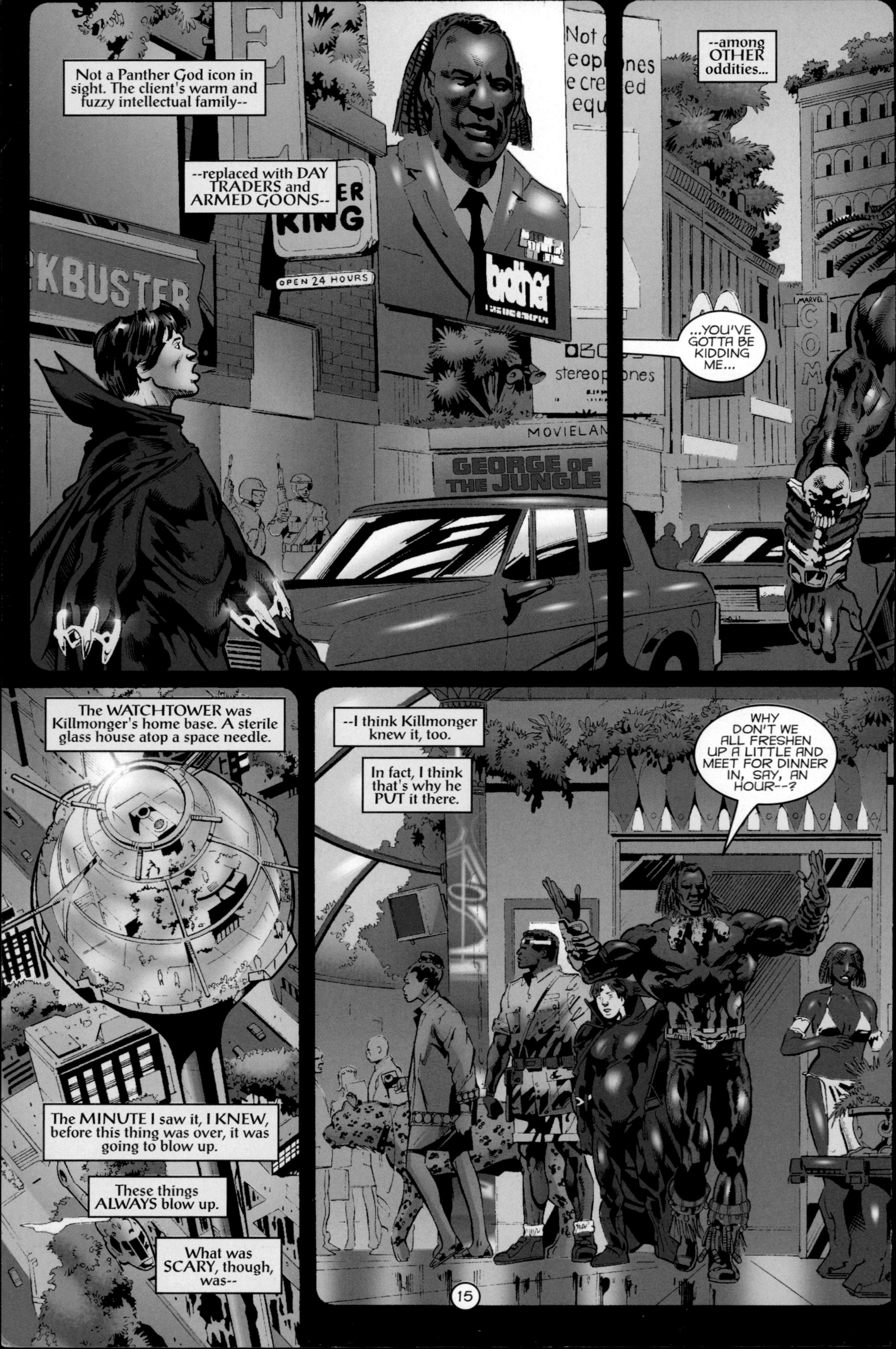

Not a Panther God icon in sight. The client's warm and fuzzy intellectual family--
--replaced with DAY TRADERS and ARMED GOONS--
ER KING
OPEN 24 HOURS
CKBUSTER
brother
stereophones
MOVIELAN
GEORGE OF THE JUNGLE
--among OTHER oddities...
...YOU'VE GOTTA BE KIDDING ME...
MARVEL
COMIC
The WATCHTOWER was Killmonger's home base. A sterile glass house atop a space needle.
The MINUTE I saw it, I KNEW, before this thing was over, it was going to blow up.
These things ALWAYS blow up.
What was SCARY, though, was--
--I think Killmonger knew it, too.
In fact, I think that's why he PUT it there.
WHY DON'T WE ALL FRESHEN UP A LITTLE AND MEET FOR DINNER IN, SAY, AN HOUR--?

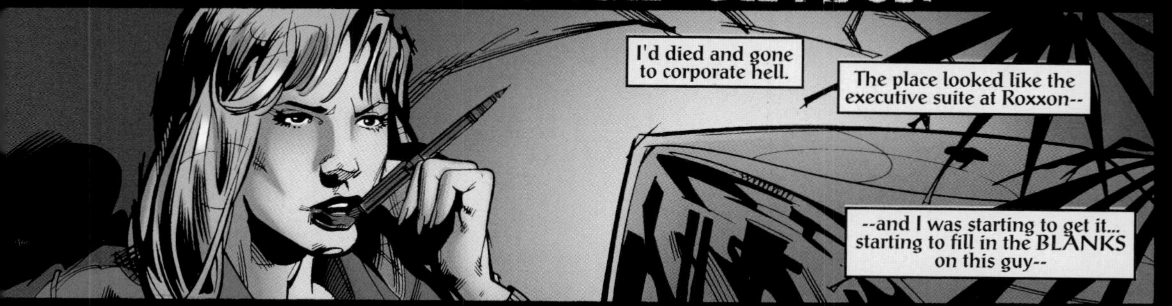
I'd died and gone to corporate hell.
The place looked like the executive suite at Roxxon--
--and I was starting to get it... starting to fill in the BLANKS on this guy--

eK (classified)

US DEPARTMENT OF STATE
CLASSIFIED

Real name: Erik Killmonger
Former Aliases: N'Jadaka (birth name)
Identity: Publicly known
Current Occupation: N/A
Legal status: Citizen of Wakanda with a criminal record (high treason)
Place of birth: N'Jadaka village, Wakanda
Marital status: Single
Known relatives: None- both parents deceased
Group affiliation: None
Extent of education: Ph.D. Engineering, MBA

Physical description
Height: 195cm, 6' 6"
Weight: 80 kg, 175 lbs.
Eyes: Brown
Hair: Black

Powers and Abilities
Intelligence: Above Average
Strength: Peak human
Speed: Athlete
Stamina: Peak human
Durability: Peak human
Agility: Athlete
Reflexes: Athlete

Fighting Skills: Killmonger is an exceptionally proficient hand to hand combatant. While he has undoubtedly been trained professionally, the exact styles and techniques that he uses are unknown.

History
When Ulysses Klaw first came to Wakanda, his mercenaries gathered the young men from the small outlying villages to be used as slaves for mining Vibranium. However Klaw was soundly defeated at that time, due largely to the actions of the young Prince T'Challa. The mercenaries fled back to America, taking some of the Wakandan slaves with them. One of those youths was a young man known as N'Jadaka whose parents had both been killed by Klaw's men.

Upon reaching America, N'Jadaka managed to escape his captives, but had no way of returning to his homeland. N'Jadaka blamed King T'Chaka for his situation, and by extension his son T'Challa. He changed his name to Erik Killmonger and swore vengeance on the Panther-king.

After spending years preparing for his eventual return to Wakanda, Killmonger recognized the Black Panther while he was with the Avengers and contacted him, telling him how he came to be in America. T'Challa arranged a transport to take him from the tenement building where he stayed in Harlem back to Wakanda at the first opportunity. Unknown to the Panther, Killmonger also smuggled the man known as Vennom back to Wakanda with him.

Killmonger returned to his village and began to sow the seeds of insurrection amongst them. He gathered a veritable army of followers, which he called his death regiments, and appointed leaders over them, giving them titles that he had learnt in the West. His followers named his small village "N'Jadaka" in honor of its new leader.

He found a place called Resurrection Altar in a remote part of Wakanda and subjected many of his followers to the unearthly radiation which flowed from it, granting some of them superhuman abilities. He also began mining out the great Vibranium mound from below with the assistance of his death regiments. The Panther, still serving with the Avengers, got word that trouble was brewing in Wakanda and returned quickly.

After Killmonger destroyed a small fishing village, the Panther confronted him atop Warrior Falls, where he battled both him and his pet leopard named Preyy. T'Challa was defeated and thrown from the Falls, only his agility and the proximity of Monica Lynne saving him.

The Panther and his army then took the fight to Killmonger, attacking his village and decimating the army that he had there. Unfortunately Killmonger wasn't there at the time, but the Panther learned from his followers that he was at Resurrection Altar. Here Killmonger once more defeated the king in physical combat, and left him for dead. The Panther survived and tracked Killmonger to the Serpent Valley, where he was capturing great prehistoric beasts to use. Killmonger left the weakened T'Challa to battle a Tyrannosaurus Rex, certain that the beast would finally finish him. However with the help of a strange imp, the Panther prevailed and went on to make it back to Central Wakanda in time for Killmonger's final attack. Killmonger then attacked Central Wakanda with his entire remaining army, along with a horde of stampeding dinosaurs. The Panther's loyal army battled valiantly, but all seemed lost when Killmonger once again held the Panther atop Warrior Falls, preparing to throw him to his death. Only the intervention of Kantu, a small child whose father had been killed by the death regiments, saved the King's life as he knocked Killmonger over the edge instead.

Current Whereabouts
Killmonger's body was found a week after his death, smashed to a pulp by the rapids.

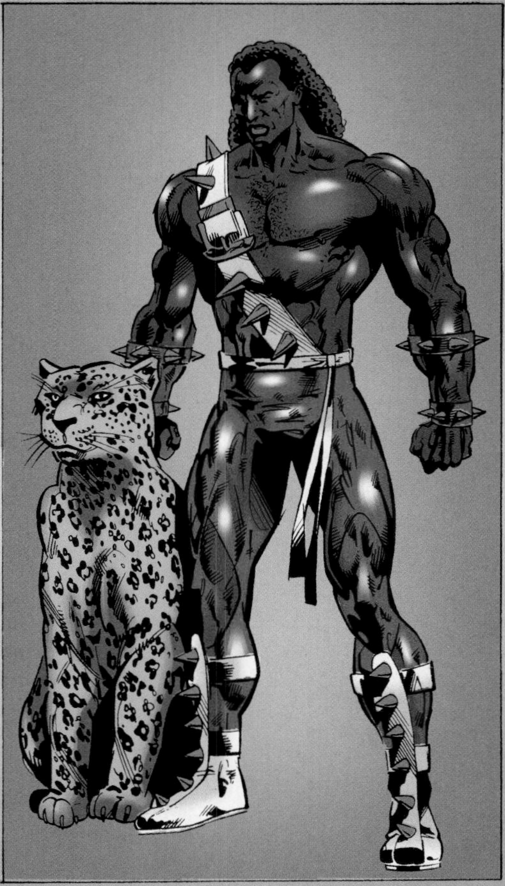

100 Page 1

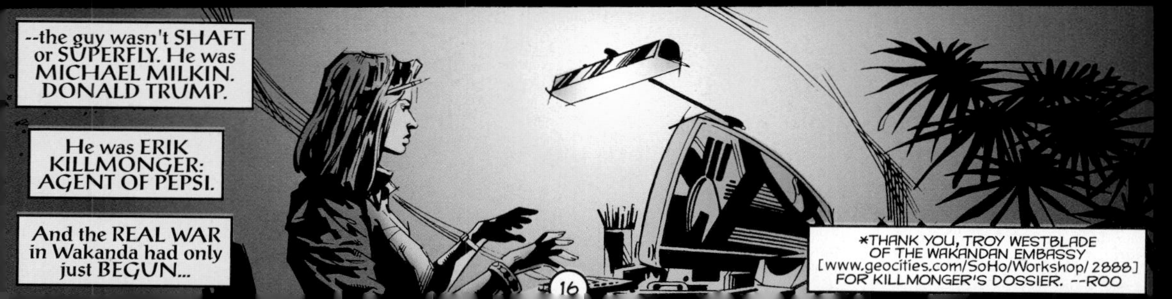
--the guy wasn't SHAFT or SUPERFLY. He was MICHAEL MILKIN. DONALD TRUMP.
He was ERIK KILLMONGER: AGENT OF PEPSI.
And the REAL WAR in Wakanda had only just BEGUN...
*THANK YOU, TROY WESTBLADE OF THE WAKANDAN EMBASSY [www.geocities.com/SoHo/Workshop/2888] FOR KILLMONGER'S DOSSIER. --ROO

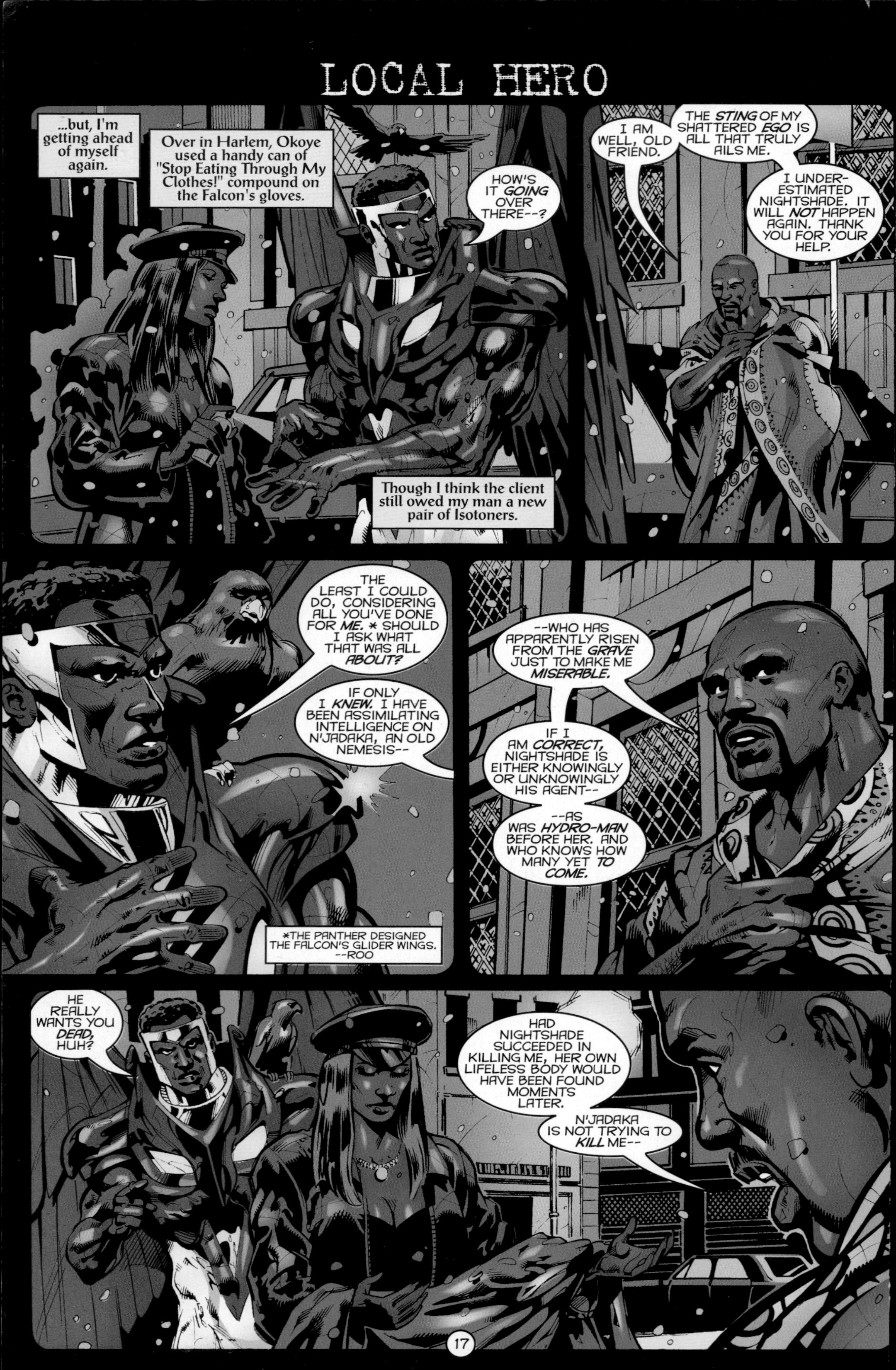

LOCAL HERO
...but, I'm getting ahead of myself again.
Over in Harlem, Okoye used a handy can of "Stop Eating Through My Clothes!" compound on the Falcon's gloves.
HOW'S IT GOING OVER THERE--?
Though I think the client still owed my man a new pair of Isotoners.
I AM WELL, OLD FRIEND.
THE STING OF MY SHATTERED EGO IS ALL THAT TRULY AILS ME.
I UNDER-ESTIMATED NIGHTSHADE. IT WILL NOT HAPPEN AGAIN. THANK YOU FOR YOUR HELP.
THE LEAST I COULD DO, CONSIDERING ALL YOU'VE DONE FOR ME. * SHOULD I ASK WHAT THAT WAS ALL ABOUT?
IF ONLY I KNEW. I HAVE BEEN ASSIMILATING INTELLIGENCE ON N'JADAKA, AN OLD NEMESIS--
*THE PANTHER DESIGNED THE FALCON'S GLIDER WINGS. --ROO
--WHO HAS APPARENTLY RISEN FROM THE GRAVE JUST TO MAKE ME MISERABLE.
IF I AM CORRECT, NIGHTSHADE IS EITHER KNOWINGLY OR UNKNOWINGLY HIS AGENT--
--AS WAS HYDRO-MAN BEFORE HER. AND WHO KNOWS HOW MANY YET TO COME.
HE REALLY WANTS YOU DEAD, HUH?
HAD NIGHTSHADE SUCCEEDED IN KILLING ME, HER OWN LIFELESS BODY WOULD HAVE BEEN FOUND MOMENTS LATER.
N'JADAKA IS NOT TRYING TO KILL ME--

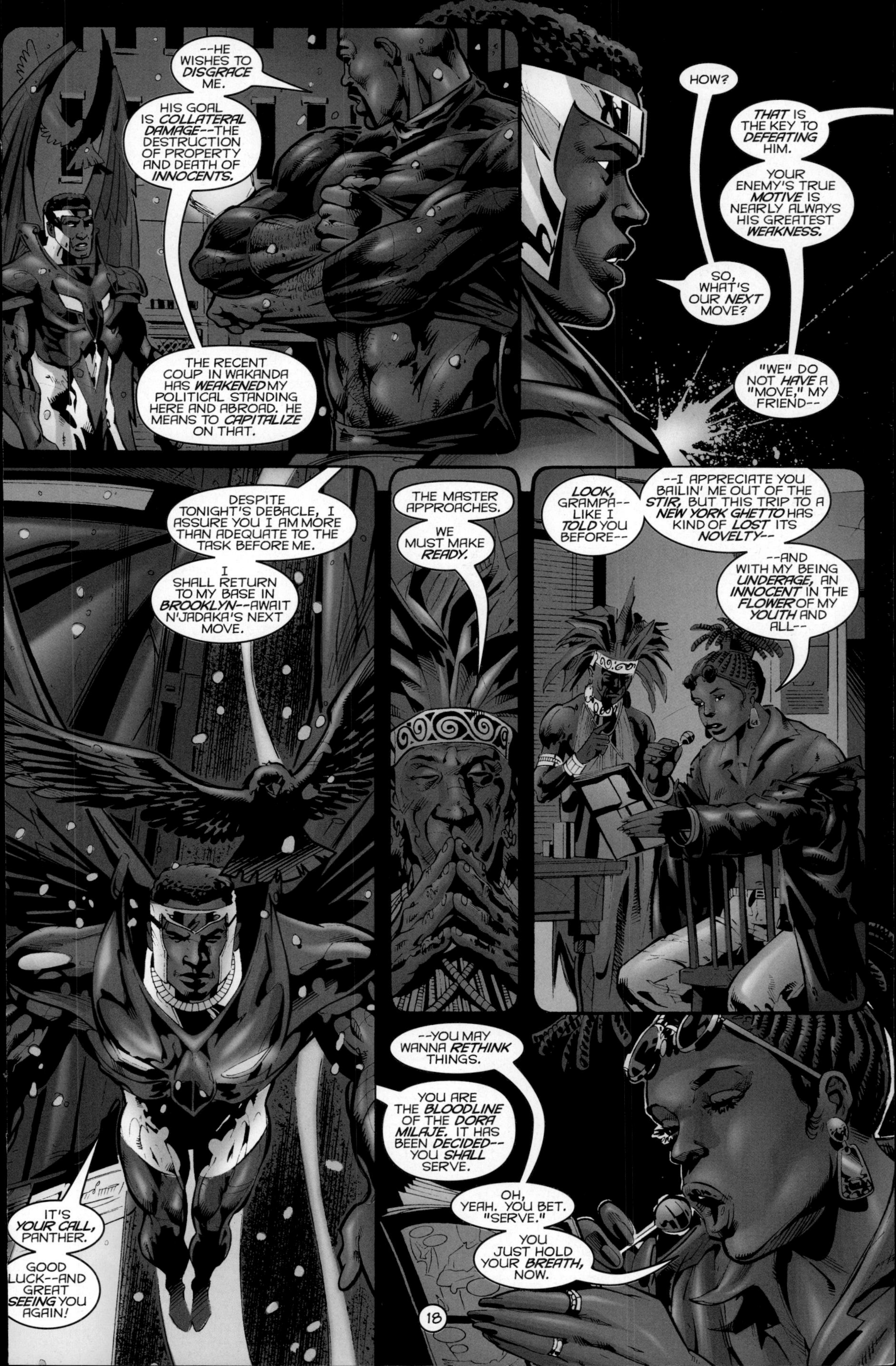

--HE WISHES TO DISGRACE ME.
HIS GOAL IS COLLATERAL DAMAGE--THE DESTRUCTION OF PROPERTY AND DEATH OF INNOCENTS.
THE RECENT COUP IN WAKANDA HAS WEAKENED MY POLITICAL STANDING HERE AND ABROAD. HE MEANS TO CAPITALIZE ON THAT.
HOW?
THAT IS THE KEY TO DEFEATING HIM.
YOUR ENEMY'S TRUE MOTIVE IS NEARLY ALWAYS HIS GREATEST WEAKNESS.
SO, WHAT'S OUR NEXT MOVE?
"WE" DO NOT HAVE A "MOVE," MY FRIEND--
DESPITE TONIGHT'S DEBACLE, I ASSURE YOU I AM MORE THAN ADEQUATE TO THE TASK BEFORE ME.
I SHALL RETURN TO MY BASE IN BROOKLYN--AWAIT N'JADAKA'S NEXT MOVE.
IT'S YOUR CALL, PANTHER.
GOOD LUCK--AND GREAT SEEING YOU AGAIN!
THE MASTER APPROACHES.
WE MUST MAKE READY.
LOOK, GRAMPA-- LIKE I TOLD YOU BEFORE--
--I APPRECIATE YOU BAILIN' ME OUT OF THE STIR, BUT THIS TRIP TO A NEW YORK GHETTO HAS KIND OF LOST ITS NOVELTY--
--AND WITH MY BEING UNDERAGE, AN INNOCENT IN THE FLOWER OF MY YOUTH AND ALL--
--YOU MAY WANNA RETHINK THINGS.
YOU ARE THE BLOODLINE OF THE DORA MILAJE. IT HAS BEEN DECIDED-- YOU SHALL SERVE.
OH, YEAH. YOU BET. "SERVE."
YOU JUST HOLD YOUR BREATH, NOW.

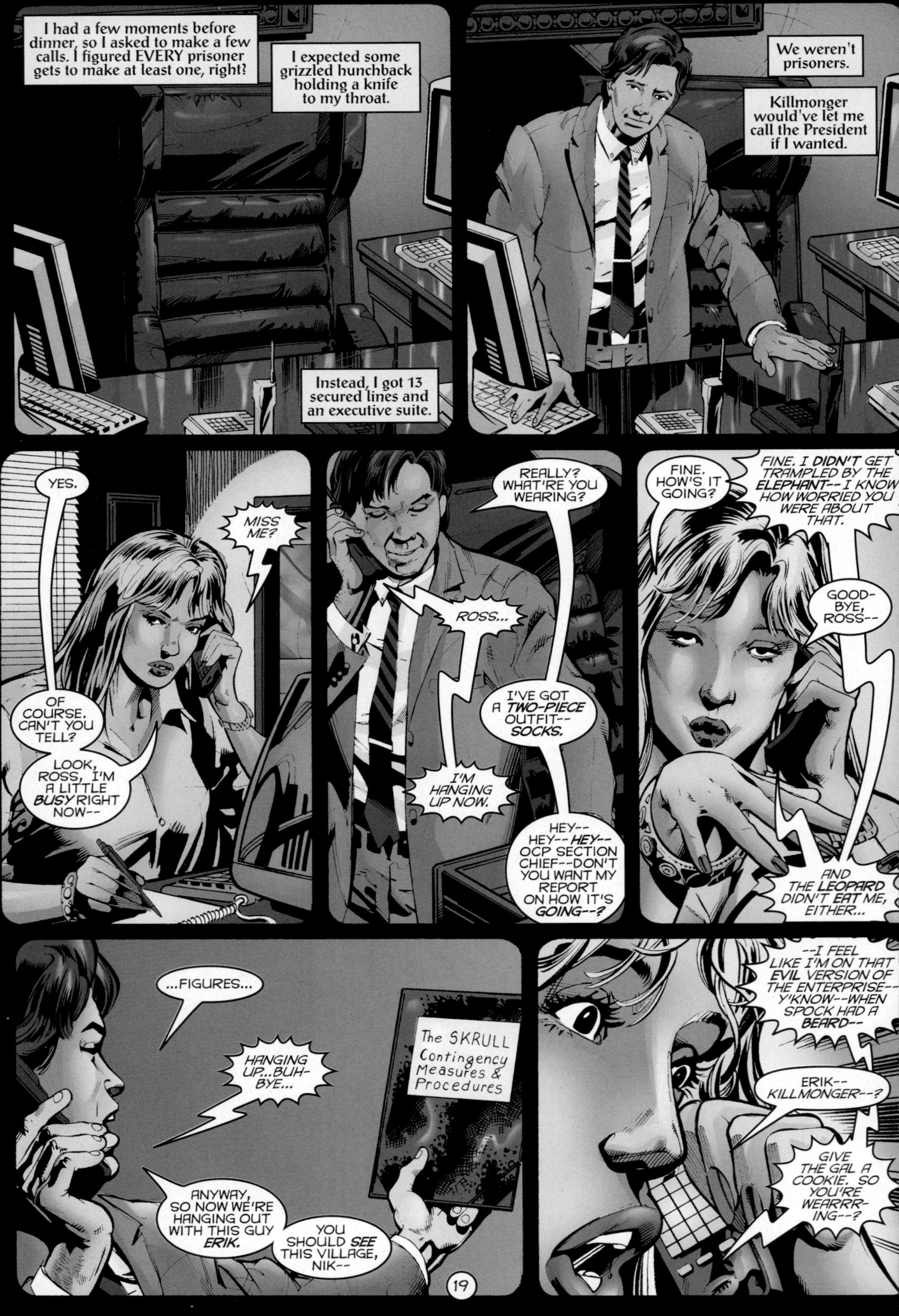

I had a few moments before dinner, so I asked to make a few calls. I figured EVERY prisoner gets to make at least one, right?
I expected some grizzled hunchback holding a knife to my throat.
Instead, I got 13 secured lines and an executive suite.
We weren't prisoners.
Killmonger would've let me call the President if I wanted.
YES.
MISS ME?
OF COURSE. CAN'T YOU TELL?
LOOK, ROSS, I'M A LITTLE BUSY RIGHT NOW--
REALLY? WHAT'RE YOU WEARING?
ROSS...
I'VE GOT A TWO-PIECE OUTFIT--SOCKS.
I'M HANGING UP NOW.
HEY--HEY--HEY--OCP SECTION CHIEF--DON'T YOU WANT MY REPORT ON HOW IT'S GOING--?
FINE. HOW'S IT GOING?
FINE. I DIDN'T GET TRAMPLED BY THE ELEPHANT--I KNOW HOW WORRIED YOU WERE ABOUT THAT.
GOOD-BYE, ROSS--
AND THE LEOPARD DIDN'T EAT ME, EITHER...
...FIGURES...
HANGING UP...BUH-BYE...
The SKRULL Contingency Measures & Procedures
ANYWAY, SO NOW WE'RE HANGING OUT WITH THIS GUY ERIK.
YOU SHOULD SEE THIS VILLAGE, NIK--
--I FEEL LIKE I'M ON THAT EVIL VERSION OF THE ENTERPRISE--Y'KNOW--WHEN SPOCK HAD A BEARD--
ERIK--KILLMONGER--?
GIVE THE GAL A COOKIE. SO YOU'RE WEARRRING--?

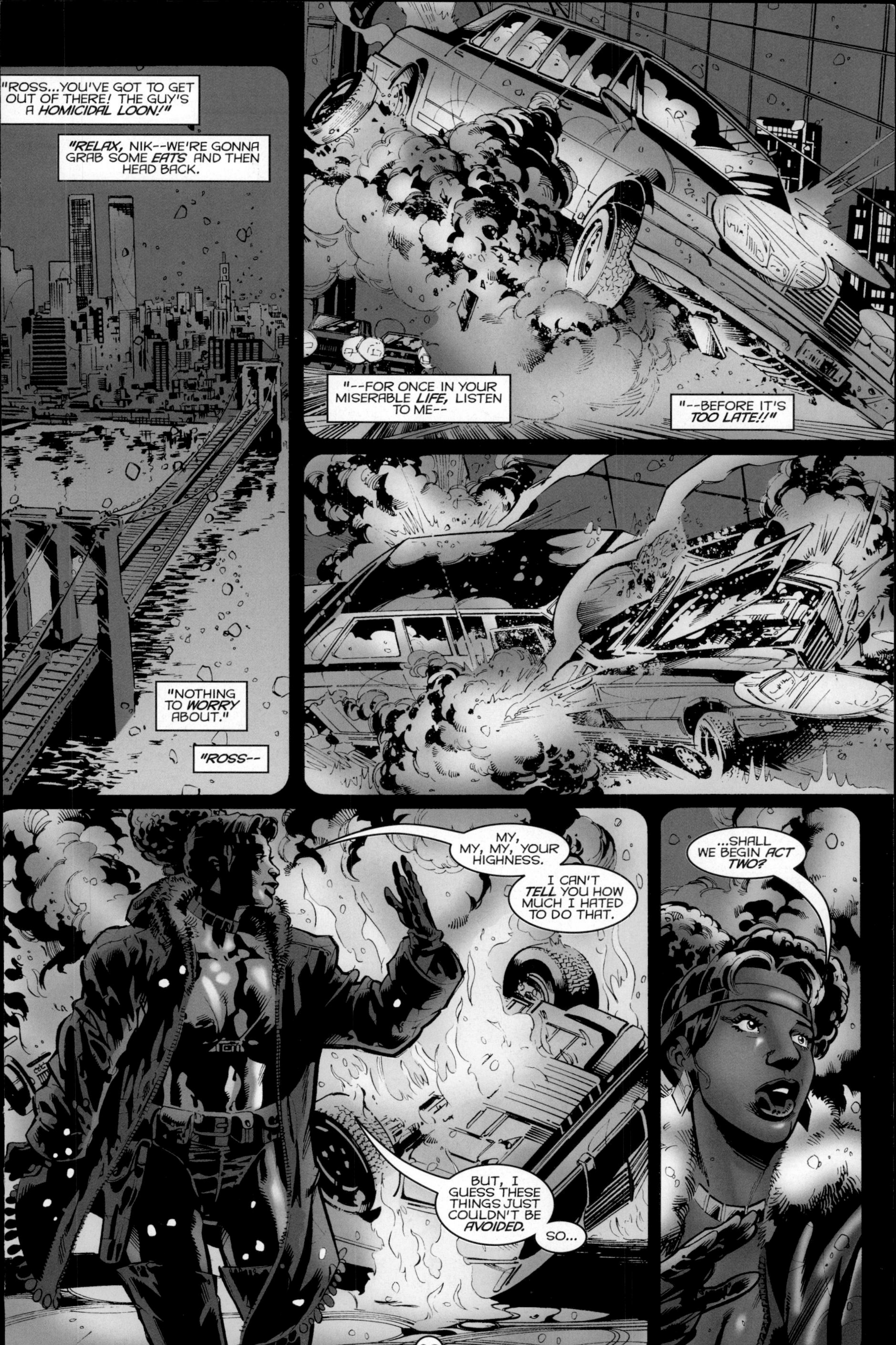
"ROSS...YOU'VE GOT TO GET OUT OF THERE! THE GUY'S A HOMICIDAL LOON!"
"RELAX, NIK--WE'RE GONNA GRAB SOME EATS AND THEN HEAD BACK.
"NOTHING TO WORRY ABOUT."
"ROSS--
"--FOR ONCE IN YOUR MISERABLE LIFE, LISTEN TO ME--
"--BEFORE IT'S TOO LATE!!"
MY, MY, MY, YOUR HIGHNESS.
I CAN'T TELL YOU HOW MUCH I HATED TO DO THAT.
BUT, I GUESS THESE THINGS JUST COULDN'T BE AVOIDED.
SO...
...SHALL WE BEGIN ACT TWO?

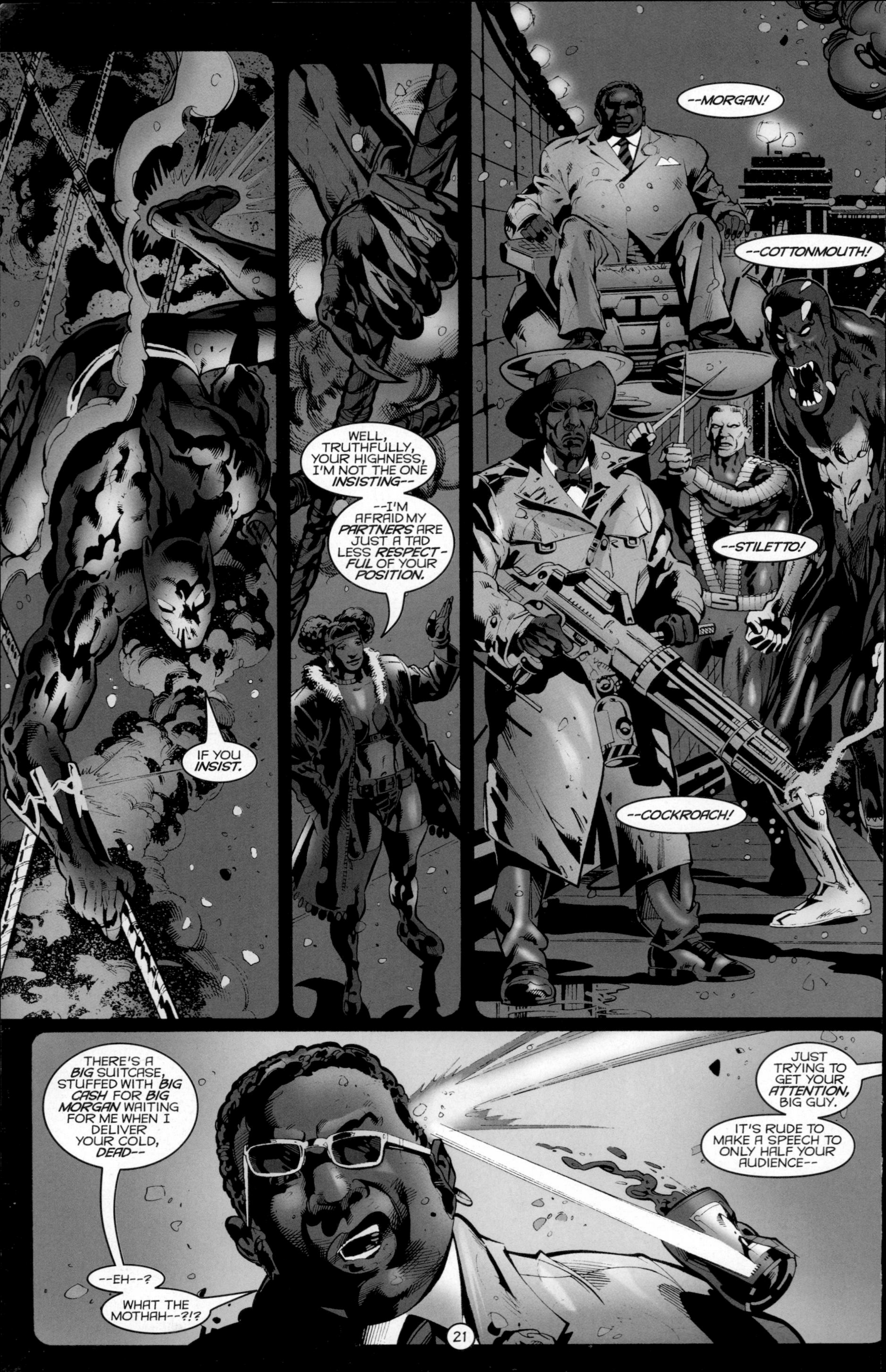

IF YOU INSIST.
WELL, TRUTHFULLY, YOUR HIGHNESS, I'M NOT THE ONE INSISTING--
--I'M AFRAID MY PARTNERS ARE JUST A TAD LESS RESPECTFUL OF YOUR POSITION.
--MORGAN!
--COTTONMOUTH!
--STILETTO!
--COCKROACH!
THERE'S A BIG SUITCASE, STUFFED WITH BIG CASH FOR BIG MORGAN WAITING FOR ME WHEN I DELIVER YOUR COLD, DEAD--
--EH--?
WHAT THE MOTHAH--?!?
JUST TRYING TO GET YOUR ATTENTION, BIG GUY.
IT'S RUDE TO MAKE A SPEECH TO ONLY HALF YOUR AUDIENCE--

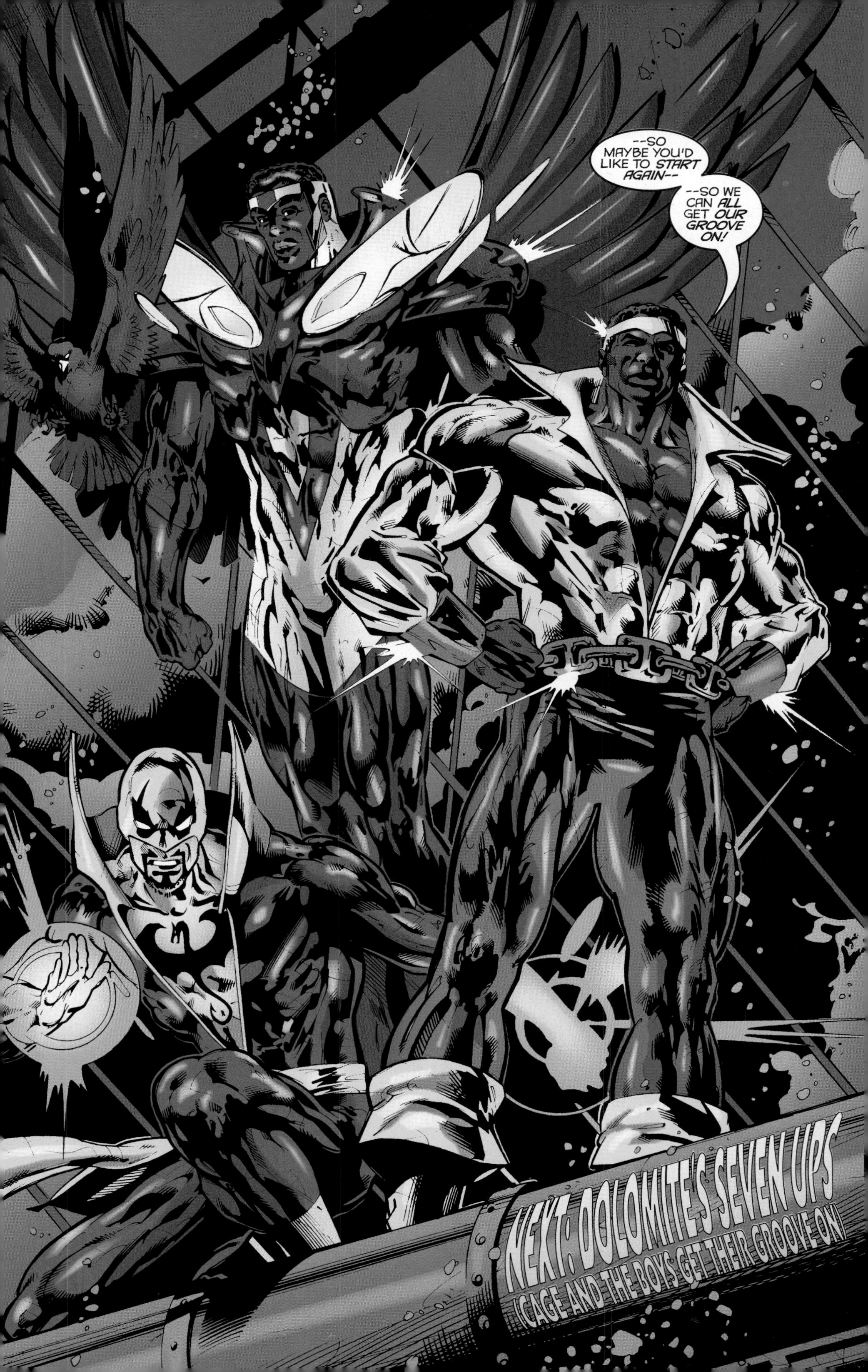
--SO MAYBE YOU'D LIKE TO START AGAIN--
--SO WE CAN ALL GET OUR GROOVE ON!
NEXT: DOLOMITE'S SEVEN UPS
(CAGE AND THE BOYS GET THEIR GROOVE ON)

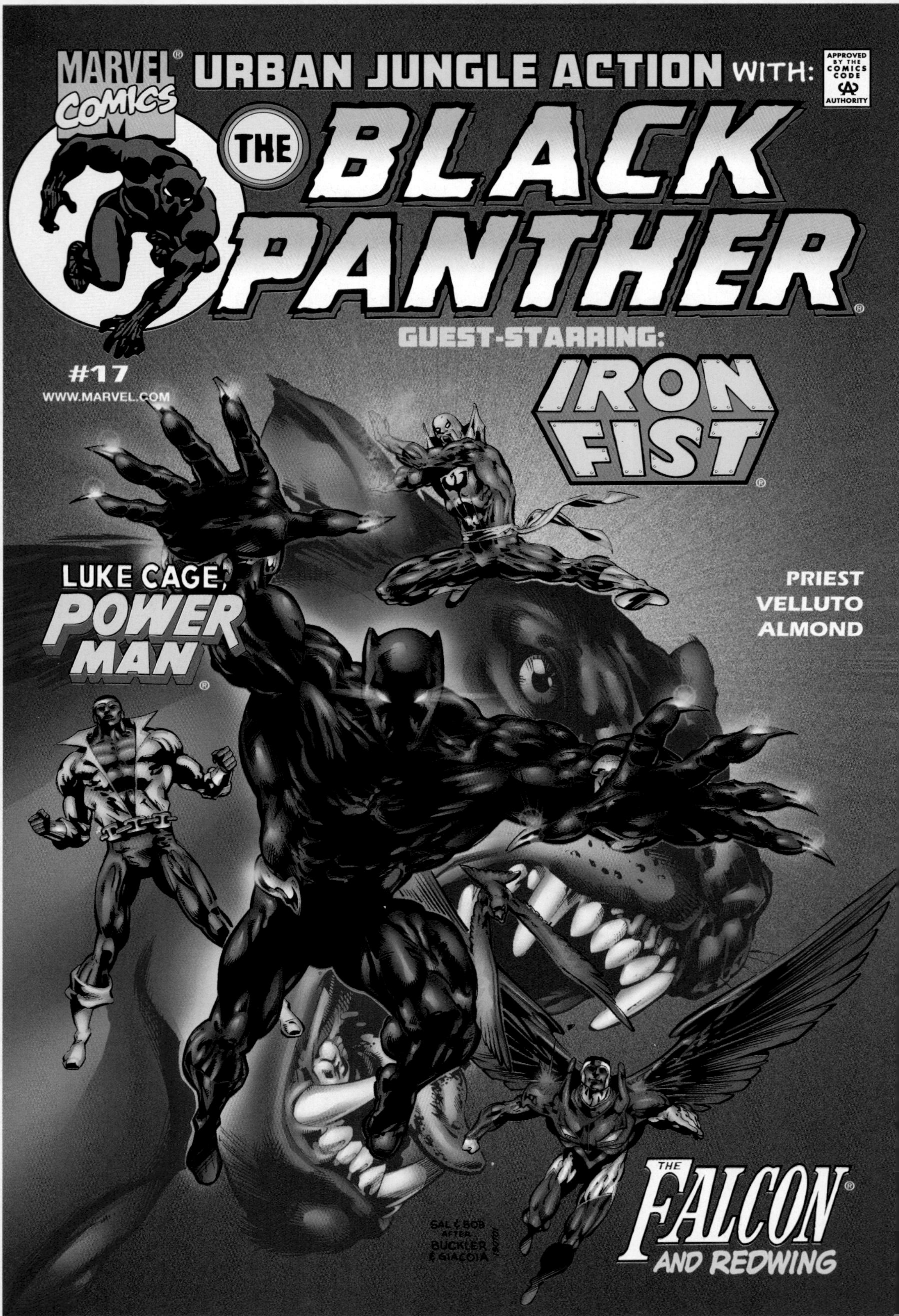
MARVEL COMICS
URBAN JUNGLE ACTION WITH:
APPROVED BY THE COMICS CODE AUTHORITY
THE BLACK PANTHER
GUEST-STARRING:
IRON FIST
#17
WWW.MARVEL.COM
LUKE CAGE, POWER MAN
PRIEST
VELLUTO
ALMOND
SAL & BOB AFTER BUCKLER & GIACOIA
THE FALCON AND REDWING

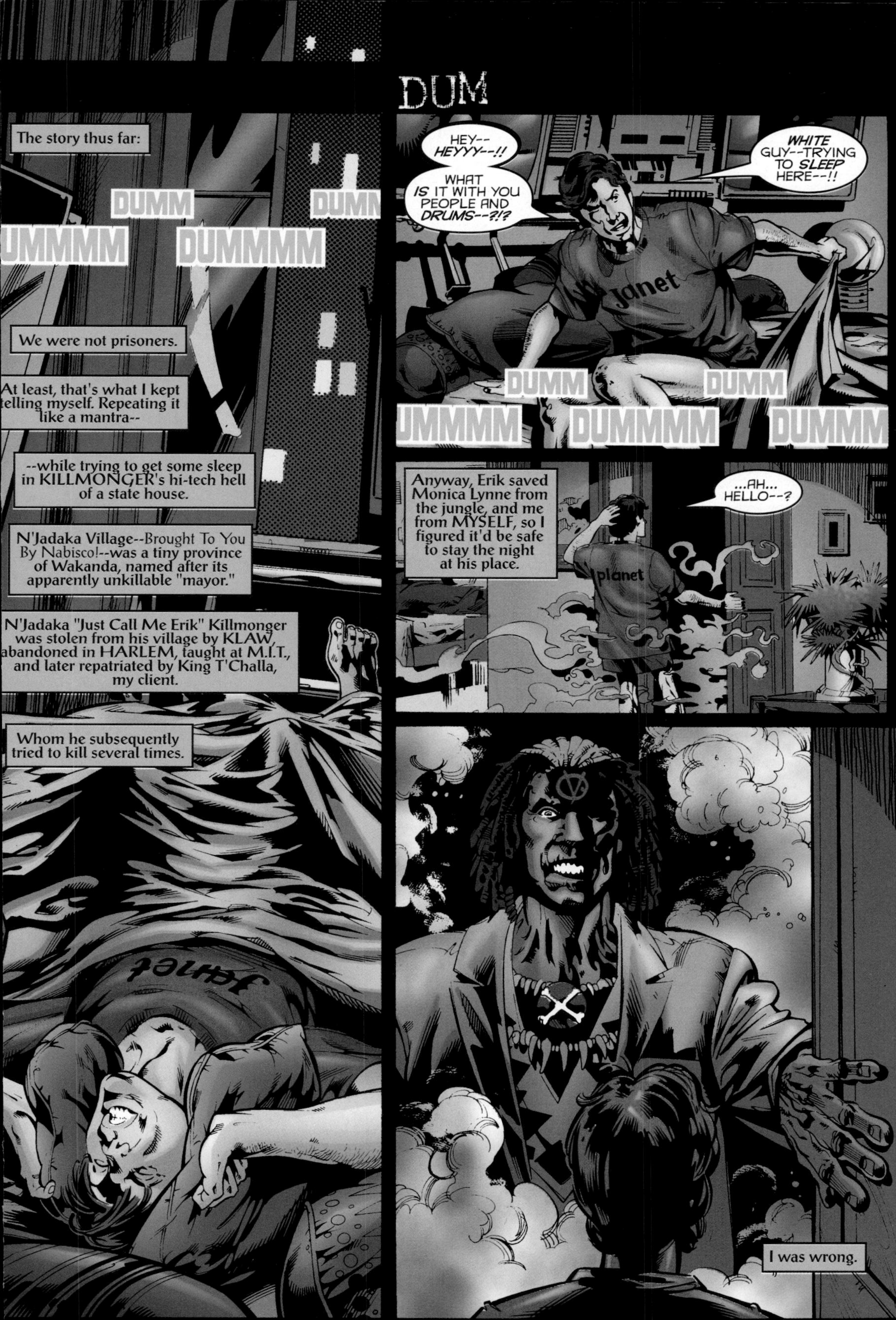
DUM
The story thus far:
DUMM
DUMM
UMMMM
DUMMMM
HEY-- HEYYY--!! WHAT IS IT WITH YOU PEOPLE AND DRUMS--?!?
WHITE GUY--TRYING TO SLEEP HERE--!!
Janet
DUMM
DUMM
UMMMM
DUMMMM
DUMMM
We were not prisoners.
At least, that's what I kept telling myself. Repeating it like a mantra--
--while trying to get some sleep in KILLMONGER's hi-tech hell of a state house.
N'Jadaka Village--Brought To You By Nabisco!--was a tiny province of Wakanda, named after its apparently unkillable "mayor."
N'Jadaka "Just Call Me Erik" Killmonger was stolen from his village by KLAW, abandoned in HARLEM, taught at M.I.T., and later repatriated by King T'Challa, my client.
Whom he subsequently tried to kill several times.
Anyway, Erik saved Monica Lynne from the jungle, and me from MYSELF, so I figured it'd be safe to stay the night at his place.
...AH... HELLO--?
planet
I was wrong.

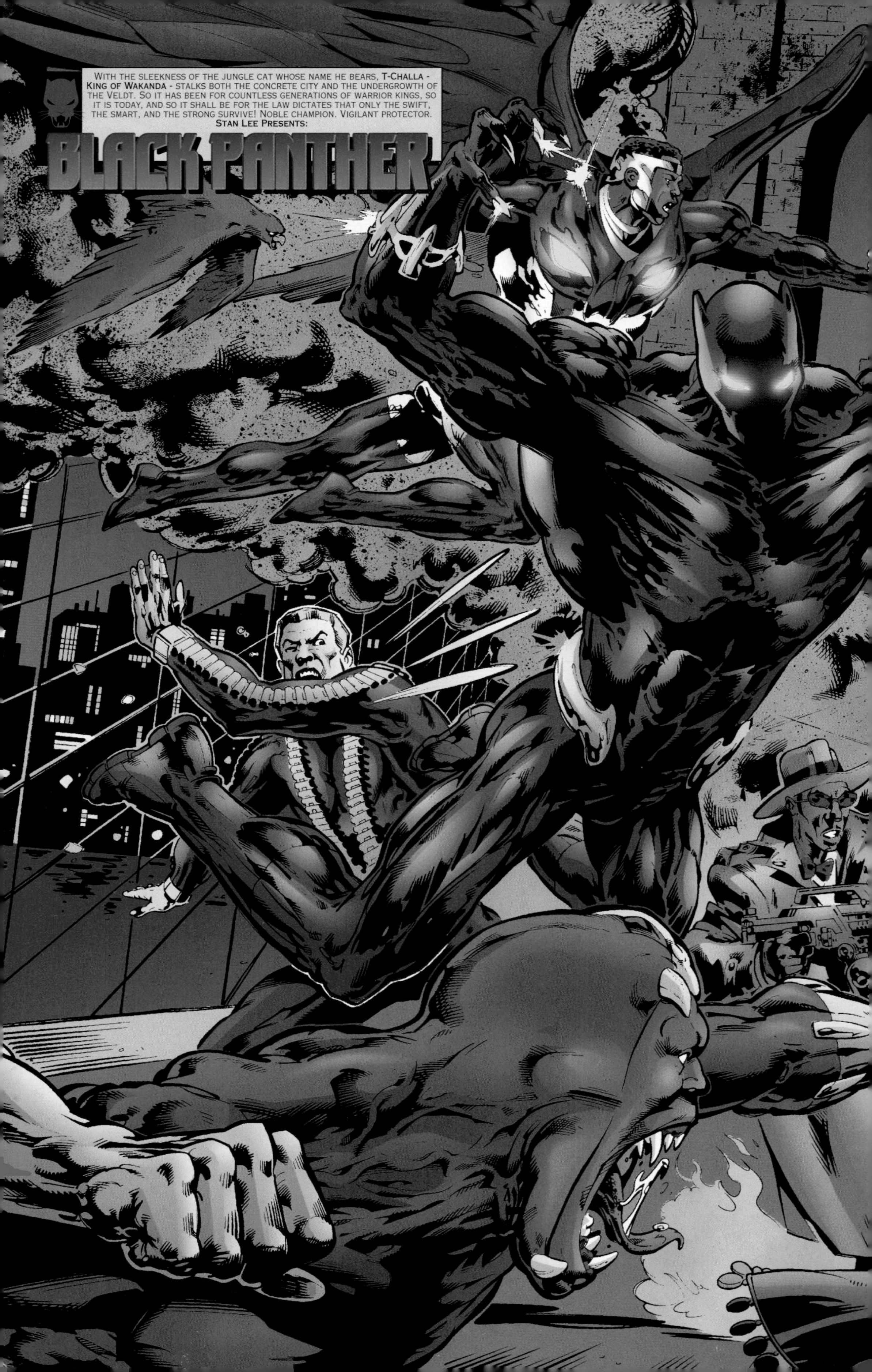
WITH THE SLEEKNESS OF THE JUNGLE CAT WHOSE NAME HE BEARS, T-CHALLA - KING OF WAKANDA - STALKS BOTH THE CONCRETE CITY AND THE UNDERGROWTH OF THE VELDT. SO IT HAS BEEN FOR COUNTLESS GENERATIONS OF WARRIOR KINGS, SO IT IS TODAY, AND SO IT SHALL BE FOR THE LAW DICTATES THAT ONLY THE SWIFT, THE SMART, AND THE STRONG SURVIVE! NOBLE CHAMPION. VIGILANT PROTECTOR.
STAN LEE PRESENTS:
BLACK PANTHER

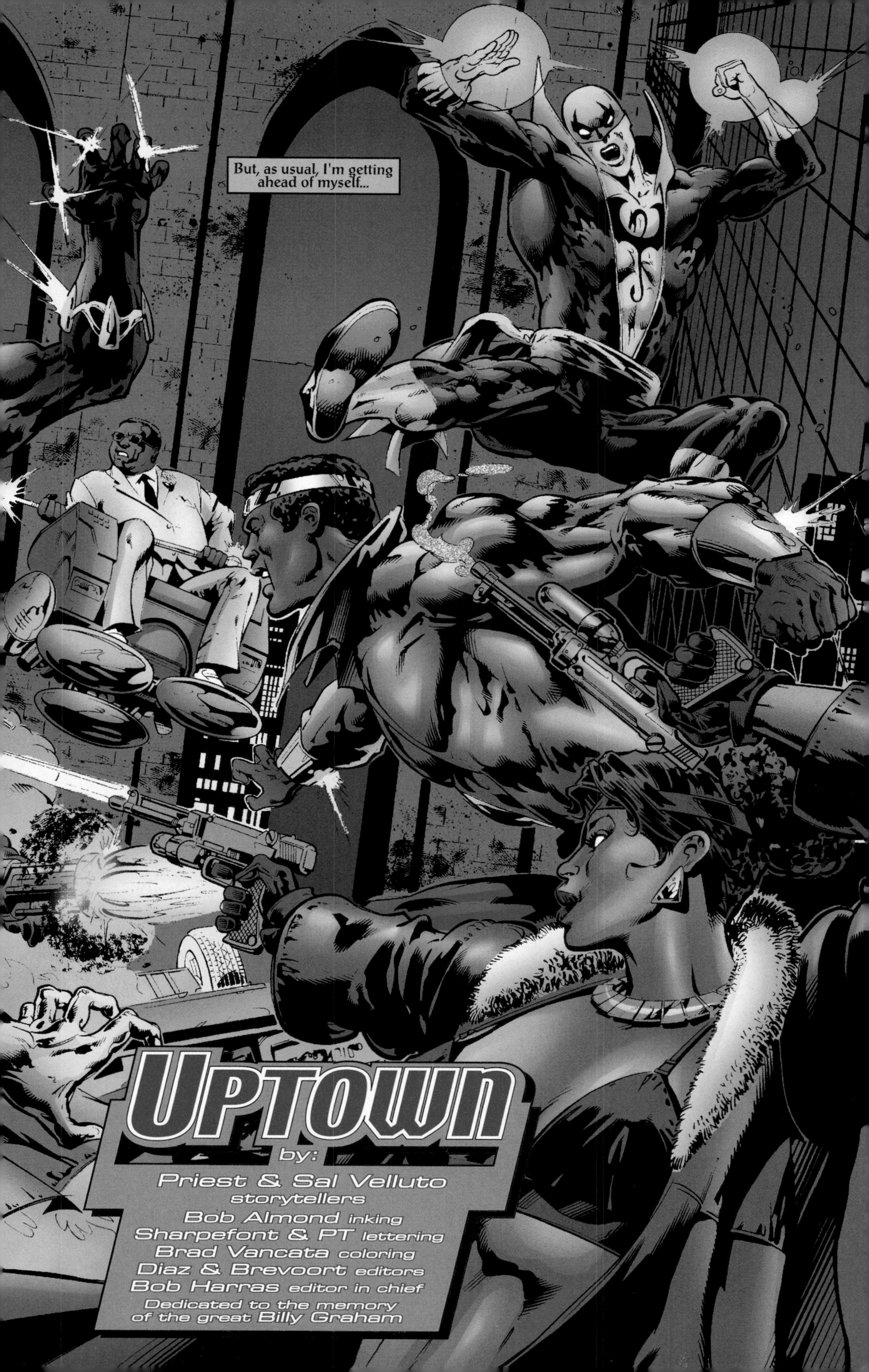

But, as usual, I'm getting ahead of myself...
UPTOWN
by:
Priest & Sal Velluto storytellers
Bob Almond inking
Sharpefont & PT lettering
Brad Vancata coloring
Diaz & Brevoort editors
Bob Harras editor in chief
Dedicated to the memory of the great Billy Graham

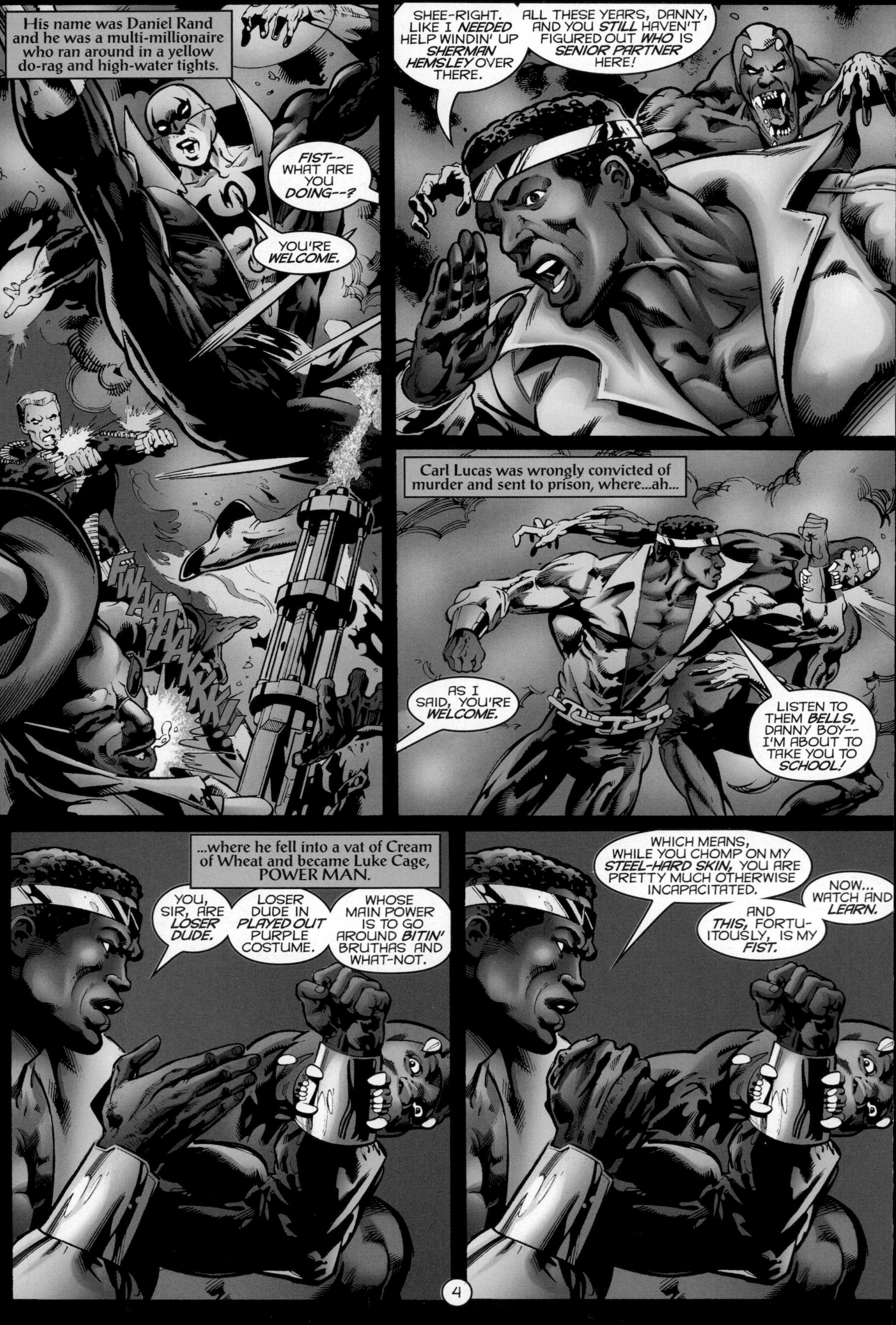
His name was Daniel Rand and he was a multi-millionaire who ran around in a yellow do-rag and high-water tights.
FIST-- WHAT ARE YOU DOING--?
YOU'RE WELCOME.
FWAAAAAAKKKK!
SHEE-RIGHT. LIKE I NEEDED HELP WINDIN' UP SHERMAN HEMSLEY OVER THERE.
ALL THESE YEARS, DANNY, AND YOU STILL HAVEN'T FIGURED OUT WHO IS SENIOR PARTNER HERE!
Carl Lucas was wrongly convicted of murder and sent to prison, where...ah...
AS I SAID, YOU'RE WELCOME.
LISTEN TO THEM BELLS, DANNY BOY-- I'M ABOUT TO TAKE YOU TO SCHOOL!
...where he fell into a vat of Cream of Wheat and became Luke Cage, POWER MAN.
YOU, SIR, ARE LOSER DUDE.
LOSER DUDE IN PLAYED OUT PURPLE COSTUME.
WHOSE MAIN POWER IS TO GO AROUND BITIN' BRUTHAS AND WHAT-NOT.
WHICH MEANS, WHILE YOU CHOMP ON MY STEEL-HARD SKIN, YOU ARE PRETTY MUCH OTHERWISE INCAPACITATED.
AND THIS, FORTUITOUSLY, IS MY FIST.
NOW... WATCH AND LEARN.

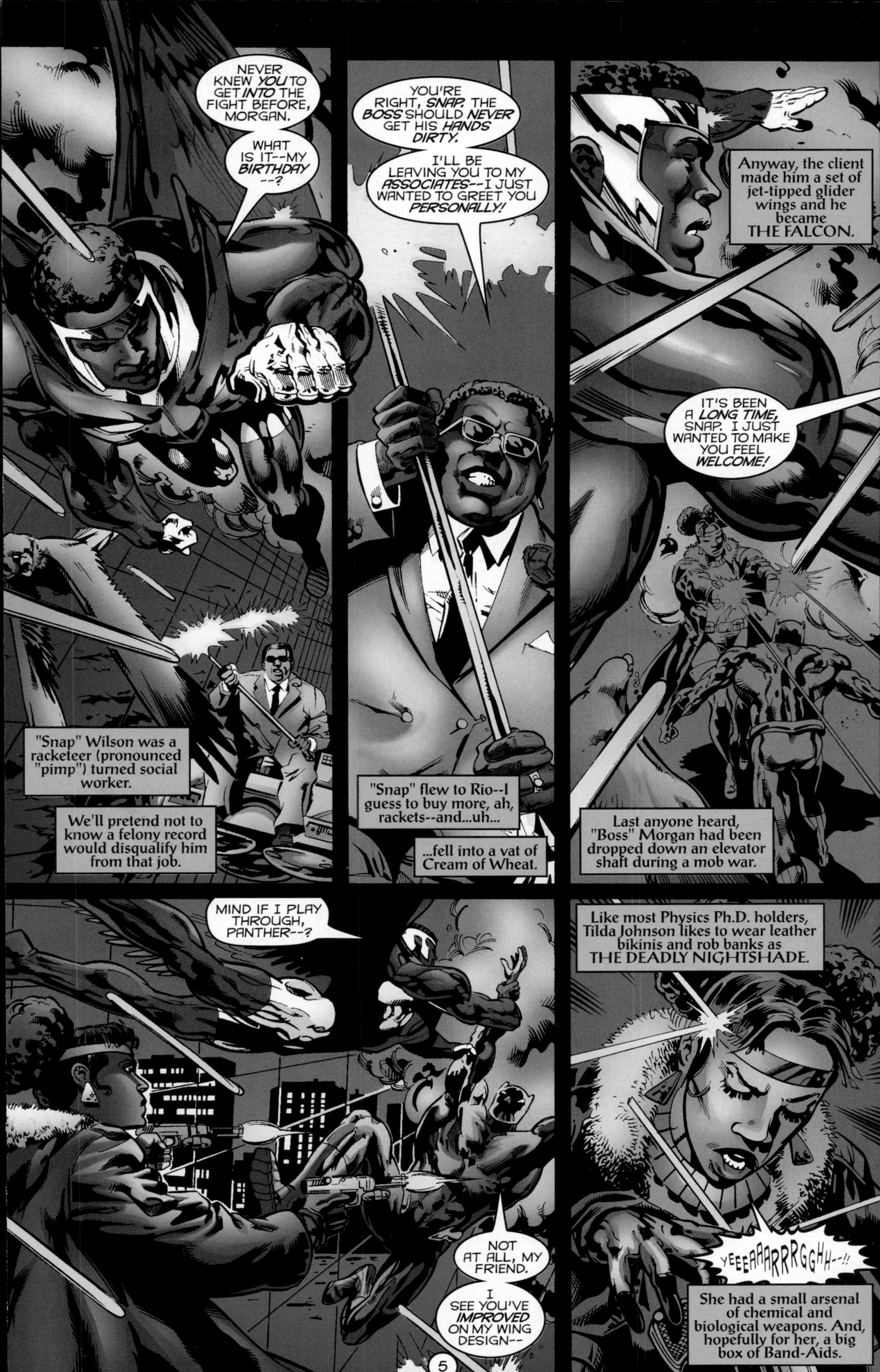

NEVER KNEW YOU TO GET INTO THE FIGHT BEFORE, MORGAN.
WHAT IS IT--MY BIRTHDAY--?
"Snap" Wilson was a racketeer (pronounced "pimp") turned social worker.
We'll pretend not to know a felony record would disqualify him from that job.
YOU'RE RIGHT, SNAP. THE BOSS SHOULD NEVER GET HIS HANDS DIRTY.
I'LL BE LEAVING YOU TO MY ASSOCIATES--I JUST WANTED TO GREET YOU PERSONALLY!
"Snap" flew to Rio--I guess to buy more, ah, rackets--and...uh...
...fell into a vat of Cream of Wheat.
Anyway, the client made him a set of jet-tipped glider wings and he became THE FALCON.
IT'S BEEN A LONG TIME, SNAP. I JUST WANTED TO MAKE YOU FEEL WELCOME!
Last anyone heard, "Boss" Morgan had been dropped down an elevator shaft during a mob war.
MIND IF I PLAY THROUGH, PANTHER--?
NOT AT ALL, MY FRIEND.
I SEE YOU'VE IMPROVED ON MY WING DESIGN--
Like most Physics Ph.D. holders, Tilda Johnson likes to wear leather bikinis and rob banks as THE DEADLY NIGHTSHADE.
YEEEAAARRRGGHH--!!
She had a small arsenal of chemical and biological weapons. And, hopefully for her, a big box of Band-Aids.

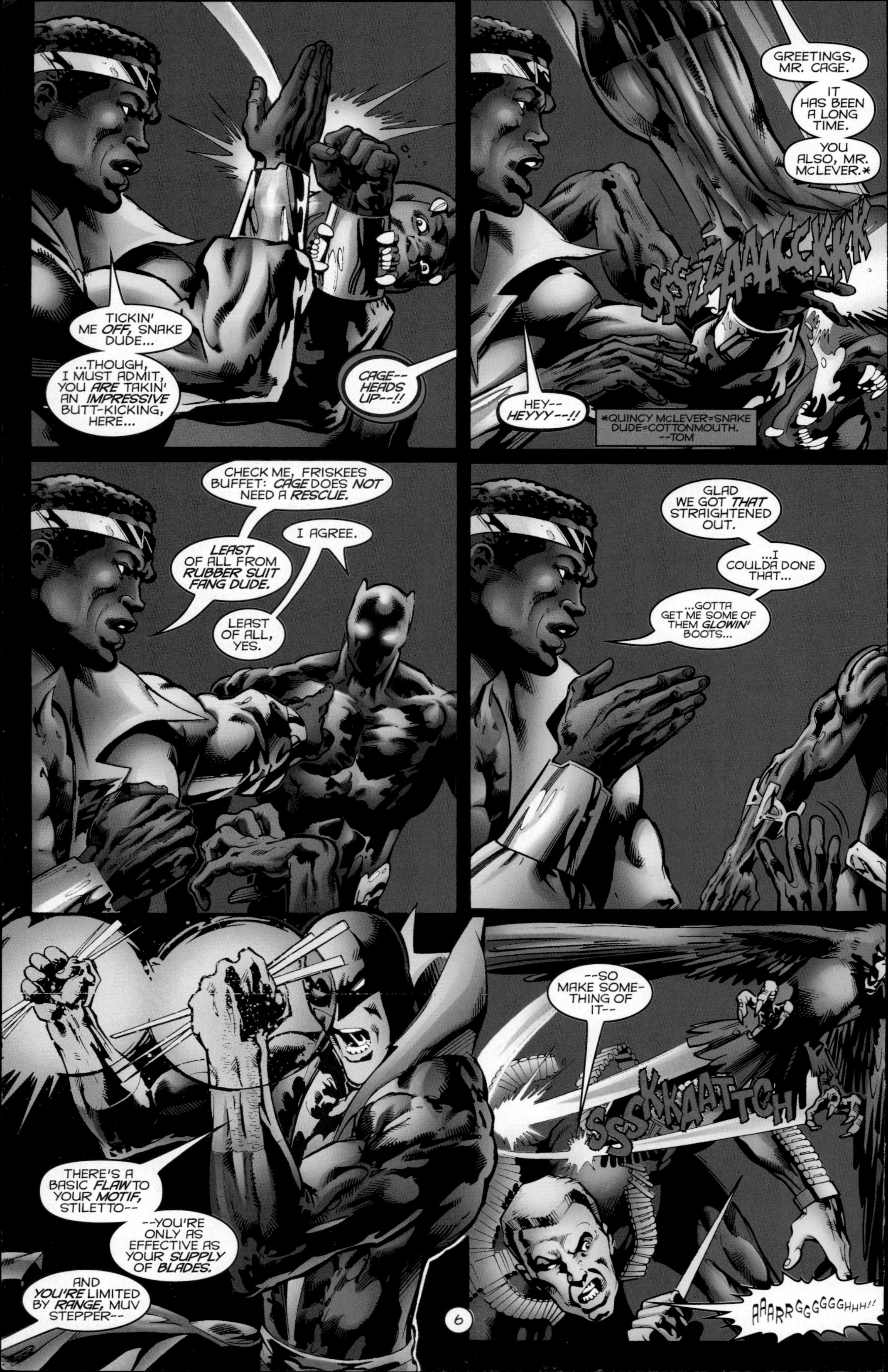

TICKIN' ME OFF, SNAKE DUDE...
...THOUGH, I MUST ADMIT, YOU ARE TAKIN' AN IMPRESSIVE BUTT-KICKING, HERE...
CAGE-- HEADS UP--!!
GREETINGS, MR. CAGE.
IT HAS BEEN A LONG TIME.
YOU ALSO, MR. MCLEVER.*
SSSZZAAACCKKKK
HEY-- HEYYY--!!
*QUINCY MCLEVER=SNAKE DUDE=COTTONMOUTH. --TOM
CHECK ME, FRISKEES BUFFET: CAGE DOES NOT NEED A RESCUE.
LEAST OF ALL FROM RUBBER SUIT FANG DUDE.
I AGREE.
LEAST OF ALL, YES.
GLAD WE GOT THAT STRAIGHTENED OUT.
...I COULDA DONE THAT...
...GOTTA GET ME SOME OF THEM GLOWIN' BOOTS...
THERE'S A BASIC FLAW TO YOUR MOTIF, STILETTO--
--YOU'RE ONLY AS EFFECTIVE AS YOUR SUPPLY OF BLADES.
AND YOU'RE LIMITED BY RANGE, MUV STEPPER--
--SO MAKE SOME-THING OF IT--
SSSKKAATTCH
AAARRGGGGGHHH!!

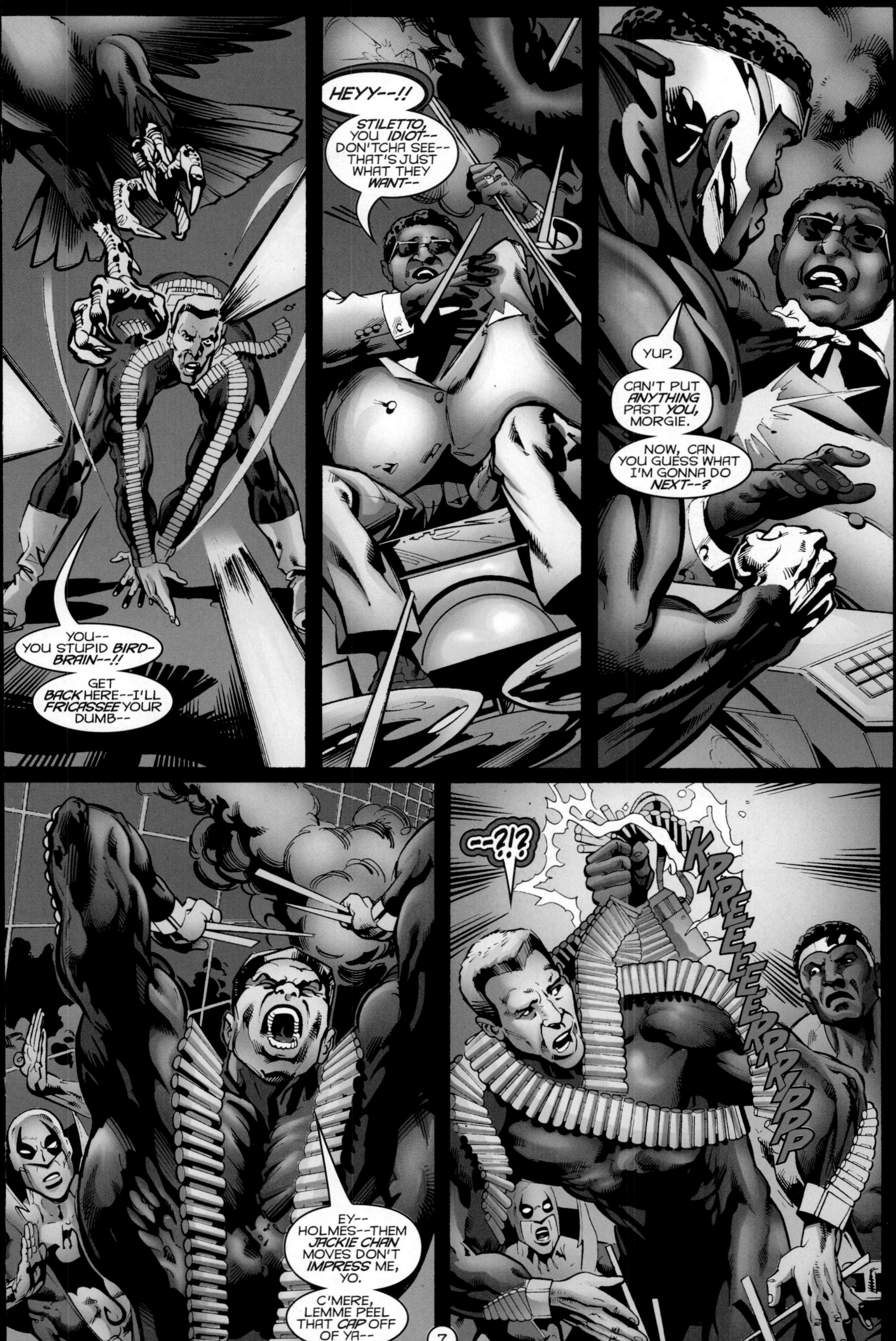
YOU-- YOU STUPID BIRD-BRAIN--!!
GET BACK HERE--I'LL FRICASSEE YOUR DUMB--
HEYY--!!
STILETTO, YOU IDIOT-- DON'TCHA SEE-- THAT'S JUST WHAT THEY WANT--
YUP.
CAN'T PUT ANYTHING PAST YOU, MORGIE.
NOW, CAN YOU GUESS WHAT I'M GONNA DO NEXT--?
EY-- HOLMES--THEM JACKIE CHAN MOVES DON'T IMPRESS ME, YO.
C'MERE, LEMME PEEL THAT CAP OFF OF YA--
--?!?
KRREEEEERRRIPPP

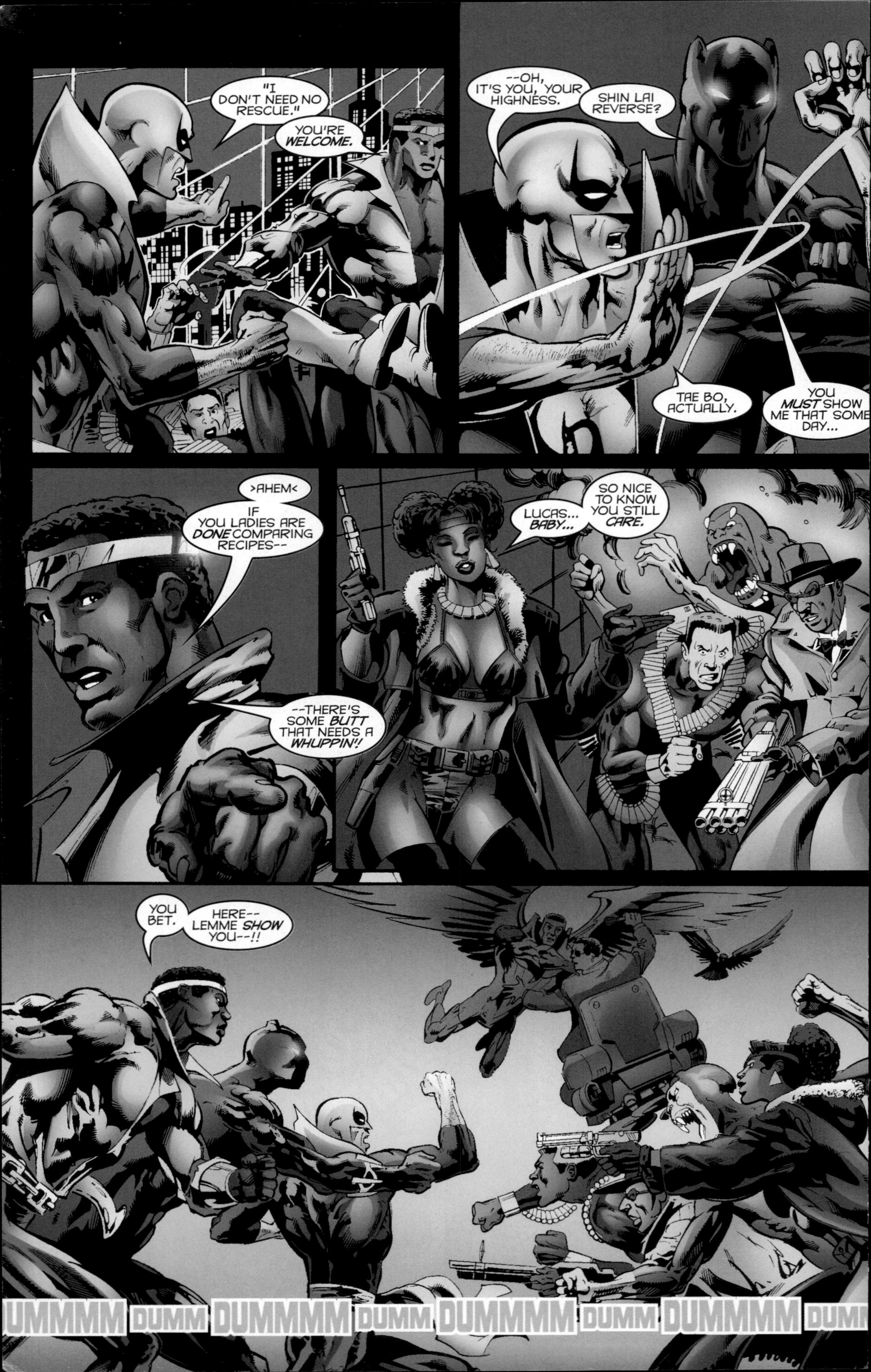
"I DON'T NEED NO RESCUE."
YOU'RE WELCOME.
--OH, IT'S YOU, YOUR HIGHNESS.
SHIN LAI REVERSE?
TAE BO, ACTUALLY.
YOU MUST SHOW ME THAT SOME DAY...
>AHEM<
IF YOU LADIES ARE DONE COMPARING RECIPES--
--THERE'S SOME BUTT THAT NEEDS A WHUPPIN'!
LUCAS... BABY...
SO NICE TO KNOW YOU STILL CARE.
YOU BET.
HERE-- LEMME SHOW YOU--!!
UMMMM DUMM DUMMMM DUMM DUMMMM DUMM DUMMMM DUM

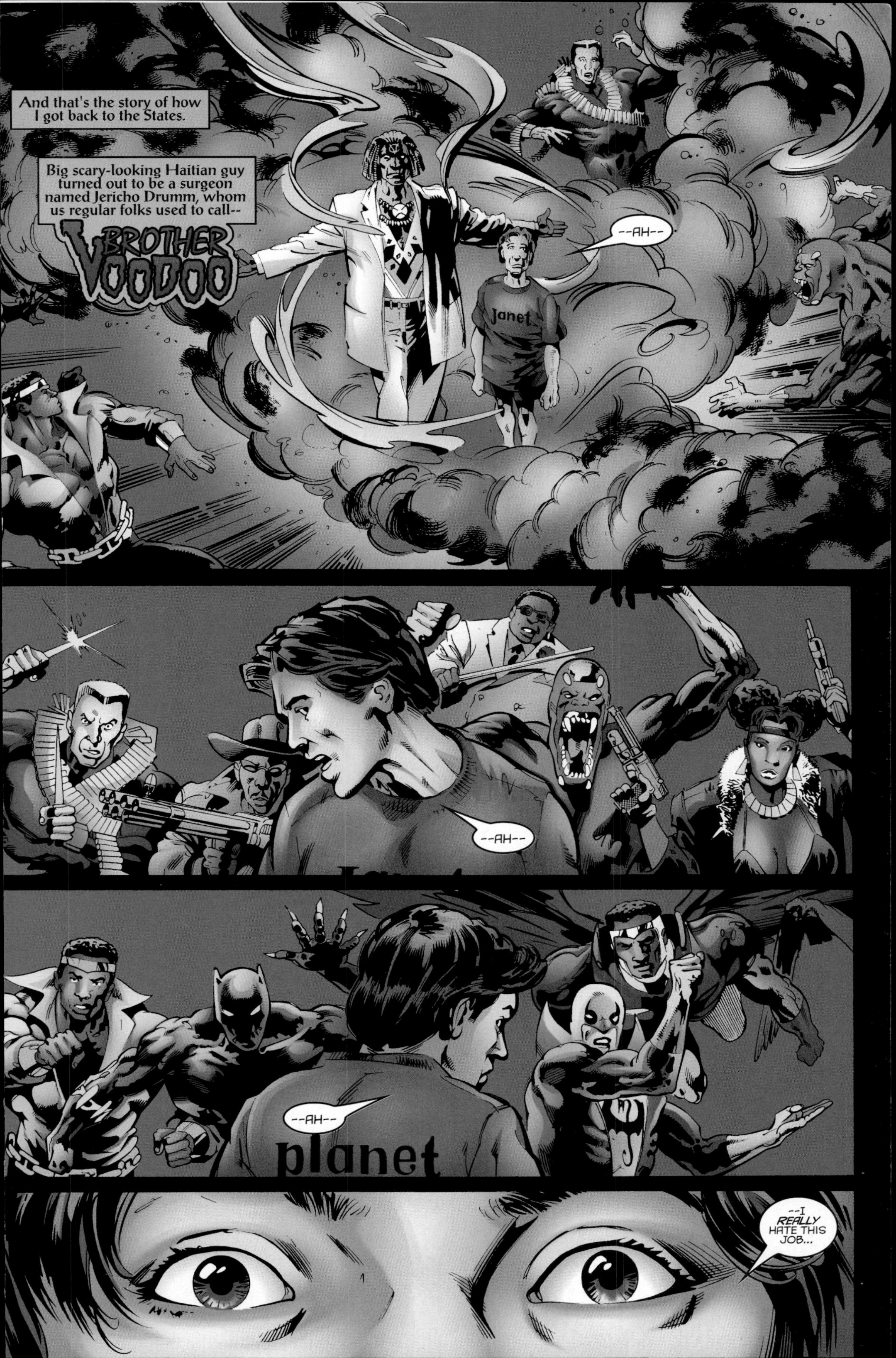
And that's the story of how I got back to the States.
Big scary-looking Haitian guy turned out to be a surgeon named Jericho Drumm, whom us regular folks used to call--
BROTHER VOODOO
--AH--
Janet
--AH--
--AH--
planet
--I REALLY HATE THIS JOB...

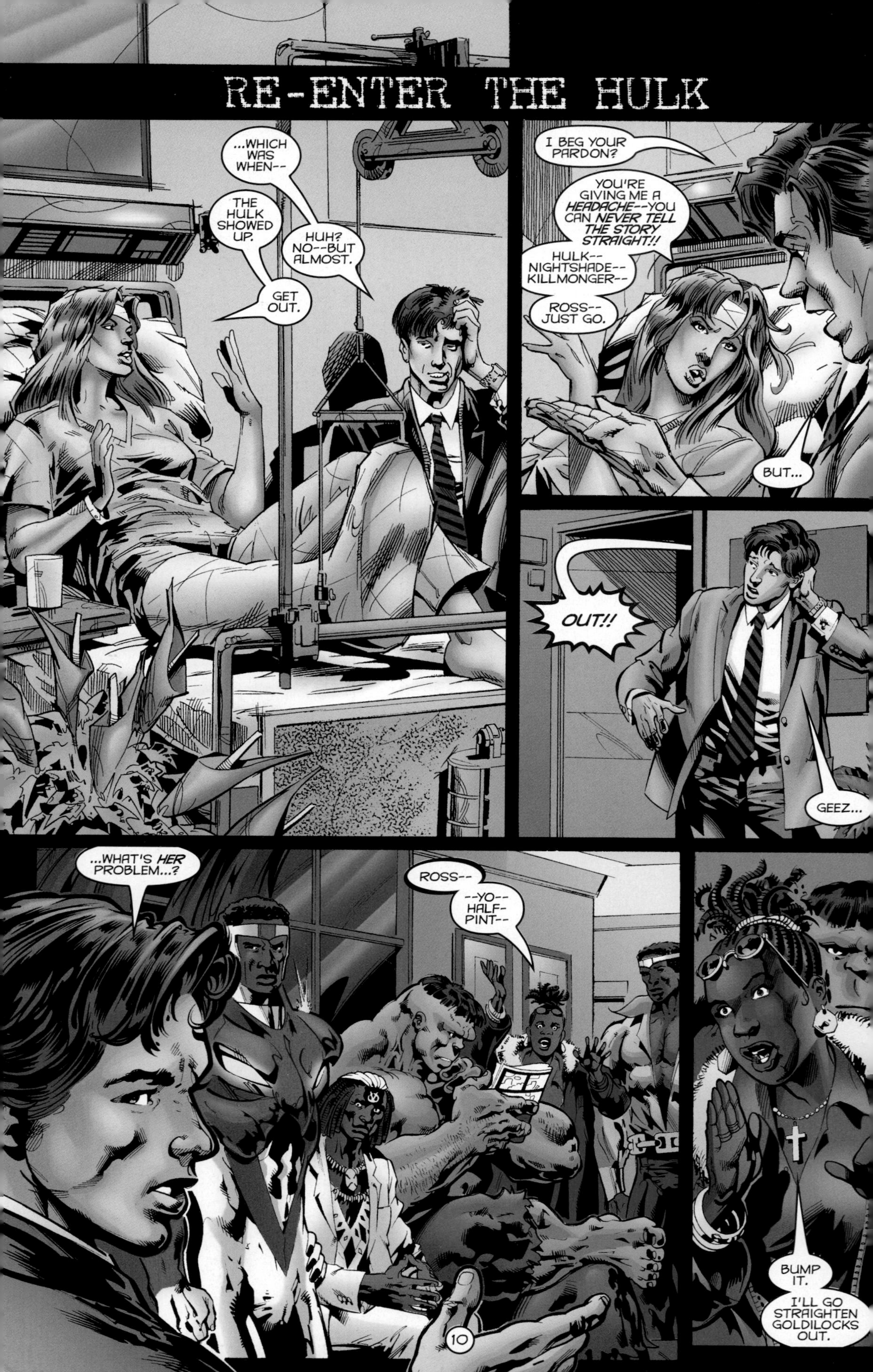
RE-ENTER THE HULK
...WHICH WAS WHEN--
THE HULK SHOWED UP.
HUH? NO--BUT ALMOST.
GET OUT.
I BEG YOUR PARDON?
YOU'RE GIVING ME A HEADACHE--YOU CAN NEVER TELL THE STORY STRAIGHT!!
HULK--NIGHTSHADE--KILLMONGER--
ROSS--JUST GO.
BUT...
OUT!!
GEEZ...
...WHAT'S HER PROBLEM...?
ROSS--
--YO--HALF-PINT--
BUMP IT.
I'LL GO STRAIGHTEN GOLDILOCKS OUT.

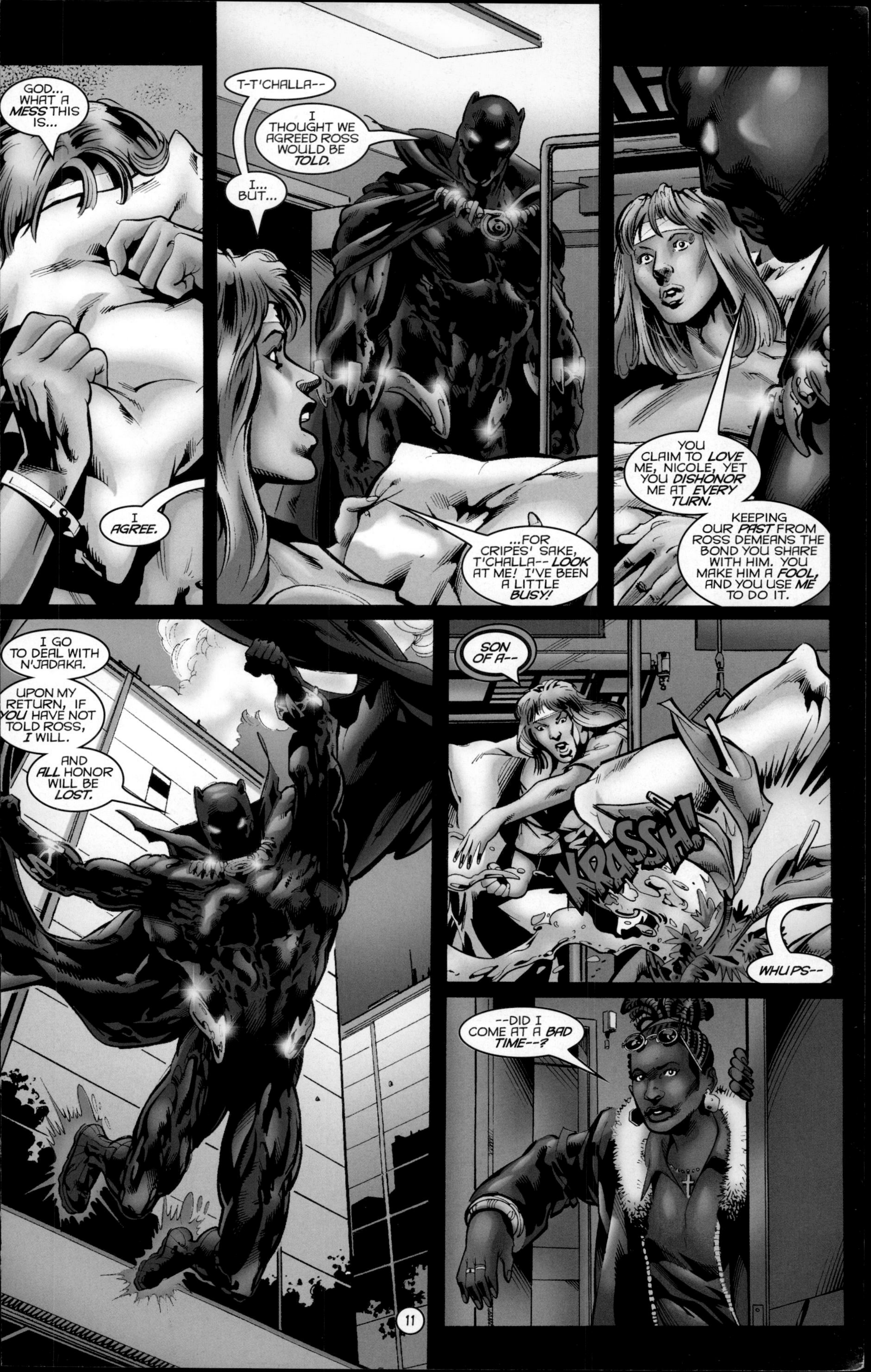
GOD... WHAT A MESS THIS IS...
I AGREE.
T-T'CHALLA--
I THOUGHT WE AGREED ROSS WOULD BE TOLD.
I... BUT...
...FOR CRIPES' SAKE, T'CHALLA-- LOOK AT ME! I'VE BEEN A LITTLE BUSY!
YOU CLAIM TO LOVE ME, NICOLE, YET YOU DISHONOR ME AT EVERY TURN.
KEEPING OUR PAST FROM ROSS DEMEANS THE BOND YOU SHARE WITH HIM. YOU MAKE HIM A FOOL, AND YOU USE ME TO DO IT.
I GO TO DEAL WITH N'JADAKA.
UPON MY RETURN, IF YOU HAVE NOT TOLD ROSS, I WILL.
AND ALL HONOR WILL BE LOST.
SON OF A--
KRASSH!
WHUPS--
--DID I COME AT A BAD TIME--?

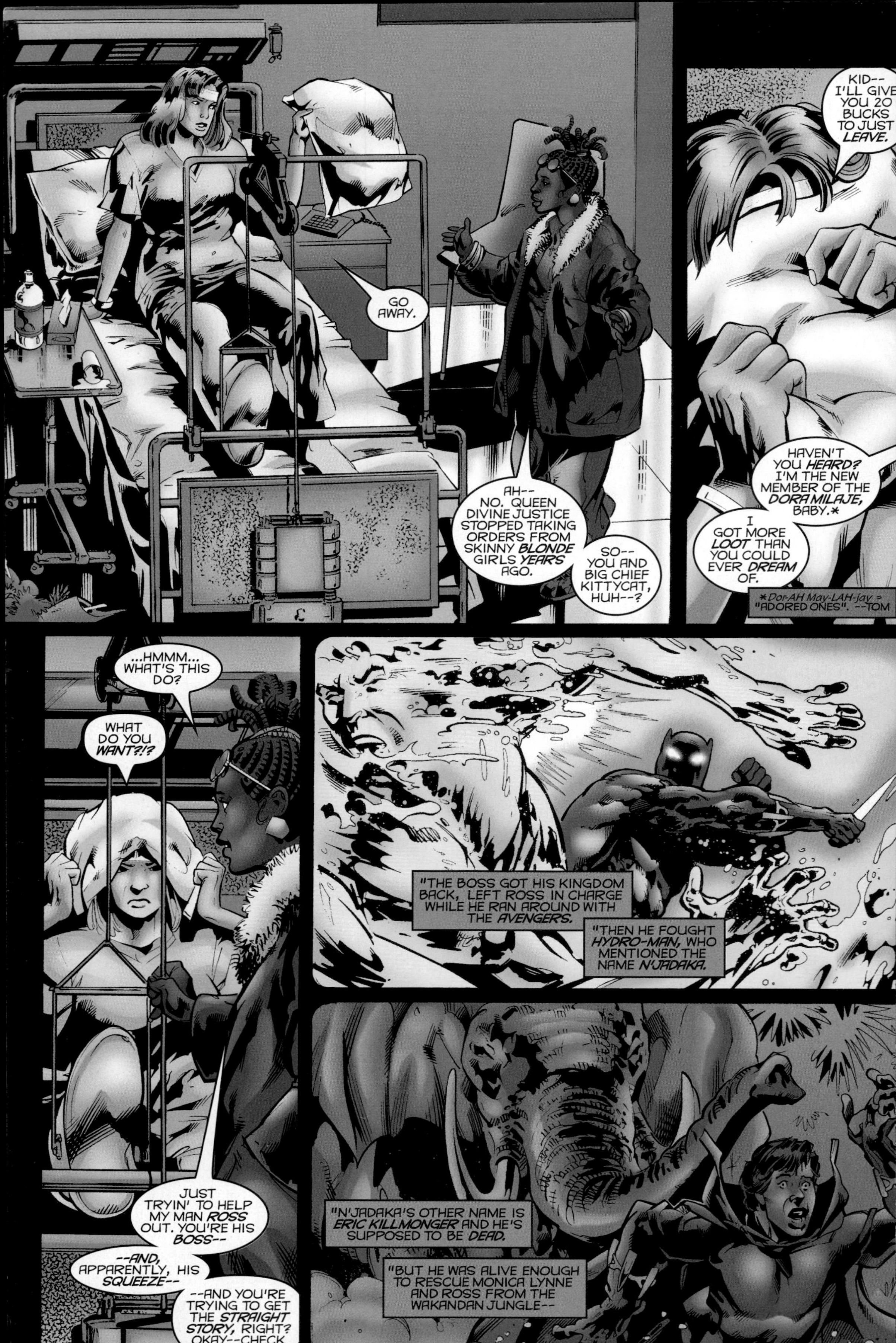
GO AWAY.
AH-- NO. QUEEN DIVINE JUSTICE STOPPED TAKING ORDERS FROM SKINNY BLONDE GIRLS YEARS AGO.
SO-- YOU AND BIG CHIEF KITTYCAT, HUH--?
KID-- I'LL GIVE YOU 20 BUCKS TO JUST LEAVE.
HAVEN'T YOU HEARD? I'M THE NEW MEMBER OF THE DORA MILAJE, BABY.*
I GOT MORE LOOT THAN YOU COULD EVER DREAM OF.
*Dor-AH May-LAH-jay = "ADORED ONES". --TOM
...HMMM... WHAT'S THIS DO?
WHAT DO YOU WANT?!?
JUST TRYIN' TO HELP MY MAN ROSS OUT. YOU'RE HIS BOSS--
--AND, APPARENTLY, HIS SQUEEZE--
--AND YOU'RE TRYING TO GET THE STRAIGHT STORY, RIGHT? OKAY--CHECK ME--
"THE BOSS GOT HIS KINGDOM BACK, LEFT ROSS IN CHARGE WHILE HE RAN AROUND WITH THE AVENGERS.
"THEN HE FOUGHT HYDRO-MAN, WHO MENTIONED THE NAME N'JADAKA.
"N'JADAKA'S OTHER NAME IS ERIC KILLMONGER AND HE'S SUPPOSED TO BE DEAD.
"BUT HE WAS ALIVE ENOUGH TO RESCUE MONICA LYNNE AND ROSS FROM THE WAKANDAN JUNGLE--

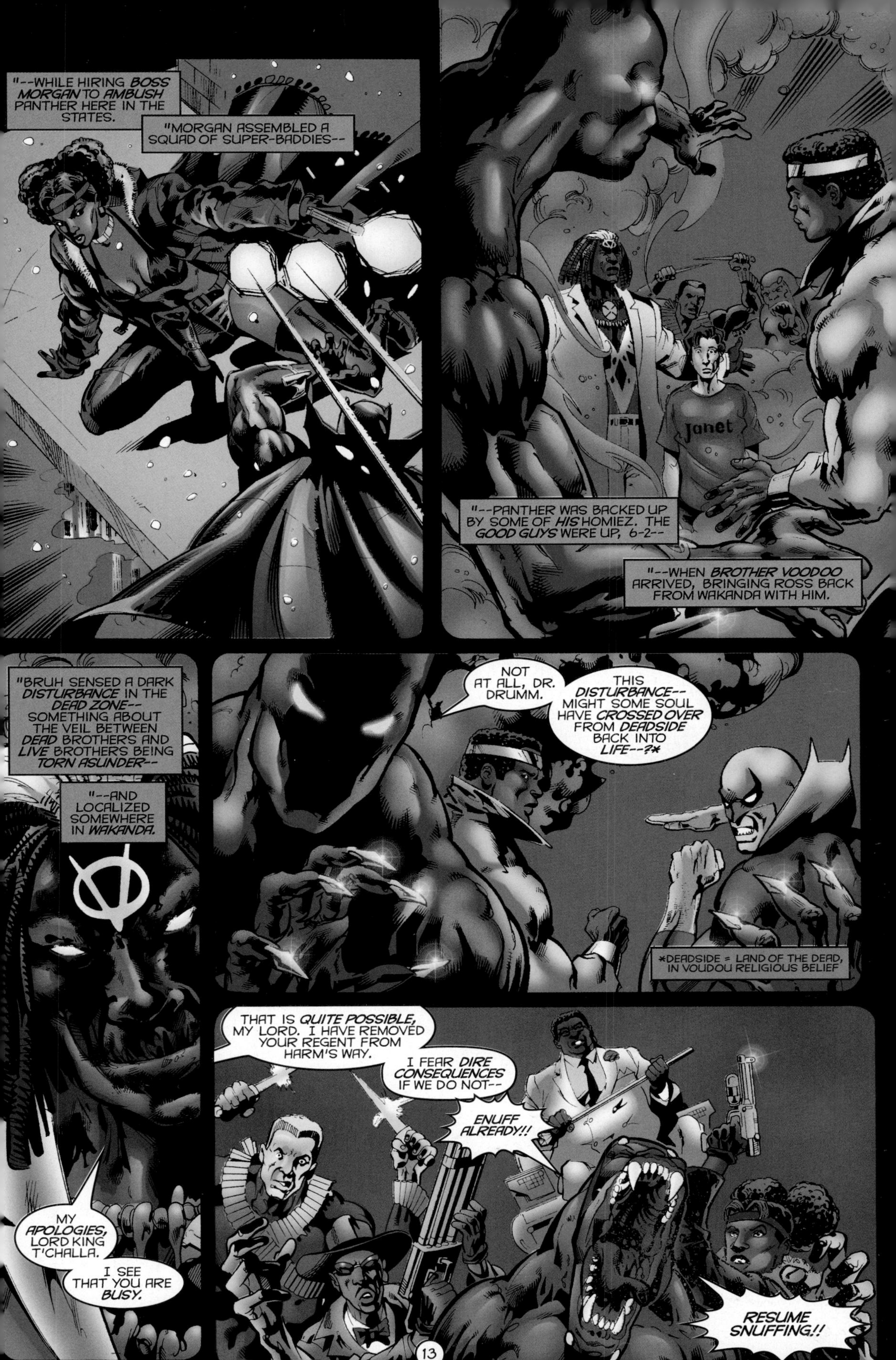
"--WHILE HIRING BOSS MORGAN TO AMBUSH PANTHER HERE IN THE STATES.
"MORGAN ASSEMBLED A SQUAD OF SUPER-BADDIES--
Janet
"--PANTHER WAS BACKED UP BY SOME OF HIS HOMIEZ. THE GOOD GUYS WERE UP, 6-2--
"--WHEN BROTHER VOODOO ARRIVED, BRINGING ROSS BACK FROM WAKANDA WITH HIM.
"BRUH SENSED A DARK DISTURBANCE IN THE DEAD ZONE--SOMETHING ABOUT THE VEIL BETWEEN DEAD BROTHERS AND LIVE BROTHERS BEING TORN ASUNDER--
"--AND LOCALIZED SOMEWHERE IN WAKANDA.
NOT AT ALL, DR. DRUMM.
THIS DISTURBANCE--MIGHT SOME SOUL HAVE CROSSED OVER FROM DEADSIDE BACK INTO LIFE--?*
*DEADSIDE = LAND OF THE DEAD, IN VOUDOU RELIGIOUS BELIEF
MY APOLOGIES, LORD KING T'CHALLA.
I SEE THAT YOU ARE BUSY.
THAT IS QUITE POSSIBLE, MY LORD. I HAVE REMOVED YOUR REGENT FROM HARM'S WAY.
I FEAR DIRE CONSEQUENCES IF WE DO NOT--
ENUFF ALREADY!!
RESUME SNUFFING!!

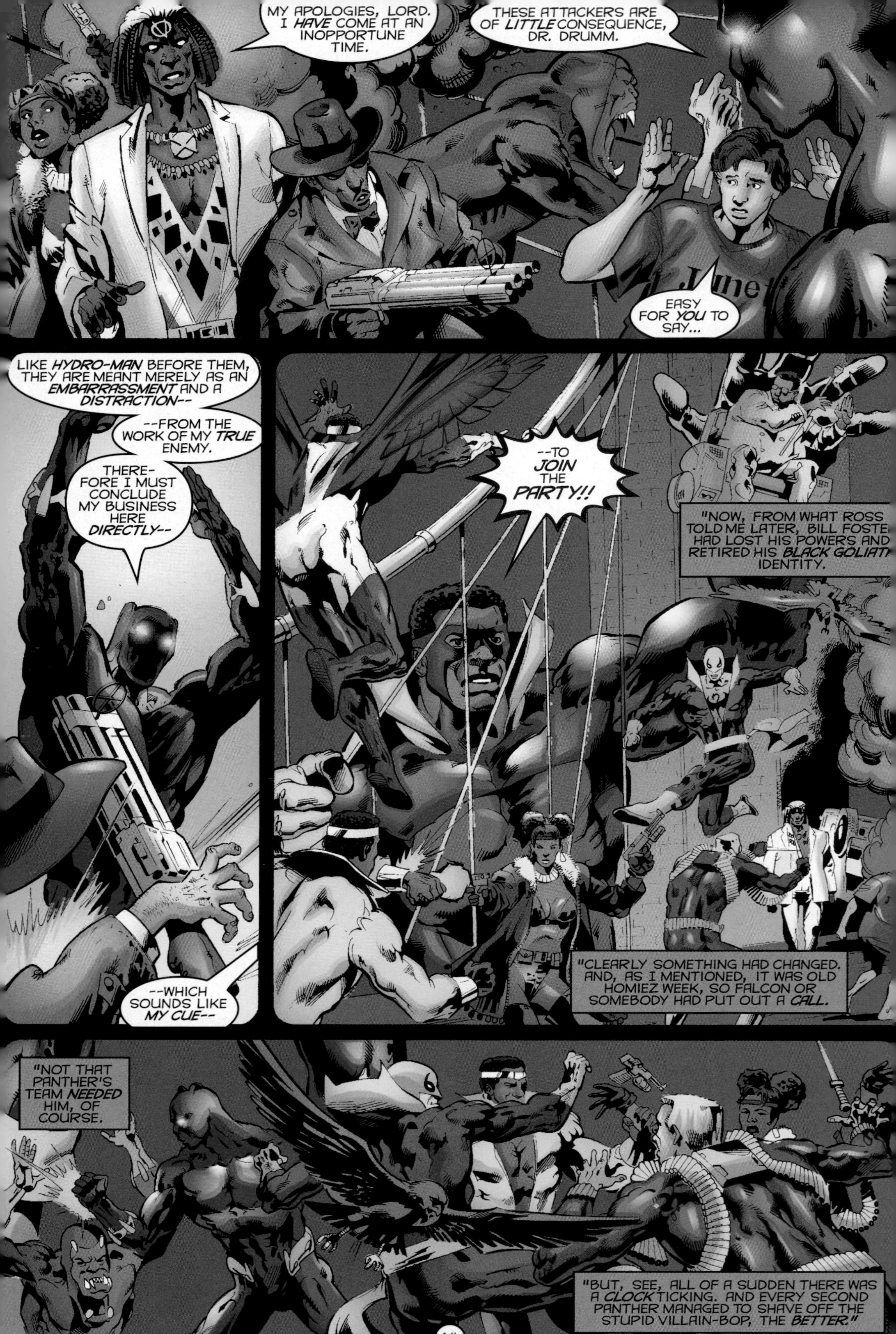
MY APOLOGIES, LORD. I HAVE COME AT AN INOPPORTUNE TIME.
THESE ATTACKERS ARE OF LITTLE CONSEQUENCE, DR. DRUMM.
EASY FOR YOU TO SAY...
LIKE HYDRO-MAN BEFORE THEM, THEY ARE MEANT MERELY AS AN EMBARRASSMENT AND A DISTRACTION--
--FROM THE WORK OF MY TRUE ENEMY.
THERE-FORE I MUST CONCLUDE MY BUSINESS HERE DIRECTLY--
--WHICH SOUNDS LIKE MY CUE--
--TO JOIN THE PARTY!!
"NOW, FROM WHAT ROSS TOLD ME LATER, BILL FOSTE HAD LOST HIS POWERS AND RETIRED HIS BLACK GOLIAT IDENTITY.
"CLEARLY SOMETHING HAD CHANGED. AND, AS I MENTIONED, IT WAS OLD HOMIEZ WEEK, SO FALCON OR SOMEBODY HAD PUT OUT A CALL.
"NOT THAT PANTHER'S TEAM NEEDED HIM, OF COURSE.
"BUT, SEE, ALL OF A SUDDEN THERE WAS A CLOCK TICKING. AND EVERY SECOND PANTHER MANAGED TO SHAVE OFF THE STUPID VILLAIN-BOP, THE BETTER."

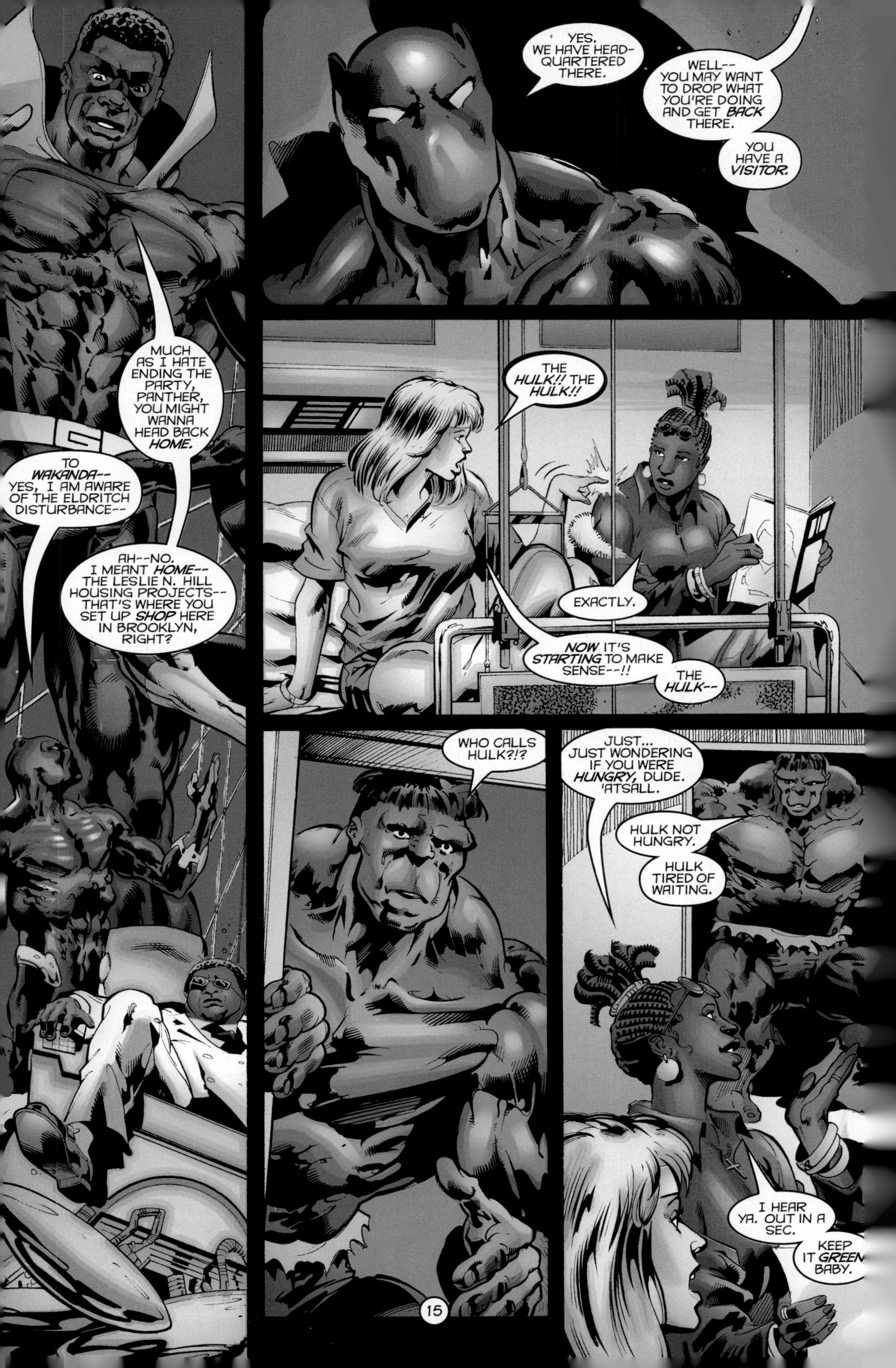
MUCH AS I HATE ENDING THE PARTY, PANTHER, YOU MIGHT WANNA HEAD BACK HOME.
TO WAKANDA-- YES, I AM AWARE OF THE ELDRITCH DISTURBANCE--
AH--NO. I MEANT HOME-- THE LESLIE N. HILL HOUSING PROJECTS-- THAT'S WHERE YOU SET UP SHOP HERE IN BROOKLYN, RIGHT?
YES. WE HAVE HEAD-QUARTERED THERE.
WELL-- YOU MAY WANT TO DROP WHAT YOU'RE DOING AND GET BACK THERE.
YOU HAVE A VISITOR.
THE HULK!! THE HULK!!
EXACTLY.
NOW IT'S STARTING TO MAKE SENSE--!!
THE HULK--
WHO CALLS HULK?!?
JUST... JUST WONDERING IF YOU WERE HUNGRY, DUDE. 'ATSALL.
HULK NOT HUNGRY.
HULK TIRED OF WAITING.
I HEAR YA. OUT IN A SEC.
KEEP IT GREEN BABY.

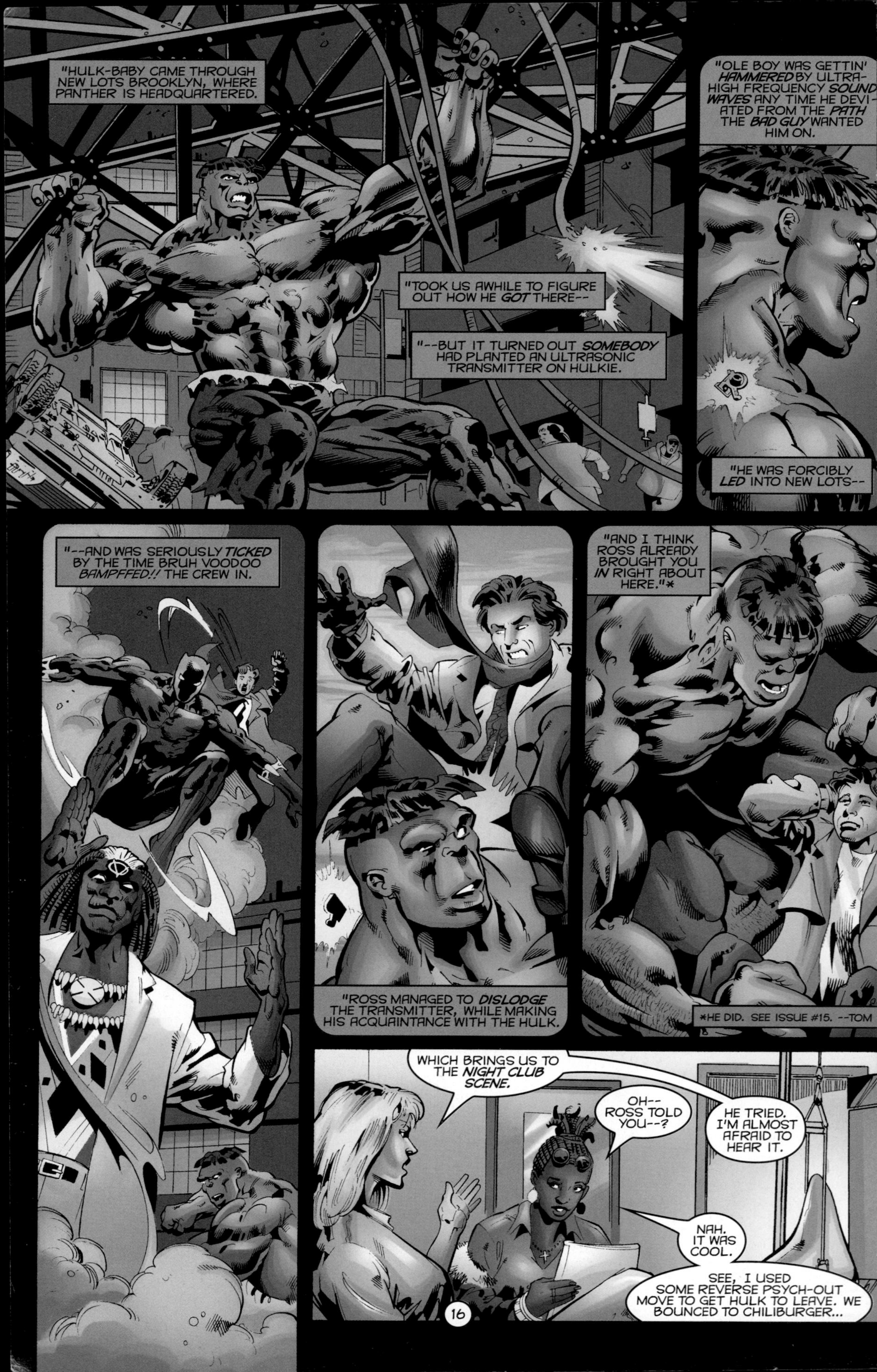
"HULK-BABY CAME THROUGH NEW LOTS BROOKLYN, WHERE PANTHER IS HEADQUARTERED.
"TOOK US AWHILE TO FIGURE OUT HOW HE GOT THERE--
"--BUT IT TURNED OUT SOMEBODY HAD PLANTED AN ULTRASONIC TRANSMITTER ON HULKIE.
"OLE BOY WAS GETTIN' HAMMERED BY ULTRA-HIGH FREQUENCY SOUND WAVES ANY TIME HE DEVIATED FROM THE PATH THE BAD GUY WANTED HIM ON.
"HE WAS FORCIBLY LED INTO NEW LOTS--
"--AND WAS SERIOUSLY TICKED BY THE TIME BRUH VOODOO BAMPFFED!! THE CREW IN.
"ROSS MANAGED TO DISLODGE THE TRANSMITTER, WHILE MAKING HIS ACQUAINTANCE WITH THE HULK.
"AND I THINK ROSS ALREADY BROUGHT YOU IN RIGHT ABOUT HERE."*
*HE DID. SEE ISSUE #15. --TOM
WHICH BRINGS US TO THE NIGHT CLUB SCENE.
OH-- ROSS TOLD YOU--?
HE TRIED. I'M ALMOST AFRAID TO HEAR IT.
NAH. IT WAS COOL.
SEE, I USED SOME REVERSE PSYCH-OUT MOVE TO GET HULK TO LEAVE. WE BOUNCED TO CHILIBURGER...

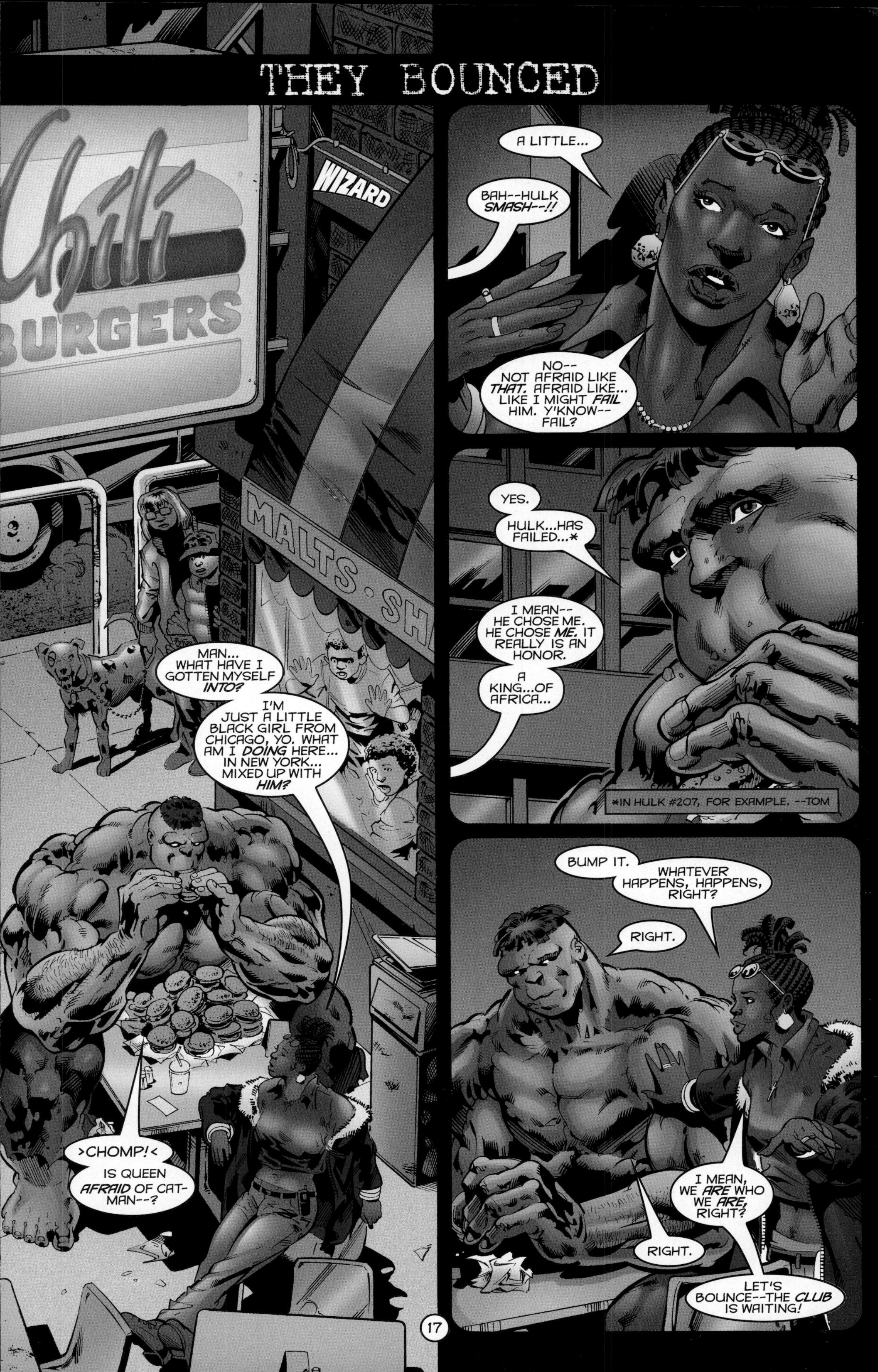
THEY BOUNCED
CHILI BURGERS
WIZARD
MALTS · SH
MAN... WHAT HAVE I GOTTEN MYSELF INTO?
I'M JUST A LITTLE BLACK GIRL FROM CHICAGO, YO. WHAT AM I DOING HERE... IN NEW YORK... MIXED UP WITH HIM?
>CHOMP!<
IS QUEEN AFRAID OF CAT-MAN--?
A LITTLE...
BAH--HULK SMASH--!!
NO-- NOT AFRAID LIKE THAT. AFRAID LIKE... LIKE I MIGHT FAIL HIM. Y'KNOW-- FAIL?
YES.
HULK...HAS FAILED...*
I MEAN-- HE CHOSE ME. HE CHOSE ME. IT REALLY IS AN HONOR.
A KING...OF AFRICA...
*IN HULK #207, FOR EXAMPLE. --TOM
BUMP IT.
WHATEVER HAPPENS, HAPPENS, RIGHT?
RIGHT.
I MEAN, WE ARE WHO WE ARE, RIGHT?
RIGHT.
LET'S BOUNCE--THE CLUB IS WAITING!

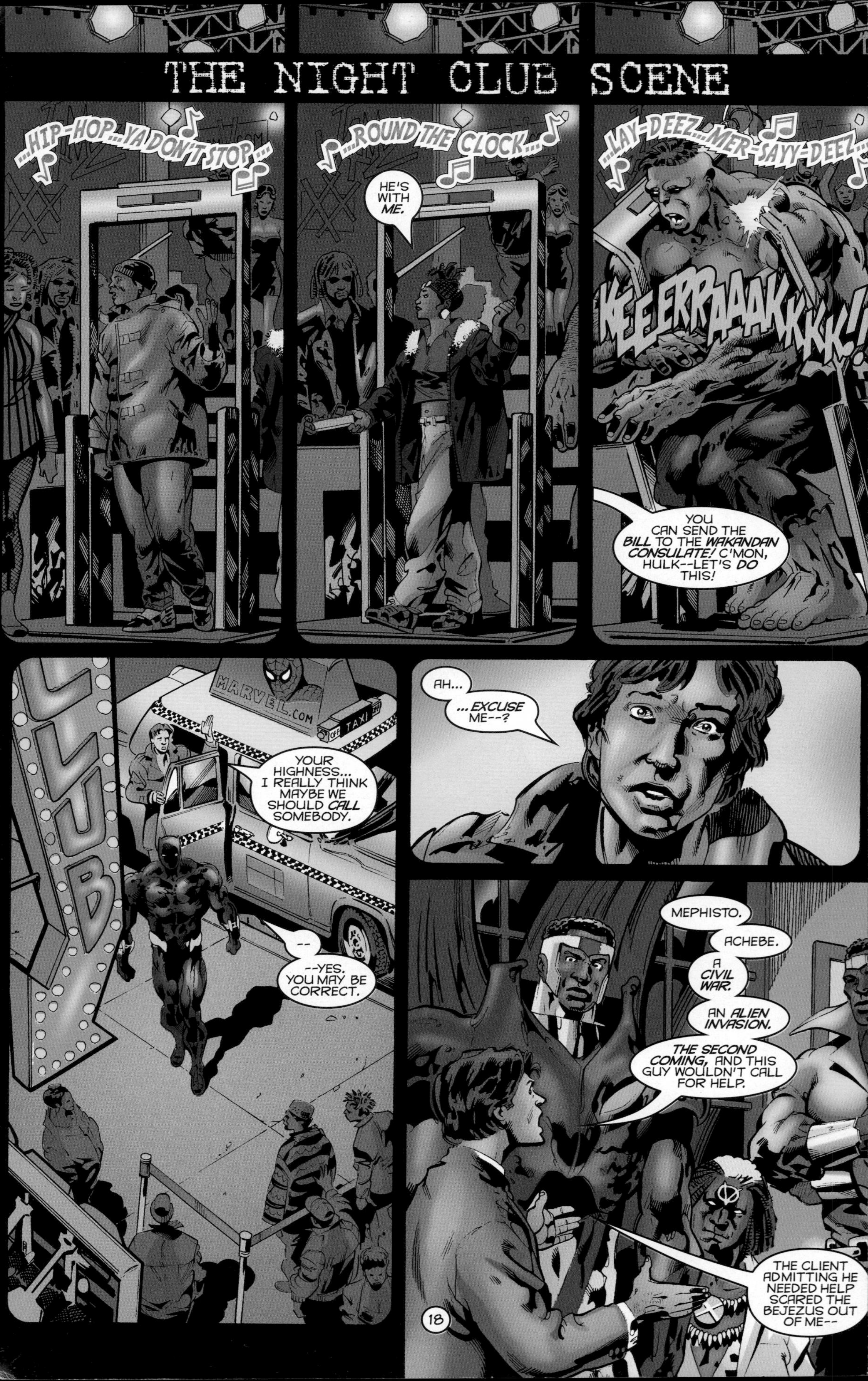
THE NIGHT CLUB SCENE
...HIP-HOP...YA DON'T STOP...
...ROUND THE CLOCK...
HE'S WITH ME.
...LAY-DEEZ...MER-SAYY-DEEZ...
KEEERRAAAKKKK!!
YOU CAN SEND THE BILL TO THE WAKANDAN CONSULATE! C'MON, HULK--LET'S DO THIS!
MARVEL.COM
TAXI
YOUR HIGHNESS... I REALLY THINK MAYBE WE SHOULD CALL SOMEBODY.
--
--YES. YOU MAY BE CORRECT.
AH...
...EXCUSE ME--?
MEPHISTO.
ACHEBE.
A CIVIL WAR.
AN ALIEN INVASION.
THE SECOND COMING, AND THIS GUY WOULDN'T CALL FOR HELP.
THE CLIENT ADMITTING HE NEEDED HELP SCARED THE BEJEZUS OUT OF ME--

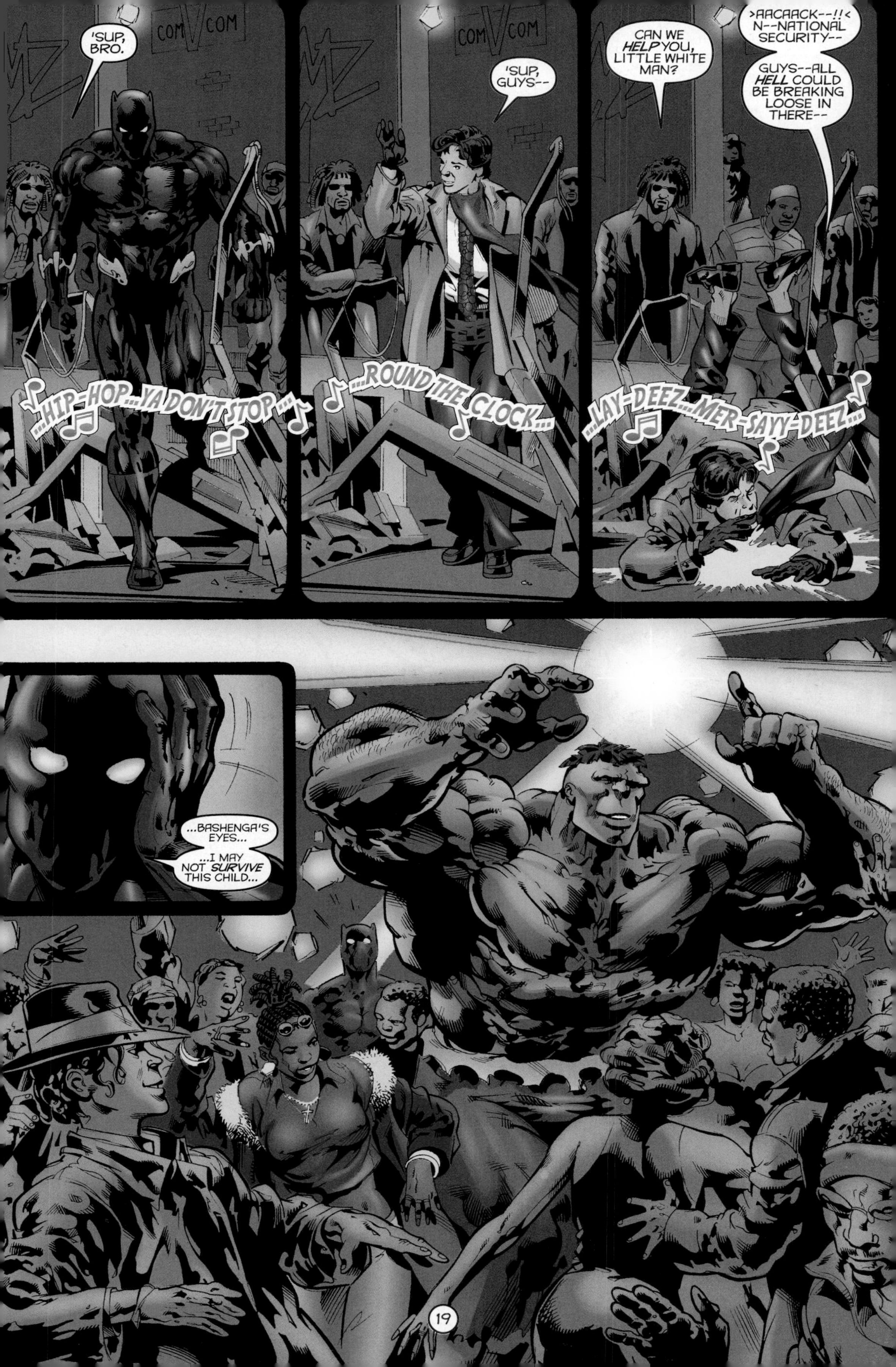
'SUP, BRO.
...HIP-HOP...YA DON'T STOP...
'SUP, GUYS--
...ROUND THE CLOCK...
CAN WE HELP YOU, LITTLE WHITE MAN?
>AACAACK--!!< N--NATIONAL SECURITY--
GUYS--ALL HELL COULD BE BREAKING LOOSE IN THERE--
...LAY-DEEZ...MER-SAYY-DEEZ...
...BASHENGA'S EYES...
...I MAY NOT SURVIVE THIS CHILD...

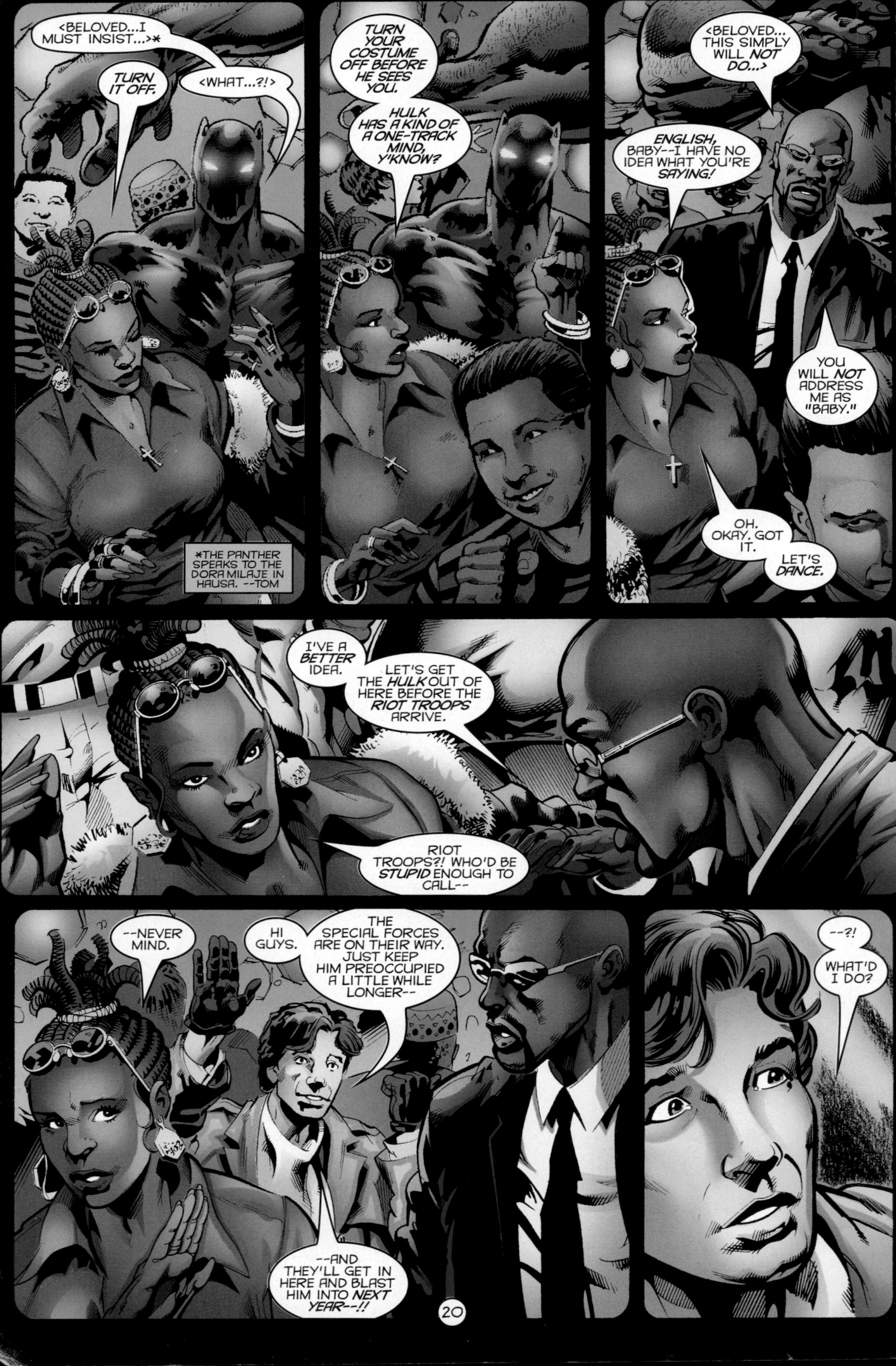
<BELOVED...I MUST INSIST...>*
TURN IT OFF.
<WHAT...?!>
*THE PANTHER SPEAKS TO THE DORA MILAJE IN HAUSA. --TOM
TURN YOUR COSTUME OFF BEFORE HE SEES YOU.
HULK HAS A KIND OF A ONE-TRACK MIND, Y'KNOW?
<BELOVED... THIS SIMPLY WILL NOT DO...>
ENGLISH, BABY--I HAVE NO IDEA WHAT YOU'RE SAYING!
YOU WILL NOT ADDRESS ME AS "BABY."
OH. OKAY. GOT IT.
LET'S DANCE.
I'VE A BETTER IDEA.
LET'S GET THE HULK OUT OF HERE BEFORE THE RIOT TROOPS ARRIVE.
RIOT TROOPS?! WHO'D BE STUPID ENOUGH TO CALL--
--NEVER MIND.
HI GUYS.
THE SPECIAL FORCES ARE ON THEIR WAY. JUST KEEP HIM PREOCCUPIED A LITTLE WHILE LONGER--
--AND THEY'LL GET IN HERE AND BLAST HIM INTO NEXT YEAR--!!
--?!
WHAT'D I DO?

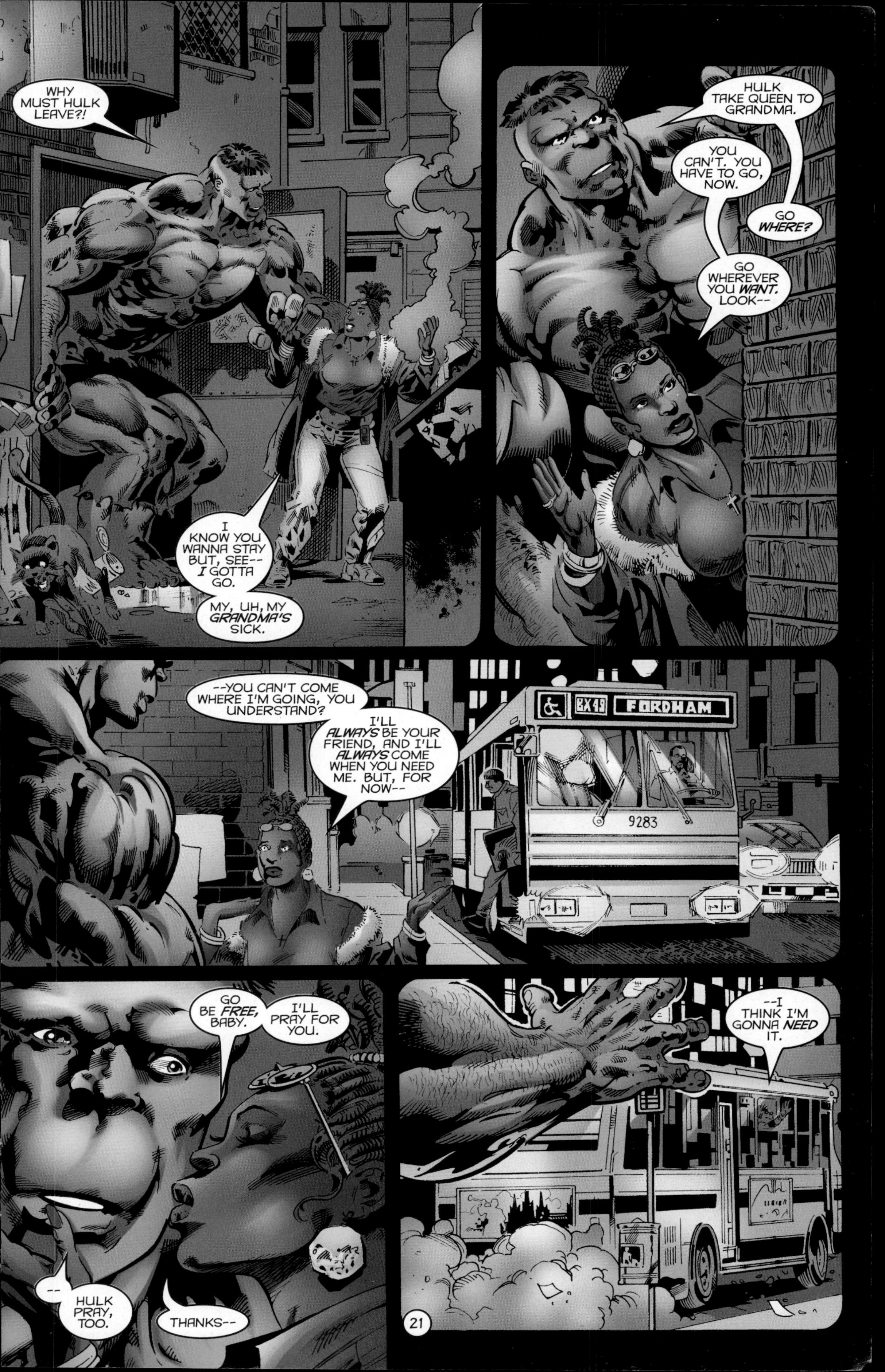
WHY MUST HULK LEAVE?!
I KNOW YOU WANNA STAY BUT, SEE-- I GOTTA GO.
MY, UH, MY GRANDMA'S SICK.
HULK TAKE QUEEN TO GRANDMA.
YOU CAN'T. YOU HAVE TO GO, NOW.
GO WHERE?
GO WHEREVER YOU WANT. LOOK--
--YOU CAN'T COME WHERE I'M GOING, YOU UNDERSTAND?
I'LL ALWAYS BE YOUR FRIEND, AND I'LL ALWAYS COME WHEN YOU NEED ME. BUT, FOR NOW--
BX49
FORDHAM
9283
GO BE FREE, BABY.
I'LL PRAY FOR YOU.
--HULK PRAY, TOO.
THANKS--
--I THINK I'M GONNA NEED IT.

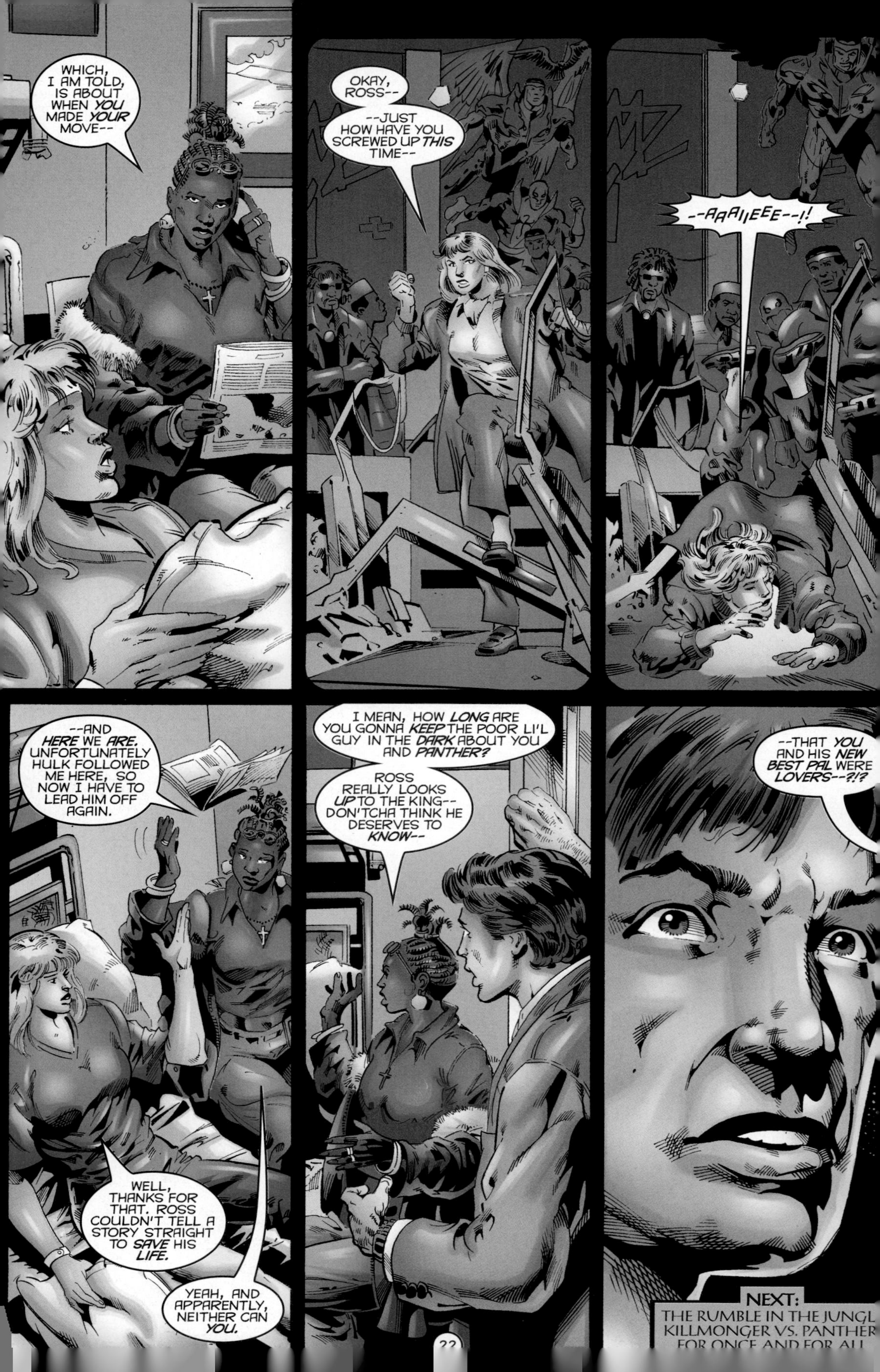
WHICH, I AM TOLD, IS ABOUT WHEN YOU MADE YOUR MOVE--
OKAY, ROSS--
--JUST HOW HAVE YOU SCREWED UP THIS TIME--
--AAAIIEEE--!!
--AND HERE WE ARE. UNFORTUNATELY HULK FOLLOWED ME HERE, SO NOW I HAVE TO LEAD HIM OFF AGAIN.
WELL, THANKS FOR THAT. ROSS COULDN'T TELL A STORY STRAIGHT TO SAVE HIS LIFE.
YEAH, AND APPARENTLY, NEITHER CAN YOU.
I MEAN, HOW LONG ARE YOU GONNA KEEP THE POOR LI'L GUY IN THE DARK ABOUT YOU AND PANTHER?
ROSS REALLY LOOKS UP TO THE KING--DON'TCHA THINK HE DESERVES TO KNOW--
--THAT YOU AND HIS NEW BEST PAL WERE LOVERS--?!?
NEXT:
THE RUMBLE IN THE JUNGL
KILLMONGER VS. PANTHER
FOR ONCE AND FOR ALL

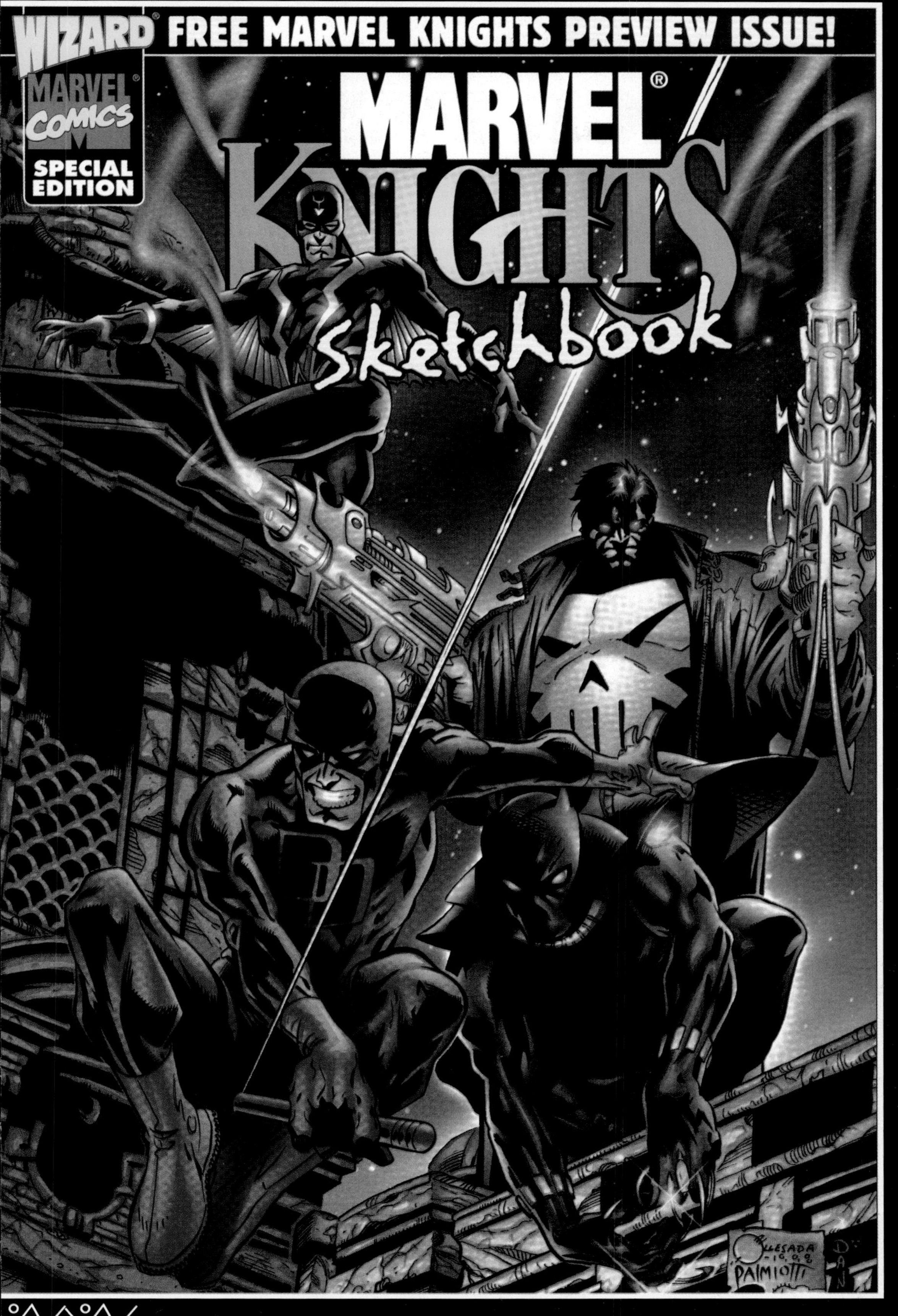
WIZARD FREE MARVEL KNIGHTS PREVIEW ISSUE!
MARVEL COMICS
SPECIAL EDITION
MARVEL KNIGHTS
Sketchbook
QUESADA
PALMIOTTI

CHRISTOPHER PRIEST ON: BLACK PANTHER

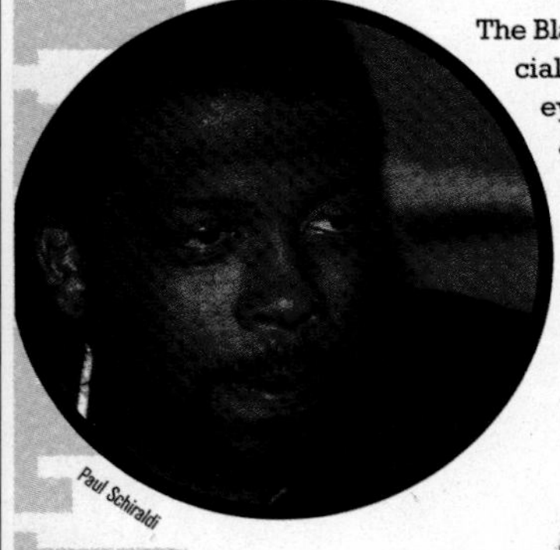

Paul Schiraldi

The Black Panther is *the* iconic superhero to the African-American community, and I feel especially flattered that Jimmy and Joe thought of me for this project. As reward for this starry-eyed optimism, Tex and I have turned the Panther concept on its ear with *Quantum and Woody*-levels of verve and irreverence, producing a dynamic, unexpected *Panther* book designed to cause creative whiplash for most anyone expecting, well, more of the same. We're inclusive and respectful of the Panther's proud legacy while forging new ground with a chainsaw and a blowtorch, giddily skewering the Panther's undeserved also-ran status and driving up the blood pressure of the Marvel honchos in the bargain.

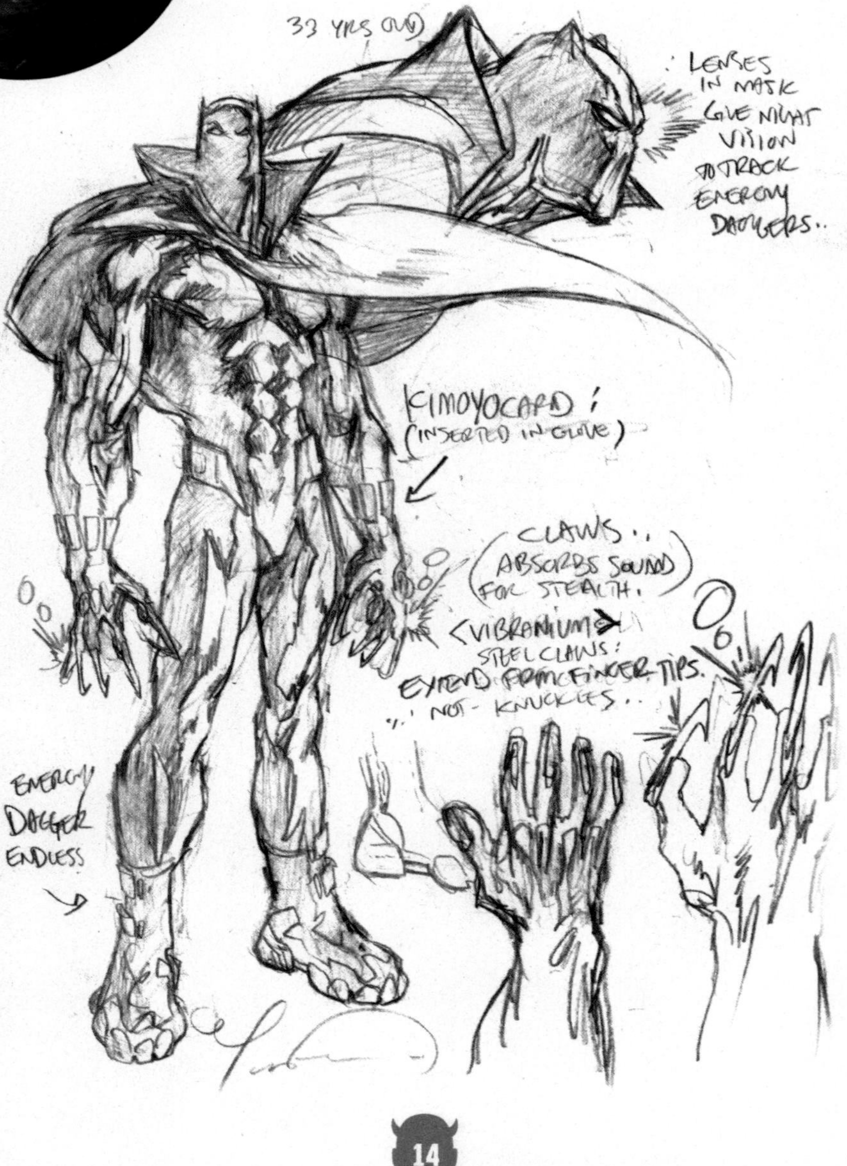
33 YRS OLD
LENSES IN MASK GIVE NIGHT VISION TO TRACK ENERGY DAGGERS..
KIMOYO CARD! (INSERTED IN GLOVE)
CLAWS.. (ABSORBS SOUND FOR STEALTH.
<VIBRANIUM> STEEL CLAWS! EXTEND FROM FINGER TIPS. NOT- KNUCKLES..
ENERGY DAGGER ENDLESS

MARK TEXEIRA ON:
BLACK PANTHER

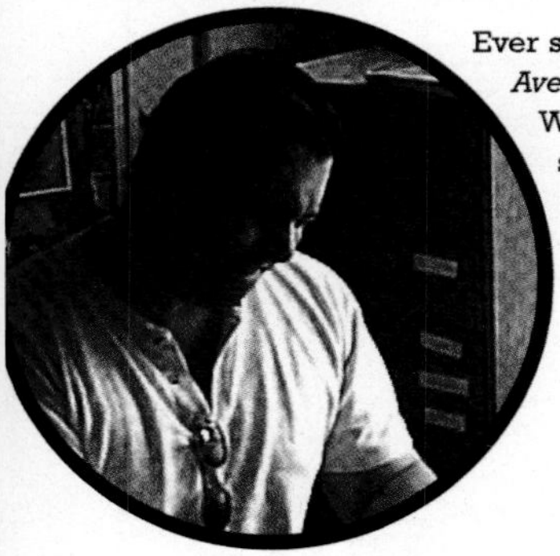

Ever since I came across artist Jim Steranko's version of Panther back in the early run of *Avengers*, I've always had an itch to try my hand at making a mark in the Panther legend. With much frustration and white-out, I've managed, with the help of Joe and Jimmy, to sculpt a formidable, fearsome image of a new '90s Panther. A kick-ass, don't-mess-with-me, take-no-crap, smack-your-mother-down-the-stairs, punch, drag-out, crack-is-whack, baddest Panther in recent history.

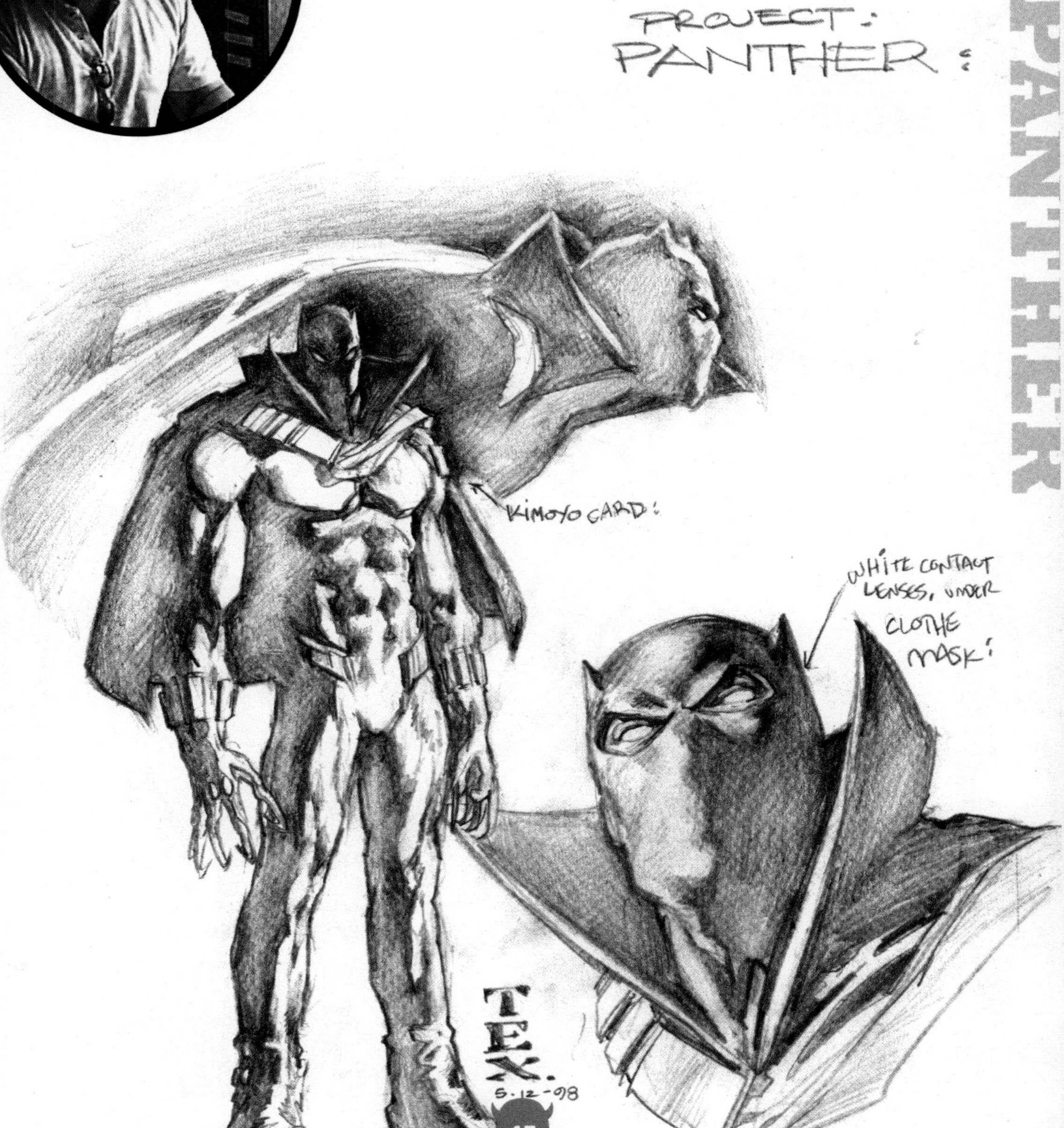
PROJECT:
PANTHER:
KIMOYO CARD!
WHITE CONTACT LENSES, UNDER CLOTHE MASK!
TEX.
5-12-98

BLACK PANTHER

BLACK PANTHER

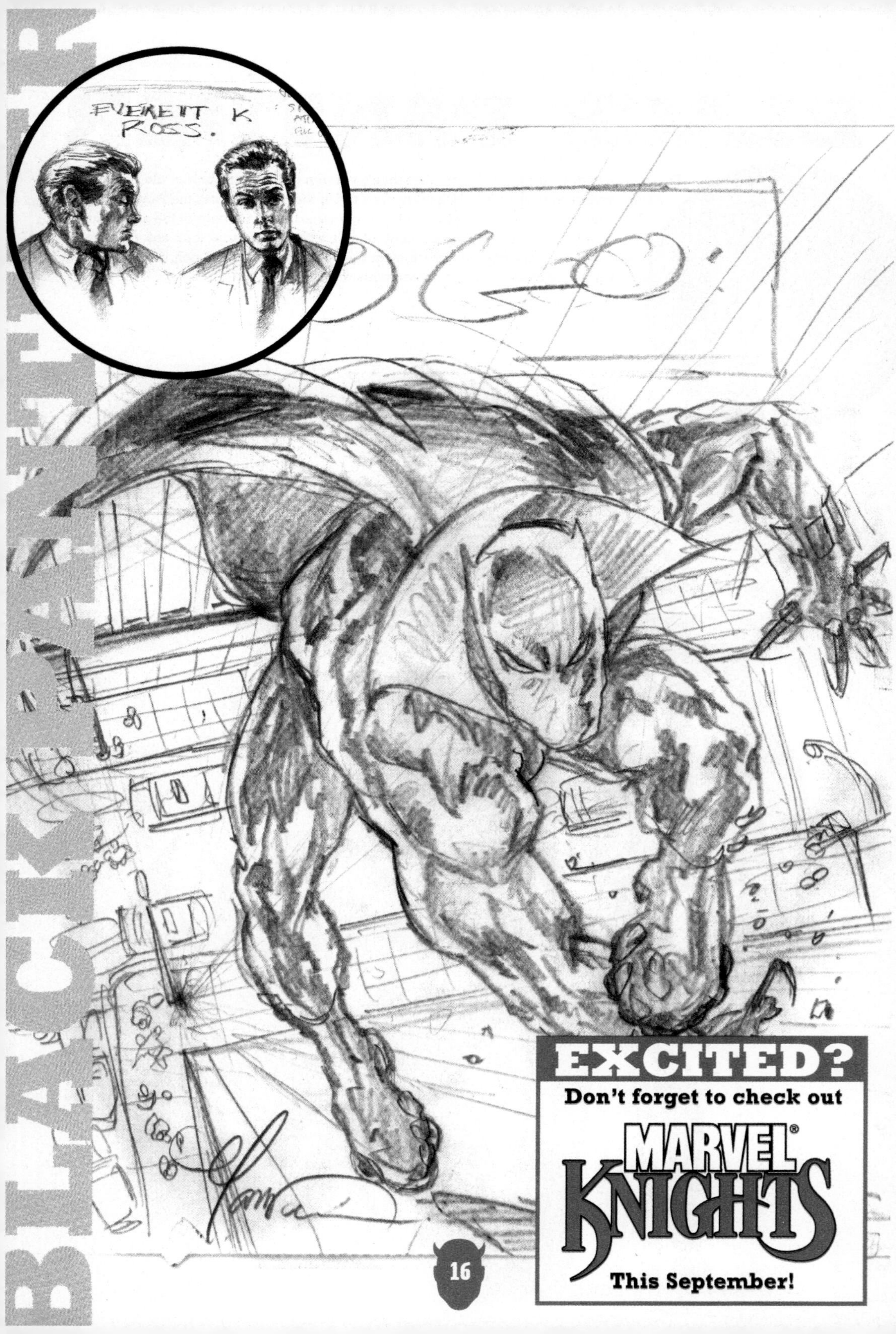
EVERETT K ROSS.

JOE JUSKO ON: BLACK PANTHER

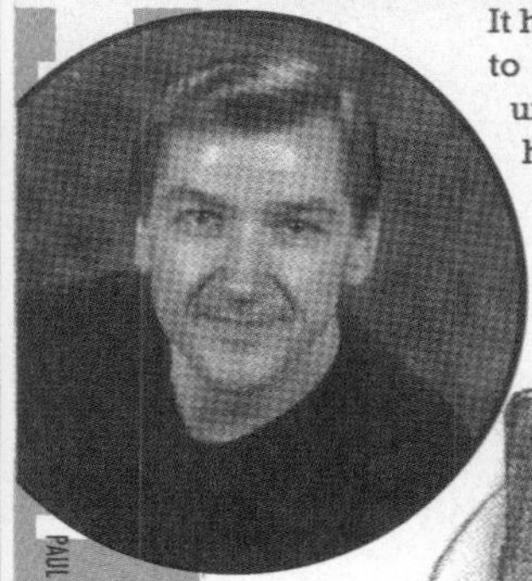

PAUL SCHIRALDI

It has to be something exciting and special to get me to sit down for the time it takes to do an entire story. The new *Black Panther* series is such a project! It's gritty, urban and dark, with just the right amount of comic relief. The downside is that I have to follow the masterful *Black Panther* work that Mark Texeira has been turning in!

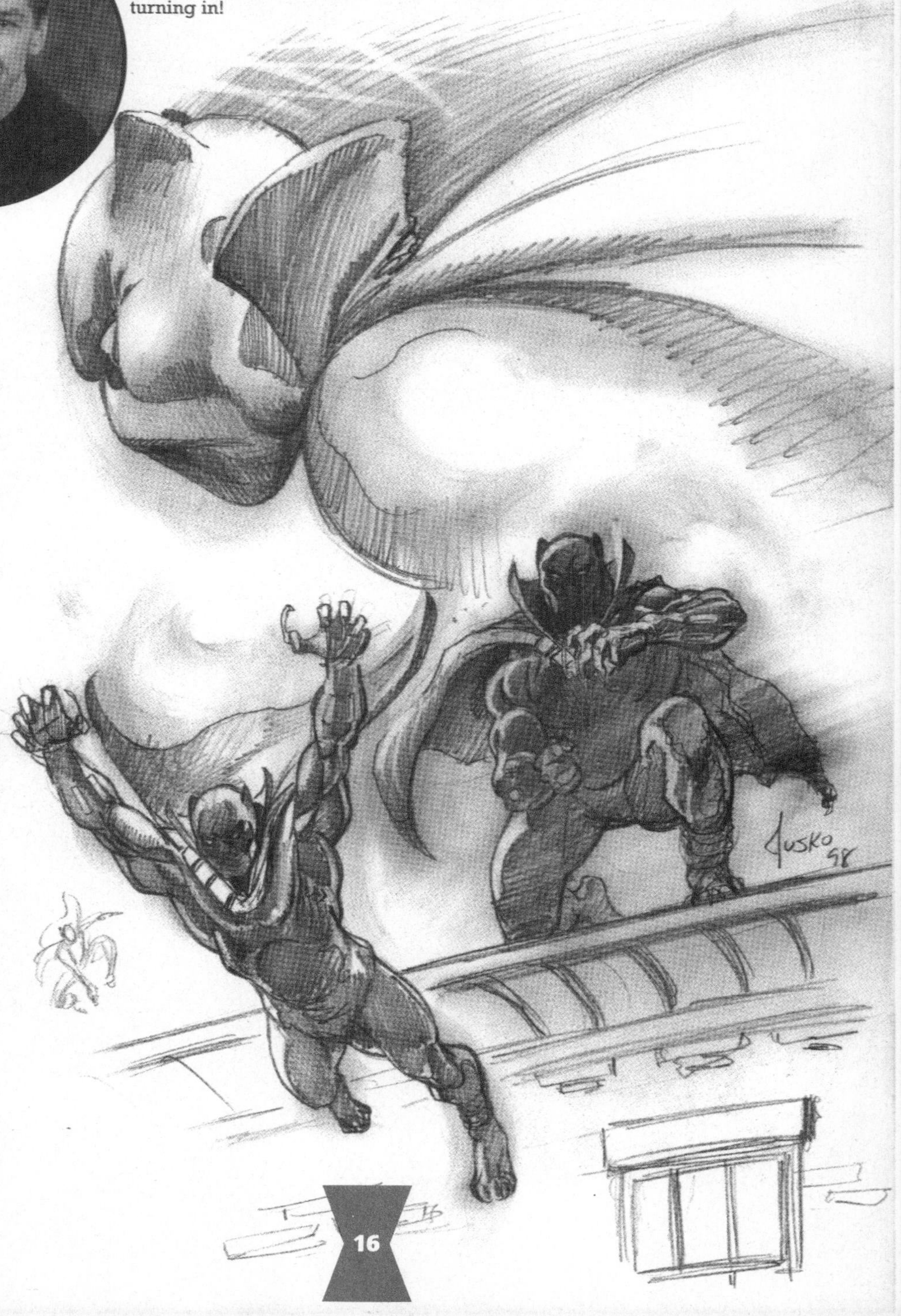
Jusko 98

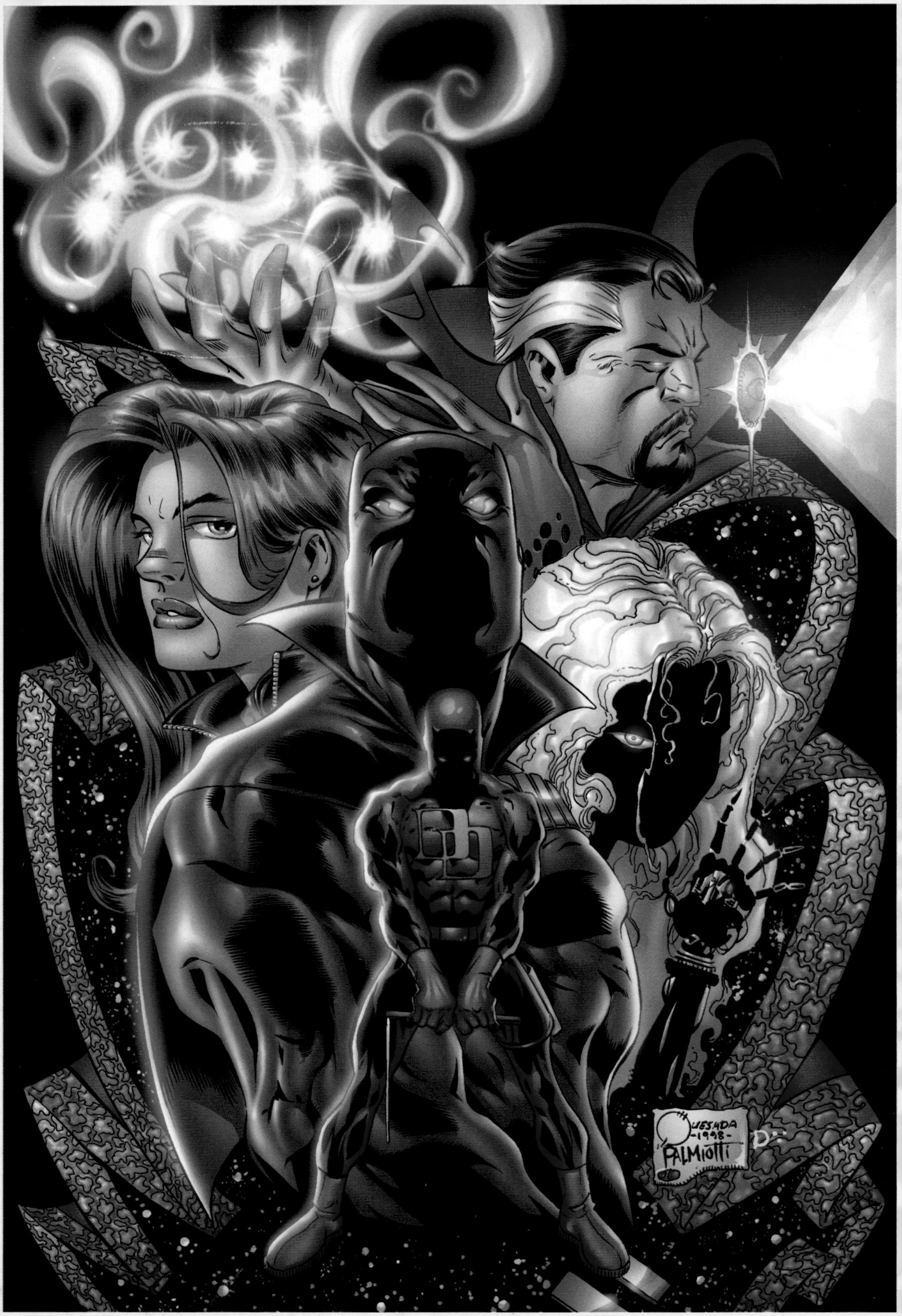
QUESADA
-1998-
PALMIOTTI

INTERVIEW
CRISTOPHER PRIEST AND MARK TEXEIRA

ANY TREPIDATION ARISING FROM WORKING ON REVITALIZING SUCH "CLASSIC" MARVEL CHARACTERS?

Tex: Look, I'm too old for that kind of thing. I've been at this for 20 years. I don't get nervous about ANYTHING.

Priest: The hardest part about doing something like the Panther is that it's about a black character, which can often throw up fences between the book and mainstream readers who may not immediately identify with the character or who may wrongly assume we're got some kind of social agenda. We don't. We're telling stories. We're not out to prove any points or turn everything into a lesson on racial tolerance and ethics. Panther is a fun book, and we want to appeal to the hip-hop nation: the youth-oriented melting pot subculture where gender and race are less significant than how baggy your pants are.

Tex: What's been established has only scratched the surface as to how large and explosive Panther can be...it'll be a blast!!

WHAT'S BEEN THE MOST ENJOYABLE PART ABOUT TACKLING THESE ESTABLISHED CHARACTERS?

Priest: Finding a fresh perspective while keeping the character totally consistent. Changing his environment around a bit so we get more resonance off him and see him in a fresh light, while clearly maintaining he is exactly the sam character he's always been.

Tex: Continuing to peel away at a Marvel icon and realize its potential. Its great joy!

IT'S BEEN SAID YOU'LL BE USING A NEW STYLE/TECHNIQUE ON BLACK PANTHER—TELL THE READERS A BIT ABOUT THIS TECHNIQUE.

Tex: I'm so pleased Joe and Jimmy let me do this book in black and white tones and allowing Brian to do his magic with this computer coloring! I'm hoping it'll catch on for my future projects.

RECENTLY, YOU'VE MADE A NAME FOR YOURSELF AS A WRITER WHO CAN TELL SOLID SUPER HEROES STORIES WITH A DECIDED HUMOROUS SLANT— HOW WILL YOU ATTEMPT TO BRING HUMOR INTO A BOOK STARRING SUCH STOIC LEAD CHARACTERS?

Priest: The Panther's stoicism and sincerity fuel this series, which is about as irreverent and politically risqué as we can get without actually having Newt Gingrich appear on-camera. I started as a comedy writer (for Marvel's Crazy Magazine), and I am infamous at DC Comics for being a writer who doesn't believe a man can fly. My disbelief provides a certain edge to my super hero writing; the work is grounded in realism and a healthy cynicism. In Panther, that cynicism is embodied in the person of Everett K. Ross, the Panther's U.S. State Department handler, who is essentially the eyes and ears and skepticism of the readership—themselves weary from the hype and doubtful a book with a black man in a kitty cat suit can hold their interest for long. Hopefully Ros's journey of discovery will mirror the readers'.

WHAT DO YOU INTEND TO BRING VISUALLY TO THE CHARACTER IN ORDER TO GARNER READER'S ATTENTION?

Tex: My fans know my work for its gritty dark intensity. I hope not to disappoint all three of them.

HOW DO YOU FEEL YOU'LL PERSONNALLY BE ABLE TO PIQUE READER/FAN INTEREST IN A CHARACTER THAT HASN'T HAD ITS OWN BOOK IN ABOUT TWO DECADES?

Priest: I can't. No, really, that's not my job. Interest-piquing is TEXEIRA's job. Interest is piqued when they flip through the thing on the racks, wondering if they should buy it. If Tex doesn't punch 'em in the face, they'll put it back and get something else. I am amazed and awed by Tex's work here. It's truly beautiful and unique stuff, and I think Tex will do a fine job of interest-piquing. My job is to bring them back. The first issue or two will be a tough read because it's told out of sequence (note to Bob Harras: they MADE ME DO IT!! Oh, and I'll be by to finish that second coat of wax on your car this weekend). But it's worth the effort and, if it grabs you, you'll be hooked.

ARTICLE EXCERPT FROM ***MARVEL CATALOG: SEPTEMBER 1998***

KNIGHT MOVES

By Michael Doran & Matthew Brady

Jungle 2 Jungle

Choosing a starring character for Marvel Knights' second ongoing series, Quesada and Palmiotti turned into a road less traveled (or a character less developed) and picked the Black Panther. Offering writer Christopher Priest the challenge of making an African King accessible to your average American comic book reader, Priest met the challenge by crafting a series that takes T'Challa out of one jungle and drops him right smack dab into another.

"The first story arc, entitled 'The Client', finds the Wakandan King coming to America on a brief fact-finding mission following a stateside scandal," says Priest. "Though a palace coup breaks out back home, circumstances we're not ready to divulge prevent T'Challa from immediately returning to deal with the home-grown problem."

Remaining in exile here in the U.S., the Panther sets up shop in the less than prosperous New Lots section of Brooklyn, NY, and is assigned to one Everett K. Ross, a U.S. State Department handler. This new character will serve a much larger role than just supporting cast member. "The Panther and these events are seen through the eyes of Ross, our totally out of his element Everyman," explains Priest. "He becomes, literally, the eyes of the skeptic reader, always underestimating the Panther's resourcefulness, strength and character. A dynamic and gifted legal vulture, Ross finds himself totally unprepared for the headlong plunge into Brooklyn's gang and criminal element the Panther takes him on. His discoveries of the Panther's character and strength serve as a guide for our own, as we subtly shift focus on the Panther to show new or underexplored sides of his character."

And just who is this T'Challa? "The Panther's a creature of the night, stalking the concrete jungle," says Priest. "He's a dark (darker, in some ways, than he has traditionally been portrayed), dangerous, cunning man who sees the most direct route between two points is a straight line. But he's figuratively handcuffed to Ross, a political spin doctor who plea-bargains everything to death. Though the Panther himself is unflappable, Ross finds himself in a world he never made, trying to keep track of a head of state who tends to pull on a cat mask and leap out the nearest window."

> THE PANTHER'S A CREATURE OF THE NIGHT, STALKING THE CONCRETE JUNGLE

Featuring painted art by South Bronx, NY native Mark Texeira, the series will strive for an authentic but unique New York feel. And Priest hopes to complement the art with a unique narrative structure. "The story is told out of sequence, in a 'Pulp Fiction-in-rewind' series of blackout sketches, and with other storytelling techniques I developed for Quantum & Woody," says the writer. "The narrative device and momentum is provided by Ross's exasperated attempts to rein in the exiled monarch (like suggesting Black Panther use a somewhat less politically risqué code name). There is a lot of humor in this book, intercut with a lot of tension and action." ■

BLACK PANTHER: THE CLIENT TPB INTRODUCTION

THE STORY THUS FAR

Introduction by Christopher Priest

I was so excited. Artist Joe Quesada and I had been missing each other's phone calls for a week, but I knew he wanted to talk to me about his new MARVEL KNIGHTS imprint. This was it, I thought: I was finally gonna get my dream shot. I was finally gonna get a chance to write DAREDEVIL.

I was a little horrified when the words "Black" and "Panther" came out of Joe's mouth. I mean, Black Panther? Who reads Black Panther? Black Panther?! The guy with no powers? The guy in the back of the Avengers class photo, whose main job was to point and cry out, "Look— A BIG, SCALY MONSTER! THOR— GO GET HIM!!" That guy?!

No, PANTHER was not the move. Panther was, by most any objective standards, dull. He had no powers. He had no witty speech pattern, bub. His supporting cast were a bunch of soul brothers in diapers with bones through their noses. King T'Challa is, by necessity, a man of secrecy and cunning, which is difficult to illustrate if he has thought balloons over his head telling the reader everything he's thinking. Or, worse, if he's narrating his own story and blathering on and on and on. Hard to convey cunning from a motormouth.

Also, Panther was a black super hero, and the most basic economic lesson this business can teach you is minorities and female super heroes do not sell (but, kudos to Marvel for trying to do both with the black female version of CAPTAIN MARVEL).

> THERE'S NO WAY MARVEL WOULD LET ME WRITE THIS.

But Joe and his partner, inker Jimmy Palmiotti, were adamant: the book can work, they insisted. If we have a fresh approach, perhaps along the lines of Eddie Murphy's *Coming To America*, where the crown prince of an African nation comes to America in search of a bride. Given that kind of energy, taking Wakanda and the Panther seriously, and concentrating on how people react to him -- that approach might have a chance in the market. Get him out of the jungle. Bring him to Brooklyn. Make him a night creature, a fearsome African warrior, a manner of black man most blacks in Brooklyn have never seen.

Nah. I was still unconvinced. "Look, guys, we're talking about a king. A black king of not just an African nation but a powerful nation with advanced technology capable of posing a threat to U.S. national security. A king who is prone to occasionally leaping out of windows dressed in a kitty cat outfit. If this guy, and his nation, actually existed, there's just no way the U.S. State Department would let this guy wander around unescorted, and the CIA would be constantly trying to figure out what's going on in Wakanda. There'd be all manner of global and domestic and racial politics involved."

For me to flesh out Joe and Jimmy's PANTHER premise, I'd need to go to the wells of snarkdom for the snarkiest snark I was capable of. Social politics as interpreted by Richard Belzer or Dennis Miller. And Marvel hasn't been the home of true snark since they sent Steve Gerber and his duck packing. I was trying to chase Joe and Jimmy away, but this stuff just excited them.

Again and again, I whined, there's no way Marvel would let me write this. It's a violation of the Fantasy Land Nice-Nice Accords, signed by both DC and Marvel, that says the U.S. government is always good all the time, everyone accepts Panther, and the Avengers hold hands and sing and what have you. Mainstream comics were demented places where heroes actually referred to themselves as "heroes," and villains as "villains." These were places run by people who have run comic book companies far, far, far too long and have completely lost touch with popular culture or with what young people today are actually about. I have had my hand slapped more times than I can count for simply pointing out the absurdity of what we do -- of these colorful men and women who fly around wearing their underwear on the outside of their clothes.

I believe Chris Claremont was the first writer I experienced who made sense out of all of this for me when he humanized the deadly Magneto. Claremont's brilliant writing had some of his heroes acting in completely unheroic ways, and resented many of his villains as conflicted, desperate souls who never, ever, referred to themselves as "villains," and certainly never thought of Xavier and his ilk as "heroes."

Frank Miller and others followed suit, bringing more dimension and plurality to the Marvel universe (while, for the most part, DC continues fairly entrenched in a kind of whitewashed estrangement from the real world, nearly all their heroes being beloved, respected and trusted by the average citizen, to whom flying men and women are a mundane and accepted practice).

The PANTHER book Joe and Jimmy were asking me to produce could not possibly exist in such a world. It would have to exist on the fringes of that world, with our book regularly hacking chunks out of it. This was fine with the guys, and they both encouraged me towards my darker side; the wittier and more gleeful the discourse, the more they enjoyed it and the harder they fought for it.

The problem with race and popular media is, in most every "black" movie or "black" music CD you'll see or hear, there is some hostility directed towards whites. Now, were I a white male, I certainly wouldn't want to spend eight bucks to go see a film where white males are portrayed as stupid and are the butt of every joke, or where I am made to feel guilty about things I had nothing to do with, or prejudices I don't actually have.

That's my pet peeve with a lot of black film and black comedians: it's all White People Bashing, fueled by our race's legacy of anger and resentment by centuries-old unreparative wrongs. But, this hostility polarizes rather than unites. There is no healing in it, and it limits our opportunities.

I feel the most profound statement I can make about race is to make Panther so cool he transcends the racial divide here in America. Rather than try and force the readers to identify with a black character, I accepted the fact a great many readers would not be able to overcome the race thing, and withdrew Panther from the reader entirely.

Borrowing a page from my mentor, legendary comics writer Denny O'Neil, I reinterpreted T'Challa in the mold of Denny's brilliant Ras Al Ghul, a villain from Batman's glory days. Nobody, not even Batman, ever knew, for sure, what Ras was thinking, what his true motives or true plans were. He was the world's greatest poker face, and only the legendary Darknight Detective had the power to challenge him. Ras was, like O'Neil himself, cool. And his coolness transcended race, gender, and even Ras' advanced age.

That was the energy I wanted for Panther. Rather than get into his head with an enforced intimacy that worked against his stealth, we withdrew altogether, pushing him to the shadows and, to some complaint, making him almost a guest star in his own book. Only, in any reasonable analysis of the series, Panther clearly drives the book. Even he has only a handful of lines per issue, he is the dominating force.

So, how do we do a book about a black king of a black nation who comes to a black neighborhood and not have it be a "black" book? Moreover, how do we deal with reader apathy and resistance to the return of one of Marvel's least appreciated and dullest characters? Do we turn Panther into WolverPanther? Do we kill him off and replace him with some kid with a crab on his face? Cut off his hand and replace it with a hook?

HOW DO WE DO A BOOK ABOUT A BLACK KING OF A BLACK NATION WHO COMES TO A BLACK NEIGHBORHOOD AND NOT HAVE IT BE A "BLACK" BOOK?

The answer came to me while watching the brilliant Matthew Perry perform a scene in the NBC hit sitcom Friends. "Gum would be perfection," a line only Friends fans would know, made me howl with laughter for days. Perry's character, an investment banker named Chandler Bing, was actually quite competent at his job. Respected and successful, Bing nevertheless was the horrified fish out of water when caught up in the machinery of his friends' complex personal lives. This was a role Perry freely adapted for the largely ignored but very funny film Fools Rush In, where he plays a brilliant corporate developer who is nonetheless The White Boob around Salma Hayek's Latino community.

I asked Joe and Jimmy, "What if we put that guy-Chandler Bing-into the series? He could be the motormouth, he could give voice to the skeptical readers and validate their doubts and fears about the series. And, best of all, he could amplify the Panther's mystery and overall enigma as his monologues would be, at best, a guess about Panther's whereabouts and motives.

The guys loved the idea, and we started hammering away at the details. This character's name was, literally, Chandler for the first couple of weeks, until I settled on an Alex P. Keaton vibe in Everett K. Ross. Most fans assumed him to be a one-off of Michael J. Fox, and Fox could certainly bring him to life, but I was writing Chandler, not Alex. I had Ross appear in KA-ZAR #17 as a warm-up of sorts, a runthrough with the quick-witted, sardonic halfpint, who effortlessly got Ka-Zar off on an attempted murder charge.

With Ross in place, the book began to take shape. Ross became the key to making the book work. He was the voice of the average Marvel reader, who no doubt wondered why Marvel was bothering with another Panther series.

Ross's monologues began to steal the show, offsetting the mysterious night creature, the man of few words whom Ross was attached to. The monologues were often outrageous, with Ross interpreting the Marvel Universe through his Everyman's eyes rather than through the eyes of someone who's been reading comics all his life. It

was a new voice, one seemingly hostile towards the Marvel Universe (and, by extension, its fans), but actually, the intent is more to be a social observer and deconstructionist.

Rather than ignore or run from the looming shadow of skepticism and low expectation, Joe and Jimmy and I turned that stuff into kindling for the fire; the secret skepticism of most every Marvel reader became grist for our humor mill, as Ross blurted out what many fans were likely thinking, but never dared to so much as commit to paper or post on a newsgroup: questions of race and values and our own insecurity about being super-hero fans well into adulthood. Ross giddily makes salad of all of the anxiety of the adult super-hero fan, kicking over many a sacred cow in the process.

Panther's ethnicity is certainly a component of the series, but it is not the central theme. We neither ignore it nor build our stories around it. One of Joe and Jimmy's earliest battles with Marvel was to get the Politically Correct handcuffs off and allow us to poke fun at race (in issue #1 Ross assumed Panther's going to 'hang out at Avengers Mansion and order up some ribs').

That was the scene that would tell us whether Marvel was prepared to allow us to do this book. And, once J&J convinced the powers-that-be to leave us alone, it opened up a floodgate of possibilities for outrageous adventure and a gleeful evisceration of some of the most cherished tenets of the Marvel Universe. Jimmy and Joe were regularly summoned to the principal's office and kept after school for our Don Imus/David Letterman snark-fest (calling the Avengers "Gaudily Dressed Fascists," and wondering, "Who appointed them to 'avenge' me?! I don't need any 'avenging'!").

Which is how the book achieved its small cult following. The core die-hard PANTHER fans regularly tune in not so much for the super-hero battles or the villain of the month as to see what Ross will say about it.

To the great surprise of most industry experts, and even to myself, BLACK PANTHER is, at this writing, still going strong. Still attracting new fans and pursuing new adventures. We're thrilled and grateful to everyone who's been along for the ride. To old friends and new: to Joe, Jimmy and Nanci, to Chris Claremont who fought the good fight, to Bob Harras who often beat up Chris for us, to our pal Ruben who brought us back into the family, the great Tom Brevoort who took us to the next level, our new pal Michael Marts, to Bill Jemas for being in our corner when it really counted, the wonderful Alitha Martinez without whom we'd have NEVER shipped on time, to colorist Brian Haberlin, letterers Siobhan Hanna and Richard Starkings (who spent many an hour with me on the phone designing the look of Panther's graphics), and the fabulous Mark Texeira— thanks, everyone, for this ground-breaking comic. And for those who are meeting the Panther, Ross and the gang for the first time— enjoy!

— Christopher Priest
JUNE, 2001

WAKANDA MAIL WE GET

THE STORY THUS FAR...

I hate to bring this up, but, yes, I'm black. Now, every time I mention I'm black, everybody at the office starts having meetings. They had meetings at Acclaim. They had meetings at DC. And, at the Marvel Knights offices, we've shared one or two conference calls about it.

The MK folks have received some bizarre letters claiming that I couldn't possibly be black because I've made ribs jokes and grits jokes and Fred Sanford jokes. These people probably haven't noticed that Ross, the whitest guy in the book, takes the brunt of 90% of the gags in here.

Sure, it's a double standard: I get to make cracks about racial issues that a white writer would be strung up for. But that's not why I do it. Nobody sat me down and told me to make BLACK PANTHER about race. And it's not.

It's about family, and loyalty, and being true to oneself. It's about devotion to country and duty, being honorable when everyone around you is not. Focusing too narrowly on race here denies the real message of the series: it's about The Noblest Guy In The World. And, hopefully, it makes you think about the world we live in.

EVERETT K. ROSS: "He comes here all the time. Hangs out at Avengers Mansion-- orders up some ribs-- "

That line made a lot of fans laugh. And it made most everybody at the office nervous. I mean, King T'Challa had been around for 30 years and no one had ever said anything like that about him. Of course, I'd bet most everyone, at one point or another, thought those things (though perhaps less pointedly), but giving voice to it just sent everybody scrambling. I mean, I was making fun of the whole race issue. And I think it deserves to be made fun of.

Race IS funny. Black people are hilarious. Look at Don King's hair. Lionel Richie's career. The word "grits" just makes me chuckle, in almost any context. Go on--you try it. Say it out loud, "Grits." Bwaaahahahahaha!! Oh, and grits didn't come from Zimbabwe, folks. It's not like Beshenga and his loyal page U'ambu, laboring over a steaming kettle, passed the recipe on from generation to generation, until it finally came to America at the turn of the century, clutched in the gnarled hand of a hunchback Armenian woman.

In a litigious, politically correct world, these kinds of observations are hot button issues, best kept in smoky sub-basements at comedy clubs or Pat Buchanan campaign ads. Mind you, comics are often full of violence and Satan-worshipping chicks in thongs (well, not so much anymore, but I just like typing the phrase, "chicks in thongs"), but Everett K. Ross's cultural awakening is something that gets everybody jumpy. To Marvel Comics' credit, they never once came down the hall to tell the MK crew to lay off of race. In this volatile comics market, and from the industry leader, that equals unparalleled bravery.

All of which is to say, yes, I'm black. The fact that it matters at all means we still have a very long way to go. And, while that's certainly sad, it does provide fodder for a lot of new Ross gags.

This isn't good-bye. The book's not cancelled. There IS a next issue. And one after that. And one after that. I know because I've already written them, and Our Pal

Christopher Priest

Sal Velluto is cranking out gorgeous work.

Joe and Jimmy are handing the book off to the mainstream Marvel line because J&J are money grubbing jackals who want to conquer the market with new #1's (hopefully one from me in the near future, more on that later). It is not a painful decision; Nanci and the boys have shepherded the Panther into a new era and introduced him to thousands of new fans. But the book no longer requires their daily hands-on efforts, efforts they could use more efficiently to launch more new, exciting projects.

I'd like to thank the crew for a wonderful dozen issues, and for encouraging, nay, insisting on the creative direction the book ultimately took. Thanks also for fighting the fights for me ("Who is Mephisto?") and for sticking your collective necks out on many, many occasions for me and for the prodigal Texeira, whom I miss more than I can tell you. Mark's vision for this book was nothing short of revolutionary. Tex, wherever you are, come back, Shane, come back!!

Thanks also to my longtime buddies Jusko (from the good ol' CONAN days!!!) and Mike Manley (from my stint as Spidey editor in the Cro-Magnon 1980's). And to Vince Evans, whom I've never had the privilege of meeting, but whose incredible art graces the cover of QUANTUM & WOODY #1's alternate edition and store poster. Vince: you're my hero.

I bow at the feet of Doc Bright, my long-time partner in crime (and no, we are not a couple, not that there's anything wrong with that, but we're not). Thanks for rescuing us all in issues #11 and 12, especially given your hectic schedule on QUANTUM & WOODY.

Thanks also to my long, longtime buddy (from way back in THE RAY days) Ruben Diaz, who takes the helm next month.

And that's about it. I've gotta get back to writing DEADPOOL #37 (I'm right in the middle of 'Pool's big fight with THOR-- shameless plugs "R" us). After that, I'm going to kick back for awhile and order up some ribs before heading out tonight to steal hubcaps and hold up liquor stores.

Y'all be cool. One love.

Priest

This is what it must be like for parents sending their children off to college. Panther has been very near and dear to our hearts and greater thanks could not be given to Mark Texeira, Joe Jusko, Vince Evans, Alitha Martinez, Bruce Timm, Mike Manley, Mark Bright and Nelson Decastro for supplying us with the most beautiful artwork this character has, in our humble opinion, ever been graced with since Jack "King" Kirby. Thanks to Richard Starkings and the crew, Brian Haberlin, Elizabeth Lewis and Chris Sotomayor for being our clutch hitters. And a special big thank you and a wet sloppy kiss to Christopher Priest, who made this book work and kept us all in good spirits with his wonderful scripts and his hearty belly laughs over the phone.

Now don't all of you just hang up the phone--Panther is not going anywhere! The only difference you'll see is that it just won't have the MK logo on it. So be back here next month as Priest and Sal Velluto and Bob Almond continue the Black Panther's wild ride into Super Hero Superstardom!

Boy, we're going to miss that idiot Ross.

Daki created by Priest and Manley

J&J

JOE QUESADA & JIMMY PALMIOTTI EDITORS

BOB HARRAS CHIEF

DESIGN BY COMICRAFT/EW

BLACK PANTHER c/o MARVEL COMICS 387 PARK AVENUE SOUTH NEW YORK, NY 10016

E-MAIL: MAIL@MARVEL.COM MARK E-MAIL "OKAY TO PRINT"

IF YOU DON'T WANT YOUR NAME AND ADDRESS PRINTED, PLEASE LET US KNOW. LETTERS MAY BE EDITED FOR CONTENT AND LENGTH.

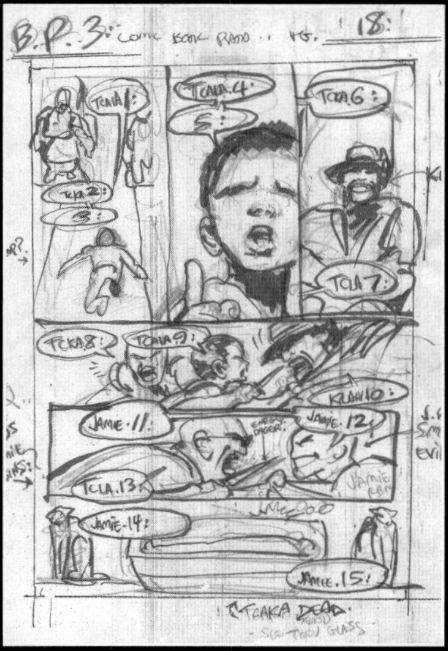
B.P. 3:
18:

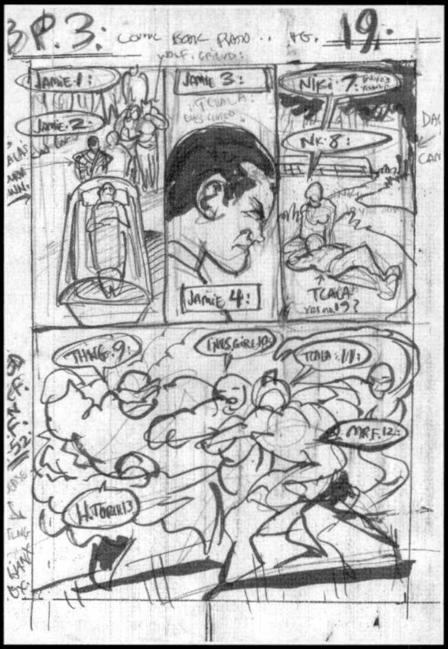
B.P. 3:
19.

BLACK PANTHER #3, PAGES 18-19 LAYOUTS BY **MARK TEXEIRA**

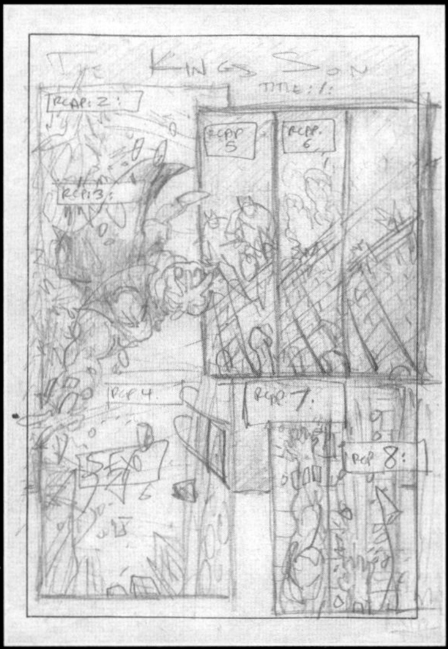

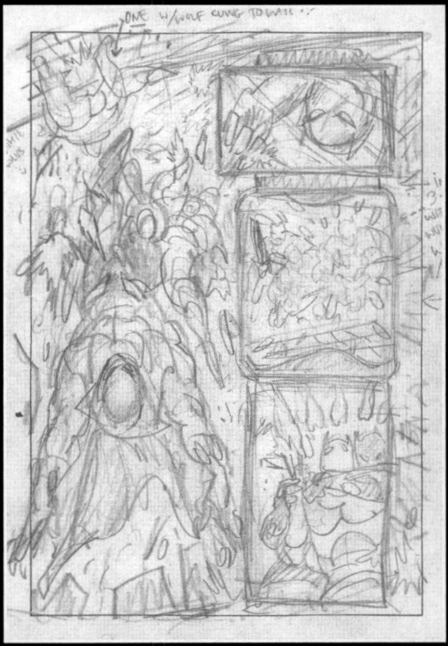

BLACK PANTHER #4, PAGES 4-5 LAYOUTS BY **MARK TEXEIRA**

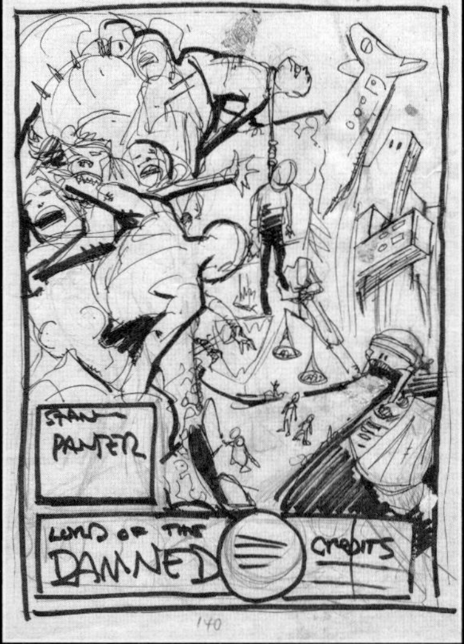
PANTER
LAND OF THE
DAMNED
CREDITS

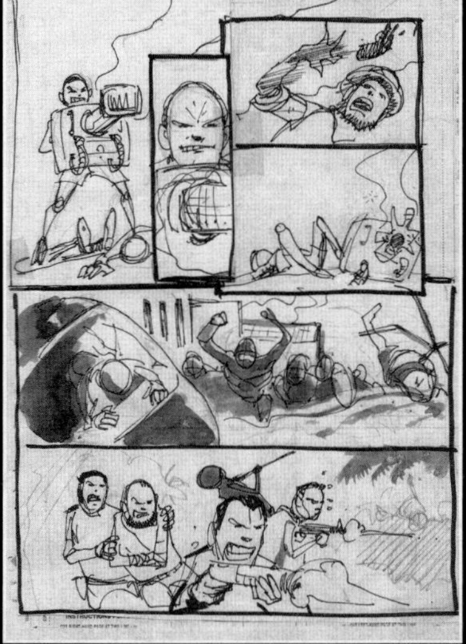

BLACK PANTHER #5, PAGES 1 & 13 LAYOUTS BY **VINCE EVANS**

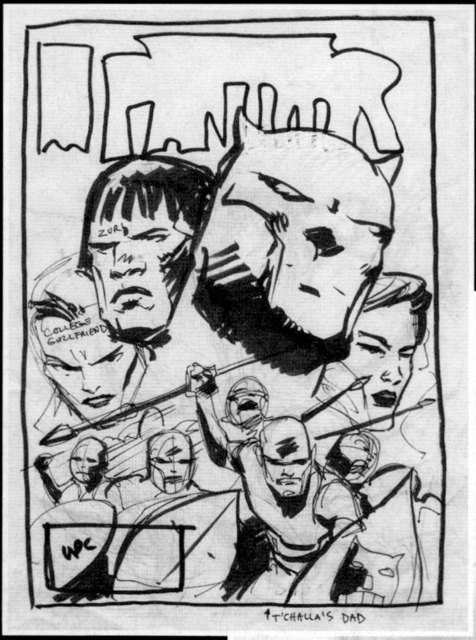
ZURI
COLLEGE GIRLFRIEND
WPC
T'CHALLA'S DAD

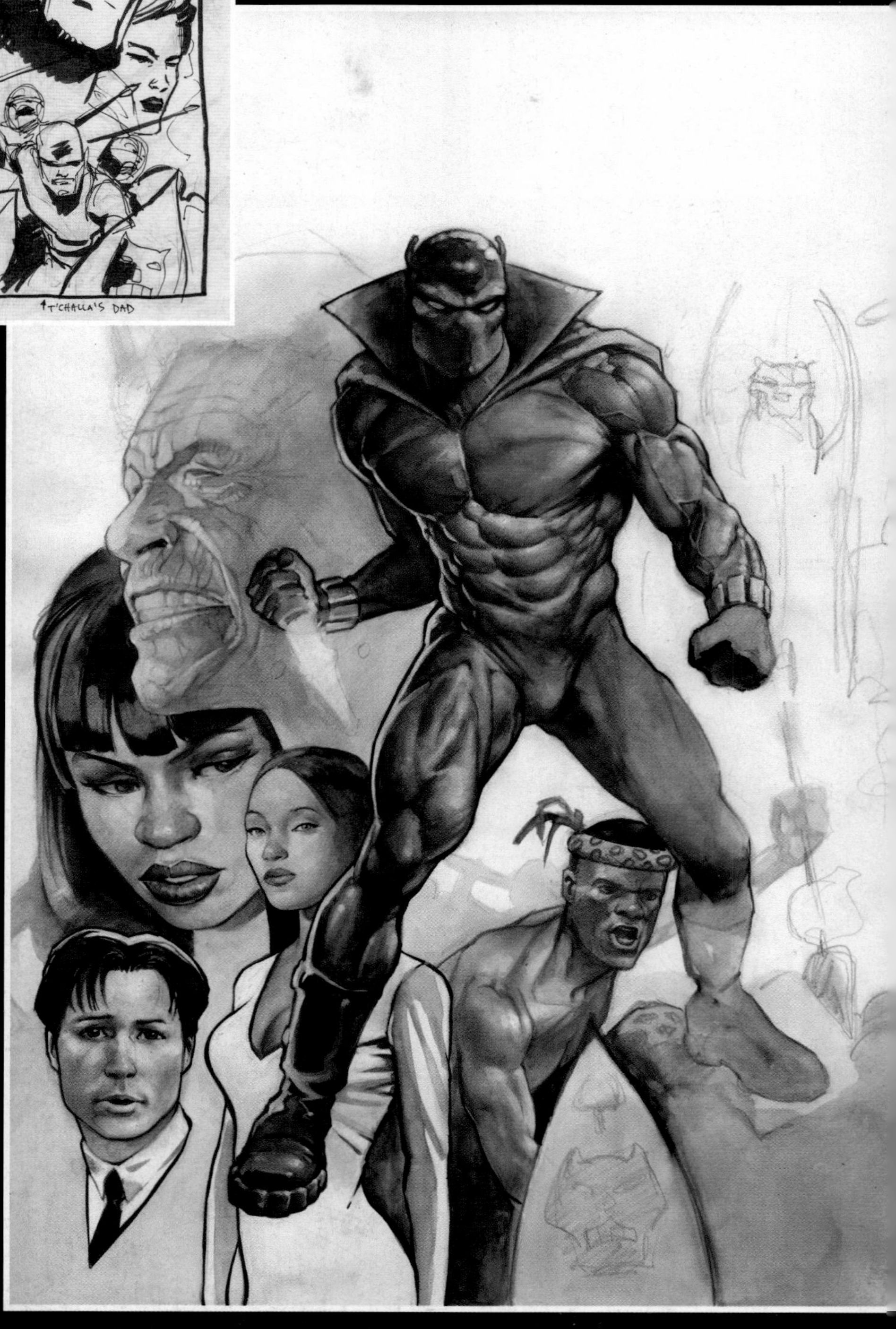

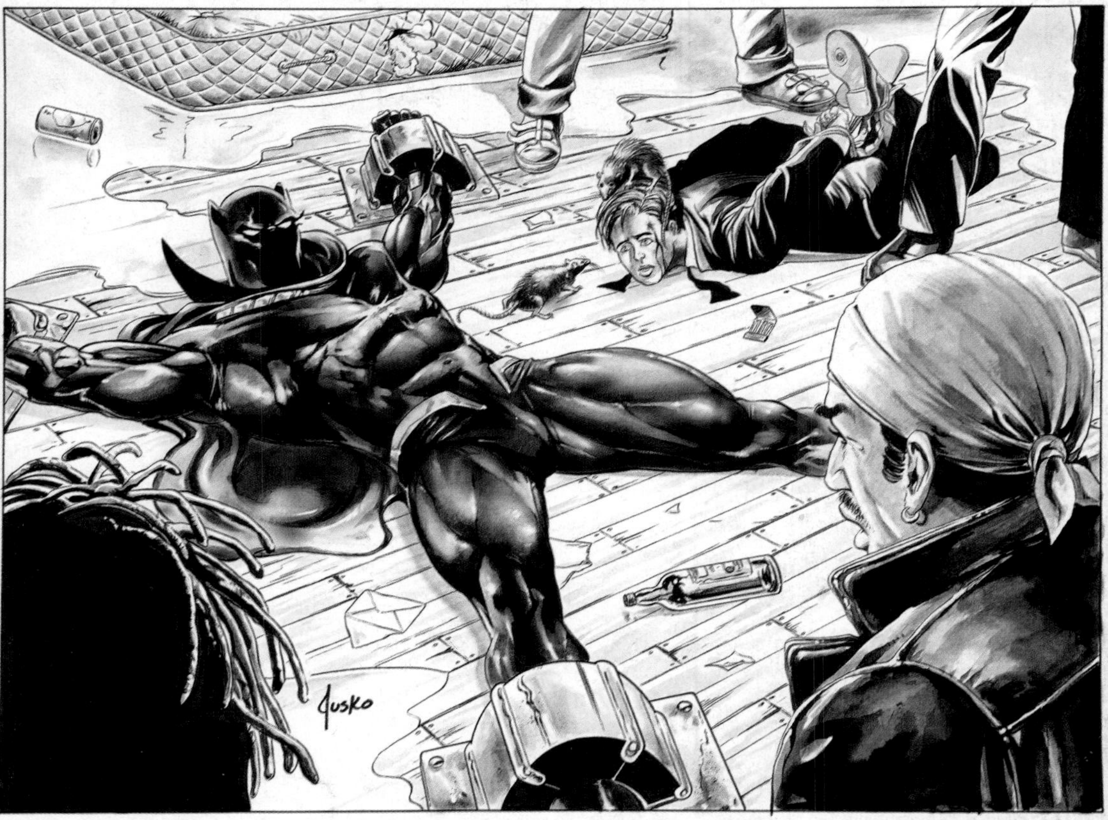
JUSKO

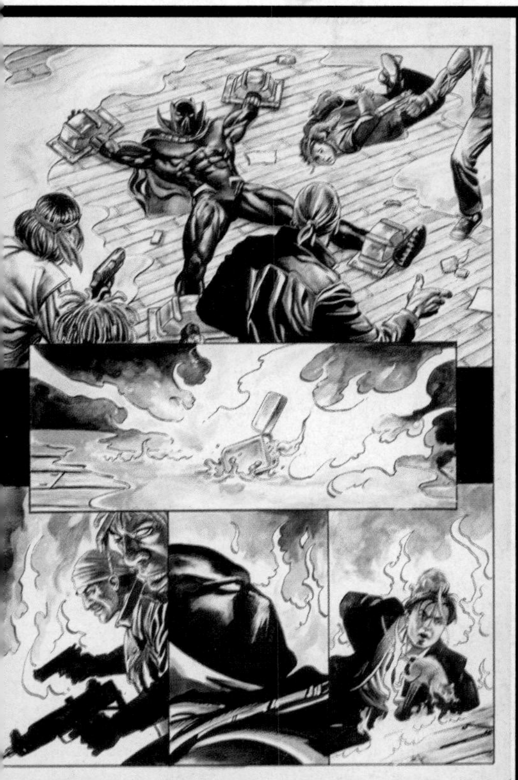

BLACK PANTHER #15, PAGE 1 PENCILS BY **SAL VELLUTO** WITH INKS BY **BOB ALMOND**

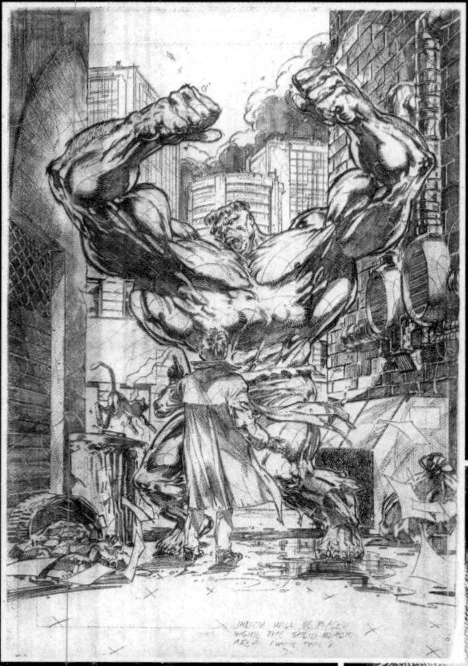

IMAGE COURTESY OF BOB ALMOND

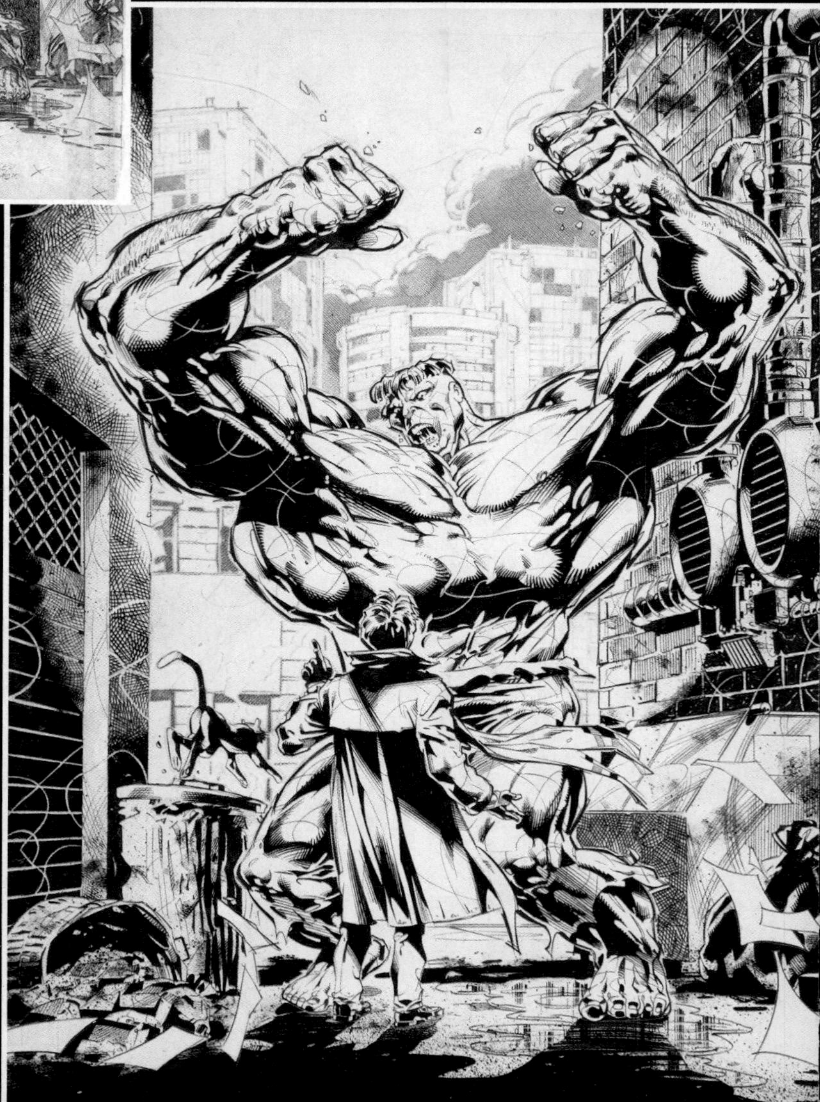

IMAGE COURTESY OF *HERITAGEAUCTIONS.COM*